1995

EAST AFRICAN HANDBOOK

With Mauritius, Madagascar and Seychelles

Editors ***Michael Hodd***
Cartographer ***Sebastian Ballard***

All the flowers that you found on the plains, or upon the creepers and liana in the native forest, were diminutive like flowers of the downs – only just in the beginning of the long rains a number of big, massive heavy-scented lilies sprang out on the plains. The views were immensely wide. Everything that you saw made for greatness and freedom, and unequalled nobility.

Karen Blixen *Out of Africa*

Trade & Travel Publications Ltd
6 Riverside Court, Lower Bristol Road, Bath BA2 3DZ, England
Telephone 01225 469141 Fax 01225 469461

ISBN 0 900751 59 2 ISSN 1352-7886

CIP DATA: A catalogue record for this book is available from the British Library

In North America, published by

4255 West Touhy Avenue
Lincolnwood (Chicago), Illinois 60646-1975, USA

ISBN 0-8442-8983-3

Library of Congress Catalog Card Number 94-66053

WARNING: While every endeavour is made to ensure that the facts printed in this book are correct at the time of going to press, travellers are cautioned to obtain authoritative advice from consulates, airlines, etc, concerning current travel and visa requirements and conditions before embarking. The publishers cannot accept legal responsibility for errors, however caused, that are printed in this book.

Maps – Publisher's note: a number of frontiers in the area covered by this Handbook are disputed and the subject of territorial claims by various countries in the region. Neither the coloured nor the black and white maps in this book are intended to have any political significance or purport to show authenticated international boundaries.

Cover illustration by Suzanne Evans

Printed and bound in Great Britain by Clays Ltd., Bungay, Suffolk

CONTENTS

TRADE & TRAVEL *HANDBOOKS*

"A travel guide business that looks set to sweep the world."

The Independent

*"The **India Handbook** (formerly the South Asian Handbook) has reminded me of how much I do not know about the sub-continent!"*

Mark Tully, BBC India correspondent

"More info - less blah."

Readers's letter, Germany

"By far the best, most comprehensive guides: in a class of their own. Unreservedly recommended - a Handbook will pay for itself many times over."

Journey Latin America

"On Bible thin paper with distinctive covers. The miraculous result is that they are, at the same time, sturdy, exhaustive and light-weight."

Fort Lauderdale Sun Sentinel

"Mines of information and free of pretentiousness: make other guidebooks read like Butlins brochures."

Bookshop review

"Accurate and reliable down to the minutest detail. Amazingly so."

Reader's letter, Canada

"By far the most informative guide to Burma published in recent years. Miraculously, the information appears to be up-to-date, rare for books in this genre."

Far Eastern Economic Review

PREFACE

Welcome to this first edition of the ***East African Handbook***. The sixteen countries and territories covered fall into four groups. There are the three great safari lands (Kenya, Tanzania, Uganda); the countries of the central mountains (Rwanda, Burundi and Eastern Zaire); the nations of the horn of Africa (Ethiopia, Eritrea, Somalia and Djibouti); and the Indian Ocean islands (Comoros, Mayotte, Madagascar, Seychelles, Réunion and Mauritius). They offer attractions ranging over wildlife, exotic beaches and history that are the equal of anywhere in the world.

But a salutory year to start. Somalia remains firmly off-limits to the traveller and Rwanda, Burundi and Eastern Zaire join it. Rwanda is a particularly sad loss – prior to this recent disaster it was friendly, safe and visitors were invariably enchanted by its startling beauty. These three countries are covered in the book – a time will come when they can be visited again, and the spirit of the entries is to indicate what was there before the current turmoil – things will be lost, but much will survive.

In general, what does this new guide offer?

- In common with all the books in the series, coverage is up-to-date, compact and carefully tailored to the needs of the independent traveller. But more than that – for half of the countries (Tanzania, Uganda, Burundi, Rwanda, Ethiopia, Eritrea, Djibiouti and Somalia), it is the most comprehensive currently available.
- One of the major attractions of travel in Africa is the unique wildlife. This guide includes a comprehensive Wildlife Section, specially commissioned, and with 200 new illustrations. In addition to the familar animals, there are reptiles, insects, birds, sea-life, trees, flowers and agricultural crops. We hope it will be of wider use to the traveller than just as an identification aid in the parks.
- The wildlife, beaches and exotic traditional life of some of the people of Africa are well known. This book also tries to introduce the traveller to the fascinating aspects of the day-to-day life of the urban-dweller and small farmer in Africa. The reader will find much emphasis on this in the special interest boxes.
- Apart from the exploits of the famous explorers, it is often thought there is little of interest in the historical record of Africa. How wrong this is. Ethiopia, for example, has a rich history that can be traced back to biblical times. Other countries have been marked by the impact of Shirazi migrants, Portuguese explorers, Dutch, British, French, German and Italian colonisers. Africa has witnessed astonishing tales and extraordinary people. This guide seeks to lay some of this background before the reader, for in many cases it is the key to understanding the Africa of today.
- A guide of any worth should point the traveller toward some special experiences and new, mostly unvisited, places. We hope we have been able to do this in Tanzania, Zanzibar, Uganda, Ethiopia and Eritrea – all fascinating countries that are steadily becoming more accessible and accommodating to travellers after periods of being withdrawn. As Pliny observed two thousand years ago:

Ex Africa, semper aliquid novi.

Travelling offers the prospect of being wonderfully uplifted by new places – witness the feelings of Alec Waugh on arriving for the first time in the Seychelles:

> I sauntered that evening along the waterfront. The honking horns, the rattling rickshaws; the local people in their Sunday

> finery; the government buildings, rectangular, two-storied, weatherworn; the mango trees; coconut palms aslant over the lagoon; streets that climb back into the hills, losing themselves in greenery; isolated white verandahed bungalows; the crotons and bouganvillea; the brilliant scarlet of the tulip tree; the mountains towering behind.
>
> I knew very well that I would find something here that I had found nowhere else. My nerves were alert and quivering; the old excitement was upon me.
>
> Where the Clocks Chime Twice (1952)

On the other hand there are *longeurs*. Here are the remarks of Alec Waugh's more famous brother, Evelyn – also an inveterate traveller – when he was stuck in Dire Dawa in Ethiopia:

> I am constitionally a martyr to boredom, but never have I been so desperately and degradingly bored as I was during the next four days.
>
> I sat in Mr Bollolakos' hotel. I had nothing to read except a first volume of a pocket edition of Pope. There are moments when one does not wish to read Pope: when one requires something bulky and informative.
>
> Most hotels, however simple, harbour some reading matter of some sort or another: brochures of advertisement, magazines or novels left by previous visitors, a few postcards on a rack. At Mr Bollolakos' there was nothing.
>
> For an hour or two I sat in the rocking chair reading Pope's juvenile poems.
>
> Most of the time I thought about how awful the next day would be.
>
> Remote People (1931)

This guide contains scores of special interest boxes, to be dipped into when the traveller is marooned at airports, waiting at a border post, or spending a night in Mr Bollolakos' hotel. Many of the boxes reflect Africa through the eyes of celebrated visitors and writers.

We hope, too, that these boxes will help transmit some of the immense enthusiasm and affection that Africa has generated in all who have contributed to this book.

The Editor
London

THE EDITOR

Michael Hodd

Mike Hodd is the author of some pretty dull stuff – three academic tomes on Africa; editor of three other books; and over sixty articles, reports and papers.

He has also been a commissioned writer for the BBC Radio 2 comedy show News Huddlines, a regular contributor to Week Ending on BBC Radio 4, and a script-writer for Rory Bremner. He is a co-owner of the Canal Café Theatre in Little Venice, London, which presents Newsrevue, a continually updated topical comedy show, winner of many awards, now in its 15th year.

He has visited Africa more than 30 times, and only hopes that some of his enthusiasm for the continent will emerge in this ***Handbook.***

ACKNOWLEDGEMENTS

A large number of people have contributed to this book. The major inputs have been from Margaret Carswell, who wrote the Wildlife Guide; Joan Callaghan-Roche who did the Wildlife illustrations; and Sebastian Ballard who drew the maps. The excellence of their contributions is apparent from the finished products.

Background material has come from several sources. Susan Murrell meticulously researched and stylishly contributed to the Kenya, Burundi, Rwanda, Eastern Zaire, Somalia and Djibouti sections. Grace Carswell employed her wide experience of the region to provide absolutely splendid material on Tanzania, Kenya and especially Uganda, where she lived for many years. Dan Collison, a horn of Africa specialist, wrote with enthusiasm on Ethiopia. Finally, Mark Povey brought his geographical and natural history expertise to bear on the six Indian Ocean territories.

Suwanna Sutakan was terrific help in typing and editing most of the manuscript, digging out maps and historical background, all the while contriving to maintain good spirits and a sense of fun.

I would like to think those cited above are entirely responsible for any errors that remain.

Angela, my wife, and my son, Jack, of course, gave absolutely no help, encouragement or support whatever, and derided the entire project from start to finish. To them and all the others I am more than a little grateful. [*Ed.*]

MAP SYMBOLS

Symbol		Symbol
International Border		Capital
Provincial Border		Other Towns
Main Roads (Rt 9)		Bus Stations (B)
Other Roads		Hospitals (H)
Jeepable Roads, Trails, Paths, Ferry Service		Key Numbers (27)
Railways, Stations		Airport
Contours (approx), Rock Outcrops		Bridges
Rivers (*Nile River*)		Mountain Pass
Built Up Areas		Mountains
Lakes, Reservoirs		Waterfall
River Flood Plain, Swamp		National Parks, Wildlife Parks, Bird Sanctuaries
Sand Banks, Beaches		Archaeological Sites
City Squares, Parks & Stadiums		Places of Worship
Fortified Walls		Muslim
		Christian

National Park Maps

Park Boundary

Park Gates

Hotel, Lodge

Campsite

Ranger Post

Volcano Crater

Escarpment

EA 0

INTRODUCTION AND HINTS

CONTENTS

General note The advice given below represents a regional summary of more detailed information provided in the *Information for visitors* section of each country entry.

Using this *Handbook*

The book is laid out as follows:

- **Overviews**
  Introduction and hints
  Health
  Regional introduction
- **Country entries**
  Introduction
  Capital city
  Regions and routes
  National Parks and Reserves
  Information for visitors
- **Wildlife guide**
- **Index**

Structure

The book begins with some overviews of general matters. The reader contemplating visiting the region for the first time might look at the **Regional Introduction** first to get a grasp of the nature and scope of what is available to the traveller. The next step might be to look at the **Country Entries** for places that are of interest. The **Health** section and the **Wildlife Guide** can be consulted for reference.

Country entries

Each Country Entry begins with an **Introduction**, highlighting the main points of interest, and goes on to review, where appropiate: environment (geography, climate and natural history); people; culture, art and crafts; history; politics and economics.

The **Capital City** is then covered as this is invariably the initial destination of the traveller, and the biggest urban area, containing the bulk of services and amenities as well as some notable tourist attractions. The various **Regions and Routes** follow the way in which most visitors are likely to explore the country. As with the Capital City, for each location, there is coverage, where appropriate, of: history; places of interest; accommodation and places to eat; entertainment; other services; and transport both local and long distance.

For many of the countries in the region, a major attraction is the wildlife, and numerous visitors make this the centrepiece of their visit. For countries with exceptional wildlife resources, a section covering **National Parks and Reserves** is included. These attractions are cross-referenced from the places where they are located, or their access points, in the Regions and Routes sections.

Finally for each country there is **Information for visitors** covering: before you go; getting there; when you arrive; where to stay; food and drink; getting around; entertainment; communications; and further reading.

Before you go

Documents

● **Passports**

You will require a passport that is valid for the entire period of your travel, and with enough pages for the visas and stamps of the countries you are visiting.

Visas are required for many countries (see 'Information for Visitors' section in each country entry) and they will normally cost somewhere between US$20 and US$100; will require passport photographs, and occasionally letters of introduction from your embassy. It is sensible to arrange a supply of photographs before departing. Visa issue for some of the smaller countries can be speeded up by insisting that the visa is required in a hurry and recourse to petty bribery. Ask if there are any 'special express services' for which you are prepared to pay. A sum of US$10-30 will usually suffice – bear in mind that a day's delay will invariably cost more that this. Embassy officials of some countries are not paid, and you should view the bribe as a part of the payment for the visa.

● **Sensitive areas**

All countries have zones where there are military or communications installations which are off-limits. These are usually well sign-posted. You must avoid taking photographs, sketching or making notes, however innocent, in these areas. To take risks in this regard invites detention by the police and untold inconvenience.

Health

See main section, page 21

EXCHANGE RATES (1 AUGUST 1994)

	US$	£	DM
Burundi (Burundi Fr)	251.20	386.00	158.11
Comoros (CFA Fr)	542.80	834.08	341.65
Djibouti (Djib Fr)	176.49	271.20	111.07
Eritrea (Ethiopia Birr)	5.45	8.38	3.43
Ethiopia (Ethiopia Birr)	5.45	8.38	3.43
Kenya (Kenya shilling)	55.56	85.38	34.97
Madagascar (MG Fr)	3346.74	5142.60	2106.50
Mauritius (Maur Rupee)	17.67	27.15	11.12
Mayote (French Fr)	5.43	8.34	3.42
Réunion (French Fr)	5.43	8.34	3.42
Rwanda (Fr)	140.70	216.20	88.56
Seychelles (Rupee)	4.82	7.56	3.10
Somali (Shilling)	2601.93	3998.12	1637.70
Tanzania (Shilling)	508.48	778.26	318.79
Uganda (New Shilling)	929.58	1419.18	581.32
Zaire (Zaire)	1050.00	1613.43	660.89

Money

Traveller's cheques in US$ are a wise precaution. Almost every country (the exceptions are Somalia, Eritrea and Eastern Zaire) has an American Express representative where US$500 of traveller's cheques can be bought against payment by personal cheque and production of an American Express card.

Some cash is desirable, held in US dollars, with some in small denomination notes for requirements such as payment of airport departure taxes.

What to take

Travellers tend to take more than they need though requirements vary with the destination and the type of travel that is to be undertaken. Laundry services are generally cheap and speedy. A travelpack, a hybrid backpack/suitcase, rather than a rigid suitcase, covers most eventualities and survives bus boot, roof rack and plane/ship hold travel with ease. Serious trekkers will need a framed backpack.

Clothing of light cotton or cotton/polyester with a woollen sweater for evenings. Alternatively a jacket with lots of pockets, although not essential, can be useful. Comfortable shoes with socks as feet may swell in hot weather. Modest dress for women including a sunhat and headscarf. See hints in country sections.

● Checklists

Air tickets
Cash
Chequebook
Credit cards
Passport including visa
Passport photographs
Photocopies of main documents (keep separate)
Traveller's cheques

Toiletries

Comb
Concentrated detergent
Contact lens cleaner
Deodorant
Elastoplasts
Insect repellent
Nailbrush
Razor and blades
Shampoo
Sleeping tablets
Soap
Sun protection cream
Talcum powder
Tissues and toilet paper
Toothbrush
Toothpaste
Vaseline/moisturiser

Other

Ear plugs
Electric insecticide vapouriser and tablets
Electric plug adaptor
Eye mask
Folding umbrella
Inflatable cushion
Lock and chain (securing luggage at night)
Multiple outlet adaptor

Plastic bags
Sewing kit
Short-wave radio and batteries
Small torch plus batteries
Sun-glasses
Swiss army knife
Traveller's heating jug
Universal washbasin plug
Water bottle

Those intending to stay in budget accommodation might also include:

Cotton sheet sleeping bag
Money belt
Padlock (for hotel room and pack)
Soap
Student card
Towel
Toilet paper
Universal bath plug

Health kit

Antiacid tablets
Anti-diarrhoea tablets
Anti-malaria tablets
Anti-infective ointment
Condoms
Contraceptives
Dusting powder for feet
First aid kit and disposable needles
Flea powder
Sachets of rehydration salts
Tampons
Travel sickness pills
Water sterilizing tablets

If you are intending to visit the region on business, include:

Business cards
Notepaper, paper, envelopes
Pen, pencil, ballpoint
Calculator
Stapler, staples, paper clips
Address book
Laptop computer and printer

Getting there

Air

It is possible to fly directly to almost all the capitals in the region from Europe. The main exceptions are Somalia and Rwanda where international flights are currently suspended, and Eastern Zaire, which can only be accessed from nearby countries.

However, many travellers will find it cheaper and often more convenient to fly to one of the well-serviced capitals, and connect from there.

Nairobi (Kenya) has many regular, cheap flights. There is little advantage in accessing Uganda or Tanzania from here unless you travel on by road or rail. However, all the Indian Ocean Islands can be reached from Nairobi, and there are good air connections from there to Rwanda and Burundi.

Addis Ababa (Ethiopia) is a natural centre for Eritrea and Djibouti (and for Somalia when access resumes), and Ethiopian Airways runs a frequent and efficient network of services.

Antananarivo (Madagascar) is served by cheap flights by Aeroflot, and is a convenient centre for onward air travel to the other Indian Ocean Islands.

If you are booking flights while in East Africa or the Indian Ocean, it is a considerable advantage to have an American Express card, which is accepted by all international and domestic carriers, both for scheduled flights and charters. Other credit cards are also readily acceptable.

● Discounts

Specialist agents will arrange economical fares from Europe, typically for fixed arrival and departure dates, and for stays of a week or longer. Among the specialist agencies offering discounted fares are: **Australia:** *Africa Travel Centre*, 456 Kent St, Sydney, NSW 2000, T (02) 267-3084; *STA Travel*, 222-224 Faraday St, Carlton,

Melbourne 3053, T (03) 347-4711. **Canada**: *Travel Cuts*, 187 College St, Toronto, ON M5T 1P7, T (416) 979-2406. **New Zealand:** *Africa Travel Centre*, 21 Remuera Rd, Newmarket, Auckland 3, T (09) 524-5118. *STA Travel* 10 High St Auckland T(09) 309-9723. **UK**: *Africa Travel Shop*, 4 Medway Ct, Leigh St, London WC1H 9OX, T (071) 387-1211, F (071) 911-0830. *Key Travel*, 92-96 Eversholt St, London NW1 1BP, T (071) 387-4933, F (071) 387-1090. *STA*, 117 Euston Rd, London NW1, T (071) 937-0486, F (071) 388-0944. **USA**: *Swan Travel*, 400 Madison Av, New York, NY, T (212) 421-11010. *STA*, 48 East 11th St, New York, NY 10003, T (212) 477-7166. *Around the World*, 2241 Polk St, San Fransisco, CA 94109, T (415) 673-9950.

● **Note**

In this Handbook, further details on air links to and from each country, arrival and departure regulations, airport taxes, customs regulations and security arrangements for air travel are outlined in the relevant *Information for visitors* sections.

When you arrive

Bargaining

Bargaining is expected in the street markets. Start lower than you would expect to pay, be polite and good humoured, enjoy the experience and if the final price doesn't suit – walk away. There are plenty more shops. Once you have gained confidence, try it on the taxi drivers and when negotiating a room.

Beggars

A number of physically handicapped persons and destitute mothers with children are present in most large towns. Clearly many are genuine and heart-rending cases of need.

Street children, however, give pause for thought. In some places they request money to guard vehicles, in others they ask for money for food. Giving to one child usually leads the donor to be surrounded and harassed by a throng. A fight may arise as to who should guard a car. Giving a bank-note to one child with instructions that it should be shared will result in violence with the whole sum going to the strongest and most ruthless child. In some places street children are clearly organised by adults.

A constructive alternative is to make a donation to an organization such as Street Kids International which provides subsistence and skill-training programmes in an attempt to provide a long-term solution. There are collection points in the departure lounges of most international airports. They are always very grateful for donations of loose coins or notes.

Conduct

Great store is set everywhere by modesty and courtesy and an effort to dress smartly. Respect toward elderly people is particularly important. If you are making a formal visit to an official, for men a tie and neat dress (or safari suit) is a minimum; a jacket helps, and a suit is desirable. Women should dress soberly and smartly.

Confidence tricksters

Particularly common in Kenya, but also found elsewhere. Be wary of anyone with a hard-luck story, soliciting sponsorship (particularly educational) or offering a deal to change money at favourable rates.

Drugs

Illegal in all countries. There are considerable risks in using drugs even where a blind eye is turned to use by local people. In such circumstances you are extremely vulnerable to extortion.

Firearms

Cannot be imported or carried, without special permission.

Jetlag and travel

Time differences, unsociable airline hours and touchdowns at intermediate points all serve to upset sleep patterns. Most doctors are happy to prescribe some sleeping tablets to help establish a sleep pattern at your destination and on your return. Inflatable pillows can be a great comfort on long journeys, especially by bus. Earplugs and eyemasks can also help with sleep on journeys.

Mosques and Temples

Make sure you follow observances as indicated by attendants. Shoes will normally need to be taken off, and there may be restriction on visits by women.

Personal security

The overwhelming majority of countries in the region are very safe, and it is rare for a traveller to have a trip marred by theft or an unpleasant incident. Visitors in supervised parties, on excursions, or staying in large hotels are particularly safe.

Nevertheless, some countries have experienced collapse into chaos and turmoil. Somalia and Rwanda in late 1994 are current examples; Burundi is teetering on the brink, and Uganda had severe breakdown prior to 1986. If there is any hint of serious instability, such as a coup attempt with armed supporters of rival factions on the streets, you should immediately leave the country. If necessary you should seek help from your national embassy, or any international agency.

Otherwise, it is sensible to take reasonable precautions by not walking in deserted, unlit areas at night, and by avoiding places of known risk during the day. Snatch thieves can be problem, particularly in Kenya, and risks can be minimised by not wearing jewellry, expensive watches, or carrying cameras in busy public places. Waist pouches are very vulnerable as the belt can be cut easily. Carry money and any valuables in a slim belt under clothing. Always lock room doors at night as noisy fans and air-conditionsing can provide cover for sneak thieves. Be wary of leaving items by open windows in hotel rooms.

Police

If you have any items stolen, you must report the occurrence to the police, and keep a record of the incident number, the police station, and the name of the officer dealing with it. This is vital if you have lost official documents, or wish to make an insurance claim. The police will often insist that you report regularly to check on how the investigations are proceeding. These visits can be very time-consuming and tedious. Property is almost always never recovered, and it is often possible to use your discretion as to whether it is worth following things up.

For petty offences (driving without lights switched on, for example) police will often try to solicit a bribe, masked as an 'on the spot' fine. Establish the amount being requested, and then offer to go to the police station to pay, at which point you will be released with a warning.

For any serious charges, immediately contact your embassy or consulate.

Prisoners Abroad

Prisoners Abroad, a UK charity, was formed to help people who fall foul of the law in foreign countries, where sentencing can be much harsher than at home. If you or a friend do get into trouble, you can contact Prisoners Abroad at 72-82 Rosebury Ave, London EC1R 4RR, T 071 833 3467, F 071 833 3467 (F +4471 833 3467 if outside the UK).

Shopping

Be prepared to bargain. It is often the case that traders will attempt to overcharge tourists who are unaware of local prices. Ask about the prices of taxis, excursions, souvenirs, and so on, at your hotel.

Tipping

In large establishments a service charge is invariably added. Elsewhere it is optional, but a modest tip for courteous and attentive service is greatly appreciated by hotel and restaurant staff, most of whom enjoy very low pay.

Where to stay

Hotels

Places to stay vary between those used by well-heeled tourists, and are expensive, at around US$100 a day, self contained with air-conditioning, hot water and swimming pools, and those used by local people (and budget travellers) at under US$5 a day, which may comprise a simple bed, shared toilet and washing facilities, irregular water supply.

Some of the small beach hotels are in splendid locations and despite having only simple facilities are excellent value.

In the parks camping in either a tented camp or a campsite is often more atmospheric and cheaper than staying in one of the lodges.

A+ Over US$100 a night. International standards and decor, air conditioning, self contained rooms, swimming pool, restaurants, bars, business services.

A US$40-100. First class standards, air-conditioning, attached bathrooms, restaurants and bars, swimming pool.

B US$20-40. Tourist class, comfortable with air conditioning or fans, attached bathrooms, restaurant, bar, public rooms.

C US$10-20. Budget, fans, shared bathroom facilities.

D US$5-10. Guest house, no fan, shared bathroom, cold water.

E Under US$5. Basic guest house, simple bed, no soap or towels, no wardrobe, shared bathroom facilities, erratic cold water supply, no fans or mosquito nets.

Insects

Be prepared for mosquitoes, particularly, and other insects. Sleep under a net treated with insecticide where mosquitoes are a problem; smear exposed skin with repellent at night; use an electric heat-pad insecticide tablet vapouriser at night; buy a can of insecticide to spray your hotel room.

Food and drink

Food

Restaurants Given the variations in price of food on any menu our restaurants are divided where possible into four simple grades:

♦♦♦♦ Over US$10 for a meal. A 3-course meal in a restaurant with pleasant decor. Beers, wines and spirits available.

♦♦♦ US$5-10 for a meal. Two courses, not including alcohol, reasonable surroundings.

♦♦ US$2-5 for a meal, probably only a single course, surroundings spartan but adequate.

♦ Under US$2. Single course, often makeshift surroundings such as a street kiosk with simple benches and tables.

Bearing in mind the suggestions in the Health section (page 25) on food best avoided in uncertain conditions, a wide choice of African food still remains. For the less adventurous, Western style food is widely available.

Drink

The most common drink is tea. Coffee is generally available too. Bottled soft fizzy drinks are found even in small settlements and are safer than water. Alcohol is widely available. You will be expected to take your own supplies on camping safaris however. Bottled water is an essential part of every traveller's baggage. However avoid buying the cheapest brand in supermarkets as, although clean, it often doesn't taste so. Safari companies usually stock bottled water for taking on camping safaris – take plenty with you.

Safaris

General note One of the main reasons for going to East Africa is the wonderful wildlife. Seeing the animals – going on Safari – can be a most rewarding experience at any time of year. However, for the vast majority of travellers it is something to be prepared for, as it will almost certainly involve a degree of discomfort and long journeys. It is also important to remember that despite the expert knowledge of the drivers, they cannot guarantee that you will see any animals. When they do spot one of the rarer animals – a leopard or rhinocerous perhaps – their pleasure is almost as enjoyable as seeing the animal. To get the best from your safari, approach it with humour, look after the driver as well as you are able (a disgruntled driver will quickly ruin your safari), and do your best to get on with, and be considerate to your fellow travellers. The advice given below represents a general summary of more detailed information provided in the *National Park* section of each country entry.

Accommodation

Hotels and lodges These vary and may be either typical hotels with rooms and facilities in one building or individual bandas or rondavels (small huts) with a central dining area. Most have been built with great care and blend very well into the environment.

Tented camps A luxury tented camp is really the best of both worlds. They are usually built with a central dining area. Each tent will have a grass roof to keep it cool inside, proper beds, and verandah and they will often have a small bathroom at the back with solar heated hot water. But at the same time you will have the feeling of being in the heart of Africa and at night you will hear animals surprisingly close by.

Camp sites There are camp sites in most national parks. They are extensively used by camping safari companies (although they often have their own 'permanent' camp sites). They are often most attractively sited, perhaps in the elbow of a river course but always with plenty of shade. Birds are plentiful and several hours can be whiled away bird watching. Some campsites have attached to them a few bandas or huts run by the park where you may be able to shower. Toilet facilities can be primitive – the 'long drop', a basic hole in a concrete slab being very common. Away from the permanent sites, you will be expected to pitch your own two-man ridge hiking tent. Sleeping mats are provided but you must bring your own sleeping bag and pillow. Sleeping bags can be hired from most companies for a modest amount. A deposit is required. Check on availability at the time of booking and reserve if necessary.

Most camps are guarded but despite this you should be careful to ensure that valuables are not left unattended. Be careful about leaving items outside your tent. Many camp sites have troops of baboons nearby. They can be a nuisance.

If you are camping on your own, you will almost always need to be totally self sufficient with all your own equipment. The campsites usually provide running water and firewood. The extent to which you will have to be self sufficient with food varies from park to park.

Safari Companies

There are a huge number of companies offering safaris. These are noted under each country section. Safaris can be booked either at home or in the country concerned – if you go for the latter it may be possible to obtain substantial discounts. If you elect to book in the country avoid companies offering cheap deals on the street – they will almost always turn out to be a disaster and may be cheap because they do not pay National Park entrance fees.

Safaris do not run on every day of the week. Trips are often timed to end on a Thursday night. Thus a six-day safari will start on a Saturday, a four-day one on a Monday. In the low season you may also find that these will be combined. If you are on a four-day safari you can expect to join another party. This can be awkward as the 'six-dayers' will already have formed into a coherent group and you may feel that you are an outsider.

Food and drink

Standards at lodges and tented sites are the same as at normal hotels. Camping safaris usually have a cook. Food is wholesome and surprisingly varied. You can expect eggs, bacon and sausages and toast for breakfast, salads at midday and meat/pasta in the evening with perhaps a fruit salad for desert. The better companies will cater for vegetarians. Tea and coffee are on hand at all times of the day.

Insects are a fact of life and despite valiant attempts by the cook it is virtually impossible to avoid flies (as well as moths at night) alighting on plates and uncovered food. Notwithstanding this, hygiene standards are high.

Game drives

There are usually two game drives each day. The morning drive sets off at about 0700 and lasts until midday. The afternoon drive starts at about 1600 and lasts until the park closes (roughly 1830-1900). In addition you may have an early morning drive which will mean getting up well before dawn at about 0500.

Transport

It is worth emphasing that most parks are some way from departure points. Consequently if you go on a four-day safari, you will often find that two days are taken up with travelling to and from the park – leaving you with a limited amount of time in the park itself. You will be spending a lot of time in a vehicle.

On a more upmarket safari these will almost certainly be of the Toyota mini van variety accommodating about eight people. Leg room can be very limited. They will have three viewing points through the roof (the really upmarket ones will also have a sun shade). In practice this means that only one or two people can view out through the roof at each point – those in the cab will therefore have problems viewing on the opposite side as the view is usually impeded by legs.

Camping safari companies tend to use converted 10-ton lorries. Although very basic, they are surprisingly comfortable being well sprung (essential on some roads), with good leg room and large windows which fully open. Views of the animals on both sides of the truck are therefore good. They can be a little cramped if there is a full party of about 20 people.

Tipping

How much to tip the driver on safari is tricky. It is best to enquire from the company at the time of booking what the going rate is. However as a rough guide you should perhaps allow a sum of about US$5-7 per adult, per night (half this for a child). Always try to come to an agreement with other members of the group and put the tip into a common kitty. Again remember that wages are low and there can be long lay-offs during the low season. If you are on a camping safari and have a cook, give all the money to the driver and leave him to sort out the split.

What to take

Room is very limited in both mini vans and lorries. You will be asked to limit the amount you bring with you. There is very little point in taking too much clothing – expect to get dirty particularly during the dry season when dust can be a problem. Try to have a clean set of clothes to change into at night when it can also get quite cold. Comfortable, loose clothing and sensible footwear is best. Bear in mind that you may well travel through a variety of climates – it can be very cool at the top of the rift valley but very hot at the bottom. It is worth having warm clothing to hand in your transport as well as a bottle of water.

The other important items are binoculars – preferably one pair for each member of your party, a camera with a telephoto lens (you will not get close enough to the animals for a compact version) and plenty of film. Take twice as much as you think you will need. Film can be purchased at the lodges but it will cost you three times as much.

The Wildlife section in this *Handbook* will enable you to identify most animals. However you may wish to take a more detailed Field Guide. The Collins series is particularly recommended. The drivers are usually a mine of information – bear in mind though that Africans often have difficulty pronouncing Ls and Rs. The Lilac-breasted Roller comes out as Rilac-breasted lolla – and this can confuse. Take a notebook and pen as it is good fun to write down the number of species of animals and birds that you have spotted – anything over a 100 is thought to be pretty good.

Getting around

Air

There are quite good regional airlines. However flights can be delayed and sometimes get overbooked. It is essential to reconfirm return flights 48 hours before departure. Allow plenty of time at departure. There is often a considerable amount of bureaucracy to go through involving lots of queuing. Make sure that you have hard currency (prefarably dollars) for departure taxes, as local currency, travellers cheques and credit cards are not accepted. You will usually be able to change travellers cheques at the airport bank but beware of commission charges – you may have to change more than you thought. Beware of public holidays and the week before and after them. Flights are often hard to find during this period.

Rail

Where rail systems exist, and haste is not of over-riding importance, this mode is thoroughly recommended. It is safe, cheap, and comfortable, albeit slow and often subject to delays.

Road

Major road networks are serviceable almost everywhere, and improving all the time. However, rain can be torrential, and sealed roads are regularly washed away and unsealed roads rendered impassable. In the wet seasons road travel can be very difficult.

For long journeys travellers should try to use big buses and coaches as first choice, on grounds of both comfort and safety. Peugeot taxis (station wagons with seats) are fast, comfortable and fairly safe. Small buses and minibuses have poor safety records, and are uncomfortable and usually overcrowded.

Own Vehicle

If you are arriving with your own vehicle, you will require a Carnet de Passage issued by a body in your own country (usually the Automobile Association) affiliated to the Alliance International de Tourisme in Geneva. An International Certificate for Motor Vehicles (ICVM) and an International Driving Permit (IDP), again from the appropriate national body, are useful additions to the documentation and can expedite clearance at borders.

You should check with the embassy of any country you are planning to visit. In some cases sureties need to be lodged with the authorities on entry, and there may be special regulations relating to insurance.

Car Hire

In most countries your national driving licence will allow you to drive for a period, usually 3 months. Nevetheless, it is a wise precaution to obtain an International Driving Permit (see above).

For motoring in town, a driver is of limited advantage. However for touring or on long journeys a driver can be invaluable in terms of providing local knowledge, experience and resourcefulness. The cost of a driver is very modest, and when touring, the driver will lodge *Swahili* at night, that is, in simple local accommodation that he will find for himself.

Hitch-hiking

In the Western sense (standing beside the road and requesting a free ride) this is not an option. However, truck drivers and many private motorists will often carry you if you pay, and if you are stuck where there is no public transport you should not hesitate to approach likely vehicles on this basis.

Communications

Language

English is widely used and understood. French is used in Rwanda, Burundi, Eastern Zaire, Djibouti, and all the Indian Ocean countries. Swahili can be a help in Tanzania, Kenya and to a degree in Uganda.

Short wave radio guide

The BBC World Service (London) broadcasts throughout the region.

HEALTH INFORMATION

CONTENTS

The following information has been compiled for us by Dr David Snashall, Senior Lecturer in Occupational Health, United Medical Schools of Guy's and St Thomas' Hospitals and Chief Medical Officer, Foreign and Commonwealth Office, London.

The traveller to East Africa is inevitably exposed to health risks not encountered in North America or Western Europe. Because much of the area is economically under-developed, infectious diseases still predominate in the same way as they did in the West some decades ago. Poor living conditions, malnutrition and inadequate medical facilities contribute to poor health in the local population in some of these countries, but the traveller or tourist need not necessarily share their unfortunate circumstances. Some diseases, however, are no respectors of persons and in some cases, malaria for example, local populations have a degree of immunity which is completely lacking in visitors. It is a myth to suppose that true tropical disease has been largely eradicated from East Africa: mosquito control is nowhere near as good as it used to be with a consequent increase in malaria. River blindness, schistosomiasis (bilharzia) are still common, specific African types of HIV infection are rampant and infections with leprosy and tuberculosis still widespread. There are obvious health differences between the countries of East Africa and in risks between the business traveller who tends to stay in international class hotels in large cities, the back packer trekking from country to country and the tourist visiting the game parks. There is a huge variation in climate, vegetation and wildlife from desert to tropical isle, from the mountains of Ethiopia to the rain forests of Zaire all with their typical disease patterns. There are no hard and fast rules to follow, you will often have to make your own judgements on the healthiness or otherwise of your surroundings.

There are well qualified doctors in many but not all of these countries. Most of them speak English or French or other European languages; others may have Russian as a second language. The quality and range of medical care is extremely variable from country to country and diminishes very rapidly as you move away from cities, although some rural mission hospitals have been able to maintain good standards. On the mainland it is generally recognised that standards of medical care are declining for a variety of reasons. In some of the countries there are systems and traditions of medicine rather different from the Western model and you may be confronted with unusual modes of treatment based on local beliefs. This is not a reference to witch doctors who certainly still exist but whose services you are unlikely to have to call upon. In general you can be reasonably sure that local medical practitioners have a lot of experience with the particular diseases of their region. If you are in a city it may be worthwhile calling on your Embassy to obtain a list of recommended doctors.

If you are a long way from medical help, a certain amount of self medication may be necessary and you will find that many of the drugs that are available have familiar names. However, always check the date stamping and buy from reputable pharmacists because the shelf life of some items, especially vaccines and antibiotics is markedly reduced in hot conditions. Unfortunately drugs are imported into Africa from many parts of the world where quality control is not good and there have been cases of drugs being supplied with the active principle substituted by inert materials.

With the following precautions and advice you should keep as healthy as usual. Make local enquiries about health risks if you are apprehensive and take the general advice of European and North American families who have lived in or are living in the area.

Before you go

Take out medical insurance including the possibility of medical evacuation by air ambulance to your own country. You should have a dental check up, obtain a spare glasses prescription and, if you suffer from a longstanding condition such as diabetes, high blood pressure, heart/lung disease or a nervous disorder, arrange for a check up with your doctor who can at the same time provide you with a letter explaining details of your disability (in English, French or both, depending on the countries you are visiting). Check the current practice for malaria prophylaxis (prevention) for the countries you intend to visit.

For a simple list of 'Health Kit' to take with you, see page 12.

Inoculations

Smallpox vaccination is no longer required. Neither is cholera vaccination officially required, despite the fact that the disease is endemic in a number of East African counties. Only Rwanda requires a yellow fever vaccination certificate from all arriving travellers but Burundi, Djibouti, Ethiopia, Kenya, Madagascar, Mauritius, Réunion, Somalia, Tanzania, Uganda and Zaire may require yellow fever vaccination certificates from travellers who have entered from other, (especially Central and West) African, countries. Even though cholera vaccination is not officially required, nor recommended by the WHO because its effectiveness is limited, travellers are occasionally asked to produce vaccination certificates if they have been in cholera endemic areas such as parts of Asia or South America. If you are concerned this may be a problem but do not want to be given an ineffective vaccine, ask your own doctor for a cholera vaccination exemption certificate. The following vaccinations are recommended:

Typhoid (monovalent): one dose followed by a booster in one month's time. Immunity from this course lasts 2-3 years. Other injectable types are now becoming available as are oral preparations marketed in some countries.

Poliomyelitis: this is a live vaccine, generally given orally and the full course consists of three doses with a booster in under-developed regions every 3-5 years.

Tetanus: one dose should be given with a booster in 6 weeks and another at 6 months and 10 yearly boosters thereafter are recommended.

Children should in addition be properly protected against diphtheria, whooping cough, mumps and measles. Teenage girls, if they have not yet had the disease, should be given rubella (german measles) vaccination. Consult your doctor's advice on BCG inoculation against tuberculosis. The disease is still common in the region. Meningitis occurs in epidemic form in a belt extending across Sub-Saharan Africa during most dry seasons. It may be worth being vaccinated against this disease or indeed if there is an epidemic occurring locally in any of the countries.

Infectious hepatitis (jaundice)

This is common throughout East Africa. It seems to be frequently caught by travellers probably because, coming from countries with higher standards of hygiene, they have not contracted the disease in childhood and are therefore not immune like the majority of adults in developing countries. The main symptoms are stomach pains, lack of appetite, nausea, lassitude and yellowness of the eyes and skin. Medically speaking, there are two main types: the less serious but more common is *hepatitis A* for which the best protection is careful preparation of food, the avoidance of contaminated drinking water and scrupulous attention to toilet hygiene. Human normal immunoglobulin (gamma globulin) confers considerable protection against the disease and is particularly useful in epidemics. It should be obtained from a reputable source and is certainly recommended for travellers who intend to live rough. The injection should be given as close as possible to your departure and, as the dose depends on the likely time you are to spend in potentially infective areas, the manufacturer's instructions should be followed. A new vaccination against hepatitis A is now generally available and provides good immunity for many years but is expensive.

The other more serious version is *hepatitis B* which is acquired as a sexually transmitted disease, from a blood transfusion or injection with an unclean needle or possibly by insect bites. The symptoms are the same as hepatitis A but the incubation period is much longer, (up to six months) and there are more likely to be complications.

You may have had jaundice before or you may have had hepatitis of either type before without becoming jaundiced in which case it is possible that you could be immune to either hepatitis A or B already. Immunity can be tested before you travel with a blood test. If you are not immune to hepatitis B already, a vaccine is available (3 shots over 6 months) and if you are not immune to hepatitis A already then you should consider vaccination (or gamma globulin if you are not going to be exposed for long).

There are other kinds of viral hepatitis (C, E etc) which are fairly similar to A and B but a bit more difficult to diagnose correctly.

AIDS

This has had a devastating effect on the population of East Africa where it is mainly spread by heterosexual intercourse. Men and women are about equally affected. Some transmission will occur through infected blood transfusions. Screening for the HIV virus in blood transfusion is not always accurately performed or even performed at all, so in some East African countries blood transfusion represents a real risk, not only of infection with HIV but with hepatitis, malaria and a few other infections. The main risk to travellers is from casual sex, heterosexual or homosexual. The same precautions should be taken as when encountering any sexually transmitted disease. Female prostitution is common throughout East Africa and an alarmingly high proportion of the prostitute population is HIV positive. There may in addition be transmission, especially in the big cities and holiday areas, via intravenous drug abuse. The AIDS virus (HIV) can be passed via unsterile needles which have been previously used to inject a HIV positive patient but the risk of this is very small indeed. It would however be sensible to check that needles have been properly sterilised or disposable needles used. Hepatitis B is a much greater risk. Be wary of carrying disposable needles as Customs officials may find them suspicious, not so much in Africa but in Europe and North America. The risk of HIV transmission in a blood transfusion is greater than from dirty needles because of the amount of fluid exchanged.

Catching the AIDS virus (HIV) does not necessarily produce an illness in itself (although it may do). The only way to be sure if you feel you have been put at risk is to have a blood test for HIV antibodies on your return to a place where there are reliable laboratory facilities. The test does not become positive for many weeks and during those weeks the person who has caught the virus may well be extremely infectious.

Common Problems

Heat and Cold

Full acclimatisation to high temperatures takes about 2 weeks and during this period it is normal to feel a degree of apathy, especially if the relative humidity is high. Drink plenty of water (up to 15 litres a day are required when working physically hard in hot, dry conditions), use salt on your food and avoid extreme exertion. Tepid showers are more cooling than hot or cold ones. Large hats do not cool you down but do prevent sunburn. Remember that, especially in the mountains, there can be a large and sudden drop in temperature between sun and shade and between night and day so dress accordingly. Clear desert nights can prove astoundingly cold with a rapid drop in temperature as the sun goes down. Loose fitting cotton clothes are still the best for hot weather, warm jackets and woollens are essential after dark in some desert areas, and especially at high altitude.

Altitude

East Africa contains two well known mountains, Kilimanjaro and Mount Kenya both of which are over 5,000 metres in height, Addis Ababa in Ethiopia is about 2,400 metres, therefore the main risks to health are to high level trekkers and mountaineers.

Acute mountain sickness can strike from about 3,000 metres upwards and in general is more likely to affect those who ascend rapidly (e.g. by plane) and those who over-exert themselves. Teenagers seem to be particularly prone. Past experience is not always a good guide: the author, having spent years in Peru travelling constantly between sea level and very high altitude, never suffered the slightest symptoms, then was severely affected climbing Kilimanjaro.

On reaching heights above 3,000m, heart pounding and shortness of breath, especially on exertion, are almost universal and a normal response to the lack of oxygen in the air. Acute mountain sickness takes a few hours or days to come on and presents with heachache, lassitude, dizziness, loss of appetite, nausea and vomiting. Insomnia is common and often associated with a suffocating feeling when lying down in bed. Keen observers may note that their breathing tends to wax and wane at night and their face tends to be puffy in the mornings – this is all part of the syndrome. If the symptoms are mild the treatment is rest, painkillers (preferably not aspirin based) for the headaches and anti-sickness pills for vomiting. Oxygen may help at very high altitudes but is unlikely to be available.

The best way of preventing acute mountain sickness is a relatively slow ascent. When trekking to high altitude, some time spent walking at medium altitude, getting fit and getting adapted, is beneficial. On arrival at places over 3,000 metres a few hours rest and the avoidance of alcohol, cigarettes and heavy food will go a long way towards preventing acute mountain sickness. Should the symptoms be severe and prolonged it is best to descend to a lower altitude and re-ascend slowly and in stages. The symptoms disappear very quickly with even a few hundred metres of descent. If a slow staged attempt is impossible because of shortage of time, then the drug Acetazolamide (Diamox) can be used as a preventative and continued during the ascent. There is good evidence of the value of this drug in the prevention of acute moutain sickness but some people do experience funny side effects. The usual dose is 500 mgs of the slow release preparation each night starting the night before ascending above 3,000m.

Other problems experienced at high altitude are sunburn, excessively dry air causing skin cracking, sore eyes (it may be wise to leave your contact lenses out) and sore nostrils. Treat the latter with Vaseline. It is unwise to ascend to high altitude if you are pregnant especially in the first three months or if you have any history of heart, lung or blood disease, including sickle cell.

There is a further, albeit rare, hazard due to rapid ascent to high altitude – a kind of complicated mountain sickness presenting as acute pulmonary oedema or acute cerebral oedema. Both conditions are more common the higher you go. Pulmonary oedema comes on quite rapidly with breathlessness, noisy breathing, cough, blueness of the lips and frothing at the mouth. Cerebral oedema usually presents with confusion, going on to unconsciousness. Anybody developing these serious conditions must be brought down to low altitude as soon as possible and taken to hospital.

Rapid descent from high places will aggravate sinus and middle ear infections and may make bad teeth ache. The same problems are sometimes experienced during descent at the end of an aeroplane flight. Do not ascend to high altitude if you are suffering from a bad cold or chest infection and certainly not within 24 hours following scuba diving.

Despite these various hazards (mostly preventable) of high altitude travel, many people find the environment healthier and more invigorating than that at sea level.

Intestinal upsets

Practically nobody escapes this one so be prepared for it. Some of these countries lead the world in their prevalence of diarrhoea. Most of the time intestinal upsets are due to the insanitary preparation of food. Do not eat uncooked fish or vegetables or meat (especially pork), fruit with the skin on (always peel your fruit yourself) or food that is exposed to flies. Tap water is generally held to be unsafe or at least unreliable throughout East Africa, although this does not generally apply to the French islands. Filtered or bottled water is generally available and if your hotel has a central hot water supply this is safe to drink after cooling. Ice for drinks should be made from boiled water but rarely is, so stand your glass on the ice cubes instead of putting them in the drink. Really dirty water should first be strained through a filter bag (available through camping shops) and then boiled or treated. Bringing the water to a rolling boil at sea level is sufficient but at high altitudes you have to boil the water for longer to ensure that all the microbes are killed. Various sterilising methods can be used and there are preparatory preparations available containing chlorine or iodine compounds. Alternatively you can use one of the portable anti-microbial water filters or pump action sterilisers.

Pasteurised or heat treated milk is widely available in some of the countries as is ice cream or yoghurt produced by the same methods. Unpasteurised milk products, including cheese, are sources of tuberculosis, brucellosis, listeria and food poisoning germs. You can render fresh milk safe by heating it to 62°C for 30 minutes, followed by rapid cooling or by boiling it but this usually makes it taste horrible. Matured or processed cheeses are safer than the fresh varieties.

Diarrhoea – Diagnosis and treatment

Diarrhoea is usually caused by eating food which is contaminated by food poisoning germs. Drinking water is rarely the culprit. Seawater or river water is more likely to be contaminated by sewage and so swimming in such dilute effluent can also be a cause. Infection with various organisms can give rise to diarrhoea, e.g. viruses, bacteria (e.g. Escherichia coli, probably the most common cause), protozoa (amoeba), salmonella and cholera. The diarrhoea may come on suddenly or rather slowly. It may or may not be accompanied by vomiting or by severe abdominal pain and the passage of blood or mucus when it is called dysentery. How do you know which type you have and how to treat it?

If you can time the onset of the diarrhoea to the minute (acute) then it is probably due to a virus or a bacterium and/or the onset of dysentery. The treatment, in addition to rehydration, is Ciprofloxacin 500 mgs every 12 hours. The drug is now widely available as are various similar ones.

If the diarrhoea comes on slowly or intermittently (sub-acute) then it is more likely to be protozoal i.e. caused by an amoeba or giardia and antibiotics will have little effect. These cases are best treated by a doctor as is any outbreak of diarrhoea continuing for more than 3 days. Sometimes blood is passed in sub-acute amoebic dysentery and for this you should certainly seek medical help. If this is not available then the best treatment is probably Tinidazole (Fasigyn) 1 tablet 4 times a day for three days. If there are severe stomach cramps, the following drugs may help but are not very useful in the management of acute diarrhoea: Loperamide (Imodium, Arret) and Diphenoxylate with Atropine (Lomotil).

Any kind of diarrhoea whether or not accompanied by vomiting responds well to the replacement of water and salts taken as frequent small sips of some kind of rehydration solution. There are preparatory preparations consisting of sachets of powder which you dissolve in boiled water or you can make your own by adding half a teaspoonful of salt (3.5 grams) and 4 tablespoonfuls of sugar (40 grams) to a litre of boiled water.

Thus the lynchpins of treatment for diarrhoea are rest, fluid and salt replacement, antibiotics such as Ciprofloxacin for the bacterial types and special diagnostic tests and medical treatment for the amoeba and giardia infections. Salmonella infections and cholera can be devastating diseases and it would be wise to get to a hospital as soon as possible if these were suspected. Fasting, peculiar diets and the consumption of large quantities of yoghurt have not been found useful in calming travellers diarrhoea or in rehabilitating inflamed bowels. Oral rehydration has on the other hand, especially in children, been a lifesaving technique and it should always be practised whatever other treatment you use. As there is some evidence that alcohol and milk might prolong diarrhoea they should probably be avoided during and immediately after an attack. Diarrhoea occurring day after day for long periods of time (chronic diarrhoea) is notoriously resistant to amateur attempts at treatment and again warrants proper diagnostic tests. There are ways of preventing travellers diarrhoea for short periods of time by taking antibiotics but this is not a foolproof technique and should not be used other than in exceptional circumstances. Doxycycline is possibly the best drug. Some preventatives such as Enterovioform can have serious side effects if taken for long periods.

Insects

These can be a great nuisance. Some, of course, are carriers of serious disease – not just malaria and yellow fever but dengue, river blindness, onchocerciasis, leishmaniasis (Kala-azar) and sleeping sickness. The best way of keeping insects away at night is to sleep off the ground under a mosquito net and to burn mosquito coils containing Pyrethrum. Aerosol sprays or a "flit" gun may be effective but best of all are insecticidal tablets which are heated on a small mat which is plugged into the wall socket (if taking your own check the voltage of the area you are visiting so that you can take an appliance that will work). Similarly check that your electrical adaptor is suitable for the insecticide bearing plug.

You can use personal insect repellent, the best of which contain high concentrations of Diethyltoluamide. Liquid may be best for arms and face (take care around eyes and make sure you do not dissolve the plastic of your spectacles, watch strap etc.). Aerosol spray on clothes, ankles and hair deters mites and ticks as well as flying insects. Liquid DET suspended in water can be used to impregnate cotton clothes and mosquito nets. Wide mesh mosquito nets are now available impregnated with an insecticide called Permethrin and are generally more effective, lighter to carry and comfortable to sleep in than the traditional variety. Permethrin is now being incorporated into some repellent sprays. If you are badly affected by insect bites try cool baths or showers and anti-histamine tablets (take care with alcohol or driving). Local anaesthetics and antihistamine creams do not have a very good reputation. Weak corticosteroid creams may help but do not use if there is any hint of sepsis. You may find that careful scratching of all your bites in a controlled fashion once a day may help. Calamine lotion and cream have limited effectiveness.

Bites which become infected (commonly in dirty and dusty places) should be treated with a local antiseptic or antibiotic cream such as Cetrimide as should infected scratches. Skin infestations with body lice, crabs and scabies are unfortunately easy to pick up. Use Gamma benzene hexachloride for lice and Benzyl benzoate for scabies. Crotamiton cream (Eurax) alleviates itching and also kills a number of skin parasites. Malathion lotion 5% is good for lice but avoid the highly toxic full strength Malathion used as an agricultural insecticide. In grassland areas where animals graze, ticks are common and if you walk in such areas, get somebody else to examine your legs and body for these small spider-like insects after you have finished walking. Ticks can be removed with tweezers or by pinching them out carefully with fingers, doing it gently so that the head end disengages and is extracted with the body.

In some parts of Africa the jigger flea commonly burrows its way into people's feet causing a painful itchy swelling which finally bursts in a rather disgusting fashion. Avoid these by not going barefoot or wearing sandals and if they do become established have someone experienced winkle them out with a sterile needle.

Malaria

Malaria occurs with varying frequency throughout East Africa and the island countries. In some countries – Djibouti, Somalia, Tanzania, Uganda and Zaire it is very common indeed. Malaria remains a serious disease and you are advised to protect yourself against mosquito bites as described above and to take prophylactic (preventive) drugs where and when there is a risk. Start taking the tablets a few days before exposure and continue to take them six weeks after leaving the malarial zone. Remember to give the drugs to babies and children and pregnant women also.

There are various different kinds of malaria of which the most important is that due to plasmodium falciparum – important because it is fatal if treatment is delayed. Even the other kinds of malaria, though not usually fatal, cause serious disease.

The subject of malaria prevention is becoming more complex as the malaria parasite becomes immune to some of the more well known prophylactic drugs. This immunity on the part of the falciparum malaria parasite is commonly termed Chloroquine resistance and the phenomenon is now widespread throughout East Africa – the first cases were in Madagascar.

No presently used regime of malaria proplylaxis is one hundred percent effective – it is still possible to catch malaria when on prophylactic drugs but you will not catch it if you are not bitten by malaria carrying mosquitoes. These usually only bite in the evening and early morning so you should redouble your precautions at these times. Taking prophylactic drugs will reduce your chances of contracting malaria if you are exposed and may make the disease less serious. There is great controversy in the medical world at the present time as to the best drugs to use for prevention. European and North American opinions often vary and frequently clash with local African opinion. Be prepared for this. Seek expert advice before you travel and stick to it religiously. No drug regime, however complicated, will work if you do not take the tablets as prescribed. Two commonly used regimes are to take either Chloroquine plus Paludrine or to take a newer drug called Mefloquine which may in any case be more effective and suitable for short journeys, though not if you are likely to be pregnant.

If you do develop symptoms of malaria (high fever, shivering, severe headache, sometimes diarrhoea) seek medical advice immediately. If this is not available, then self treatment of Chloroquine resistant malaria can be tricky. Halofantrin is the drug most easily carried and self administered but side effects do occur and it must be taken with advice from a knowledgeable doctor at the time of prescription and in the right dosage.

Sunburn and heat stroke

The burning power of the sun in East Africa is phenomenal especially at high altitude. Always wear a wide brimmed hat and use some form of suncream or lotion on untanned skin. Normal temperate zone suntan lotions (protection factor up to 7) are not much good. You need to use the types designed specifically for the tropics or for mountaineers or skiers with a protection factor (against UVA) between 7 and 15. Certain creams also protect against UVB and you should use these if you have a skin prone to burning. Glare from the sun can cause conjunctivitis so wear sunglasses, especially on beaches or on snow.

There are several varieties of heat stroke. The most common cause is severe dehydration. Avoid this by drinking lots of non alcoholic fluid, adding some salt.

Snake bite and other bites and stings

If you are unlucky enough to be bitten by a venomous snake, spider, scorpion, lizard, centipede or sea creature, try (within limits) to identify the animal. In general the reactions to be expected are fright, swelling, pain and bruising around the bite, soreness of the regional lymph glands, nausea, vomiting and fever. If in addition any of the following symptoms supervene, get the victim to a doctor without delay: numbness, tingling of the face, muscular spasms, convulsions, shortness of breath or haemorrhage.

Commercial snake bite or scorpion sting kits may be available but are only useful for the specific type of snake or scorpion for which they are designed. The serum has to be given intravenously so is not much good unless you have had some practice in making injections into veins. If the bite is on a limb immobilise it and apply a tight bandage between the bite and body releasing it for 90 seconds every 15 minutes. Reassurance of the bitten person is very important because death by snake bite (or any other kind of bite) is in fact very rare. Do not slash the bite area and try and suck out the poison because this kind of heroism does more harm than good. Hospitals usually hold stocks of snake bite serum appropriate to the local area. Do not walk in snake territory with bare feet, sandals or shorts and if you are confronted by a snake, keep still until it slithers away.

If swimming in an area where there are poisonous fish such as stone or scorpion fish (also called by a variety of local names) or sea urchins on rocky coasts, use footwear. The sting of such fish is intensely painful and this can be helped by immersing the stung part in water as hot as you can bear for as long as it remains painful. This is not always very practical and you must take care not to scald yourself but it does work. Avoid spiders and scorpions by keeping your bed away from the wall and look under lavoratory seats and inside your shoes in the morning.

Other afflictions

Rabies is endemic throughout Africa. If you are bitten by a domestic animal, try to have it captured for observation and see a doctor at once. Treatment with human diploid vaccine is now extremely effective and worth seeking out if the likelihood of having contracted rabies is high. A course of anti-rabies vaccine might be a good idea before you go.

Dengue Fever is a problem in some East African countries but particularly in the Seychelles. It is transmitted by the bite of mosquitoes and causes a severe headache, fever and body pains. There is no treatment. You must just avoid mosquito bites.

Intestinal worms are difficult to avoid but on the whole fairly easy to treat and usually you can leave this until you come home. The more serious ones such as hook-worm can be contracted by walking bare foot on earth or beaches.

Filariasis causing such diseases as elephantiasis occurs in many East African countries.It is also transmitted by mosquitoes.

Hydatid disease is common in Ethiopia but can be avoided by keeping well clear of dogs which is good advice in any case.

Leishmaniasis causing a skin ulcer which will not heal occurs in many East African countries. It is transmitted by sand flies. A more serious form, visceral leishmaniasis or kala-azar affects mainly children, rarely tourists but occurs all over East Africa.

Schistosomiasis (Bilharzia) is a parasite harboured by snails which live in fresh water lakes. The parasites enter through the skin and are responsible for serious, ongoing disease in the gastrointestinal tract or bladder. Do not swim in freshwater lakes. Most lakes in East Africa are probably contaminated in this way whatever local people say.

Trypanosomiasis (sleeping sickness). This disease, essentially a brain infection causing drowsiness, is transmitted by a large, tenacious insect – the tsetse fly. This is a fly not always repelled by DET but very susceptible to Pyrethroid fly spray and Permethrin. The main risk is in game parks where these rather aggressive flies are common.

Prickly heat is a common itchy rash which can be avoided by frequent washing of clothes and body and by wearing non restrictive clothing. The regular use of talcum powder also helps. A bad attack of prickly heat can be most distressing. The best treatment is probably a couple of nights in an air conditioned hotel.

Athlete's foot and other fungal infections of the skin, especially the groin area, are best treated by exposure to sunshine and fresh air and the use of a preparatory preparation such as Tolnaftate. Regular dusting of the feet, armpits and groin is worthwhile.

Psychological disorders

First time exposure to countries where sections of the population live in extreme poverty or squalor and may even be starving can cause odd psychological reactions in visitors. So can the exceptional curiosity extended to visitors, especially women. Simply be prepared for this and try not to over-react.

When you return home

Remember to take your anti-malarial tablets for six weeks. If you have had attacks of diarrhoea, it is worth having a stool specimen tested in case you have picked up amoebic dysentery. If you have been living rough, a blood test may be worthwhile to detect worms and other parasites. If you have been exposed to bilharzia by swimming in lakes etc. check by means of a blood test when you get home but leave it for six weeks because the test is slow to become positive. Report any untoward symptoms to your doctor and tell the doctor exactly where you have been and, if you know, what the likelihood of diseases to which you were exposed is.

Further information

Further information on health risks abroad, vaccinations etc., may be available from a local travel clinic. If you wish to take specific drugs with you such as antibiotics, these are best prescibed by your own doctor. Beware however that not all doctors can be experts on the health problems of tropical countries. More detailed or more up to date information than local doctors can provide are available from various sources.

In the UK there are hospital departments specialising in tropical diseases in London, Liverpool, Birmingham and Glasgow and the Malaria Reference Laboratory at the London School of Hygiene and Tropical Medicine provides free advice about malaria, telephone no: 071 636 7921. In the USA the local public health services can give such information and information is available centrally from the Centres for Disease Control in Atlanta, telephone no: (404) 332 4559.

There are in addition computerised databases which can be accessed for specific destination, up to the minute information. In the UK there is MASTA (Medical Advisory Service to Travellers Abroad) telephone no: 071 631 4408, telex: 895 3474. fax: 071 436 5389 and Travax (Glasgow, telephone no: 041 946 7120, extension 247).

Further information on medical problems overseas can be obtained from the book by Richard Dawood (Editor) – Travellers Health, How to Stay Healthy Abroad, Oxford University Press, 1992, cost: £7.99. We strongly recommend this revised and updated edition, especially to the intrepid traveller heading for the more out of the way places. General advice is also available in the UK in "Health Advice for Travellers" published jointly by the Department of Health and the Central Office of Information available free from your UK Travel Agent.

REGIONAL INTRODUCTION

Contents

The countries covered by this handbook can be placed into four main groupings.

Firstly there are the great **Safarilands**, centred on the three former British territories of Kenya, Tanzania and Uganda.

The territories of the **Mountains,** surrounding the Rift Valley lakes in the centre of the continent, make up the second group. Comprising Burundi, Rwanda and the eastern part of Zaire, they were all at one time administered by Belgium.

To the north are the countries of the **Horn** of Africa comprising Ethiopia, Eritrea, Djibouti and Somalia. Italian influence has been strong here in all the territiories except the port of Djibouti which was a French colony.

Finally there are the six **Indian Ocean** territories. France has, at one time or another, administered all of these islands, and the cultural legacy is everywhere apparent.

Stability

Safe countries

The majority of territories (12) in the region can be visited with confidence. Circumstances can change suddenly, however, and if you have any doubts, a source of reliable up-to-date information is to contact the appropriate country desk of your national External Affairs Ministry or Foreign Office.

Safarilands

Tanzania has an enviable record of stability, and it has established a consensus among its many peoples that is allowing it to move peacefully toward a multiparty parliamentary democracy.

Kenya had some disturbances following the introduction of a multi-party system in 1993, and there have been odd incidents involving tourists. With normal precautions, however, it is quite safe to visit.

Uganda, since 1986, has made a remarkable recovery since the turmoil of the Amin period and its aftermath. It is not really safe to visit the north of the country, where there is still some unrest. Fortunately, the main tourist attractions are in the other, quite secure, regions.

Horn

Ethiopia has made great strides since the fall of the Mengistu regime, and political accommodation has been made with the main rebel groups. There are some remote areas where there is danger, and it is important to take local advice on this.

Eritrea, having made an amicable break with Ethiopia, is now peaceful for the first time in many years.

Djibouti, bolstered by its links with France, and the commercial interests in the port, has always been very stable.

Indian Ocean

Réunion is a Departement of France, and this status ensures tranquility.

Mayotte is also formally part of France, and stability stems from the link.

Mauritius has had a mature multi-party political system since Independence. It is a sophisticated middle-income country and very secure.

Seychelles has experienced its minor political dramas, but throughout these, although tourists might have been inconvenienced, they were never in any risk.

Comoros has had a struggle to establish stable and viable governments, but such upsets as have occurred have not inconvenienced visitors to any significant degree.

Madagascar looks to have come through the recent political impasse, marked by demonstrations and disturbances. Even in the most uncertain times, however, travellers were unaffected, welcomed as warmly as ever, and treated well.

Unsafe countries

At the time of writing (late 1994), four countries are effectively off limits to travellers. Circumstances will change with time, and up-to-date information can be obtained from the appropriate country desk of your national External Affairs Ministry or Foreign Office.

Mountains

Rwanda, a beautiful country (the "Switzerland of Africa") and for many years, well-organised and efficient, has plunged into the most horrific chaos. The death of the president, shot down in a plane returning from peace talks early in 1994, has sparked conflict and genocide between the country's two main groups, the Tutsi (15%) and the Hutu (80%). A massive exodus of over 1 million refugees to neighbouring countries, has taken place.

Burundi, Rwanda's neighbour to the south, and with an identical ethnic mix of Tutsi and Hutu, is teetering on the brink. Rivalry between the Tutsi and Hutu has, in the past, been bitter and violent. The multi-party election of 1993 resulted in the first president from the Hutu, the overwhelming majority, coming to power. Efforts to form a broadly-based government were shattered when the president was assassinated by Tutsi army officers late in 1993. A new Hutu president was installed only for him to perish in the same plane as the Rwandan president. In the context of the blood-letting in nearby Rwanda, it is touch-and-go as to whether Burundi can avoid the same fate.

Eastern Zaire has been swamped by over a million Rwandan refugees, many still settling scores in the emergency camps. Preoccupation with these problems effectively rules out any tourism. Although it is undoubtedly beautiful, with mountains, lakes, colonial charm in the lake resorts, and the attraction of the mountain gorillas, even prior to the Rwandan crisis travel in Eastern Zaire was problematical. The public sector in the east, cut off from the seat of government in the west of the country, has effectively collapsed. Public servants are not paid, petty corruption is rife, and there can be little confidence in the maintenance of law and order.

Somalia has sunk into a desperate civil war between rival gangs of armed clans that has proved beyond the international community to resolve. In recent months the ferocity of the conflict has abated somewhat, and the northern part of the country (the former British Somaliland) is reported to be have established its own government, claimed *de facto* secession, and to be reasonably peaceful. Nevertheless, it will be some time before it is safe to travel there.

Tourist Highlights

Wildlife

Quite superb natural attractions offer some very special experiences. In **Kenya** the Parks have a range of spectacular lodges, tented camps and ballooning. The big game in the Maasai Mara and the flamingoes on the Rift Valley lakes are unforgettable. **Tanzania** has perhaps the best wildlife in the region. The Serengetti, Ngorongoro Crater, Lake Manyara and the Selous reserve are outstanding. The lodges are not as luxurious as in Kenya, but they are improving, and there are some first-rate small establishments. Above all, the great game areas of Tanzania are less crowded than those in Kenya. **Uganda** has two fine Parks in Queen Elizabeth and Murchison Falls, and, at the current time, the only viable prospect for viewing mountain gorillas in the Virunga Mountains. **Rwanda**, before its current problems offered access to mountain gorillas, as did **Eastern Zaire**.

Madagascar has a unique range of wildlife, not as spectacular as on the mainland, but nevertheless quite fascinating.

The other **Indian Ocean** islands have a fine and plentiful selection of bird species on view, and the marinelife in clear waters by coral reefs is one of the highlights.

Climbing and Trekking

Both **Kenya** and **Tanzania** have challenging peaks in Mt Kenya and Mt Kilimanjaro. **Uganda** offers the prospect of the Ruwenzori Mountains and the Virungas, as well as Mt Elgon, which can also be climbed from Kenya. The Indian Ocean islands are hilly – most of them are volcanic – and there is excellent hill-walking to be enjoyed, particularly in **Réunion** and **Mauritius**.

Beaches

The coasts of the Indian Ocean islands are among the finest in the world. The **Seychelles**, though expensive, has quite suberb coasts, with splendid accommodation. **Mauritius** also offers good beaches, and can be enjoyed by all categories of traveller. The real bargain among the Indian Ocean islands, however, is **Madagascar**, where it is quite possible to stay inexpensively on marvellous uncrowded shores.

On the mainland, **Kenya** has an excellent range of beach hotels and some really fine places to stay. Diani beach south of Mombasa is miles of white sand, blue seas and palm trees. **Tanzania's** coast is less developed, but there are good beaches and simple, charming accommodation at Pangani and Bagamoyo. The two most popular islands off the mainland, Lamu in Kenya, and Zanzibar in Tanzania, both have good beaches.

Historical Interest

Olduvai Gorge in **Tanzania** has revealed the evolution of early man from fossils going back three million years, and many discoveries there have led to the site being called the "Cradle of Mankind".

Ethiopia has a recorded past going back two thousand years. There are the ancient cities of Axum, Gondar, and Harar, as well as a wealth of monasteries and early Christian churches.

Remnants of Shirazi settlements on the coast of mainland Africa and in the Comores islands are thought to date from perhaps as early as the tenth century. The marvellous old town sections of Mogadishu, Zanzibar, Mombasa, Bagamoyo and Lamu began to be developed somewhat later, from the end of the fourteenth century. They contain fine houses with balconies and verandahs around courtyards designed to stay cool by catching the ocean breezes, richly carved doors, elaborately decorated mosques, narrow winding streets of cobblestones.

The first European impact was with the arrival of the Portuguese in the fifteenth century. The strategic forts they built to consolidate their trading presence remain, most notably in Mombasa and Zanzibar.

The earliest settlers in Madagascar are presumed to have come from Indonesia before the fourth century, and to have established a civilisation in the interior in the highlands, and some archaeological finds date from these first migrants. As with all the Indian Ocean islands, however, the earliest structures effectively date from the beginning of French settlement which got under way from the start of the eighteenth century, and there are many fine public buildings, mansions, and plantation houses surviving from this period.

Of the eventual colonisers of the mainland, the Germans left by far the most impressive architecture, a distinctive style adapting European technique to local materials climatic conditions, and examples are scattered throughout what is now mainland Tanzania, Rwanda and Burundi. Railways were built by the British in Kenya and the Germans in Tanzania at the beginning of the twentieth century. The stations are still in use, and examples of the early rolling stock and locomotives survive. In the Horn of Africa, Italy has left its mark, with a Mediterranean style of architecture, which is most marked in Eritrea, but is also noticeable in Somalia and Ethiopia,

Traditional life and culture

Many of the mainland people have spectacular traditional lifestyles. The dress, decoration and ceremonies of the Maasai are perhaps best known. However, on mainland East Africa over three hundred distinct communities have their own traditional dress, fables and stories, dances, ceremonies, customs and styles of dwelling.

Modern life

Urban Africa has a style and excitement all its own. Intricately laid-out goods at markets. Gaudily painted, sloganed and crowded minibuses with swashbuckling conductors. Churches packed to overflowing. Weddings with exuberant processions. Vibrant local bars, dance halls and discos, with men in dress ranging from silk suits to baseball caps and lycra cycling shorts; girls in second-hand wedding dresses, mini-skirts, designer jeans, wide-brimmed hats; hair natural, straightened, plaited. Exciting music with sophisticated rhythms and delicate melodies.

Environment

Geography

The great **Safarilands** have extensive spreads of grassland, dotted with thorn trees, home to much of the wildlife. They are bordered by the great lakes of the Rift Valley, and Kenya and Tanzania have long coastlines on the Indian Ocean. All the countries have highland areas where the altitude makes for moderate temperatures, and peaks with glaciers and snow all the year round, despite the tropical location. Uganda and Kenya have extensive arid areas to the north.

The **Mountain** countries are clustered around lakes, and the terrain is hilly, covered with dense vegetation and cultivation, and the peaks often wreathed in mist.

Great areas of the countries of the **Horn** are arid. However, Ethiopia and Eritrea have extensive areas of highland with reasonable rainfall and vegetation and well able to support cultivation. Most of Somalia is desert, with some grassland dotted by scattered bushes and trees in the north and in the south, and mangroves along the coast.

In the **Indian Ocean**, the small islands are volcanic with sandy beaches, palms and invariably hills and mountains, covered in vegetation, rising up behind the coast. The exception is Madagascar, which is not volcanic, but is thought to have been at one time part of the mainland. It is mountainous with a narrow eastern coastal strip, central highlands and wide western plains. Most of the island is grassland with areas of woodland and some tropical rainforest.

Peoples

The population of the **Safarilands** is largely of Bantu origin, comprising several hundred identifiable communities. Most are settled cultivators, but there are many pastoralists, often nomadic. Kenya and Tanzania have Swahili people along the coast that are the product of intermarriage between Africans and Arabs. These two countries also have communities from the Indian sub-continent, mostly involved in commercial life and the professions. In Uganda, almost all Asians were expelled under Amin, and it is only now that they are beginning to return. Small communities of Europeans have remained in farming and business.

The **Mountain** countries of Rwanda and Burundi are riven by the division into the majority Hutu (80%) and the Tutsi (15%). The Tutsi are tall pastoralists from the north who traded cattle for land and established themselves as a land-owning class, dominating government, the armed forces and access to education. The Hutu are physically smaller, and engaged mostly in cultivation. Eastern Zaire is a mixture of mostly Bantu people.

The inhabitants of the **Horn** have distinctive features with a more Arabic appearance and, except in Ethiopia, lighter skin colour. In Somalia there are many pastoralists, following Islam. The Ethiopians have a strong cultivating tradition and their own form of Christianity.

Of the **Indian Ocean** territories, Seychelles, Réunion and Mauritius were uninhabited until the eighteenth century, when they were settled by Europeans. African slaves were imported to work on the plantations, and when slavery was abolished, people were brought in from the Indian sub-continent to provide labour. Comoros and Mayotte were first settled by peoples of Arabic origin at some stage between the tenth and fifteenth centuries, and later there was the arrival of Europeans, African slaves and some traders from Asia. Madagascar has people in the interior who are thought to have originated in South East Asia before the fourth century, and there has been immigration of people from mainland Africa.

The history of East Africa

Mainland

Archaeological sites at Olduvai Gorge in Tanzania and at Lower Awash river in Ethiopia suggest that man began to evolve in the Rift Valley more than 3 million years ago, and hunter-gatherer communities were established.

The area then experienced an influx of people from West Africa, which has become known as the Bantu Expansion, beginning around 500 BC. In the Horn it is thought that Cushtic immigrants came from Mesopotamia (now Iraq) around 300 BC. The newcomers were cultivators and pastoralists, and they began to change the pattern of subsistence away from hunting and gathering.

Contact with other areas began as sea-going traders arrived from the north, sailing down the East coast of Africa and coming from as far as India, China and South East Asia. A sprinkling of settlements by Islamic people from Shiraz in Persia (now Iran) were established along the coast from about 1000 AD.

European contact began with the arrival of the Portuguese who sailed round the southern tip of Africa and passed up the East coast from 1500 on. They set up fortified settlements to consolidate their trading presence, several of which remain, most notably Fort Jesus in Mombasa.

A struggle for dominance of these coastal strips began between Arab groups drawing support from the Persian Gulf and vying with the Portuguese for the trade in gold, ivory and slaves. By the end of the 17th century the Portuguese found themselves stretched to retain their hold in East Africa, and Fort Jesus fell to the Arabs in 1698. For most of the next two centuries Arab rule prevailed at the coast, and they began to penetrate the interior with caravans to capture slaves and ivory. These set out from Bagamoyo and Kilwa on the coast of present-day Tanzania, following routes that stretched over 1000 km to the Great Lakes and beyond.

In the interior, meanwhile, pockets of centralised rule and formalised social structures emerged, particularly to the west of Lake Victoria. In the Horn of Africa, the dynasty that traces its origins to Biblical times was establishing cities at Axum, Gondar and Harar.

European exploration began in the eighteenth century. A Scot, James Bruce in 1768-73 travelled from Suskin on the Red Sea up the Abara River to join the Nile. Lacerda, a Portuguese explorer travelled up the Zambesi in 1798-9, and then headed north to reach Lake Tanganyika. Burckhardt in 1809-17 journeyed from Massawa to Lake Tana and down the Blue Nile to Khartoum. The brothers Antoine and Arnaud Abbadie in 1837-48 pressed further south from Gondar in Ethiopia. Kraf and Rebmann, two Germans, in 1848 travelled from the Kenya coast up through the highlands. Richard Burton in 1854-5 managed an excursion from Zaila on the Red Sea coast to Harar in Ethiopia.

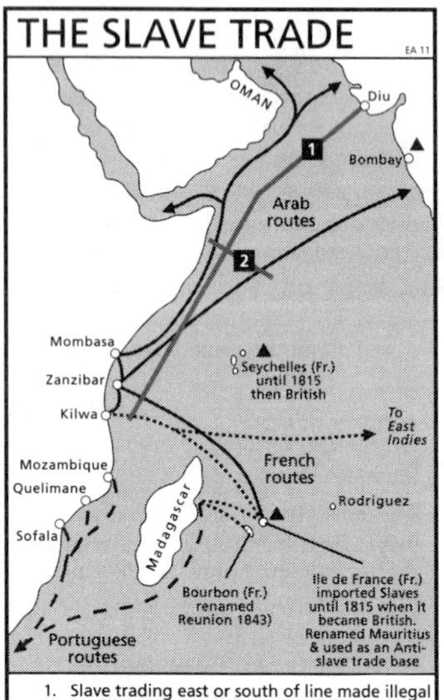

The origins of the White Nile (which joins the Blue Nile at Khartoum) began to exercise the imagination in Europe, and the source was eventually traced to Lake Victoria by Burton and Speke in 1860. The two great journeys by David Livingstone in 1858-64 and 1866-73 reached to Lake Tanganyika and beyond, and were followed by Stanley's expedition in 1874-77 which crossed the continent from east to west.

The activities of the explorers were followed by missionary activity and a campaign to end the slave trade. Although slavery was made illegal in 1873, it was some time before it was finally eliminated.

The European nations formalised their presence with the British occupying Kenya, Uganda and Zanzibar, and the Germans established themselves in what is now mainland Tanzania, Rwanda and Burundi. Eastern Zaire was part of the Belgian Congo. Eritrea and southern Somalia were Italian, and northern Somalia was British. The French held the port of Djibouti. Only Ethiopia retained its independence, holding off the attentions of Italy.

Economic progress had taken place in the interior as iron implements replaced more primitive stone and wooden tools, and cultivators accumulated farming knowledge. However, droughts, locusts, rinderpest and local

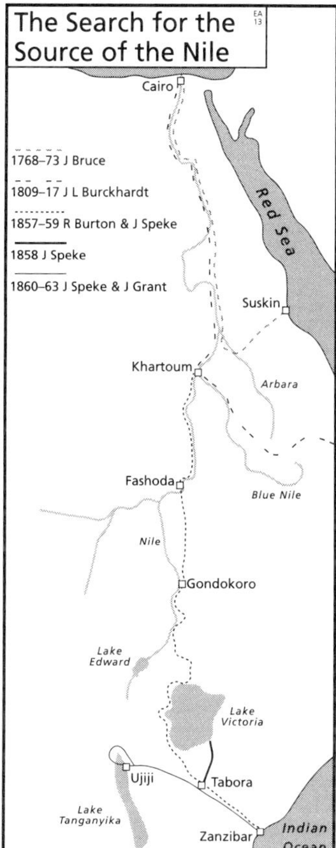

conflicts contrived to keep populations fairly stable. Progress accelerated with the advent of European occupation. Diseases were controlled, new crops introduced, roads and railways were built. Death rates fell, birth rates remained high and the population began a steady expansion. Living standards improved and significant sections of the population received basic education.

After WW1 the British took over the part of German East Africa that became Tanganyika, and Belgium absorbed Rwanda and Burundi. Italy occupied Ethiopia for a period from 1936-42. Settler presence increased, particularly in Kenya, and the Asian communities consolidated their positions in commerce and the skilled trades.

Nationalist movements began to emerge as significant political factors after WW2. Ethiopia federated with Eritrea in 1952. In Kenya, where there was by now a substantial settler population, there was an armed conflict in the 1950s (the Mau Mau uprising) over land grievances and generally in support of self-determination. Most countries obtained their independence in the early 1960s, although Djibouti did not break from France until 1977.

Tanzania was created when Tanganyika formed a union with Zanzibar in 1964. The immediate post-Independence period typically saw the establishment of single-party regimes, and in many cases government was unstable (although Tanzanian, Kenya and Djibouti have proved exceptions). In Uganda, Somalia, Rwanda, Burundi, and Ethiopia there have been disastrous collapses of peace and security.

Economic development was pursued by the adoption of socialist development strategies with heavy reliance on the public sector. A deceleration of economc progress followed, and in the 1980s most countries reversed their economic policies and by 1994 had either undertaken, or were planning, multiparty elections.

Indian Ocean

The East African coast was visited by mariners from the Red Sea area after about 3000 BC, and by 1000 BC the Phonecians had begun trading with the mainland settlements. Whether they visited the Comores or Madagascar is not known – certainly the islands appear to have been uninhabited at this stage.

At some time before the fourth century AD peoples thought to have originated in Indonesia arrived and settled in Madagascar. The exact route they took is not clear, but it is likely that they followed the coastline round the Bay of Bengal, the Arabian Sea, and then south down the African coast.

From perhaps the seventh century AD, and certainly after the tenth century, Arab migrations from Shiraz in Persia led to settlements in the Comores and Madagascar. Arab seafarers almost certainly sighted the Seychelles and the Mascarenes (Mauritius, Réunion and Rodrigues) but did not settle.

The Portuguese were the first European visitors following the rounding of the south tip of Africa by Bartholomew Diaz in 1487. Portuguese settlements followed on the mainland, but there was no attempt to establish a presence on the islands.

The Dutch and the British began to frequent the Indian Ocean from about 1600, passing through on their way to India and the Far East. The Dutch established a post on Mauritius in 1638. In the same year France claimed Réunion and in 1643 established a community in Madagascar. The Dutch left Mauritius in 1674 to concentrate their interests on southern Africa. A French settlement was set up in Rodrigues in 1691, Mauritius was claimed in 1715 and the Seychelles in 1756.

With valuable cargoes passing through to the Indies, pirates began operating in the area, and several locations, most notably Ile Ste Marie off the east coast of Madagascar, became pirate bases.

Rivalry in Europe led Britain to attack French possessions in the Indian Ocean, and by 1810 Britain had occupied all three Mascarene islands, although Réunion was returned to France in 1815. These losses caused France to turn its attention to the Comoros, (occupied in 1841), and to redouble its efforts to establish control over Madagascar in the face of local resistance, which was finally achieved in 1896.

The opening of the Suez Canal in 1869 led to the end of the strategic role of the islands as watering and provisioning points on the route to the Indies. Settlement concentrated on plantations to grow spices and sugar for export to Europe, using slaves until 1873, and contracted labour from India thereafter.

The steady introduction of education led to pressure for self-determination. Madagascar became independent in 1960 with most of the other French possessions in Africa, Mauritius in 1968, the Comoros in 1975 and Seychelles in 1976. Réunion and Mayotte (one of the islands of the Comores) opted to remain with France.

Mauritius has been outstandingly successful as an independent nation, achieving a rapid rate of economic development with liberal economic policies and maintaining a multi-party democracy. Réunion and Mayotte have prospered through their links with France. Seychelles has taken advantage of its location to establish a successful tourist industry, despite some political instability. Madagascar and Comoros have found it difficult to establish secure, representative government, and development has been hampered by socialist development strategies. There are now moves to liberalise these economies, and multi-party elections have recently taken place.

KENYA

Contents

Maps

Introduction

Any visit to Kenya will be amply rewarded as there is such a diverse range of things to do and places to see. Kenya's coastline is beautiful, with miles of white sands, and a warm sea protected from sharks by a coral reef just off the coast. The Kenya highlands are always popular with visitors interested in a more energetic holiday, particularly Mount Kenya. However, it is probably the wildlife for which Kenya is most famous, particularly the big 5 (lions, elephants, buffalo, leopard and rhino). Kenya is the most popular tourist vacation spot in East Africa and tourism has become Kenya's largest source of foreign exchange. Its long experience with visitors means the country has something to offer all types of travellers. The importance of tourism to the Kenyan economy is reflected in the quality of services: throughout the country there are first class hotels, and good quality western-style food is easy to find.

With common sense Kenya is a safe place to travel. A recent spate of disturbances has caused worry in people's minds, but the country has not experienced much trouble since 1992 and appears to have overcome its political problems for the time being.

Exchange Rate Aug 1994 KSh 55.56 = US$1

Environment

Geography

Kenya is 580,367 sq km in area with the equator running right through the middle. Physically, the country is made up of a number of different zones. The Great Rift Valley runs from the N to the S of the country and in places is 65 km across, bounded by escarpments 600-900m high. This is probably the most spectacularly beautiful part of country, dotted with soda lakes teeming with flamingos. To the east of the Rift Valley lies the Kenya highlands with Mount Kenya, an extinct volcano, which at 5,199m is Africa's second highest mountain. This is the most fertile part of the country, particularly the lower slopes of the mountain range. Nairobi sits at the southern end of the central highlands. The N of Kenya is arid, bounded by Sudan and Ethiopia. To the W lies Uganda and the fertile shores around Lake Victoria. Further S, the land turns into savannah which typifies Kenya and is mainly used for grazing.

The Indian Ocean coast to the east of the country runs for 480km and there is a narrow strip of fertile land all along it. Beyond this, the land becomes scrubland and semi-arid. Somalia borders Kenya in the NE, and this is also a fairly arid area.

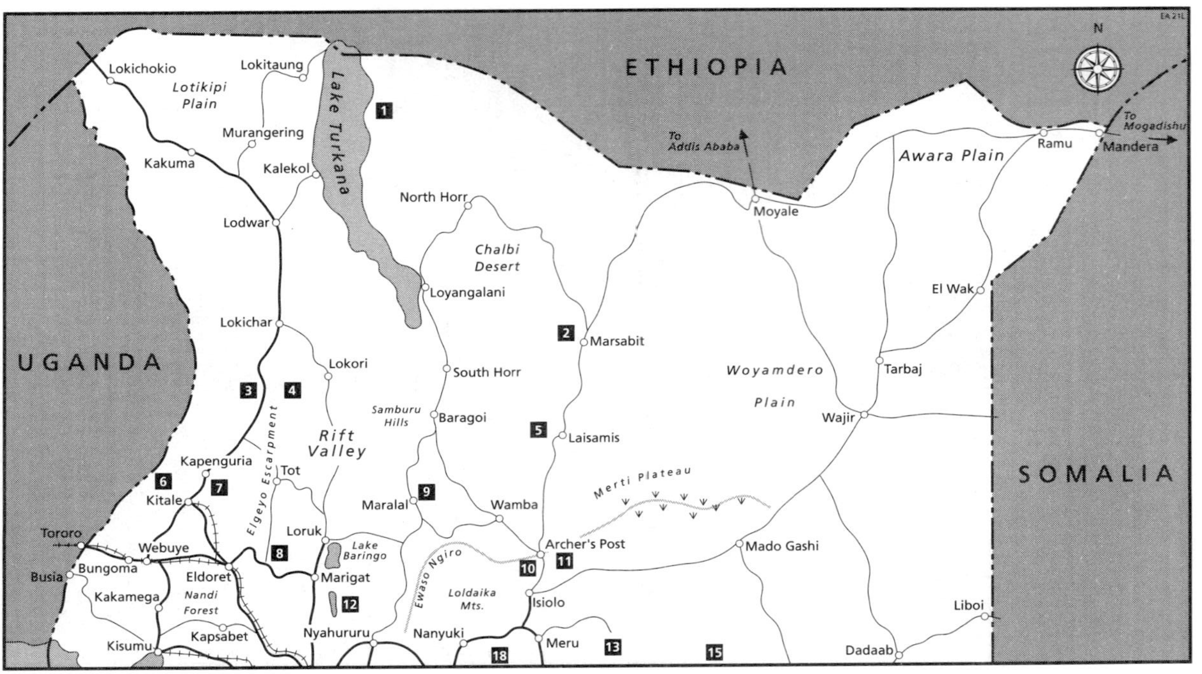
N
ETHIOPIA
SOMALIA
UGANDA
Lokichokio
Lotikipi Plain
Lokitaung
Lake Turkana
Murangering
Kakuma
Kalekol
Lodwar
North Horr
Chalbi Desert
Loyangalani
To Addis Ababa
Moyale
Awara Plain
Ramu
To Mogadishu
Mandera
El Wak
Lokichar
Lokori
Marsabit
South Horr
Woyamdero Plain
Tarbaj
Wajir
Samburu Hills
Baragoi
Rift Valley
Laisamis
Elgeyo Escarpment
Kapenguria
Tot
Merti Plateau
Kitale
Maralal
Wamba
Tororo
Webuye
Loruk
Lake Baringo
Archer's Post
Mado Gashi
Busia
Bungoma
Eldoret
Ewaso Ngiro
Marigat
Kakamega
Nandi Forest
Loldaika Mts.
Isiolo
Liboi
Kapsabet
Nyahururu
Nanyuki
Meru
Kisumu
Dadaab
1
2
3
4
5
6
7
8
9
10
11
12
13
15
18

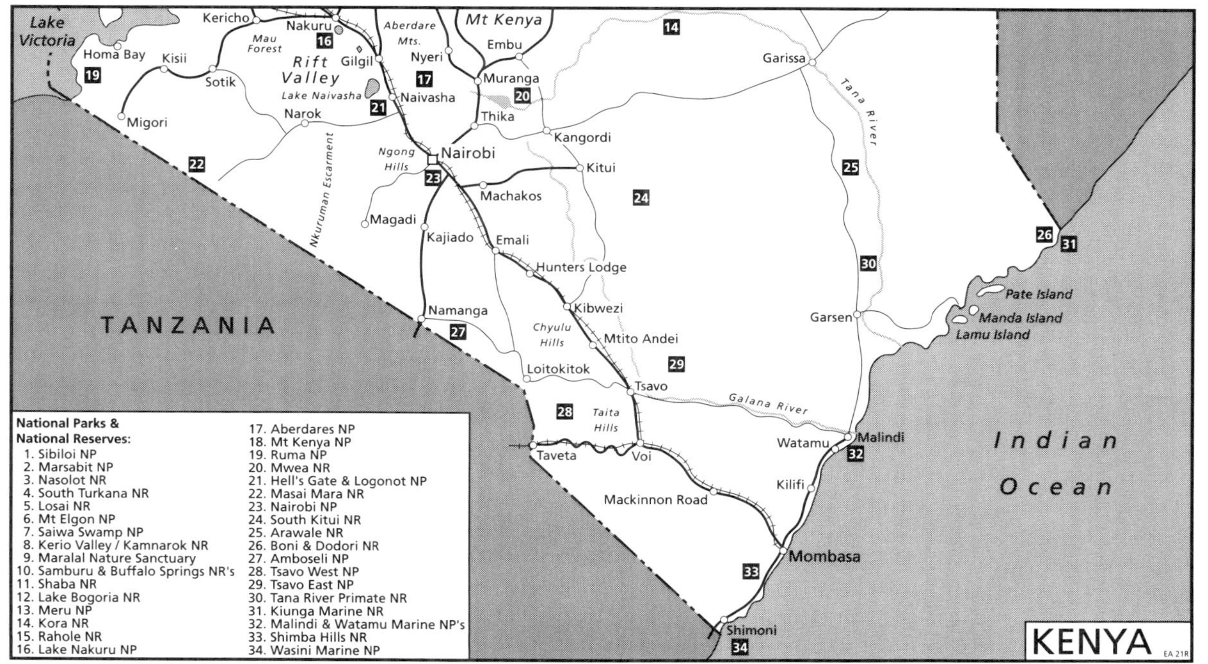
KENYA
EA 21R
Indian Ocean
TANZANIA
Lake Victoria
Pate Island
Manda Island
Lamu Island
Tana River
Galana River
Mt Kenya
Aberdare Mts.
Rift Valley
Lake Naivasha
Mau Forest
Ngong Hills
Nkuruman Escarment
Chyulu Hills
Taita Hills
Malindi
Mombasa
Watamu
Kilifi
Shimoni
Garsen
Garissa
Tsavo
Voi
Mackinnon Road
Mtito Andei
Kibwezi
Hunters Lodge
Emali
Kitui
Kangordi
Machakos
Nairobi
Thika
Muranga
Embu
Nyeri
Naivasha
Gilgil
Nakuru
Narok
Kericho
Sotik
Kisii
Homa Bay
Migori
Magadi
Kajiado
Namanga
Loitokitok
Taveta
National Parks &
National Reserves:
1. Sibiloi NP
2. Marsabit NP
3. Nasolot NR
4. South Turkana NR
5. Losai NR
6. Mt Elgon NP
7. Saiwa Swamp NP
8. Kerio Valley / Kamnarok NR
9. Maralal Nature Sanctuary
10. Samburu & Buffalo Springs NR's
11. Shaba NR
12. Lake Bogoria NR
13. Meru NP
14. Kora NR
15. Rahole NR
16. Lake Nakuru NP
17. Aberdares NP
18. Mt Kenya NP
19. Ruma NP
20. Mwea NR
21. Hell's Gate & Logonot NP
22. Masai Mara NR
23. Nairobi NP
24. South Kitui NR
25. Arawale NR
26. Boni & Dodori NR
27. Amboseli NP
28. Tsavo West NP
29. Tsavo East NP
30. Tana River Primate NR
31. Kiunga Marine NR
32. Malindi & Watamu Marine NP's
33. Shimba Hills NR
34. Wasini Marine NP

Climate

Kenya's different altitudes mean that climate varies enormously around the country. Probably the pleasantest climate is in the central highlands and the Rift Valley, though the valley floor can become extremely hot and is relatively arid. Mount Kenya and Mount Elgin both become quite cool above 1,750m and the top of Mount Kenya is snow-covered. Mount Kenya and the Aberdares are the country's main water catchment areas.

Western Kenya and the area around Lake Victoria is generally hot around 30-34°C all year with high humidity and rainfall evenly spread throughout the year. Most rain here tends to fall in the early evening.

The country is covered in semi-arid bushland and deserts throughout the N and east of the country. Temperatures can go up to 40°C during the day and fall down to 20°C at night in the desert. Rainfall in this area is sparce, between 250mm and 500mm per annum.

The coastal belt is hot and humid all year round, though the heat is tempered by sea breezes. Rainfall varies from as little as 20mm in Feb to 240mm in May. The average temperature varies little throughout the year but is hottest in Nov and Dec at about 30°C.

Flora and fauna

Kenya is justifiably famous for its flora and fauna. In areas of abundant rainfall, the country is lush, supporting a huge range of plants, and the wide variety of geographical zones houses a corresponding diversity of flora. The majority of the country is covered in savannah-type vegetation characterised by the acacia. The slopes of Mount Elgon and Mount Kenya are covered in thick evergreen temperate forest from about 1,000m to 2,000m; then to 3,000m the mountains are bamboo forest; above this level the mountains are covered with groundsel trees and giant lobelias. Mangroves are prolific in the coastal regions.

Kenya's wildlife is as diverse as its flora. On the savannahs you will be able to see the 'Big 5' of lion, leopard, buffalo, elephant and rhino as well as cheetah, gazelle, giraffes, zebra, wildebeest, wart-hog and a host of other species. Apart from these animals, there are flamingos on the soda lakes and crocodiles in other waterways, many species of monkeys in the forests both by the coast or inland the amazingly tame rock hyraxes in Hell's Gate and many more. The birdlife is equally as varied including ostriches, vulture and many types of eagle and even parrots up in Mount Kenya.

History

Earliest times

There is evidence that the forefathers of *Homo sapiens* lived in this part of East Africa 10-12,000 years ago. In the 1960s the Leakeys, Kenyan-born Europeans, began a series of archaeological expeditions in East Africa, particularly around Lake Turkana in the N. During these excavations they traced man's biological and cultural development back from about 50,000 years to 1.8 million years ago. They discovered the skull and bones of a 10,000 year old fossil which they named *Homo habilis* who they argued was an ancestor to modern man. Since the 1970s, Richard Leakey, Louis and Mary Leakey's son, has uncovered many more clues as to the origins of mankind and how they lived, unearthing some early Stone Age tools. These findings have increased our knowledge of the beginnings of earth, and establish the Rift Valley as the Cradle of Mankind. Many of the fossils are now in the National Museum of Narobi. Little evidence exists as to what happened between the periods 10,000 -12,000 BC and 5,000 -3,000 BC except that *Homo erectus* stood upright and moved farther afield spreading out over much of Kenya and Tanzania. It is known that from 5,000 - 3,000 BC Kenya was inhabited by hunter-gatherer groups, the forefathers of the Boni, Wata and Wariangulu people.

Bantu expansion

Later still began an influx of peoples from all over Africa which lasted until about the 19th century. The first wave came from Ethiopia when the tall, lean Cushitic people gradually moved into Kenya over the second millennium BC settling around Lake Turkana in the N. These people practised mixed agriculture, keeping animals and planting crops. There is still evidence of irrigations systems and dams and wells built by them in the arid northern parts of Kenya. As the climate changed, getting hotter and drier, they were forced to move on to the hills above Lake Victoria.

The Eastern Cushitics, also pastoralists, moved into central Kenya around 3 thousand years ago. This group assimilated with other agricultural communities and spread across the land. The rest of Kenya's ancestors are said to have arrived between 500 BC and 500 AD with Bantu-speaking people arriving from West Africa and Nilotic speakers from Southern Sudan attracted by the rich grazing and plentiful farmland.

The Kenyan coast attracted people from other parts of the world as well as Africa. The first definite evidence of this is a description of Mombasa by the Greek Diogenes in 110 AD on his return to Egypt. He describes trading in cloth, tools, glass, brass, copper, iron, olives, weapons, ivory and rhinoceros horn at Mombasa. In 150 AD Ptolemy included details of this part of the coast in his Map of the World. It was to be another few hundred years before the arrival of Islam on the coast and the beginning of its Golden Age.

Arab and Persian settlers developed trade routes extending across the Indian Ocean into China establishing commercial centres all along the East Africa coast. They greatly contributed to the arts and architecture of the region and built fine mosques, monuments and houses. Evidence of the prosperity of this period still are evident in the architecture in parts of Mombasa, Malindi and Lamu and particularly in the intricate and elegant balconies outside some of the houses in the old part of Mombasa. All along this part of the coast, intermarriage between Arabs and Africans resulted in a harmonious partnership of African and Islamic influences personified in the Swahili people. This situation continued peacefully until the arrival of the Portuguese in the 16th century.

Portuguese

Mombasa was known to be rich in both gold and ivory making it a tempting target for the Portuguese. Vasco da Gama, in search of a sea route to India, arrived in Mombasa in 1498. He was unsuccessful at docking there at this time, but 2 years later sacked the town. For many years the Portuguese returned to plunder Mombasa until finally they occupied the city. There followed one hundred years of harsh colonial rule from their principle outpost at Fort Jesus overlooking the entrance to the old harbour. Arab resistance to Portuguese control of the Kenya coast was strong, but they were unable to defeat the Portuguese who managed to keep their foothold in East Africa.

The end of Portuguese control began in 1696 with a siege of Fort Jesus. The struggle lasted for nearly 2½ years when the Arabs finally managed to scale the fortress walls. By 1720, the last Portuguese garrison had left the Kenya coast. The Arabs remained in control of the East African coast until the arrival of the British and Germans in the late 19th century. In this period the coast did not prosper as there were destructive in-

The Uganda Railway

What it will cost no words can express
What is its object no brain can suppose
Where it will start from no one can guess;
Where it is going to nobody knows;

What is the use of it none can conjecture;
What it will carry there's none can define;
And in spite of George Curzon's superior lecture,
It clearly is naught but a lunatic line.

London Magazine *Truth* 1896

trigues amongst rival Arab groups and this hampered commerce and development in their African territories.

The British influence in Kenya began quite casually following negotiations between Captain Owen, a British Officer, and the Mazruis who ruled the island of Mombasa. The Mazruis asked for British protection from attack by other Omani interests in the area. Owen granted British protection in return for the Mazruis abolishing slavery. He sent to London and India for ratification of the treaty, posted his first officer together with an interpreter, 4 sailors and 4 marines and thus began the British occupation of Kenya. At this time, interest in Kenya was limited to the coast and then only as part of an evangelical desire to eliminate slavery. However, fifty years later attitudes towards the country changed.

In 1887 the Imperial British East Africa Company (IBEAC) founded its headquarters in Mombasa with the purpose of developing trade. From here it sent small groups of officials into the interior to negotiate with tribesmen. One such officer Frederick Lugard made alliances with the Kikuyu en route to Uganda.

The final stage in British domination over Kenya was the development of the railway. The IBEAC and Lubard believed a railway was essential to keep its posts in the interior of Kenya supplied with essential goods, and also believed it was necessary in order to protect Britian's position in Uganda. Despite much opposition in London, the railway was built at a cost of £5mn.

Nairobi was created as the centre of operations as a convenient stopping point midway between Mombasa and Lake Victoria where a water supply was available. Despite many problems, the railway was completed in 1901 and was the catalyst to British settlers moving into Kenya as well as to African resistance to the loss of their lands.

From 1895 to 1910 the government encouraged white settlers to cultivate land in the central highlands of the country around the railway, particularly the fertile western highlands. It was regarded as imperative to attract white settlers to increase trade and thus increasing the usefulness of the railway. The Maasai bitterly opposed being moved from their land but years of war combined with the effects of cholera, smallpox, rinderpest and famine had considerably weakened their resistance. The Maasai were moved into 2 reserves on either side of the railway, but soon had to move out of the one to the N as the White settlers pressed for more land. Kikuyu land was also occupied by white settlers as they moved to occupy the highlands around the western side of Mount Kenya.

The number of Europeans in Kenya steadily increased from only about 3,000 at the beginning of World War I to 80,000 by the early 1950s. The rise in numbers of people entering Kenya was helped by the British government's decision to offer war veterans land in the Kenya highlands. In order to increase the pool of African labour for white settler development (most Africans were unwilling to work for the Europeans voluntarily), hut taxes and other levies were imposed. Furthermore, Africans were prevented from growing coffee, the most lucrative crop, on the grounds that there was a risk of coffee berry disease with lots of small producers. Thus many Africans were forced to become farm labourers or to migrate to the towns in search of work to pay the taxes. By the 1940s the European farmers had prospered in cash crop production.

Independence

As the number of Europeans moving into the country increased, so too did African resistance to the loss of their land and there was organised African political activity against the Europeans as early as 1922. The large number of tribesmen, particularly Kikuyu, moving into the growing capital Nairobi formed a political community supported by sections of the influential Asian community. This led to the formation of the East African Association, the first pan-Kenyan nationalist movement led by Harry Thuku. His arrest and the subsequent riots were the first challenge to the settlers and the colonial regime.

Jomo Kenyatta led a campaign to bring Kikuyu land grievances to British notice. In 1932 he gave evidence to the Carter Land Commission in London which had been set up to adjudicate on land interests in Kenya, but without success. During the war years, all African political associations were banned and there was no voice for the interests of black Kenyans. At the end of the war, thousands of returning soldiers returned demanding to be heard, and discontent grew. Kenyatta had remained abroad travelling in Europe and the Soviet Union and returned in 1946 a formidable statesman.

In 1944 an African nationalist organisation, the Kenya African Union (KAU) was formed to press for African access to settler occupied land. The KAU was primarily supported by the Kikuyu. In 1947 Kenyatta became president of KAU and was widely supported as the one man who could unite Kenya's various political and ethnic factions.

At the same time as the KAU were looking for political change, a Kikuyu group, Mau Mau, began a campaign of violence. In the early 1950s the Mau Mau began terrorist activities, and several white settlers were killed as well as thousands of Africans thought to have collaborated with the colonial government.

The British authorities declared a state of emergency in 1952 in the face of the Mau Mau campaign and the Kikuyu were herded into 'protected villages' surrounded by barbed wire and people were forbidden to leave during the hours of darkness. From 1952 to 1956 the terrorist campaign waged against colonial authority resulted in the deaths of 32 European civilians and 13,000 Africans. Over 20,000 Kikuyu were placed in detention camps before the Mau Mau finally were defeated. The British imprisoned Kenyatta in 1953 for 7 years for alleged involvement in Mau Mau activities, and banned the KAU, though it is dubious whether Kenyatta had any influence over Mau Mau activities.

The cost of the supressing Mau Mau, the force of the East African case, and world opinion, convinced the British government that preparation for Independence was the wisest course. The settlers were effectively abandoned, and were left with the prospect of making their own way under a majority-rule government. A number did sell up and leave, but many, encouraged by Kenyatta, stayed on to become Kenyan citizens.

The state of emergency was lifted in Jan 1960 and a transitional constitution was drafted allowing for the existence of political parties and ensuring Africans were in the majority in the Legislative Council. African members of the council subsequently formed the Kenya African National Union (KANU) with James Gichuru, a former president of KAU, as its acting head and Mboya and Oginga Odinga, 2 prominent Luos, part of the leadership. KANU won the majority of seats in the Legislative Council but refused to form an administration until the release of Kenyatta.

In 1961 Kenyatta became the president of KANU. KANU won a decisive victory in the 1963 elections, and Kenyatta became prime minister as Kenya gained internal self-government. Kenya became fully independent later that year, the country was declared a republic, and Kenyatta became president. Kenya retained strong links with the UK, particularly in the form of military assistance and financial loans to compensate European settlers for their land some of which was redistributed among African landless.

Kenyatta

The two parties that had contested the 1963 with KANU were persuaded to join KANU and Kenya became a single-party state. In 1966 Odinga left KANU and formed a new party, the Kenya People's Union, with strong Luo support. Tom Mboya, a Luo, was assassinated by a Kikuyu in 1969. There followed a series of riots in the W of the country by Luos, and Odinga was placed in detention where he remained for the next 15 months. At the next general election in 1969 only KANU members were allowed to contest seats, and two-thirds of the previous national assembly lost their seats.

The East African Community (EAC) comprising Kenya, Tanzania and Uganda, which ran many services in common such as the railways, the airline, posts and telecommunications, began to come under strain. Kenya had pursued economic policies which relied on a strong private sector; Tanzania had adopted a socialist strategy after 1967; Uganda had collapsed into anarchy and turmoil under Amin. In 1977, Kenya unilaterally pulled out of the EAC, and in response Tanzania closed its borders with Kenya.

Kenyatta was able to increase Kenya's prosperity and stability through reassuring the settlers that they would have a future in the country and that they had an important role in its success at the same time as delivering his people limited land reform. Under Kenyatta's presidency, Kenya became one of the more successful newly independent countries. However, he became increasingly autocratic, and he was biased in favour of his own tribe over other interests.

Moi

Kenyatta died in 1978 to be succeeded by Danial arap Moi, his vice president. Moi began by relaxing some of the political repression of the latter years of Kenyatta's presidency. However, he was badly shaken by a coup attempt in 1982 that was only crushed after several days of mayhem, and a more repressive period was ushered in.

Relations between Kenya and its neighbours began to improve in the 1980s and the 3 countries reached agreement on the distribution of assets and liabilities of the EAC by 1983. At this time the border between Kenya and Tanzania was re-opened.

People

Kenya has long been a meeting place of population movements from around the continent. This has resulted in there being as many as 70 different tribes living in Kenya. There are 3 main groupings based on the origins of these groups.

The **Bantu** came from W Africa in a migration, the reasons for which are not clearly understood. The **Nilotic** peoples came from the NW, mostly from the area that is now Sudan. They were mainly pastoralists, and moved S in search of better grazing on more fertile land. Finally there is the **Hamitic** group, made up of a series of relatively small communities such as the Somali, Rendille, Boran, Ogaden and others, all pastoralists, who have spread into Kenya in the N and NE from Ethiopia and Somalia.

Kikuyu (Bantu)
Primarily based around Mount Kenya. This is the largest ethnic group with 21%. They are thought to have originated from the east and NE Africa around the 16th century. Land is the dominant social, political, religious and economic factor of life for Kikuyus and this attitude soon brought them into conflict with colonial interests when settlers occupied their traditonal lands,

The administration of the Kikuyu was undertaken by a council of elders based on clans made up of family groups. Other important members of the community were witch doctors, medicine men and the blacksmiths. The Kikuyu God is believed to live on Mount Kenya and all Kikuyus build their homes with the door facing the mountain. In common with most tribes in Kenya, men and women go through a number of stages into adulthood including circumcision to mark the beginning of their adult life. It is not so common for women to be circumcised today.

It is said the Kikuyu have adapted more successfully than any other tribe to the modern world. Kikuyu are prominent in many of Kenya's business and commercial activities. Those still farming in their homelands have adapted modern methods to their needs and benefit from cash crop production for export, particularly coffee and tea. They have benefited by occupying a fertile area close to the capital, Nairobi.

Meru (Bantu)
Arrived to the NE of Mount Kenya around the 14th century, following invasions by Somalis in the coast. This group is not homogenous being made up of 8 different groups of people, making up 5% of Kenya's population. Some of the Meru were led by a chief known as the *mogwe* until 1974 when the then chief converted to Christianity and ended the tradition. A group of tribal elders administer traditional justice along with the witch doctor.

The Meru occupy some of the country's richest farmland which is used to produce tea, coffee, pyrethrum, maize and potatoes. Another highly profitable crop grown by the Meru in this region is miraa, a mild stimulant particularly popular amongst Islamic communities and Somalis.

Kalenjin (Nilotic)
It is a name used by the British to describe a cluster of tribes, the main being the Kipsigis (4% of total population), Nandi 2%), Tugen (1%), and Elgeyo (1%), who speak the same language but different dialects. They mainly live in the western edge of the central Rift Valley and are thought to have migrated from southern Sudan about 2000 years ago. Most Kalenjin took up agriculture though they are traditionally pastoralists. Bee-keeping is common with the honey being used to brew beer. Administration of the law is carried out at an informal gathering of the clan's elders. Witch doctors are generally women, which is unusual in Africa.

Luyha (Bantu)
Based on Kakamega town in western Kenya, and making up 14% of the total. They are Kenya's third largest grouping after the Kikuyu and the Luo. They are cultivators, and small farmers are the mainstay of sugar-cane growing in the W. They occupy a relatively small area, and population densities are the highest

anywhere in Kenya's countryside, with plot sizes becoming steadily smaller with the passing of each generation.

Luo (Nilotic)
Live in the W of the country on the shores of Lake Victoria. The second largest ethnic group with 14% of the total. They migrated from the Nile region of Sudan in around the 15th century. Originally the Luo were cattle herders but the devastating effects of rinderpest on their herds made it necessary to diversify into fishing and subsistence agriculture.

The Luo were also prominent in the struggle for independence and many of the country's leading politicians including Tom Mboya and Oginga Odinga were Luos.

The Luos have a different coming of age ritual to other tribes in the region which involved extracting the bottom 4 or 6 teeth, though this practice has fallen into disuse.

Kisii (Bantu)
Based on Kisii town in the W, S of Kisumu. Traditional practices have been continued, with sooth-sayers and medicine men retaining significant influence, despite the nominal allegiance of most Kisii to Christianity. Trepanning, the drilling of a hole in the skull, has been a time-honoured remedy for mental illness and headaches, and is still used occasionally today.

Kamba (Bantu)
Traditionally lived in the area now known as Tsavo National Park. They comprise 11% of the total population. Originally hunters, the Kamba soon adopted a more sedentary lifestyle and developed as traders because of the relatively poor quality of their land. Ivory was a major trade item as were beer, honey, ornaments and iron weapons which they traded with neighbouring Maasai and Kikuyu for food.

The Akamba were well regarded by the British for their intelligence and fighting ability and they made up a large part of the East African contingent in the British Army during World War I.

Akamba adolescents go through initiation rites at around 12 including male circumcision. In common with most Bantu tribespeople, political power lies with clan elders.

Swahili (Bantu)
Dwell along the coast, and make up less than 1% of the total population. Although they do not have a common heritage, they do share a common language, religion and culture. Ancestry is mainly a mixture of Arabic and African. Today the majority of coastal people are Muslims.

Maasai (Nilotic)
Probably the best known tribe to people outside Kenya with their striking costume and reputation as fierce and proud warriers. They comprise 2% of Kenya's people. The Maasai came to central Kenya from the Sudan around a thousand years ago, where they were the largest and one of the most important tribes. Their customs and practices were developed to reflect their nomadic lifestyle and many are still practised today, though change is beginning to be accepted. The basic Maasai diet, for instance, is fresh and curdled milk carried in gourds. Blood tapped from the jugular vein of cattle is mixed with cattle urine and this provides a powerful stimulant. Cattle are rarely killed for meat as they represent the owners' wealth.

Turkana (Nilotic)
Like the Maasai, this group has retained its rich and colourful dress and have a reputation as warriors. They are 2% of total population. They are mainly based in the NW part of Kenya living in the desert near the Uganda border. This is the most isolated part of the country and as a consequence the Turkana have probably been affected less by the 20th century than any other tribe in Kenya.

The Turkana are pastoralists whose main diet consists of milk and blood. Cattle are important in Turkana culture, being herded by men. Camels, goats and sheep are also important and are looked after by boys and small girls. Recently some Turkana have begun fishing in the dry season or during famine

The traditional dress of the Turkana is very eye-catching and is still fairly commonly worn. Men cover part of their hair with mud which is then painted blue and decorated with ostrich feathers. The main garment is a woollen blanket worn over one shoulder. Women wear a variety of beaded and metal adornments many of which signify different events in a woman's life. Women wear a half skirt of animal skins and a piece of black cloth. Both men and women sometimes use the lip plug through the lower lip. Tattooing is still fairly common. Men are tattooed on the shoulders and upper arm each time they kill an enemy. Witch doctors and prophets are held in high regard.

Culture and life

Tribal identity is still important in Kenyan life though this is changing as more people move into towns and tribal groups become scattered. Polygamy is still practised, though it is not officially condoned. The custom of a man taking more than one wife, is only recognised in the traditional systems, and not by official Kenyan family law. There is much resistance to western censure of polygamy. However, the practice is dying under the twin influences of economic realities and social pressure. Few men can now afford to take more than one wife. Among the better off, it is frowned upon for anybody in public life as it causes embarrassment when mixing with the international community. The Christian churches strongly disapprove.

Modern Kenya

Politics

Danial arap Moi was elected to the Presidency in Oct 1978 following the death of Jomo Kenyatta, began a programme to reduce Kenya's corruption and released all political detainees. Moi, a Kalenjin, emphasised the need for a new style of government with greater regional representation of tribal groups. However, he did not fully live up to his promises of political freedom and Oginga Odinga (the prominent Luo who had been a voice of discontent in KANU under Kenyatta) and 4 other former KANU members who were critical of Moi's regime were barred from participating in the 1979 election. This led to an increase in protests against the government, mainly from Luos. Moi began to arrest dissidents, disband tribal societies and close the universities whenever there were demonstrations. This period also saw the strengthening of Kenya's armed forces.

On 1 Aug 1982 there was a coup attempt supported by a Luo-based section of the Kenya air force and supported by university students. Although things initially appeared to be touch-and-go, the coup was eventually crushed, resulting in an official death toll of 159. As a result of the coup attempt, many thousands of people were detained and the universities again closed. The heavy Luo involvement led to Odinga being placed under house arrest and the Information minister, also a Luo, being dismissed. Conciliatory moves from Moi followed these measures including an amnesty for political prisoners sentenced to death and an investigation of the civil service. The constitution was changed to make Kenya a *de jure* one-party state.

Moi decided to reassert his authority over KANU by calling an early election in which he stood unopposed. Inevitably he was re-elected but less than 50% of the electorate turned out to vote. Various measures were introduced to try to purge the political system of corruption and inefficiency though none resulted in any major changes. Students were seen as potential agitators and Nairobi

University was regularly closed. By 1986 there were rumours of underground agitation from a group known as Mwakenya.

Mwakenya was a group formed of members from a wide spectrum of tribes and political interests, mostly well-educated, all brought together in opposition to the Moi presidency. The National Council of Churches became increasingly critical of political events as well, in particular voicing opposition to a new electoral system whereby voters were to queue publicly in line behind the candidate of their choice, replacing the secret ballot.

Moi's response to political criticism was to increase his power by transferring control of the civil service to the president's office and reduce the independence of the judiciary by giving the president the power to dismiss the attorney-general and the auditor-general without endorsement by a legal tribunal. He also expanded his cabinet to 33 ministers, many posts being filled on the basis of political patronage. With the fall of a couple of outspoken politicians, parliamentary opposition to Moi evaporated.

By 1987 international criticism of Moi's government was intensifying, particularly as allegations of human rights abuses increased. 1988 saw more student demonstrations, protesting against the arrest of 7 student leaders. Nairobi university was closed and its student organisation banned. At the same time Moi made some minor concessions by releasing 9 political detainees and dismissing some police officers. Later that year a general election, using the queue voting system, saw Moi re-elected for a third term of office. Of the successfully re-elected 123 (of 188), 65 were unopposed, and there were allegations that opponents had been intimidated or bribed into withdrawing. Following the election there was a government reshuffle. Mwai Kibaki, the vice-president, was replaced by Josephat Karanja, a relatively unknown politician.

In 1988 Moi again increased his control over the legal system by a new set of constitutional amendments. This time, the national assembly assented to allow the president to dismiss judges at will. Also, periods of detention were increased from 24 hrs to 14 days. These latest changes were greeted with criticism by both foreign observers, the church, and the judiciary in Kenya but went through parliament unopposed. Moi greeted these reproaches with proposals to arrest any 'roaming foreigners' and threatened to curtail freedom of worship.

In Feb 1990, the popular and internationally influential Luo Minister of foreign affairs and international co-operation, Dr Robert Ouko was found murdered after his return from a visit to Washington DC, USA. There followed riots in Nairobi and Kisumu resulting in some 20 people being killed and thousands were arrested. Moi asked the British police to investigate Ouko's death, and the report named a minister, a Kalenjin kinsman of Moi, as one of the prime suspects. Pressure on the government to move to a multi-party sytem intensified, but Moi argued that this would play into the hands of tribalists in the pay of foreign masters seeking to undermine Kenyan unity.

A former cabinet minister Kenneth Matiba and Ogonga Odinga's son Raila Odinga were arrested for forming an alliance of people seeking to legalise political opposition. The US embassy intervened to grant refuge to one of the dissident leaders which caused a breakdown of accord between the Kenyan and US administrations. The US and British suspended aid disbursements, and within a matter of weeks, the Moi administration announced the introduction of a multi-party system. Several new political parties were registered in early 1992, the most important of which was the Forum for the Restoration of Democracy (FORD) in which

Oginga Odinga was involved.

Tribal clashes abounded throughout Kenya in 1992, but were particularly violent in western Kenya resulting in as many as 2,000 people being killed and 20,000 being made homeless. In May the government banned all political rallies ostensibly to suppress the unrest, they also placed restrictions on the press. The opposition parties accused the government of inciting the violence as a means of discrediting multi-party politics.

The opposition to KANU split, the main parties being FORD-Asili, led by Kenneth Matiba; FORD-Kenya, under Oginga Odinga; and the Demoocratic Party of Mwai Kibaki. The elections, at the very end of 1992, monitored by a commonwealth group, saw Moi re-elected but with only 36% of the popular vote. KANU won 100 of the 188 seats in the national assembly.

Moi's relationship with his neighbours has not been an easy one. Although Moi offered full co-operation with Museveni and the National Resistance Army (NRA) when they came to power in 1986, relations between Kenya and Uganda have often been strained. Moi was nervous that Uganda might supply arms to the Mwakenya movement. In 1987 the Kenya/Uganda border was temporarily closed as the 2 armies clashed, though the 2 countries later signed a treaty for co-operation.

Economics

Kenya's economic strategy maintains reliance on a strong private sector in manufacturing and services as well as in the farm sector. Foreign investment is encouraged, although the regulations have recently been uncertain, and there are periodic efforts to increase local participation in foreign-owned enterprises. In the East African context, Kenyan economic management has been successful, and has achieved as much as can reasonably be expected of a country with no oil and without any major mineral deposits.

Economic and social structure

Estimates for 1994 indicate a population of 27.7 mn. The density of population is 47.8 per sq km which is high for the region. The density is unevenly distributed with very high rates in the areas which are suitable for cultivation so about 75% of the population live in 10% of the land space. At least 24% of the population live in urban areas and rural to urban migration continues at a rapid pace. Population growth in Kenya over the period 1980-91 was one of the highest in Africa at 3.8% a year and is of serious concern, especially with the increase in agricultural production of only 3.2% over the same period.

GDP in 1991 was estimated at US$7,125mn, making it one of the larger economies in Africa. GNP per head was US$340, and this places Kenya firmly in the low-income group.

Agriculture generated about 27% of GDP in 1991, and this is well below the regional and African averages. Industry generated 22% of GDP and services 51%, and these are above the regional averages. On the demand side, private consumption accounted for 63% of GDP, below the regional and African averages. Investment was 21% of GDP, high by African standards, where investment averaged about 16% of GDP. Government consumption was 17% of GDP, and again this is above the East African average of 15%. Dependence on foreign trade, with exports comprising 27% of GDP and imports 28% of GDP, is fairly high. The main sources of foreign exchange earnings are tourism, coffee and tea.

Adult literacy was estimated at 69% in 1990, markedly better than the regional and African averages, and will improve with 94% primary school enrolments, one of the best rates of provision of basic education in Africa. Secondary school enrolments at 23% are significantly better than the regional average. Tertiary enrolments in are 2%, which puts Kenya on an equal footing with the rest of Africa.

Life expectancy is 59 years and significantly above the East African average of 50 years. Average daily calorie supply is above the East African average, and provision of doctors and nurses per head of population is over twice as good.

Overall, although it is a low-income country, Kenya has one of the larger economies in Africa, and better developed industrial and service sectors than the level of income per head alone might indicate. Educational and health provisions are above average for Africa.

Economic performance

GDP grew at 4.2% a year in the period 1980-91, and with population growth at 3.8% a year, GNP per head increased at 0.3% a year. This is a very creditable performance, even though the increase in average living standards was slight, as for most of Africa living standards fell in the same period.

Growth in the 1980s has been reasonably evenly spread across the sectors. Agriculture has expanded at 3.2% a year, industry at 4.0% and services at 4.9%. These are all very much better than African averages, but there must be some concern that agriculture has not expanded as fast as population. Export volumes grew at 2.9% a year, but import volumes, affected by increasing debt service payments and terms of trade falling by 13% since 1987, have only grown at 1.0% a year. Inflation has been around 9% a year, 1980-91, and this is a slight improvement compared with 11% in the 1970s, and much better than the rest of Africa, where inflation was 17% a year in the same period.

Overall, Kenya's economic performance has allowed a small increase in average living standards, and this is significantly better than elsewhere in Africa. Inflation has been moderate, at just above single figure annual price rises.

Recent economic developments

Kenya is in receipt of structural adjustment loans from the World Bank and an enhanced structural adjustment arrangement was agreed with the IMF for US$ 301m in 1989. Policy changes involve gradual changes to bring domestic prices in line with world prices, although this has stopped short of floating the exchange rate. Moves to end marketing board monopolies and to undertake widespread privatisation of parastatal enterprises have been resisted, and the donor community is beginning to lose patience over this issue.

The financial sector has been subject to a series of failures by privately-owned domestic institutions. There have been collapses of 5 financial groups, where 3 have shown evidence of irregularities, and 2 have suffered from the ensuing lack of confidence. Banking regulations have been tightened, and banks with foreign ownership and control, namely Barclays and Standard Chartered, have increased their share of banking business, realising higher profits.

Efforts are being made to reform and improve the performance of the parastatal sector with changes in management personnel. The grain purchasing body, the National Cereals and Produce Board (NCPB), provides a continuing problem as maize is bought at well above the world price, and in recent years of good harvests, the Board is accumulating stocks and runs at a continual loss. Kenya seems inclined to solve problems in the parastatal sector by reforms rather than privatisation, although there are moves to end the monopoly of the NCPB by making it a purchaser of last resort.

Kenya's trade balance has been affected by world commodity prices in the 1980s, particularly the prices for coffee and tea. Imports stand below the level achieved in 1980, when US$ 2.3b of goods were imported. Some US$7 bn of external debt was estimated outstanding in 1989. Debt service takes up just under a third of export earnings and at present this is within Kenya's ability to service, providing export revenues can be maintained.

Kenya's exchange rate policy involves periodic adjustments such that the official rate responds to the market rate. The black market in foreign exchange is not particularly vigorous, but there is evidence of some measure of currency overvaluation.

Kenya continues to be a major aid recipient with USAID adding US$ 5m to the US$ 25m already committed to housing, and lending a further US$ 15m to rural enterprise schemes. Finland has allocated US$ 74m over 4 years to dairy, water, health and electrification projects.

Comparative Economic and Social Data

	Kenya	East Africa	Africa	Industrial Countries
Population and land				
Population, mid year, millions, 1994	27.7	12.2	10.2	40.0
Urban Population, %, 1991	24	30.5	30	75
Population Growth Rate, % per year, 1980-91	3.8	3.1	3.1	0.8
Land Area, thou. sq. kilom.	580	486	486	1,628
Population Density, persons per sq kilom., 1994	47.8	24.2	20.4	24.3
Economy: production & income				
GDP, US$ millions, 1991	7,125	2,650	3,561	550,099
GNP per head, US$, 1991	340	250	389	12,960
Economy: supply structure				
Agriculture, % of GDP, 1991	27	43	35	3
Industry, % of GDP, 1991	22	15	27	35
Services, % of GDP, 1991	51	42	38	61
Economy: demand structure				
Private Consumption, % of GDP, 1991	63	77	73	62
Gross Domestic Investment, % of GDP, 1991	21	16	16	21
Government Consumption, % of GDP, 1991	17	15	14	17
Exports, % of GDP, 1991	27	16	23	17
Imports, % of GDP, 1991	28	24	26	17
Economy: performance				
GDP growth, % per year, 1980-91	4.2	1.6	-0.6	2.5
GDP per head growth, % per year, 1980-91	0.3	-1.7	-3.7	1.7
Agriculture growth, % per year, 1980-91	3.2	1.1	0.0	2.5
Industry growth, % per year, 1980-91	4.0	1.1	-1.0	2.5
Services growth, % per year, 1980-91	4.9	2.5	-0.5	2.6
Exports growth, % per year, 1980-91	2.9	0.7	-1.9	3.3
Imports growth, % per year, 1980-91	1.0	0.2	-6.9	4.3
Economy: other				
Inflation Rate, % per year, 1980-91	9.2	23.6	16.7	5.3
Aid, net inflow, % of GDP, 1991	10.6	11.5	6.3	-
Debt Service, % of Exports, 1991	32.7	18	20.6	-
Budget Surplus (+), Deficit (-), 1991	-5.8	-3.0	-2.8	-5.1
Education				
Primary, % of 6-11 group, 1989	94	62	76	102
Secondary, % of 12-17 group, 1989	23	15	22	93
Tertiary, % of 20-24 group, 1989	2	1.2	1.9	39
Adult Literacy Rate, %, 1990	69	41	39	99
Health and nutrition				
Life Expectancy, years, 1991	59	50	50	76
Calorie Supply, daily per head, 1989	2,163	2,111	2,096	3,357
Population per doctor, 1990	10,130	35,986	24,185	550

Notes: 'Africa' excludes South Africa. Dates are for the country in question, and do not always correspond with the Regional, African and Industrial averages.

The UK has allocated US$ 9.4m to telecommunications, the Netherlands US$ 7m to sugar rehabilitation, the East African Development Fund and OPEC US$ 29m to rice schemes, and the World Bank US$ 28m to railway improvements. Japan is contributing US$ 20m to balance of payments assistance to support the structural adjustment programme and a further US$ 20m for various projects.

Foreign investment has been steady despite uncertainty regarding local ownership provisions, and the UK's Mirror Group is investing US$43mn in publishing, printing and newspapers. Phillips is expanding its involvement in assembly of electrical goods, and the World Bank's International Finance Corporation has lent up to US$29mn for private sector paper production.

Economic outlook

Despite the good economic performance since independence, and the avoidance of major stability problems, there are reasons to be cautious about Kenya's prospects. The tourism sector is now the main source of foreign exchange earnings, and this is very vulnerable any deterioration of law and order in the country. The political situation has undoubtedly improved with the introduction of a multi-party system and a large contingent of opposition MPs in the national assembly. However, the outbreaks of violence before the 1992 elections were worrying, and it remains to be seen if the present political system can deliver stability and security on a long-term basis.

NAIROBI

CONTENTS

MAPS

A lively, cosmopolitan and bustling city, the centre is modern and prosperous, and services are well-organised and efficient. Kenya's burgeoning population, however, combined with migration to the towns has resulted in the population of Nairobi increasing at an enormous rate. Housing and other facilities have failed to keep up and shanty towns in the outskirts are the inevitable result. The population is currently over 2 mn and it is estimated that it will exceed 3.5 mn by the year 2000.

The city sits at 1870 m above sea level – from here it is a long and steady fall to the coast 500 km away.

Central Nairobi is bounded by Uhuru Highway to the W, Nairobi River to the N and E and the railway to the S. Across the Uhuru Highway is Uhuru Park and Central Park. In the southwest of this central triangle of about 5 square km are most of the government buildings, offices, banks, hotels and shops. In the northern section the buildings are closer together and there are many less expensive shops and restaurants and to the east of the triangle is the poorer section where there are cheaper hotels and restaurants, shops and markets. This is the area around River Rd, very lively, full of character and has the authentic atmosphere of the East African section of a great city.

The altitude makes for a marvellous climate with sunny days and cool nights. Sep to Apr are the hottest months, with maximum temperatures averaging 24°C, but falling at nights to around 13°C. May to Aug is cooler, with maximums averaging of 21°C, and minimums of 11°C at night. It can be quite chilly in the evenings. The heavy rains are in Mar-May, and smaller rains in Nov and Dec, although the timing of the rains has been less regular in recent years. Even on days of heavy rain there will invariably be some hrs of sunshine.

History

The name Nairobi comes from the Masai words *enkare nyarobe* meaning sweet water for originally this was a watering hole for the Masai and their cattle. Just one hundred years ago Nairobi hardly existed at all. It began life in 1896 as a railway camp during the building of the railway from the coast to the highlands. It grew steadily and by 1907 had become a town sufficient in size to take over from Mombasa as capital of British East Africa. Its climate was considered healthier than that of the coast and its position was ideal for developing into a trading centre for the settlers who farmed the White Highlands. Since then the city has continued to grow and is now the largest in East Africa.

Local festivals

The big event of the year is the annual *Safari Rally* which begins and ends in Nairobi. It is held around Easter time and is a great spectacal for local people. The route is over 4,000 km – it used to be the East African Safari but now just covers Kenya. The *Nairobi International Show*, an agricultural fair, is held at the end of September.

Places of interest

Kenya National Museum Located on Museum Hill this presents an overview of Kenya's history, culture and natural history. The section on Pre-history is particularly strong with exhibits of archaeological findings made so famous by the work of the Leakeys. The museum also has an excellent collection of butterfly and bird species found in Kenya. The Kenya Museum Society offers guided tours of certain exhibitions which are recommended. The museum is open from 0930 to 1800 and the entrance fee is US$4.

Snake Farm is found opposite the National Museum and houses most of the snake species found in Kenya as well as crocodiles and tortoises. Some are in glass tanks and others in open pits. The opening hours and charge are the same as for the National Museum.

Railway Museum Located next to the railway station on Station Rd. Among the exhibits are a number of the old steam trains. Perhaps the most interesting is the carriage from which a man-eating lion dragged a victim as the line was being constructed through what is now Tsavo National Park. There is also a model of *MV Liemba*, the vessel, built by the Germans and which still plies up and down Lake Tanganyika, see page 323.

National Archives This is more interesting than it might sound to the non-historian. The building originally served as the Bank of India and is located on Moi Ave opposite the *Hilton Hotel*. It contains various exhibitions of arts and crafts as well as photographs and, of course, hundreds of thousands of documents.

McMillan Memorial Library Located close to the Jamia Mosque and has an excellent collection of books, newspapers and parliamentary archives. The neo-classical building was built in 1928 and has huge lions on each side of the steps going up to the building. Books can be borrowed from here for a small charge. On the first floor is a collection of furniture from the house of Karen Blixen, several of the pieces can be recognised from descriptions in *Out of Africa*.

Parliament House On Parliament Rd and is recognisable by its clock tower. When Parliament is in session you can watch the proceedings from the public gallery, otherwise you can usually arrange to be shown around the building – ask at the main entrance.

Kenyatta Conference Centre This building is the tallest in the city with 28 floors and was built in 1972. At the top is the revolving restaurant which functions only periodically. However you can usually go up to the viewing level from where you can take photos – ask at the information desk on the ground floor. It is free but it is usual to tip the guide.

Karen Blixen Museum (T 882779) The museum is found in the house of Karen Blixen (Isak Dinesen) and many people who have read her books or seen *Out of Africa* will want to savour the unique atmosphere. Most of the original furniture is housed in the Macmillan Libray (see above). Exhibits include various agriculture implements. It is open daily from 0900 to 1800 and entrance costs US$4.

African Heritage Gallery Located on Kenyatta Ave opposite the *680 Hotel*. Arts and crafts are both exhibited and sold here.

Bomas of Kenya These are found in the Nairobi suburb of Langata. Here programmes based on traditional dances of the different tribes of Kenya are presented. They are not in fact performed by people of the actual tribe but are a professional group of dancers. The dancers finish with a lively display of acrobatics and tumbling. There is also a open air museum showing the different life styles of each tribe. The

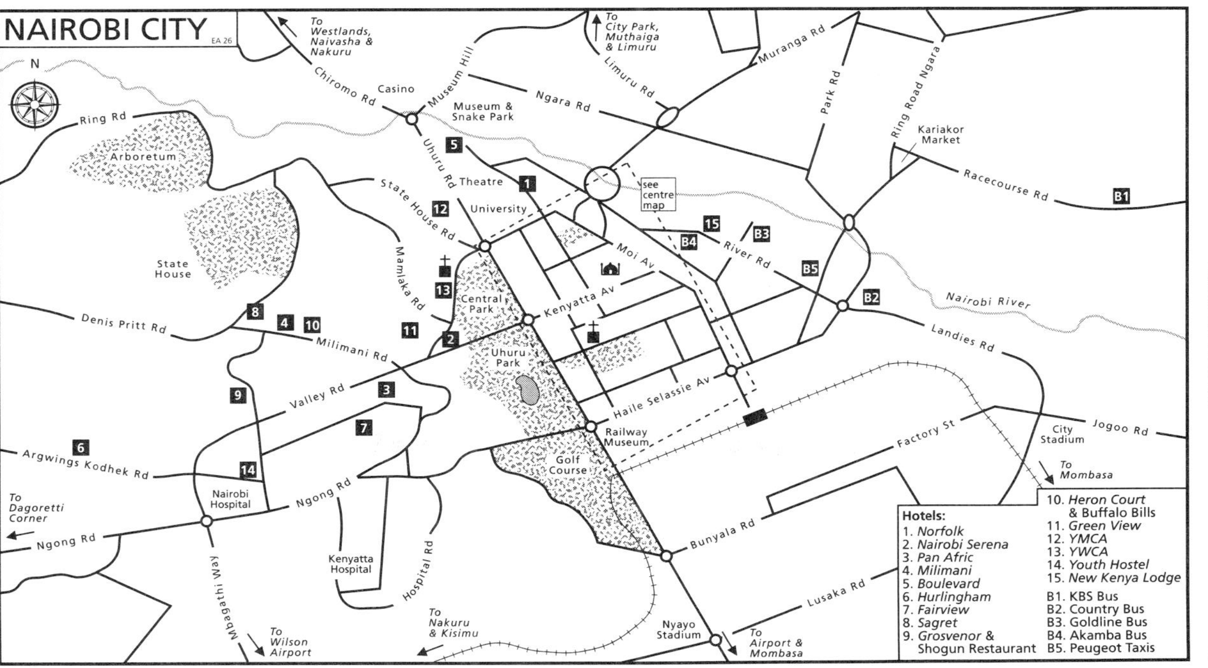
NAIROBI CITY
EA 26
N
To Westlands, Naivasha & Nakuru
To City Park, Muthaiga & Limuru
Muranga Rd
Park Rd
Ring Road Ngara
Kariakor Market
Racecourse Rd
B1
Chiromo Rd
Casino
Museum Hill
Museum & Snake Park
Ngara Rd
Limuru Rd
Ring Rd
Arboretum
Uhuru Rd
Theatre
University
see centre map
State House Rd
State House
Mamlaka Rd
Central Park
Kenyatta Av
Moi Av
River Rd
Nairobi River
Landies Rd
Denis Pritt Rd
Milimani Rd
Uhuru Park
Haile Selassie Av
Valley Rd
Railway Museum
Golf Course
Factory St
City Stadium
Jogoo Rd
To Mombasa
Argwings Kodhek Rd
Nairobi Hospital
Ngong Rd
To Dagoretti Corner
Mbagathi Way
To Wilson Airport
Kenyatta Hospital
Hospital Rd
To Nakuru & Kisimu
Bunyala Rd
Nyayo Stadium
Lusaka Rd
To Airport & Mombasa
Hotels:
1. Norfolk
2. Nairobi Serena
3. Pan Afric
4. Milimani
5. Boulevard
6. Hurlingham
7. Fairview
8. Sagret
9. Grosvenor & Shogun Restaurant
10. Heron Court & Buffalo Bills
11. Green View
12. YMCA
13. YWCA
14. Youth Hostel
15. New Kenya Lodge
B1. KBS Bus
B2. Country Bus
B3. Goldline Bus
B4. Akamba Bus
B5. Peugeot Taxis

shows begin at 1430 and cost US$2. If you are travelling independently you can get here on the matatu from outside Development House on Moi Ave which takes about half an hr.

Langata Giraffe Centre Set in 15 acres of indigenous forest the Langata Giraffe Centre is located about 20 km out of the city centre near the Hardy Estate Shopping Centre. If you do not have transport you can get there on the No 24 bus. The Centre is funded by the East African Fund for Endangered Wildlife and it houses a number of Rothchild's giraffes. There is information about them on display and it is designed to be interesting to children. You can watch and feed them from a raised wooden structure. The centre is also an excellent spot for bird-watching. During school holidays and public holidays it is open from 1100 to 1730, and at other times it is only open 1400 to 1730 on weekdays and 1000 to 1730 on weekends. Admission is free for children and US$4 for adults.

Langata Bird Sanctuary This is a private sanctuary and has a splendid range of birds. You must book in advance and parties are accompanied by an ornithologist with a well-trained eye. Binoculars will add greatly to the pleasure of a visit. (T 25255) Admission is US$5.

Nairobi National Park See Section on National Parks, page 190.

Animal Orphanage This is part of the Nairobi National Park and was opened in 1963 for orphaned or sick animals. Located close to the main entrance of the Nairobi National Park.

Excursions

Gikomba Village This village is well known for wood carving and you can come here to see wood carvers learning their trade. It is found a few km to the east of Nairobi toward Thika and is a popular stopping off point for tours.

Ngong Hills These hills are located about 25 km to the southwest of Nairobi on the edge of the Great Rift Valley. Plan for at least half a day for the round trip. It is advisable to go in a group and to take care over security. Take the Langata Rd out through the suburbs of Langata and Karen until you reach the town of Ngong. Just after this town turn right up the Panorama Rd which should be well signposted. The road winds up fairly steeply in places. The route is about 100 km in full and you climb up 1000 m. From the top you can look back from where you have come to see the skyline of Nairobi. The city centre with its sky scrapers is clearly visible and gradually peters out to the suburbs and farms. On a very clear day you can see Mount Kenya in the distance. Looking over in the other direction, towards the Great Rift Valley is a view of about 100 km.

Lake Magadi is a lake on the base of the Rift Valley at 580m altitude which makes it the second lowest of the Rift Valley lakes. It is only 110km from Nairobi but the climate is very different to that of the capital – it is semi-desert and the temperatures are around 38°C. As with many of the other Rift Valley Lakes this is a soda lake and because of the high temperatures it is particularly rich in the mineral. A soda factory has been built on the lake shores. It is fairly remote and inaccessible for those without their own transport. There is no public transport at all and the railway line which serves the factory does not take passengers.

To get there take the Langata Rd out past Wilson Airport and the National Park. Soon after the Park entrance there is a left fork. Take this road, it peters out to murram for about 10 km before the tarmac returns. The road goes through the village of Kiserian and then climbs from where you will get some good views of the Rift. It then drops down into the Rift and as it does it gets hotter and drier.

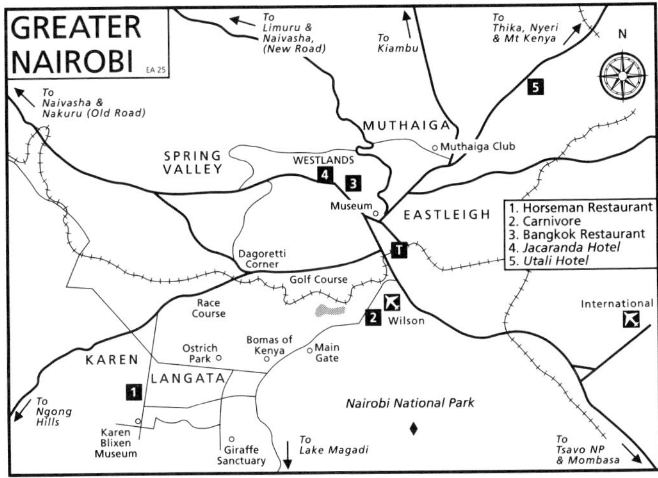

Lake Magadi is about 110 km from Nairobi. As you approach the views are splendid and you will probably see Masai grazing their cattle. There is an abundance of bird life – in particular lesser flamingoes, ibis and African spoonbills. At the southern end of the lake are hot springs.

Olorgesailie Prehistoric Site A trip to this important prehistoric site can be combined with a visit to Lake Magadi. It is located 65 km from Nairobi and is 2 km off the road to Lake Magadi. It is well signposted. The National Museums of Kenya administer the site and arrange tours. At the site is a small museum with a number of exhibits including animal bones and hand axes believed to date from 700,000 years ago. The site was discovered in 1919 by a geologist J. W. Gregory and later in the 1940's excavated by Kenya's most famous archaeologists, Mary and Louis Leakey. In 1947 it was given National Park status. There is limited accommodation at the site. For further information of tours and also for details of accommodation contact the Nairobi Museum (T 742161).

Local information

● Where to stay

Price guide: A+ Over US$100; **A** US$40-100; **B** US$20-40; **C** US$10-20; **D** US$5-10; **E** Under US$5.

There is an enormous range of hotels from the most expensive to the most basic. Those at the top of the range have all the facilities that you would expect of 5 star hotels and are of an international standard.

A+ *Norfolk*, PO Box 40075, Harry Thuku Rd, T 335422. Built in 1904 this is a world-famous hotel and as a result many people who cannot afford to actually stay, drop in for a drink. It suffered some damage in 1980 when a bomb, believed to be being carried by a terrorist in transit, went off in the hotel. However it was repaired and in 1991 it underwent extensive renovations. There are about 100 rooms and 20 luxury cottages. The Lord Delemare Bar is a popular drinking spot and has a series of caricature cartoons of early settlers. You can also sit on the terrace or in the gardens near the aviary. Other facilities include a swimming pool, shops, 2 restaurants and bars and a ballroom. **A+** *Nairobi Safari Club*, PO Box 43564, University Way at Koinage St, T 330621. This is one of the newest of the Nairobi Hotels and probably the most expensive. It was originally known as the Mount Kenya Safari Club and is one of the few places

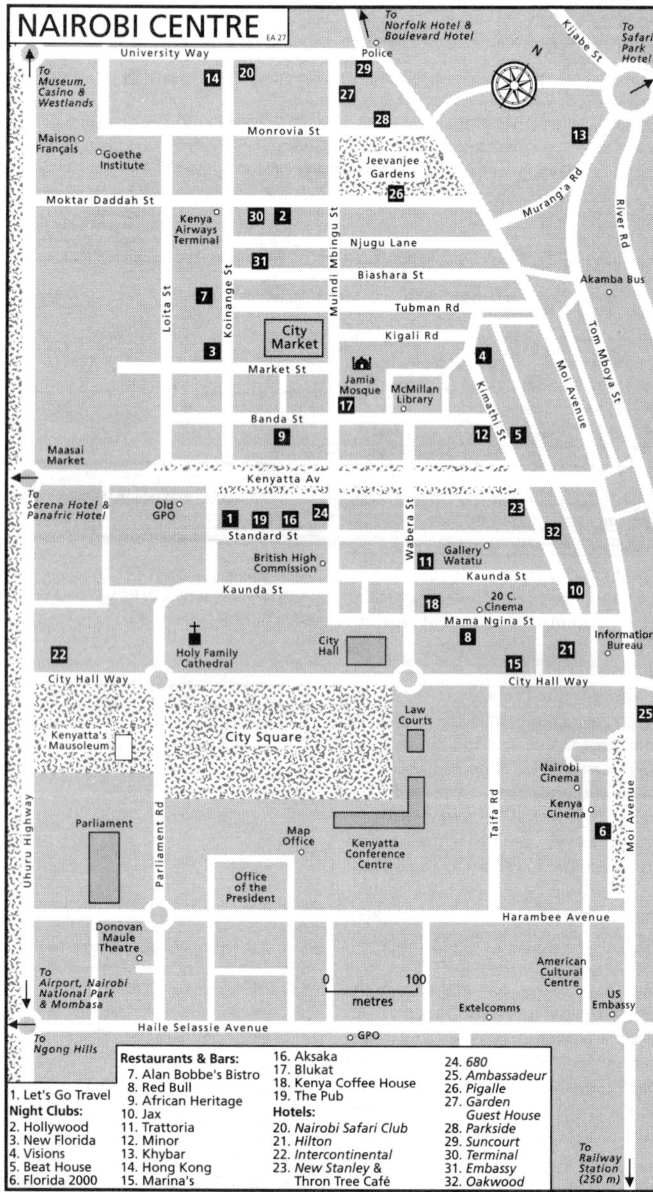

1. Let's Go Travel

Night Clubs:
2. Hollywood
3. New Florida
4. Visions
5. Beat House
6. Florida 2000

Restaurants & Bars:
7. Alan Bobbe's Bistro
8. Red Bull
9. African Heritage
10. Jax
11. Trattoria
12. Minor
13. Khybar
14. Hong Kong
15. Marina's
16. Aksaka
17. Blukat
18. Kenya Coffee House
19. The Pub

Hotels:
20. *Nairobi Safari Club*
21. *Hilton*
22. *Intercontinental*
23. *New Stanley & Thron Tree Café*
24. *680*
25. *Ambassadeur*
26. *Pigalle*
27. *Garden Guest House*
28. *Parkside*
29. *Suncourt*
30. *Terminal*
31. *Embassy*
32. *Oakwood*

where you are expected to wear a tie and jacket. It also does not welcome children under the age of twelve. It has been described as palatial which is not far wrong – marble, fountains and lots of greenery. It has a swimming pool, sauna, health centre, hairdresser and meeting rooms. You will also have to pay temporary membership to stay. **A+** ***Safari Park***, North of Nairobi on the Thika Rd, T 802561, F 802477. Completed in 1990. It has 125 rooms, 2 restaurants, 3 bars, a swimming pool, tennis and squash courts and meeting rooms. **A+** ***Windsor Golf and Country Club***, North of Nairobi on Garden Estate Rd, T 726702/726505, F 726328. Built in 1991 and is one of Nairobi's newer hotels. There are about 100 rooms and 15 luxury cottages. It has extensive facilities including 2 restaurants, meeting rooms, a health club, an 18-hole golf course, squash and tennis courts, and riding facilities. **A+** ***Hilton***, PO Box 30624, Watali St just off Mama Ngina St, T 334000. It is rather like any other Hilton anywhere in the world although the large wildlife mural in the foyer does remind you that you're in Africa. It has over 300 rooms and facilities include a roof top swimming pool, shops, meeting rooms and a health club. It does an excellent buffet breakfast which is very good value and is open to non-residents. **A+** ***Inter-Continental Nairobi***, PO Box 30667, City Hall Way and Uhuru Highway, T 335550. Nairobi's largest hotel with over 400 rooms. Facilities include a heated swimming pool, shops, casino and an excellent roof top restaurant Le Chateau that is popular in particular for its dinner dance evenings. This hotel welcomes children.

A ***Nairobi Serena***, PO Box 46302, Kenyatta Ave and Nyene Rd close to All Saints Cathedral, T 725111. Set in beautiful gardens it has plenty of parking space and runs a shuttle service into town. The Serena has a good reputation and is popular with business travellers and tourists. It has about 200 rooms and facilities include a swimming pool, health club, meeting rooms and shops. **A** ***Panafric***, PO Box 30486, Kenyatta Ave, T 720822. It is a modern practical hotel of 200 rooms, but without an enormous amount of atmosphere. Facilities include a swimming pool, shop, hairdressers and meeting rooms. There is a cafe by the pool and the Simba Grill is popular, with a live band most nights.

B ***Milimani***, PO Box 30715, Milimani Rd, T 720260. Large hotel popular with expatriates working in Kenya. Prices include breakfast. **B** ***New Stanley***, PO Box 30680, corner of Kenyatta Ave and Kimathi St, T 333233. It is actually the oldest hotel in Nairobi although originally it was not located here.The celebrated outdoor Thorn Tree Café is found here as well as the Nation Bookshop. The Thorn Tree is famous for its notice board where travellers leave messages for each other. The board can be used by anyone at no cost, but not for any advertisements. It has about 240 rooms and facilities include meeting rooms, shops and a moderate restaurant. **B** ***Jacaranda***, PO Box 14287, T 742274. About 5 km out of town on Chiromo Rd close to the Westlands shopping centre this is a popular family hotel. It has about 135 rooms and facilities include a swimming pool, tennis court, and playground.

C ***Six Eighty***, PO Box 43436, Muindi Mbingu St, T 332680. Very central. It has 380 rooms and facilities include a Japanese restaurant, shops and a bar. **C** ***Boulevard***, PO Box 42831, Harry Thuka Rd, T 27567. Good value. Facilities include a swimming pool, tennis courts, gardens and restaurant. **C** ***Ambassadeur***, PO Box 30300, Moi Ave, T 336803. This has a good central location. It is fairly ordinary – nothing special and there are better value hotels in the same range. **C** ***Utalii***, PO Box 31067, located a bit out of town on the Thika Rd, T 802540. Utalii is the Swahili word for tourism and this is the government-run training centre for people entering hotel and catering. As a result it is really very good. There are 50 rooms and facilities include swimming pool, lovely gardens, tennis courts and restaurant. **C** ***Hurlingham***, PO Box 43158, Argwings Kodhek Rd, T 721920/723001. This is a small hotel with only 14 rooms, located on in western Nairobi. It has a definite charm and is popular with local residents.

● D Central

In this price range it is particularly noticeable that for the same price the hotels out of town tend to be of a higher standard than those in the centre. In particular those in the centre often suffer from the noise.

D ***Africana***, Dubois St off Latema Rd, T 20654. One of the best in this category. It is clean, safe and fairly quiet and rooms all have bathrooms with hot water. **D** ***Hermes***, a little way out on the corner of Tom Mboya St and Haile Selassie Ave this is a good value hotel. It is clean and has a fairly good restaurant. **D** ***Pigale***, in the northwest of the town centre on Daddah St off Moi Ave, facing the Jeevanjee Gardens, T 331403. Small but popular hotel. Rooms have bathrooms with hot water. Good value. **D** ***New***

Garden, Muindi Mbingu St. Most rooms have bathrooms with hot water (some shared bathrooms) and the price includes breakfast. **D** ***Parkside***, Monrovia St. Rooms have bathrooms and hot water and the price includes breakfast. It is friendly and clean and there is a restaurant attached. **D** ***Terminal***, Moktar Daddah St in the NW of town, T 28817. Popular hotel although it has seen better days. It is however clean, safe and friendly and rooms have bathrooms with hot water. **D** ***Embassy***, Biashara St, T 24087. Clean, safe and friendly and rooms have bathrooms with hot water. **D** ***Oakwood***, PO Box 40683, Kimathi St opposite the *New Stanley Hotel*, T 20592. Good value. There are only 23 rooms and the price includes breakfast. Facilities include a bar, restaurant and a roof terrace. **D** ***Sirikwa Lodge***, corner of Accra Rd and Munyu St, T 26089. Not too noisy. Rooms have bathrooms with hot water and are clean. Breakfast is included in the price. **D** ***Salama***, corner of Tom Mboya St and Luthuli Ave, T 25899. Suffers from the noise. Price includes breakfast but it is not terribly good value. **D** ***Solace***, Tom Mboya St, T 331277. Has noise problems. Reasonable value.

● D Out of city centre

D ***Fairview***, PO Box 40842, a little way out of the centre close to the *Panafric Hotel* on Bishops Rd, T 723210. Very peaceful. It is a wonderful family hotel and is extremely popular with up-country people visiting Nairobi. It has very well kept gardens and a sort of colonial charm. Residents can use the swimming pool at the *Panafric*. **D** ***Sagret***, PO Box 18324, Corner of Milimani Rd and Ralph Bunche Rd, T 720933. Not bad value. Price includes breakfast and facilities include a bar and restaurant. **D** ***Grosvenor***, PO Box 41038, Ralph Bunche Rd between Milimani Rd and Valley Rd, T 722080. Set in gardens and is a popular family hotel. It is good value and price include breakfast. Facilities include a bar, 2 restaurants (one Japanese and one Ethiopian), a playground and a swimming pool. **D** ***Heron Court***, PO Box 41848, Milimani Rd, T 720740. Popular. It is safe and has a guarded car park. Rooms vary – all have bathrooms and hot water, and some are self contained with kitchens. Facilities include swimming pool, sauna, shop and laundry service. Some rooms can however be noisy as the celebrated Buffalo Bill's restaurant and bar is attached. **D** ***Green View Lodge***, situated off Nyerere Rd, T 720908. Nice surroundings. There are both private and shared bathrooms. There is a bar and restaurant and prices include breakfast.

● E Central

E ***Gloria***, Ronald Ngala St, T 28916. Rather noisy place to stay but as all rooms have bathrooms and hot water and the price includes breakfast it is really quite good value. **E** ***Terrace***, Ronald Ngala St, T 21636. This is close to the *Gloria* and is similar. It can be rather noisy; also the staff don't appear to make much of an effort. **E** ***Eolat*** Mfangano St, T 22797. Relatively quiet and friendly. Very clean, secure and rooms all have bath and hot water. **E** ***Iqbal***, Latema Rd, T 20914. It has however seen better days although it does remain one of the most popular places in central Nairobi. If you want to stay you will have to arrive early. There is sometimes hot water in the mornings and although its only basic it is friendly and you will meet lots of other travellers here. All rooms have shared bathrooms. It has baggage storage facilities and a notice board. **E** ***New Kenya Lodge and Annex***, River Rd by the junction of Latema St, the annex is just around the corner, T 22202. Another very popular budget hotel. Again it is basic, bathrooms are shared and there is only hot water in the evenings, except in the Annex which only has cold water. However it is reasonably clean and friendly and has baggage storage facilities and a notice board. **E** ***Sunrise***, Latema Rd. Another basic but clean place with shared bathrooms which have hot water mornings and evenings. Some of the rooms are rather noisy as it is next door to the *Modern 24 Hr Green Bar* which is, as its name implies, opens all day and all night. **E** ***New Safe Life Lodging***, Dubois Rd just off Latema Rd. It is clean, basic with shared bathrooms but has the usual hot water problems. As with many of these places the single rooms are not very good value. **E** ***NyanEarwa Lodging***, Dubois Rd just off Latema Rd. Shared bathrooms and hot water. **E** ***Bujumbura Lodge***, Dubois Rd just off Latema Rd, T 28078. Near *New Safe Lodging*. Basic with shared bathrooms and unpredictable hot water supplies. **E** ***YMCA***, State House Rd, T 337468. It is good value but caters for the long term visitor. Many of the residents are Kenyan students who live there semi-permanently. Swimming pool. **E** ***YWCA***, Mamlaka Rd off Nyerere Rd, T 338689. Does take couples. Good value.

● E Out of city centre

E ***Mrs Roche's***, it is a little way out, situated opposite the Aga Khan Hospital on Third Parklands Ave. This is a legend amongst travellers and remains popular. Campers are also welcome and use the garden which can get rather crowded. If you get there late you will have to sleep on the floor until a bed is free. You can safely leave baggage. Can be reached on matatu (which will say Aga Khan on the front) from outside the Odeon Cinema at the junction of Tom Mboya St and Latema Rd. Ask the driver to tell you where to get off. **E *Nairobi Youth Hostel***, about 2km out of town on Ralph Bunche Rd (which runs between Ngong Rd and Valley Rd), T 21789. You must belong to the Youth Hostels Association to stay here but can join on the spot without any problem. Bathrooms are shared but there is hot water all day. It is clean, friendly and safe. Take the No 8 matatu from outside the *Hilton Hotel* or at the junction of Kenyatta Ave and Uhuru Highway down Ngong Rd and ask to be dropped off at Ralph Bunche Rd. Do not walk back to the youth hostel at night – always take a taxi or matatu.

● Places to eat

Price guide:
♦♦♦♦Over US$10; ♦♦♦US$5-10; ♦♦US$2-5; ♦Under US$2

There are wide range of restaurants to suit all tastes and budgets. All the top hotels have restaurants.

● General

♦♦♦♦***Ibis Grille***, *Norfolk Hotel*, T 335422. This specializes in nouvelle cuisine and is really excellent. The food is very good, it has a lovely setting and a good atmosphere. Jacket and tie recommended. The *Norfolk* also does a wonderful buffet breakfast which is open to non-residents. ♦♦♦♦***The Tate Room***, *New Stanley Hotel*. Very plush and the food is good. Sun buffet is very popular here. ♦♦♦♦***Cafe Maghreb***, *Serena Hotel*. Another popular buffet place this is next to the swimming pool and is particularly busy on Fri evenings. ♦♦♦♦***Le Chateau***, *Intercontinental Hotel*. Rooftop restaurant is the only one of its kind in Nairobi and serves excellent food. Dinner dancing at weekends. ♦♦♦♦***The Tamarind***, National Bank building on Harambee Ave. T 338959, 20473. Probably Nairobi's finest fish restaurant – helped in part by their own fish farm. It is highly recommended. ♦♦♦♦***Alan Bobbe's Bistro***, this small restaurant is located on Koinange St, T 21152. It is advisable to come here in something more than shorts and a T-shirt. It specialises in sea-food and the food and atmosphere are both excellent. Reservations are recommended. ♦♦♦♦***Red Bull***, located in Silopark House on Mama Ngina St this has long been one of Nairobi's most popular restaurants – for residents, business people, and tourists alike, T 335717. Portions are generous and the food high quality. ♦♦♦♦***Horseman***, in Karen and is highly recommended, T 882033. There is a blazing fire in the bar and you can also eat outside in the garden.

♦♦♦***Carnivore***, Langata Rd about 20 minutes out of town past the airport this was set up by the owners of the Tamarind, T 501775. As is clear from the name it specializes in meat dishes including game (wart-hog, gazelle, crocodile, wildebeest etc) which are grilled over a huge charcoal fire. The waiters bring the skewer of meat to your table and carve until you say stop. It has become very popular with all types of travellers and is often included as part of tours. There is also a vegetarian menu. Portions are huge and it works out as fairly good value. ♦♦♦***Revolving Restaurant*** Top of the 27 storey tower of the Kenyatta International Conference Centre – the floor does not always rotate but the view is exceptional.

♦♦***Buffalo Bill's***, *Heron Court Hotel* on Milimani Rd, T 720740. You can eat here although the main pastime is drinking. Lively atmosphere. The food is okay but not very good value. ♦♦***Thorn Tree Cafe*** *New Stanley Hotel*. Very popular place to meet people although the service is notoriously slow. ♦♦***African Heritage Cafe***, Banda St, T 333157. African food. Selection of dishes from a buffet, so it is possible to sample the various examples. Highly recommended. There is also a garden. ♦♦***Jax***, Kimathi St, T 23427. Popular with business people for quick cheap lunches. It is self-service and usually busy and includes a number of Indian dishes.

Cheap eating There are lots of cheap places in the River Rd area selling African and Indian food and snacks. The ♦***Iqbal*** is particularly popular with travellers. ♦***The Coffee Bar*** on Mama Ngina St is busy for lunches and does filling meals. The ♦***Jacaranda*** is pleasant for a drink and snack and is al favourite with business people. Other places to try are the ♦***Malindi Restaurant*** on Gaborone Rd. ♦***Beneva Coffee House*** on the corner of Standard and Koinange Sts. ♦***Bull Cafe*** on Ngariama Rd.

Italian

♦♦♦♦***Foresta Magnetica***, Mama Ngina St, T 728009. Has a piano bar. The menu is probably better at lunchtime than in the evenings because the cafeteria does not operate in the evenings. But it has a very pleasant atmosphere in the evenings when the pianist is playing. ♦♦♦***La Galleria*** and ♦♦***The Toona Tree*** are both in the International Casino, T 742600. *La Galleria* has good Italian food including some excellent seafood dishes. The *Toona Tree* is a cheaper outdoor restaurant which is especially good for drinks and snacks. It has live bands about 3 days a week. *Toona Tree* is closed on Mondays and both close during the afternoon.

♦♦***Trattoria***, situated on Kaunda St and Wabera St. Rather bustling if chaotic place. The food is fairly good which is more than can be said for the service. It does good cappuccinos and ice cream. Reservations are recommended especially if you want one of the tables with a view. ♦♦***Twiga***, Nkrumah Rd, T 335864/ 336308/ 335243. Menu is part Italian, part French as well as quite a lot of seafood. The food and service are both very good. Downstairs is an ice-cream parlour. ♦♦***Marinos***, situated next to the American Embassy on Aga Khan Walk, T 337230. You can eat inside or outside, and there is a fairly extensive menu. It is open from 0900 to 1400 and from 1900 to 2200.

Others include ♦♦♦***Jardin de Paris***, T 336435, ♦♦♦***Arturos***, T 26940 and ♦♦♦***Casino***, T 742600.

Indian

♦♦♦♦***Minar***, there are 2 *Minar's*, one located on Banda St in the city centre and the other in the Sarit Centre in Westlands, T 29999/748340. They are both popular and reservations are recommended. They do a buffet lunch and the service is friendly. Their tandoori dishes are especially good. ♦♦♦***Rasoi***, located on Parliament Rd, T 25082/26049. Excellent standard. ♦♦♦***The Golden Candle***, Ralph Bunche Rd, T 720480. Extensive menu, all of which is very good. Closed on Mon. ♦♦♦***Khyber Restaurant***, located at the *Meridian Hotel* on Murang'a Rd, this restaurant has an excellent buffet lunch, T 25595. Tandoori chicken a speciality.

♦♦***Dhaba***, Tom Mboya St, T 334862. Specializes in North Indian food. It is particularly popular with Nairobi Indians. Their speciality is *taka taka* dishes. *Taka taka* means rubbish in Swahili – although what that has to do with these delicious dishes is not totally clear – may be they were originally the left-overs. ♦♦***Mayur***, corner of Tom Mboya St and Keekorok Rd. Specialises in vegetarian Indian food. Has seen better days, but the food is still good.

♦♦***Durgar***, Ngara St, T 742781. Although the decor is certainly not fancy this has good cheap food, with a good range of vegetarian dishes. Also lots of Indian snacks which are very popular. ♦♦***Supreme***, located in the River Rd area this Indian restaurant is excellent, T 25241. It also does takeaways and has an extensive dessert menu. ♦♦***Satkar***, Moi Ave. Specializes in southern Indian food.

Others include ♦♦***Safeer***; ♦♦***Ambassadeur***; ♦♦***New 3 Bells***, T 20628; and ♦♦***Nawab Tandoori***, T 740209.

Chinese

♦♦♦***China Plate***, Taveta St, T 20900. Expensive, but the food is very good, the decor authentic Chinese and the services attentive. ♦♦♦***Hong Kong***, Koinange St, T 28612. Specializes in Cantonese dishes and has a good reputation. ♦♦♦***Panda***, located in Imenti House on Tom Mboya St, T 331189. Good food and friendly staff. ♦♦♦***Dragon Pearl***, Kenyatta Ave, in Bruce House, T 340451. Deservedly very popular. ♦♦♦***Rickshaw***, in the Fehda Towers on Standard and Muindi Mbingu St, T 333229. Extensive menu. ♦♦♦***Mandarin***, Tom Mboya St, T 20600. Reasonable standard.

Japanese

♦♦♦♦***Shogun***, located at the *Grosvener Hotel* on Ralph Bunche St this is one of Nairobi's 3 Japanese restaurants, T 720563. They are fairly similar with comparable menus although the Shogun is not so good for lunches.

♦♦♦***Akasaka***, located next to *The Pub* on Standard St, T 20299. This also does take-away lunch boxes. ♦♦♦***Six Eighty*** Very central. Reasonable standard.

Thai

♦♦♦***Bangkok***, located in the Westlands Shopping centre this is Nairobi's only Thai restaurant, T 751311. It is popular and deservedly so.

● Bars

Eating, drinking and dancing are the most popular evening entertainments in Nairobi. There are a number of popular bars and clubs, and 3 casinos. For most of these clubs entrance for women is cheaper than for men. Single men should expect a lot of attention. As with most establishments in Kenya, dress is casual in all these clubs. The only exception to this rule are the ***Nairobi Safari Club*** and the ***Windsor Golf and Safari Club***.

Popular hotel bars include the ***Norfolk***, ***Fairview*** and the ***Grosvenor***. The ***Thorn Tree*** is a good meeting place but the service is notoriously slow.

If you are there at lunch time (1100 to 1400) or supper time (1700 to 1900) you will have to order food as well. *Buffalo Bill's* Bar in the *Heron Court Hotel* on Milimani Rd is popular and it is certainly one of the liveliest places in town. *The Pub* on Standard St is open from 1100 to 2300 and is also popular. If you want to drink all day and night and are not too fussy about your surroundings you can try the ***Modern 24-Hr Green Bar*** on Latema Rd. This is the authentic African city side of Nairobi.

Airlines

International **Aeroflot** Corner House, Mama Ngina St, T 20746. **Air Canada**, Kimathi House, Kimathai St T 339755. **Air France**, Chai House, Koinange St. T 726265. **Air India**, Jeevan Bharati Building, Harambee Ave, T 334788. **Air Madagascar**, *Hilton Hotel*, City Hall Way, T 25286. **Air Malawi**, Cotts House, Cnr City Hall Way & Wabera St, T 333683. **Air Mauritius**, Union Towers, Cnr Mama Ngina St and Moi Ave, T 29166. **Air Tanzania**, Kimathi St, T 336397.

Air Zaire, Kimathi St, T 25626. **Air Zimbabwe**, Koinanage St, T 339499. **Alitalia**, *Hilton Hotel*, City Hall Way, T 24361. **British Airways**, 11th Floor, International House, Mama Ngina St, T 334440. **Cameroon Airlines**, Kenyatta Ave, T 337788. **EgyptAir**, Shankardass House, Moi Ave, T 26821. **El Al**, Sweepstake House, Mama Ngina St, T 28123/4. **Ethiopian Airlines**, Bruce House, Muindi Mbingu St, T 330837. **Gulf Air**, Global Travel, International House, Mama Ngina St, T 728401/3. **Iberia**, *Hilton Hotel*, Mama Ngina St, T 331648/338623. **Kenya Airways**, Airways Terminal, Koinange St, T 332750/29291. **KLM**, Fedha Towers, Muindi Mbingu St, T 332673. **Lufthansa**, Kimathi St, T 26271. **Olympic Airlines**, *Hilton Hotel*, City Hall Way, T 338026. **Pakistan International Airlines**, ICEA Building, Banda St, T 333901. **Royal Swazi National Airlines**, Taifa Rd, T 729475. **Sabena**, International House, Mama Ngina St, T 22185. **Saudia**, Banda St, T 331456. **Scandinavian Airlines**, Grindlays Building, Kimathi St, T 338347. **Somali Airlines**, Bruce House, Muindi Mbingu St, T 335409. **Sudan Airways**, UTC House, General Kagao St, T 25129. **Swissair**, Mama Ngina, St, T 340231/2/3. **Uganda Airlines**, Phoenix house, Kenyatta Ave, T 21354. **Zambia Airways**, Hamilton House, Kuanda St, T 21007.

Domestic and charter: **Africair**, PO Box 45646, T 501210. **Air Kenya Aviation**, Wilson Airport, T 501601. **Equator Airlines**, Wilson Airport, T 21177/501399. **Kenya Airways**, Airways Terminal, Koinange St, T 332750/29291.

Embassies, High Commissions and Consulates

Argentina, PO Box 30283, T 335242. **Australia**, PO Box 30360, T 22203. **Austria**, PO Box 30560, City House, Wabera Street, T 228281. **Bangladesh**, PO Box 41645, T 562815. **Belgium**, PO Box 30461, Limuru Road, T 222269. **Brazil**, PO Box 30751, Jeevan Bharati Bldg, Harambee Ave, T 337722. **Burundi**, PO Box 44439, Development Hse, Moi Ave, T 218458. **Canada**, PO Box 30481, Comcraft Hse, Haile Selassie Ave, T 214804. **Chile**, PO Box 45554, International House, Mama Ngina St, T 331320. **China**, PO Box 30508, Woodlands Road, T 722559. **Colombia**, PO Box 48494, Muthaiga Road, T 765927. **Costa Rica**, PO Box 30750, T 501501. **Cyprus**, PO Box 30739, Eagle Hse, Kimathi St, T 220881. **Denmark**, PO Box 40412, HFCK Bldg, Koinange St, T 331008. **Djibouti**, PO Box 59528, T 229633. **Egypt**, PO Box 30285, Harambee Plaza, 7th Floor, T 225991. **Ethiopia**, PO Box 45198, State House Ave, T 723027. **Finland**, PO Box 30379, International Hse, City Hall Way, T 334777. **France**, PO Box 41784, Embassy House, Harambee Ave, T 339783. **Germany**, PO Box 30180, Williamson Hse, Ngong Ave, T 712527. **Greece**, PO Box 30543, IPS Bldg, Kimathi St, T 340722. **Holy See**, PO Box 14326, Apostolic Nunciature, Manyani Rd West, T 442975. **Hungary**, PO Box 30523, Agip Hse, 2nd Floor, T 226914. **India**, PO Box 30074, Jeevan Bharati Bldg, Harambee Ave, T 222361. **Indonesia**, PO Box 48868, Utalii Hse, Uhuru Highway, T 215873. **Iran**, PO Box 49170, T 720343. **Iraq**, PO Box 49213, Matungulu House, T 580262. **Israel**, PO Box 30354, T 722182. **Italy**, PO Box 30107, International Life Hse, Mama Ngina Street, T 337356. **Japan**, PO Box 60202, Kenyatta Ave, T 332995. **Korea**, PO Box 30455, Anniversary Towers, University way, T 333581. **Kuwait**, PO Box 42353, Muthaiga Rd, T 767144. **Lesotho**, PO Box 44096, International Hse, Mama Ngina St, T 337493. **Malawi**, PO Box 30453, Standard St, T 221174. **Mexico**, PO Box 14145, T 582850. **Morocco**, PO Box 61098, T 222264. **Mozambique**, PO Box 66923, T 581857.

Netherlands, PO Box 41537, Uchumi Hse, Nkrumah Av, T 227111. **Nigeria**, PO Box 30516, Hurlingham, T 564116. **Pakistan**, PO Box 30045, St Michel Rd, Westlands, T

443991. **Poland**, PO Box 30086, Kabernet Rd, T 566288. **Portugal**, PO Box 34020, T 338990. **Romania**, PO Box 48412, T 227515. **Russia**, PO Box 30049, Lenana Rd, T 722559. **Rwanda**, PO Box 48579, International Life House, Mama Ngina St, T 334341. **Saudi Arabia**, PO Box 58297, T 762781. **Slovak Republic**, PO Box 30204, Milimani Rd, T 721896. **Spain**, PO Box 45503, Bruce House, Standard St, T 336330. **Sri Lanka**, PO Box 48145, International Life House, Mama Ngina St, T 227577. **Sudan**, PO Box 48784, Minet ICDC House, 7th Floor, T 720853. **Swaziland**, PO Box 41887 Nbi, T 339231, Silopark house. **Tanzania**, PO Box 47790, Continental House, T 331056. **Thailand**, PO Box 58349, T 715800. **Turkey**, PO Box 30785, Gigiri Rd, off Limuru Rd, T 520404. **Uganda, PO Box 60855, T520404, T520404.** **United Kingdom**, PO Box 30465, Bruce House, Standard St, T 335944. **USA**, PO Box 30137, Cnr Moi and Haile Selassie Ave T 334141. **Venezuela**, PO Box 34477, International Hse, Mama Ngina St, T 341078. **Yemen**, PO Box 44642, Ngong Rd, T 564379. **Zaire**, PO Box 48106, Electricity House, Harambee Ave, T 229771. **Zambia**, PO Box 48741, Nyerere Road, T 724850. **Zimbabwe**, PO Box 30806, Minet ICDC House, Mamlaka Rd, T 711071.

● Entertainment

Casinos The 3 casinos in Nairobi are government-supervised and foreigners must use foreign currency. They are open until 0300 on weekdays and 0330 on weekends. The oldest is the ***International Casino*** which also houses the Bubbles nightclub. The other 2 are found in the ***Intercontinental***, located on Uhuru Highway and the ***Safari Park*** located on Thika Rd.

Cinemas There are a number of cinemas in Nairobi – including 2 drive-ins the ***Fox*** and ***Belle-Vue***. If you have a vehicle an evening at the drive-in is well worth it. Other good cinemas are the ***Nairobi*** and ***20th Century*** on Mama Ngina St. There are other cheaper ones on Latema Rd but the quality of the films is less good. Films on show include British, American and Indian productions and there are often fairly recent releases.

Cultural centres Other places that have films, concerts and talks include the ***British Council*** ICEA Building, Kenyatta Ave. (T 334855); the ***French Cultural Centre*** Maison Francais, Loita St. (T 336263); ***Alliance Francais*** ICEA Building, Kenyatta Ave (T 340054); ***Goethe Institute*** Maendeleo House, Monrovia St (T 24640); ***American Cultural Centre*** National Bank Building, Harambee Ave. (T 337877); ***Italian Cultural Institute*** Prudential Building, Wabera St. (T 21615); ***Japan Information Centre*** Matungulu House, Mamlaka Rd, T 331196.

Programmes are announced in the local press. If you want to see some newspapers from home they can be seen your particular cultural centre. All are free (except the American which is open to members only).

Music (classical) Choral Concerts are held at All Saints Cathedral by the ***Nairobi Music Society***, which also gives evening recitals at the British Council. There are occasional classical concerts held by the ***Nairobi Orchestra***.

Music (popular) can be heard at the ***African Heritage Cafe*** on Banda St who have live bands most weekends. Another place to try is ***Bombax Club*** which is located on Dagoretti Corner on the Ngong Rd. This has live bands from Thu to Wed. It is a bit out of town so take a taxi, or else a minibus from outside Nyayo House on Kenyatta Ave. Quite a few of the hotels have bands from time to time – see the local press.

Theatre There are 2 main theatres in Nairobi. ***The Professional Centre*** has performances at the Phoenix Theatre on Parliament Rd. Although a small group they are the most active and produce a range of drama of a very high standard. The other is the ***Kenya National Theatre*** located opposite the *Norfolk Hotel* on Harry Thuka Rd close to the University. Concerts are also held at the National Theatre. There are 2 high standard amateur groups, Lavington Players and Nairobi Players, who present a range of comedies, musicals and pantomimes, all of which are very popular. The local papers have notices of what's on.

● Hospitals and medical services

There are 2 private hospitals which have good facilities and staff. The first is the ***Nairobi Hospital*** (T 722160) located on Argwings Kodhek Rd and the other is the ***Aga Khan Hospital*** (T 742531) located on Limuru Rd in Parklands. If you can help it, avoid the Kenyatta Hospital, although it is free it is not worth trying to save the money as the wait can be so long.

● Night Life

The ***New Florida*** and ***Florida 2000*** on Koinange St and Moi Ave respectively are both very popular. They have fairly good sound systems and lights and stay open until 0500. ***Visions*** Kimathi St is also popular. It is smaller but otherwise fairly similar and is open from 1200 Other places include ***Hollywood*** Moktar Daddah St; ***Milano***

Club Ronald Ngala Rd; ***Beat House*** Kimathi St; ***Bubbles*** Westlands Rd; ***Kenya International*** Murang'a Rd; ***JKA Resort Club***, located on Mombasa Rd just after the turn-off to the airport, which has an open air dance floor; and ***Hillock Inn*** Enterprise Rd. There is a live band and disco at the ***Carnivore*** in Langata every night which is increasingly popular. For a very civilised dinner-dancing you cannot beat ***Le Chateau*** at the Intercontinental.

● Shopping

There are a huge number of curio and souvenir shops in Nairobi. They vary enormously in terms of more price range and quality. At stalls you will be able bargain the prices down to between a third and a half of the original asking price, although not in the more formal shops which tend to be fixed price. Shops that are part of hotels are always much more expensive. Be sure to have a good look at any purchases – wood that may look like ebony may in fact just have been polished with black shoe polish – it is a popular trick. Also cracks may appear in the wood (particularly when it is placed in a centrally heated room) if it has not been properly seasoned.

City Market, Muindi Mbingo St. Around the Market and the Jamia Mosque there are numerous stalls selling baskets, wooden and soapstone carvings, bracelets and lots of other souvenirs. Be prepared to look around and bargain.

Perhaps the best place for baskets is the ***Kariakor Market*** located on the Ring Rd at Ngara. ***Antique Gallery***, Kaunda St, T 27759 and ***Antique Auction***, Moktar Daddah St, T 336383, have antiquEast Africana collections. For paintings, batiks carvings and other higher quality crafts try ***African Heritage*** on Kenyatta Ave. ***Gallery Watatu*** and ***Roland Ward***, both on Standard St. There is a cluster of shops selling material and cloth squares (kangas and kikois) on Biashara St quite close to the market. Here you can also watch tailors on their foot-propelled machines sewing clothes, cushions etc and stitching some of the most elaborate embroidery at amazing speed. ***Lucky Wear*** has a good range of clothes and fabric as does ***Maridadi Fabrics*** which is further out of town on Landies St. There are lots of places which will kit you out in safari gear. ***Colpro*** on Kimathi St is recommended as good quality and reliable. ***Spinners Web*** located on Kijabe St close to the *Norfolk Hotel* is a good craft shop, in particular for fabrics and baskets. Its merchandise comes from various self-help groups around the country and the staff are very helpful. For jewellery and semi-precious stones try ***Al-Safa Jewellers*** at the *New Stanley Hotel* and ***Treasures and Crafts*** on Kaunda St.

Bookshops ***The Nation*** is located on Kenyatta Ave next to the *Thorn Tree Cafe* and has a good selection of books (fiction and non-fiction) and maps. ***Select*** on Kimathi St is opposite the *New Stanley Hotel* and is larger although rather run down. There is a good but small antiquEast Africana section. Other bookshops which stock a fairly good Africana selection include the ***Book Corner*** and ***Prestige*** both located on Mama Ngina St, while the ***Text Book Centre*** has text books as well as other Africana and fiction. There are a number of book stalls along Tom Mboya St and Latema Rd where you may be able to pick up a few bargain secondhand books. There is also a secondhand bookshop on Banda St.

The best maps of Nairobi are the *City of Nairobi: Map and Guide* published by the Survey of Kenya in English, German and French. If you want more detail or are staying a while it may be worth getting *A to Z Guide to Nairobi* by D T Dobie (Kenway Publications).

Pharmacies are found in all shopping centres but are generally expensive. If you know you will need anything then be sure to bring an adequate supply. The major hospitals (see above) have pharmacies which are open 24 hrs a day. Vaccinations are available from ***City Hall Clinic*** on Mama Ngina St, open only in the mornings.

Photography ***Camera Maintenance Centre*** located in the Hilton Arcade, Mama Ngina St, T 26920 and ***Camera Experts*** on Mama Ngina St, T 337750. Get a quote as repairs can be quite expensive.

If you need passport size photos there are a few booths. One is on the corner of Tom Mboya St and Accra Rd, another is a few doors up from the Thorn Tree Cafe on the corner of Kenyatta Ave and Kimathi St.

● Post Office

Kenyatta Ave. There is also a post office on Haile Selassie Ave where you will find the fairly reliable, and free, Poste Restante. Post Offices are open from 0800 to 1230 and 1400 to 1700.

● Religion

All Saints Cathedral is located on Kenyatta Ave close to Uhuru Park and the **Catholic Holy Family Minor Basilica** is situated on the corner of Parliament Ave and City Hall Way. Perhaps the most beautiful of all the places of worship is the **Jaima Mosque**, located near the City Market. This was built in 1925 in the Indian style and is set in a lively part of town close to the City Market.

● **Safety**

There are increasing reports of muggings, snatchings and robberies in Nairobi. This can certainly be a problem if you are not sensible. If you walk around with a camera around your neck, an obviously expensive watch, jewellery or a money belt showing then you are vulnerable. If you are unsure take a taxi. Places to definitely avoid walking around at night include Uhuru Park, along Uhuru Highway and the road past the National Museum. Some thieves specialise in jostling, robbing and snatching from new arrivals on buses and *matatus* from the airport.

● **Societies**

Nairobi Photographic Club Meet twice a month on Thu evenings at the St Johns Ambulance Centre which is found behind the Donovan Maule Theatre off Parliament Rd. ***Nairobi Chess Club*** Meet weekly on Thu evenings at the French Cultural Centre (PO Box 50443, T 25007). ***East African Wildlife Society*** PO Box 20110 (T 27047). This society is worth joining if you are going to be in Kenya for a while. Although membership is quite expensive you do get reductions on some national park entrance fees and they produce a monthly newsletter. They are active in the struggle to save East Africa's wildlife.

● **Sport (participant)**

Climbing Each Tue evening the ***Kenya Mountaineering Club***, PO Box 45741, meets at its clubhouse at Wilson Airport to arrange expeditions and get high on Kendal Mint Cake. T 501747.

Golf There are a number of very well kept golf courses in the suburbs of Nairobi. These include ***Karen Country Club***, Karen Rd, T 882801; ***Muthaiga Golf Club***, Muthaiga Rd, T 27333; ***Limuru Country Club***, Limuru, T Karuri 40033; ***Railway Golf Club***, Ngong Rd, T 22116; and the ***Windsor Golf and Country Club***, T 726702.

Riding Lessons and safaris can be arranged through the ***Arifa Riding School***, bookings T 25255/21845/20365.

Running ***Hash House Harriers***, meet regularly. See notices in British Council, or at British High Commission.

Sailing The ***Nairobi Sailing Club***, sails on Nairobi Dam which is found off Langata Rd. Details T 501250.

Swimming Most of the big hotels have swimming pools which can also be used by non-residents for a daily fee.

Tennis and squash Many of the major hotels have courts. Other clubs include the ***Karen Club***, Karen Rd, T 882801; ***Limuru Country Club***, Limuru, T Karuri 40033.

● **Sport (spectator)**.

Horse racing The ***Ngong Racecourse***, holds meetings most Sundays from Jan to Jun. It is a wonderful setting as well as being a great place to observe all sections members of Nairobi society.

Polo is played on Saturdays and Sundays at Jamhuri Club, Ngong Rd, weather permitting.

● **Telecommunications**

Almost opposite the Post Office on Haile Selassie Ave is the Extelcoms office from which you can make international phone calls, send faxes and telexes. You can also make calls from the Kenyatta Conference Centre – the telephone exchange is on the ground floor and it is usually much quieter than the Post Office.

● **Tourist information centre**

Located at the junction of Moi Ave and Mama Ngina St opposite the Hilton. There is also a free publication called ***Tourist's Kenya*** which is published fortnightly and which gives a run down on things going on. There is another publication called ***What's On*** which comes out monthly.

● **Tour operators and travel agents**

There are numerous tour operators based in Nairobi where you should be able to get fairly reliable information and book safaris etc. They include ***Abercrombie and Kent***, Sixth Floor, Bruce House, Standard St, T 334955/6/7, who arrange some of the most luxurious safaris in Kenya; ***Express Kenya Co (American Express Representative)***, PO Box 40433, Standard St, T 334722. Others include ***AA Travel***, Hurlingham Shopping Centre, PO Box 14982. T 339700); ***Bunson Travel Service***, PO Box 45456, Standard St, T 21992; ***Lets Go Travel***, Caxton House, Standard St, T 29539/29540/340331; ***United Touring International***, PO Box 42196, Muindi Mbingu St, T 331960).

● **Tours**

Most operators will be able to arrange a tour of Nairobi itself and this is a very useful way of familiarizing yourself with the layout of the city, as well as seeing some of the sites that are further out. The tours will usually include a trip to the *City Market*, which you may well want to return to later, the *Parliament Buildings*, and the *National Museum*.

● Transport

Local Road There are plenty of buses, *matatus* and taxis, all of which are very cheap by Western standards. Buses and *matatus* are almost always very crowded and beware of pickpockets when travelling in them.

The main city **bus** terminal is located at the end of River Rd and there are main bus stops outside the *Hilton Hotel* on Moi Ave, outside Nation House on Tom Mboya St and outside the General Post Office on Kenyatta Ave. Taxis are available outside cinemas, restaurants, hotels and at official taxi stands. Your hotel will order one for you. They cannot be hailed in the street. It is recommended that you should always take a taxi if you want to get around at night.

Car hire Cars can be rented easily in Kenya, with or without a driver. Companies include **Hertz**, PO Box 42196, T 331960; **Avis Rent a Car**, PO Box 49795, T 336794. **Europe Car**, PO Box 49420, T 332744. **Budget**, PO Box 59767, Parliament lane, Haile Selassie Ave, T 337154; **Let's Go Travel**, PO Box 60342, Caxton House, Standard St, T 29539; **Central Hire a Car**, PO Box 49439, Fehda Towers, Standard St, T 22888/332296; **Habib's Cars**, PO Box 48095, Agip House, Haile Sealassie Ave, T 20463/23816, F 339357; as well as a number of other local companies. You will often be able to collect your car in one town and drop it off in another. A cash deposit of about US$100 will be necessary unless you have a major credit card. You can expect to pay between US$20 and US$30 per day plus a mileage charge of about US$0.20 per km but it is worth asking around to compare prices.

Driving in Nairobi is a bit of an art and you will have to get used to a large number of roundabouts with rather bizarre lane systems. Be prepared for a lot of hooting, traffic light jumping and the odd potholes. Parking in Nairobi is a problem and you will be pestered by parking boys.

Policies toward these vary although there is no evidence that it is necessary to pay them to ensure the safety of your vehicle.

Central Police Station is located on University Way, T 22222. Always inform the police of any incidents – you will need a police form for any insurance claims. In emergencies dial 999.

Air The main airport is ***Jomo Kenyatta International Airport***, located about 13 km SE of the city connected by a good dual carriageway, T 822111. There is also ***Wilson Airport*** on Langata Rd from which smaller planes, including many internal charter flights, leave.

If you are travelling on an arranged tour you will probably be met at the airport by your driver who will hold up a notice with your name or the name of the tour company on it. If you are travelling independently you can either take a taxi or bus into Nairobi. Be sure to agree on the price into town – it should be around US$12. You can change money at the airport 24 hrs a day. Kenya Airways runs an hourly shuttle to the airport and picks up from Koinage St as well as from the main hotels. It costs US$3.

For international services into Nairobi see Information for Visitors, page 200.

Kenya Airways has daily flights to ***Kisumu*** and ***Mombasa*** from Kenyatta Airport. Charter fly to Maasai Mara, Malindi, Lamu and other destinations.

Train Taking the train is a splendid experience. They run overnight (it is said this is to avoid the heat of the day). There are plans, however, for a daytime departure to the coast, which will allow some sight-seeing through Tsavo National Park. Of the current rolling-stock, the 1st class carriages were built in the 1960s in the UK, the 2nd class in the 1920s (UK), and the 3rd class in 1980s in Sweden. 1st class cabins are 2-berth with wash basins. 2nd are 4-berth, and the wash basins are pretty unreliable as the carriages are around 70 years old. Ear-plugs can be a boon. Bedding is provided in 1st class. 3rd class is seated, and can get very crowded. 1st class is recommended. 1st and 2nd class should be booked in advance – it is necessary to go down to the Railway Station to do this. Dinner can be taken on the train, and is very good. Wines, beers and spirits available.

2 trains leave daily each way for **Mombasa** at 1700 and 1900 and the journey takes about 13 hrs. As it gets dark the train crosses the plains – looking out of the window you can get a real feeling of emptiness with just a glimpse of the occasional pair of glowing eyes. It costs US$19 for 1st class, US$9 for 2nd and US$5 for 3rd.

Trains to **Kisumu** leave at 1800 each day and take 14 hrs. Return to Nairobi at 1830. Extra trains sometimes run at periods of peak demand. It costs US$14 for 1st class, US$7.00 for 2nd and US$3.50 for 3rd.

There is also a train to **Malaba** on the Ugandan border twice a week. This takes over 17 hrs – it leaves Nairobi at 1500 on Fri and Sat, arriving early the next day, and leaves Malaba for Nairobi at Sat and Sun at 1600. A one-way ticket costs US$20 for 1st, US$10 for 2nd and US$5 for 3rd.

There are through trains running once a week between Nariobi and Kampala.

Departs **Nairobi** on Tue at 1000; **Naivasha** 1323; **Nakuru** 1510; **Eldoret** 2145; **Webuye** 2356; **Bungoma** 0043; **Malaba** 0155; **Tororo** 0305; **Inganga** 0518; **Jinja** 0615; **Kawolo** 0724; arrives **Kampala** 0850.

Departs **Kampala** on Wed at 1600; **Kawolo** 1731; **Jinja** 1842; **Iganga** 1932; **Tororo** 2230; **Malaba** 2305; **Bungoma** 0011; **Webuye** 0057; **Eldoret** 0355; **Nakuru** 0940; **Naivasha** 1123; arrives **Nairobi** 1425.

Road The long distance bus station is on Landies Rd. There are at least daily departures to almost every destination. The timetable is fairly flexible. For a long journey you will be told to arrive at 0700 or earlier, but if the bus is not full it will usually not go until it is. For information and bookings there are a number of coach company offices along Accra Rd.

There are many companies to choose for buses between **Nairobi** and **Mombasa** and they go frequently taking 8 hrs, costing around US$9. Since 1983 when the Kenya/Tanzania border was reopened there has been increasing traffic crossing to take advantage of the game parks in Tanzania – in particular the Serengeti and Ngorongoro Crater. You can take a bus run by Kilimanjaro Bus Service from Nairobi to **Arusha** which departs Nairobi 3 times a week at 2100 on Tue, Fri and Sat. Fares are about US$8. To the Uganda border at **Busia** take about 10 hrs and cost about US$9.

Shared taxis and matatus Shared taxis, usally Peugeot station wagons, are more expensive than matatus (mini-buses) but are quicker and safer. They usually take 7 people and leave when full, usually early in the morning. Offices in Nairobi are around Accra Rd and River Rd. Some examples of fares and costs are Kisumu US$12, 4 hrs; Nakuru US$6, 2 hrs; and Tanzanian border US$6, 2 hrs.

CENTRAL HIGHLANDS: MOUNT KENYA

CONTENTS

MAPS

The Central Highlands of Kenya is the area that was known as the 'White Highlands', to the N of Nairobi. The area includes 2 national parks (Mount Kenya and the Aberdares) and forms the eastern boundary to the Rift Valley. It is a very densely populated area, being fertile and well watered – for this reason it was here that many of the White settlers chose for their farmland. This area is the heartland of the Kikuyu people who make up the largest tribal group in Kenya.

There is a railway going up into the highlands to Nyeri and on to Nanyuki and a whole network of roads. There are a number of towns in the Central Highlands – including Nyeri, Embu, Meru, Nanyuki and Isiolo. People come to the Central Highlands to visit the Aberdare National Park (which is home to the famous hotels, the *Ark* and *Treetops*), and also to climb Mount Kenya which is also part of a National Park. (National Parks are dealt with separately in the National Park section, see page 172.

This area is very high – with peaks in the Aberdares of up to 4,000m, and Mount Kenya which is 5199m. You should therefore expect it to get fairly chilly especially at night. The maximum temperatures range from 22-26°C, and the minimum from 10-14°C. It is also very wet here with annual rainfalls of up to 3000 mm not unusual.

History

The settlers

The first settlers to come to Kenya came in search of wealth and adventure and were encouraged by the Colonial Government, who were desperate to make the colony pay for itself. The White Highland Policy was established in the early 20th century. By 1915 there were 21,400 sq km set aside for about 1,000 settlers. This number was increased after the Second World War with the Soldier Settlement Scheme. Initially the settlers grew crops and raised animals with which they were familiar with such as wheat, wool, dairy and meat, but by 1914 it was clear that these had little potential as export goods and they changed to maize and coffee. Perhaps the most famous of the early settlers was Lord Delamere. He was important in early experimental agriculture and it was through his mistakes that many lessons were learnt about agriculture in the tropics. He experimented with wheat varieties until he developed a variety resistant to wheat rust.The 1920's saw the rapid expansion of settler agriculture – in particular coffee, sisal and maize and the prices for these commodities rose, giving the settlers reason to be optimistic about their future.

However when the prices plummeted in the Depression of the 1930's the weaknesses of settler agriculture were revealed. By 1930 over 50% by value of settler export was accounted for by coffee alone, making them very vulnerable when prices fell. Many settlers were

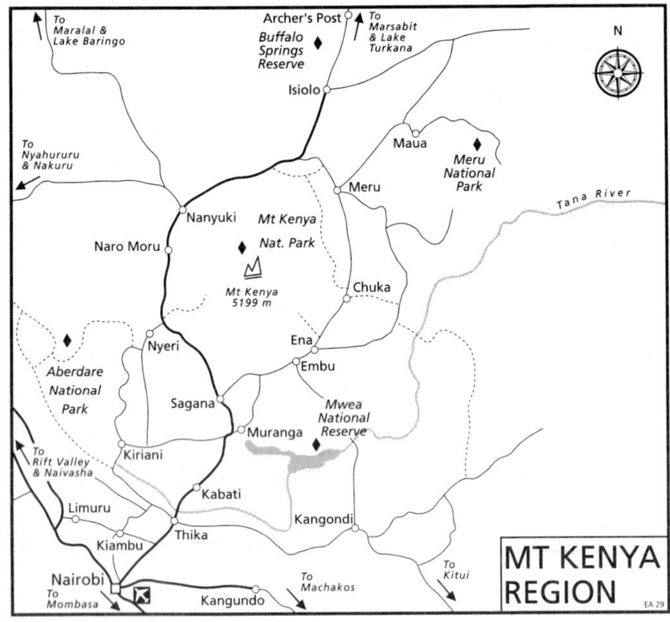

heavily mortgaged and could not service their debts. About 20% of the white farmers gave up their farms, while others left farming temporarily. Cultivated land on settler farms fell from 644,000 acres in 1930 to 502,000 acres in 1936, most of the loss being wheat and maize.

About one third of the colonial government's revenue was from duties on settlers' production and goods imported by the settlers. Therefore the government was also seriously affected by the fall in prices. In earlier years the government had shown its commitment to white agriculture by investment in infrastructure (eg railways and ports), and because of its dependence on custom duties for revenues it felt it could not simply abandon the settlers. Many were saved by the colonial government who pumped about £1 million into white agriculture with subsidies and rebates on exports and loans, and the formation of a Land Bank.

Following the Depression and the Second World War the numbers of settlers increased sharply so that by the 1950's the White population had reached about 80,000. The main crops that they grew were coffee, tea and maize as well as diary farming. However discontent among the East African population over the loss of their traditional land to the settlers was growing. the East Africans had been confined to Native Reserves, and as their population grew, the pressure on these areas increased. Some of the East Africans lived as squatters on White land, and many migrated and worked as wage labourers for the settlers.

Political demands by Kenyans accelerated throughout the late 1940s and 1950s and the issue of land was critical (see section on **Independence**, page 45. Although there are still many White

Kenyans in this area the size and number of their land holdings has been reduced considerably and land transferred to the Kikuyu. The allocation of land at and around the time of independence was a controversial issue – the aim was to distribute land bought by the British government from settlers as equitably as possible. However there is evidence that a few richer Kenyans managed to secure large areas. The issue of the polarisation and concentration of land ownership amongst a privileged few is one that continues today – it is not something that independence has solved.

Kikuyu in the Colonial Period

Up until the 1930's African agriculture had been largely ignored by the Government. Africans were in fact banned from growing, coffee, the most valuable crop. The reason given for this was that production by thousands of small farmers would make it impossible to control coffee berry disease. It had the side effect of ensuring a labour supply for European farms as Africans could then only pay their hut and poll taxes by working as wage labourers.

When the effects of the Depression reached Kenya it became clear that African producers were more easily able to survive difficult years, and in particular were able to produce cereals more cheaply than the settlers. As European agriculture contracted, squatters on white land increased production of food crops and maize in particular, and found they could make a profit despite the low prices of the 1930's. The need to boost exports as prices fell undermined both official and settler opposition to African production and the East African share of production increased from 9% in 1931 to between 15 and 20% in 1933 as a result of increased maize production and the expansion of the cultivation of wattle by the Kikuyu.

Wattle production, encouraged by the Department of Agriculture, was expanded dramatically and earnings from wattle increased from £35,000 in 1929 to £79,500 in 1932. It was in many ways an ideal crop – it could be used or sold for fuel, or sold to expatriate firms for the extraction of tannin. It needed little attention after the initial planting, and so could be grown without interrupting the normal agricultural cycle. The areas most affected were Kiambu, Kikuyuland and Embu and many peasant producers made substantial profits.

Meanwhile, during the late 1920's and early 1930's there were a series of droughts which affected the lowland pastoral areas of the Rift Valley much more severely than Kikuyuland. Livestock prices fell dramatically as the pastoralists sold stock to buy food and Kikuyu agriculturalists took advantage. This was a structural change at the expense of the pastoralists from which they have never recovered. There is little doubt that the Kikuyu acted with great economic acumen. The situation also increased the inequalities within Kikuyu society as those with secure access to land not only made a comfortable living from maize and wattle, but were able to increase their livestock, land and wives.

Observers have argued that the Kikuyu not only showed great resilience in the time of the Depression but (particularly those with assured access to land) managed to seize the opportunity given to them by the Depression and benefit greatly. The contraction of European production of maize, and the reassessment by the government of the importance of African agriculture, together with the favourable trading conditions with their neighbours meant that the Kikuyu were given a real opportunity to increase their economic position, and ultimately their political power. The Depression can be seen therefore as a turning point in the fortunes of the Kikuyu – by stimulating production of both food and wattle.

People

Kikuyu, see page 47, are the largest tribal group in Kenya and make up an estimated 21% of the population, with a population of around 6mn. They are believed to have migrated into this area around the 16th century from the east and northeast of Africa as part of the Bantu expansion, and to have intermarried with the groups that occupied the area. These groups were largely hunter-gatherer peoples (unlike the Kikuyu who were kept livestock and cultivated the land) and included the Athi and the Gumba.

The Kikuyu belong to age-sets and as they get older they advance in terms of status. One of the most important of the cultural aspects of the Kikuyu is circumcision which traditionally applied to both men and women. Circumcision of women, known as clitoridectomy, is now illegal (there was a campaign against the practice during the colonial period), but there is still evidence of some continuation of the practice. For men however the ritual is an important part of the transition from boyhood to manhood.

The Kikuyu are made up of clans, the 2 most important being based on Kiambu and Nyeri, and rivalry between the 2 is intense. In the 1992 multi-party elections, the Ford-Asili party, headed by Kenneth Matiba, effectively represented Kiambu interests, while the Democratic Party was led by Mwai Kibaki from Nyeri. Fragmentation of the opposition allowed the incumbent KANU party to retain power.

The **Embu** and the **Meru** are 2 groups, each with their own main town of the same

Kikuyu Proverbs

Kikuyu proverbs are revealing about a number of elements of Kikuyu culture. In particular you will notice the position and influence of women; the status of the old; the strength of the more powerful against the weak; and the importance of children - something which helps explain the very high birth rate that is found here.

Brought up among boys, the young girl weakens
(The weak cannot compete with the strong. Boys are better nourished than girls.)

Women and the sky cannot be understood.

The man may be the head of the home; the wife is the heart.

Two wives, two pots of poison.

An old goat never sneezes for nothing.
(The old do not speak without reason, they speak the truth.)

A women whose sons have died is richer that a barren woman.

Who will draw water for the childless old woman?

He who asks for mashed food has someone to mash it.
(Only a married man can expect home comforts.)

Women have only crooked words.
(Women cannot keep secrets and seldom tell the truth.

Women's quarrels never end.
(Women are relentless in their disputes).

A woman and an invalid man are the same thing.

The law of the fishes: the big ones eat the small ones.

Frowning frogs cannot stop the cows drinking from the pool.

They are friends when you have your beer party, they were not friends when your house had to be built.

name, which have strong affinities with the Kikuyu. In the 1970s a pressure group called the Gikuyu, Embu and Meru Association (GEMA) was active in advancing the interests of these 3 peoples.

NAIROBI TO NYERI

Thika

From Muthaiga the road, which is 4 lanes and a good surface, continues up towards Thika which is actually off the main road N. This is the town which was made famous by the book (and later the television series) *The Flame Trees of Thika* by Elspeth Huxley. It is about her childhood when her parents came out to Kenya as one of the first families, and their attempts to establish a farm. The route cross the Thika River which joins the Tana River further down stream. The **Blue Posts Hotel** is a famous colonial landmark. Nearby is the **Ol Doinyo Sabuk National Park** which is located about 25 km from Thika on the A3, the road leading east toward Garissa. In this area there are also the **Fourteen Falls** which are particularly splendid during the rainy season (see National Parks). Thika itself has a fair amount of manufacturing activity, particularly fruit canning for export.

● **Where to stay** **C** *New Blue Posts*, PO Box 42, Thika, T 22241. Just N of Thika, on the road to Murang'a. This has been renovated fairly recently and remains popular. It has a very good view over the Falls, and it is a good place to break a journey, and quite the nicest place to stay in the area. **D** *White Line*, this is located on the same road as the Post Office in the centre of Thika, and is not a bad place to stay. The rooms have bathrooms and there is sometimes hot water. There is a restaurant.

From Thika the road (A2) continues northwards through the green and verdant countryside. Almost every inch of ground is cultivated and you will see terraces on some of the steeper slopes. You will soon notice that this is pineapple country and many acres are taken up with plantations. They look similar to sisal plantations with spiky plants. There are a number of choices: you can go N to Nyeri and the Aberdare National Park; clockwise round the mountain via Naro Moru or anticlockwise via Embu. This section will cover the route clockwise around Mount Kenya, taking in Nyeri, Naro Moru, Nanyuki, Meru and then finally Embu.

Murang'a

The first town that you will reach is Murang'a. This is a small bustling town that is situated just off the main road N. At the turn of the century there was very little here – it was initially established as an administrative centre and as it was located in the Kikuyu Reserves rather than in the White Highlands it never became a settler town.

The town has become known as the Kikuyu Heartland because it is close to **Mugeka**, the *Mukuruwe wa Gathanga* (Garden of Eden of the Kikuyu) – which is an important place in Kikuyu mythology. The legend is that it was here that God found 9 husbands under a fig tree for the 9 Gikuyu and Mumbi daughters, who in mythology are the ancestors of all Kikuyu. These 9 became the forefathers of the 9 Kikuyu clans. At one time there was a museum at the site of the original fig tree.

In Murang'a is the **Church of St James and All Martyrs**, also known as CPK Cathedral. This is not particularly old but has some interesting decorations painted in 1955 by a Tanzanian artist named Elimo Njau. It shows various scenes from the bible with an African Christ and in African surroundings. The Church was founded in memory of the Kikuyu who died in the Mau Mau Emergency.

● **Where to stay & eat** **E** *Ngurunga Bar*, close to the bus station. Simple lodging. **E** *Rwathia Bar and Restaurant*, PO Box 243, located opposite the market, T 22527. Reasonable meals.

From Murang'a the main road continues N towards Nyeri, Naro Moru and Nanyuki. It is possible to take a detour into the **Aberdare Forest**. To take the route into the Aberdare Range, follow one of the minor roads from Murang'a which eventually leads to Othaya and on to Nyeri – the turning for this is to the left just before you get to Murang'a.

On the main road N the next town you will reach is **Karatina** where there are baskets for sale from the Kikuyu women who sit on the road side. It is often the vendors themselves who make the baskets, and they are good value.

Just beyond Karatina there is a track to the right which goes to the **Mountain Lodge** which is located in the foothills of Mount Kenya (See section on National Parks, page 187). About another 20 km from Karatina is the turning off to Nyeri which is the largest town in the Province.

Nyeri

Nyeri is the administrative centre of the Central Province and is located about 120 km from Nairobi. It is at the base of the Aberdares, close to the boundary of the Aberdare National Park. It is situated a few km off the road that goes around Mount Kenya – the turning is signposted.

The surrounding area is fairly densely populated. On a clear morning you can see Mount Kenya in the distance. It is one of the wettest parts of Kenya and can be cold in the evenings.

During the British colonial period Nyeri developed as an army base and then as an important trading centre for farmers in the surrounding countryside. It surrounding land is very fertile and as you drive into Nyeri you will see the many *shambas* (farms) growing maize, bananas and coffee as well as many varieties of vegetables.

Useful information

The town has a main street, Kimathi Way on which you will find banks, the Post Office, the Clock Tower, and several the hotels. A little to the S of this cluster is the market and the bus stand. The Cemetery, with the grave of Baden-Powell and his wife, is just to the N of the Clock Tower.

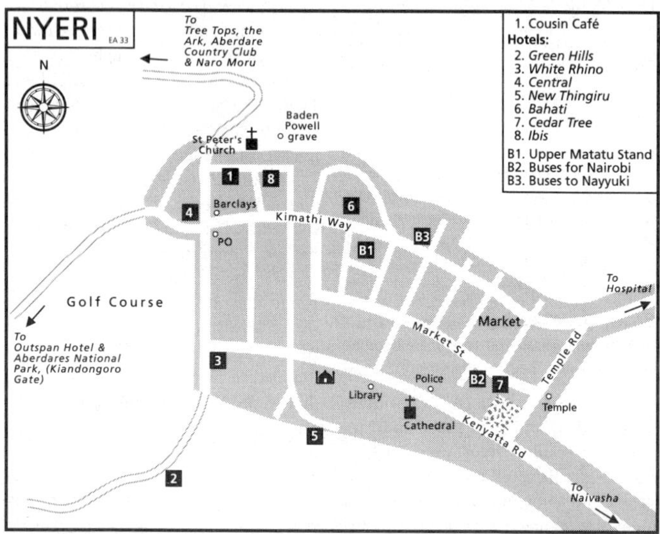

Places of interest

On the main road – Kimathi Way – you can see a memorial to those that died during the Mau Mau. It has the inscription: To the Memory of the Members of the Kikuyu Tribe Who Died in the Fight for Freedom 1951-57.

Local information

● Where to stay

A+ *Aberdare Country Club*, PO Box 449, Nyeri, T Mweiga 17. This is located about 12 km to the N of Nyeri itself and is now managed by the *Lonhro Group*. It is another old colonial type of country hotel, and is very luxurious. You can hire self-drive cars here, as well as arrange game drives into the National Park. **A+** ***Outspan Hotel***, PO Box 24, Nyeri, T 2424, Nyeri – Bookings: PO Box 47557, Nairobi, T 335807. This hotel is located a little out of town (about 20 mins walk or a taxi ride) opposite the golf course. It is set in some of the most beautiful gardens and has the full facilities of a country hotel. There are a range of rooms and prices depend on the season. The rooms are very spacious and the hotel has a wonderful atmosphere. If you are staying at *Treetops* you will come here to be picked up for the final drive. The *Outspan* is a good place to stop for breakfast or lunch – you can admire the gardens and, as long as the clouds are not down, you will get a good view of Mount Kenya. There is also a swimming pool. You can rent self-drive vehicles from the *Outspan*, and they also arrange game drives for the day into the Aberdare National Park which are good if you cannot afford the cost of accommodation in the Park itself.

C *Green Hills*, PO Box 313, Nyeri, T 2017. This hotel is located close to the golf course on the top of a hill, it is spread over fairly extensive gardens and lawns and is large with over 100 rooms. It has excellent facilities including 2 restaurants, bar, swimming pool, and sauna and is safe and friendly.

D *White Rhino* This hotel is located fairly centrally in Nyeri and is one of the old colonial hotels that are found scattered all over the White Highlands. The facilities are not that extensive, but it has a atmosphere that makes it worth it. It has a bar, restaurant, and lounge. **D** *Central*, this is a modern hotel that is located close to the Post Office in the N of the town. It is good value and all the rooms have bath-

BADEN-POWELL

Lord Baden-Powell distinguished himself in the Boer War during the seige of Mafeking. At the time he was the youngest General in the British Army at 45 years old.

Baden-Powell is best known as the founder of the Boy Scout movement. Guides were soon to follow and, for younger children, Cubs and Brownies. The movement is immensely successful, and is popular around the world with millions of children.

Baden-Powell once visited a small boarding school in the Rift Valley which was popular amongst British settlers and missionaries. Some of the children there were as young as six, and considered to be too small to join the Brownies or the Cubs. Baden-Powell therefore decided to establish something for the youngest children - and so the "Chippets" were born. The Chippets have continued there to this day and the school (St Andrew's School, Turi, see page 93) remembers Lord Baden-Powell each year. They also have a flag mounted in one of the corridors which was presented to the school by Baden-Powell's wife after his death.

Nyeri was Baden-Powell's great love and he once wrote that "The nearer to Nyeri the nearer to bliss". In the grounds of the *Outspan Hotel* is the cottage, *Paxtu*, meaning "Just Peace", built with money collected by guides and scouts from around the world, where Baden Powell spent his final years. He died in 1941 and his obituary states: "No Chief, no Prince, no King, no Saint was ever mourned by so great a company of boys and girls, of men and women, in every land." He is buried in Nyeri cemetery, and his wife is buried beside him.

rooms with hot water. It has a bar and restaurant, and a disco at weekends. **D** *New Thingira Guest House*, PO box 221, Nyeri, T 4769. Another modern hotel this is very good value. Rooms have bathrooms with hot water, it is clean, friendly and secure, and there is a restaurant attached.

E *Bahati Boarding and Lodging*, located close to the northern-most matatu and bus stand this hotel is good value. It has a range of rooms – with and without bathrooms (hot water at certain times of the day only) – which are basic, but it is clean and reasonably friendly. There is a bar and restaurant attached. There are a number of other cheap places but none particularly pleasant for more than the minimum stay. They include the **E** *Cedar Tree Board and Lodging* close to the southern Post Office which is not bad and the **E** *Ibis*.

● Places to eat

If you staying in one of the top range hotels you will probably eat there. Otherwise the ♦♦*Central* and ♦♦*White Rhino* have restaurants which are both good value. For very basic, but cheap food, try the ♦*Cousin Café* which is located in the town centre just round the corner from Barclays Bank.

● Shopping

There are a number of good shops in Nyeri including bookshops, grocers, and hardware shops. There is also the market which is very good for fruit and vegetables.

● Tours

Nyeri is the gateway to the Aberdare National Park and you will come here before you go to the Park. If you do not already have a trip arranged you can organise one through the *Outspan*. You will need a group of at least 3 people (the more people the cheaper it should work out) and they are just for the day. They are therefore ideal if you cannot afford the lodges in the Park itself. They are fairly good value and the price varies depending on where you want to go in the Park.

● Transport to and from Nyeri

Air Nyeri is served by *Kenyan Airways* – flights to Nanyuki (10 mins), Samburu (50 mins) and Nairobi (about an hr) daily. It is not worth the bother of flying Nyeri-Nanyuki – by the time you have checked in and so on you could have driven there.

Rail Although there is a railway line up to Nyeri, this no longer takes passengers, but is freight only.

Road Nyeri is located about 130 km to the N of Nairobi and is on the very good A2 road. From here it is about 60 km to Nanyuki. The bus stand is on Kimathi Way in the centre of town.

MOUNT KENYA

There are a number of towns located along the Kirinyaga Ring Road, at the base of Mount Kenya which serve as starting points for the climb up the mountain. This section deals with these towns going clockwise – Naro Moru, Nanyuki, Meru and Embu. Details of the mountain and the actual routes up it, is dealt with in the Game Parks section (see page 187). The route is becoming increasingly popular as a tourist circuit which is not surprising for it is a beautiful part of the country, and the mountain and the game parks nearby are an added attraction. The base of the mountain is about 80 km across making it one of the largest volcanic cones in the world. As you drive along this route you will spend much of the time looking towards the mountain – however, much of the time it is shrouded in cloud. There are some clear days – otherwise very early in the morning or just before nightfall the cloud will often lift suddenly revealing the 2 peaks for a few minutes.

Naro Moru

The road from Nyeri climbs gradually up to Naro Moru which is little more than a village located at the base of the mountain. It has a few shops, guesthouses and a post office and is clustered around the railway station which no longer functions as a passenger terminal. Bear in mind before you arrive here that there are no banks in the village. There are no restaurants apart from the one at the *Naro Moru River Lodge*, and if you are cooking your own food you would be advised to stock up before you get here. However, the village does receive quite a few visitors as it serves as the starting point of the Naro Moru

Trail, one of the most popular routes up the mountain. Before you set off on this route you have to both book and pay for the mountain huts that you will stay in on the way up. This can all be done through the *Naro Moru River Lodge*.

● **Where to stay A** ***The Naro Moru River Lodge***, PO Box 18, Naro Moru, T 22018. This is located about 2 km from the village itself off the main road. This hotel is the most popular place to stay as it organises climbs up the mountain. The facilities are good including a swimming pool, restaurant, bar and roaring log fire which is perfect for the chilly evenings.

C ***Bantu's Mount Kenya Leisure***, PO Box 333, Nanyuki, T 22787. Lodge. This is located on the road to Nanyuki – you will see a signpost off the main road. It is in lovely surroundings and has a range of self-contained cottages with full facilities. They even have fire places in each cottage which is very nice on a cold evening. The hotel also arranges a wide range of activities including riding, fishing, bird-watching and evening entertainment. The hotel is well known for its very well run treks up the mountain (taking the Naro Moru, Sirimon or Burguret routes). You can choose an itinery to suit you – for more details see Mount Kenya section, page 187.

E ***Mount Kenya Hostel***, this is located about 12 km down the track towards the Park entrance off the main Nanyuki road, about 4 km from the Park entrance gate. It is popular with budget travellers. Hot showers and cooking facilities. Construction work should be being undertaken for a more substantial building – the original building burnt down in 1988 and as they were not insured rebuilding has been delayed. **E** ***Camping***, there is a site attached to *Naro Moru River Lodge*, and if you do not have the necessary equipment you can hire everything. You can use all the hotel facilities, and the campsite sometimes has hot showers. There are also bunk beds available in huts – but these are not very good value. Also at *Bantu's Mount Kenya Leisure*, good facilities available and *Mount Kenya Hostel*, where you can hire a tent.

Nanyuki

Nanyuki is a small up-country town located to the northwest of the mountain that dates back to about 1907 when it was established and used by white settlers as a trading centre and for socialising. The town today is home to the Kenyan air force as well as a British Army base. Despite this it is a fairly sleepy kind of up-country town and retains some of its colonial character. The town is visited by people planning to use the Sirimon or Buguret trails up the mountain. It has a good range of shops, banks including Barclays, Standard

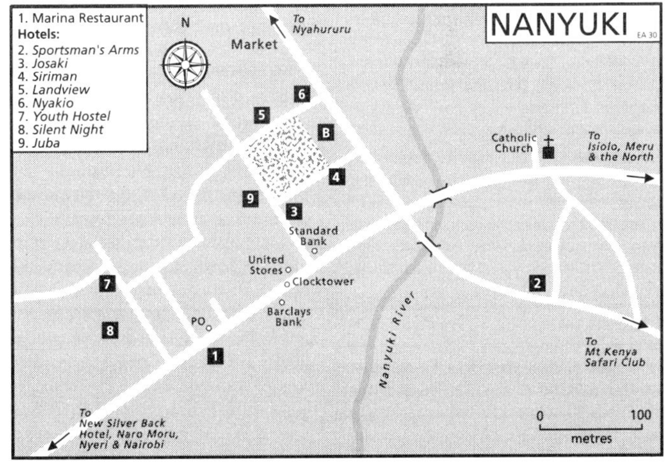

Chartered and Kenya Commercial Bank. The District Hospital is located about a kilometre out of town to the east.

On the main road to Nanyuki there are signposts marking the equator, and souvenir sellers.

Local information

● Where to stay

A+ ***Mount Kenya Safari Club***, PO Box 35, Nanyuki, T 2141/2142. This is Nanyuki's most exclusive hotel.

C ***Sportsman's Arms***, PO Box 3, Nanyuki, T 22598. Located across the river and is probably the best value hotel in Nanyuki. Surrounded by gardens and in a lovely setting. Rooms are self contained and the price includes breakfast. It is clean and friendly. **C** ***New Silverbeck***, T 2740. This hotel is rather shabby. It offers a range of rooms but the facilities are poor and there are frequently problems with the water supply. However the cottages all have fireplaces and there is an Equator sign in the grounds. Facilities include bar, restaurant and shops.

D ***Josaki***, T 2181. Located close to the Park in the centre of town and popular. All rooms have bathrooms and it has a bar and restaurant, and good views around. It has a disco and can be noisy. **D** ***Sirimon Guest House***, situated facing the Park this hotel is very good value, T 22243. It has a range of rooms with bathrooms – with hot water. It is secure and friendly and there is parking space available. **D** ***Landview Boarding and Lodging***, located on the N side of the park. All rooms have bathrooms and it has a bar and restaurant. **D** ***Nyakio Boarding and Lodging***, north side of the park. All rooms have bathrooms and a bar and restaurant.

E ***Youth Hostel***, T 211, which is located on Market Road and is very cheap. It is clean and friendly and has shared facilities. **E** ***Silent Guest House***, Market Road. Simple but perfectly acceptable. **E** ***Juba Boarding and Lodging***, near Park. Very cheap. **E** ***Camping***, site at *Sportsman's Arms*.

● Places to eat

Apart from the restaurants attached to the hotels there are few places to eat in Nanyuki. ♦***Marina Bar and Restaurant***, opposite the Post Office. Convenient for a cold beer and a snack. ♦***Maridadi Cafe***, near bus stand. Good value.

● Transport

Road Nanyuki is located about 60 km from **Nyeri** and 190 km from **Nairobi** – a drive that will take you about 3 hrs. There are frequent buses and *matatus* running between Nanyuki and Nairobi. If you are heading N of Marsabit and Northern Kenya you can get buses and matatus from Nanyuki to **Isiolo** (which is the last town on the good road heading N) and from there continue N. The matatu station is located next to the Park.

● Useful addresses

On the main street there is the ***Post Office*** and branches of ***Barclays Bank***, ***Standard Chartered Bank*** and ***Kenya Commercial Bank***. There is also ***Settlers Stores*** which is one of the oldest shops in town having been founded in 1938 and selling hardware and groceries. Other shops include the ***United Stores*** and ***Modern Sanitary Stores*** where you should be able to stock up on all your supplies. If you are interested in buying hand woven rugs and other items you may want to visit the ***Nanyuki Spinners and Weavers Workshop***. This is run by a women's group who sell to the Spin and Weave Shop in Nairobi.

NANYUKI TO NYAHURURU

From Nanyuki you can take the road W towards **Nyahururu**. This town is closer to Nakuru and more easily reached from there. The road between Nanyuki and Nyahururu is not good – particularly during the wet season. On the road to Nyahururu there are a number of game ranches, some of which, including the **Laikipia Ranch**, have been important in the battle to save the rhino. The efforts have involved keeping the rhino as part of an integrated grazing system – they seem to do well and do not interfere in the cattle who graze the same land. The **Ol Pejeta Game Reserve** which covers an area of about 400 km is also open to the public – it has a luxury lodge called Sweetwaters Camp (located about 40 km from Nanyuki) PO Box 585 81, Nairobi, T Nairobi 216940, F Nairobi 216796 and much of the Reserve is a rhino sanctuary. They organise night game viewing trips and you are likely to see rhino. Another ranch that is open to the public is the **El Karama Ranch** (book through *Let's Go Travel*, PO Box 60342, Nairobi, T Nairobi 340331, F Nairobi 336890) located about 40 km to the N of Nanyuki. They have a range of good value accommodation and also organise horse riding game viewing.

Nyahururu (Thomson's Falls)

Small town at high altitude (2,360m) with a splendid climate. Although only a few kilometres north of the equator, there are bracing nights with occasional frosts in the early months of the year. There is good rainfall, the surrounding area is well timbered, and a variety of vegetables and grains are grown. The town served settler farmers in the area during the colonial period, and was boosted when a branch line of the railway reached the town in 1929. It still runs, but only carries freight. In the postwar period the town was prosperous enough to boast a racecourse.

Joseph Thomson, an explorer, came across the waterfall to the north of the town in 1883 which he named **Thomson's Falls** after his father. The cascade plunges 75m, and is a pretty area to walk around.

Local Information

● Where to stay

C *Thomson's Falls Lodge*, PO Box 38, just off the road out of town toward Nyeri and Nanyuki. T 22006. Very charming colonial atmosphere. There is a choice of rooms in the main building, or cottages. Built in 1931, and initially called Barry's Hotel. **C** *Baron Hotel*, Ol Kalou Rd. Own bathrooms. Bar-Restaurant. More modern building. Disco at weekends.

E *Good Shepherd Lodge*, just north of centre. Own bathrooms. Good value. **E** *Manguo* (Stadium Lodging). Next to open market. Simple, but clean and secure. **E** *Cyrus*, Ol Kalou Rd Nothing elaborate, but sound. Good

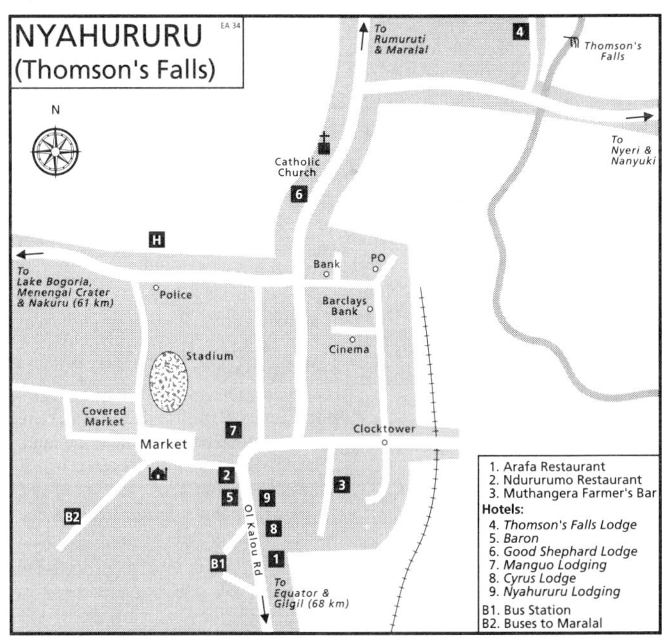

reataurant (Arafra) attached. **E** ***Nyahururu Lodging***, Ol Kalou Rd. Shared bathrooms. Basic, but adequate.

● Places to eat and drink

♦♦*Arafa Ol Kalou Rd*, attached to Cyrus Hotel. Good standard.

♦*Ndururumo*, close to open market. Rough and ready, but reasonable value.

● Entertainment

Disco at Baron Hotel at weekends. **Cinema** just north of clocktower. **Bar** Lively atmosphere at Muthengera Farmer's Lodge, just east of Ol Kalou Rd.

● Transport

Regular buses and minibuses linking to **Nakuru** to the west and **Nyeri** to the east. One departure north each day for **Maralal**, leaving at 0700 and costing $3.

NANYUKI TO MERU

North east from Nanyuki the road continues around Mount Kenya. The next village that you will reach after Nanyuki is **Timau** – there is very little here. Another 35 odd km down the road is the turning off to the left that goes on up to Marsabit and northern Kenya. The first town on this road is **Isiolo** which is located about 30km off the Nanyuki-Meru road and is where the good road ends. (See Northern Kenya Section). Continuing around the mountain you will reach the town of **Meru**, about 30 km on from the turning to Isiolo, which is a thriving and bustling trading centre. The journey from Nanyuki to Meru is very beautiful – and shows the diversity of Kenya's landscape. To the S is Mount Kenya, to the N (on a clear, haze-free day) you can see miles and miles of the northern wilderness of Kenya.

Meru

Meru is located to the northeast of the Mountain and has a population of about 75,000. Although it serves as an important trading centre it is not visited by many tourists. It also does not have the advantage of proximity to any of the trails up the mountain and so has not been developed for this. It is however the base for visits to the **Meru National Park** the entrance of which is about 80 km from the town – See Game Parks section, page 185. It is set at an altitude of about 3000m and in the rainy season is cold and damp. If you are there on a clear day you may get good views around – it is heavily cultivated and forested. The town developed as a trading centre and is strung out along the main road.

The Meru National Museum PO Box 592, T 20482. Entrance US$0.50 Located down the road roughly opposite the *Meru County Hotel* off the main road and in what is the oldest building in the town, originally the District Commissioner's office. The most interesting section of the museum is that related to the customs and culture of the local Meru people: various ethnographic exhibits, examples of local timber and stone and tools from the prehistoric site at Lewa Downs. There is a Meru homestead which gives a good idea of how the Meru people live. Outside there is a display of

MIRAA

Miraa is also known as "qat" and "gatty" and is produced in large quantities around Meru. It is a leaf which is chewed and is a mild stimulant as well as acting as an appetite suppressant. You will see people all over Kenya (but particularly in the N and NE) holding bunches of these leaves and twigs and chewing them. In the town centre there is a street corner that is devoted to the selling of miraa - in case you want to try some. It is a small tree that grows wild here and is also grown commercially. It is produced legally and it is also sold to the northeast of Kenya and exported to Somalia, Yeman and Djibouti.

various herbal and traditional medicinal plants – including an example of a miraa plant. There is also a display of stuffed birds and animals.

The **Post Office** is on the main road on the left as you come in from Nanyuki. There are branches of **banks** situated just off the main road. There is an excellent well stocked supermarket on the road out towards Nanyuki called **Supermart**. There are 2 **markets** at Meru – one is situated on the main road towards Nanyuki and the other is the other side of town. The merchandise on sale are very cheap and include not just agricultural produce from the farms around Meru, but also baskets and household goods.

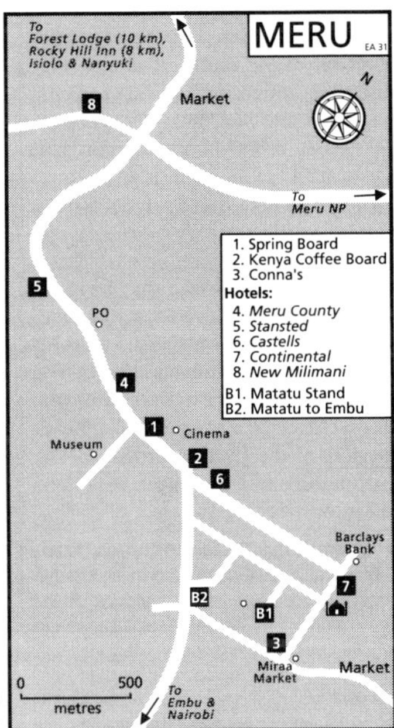

Local information

● Where to stay

B *Forest Lodge*, about 10 km out, to the N of the town and has a range of comfortable cottages. Facilities include bar, restaurant and swimming pool and it is set in fine gardens.

C *Rocky Hill Inn*, located 8 km out of town in the same direction as the *Forest Lodge*. It has simple cottages for rent – unfortunately the water supply is not very reliable. There is a bar and they have a barbecue which is good value.

D *Meru County*, PO Box 1386, T 20427. This is situated on the main road and is probably the best hotel in the town itself. It is simple but clean, safe and friendly. It has a restaurant, bar and video lounge and there is plenty of parking space.

E *Stansted*, PO Box 1337, T 20360. This is a very good value hotel – clean, comfortable and friendly. **E** *Castells* Simple and good value. **E** *Continental*, fairly basic. **E** *New Milimani*, disco at weekends – plenty of parking space but often has water supply problems.

● Places to eat

♦♦*Meru County*, good snack bar. ♦♦*New Milimani*, wide-ranging menu including curries. ♦♦*Canopy Restaurant*, Main road near to *Castells Hotel*. Good standard and value. ♦♦*Springboard Quality Cafe*, Main road is good for snacks and the ♦♦*Kenya Coffee Board*, excellent coffee and snacks.

♦*Conna's Hygienic Food Centre*, generous helpings of simple fare.

● Transport

Air There is an airstrip serving Meru.

Road There are daily buses to Meru from **Nairobi** including the luxury service. The journey to Nairobi takes about 5 hrs, to **Chogoria** about an hr and a half and to **Embu** about 2 and a half hrs. Matatus are not very safe as they are often involved in accidents on this route and the bus is definitely better option. Meru is located about 70 km from Nanyuki.

South from Meru the road to Embu is good.The scenery here is well worth spending the time to appreciate. If you can sit on the right you will be able to look out for glimpses of the mountain peaks. About 5 km S of Meru you will again cross the equator.

Chogoria

Between Meru and Embu is the village of Chogoria which is the starting point for the Chogoria trail. This is the only eastern trail up the mountain and it is generally considered to be the most beautiful of the routes. It is also supposed to be the easiest as far as gradients are concerned. See Mount Kenya, page 187 for detail. The buses to Embu usually stop off at Chogoria (it takes about an hr and a half) so it is easily accessible.

Embu

This is the final town in the clockwise circuit around Mount Kenya, before rejoining the road S to Nairobi. The town is strung out along the main road. The town, named after the Embu people who live in this area, is the provincial headquarters of the Eastern Province. The surrounding area is densely populated and intensively cultivated.

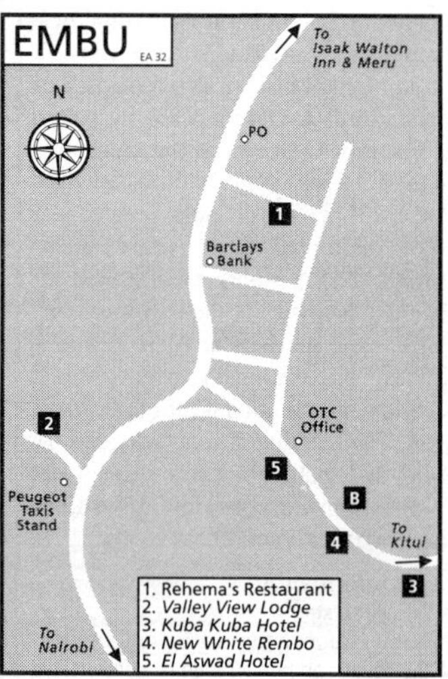

● **Where to stay B** *Izaac Walton Inn*, PO Box 1, Embu, T 20128/9. This is the best hotel in Embu. Situated about 2 km out of town on the road that heads N towards Meru. It is an old colonial hotel – set in gardens with a comfortable lounge with a log-burning fire. Rooms all have bathrooms with hot water and each room has a balcony. The price includes breakfast and there is a good bar and restaurant. It is very friendly and the staff helpful. **D** *Valley View Lodge*, PO Box 563, T 20147. Located away from the centre of town. It is quiet, clean and friendly. It has a range of rooms – all with hot water, and has a bar and good restaurant. **E** *Kuba Kuba*, situated down the hill from the centre of town. Reasonable – basic with small rooms but clean and simple. **E** *New White Rembo*, opposite the bus and matatu stop. Range of self-contained rooms and is conveniently located. It also has a good restaurant. **E** *Al-Aswad*, situated a little up the hill. It has a popular restaurant attached, serving simple fare.

● **Places to eat** ♦♦*Izaac Walton Inn*, good meals, and fine atmosphere. ♦*Rehema's Cafe*, north part of town, off the main road, up the hill. Good snacks.

● **Services** The **Post Office** is located on the Meru road that heads N, as is the town **library**. There is a branch of **Barclays Bank** located on the roundabout where the roads meet.

● **Transport** The road from Nairobi to Embu is a very good surface but is probably one of the most dangerous roads in Kenya and there are frequent accidents. *Matatus* are therefore not to be recommended. Instead take the OTC bus, if possible, which goes everyday and is reasonably safe.

THE RIFT VALLEY

Contents

Maps

The Great Rift Valley is one of the most dramatic features on earth, stretching some 6,000 km from the Dead Sea in Jordan down to Mozambique in the South. In Kenya, the Rift Valley starts at Lake Turkana in the North, and runs right through the centre of the country to Lake Natron just across the southern border in Tanzania. It is up to 100 km wide in places and a fascinating place of cliffs, escarpments, rivers and arid plains housing an enormous diversity of wildlife, and trees and plants. The valley floor rises from around 200m at Lake Turkana to about 1,900m above sea level at Lake Naivasha to the South. The walls rise where the valley floor is at its highest, and reach their peak in the Aberdares above Naivasha.

There are some 30 active and semi-active volcanoes in the Rift Valley and countless springs bringing sodium carbonate up to the surface of the earth, forming the soda lakes. Soda lakes are a result of the poor drainage system in the valley resulting in a number of shallow lakes on the valley floor. Evaporation has left a high concentration of alkaline volcanic deposits in the remaining water. The algae and crustaceans which thrive in the soda lakes are ideal food for flamingos and there are many here, and they are quite spectacular.

The Rift valley is one of the few ecosystems which has remained unchanged for centuries, holding a great array of Africa's wildlife. It is the site of 2 of the most significant digs in palaentological history the **Koobi Fora** on the eastern shores of Lake Turkana and **Olduvai Gorge** in the Tanzania section of the Rift. No visit to Kenya is complete without spending some time in the Rift Valley.

Your first glimpse of it is likely to be from the viewpoints along the Nairobi-Naivasha new road just past Limuru, at the top of the escarpments of the Valley. Mount Longonot is directly in front, while the plains seem to sweep on for ever to the S. There are a number of tourist stalls here selling curios. A reasonably good buy, however, are the lambskins, though they are not particularly well cured.

Naivasha and environs

Naivasha is a small trading centre just off the main road from Nairobi to Nakuru. It used to be more popular with tourists as the old road passed through it, now the best reason to visit is for the excellent Belle Inn fruit juices and pastries. It is a stop on the way to **Lake Naivasha**, **Mount Longonot** and the **Hell's Gate National Park**. Naivasha is sufficiently close to Nairobi to be used as a weekend retreat for people working in the capital. There are still a number of White Kenyans farming the land around the lake.

Places of interest

The most likely reason for stopping here is en route to either Lake Naivasha or Hell's Gate, see National Parks section, page 187. The lack of facilities for budget travellers around the lake make staying in Naivasha a useful option. **Kamuta Ltd**, T 0311 30091 is the base of Air Naivasha which offers flights at US$150 an hr. Of particularly good value is the flight around Lake Naivasha and over Hell's Gate at US$25 each for 2 people for half an hr. It is on the same entrance as Lakeside House by Lake Naivasha.

Local information

● Where to stay

B *La Belle Inn*, T 20116. Selection of rooms at different prices.

D *Kenvash*, just up from Moi Ave, T 30256. Naivasha's newest hotel. **D** *Four Seasons Naivasha*, T 20377. Very cheap rooms. Clean.

● Places to eat

♦♦*La Belle Inn*, Moi Ave. Has excellent fresh

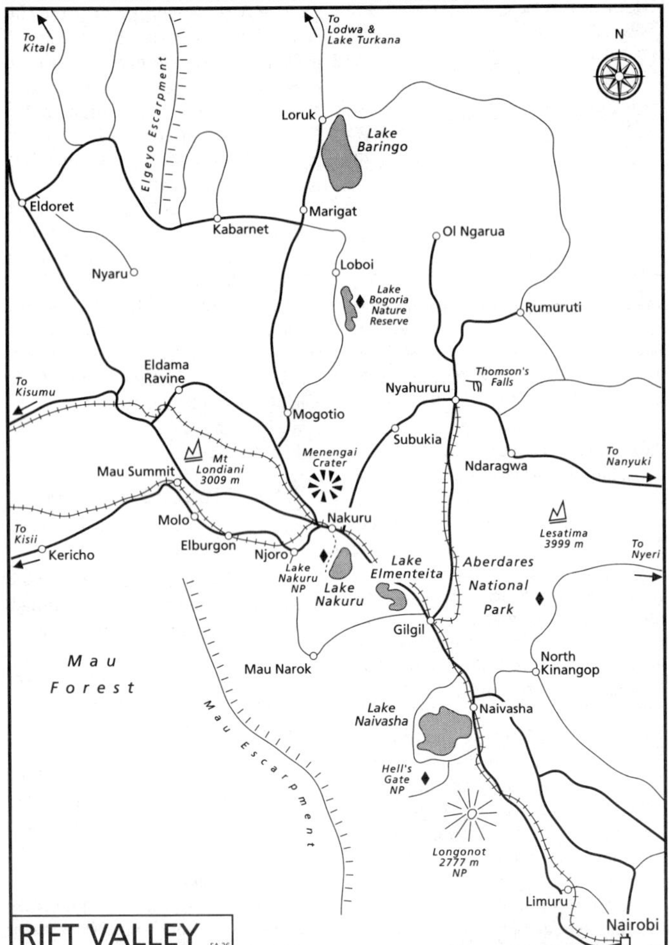

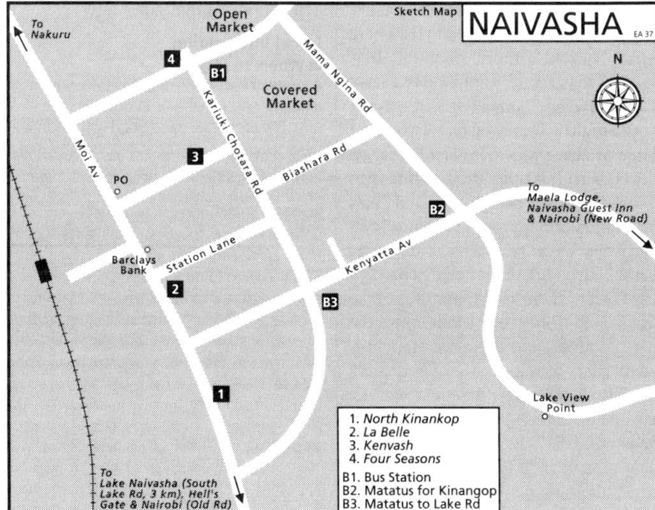

fruit juices served ice-cold. It also does very good (and huge) breakfasts including fruit juice, croissants, home made jam, butter, bacon, eggs and lots of coffee. Also a good place to stop for a drink and a break from driving. It has a selection of pastries (many vegetarian which is unusual for Kenya) and meals for lunch or dinner. ♦♦*North Kinangop*, Moi Ave, a little further towards the Lake. Serves very good snacks and simple meals. Good value.

● Transport

Rail Naivasha is on the main railway running from **Kisumu** on Lake Victoria in the W to **Mombasa** on the coast in the east. The train leaves Nairobi each evening at 1800 and arrives at 2100. From Naivasha W, the train leaves soon after it arrives 2100, gets to Nakuru at about 2300 and reaches Kisumu at 0800 the next morning. On the way back the Kisumu train to Nairobi leaves at 1830, reaches Nakuru at 0200, Naivasha at 0400, and Nairobi at about 0700.

Road If you are coming by road from Nairobi there are 2 routes. The first is along the old road which nowadays is the preserve of hundreds of lorries driving between Mombasa and Uganda. The road is poor, though the views are great and you are likely to see herds of zebra and other wildlife roaming the vast valley floors. The other route is along the new road which does not come into Naivasha town itself. It is in good condition and has the added advantage of having the most wonderful views of the Rift Valley, particularly at the equator. Peugeot taxis run to Naivasha throughout the day taking about an hr and a half. You can also take many of the buses heading further W to Nakuru or Kisumu. Remember to ask the driver to let you off at the Naivasha turning, as he is unlikely to stop automatically. The road from the dropping off point to Naivasha town is a few km to which you can either walk or flag down a matatu.

● Useful addresses

The main street running through the town is called Moi Avenue and it is along here that you will find almost everything you need in town including the **Post Office** and a branch of **Barclays Bank** where you can change money. Moi Avenue is also where you should stock up of groceries if you intend to do your own cooking while staying round Lake Naivasha, there is a supermarket called **Multiline** which has the best selection and there are some fruit stalls just opposite.

Lake Naivasha

Lake Naivasha is a lovely place to come for a weekend if you are staying in Nairobi as it is only an hour and a half's drive. The flying boats used to land here before Nairobi airport was built. It is possible to come to spend a day at one of the Lakeside hotels without staying for the night – it may be free if you take meals or there may be a small charge. The lake itself is quite picturesque with a mountain in the background and floating islands of papyrus. The water level fluctuates as a result of underwater springs, although the actual mechanism is not clear. There are hippos in the lake which sometimes come out onto the shore at night, and there are many different types of water birds. There are a number of activities. A motorboat can be hired for US$20 per hr; a rowing boat for about US$7 an hr. There is a fish eagle nest near to the Yacht Club. The twin-hulled launch from the country club on its 'ornithological cruise' often tries to entice the birds with fish. The evening cruise at about 1800 is a good time to see them. Visits can be made to the **Crescent Island Game Sanctuary** via the Lake Naivasha Country Club.

On the way Fisherman's Camp, the road goes through a major cut-flower growing area. Owned by Brooke Bond it is a major exporter and employs thousands of local people. The flowers are chilled and then airfreighted to Europe.

Just past Fisherman's Camp is **Elasmere**, the home of George and Joy Adamson. It is easy to miss - look out for the sign to Hell's Gate: it is a few hundred yards after it on the right-hand side. There is a small museum (not as interesting as the display of her paintings in the National Museum) and the gardens are very pleasant with lots of birds flying amongst the trees. The entrance fee of US$3 includes a copious tea. A film shows the life (and death) of Joy. Beware though, it lasts well over one hour! You can stay here as well - book in advance.

Green Crater Lake is about 17 km past Fisherman's Camp where the jade-coloured waters are quite breathtaking. There is an animal sanctuary.

Local information

● Where to stay

A *Lake Naivasha* (T 20013) Has wonderful gardens which gently lead down to the lakeside. The rooms are quite good with all amenities including a swimming pool. This hotel welcomes children and has a small adventure playground for them. Good food and does an excellent buffet lunch on Sundays which is very popular – eat as much as you like for around US$8. **A** *Safarilands Lodge* Slightly further round the road beside the Lake. Rambling colonial lodge of great charm, with log fires in the evening, splendid gardens swimming pool, horse-riding, tennis. Excellent food with vegetables grown in the hotel gardens. **A** *Lakeside House* (T 20908 or Nbi 567 424). Package deal includes food and drink in the house of the Anglo-Kenyans who have lived here for many years. They also offer safaris at an extra cost. The prices are considerably less for residents.

D *Fisherman's Camp* further along the lakeside road. This is set in beautiful surroundings, deeply shaded by huge trees. There are 2 types of accommodation. Bandas are the most comfortable with reasonable facilities including showers and bedlinen. All the bandas have electricity. Cheaper is the spartan youth hostel of dormitory type bunks.

E *YMCA* is the cheapest place to stay It is further along the road from Fisherman's Camp. Unfortunately over time the YMCA has lost some of its land to farming. Nowadays it is a good 15 minutes from the lakeside, though still set in beautiful gardens. It is sometimes possible to buy provisions, though these are not reliable. **E** *Camping* at a site close to the water's edge at Fisherman's camp (need to bring provisions), or at YMCA.

Hell's Gate is a major attraction (see National Parks section, page 178).

Mount Longonot Can be climbed. Costs US$15 to do so (there are student reductions). You need to get to Longonot village along the old road, from there it is about 6km to the base of the mountain. You can be escorted up by Kenya Wildlife Service rangers and the fairly straightforward climb takes about an hr. A wander round the rim of the mountain takes a further 2-3 hrs.

Mount Longonot is a dormant volcano standing at 2,886 m The mountain cone is make up of soft volcanic rock which has eroded into deep clefts and ridges. There are fine views over the Rift Valley on one side and into the enormous crater on the other.

The best places to stay are by the lakeside, there is nowhere in the immediate vicinity of Mount Longonot.

Lake Elmenteita

This is a shallow soda lake, similar to Lake Nakuru though it does not attract the enormous numbers of flamingos. As it is not a national park, you can walk around it easily and you don't have to pay. It is between Naivasha and Nakuru, just off the main road.

Kariandusi is a prehistoric site to the right of the Naivasha/Nakuru road. There is a small museum here, but the last excavations were carried out in the 1920s.

Nakuru

Nakuru is the next major town along from Naivasha. It is Kenya's fourth largest town in the centre of some of the country's best farming land. It is a nice agricultural town with of shops mostly selling farming equipment and supplies. The town itself came into existence when the building of the railway opened up access to the surrounding lush countryside attracting many white settlers to the area. Lord Delamere, one of the most famous figures in colonial times, collected around 600 sq km of land here and developed wheat and dairy farming.

Places of interest

Menangai Crater is on the northern side of Nakuru. Despite the fact that this extinct volcano is 2,490 m high, it is not easy to see from the town itself. To get there you can walk (it takes a couple of hrs but is pleasant enough) or motor along Menengai Drive out through the suburbs. It is fairly well signposted. There is no public transport from the town to the Menangai Crater, and as few people visit it there is scant hope of hitching a lift. There are a number of kiosks en route to the top where you can get a drink and basic local foods.

The views over Lake Nakuru are excellent (although the lake dried up completely in Spring 1994 but has now refilled) as are the views towards Lake Bogoria over the other side. The crater itself is enormous, about 12km across and 500 m deep. Traditionally this was Maasai land, and the site of some famous clan wars. The place still retains a reputation amongst local people as an unsavoury place.

Hyrax Hill Prehistoric Site is a small settlement dating back about 3,000 years. This site was first investigated by the Leakeys in the 1920s and work has been going on there, periodically, ever since. The excavations have found evidence of settlements from 3,000 years ago, and there are signs of habitation here up until about 300 years ago.

The North-east village has some enclosures where the digging was carried out though only one is not overgrown. It dates back about 400 years and the finds have been pieced together and are exhibited in the museum. There is no evidence of human dwellings suggesting this may have been used for livestock but not humans, though the evidence is not conclusive.

Up at the top of Hyrax Hill are the remains of the stone-walled fort and on the other side of the hill it is possible to see the position of 2 huts in a settlement which have been dated back to the Iron Age. A series of burial pits with 19 skeletons were found, most of them decapitated, dating back to the same time. The remains are all in a heap and all appear to be young men suggesting they were buried in a hurry – possibly the remains of the enemy after a battle.

Underneath the Iron Age site, a neolithic site was found and the neolithic burial mound has been fenced off as a display, the stone slab which sealed the

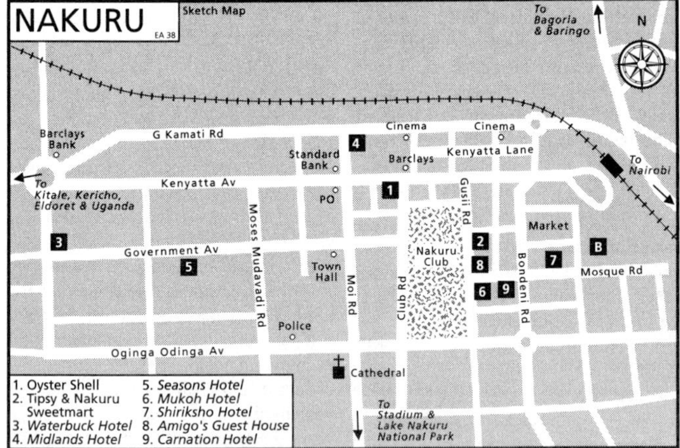

mound having been removed. The neolithic burial site has produced some very interesting things including 9 female skeletons. Unlike the male remains, the females have been buried with grave goods including dishes, pestles and mortars. No-one can be sure why the women were buried with grave goods and not the men, but it could indicate that women were far more powerful in former times. Oral history in the region suggests this may have been the case. A further mystery is why the Iron Age burial site is directly on top of the neolithic one.

On the path back to the museum, a bau board (a game with pebbles in cups) has been carved into the rock. One very curious find was 6 Indian coins dating back 500 years – no-one knows how they got here.

The site is open each day between 0930 and 1800 and there is a small entrance fee. It is just off the Nairobi road so it is easy to get to. Just take a matatu heading for Gilgil and ask them to drop you at the turning for Hyrax Hill. It is about 1km from here to the museum. You can camp here if you wish, though there are no facilities except those for the museum staff.

Lake Bogoria is a shallow soda lake just N of the Menengai Crater. It is easy to get to along the B4 sealed road. The road is pleasant enough, passing sisal plantations as it goes deeper into the Valley. A sign marks the equator and you can be treated with a demonstration. 10m to the N of the line and water turns clockwise; 10m to the S and it turns anti-clockwise; on the line it goes straight down!

It is a peaceful area with some wildlife, though most have migrated over recent years to the more fertile regions of Lake Nakuru. However as Lake Nakuru almost dried up in 1994, the lake was home to many thousands of flamingoes. About three-quarters of the way down the lake there are a number of hot springs and geysers. This is a good place to watch the flamingoes feed in the very hot water. Take care, you can get badly burnt. Along the eastern end of the lake you can see the northernmost part of the Aberdares. As this is a national park, there is an entrance fee of US$10. You can camp here but be prepared it can get very hot at night.

Lake Baringo If you continue driving N past Lake Bogoria, you will come to this peaceful and beautiful lake. (See National Parks, page 180) which is easy to get to from Nakuru. Buses leave twice daily to Kampi ya Samaki (Fisherman's Camp) and matatus go to the small town of Marigat. From either place you will be able to get a local matatu to the lake itself. The journey only takes a couple of hrs on good roads.

● Where to stay

A ***Waterbuck***, Government Ave, T 40081 and 44122. Modern hotel offering some of the best hotel facilities in town including a huge and reasonably priced buffet style lunch and an excellent breakfast.

B ***Midland***, on Kamati Road and is a long established hotel which used to be the most popular place in town for the more upmarket travellers, though it has been supplanted by the *Waterbuck* of recent years, T 43954. The rooms have en suite bathrooms and breakfast is included in the price. **B** ***Stem***, about 8km outside the town itself, close to Nakuru National Park, T 85391.

C ***Seasons***, Government Ave, T 45218, but overpriced for the facilities on offer.

D ***Mukoh***, corner of Mosque and Gusii Rd. Popular place offering clean, quiet and comfortable accommodation. It has some rooms with baths. Breakfast is a bit overpriced. **D** ***Shiriksho High Life***, Mosque Road is close to the bus stand. Reasonable. **D** ***Amigos Guest House***, Gusii Road is the best value place in this price range, and is very popular with budget travellers. The toilet and shower are clean and there is hot water. **D** ***Carnation***, Mosque Rd, T 43522. Large hotel offering very good value in the centre of town.

● Places to eat

♦♦♦***Oyster Shell Restaurant***, Kenyatta Ave is considered to be the best restaurant in town with an extensive menu for breakfast, lunch and dinner.

♦♦***Tipsy Restaurant***, Gusii Rd is popular with local people and is good value. They have western dishes as well as good curries and tilapia (fish). ♦♦***Mukoh***, best breakfast in town and is also good for snacks. ***Waterbuck***, Kenyatta Ave has an outside restaurant with a barbecue bar at the back. ♦♦***Nakuru Sweet Mart***, vegetarian Indian food.

● Banks

Barclays and ***Standard Chartered*** on Kenyatta Ave.

● Chemist

Fades, Kenyatta Lane, T 212627.

● Entertainment

Discos *Illusions* Kenyatta Ave; ***Pivot*** (weekends).

Cinema There are 2 cinemas in Nakuru both on GK Kamau Highway; screenings are twice a night,usually. The better of the 2 is ***Eros***.

● Shopping

There is a branch of the food chain ***Uchumi*** on Kenyatta Lane which is open 7 days a week. There is also a supermarket at the ***Sita Shopping Centre*** to the east of the town centre.

● Travel Agents

Crater Travel, T 45409, just off Kenyatta Ave can arrange air tickets. ***Blackbird Tours***, T 45383, at the *Carnation Hotel* are very helpful and can help you with visits to nearby national parks and other safaris.

● Transport

Road There are regular matatus, buses and Peugeot taxis to Nakuru from Nairobi (3 hrs), Nyahururu, Naivasha (1½ hrs) and all points W including Kisumu (4½ hrs), Eldoret (4 hrs) and Busia (8 hrs). The main bus station is on the eastern edge of town.

Rail Bookings need to be made to be sure of a seat with Kenya Railways at their Nakuru office (T 40211).

From **Nairobi** there is a train passing through Nakuru to **Malaba** on the Ugandan border twice a week. It leaves Nairobi at 1500 on Fri and Sat, arriving at Nakuru around 2000 to travel on to Malaba. It leaves Malaba for Nairobi on Sat and Sun at 1600, reaching Nakuru at about 0230. Nakuru to Malaba costs about US$14 1st, US$7 2nd; US$3 3rd., Nakuru to Nairobi US$7, US$4 US$2.

There are through trains passing through Nakuru running once a week between ***Nariobi*** and ***Kampala***. Departs Nairobi on Tue at 1000; Nakuru 1510; arrives Kampala 0825. Departs Kampala on Wed at 1600; Nakuru 0940; arrives Nairobi 1425.

NORTHERN RIFT VALLEY

Much of the northern part of the Rift Valley is unexplored by travellers and facilities are few and far between. The landscape is quite different from the central and western parts of the Rift. It is hot and arid, and only sparsely inhabited, but it has a stark beauty and is the home of the spectacular **Cherangani Hills**.

Once past the lakes of Bogoria and Baringo which can easily be reached from Nakuru within a few hrs, you are heading up into the less frequented regions of Kabarnet. **Kabarnet** is set on the Tugen Hills which are virtually impenetrable, and looks down into the **Kerio Valley**. The town itself is very unpreposing despite the fact it is the capital of Baringo district. It is a useful place to shop for food if you intend to go camping later in the Hills, and there are a few hotels which offer reasonable accommodation in the area including C *Kabarnet*, T 0328 2035, which has a pool. The Kerio Valley is home to many Kalenjin herders and their livestock, but little else. The unspoilt beauty and quiet of the place is hardly disturbed by vehicles, though this does make it hard to explore except by hiking. It is best to visit in Jun, Jul, Aug after the long rains when the land is at its greenest and the temperatures are comfortable. At other times, the environment is hot and very dry.

The largest town in the valley is **Kimwarer**, a company town developed for the fluorspar mine at the head of the Kerio River. Fluorspar, used in the manufacture of steel, aluminium and cement, is an important industry here and the company which extracts it is evident everywhere with its own housing, schools, playgrounds and clinics.

Elgeyo Escarpment. Presents one of the most astonishing vistas in the Rift Valley. About 1,000m below the sheer cliff face S of the village of **Tot**, stretches the hazy scrublands extending as far as the eye can see to Turkana and Pokot. This region is not easy to access, nothing short of a 4-wheel drive and calm nerves are needed to drive up the escarpment road. An easier approach is to walk from Tot (about 25 km). If you intend to stay in the area, Tot offers a delightful peaceful atmosphere with small local hotels.

The Elgeyo Escarpment has been inhabited for centuries. The Marakwet who live here arrived around 1,000 years ago and claim they took over existing irrigation systems which zigzag all over the escarpment from the Cherangani Hills over 40km away. The waterways make this area a lush land of agriculture with back-to-back *shambas* (small farms) everywhere.

The Cherangani Hills These wild, thickly forested hills are miles away from the popular tourist circuit with fine mountain landscapes. The Cherangani range rises to 3,500m at the northern end of the Elgeyo Marakwet Escarpment and is Kenya's only range of fold mountains. The range offers some of the best walking in Kenya in a pleasant climate, the northern end being particularly attractive.

You should be able to reach the Hills easily enough by public transport as there are a number of matatus running between Cheptongei and Chesoi. There are a number of suitable campsites where you can stay. The town of **Kapenguira** is in these hills, the place where the colonial government held the trial of Jomo Kenyatta during the 1950s when he was convicted of being involved in Mau Mau activities.

WESTERN RIFT

The main road W taking you towards Kisumu is in good condition and is therefore quite fast. The more scenic route is the C56 which passes through the towns of Njoro, Elburgon and Molo over the Mau Escarpment, before joining the Kisumu Rd. Few tourists travel this route mainly because there is little to visit, but the scenery is lovely, and quite varied.

The first town is **Njoro** by the Mau Escarpment about 5km W of Nakuru. It is home to **Egerton University** (about 5km out of town). The main street is an unpaved road lined with jacaranda and hotelis serving basic Kenyan fare. You will find a post office and bank here if you need them.

The road goes up into conifer country from here reaching the town of **Elburgon**. Elburgon is quite a lot bigger than Njoro, and is quite a prosperous little town owing its wealth to the logging industry. Evidence of logging is everywhere with most buildings being constructed of wood. The railway stops here between Nakuru and Kisumu. Again you will find a post office and bank in town as well as a number of small hotels offering extremely cheap accommodation. There is also a very good new hotel here called C *Eel*, T 0363 3127, set in a lovely garden. Apparently plans are underway to develop an adventure playground and disco here. If you are staying in the area it is worth knowing about the teacher's club at **St Andrew's School, Turi** which each Thu night is open for meals and a drink. It is also sometimes open at weekends.

Just W of Elburgon, you will pass through the **Mau Forest.** This dense forest of huge gum trees has yet to be exploited for tourism, particularly by the Okiek people (hunter-gatherers) who have lived here for generations. The road emerges from the forest among fields of crops, primarily pyrethrum and cereals which border the town of **Molo**. There is a post office and bank along the main street, and plenty of places to stay including D *Molo Highlands Inn*, T 0363 21036. Lovely wooden rooms with a log fire and a good restaurant. There is also the D *Green Garden Lodge* which is a nice enough place to stay, but very quiet.

West of Molo, between **Londiani** (a small town near the junction of the C56 with the B1 – the main road going into Kisumu) and **Kipkelion** is the **Cistercian Monastery**. This monastery, stuck in the middle of nowhere in the Kenyan countryside, is the only Cistercian monastery in Africa. It is a wonderful place to stay if you need a break from the outside world – donations for board and lodging are gratefully received. The monastery was founded in 1956 originally as a Trappist monastery but changed to being Cistercian. The monks still only talk when necessary, but are happy to receive guests and have rooms and dining facilities available. The monastery provides an important service for the local community through its hospital (the only one in the area) and its school. If you do wish to stay, you should write to them first to: Our Lady of Victoria, PO Box 40, Kipkelion.

The monastry is about 11km from **Baisheli** to the N of Londiani. If approaching from Kipkelion, you need to head off the main highway up the C35 unsurfaced road. Few matatus or cars go along this route, but you may be lucky. It is fairly well signposted, so you are unlikely to get lost.

St Andrew's School, Turi

The school has an interesting history. It was founded in 1932 and was, and still is, popular for children of farmers, missionaries, and aid workers of all nationalities from all over E Africa. It was home to Italian prisoners of war during the Second World War and their presence is still felt, for while they were there, they decorated many of the walls with paintings. The dining room, dormitories, bathrooms and corridors are covered in pictures of children's stories and fairytales such as Winnie in Pooh, the Pied Piper, and other such tales.

WESTERN KENYA

CONTENTS

MAPS

Western Kenya is the most fertile and the most populous part of the country, teeming with market towns and busy fishing villages. For some reason it is not that popular with the big tour operators which is all to the benefit of the adventurous. In fact, conditions for independent budget travellers are perfect; over half the population of the whole country lives here so public transport is excellent (though slightly unpredictable) and the road surfaces tend to be above average; there are numerous cheap hotels and restaurants; people are generally helpful and friendly, not having become weary of tourists, and there is plenty to see and do. Facilities for tourists wanting slightly more upmarket services are less well catered for, their best bet being to stay in one of the better hotels in Kisumu and hire a car to explore other parts of the region.

There are a number of National Parks in this region. The Kakamega Forest is the only tract of equatorial rainforest in Kenya with many animals found nowhere else in the country; the Saiwa Swamp is near Kitale; Mount Elgon with good climbing accessed from Kitale; Ruma National Park in South Nyanza; and Lake Victoria.

The climate is far warmer to the S, round Lake Victoria. This is traditionally Luoland and is quite a poor part of the country. The pace of life is slow and extremely friendly. The northern part of Western Kenya is lush and green and fertile, the climate is more temperate and there are more Europeans around.

Kisumu

Kisumu is the principle town in Western Kenya and the third largest in the country. It is a very pleasant place with a slow, gentle pace of life and a relaxed ambience, with the whole town coming to a standstill on Sundays. The sleepy atmosphere is as much due to lack of economic opportunities experienced here as to the extremely hot dry weather, which makes doing almost anything in the middle of the day quite hard work.

The town has been by-passed by post-independence development, and the signs are all too visible. Warehouses by the docks remain empty and the port does not have the bustling atmosphere you would expect in such an important town. Many of the wealthier people have moved out of Kisumu hence the number of large houses lying empty or rundown.

History

Kisumu developed during the colonial era into the principal port in the region. The railway line reached Lake Victoria in 1902 opening up trade opportunities. By the 1930s it had become the hub of administrative and military activities

on the Lake. Kisumu was a difficult place at this time, bilharzia was endemic, malaria and sleeping sickness were common and the climate was sweltering. However, the area attracted investment from many different quarters, including Asians ending their contracts to work on the railway.

The Luo felt they were neglected immediately after independence, and that political life was dominated by Kikuyu who centred development on Central province. The breakdown of trade between Kenya, Uganda and Tanzania and the collapse of the East African Community in 1977 badly affected Kisumu and there has been no compensating expansion of manufacturing in the area.

The murder of Robert Ouko, a Luo, led to riots where many died and much property was destroyed. Later, in the build-up to multi-partyism in Kenya, the nearby area was the scene of outbreaks of ethnic violence and thousands of people fled their shambas, coming into Kisumu or heading up to Eldoret.

Places of interest

Kisumu Museum is to the east of the market. There are a number of stuffed birds, mammals, reptiles and fish. They include a lion bringing down a wildebeest. A 190kg Nile perch is about to be added to these exhibits when the taxidermist has finished his work. The ethnographic exhibits centre on the customs and traditions of the tribal groups who lived in this area – the Luo, Maasai, and Kalenjin (see page 47 and page 48). The curator is both imaginative and energetic, and intends to develop the scope and range of the museum including the traditional Luo homestead. Opening times are 0830 – 1800 and there is a nominal entrance fee of about US$4.

Dunga is a small village just 3km outside Kisumu. It is a lovely place to visit on the shores of Lake Victoria, peaceful and timeless. There are hippos here, but they are elusive. *Dunga Refreshments* has great views over the lake where you can get a cold soda and something to eat whilst watching fishermen bring their catch in. Watching the sun set over

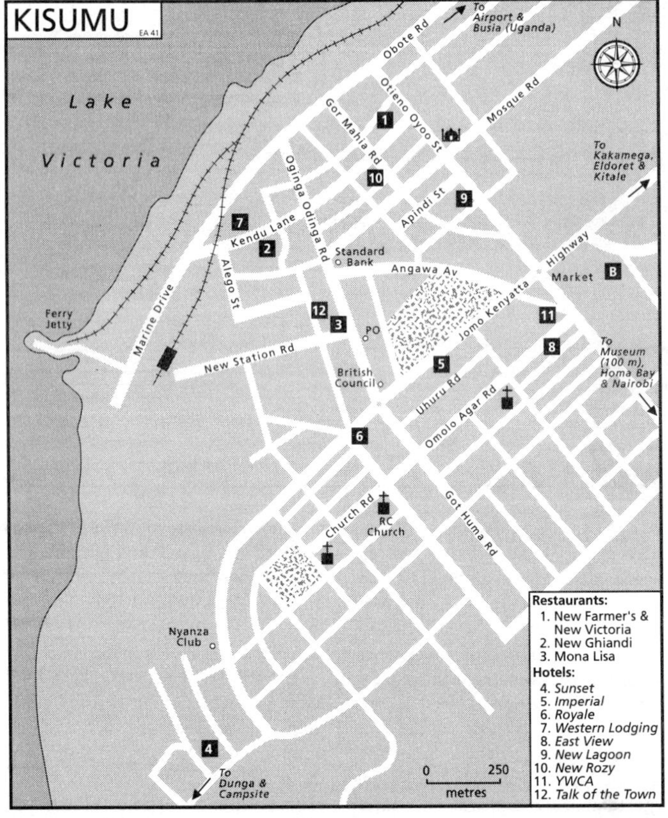

the lake is a very pleasant way to end the day. It is possible to negotiate with the fishermen to join a night fishing trip. On the way up the dirt track to Dunga you pass the **Impala National Park** with a small herd of antelope.

Kisumu Bird sanctuary is off the main A1 on the way to Ahero about 8km out of Kisumu. You need to follow the track round the lake for the best sites. This is a nesting site for hundreds of birds including herons, ibises, cormorants, egrets and storks. The best time to visit is from Apr to May.

Local information

● Where to stay

Kisumu is swarming with mosquitos, so it is important to look for a room with mosquito nets if you don't have one with you. A fan is also a boon. **A** *Sunset*, to the S of the town itself, T 035 41100 or 42534, has a verandah looking over beautiful lawns and a good swimming pool.

B *Imperial*, Jomo Kenyatta Ave, T 035 41485, is probably the best value in this price range. **B** *Royal*, Jomo Kenyatta Ave, T 035 44240, average rooms. Good Indian menu.

C *Western Lodging*, Kendu Lane, T 035 42586. New hotel with good rooms at cheap prices. There is good security in the hotel with a safe in each room. **C** *East View*, Omolo Agar Rd, near the bus station. The hotel is reasonable and has a secure car park attached.

D *New Lagoon Motel*, Otieno Oyoo St, T 035 42118. Simple but reasonable. **D** *New Rozy Lodge*, Oganda St, T 035 41990. Good value and clean. **D** *Safari*, Omino Crescent. Best value in this price category. **D** *YWCA*, off Ang'awa Ave. Reasonable, although there is not always water. **D** *Talk of the Town*, Otuma St. Used by the Peace Corps volunteers, so it is not the most quiet of places.

● Places to eat and drink

It is quite easy to get good cheap food in Kisumu. Of particularly good value are the fish dishes. The large Asian community that has settled here means it is possible to get excellent Indian meals, including vegetarian, very cheaply. There are several very cheap kiosks near bus station selling grilled meat on skewers or tilapia fish with ugali (maize dough). ♦♦♦*Dunga Refreshments*, on the lake shore to the S of town. A bit of a trek from the town centre. Great buffet lunch on weekends with curries. ♦♦♦*Sunset*, out of town to the S. Does a weekend buffet which is plentiful in slightly grand surroundings. ♦♦♦*Talk of the Town*, Otuma St. Popular place with good food. ♦♦♦*Bodega's*, just off Accra St. Good fresh fish. Happy hr between 1900-2100.

♦♦*New Farmers' Bar & Restaurant* has a good, if predictable, menu. ♦♦*New Ghiandi Paradise Bar & Restaurant* is a popular local hangout with a juke box.

♦*Kisumu Sweet Mart*, Oginga Odinga Rd Sodas, bhajias and cheap Indian food. ♦*Mona Lisa*, Oginga Odinga Rd sound far and good breakfasts. ♦*New Victoria*, Gor Mahia Rd. Does a substanital breakfast from 0700 to 0900 and snacks at other times.

● Banks

Barclays, Kampala St or *Standard Chartered*, Ogingaa Odinga Rd are the most efficient for changing money Banking hrs are Mon to Fri 0830 to 1300 and Satu 0830 to 1100.

● Car hire

Shiva Travels, T 43420. *Kisumu Travels*, T 44122. Only have a limited number of cars available and are more expensive than hiring a car from Nairobi.

● Entertainment

There are many African bars which play music, mainly Lingala, which are open till late. A particularly popular one is just outside Kisumu to the W near the molasses refinery. It is a bit rough and ready with only warm beers served from behind a metal grille, but the atmosphere on Fri nights is lively and it often has live bands. In town there is the far more sophisticated **Octopus** on Oganda St which plays western music. Good fun. It gets very crowded late in the evening.

● Library

British Council on Oginga Odinga Rd (T 035 45004) Library (open Mon to Fri from 0930 to 1700 with an hr for lunch and Sat from 0830 to 1245. Papers and magazines and occasional videos of BBC news.

● Post Office

This is in the centre of town on Oginga Odinga R and has a reliable poste restante service. Hrs are Mon to Fri 0800 to 1700 and Sat 0900 to 1200.

● Religion

Majority of people here are Christian (mainly

Roman Catholics), but there are a significant number of Muslims. **Jamia Mosque** on Otieno Oyoo St is testamant to the long tradition of Islam here, built in 1919 this green and white building has 2 imams and calls to prayer can be heard in much of the town.

● Shopping

For curios and crafts is quite good here as there are many artefacts from other parts of the country also available. Kisii stone is a particularly good buy as are kikois (woven cloth). The **Wananchi Crafts** shop is reasonable selling things made by local women. Street vendors are outside the post office and at stalls on the northern side of Oginga Odinga Rd.

● Sport

Golf Club just outside the town where you can hire equipment and a caddy. You need to pay a day's membership fee and the whole lot will come to around US$6. **Swimming** Use pools rather than the lake as bilharzia is rife. There are 3, the best is at the *Sunset*, there are also pools at *Royale* and the *Imperial*.

● Telecommunications

Direct calls from the card phone outside the post office.

● Transport

Air *Kenya Airways* There are daily flights from Nairobi taking 1 hr and costing US$54. There are also 5 flights a week from Mombasa (stopping at Nairobi) taking 2¾ hrs and costing US$136.

Road There are countless Peugeots, matatus and buses travelling between Kisumu and most major towns in Western Kenya leaving from the bus station. There are also many leaving for Nairobi passing through Nakuru, Kericho on the B1. Approximate times: **Nairobi** to Kisumu. express 6 hrs or normal 8hrs. It approximately 2 hrs to **Kericho**, 5 hrs to **Nakuru**, 2 hrs to **Eldoret**, 1 hr to **Kakamega**.

Boat Motor ferries run between Kisumu and a number of lakeshore towns. Tickets can be got from Kisumu wharf (it opens at 0800) and it is a good idea to board your boat as soon as possible as they are very popular and get full. Tickets are very cheap and this is a nice way of seeing around Lake Victoria.

Outward: **Kisumu** 0900; **Kendu Bay** 1100; **Kuwur Bay** 1300; **Homa Bay** 1400; **Asembo Bay** 1700.

Return: **Asembo Bay** 0800; **Kuwur Bay** 1000; **Homa Bay** 1040; **Kuwur Bay** 1150; **Kendu Bay** 1400; **Kisumu** 1600.

There is also a ferry going from Kisumu to Mbita, Mfangano, Homa Bay and Kuwur Bay leaving Kisumu on Tue and returning on Sun.

Unfortunately there are no ferries between Kenya, Uganda and Tanzania at present, though this situation is expected to change as relations between the 3 countries improve.

Rail Trains from **Nairobi** leave at 1800 each day and take 14 hrs. Return from Kisumu at 1830. Extra trains sometime run at periods of peak demand. It costs US$14 for 1st class, US$7.00 for 2nd and US$3.50 for 3rd. The booking office in Kisumu is at Kenya Railways (T 035 42211).

South Nyanza

This is an easy area to explore by public transport either by using the ferry from Kisumu, or the matatu services, which are excellent. There are also a few attractions for the more active tourist such as the **Lambwe Valley National Reserve, Ruma National Park** and **Thimlich Ohinga** archaeological site all near Homa Bay. Fishing (a male activity) and the smoking of fish (a female activity) are important occupations around here.

Homa Bay

The biggest town in this area. Very busy at the end of the month when workers are paid and flock to town

● **Where to stay** **B** *Homa Bay*, on the lake shore. Rarely many guests here. **D** *Masawa*, simple but good value. **D** *Nyanza*, reasonable value. **D** *New Brothers*, fairly basic.

Thimlich Ohinga

Quite near Homa Bay (60km) is one of the most significant archaeological sites in East Africa. The name means thick bush with stone enclosures in Luo and is an impressive example of a style of architecture whose remnants are all over the district. The main structure consists of a compound about 150m in diameter with 5 smaller enclosures in each and at least 6 house pits. The walls are about 2½ to 3½ m high. Outside the compound, there is evidence of ironworks.

They are similar to the stone ruins in Zimbabwe of the 17th century. It is believed the enclosure dates back to the 15th century, and the same style is used in some places by Luos today. There is no public transport to get here. You need to follow the Rongo-Homa Bay road as far as Rod Kopany then head southwest to Miranga. From Miranga there are sign posts to Thimlich Ohinga.

Homa Bay is the nearest town to **Lambwe Valley National Reserve** and **Ruma National Park** described in the section on National Parks (see page 191).

Rusinga Island

Access from Homa Bay is better by ferry than by road (it is now linked by causeway to the mainland) due to the poor state of the highway. The main town on Rusinga Island, Mbita, is unexceptional. Inland foreigners are rare and you are sure of a welcome. The traditional way of life is threatened here as drought coupled with environmental degradation (mainly tree clearance for fuel or land) has reduced agricultural productivity. This was the birthplace of Tom Mboya, an important Kenyan political figure during the fight for independance, who was assassinated in 1969 by a Kikuyu, sparking off ethnic violence. On the shores of the island you may see the rare spotted-necked otter. If you do intend to walk around the island take plenty of water as it is hot here; there is little danger of getting lost.

Mfangano Island Further along Lake Victoria, slightly bigger than Rusinga Island where hippos are very much in evidence as are monitor lizards basking in the sun. There are rock paintings here showing signs of centuries of habitation. The rock paintings are in a gently scooped cave on the N coast of the island and are reddish coloured shapes. It is not known who drew them, when or why. This is off the beaten track and there are few facilities for tourists apart from the newly-built luxurious A *Lake Victoria Game Safari*, PO Box 188, Kisumu (T 035 43141), which mainly takes package tourists flying to Kisumu from the Maasai Mara.

There are large wooden boats available to shuttle people between Mbita and surrounding places. It leaves Mbita at 0900 and takes about 90 minutes to Sena. There is a government rest house (officially free though ask for permission to stay) and local people are usually willing to put up travellers.

Kendu Bay Another stop on the ferry from Kisumu. The main reason for coming here is to visit the curious **Simbi Lake** which is bright green opaque water only a few km from Lake Victoria. No-one knows what the source of the lake is and its size is constantly changing. Local people believe it to be unlucky and the surrounding area is certainly devoid of vegetation. It is not fished and the area is uninhabited. Legend has it the area was flooded by a woman who was ill-treated by villagers living there in the past.

Kendu Bay is a tiny village with a number of small cheap hotels D *South Nyanza* is said to be the best and it has a disco each night. If you are in town, it is worth checking out the *Masjid Tawakal Mosque*, a beautiful old building in town. If you are travelling by road, take the newly tarred lakeshore road which meets the A1 Kisumu road going via Katito. The drive is great through countryside which is just opening up.

Migori The last town along this stretch, on the Tanzanian border. It is a transit stop for people travelling to Musoma in Tanzania, finding it quicker through Kenya. The town has a rough reputation. If you wish to get to Nairobi quickly, there are a number of buses going direct, one at 0600, one at 0700 and a few in the evening.

Busia and Siaya District

Northwest out of Kisumu towards the

border town of Busia, is Siaya District a heavily-populated agricultural region. About 20km out of town is small hill, **Got Ramogi**. From the top of this are great views over the lake on one side and of shambas on the other.. The hill is significant to Luos as it is the site where Luos fought for their right to settle here.

Busia

A small town on the border with Uganda. It primarily consists of one road lined with shops, kiosks and cafés. The border crossing itself is fairly straightforward, but quite thorough. The best hotel here is about 1km from the border, on the S side of the road slightly set back next to a small market. It costs around US$5 per night. The rooms are clean and have en suite bathrooms and there is a bar which is popular with local people. The restaurant is very good and cheap and serves mashed potatoes, a rarity in Kenya.

Kisii and Western Highlands

The Western Highlands are the agricultural heartland of Kenya separating Kisumu and environs from the rest of the country. They stretch from Kisii in the S up to the tea plantations around Kericho through to Kitale and Mount Elgon and Eldoret.

Kisii

Set in picturesque undulating hills in some of the most fertile land of the country with abundant sunshine and rainfall. The town itself is growing fast and is very lively. As with so many other towns in agricultural areas, the market here is buzzing and has an excellent array of fresh fruit and vegetables. The town lies on a fault line, so earth tremors are not uncommon.This is the home of *Kisii soapstone* though you may look to buy some in vain as most is bought up by traders.

Tabaka

About 25km from Kisii this village is the most important producer of soapstone and the centre of carvings in the country. To visit the quarries or the carvers, you need to go past the Tabaka Mission Hospital to the Kisii Soapstone Carvers Co-operative. The stone comes in a variety of colours from orange (the softest) to deep red (the heaviest).

Local information

● Where to stay

D *Sakawa Towers*, PO Box 541, by market, T 21218. Own bathrooms. Newish highrise buildings. **D** *Safe Lodge*, just to the S of the market, T 0381 21375. Own bathrooms. Clean and friendly, though quite noisy. **D** *Kisii*, N of town centre, T 0381 20954. Own bathrooms. Best of the slightly more expensive places, though the rooms are quite basic. Comfortable colonial atmosphere.

E *Njau Guest House*, T 0381 21375, comfortable. **E** *Highway Lodge*, T 0381 21213, cheapest in town and is clean but nothing special. Try to get a room at the back – rooms at the front are very noisy as they are over the main road. **E** *Sabrina Lodge*, just around the corner from the matatu park and is a friendly place with communal facilites. The hotel also

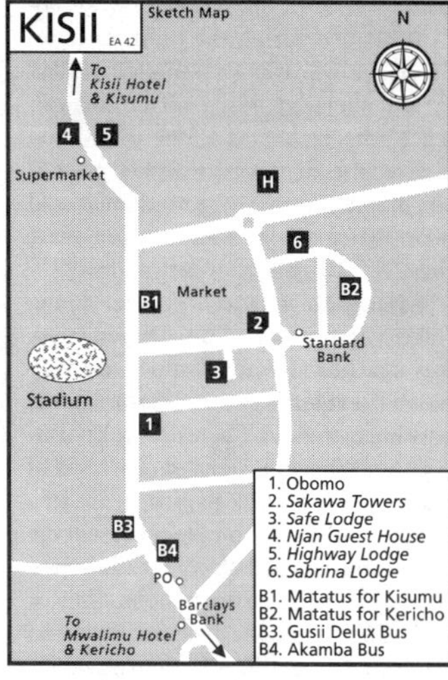

has a bar and restaurant.

● **Places to eat and drink**
♦♦*Sakawa Towers*, close to market. Good restaurant, probably the best in town.

♦*Safe Lodge*, reasonable grilled meat skewers and a good breakfast. ♦*Obomo*, popular with good basic food and fresh fruit juices. *Satellite Inn*, busy drinking den, though not very savoury.

● **Banks**
Both *Standard Chartered*, near market, and *Barclays*, on main road, have branches here open Mon to Fri 0830 to 1300and Sat from 0830 to 1100.

● **Entertainment**
Centred around bars. There is a disco at *Mwalimu*, at the southern end of town. *Kisii Sports Club*, behind Barclays Bank on the main road, is worth joining if you are here for a few days. It has a friendly atmosphere and facilities for swimming, pool, tennis, squash, darts and bingo. There is a good bar to relax in afterwards. Kisii's football team, *Shabana FC*, is in the first division and the stadium just to the W of the main road.

● **Transport**
Road Matatus for Kisumu, takes 3 hrs, leave in front of the market. All others leave from the station the stand to the east of the main street. Nairobi is 8½ hrs.

Kericho

Perched on the top of a hill, the tea plantations stretch for miles on either side of the road their bushes neatly clipped to the same height with paths running in between, in straight lines, for the pickers to walk down. The predictable weather, (it rains each afternoon here) and the temperate climate makes this the most important tea-growing region in Africa. This is an orderly part of Kenya, very different from the shambas further down the slopes, and very English exemplified by the *Tea Hotel* with its lovely gardens. The town's main purpose is to service the enormous tea plantations, so it has all basic amenities; branches of the main banks, post office, market, library, English-style church, cemetery, Hindu Temple.

Plantation tour If you have a vehicle, this can be arranged through the *Tea Hotel*. The growing and picking procedures are explained, and there is a tour around the tea factory where the leaves are processed.

Chagaik Dam and Arboretum About 8km to the NE of Kericho off the road to Nakuru. Established after the second war by a Kericho teaplanter, John

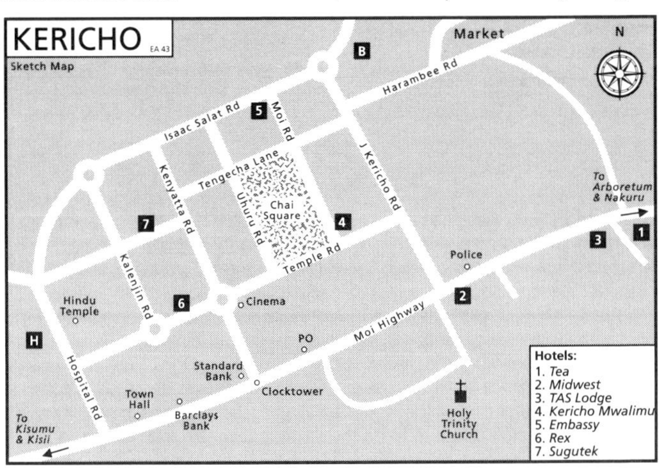

Grumbley, now retired to Malindi on the coast. Exceptionally attractive, well-tended, with lawns running down to the water's edge.

Trout fishing This is available in the Kiptariet River. The *Tea Hotel* will arrange for permissions and equipment hire. The river runs close-by the hotel.

Local information

● Where to stay

B *Tea*, PO Box 75, to NW of town centre, on Moi Highway, on road to Nakuru, T 0361 20280. Own bathrooms. Comfortable and well-appointed. Swimming pool.

C *Midwest*, PO Box 1175, Moi Highway opposite Police Station, T 20611. Own bathroom. Modern, central, functional.

D *TAS Lodge*, PO Box 304, to NW of town centre, on Moi Highway, on road to Nakuru, close to *Tea Hotel*, T 21112. Own bathroom. Very good value. Bar. Restaurant. Attractive garden setting. **D** *Kericho Mwalimu*, PO Box 834, Temple Rd, just to N of Chai Square in the town centre. T 20601. Own bathroom. Restaurant and bar.

E *Embassy*, Isaac Salat Rd, close to bus stand. Central, and reasonable value. **E** *Rex Inn Lodge* Temple Rd. Simple, but fairly central. **E** *Sugutek* Tengecha Rd. Shared bathroom. Restaurant. Fairly basic, but quite central. *Camping* at TAS Lodge.

● Places to eat and drink

♦♦♦*Tea*, solid and dependable English-style menu, with some Indian dishes.

♦♦*Midwest*, good value set menu.

♦*Sugutek*, Tegecha Rd. Very simple, but sound value.

● Transport

Road The matatu station, at the northern end of Isaac Salat Rd is well organised, and there is plenty of transport, both buses and matatus.

Kakamega

Pleasant lively place, and the main town of the of the Luhya people. A major attraction is the **Kakamega Forest** (see section on National Parks, page 179), and the town is the place to buy provisions for and excursion there. At the end of Nov is the **Kakamega Show**, with agricultural festival, at the showground just to the N of the town, on the Webuye Rd.

Local information

● Where to stay

B *Golf*, PO Box 118, just off main road, behind Sports Club, T 20460. Own bathrooms. Swimming pool. Facilities for golf, tennis and squash at the Sports Club.

E *Kakamega Wayside House*, PO Box 900, close to Town Hall, T 20128. Central and inexpensive. **E** *Bendera*, just to the W of the main road. Good value and comfortable accommodation. **E** *New Garden House*, close to the main bus stand. Lively establishment, and reasonable standard and value.

● Places to eat

♦♦♦*Golf Hotel*, solid fare, English-style cooking with some Indian dishes.

♦*New Garden House*, basic food. Fairly busy atmosphere. ♦*Soweto*, close to main bus station and market. Mostly grilled skewered meats. Simple and sound.

Kakamega Gold

During the 1930s, Kakamega was the centre of Kenya's gold-mining industry, and many coffee growers left their impoverished farms to become prospectors. Most gold was extracted by large South African-owned companies, mining the ore, crushing it, using steam-powered stampers, and sluicing out the gold.

The British mining engineers contrived to avoid the vulgarity associated with gold-rush towns and continued to dine in dinner-jackets at the *Golf Hotel*. When the Empire Airlines sea-plane service from London to Cape Town was introduced, hopping across Africa from lake to lake, one of the overnight stops was at Kisimu. The passengers were driven the 50 km to Kakamega where they danced till dawn before returning to Kisumu to fly on the next leg down to Lake Naivasha.

● **Transport**

Road The town is less than an hr from Kisumu (about 50 km) along the excellent though very busy A1 and there are plenty of buses and matatus travelling this route. The main bus stand is close to the market. The Akamba bus service has its stand opposite the Hindu Temple, off the Mumias Rd

Kericho to Eldoret

The journey from Kericho to Eldoret passes through the Nandi Hills, which provide some of the most spectacular scenery in this part of the country, and the Kano plains, bleak mountainous scrubland and ravines. The only town of note on this route is:

Kapsabet

Small town about 60 km N of Kisumu.

● **Where to stay** **E** *Kapsabet*, PO Box 449, T 2176. Inexpensive. Restaurant and bar. **E** *Keben*, has a restaurant, bar and disco. Rather lively. **E** *Bogol Inn*, fairly basic. Reasonable restaurant.

Eldoret

Pleasant, busy and fairly prosperous highland town surrounded by fertile countryside growing a mixture of food and cash crops. It is home to **Moi University** and this appears to be benefiting the town and expanding its economic potential.

Local Information

● **Where to stay**

B *Sirikwa*, PO Box 3361, Elgeyo Rd, T 0321 31655. Own bathrooms. Swimming pool.

C *New Wagon Wheel*, Elgeyo Rd, PO Box 2408, T 32271. New and comfortable.

D *New Lincoln*, PO Box 551, Oloo Rd, T 22093. Own bathrooms. Colonial-style hotel, with some character. **D** *Highlands Inn*, PO Box 2189, Elgeyo Rd, T 0321 22092. Quiet place and good value.

E *New Mahindi*, PO Box 1964, Uganda Rd, T 31520. Own bathrooms. Lively atmosphere. **E** *Eldoret Valley*, Uganda Rd. Well-run and quiet, but rather puritanical. **E** *Kubathayu Board & Lodging*, PO Box 832, Tagore Rd, to W side of centre, T 22160. Comfortable, pleasant, inexpensive. **E** *Top Lodge*, corner of Nandi and Oginga Odinga Road is more used

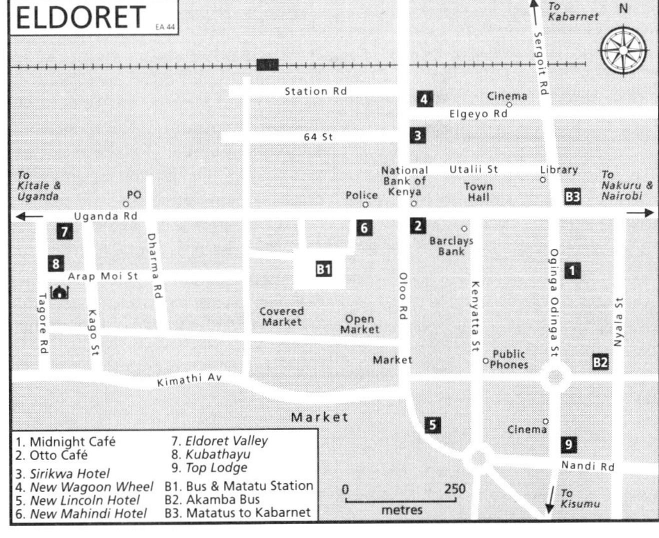

to renting rooms by the hour, but has clean rooms available for the night if you wish

● **Places to eat**

♦♦♦*Sirikwa*, also on Elgeyo Road has a buffet lunch at weekends including a barbecue.

♦♦*Eldoret Valley*, Uganda Rd. Mostly grills, skewered meat. Good standard.

♦♦*New Wagon*, Elgeyo Rd. Good value meals. ♦*Midnight Cave*, Oginga St. Cafeteria style. ♦*Otto Cafe*, Uganda Rd Simple, with good range of dishes.

● **Entertainment**

The best disco, and the newest, is *Sparkles Disco* on Kenyatta St. *Woodhouse Disco* on Oginga Odinga Street is also popular and very lively.

● **Getting there**

Air There are 2 flights a week from **Nairobi** departing Wilson Airport Tue and Thu at 0700 and 1545 respectively and returning at 2015 and 1700 on the same days.

Road The matatu stand is in the centre of town just off Uganda Rd and there are a number of peugeots, matatus and buses throughout the day. The journey direct to Nairobi takes just 3½ hrs.

Rail There is a service 3 times a week from Nairobi on Wed, Sat and Sun leaving at 9pm and arriving at 9.30am the next day. It goes onto the Ugandan border at Malaba. Trains going back to Nairobi depart on Wed, Sat and Sun at 4pm.

From **Nairobi** there is a train passing through Eldoret to **Malaba** on the Ugandan border twice a week. It leaves Nairobi at 1500 on Fri and Sat, arriving at Eldoret around 0200 to travel on to Malaba. It leaves Malaba for Nairobi on Sat and Sun at 1600, reaching Nakuru at about 2015. Eldoret to Malaba costs about US$6 1st, US$3 2nd; US$2 3rd., Eldoret to Nairobi US$15 1st; US$8 2nd; US$4 3rd.

There are trains passing through Eldoret running once a week between **Nariobi** and **Kampala**. Departs Nairobi on Tue at 1000; Eldoret 2100; arrives Kampala 0825. Departs Kampala on Wed at 1600; Eldoret 0310; arrives Nairobi 1425.

Eldoret to Malaba

From Eldoret the A104 passes through **Webuye** and **Bungoma** to reach **Malaba**, the most common border crossing into Uganda. These are all geared toward the transit traffic heading for Uganda. **Webuye Falls** are about 5km from the road, and provide the water for **Panafric Paper Mills**. It is possible to visit the mills PO Box 535 (T 16 Bungoma). **Chetambe's Fort** is a further 8km from the Webuye Falls, and is the site of the last stand of the Luhya against the British in 1896.

Kitale

Pleasant, small town in the middle of lush farmland between Mount Elgon and the Cherangani Hills. Originally this was Maasai grazing land, but it was taken over by European settlers after the First World War. The town did not really develop until after 1925 and the arrival of a branch line of the railway. The region is known for its fruit and vegetables, including apples which are rare in East Africa. Its main attraction for tourists is as a base from which to explore the **Cherangani Hills** (see section on Rift Valley, page 92) or **Mount Elgon** and **Saiwa Swamp National Park** (see National Parks, page 186).

Kitale Museum Eldoret Rd, just to the east of town centre. PO Box 1219 (T 20690) Open 0930-1800 Entrance US$4. Has ethnographic displays of the life of the people of Western Kenya, butterfly and wildlife exhibits. Murals on local life in the Museum Hall. Excellent nature trail trough local forest, with some pleasant picnic sites.

Kitale Show is at the beginning of Nov and is an agricultural festival.

Local information

● **Where to stay**

B *Kitale Club*, PO Box 30 , Eldoret Rd, just beyond the Kitale Museum, T 20030. Own bathroom. Comfortable rooms with hot water. Swimming pool.

D *Bongo Hotel*, PO Box 530, Moi Ave, T 20593. Communal facilities. Comfortable.

E *Star Lodge*, South of Moi Ave. Inexpensive. Large rooms. Communal facilities. Bit noisy. **E** *Executive Lodge*, Kenyatta St. Communal facilities. Good rooms. Hot water.

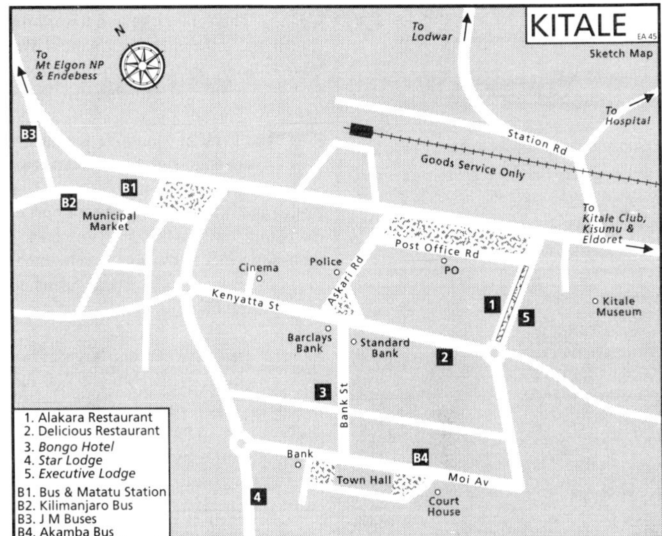

● Places to eat

♦♦♦*Kitale Club*, solid English fare, with some Indian dishes.

♦*Alakara*, Kenyatta St. Fairly simple food, but good value. ♦*Delicious Restaurant*, Kenyatta St. Mostly ice cream and snacks.

● Transport

Rail Although a branch of the railway comes to Kitale, it does not take passengers.

Road Various bus stands and matatu stops are at the western end of the road to Mt Elgon Getting to and from Kitale is relatively easy as it is on the A1 heading for Kakamega and Kisumu in the S, and is the main route to Lake Turkana in the N. Thee are regular buses and matatus.

COAST

CONTENTS

MAPS

MOMBASA

The town of Mombasa is situated on an island on the southern coast of Kenya. It is the oldest town in Kenya and is the most significant port in the country with a history going back 2 thousand years. It owes its development to its location, for the island forms an ideal natural harbour.

Mombasa is Kenya's second largest town with a population of about 550,000 and has large communities of Indian and Arabic origin. It has greatest concentration of Muslims in Kenya and the influence on the culture is strong. The town is centred on an island about 4 km across and 7 km wide, but has now begun to sprawl onto the mainland. The island is now linked to the mainland at 3 points as well as by the Likoni Ferry.

History

The earliest known reference to Mombasa dates from 150 AD when the Roman geographer Ptolemy placed the town on his map of the world. Roman,

LUNATIC EXPRESS

Construction of the railway that was to be dubbed the "Lunatic Express" (see page 44) began in 1896. Until the railway was built the only means of getting inland was by foot and this was how the early explorers and missionaries travelled. It was soon realised that it was not economical for cash crops such as cotton to be grown in Uganda if they then had to face this protracted journey to the coast before they could be exported.

The railway was built using indentured labour from Punjab and Gujarat in India and many of these remained to form the Asian population that is found in E Africa today. The railway was built through some extremely harsh environments and across some very difficult terrain. A further problem was the wildlife in the area and it was the "Man-Eating Lions of Tsavo" that really caught the public's imagination. During construction these lions attacked the camps, mauling and killing some of the workers.

Despite the problems - including the difficult engineering problems that were involved in climbing the Rift Valley escarpment - the railway reached Nairobi in 1899, Kisumu on Lake Victoria in 1901, but did not finally reach Kampala until 1928.

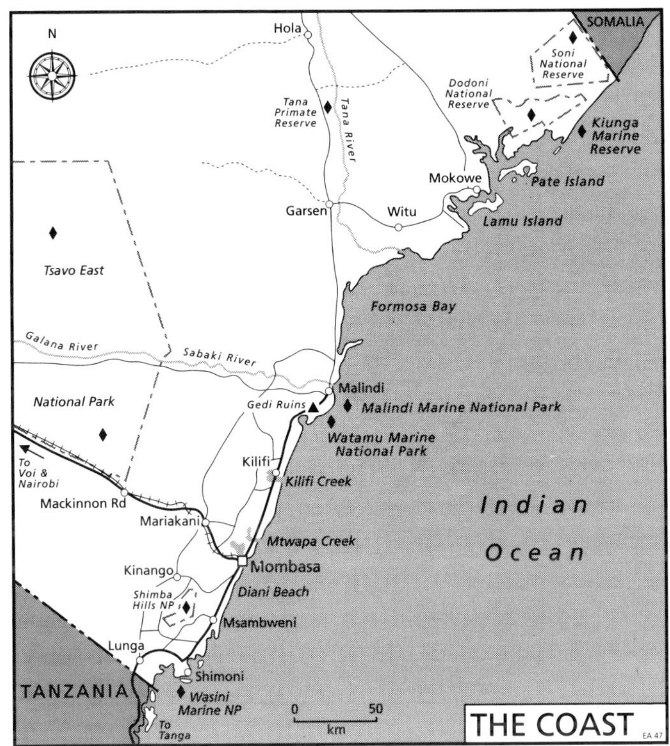

Arabic and Far Eastern seafarers took advantage of the port and were regular visitors. The port provided the town with the basis of economic development and it expanded steadily.

By the 16th century Mombasa was the most important town on the east coast of Africa with a population estimated at 10,000. By this time a wealthy settlement, it was captured in the 16th century by the Portuguese who were trying to break the Arab trading monopoly – particularly in the lucrative merchandising of spices. The town first fell to the Portuguese under the command of Dom Francisco in 1505. He ransacked the town and burnt it to the ground. It was rebuilt and returned to its former importance before it was sacked again in 1528. However, the Portuguese did not remain and having again looted and razed the town, they left.

The building of Fort Jesus in 1593, the stationing of a permanent garrison there, and the installation of their own nominee from Malindi as Sultan, represented the first major attempt to secure Mombasa permanently. However, an uprising by the townspeople in 1631 led to the massacre of all the Portuguese. This led to yet another Portuguese fleet returning to try to recapture the town. In 1632 the leaders of the revolt retreated to the mainland leaving the island to the Portuguese. Portuguese rule lasted less than a hundred years and they were

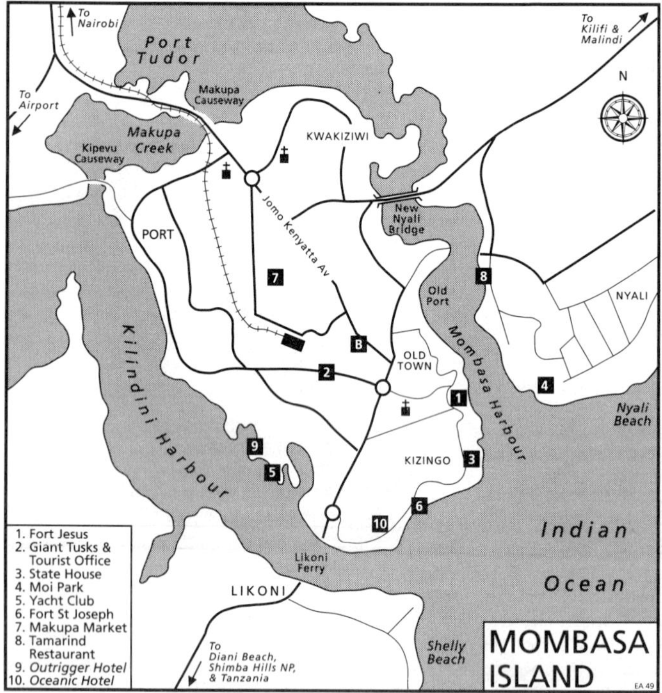

eventually expelled by the Omanis in 1698. The Omanis also held Zanzibar and were heavily involved in the slave trade. Their rule was in turn supplanted by the British in 1873.

The British efforts to stamp out the slave trade, and anxiety about German presence in what is now Tanzania, led, in 1896, to the beginning of the construction of the railway that was to link Uganda to the sea. One of the railway camps that was established before the construction of the line across the Rift Valley was at Nairobi. This town grew rapidly so that by 1907 it was large enough for the administrative quarters to move inland. The climate of Nairobi was considered to be healthier than the coast. Meanwhile, with the railway the importance of the port of Mombasa increased rapidly and it became known as the Gateway to East Africa, serving Kenya, Uganda, Rwanda and Burundi.

Places of interest

City Market The Mombasa market is lively, bustling and colourful. The main section of the market is situated in an enormous shed but numerous stalls have spilt out onto the streets. Obviously the number of tourists has affected the prices and the market is no longer the bargain that it used to be. However if you prepared to haggle and bargain in a good-natured manner you can usually bring the price down quite considerably. Apart from fresh fruit and vegetables you will be able to buy baskets, jewellery and other souvenirs. For kikois and kangas (brightly coloured cloth squares) the best place is Biashara St. This is also the place to come if you want your clothes repaired quickly and cheaply.

Fort Jesus (T 312839) Mombasa Old Town's major attraction. It is located on Nkrumah Rd and the Fort and Museum are open every day from 0800 to 1830. Entrance is US$2 for non-residents. **NB** if you are not part of a tour, local guides will attempt to pick you up. They are very persistent and will expect payment.

The fort was designed by an Italian architect called Cairati who had also done some work for the Portuguese at Goa on the other side of the Indian Ocean. It dominates the entrance to the Old Harbour and is so positioned so that even when it was under siege it was still possible to bring supplies in from the sea.

Despite this apparently secure position the Portuguese lost possession of the fort in 1698 following an uprising by the towns people who had formed an alliance with the Omanis. The fort had been under siege for 15 months before it finally fell. During the battle for the Fort a Portuguese ship named *Santo Antonio de Tanna* sank off the coast and the museum displays some of the relics that were recovered from the ship. The British took control of the Fort in 1825 and from then until 1958 the Fort served as a prison. In 1958 the money was raised to restore the fort and convert it into a museum.

In the late 18th century the Omanis built a house in the NW corner of the fort in what is known as the San Felipe bastion. Since then this has served various purposes including being the prison warden's house. The Omani's also raised the walls of the fort, built turrets and equipped the fort with improved guns and other weaponary to increase its defensive capabilities. At the main gate are 6 cannons from the British ship the *Pegasus* and the German ship the *SS Konigsberg*. The walls are particularly impressive being nearly 3 m thick at the base.

Close to the Omani house one of the trolleys that used to be the mode of transport around town can be seen. There is also an excellent view over the fort and Old Town from here.

The museum is situated in the southern part of the Fort and has an interesting collection. Exhibits include a fair amount of pottery as well as other archaeological finds from other digs on the coast. The diversity of the exhibits is a good illustration of the wide variety of influences that this coast saw over the years. Within the Fort are wall paintings and some of the oldest graffiti in Mombasa.

Old Town

The best way to see Old Mombasa is by walking around. You will pass women dressed in *bui buis* which cover them from head to toe, sometimes with just their eyes peeping through. The buildings in this part of town clearly reflect the Indian influences. Most of the buildings are not actually more than about one hundred years old although there are some exceptions. The finer buildings may have a balcony and one of the elaborate doors which are now so prized. These were once much more numerous than they are now and are a reflection of the wealth and status of the family.

One of the older buildings on the island is **Leven House** located just off the top end of Ndia Kuu. This was built around the beginning of the 19th century and has served many different purposes since then. It was originally occupied by a wealthy trading family and later was the headquarters of the British East Africa Company. It also housed a German Diplomatic Mission and more recently has been used by the Customs Department. Among its most famous visitors were the explorers and missionaries Burton, Jackson and Ludwig Krapf. In front of Leven House are the Leven steps – here a tunnel has been carved through to the water edge where there is a freshwater well. Burton actually mentions climbing up here through this tunnel but you do not need to follow

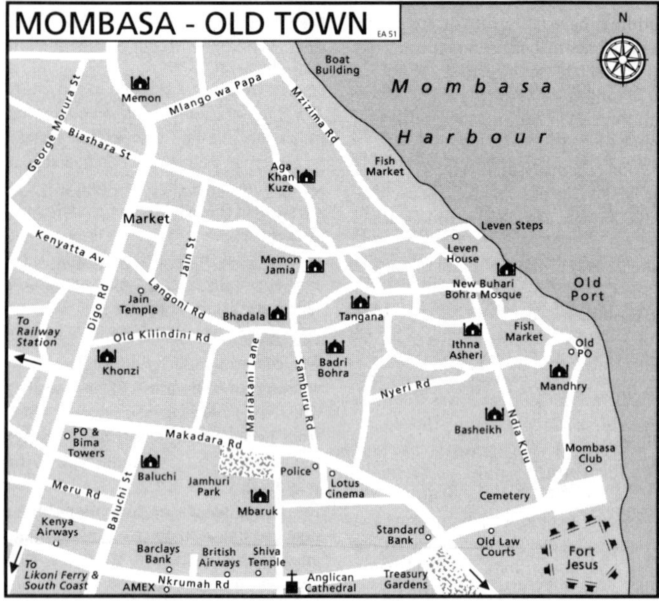

his example – there are steps nearby. Photography in the area of the old harbour is forbidden, so take care.

The **Old Law Court** is located close to Fort Jesus on Nkrumah Rd. The building dates from the beginning of this century Near the Law Courts on Treasury Square is another building of approximately the same age. This was the District Administration headquarters. The roof is tiled and there is a first floor balcony.

Mzizima

The Old Town is probably not the oldest part of Mombasa – the earliest settlement was probably around what is known as Mzizima to the N of the Old Town. The evidence for this is the discovery of pottery dating from the 11th to the 16th centuries. There is, however, very little left of this early settlement

Mbaraki Pillar

On the other side of the island at Mbaraki is the **Mbaraki Pillar** which is believed to have been built largely of coral as a tomb in the 14th century. There was also a mosque next to it which was used by a nearby village. Although this village has long since been abandoned, people still visit the pillar, pray to the spirits of the dead, burn incense and leave offerings.

Kizingo

This area in the southern part of the island around the lighthouse has some very fine buildings, whose style has been called Coast Colonial. These building are spacious and airy and built to keep the occupants as cool as possible. There are wide balconies and shutters which ensure that the sun's rays do not enter, and the buildings are designed to take advantage of every breeze. Many of the building materials were imported from Europe and Asia and hardwoods were used. Unfortunately many of these buildings have fallen into disrepair and you will have to look beyond the exterior to appreciate architecture. Some of these buildings are now used as public buildings such as the Aliens Office on State House Rd.

Along Mama Ngina Drive at the S of the island it is possible to look over the cliffs that rise above Kilindini Channel and out towards the sea. Inland, at the Likoni end of Mama Ngina Drive close to the *Oceanic Hotel* is the Golf Course. At the other end of the road is State House – this is a sensitive area so do not take photos or you risk being arrested. On the golf course is **Fort St Joseph** – this was also built by the Portuguese and can be reached by following the path from the lighthouse that runs between the Mombasa Golf Club and the Police Headquarters.

Other buildings on the island that date from the early 20th century include the **Anglican Cathedral** on the southern side of Nkrumah Rd, which was built by the Universities Mission of Central Africa. **Datoo Auctioneers** is located on Makadara Rd and **Dodwell House** on Moi Ave was home to a shipping company. It has a splendid example of a Mangalore tiled roof which would have been imported from India. The large entrance hall has splendid columns and a fantastic hardwood counter. There are 2 hotels which date from the beginning of the century. The **Castle Hotel** is one of these located on Moi Ave. The **Manor Hotel** on Nyerere Ave, built in 1920s is similar with balconies, pillars and verandas.

Mosques

There are many mosques, over a hundred on the island, some of which dates back over 150 years. On Mbarak Ali Hinawy St, close to the Old Port is **Mandhry Mosque**, with a white minaret. Close to the Leven Steps and the Fish Market is **New Burhani Bohra Mosque** with a tall minaret, built in 1902, and is the third mosque to have been built on this site. One Kuze Rd is the **Jamat-khana Mosque** of the Ismaili community. From the upstairs are good views over the Old Harbour where the dhows are docked. The **Bhadala Mosque** is on Samburu Rd, with a fine dome and minaret. The Bhadala are a sea-faring people, and were among the first settlers. Near the Post Office on Digo Rd is the **Baluchi Mosque.** The Baluchis were a fierce fighting people who served as mercenaries for various Sultans. The **Jundani Mosque** is on Gusii St, and was rebuilt in 1958 on the site of mosque that was established in 1870. Before you enter any of these mosques be sure you are properly dressed, ask for permission to enter, and remove your shoes. As well as mosques there are also a number of Hindu Temples.

Moi Ave

This is Mombasa's main road and is about 4 km long. Along Moi Ave there are many shops that the tourist will want to visit including souvenir shops, travel agencies and the tourist information office. The **Tusks** are found on Moi Ave and were were built in 1952 to commemorate the visit of Queen Elizabeth (Princess Elizabeth as she was then.) They are ctually rather disppointing close to. There are curio shops for about 50 yards in both directions - the goods are not very good quality and are rather expensive.

Nyali

One of the wealthier suburbs of Mombasa. There are a number of good restaurants as well as the Ratna Shopping Centre. It was in this area that newly freed slaves settled, and a bell tower is erected in memory. Across the bridge there is a fork in the road. The right goes towards the village of **Kongowea** which is believed to date back to the 11th century. It is a fishing village and the influence of the missionaries in the 19th century remains strong. It is also near here that the graves of the wife and daughter of the missionary Ludwig Krapf are to be found.

Ludwig Krapf

Krapf was born in 1810 in the foot hills of the German Black Forest. He was the son of a prosperous farmer and during a period of convalescence he spent many hours reading the Bible. He also spent much of his childhood showing a keen interest in geography looking at maps of the world and reading travel books, and by the age of 14 had decided to become a sea captain in order to be able to see the countries that he had read about. His interest in the Church had not waned and he was soon to realise that joining the Church was the most feasible, and affordable, way to travel. He therefore set his mind on being a missionary and soon after his ordination he joined the Church Missionary Society (CMS).

He was appointed to a posting in Abyssinia but only stayed there 2 months. Krapf was married in 1842 to Rosine Dietrich - the couple had not met before they were married. The couple travelled down the coast and spent some time on Zanzibar. Krapf then set off alone to see some of coast and during these travels he decided to work amongst the Wanyika people who were to be found inland from Mombasa. He returned to Zanzibar to collect his pregnant wife and they set off. However tragedy struck in Mombasa when both the Krapf's suffered from a severe fever, and Rosine died 3 days after giving birth and the child, a girl, lived for just a week. He was to write in his diary "I was obliged by the climate to conduct this second victim of the king of terrors to the grave of my beloved Rosine as soon as possible."

Having regained his health Krapf continued with his work translating the Bible into the Swahili and Wanyika languages. Two years later he was to be joined by Johann Rebmann and they set off inland and established themselves amongst the Wanyika peoples. Over the next few years the two made trips inland and it was in May 1848 that Rebmann became the first white man to set eyes on Mount Kilimanjaro. His reports of snow on the equator were greeted in Europe with disbelief.

Krapf's basic objective was to improve geographical knowledge of the "Dark Continent" which would in turn facilitate the stamping out of the slave trade, and allow the spread of Christianity. In 1849 Krapf set off on another journey inland; he went further than any white man before, crossing the Tsavo River and setting eyes on Mount Kenya in the distance. His next trip was along the coast as far S as Cape Dalgado situated on the NE of Mozambique.

After this he returned to Europe for about a year as his health had suffered from his time in the tropics. Whilst in Europe he persuaded the CMS that they should aim to set up a string of missions stretching from one side of Africa to the other. He returned to Africa with five volunteers but one absconded, one died of fever, two returned to Europe having been struck down by fever, and Krapf was left with just Brother Hagerman, a carpenter.

Krapf began what was to be his last expedition into the interior in 1851. It was to be a difficult journey. They were attacked by robbers, most of his porters deserted and he was held prisoner before he escaped and returned to the coast. Although only 43 years old his health was failing him, and in 1853 he was persuaded to return to Europe. He returned to Africa for a brief visit in 1861 and but continued his work in Europe. His greatest contribution was perhaps in the field of linguistics - he translated the Scriptures into six vernacular languages, prepared a Swahili dictionary as well as the basic vocabulary of the Maasai, Galla, Pokomo and Ki-Nyika languages. He died at the age of 71 in Nov 1881.

Local information

● Where to stay

Price guide: A+ Over US$100; **A** US$40-100; **B** US$20-40; **C** US$10-20; **D** US$5-10; **E** Under US$5.

A *Castle*, PO Box 84231, Moi Ave, T 23403/21683/312296. Centrally located this is particularly popular with visiting businessmen. It was renovated in the mid-1980's and has about 65 rooms, all with air-conditioning and bathrooms. Many rooms also have balconies. Other facilities include meeting rooms, garden, terrace, restaurant and bar. The terrace bar looking out onto the street, is a sight to behold when an American aircraft-carrier is in port. **A** *New Outrigger*, PO Box 82345, Ras Liwatoni right on the beach, T 20822. Excellent hotel run by Belgians. There are about 50 rooms all of which are airconditioned with a bathroom and balcony. Other facilities include a swimming pool and the price includes breakfast. **A** *Oceanic*, PO Box 90371, Mama Ngina Drive in the S of the island, T 311191/311192. Large hotel that has been renovated fairly recently. Facilities include 3 restaurants, swimming pool, health centre, meeting rooms and transport into town is provided.

B *Manor*, Nyerere Ave, PO Box 84851, T 314643. An older hotel dating from the 1920's set in gardens. All rooms have bathrooms, most have air-conditioning and the price includes breakfast. Facilities include meeting rooms, bar and restaurant. **B** *Lotus*, PO Box 90193, Mvita Rd, close to Fort Jesus, T 313207. Recently renovated. It has a charming central courtyard and a lovely atmosphere. The rooms are all air conditioned and there is a good restaurant.

C *Splendid*, PO Box 90482, Msanifu Kombo St, T 20967. Large modern hotel. It is clean but the rooms are rather small and pokey. Facilities include a roof top restaurant and bar.

D *New Carlton*, PO Box 86779, Moi Ave, T 23776/315116. Comfortable, reasonably priced hotel. All rooms have bathrooms and there is a restaurant which is fairly good. **D** *Miramer*, PO Box 84819, Tangana Rd close to the railway station, T 313599. Located on this is fairly good value and has an excellent restaurant attached. **D** *Hermes*, PO Box 94819, Haile Selassie Rd, T 313599. All rooms have bathrooms attached and there is very good restaurant. **D** *New Palm Tree*, PO Box 90013, Nkrumah Rd, T 311756/312169/312296. Simple, quiet hotel, that is highly recommended. There is a restaurant which serves basic dishes. **D** *Hotel Relax*, Meru Rd, T 311346. Range of rooms both with and without bathrooms. It is clean, friendly and good value – the price includes breakfast. **D** *Glory Guest House*, Shibu Rd, T 314557. All rooms in this hotel have bathrooms and some have airconditioning. It is very clean although a bit pokey. **D** *Continental Guesthouse*, Haile Selassie Rd, T 315916. Popular hotel. Rooms have bathrooms and the price includes breakfast. It is clean and well run. **D** *Visitors Inn*, corner of Haile Selassie Rd and Shibu Rd. Price includes bathrooms and breakfast. Some rooms are noisy.

E *Fortuna* and *Annex*, Haile Selassie Rd. Main hotel has rooms with own bathrooms while the rooms in the Annex across the road are cheaper and share bathrooms. **E** *ABC Lodge*, Shibu Rd. Fairly good value hotel. The rooms are comfortable and reasonably clean and have bathrooms. **E** *New Britannia Boarding and Lodging*, Gusii St. Popular and friendly hotel Bar downstairs and can be a bit noisy. **E** *Hydro*, PO Box 85360, corner of Digo Rd and Langoni Rd, T 23784. Variety of rooms, from dorms upwards. It has seen better days but remains popular. It has a restaurant. **E** *New Peoples*, PO Box 95342, Abdel Nasser Rd, T 312831. Popular budget hotel. However, it has also seen better days and some rooms are rather noisy. There are a variety of rooms some with own bathrooms and some with shared bathrooms. It is generally safe, reasonably clean and is friendly. It has its own restaurant. **E** *Mvita*, bathrooms are shared although all rooms have a basin. It is clean and friendly, meals are available and there is a bar downstairs. **E** *Midnight Guest House*, Haile Selassie Rd, T 26725. Shared bathrooms. **E** *New Al Jazira*, Shibu St, just off Haile Selassie Rd. Double and triple rooms with shared bathrooms but no singles. **E** *Al Nasser Lodgings*, Abdel Nasser Rd, T 313032. Budget hotel. The rooms have their own bathrooms. **E** *Cosy Guest House*, Haile Selassie Rd, T 313064. Popular with budget travellers and all rooms have fans with shared facilities. It is however a bit run down and often there is no water. **E** *Balgis* Digo Rd, T 313358. Very cheap it has a range of rooms from dorms upwards. Some of the rooms are hot and noisy but it is probably the cheapest place you will find. **E** *Down Town Lodge*,

Hospital St. Range of rooms. Very cheap but can be hot and noisy.

● **Places to eat**

Price guide:
♦♦♦♦Over US$10; ♦♦♦US$5-10; ♦♦US$2-5; ♦Under US$2

There are a number of eating place in Mombasa to choose from apart from hotel restaurants. With its large Indian population there is a lot of excellent indian food in Mombasa as well as fresh fish and shellfish.

International ♦♦♦♦*Tamarind*, Silo Rd at Nyali this is a 15 minute drive from central Mombasa, T 471747. It is well worth the journey for it has marvellous views looking over a creek that flows into the ocean. The Moorish design of the building is well thought out – it has high arches and it cool and spacious. The food and

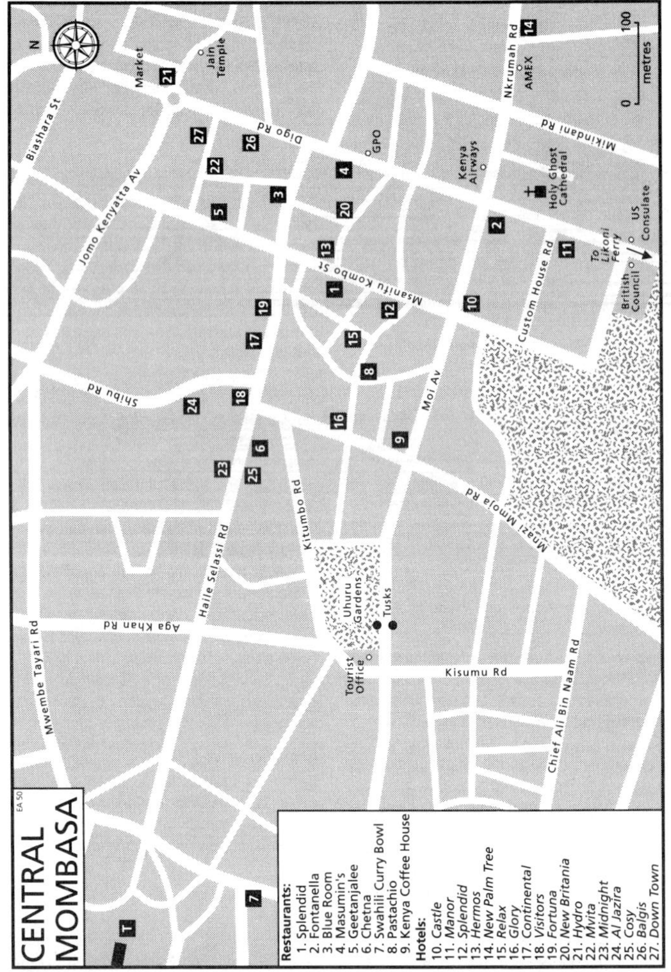

service are both excellent – it specialises in seafood. If you can't chose between dishes try the seafood platter. Be sure to phone and reserve a table.

♦♦♦*Bella Vista*, located on the corner of Moi Ave and Liwatoni above a petrol station, T 313572/25848. Air conditioned. Serves good value, well-prepared food. ♦♦♦*Splendid*, Msanifu Kombo St. Roof-top restaurant of the Hotel Splendid. Pleasant and not too expensive. ♦♦♦*Fontanella Restaurant*, corner of Moi Ave and Digo Rd. Quiet shady courtyard. It has a fairly extensive menu with everything from snacks upwards.

♦*Blue Room Restaurant*, Haile Selassie Rd. Cheap basic restaurant. It serves fish and chips, burgers, chicken and all the usual Indian snacks. *Masumin Restaurant*, located on Digo Rd this is especially for its good value breakfast. It also does the standard menu and the food is not bad.

Italian ♦♦♦♦*Capri Restaurant*, Ambalal House, on Nkrumah Rd, T 311156. This Italian restaurant is one of Mombasa's most sophisticated restaurants. It is well air-conditioned, the food is superb – especially the seafood dishes – and it has a wonderful atmosphere. It is infamous for its slow service.

♦♦♦*Cinabar*, located in Nyali close to the new Nyali Bridge, T 472373. Italian cuisine. Good value.

Chinese ♦♦♦*Galaxy Chinese Restaurant*, Archbishop Makarios St, T 26132. Popular Chinese restaurant and is probably one of the best in town. It has especially good seafood dishes. ♦♦♦*Chinese Overseas*, Moi Ave just N of the tusks, T 21585 Popular Chinese. It is family run, friendly and the food is pretty good. ♦♦♦*Hong Kong*, Moi Ave, T 26707. Another fairly good Chinese restaurant.

Indian ♦♦♦*Hermes*, Msanifu Kombo Rd, T 313599. A bit shabby and the surroundings are not anything special but it is air conditioned and the food is good. ♦♦♦*Singh*, Mwembe Tayari Rd, T 493283. Good air conditioned restaurant. Although the menu is not very extensive the food is freshly prepared and very tasty. ♦♦♦*Nawab*, Moi Ave, T 20754. Air-conditioned restaurant. Good value. The staff are reasonably friendly but the service is slow.

♦♦*Shehnai*, Fatemi House, Maungano St, T 312482. Sound cuisine. ♦♦*Indo Africa*, Haile Selassie Rd, T 21430. Reasonable value. ♦♦*Geetanjalee*, Msanifu Kombo St. Very good for thalis which are a South Indian speciality. You basically get a bit of everything and they are usually very good value. ♦♦*Chetna*, Haile Selassie Rd. South Indian.

African ♦♦*Recoda*, Nyeri St in the Old Town. This serves Indian and African food and is popular with locals as well as budget travellers. The food is basic but cheap. It is only open in the evenings. ♦♦*Swahili Curry Bowl*, Tangana Rd off Moi Ave. Very good for traditional coastal African dishes. Closed on Suns. The icecream is also very good.

Cafés ♦♦*Castle*, centrally located on Moi Ave. Very popular and is ideal for a snack and cold drink. ♦♦*Pistacchio Ice Cream and Coffee Bar*, Msanifu Kombo St. Wonderful ice cream and fruit juices. It serves snacks and you can also have proper meals – including a buffet lunch.

♦*Kenya Coffee House*, Moi Ave. The best in Kenyan coffee.

● Banks

There is a *Barclays Bank* on Moi Ave where you can change travellers cheques from 0900 to 1630 on weekdays and 0900 to 1400 on Sat. Out of hrs you will be able to change money at the *Castle* although there is a charge for this.

● Embassies (E), High Commissions (HC) and Consulates (C)

Austria (C), PO Box 84045, T 313386. **Belgium** (C), PO Box 99697, T 316051. **Denmark** (C), PO Box 95119, T 316051. **Finland** (C), PO Box 99543, T 316051. **France** (C), PO Box 82804, T 21008). **Germany** (C), PO Box 90171, T 21273). **Greece** (C), PO Box 99211, T 315478). **India** (C), PO Box 90614, T 311051. **Italy** (C), PO Box 80033, T 26948. **Netherlands** (C), PO Box 80301, T 311043. **Norway** (C), PO Box 86954, T 471771. **Rwanda** (C), PO Box 87676, T 20466. **Sweden** (C), PO Box 86408, T 20501. **Switzerland** (C), PO Box 84255, T 316684. **United Kingdom** (C), PO Box 90680, T 25913. **USA** (C), PO Box 88079, T 315101.

● Entertainment

Bars and Clubs *Istanbul*, Moi Ave. Lively place; *Rainbow House Night Club*, Corner of Moi Ave and Meru Rd. Popular disco and reggae club; *New Florida*, Mama Ngina Drive; *Rainbows*, Mnazi Moja Rd; *Sunshine*, Moi Ave; *Toyz* on Baluchi St; *Tiffany's* Ambalal House.

Gambling *International Casino Oceanic Hotel*, Lighthouse Rd, T 312838.

Cinemas *Lotus* and the *Kenya*, which are both located fairly centrally as well as the ***Drive In***. See what's on in *Coastweek* which is the local paper.

● Hospitals

Aga Khan Hospital Vanga Rd T 321953 ***Mombasa Hospital*** Mama Ngina Drive T 312190 / 312099.

● Police Station

Makadara Rd, T 311401.

● Post Office

Digo St. Mon-Fri 1800 to 1630; Sat from 8.00 to 1200.

● Religion

For Mosques see page 111 above. ***Jain Temple***, on Langoni Rd, built in 1963 which is a splendid sight with a pair of lions flanking the entrance. The most important religious centre for Mombasa's Hindus is the ***Lord Shiva Temple*** which is located on the edge of the Old Town. The ***Holy Ghost Cathedral*** is located on the corner of Nkrumah Rd and Digo Rd and dates from 1918. There has been a church on this site since 1891.

● Shopping

Sea shells Do not buy any shells at all. As a result of killing the animals that live inside the shells to sell them to tourists, populations have declined dramatically and many are seriously threatened. The vendor may tell you he has a licence – but if you want these species to survive into the next century you will not encourage this trade.

Souvenirs that you will find in Mombasa are wooden carvings including Makonde carvings from Tanzania, soap stone carvings and chess sets, baskets, batiks and jewellery. There are lots of stalls in and around the market and around the junction of Digo Rd and Jomo Kenyatta Ave. There are also lots along Msanifu Kombo St; along Moi Ave from the *Castle Hotel* and down to the roundabout with Nyerere Ave; and around Fort Jesus. For kikois, kangas and other material or fabric go to Biashara St which runs off Digo St parallel to Jomo Kenyatta Ave.

Pharmacies *Digo Chemist*, Meru Rd, T 316065. Open 0800 to 1900 on weekdays; 0800 to 1500 on Sat and 0900 to 1300 on Sun. *Coast Medical Stores*, Digo Rd, T 25600/26435. Open from 0800 to 1230 and 1400 to 1600.

● Sports (participant)

Mombasa Sports Club is located on Mnazi Mosi Rd. It offers a fairly wide range of activities.

Yacht and Rowing Club in the southwest of the island close to the *Outrigger Hotel*. They have a busy program – both races and social events.

● Tourist Office

Moi Ave near the Tusks T 311231. Open from 0800 to 1630 with 2 hrs off for lunch. It sells a map of Mombasa as well as guide books of Mombasa Old Town and Fort Jesus.

● Travel agents and tour operators

Across Africa Safaris, PO Box 82139, Moi Ave, T 315360/314394. ***African Tours and Hotels***, PO Box 90604, Moi Ave, T 23509/20627. ***Airtour Suisse***, PO Box 84198, Moi Ave, T 312565. ***Archers***, PO Box 84618, Nkrumah Rd, T 25362/311884. ***Big Five Tours and Safaris***, PO Box 86922, Nkrumah Rd, T 311462/311524. ***Express Safaris***, PO Box 86031, Moi Ave, T 25699. ***Flamingo Tours***, PO Box 83321, Ambalal House, Nkrumah Rd, T 315635. ***Glory Tours and Safaris***, PO Box 85527, Moi Ave, T 313561. ***Highways***, PO Box 84787, T 26886/20383. ***Kuldips Touring***, PO Box 82662, Moi Ave, T 25928/24067. ***Leisure Tours and Safaris***, PO Box 84902, Moi Ave, T 24704/314846. ***Marajani Tours***, PO Box 86103, Moi Ave, T 314935/315099. ***Pollman Tours and Safaris***, PO Box 84198, Moi Ave, T 316732/3. ***Private Safaris***, PO Box 85722, Ambalal House, Nkrumah Rd, T 316684/5. ***Rhino Safaris***, PO Box 830050, Nkrumah Rd, T 311755/311141/311536. ***Rusco Tours and Safaris***, PO Box 99162, Maungano Rd, T 313664/21137. ***Sawa Sawa Tours***, PO Box 80766, Nkrumah Rd, T 313187/3114790. ***Southern Cross Safaris***, PO Box 90653, Nkrumah Rd, T 311627/26765. ***Sunny Safaris***, PO Box 87049, Moi Ave, T 23578/20162. ***Thorn Trees Safaris***, PO Box 81953, Nkrumah Rd. ***Transafric Tours and Travel Services***, PO Box 82829, Haile Selassie Rd, T 26928. ***Turkana Safari***, PO Box 99300, Moi Ave, T 21065. ***United Touring Company***, PO Box 84782, Moi Ave, T 31633/4.

● Tours

It is possible to do a cruise of the Old Harbour and Kilindini Harbour. Ask at the ***Castle Hotel*** on Moi Ave, T 315569, who arrange them. They take about 4 hrs and you can either do a lunchtime or evening cruise leaving at 1030 and 1800. They are not cheap, but the price includes food and live music. ***Tamarind Restaurant***, T 472263, also arrange lunch cruises which are excellent although, again, not cheap.

● Transport

Local Car hire *Avis*, PO Box 84868, Moi Ave, T 23048 and at the airport T 43321. ***Coast Car Hire***, PO Box 99143, Ambalal House, Nkrumah Rd, T 311752. ***Glory Car Hire***, PO Box 85527, Moi Ave, T 313561. ***Leisure Car Hire***, PO Box 84902, Moi Ave, T 314935. ***Ocean Car Hire***, PO Box 84798, Digo St, T 313559/ 313083/ 23049. ***Avenue Motors***, PO Box 83697, Moi Ave, T 25162/315111.

Likoni Ferry Joins the mainland with the island. They go about every 20 minutes and are free for pedestrians and cyclists. Matatus to the ferry leave from outside the Post Office on Digo Rd – ask for Likoni.

Air Mombasa is served by a number of different airlines, as well as by chartered planes for safaris etc. ***Kenya Airlines*** does the Nairobi-Mombasa-Malindi route once a day in both directions (except Sat). It is a popular route so be sure to book well ahead and confirm your seat. The problem of double booking can be serious. Also serving this route are ***Eagle Aviation***, T Mombasa 316054. ***Equator Airlines***, T Malindi 2053. ***Prestige Air Services***, T Malindi 20860. ***Skyways Airlines***, T Mombasa 432167. All have 2 flights per day in both directions between Malindi and Mombasa. Baggage allowance is only 10 kg, and check in time is 30 mins before take off. Airport tax is around US$1.

Moi International Airport is located on the mainland about 10 km out of the centre of town. Kenya Airways operates a shuttle bus, about US$2. Taxi about US$9. Also public buses and matatus. Airport departure tax must be paid – currently US$1.50.

Train There are 2 overnight trains daily between Mombasa and Nairobi. They leave at 1700 and 1900 and arrive in Nairobi at 0800 and 0830. Be sure to book in advance as this is a popular route. On the earlier train you see more of the plains before it gets dark. The booking office in Mombasa is open from 0800 to 1830 with 2 hrs off for lunch. Fares to Nairobi are US$19 for 1st class, US$9 for 2nd and US$5 for 3rd.

Road There are lots of bus companies that go to Nairobi whose offices are to be found on Jomo Kenyatta Ave. They usually leave early morning and evening and take about 8 hrs. Fares vary and are about US$8.

Buses and matatus depart for Malindi frequently throughout the day and take about 3 hrs. They leave Mombasa from Abdel Nasser Rd outside the *New People's Hotel*. Alternatively you can get together with a group and hire a Peugeot 504 station wagon as a share-taxi. They take 7 people and leave when full so get there early. They work out about the same price as the bus.

Heading S to Tanzania there are buses run by a company called ***Cat Bus***, 3 times a week on Mon, Wed and Fri. They leave at 1600, and take about 8 hrs to Tanga and 20 hrs to Dar es Salaam.

Boat There have been boats (hydrofoils) from Mombasa to **Tanga**, **Zanzibar** and **Dar es Salaam** (see page 202). Although these have not been operating for a while, resumption of the service is expected. The cost to Dar es Salaam was about the same as the air fare (US$45).

It is possible to take a dhow from Mombasa to **Tanga** and **Dar es Salaam** (**see page 202**). However, you must expect to wait around for a week or more for one to depart. It will take one or two days depending on the weather. Expect to pay about US$15 to Dar es Salaam, bring all your own food, and you will sit and sleep on the cargo. At one time it was also possible to get dhows to **Kismayo**, **Mogadishu**, **Berbera** and **Djibouti**. These are not currently an option with the civil war in Somalia.

SOUTH COAST

You are unlikely to visit Mombasa without going to the beach – this is the reason, that most people come here and with good reason for these beaches are some of the best in the world. The sand is white and some of the beaches seem endless. The sand is very fine – it is actually coral that has been broken down by pounding waves over the centuries.

The coast is hot and humid all the year round although the rainfall varies. From Apr to Jun is the quietest season – this is when it is often overcast and muggy. However there is the definite advantage of cheaper accommodation and greater availability of places to stay.

Running from Mombasa S, the main

beaches are **Shelley**, **Tiwi** and **Diani.** The most popular beach on the S coast is Diani – it is also the most built up and not surprisingly is now the most expensive. However, most of the buildings have been designed well and local materials have been used so the hotels do not intrude too much. The hotels all have their own restaurants and bars and most of them arrange regular evening entertainment such as traditional African dancers and singers.

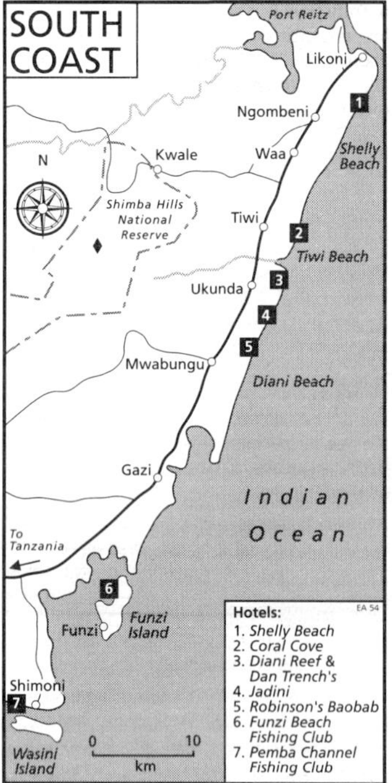

Shelley Beach

This is the closest beach to Mombasa, ideal for a day trip if you are staying in the town.

• **Where to stay A** *Shelley Beach* PO Box 96030, T 451011/2/3/4, F 315743. This is the only place to stay on this beach. It is located about 3 km from the Likoni ferry and is well signposted. The hotel has over 100 rooms as well as some cottages that are ideal for families. There is a swimming pool very close to the sea. Other facilities include tennis courts, water sports, glass bottom boat trips, restaurant, coffee shop and verandas and the hotel has wheelchair access.

Tiwi Beach

Going S from Likoni, Tiwi Beach is the next that you come to. It is about 20km from Likoni Ferry and is 3 km off the main coastal road down a very bumpy track. It is wise not to walk down this track – there have been muggings. This beach is wider than that at Shelley and it is particularly popular with families and with budget travellers as it has camping facilities and budget accommodation. It is ideal for children – the reef is quite close to the mainland which keeps the waves smaller than those at Diani. There is also lots for small children to do – hundreds of pools are exposed when the tide is out all with plenty of marine life in them. There is also some quite good snorkelling here.

Before you go exploring on the reef check up on the tides (they are published in the local papers) and set out with plenty of time. It is very easy to get cut off when the tide comes in and it does turn quite rapidly. Also be sure you have a good pair of thick rubber soled shoes to protect you feet against the coral and sea urchins.

• **Where to stay B-D** *Coral Cove Sea Cottages*, T 0127 4164. Has bandas (round thatched cottages) which vary in price – the most expensive have bathrooms while the others are cheaper and more basic. **D** *Twiga Lodge*, PO Box 96005, Mombasa, T 0127 4061. This is one of the oldest of the lodges on this beach. There are rooms and bandas or you can camp. **E** *Camping*, facilities here are fairly basic but it is right on the beach and there is plenty of shade. There is a restaurant which does fairly good meals and snacks and a shop with most supplies that you will need.

● **Transport** Take a bus or matatu from Likoni and ask to be dropped off at Tiwi Beach. It is about 3 km from the main road to the beach and unless there is a fairly big group of you then it is advisable to wait for a lift as there have been attacks on people walking down this road. You should not have to wait too long – and it is not worth the risk of going alone. There is also a newly established taxi service doing this route.

Diani Beach

At about 20 km this is the longest beach in Kenya and has a whole string of hotels. It is also the place to come if you want to do a bit of windsurfing or water sports including sailing, wind surfing, snorkelling and scuba diving. You can also go water-skiing or parascending, or can hire a bike or a motor bike. It is very geared to the big spender which obviously has some disadvantages. However it is a classic paradise beach with endless dazzling white sand, coconut trees and clear sea.

The reef and tides At low tide you can go out to the reef which is worth doing at least once. At Diani you will need to take a boat if you want to go out to the main reef, although you should be able to wade out to the sand bank which is not too far. Of course this depends on the tides. The tides are controlled by the moon, in a monthly cycle. At full moon there are spring tides which means high High Tides and low Low Tides, while a fortnight later there will be neap tides with low Highs and high Lows. There are advantages to both – wind surfers may prefer neap tides as you will be able to go out for longer, while those who want huge waves at high tide, as well as going out to the reef during the low tide, the spring is probably better as it has the biggest contrasts. The timing of the tides changes and are published in local papers. Obviously if you are only at the coast for a few days there will not be much difference – but if you particularly want to do something (such as going out to the reef) it is worth looking up the tides and planning ahead so to make the best of your time.

Vendors There are now hoards of hawkers who walk up and down the beach selling all sorts of things as well as offering themselves as models for photos. Most of the goods are hugely overpriced and are often of very poor quality. They may also try to sell you ivory and elephant hair bracelets. These are probably fake and anyway should not be bought if the elephant is not to go the way of the dodo. It may also surprise you to learn that some of the Maasai who come round offering themselves for a photo (at a charge of course) are not Maasai at all but are of other tribes.

Places of interest

At the far N of Diani beach is the **Kongo Mosque** (also known as the Diani Persian Mosque). It is rather a strange place – it is very run down but not really a ruin – and still has some ritual significance. The building is believed to date from the 15th century and is the only remaining building from a settlement of the Shirazi people (see page 278) who used to live here. There are a number of entrances and you should be able to push one of the doors open and have a look inside.

Apart from the beach and the sea the other major attraction on this stretch of coast is the **Shimba Hills National Reserve** (see page 192). There are also the marine reserves, and you will see plenty of notices about trips in glass bottom boats. These can be excellent if you go to a good section of reef but on some of the trips you see little more than sand and seaweed (see Marine Parks under Game Parks, page 132). Closer to the hotels is the **Jadini Forest** which is a small patch of forest that used to cover the whole of this coastal area. There are colobus monkeys and porcupine as well as other animals.

Local information

● **Where to stay**

The better hotels are all good value compared,

say with similar standard hotels in the Seychelles or Mauritius. Prices vary with the season ***Low*** is Apr-Jun; ***Mid*** is Jul-Oct; ***High*** is Dec-Mar. **A+** ***Diani House***, PO Box 19, Ukunda, T 1261 2412. This is an extremely exclusive hotel that only takes 8 guests at any one time. It was a private house and is set in 12 acres of gardens and forest right on the beach. The price includes all meals and a trip to the Shimba Game Reserve.

A ***Africana Sea Lodge***, PO Box 84616, T 01261 2021, Tex 22591. This is linked to the Jardini Beach Hotel and you can use the facilities of both – this is marginally cheaper than the Jardini. Instead of standard rooms the East Africana has bandas, some of which are divided into 2. They are set in gardens, each have a little verandah and all are air conditioned with bathrooms. The facilities are the same as for the Jardini – some are shared although it has its own swimming pool.

A ***Diani Reef*** PO Box 35 Ukunda, T 01261 2175/6/7. This is a comfortable hotel, all the rooms are airconditioned and the hotel has all the usual facilities including a craft shop, shops, doctor, bar, restaurant and disco. **A** ***Diani Sea Lodge***, PO Box 37, Ukunda, T 01261 2114/5. These are self catering cottages that are ideal for families and are popular with expatriates. They vary in size and price – but you hire the cottage and can get as many people in as you want. They all have a balcony and are simple but very pleasant and excellent value. **A** ***Jadini Beach***, PO Box 84616, T 01261 2121/5. This is linked to the *Africana Sea Lodge*, and you can use the facilities of both of the hotels. The Jadini has about 150 normal hotel rooms, while the East Africana has individual bandas. All rooms are air conditioned and have a balcony or terrace. Facilities include swimming pool, squash courts, tennis courts, health club, water sports, bar, restaurant, meeting rooms, shops and evening entertainment including live dancing, films and disco. **A** ***Robinsons Baobab***, PO Box 32, Ukunda, T 01261 2026/7/8 Tlx 21132. Set up on the cliff at the southern end of Diani this looks out across the sea. To get to the beach you have to climb down the steep steps. It used to be a very popular hotel with package tours who seemed to have their whole day planned out for them: 0800-0900 Early Morning Jog; 0900-1000 Breakfast; 1000-1030 Aerobics; 1030-1100 Coffee; 1100-1200 Postcard Writing and so on. It has about 150 air conditioned rooms as well as a number of bungalows suitable for families or groups. Facilities include a library, restaurant, swimming pool, bar, water sports and diving facilities, shops, hairdresser and lots of organised activities. You can learn Swahili here. **A** ***Safari Beach***, PO Box 90690, T 01261 2726/ 2131/2088. This is a large hotel with about 180 rooms. They are in round bandas which are grouped into villages set in wonderful gardens. All are air conditioned and very comfortable. Facilities include meeting rooms, tennis courts, squash courts, swimming pool, bar, restaurant and water sports. **A** ***Trade Winds***, PO Box 8, Ukunda, T 01261 2016/2116, Tex 21139. One of the most northerly of the big hotels this is also one of the older ones on Diani. It has about 100 rooms all of which are air-conditioned. It was well designed and is one of the most attractive of the hotels. Facilities include swimming pool, water sports and very attractive gardens. **A** ***Two Fishes***, PO Box 23, Ukunda, T 01261 2101/2/3, Tlx 21162. This is the hotel with the swimming pool that goes under part of the hotel and into the bar. It is one of the oldest hotels on Diani and for a long time had the most imaginative swimming pool – all the other hotels had straightforward rectangular pools. Children love the idea of swimming under the hotel and there are a few water chutes and slides. Non-residents can swim here but at a daily fee. It has been done up fairly recently

B ***Leopard Beach***, PO Box 34, Ukunda, T 01261 2110/1/2/3. This is one of the cheaper hotels on this stretch of beach and is not bad value. Rooms are comfortable although perhaps a little shabby. **B** ***Nomad Beach Bandas***, T 01261 2155) Banda accommodation, good value and probably (with *Diani Sea Lodge*) the cheapest place to stay on Diani if you are not camping. There is a very good seafood restaurant here and water sports are available.

C ***Golden Beach***, PO Box 31, Ukunda, T 01261 2054/2059/2066 /2067. This is one of the less attractive hotels and the architect would not get any prizes for blending into the surroundings. It is modern and very large with about 150 rooms all with bathrooms. Facilities include meeting rooms, swimming pool, shops, restaurant, bar, tennis courts, gym, water sports facilities and wheelchair access.

D ***Diani Beachalets***, South Diani, T 01261 2180. Also located at the southern end of the beach this has a range of facilities including camping. Some of the bandas have shared facilities while others have their own bathrooms and kitchens. There is a tennis court but no swimming pool or restaurant. There is also no shop so you will have to stock up before you get here. **D *Four Twenty South Cottages***, South Diani, T 01261. Located at the southern end of these cottages sleep 4 and have all facilities. You will need to bring bed linen. There is no shop on the site so you will have to buy food at Mombasa or else at the Diani shopping centre or Ukunda. **D *Larry Peacock's***, close to Tradewinds is Larry Peacock's which has 3 rooms. The owner, a real eccentric, has been swanning around Diani for years and has always been known as 'The Peacock'. The rooms are comfortable and the security is good. It is clean and friendly and you can use the facilities at Trade Winds.

E *Dan Trench's*, just behind the *Trade Winds Hotel* is famous amongst budget travellers. Unfortunately it has seen better days but it remains popular being the only cheap place to stay on Diani. The facilities are basic and unfortunately it is not very safe so watch your belongings like a hawk. There is a small dorm and one banda. If you are staying here you can use most of the facilities at Trade Winds. **E *Camping*** at Dan Trench's; Diani Beachalets.

● Places to eat

Apart from the hotel restaurants there are a number of others. All do very good fish and seafood and you can rely on it being very fresh. Many of the hotels do special buffet lunches and dinners and these are usually very good value. ♦♦♦♦***Ali Barbours***, between *Diani Sea Lodge* and *Trade Winds*, T 1261/2033. One of the most popular. You can either eat in the open air or else in a sort of underground cave. It does excellent seafood as well as French food.

♦♦♦***Bush Baby Restaurant***, opposite the *2 Fishes Hotel*. Open air restaurant. Later on in the evening it develops into a disco and usually has quite a lively crowd. ♦♦♦***Nomads Seafood Restaurant***, at *Nomads Beach Bandas*, just S of Jadini and is probably one of the best restaurants on Diani. It does a very popular Sun buffet lunch which is good value. ♦♦♦***Vulcano***, T 1261/2004. Italian food and is not too expensive. ♦♦♦***Cheers*** is also located at Diani Shopping Centre but is a bit more expensive.

♦♦***South Coast Fitness Centre***, has a restaurant which is fairly good value.

● Entertainment

Most of the hotels arrange entertainment in the evenings. This includes traditional dancers who are usually a group who do a range of dances from around Kenya. The hotels will often combine this with an evening barbecue. They also hold films shows. Almost all the hotels have discos which are of varying quality.

● Transport

Air There is also a small airfield at Ukunda which is used for small planes – usually charters for safaris.

Road To get to the S coast, take the Likoni ferry from Mombasa Island. There are 2 ferries and they go about every 20 minutes throughout the day, although there are many fewer late in the evening. You will be charged according to the length of your vehicle. Pedestrians go free.

● Useful addresses

If you are self-catering it is worth buying most of your supplies in Mombasa where it is cheaper. There are however a couple of places closer to the beach. Firstly there is the small village of **Ukunda** which is on the main road close to the Diani turnoff. There is a post office here and a shop which before the **Diani Shopping Centre** was built was the best around. You can get most things here. Off the main road, on the road with all the hotels, is the much newer shopping area. This has sprung up in the last ten years very quickly and has a couple of good supermarkets, banks (open 10am to 3 pm), souvenir shops, petrol stations and you can hire a car here. There is also the South Coast Fitness Centre gym. You can also hire go-karts here. For fresh fruit, vegetables and fish you will be able to buy off the vendors who come round all the self catering places with their stock on their bicycles.

● Transport

From Likoni drive S on the A14, the main Kenya-Tanzania coastal road. All the turnings off are well signposted. For Diani, go as far as Ukunda village (about 22 km) where there is the turning off to the smaller road that runs along Diani beach. At the T-junction, some hotels are to the left, while all the others are to the right.

South of Diani

For many people Diani is the furthest S that they will go. In fact there are a few places to stay including the Funzi Island

Fishing Club and the *Shimoni Reef Fishing Lodge* which are both located very close to the Tanzanian border. Both are very exclusive and in the A+ price range although Shimoni is marginally the cheaper of the 2. They both cater largely for keen fishermen. Before these 2 are reached, at the southern end of Diani is a small bay and Chale Island. This is a popular spot for day trips from Diani – boats take you out for swimming, snorkelling and beach barbecues on the island. Contact Nomad Safaris on Diani Beach for more details. Along this route you will not be able to miss the coconut plantations which cover a wide area.

Gazi

A village the southern end of Diani, once significantly more important than it is now as it was the district's administrative centre. Here you will see the **House of Sheik Mbaruk bin Rashid.** There are said to be the bodies of 8 men and 8 women buried in the foundations of the house to give the building strength. He was also notorious for torturing people, and suffocating them on the fumes of burning chillies. In the Mazrui Rebellion of 1895 Mbaruk was seen arming his men with German rifles and flying the German flag. British troops did eventually defeat him and he ended his days in exile in German East Africa (mainland Tanzania). However, the house is now used as a school. It is looking rather run down. It once had a very finely carved door but this has been moved to the Fort Jesus Museum. You will have to ask directions for Gazi as it is not signposted on the main road.

Msambweni

About 50 km S of Likoni is the village of Msambweni which is home to what is one of the best hospitals on the coast as well as a famous leprosarium. The beach here has recently been developed for tourists and there are some bungalows and a hotel. The beach here is nice and there are some ruins in this area which are believed to have been a slave detention camp.

• **Where to stay** **A+** *Funzi Beach Fishing Club*, PO Box 90246, South of Msambweni, Mombasa, Tlx 21126. Only takes 12 people accommodated in tents on a beautifully secluded island to a very high standard. Facilities for all water sports are available and are included in the price, as are all meals, drinks and transport. **B** *Beachcomber Club*, c/o *Let's Go Travel*, Caxton House, Standard St, Nairobi, PO Box 60342, T 340331 F 336890. **B** *Black Marlin*, PO Box 80, Msambweni, T Msambweni 90.

Shimoni

A a small fishing village whose name means Place of the Hole. This is from the system of **Slave Caves** located to the W of the village. It is said that these caves were used by slave traders to hide the slaves before they were shipped out and sold to overseas markets. The other story associated with them is that they have been used as a refuge from various marauding tribes through the ages. To reach the caves take the path that begins opposite the jetty and walk up through the forest. When you get to the entrance you take a ladder down through a hole in the ground. The cave system is believed to extend about 20 km underground.

In the far S is the **Kisite-Mpunguti Marine National Park** which has superb coral gardens and lots of sea life. You can take trips out to the Park – and this is one of the glass bottom boat trips that are very good. For details contact *Kisite Dhow Tours*, T 01261 2331 or T Mombasa 11 311752. Apart from the fish, coral and shells you may also see dolphins. This stretch of the coast line is also a bird watchers paradise.

• **Where to stay** **A+** *Shimoni Reef Fishing Lodge*, South of Msambweni, beyond Funzi Beach, overlooking Wasini Island. c/o *Reef Hotel*, PO Box 82234, Mombasa, T 471771. High standards. **A+** *Pemba Channel Fishing Club*, PO Box 44, Msambweni, T 572 Msambweni, which is older than the Shimoni Reef Fishing Lodge. It caters almost exclusively for keen anglers Closed Apr-Jun (after fishing season).

Wasini Island

A wonderful place measuring one kilometre across and 6 along. It is totally undeveloped and there are no cars, no mains electricity, and no running water. There is no reliable fresh water supply on the island (it relies on the collection of rain water) which is the major factor that has limited the growth of the island's population and pace of development. There is a small village on the island that includes the remains of an Arab settlement. There are the ruins of 18th and 19th century houses as well as a pillar tomb which has Chinese porcelain insets that have, so far, survived. The beach is worth exploring – you might well find bits of pottery and glass. Also interesting are the dead coral gardens which are found behind the village. They are above the sea although during the Spring tide they are covered.

From Wasini Island you may want to organise a trip to the Marine Park (if you have not arranged this from Mombasa or Diani). Get a group together and ask at the *Mpunguti Restaurant*, who will be able to arrange a trip for you. This is said to be the best snorkelling in Kenya. It is not too expensive – especially as the price includes an excellent lunch. You can if you wish also hire a canoe and do it yourself but obviously will not know the best places to go.

• **Where to stay** **C** *Mpunguti Lodge*. This has a number of bandas and the food here is excellent – it is also very friendly. Alternatively you can camp but if you want to be totally self-sufficient be sure to bring plenty of supplies from Mombasa as there is not much here. Bring as much drinking water with you as you can carry.

• **Transport** To get to Wasini Island under your own steam either hire a taxi or take a KBS bus from Likoni to Shimoni (there are not very many). Alternatively take a matatu to Lunga Lunga and ask to be let off at the turning for Shimoni which is about 15 km off the main road. From here you will have to hitch. From Shimoni, there is a dhow run by the Mpunguti Restaurant, otherwise a matatu boat.

Lunga Lunga

A village located about 95 km S of Mombasa and is the nearest village to the border with Tanzania. It is about 5 km from the actual border itself and can be reached by bus from Mombasa. Buses between Mombasa and Dar es Salaam or Tanga go about once a week in both directions taking about 20 hrs to Dar and 8 to Tanga. The border post is slow so you will have to be patient – it can take up to 4 hrs. If you do not get a through bus you can take matatus but this involves a fair bit of walking. Coming from Kenya you cross through the Kenyan formalities and from here, unless you have your own transport, you will have to walk the 6 km to the Tanzanian border at Horohoro. From here there are about 2 buses a day to Tanga, but several *dala dala* (Tanzanian matatus).

NORTH COAST

There is a whole string of beaches with lots of hotels on them to the N of Mombasa, including the major attractions of Malindi and Lamu. At these latter places there is much more choice for the budget traveller, and anyone who wants to avoid the package tours. There are major historical sites at Kilifi, Malindi and Lamu.

Mombasa to Kilifi

The strip of beach immediately to the N of Mombasa Island is well developed and there are lots of hotels. Most of them cater for package tours from Europe and usually each hotel caters for one nationality or another. None of them is cheap. All have facilities such as swimming pools, tennis courts, water sports etc and they all do their best to look after their guests very well, organising all sorts of activities and trips.

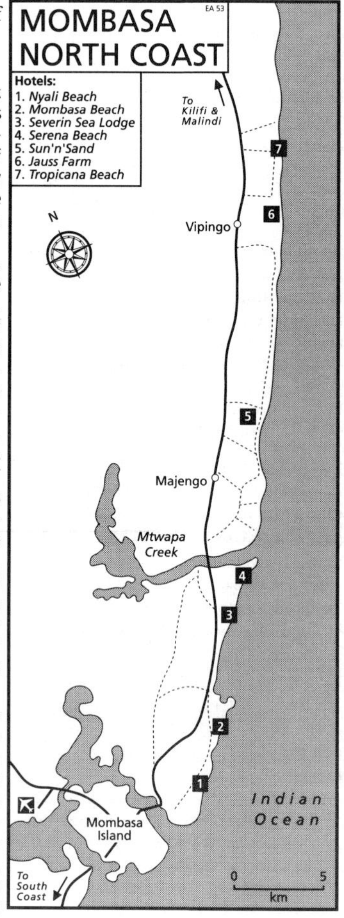

● Where to stay

Nyali Beach A+ ***Mombasa Beach***, PO Box 90414, Mombasa, T 471861. This hotel has about 150 rooms all of which are air conditioned with balconies. It is set up on a cliff looking over the beach and the sea. It is very well managed and facilities include conference rooms, tennis courts, golf, water sports, bar, restaurant and grill room.

A ***Nyali Beach***, PO Box 90414, Mombasa, T 471551/471861. This hotel is located close to Mombasa and is popular for conferences. It is very large with over 200 rooms some of which are in a newer section of the hotel called the Palm Beach annex. They are all air conditioned and most have balconies. There are also some cottages. Facilities include meeting facilities, restaurant and grill room, tennis courts, swimming pool, snack bar and night club. **A** ***Nyali Reef***, PO Box 82234, Mombasa, T 471771. This recently renovated hotel has about 160 rooms all of which are airconditioned and have balconies. Facilities include meeting rooms, swimming pool, tennis court, sauna, restaurant and bar. **A** ***Silver Beach***, PO Box 81443, Mombasa, T 471771. This hotel is located fairly close to Mombasa and is popular with package tours. It has the usual range of facilities including swimming pool, restaurants and bar.

Bamburi Beach A ***Bamburi Beach***, PO Box 83966, Mombasa, T 485611 Tlx 21181. Another of the older hotels this has recently been renovated. It has about 120 rooms and 25 suites all of which are air conditioned and have sea facing balconies. Facilities include conference facilities and extensive sports provision-including tennis, squash, gym, sauna, golf, horse riding, and various water sports. There is a roof top bar and night club. **A** ***Giriama Apartments***, PO Box 86693, T 485726. Located on Bamburi Beach these apartments are very comfortable and set in lovely gardens. Swimming pool and restaurant. **A** ***Whitesands***, PO Box 90173, Mombasa, T 485926. One of the older hotels this has been refurbished recently. It is set in gardens and has meeting rooms, a swimming pool, and tennis courts. **A+** ***Severin Sea Lodge***, PO Box 82169, Mombasa, T 485001. This lodge consists of about 180 bungalows all of which are airconditioned and are very comfortable. Facilities include 2 swimming pools, tennis courts, excellent water sports and sailing.

B ***Kenya Beach***, PO Box 95748, Mombasa, T 485821. A number of cottages, all air conditioned, set in gardens with a communal swimming pool. Various water sports are available including deep sea diving. **B** ***Ocean View Beach***, PO Box 81127, Mombasa. A rather old-style hotel. Although most of the rooms are air conditioned it has no phone. However it does have a number of very modern facilities consisting of swimming pool, water sports including deep sea diving, bar, restaurant and disco. **B** ***Plaza Beach***, PO Box 88299, Mombasa, T 485321/485212. This hotel is reasonably good value. The rooms all have views of the sea and the restaurant, which specialises in Indian food, is especially good.

Shanzu Beach A+ ***Dolphin***, PO Box 81443, Mombasa. A very pleasant hotel. It has the full range of facilities. **A+** ***Intercontinental***, PO Box 83492, Mombasa, T 484811. A large hotel with nearly 200 rooms. All are airconditioned and have balconies. It has extensive meeting facilities, 2 swimming pools, 2 tennis courts, 2 squash courts and health club, bars, restaurants, night club and casino. It is set in large grounds and has a long beach front. **A+** ***Serena Beach***, PO Box 90352, Mombasa, T 485721. A very pleasant luxury hotel which has been designed to resemble Lamu architecture and it is clear that great care has been taken in its construction. It has about 120 rooms all of which are air conditioned. Facilities include meeting rooms, tennis courts, swimming pool, water sports, bar, and restaurant.

Kikambala Beach A+ ***Sun 'n' Sand Beach***, PO Box 2, Kikambala, T Kikambala 8. A very pleasant hotel.Good facilities. The beach here is particularly fine. **A** ***Whispering Palms***, PO Box 5, Kikambala, T Kikambala 3/4/5/6. This is located on a quiet piece of beach and has been built with a high roof made of palm leaf thatch known as *makuti*. It has all the usual facilities including a swimming pool, water sports, restaurant, bar and entertainment.

C ***Continental Beach Cottages***, PO Box 124, Kikambala, T Kikambala 77. These are simple cottages that are rather out of the way set in peaceful gardens. Some of them have air conditioning but they have seen better days and are rather grubby. You are charged for the cottage so can cram in as many people as you want. They are difficult to get to unless you have your own transport. However there is a swimming pool and a good beach. Meals are available fairly cheap and basic.

C-E ***Jauss Farm***, T 01251 2218. This is located about 40 km N of Mombasa and is a popular place for budget travellers. It offers a range of accommodation from camping to luxury cottages. The site is well-managed it has excellent facilities including a swimming pool, shop, video lounge and camping gear and diving gear is available to rent. It is secure, there are meals available and it is friendly. There are budget cottages which share the facilities with the camp site, or else luxury ones which are fully self contained. They also arrange budget camping safaris. The whole site is set in a fruit and dairy farm and has its own beach. To get there take a matatu to the sign post for Jauss Farm, about 2 km N of Vipingo and from there it is a walk of about 1 km. If you ring from the Post Office at Vipingo they will probably come and pick you up.

E ***Kanamai Centre***, PO Box Kikambala 208, T Kikambala 46. This centre used to be a youth hostel but you no longer need to be a member of the International Youth Hostel Association to stay here. It has a range of rooms including dormitories, doubles and singles. There are also a couple of self-catering cottages. They are basic but are good value and the beach is lovely. It is very clean and friendly and there is a dining room serving basic food. It is difficult to get to if you do not have your own transport you need to take a matatu as far as Majengo on the main road where you will see a sign saying Camping Kanamai. From here you will have to walk follow the road until you get to a fork take the left fork and then it is a little over 3 km down a dusty track.

E ***Camping***, at Kanamai Centre and Jauss Farm.

● Places to eat

If you are staying in one of the big hotels then the chances are that you will eat there most evenings. If you wish to try other places, you will usually need to have your own transport or else take a taxi. ♦♦♦♦***Harlequin Restaurant***, T 472373. This is an excellent seafood restaurant. It has a wonderful position located overlooking Tudor Creek and the food is guaranteed to be very fresh. ♦♦♦♦***Le Pichet***, T 585923. Another excellent seafood restaurant, this is located overlooking Mtwara Creek about 20 km out of Mombasa in Kikambala. It is very popular so you are advised to reserve a table. There are lots of craft stalls surrounding the restaurant in response to the tourists who patronise it. They also organise an evening trip on a dhow – you go across the creek to a nearby beach and have your dinner under the stars. The trip includes the evenings entertainment of traditional African music and dancing. This trip of particularly popular so be sure to book ahead.

♦♦♦***Galana Steak House***, T 485572. As the name suggests this restaurant is a carnivore's delight. It is located near Jomo Kenyatta Beach and is good value. ♦♦♦***Libbas Restaurant***, T

471138. Located in the Ratna Shopping Mall in Nyali this is a popular family restaurant. It specialises in Italian food – pizza and pasta. ♦♦♦*Rene's Restaurant*, T 472986. Another Italian this is also good value. It is located in Nyali on Links Rd and in the evenings develops into a disco. ♦♦♦*Imani Dhow*, this is a superb grill restaurant located on Bamburi Beach.

● Sports

Sun Line Tennis School and Club, Jomo Kenyatta Beach. The courts are excellent quality and you will be able to arrange lessons if you wish.

As you head N the road crosses Tudor Creek, then reaches Mamba Village and Bamburi Nature Reserve. The road then runs parallel to Jomo Kenyatta Beach before crossing Mtwapa Creek. In this area is the Jumba la Mtwana site and Majengo village. A little further on is the Kurita Cottage Complex and the Vipingo Sisal estates. The next beaches are Bamburi Beach, and Kikambala Beach.

Mamba Village

This is a crocodile farm located to the N of Mombasa close to the Nyali Golf Course on Links Rd. Here you can see crocodiles of all ages and sizes from newborns to huge fully grown adults. There are film shows explaining some of the conservation efforts as well as the financial side of the venture. You can go for a camel ride here and it is a day trip in a pleasant setting which children in particular will enjoy. There is a very good restaurant. It is open all day during the week and on Sat afternoons. For details contact PO Box 85723, Mombasa, T 472709/472341/472361.

Further N along the main road is the **Bombolulu Craft Centre** which you might want to stop off at to do some of your souvenir shopping. PO Box 83988, Mombasa, T 471704. The crafts are produced by the handicapped in the area and are generally of good quality and good value. A secondary school for the Physically Disabled is near here. You can also do a tour of the workshops.

Bamburi Quarry Nature Reserve

When you are at Likoni waiting for the ferry you will be able to see the Bamburi Cement factory. When quarrying of coral to make lime for the cement stopped in 1971 an effort was made to reclaim the land by reafforestation and a nature trail was then created. The reclamation scheme was ahead of its time and it attracted the attention of ecologists from all over the world. Part of the process include the introduction of hundreds of thousands of millipedes which helped convert the soil from infertile sand to soil able to support a forest in which the centre is now situated. Despite this, the whole area is still dominated by the Simbarite Ltd quarry.

A fish farm produces tilapia; a reptile pit, a hippo called Sally which featured in one of the Root films, various antelope, monkeys, wart hog, buffalo and lots of different birds. Feeding time is at about 1600 and the trail is open from 1000 to 1800 during the week, 1000 to 1700 on Saturdays and 1200 to 1700 on Sundays. Entrance US$3.50, children US$1. For further details contact Bamburi Farm, PO Box 90202, Mombasa, T 48529. It is signposted on the main road towards Malindi and is 10 km N of Mombasa, easily accessible by bus (bus stop outside).

Kipepee Aquarium

Located opposite the Bamburi Quarry Nature Reserve. There are about 15 large tanks filled with an estimated 150 different species of colourful fish, as well as the deadly stonefish. This is an extraordinarily well-camouflaged fish which lies at the sea completely still and is extremely painful if you tread on it. The collection has been put together by Jacques Allard who is often available to talk to visitors.

Kenya Marineland PO Box 15050, Kikambala, T 485248/ 485738/ 385866) Located in Mtwapa Creek this centre has an underwater viewing rooms from where you can see turtles, barracudas, etc and watch sharks being fed. There are also boats for hire.

Jumba la Mtwana

About 13 km from Mombasa is the Jumba la Mtwana site, a national monument located N of the Mtwapa Creek. The name means the house of the slave and this was once a slave-trading settlement believed to date from the 15th century. The site has only fairly recently been excavated and is now run by the National Museums of Kenya. At the entrance, fee (US$4), you can buy a short guidebook to the site, or else hire a guide. Within the site, which is spread over several acres there are 3 mosques, including the **Mosque by the Sea**, a number of tombs and 8 houses. You will notice that architecturally they look little different from the houses of today in the area. This was a successful design that there was no need to change. The people of this town appear to have been very concerned with ablutions for there are many remains showing evidence of cisterns, water jars, latrines and other washing and toilet facilities.

Building with coral rag (broken pieces of coral) was something reserved for the more privileged members of the community, and it is their houses that have survived. Those that belonged to the poorer people would have been built of mud and thatch.

It is a lovely setting – close to the beach with shade provided by baobabs. To reach the site ask to be dropped off at the sign about a 1km beyond Mtwapa Bridge and from there it is a walk of about 3 km. However you will probably be offered a lift as you walk down the track.

About a kilometre N of the Jumba site there is the Porini Village Restaurant which serves local dishes and puts on displays of traditional African dancing. The road continues N with the Kikambala beach running parallel to the right. You will then notice the very green, lush looking fields with hundreds of thousands of spiky plants growing in straight lines. This is sisal and much of this that

SISAL

Sisal is used to make sacking and rope and before the invention of nylon was a particularly vital raw material. It requires a large amount of capital investment and for this reason is produced on large estates using wage labourers rather than on small-scale farms using family labour. It also has a very long maturation period requiring about 6 years from the time it is planted until it can be harvested. During the prosperous 1920s the demand for sisal was high, supply was inadequate and so prices were also high. As a result huge areas of sisal were planted but by the time they had matured the world economy was in slump and supply far outweighed demand. This lag in the supply of sisal makes it a difficult crop to manage. The harvesting of sisal is very demanding, and it requires a large labour force.

One of the biggest advantages of sisal is its ability to cope with a fluctuating and unreliable water supply and infertile soil. For this reason it has been grown in areas of the world where no other crops can survive.

During the Second World War the Americans were desperate to maintain their supply of sisal as sisal twine was vital for harvesting. As a result prices were controlled and the sisal farmer maintained a steady and healthy income during the war. However sisal is of less importance now compared to 50 years ago as the petroleum industry has produced substitutes such as nylon. This greatly reduced the world demand for sisal, although it recoverd slightly when oil prices rose in the 1970s. It remains of local importance in Kenya. and many of the goods that you take home from Kenya have sisal in them - table mats, baskets, bags. etc.

you see is part of the **Vipingo Sisal Estates**. The estate covers an area of about 50,000 ha, and has not just fields, but factories, a railway and housing for the workers. You can do a tour of the estate and will see the spiky leaves being cut by hand and loaded onto a trolley and taken to the factory where the fibre is removed and dried.

There are also plantations of cashew nuts, mango trees and coconut trees. A few km N of the sisal estate is the Kuritu Cottage Complex an example of a modern Swahili village. It is near to here that Denys Finch-Hatton had a beach cottage. He was hunter and pilot and lover of Karen Blixen, described in *Out of Africa*. As you get to the end of sisal estates you will reach the village of Takaunga located on the banks of a small creek.

Takaunga

This is a small village located 10 km S of Kilifi about 5 km off the main road. This is a sleepy kind of place located above the Takaunga Creek. It has white-washed houses, and a few shops. About a kilometre to the east there is a lovely beach which is only revealed at low tide. The swimming here is very good, and even when the beach is covered you can swim off the rocks – the water is beautifully clear. There are also some old ruins, and it is said to be the oldest slave port on the Kenyan coast.

There are no hotels as such, but it is possible to obtain a room to rent. You should also if possible bring your own supplies and ask the family if they will cook them for you.

To get to Takaunga you can either take a matatu from Mombasa (there are 2 a day), or else take one to Kilifi and ask to be dropped off at the turning for Takaunga. From here it is a walk of about 5 km – you are unlikely to get a lift as there is little traffic along this road.

Kilifi

Kilifi Creek is located about 60 km N of Mombasa. The town of Kilifi is situated to the N of the creek, while Mnarani village is to the S. In the time of the Portuguese era the main town was located at to the S of the creek at Mnarani. Until very recently one had to cross the creek by ferry. A bridge, complete with street lights, has now been built with Japanese funding. There is a Ksh 10 toll - keep the receipt as you may be stopped by the police and asked for it.

The town has a interesting mix of people with quite a number of resident expatriates. The main industry in the town is the cashew nut factory which employs about 1,500 people. To the S there are the Mnarani Ruins. It is an easy going town with a nice beach.

Mnarani Ruins

The Mnarani Ruins was first excavated

Baobab Trees

These huge trees have enormous girths - which enable them to survive during very long dry patches. They live for up to 2,000 years. You will see some extremely large ones - there is one at Ukunda which has a girth of 22m and which has been given "presidential protection" to safeguard it.

The legend is that when God first planted them they kept walking around and would not stay still. So He decided to replant them up-side-down which is why they look as if they have the roots sticking up into the air. During droughts people open up the pods and grind the seeds to make what is known as "hunger flour".

in the 1950's but renewed interest in the site has led the British Institute in Eastern Africa to work on the site again. The town was the place of one of the ancient Swahili city-states that are found along this coast. It is believed that the town was inhabited from the latter half of the 14th century until about the early 17th century, when it was ransacked and destroyed by a group of Galla tribesmen. It is thought that the inhabitants of the town locked themselves into the Great Mosque as they were attacked.

The ruins include one of the deepest wells (70m) along the coast, 2 mosques, part of the town wall and city gates and a group of tombs including a pillar tomb decorated with engravings of a wealthy sharif. Note particularly the tomb of the doctor which is easily the most ornate. At the ruins of the larger or **Great Mosque** can be seen the *mihrab* (which points towards Mecca) surrounded by carved inscriptions. There are many niches in the walls. To the left of the entrance, the smaller mosque is believed to date from the 16th century. There is a huge boabab tree nearby with a circumference of over 15m. The ruins are best known for the inscriptions carved into them – many of them remaining untranslated. However, in general they are much smaller and less impressive than the ones at Gedi.

To get to the ruins, turn off the main road to the S of the creek by the toll booth and go through Mnarani village. Turn left on to the old road and pass the now rusty ferry sign. There is a path signposted ("3 minutes and a short climb") and the ruins are a few hundred metres down this path and then a climb of about 100 steps. You also get a wonderful view of the creek from the ruins. Entrance US$1.75. Open 0700-1730.

There are also ruins nearby at **Kitoka** about 3 km S of Kilifi. This is a smaller site – there is a small mosque and a few houses.

Local information

● Where to stay

A *Mnarani Club*, PO Box 81443, Mombasa, T Kilifi 18/26. Located overlooking Kilifi Creek on Malindi Rd, this hotel is one of the oldest in the country. It has been designed very well, is set in marvellous gardens and has wonderful views. Facilities include water sports, including sailing, wind surfing and water skiing, a bar, a good value restaurant overlooking the creek, and evening entertainment such as traditional dancing and music. **A** *Seahorse*, PO Box 70, Kilifi, T Kilifi 64/90. Located looking out across Kilifi Creek on the northern side of the creek this also has good views and is a popular drinking spot for the resident expatriates and is considered to be Kenya's sailing centre. If you are hoping for some crewing this is the place to try your luck.

D *Dhows Inn*, this small hotel is located on the S side of the creek on the new road leading to the bridge. Rooms have bathrooms and mosquito nets are clean and fairly basic but good value. The hotel has nice gardens and there is a popular bar and restaurant.

E *Tushaurine Boarding and Lodging*, this is a fairly new hotel located in the town centre. Facilities are mostly shared, it is simple but it is clean and friendly and mosquito nets are provided. There are a number of inexpensive hotels located in the town centre including the **E** *Kilifi*; **E** *Hotel '36*; **E** *New Mwangea Lodge*; **E** *Top Life Board and Lodging*.

● Eating

♦♦♦♦*Mnanari Club*, high standard, superb seafood, excellent atmosphere.

♦♦♦*Seahorse*, Reliable international menu.

♦♦*Dhows Inn*, reasonable food. ♦♦*Jay's Coffee House*, Main road opposite the Kenya Commercial Bank.

♦*Kilifi*, at the bus station, open air and very basic, excellent fruit juices. ♦*Kilifi Cafeteria*, near bus stand. Inexpensive.

● Useful addresses

There are 2 *banks*, in Kilifi which are open from 0830 to 1300 on weekdays and until 1130 on Saturdays. Dr Bomo has a *clinic* on the old Kilifi Road in Mnarani. There is a *Post Office*, next to the market. You can hire cars at *Azzura Tours*, PO Box 2, Kilifi, T 2385, where you can also buy bus tickets and organise various trips. There is a small *bookshop*, just off the main street. **Watersports** from the *Pink Shark Diving School*.

● Transport

Kilifi is about 50 km from ***Mombasa***, and 45 km from ***Malindi***. The buses which go between the 2 towns do pick people up here although they may be full. You may find it easier to get a matatu. Enquiries and bookings can be made at ***Azzura Tours***, T 2385, whose office is on the Kilifi's main road.

To get to and from ***Nairobi*** from Kilifi the Tara Bus Company goes twice a day taking about 9 hrs. The buses leave at 0730 and 1930.

KILIFI TO MALINDI AND LAMU

This area is rather more remote than the southern section of the coast. However communications have improved in recent years and much of this part of the coast has been developed for tourists.

Kilifi to Malindi

The road from Kilifi continues N running parallel to the coast. As with much of the road from Mombasa it runs straight and true and is in quite good condition. Leaving Kilifi the road passes small villages dotted between lots of cashew nut trees which are surprisingly green-leafed at the end of the dry season. There are occasional stands of eucalyptus trees. Don't expect tropical rain forest as you approach the **Arabuko Sokoke Forest** – from the road the only discernible difference is that the scrub disappears and the trees are noticeably closer together. It is home to many species of birds – some of which are rare. Efforts to prevent the forest being cut down completely are being made but the constant needs for fuel and land in a country whose population is increasing so rapidly makes this difficult. The forest is home to a number of animals including the very small Zanzibar duiker which is only 35cm high and is usually seen in pairs. Also found in this forest is the Golden-rumped elephant shrew. Both these animals are rare. The Forest Office is about 1 km from the Watamu turning – obtain permission if you wish to explore the forest. They will also be able to advise whether the tracks which join the Tsavo National Park road to the N are passable.

The road heads inland to skirt around the Mida Creek before coming to the village of Watamu. This is the location of **Watamu Marine Park**. A little further on and to the W of the road you will pass the Gedi National Park. This is located to the S of Malindi (see Game Parks Section). Close to the village of Watamu is the turnoff for the **Gedi ruins**. Beyond the Watamu turning, the road again passes through scrub with small villages interspersed. At the end of the dry season you will notice, both from the road and from the air, lots of bonfires. This is the villagers clearing their land ahead of the long rains when they will plant their crops. You will also notice termite mounds - some are well over 2m high and often fantastically shaped. Finally before reaching Malindi you will see signs to the **Malindi Marine Park** and the **Snake Park**.

Watamu

A small fishing village which in recent years has been seeing some fairly rapid tourist development. The atmosphere of the village itself is mixed – it is certainly feeling the impact of tourists. Apart from the beach and the sea, the attractions of staying here are the nearby **Watamu Marine Park** and the **Gedi Ruins**. There are a number of resort hotels situated in the 3 coves that make up this part of the coast. It is scenically quite attractive as there are a number of small islands just offshore – those at Turtle Bay are quite good for snorkelling as they are only about 50m offshore at low tide. Watch out for speed boats ferrying fishermen to the large game boats. A passable alternative if you haven't the time or money to take a glass bottom boat. The water is much clearer here

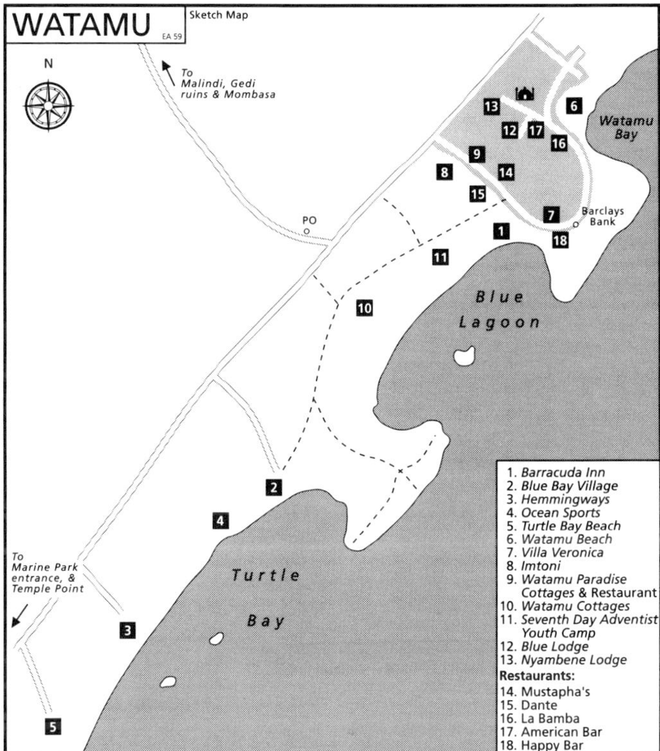

than at Malindi during the wet season. The beach is also free of seaweed. Avoid the camel rides along the beach. If you can't afford deep sea fishing, be at *Hemmingways* at 1600-1700 when the days catch is recorded and the fishermen photographed. Tagged fish are apparently returned to the sea.

Local information

● Where to stay

A+ *Barracuda Inn*, PO Box 59, Watamu, T Watamu 61/70/74. Located just to the S of the village this new hotel is Italian-owned and managed and attracts a large proportion of Italians amongst their clientele. It is a wonderful building with fantastic thatched *makuti* roofs. The gardens are also very pretty and the staff friendly. **A+** *Blue Bay Village*, PO Box 162, Watamu, T 32626. Located a couple of km to the S of the village in the most southerly of the 3 coves, this hotel is also popular with Italians. Good facilities. **A+** *Hemingway's* (Formerly known as *Seafarers*), PO Box 267, Watamu, T Watamu 32624, Nairobi 225255, F Watamu 32256. This has more of a mix of clientele although perhaps British, and expatriates living in Kenya, dominate. The hotel has been renovated recently and is highly recommended. Facilities include 2 swimming pools, bar, an excellent restaurant, and water sports facilities including deep sea fishing fleet. Trips to Tsavo National Park can also be arranged.

A *Ocean Sports*, PO Box 340, Malindi, T Watamu 8. Located a little further S this has a series of cottages set in gardens. There is a large bar and restaurant and all the other usual facilities. The Sun lunch is a huge buffet, popular with expatriates and particularly good value. **A** *Turtle Bay*, PO Box 457, Watamu, T Watamu 32622. This hotel also has a mixed clientele. It is very relaxed and has all the facilities including water sports. It has a variety of rooms with or without airconditioning.

B *Watamu Beach*, PO Box 81443, Mombasa T 32001/32010. This hotel is the northern most of the all the Watamu hotels. It is located behind the village on the northern cove. It is a large hotel and is popular with German tourists. It is set in generous grounds, and facilities include swimming pool, bar, and restaurant. The beach in this cove is lovely and there are lots of fishermen offering to take you out to the reef in their boats.

D *Villa Veronica (Mwikali Lodge)*, PO Box 57, Watamu, T Watamu 83. This is one of the best of the budget hotels in Watamu. Rooms have bathrooms attached, mosquito nets provided and are clean. It is friendly and the price includes breakfast.

E *Iritoni Lodge*, only has 2 rooms. but is clean and friendly. **E** *Watamu Paradise Cottages*, PO Box 249 Watamu, T 32062. These cottages are situated close to the village near Mustafa's Restaurant. There is a swimming pool in the grounds and they are very pleasant. **E** *Watamu Cottages*, not to be confused with the *Watamu Paradise Cottages* these are located about a kilometre out of town and are very popular. There is a swimming pool in the complex and they are used a lot by expatriate families. The price includes breakfast and they are really excellent value. **E** *Seventh Day Adventists Youth Hostel*. This is not a proper hostel and you can only stay here occasionally. Facilities are basic. **E** *Blue Lodge*, In village. Shared bathrooms. Inexpensive and basic. **E** *Nyambene Lodge*, in the village, basic rooms with shared facilities. **E** *Private Houses*, you can also usually rent a room very cheaply in a house in town if you ask around.

● Places to eat

You can eat at all the big hotels which do various set menus and buffets – look around as there are sometimes real bargains. ♦♦♦*Watamu Paradise Restaurant*, part of the cottages of the same name as this serves good food including seafood and is good value. The nearby ♦♦♦*Mustafa's Restaurant*, particularly popular at night when it can get quite lively. ♦♦♦*Hotel Dante*, opposite *Mustafa's Restaurant*. Italian cuisine. ♦♦♦*La Bamba Country Lodge*, North of village.

♦♦*American Bar*, North of village. Hamburgers and grills. ♦♦*Coco Grill Bar and Restaurant*, North of village. Grills and seafood.

♦*Happy Night Bar and Restaurant*, serves snacks and beers and is good value.

● Useful addresses

There is a small branch of ***Barclays***, in the village which is open in the mornings on Mon, Wed and Fri. The big hotels will change money out of these hrs, although the rate will not be very good. There is a place to ***hire bicycles*** in the village near the *Nyambene Lodge*.

From Malindi to Watamu takes about half an hr, there are plenty of matatus and it will cost you about 15 KSh.

Watamu Marine Park

Along this coast close to Watamu village there is an excellent marine park which has been made a total exclusion zone. Obviously this was not all good news for some fishermen – but they seem to have adapted quite happily, and the influx of tourists has increased the incomes of the village.The park headquarters are someway south of Watamu at the end of the peninsula which guards the entrance to the creek. Unfortunately the road goes a little inland, hiding views of the sea. This is somewhat compensated by views of the creek - it is not that attractive though. You go out in a glass bottom boat to the protected area and some of the hundreds of fishes come to the boat to be fed. The coral reef or garden lies about 2 km offshore. Glass bottom boats may seem rather expensive but are really well worth it and can be arranged at any of the hotels, or else at the entrance to the actual Park. You can also swim amongst the fish which is a wonderful sensation. There are lots of shells and live corals which are a splendid range of colours. If short of time, try the islands just offshore from *Hemingways*.

Gedi Ruins

These are one of Kenya's most important archaeological sites and is believed to contain the ruins of a city that once

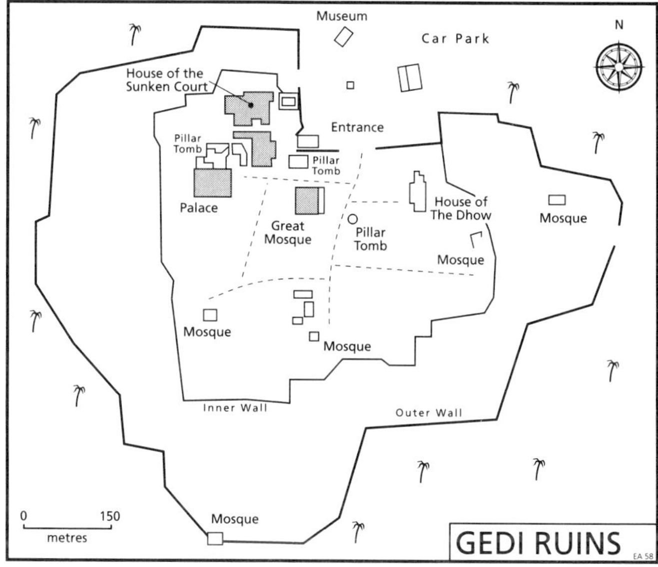

had a population of about 2,500. It was populated in the latter half of the 13th century, and the size of some of the buildings, in particular the mosque suggest that this was a fairly wealthy town for some time. However, it is not mentioned in any Arabic or Swahili writings and was apparently unknown to the Portuguese although they maintained a strong presence in Malindi just 15 km away. It is believed that this was because it was set away from the sea, and deep in the forest. Possibly as a result of an attack from marauding tribesmen of the Oromo or Galla tribe, the city was abandoned at some time during the 16th century. Lack of water may have also been a contributing factor as wells of over 50m deep dried out. It was later re-inhabited but never regained the economic position that it once had held. It was then finally abandoned in the early 17th century and the ruins discovered in 1884. The site was declared a national monument in 1948 and has been excavated since then. It has been well preserved. There is a small museum and visitors are welcome. You can buy a guide book and map of the site at the entrance gate. There are also informative guides – ask for Ali.

The site was originally surrounded by an inner and outer wall (surprisngly thin). Most of the most interesting buildings and features are concentrated around the entrance gate, although there are others. Most that remain are within the inner wall although there are some between the 2 walls. All the buildings are built using coral rag and lime, and some had decorations carved into the wall plaster. You can still see the remains of the bathrooms – complete with deep bath, basin and squat toilet. There are a large number of wells in the site, some being exceptionally deep. The main buildings that remain are a sultan's palace, a mosque and a number of houses and tombs, a water system and a prison. Other finds include pieces of Chinese porcelain from the Ming Dynasty, beads from India and stoneware from Persia – some are displayed in the musuem, others in Fort Jesus, Mombasa.

The **Palace** can be entered through a rather grand arched doorway which brings you into the reception court and then a hall. This is the most impressive building on the site. Off this hall there are a number of smaller rooms – including the bathrooms. You can also see the remains of the kitchen area which contains a small well.

The **Great Mosque** probably originally dates from the mid 15th century, and is the largest of the 7 on this site. It is believed to have been rebuilt fairly substantially more recently. Look out for the *mihrab* which indicates to the faithful the direction of Mecca, and being built of stone (rather than wood) has survived well. As you leave notice the carved spearhead which is located above the northeast doorway.

A great amount of trade seems to have been established here – silk and porcelain were exchanged for skins and most importantly ivory. China was keen to exploit this market and in 1414 a giraffe was given to the Chinese Emperor and shipped from Malindi. It apparently survived the trip. There was also trade with European countries – a glass bead has been found which originated in Venice.

There are in total 14 houses on the complex which have so far been excavated. Each one is named after something that has been found at its site – for example House of Scissors, House of Ivory Box. There is also one named after a picture of a dhow which is on the wall. In the houses you will again be able to see the bathrooms facilities. Deep pits were dug for sewage, capped when full and then used for fertilizer. Such techniques are still used in the Old Town district in Malindi.

The tombs are located to the right of the entrance gate and one of them is of particular interest to archaeologists as it actually has a date engraved on it – the Islamic year 802 which is equal to the year 1399 AD. This is known as the Date Tomb and has enabled other parts of the site to be dated with more accuracy. There is also a tomb with a design that is common along the Swahili coast – that of a fluted pillar. Pillar tombs are found all up the coast and were used for men with position and influence.

The site is in very pleasant surroundings – it is green and shady but can get very hot (cool drinks are available at the entrance). You may hear a buzzing noise. This is an insect that lives only for 3 or 4 days until it literally blows itself to pieces! There are usually monkeys in the trees above which are filled with the noise of many different types of birds. It is in fact also a wildlife sanctuary and is home to the magnificent, and now sadly rare, black and white colobus monkey. This monkey has suffered at the hand of poachers for their splendid coats but a few remain and you may see some here. Also in the sanctuary are the golden-rumped elephant shrew (only seen at dawn and dusk) and various birds such as the harrier hawk and palm tree vulture.

● **Transport**

To get to the site, take the main Malindi-Mombasa road. The site is located about 4 km to the N of Watamu. It is signposted from the village of Gedi and if you came by matatu you will have to walk the last 1 km. You can hire a taxi from Malindi – it will cost about US$8. Entrance will cost around US$3.75, children US$1 and is open from 0700 to 1800 daily.

Malindi

Malindi is the second largest coastal town in Kenya after Mombasa. Although the history of the town dates back to the 13th century there are few remains of the ancient town. The beach is excellent and popular as it suffers less from the problem of seaweed compared to the beaches around Mombasa. Seaweed seems worse before the spring equinox and can make it impossible to swim. Some hotels employ labourers to remove it from their patch of sand! The surf is good during Jul-Aug and the only problem is that silt from the Galana River can make the water a rather red, muddy colour during the rainy season.

SAFETY Parts of Malindi are notorious for muggings so do not walk around at night unless you are in a group, know where you are going, and know that it is safe. If in doubt always take a taxi. Take a guide if you wish to visit the Old Town district even during the day.

History

The earliest known reference to Malindi is found in Chinese geography in a piece published in 1060 written by a scholar who died in AD 863. This refers to Malin, its people are said to be black and their nature fierce. However details in the piece are inaccurate and suggest that the writer was possibly referring to another town to the N of Malindi. The next reference, in 1150 is also thought to be inaccurate and actually to be Manda, a town to the S of Lamu. The first accurate description of the town is believed to be written by Prince Abu al-Fida who lived from 1273 to 1331. Archaeological evidence supports the theory that the town of Malindi was founded in the 13th century by Arabs. In any event, locals claim that there was a big Chinese trading influence. This is evidenced even today by the faces of the local people who still retain traces of Chinese features.

In 1498 Vasco da Gama, having rounded the Cape of Good Hope stopped off at various ports along the coast. At Mombasa he was not made welcome – indeed attempts were made to sink his ships. He quickly left and continued N stopping at Malindi where he found a friendly reception. Why the response of the 2 towns should be so different is not clear – it may have been because of an on-going feud between the 2 towns. The good relations between Malindi and the Portuguese continued throughout the 16th century. In about 1500 the population of within the town walls was about 3,500, with another 2,000 Africans living in surrounding plantations. The town was governed by the Arabs who were the wealthiest group, owning the surrounding plantations. It was a wealthy town during the 15th century as was shown by the number of multi-storied buildings. The wealth came from the trade with India and the supply of agricultural produce, grown in the surrounding plantations largely by slaves, for passing ships. One of the visitors in this period was St Francis Xavier who passed though Malindi in 1542.

The town went into a period of decline in the 16th century and in 1593 the Portuguese administration was transferred from Malindi to Mombasa. Traders and labourers followed but the Arabs who remained behind had become too dependent on the Portuguese to manage without them. The decline was in part a consequence of the superiority of the harbour facilities at Mombasa. Neighbouring tribes, in particular the Galla, overran the town, and it is believed that Malindi was abandoned in the late 17th century. It lay in an ruined state for many years and it was not until 1861 that it was re-founded by the Sultan of Zanzibar and again became prosperous.

In the period of the latter half of the 19th century Malindi was dominated by Zanzibar. Although Malindi continued to suffer as Mombasa expanded and took more trade, the town's prosperity did improve during this period and the use of slaves was undoubtedly an important factor. To get an idea of the scale in the first year of resettlement in 1861 there were a thousand slaves working for just fifty Arabs. Malindi was not a major exporter of slaves as the demand within the town did not allow it. Malindi had a particularly bad reputation for its treatment of slaves.

The period under the Imperial British East Africa Company (IBEAC) began in 1887 when the Company acquired a fifty-year lease from the Sultan of Zanzibar for territories in East Africa. The Company administered the area, collected taxes and had rights over minerals found. Bell Smith was sent to the town as officer for the Company and he began carrying out the abolition of the slave trade. From around 1890 slaves who wished and were able to, could buy their freedom. For those who could not, the the Company offered jobs, or found paid employment. Interestingly relatively few took up the opportunity and the process was a gradual one. It has been estimated that from 1888 to 1892 2,387 slaves were freed on the coast by the IBEAC and by 1897 there were still 5,442 slaves in the Malindi district.

In 1895 the British government purchased the assets of the IBEAC and established formally the East African Protectorate. The same year the Sultan of Zanzibar transferred the lease of the ten-mile coastal strip to the British Government for the sum of £11,000 per year. The Arabs, who had grown used to having slave labour, found it very difficult to adapt to actually paying workers, and the final blow was dealt in 1907 when the Protectorate government abolished the status of slavery. Merchandise trade developed, and in the early 20th century the most important exports were rubber, grain, ivory, hides and horns. Rubber was grown on European-owned plantations in response to a dramatic increase in the world price around the First World War. However, it was short lived as the world price subsequently fell and most of the plantations were abandoned.

During the second half of the British period the foundations were laid for what is now Malindi's most important industry – that of tourism. During the depression years Malindi's trade and agriculture had suffered not just from low world prices but also from drought. There also continued to be a shortage of labour and the only crop that experienced an increase in production was cotton. The 1930s also saw the beginning of the tourist industry with the first hotel *Brady's Palm Beach Hotel* opening in 1932 – famous visitors include Ernest Hemingway who visited in 1934. Most of the tourists at this time were settlers from the White Highlands. Expansion continued after the Second World War and Malindi became popular as a retirement town for European settlers. With the increase in air travel and affordability of holidays abroad the growth of Malindi as a tourist resort spiralled, spurred on by the popularity of package tours.

Today, Malindi is heavily influenced by the Italians who have been encouraged to invest by the Government. Many are attracted by the "cheapness" of the area and many retirement villas have been built. This has not been altogether welcomed by the local people despite the obvious increase in jobs. A number of expensive shopping malls have sprung up recently which are full of expensive Italian goods and overpriced curios.

Places of interest

Although there is little left of the ancient walled town of Malindi, there are a couple of remains in the town itself that are worth seeing. The oldest part of the town is clustered around the jetty – here you can see the main mosque and some tombs that date from the 14th century. The Malindi Curios Dealers Associations have a huge market here. Bargain hard! Behind the mosque are a maze of small streets that form the Old Town district.These are interesting although there are no outstanding buildings. It is easy to get lost, take a guide (ask around for Adam) and be careful as drugs are reported to be widespread.

In the centre of town, the Uhuru gardens are being relaid. Close to them is a modern monument: it is not obvious from the roadside but is in fact shaped like Vasco da Gama's ship when viewed from the front. Close to the bus and matatu stand is the Malindi Wood Carvers Cooperative Society. There is a fully stocked shop with reasonable prices. Ask to visit the workshops which are behind the shop. This is very interesting as many of the society's 350 members work in very poor conditions on a variety of wood. You will be able to see how some of the finely carved pieces are manufactured from the most unlikely looking pieces of wood. Also in this area is the main market. Once again it is interesting to wander through as apart from clothing, vegetables and

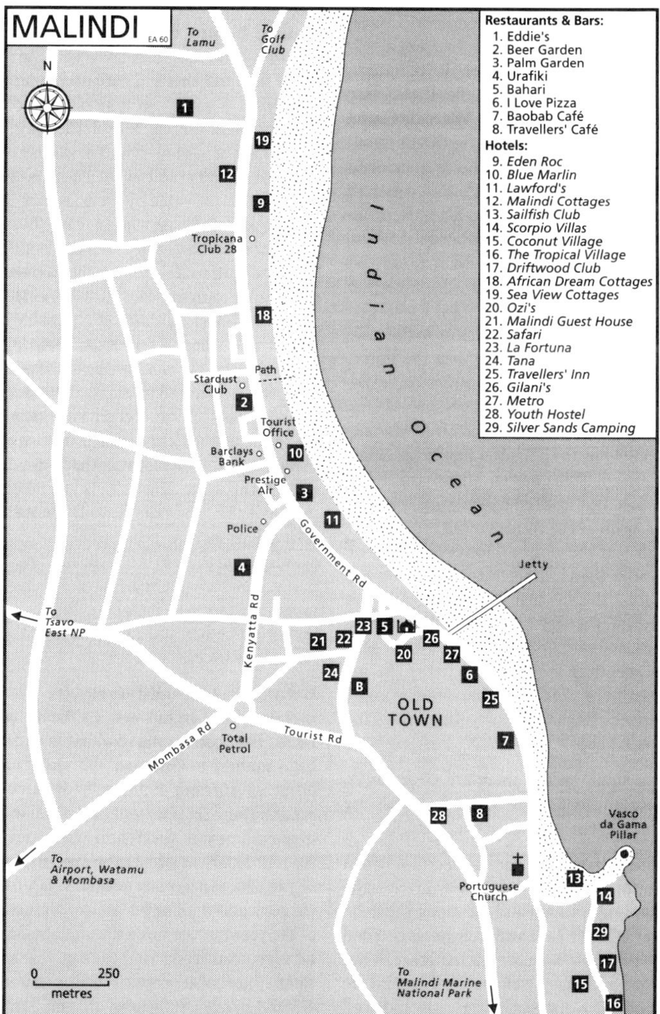

charcoal, you can see old cars being converted into pots and pans and other hardware. The area between here and Kenyatta Road to the NW is the trading quarter – a hive of activity. Beyond it are the hotels and modern shopping malls – a dusty and uninteresting part of town. Note access to the beach can be gained by a footpath just beyond the Tourist Office and Galana shopping centre.

There are also a couple of monuments that date from the Portuguese period, in particular the **Vasco da Gama Cross**. This is situated on the promontory that is located at the southern end of the bay. It was erected to assist in navigation. The actual cross is the original and is made of stone from Lisbon, although the pillar on which it stands is constructed of local coral. You can reach it by turning down Mnarani Road. The small **Catholic Church** close to the cross is also believed to date from the Portuguese period and is thought to be the same one that St Francis Xavier visited in 1542 when he stopped off at Malindi on his way to India. It is one of the oldest Catholic churches in Africa still in use today (but is often locked).

Both these monuments are about 1 km S of the centre. However, it may be worth hiring a bicycle to visit them. You could then continue along the beach (follow the sign to Vasco da Gama Cross but carry on up the hill - there is a path descending to the beach) to the Marine Park. The sand is hard and flat - a much better alternative to cycling along the main road.

Outside Malindi there are Gedi Ruins, located 16 kms S Malindi, which are more extensive (see above, page 132).

Tana River You can take a cruise whilst in this part of Kenya. They are usually for 2 or 3 nights and are along the delta of the River Tana and tributaries situated to the N of Malindi. It is expensive – but you will be very well looked after and the food is excellent. The price includes all food, transport and day trips. You can be picked up from the airport or from Malindi, and will be taken by landrover to the camp on the river bank. While you are there you can swim, go on river trips, bird watching and animal tracking. For details and reservations: *Tana Delta*, PO Box 24988, Nairobi (T 882826).

Malindi Marine Park This is popular and with good reason. It has a wide variety of fish and shells. There are 2 main reefs with a sandy section of sea bed dividing them. You can hire all the equipment that you will need and a boat here. The fish are very tame as they have been fed on bread provided by the boatman. If you see any shells be sure to leave them there for the next visitor – the shell population has suffered very severely from the increase in tourism. The Park is located to the S of Malindi, and it is probably easiest to arrange a trip from Malindi. The price should include park entrance fees, transport to and from your hotel and the boat itself. Try and go at low tide as the calmer the sea, the better; also be sure to take some sort of footwear that you can wear in the water. You will also be taken to one of the sand bars just off the reef: take plenty of sun protection. You can also organize the trip through your hotel, many of which seem to have arrangements with local boat owners. Be sure to enquire whether the rate includes the National Park entrance fee.

Lake Chem Chem Rhino reserve This is about 8 km from town on the Tsavo Road. The road is quite bad but you can get a matutu to Ghardan. Get dropped off at the turning and then walk about 200m. There is only one rhino at the moment but you can go on a bird watching tour for about US$25 although it may be possible to negotiate a better rate with the park guards. The lake is dry for most of the year but the birds are supposed to be very good from May to Aug. Camel safaris are also organized for about US$60. Further information from Marcus Russell, Galdesa Office, T 31084.

Malindi Falconry This is located a little to the N of the town on the Lamu Rd, and is said to be the only falconry in the country.

Snake Park Situated close to the Falconry on Lamu Rd. Avoid feeding time at 1600 Wed and Fri if you will be upset at the sight of live mice being fed to the snakes.

Gedi Ruins and National Park Located 16 km S of Malindi the National Park contains the ruins of this ancient village (see above, page 132). A visit can be combined with a trip to the Watamu Marine Park (see above, page 132).

Dhows Trips can be arranged through *Prince Safaris*, Silver Sand Road, PO Box 966, T 20596, by the main jetty. There are several options: safaris, fishing or just sailing and involve a variety of activities including bar-b-cues on the beach. Prices are around US$60 per person, min 4-6 people.

Deep Sea Fishing These can be arranged through your hotel or contact one of the following: *Malindi Sports Fishing Club*, PO Box 163, T 20161; *Malindi Sea Fishing Club*, PO Box 364, T 20410; *Kingfisher Safaris*, PO Box 29, T 20123; *Slaters*, PO Box 147, Watamu, T Watamu 12; *Peter Ready*, PO Box 63, T 21292; *Von Menyhart*, PO Box 360, T 20840; *Baharini Ventures*, PO Box 435, T 20879.

Scuba Diving *Drift Wood Club*, at Silver Sands which charges about US$8 per dive. They also have a diving school for those who have never done it before – learning to scuba dive is not cheap anywhere in the world and Kenya is no exception.

Windsurfing Arrange through the centre next to the *White Elephant Hotel* at the S end of the beach.

Local information

● Where to stay

The great advantage that Malindi has over Mombasa is that there are inexpensive hotels located close to the beach. There are also plenty of luxurious hotels.

Price guide: A+ Over US$100; **A** US$40-100; **B** US$20-40; **C** US$10-20; **D** US$5-10; **E** Under US$5.

Town Centre The places in the town centre are mainly for the budget traveller. They often suffer from having more mosquitoes and being hotter as they do not get the sea breezes. They can also be noisy. They include the **E** *Safari*; the **E** *Malindi Guest House*; **E** *La Fortuna*; the **E** *Lamu Hostel*; and the **E** *Tana*. They are all fairly similar – having dormitories or doubles and are basic with shared bathrooms but are usually fairly clean. There is also a **E** *Youth Hostel*, which is very clean and friendly.

North of Malindi These hotels are strung out on the Lamu Rd to the N of the town. **A+** *Club Che-Shale*, PO Box 492, T 20063 F 21257. Located about 8 km N of Malindi this has 12 thatched bandas with bathrooms and verandas. They vary – some are a bit run down. However it is a pleasant atmosphere and is located on a lovely secluded beach. There is plenty to do here sailing, deep sea fishing and snorkelling, and there is a bar and very good restaurant. **A+** *Eden Roc*, PO Box 350, T 123/20480. This hotel is located on a cliff top overlooking the bay in generous grounds. There are over 150 rooms, all air conditioned with bathrooms as well as some cottages. It has its own beach and facilities include swimming pool, tennis courts, water sports, scuba diving, deep sea fishing, golf, and disco. **A+** *Indian Ocean Lodge*, PO Box 171, T 123/123/20394. This is a very exclusive hotel with just 5 rooms and a private beach. It has been built of local materials in the Lamu Arab style and tastefully decorated and is set in marvellous gardens. The price includes meals and there are trips arranged, such as fishing, snorkelling and bird watching. You can also go on a trip to the Gedi Ruins.

A *Blue Marlin*, PO Box 54, T 20440/1. This hotel was originally named *Brady's Palm Beach Hotel* and was the first hotel to open in 1932. It is excellently run, very friendly and has splendid facilities. **A** *Lawford's*, PO Box 20, T Malindi 6. This was the second hotel to open in this part of the coast being established in 1934 by Commander Lawford. He was not just a hotelier, he was also a pioneer in the dairy industry of Kenya. He brought out a herd of Jersey cattle and, despite the presence of tsetse fly, succeeded in producing milk in this part of Kenya. Located very close to the town. A new wing was built in the late 1970's and the hotel has singles, doubles and cottages. The rooms are nice although the restaurant only fair. There are 2 swimming pools, meeting rooms and the hotel organises trips out to the reef in the glass bottom boat. **A** ***Malindi Cottages***, PO Box 992, T 20304/21071. These cottages are self-contained and fully furnished with excellent facilities. Each sleep 5, and everything is provided. There is a swimming pool in the complex.

B ***African Dream Cottages***, PO Box 939, T 21296. These are self contained cottages which each sleep 4. There is a swimming pool and a newly built restaurant and bar. **B** ***Sea View Cottages***, these cottages are all self-contained with their own bathroom. The place has seen better days and this really is not very good value. The swimming pool has had problems although these may have been solved by now.

C ***Zinj Beach Cottages***, fully equipped and good value.

E ***Lutheran Guest House***, T 21098. Located to the N of the town off the Lamu Rd this is good value and popular. There are a range of rooms singles and doubles with or without own bathroom. There is also a self-contained cottage. It is clean and the staff are very friendly.

South of Malindi **A+** ***African Dream Village***, PO Box 939, T 20442/3/4. Run by the same group that run the East African Dream Cottages further N. This caters for a slightly different type of holiday maker being a top quality beach resort with full facilities. These include swimming pool, gym, bars and restaurant. All rooms are air conditioned with bathroom and verandah. **A+** ***Sailfish Club***, PO Box 243, T 20016. This is a very small and exclusive hotel with just 9 rooms. It is very much geared to big-game fishing.

A ***Coconut Village***, PO Box 868, T 120928/20252. A popular family hotel with good facilities. The bar has been cleverly built into and around a growing tree, and the disco is under a thatched roof on the beach. **A** ***Kivulini***, PO Box 142, T 20898. This is a relatively new hotel and is highly recommended. Again it has cottages set in wonderful gardens, and it has it's own private beach. The food is superb and the hotel is very well managed. **A** ***Scorpio Villas***, PO Box 368, T 20194/20892. This collection of about 17 villas is set in magnificent gardens. There are 3 swimming pools, a restaurant and bar and the beach is very close. The cottages are all fully furnished and self-sufficient and you even get your own cook. It is an excellently managed complex and caters mainly for Italians. **A** ***Silversands Villas***, PO Box 91, T 20842. This hotel has a range of rooms and villas. The cottages are thatched with *makuti* and are set in wonderful gardens. It is tastefully decorated with bits and pieces from across Africa. It is very friendly and well managed, and has a very good restaurant attached. **A** ***Tropical Village***, PO Box 736, T 20888. High standard hotel this caters largely for package tours, with good facilities. **A** ***White Elephant Sea Lodge***, PO Box 948, T 20528/20223. This is a lovely hotel and good value. The cottages are decorated tastefully and are set in magnificent gardens on a beautiful stretch of beach. There is a swimming pool and very good restaurant.

A-C ***Driftwood Club***, PO Box 63, T 20155. One of the older hotels in Malindi this has managed to retain some of the pre-package tour atmosphere. It has a range of rooms including luxury cottages, doubles and singles (with own or shared bathroom). Breakfast is included in the price and some of the rooms work out at very good value. Facilities include snack bar, water sports including wind surfing and a squash court.

D ***Ozi's***, T 123/20218, situated overlooking the beach very close to the jetty this hotel has a range of rooms. It is simple, but clean and good value and is one of the most popular of the budget hotels. The price includes a very good breakfast.

E ***Gilani's***, this hotel is located close to the jetty where most of the budget hotels are located. It is cheap but is not very good value as it is rather grubby and you can stay at much nicer places for the same price. **E** ***Metro***, PO Box 361, T 20400. This is good value and popular and is located close to the Gilani's. The rooms are, however, poky and stuffy and the water is unreliable. The people that run it are friendly. **E** ***Silver Sands Camp Site***, T 236, located nearly 2 km out of town this camp site is popular with overlanders and other campers. The facilities are fairly good although there are sea-water showers only and if you do not have a tent you can rent one. There is also a small tented camp (these are tents with a thatched roof over them to keep them cool) and a bathroom and electric lights. There are also bandas with beds and mosquito nets which have shared bathrooms. It is a lovely stretch of beach and a friendly atmosphere. There is a bar and a snack bar and restaurant, and a well stocked shop. You can also hire bicycles here. For a proper shower and a swim you can join the Driftwood Club for the day. **E** *Travellers Inn*, this is very popular amongst budget travellers and is good value. It is located just to the S of the fishing jetty and is clean and friendly. There are drinks and food available.

● Places to eat

Price guide:
♦♦♦♦Over US$10; ♦♦♦US$5-10; ♦♦US$2-5; ♦Under US$2

There is a range of restaurants and most of the restaurants in the hotels are open to non-residents – especially good value are their set menus and buffets. ♦♦♦♦***La Malindina***, T 20045. This is located near the *Eden Roc Hotel* and is popular so book ahead. The food is good and very fresh.

♦♦♦***Driftwood Club***, this is a nice way to spend a lazy day. You will need to join the Club as a temporary member – you will then be able to eat here as well as use their pool. The restaurant has a set menu, a huge buffet, an a la carte menu as well as a snack menu. ♦♦♦***Eddie's***, T 123/20283. This is a relatively new restaurant and is set in very pleasant surroundings with a swimming pool. It specialises in seafood which is delicious, and is open for lunch and dinner. ♦♦♦***I Love Pizza***, T 123/20672. This Italian restaurant is located on the Vasco da Gama Rd and is good value. It serves pizza, pasta, seafood dishes and other food. ♦♦♦***German Beer Garden***, T 123/20533. This bistro, located to the N of the shopping centre, is good for snacks and a beer. It is particularly popular in the evenings.

♦♦***La Galateria***, T 123/20710. Located on Lamu Rd this is the best place in town for ice creams – they are excellent. Good for a coffee and a snack. ♦♦***Palm Garden Restaurant***, T 123/20015. Also located on Lamu Rd, opposite the Shell petrol station, you can sit in the shade of bandas. The food is fine – curries, chicken, seafood and so on – and it is very good value. There is also a bar and ice cream parlour which are rather run down. ♦♦***Ozi's***, located near the Juma Mosque, this is good for curries as well as for sea food and is good value.

♦***Malindi Fruit Juice Garden***, is ideal for a break on a hot day, located close to the market. As the name suggests they do very good fruit juice as well as milk shakes. ♦***Baobab Cafe***, this is located close to the Portuguese Church and has a wide ranging menu. You can have breakfast here, snacks and a beer or fruit juice, as well as full meals. ♦***Travellers Cafe***, this is very popular with budget travellers and is close to the Baobab Cafe. It serves both Western and African food all of which are cheap, tasty and good value.

There are a couple of places in the town centre which are good for Indian and traditional African food – such as ugali and stew. These include the ♦***Urafiki Bar and Restaurant***, located on Kenyatta Rd and the ♦***Bahari Restaurant***, close to the Juma Mosque.

● Entertainment

There is plenty to do in the evenings in Malindi and there are a number of bars and discos. The bigger discos are found at the larger hotels. There is also occasionally live music – ask around at the different hotels.

Bars include the ***Beer Garden***, located just N of the shopping centre, the ***Baobab Cafe***, located at the other end of town near the old Portuguese Church.

Discos Close to the Beer Garden is the ***Stardust Club***, which starts fairly late in the evenings but is nevertheless very popular. The ***Tropicana Club 28***, is situated up near *Eden Roc Hotel* and is small, friendly and popular. The ***Lawford's***, has a disco, as does ***Coconut Village***, (open-air on the beach) and a number of the other large hotels. The bar at the Coconut Village is well worth seeing – it has been cleverly constructed into and around a tree.

Video films If you want to see a film while you are here ask around at the hotels who often have video shows. Also the Malindi Fishing Club which has regular showings.

● Useful addresses

There are a number of banks in Malindi. ***Barclays***, is located on the main coastal road (the Lamu road) opposite the *Blue Marlin Hotel* and is open on weekdays from 0830 to 1700 with a break for lunch from 1300 to 1430, and on Saturdays from 0830 to 1200. There is also a ***Standard Chartered Bank***, close to the police station and post office. The ***Tourist Office***, and ***Kenya Airways***, office are located on the same road opposite the shopping centre.

● Shopping

Craft shops have been forced to move due to works on the towns sewage system. They are mostly now located close to the beach and the jetty. In general the quality is reasonably good as are the prices – although you must expect to bargain. The *Kongoni Shop*, is located on the main coastal road, and although rather expensive, sells good quality items. There is a **bookshop** next to Barclays Bank at the Sitawi Shopping Centre – very limited choice.

● Transport

Local You will be able to walk around the town itself with out any problems. If you want to go out at night then be prepared to take a taxi or ask your hotel to arrange transport. For day trips you can either organise them through the hotel, hire a car or else try the public transport.

Car Hire *Kotsman Car Hire*, PO Box 262, Malindi, T 20777/20988. Some hotels also have mini-mokes for hire (about US$35 per day). Arrange on a daily basis as there are not many places to visit.

Bicycle hire The *Silver Sands Camp Site* and a stall just outside the *Tropicana Club 28*. The quality of the bikes varies – so check thoroughly before you choose one.

Air The airport at Malindi is served by a number of different airlines, as well as by chartered planes for safaris etc. The airport is located about 3 km S of the town – taxi to the centre costs about US$3; the hotels to the S will be about US$6. *Kenya Airlines*, does the Nairobi-Mombasa-Malindi route once a day in both directions (except Sat). It is a popular route so be sure to book well ahead and confirm your seat. The problem of double booking can be serious. Also serving this route are *Eagle Aviation*, T Malindi 21258; Mombasa 316054; Lamu 3119, *Equator Airlines*, T Malindi 2053; *Prestige Air Services*, T Malindi 20860; *Skyways Airlines*, T Malindi 21260; Mombasa 432167; Lamu 3226. All their offices are situated on the Lamu road in Malindi. All have 2 flights per day in both directions between Malindi and Mombasa and Malindi and Lamu. Baggage allowance is only 10 kg, and check in time is 30 mins before take off. Airport tax is around US$1.

Train There is no railway line to Malindi, but it is possible that you may want to reserve a sleeper on the Mombasa-Nairobi train. You can ask your hotel or a travel agent in Malindi to do this for you – but they will charge. Just as easy, and about a tenth of the price, is to ring and do it yourself, T 011 312221.

Road There are plenty of buses between *Malindi* and *Mombasa* – there are 3 companies (Malindi Bus Service, Garissa Express and Tana River Bus Service) all of which have a number of departures each day. They all have offices in Malindi, Mombasa and Lamu but booking is not usually necessary. They mostly leave early in the morning and take about 2 hrs, they cost about US$1. If you are in a real hurry you can take a matatu which go even faster and take under 2 hrs. They leave when full throughout the day and cost about US$2.

To *Lamu* there are also buses but the route is popular so you should book in advance. The trip takes about 5 hrs and costs about US$4. They leave in the morning at between 0700 and 0800. If you miss these you might be able to get onto one of the Mombasa buses which get to Malindi about 0830 and go on at 0930 – but there is no guarantee that you will get a seat. The bus will take you to the jetty on the mainland from where you get a ferry across to Lamu (see page 153).

Share-Taxi Peugeot 504 share-taxis do the Mombasa-Malindi route. These take 7 passengers and go in the mornings when full. They cost about the same as a matatu (US$2).

Malindi to Lamu

Soon after leaving Malindi you cross the Sabaki River, and then the turning for the village of **Mambrui**. This village is believed to be about 600 years old and all that remains of the ancient town is a mosque and a pillar tomb, which has insets of Ming porcelain. Further on you will eventually pass **Garsen,** a small town at the crossing of the Tana River where there is petrol and a drinks. From here the road turns back towards the coast towards the town of **Witu,** another small old town. As you drive in this area you may see people of the Orma tribe as well as Somalis for this is getting close to the border. Both groups are pastoralists, and you will see their cattle which represent their wealth. Finally, about 5 hrs after leaving Malindi, you will get to **Mokowe** and you will see the Makanda channel which separates Lamu from the mainland.

Lamu

A wonderful old stone town with its distinctive architecture, the carved doors, the narrow streets, the lack of vehicles, the many mosques, the fishermen, the women dressed in dressed in black and wearing the *bui bui*. The town takes tourism seriously as this is the major source of income. Conservation and preservation all cost money and tourists are an excellent source of foreign exchange. Whatever the changes in the last few years Lamu remains very popular with budget travellers and with good reason.

The island has a population of about 12,000 people – almost half of whom are Bajun immigrants from the N. It is suffering not just from the growth in the tourist population, but also the rapid growth of the population of the local peoples which has made population pressure a problem. The vast majority of the population are Muslim, and it is courteous for visitors to respect this during their stay. Aid from Saudi Arabia has been directed to the island in the form of a hospital, various schools and religious centres.

Swahili Culture

The coastal region is the centre of this distinct and ancient civilisation. The Swahili are not a tribe as such - they are joined together by culture and a language - Ki-Swahili - which is the most widely spoken language in E Africa. It is one of the Bantu languages and was originally most important as a trading language. It contains words derived from Arabic, Indian as well as English and Portuguese.

The Swahili civilisation emerged from the meeting of E Africa, Islam, the classical world and eastern civilisations. Traders, as well as immigrants, from Asia and Arabia have had a gradual influence on the coast shaping society, religion, language as well as literature and architecture. These traders arrived at the ports of the east coast by the NE monsoon winds which occur in Mar and Apr (the *Kaskazi* wind) and left around Sep on the southerly wind (the *Kusi* wind). Inevitably some stayed or were left behind and there was intermarriage between the immigrants and the indigenous people. Many families trace their roots back to traders from foreign shores and there is a complex social system.

Slavery was important to the coastal region and was not entirely an alien phenomenon. For long before slaves were being rounded up from the interior and shipped overseas, there was an important although rather different "slave trade". This involved a family "lending" a member of the family (usually a child) to another richer family or trader in exchange for food and other goods. That child would then live with the family and work for them - essentially as a slave - until the debt had been paid off. However, in the same way as with bonded child labourers in India today, the rates of interest demanded often ensured that the debt could never be paid off and the person would remain effectively a slave. Later slavery became an important part of trade and commerce and the old system was replaced with something much more direct. Many slaves were rounded up from the interior (some of them "sold" by tribal chiefs and village elders) and taken to the coast. Here they would either be sold overseas to Arabia via Zanzibar or put to work on the plantations that were found all along the coast. In 1907 the British formally ended the slave trade although it did continue underground for many years. When slaves were released they were gradually absorbed into the Swahili culture although their antecedents are known it means it is almost impossible to be rid of the stigma associated with being a slave.

The island is about 9,000 acres in size. The coral rock is covered with sandy soil, and about a third of the island is covered with sand dunes. Although these render this part uncultivable the dunes serve an important purpose for they act as a filter for the water. Despite this, Lamu does often suffer from severe water shortages and supplies are often limited to certain times of the day. The island also has a fairly extensive area of mangrove swamps, and the only cultivable part of the island lies between the dunes and the marshy swamps. The conditions of Lamu are most suitable for coconut plantations and mango trees.

The Beach The southern shores of Lamu island have the best beach – 12km of almost deserted white sand which back onto the sand dunes. As there is no reef the waves get fairly big. To get there you have to walk through the southern part of the town towards Shela which will take you about 45 mins and on to the beach. If you do not feel like walking you can take the dhow or motor boat which goes to Peponi's for US$0.30. It is possible to strike off directly S W, but although it is shorter, the walk through the dunes can be hard work.

Cautions

Safety Until very recently it would not have been considered necessary to include this section. As long as you are sensible there should not be a problem. However, a number of incidents over the last few years has meant that it is important to stress that there are certain dangers. Do not walk around after dark alone in secluded parts of town. Do not go to remote parts of the island alone (for example jogging) – always go with a group and ask your hotel whether there are any particular risks. On the beach if you are alone (especially women) you should not go out of shouting distance from other people.

Health Stomach upsets are fairly common, and it is wise to stick to bottled water or soft drinks. More serious is hepatitis – make sure you have a gamma globulin injection, or else the new treatment Havrix, which once completed, will lasts ten years.

History

The town of Lamu was founded in the 14th century although there were people living on the island long before this. Throughout the years, and as recently as the 1960s, the island has been a popular hide-out for refugees fleeing from the mainland.

By the 15th century it was a thriving port, one of the many that dotted the coast of East Africa. However in 1505 it surrendered to the Portuguese, began paying tributes, and for the next 150 years was subservient to them, and to the sultanate of the town of Paté on the nearby island, part of the Omani dynasty that ruled much of the East African coast.

By the end of the 17th century Lamu had become a republic ruled by a council of elders called the Yumbe, who were in principle responsible to Oman. In fact the Yumbe were largely able to determine their own affairs, and this period has been called Lamu's Golden Age. It was the period when many of the buildings were constructed and Lamu's celebrated architectural style evolved. The town became a thriving centre of literature and scholarly study and there were a number of poets who lived here. Arts and crafts flourished and trade expanded.

Rivalries between the various trading settlements in the region came to a head when Lamu finally defeated Paté in the battle of Shela in 1813. However, Lamu soon found itself dominated by Zanzibar which had been now developed to become the dominant power along the East African coast. At a local level there were factions and splits within the town's population – in particular rivalries between different clans and other interest groups.

Lamu Weddings

In the traditional Lamu culture children are often promised in marriage at an early age. A women is not supposed to marry a man who is socially inferior, although a man can marry a woman who is socially inferior. Once the marriage has been agreed, the couple are not meant to meet. Bridewealth must be paid by the groom to the girl's parents. The bride spends the period in the run up to her wedding with the *somo*, usually a close friend of her mother's, who advises the bride.

Weddings themselves are held in the month preceding Ramadhan. In the days before the wedding the bride must go though a series of rituals which last about 3 days - including the washing of hair, the painting of the hands and feet with henna and the shaving of the skin. After this there are a series of ceremonies and celebrations which last about 4 days. The third day is perhaps the most important and has a number of ceremonies. The relatives of the groom go in a procession through the town until they reach the house of the bride. Here more singing and dancing occurs, gifts are exchanged and finally the "nikaha" takes place at which the marriage is formally contracted. More rituals take place before the groom may lift the curtain of the bride's sleeping alcove and then lift the veil that covers her face. In due course the *somo* takes the bride for another ritual to remove the "impurity" of intercourse and the sheet is shown to the women of the family evidence of the girl's virginity. After the the bride has been presented publicly the couple return to the bride's sleeping alcove to remain in seclusion there for 7 days.

One interesting feature that is fairly common in Lamu are "secret marriages". These are marriages that are kept from the parents or the first wife. They are often made between a young divorced women who has some wealth of her own, or women of a lower rank who would not be approved by the husband's family. The ceremony is different and no property changes hands but such marriages gradually become general knowledge and become recognised, and children born to such alliances are legitimate.

Divorce is reasonably common. It is easiest for a man to get a divorce - on grounds such as a woman's sterility, her adultery or persistent quarrelling. He simply needs to make it known to the *Kadhi* (Islamic judge) or *Mwalimu* (teacher or Muslim healer) that he wants a divorce and on what grounds. If the marriage does not involve property, he may simply pronounce the triple repudiation or "talaka". It is much harder for a woman to get a divorce - she must give detailed reasons and provide substantial evidence. Otherwise she can try to provoke her husband so that he will initiate the divorce himself.

Towards the end of the 19th century Lamu began a slow economic decline as Mombasa and Zanzibar took over in importance as trading centres. The end of the slave trade dealt a blow to Lamu as the production of mangrove poles and grains for export depended on slave labour. Additionally communications between the interior and Mombasa were infinitely better than those with Lamu – particularly after the building of the railway. In recent decades the tourist trade has helped improve Lamu's economic prospects.

Peoples of Lamu

The people of Lamu are a mixture of Swahili-speaking people of Arab and African ancestry – with much of the East African blood being brought in by the movement of slaves through this area. Some broad distinctions can be made:

Swahili and Bajun Taking advantage

of the monsoon winds, traders visited these shores annually in search of ivory, gold and slaves. Arabs, Indians, Persians and Chinese visited the coast and over the years some remained, intermarried with the local people and built up city states. The Afro-Arab peoples, who shared their Islamic faith and way of life became known as the Swahilis. Both the Swahili and the Bajun people claim Arab ancestry, although it is very much mixed with African blood. There is a rural-urban distinction between Bajun and Swahili with the Swahili mainly in the towns. The Bajun people also often claim Somali ancestry as well as Arabic origins.

Oromo or Galla The Oromo people (or Galla as they are also known), are nomadic pastoralists and mainland dwellers who for many years were a great influence on Lamu. While the Arabs and the Swahili speaking people of the islands and mainland were all Muslims, the Oromo retained their traditional beliefs. They were an aggressive people and a number of towns were abandoned as a result of their incessant pillaging. The ways of the Oromo have changed considerably since the 19th century and in the present they are suffering from pressure on their land.

Omani Arabs At the turn of the 19th century the Swahili and Bajun, including descendants of slaves, formed the majority of the population, with the *wangwana* (free or nobly born) ruling the communities. During the 19th century Omani Arabs started to arrive until eventually they became the most politically powerful group, despite being outnumbered a thousand to one by the Swahili and Bajun. A governor was appointed to the island who was usually closely related to the Sultan of Zanzibar, and he and other officials settled with their families.

Asians During the 19th century Asians, both Muslims and Hindus, came to Lamu to work as merchants and traders. While the Hindus often came on a more temporary basis and returned to India, many of the Muslim Asians came with their families and formed more permanent communities.

Places of interest

Old Town or Stone-Town Known to the local people as *Mkomani*. It is the largest stone-town on the East African coast. The town dates back to the 14th century although most of the buildings are actually from the 18th century and Lamu's Golden Age. The streets are very narrow,

Swahili Proverbs

A good house is not judged by its door.

What God has written cannot be erased.

The first wife is like a mother
(Used by polygamists to justify a second wife; also refers to the important part that the first wife plays in running the household)

A bird can be guarded, a wife cannot.

A woman you love for her being, not for her beauty.

A new mat is no pleasure to sleep on.
(A young wife has a lot to learn).

Without children the house is sad and silent.

You cannot turn the wind, so turn the sail.

When the crocodile smiles, be extra careful.

A wise man talks about secrets only to his heart.

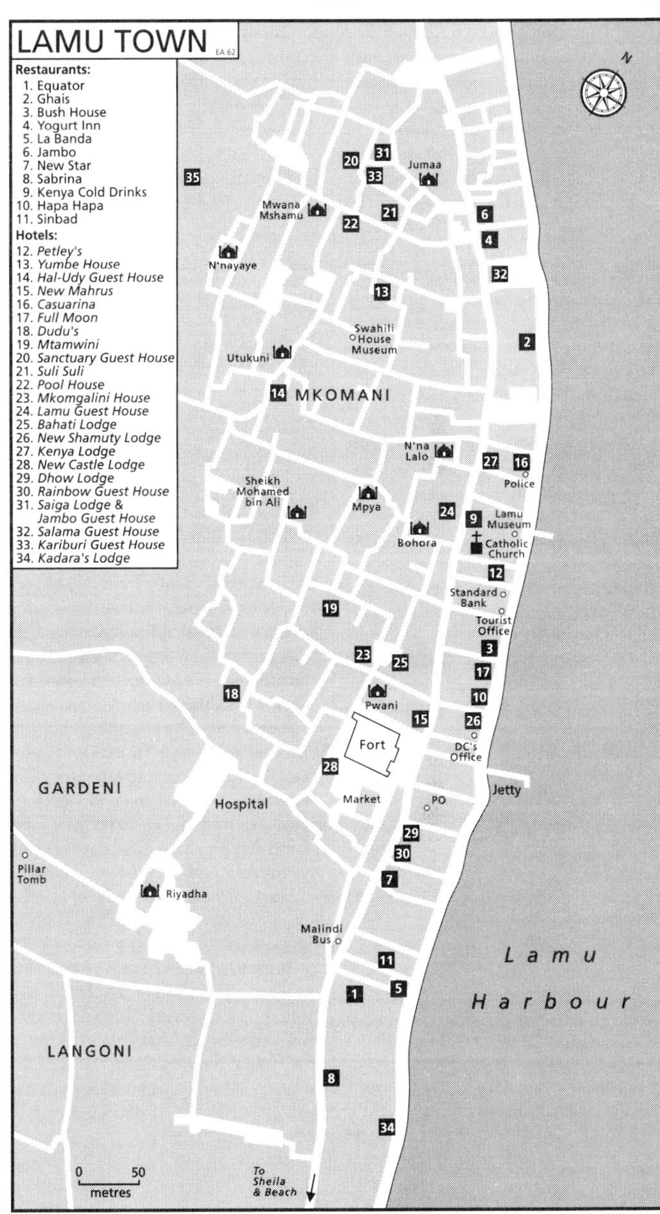
LAMU TOWN
EA 62
Restaurants:
1. Equator
2. Ghais
3. Bush House
4. Yogurt Inn
5. La Banda
6. Jambo
7. New Star
8. Sabrina
9. Kenya Cold Drinks
10. Hapa Hapa
11. Sinbad
Hotels:
12. Petley's
13. Yumbe House
14. Hal-Udy Guest House
15. New Mahrus
16. Casuarina
17. Full Moon
18. Dudu's
19. Mtamwini
20. Sanctuary Guest House
21. Suli Suli
22. Pool House
23. Mkomgalini House
24. Lamu Guest House
25. Bahati Lodge
26. New Shamuty Lodge
27. Kenya Lodge
28. New Castle Lodge
29. Dhow Lodge
30. Rainbow Guest House
31. Saiga Lodge &
Jambo Guest House
32. Salama Guest House
33. Kariburi Guest House
34. Kadara's Lodge
N
Jumaa
Mwana Mshamu
N'nayaye
Swahili House Museum
Utukuni
MKOMANI
N'na Lalo
Police
Sheikh Mohamed bin Ali
Mpya
Lamu Museum
Bohora
Catholic Church
Standard Bank
Tourist Office
Pwani
Fort
DC's Office
Jetty
GARDENI
Hospital
Market
PO
Pillar Tomb
Riyadha
Malindi Bus
Lamu Harbour
LANGONI
0 50
metres
To Sheila & Beach

and the buildings on each side are 2 or 3 stories high. The streets are set in a rough grid pattern running off the main street which is called the *Usita wa Mui* (street of the town) now known as Harambee Ave. *Usita wa Mui* runs parallel to the harbour and used to open out to the sea, although building from the mid 1800s onwards has cut it off from the quayside.

Mkomani is a very secluded place – the houses face inwards and privacy is carefully guarded. The families who live in these houses are mainly the patrician *wangwana* who keep themselves to themselves. The non-patricians who reside in *Mkomani* live there as clients of the patricians and are often descendants of their patron's slaves. The importance of the patron-client relationship is paramount. At the edges of the town live people of slave and immigrant ancestry.

Carved doors which are one of the attractions for which Lamu has become known. The skill continues to be taught, and at the N end of the harbour you can see them being made in workshops by craftsmen and apprentices.

It is easy to get lost – just bear in mind that Harambee Ave runs parallel to the waterfront and the all the streets leading into town from the shore slope uphill slightly.

Mosques There are a number of mosques on the island (over 20) but they are usually not very grand affairs and you may not even be able to tell what they are as some are little different from other buildings. You will need to seek permission before entering to look around.

The oldest mosque in Lamu is believed to be the **Pwani Mosque**, situated near the Fort which dates back to the 14th century. One of Lamu's newest mosques is the **Riyadha Mosque** located in the S of town. It was built at the turn of the century and represented a shift in Lamu's style of Islam. Near to this mosque is the **Muslim Academy** – funded and supported by Saudi Arabia this attracts muslim students from around the world.

Women did once have a mosque for themselves – **Mwenye Alawi Mosque** located in the N of Lamu – however this has since been taken over by the men.

Lamu Museum incorporates a library and is located on Kenyatta Rd. It is run by the National Museums of Kenya, and plays an important role in the conservation of old Lamu. A model of an 18th century Swahili house is on display as well as other exhibits of Swahili life and culture through the ages. 2 siwa horns, one of which is from Lamu and is made of brass, the other from Pate is of ivory, are thought to be the oldest surviving musical instruments in black Africa with the Pate horn dating from the mid-17th century. There are models of various dhows (at the village of Matondoni you can see dhows being made and repaired). A slide show can be seen on request. Inland from the Museum is the small House Museum – ask at the Museum for directions. It is a traditional Swahili house, restored, with all the traditional furniture.

Lamu Fort The construction of the Fort was begun in 1809 and completed in 1821. The Fort initially faced over the quayside, but there are now buildings between it and the sea. In the past it has served as both a fort and as a prison. Now it contains an exhibition hall, a shop and a library, while on the top there is a roof top restaurant which has fine views of the harbour.

Tombs In the southwest part of town is a fluted pillar tomb, thought to date from the 14th century. It can be reached by going S and turning inland just after the Halwa Shop towards the Riyadha Mosque, and continuing beyond the mosque. It is not in particularly good repair.

Another tomb is that of Mwana Hadie Famau, a local woman believed to have lived here in the 15th or 16th century. This is situated a little inland from the museum.

Donkey Sanctuary This is located in the northern part of the town close to the waterfront. It is run by the International Donkey Protection Trust, based in the UK.

Excursions

Matondoni Village Here, on the western side of the island, about 8km from town, you can see dhows being built and repaired. The easiest way is to hire a dhow between a group – you will have to negotiate the price and can expect to pay around US$10 for the boat. Alternatively you can hire a donkey – ask at the *Pole Pole Lodge* (situated up near the Jumaa Mosque – turn inland at the Pole Pole Restaurant). Finally you can walk – although leave early as it gets very hot. The walk will take a couple of hrs and is quite complicated. You want to turn off the main street roughly opposite Petley's and keep walking W inland. Ask for directions from there – basically you want to keep going in the same direction of the telephone wires which go to Matondoni – if you follow these you should get there eventually.

Shela This village is another of the old stone-towns and is located to the S of Lamu town. It is a popular destination for beach lovers as it is just a 40 minute walk from Lamu. In the town are a number of old buildings including the **Mosque** which is situated behind Peponi's. The people of Shela were originally from the island of Manda and speak a dialect of Swahili that is quite different to that spoken in Lamu. The **Friday Mosque** was built in 1829 and is noted for its rather unusual minaret.

If the tide is low it is an easy walk, about 3 km – down to the end of the harbour – and then along the beach. There is also a route inland, basically you need to head SW and hug the shore. You can always hire a dhow which will take you for about US$0.50 a person, or get a group together and hire a motor boat run by Peponi's.

Dodori and Boni National Reserves In the far N of the Kenya coast close to the Somali border and are covered in the section on National Parks (see page 177). Because of the recent troubles in Somalia parts of this area have been out of bounds to tourists for a while. If you want to go up here be sure to check with the local authorities and tour agencies.

Kiunga Marine National Reserve Located in the far northern part of the Kenyan coast, adjoining the Somali border, this Marine park suffers from being rather remote. It is possible to arrange a trip there through *Peponi's* at Shela, T 3029.

Nearby islands

Manda Island is quite close, **Pate Island** about 20 km away, and **Kiwaiyu Island** 50 km off. These island are described in detail below, see page 153, 154 and page 155. You will see notices advertising trips and will, undoubtedly, be offered trips from various people who usually act as a go-between for the dhow owners. Day trips are popular and because competition is tough the prices are almost standard. For longer trips you will need to be sure that everyone is clear who is arranging the food and drink (you or the dhow owner). Be sure to take lots to drink as it can get very hot. Another thing to remember is that the dhow is dependent on the tides and, if it has no outboard motor, on the winds. So bear in mind that a trip could easily turn into something longer through no fault of the dhow crew. You would be foolish to set off with a very tight schedule. You would be advised to bring your own soft drinks or beer, buying the latter at the Kenya Breweries depot on the waterfront. The price will probably work out at about US$10 per person including food for a 3 day trip for a party of 8. You need to know that you will spend the odd night on the boat, so make sure you will be comfortable. Staying in any temporary lodging on one of the islands will be an extra (but nominal) expense.

Local information

● Where to stay

Price varies with the season. The peak periods are Dec and Jan for up-market travellers, and Jul, Aug and Sep for family visitors and budget travellers.

Most of the more expensive hotels are not actually located in the Old Town, but are around the island or on nearby islands. At the lower end of the price range the main problems with the hotels in Lamu are twofold: firstly there are frequently problems with the water supply, you should expect to have cold bucket showers much of the time; secondly many are very hot. The worst are those that do not catch the breeze, such as the ones on Harambee Ave. If possible get a room as high up as possible or on the waterfront. With many of these places you may be able to get a cheaper price if you agree to stay for a while. If you want, you can often sleep on the roof which is very cheap.

House rentals If you are planning to stay here for a while then it is probably worth getting together with a group to rent a house. Ask around. Many of the houses have been bought up by foreigners and they can be very good value. Some of them are really quite luxurious.

Lamu Town A+ *Kipugani Sea Breezes*, PO Box 55343, Nairobi, T Nairobi 503030, F Nairobi 503144. This new lodge, with just 12 *makuti* thatched cottages, is located at the southern tip of Lamu Island. They are all extremely spacious and comfortable and each has a verandah. They organise various excursions and snorkelling trips. There is a good restaurant and bar outside, and non residents can visit for lunch, boats leaving from Peponi's. **A+** *Blue Safari*, PO Box 41759, Nairobi, T Nairobi 338838. A small and exclusive hotel this is located on Manda Island. Thatched bungalows provide extremely comfortable accommodation and the hotel caters in particular for those interested in water sports, scuba diving in particular. It is closed from May to Sep. **A+** *Kiwaya Safari Village*, PO Box 55343, Nairobi, T Nairobi 503030, F Nairobi 503144. Located to the N of Lamu on the Kiwaya Peninsula. This is managed by the same people as the Kipungani Sea Breezes and has been recently refurbished. It consists of thatched cottages, swimming pool, restaurant, bar and shops and has its own private airstrip. The hotel has a fleet of deep sea fishing vessels and is ideal for the enthusiast. The beach is also wonderful, and there is a full range of water sports on offer, and boat trips into the mangrove swamps. The food is excellent.

A *Manda Island Village Resort* PO Box 78, Lamu, T 2751. As its name suggests this is located on Manda Island looking across to the village of Shela on Lamu. It has self sufficient cottages, a restaurant, bar and shop. Excursions that the hotel organises include trips to Lamu, deep-sea fishing and snorkelling trips. **A** *Petley's Inn* PO Box 4, Lamu, T 7. This is the only top range hotel in the actual town of Lamu, located on Kenyatta Rd next to the Lamu Museum on the harbour front. It was founded by an Englishman called Percy Petley in 1962 and only has 15 rooms. It is looking rather shabby these days but has a certain atmosphere. However it is really rather expensive for what you get. Many of the rooms are very hot and stuffy. It has 2 restaurants and a bar, the only hotel bar in the town, which of course makes it fairly popular. It has a swimming pool and sometimes holds a disco.

C *Yumbe House*, PO Box 81, Lamu, T 3101. This is a wonderful hotel full of atmosphere and excellent value. It is located in the heart of the old town and is a traditional house of 4 storeys that has been superbly converted into a hotel. It has a courtyard, and is airy and spacious. It is clean, friendly, has a good water supply and the price includes breakfast.

D *Hal-Udy Guest House*, located in the heart of the old town, back from the harbour, this is a small hotel with 4 self contained suites. Each has a bedroom, sitting room, with some lovely furniture, and cooking facilities. There is also a house boy, and this is particularly popular with expatriate families. It is especially good value if you are planning on staying for a few weeks. **D** *New Mahrus*, PO Box 25, Lamu, T 3001. This has a range of rooms with and without bathrooms, as well as one fully self contained Arab house for rent. It is modern and rather rundown and not very well run. The price includes breakfast.

E *Casuarina Rest House*, PO Box 10, Lamu, T 132. Great location on the waterfront to the N of the Tourist Office. It is very clean, the rooms are spacious and it is well run and friendly. Also has self-contained apartments. There is a large roof top area. **E** *Full Moon*

Guest House, small hotel located right on the waterfront. It only has 4 rooms with shared bathroom, but they are large, it is very friendly and is in an excellent position. **E** *Dudu's Guest House*, one of the nicest hotels in this range. It is located behind the Fort, and is a wonderful old house. The rooms are spacious and airy, and include bathrooms. There is a kitchen that you can use. **E** *Mtamwini Guest House*, located close to fort. Large cool rooms, all with bathrooms. **E** *Sanctuary Guest House*, situated in the northern part of town this has a range of self contained rooms and suites. It has good facilities: kitchen, garden and rooftop. **E** *Suli Suli House*, also located in the northern part of town this is another old house that has been converted into a lodge. It has 8 rooms around a courtyard. It is very clean and friendly and you can get meals. **E** *Pool House*, close to Jumaa Mosque, a bit further inland. This is probably the only hotel in this range with a swimming pool. It is small with only 4 rooms, each with bathroom. **E** *Mlangilangi House*, this is located behind the fort, and has a number of rooms. You can use the kitchen and it is a very friendly. **E** *Lamu Guest House*, situated at the back of the Lamu Museum and is good value. There are a range of rooms the general rule is that top ones are usually the best because they catch the sea breezes. It is clean and friendly. **E** *Bahati Lodge*, situated to the N of the fort some of these rooms are better than others. The ones on the top floor are much cooler because they get the sea breezes and they also have good views. However it is fairly basic and perhaps not the cleanest. **E** *New Shamuty Lodge*, positioned close to the jetty on the waterfront this is a popular cheap hotel. Bathroom facilities are shared and there is a rooftop. **E** *Kenya Lodge*, located a little inland from the waterfront this is one of the very basic hotels. It is reasonably clean but rather shabby and sometimes has problems with water supply although other times it can be 24 hrs. Some of the rooms are hot and stuffy so try and get one with a breeze. **E** *New Castle Lodge*, PO Box 10, Lamu, T 3123/3132. This is situated next to the fort. It has a good position and is kept cool by the sea breezes. It has recently been done up so the prices may rise accordingly. It has both a dormitory on the roof and rooms with shared facilities.

Other similar hotels basic, cheap and with shared facilities include: **E** *Dhow Lodge*, on the waterfront to the S of the jetty; **E** *Rainbow Guest House*, on the waterfront to the S of the jetty; **E** *Saiga Lodge*, **E** *Salama Guest House*, **E** *Jambo Guest House*, **E** *Karibuni Guest House*, all in the N of town; **E** *Kadara's Lodge*, in the far S of the town; **E** *Peace Guest House*, a bit inland, set in gardens with *camping* facilities.

Shela Village (about 3 km S of Lamu Town). **A+** *Peponi's*, PO Box 24, Lamu, T 3029. This is located on the beach next to the village of Shela and is highly recommended. It faces the channel that runs between Lamu and Manda and is a really wonderful setting with about 5 km of private beach. The hotel is made up of a series of cottages each with a verandah and full facilities. There is an excellent restaurant which is for residents only, as well a bar and grill for non-residents. The hotel provides full water sports facilities probably the best and most extensive on the island and organises various excursions. It is very efficiently run by the Korschen's who are Danish. Booking well ahead is definitely advised. It is closed from mid Apr to end of Jun.

B *Shela Rest House*, PO Box 199, Malindi; or PO Box 255, Lamu, T 20182, or 121/3251. This small hotel is located in the village of Shela close to Peponi's. It is a wonderful converted house and there are rooms as well as several self-contained suites.

E *Samahani Guest House*, PO Box 59, Lamu, T 3100. Located in the village of Shela this is particularly popular with budget travellers who want to be closer to the beach. It is basic but clean and friendly. **E** *Stop Over*, located right on the beach. Clean and simple but basic.

● Places to eat

There are lots of places to eat in Lamu which has responded magnificently to the demand for tourist menus. You will find lots of yoghurt, pancakes, fruit salads, and milk shakes as well as good value sea food. If you are looking for the traditional food that you find in up-country Kenya, such as ugali, beans, curries, chicken and chips, there are also a number of places that do these. They are mainly on Harambee Ave – particularly in the southern end of town.

Lamu Town ♦♦♦*Equator Restaurant*, south of the town and is a very popular restaurant. It has a very nice atmosphere and a good range of food on the menu. Make you sure you pop in and book before you go as it can get very full. The food is good – and there is also excellent ice cream. ♦♦♦*Ghai's Restaurant* is named after the owner and cook. It is located up in the N of town close to the donkey sanctuary. Its speciality is seafood although the quality of the food can vary. ♦♦♦*Petley's Inn*, restaurant and a grill house. The food at both of these is variable – snacks generally seem to be better than the full meals. ♦♦♦*Bush Gardens*, on the waterfront and is a very good seafood and fish restaurant. It is friendly although can be extremely slow, especially when it gets full.

♦♦*Yoghurt Inn* (also known as *Coral Inn*). North of the town and is popular for snacks and a drink although it also does more substantial meals. It is good value and has a pleasant atmosphere set in gardens. It is particularly popular for breakfasts. ♦♦*Labanda*, this is a new restaurant located in the far S of town which is very good – especially the seafood. Prices are very reasonable.

♦*Jambo Cafe*, Harambee Ave, northern end. Popular with locals and is very cheap. It serves mainly traditional African food and also does good breakfasts. ♦*New Star Restaurant* in the southern end of town is reasonable and is very cheap. It has good breakfasts and opens very early. ♦*Sabrina Restaurant*, southern end of town, is very cheap, has a reasonably wide range of food on the menu, and does breakfasts. ♦*Kenya Cold Drinks*, located on Harambee Ave close to the museum this is very good for a milkshake and a snack. ♦*Hapahapa Restaurant*, on the harbour front. Good fruit juices and snacks. ♦*Sinbad Restaurant*, (Olympic) S of the town also on the harbour front. Excellent pancakes and seafood.

Shela Village (about 3km S of Lamu Town) ♦♦♦*Barbecue Grill* at *Peponi's*. Excellent and open to non-resident's. The food is very good value and is probably the best on the island.

♦♦*Stop Over Restaurant* which serves simple, basic but good value food. It also has a great location right on the beach.

● Bank

Only one on the island, *Standard Chartered*, located on the harbour front. It is only open in the mornings 0830 to 1300 on weekdays, and until 0830 to 1100 on Saturdays, and can get busy. It can also be painstakingly slow.

● Entertainment

Bars There are in fact only 3 places in Lamu Town – *Petley's*; the *Civil Servants Club* (S end of town); and the *Police Club* (S on Harambee Ave, turn right after after the bus booking office and proceed inland. It's on the outskirts of town). You don't have to be into red-tape or law enforcement to use these clubs, although you made feel obliged to buy the officials a drink. Also there is *Peponi's* at Shela, which is most pleasant.

Discos The *Civil Servant's Club* (S end of town) has a disco most weekends.

Cinema The open-air *Coast Cinema* inland from roughly behind the Museum, on the edge of town. There are films most nights in the peak period, and the programme is posted at the Museum.

● Hospital and medical services

Hospital Located in the southern end of the town to the S and inland from the fort.

● Shopping

Books The *Museum* has a very good collection of books on Lamu, its history and culture. There is also the *Lamu Book Centre* which has a reasonable selection as well as the local newspapers.

Souvenirs Hand-built model dhows. They are not too easy to carry around so try and get them at the end of the trip. Other woodcarvings are also good value here – chests, siwa horns, Lamu candlesticks, and furniture. Also in Lamu you will be able to get jewellery – silver in particular – as well as curios. You can get things made for you but be prepared to bargain.

● Tourist office

Harbour front, next door to the bank. While the staff are friendly they have little information to give out.

● Post Office

Just to the S of the jetty Mon-Fri 0800-1230 and 1400-1700; Sat 0900-1200. There is a poste restante service.

● Local transport

Except for the District Commissioner's Land Rover, there are no vehicles on the island. Even if they were allowed, the narrow streets would make driving impossible in town. Instead there are donkeys and bicycles.

● Transport

Air There are flights to the airstrip on Manda Island and then get boat taxi or a dhow across. The companies serving this route are *Eagle Aviation*, T Malindi 21258; Mombasa 316054; Lamu 3119; *Equator Airlines*, T Malindi 2053; *Prestige Air Services*, T Malindi 20860/1; Mombasa 21443; *Skyways Airlines*, T Malindi 21260; Mombasa 432167; Lamu 3226. Prestige and Equator both have offices on Lamu close to the Standard Chartered Bank. All the companies have 2 flights per day in both directions between Malindi and Mombasa and Malindi and Lamu. Baggage allowance is only 10 kg, and check in time is 30 mins before take off. There is no airport tax when you leave Lamu (although there is from Malindi).

Fares are: Malindi US$35; Mombasa US$55; Nairobi US$100.

Road Buses to Lamu go fairly regularly but the route is popular so you should book in advance. The trip takes about 5 to 6 hrs from Malindi and costs US$4. They leave in the morning at between 0700 and 0800. You might also be able to take one of the buses from Mombasa that stop off at Malindi on the way, but these are often full so you will have to stand all the way which is not much fun. If possible sit on the left side of the bus (in the shade) and keep your eyes open for wildlife. The bus will take you as far as the jetty at Makowe on the mainland from where you get a ferry across to Lamu which costs about US$0.50.

● Water Sports

Organised from *Peponi's* at Shela, T 3029. Includes windsurfing, surfing, snorkelling, deep sea fishing, sailing, and scuba diving.

Manda Island

This is the island which is located just to the N of Lamu and has the air strip on it. It is very easy to get to and is a popular day trip to see the ruins at Takwa.

The island is approximately the size of Lamu but has only a small permanent population – partly because of a shortage of fresh water and also because of the shortage of cultivable land. About a fifth of the island is made up of sand dunes and sandy flat land with just thorn bushes and palms. Another 3 fifths of the island is mangrove swamps and muddy creeks. Thus only about a fifth of the island's surface area is suitable for agriculture. The creek that Takwa is located on almost cuts the island in half during high tide. The main port is Ras Kilimdini which is located on the northern side of the island. In the 19th century this deep water harbour was considered to be superior to Lamu and was used by ocean-going vessels who would then take dhows across to Lamu.

The **Takwa Ruins** are those of an ancient Swahili town which is believed to have prospered from the 15th to the 17th centuries, with a population of between 2 and 3 thousand people. For some reason it was abandoned in favour of the town of Shela on Lamu – it is not altogether clear why. The ruins consists of the remains of a wall which surrounded the town, about 100 houses, a mosque and a dated tomb from 1683. As with many of the other sites on the coast, the remains include ablution facilities. The houses face N toward Mecca as does the main street. There is a mosque at the end of the street which is thought to have been built on the site of an old tomb. The other feature of the ruins is the pillar tomb. It is situated just outside the town walls and has been dated from 1683. The ruins have been cleared but little excavation has been done here. Only relatively little is known about the town – the biggest question that remains is if it was so well defended (as it clearly was with town walls, the sea and mangrove swamps as protection) why did the inhabitants leave so quickly? Entrance fee of US$2.

There are a number of good **snorkelling** sites off Manda Island. Perhaps the best is actually off the small island to the N of Manda, named Manda Toto. You will have to take a dhow to get here.

● Where to stay

There are 2 hotels on Manda Island in the upper price brackets **A+** *Blue Safari Hotel* and **A** *Manda Island Village Resort*: (see Lamu Accommodation, page 150) as well as **E** *Camping* close to the ruins.

● Transport

You can get to Manda Island and the towns by way of motorised ferry as well as by dhow. However dhow is the easiest as it will take you closest to the ruins, otherwise you will have to walk across the island. The dhow will cost you about US$15 for a party of up to 8. Be sure you know what is included in the price. It takes about an hr and a half and is dependent on the tides. You may have to wade ashore through the mangrove swamp.

Pate Island

About 3 times the size of Lamu and located about 20 km to the northeast. Unlike both Lamu and Manda, it does not have a large area taken up by dunes. The island is divided into 2 parts – indeed it may have once been 2 islands but the channel dividing the 2 is so shallow that only the smallest boats can go down it. The land is very low lying and the towns are situated on shallow inlets which can only be reached at high tide. The only deep water landing point is at Ras Mtangawanda in the W of the island, but as it is not a sheltered harbour it has never had a major settlement. Although it is fairly easily accessible it does not receive many visitors.

Pate Town

The town of Pate is only accessible from the sea at the right tide – otherwise you will have to walk from the landing place. It is situated in the southwest corner of the island and is one of the old Swahili towns that dot the coast. The town shows strong Arabic and Indian influences, and was once most famous for the silk that was produced here. The old stone houses are crumbling and tobacco has been planted amongst the ruins. The main ruins are those of **Nabahani** which are found just outside the town. Although they have not yet been excavated you should be able to make out the town walls, houses, mosques and tombs.

The age of the town is disputed – the earliest remains that have been found are from the 13th century – although according to some accounts the town dates back to the 8th century. The town was reasonably prosperous for up to 1600, although by the time the Portuguese first arrived it had begun to decline. The Portuguese did not have much success and by the 17th century had withdrawn to Mombasa. The final decline of Pate was the war with Lamu. There had been an ongoing dispute between the 2 islands. Over the years the port at Pate silted up, Lamu was used instead by the bigger dhows, and the tensions increased. The situation reached a climax in 1813 when the army from Pate was defeated at Shela and the town went into a decline from which it has never recovered.

● Transport

To get to Pate fromm Lamu, you will have to take the motor launch to **Faza** or to **Mtangawanda** and walk from there. To Faza the boat goes 3 times a week, Mon, Wed, and Fri and takes about 4 hrs. To Mtangawanda the trip takes about 3 hrs. Once you get to Mtangawanda the walk will take you about an hr – the track is clear and you will probably be accompanied by other people from the boat. To get back to Lamu the boat leaves Faza on Tue, Thu and Sat. It does not always call at Mtangawanda so you may have to walk to Faza via Siyu (quite a hike) and catch it from there. You would be advised to take a guide (at least as far as Siyu).

Siyu

A stone-built town dating from about the 15th century. It became most well known as a centre for Islamic scholarship and is believed to have been an important cultural centre during the 17th and 18th centuries. At one time is said to have had 30,000 inhabitants. Today there are probably fewer than 5,000 people living in the town and the inhabited part of the town is slightly apart from the ancient ruined area. A creek separates the residential part of the town from the **Fort** which is believed to date from the mid-19th century when the town was occupied by forces of the Sultan of Zanzibar. The Fort has some impressive canons and has been partly renovated. The town itself is fairly dilapidated and outside the town are coconut plantations. It is a small fishing village which has a thriving crafts industry – you will be able to see leather goods being made as well as doors, furniture and jewellery.

About one hrs walk from Siyu there are the **Shanga Ruins**. There have been excavations in recent years and they show signs of unearthing impressive remains. There are buildings from the 13th and 14th century and many artifacts have been found dating back to the 8th and 9th centuries. There is a pillar tomb, a large mosque, a smaller second mosque, about 130 houses and a palace. The whole town was walled with 5 access gates and outside the wall is a cemetery containing well over 300 tombs. If you are visiting the islands by dhow and would rather not walk you can ask your boatman to take you to Shanga direct.

The channel which Siyu is sited on is so silted up that only the smallest boats can reach Siyu. It is therefore necessary to approach the town by foot – either from Shanga (about an hr), from Faza (about 2 hrs), or from Pate (about 8 km). In the case of the latter 2, unless you are happy to get lost and therefore walk for hrs, you would be advised to take a guide, as the route (particularly from Pate) is complicated.

About a 2 hr walk to the northeast of Siyu is the town of **Chundwa** which is situated in the most fertile part of the island. Being agriculturally productive the island is perhaps the most capable of self-sufficiency of all the islands in the archipelago, however, it does suffer from problems with the supply of fresh water.

• **Where to stay** It is possible to rent rooms in local houses – there are no formal guest houses.

• **Transport** The inlet is very shallow, and sea-going dhows and the motor launch from Lamu by-passes Siyu en route to Faza. It may be possible to persuade a small boat to sail or pole you round from Pate or Faza. Otherwise it is about a 10 km hike to each of these places, and you probably need to hire a guide.

Faza

About 20 km from Pate Town, and 10 km northeast of Siyu. Although the town of Faza is believed to date from the 13th century and possibly as early as the 8th century, there is little in the way of ruins left here. However the town is important in that it is the district headquarters of Pate Island and some of the mainland. It therefore has a number of modern facilities that are not found elsewhere on the island – such as post office, telephone exchange and some shops, restaurants and simple guest houses.

The town is believed to have been completely destroyed in the 13th century by the nearby town of Pate, rebuilt, and destroyed again in the late 16th century this time by the Portuguese. It was again rebuilt and joined forces with the Portuguese against Pate. However, its significance declined until recently when, being the district headquarters, it resumed its position of importance.

Close to where the ferries anchor are the ruins of the **Kunjanja Mosque**. You can see some the mihrab which points to Mecca and which is a beautiful example with fine carvings. There are some rather splendid Arabic inscriptions above the entrance. Outside the town there is the tomb of the commander of the Sultan of Zanzibar's army who was killed here, in action, in 1844.

• **Where to stay and eat** There are 2 guesthouses in the town. **E** *Shela House* and **E** *Lamu House*, they are simple, basic and family run. Alternatively you can ask around to stay at a family house. You will probably be offered food at the place that you are staying – otherwise there is a simple restaurant in the village.

• **Transport** To get to Faza from **Lamu** take the motor launch which goes 3 times a week (on Mon, Wed and Fri) and takes about 4 hrs. To get back to Lamu the boat leaves Faza at about 0600 on Tue, Thu and Sat. You have to take a small boat out to the launch so be sure to get there early. The journey to Lamu takes about 4 hrs and will cost you about US$1.50. From Faza to any of the other towns you will probably have to walk – it is advisable to take a guide or ask around to see if anyone else is going who can show you the route. Generally when visiting Pate Island the best thing to do is to start at Pate Town, and walk through Siyu to Faza from where you will be able to get a boat back to Lamu.

Kiwaiyu Island

This island is located on the far NE of the archipelago and is part of the **Kiunga Marine National Reserve**. Unfortunately this area has suffered from the problems to the N in Somalia, and so visitors are fewer than in previous years. The Marine Park has a reputation for being some of the best reef in Kenya.

• **Where to stay** There is an airstrip which serves the 2 luxury lodges below, as well as a launch which takes an hr to Lamu. **A+** ***Kiwaiyu Safari Village***, PO Box 55343, on the mainland, Nairobi, T Nairobi 503030. **A+** ***Kiwaiyu Mlango Wa Chanu Lodge***, on the Island, PO Box 48217, Nairobi, T Nairobi 331878, Tlx Nairobi 22678. **D-E** ***Kasim's***, has a number of bandas, located on the western shore of the island. The facilities are good and there is a dining and cooking area. **E** ***Camping***, if you have a tent you can camp at Kasim's.

• **Transport** To get there you can either take a regular boat or (and probably easier) you can get a group of 5 or 6 together and charter a dhow. This should include food and water as well as snorkelling gear and should work out at around US$15 per person. The journey is dependent on the winds and the tides and so be prepared for the journey in each direction to be anything between 8 and 36 hrs.

NORTHERN KENYA

CONTENTS

MAPS

This is a vast area of forested and barren mountains, deserts and scrubland occasionally broken by oases of vegetation and the huge Lake Turkana. Northern Kenya accounts for almost half of the country and yet only a fraction of the population live here. The people who do inhabit the area, the Samburu, Rendille, Boran, Gabbra, Turkana and Somali, are nomadic peoples crossing the region using ancient migration routes, existing as they have done for generations hardly affected by the modern world. The main reason tourists come up here is to see the wonders of Lake Turkana—the jade sea.

Lake Turkana, the largest lake in the country, runs about 250 km from the Ethiopian border in a long thin body of water which is never more than 50 km wide. This lake used to be far larger than it is today. Around 10,000 years ago it is believed the water level of the lake was about 150m higher and considered to be one of the sources of the Nile. At that time it supported a far greater number and diversity of plant and animal life. Now a combination of factors including evaporation and major irrigation projects in southern Ethiopia have brought the water level to its lowest in memory. As a result, the water is far more alkaline than in the past. The lake still supports a huge number of hippos and the largest population of Nile crocodiles in the world, about 20,000. There is also a profusion of birdlife including many European migratory species. Do not be fooled by its calm appearance, the lake's waters are highly unpredictable; storms builds up out of nowhere and are not to be dismissed lightly as they are capable of sinking all but the most sturdy craft.

The climate up here is extraordinary. It can easily reach 50°C during the day with not a cloud in sight, then out of nowhere a storm will break whipping up a squall on Lake Turkana. For most of the year, the area is dry but when the rains do come, the rivers and ravines become torrential waterways sweeping over the parched plains. It is quite a sight, and it can leave you stranded until the water levels drop.

The environment in Northern Kenya supports many species not seen in other parts of the country such as the Grevy's zebra with saucerlike ears and narrower stripes. There are only about 10,000 left as they are hunted for their skins. The reticulated giraffe is found only here.

There are plenty of National Parks in this part of Kenya. On the eastern shores of Lake Turkana is the Sibilois National Park, just N of Isiolo you will find Samburu, Buffalo Spring and Shaba National Reserves, all 3 along the banks of the Ewaso Nyiro River covering an area of some 300 sq km. Further N still are the Parks at Maralal, Losai and Marsabit.

Travelling in Northern Kenya is a real adventure as there is almost no public transport in this desolate region. In fact, there is little traffic of any kind making hitching an option only for those with plenty of time on their hands. The western approach from Kitale is the simplest way for independent travellers without

vehicles as there is transport to Kalokol on the lake on a fairly regular basis. Driving yourself is a possibility (a 4-wheel drive is imperative), though this is not exactly trouble free. You will need to bring a number of tools in case of breakdown or getting stuck in the sand: a jack, sand ladders, a shovel and a rope. Also, you need to bring plenty of petrol, as it is in particularly short supply.

An alternative method of exploring Northern Kenya is to go on an organised tour. There are a number of organisations running tours, among them: *Best Camping*, PO Box 40223, Nairobi, T 28091; *Birds Paradise Tours Ltd*, PO Box 22121, Nairobi, T 25898. Offers both overland and flying safaris; *Safari Camp Services* PO Box 44801, Nairobi, T 28936; *Special Camping Safaris*, PO Box 51512, Nairobi, T 338325; *Zirkuli Expeditions*, PO Box 34548, Nairobi, T 23949; *Turkana Air Safaris*, PO Box 41078, Nairobi, T 26623. Air safaris only.

Most operators offer a 8-9 day tour heading up the Rift Valley to stop at Lake Baringo going on to Maralal and then to Lake Turkana via Baragoi and South Horr. The return journey goes via Samburu National Park and Buffalo Springs National Reserve. Some go via the Marsabit National Reserve crossing the Koroli Desert. Safaris cost between US$150 and US$180 which include transport, food and camping. Most use open-sided 4-wheel drive trucks, not built for comfort but sturdy and reliable. If you have a bit more money to spend, some companies arrange flying safaris. The flying safaris usually go to the western shores of the lake using the *Lake Turkana Lodge* on Ferguson's Gulf as a base. The cost is around US$320 for 5 days.

Another consideration when exploring this region is the time of year. The majority of the inhabitants are Muslim and will adhere to Ramadan, a month of fasting. During Ramadan most stores and hotel is are closed through daylight hrs, though public transport and official business should continue as normal. The times of Ramadan vary each year but in 1995 it starts 31st Jan, and in 1996 on 21st Jan.

The recent problems in Sudan and

Somalia, and the influx of refugees into Kenya from these countries, means there is a high military presence in the N. Vehicles are escorted by armed guards, road blocks are common and vehicle searches are a part of everyday life. However, it is rare that this level of precaution is required. On the whole it is a safe area to travel, and you are assured a warm welcome whereever you go. The only area for which this may not be true is travelling N of Isiolo into the far northeast.

Marich Pass

If you are coming up into Northern Kenya from Kitale, you travel a glorious route through the highlands, past the **Saiwa Swamp National Park** (see section on National Parks, page 172), through the northern gorges of the **Cherangani Hills**, coming into the desert plains through the **Marich Pass**. The views are incredible, looking down onto the plains from the lush highlands. There isn't much happening around here, the only town in these parts is **Ortum** where you should be able to find accommodation though it is pretty basic. If you do intend to stop and explore the area, the best place to stay is the **Marich Pass Field Studies Centre** (see below). This is an educational facility set up for groups to study various aspects of the environment in this area but it welcomes independant travellers. The centre has cordoned off about 12 ha of wilderness and acts as a haven for species in the region including monkeys and baboons (who now live here) and has visits from wart hog, antelope, elephants and buffalo, as well as several species of birds.

Places of interest

Mount Sekerr is a few km from the Study Centre and is a fairly easy climb. The views of the top (3,326m) are great looking onto forest glades and open moors.

Cherangani Hills is a good place to base yourself to explore (see Northern Rift Valley, page 91, offering some of the best walking in Kenya away from other tourists.

Elgeyo Escarpment About 1½ hrs from the centre, with spectacular views out over the Kerio Valley.

South Turkana National Reserve is just NE of the Marich Pass Field Studies Centre. Used by Turkana herdsmen as grazing land.

Local information

● Where to stay

E *Marich Pass Field Studies Centre*, T 0321 31541. Banda accommodation. There are toilets, showers, firewood and drinking water, a basic restaurant, and local shops for provisions. There is no petrol available. **E** *Camping*, also available at the Field studies Centre (above).

● Transport

Road The Pass is about 70km from *Kitale* going N. You can also reach it from *Eldoret* via Kabarnet and then on through the Kerio Valley joining the Kitale-Lodwar road near Kapenguria. The other way is from *Lake Baringo* across the Kerio Valley though this way involves travelling a track through the northern face of the Cherangani Hills which becomes impassable after heavy rains when the streams which cross the track flood the road. The centre itself is off the main Kitale-Lodwar road to the N. It is clearly signposted N of the Sigor-Tot junction at Marich Pass. There is no public transport.

Lodwar

The only town of any size in the NW of the region is Lodwar, the administrative centre. It is not nearly so isolated as in the past due to the opening of a surfaced road from the highlands and air connections to Nairobi, but it is still very much a backwater town with a pleasant enough atmosphere. It is currently the boom town in the region because of the possibility of oil discoveries, the development of the fishing industry at the lake, and the extension of a surfaced road from Kitale. This is a useful base if you intend to explore the lake from the western side. There is both a bank, though do not rely on it taking travellers cheques, and a Post Office in town. The local people, predominately Turkana, are persistent in attempt to sell their crafts, but it is generally done in a friendly spirit.

Local information

● Where to stay

At the moment most is at the bottom end of the market, though a luxury hotel is planned just outside the town by the Turkwel River. You will need a room with both a fan and mosquito protection if you intend to get any sleep. **D** *Turkwel*, T 21201. Best accomodation in town. Rooms come with a fan and bathroom. For slightly more you can hire a self-contained cottage with a full breakfast included in the price. Bar is popular with Lingala music playing into the small hours

E *Mombasa* next to the JM Bus office is the best in this price range. **E** *Mawoitorong Guest House and Conference Centre*, just outside of town to the S. The centre was set up to support single mothers and drought victims but will take travellers.

● Transport

Road Buses go between here and *Kitale* daily, taking around 7 hrs. There are also a few matatus which work the route though whether they reach their final destination depends on the number of passengers. The bus leaves from Kitale at 1500 and leaves Lodwar for Kitale at 0700. It is wise to take water and food for the trip as breakdowns and delays are common on this trip. Another point worth remembering is to book your seat on the return to Kitale the night before as the bus gets very full.

Lake Turkana – West

From this side of the Lake it is possible to access Central Island National Park. The main virtue of this approach to the Lake is accessibility, as it is only 35km from Lodwar.

Kalokol

This is the nearest town to the lakeshore, a small and simple place, and the heat is quite oppresive. It is a few km from here to the lakeshore itself.

To get to the lake itself you will need to walk out to the Italian-sponsored fish processing plant (you can ask for a guide form *Oyavo's Hotel* if you want one). **Ferguson's Gulf** is the most accessible part of the lake, but not the most attractive. There are loads of birds here particularly flamingos, and a number of hippos and crocodiles making swimming a fairly exciting activity. If you do intend to swim, ask the local people where to go.

To get onto the lake you can hire a boat from *Turkana Lodge* at Ferguson's Gulf to take you to the **Central Island National Park**. This is expensive: a cruiser costs around US$100 for 8 or a long-boat for 4 costs US$45, but is well worth the trip. You will also be asked for a US$15 entrance fee by the park game wardens. The island is just 5km sq with 3 small volcanoes on it. There are many reptiles on the island and if you arrive around Apr-May, you can witness crocodiles hatching and sprinting, squealing, down to one of the crater lakes. It is possible to negotiate with a local fisherman to take you out on his craft, though remember that the lake's squalls are a real danger, and there are crocodiles.

En route to Kalokol look out for the standing stones of **Namotunga** which are have a spiritual meaning to the Turkana who gather here in Dec.

● Where to stay & eat A *Lake Turkana Fishing Lodge*, just across Feruson's Gulf from Kalakol, PO Box 74609, Nairobi, T 760226, F 760546. Aimed at the top end of the market with self-contained bandas. This has a beautiful view across the lake and gets quite busy at weekends when parties from Nairobi are flown in, but is pretty deserted the rest of the time. Set menu, which is changed regularly. Good fish. **E** *Oyavo's*, in Kalokol. Best of the cheaper places. The rooms are clean and cooler than you would expect, with palm leaf thatch roofs. Food is basic, fish and rice, but sufficient, and there are warm beers and sodas.

● Transport Road Buses go from **Lodwar** at 0500 (the driver honks his horn to announce his departure) arriving at Kalekol an hour and a half later.

Eliye Springs

A far pleasanter place to see the Lake from and the springs themselves under the palm trees bubble up warm water. However, you will need a vehicle to get here. Also, there is nowhere to stay, the only lodge being closed, and facilities are virtually non-existent. There is a small village nearby where you can get some food and drink. The turn off for Eliye Springs is about halfway along the Lodwar to Kalekol road. As it is only 35 km from Lodwar, your best bet would be to base yourself there, and travel up to the Springs.

Lake Turkana – East

Exploring the Lake from the east is far more exciting than the W, and you pass through a number of national reserves. Driving here takes skills and steel nerves and you will need a 4-wheel drive vehicle. Few of the roads are surfaced, and the main A2 road is tricky to say the least. Avoid the rainy season as some routes become impassable. Public transport is available for most of the way, though not as easy as on the W.

Isiolo

Your starting point for travelling this way is likely to be from Isiolo, 50 km N of Meru, which is why it is included it in this section though strictly it is in the Central Highlands. It is a lively market town and is the last place with good facilities on your journey further N. There are a number of petrol stations, a bank and a post office (the last town to have these facilities until you reach either Maralal or Marsabit). It is also the last place to have a good supply of provisions, including an excellent fruit and vegetable market.

Isiolo is the nearest town to explore the **National Reserves** at **Samburu**, **Buffalo Springs** and **Shaba,** all grouped together 40 km to the N (see National Park Sections, page 191).

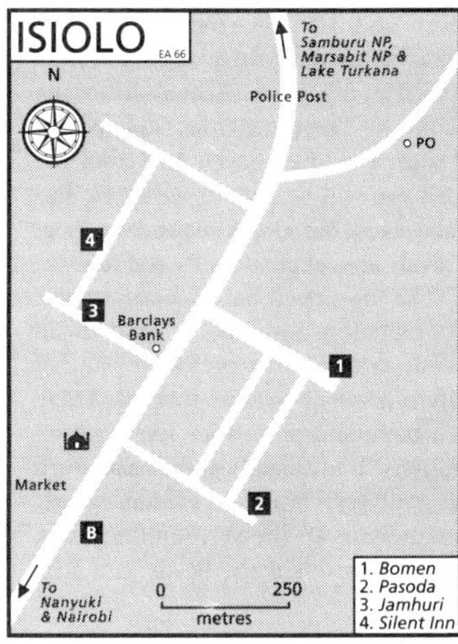

• **Where to stay & drink** **C** *Bomen*, T 0165 2225. Offers excellent value, relative luxury before roughing it trekking further N. All rooms have en suite bathrooms and they are well furnished. The hotel does excellent food and cold beers. **D** *Pasoda Lodge*, good double rooms with bath. Restaurant. **E** *Jamhuri Guest House*, best of the cheap hotels and has been popular with travellers for years. The rooms are clean, have mosquito nets and the communal showers have hot water. You are ensured a warm welcome by the hosts here. **E** *Silent Inn* Good value and it is quite quiet.

• **Transport Road** Buses leave from Nairobi daily at 0700 and 1900 taking around 7 hrs. Buses run from Isiolo to Marsabit and Moyale on Tue, Thu and Sat taking around 6 hrs to Marsabit and a further 6 hrs on to Moyale.

Wamba

A small town 90 km NW of Isiolo, and 55 km from the Samburu National Reserve. It is a useful place to stock up on fresh meat and other provisions. Also, there is **E** *Saudia Lodge* off the main street where you can get sound food and lodging.

Maralal

High up in the hills looks down onto the Lerochi Plateau, about 240 km from

Meru and 160 km from Nyahururu. Long before the British administrators moved in, this was a spiritual site for the Samburu. The route from Isiolo passes though a wildlife haven and from the road you will be able to see zebra, impala, eland, buffalo, hyena and warthog, a lovely area of gentle hills and forests.

The town itself has all basic amenities including a number of good cheap hotels as this is the preferred route of safaris going up to Lake Turkana. There is a bank and post office and 2 petrol stations. Traditionally garbed Samburu are still very much in evidence here, brightening up the surroundings with their skins, blankets, beads and hair styles.

You can arrange to join a safari to Lake Turkana from here costing US$300 all in and taking 8 days.

• **Where to stay and eat** **A** *Maralal Safari Lodge*, PO Box 45155, Nairobi, T Nairobi 211124, F Nairobi 214261. A series of cottages with a main bar and restaurant. There is also a souvenir shop. The lodge is by a water hole which attracts a wide range of wildlife, and it is a nice place to go and have a beer (you don't need to be a resident to eat or drink here). **C-E** *Maralal Hostel*, About 3km out of town with excellent facilities (a library, self-service restaurant and bar, shop and a lounge). Comfortable bandas or dormitory accommodation. **D** *Buffalo Lodge*, good value. The bar here is lively. Video room. **E** *Camping*, available at the *Maralal Hostel*, with good facilities.

Baragoi

This next largish settlement on the route up to the Lake and marks the end of the Elbarta plains, climbing into the mountains. There are a few shops here and you should be able to get petrol (sold out of barrels). There is **Camping** about 4km N of town through a small gully. There are toilets and showers, and Samburu warriors will guard your possessions for around US$2 a night. You can get food in the town itself from ♦*Wid Wid Inn* on the main street.

South Horr

The nearest village to the southern end of Lake Turkana. The village itself is set in a beautiful canyon and is an oasis of green between 2 extinct volcanos (Mount Nyiro and Mount Porale). There is a Catholic Mission here with a nice site for **Camping** nearby. There are a few **hotels** offering accomodation and food, though you will need to order your meal well in advance of actually eating it. There is also a **bar** with plenty of atmosphere, though there are only warm drinks. It would appear there is no petrol for sale here. There are some great walks in the mountain forests all around you and you could either hike through (it's a good idea to take a guide) or go on a camel trek (US$5-10 a day for a camel).

Loyangalini

One of the biggest villages on the lake shore, and is a collection of traditional huts, with thatched grass and galvanised iron roofs. The barren lava beds at the southern end of Lake Turkana peter out into the waters of the lake itself. The high salinity and soda mean nothing much grows around the shores.

• **Where to stay** **A +** *Oasis Lodge*, PO Box 34464, Nairobi, T 339025, Nairobi 750034 F Nairobi 750035. Bungalows with electricity. It has a beautiful swimming pool and cold beers. Non-residents are charged US$9 entrance. **A** *El-Molo Camp*, well equipped with a swimming pool and a bar. There is also a restaurant which appears to open when you want. Camping costs US$3 or there are bandas with full board available. You will need to bring your own fuelwood. The **E** *Camping*, at El-Molo Camp. You need to supply your own cooking fuel.

• **Useful addresses** The village itself has a Post Office though no bank and no garage.

MARSABIT TO MOYALE

Matthew's Range Off the Isiolo to Marsabit road, is just N of Wamba. This mountain range is thickly forested with its highest point reaching 2,375m. The area supports elephants, rhino, buffalo and other species and is in the process of being turned into a national reserve for rhino. There are also a spectacular array of butterflies and some unusual vegetation including cycad plants and giant cedars. There is **Camping** nearby on the grounds of a derelict research centre, with no facilities, by a river, a beautiful spot. You are likely to be met by Samburu who will offer to guide you around the range for a small fee. The campsite is not easy to find, so ask for directions as there are tracks going all over the place. You will need to be self-sufficient here, so bring drinking water, food and fuelwood.

Marsabit

Rising to a 1,000m above the surrounding plains, Marsabit is permanently green. The hills around the town are thickly forested making a nice change to the desert which surrounds the area. The main inhabitants of the town are the Rendille who dress in elaborate beaded necklaces and sport wonderful hair styles. They are nomadic people keeping to their traditional customs of nomadism only visiting the town to trade. **Marsabit National Park** is nearby and houses a wide variety of wildlife though it is difficult to see much through the thick forest (see National Parks section, page 185).

There is a bank and post office here, shops, bars, restaurants, hotels and 3 petrol stations. This is also a major trading centre in the area of livestock and the administrative capital in the district.

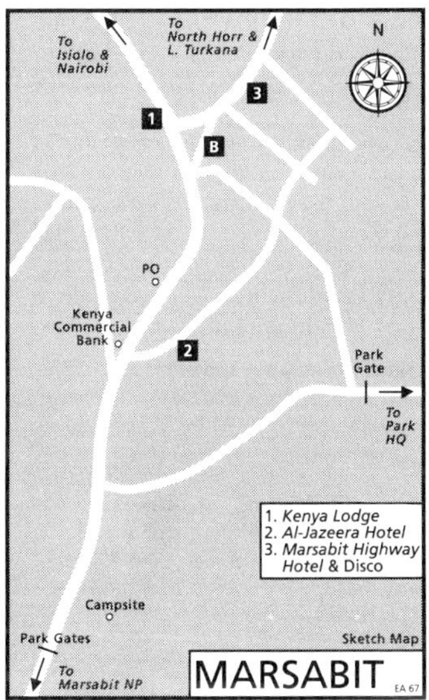

• **Where to stay, food and drink** **E** *Kenya Lodge*, good value. There is a good restaurant attached serving Ethiopian style food including ngera (pancakes made from fermented batter) and stews. The cheapest place in town is **E** *Al-Jazeera*, very inexpensive. Communal showers. Bar and restaurant.

• **Entertainment** Disco at *Marsabit Highway Hotel* on Fri and Sat nights. Bar stays open every night until 0200.

• **Transport Air** It is possible to charter a plane from Wilson Airport, Nairobi or take one of the small private airlines directly to Marsabit (see Airlines Domestic and Charter, see page 205). **Road** Buses run from Isiolo to Marsabit on Tue, Thu and Sat taking around 6 hrs. They return on Wed, Fri and Sun though they may be delayed if there aren't enough passengers. All vehicles travelling around Marsabit, Isiolo and Moyale must travel in convoy to minimise the likelihood of being attacked. The journey to Moyale can take up to 9 hrs passing through the Dida Galgalu Desert.

MARSABIT TO LAKE TURKANA

Maikona is a larger village with shops, but no lodges, though the Catholic Mission here is very friendly and is fairly sure to let you stay (donations gratefully received).

North of Loyangalani you come to **North Horr**. The Catholic Mission here may be able to supply you with petrol (at a price) or lodgings if necessary.

It is possible to strike S W from North

Horr to El Molo Bay on Lake Turkana (see above, page 157).

Moyale

Lies about 250km N of Marsabit and is on the Kenyan-Ethiopian border. This is a small town with a post office, basic shops and a police station which has only recently been supplied with electricity. It is developing slowly and there is now a bank here and 2 petrol stations.

• **Where to stay, eat and drink** E *Barissah*, where you can rent a bed for the night in an unlockable room for less than US$2. There are no showers, but you can have a bucket wash. If this is not available, try the E *Bismillahi Boarding & Lodging*, which has the same basic level of facilities but is slightly more expensive at US$2.50 per night. The ♦*Barissah Hotel*, has the only bar in town and has a simple restaurant attached.

• **Transport** Buses run from Isiolo to Marsabit and Moyale on Tue, Thu and Sat taking around 6 hrs to Marsabit and a further 6 hrs on to Moyale.

It should be possible to cross from here into Ethiopia, and it is reported that procedures are now much easier. In the past, officially only Kenyans and Ethiopians have been able to cross here. In practice a day crossing has been possible – the customs officials have been persuadable. On the Ethiopian side you used to have to go through the same rigmarole and were asked to leave your camera behind.

NORTH-EAST KENYA

The most remote part of the country is the NE, a vast wilderness with almost no signs that humans have ever been here. The attraction is the scale of the place. Endless blue skies and flat landscapes hardly broken by anything, produce a sense of solititude that is hard to experience anywhere else. The landscape is made up of tracts of desert and semi-desert barely broken by settlements and with almost no public transport. Its inaccessibility combined with security problems around the Somali border to make this area unappealing to even the most intrepid travellers – no tour companies operate in this region. Physically, the area is very flat with 2 important rivers flowing through, the Tana River and the Ewaso Nyiro. As you would expect, it is around these waterways that settlement is greatest and the national parks are based. The **Tana River Primate Reserve**, is based near Garsen though it is hard to get to. It was set up to protect the red colobus and crested mangabey monkeys (both endangered species). The other major national park in this region is **Meru National Park** based on the lowland plains east of the town of Meru (see National Parks section, see page 185). It is advisable to check on the security situation before visiting the park as there have been some unpleasant incidents between tourists and poachers who have decimated the elephant and rhino population here.

This area has a long-standing bad reputation, though much of it would seem to have more to do with prejudice than justified danger. The majority of people living in this area are ethnically Somali and before the creation of country boundaries pastoralists roamed the area freely. In fact in colonial days, the area was known as Somali country. As countries in the region gained independence, Somalis unsuccessfully tried to claim this area as part of Somalia. Shortly after, the area was closed to visitors by the Kenyan authorities who wished to drill for oil. Years of neglect and almost no development leave it one of the poorest areas of the country. These problems have been exacerbated more recently by the civil war in Somalia resulting in a huge influx of refugees into NE Kenya. There are a number of refugee camps now set up for them (and for Somali-Kenyans who can no longer support their way of life in this barren area). Somalis are blamed for most of the poaching in the region. Poachers pose a real threat to tourists being heavily armed and quite willing to attack if they feel it is justified.

Garissa

This is the town in the NE that is closest to Nairobi both geographically and culturally. It is on an alternative route back from Lamu to Nairobi. There are shops for provisions, and petrol a bank. It is the administrative centre for the district. The heat is fierce and there is high humidity making it an unpleasant climate to stay in for long.

• **Where to stay & eat** **E** *Safari*, Clean rooms and running water. There is a restaurant attached with reasonable food. **E** *Garissa Guest House* Just outside of town. Simple but adequate.

• **Transport** **Air** There is a flight from Nairobi's Wilson Airport direct to Garissa if there is sufficient demand (see Airlines: Domestic and Charter, page 200). **Road** There are 3 bus routes travelling to and from Garissa. A bus goes from Eastleigh, **Nairobi** to Garissa direct on Mon, Wed, Fri and Sun leaving at 0800. The journey takes about 8 hrs. There is a bus from **Lamu** to Garissa leaving at 0700 and taking 8 – 10 hrs. The other route is between Garissa and **Mandera** at the junction of the Kenya, Ethiopia, Somalia border, going on to **Wajir** on Tue, Thu and Sat and travelling on the next day to Mandera. Returns from Mandera Thu, Sat and Mon, to Wajir, and on to Garissa the next day.

Wajir

This is 300 km from Isiolo along the most remote route in the country. The area is a vast scrubland which seems to go on for ever. Due to security problems in this area following the Somali war, this unappealing journey becomes even more difficult. If you are going to try it, check the route has not been closed before setting out.

The town of Wajir itself is growing. The population and atmosphere of the place has more Arab than African influences and is far more interesting to visit than Garissa. The settlement developed around wells have been fought over by rival clans for generations, water being such a valuable commodity in this area. In 1984, the rivalry between clans became more fierce than usual forcing the regional administration to act. It announced an amnesty for all those who surrendered their arms, but thousands of men and boys of one of the clans, the Degodia, did not avail themselves of this opportunity. They were rounded up to be interned by the government authorities in a military airstrip with no facilities where many died of exposure or dehydration. This tragedy has made the relationship between local people and the administration poor to say the least.

The **market** here is quite different from anything else you are likely to see in Kenya. It consists of a section of grass huts with a wide assortment of produce. Fruit and vegetables are not common, but you will find some beautiful pottery. A visit to the wells just outside of town to the N also also be quite interesting. A popular past time is to chew *miraa*, an appetite suppressant and mild stimulant very popular among Somali men.

• **Where to stay, eat and drink** **D** *Nairobi Hotel* Showers, bar and a restaurant. Good value. **E** *Malab*, by the bus station. Has a good reputation with fans and mosquito nets.

• **Transport** **Air** There is an airstrip (see Airlines: Domestic and Charter, page 200). **Road** Buses from **Garissa** to Wajir on Tue, Thu and Sat and travelling on the next day to **Mandera**. Returns from Mandera Thu, Sat and Mon, and on to Garissa the next day.

Mandera

The furthest point in Kenya, 370 km NE further on from Wajir, on the Ethiopian, Somali and Kenyan border. The war has made this a particularly foolhardy expedition at the moment with marauding rival Somali clans. The main line of contact is on the private aircraft who fly in shipments of miraa. In the past, trade and communication with Somalia was more important than with Kenya as Mandera is far closer to Mogadishu, the capital of Somalia, than to Nairobi.

Until recently Mandera was a fairly small border town servicing the local community. Since the Somali civil war, it has become the home to literally tens of thousands of Somalians putting an impossible strain on resources. The lack of water, always been a problem, has become critical. Also, the stability of the place is severely tested by the prevailing conditions. *Miraa* is the big business in town.

• **Where to stay, eat and drink D** ***Mandera County Council Resthouse***, just to east of centre, fans, showers, own bathrooms. **E** ***Jabane***, town centre. Has showers and fans and reasonable restaurant. **E** ***Mombasa Inn***, town centre. Simple. Basic restaurant.

• **Services** There is a Post Office, Police Station and bank.

• **Transport Air** There is an airstrip with several flights a day transporting *miraa* (see Airlines: Domestic and Charter, page 200). A flight costs US$50 to US$100 to Nairobi, depending on demand, and is negotiated with the *miraa* charterer. **Road** Buses from ***Wajir*** on Wed, Fri and Sun Return to Wajir Thu, Sat and Mon, and on to ***Garissa*** the next day.

SOUTH TO TANZANIA

CONTENTS

This section looks at Southern Kenya from Nairobi down to the Tanzania border, and Southeast to Kenya's coastline on the Indian Ocean. It is one of the most visited regions of the country with 4 of the country's major game parks. The Maasai Mara towards the W of the region bordering onto the Serengeti in Tanzania, is one of the most exciting game parks in the world, teeming with wildlife and the site of the quite spectacular wildebeest migration. It is also the most likely place to see lions in Kenya. The scenery here is wonderful, with Mount Kilimanjaro in the background acting as the perfect backdrop to miles and miles of arid savannah plains covered with fragile grasslands and scrub bush. Tsavo West and Tsavo East on either side of the Mombasa-Nairobi road make up the largest park in the country, and Amboseli National Park, is one of the most visited in the country. All the parks are described in detail in the section on the National Parks, page 172).

There are many points of interest off the Mombasa road. This road is one of the most important thoroughfares in the East Africa region as it runs the length of the country to Nairobi and then to Uganda, where it continues on to Kampala.

MOMBASA ROAD

NB Ensure you have sufficient fuel for your journey – some petrol stations often run out.

The Mombasa road starts as a continuation of the Uhuru Highway in Nairobi, passing the city's drive-in cinema and a number of housing estates. The first small town is **Athi River**, about 3km from Nairobi. There are abattoirs here for the Kenya Meat commission. C *Small World Country Club*, PO Box 78, (T 239) is open 24 hrs and is a lively spot; also D *Congress Club*, with accommodation, a restaurant and discos at the weekends. The turning for **Machakos** is on the left just before the toll station across the Athi River.

Continuing along the road, the route passes through the **Kaputei Plains** with the Ngong Hills in the far distance. Most of this area is large scale cattle ranches with herds of gazelle and antelope. It is along here that you turn right for **Kajiado** and **Magadi**. The next section of the route is through semi-arid country broken by the **Ukambani Hills**. The road up this long steep slope is poor, as years of heavy trucks making the laborious climb have dug deep ruts into the road. The only town you pass along here is **Kima**, meaning mincemeat in Kiswahili. Kima was so named after a British Railway Police Assistant Superintendent who was eaten by a lion. Charles Ryall, using himself as bait, was trying to ambush a lion which had been attacking railway staff and passengers. Unfortunately the ambush went horribly wrong when he fell asleep on the job.

Past Kima is the town of **Sultan Hamud**. It sprung up during the making of the railway at Mile 250 where it was visited by the then ruler of Zanzibar and named after him. It has hardly changed since that time and is a pleasant enough place to stop off for a soda and snack. Just to the SE lie the alluvial **Maasai Plains** and the road for **Amboseli National Park**. To get to Amboseli, you need to take the road towards Kibiki where there is a cattle market on Fridays visited by hundreds of Maasai and Akamba herders. The route continues S to Olitokitok on the slopes of Kilimanjaro.

Back on the Mombasa road, you are now passing through Maasai country, which is primarily featureless scrubland. There is a lodge at Kiboko which is about a third of the way through the journey (160km from Nairobi) and a good place to stop off for some refreshment. **C** *Hunter's Lodge* is run by the wife of J A Hunter, a professional hunter with the Game Department. The gardens are quite pleasant with hundreds of species of birds, and there are wonderful views out over the Koboko River. There is a swimming pool at the lodge though there is rarely any water to go in it.

If you fancy a break in your journey, an excellent place to stay is at **Makindu**, about 40 km from Kiboko where a Sikh temple of the Guru Nanak faith offers free accommodation and food for travellers (offerings gratefully received). This is particularly handy on the return from Mombasa if you do not want to get back in to Nairobi late at night. Slightly further along the road (in the direction of Mombasa) is the *Makindu Handicrafts Co-operative* where around 50 people handcraft carvings for the tourist market, mostly of animals.

The road continues its route passing into more lush pastures with a proliferation of the wonderful and rather grotesque baobabs (see **Wildlife Section**, page W49). The main trading centre at **Kibwezi** has some cheap places to stay including the E *Riverside Lodge*. There is no electricity in town as yet. This is the most important region in the country for sisal growing. Honey production is also much in evidence and you are likely to be offered some from sellers at the side of the road. Do try it before you buy to check its quality as sometimes it is adulterated with sugar. From Kibwezi the road passes through heavily cultivated land to the boundary of Akamba country at **Mtito Andei** – meaning vulture forest – about half way between Nairobi and Mombasa. There is a petrol station, a few places to eat and a curio shop. It is also the main gate to Tsavo West (see National Parks, page 194). Places to stay include the A *Tsavo Inn*, and the D *Okay Safari Lodge*.

From here the road runs through the centre of the parks Tsavo West and Tsavo East for around 80 km. In the past, herds of elephants could be seen crossing the road in the grasslands making progress along this route slow. Now the grasslands are reverting back to thick brush and scrublands as there are so few elephants left (a combination of hunting and drought). On the right you will pass the Mbololo Hills Prison, formerly Manyani Detention Camp where the colonial forces incarcerated Mau-Mau freedom fighters. Today there is a prison industry showroom with handcrafted furniture and a prison farm shop with a selection of produce.

Voi

The capital of this region, a rapidly developing industrial and commercial centre. This was the first upcountry railhead on the railway where passengers would make an overnight stop. There are a number of bungalows which were built in the early years of the century to accommodate passengers and provide dinner, bed and breakfast, this is no longer offered as you can dine, sleep and breakfast on the train. Voi is a good place to look for lodgings if you are visiting Tsavo East as it is not far from the gates and has many excellent cheap places.

• **Where to stay D** *Jambo Guest House*, near the bus station has cheap rooms with bath though it can be a bit noisy. **D** *Vuria Lodging*, fans and mosquito nets in all rooms and flush toilets.

• **Transport Rail** This is a major stop on the railway, though the train pulls into Voi from Nairobi at around 0300 and from Mombasa at 1200. **Road** There are also buses coming and going all day long between Mombasa and

Nairobi. Buses leave to connect Voi with the border town of **Taveta** at 0930 and 1500.

Voi to Mombasa

From Voi the road runs through the Taru Desert for another 150 km down to Mombasa. This area is an arid, scorched wilderness and there is little sign of life. You will see several small quarries. These supply many of the hotels on the coast with natural stone tiles used in bathrooms and patios. The main settlement is **Mackinnon Road** with the Sayyid Baghali Shah Mosque as its only landmark. 30 km along the route you come to **Samburu** where to the left is a road to the **Shimba Hills**. Another 30 km brings you to the busy market centre of **Mariakani**, a place of palm groves and an atmosphere quite different from up-country Kenya. For the next 90 km the scenery becomes progressively more tropical, the heat increases, as does the humidity and the landscape changes to coconut palms, papaya and other coastal vegetation. Eventually you enter the industrial suburbs of Mombasa.

Machakos

Machakos has a long history as the capital of the Ukambani – the Akamba – who have lived in this part of Kenya for around 500 years. The town is named after Masaku, the Akamba chief who predicted the coming of the railway the iron snake and the plagues which followed (both smallpox and rinderpest decimated animal and human populations in the region). He died at the turn of the century.

Machakos was also important in colonial times. John Ainsworth, Britain's first upcountry administrator made his headquarters here in 1889 and built a mudbrick fort, the site of which is on the right of the main road just N of town toward Nairobi. Reverend Stuart Watt and his wife arrived soon after and set up a mission which is now the Kenya Orchards Mua Hills Jam Factory. In 1895 the Church Missionary Society arrived and introduced wheat into the area. The importance of this area to the Imperial British East Africa Company made Machakos the ideal place to set up the first inland African Training Centre.

Little sign of its past remains to be seen except the clock tower which was erected in 1956 to mark a visit from Princess Margaret, sister of the British Queen. The clock no longer works. However, the tree lined streets and attractive old buildings make it a pleasant town set in the Mua Hills, and the local people (who are predominantly Kamba) are very friendly. The colourful market selling locally grown produce as well as sisal baskets and other handicraft gives the town a bustling atmosphere.

The weaving of sisal baskets is a major occupation of women in this area. A good place to get one is from the Machakos Handicrafts Centre, a self-help women's group. There is a small shop full of finished and half-finished baskets. The ones without leather straps are far cheaper, but all are considerably better value than in Nairobi and there is more choice.

About 75km out of Machakos along the road towards Kitui you come across the small village of **Wamanyu** which is the centre of wood carving activities in the country. A great grass rectangle in the centre of the village is surrounded by huts sitting in an ocean of wood shavings accumulated from years of work. Most of the wood carvings end up in Nairobi, but are considerably cheaper if bought here.

• **Where to stay, eat and drink D** *Kafoca Club*, T 0145 21933. Near the market. Pleasant, though quite basic. Good restaurant. **D** *Masaku Motel*, T 0145 21745. Close to town centre. Inexpensive but adequate. ♦♦*Ivory Restaurant*, grills and some local dishes.

• **Transport** There is no shortage of transport between **Nairobi** and Machakos, you can take your pick from buses, matatus or the Peugeot taxis which run from Nairobi's country bus station on Pumwani Rd at the SE end of River Rd. You should not have to wait more than half an hr for something. There is also transport from **Mombasa**, though not as frequent.

Kitui

Kitui is in the middle of a semi-arid area which is frequently affected by drought causing malnutrition in this poor part of the country. Despite it being so close to Nairobi, it is quite undeveloped, and there is not much here of interest to travellers. Kitui used to be on the trade route of Swahili poeple in the nineteenth century, though there are few signs of this now apart from the mango trees planted in the town and the presence of the descendants of the Swahili traders.

• **Where to stay** **E** *Gold Spot*. Just to the east of the market. Own bathrooms. **E** *Kithomboani* Close to the market. Quite adequate.

• **Transport** There are 3 buses a day to and from **Nairobi**, and one bus to **Mombasa** leaving at 1900.

Kajiado

Directly S of Nairobi on the road to the Namanga border crossing to Tanzania. It is the administrative headquarters of southern Maasai-land at the southern corner of the Kaputei Plains which run between Machakos and Kajiado. The town is in the middle of bleak grasslands which show little sign of the abundance of zebra, wildebeest and giraffe which used to roam here. The town is very Maasai and shows signs of their preoccupation with cattle. Simple accommodation and food and drink are available.

• **Transport Road** The road to Kajiado forks right off the Mombasa highway just east of the Athi River crossing the Athi Plains. There are plenty of buses and matatus to Kajiado running between **Nairobi** and **Namanga**.

Oloitokitok

This is a busy Maasai town between the parks off the main road that runs from Amboseli in the SE through to the Kimana Gate of Tsavo West. It is a useful place to stay between the parks, has a busy thriving atmosphere and the best views of any town in the area of Kilimanjaro. It is also a border crossing to the Tanzanian town of Moshi. The town has a bank and a Post Office, and there are market days on Tue and Sat.

• **Where to stay, eat and drink** As you would expect in a busy market town, there are plenty of cheap and clean lodgings and places to eat and drink. **E** ***Mwalimu Lodge*** is popular.

• **Transport Road** There are buses and matatus along the road that links Oloitokitok with **Taveta**, running through Rombo (not marked on some maps), and thence to Voi. Transport is more available on Tue and Sat, the market days. There are matatus and buses, but less frequent, W to **Tsavo** on the Mombasa Rd; east to **Namanga**; N to **Emali** on the Mombasa Rd. A route S runs into **Tanzania**, crossing the border at Kibouni, and on to Moshi. However, it is better to take the road through Kenya to Taveta and cross at Himo.

Taveta

Taveta is a small town on the Tanzanian border next to Tsavo West National Park. It is fairly remote and inaccessible, but electricity was recently brought to the town and a bank has opened.

Places of interest

The town is near the privately run **Taita Hills Game Sanctuary**, which are actually S of the Taita Hills about 15km W of Mwatate. The Sanctuary is run by the *Hilton Hotel* chain who have 2 upmarket lodges here for visitors on flying safari visits from the coastal resorts. The sanctuary is a pleasant place to visit with a good selection of wildlife for most of the year. Unfortunately it is extremely difficult to get to without your own transport as there is no public transport and it is rather off the regular tourist track and therefore not good hitching territory.

The **Taita Hills** are quite beautiful, densely cultivated and highly populated

– in total contrast to the vast empty plains below. The fertile hills have made the Taita-speaking population relatively prosperous compared to other parts of the region. **Wundanyi** is the district capital here and the best accommodation is just outside town at the D *Mwasungia Scenery Guest House*. This is popular with people throughout the hills and consequently has a lively atmosphere and good food. On market days, Tue and Fri, it gets particularly busy.

Just outside Wundanyi is the **Cave of Skulls**, where the Taita would put the skulls of their ancestors. Traditionally, people would visit these caves if they needed to contemplate issues that were troubling them. The tradition is dying down as Christianity takes over from older beliefs, though the spot is left undisturbed. Its possible to ask someone from Wundanyi to guide you there.

Lake Chala is just N of Taveta, part of the lake being in Kenya and part being in Tanzania. This deepwater crater lake is about 4 sq km and is totally clear. It is a tranquil, beautiful place to explore by foot with **Camping** possible, though you will need to bring all your own supplies. Getting there is not hard as there is a bus once a day from Oloitokitok, or Taveta.

Grogan's Castle is an extraordinary construction on an isolated hill quite near the main road. It was built in the 1930 by Ewart Grogan, a settler from South Africa, a complicated man with some good and some unattractive qualities. In order to prove his worth to his prospective father-in-law, he walked from the Cape to Cairo. He later brutally flogged 3 of his servants for showing disrespect to a white woman, and received a conviction for this from a local magistrate. He amassed considerable wealth, some of it in sisal, and the castle was planned as a resort for the sisal estate managers in the area. It has now fallen into disrepair, but retains spectacular views over Kilimanjaro and Lake Jipe.

Local information

● Where to stay

B *Chala*, T 0149 2212. On the right hand side of the railway level crossing is the most comfortable hotel in town with a good restaurant and bar. Staff will be able to help arrange excursions for you to points of interest in the area.

D *Kuwoka Lodging House*, T 0149 228. Clean and pleasant and the best in this price bracket.

● Places to eat

The best places to eat in town are ♦♦*Taveta*, near the bus station, and the ♦♦*Taveta Border*, which has good fresh samosas, though food in Taveta is quite good on the whole, and relatively varied.

● Transport

Road There are irregular matatus going to and from **Voi**, public transport being at its best on market days, Wed and Sat. The road passes S of the Taita Hills past Wundanyi through Tsavo West.

Rail The 1993 accord between the leaders of Kenya, Tanzania and Uganda included a resolution to reopen the rail link between **Voi**, through Taveta, on to **Moshi** in Tanzania, and then to Tanga and Dar es Salaam. When the service does start, it will probably be weekly.

Lake Jipe

Straddles Kenya and Tanzania fed from streams on the Tanzanian side and from Mount Kilimanjaro. There are a number of small fishing villages around the Kenyan side, and its SE shores lie inside Tsavo West National Park. Again, this is a peaceful place to stop off where you will be able to see hippos and crocodiles, and plenty of bird life. You can hire a boat to take you round the lake.

● **Where to stay** **A** *Lake Jipe Safari Lodge*, PO Box 31097, Nairobi, T Nairobi 227623, Tlx Nairobi 25508, provides accommodation in bandas, and arranges trips on the Lake. **E** *Bandas* and **E** *Camping* are available by the park entrance. The nearest settlement is **Mukwajoni**, a fishing village about 2 km away from Tsavo West National Park. Supplies in the village are limited, except for fish, so bring everything you want from Taveta.

● **Transport** Limited services, basically confined to a few matatus on Taveta's market days on Wed and Sat. Depart Taveta 0600 and 1500 and leaves Jipe at 0730 and 1630.

NATIONAL PARKS & RESERVES

Contents

Maps

Kenya has many national parks and game reserves in which live a dazzling array of animals, birds, reptiles and plant species. They rate as amongst the best parks in the whole of Africa, and are certainly the most accessible in East Africa. Marine life is also excellent and is preserved in the marine national parks off Malindi and Watamu. Along with the wildlife, some of the parks have been gazetted to preserve the vegetation and unique locations such as Mount Kenya or the Kakamega Forest.

The Kenyan government has long been aware that the attraction of the country to tourists is its wildlife and since 1989 have been keen to ensure it is available in abundance for tourists to see. Richard Leakey was appointed head of the Ministry of Wildlife in 1989 and put in force some drastic methods to reduce poaching. Poaching patrols are well trained and well equipped with Land Rovers and guns and there are extremely stiff penalties for anyone found poaching. In 1990, 200 US-trained paramilitary personnel were deployed on shoot-to-kill patrols. The battle against poachers is a hard one. It is easy to see why people faced with poverty would resort to an occupation which appears to have such high risks, but also such high rewards (up to US$300 for a kilo of elephant tusk and US$2,000 for rhino horn).

The Kenyan government's policies have been controversial, and it has struggled to strike a balance between the demands of conservation and the needs of local people. Notwithstanding these problems Kenya's wildlife is one of its greatest assets and many of the parks and reserves offer a glimpse of a totally unspoilt, peaceful world.

Most of the game parks have to be explored from inside a vehicle, for safety reasons. The exceptions to this are Hell's Gate, parts of Nakuru and Saiwa Swamp National Park near Kitale.

The following is a guide to most of the parks and reserves, with just a paragraph on the smaller places saying where they are and what you are likely to see in them. For more details on nearby facilities such as transport, food and accommodation please look under the relevant regional section.

GENERAL INFORMATION

Park classifications

A number of different terms are used to describe the parks and reserves of Kenya.

National Parks are wildlife and botanical sanctuaries and form the mainstay of Kenya's tourist industry. They are conservation points for educational and recreational enjoyment.

National Reserves are similar to parks but under certain conditions the land may be used for other purposes than nature conservation. Thus, some controlled agriculture may be allowed; in marine reserves there may be monitored fishing.

Biosphere Reserves were set up in 1989 and are protected environments which contain unique landforms, landscapes and systems of land use. There are 4 in Kenya, and only 271 in the rest of the world. Specific scientific research projects are attached to them, funded by UNESCO. They are protected under national and international law

World Heritage Sites are even more strictly protected under international law. Kenya signed the convention in 1989 but as yet no sites have been scheduled. Sites being considered are the Gede ruins, the Koobi Fora fossil beds, Mount Kenya, Hell's Gate and the Maasai Mara.

Costs

Theoretically, the pricing of each of the national parks is the same at around US$20 per person. The only different ones are the Maasai Mara and the Samburu—Buffalo Springs—Shaba complex which are administered locally as national reserves and set their own prices.

When to visit

You are likely to see more animals during the dry seasons as they will congregate round water ways. Also, driving during the wet season becomes far harder in deep mud as none of the park roads are paved. However, prices can be up to a third lower in lodges during the rainy seasons.

Where to stay

Accommodation in the parks tends to be of 2 types, the ultra-expensive lodges or camp sites. There is little or nothing in between. If you do not fancy camping and cannot afford the lodges, you may be able to stay in a nearby town and enter your chosen park daily though this is not an option for all parks such as the Masai Mara or Amboseli in the S. If you are on a luxury holiday, accommodation is excellent and there are a number of hotels in each of the major parks offering superb facilities. Camping is possible in designated sites (for obvious reasons it is not wise camping outside these areas in a park full of wild animals). You will need to bring your own tent and facilities tend to be extremely limited.

Self-drive This is the most convenient method of getting around the parks offering you greater freedom of movement, though it can be quite expensive. You will usually need to have a 4-wheel drive vehicle, but it is not absolutely essential in many parks and outside the rainy season. If you are driving yourself, it is invariably an advantage to hire a local guide – the habits of the animals change, and the guide will know where to find them. Driving at night in the parks is prohibited.

Tours

Arranged by many different companies and can be booked in Europe or in Kenya. There are a number of different types ranging from the luxurious to budget (see Tour Agents, page 199).

ABERDARES NATIONAL PARK

The Aberdares is a range of mountains to the W of Mount Kenya in the central highlands of Kenya, and the national park encloses around 60 sq km and is one of Kenya's only virgin forest reserves. The Aberdares come to a peak at about 4,000m and the middle and upper reaches are densely forested with bamboo thickets and tangled jungle. The Kikuyu call these mountains *Nyandarua* (drying hide) and they were the home to guerillas fighters during the struggle for independence. Nowadays the mountains house leopard, bongo, buffalo and elephant. At about 3,500m, where the landscape opens up, you may see lions, serval cats and even bushbucks. Wildlife is comparatively scarce, but the views in the park are spectacular. Particularly good walks include hiking up the 3 peaks, Satima, Kinangop and Kipipiri. You can hire a guide to take you if you so wish.

This park is not often visited either by individual travellers or tour companies primarily because of the weather. It rains often and heavily making driving difficult and seeing things impossible. The park is often closed during the wet season as roads turn into mud slides.

Places of interest

The park is split into 2 sections, the high moorland and peaks and the lower salient which is dense rainforest and where much of the wildlife lives. The Salient slopes are closed to casual visitors, you will need to apply for keys to enter this area from the warden. There are a number of spectacular waterfalls in the park including the **Chania Falls** and the **Karuru Giant Falls**.

Costs

Daily fees are US$20 per person, US$4 to camp. Entry on foot is allowed only with the permission of the warden as is any mountain climbing.

Park information

● Where to stay

As accommodation is expensive and limited at the park, a sensible option is to stay at Nyeri (see page 76) and travel to the park from there by matatu. **A** *The Ark*, centre of the park. The costs include full board, transfer to the hotel but exclude park entry fees. Children under 7 are not allowed. You need to book in advance from *Lonrho Hotels*, Bruce House, Standard St, PO Box 58581, Nairobi, T Nairobi 723 776). **A** *Treetops* The main appeal is that Queen Elizabeth had her honeymoon here. The design – essentially a large tree house – is unique, but the small rooms are small with shared bathroom facilities. You will need to book in advance from *Block Hotels*, Rehema House, Standard St, PO Box 47557, Nairobi, T Nairobi 335 807).

D *Fishing Lodge*, T Mweiga 24. Offers self-catering accommodation in the high park. There are 2 stone-built cottages each with 3

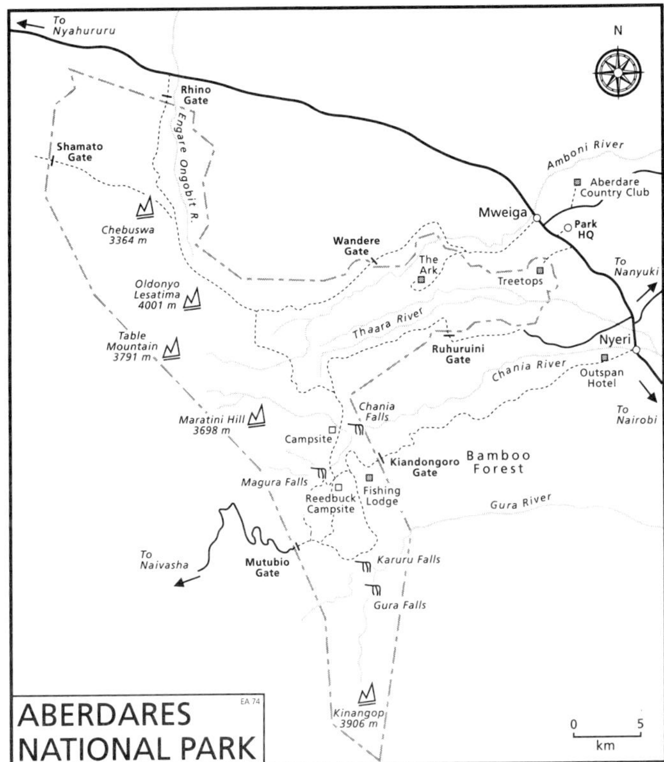

separate bedrooms of 2, 4 and 6 beds. You book your space with the warden at the front gate of the park. Facilites are shared by everyone and include an open-fire for cooking and a communal eating area. You will need to take everything with you except water, including firewood.

E *Camping*, there is a site near the fishing lodge though it is extremely basic.

● **Transport**

The nearest bases are at Naivasha or Nyeri and it is easy enough to get a matatu to the gates of the park. From **Naivasha** follow the signs along the Upland road until you reach Ndunyu Njeru. From here the road only continues to the park, there are no services (food, petrol etc) from this point onwards. From **Nyeri** there are a number of matatus to the park, or you can rent a car and drive yourself. If you hire a vehicle, you will need a 4-wheel drive.

AMBOSELI NATIONAL PARK

Background

This park has long been one of the most visited in Kenya, and rightly so. It was first established as a natural reserve in 1948 and all 3,260 sq km of it was handed to the Maasai elders of Kajiado District Council in 1961 to run with an annual grant of £8,500. After years of the de-

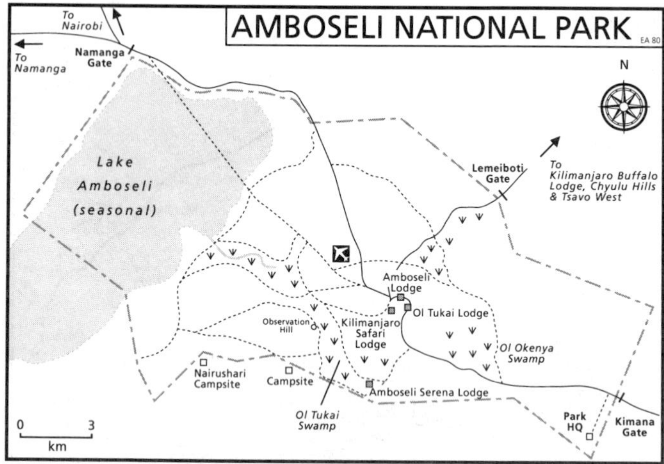

structive effects of cattle grazing and tourists on the area, 392 sq km of it were designated as a national park in 1973 which the Maasai were not allowed to use for grazing.

Decades of tourism have left well-worn trails, and much off-road driving has made the park look increasingly dusty and rather bleak. The late 1980s saw the start of an environmental conservation programme to halt erosion and this park now has the toughest policy on off-road driving. Many new roads are being built which should improve access. The Kenya Wildlife Service has committed US$2 million to rehabilitation.

Amboseli is in a semi-arid part of the country and is usually hot and dry. The vegetation is typical of savannah covered with the beautiful acacias which are so much a feature of East Africa. The main wildlife you are likely to see here are herbivores such as buffalo, gazelle, wildebeest, wart hog, giraffe and zebra and there are lots of baboons. One of the most spectaular sites is the large herd of elephants here (some 700 live in the park) and you may be able to see the very rare black rhino which has nearly been poached out of existence. There are a few predators: lions, cheetahs, hyenas and jackals.

There have been environmental changes over recent years. Lake Amboseli, which had almost totally dried up, reappeared during 1992/93. The return of water to the Lake flooded large parts of the park including the area around the lodges. Since then, flamingos have returned, and the whole park is far greener.

A main feature of the place is the back-drop of Kilimanjaro. At dusk or dawn, the cloud cover breaks to reveal the dazzling spectacle of this snow-capped mountain, the highest in Africa. Accessability from Nairobi has made the park busy.

Places of interest

Near the park is the town of **Isinya** where you will find the *Maasai Leather-working and Handicrafts Centre*. Good buys are the handmade shoes and big leather bags. You will also be able to find some unusual Maasai crafts such as marriage necklaces or beaded key-rings.

Best time

Best time to visit is just after the long

rains in Apr-May as this is when the park is lush and green and you should be able to see more wildlife.

Park information

Daily park fees US$20 payable to the warden at the park gate.

● Where to stay

A+ ***Kilimanjaro Safari Lodge***, bookings through *Kilimanjaro Safari Club*, PO Box 30139, Nairobi, T Nairobi 227136, F Nairobi 219982. Pleasant setting with white thatched cottages. Good views of Mt Kilimanjaro. **A+** ***Amboseli Lodge***, bookings through Kilimanjaro Safari Club, PO Box 30139, Nairobi, T Nairobi 227136, F Nairobi 219982. Good accommodation with pleasant gardens and a swimming pool. Offer spectacular views out towards Kilimanjaro. **A+** ***Amboseli Serena Lodge***, bookings through *Serena Lodgings and Hotels*, PO Box 48690, Nairobi, T Nairobi 751511, F Nairobi 718103. A very attractive design, drawing on elements of Masai traditional dwellings, blending into the landscape. Quite the nicest place to stay. It is near the Enkongo Narok Swamp which means there is always plenty of wildlife to see.

D ***Ol Tukai Lodge***, located near the *Amboseli Serena Lodge*. These were renovated in 1992 and are equipped with electricity. They occupy one of the finest viewing points in the park and are good value.

E ***Camping***, there is a poorly equipped camp site in the park is on the southern boundary. Its only facilities are a hole-in-the-ground toilet and a kiosk selling unrefridgerated drinks. The water supply is unreliable, so bring some with you.

● Where to eat and drink

If you intend to go camping or use the bandas, you will need to bring your own supplies of most things, though there is a kiosk at the campsite selling drinks. The lodges do allow non-residents to use their facilities and the *Amboseli Safari Lodge* is a nice place to stop off for a cold drink towards the end of the day.

● Transport

Air There is a daily flight from the private aerodrome at Wilson Airport to Amboseli on Air Kenya Aviation. It costs US$50 one way and leaves Nairobi at 7.30am and Amboseli at 8.30am. The journey takes 45 minutes.

Road The most common route is to drive from Nairobi along the A104 to Namanga (165km S), which is the border post between Kenya and Tanzania. The road is in good condition and there is a fuel stop here as well as a couple of shops selling Maasai crafts. The prices are high but negotiable. From here to the park is 75 km down an appalling road and there are no more petrol stations. The whole journey from Nairobi to Amboseli takes about 4 hrs.

If travelling by public transport, there is a bus from Nairobi bus station to Namanga. From there on in you will have to hitch.

ARAWALE NATIONAL RESERVE

North of Malindi, the Reserve is in North Eastern Province and is the only area in Kenya where Hunter's hartebeest can be found with their lyre-shaped horns. The thorny bushland also has zebra, elephant, lesser kudu, buffalo, hippo and crocodiles. There are no tourist facilities and as there is no gate into the reserve, there is no charge to visit.

BIANADI NATIONAL RESERVE

This is adjacent to the NE boundary of Meru National Park and is about 600 sq km. The area is mainly thorny bushland and thicket merging into wooded grasslands with dense riverine forests of raffia palm along the watercourses. You are likely to see the same sort of wildlife as in Meru National Park as it acts as a dispersal area during the rains. It is a particularly good place to find elephant and buffalo in the wet season.

The reserve forms part of a chain of parks running from Meru NE to Kora in the east. Kora is bounded by North Kitui National Reserve to the S and by Rahole National Reserve to the NE. There are no facilities for visitors.

BONI NATIONAL RESERVE

This is one of the large, remote parks in the NE of the country along the coast in North Eastern province. It is 1,340 sq km of the only coastal lowland groundwater forest in Kenya and has large concentrations of elephant and Harvey's and Ader's duiker in the dry season. It borders onto the better served Kiunga Marine National Reserve. No facilities for tourists.

DODORI NATIONAL RESERVE

The Dodori National Reserve is in Coastal Province and is 877 sq km extending from NE Lamu District up to the Somali border. The vegetation consists of mangrove swamp, lowland dry forest, marshy glades and groundwater forest and is bisected by the Dodori River. It is a major breeding ground for topi and there are also elephant and lesser kudu. There are also a substantial numbers of dugong and green turtle. Pelicans are particularly common birds here. There is E *Camping* for visitors but it is essential to check with the police before choosing to stay as the park is often refuge to armed bandits or desperate Somali refugees.

HELL'S GATE NATIONAL PARK

This is to the S of Lake Naivasha in the Rift Valley and is one of the few parks you are allowed to enter on foot. The walk through the park is spectacular leading through a gorge lined with sheer red cliffs. The Park is small, only 68 sq km and despite the wide variety of wildlife which inhabits the park, including eland, giraffe, zebra, impala, gazelle you may see very little as there do not appear to be too many of them. What you will see, though is the incredibly tame hyrax which looks like a type of guinea pig but is actually more closely related to the elephant, and a host of different birds of prey.

There are no visitors facilities here but there is a campsite up the road by Lake Naivasha (see page 88) which also has bandas and is set in a beautiful shady garden.

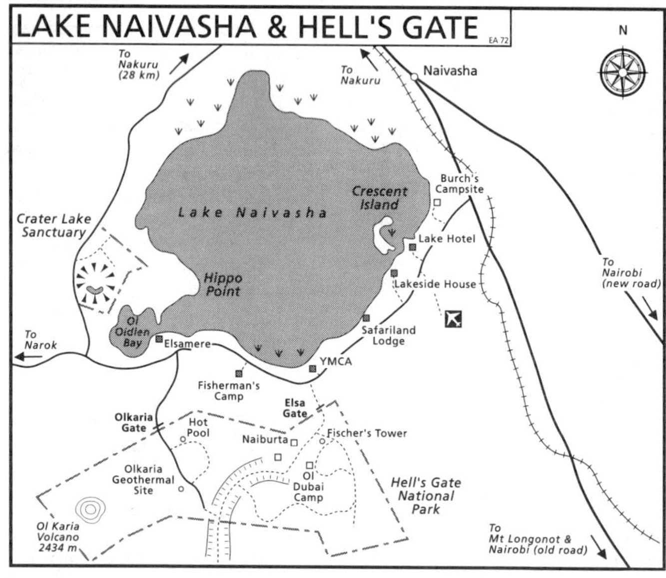

KAKAMEGA FOREST NATIONAL RESERVE

This forest is only 45 km sq and is the easternmost corner of the Congo-West African equatorial rainforest. It is extraordinarily beautiful with at least 125 species of trees. There are a number of animals which are found in no other part of the country, including the bush-tailed porcupine, giant water shrew, and hammer-headed fruit bat. There are also several primates including the colobus and blue monkey. For a small fee a guide will take you round the forest and this is well worth it as they are very knowledgeable about the forest flora and fauna. Look out for the Gabon viper, a particularly nasty snake which lives in the forest. The forest is also home to the hairy-tailed flying squirrel which can 'fly' as far as 90m.

Park information

● **Where to stay**

E *Forest Rest House*, PO Box 88 Kakamega. Located within the forest reserve. It is small, having only 4 bedrooms, all with their awn bathrooms. You will need to take your own food, but it is clean and friendly. Advisable to book at weekends and during school holidays (Christmas, Easter and Jul-Aug).

● **Transport**

Road Take the Kisumu road S of Kakamega for about 10 km and turn left at the sign opposite the service station. Carry on down this road for about 7km when you will reach the village of Shinyalu. Take a right and after about another 5km you will reach the forest reserve.

KIUNGA BIOSPHERE NATIONAL PARK

Is 250 sq km from the NE coastal border of mainland Kenya to the Pate Islands in the Indian Ocean in the district of Lamu. The coastal area is made up of scrublands and mangroves surrounded by microscopic marine plants and dugong grass. The vegetation is home to both the dugong and green turtle and an wide selection of reef fish. The coral here is extensive. As you would expect, there is a good variety of marine birds with colonies of various gulls and terns. The whole area contains more than 50 off-shore islands some of which house lesser kudu, bushbuck, monkeys, porcupines and wild pig. Poaching of the turtles and their eggs has been greatly reduced thanks to the efforts of the game wardens of Lamu.

There are a number of facilities for visitors despite the fact that this is one of the least developed of Kenya's marine reserves. There is swimming, sailing, water-skiing and diving here.

Park information

Accommodation and Travel See under Lamu section, page 113. There are also some simple places to stay in **Kiunga**, the administrative centre of this area about 12km from the border with Somalia, a village unspoilt by tourism.

KORA NATIONAL RESERVE

On one of Kenya's most important waterways, the Tana River, the Reserve is 125km east of Mount Kenya in Coastal Province and covers 1,787 sq km. The land is mostly acacia bushland with riverine forests of doum palm and Tana River poplar. There is a wide variety of animal species here including elephant, black rhino, hippo, lion, leopard, cheetah, serval, caracal, wildcat, genet, spotted and striped hyena, and several types of antelope. The rivers hold lizards, snakes, tortoise and crocodiles. This was once the home of George Adamson who was murdered in 1989. There are no tourist facilities.

LAKE BOGORIA NATIONAL RESERVE

This reserve is in the Rift Valley near Baringo, 50 km N of Nakuru. It is mainly bushland with small patches of riverine forest. The shoreline of the lake is surrounded by grasslands where there are

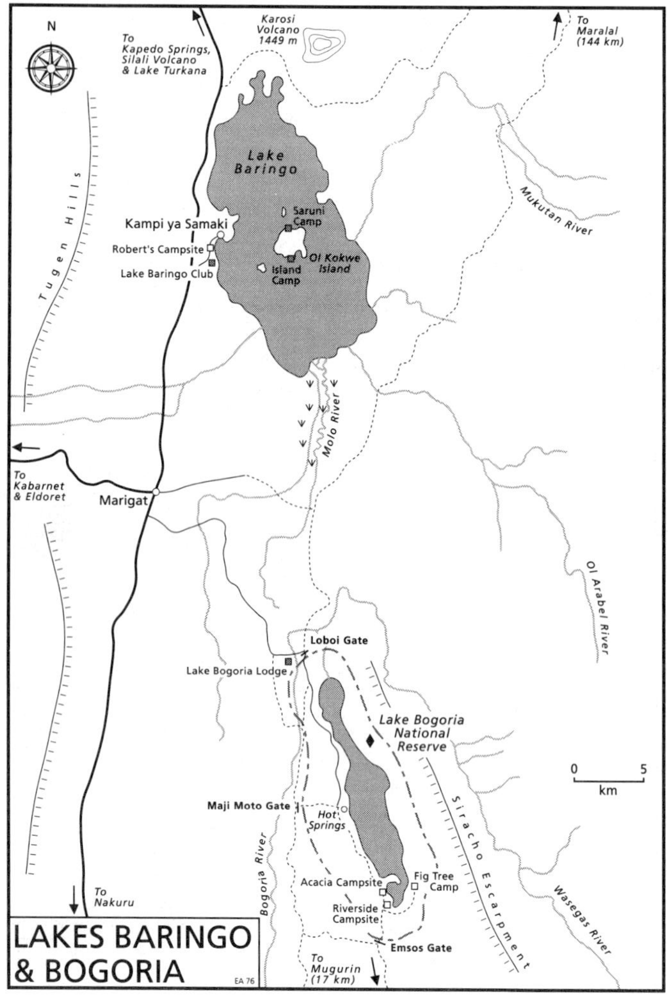

a number of greater kudu. The main reason people visit Lake Bogoria is to see the thermal areas with steam jets and geysers and the large number of flamingos which live here.

This is the least-visited of all Kenya's Rift lakes, but it can conveniently be included in a visit to Lake Baringo and the Kerio Valley, all of which are in this extremely hot area of the Rift Valley. The Lake itself lies at the foot of the Laikipia Escarpment and its bottle-green waters reflect woodlands to the east.

Park information

● Where to stay

There is also accommodation at nearby Nakuru

(see page 91). **A** *Lake Bogoria Lodge*, recently been built inside the reserve near its northern entrance, which has a swimming pool. Charge for use by non-residents.

● **Camping**

E *Fig Tree Campsite*, on the southern shore is pleasant and quite quiet. There is a freshwater stream running through the campsite which is just big enough to get into. Baboons can be a problem. **E** *Acacia Tree* and **E** *Riverside* are both on the western shore. No facilities, and you need to bring all equipment, supplies and water.

● **Transport**

It is an easy drive from **Nakuru** taking less than an hr along the Baringo road. There are 2 entrances: at the southern end Mogotio Gate, which has some difficult road; at the northern end there is a better access via Loboi Gate.

LAKE NAKURU NATIONAL PARK

The park is just outside Nakuru town in central Kenya, 140km northwest of Nairobi. It is about 188 sq km and the lakes are fringed by swamps surrounded by dry savannah. The upper areas are forested. There is a wide variety of wildlife: bats, colobus, spring hare, otter, rock hyrax, hoppo, waterbuck, leopard, hyena, and giraffe but the most popular reason for visiting is the flamingoes. At one time there was thought to be to be around 2 million flamingoes here, about one third of the world's entire population, but the numbers have diminished

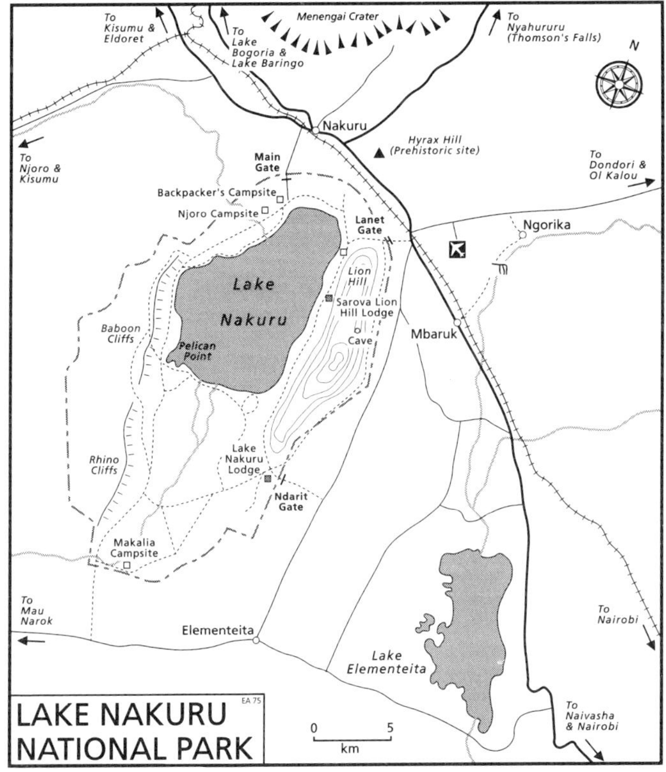

in recent years. There are also more than 450 other species of other birds here.

Park information

● Where to stay

There is also accommodation at nearby Nakuru (see page 91). **A** ***Lake Nakuru Lodge***, PO Box 70559, Nairobi, T Nairobi 224998, Tlx Nairobi 22658. Access from Ndarit Gate. Banda accommodation. Swimming pool. Good views. **A** ***Sarova Lion***, PO Box 30680, close to eastern shore of Lake, Nairobi, T Nairobi 333248, F Nairobi 211472. Access from Lanet Gate. Swimming pool. Sauna and boutique. Good views. Popular with group tours. **E** ***Florida Day and Night Club***, close to main Gate, just beyond the outskirts of Nakuru.

● Camping

This is available at **E** ***Backpackers's Campsite***, just inside the Main Gate; **E** ***Njoro Campsite***, about 1 km into the park on the NW side of the lake; and at **E** ***Makalia Campsite***, by the southern boundary of the Park. You will need a vehicle for these last 2 campsites.

● Transport

This is one of the easiest parks to visit being just outside Nakuru. You will need to be in a vehicle though you are allowed to get out at the lakeside.

LOSAI NATIONAL RESERVE

This is 1,800 sq km of thorny bushland situated in the Losai Mountains S W of Marsabit National Reserve and about 175 km N of Mount Kenya, in northern Kenya. The Reserve is a lava plateau with scattered volcanic plugs. No tourism is allowed at the moment as the area is trying to rehabilitate its elephant and black rhino populations which have been decimated by poachers. It is also unlikely tourism will develop for some time to come as it is virtually impenetrable even with a 4-wheel drive.

MALINDI BIOSPHERE RESERVE

This strip along the coast is 30km long and 5km wide and includes Mida Creek. It lies about 80km N of Mombasa, around the Malindi and the Watamu Marine area, and includes the Watamu Marine National Reserve and National Park. The vegetation includes mangrove, palms, marine plants and various forms of algae which are home to various crabs, corals, molluscs, cowrie and marine worms. Coral viewing is popular here, as are boat trips and watersports. Whale Island is a nesting ground for roseate and bridled tern, and there are a number of other shore birds here.

MAASAI MARA GAME RESERVE

Background

The Maasai Mara National Reserve covers some 1,672 sq km at between 1,500 and 2,100m above sea level. It is an extension of Tanzania's Serengeti National Park, a small part of the Serengeti ecosystem covering some 40,000 sq km between the Rift Valley and Lake Victoria. It is the most popular of Kenya's parks with good reason. Almost every species of animal you can think of in relation to East Africa live on the well-watered plains in this remote part of the country. One of the most memorable and spectacular sites is the migration of hundreds of thousands of wildebeest, gazelle and zebra as they move from the Serengeti plains in Jan on their way northwards arriving in the Maasai Mara by about Jul-Aug as the dry weather sets in. They begin to return S in Oct.

The Maasai Mara is not a national park but a game reserve the difference being that people (the Maasai) have the right to graze on the land and shoot animals if they are attacked.

The landscape is mainly gently rolling countryside with rainfall in the N being double that of the S. The Mara River runs from N to S through the park and then turns westwards to Lake Victoria. Most of the plains are covered in

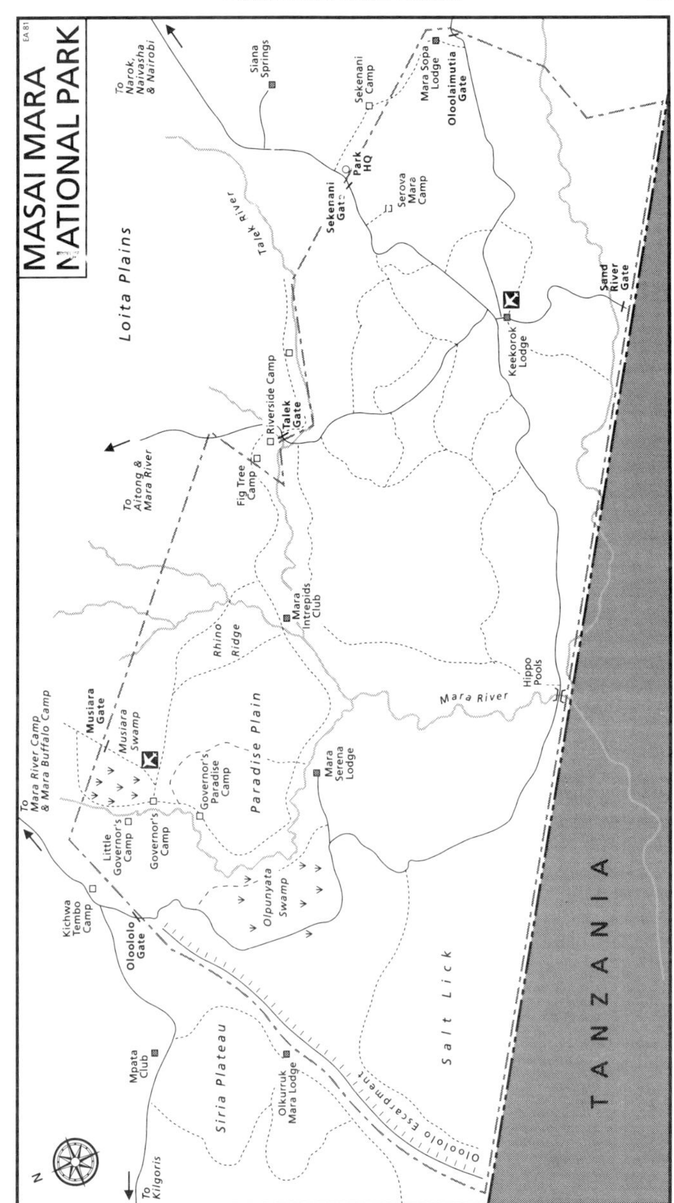
MASAI MARA NATIONAL PARK
EA 81
To Narok, Naivasha & Nairobi
Siana Springs
Sekenani Camp
Mara Sopa Lodge
Ololaimutia Gate
Park HQ
Sekenani Gate
Serova Mara Camp
Talek River
Loita Plains
Sand River Gate
Keekorok Lodge
Riverside Camp
Talek Gate
Fig Tree Camp
To Aitong & Mara River
Mara Intrepids Club
Rhino Ridge
Hippo Pools
Mara River
Musiara Gate
Musiara Swamp
To Mara River Camp & Mara Buffalo Camp
Governor's Paradise Camp
Paradise Plain
Mara Serena Lodge
Little Governor's Camp
Governor's Camp
Kichwa Tembo Camp
Olpunyata Swamp
Oloololo Gate
Salt Lick
Mpata Club
Siria Plateau
Olkurruk Mara Lodge
Oloololo Escarpment
TANZANIA
N
To Kilgoris

a type of red-oat grass with acacias and thorn trees.

The reserve is teeming with herbivores – numbering around 2.5 mn including: wildebeest, gazelle, zebra, buffalo, impala, topi, hartebeest, giraffe, elant, elephant, dik-dik, klipspringer, steinbok, hippo, rhino, wart hog, bushpig. There is also a large amount of lion, leopard, cheetah, hyena, wild dog, jackal as well as smaller mammals and reptiles. The number of animals suited to grasslands living in this area has increased enormously over the last thirty years due to woodland being cleared.

The Oloololo Escarpment on the western edge of the park has the highest concentrations of game, though it is also the hardest part to get around, particularly after heavy rain, when the swampy ground becomes impassable.

The accommodation in the Reserve is superb, and a stay in one of the high standard tented camps, with perhaps a dawn hot-air balloon safari (around US$200), is an unforgettable experience. Several of the tented camps are really very special.

Places of interest

Just outside the Oloolaimutia Gate there is a Maasai village, open to the public, which you can wonder round taking as many photographs as you wish for US$7 per person.

Park information

● Where to stay Lodges

A+ ***Mara Sopa Lodge***, T Nairobi 336 088. One of the newer hotels with great views. Balloon safaris. Boutique and shop. **A+** ***Mara Serena Lodge***, T Nairobi 339 800. Well designed. Wildlife films, Maasai dancing, balloon safaris. Superb view over the Mara River. **A+** ***Rekero Farm***, outside Reserve to NW, in Maasai Mara Conservation Area. PO Box 56923, Nairobi, T Nairobi 506139, F 502739. Expensive – only 4 guests in total. Personally conducted safari walks available.

A ***Keekorok***, PO Box 47557 Nairobi, T Nairobi 335807, F Nairobi 340541. Oldest lodge, set in a grassy plain. Swimming pool. Wild life and local culture lectures. Shop. Will arrange game drives, and dawn hot-air balloon trips. **A** ***Olkurruk Mara Lodge***, outside Reserve, near Oloololo Gate, PO Box 30471, Nairobi, T Nairobi 336858, F 218109. Good views from elevated site.

B ***Bush Tops***, outside reserve, nearest to Sekanini Gate, PO Box 44191, Nairobi, T Nairobi 882408. Fairly simple, but quite comfortable

● Tented camps

A+ ***Governors' Camp***, in area to N of park, accessed from Musiara Gate, PO Box 48217, Nairobi, T Nairobi 331871, F 726427. Solid floors for tents. Bar louge, candlelit dinners, small museum. Balloon safaris. No swimming pool. Beautiful site by the Mara River. **A+** ***Little Governors' Camp***, in area to N of park, accessed from Musiara Gate. PO Box 48217, Nairobi T Nairobi 331871, F 726427. Solid floors for tents. Access by boat ferry, pulled across the Mara River. Really something special, on a splendid site, very high standards. **A+** ***Governors' Paradise Camp***, in area to N of park, accessed from Musiara Gate, PO Box 48217, Nairobi, T Nairobi 331871, F 726427. Located in bush along Mara River. Tents not on permanent floors. High standards. **A+** ***Governors' Private Camp***, in area to N of park, accessed from Musiara Gate, PO Box 48217, Nairobi, T Nairobi 331871 F 726427. Site can be booked for exclusive use, up to 16 people. Minimum of 3 nights. **A+** ***Mara Intrepids Club***, by the Talek River. PO Box 74888, Nairobi, T Nairobi 338084, F Nairobi 217278. Balloon safaris, swimming pool, shop. High standards. **A+** ***Sekanini Camp***, close to Sekanini Gate, PO Box 61542, Nairobi, T Nairobi 333285, F Nairobi 228875. A place of much charm, with high standard tented accommodation with polished wooden floors, grand baths, hurricane lamps, quite excellent food.

A ***Diners Tented Camp***, PO Box 46466, Nairobi, NE corner, access from Olemutial Gate, T Nairobi 333301, F 224539. A touch more spartan than some of the other tented camps. Excellent food. **A** ***Fig Tree Camp***, PO Box 40683, Nairobi, T Nairobi 221439, F 332170. Just outside Reserve close to Talek Gate. Quite large, and also has some timber cabins. Swimming Pool, shop, balloon safaris. **A** ***Kichwa Tembo Camp***, PO Box 74957, Nairobi, T Nairobi 219784, F Nairobi 217498. At the base of the Oloololo Escarpment by the Oloololo Gate. Does have some banda accommodation as well. Balloon safaris. Nature walks, visits to Masai village. Swimming Pool. **A** ***Mara River***

Camp, PO Box 48019, Nairobi, outside the reserve, beside river, in pleasant site, T Nairobi 335935, F Nairobi 216528. Specialist ornithologist for tours. Game drive. No swimming pool. **A** ***Sarova Mara Camp***, PO Box 30680, Nairobi, near the Sekenani Gate, T Nairobi 333248, F 211472. Good accommodation, beautiful views. Swimming pool. **A** ***Siana Springs*** (formerly *Cottars' Camp*), PO Box 74957, Nairobi, just outside the Reserve, T Nairobi 219784, F Nairobi 217498. Unspoilt site. Specialist naturalist for walks and lectures. Swimming pool. **A** ***Talek River Camp***, inside the Reserve, by the River, PO Box 74888, Nairobi, T Nairobi 338084, F 217278. Sound facilities (but no pool). Good value.

● Camping

The only option for budget travellers. You can camp outside any of the **E** ***Park Gates***, (there are 5) for a small fee. The best of these location are **E** ***Sand River Gate***, with lavatories, water and a shop; and **E** ***Musaria Gate***, there are no facilities but you should be able to get water from the wardens. The most lively place to stay is the Maasai run. **E** ***Oloolaimutia Campsite*** at the western side of the park where budget safari outfits usually stay. Water here is limited and you will have to buy it if you need it. The nearby *Mara Sopa Lodge* serves food and drink (warm beers) and has a lively atmosphere. There are camping facilities near **E** ***Keekorok Lodge*** and a place to buy food and drink. This is the only offical camp site in the reserve. **E** ***National Park Campsites***, without any facilities are at 3 locations outside the Reserve beside the Mara River N of Mara River Camp. There are **E** ***Talek River Campsites***, close to the Talek Gate, at 12 locations.

● Transport

Air Flights leave twice-daily from Wilson Airport in Nairobi and take 45 minutes. They leave Nairobi at 1000 and 1500 and from the Maasai Mara at 1100 and 1600. The fare is US$72 one way.

Road The journey to the Maasai Mara is fascinating in itself crossing through the Rift Valley over dry range lands.

The 2 major routes to the park are from Narok which is a small town to the W of Nairobi. From here to the park is 100 km along unsurfaced roads. Narok is your last chance of refuelling. The other way is from Kisii, the road to the park being OK. Opportunities for hitching are very limited, you will really need transport to explore this park properly.

MARSABIT NATIONAL RESERVE

Marsabit National Reserve is in Eastern Province 560km N of Nairobi in the district of Marsabit. Its altitudes stretch from 420m where thorny bushland dominates the scenery to 1,700m above sea level. The upper reaches are covered in forest which merge into acacia grasslands. A number of birds and animals live here including 52 different types of birds of prey. You are likely to see elephants, greater kudu, various species of monkeys, baboons, hyena, aardwolf, caracal, cheetah, lion, gazelle, oryx and reticulated giraffe. A special feature of the area is the volcanic craters several of which contain fresh water lakes.

Park information

● Where to stay

There is also accommodation in nearby Marsabit (see page 163). **B** ***Marsabit Lodge***, PO Box 45, Marsabit, T Marsabit 2044. Bookings: Msafari Inns PO Box 42013, Nairobi, T Nairobi 330820, F 227815. Excellent location overlooking a waterhole. **E** ***Camping***, site near the main gate.

● Transport

See under Marsabit, page 163.

MERU NATIONAL PARK

Meru National Park is NE of Mount Kenya and is mainly covered with thorny bushland and wooded grasslands to the W. Dense riverine forests grow along the watercourses surrounded by the prehistoric-looking doum palms. There are hundreds of species of birds including the Somali ostrich and animals include lion, leopard, cheetah, elephant, zebra, black rhino, giraffe, hippo, oryx, hartebeest and Grant's gazelle. There are few tourist package tours to this park making it one of the least trampled and unspoiled parks.

Park information

● Where to stay

A ***Meru Mulika Lodge***, Booking: Msafiri Inns,

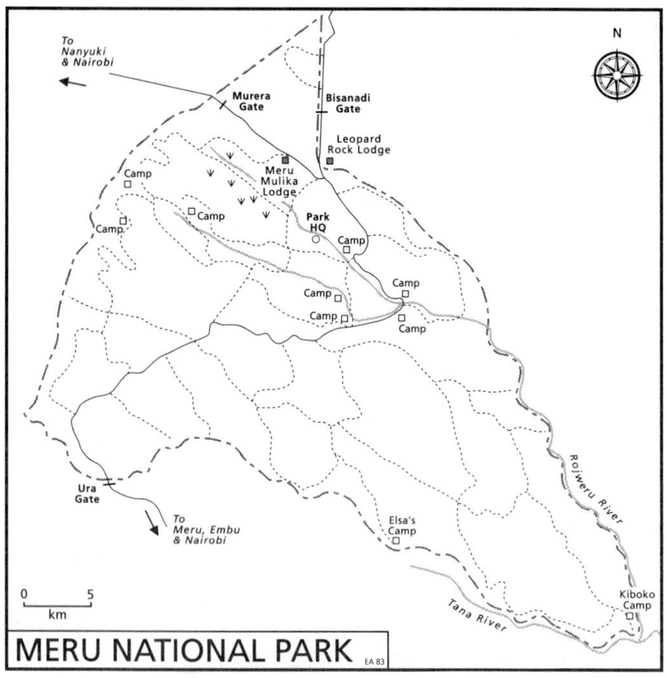

PO Box 42013, Nairobi, T Nairobi 330820, F Nairobi 227815. Pool and a lovely terrace from which you can watch elephants, oryx and other animals at the Mulika Swamp. The Lodge has become somewhat rundown due to lack of custom. The food is not particularly good and the rooms are quite shabby, you may even be asked for petrol as there is no regular fuel supply.

D ***Leopard Rock Safari Lodge***, Booking: PO Box 45456, Nairobi, T Nairobi 742926. Excellent value bandas with electricity, warm showers, fully equipped kitchens including a fridge and mosquito nets. It is best to bring your food and drink. Though there is a shop at the *Leopard Rock Safari Lodge* it is not very often open and when it is, has limited stocks.

● Transport
You will need your own vehicle. Head from Meru town to Maua which is the last place to stock up on petrol and supplies. Murera Gate is about 30 km from Maua down an unpaved road, with magnificent views over shambas.

MOUNT ELGON NATIONAL PARK

In the Rift Valley on the western border of Uganda, covering 169 sq km. The peak of the extinct volcano Mount Elgon reaches 4,322m, the topmost heights form the Kenya, Uganda border. The park's boundaries go down to 2,336m. This areas is known as Koitobos meaning table rock by virtue of its flat-topped basalt columns. There are a number of lava-tube caves, some over 60m wide which attract elephants in search of salt. Elgon is estimated to be more than 15 million years old.

The changes in altitude means there are a number of ecological zones going from bamboo forest to afro-alpine moorlands. Animals likely to be seen here are: colobus monkey, elephant, leopard, giant forest hog, bushbuck, eland, buffalo, duiker and golden cat.

Climbing Mount Elgon

Although it is possible to climb Mount Elgon at any time of year, the crater gets very cold and snow and hail are quite common so the best times are between Dec and Mar. It is possible to reach the summit and back in a day in dry weather when it is possible to drive to within a few hrs hike of the highest point. There is not such a severe problem with altitude sickness as on Mount Kenya, but a night spent en route will lessen any problems that might arise. If you do not have a 4WD vehicle, the ascent can be hiked in a fairly leisurely manner, spending 3 days on the way up and 2 down.

Equipment, porters, guides Camping gear and appropriate clothing can be hired in Nairobi at *Atul's*, Biashara St PO Box 43202, T 25935. Cost about US$20 per day, with about US$200 in deposits. You should obtain one of the maps of the mountain showing the trails in some detail (see page 199). Porters for your gear, and guides, cost about US$3 a day, and are a sound investment, and can be recruited at any of the climb departure points. It is wise to ensure that the agreement with any guides or porters is clear.

Park route, entry through the main Chorlim Gate to the park and then driving through the park to the end of the road track at Koroborte (3,580m). There is a campsite and water here. It is then about 3 hrs to the Koitoboss summit.

Kimilili route This runs S of the route through the Park. Starting from the village of Kimilili, there is a track to Kapsakwany, 8 km away. Another 2km on is the turning to the forest Gate, which is a further 2.5km. It is then 26 km, which can be driven comfortably in dry weather, to the Austrian Hut (3,350m) where it is possible to stay or camp, with water nearby. There is a further 3 km of driveable track. From here it about a 4 hr hike to Koitoboss summit.

Kimithon route This runs N of the Park route. Starting from Endebess, it is 16 km to Masara village. About 1km further on take the right fork (not the left to the Kimithon Gate). The middle of 3 tracks leads to Kimithon Forest Station, where it is possible to camp. Koitoboss is then about 6 hrs hike away. There may be problems with the Forest Station about using this route, but they can usually be negotiated.

Park information

● **Where to stay**

C *Mount Elgon Lodge*, just outside the main Chorlim Gate. Bookings: Msafri Inns, Utali House, Uhuru Highway, Nairobi, PO Box 42013, T 330820, Tlx 23009. It is not certain whether this lodge will remain open. **E** *Jasho Lodgings*, in Kimilili. Basic but sound.

● **Transport**

Road The easiest way is from Kitale, the most popular being Chorlim Gate off the Endebess road. The other gates can be reach from Kakamega (81 km) or Kimilili (50 km). You will be able to get a matatu from Kimilili.

MOUNT KENYA BIOSPHERE RESERVE

This reserve includes the Mount Kenya National Park which straddles the equator about 200km NE of Nairobi in Central province. The snow-capped peak is rarely visible during the day being surrounded by clouds, but it is usually clear at dawn and is quite an awesome site. The upper base of the mountain is nearly 100km across and has 2 major peaks Nelion at 5,199m and Batian at 5,189m. Mount Kenya has a vital role in ecosystems in the area. It is Kenya's most important watershed and its largest forest reserve and the lower slopes make up the country's richest farmlands.

The area has a variety of different vegetations over altitudes ranging from 1,600 to 5,199m. From bottom to top, it goes from rich alpine and sub-alpine flora to bamboo forests, moorlands and

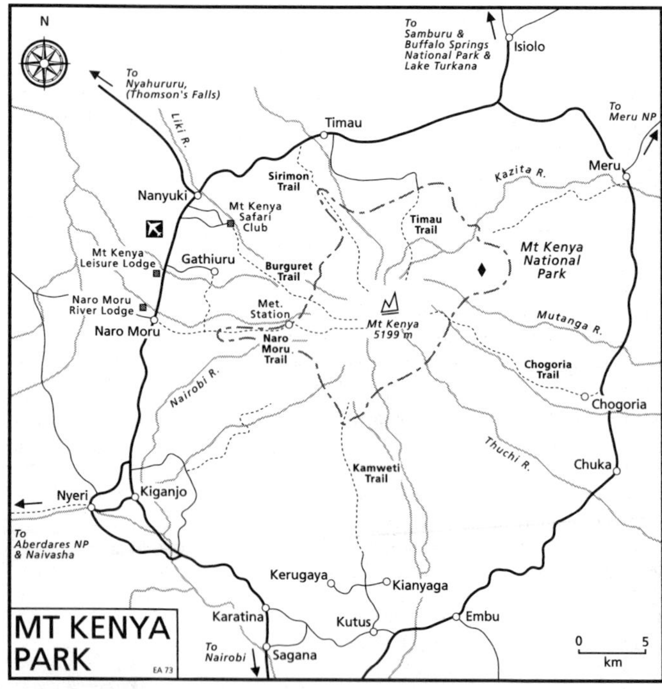

tundra. Over 4,000m there is some extraordinary vegetation including the giant rosette plants.

In the lower forest and bamboo zones, giant forest hog, tree hyrax, white-tailed mongoose, elephant, suni, duiker and leopard roam. Further up in the moorlands there are hyrax, duiker and Mount Kenya mouse shrews. In higher altitudes still there are the fairly common mole rat and the very rare golden cat.

Climbing Mount Kenya

Point **Lenena** at 4,986m is strenuous hike, but quite manageable. It is possible to reach to **Mackinder's Camp**, about 4,175m, and back in a day. – it requires going as far as the Meteorological Station (3,050m) on the Naro Moru route by 4WD vehicle. This can be arranged through *Naro Moro River Lodge* (see below) for about US$20 plus park fees. The 2 peaks, **Nelion** and **Batian**, are only possible for experienced climbers.

Take great care over equipment and altitude sickness precautions: otherwise the climb can be several days of sheer misery. The 3 most popular routes up the mountain are described here, and are best taken leisurely in 6 days, although they can be done in 4. It is an interesting variation to ascend by one route and descend by another – it is important to keep the park fee receipts for the exit.

An expedition to Point Lenena can be arranged for a group of 4, including equipment, transport and food, for about US$120 per person through *Mount Rock Hotel* (see below).

Equipment, Porters, Guides Camping

gear and appropriate clothing can be hired in Nairobi at *Atul's*, PO Box 43202, Biashara St, T 25935. Cost about US$20 per day, with about US$200 in deposits. Alternatively hire at *Naro Moro River Lodge*, PO Box 18, Naro Moro, T 0176 22018, at rates that are approximately 50% higher than in Nairobi. You should obtain one of the maps of the mountain showing the trails in some detail (see page 199). Porters for your gear, and guides, cost about US$3 a day, and are a sound investment, and can be recruited at any of the climb departure points. It is wise to ensure that the agreement with any guides or porters is clear.

Health It is important to plan the climb to allow enough time for altitude acclimatisation. See Health section, page 24.

The climb Naro Moru Approaches from the W and is the most direct route. Naro Moro and Burguret are suitable starting bases. **Day 1**, from Naro Moro, is best spent travelling to the Meteorological Station at 3,050m. A ride can be hired from *Naro Moro River Lodge* part or all of the way. There are some bandas here or some permanent tents. **Day 2** is to Mackinder's Camp, through terrain that is often very wet underfoot. The camp has a bunkhouse and some tents. **Day 3** it is possible to make the final leg to Point Lenena, although it is more comfortable to spend Day 3 in and around Mackinder's Camp, getting acclimatised to the altitude, and **Day 4** climb to Point Lenena. **Day 5** it is possible to descend all the way down to Naro Moro, (with a lift from the Meteorological station), but it is more leisurely to return to Mackinder's Camp for a night, and then on to Naro Moro on **Day 6**.

Chogaria Approach is from the east, and is the most scenically attractive of the routes, although it can be wet. Chogaria village is the starting base. **Day 1**, from village to the Park gate by vehicle, and then it is about an hr of hiking to Urimandi Hut for the night. **Day 2** is a 6 hr hike to Minto's Hut. **Day 3** it is possible to reach Point Lenena, but it is more comfortable to spend the day getting acclimatised in and around Minto's Hut, and **Day 4** climb to Point Lenena. **Day 5** it is possible to descend all the way down to Chogaria, (with a lift from the Park gate), but it is more leisurely to return to Minto's Hut for a night, and then on to Chogaria on **Day 6**.

Sirimon Approaches from the N, and has a good repution for wildlife along the route. Naro Moro, Burguret or Nanyuki are possible starting bases. The trail start 13 km N of Nanyuki. **Day 1** from the trail start to the Park gates (about 10km) and then up to the end of the road track (a further 9 km) at 3,150m, where there is a bunkhouse and a campsite. **Day 2** is to Liki North Hut at 3,993m. **Day 3** it is possible to carry on past Kami Tarn, joining the Chogaria Trail about less than 1km from Point Lenena. However, if you are finding the climb and the altitude a strain, it is a good idea to spend a day acclimatising at Liki North Hut, or climb to Kami Hut, and on **Day 4** on to Point Lenena. **Day 5** it is possible to descend all the way with a lift from the end of the road track. However it is probably best to spend a night at Liki North Hut, and then to Nanuyki on **Day 6**.

Park information

● Where to stay

Naro Moro A *Naro Maro River Lodge*, about 2km N of town centre, PO Box 18, Naro Moro T Nanyuki 22018. Some cheaper self-catering cottages available. **E** *Naro Moro Hotel '86*, town centre. Some self-contained rooms. **E** *Youth Hostel*, some dormitory accommodation. **E** *Camping*, possible at *Naro Maro Lodge*, and at the Youth Hostel.

Burguret C *Mount Rock*, (formerly *Bantu Lodge*), 8km N of Naro Moru on the Nanyuki road. PO Box 33, Nanyuki, T Nanyuki 62625) Log fires. Good restaurant and bar. Horseriding at about US$4 an hr. Escorted forest walks.

Chogoria D *Meru Mount Kenya Lodge*, Just inside park. Reasonable bandas with showers and log fires. **E** *Transit Motel*, in Chogaria village. Fairly basic.

Transport

Road For **Naro Moru** and **Burguret**, Nyeri is the nearest major town, along the main Nairobi-Nanyuki road. For **Chogaria** the most direct route from Nairobi is through Embu. There are plenty of buses and matatus.

MOUNT KULAL BIOSPHERE RESERVE

7,000 sq km of land to the SE of Lake Turkana in Eastern province has been made into one of Kenya's 4 biosphere reserves. The area includes many different types of environments ranging from mountain forest about 2,400 m above sea level to desert with grasslands, dry evergreen forest, woodlands, bushlands and saltbush scrublands in between. It covers most of Lake Turkana, its volcanic southern shores, the Chalbi desert and the South Island National Park. There are 2 outstanding volcanoes in the reserve, **Teleki** and **Mount Kulal** which stands at 2,285 m high. Both are a pretty straightforward climb if you are suitably equipped.

Animals likely to be found here include giraffe, zebra, dik-dik, gazelle, elephant, cheetah, lion, black rhino, leopard, ostrich and crocodile as well as less common species such as gerenuk and greater kudu.

This area shows increasing evidence of human occupation from 10,000-12,000 years ago. Today the area is home to Samburu, Turkana and el-Molo around Lake Turkana all of whom are pastoralists.

There are no facilities for visitors to date.

NAIROBI NATIONAL PARK

This park is just outside Nairobi and despite its closeness to the city is home to over 80 recorded species. It is Kenya's oldest park having been set up in 1946. You are very likely to see zebra, giraffe, gazelle, baboons, buffalo, ostrich, vultures, hippos and various antelope. This is one of the best parks for spotting rhinos – the area is not remote enough for poachers. The concentration of wildlife is greatest in the dry season when areas outside the park have dried up. Water sources are greater in the park as a number of small dams have been built along the Mbagathi River. There are also

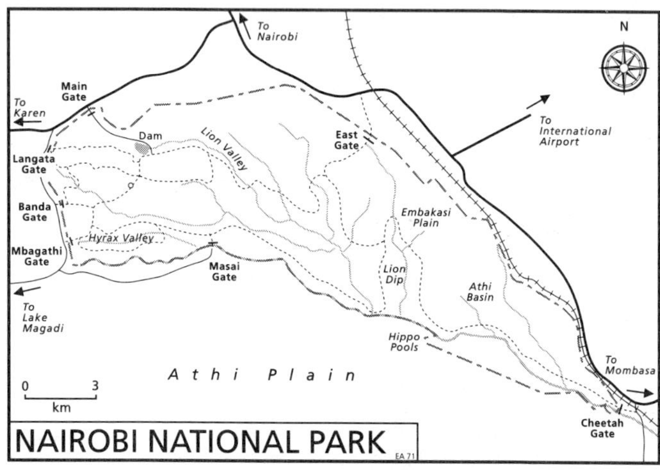

many bird species, up to 500 different types. The park is small, only 117 km sq but is well worth visiting if you are staying in Nairobi, there are a number of minibus tours for either a morning or an afternoon.

Costs If you have a vehicle, it costs US$20 per person plus US$5 for the vehicle. A tour into the park is about US$20 per person, plus the park fee, but is often negotiable.

NORTH KITUI NATIONAL RESERVE

Adjacent to Meru National Park is North Kitui National Reserve in Eastern Province. It measures 745 km sq and is mainly bushland and riverine forest. The Tana River runs through where you are likely to see crocodile and hippos. It forms part of a chain from Meru National Park to Bisanadi National Reserve E to Kora National Reserve then S to North Kitui National Reserve which itself is bounded in the NE by Rahole National Reserve.

There are no tourist facilities.

RAHOLE NATIONAL RESERVE

An enormous stretch of dry thorny bushland in Garissa district of North-Eastern Province about 150 km ENE of Mount Kenya. It is home to elephant, Grevy's zebra and beisa oryx. There are no tourist facilities.

RUMA NATIONAL PARK

This park is 10km east of Lake Victoria in the South Nyanza district of western Kenya. The land is a mixture of tall grassland and woodlands of acacia, housing roan antelope, leopard, buffalo and topi. Giraffe, zebra and ostrich have recently been introduced. Camping is possible in the grounds. The Lambwe region is infested with tsetse fly which is fatal to man (sleeping sickness) and domesticated animals, but not to wild game. There are no camping facilities here and given the tsetse fly situation, you may want to give camping a miss.

This area is fascinating with a mixture of small islands and peninsulas and is rarely visited by tourists.

SAMBURU/BUFFALO SPRINGS NATIONAL PARK

Samburu

This was set up 20 years ago in this hot, arid lowland area just to the N of Mount Kenya. The permanent water and forest shade on the banks of the Ewaso Nyiro River attract plentiful wildlife from the region including elephant, cheetah, giraffe, oryx, vervet monkeys, zebra and crocodiles. Leopards are regularly spotted. This is one of the pleasantest parks in Kenya and is not too crowded.

Buffalo Springs

Elephant, zebra, giraffe, oryx, cheetah and crocodile can be found in the riverine forest of acacia and doum palm in this reserve 85km N of Mount Kenya in Eastern Province, adjoining Samburu.

Park information

● **Costs**

Each reserve costs about US$7.50.

● **Where to stay**

There are a surprising amount of facilities considering the 2 reserves put together only cover some 400 km sq, catering for both luxury and budget tourists. Many of the more upmarket lodges offer discounts of up to 50% in the off-season between Apr and Jul excluding Easter. **A+** *Larsens Tented Camp*, PO Box 47557, Nairobi, T Nairobi 335807, F Nairobi 340541. E of *Samburu Lodge*, located by the river, small and highly recommended. Offers game drives and excellent food. Use of *Samburu Lodge* pool. They do not take children under 10.

A *Buffalo Springs Lodge*, T Isiolo 0165/2259. Bookings: PO Box 30471, Nairobi, T Nairobi

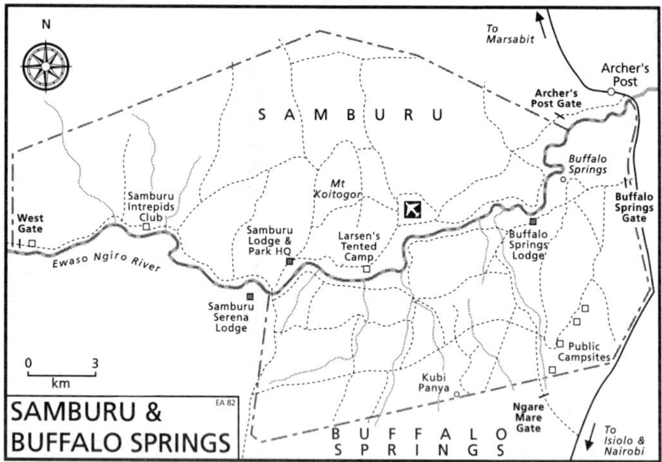

336858, F 218109. A pleasant relaxed lodge with good value bandas. Swimming pool. Excellent location. **A** *Samburu Lodge*, T 2051 radiocall Nairobi. Bookings: PO Box 47557, Nairobi, T Nairobi 335807, F Nairobi 340541. The oldest lodge in the reserve situated in the bend of the river. This place is a wonderful place to stop off for a drink on the riverside terraces even if you do not stay. Relaxed atmosphere in a beautiful setting. Swimming pool, shop.

E *Camping* is possible in *Buffalo Springs Reserve*, Ngere Mara, Ewaso Nyiro Bridge, and Maji ya Chumvi Stream near Buffalo Springs. The best is the one by Buffalo Springs Reserve which has showers and toilets. Baboons are a real nuisance here stealing anything not nailed to the ground. It is wise to have guard provided by the Reserve, as there can be problems with theft and unwelcome vistors.

● Transport

Samburu is a couple of hrs N of Nanyuki. Buses run here from Isiolo in the plains below on a regular basis.

SHABA NATIONAL RESERVE

70km N of Mount Kenya the Shaba National Reserve in Isiolo District of Eastern Province is home to a number of gerenuk, gazelle, oryx, zebra, giraffe, cheetah, leopard and lion which roam around acacia woodlands, bushlands and grasslands. The riverine areas are dominated by acacia and doum palms. There is one luxury lodge and 3 campsites. This is an extension of Buffalo Springs and Samburu National Reserve which lies to its W. The naturalists Joy and George Adamson who reared lions and returned them to the wild (the subject of *Born Free*, a book and film) had a campsite in Shaba Reserve.

● Where to stay

A *Sarova Shaba Lodge*, PO Box 30680, Nairobi, T 333248 F 211472. A new luxury lodge, opened in 1989, offering excellent facilities, just to the east of Archer's post. Overlooks river, well designed. Swimming pool.

● Transport

Buses to Archer's Post from Isiolo are fairly frequent.

SHIMBA HILLS NATIONAL RESERVE

This is a small reserve 30km SW of Mombasa and quite possible to access on a day trip from Mombasa. The area is 192 sq km and is covered with forests and grasslands, riverine forest and scrubland. Due to strong sea breezes, the

0
200
400 km
0
100
200
SUDAN
ETHIOPIA
ERITREA
DJIBOUTI
SOMALIA
YEMEN
Ed Debba
Atbara
Ed Damer
Derudeb
Karora
Nak'fa
Eriba
Shendi
Goz Regeb
W. el Milk
Abu'Urug
Nile
Omdurman
Khartoum North
Khartoum
Kassala
Khashm el Girba
El Kamlin
Blue Nile
El Geteina
Wad Medani
El Gezira
Sodiri
Umm Bell
Bara
Ed Dueim
Gedaref
Qala'en Nahl
Sennar
Singa
El Hawata
Gallabat
Rahad
Dinder
Khuwei
El Obeid
Kosti
En Nahud
Er Rahad
Umm Ruwaba
El Jebelein
Abu Zabad
Dilling
aweisha
El Fula
Nuba Mts
Rashad
Renk
El Lagowa
Kadugli
White Nile (Bahr el Abiad)
Bahr el Azraq
l Muglad
Kaka
Paloich
Kodok
Malakal
Bahr el Arab
Abyei
Nyamlell
Bentiu
Bahr el Ghazal
Aweil
Fangak
Abwong
Sobat
Nasir
Jur
Pongo
Meshra'er Req
Ayod
Wau
Sudd
Duk Faiwil
Akobo
Tor
Tonj
Shambe
Rumbek
Yirol
Pibor
Pibor Post
Numatinna
Sue
Bor
Tali Post
Tambura
Amadi
Kenamuke Swamp
Lotikipi Plain
Maridi
Mongalla
Juba
Doruma
Yambio
Torit
Laylo
Kinyeti 3187
Lokitaung
Yei
Niangara
Dungu
Aba
Lake
Sebderat
Keren
Massawa (Mits'iwa)
Dehalak Archipelago
Farasan Is
Asmara (Asmera)
Adi Ugri
Barentu
Om Hajer
Mareb
Takkaze
Adwa
Aksum
Adigrat
Ras Andadda
Mersa Fatma
Ed
Mek'ele
Tigre
Ras Dashan 4620
Dabat
Gonder
Amhara
Sek'ot'a 3657
Aseb
Tendaho
Dunkur
L. Tana
Debre Tabor
Bahir Dar
Guna 4231
Weldiya
Er Roseires
Dangila
Choke Mts
Abbai
Bure
Belfodiyo
Abbai (Blue Nile)
Debre Mark'os
Dese
4000 Abuye Meda
Debre Birhan
Asosa
Fiche
Nejo
Nek'emte
Dendi 3298
Addis Ababa (Adis Abeba)
Dembi Dolo
Koma
Sodo
Gore
Jima
Gojab
Awash
Nazret
Ahmar Mts
Dire Dawa
Harer
Asela
Gololcha
Shibeli
Shashemene
Goba
Ginir
Abera
Mizan Teferi
Omo
Yirga 'Alem
Mendebo Mts
Gughe 4200
Abaya
Maji
Arba Minch
Gidole
Bako
Hara Fanna
Gestro
Negele
Ganale Dorya
Dawa
Melka Guba
Mega
Mandera
Dolo Odo
Obock
Tadjoura
Djibouti
Dikhil
L. Abbe
Zeila
Biyo Kaboba
Bab al Mandab
Gulf of Aden
Sabya
Sa'dah
Jizan
Midi
San'a
Al Hudaydah (Hodeida)
Ta'izz
Al Mukha (Mocha)
Shaykh 'Uthman
'Adan
Hadramawt
Saywun
Ash Shihr
Al Mukalla
Caluula
Raas Caseyr
Qandala
Laasqoray
Boosaaso
Ras Khanzira
Karin
Ceerigaabo
Laas Dawaco
Hordiyo
Ras Xaafuun
Berbera
Carcar Mts
Bandarbeyla
Guban
Burao
Hargeysa
Caynabo
Nugaal
Eyl
Haud
Laascaanood
Degeh Bur
Aware
Damot
Ogaden
Werder
Geladi
Jirriiban
Gaalkacyo
Fafan
Imi
Danan
Dabaro
Shebele
Sina Dhaqa
Hobyo
El Goran
Ceelbuur
Beledweyne
Derri
Xuddur
Tayeeglow
Buulobarde
Mareeq
10

SUDAN
ETHIOPIA
SOMALIA
UGANDA
KENYA
RWANDA
BURUNDI
TANZANIA
INDIAN
MAURITIUS
Port Louis
Round I.
St Denis
Réunion
(Fr.)
20S
60E
Equator
0
100
200
300 mls
0
200
400
600 km
Mogadishu
(Muqdisho)
Nairobi
Kampala
Kigali
Mombasa
Jīma
Juba
Wau
Kismaayo
Jamaame
Jilib
Jowhar
Warshiikh
Afgooye
Marka
Baraawe
Beledweyne
Buurhakaba
Baydhabo
Luuq
Mandera
Moyale
Wajir
Garissa
Malindi
Lamu
Patta I.
Kilifi
Kwale
Tanga
Wete
Pemba I.
Pangani
Zanzibar
Kilimanjaro
5895
Meru
4565
Loolmalasin
3648
Ngorongoro
Crater
Serengeti
Nat.Pk
Tsavo
Nat.
Pk
Kirinyaga (Mt. Kenya)
5200
Mt Elgon
4321
Mt Kulal
2293
Mt Nyiru
2805
Kinyeti
3187
Gughe
4200
Mt
Karisimbe
4507
Mendebo
Mts
Ruwenzori
Ra.
Lake
Turkana
Lake
Victoria
Ukerewe
I.
L. Albert
L. Edward
L. Kivu
L. Natron
L. Eyasi
L. Kyoga
Lake Tanganyika
Kenamuke
Swamp
Lotikipi
Plain
Ogaden
Sudd
Masai
Steppe
Mitumba Mts
Shabeelle
Juba (Giuba)
Tana
Galana
Pangani
(Ruvu)
Umba
Victoria Nile
Albert Nile
Shebele
Ganale Dorya
Dawa
Gestro
Fafan
Omo
Gojab
Kerio
Turkwel
Akobo
Pibor
Sue
Numatinna
Uele
Bomokandi
Lindi
Lukuga
Luama
Bubu
Ugalla
Aswa
Abaya
Shibeli
Arusha
Moshi
Voi
Same
Lushoto
Korogwe
Handeni
Kibaya
Kondoa
Babati
Mbulu
Singida
Sekenke
Nzega
Tabora
Kaliua
Uvinza
Ujiji
Kigoma
Kalémié
Kongolo
Kabambare
Fizi
Rutana
Kibondo
Kahama
Shinyanga
Nyakabindi
Geita
Biharamulo
Mwanza
Nansio
Ushashi
Musoma
Tarime
Bukoba
Kibungu
Muyinga
Butare
Gitega
Bujumbura
Uvira
Mwenga
Bukavu
Cyangugu
Goma
Masisi
Walikale
Shabunda
Pangi
Kingombe
Lubutu
Angumu
Lubero
Beni
Kasese
Kabale
Mbarara
Masaka
Entebbe
Jinja
Kakamega
Kisumu
Kisii
Kericho
Narok
Nakuru
Nyahururu Falls
Nyeri
Naivasha
Thika
Embu
Machakos
Kajiado
Makindu
Nanyuki
Isiolo
Mado
Gashi
Afmado
Baardheere
Wanlaweyne
Eldoret
Kitale
Tororo
Mbale
Soroti
Kakamega
Bombo
Mubende
Kabarole
Mambasa
Bafwasende
Nia Nia
Bunia
Hoima
Masindi
Djugu
Pakwach
Lira
Gulu
Kitgum
Moroto
Lodwar
Kangetet
Maralal
Marsabit
Buna
Lokitaung
Mēga
Melka Guba
Negelē
Hara
Fanna
Arba Minch
Gīdolē
Bako
Maji
Mīzan
Teferī
Abera
Yirga
Alem
Shashemenē
Asela
Goba
Gīnīr
Imi
Danan
El Goran
Dolo
Odo
Xuddur
Tayeeglow
Buulobarde
Derri
Ceelbuur
Sina Dhaqa
Hobyo
Mareeq
Geladī
Gaalkacyo
Dabaro
Jirriiban
Werder
Damot
Tor
Gore
Akobo
Ayod
Duk
Faiwil
Pibor
Post
Bor
Shambe
Rumbek
Yirol
Tali
Post
Amadi
Mongalla
Torit
Laylo
Yei
Moyo
Nimule
Arua
Aru
Mungbere
Isiro
Watsa
Faradje
Aba
Dungu
Niangara
Doruma
Yambio
Maridi
Tambura
Tonj
Obo

OCEAN
SEYCHELLES
Aldabra Is
Cosmoledo Is
Assumption
Is Glorieuses
COMOROS
Moroni
Grande Comore
Mohéli
Mutsamudu
Anjouan
Mayotte (Fr.)
Dzaoudzi
Mozambique Channel
Juan de Nova (Fr.)
MADAGASCAR
(MALAGASY REP.)
Tanjona Bobaomby
Antsirañana (Diego Suarez)
Tanjona Anorontany
Ambilobe
Nosy Bé
Ambanja
Massif du Tsaratanana
Vohimarina (Vohémar)
Sambava
Antalaha
Analalava
Bealanana
Antsohiny
Befandriana
Maroantsetra
Mandritsara
C. Masoala
Mampikony
Mananara
Nosy Boraha
Ambodifototra
Fenoarivo Atsinanana
Toamasina (Tamatave)
Ampasimanolotra (Vohibinany)
Antananarivo (Tananarive)
Moramanga
Ambatondrazaka
Ankazobe
Anjozorobe
Ivongo Soanierana
Maevatanana
Tsaratanana
Ambato Boeny
Marovoay
Mahajangao (Majunga)
B. de Mahajamba
B. de Bombetoka
Tanjona Vilanandro
Besalampy
Morafenobe
Maintirano
Nosy Barren
Tsiroanomandidy
Miandrivazo
Ambatolampy
Betafo
Antsirabe
Mahanoro
Morondava
Manabo
Malaimbandy
Atofinandrahana
Nosy Varika
Ambositra
Manakara
Mananjary
Ifanadiana
Ambalavao
Fianarantsoa
Ambohimahasoa
Manja
Morombe
Ankazoabo
Massif de L'Isalo
Ihosy
Ivohibe
Farafangana
Vangaindrano
Sakaraha
Toliara
Betroka
Betioky
Midongy Atsimo
Tropic of Capricorn
Bekily
Isoanala
Ampanihy
Beloha
Ambovombe
Amboasary
Tôlañaro
Tsiombe
Tanjona
Dar es Salaam
Morogoro
Kisiju
Kilindoni
Mafia I.
Mohoro
Kilwa Kivinje
Kilwa Kisiwani
Lindi
Mtwara
C. Delgado
Palma
Mocimboa da Praia
Ibo
B. de Pemba
Pemba
Mecufi
Memba
Nacala
Moçambique
Nampula
Angoche
Moma
Pebane
Vila da Maganja
Quelimane
Chinde
Blantyre
Zomba
Lilongwe
MALAWI
L. Nyasa (L. Malawi)
L. Chilwa
Mbeya
Iringa
Ifakara
Mahenge
Liwale
Sumbawanga
L. Rukwa
Ruaha Nat.Pk
Muchinga Mts
ZAMBIA
Kasama
Mansa
L. Bangweulu
Lubumbashi (Elisabethville)
Likasi
Ndola
Kitwe
Mufulira
Luanshya
Kabwe
Chipata
Mbamba Bay
Songea
Tunduru
Newala
Masasi
Nachingwea

hills are much cooler than the rest of the coast making it a very pleasant climate. The rainforest itself is totally unspoilt and opens out into rolling downs and gentle hills.

There are a number of antelope, buffalo, waterbuck, reedbuck, hyena, wart hog, giraffe, elephant, leopard, baboon and bush pig in the reserve. It is the only place in Kenya where you can see sable antelope. There is a nature trail which is pleasant to take and a picnic area.

It is possible to take a a half-day trip form Mombasa for US$25 (booking through travel agents, see page 199).

Park information

● Where to stay

A *Shimba Hills* PO Box 47557, Nairobi, T Nairobi 335807 F Nairobi 340541. Well designed round a water hole, which is illuminated at night for viewing. Shop.

E *Bandas*, located at a site about 3 km from the main gate to the Reserve. Communal showers and lavatories. **E** *Camping* at at the Banda site.

● Transport

Regular buses from Mombasa for Kwale, about 30km distant. From Kwale the Reserve is only 5km along a murram track.

SIBIOLI NATIONAL PARK

Sibiloi National Park is one of the less known of Kenya's national parks despite its large size of 1,575 sq km. This is probably because of its isolated geographical location on the eathern shores of Lake Turkana, 720km from Nairobi in Eastern province. The landscape is grassy plains with yellow spear grass and doum palms. Within the park is Central Island holding the world's largest crocodile population about 12,000. Other mammals include zebra, gazelle, oryx, hartebeest, topi, lion and cheetah. There are around 350 recorded species of birds.

In 1968 the Leakeys made many remarkable fossil finds of humans from 10,00-12,000 years ago. The Koobi Fora palaeontological site is here, as is a museum near the parks headquarters which houses the remains of prehistoric elephants among other things. This site has also yielded information about the environment one to 3 million years ago.

Park information

● Camping

E *Camping*, there are several campsites in the Park but you will need to bring all your own supplies, including petrol.

● Transport

It is about 120km from Lioyangalani along an unpaved trail through the desert to North Horr and then NW to Alia Bay, the park headquarters. The most practical way of getting here is by air from Nairobi, or by boat from Ferguson's Gulf.

SOUTH KITUI NATIONAL RESERVE

This is the second national reserve in Kitui district. It is 1,800 sq km adjacent to Tsavo E National Park but unfortunately no tourism is allowed at present.

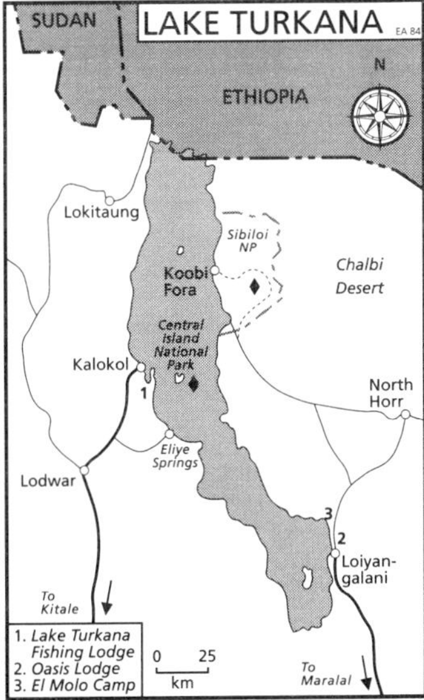

SOUTH TURKANA NATIONAL RESERVE

Situated in the Rift Valley in Turkana District, this remote reserve is rarely visited and has no tourist facilities. It is 100km N of Kitale and if you do venture up here you are likely to see elephant or greater kudu in the dense thorn bush, riverine forest and scattered forest which make up its 1,000 sq km.

TANA RIVER PRIMATE NATIONAL RESERVE

120 km N of Malindi on the Tana River between Hola and Garsen. The highly diversified riverine forest has at least 7 different types of primate including the red colobus and mangabey monkeys, and baboon. A number of other animals roam here including elephant, hippo, gazelle, duiker, river hog, giraffe, lion, waterbukc, bush squirrel and crocodiles. There is a research station for study of the primates.

● Camping

E *Camping* Available at Mchelelo camp in an attractive site.

● Transport

There are buses running between Lamu and Garissa, and some of them detour to Mnazini village just to the S of the Reserve, from where it is possible to walk N along the River (there is a small boat ferry just before Baomo Village) to the campsite.

TSAVO NATIONAL PARKS – EAST AND WEST

This is the largest national park in Kenya at around 21,000 sq km. It lies in the southern part of the country and is bissected by the Mombasa-Nairobi railway and road link. For administrative purposes it has been split into 2 sections, E (11,000 sq km) and West (8,500 sq km). The remoteness of much of the park makes it a haven for poachers but recent anti-poaching measures are having an effect. As a consequence, much of the northern area (about 2 thirds of E Tsavo) is off limits to the public in an attempt to halt poaching here which has decimated the rhino population from 8,000 in 1970 to around 100 today. Recent strict anti-poaching laws have been particularly successful in Tsavo and number of elephants in increasing again. Both parts are fairly easily navigated with a good map as all tracks are clearly defined, and junctions are numbered.

Tsavo East is the much less-visited side of the park where you will be able to see the wildlife without the usual hordes of other tourists. It mainly consists of vast plains of scrubland home to huge herds of elephants. The landscape is vast, and empty of any sign of humans dotted with baobab trees. The Kanderi Swamp, not far from the main entrance at Voi Gate, has the most wildlife in the area. The main attraction of this part of the park is the Aruba dam built across the Voi River where many animals and bird congregate. Mudanda Rock towers above a natural dam and at certain times during the dry season draws hundreds of elephants.

As time goes on, Tsavo E is opening itself up to package tourism, particularly the budget camping safaris. The wardens have even started to open up parts of the northern sector to upmarket low-profile camping and walking parties. This means the overwhelming feeling of solititude is slowly disappearing, though its vast size means you are likely to be alone for most of the time.

Tsavo West is the more developed part of the park combining good access, good facilities and stunning views over the tall grass and woodland scenery. The environment is well-watered and this combined with volcanic soils supports a vast quantity and diversity of plant and animal life. The main attractions are the watering holes by Kilaguni and Ngulia Lodges which entice a huge array of wildlife particularly in the dry season. During

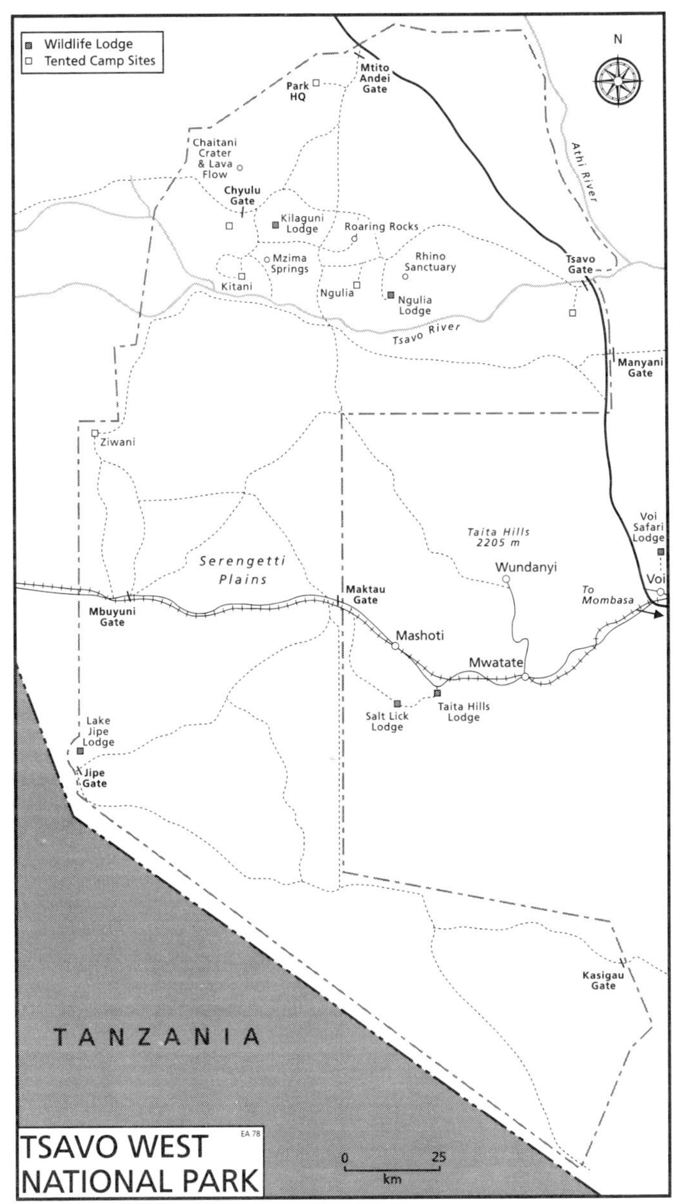

TSAVO WEST NATIONAL PARK

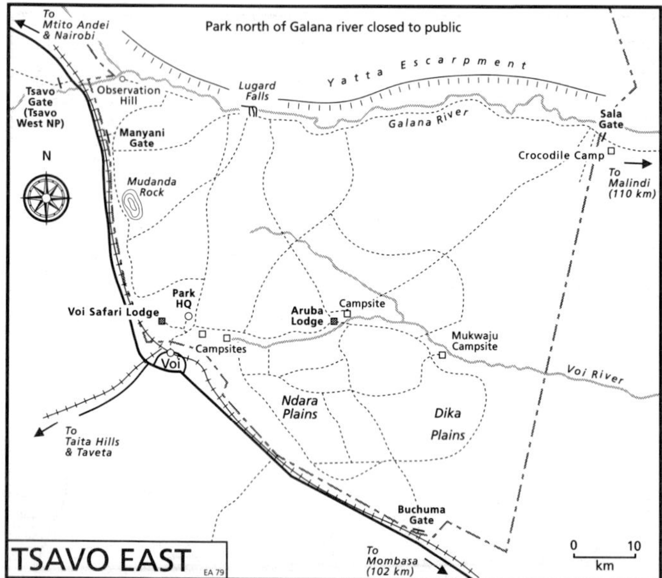

the autumn the areas around *Ngulia Lodge* are a stopover for hundreds of thousands of birds from Europe in their annual migration S.

Not far from the *Kilaguni Lodge* is the Mzima Springs, a favourite haunt of hippos and crocodiles. There is an underwater viewing chamber here, but the hippos have obviously decided against being studied so closely by moving to the other side of the pool. Also around the lodges are the spectacular Shaitani lava flow and caves which are well worth visiting. You will need to bring a good torch to explore them. Chaimu Crater to the S of *Kilaguni Lodge* can be climbed and though there is little danger of animals here, it is best to be careful.

Wildlife you are likely to spot include: hyrax, agama lizards, dwarf mongooses, marabou storks, baboons, antelope, buffalo, zebra, giraffe, jackals and hyenas, crocodiles, hippos, leopards, lions, cheetahs. This part of Tsavo has some black rhino though most have been moved to the Rhino Sanctuary now.

Park information

● Costs

Each park US$20 per day

● Where to stay (Tsavo West)

A ***Kilaguni Lodge***, PO Box 30471, Nairobi, T Nairobi 336 858, F Nairobi 218109. Best lodge in the park and also the most expensive. Every room faces the waterhole and has a verandah. Swimming pool. **A** ***Ngulia Lodge***, PO Box 30471, Nairobi, T Nairobi 336 858, F Nairobi 218109, is slightly cheaper but still very good. The waterhole, again, is a big draw both for the animals and tourists. Swimming pool. Good location. **A** ***Lake Jipe Lodge***, PO Box 3107, Nairobi, T Nairobi 227623, Tlx 25508. Near the Tanzanian border on the western border. Swimming pool. Isolated position. Usually not crowded. Views of the Lake and the Pare Mountains.

D ***Ngulia Safari Camp*** and ***Kitani Safari Camp***, T Nairobi 340 331, offer self-service accommodation in the park in fully equipped bandas including bathrooms with hot water. Both places have a good friendly atmosphere and are popular with Kenyans and tourists alike. **E** ***Camping***, each of the gates at Tsavo,

Mtito Andei and Chyulu have camp sites. There is also a campsite at Ziwani on the western boundary of the park with full-size permanent tents and excellent food available.

● Where to stay (East)

A *Voi Safari Lodge*, PO Box 30471, Nairobi, T Nairobi 336 858, F Nairobi 218109. Slightly cheaper than the lodges of equivalent standard in West Tsavo and is much less crowded. It is 5km into the park from Voi Gate. Swimming pool. Good location.

D *Aruba Lodge*, PO Box 298, Voi, T Voi 2647) Bookings: PO Box 14982, Nairobi, T Nairobi 720382. Close to the dam. Banda accommodation, and very good value. There is a small shop nearby selling basic provisions.

E *Camping*, there are sites at Voi Gate, Kanderi Swamp, Aruba Lodge and at the Makwaju Campsite on the Voi River about 50km from Voi Gate. All have toilets, showers and running water.

● Where to eat and drink

As usual, you should bring all your own provisions in to the park including petrol and water. You should be able to eat or drink at any of the lodges if you so desire. There is a shop at Voi gate in the east selling warm beers, sodas, bread and some vegetables and another shop in West Tsavo selling basic provisions.

● Transport

The park headquarters are off the Mombasa-Nairobi road at the northern end of the park through the Mtito Andei Gate. It is 30 km from here to *Kilaguni Lodge* in the park. This is the busiest entrance to the park, and therefore the best one to aim for if you intend to hitch your way through the park. If you drive along the same Mombasa-Nairobi road for 48km you come to Tsavo Gate. Tsavo West is probably the easiest park to get around if you do not have your own car as there are plenty of buses from Nairobi to Mtito Andei, and your chances of getting a lift are fairly good.

To get to the park from Voi, the easiest entrance is at Makatau near the Tailta Hills and Salt Lick lodges. This road cuts across the park exiting at the Mbuyuni Gate in the West. It is easy to get to Tanzania from here via Taveta (see page 171).

● Transport

You follow the same road as for Tsavo West (Nairobi-Mombasa road) and enter at the Park HQ at Voi Gate. There is a small educational centre at Voi Gate.

If you are coming from Malindi, it is 110km up to Sala Gate on the eastern side of the park. There is a road cutting across to the Galana river and on up to Manyani Gate on the Mombasa-Nairobi road.

INFORMATION FOR VISITORS

Contents

Before you go

Entry requirements

● Visas

The nationals of the following countries **do not require visas:** all members of the British Commonwealth (**excluding** Australians, Nigerians and Sri Lankans); Eire, Germany, Denmark, Finland, Ethiopia, Sweden, Spain, Turkey and Uruguay.

If you do not need a visa, you will be issued with a visitor's pass on arrival which allows you to travel freely for up to 3 months. You will need to negotiate this with the official on arrival. If you want to get this extended, you can stay a maximum of 6 months in the country fairly easily. In Nairobi this can be done at Nyayo House, corner of Kenyatta Ave and Uhuru Highway (Mon-Fri 0830-1230 and 1400-1530); it can also be done at the Provincial Commissioner's Offices in Embu, Garissa, Kisumu, Mombasa and Nakuru. Do check your visitor's pass as it has been known for people who have overstayed their time in the country to be fined quite heavily.

For people who do need a visa, they can be obtained in advance from any Kenyan embassy, consulate or high commission or from a British embassy in any country with no Kenyan diplomatic representation. It normally takes 24 hrs to be issued with your visa, you will need 2 passport photographs and either proof of financial status or a ticket out of the country. Visas are issued for 6 months, though this does not necessarily mean you can stay in the country for 6 months. The length of your stay is at the discretion of the immigration officer on entry, and usually depends on how much money you have and your appearance. You are asked how long you want to stay. You will then be issued with a visitors' pass, usually for 3 months. You can arrange visa extensions in Nairobi or any of the Provincial capitals: see above for visitor's pass extensions.

It is possible to get a visa on arrival, but this takes ages and if you arrive at night, you may have to wait until the next day.

● Vaccinations

None are required by law but if you are entering the country overland, you may be asked for a yellow fever and/or a cholera certificate. You should have these done before arrival as a sensible health precaution anyway.

● Kenyan representation overseas

Australia, PO Box 1990, 33 Ainslie Ave, GPO Canberra, T 062 474748; **Austria**, Rotenturmstrasse 22, 1010 Vienna, T 01 633242; **Belgium**, Av Joyeuse Entree 1-5, Brussels, T 02 2303065; **Canada**, Gillia Building, Suite 600, 415 Laurier Ave, West Ottawa, Ontario, T 613 563 1773; **Egypt**, PO Box 362, 20 Boulos Hanna St, Dokki, Cairo, T 02 70455; **Ethiopia**, PO Box 3301, Hiher 16, Kebelle 01, Fikre Mariam Road, Addis Ababa, T 180033; **France**, 3 rue Cimarosa, 75116 Paris, T 1 4 553 3500; **Germany**, Villichgasse 17, 5300 Bonn 2, T 0228 356041; **India**, 66 Vasant Marg, Vasant Vihar, New Delhi, T 11 672280; **Italy**,

Consulate, CP 10755, 00144 Rome; **Japan**, 24-20 Nishi-Azabu 3-Chome, Minato-Ku, Tokyo, T 03 479 4006; **Netherlands**, Konninginnegracht 102, The Hague, T 703 504215; **Nigeria**, PO Box 6464, 53 Queens Drive, Ikoyi, Lagos, T 01 682768; **Russia**, Bolshaya Ordinka, Dom 70, Moscow, T 237 4702; **Rwanda**, Blvd de Nyabugogo, PO Box 1215, Kigali, T 772774; **Saudi Arabia**, PO Box 95458, Riyadh 11693, T 01 488 2484; **Sudan**, Street 3, Amarat, PO Box 8242,Khartoum, T 40386/ 43758; **Sweden**, Birger Jarlsgatan 37, 2st 11145 Stockholm, T 08 218300; **Tanzania**, 4th Floor, NIC Investment House, Samora Ave, PO Box 5231, Dar-es-Salaam, T 51 31502; **Uganda**, 60 Kira Rd, PO Box 5220, Kampala, T 41 231 861; **United Arab Emirates**, PO Box 3854 Abu Dhabi; **United Kingdom**, 45 Portland Place, London W1N 4AS, T 071 636 2371; **USA**, 2249 R St NW, Washington DC 20008, T 202 387 6101; or 9100 Wilshire Blvd, Beverly Hills, CA 90212, T 213 274 6635; **Zaire**, Plot 5002, ave de l'Ouganda, BP 9667 Zone Gombe, Kinshasa, T 12 30117; **Zambia**, 5207 United Nations Ave, PO Box 50298, Lusaka, T 01 212531; **Zimbabwe**, 95 Park Lane, PO Box 4069, Harare, T 04 792 901).

● Overseas representation in Kenya

See Nairobi, page 65; Mombasa, page 115.

● Tourist Information

Tourist information centre Located at the junction of Moi Ave and Mama Ngina St opposite the Hilton in Nairobi. There is also a free publication called *Tourist's Kenya* which is published fortnightly and which gives a run down on things going on. There is another publication called *What's On* which comes out monthly.

You should be able to buy most maps you need in Nairobi though you are quite likely to have a better choice of information and maps in your own country than in Kenya itself. A good source is *Stanford's Map and Travel Bookshop*, 12-14 Long Acre, London WC2E 9LP, T 071 836 1321. The Survey of Kenya park maps are well worth getting and are inexpensive in Nairobi (they are double the price if you get them at the park gates). *The Nation*, located on Kenyatta Ave next to the *Thorn Tree Cafe* has a good selection maps.

● Tourist information overseas

France 5 rue Volnay, Paris 75002, T 42 60 66 88; **Germany** Hochstrasse 53, 6000 Frankfurt 1, T 69 28 25 51); **Hong Kong** 1309 Liu Chong Hing Bak Building, 24 Des Voeux Rd, Central GPO Box 5280, Hong Kong, T 236053; **Japan** Rm 216, Yurakucho Building, 1-10 Yurakucho, 1-Chome, Chiyoda-Ku, Tokyo, T 214 4595; **Sweden**, Birger Jarsgatan 37, 11145 Stockholm, T 21 23 00; **Switzerland**, Bleicherweg 30, CH-8039, Zurich T 202 22 44; **United Kingdom** 25 Brooks Mews, London W1Y 1LF, T 071 355 3144; **USA** 424 Madison Ave, New York, NY 10017, T 212 486-1300; 9100 Wilshire Blvd, Doheny Plaza Suite 111, Beverly Hills, CA 90121, T 213 274 6634.

● Travel and tour agents

Kenya See Nairobi, page 68; Mombasa, page 116.

Overseas *Abercrombie & Kent*, Sloane Sq House, Holbein Place, London SW1W 8NS, T 071 730 9600. Range of packages. *Africa Travel Centre* 4 Medway Court, Leigh St, London WC1H 9QX, T 071 387 1211, F 383 7512. Inexpensive package trips. *Art of Travel* 286 Lavender Hill, London SW11 1LJ, T 071 738 2038. Customised safaris. *Dragoman* Camp Green Kenton Rd, Debenham, Suffolk IP14 9LA, T 0728 861133. Overland expedition specialist. *Exodus* 9 Weir Rd, London SW12 0LT, T 081 675 7996. Overland expeditions. *Flamingo Tours* 167 Acton Lane, London W4 5HN, T 081 995 3505. Inexpensive packages. *Guerba* 101 Eden Vale Rd, Westbury. Wiltshire BA13 3QX, T 0373 827046, F 0373 858351. Overland expedition specialist. Range of packages. *Hayes & Jarvis* 152 Kings St, London W6 0QU, T 081 748 5050. Inexpensive packages. *Kumuka Africa* 42 Westbourne Grove, London W2 5SH, T 071 221 2348. Inexpensive packages. *Kuoni Travel* 33 Maddox St, London W1R 9LD, T 071 499 8636. range of packages *Select Travel* 24 Culloden Rd, Enfield EN2 8QD, T 081 363 8202. *Tracks Africa* 12 Abingdon Rd, London W8 6AF, T 071 937 5964. Package and specialist safaris. *Twickers World* 22 Church St, Twickenham TW1 3NW, T 081 892 7606. Special packages.

When to go

● Best time to visit

There are 2 rainy seasons in the country, the long rains Mar-Apr and the short rains Oct-Dec. However, even during the rains there is invariably sunshine each day.

Health

● Staying healthy

On the whole, Kenya is a healthy country to visit but as with all tropical countries, it is best to take certain precautions. Firstly, malaria is a real problem in most areas of the country except way up in the highlands. Do not be fooled into thinking it is not very serious, it is one of the major killers in tropical Africa today. This means you will need to protect against it by taking tablets before, during and after your visit. Ask your doctor for advice on which anti-malaria tablets you should take as the parasite which passes on malaria becomes resistent to tablets from time to time.

Secondly, sexually transmitted diseases and HIV are widespread throughout the country.

● Water

To avoid Hepatitis A, it is best to be careful about water, particularly if you are travelling in areas where a lack of water is a common problem. This may sound easier said than done, but most places will have sodas to drink as an alternative to water. Bilharzia, which you usually get from being in stagnant waters, the home of freshwater snails which harbour the bug, is not a common problem with travellers. To avoid it, avoid stagnant waters.

● Insurance

It is important to get medical insurance whilst travelling as the only hospitals worth going to in Kenya are expensive. If you intend to spend any time in more remote areas, it may be worth subscribing to the flying doctor service at PO Box 30125, Nbi T 02 501301 or 501280. They will fly you back to a medical centre if necessary.

● Further health information

To be on the safe side, you can get a travel pack from British Airways Travel Clinic and other places which includes syringes. You could also take pain killers, anti-diarrhoea pills, antiseptic cream and swabs, plasters and lipsalve all of which are very expensive in the country compared to Europe, North America or Australia. If you ever do have a bad stomach upset with diarrhoea and vomiting, weak black tea or water mixed with sugar and salt for 24 hrs can help against dehydration. Also see Health Section, page 21

Money

● Currency

The currency in Kenya is the Kenya shilling. As it is not a hard currency, it cannot be brought into or out of the country. If you have any Kenya shillings left when leaving the country, do not be tempted to destroy them – people have been arrested for doing this. There are banks and bureau de change at both Nairobi and Mombasa airports. There are inevitable queues but at Nairobi it is marginally quicker to change your money after you go through customs.

● Credit cards

Many are widely accepted around the country, particularly Diner's Club and American Express with Visa as a poor third. Access and Mastercard acceptability more limited.

● Cost of living

It is getting cheaper and cheaper for budget visitors as the Kenya shilling devalues. It is quite possible for budget visitors to travel by public transport, eat and stay for US$20 a day. Services specifically designed for tourists, such as the safaris, car hire, access to national parks etc can be expensive, and prices are adjusted as the currency depreciates. Moderate hotel accommodation and meals can be had for US$40 a day.

● Exchange rate

The exchange rate floats and is likely to have changed from that quoted here. As of August 1994 the rate was: Ksh 55.56 = US$1.

● Travellers' cheques

You should be able to change money or travellers' cheques throughout the country, particularly British pounds and American dollars. Most large hotels exchange money 24 hrs a day, the rate usually less good than the rate in the banks.

● Banking

Hours are Mon to Fri 0830 -1300. Sat 0830-1100. Bank Foreign Exchange Bureau are usually open longer hrs.

There is a black market in Kenya but it seems hardly worth the effort. Not only is it risky (you may be treated unpleasantly and deported if caught), but the rate you will achieve is hardly more than bank rates.

Getting there

● Air

Kenya is the cheapest country in East Africa to get to by air and consequently is a good place to start off a tour of the region.

London is by the far the cheapest place in

the western world to get to Kenya from and there are loads of discounted flights and package holidays. In the past, the only discounts were for unsold seats but now there is an enormous range of deals for students, academics or people under a certain age (usually either 26 or 32). Although not all the deals may mean cheaper flights, they usually do mean flexible flight arrangements and flight dates which is very helpful if you are planning a longish trip and do not know when you want to go back. A very good deal is to look for a package deal to Mombasa and travel on from there. All flights either go to Nairobi, the capital (about 9 hrs from London) or Mombasa on the Indian Ocean coast (about 11 hrs).

The cheapest plane tickets are in the 'off-season' from Feb to Jun and again from Oct to early Dec. If you do have to go during peak times, book as far in advance as you can, particularly if you aim to get there in mid-Dec when flights get full very quickly. ***Aeroflot*** offers the cheapest deals, but the flight makes stops all over the place including a 6 hr stop in Moscow. If you can afford slightly more, it is well worth it. ***Balkan Bulgarian*** or ***EgyptAir*** offer very good deals, the latter being the more reliable and offering a stop over in Cairo for as long as you like at no extra costs. ***Air France***, ***KLM***, ***Kenya Airways***, ***British Airways*** all have surprisingly good deals as do ***Saudia*** and ***Ethiopian Airlines***.

If you are short of time, a package holiday could well be a useful option particularly if you go out of the peak season when you can get excellent deals. Beach holidays are far cheaper than safaris. It is a good idea to find out as much as you can about the hotel in the package deal before going, though you can always stay elsewhere if necessary. It is sometimes the case that a package trip to the coast will be cheaper than a flight alone.

Specialist Agencies for discounted fares, see page 200.

From Europe Access by air to Kenya is from all over Europe.

From Africa There are a number of flights flying direct from around Africa: **Abidjan** (Ivory Coast); **Accra** (Ghana); **Addis Ababa** (Ethiopia); **Antananarivo** (Madagascar); **Bujumbura** (Burundi); **Cairo** (Egypt); **Dakar** (Senegal); **Dar-es-Salaam** (Tanzania); **Douala** (Cameroon); **Dzaoudzi** (Comoros); **Entebbe** (Uganda); **Gaborone** (Botswana); **Harare** (Zimbabwe); **Johannesburg** (South Africa); **Khartoum** (Sudan); **Kigali** (Rwanda); **Kinshasa** (Zaire); **Lagos** (Nigeria); **Lome** (Togo); **Luanda** (Angola); **Lusaka** (Zambia); **Moroni** (Comoros); **Ouagadougou** (Burkina Faso); **Zanzibar** (Tanzania).

Road

Quite a popular option with travellers is the overland tours to Kenya from Europe. There are plenty on offer, though itineraries may change taking account of political and military events around Africa. A popular route is from Western Africa passing through Zaire around Lake Victoria and cutting through Tanzania to get to Kenya. Another option would be to team up with other people and hire a vehicle or use public transport to cross Africa. This is perfectly feasible but does take some organising and a lot of time.

Ethiopia The crossing is is at **Moyale**, between Marsabit and Addis Ababa. The restricting that only Kenyans and Ethiopians can make this crossing now apears to have been lifted. It is a matter of hiring lifts from truck drivers on the route.

Somalia In more tranquil times it has been possible to take a bus from Kismayo to the border at **Liboi**, and then on to Garissa; or from Mogadishu to **Mandera**, and then on to Wajir. These crossings are currently not an option for travellers as a result of the civil war in Somalia.

Sudan In principle it has in the past been possible to to cross from Lodwar to Juba, although there was never any public transport on this route, and it was a matter of hiring rides from truck drivers. This is not currently an option for travellers as a result of civil war in the S of Sudan.

Tanzania The main road crossing is at **Namanga** (see page 170) on the road between Arusha and Nairobi. This is reasonably quick and efficient and there are through buses and good roads all the way. Other crossings are at **Lunga Lunga** (see page 123) between Mombasa and Dar Es Salaam. The road on the Tanzanian side is less good, but there are overnight through buses between the 2 cities. There are also crossings at **Taveta** (see page 170) between Moshi and Voi; at **Isebania** (see page 397) between Kisumu, Tanzania section page 308) and Musoma; and across the border from Maasai Mara Park into the Serengetti.

Uganda There are buses that run from Nairobi to Kampala, crossing at **Malaba** and **Tororo**, taking about 15 hrs and costing around

US$15. There is a variety of standards of service. It is possible to do the journey in stages in minibuses or peugeot taxis, but buses are more comfortable and safer.

There are also a border crossings at **Busia**, but no through buses, but convenient for Kisumu; and at **Suam** to the N of Mt Elgon.

● Sea

There have been boats (hydrofoils) from Mombasa to **Tanga, Zanzibar** and **Dar es Salaam** (see page 117). Although these have not been operating for a while, resumption of the service is expected. The cost was about the same as the air fare from Mombasa (US$45).

It is possible to take a dhow from Mombasa to **Tanga** and **Dar es Salaam** and (see page 262). However you must expect to wait around for a week or more for one to depart. It will take one or 2 days depending on the weather. Expect to pay about US$15, bring all your own food, and you will sit and sleep on the cargo. At one time it was also possible to get dhows to **Kismayo, Mogadishu, Berbera** and **Djibouti**. These are not currently an option with the civil war in Somalia.

There are a few companies which will take you by boat from Europe to Kenya, though this is certainly not a budget option. ***Strand Cruise Centre***, Charing Cross Shopping Centre, The Strand, London T 071 836 6363 specialises in cruises from England through the Mediterranean down the Suez Canal to Djibouti and on to Mombasa. It costs around US$3,000 one way and takes a month.

● Customs

You are expected to pay duty on items brought as gifts or for sale in Kenya, though not if they are for your personal use. You are more likely to be asked if you have anything to declare at airports than at the border crossings from neighbouring countries.

When you arrive

● Airport information

Departure tax You will need to pay a departure tax of US$20 when leaving the country by air. This has to be paid in a hard currency. If you do not have the correct money, your change will be given in Kenya shillings which you are not allowed to take out of the country.

Transport to town **Nairobi** Jomo Kenyatta International Airport, located 15 km from the centre to the S of the city. Kenya Airways run a bus to and from their office on Koinange St, and the fare is around US$3. Service is hourly 0700 to 2000. A taxi is roughly US$12. There are set rates to particular hotels – check with the dispatcher before entering taxi.

Mombasa Moi International Airport is located on the mainland about 10 km out of the centre of town. Kenya Airways operates a shuttle bus, about US$2. Taxi about US$9.

● Beggars

Most common in Nairobi and Mombasa. Many are clearly destitute and or disabled. Many Kenyans give money to beggars who in a country with no social welfare have few alternative means of livelihood. A fairly recent phenomena has been the rise of street children in Nairobi who swarm on tourists who give money. A more constructive approach is to make a donation to a organisation rehabilitating street children (see page 13).

● Conduct

Stand for the national anthem and show respect if the national flag is being raised or lowered. Do not take photographs of military or official buildings or personnel, especially the President. Respect the national currency (do not tear it) and the currency laws of the country and if you have to have any dealings with the police be polite. Another useful thing to remember is to comply with the country's drug laws. There is an ambivalent attitude to both cannibis (*bhangi* – which is readily available) and *miraa* both of which are illegal, but appear to be tolerated by the authorities. However if you are caught your embassy is unlikely to be sympathetic.

● Electricity

220-240 volts supply. Square 3-pin plugs in modern buildings. Great variety in older places. An adapter is advised.

● Hours of business

Banks Mon to Fri 0830 to 1330 and from 0830 to 1100 on Sat.

Embassies Usually open in the mornings only.

Kiosks Will often open all hrs, as the owner frequently lives at the kiosk.

Post Offices Mon to Fri 0800 to 1300 and 1400 to 1630. Some are also open on Saturdays.

Shops Generally from 0800 to 1700 or 1800, and on Saturdays.

● Official time
Kenya is 3 hrs ahead of GMT.

● Safety
A general rule to follow seems to be that the more prevalent tourists are, the greater the need to be on your guard. Nairobi and Mombasa seem to have the worst reputations, and the most popular National Parks have their fair share of robberies. Basically, you just have to be sensible and not carry expensive cameras, open bags or expensive jewellry and be careful about carrying large sums of money when you are rubbing shoulders with local people. Also, do not automatically expect your belongings to be safe in a tent. In built up areas, lock your car, and if there is a security guard (askari) nearby, pay him a small sum to watch over it. There is no need to pay street children (see page 13) to guard a vehicle. Avoid walking around after dusk, particularly in the more rundown urban areas – take a taxi. The majority of people you will meet are honest and ready to help you so there is no need to get paranoid about your safety.

● Shopping
Kenyan **baskets** are popular and cheap made from sisal and leather. They are particularly cheap around Kitui. **Soapstone** sculptures and objet-d'arts are good value (Kisumu) as are the wooden carvings which are for sale everywheve around the country. **Jewellry** is also popular with beaded necklaces and bracelets of turquoise and garnets or other semi-precious stones being good value.

Many tribal people sell traditional objects including weapons, stools, jewellery and musical instruments. The authentic articles are considerably more expensive than items made for the tourist market. Antique masks are very rarely from Kenya, most have been imported from Zaire or West Africa.

There are many different types of **cloth** peculiar to Kenya. **Kangas** are cotton wraps used by women, designed in hundreds of different styles, often with Kenyan proverbs often printed onto them. **Kikois** are men's loincloths and are more sedate prints in wonderful reds, oranges and yellows. They are particularly good value along the coast.

Bargaining There is an enormous difference between a 'tourist' price and a local price. Until you get a feel for what the local prices might be it is hard to bargain effectively, but you will soon realise most prices are negotiable.

● Tricksters
Suspect anyone who has a hard-luck story. Do not change money on the black market, as this invites a confidence trick. Popular ploys are schoolboys with sponsorship forms, or being bumped into by some-one who drops something, you bend to pick it up for them – only to be taken by 2 men from behind who will relieve you of your possessions.

● Weights and measures
Metric. In country areas items are often sold by the piece.

● Women
Women do have to be more wary than men, though Kenya seems to be a pleasanter place for lone women travellers than many countries. If you are hassled, it is best to ignore the person totally whatever you feel, expressions of anger are often taken as acts of encouragement. Women in Kenya dress very decorously, and it is wise to follow suit particularly in small towns and rural areas. Kenyan women will generally be very supportive if they see you are being harassed and may well intervene if they think you need help, but the situation is very rarely anything more than a nuisance. You are more likely to be approached at the coast, as the number of women coming for sexual adventure has encouraged this type of pestering. The key is to keep patient and have a sense of humour about it.

Where to stay

● Where to stay
Hotels Kenya has a huge range of hotels from the ultra-luxurious lodges and beach hotels to local board and lodgings. At the cheaper end of the market, a double room should cost you around US$3-5 going up slightly if it is with washing or toilet facilities.

Almost every town will have some form of accommodation even if it is a room hired in a local house, so you should rarely be stuck for somewhere to stay.

Prices of hotels are not always a good indication of their quality, and it is sensible checking what you will get before commiting yourself to stay. You can expect to pay more in the high season particularly mid-Dec to mid-Feb and prices are often negotiable, even in large hotels.

● Self-catering
This is an increasingly popular option on the

Hotel Classifications

A+ Over US$100 a night. International standards and decor, air conditioning, self-contained rooms, swimming pool, restaurants, bars, business services.

A US$40-100. First class standards, air-conditioning, attached bathrooms, restaurants and bars, swimming pool.

B US$20-40. Tourist class, comfortable with air conditioning or fans, attached bathrooms, restaurant, bar, public rooms.

C US$10-20. Budget, fans, shared bathroom facilities.

D US$5-10. Guest house, no fan, shared bathroom, cold water.

E Under US$5. Basic guest house, simple bed, no soap or towels, no wardrobe, shared bathroom facilities, erratic cold water supply, no fans or mosquito nets.

coast and is often surprisingly good value if you intend to stay for a while. For more information contact ***Kenya Villas*** Westminster House, PO Box 57046, Kenyatta Ave, Nairobi T 338 072.

● Hostels

The youth hostel in Nairobi is not only an excellent place to stay, but also a good place to meet other travellers. Apart from this one, there are very few hostels around the country. There are a number of YMCAs and YWCAs, most of which are clean and safe and of course very cheap. The ones in Nairobi tend to cater for long-term residents and many people from the university stay at the YMCA, so it is a good place to meet Kenyans. The Naivasha YMCA has a deservedly good reputation.

Camping

There are many camp sites all over the country, they are usually very cheap with basic amenities and some are very good. Camping can be a very useful option as it allows you to stay wherever you want, and is an essential if you are on a tight budget but want to explore the national parks. You should always have your own tent and basic equipment as these cannot always be hired at the sites.

● Work Camps

The Kenya Voluntary Development Association set these up in 1962. Their aim is to bring Kenyans and other nationals together to work on local projects ie irrigation ditches, building schools etc. The work is quite hard, but most people seem to enjoy them. The average length of stay is 4 weeks costing US$170. You will share local conditions implying pretty basic amenities. The average age is under 25. If you are interested contact *KVDA*, PO Box 48902, Nairobi, Kenya T 225 379.

Food and drink

● Food

Market liberalisation of the the Kenya economy and deregulation of price controls means the price of food has increased over recent years. This has caused hardship on many Kenyans but for tourists the prices are very low, mainly because devaluation of the Kenyan shilling means you get more shillings for your own currency than before. The quality of the food in Kenya is generally excellent. The fruit and vegetables taste very different, (invariably better) from produce you get at home (particularly avocados, mangos, pineapples and passion fruit). Kenya's meat is very good – you might get some tough cuts in the countryside at small restaurants. Kenyan buffets sometimes include some unusual meats such as zebra, crocodile, ostrich, wart-hog and giraffe. Salads tend to be fairly basic and are generally tomatoes, white cabbage and onions with no dressing.

Restaurant prices are low; it is quite possible to eat a meal in a basic restaurant for US$2 and even the most expensive places will not be often be more than US$20 per person. The quality, standard and variety of food depends on where you are and what you intend to pay. However, even the smallest most remote *hoteli* meal will fill you up. Rice, potatoes, chapatis and ugali eaten with chicken, goat or beef are staple foods and in some restaurants you may be able to get spinach or *sukumawiki* (a type of green vegetable a bit like cabbage). Otherwise, vegetables and salads do not figure

Eating Classifications

♦♦♦♦ Over US$10 for a meal. A 3-course meal in a restaurant with pleasant decor. Beers, wines and spirits available.

♦♦♦ US$5-10 for a meal. Two courses, not including alcohol, reasonable surroundings.

♦♦ US$2-5 for a meal, probably only a single course, surroundings spartan but adequate.

♦ Under US$2. Single course, often makeshift surroundings such as a steet kiosk with simple benches and tables.

highly in cheaper restaurants where there is rarely much choice of dishes. Various western-style fried foods are becoming ever more popular such as chips, hamburgers, sausages and eggs. Roadside stalls selling *mandazi* (a kind of sweet or savoury donut), roasted maize, grilled skewered meat, or samosas are ever more popular and very cheap.

There are a number of Kenyan dishes of note. Swahili cuisine is the most interesting in the country with coconut and tamarind figuring heavily in menus. In Kikuyu areas you will find *irio* of potatoes, peas and corn mashed together. A popular Luo dish is fried *tilapia* (fish) with a spicy tomato sauce and *ugali* (maize porridge). *Githeri* is a bean stew. Eating out is not common in Kenya (hardly surprisingly as most of the population are so poor), and if people do go out they want to eat something they would not normally have at home – which is meat. Consequently, the most popular places for Kenyans to eat out at are *nyama choma* bars where you order your meat by the half kilo. They are popular places at weekends and very good value. The meat is usually goat or beef and you can choose what you want to eat before it is cooked.

Asian food is extremely good in Kenya and cheap, and an important option for vegetarians travelling in the country. Many Indian restaurants have a lunch time buffet where you can eat as much as you want for less than US$8 a head. Other cuisines include Italian, French, Chinese, Japanese and even Thai, though only in the larger towns.

● Drink

Sodas, are available everywhere and are very cheap, bottles are refundable. The other common drink throughout the country is chai, milky sweet tea which is surprisingly refreshing. Fresh fruit juices when they are available are good as they really are freshly squeezed. Bottled water is expensive, costs around US$1 per 1.5 litre and is available in all but the smallest villages. Tap water is perfectly safe in most parts of the country, but it is best avoiding borehole or rainwater unless your stomach is quite hardy.

Kenyan beer is very good, *Tusker*, *White Cap* and *Pilsner* are the main brands sold in half-litre bottles. Fruit wines are also popular, they come in a variety of different flavours but are tend to be sweet. Papaya wine is widely available, but is a little harsh.

Spirits tend to be extremely expensive and most local people will buy them in tiny sachets. Local alternatives are ***Kenya Cane*** a type of rum and the sweet ***Kenya Gold*** coffee liqueur.

Traditional Kenyan drinks include *chang'aa*, a fierce spirit made from maize and sugar and then distilled. Sentences for distilling and possessing *chang'aa* are severe and it is sometimes contaminated. Far more pleasant and more common are *pombe* (beer) brewed from sugar and millet or banana depending on the region. It is quite legal, tastes a bit like flat cider and is far more potent than it appears at first. Palm wine is drunk at the coast.

Getting around

● Air

Internal travel in Kenya is quite cheap and efficient. There are daily flights between Nairobi (the main international airport) and Mombasa and Kisumu on Kenya Airways. There are also several flights daily from Wilson Airport, Nairobi to Maasai Mara, Malindi, Lamu and other upmarket destinations. There are daily scheduled flights along the coast between Mombasa, Malindi and Lamu. You may also be able to get onto private flights going up to the NE of Kenya at very reasonable prices – these flights are primarily for carrying *miraa*, a popular herbal drug which is a mild stimulant.

● Bicycle

There are a number of specialist bicycle tours available. ***Paradise Bicycle Tours*** in the US (PO Box 1726, Evergreen, Colorado, 80439, USA) offers 12 day trips including a trip to the Maasai Mara. ***Leisure Activity Safaris*** in the UK (164 Ellicks Close, Bradley Stoke North, Almondsbury, Bristol BS12 0EU) offers long or short safaris leaving from London.

● Bus

There are lots of private bus companies operating in Kenya, and the system is very good on the whole, being reliable, running on time and cheap. Generally, you will be able to reserve a seat a day in advance and are quite comfortable. If you have problems locating the bus station, or finding the right bus in the bus station ask around. The government has recently started its own service called **Nyayo buses**. These are the cheapest buses around and very good.

● Car hire

Renting a car has certain advantages over

public transport, particularly if you intend visiting any of the national parks or remoter regions of the country, or there are at least 4 of you to share the costs. One way of keeping the cost down is to link up with other people and share the expense. You should be able to rent either a fixed price per day or by mileage. 4-wheel drive Suzuki jeeps are a popular car if going on safari – they do not hold much petrol, so remember to carry a spare can.

To hire a car you generally need to be over 23, have a full driving licence (it does not have to be an international licence, your home country one will be do), and will be asked to leave a large deposit (or sign a blank American Express voucher). Always take out the collision damage waiver premium as even the smallest accident can be very expensive.

Driving in Kenya can be alarming. Although driving is on the left, actual practice is dictated by the state of the road to avoid potholes, debris or people and animals. Keeping to any formal 'rules of the road' is further handicapped by many drivers ignoring traffic lights at night (they argue that this is to avoid being robbed while stationary) and the high speed of most motorists. The accident statistics in Kenya are very high, so be warned. If you break down, the common practice throughout Africa is to leave a bundle of leaves some 50 m behind, and in front of the vehicle.

● Ferry

There is a ferry running between the islands of the Lamu archipelago. Motor ferries run between Kisumu and a number of lakeshore locations: Kendu Bay, Kuwur Bay, Homa Bay, Asembo Bay, Mbita, Mfangano. Tickets are very cheap and this is a nice way of seeing around Lake Victoria.

● Hitching

Common in rural areas of Kenya as it is the easiest way for the majority of people to travel, making hitching a simple and safe method of travelling the country. If you intend to hitch, you will be expected to pay something to the driver though if you cannot afford to, and make this known at the outset, you will rarely be turned away. To gain a driver's attention, put out your arm, a thumb stuck in the air is unlikely to be noticed. On routes not served by much public transport it is invariably possible to hire a ride with truck drivers.

● Matatus

These are everywhere. Almost any vehicle will be used, but the most common is a pick-up van with wooden benches inside. They are the fastest and most prolific form of transport in the country. They are also the most dangerous, driving terrifyingly fast and often totally overloaded. The drivers often look about 13 and are chewing *miraa* to stay awake longer. However, as they are often the only means of travelling in remote areas, you may have to use them and they are the most convenient method of travelling around town because there are so many.

● Peugeot taxis

These are popular on long routes when you want to travel quickly. They are estate cars with an extra row of seats fitted in the back and are fast, comfortable and reliable. They are also quite expensive compared to matatus and buses. If you want to travel in the front by the driver, you will have to pay a premium.

● Train

By far the most romantic method of travelling in Kenya is by train, not much used by travellers. The train leaves very punctually a few hrs before dusk to gently chug its way through the country. The restaurant car is very old fashioned and offers good quality, cheap meals and the single sex carriages generally have a friendly chatty atmosphere. First class is 2-berth, second class is 4-berth, third class is uncomfortable wooden benches with no sleeping facilities. You will be given clean bed linen and blankets and wake refreshed. It travels to many of the most popular places; Mombasa, Nairobi, Naivasha, Nakuru, Kisumu and Malaba on the Ugandan border.

Communications

● Language

English is widely spoken throughout the country and is the language of all higher education. Swahili, however is the official language and it is worth the effort to learn some basic phrases as a courtesy gesture. The more remote the area you visit, the less likely you are to find anyone who speaks anything but their tribal language.

● Postal services

Sending post out of the country is cheap and efficient, it generally takes a week to Europe and about 10 to Australia and USA. Receiving post also is easy, though not parcels. All parcels need to be checked by officials for import duty also, it is not uncommon for them to go astray unless they have been sent by registered post or a similar scheme. If you are sending things out of the country they must be wrapped in brown paper with string. There is no point doing this before getting to the post office as you will be asked to undo it to be checked for export duty. Parcels must not weight more than 20kg or be more than 100 cm long.

The **poste restante** service, particularly in Nairobi, Mombasa, Malindi and Lamu, is reliable and free.

● Telephone services

Generally speaking, the telephone system in Kenya is very good. You should be able to make international calls from public calls boxes and the easiest way of doing this is if you get a phone card (available from most post offices). If this is not possible, you can book your call through post offices where you get your money back if you fail to get through. The rate is roughly US$4.50 per minute to Europe or North America and if you dial through the operator, there is a 3 minute minimum. The number for the international operator is 0196.

Local calls also are very easy, the main problem is finding a box. You can generally make phone calls from hotels, though they will usually charge you double the price for the privilege.

Entertainment

● Cinema

There are cinemas in the larger towns throughout the country. Some show good reasonably current films, but the most popular films appear to be action, martial arts or adventure movies.

● Music and dance

There are displays of dancing put on for the tourists all over the country including the Bomas of Kenya just outside Nairobi. The best known are the Maasai and Samburu dances. Traditional Kenyan music is most likely to be performed by the drummers of Akamba and the Mijinkenda.

Zairean music (*Lingala*) is extremely popular and the type you are most likely to hear on matatus, in the streets, in bars and clubs, in fact anywhere and everywhere. Western music also has had its influence here. Many of the more upmarket discos and clubs play western music and there are a few reggae clubs in Nairobi.

● Newspapers

There is a range of locally produced papers and magazines. The best of the 3 English-language papers is the ***Nation*** which is the most daring in its editorial. The ***Kenya Times*** is the government owned paper, and ***The Standard*** owned by Lonrho is dull. Of the magazines, ***Law*** is usually worth reading (if it has not been confiscated) and the ***Weekly Review*** carries very detailed reports on local political and social issues.

Of the international press, *Time* and *Newsweek* regularly available, as is the *International Herald Tribune* UK daily newspapers arrive a day or two late in larger towns.

● Radio

This is the most common method with which Kenyans keep informed. KBC broadcasts in Kiswahili, English and some local languages.

● Social events

A major event in the social calendar is the Agriculture Society of Kenya's ***Agricultural Shows*** which are all over the country at different times of the year. They can be quite interesting, as well as the normal animal shows and beer tents are women's groups, beekeeping, soil conservation booths and others.

● Sport (spectator)

The biggest event in the year, for the international media at least, is the ***Kenya Safari Rally*** which normally takes place over the Easter weekend. It goes all over the country on some of the worst roads and often in appalling weather. The Asian community in particular comes out for this event, though it seems to attract large crowds everywhere.

Football is a popular sport throughout the country and the quality is excellent, Kenya having some of the best teams in the continent. Matches are well attended and are great fun to go to even if you are not a keen football supporter just to soak up the friendly atmosphere.

Horse Racing Regular meetings in Nairobi.

Golf, Tennis, Squash Annual international tournaments at Nairobi Club.

● Sport (participant)

Riding It is possible to hire horses in the Central Highlands and camels in northern Kenya.

Fishing is not a particularly popular pastime in Kenya's rivers, though it is possible and an interesting trip is to go out with local fishermen, either on the coast or on Lake Victoria.

Climbing is extremely popular among visitors, particularly up Mount Kenya where you will find many guides to help you. Other good climbing is possible in the Aberdares, Cheranganis Hills, Mathews Range, Hell's Gate and Rift Valley volcanoes. Each is described in the relevant section. The Mountain Club of Kenya at Wilson Airport T 02 501 747) is a good source of advice and contacts.

Caving has been growing in popularity in Kenya and there is enormous potential for it in the country. Contact Kenya Caverns and Lodges, PO Box 47363, Nairobi if you want to know more about this.

Water sports Widely available at the coast.

Running Hash House Harriers meet regularly. Contact British Council in Nairobi.

Cricket, *Hockey*, *Rugby* Played regularly by the Universites and local clubs.

Television

There are 2 television channels: ***Kenya Broadcasting Corporation*** (KBC, which replaced Voice of Kenya), broadcasting in Swahili and English with a number considerable import of foreign programmes; and ***Kenya Television News***, based on CNN material.

Holidays and festivals

1 Jan:	New Year's Day
Mar/Apr:	Good Fri and Easter Mon
1 May:	International Labour Day
1 Jun:	Madaraka Day, celebrates the granting of self-government
10 Oct:	Moi Day
20 Oct:	Kenyatta Day
12 Dec:	Independence Day
25 Dec:	Christmas Day
26 Dec:	Boxing Day

All along the coast and in the northeast the Islamic calendar is followed, and festivals are celebrated. These include Feb (Beginning of Ramadan); Mar (End of Ramadan); Jun (Islamic New Year); Aug (Prophet's Birthday).

Further reading

History

Miller, C. *Lunatic Express* Highly readable history of East Africa, centring around the building of the railway. Hibbert, C. 1984. *Africa Explored: Europeans in the Dark Continent* 1769-1889. London: Penguin. Describes the exploits of the main explorers, including the search for the source of the Nile. Murray Brown, J. *Kenyatta* Biography of the man who became the first president of Kenya. Patterson, J. *The Man-Eaters of Tsavo* First-hand account of problems in building the railway.

Reminiscences

Blixen, K. *Out of Africa* Wonderfully written. Impressions of the author's life in Kenya. Huxley, E. *Flame Trees of Thika* Stories of the lives of early pioneers. Markham, B. *West with the Night* Marvellous autobiography of the woman who made the first solo E-W. Atlantic flight.

Fiction

Hemingway, E. *Green Hills of Africa* Masterly short stories based on the author's African visits in 1933-4. Mwangi, M. *Going Down river Road* Entertaining stories of African urban life.

Climbing Guides

Wielochowski, A. *Mount Elgon Map and Guide*. Savage, M. and Wielochowski, A. *Mount Kenya Map and Guide* (both obtainable in Nairobi at ***The Nation*** bookshop next to Thorn Tree Café on Kenyatta Ave; or from: 1 Meadow Close, Goring, Reading, Berks RG8 9AA, England).

Other guides

Glenday B., etc. *Kenya's Best: Hotels, Lodges and Homestays*. Nairobi: Kenway Publications. Detailed descriptions of facilites available in over 200 up-market establishments. Very nicely produced with line drawings. Oberlé, P 1991. *On Safari: 40 Circuits in Kenya*. Very good for hikes and walking routes, with plenty of sketch-maps.

TANZANIA AND ZANZIBAR

CONTENTS

MAPS

INTRODUCTION

Tanzania has unrivalled tourist attractions in its glorious game parks; the Indian Ocean coast; and a fascinating history embracing the earliest relics of man's evolution, the exotic influence of Zanzibar, early explorers, and the colonial presence of the Germans and British which began over a century ago. Tanzanians are friendly, warm-hearted and relaxed, the country is free from any serious tensions between ethnic groups and it has an enviable political stability.

Present-day Tanzania comprises a union between the former mainland Tanganyika and the islands of Zanzibar. Its modern history has involved three profound changes of direction from colonialism to socialism to capitalism. Like a traveller forced to change route or uncertain of the way, these diversions have slowed progress. As a result Tanzania has not developed as rapidly as its northern neighbour, Kenya. Its cities have few modern buildings, living standards have remained more-or-less unchanged since independence in 1961, and the considerable mineral, agricultural and tourist resources of the country have been only partially exploited.

Exchange Rate Aug 1994 TSh 508.48 = US$1

Environment

Geography

Tanzania, in the East Africa region is a large coastal country which lies just below the Equator and includes the islands of Pemba and Zanzibar. It is bounded by Kenya and Uganda to the N, Rwanda, Burundi and Zaire to the W, Zambia, Malawi and Mozambique to the S. Temperatures range from tropical to temperate moderated by altitude. Most of the country consists of high plateaux but there is a wide variety of terrain including mangrove swamps, coral reefs, plains, low hill ranges, uplands, volcanic peaks and high mountains, as well as depressions such as the Rift Valley and lakes. Dar es Salaam is the main port and there are hydro-electric schemes on the River Rufiji. Mineral deposits include diamonds, gold, gemstones, gypsum, kaolin and tin.

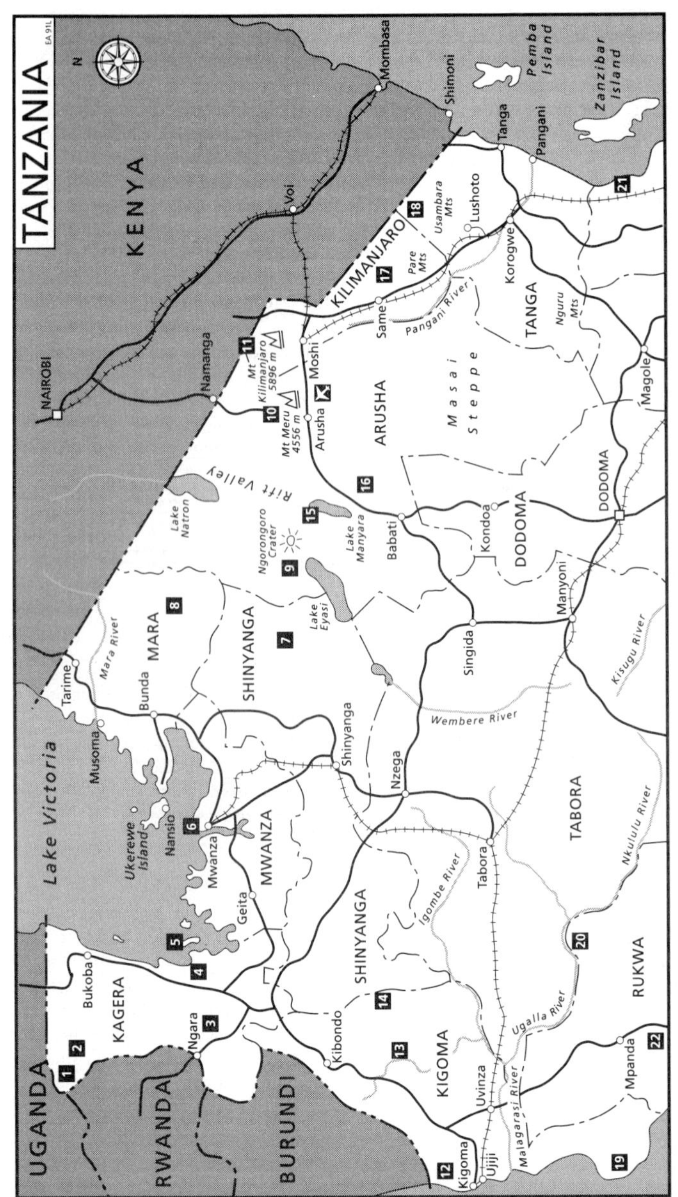
TANZANIA
EA 91L
N
KENYA
NAIROBI
Namanga
Voi
Mombasa
Shimoni
Pemba Island
Zanzibar Island
Tanga
Pangani
Lushoto
Usambara Mts
KILIMANJARO
Pare Mts
Same
Pangani River
Korogwe
TANGA
Nguru Mts
Magole
Moshi
Mt Kilimanjaro 5896 m
Mt Meru 4556 m
Arusha
ARUSHA
Masai Steppe
DODOMA
Dodoma
Rift Valley
Lake Natron
Ngorongoro Crater
Lake Manyara
Babati
Kondoa
Lake Eyasi
MARA
Mara River
SHINYANGA
Singida
Manyoni
Kisugu River
Tarime
Bunda
Musoma
Lake Victoria
Ukerewe Island
Nansio
Mwanza
Shinyanga
Wembere River
Nzega
MWANZA
Geita
Tabora
TABORA
Igombe River
Nkululu River
Bukoba
KAGERA
Ngara
Kibondo
KIGOMA
Uvinza
Ugalla River
RUKWA
Mpanda
Malagarasi River
Kigoma
Ujiji
UGANDA
RWANDA
BURUNDI
1
2
3
4
5
6
7
8
9
10
11
12
13
14
15
16
17
18
19
20
21
22

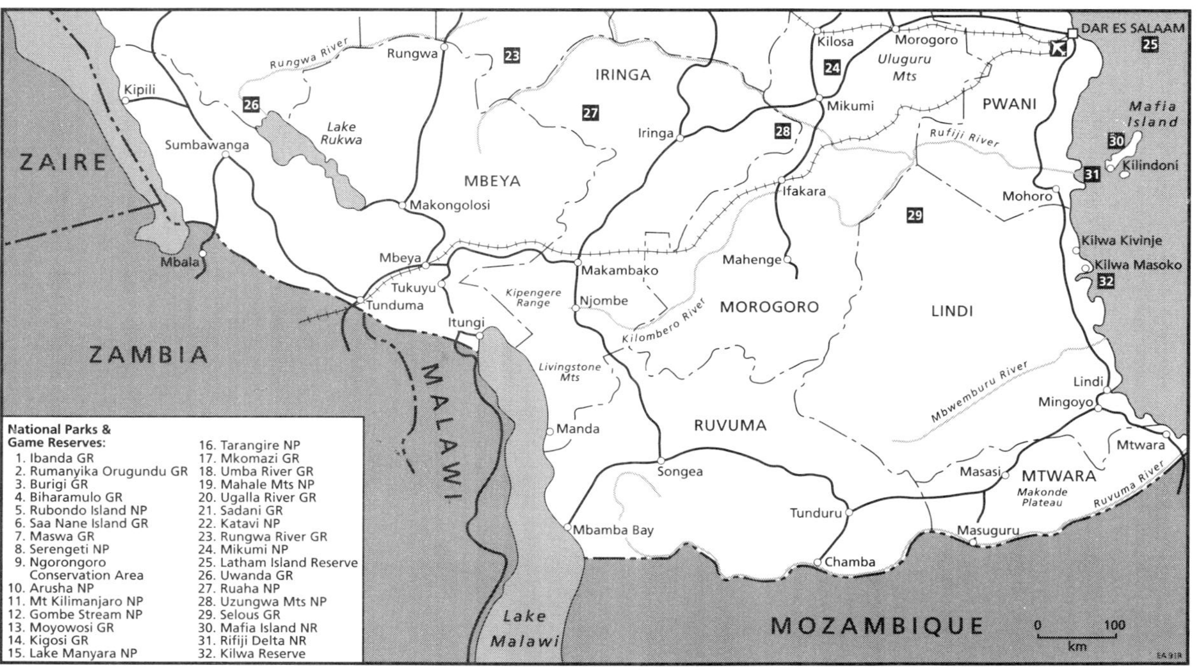
DAR ES SALAAM
25
Mafia Island
Kilindoni
30
31
Kilwa Kivinje
Kilwa Masoko
32
Lindi
Mingoyo
Mtwara
Ruvuma River
MTWARA
Makonde Plateau
0
100
km
Masasi
Masuguru
MOZAMBIQUE
PWANI
Rufiji River
Mohoro
LINDI
29
Mbwemburu River
Morogoro
Uluguru Mts
Mikumi
Kilosa
24
Ifakara
28
Mahenge
MOROGORO
RUVUMA
Tunduru
Chamba
Songea
Mbamba Bay
Kilombero River
Makambako
Njombe
Iringa
IRINGA
27
Livingstone Mts
Manda
Kipengere Range
Lake Malawi
Itungi
MBEYA
23
Makongolosi
MALAWI
Rungwa
Mbeya
Tukuyu
Tunduma
Lake Rukwa
Rungwa River
26
Sumbawanga
Mbala
ZAMBIA
Kipili
ZAIRE
National Parks & Game Reserves:
1. Ibanda GR
2. Rumanyika Orugundu GR
3. Burigi GR
4. Biharamulo GR
5. Rubondo Island NP
6. Saa Nane Island GR
7. Maswa GR
8. Serengeti NP
9. Ngorongoro Conservation Area
10. Arusha NP
11. Mt Kilimanjaro NP
12. Gombe Stream NP
13. Moyowosi GR
14. Kigosi GR
15. Lake Manyara NP
16. Tarangire NP
17. Mkomazi GR
18. Umba River GR
19. Mahale Mts NP
20. Ugalla River GR
21. Sadani GR
22. Katavi NP
23. Rungwa River GR
24. Mikumi NP
25. Latham Island Reserve
26. Uwanda GR
27. Ruaha NP
28. Uzungwa Mts NP
29. Selous GR
30. Mafia Island NR
31. Rifiji Delta NR
32. Kilwa Reserve

Climate

There is a long dry season, Jun to Oct, followed by short rains in Nov and Dec. Jan to Mar can be very hot, and are followed by heavy rains in Apr and May. The timing of the rains has been less regular in recent years and the volume also varies from year to year, and from region to region. A quarter of the country receives an annual average of 750 mm of rain, but in some areas it can be as high as 1250 mm. The central area of the country is dry with less than 500 mm per annum. In many areas 2 harvests can be grown each year.

History

Without any written records, relatively little is known about the early history of Tanzania. However, with the use of oral history, archaeology, linguistic analysis and anthropology, a certain amount can be deduced. Archaeological finds at Olduvai Gorge have provided evidence of human evolution. At this site bones from the australopithecine stage of human development have been found of 2 types. These are *Zinjanthropus* known as Nutcracker Man and *Homo Habilis* known as Handy Man. They lived together about 2 million years ago and it is thought that Homo Habilis, capable of using tools, is the ancestor of modern man – Homo Sapiens. Olduvai Gorge has become known as the cradle of mankind. The era of australopithecine man probably lasted several million years.

By about 500,000 years ago the *Homo Erectus* stage came into being which was somewhere between Australopithecine and *Homo Sapiens*. The brain was larger and the hands more nimble and therefore better capable at making tools. The development of tool-making is clearly seen at Olduvai Gorge. The different layers of rock contain tools of different ages which show the development from crude tools to more efficient and sharper implements. Another collection of such tools can be found at Isimila near Iringa, see page 329.

The middle stone age saw the further development of tools, advances in human ingenuity and craftsmanship and the use of fire. Progress accelerated into the late stone age which began about 100,000 years ago. There are a number of sites from the late stone age in Tanzania which are particularly well known as they are sites of rock painting. These hunter-gatherers were probably related linguistically and racially to the Bushmen and Hottentots of S Africa. Interestingly the Sandawe that now live in the area of the rock paintings speak a form of the Khoisan or 'click' language which otherwise is not spoken in East Africa and which is characteristic of the Bushmen.

The virtual disappearance of these people was a result of the migration and expansion of other people who were more numerous and more advanced. The most significant factor about these migrating people was that instead of being hunter-gatherers they were food producers – either by agriculture or by keeping livestock. They spoke the language of the Cushitic group (legendary biblical descendants of the Cush in Ethiopia, Somalia and N Sudan) and came from the N from around 1000 BC onwards. They did not have iron-working skills and this meant that the efficiency of their agriculture was limited.

Later still, during the past 1,000-2,000 years, 2 other groups migrated into the area. These were both Negroid but were of different linguistic groups – the Bantu from the W and the Nilo-Hamite pastoralists from the N. A process of ethnic assimilation followed and the Cushitic intermarried with the newcomers and adopted their languages. The Bantu possessed the important iron-processing skills which greatly improved agricultural efficiency and enabled population growth. There was not one single migration but a series of waves of various groups, expanding and contracting, assimilating and adapting. The present ethnic mix is as a result of this process over many centuries.

The most recent of the Nilotic migrations was by the Maasai. By about 1800 AD they had reached the area around Dodoma where their advance was stopped by the Gogo and the Hehe, see page 232. Their reputation as a warrior tribe meant that the N part of Tanzania was largely avoided by slave traders and caravan routes.

As a result of these migrations N and central Tanzania has great ethnic diversity. In this part of the country there are Khoisan, Cushitic, Nilotic and Bantu speaking peoples. The rest of the country is entirely Bantu speaking; indeed about 95% of Tanzanians born today are born into a family speaking one of the Bantu dialects. Swahili itself is a Bantu tongue and this has developed into the national language and as such is a significant unifying force.

Initially Swahili was a coastal language and developed as the language of trade. The earliest visitors to Tanzania were Arab traders who arrived on the coast, and the influence of these traders can be seen by the coastal settlements such as Kilwa.These coastal towns were very much orientated to sea-going trade and away from the interior and until the beginning of the 16th century the coast and the interior had very little contact with each other. However the development of long-distance trade led to the integration of the two. Caravan routes went from the coast to the Congo and Buganda. By the 13th century there was a bustling trade on the coast with the gold and ivory trades becoming particularly important. Initially the trade was dominated by the Persians, Arabs, Egyptians, Indians and Chinese. The Arab influence increased and with it the spread of Islam. The major trading objects were gold, ivory and rhino horns in exchange for guns, textiles and beads.

By the mid 15th century the Portuguese had arrived on the scene. Vasco da Gama noted the beauty of the town of Kilwa, and attempted to take control of the gold trade from the interior. The Portuguese were later expelled by the Arabs and the influence of the Arabs increased again. A period of reduced trading activity followed until the latter half of the 18th century when trade flourished again and the commodity traded was slaves. Around 1776 the only trading route inland went SW from Kilwa to the area around Lake Nyasa and this became increasingly important through the slave trade. During the 18th century Kilwa became East Africa's major slave-trading port, drawing first on the peoples of SE Tanganyika and then on the Lake Nyasa area.

During the 19th century the trade pattern shifted. This was as a result of the changes to the ivory trade. During the first half of the 19th century, most of the ivory came from within what was to become Tanganyika. However as Tanganyika's elephants were destroyed, so the price of ivory rose rapidly. Prices at Tabora are reported to have increased tenfold between 1846 and 1858. Thus the hunters looked further afield and eventually left Tanganyika altogether. As the hunters moved away the chiefs in these areas lost their major source of revenue. It was this that led some of them to look to the new trade in slaves.

The Slave Trade

Caravan routes into the interior developed by the 19th century and trade centres developed at places such as Ujiji and Tabora. Humans and ivory were exchanged for guns, beads and cloth. The slaves were largely obtained by bartering with the local chiefs rather than by force. Some of the more militarized tribes raided their neighbours and 'prisoners of war' were then sold on to the Arabs as slaves. Convicted criminals were often sold as slaves and this penalty was sometimes extended to include their families.

Estimates of the size of the slave trade remain speculative. However it has been estimated that in the period of the slave trade approx 1.5 million slaves from the interior reached the coast and 10 times that number died en route. Bagamoyo was a terminus of the trade and from there they were taken to Zanzibar which developed into a important trading centre. The slaves were either put to work in the plantations of Pemba and Zanzibar or were shipped to the Middle East.

By the 1830's Zanzibar had become sufficiently prosperous from the slave trade and spice trade for the Omani Sultan Seyyid Said to move his capital from Muscat to Zanzibar itself. For some time Britain tried to suppress the slave trade by signing various agreements with the Omani Sultans. However it was not until 1873 that the slave trade was officially abolished when an agreement was signed between Sultan Barghash (Seyyid Said's successor) which forbad the seaborne trade. However this prohibition was implemented only slowly and the practice continued in the mainland for some years. By the 1880's the internal market for slaves had become more important than the external.

The first Europeans

The first Europeans in this part of Africa were missionaries and explorers. In 1844 John Krapf, a German missionary working for the Church Missionary Society of London arrived in Zanzibar. He was joined by John Rebmann who was to become the first European to set eyes on Mount Kilimanjaro in 1848. The two British explorers Burton and Speke, sent by the Royal Geographical Society, arrived in Zanzibar in 1856 and journeyed along the caravan routes into the interior. In 1858 Speke came across the huge expanse of water which he named Lake Victoria. Dr Livingstone was perhaps the most celebrated of all the missionaries, being found, after no news of him for several years, by HM Stanley, a newspaper reporter.

By the 1880's numbers of Europeans were arriving in East Africa as missionaries, big game hunters, traders and adventurers. There were some with political ambitions including two Germans Carl Peters and HH Johnson, who wanted to see this part of Africa under the control of Germany. They formed the Society for German Colonization from which emerged the German East Africa Society. Emissaries of the Society signed 'protective treaties' with unsuspecting and often illiterate chiefs from the interior. These so-called treaties of friendship were then used by the German East Africa Company to exploit the areas that they covered with the apparent agreement of the chiefs.

Both Germany and Britain made claims over East Africa which were resolved by a series of agreements between the two countries. The Berlin Conference of Nov 1884 to Feb 1885 was convened by Bismarck and was important in demarcating European spheres of influence in Africa. This saw the recognition of the German 'protective treaties' and by early 1885 several chiefdoms were formally placed under the control of the German East Africa Company. Three years later the Germans were shaken by an uprising of both Arabs and Africans and the German government took control in 1891. The Anglo-German Agreement of Nov 1886 defined the N boundary from the coast inland to Lake Victoria. A month later another agreement saw the defining of the boundary with Mozambique. These and various other treaties saw Zanzibar, Pemba and a 16-km coastal strip go to the Sultan under British Protectorate rule in 1890, while what is now mainland Tanzania, Rwanda and Burundi became German East Africa. It was not until 1898 that German rule was secured and consolidated with the death of Mkwawa, chief of the Hehe.

Mount Kilimanjaro

Whilst Germany and Britain were deciding the N boundary, Kaiser William I insisted that Mount Kilimanjaro should be German because it had been discovered by a German, John Rebmann. Queen Victoria generously 'gave' the mountain to her grandson, the future Kaiser William II on his birthday in 1886. Although no official record exists the Queen is supposed to have explained, by way of justification for her royal 'gift', that 'William likes everything that is high and big'. The boundary was thus moved so that Kilimanjaro is now found within Tanzania. As can be seen on the present map, instead of marking the boundary by pencilling it in with a ruler from the coast to Lake Victoria in one go, a freehand detour was made when the ruler hit the mountain,

Dr Livingstone

David Livingstone was born on 19 Mar 1813 in Blantyre in Scotland. He had a strict Scottish upbringing, and his first job was in a factory. He studied during the evenings and at the age of 27 finally qualified as a doctor. In 1840 he joined the London Missionary Society, was ordained as a missionary in the same year and set off for Africa. On the voyage out he learnt to use quadrants and other navigational and mapping instruments which were to prove vital skills during his exploring of uncharted parts of Africa. In 1841 he arrived in South Africa and journeyed N from the mission in the search for converts. In the first few years as a missionary he gained a reputation as a surveyor and scientist. His first major expedition into the African interior came in 1853 and lasted 3 years. It was in 1855 that he discovered Victoria Falls. When Livingstone returned to England in 1856 he was greeted as a national hero, was awarded a gold medal from the Royal Geographical Society, and honoured by the City of London, by making him a Freeman of the City.

He returned to Africa 2 years later in 1858 and began his quest for the source of the Nile in 1866. This trip was funded by a grant from the British Government which enabled Livingstone to be better equipped than during his previous expedition. During this journey little was heard of from Livingstone and rumours reached Britain of his apparent death. Henry M Stanley, a newspaper reporter for the New York Herald was sent by James Gordon Bennett, his publisher, to find Livingstone. On 1871 Stanley found Livingstone's camp at Ujiji, a small town on the shores of Lake Tanganyika and the famous phrase 'Dr Livingstone, I presume?' was Stanley's greeting. At the time of the meeting Livingstone had run short of supplies, in particular quinine which was vital in protecting him and his companions from malaria.

Livingstone set out on his last trip from near Tabora in Tanzania and continued his explorations until his death at Chitambo in what is now Zambia. His heart was buried at the spot where he died, his body embalmed and taken by Susi and Chumah, his 2 servants, to the coast from where it was shipped back to England. He was buried at Westminster Abbey and a memorial was erected at Chitambo. After Livingstone's death Stanley returned to Africa to complete Livingstone's expeditionary work. He began in Bagamoyo in 1874 and travelled inland reaching Lake Victoria and Lake Tanganyika as well as Uganda and the Congo.

before carrying on again with the ruler and pencil on the far side.

The German colonial period

There were a number of phases of German colonial rule. The first around the turn of the century saw attempts at establishing a settler economy. This was to be based in the N highlands and agriculture was to be the basis of the economy. However this was initially not a great success. Revolts occurred in Bagamoyo, Pangani and Tanga which were all crushed. The best-known uprising was the Maji Maji rebellion (*maji* means water in Swahili) which occurred in the S of the country from 1905 to 1906. Discontent was initially aroused over a cotton scheme which benefited the Africans little although they were obliged to become involved. The uprising was unique in Eastern Africa for it was cross-tribal and included a large area – almost the whole of the country S of Dar es Salaam. With only spears and arrows, but believing themselves to be protected by sacred water (hence Maji Maji), the rebels were up against German troops equipped with rifles.

The uprising led to a major reappraisal of German colonial policy. The administrators realised that development would be almost impossible without a contented local population. This period saw the building of the railway to Tabora to open up the area to commerce, and crops such as coffee and groundnuts were encouraged. Economic activity increased and a world boom led to the reemergence of a settler cash crop economy as the most significant part of colonial policy. In particular the boom saw prices of sisal and rubber soar. Most farming took place along the coast and on the slopes of Mount Kilimanjaro and Mount Meru. Inland the threat of the tsetse fly hindered development as domestic animals could not be raised in affected areas. Missionary activity led to the growth of clinics and schools.

With the outbreak of hostilities in Europe, the German commander General Paul von Lettow Vorbeck realised that his meagre forces could not defeat the British. He resolved to aid Germany's efforts in the European theatre of war by tying up as many British military resources as possible. Von Lettow, his German officers and African troops conducted an astonishing rearguard campaign, retreating from Kenya through what is now Tanzania and Mozambique, being undefeated when Germany surrendered in Europe.

Major General von Lettow Vorbeck

Paul Von Lettow arrived in Dar es Salaam at the start of 1914 to take command of the German forces. He was 44 years old, son of a general, a professional soldier and experienced in bush warfare from service in German South West Africa (now Namibia).

His forces consisted of around 2,500 Schutztruppe *askaris* in 14 field companies, and he promptly signalled his intentions by capturing Taveta across the border in Kenya. The British assembled a force of 5,000 mainly British, South African, and Indian troops, and von Lettow withdrew to begin his epic, 4,000 km, 4-year campaign. When faced by overwhelming odds von Lettow fell back, but at defendable positions, although always hopelessly out-numbered, he inflicted fearful losses on his adversaries, most notably at Tanga and Kibata. The British fared better when commanded by the South African, Jan Christian Smuts, for 11 months in 1916. A rare combination of intellectual, politician and soldier, Smuts was later to be Prime Minister of South Africa. Smuts found himself pursuing an infuriatingly elusive foe. He was convinced that he would trap and destroy von Lettow's troops in Morogoro, where retreat was blocked by the Ulunguru Mountains. But as his forces marched into the town they heard a mechanical piano playing

Deutschland Uber Alles in the *Bahnhof Hotel*, and in the empty Schutztruppe barracks, on every item of furniture, was a piece of human excrement.

Never defeated, at the end of the campaign von Lettow and his force numbered 155 Germans 1,156 Schutztruppe *askaris* and about 3,000 camp-followers made up of porters and *askari* wives and children, many of the latter born during

Central And Northern Railways

The first railway to be constructed in Tanganyika was the Tanga (Northern) line which began when the German authorities decided in 1891 that a metre-gauge line should be built from Tanga to Muheza, and then on to Korogwe. Eventually this line would be continued on to Moshi and Arusha. A small port was built at Tanga to land equipment and material and the construction of the line began in 1893. Labour was scarce and at times had to be imported from Mozambique and progress was slow. It took 2 years for the laying of just 40 km as far as Muheza. Financial difficulties caused the construction to be halted periodically and the line finally reached Korogwe in 1902 and Moshi in 1911. Unfortunately much of this line, built at great expense over a long period of time, was destroyed by the Germans as they retreated in 1914.

Meanwhile the central route of the old slave trail to Lake Tanganyika was receiving attention. Dar es Salaam had been made the capital of the German protectorate in 1891 and talk of the construction of a railway began soon after. However, delays again ensued and it was not until 1905 that construction began on a line from Dar es Salaam to Morogoro. This was to be built by a private company with a grant from the Imperial German Government. The Maji Maji created problems with the supply of labour, but the line reached Morogoro in Dec 1907. By 1914 the line had been extended as far as Kigoma although it was clear that this line had little commercial value and traffic was extremely light.

Planning continued for other lines but WW1 intervened and much of the work already carried out was destroyed. Most of the bridges between Dar es Salaam and Kigoma were blown up, and the rolling stock destroyed. A line was built during the war, linking the Tanga line to the Kenya railway system which facilitated the advance and occupation of Tanga by the British.

Following the war many repairs were carried out so that the goods traffic on the railways increased. However the problems returned with the depression of the 1930's which severely affected revenues. The non-metre gauge lines were closed and about 40% of the staff were laid off. WW2 saw an increase in the activities of the Railways, and following the war the "Groundnut Scheme", **see box, page 220**, involved the hasty construction of a branch line from Lindi on the coast to Nachingwea, one of the areas where groundnuts were to be grown. However the scheme was a monumental failure, the expected traffic never materialised, and the line was abandonned.

In 1948 the railway and port services in Tanganyika were amalgamated with the Kenya and Uganda railways under the East Africa High Commission. At the time of independence it was considered that the railways in Tanzania were in a position of excess capacity and well in advance of the needs of the country. This is not to belittle their importance for the provision of the railways provided Tanzania with a solid foundation and firm infrastructure from which further economic development could take place.

The Schutztruppe – An African Fighting Elite

It was recognised by the Germans from the start that white troops in East Africa would be nothing more than a 'walking hospital'.

Under German officers, an African fighting force of *askaris* was recruited, thoroughly drilled, trained, disciplined, and well paid – 30 rupees a month for privates (about US$80 in present-day values) and 150 rupees for non-commissioned officers.

The Shutztruppe became an elite. The uniform was a khaki jacket, trousers and puttees and a black leather belt with ammunition pouches. Head gear was a *kepi* – rather like a khaki fez with a chin-strap and a gold Imperial eagle on the front. The non-commissioned officers decorated their kepis with feathers. Each soldier had his own servant (an *askari-boy*). When travelling, a Schutztruppe private would send his *askari boy* ahead to a village with a cartridge. This was an order to the local headman to have ready 4 beds (one for the askari, one for his rifle, one for his ammunition pouch and one for his uniform) – and some 'blankets' – a selection of the village girls.

Tough, resilient, and brave, around 150 *askaris* made up a field company that included 2 machine-gun teams. With several hundred porters carrying food and ammunition, it was highly mobile. During the WW1, the British were contemptuous of these African troops, considering they would collapse when faced with European and Indian forces. In the event, the Schutztruppe was never defeated, and inflicted fearful losses on the British and their allies.

the campaign. Over 250,000 Allied troops had been thrown against them at one time or another during the 4 years.

Von Lettow returned to Germany, in 1920 entered politics and for 10 years was a Deputy in the Reichstag. In 1929 he was guest of honour in London, with Smuts, at the anniversary dinner of the British East African Expeditionary Force. In 1930 he resigned from the Reichstag and in 1935 Hitler suggested he become Ambassador to Britain. Von Lettow declined. It is said he told Hitler to 'go fuck himself', but von Lettow subsequently denied he had ever been that polite.

In 1958, at the age of 88, von Lettow returned to Dar es Salaam. He was met at the dockside by a crowd of elderly Schutztruppe askaris who carried him shoulder-high to an official reception at Government House.

In 1964 the German Bundestag finally voted the funds to settle the back-pay owing to the Schutztruppe at the surrender in 1918. Over 300 veterans, some in faded and patched uniforms presented themselves at Mwanza. Only a handful had their discharge papers. Those that didn't were handed a broom and taken through arms drill, with the orders given in German. Not one man failed the test. The same year, at the age of 94, von Lettow died.

After WW1 the Germans lost control of German East Africa. The NW, now Rwanda and Burundi, went to the Belgians. The rest was renamed Tanganyika, and the British were allocated a League of Nations mandate.

The British period

From about 1925 Britain introduced the policy of Indirect Rule which had proved effective in other parts of colonial Africa. This involved giving a degree of political responsibility to local chiefs and ruling through them. Economic development between the wars was negligible. Tanganyika had few exportable products. Unlike Uganda,

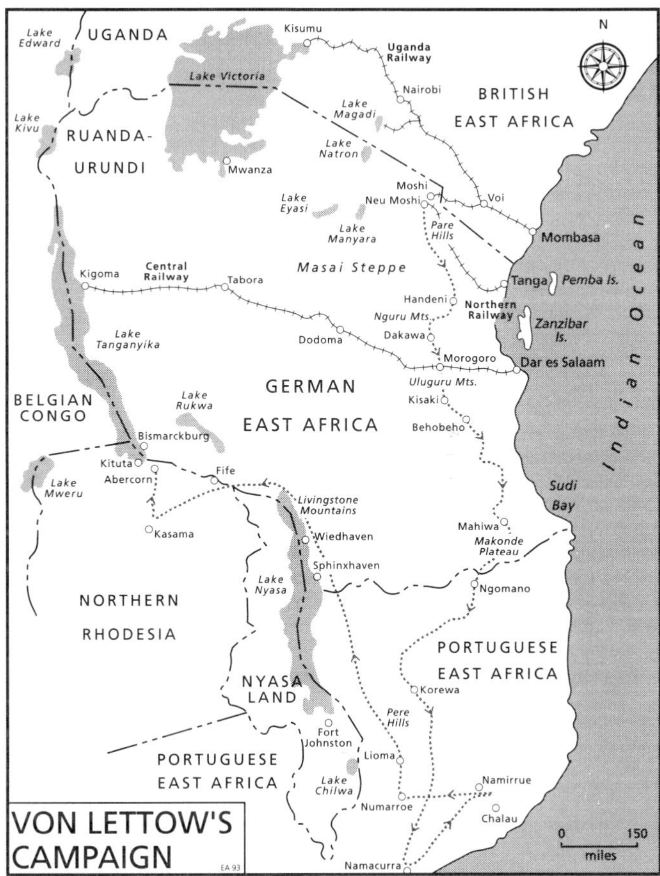

VON LETTOW'S CAMPAIGN

there was no major cash crop such as cotton suited to production by small African farmers. The most significant cash crop was sisal but this required long-term large-scale capital-intensive investment and was not suitable for small scale African production. It was produced almost entirely by British and Asian companies with a local workforce. The most successful African-grown cash crop was coffee grown by the Chagga on the slopes of Mount Kilimanjaro.

Most British settlers went to Kenya where there was already a sizeable settler community and the highlands provided an attractive climate. Moreover, British presence seemed more secure in Kenya, which was a colony. The League of Nations mandate required Britain to prepare Tanganyika for eventual self-government, and the British kept expenditure on administration, infrastructure and education to a minimum.

The 1920's saw the emergence of the first

THE GROUND NUT SCHEME

Immediately after WW2 there was an attempt by the British Labour government to grow ground nuts on an enormous scale. Three sites, were chosen, in the S, near Lindi, at Nachingwea; just N of Morogoro at Kongwa, and at Urambo W of Tabora on the central railway line. The scheme aimed to alleviate the world-wide shortage of edible oils following the war. The operation was to be capital-intensive, with a military style approach to planning, and there was immense enthusiasm among the British who went out to run the programme and became known as "ground-nutters". It was thought that with modern methods and enough machinery it would be impossible for the scheme to fail. However, it was a complete disaster. When finally abandoned a total of £36.5 million was written off. This huge sum was equal to a little less than the entire Tanganyikan government expenditure from 1946-50.

The reasons for failure were numerous and included inadequate planning which meant the environmental and climatic problems were not properly considered; unsuitable machinery; and failure to test the scheme by way of a pilot project. Other difficulties included insufficient rain in the area to support the ground nuts and inadequate capacity in the transport system to keep the tractors supplied with fuel. Although it was supposed to be a capital-intensive project the inappropriateness of the machinery meant that it actually was more efficient to clear the land by hand. The project is held up as an example of everything that was wrong with attempting to impose European agricultural techniques without adequate consideration of local African conditions.

Kongwa is now a ranch, Urambo has been given over to tobacco, and at Nachingwea, oilseeds and cereals are grown.

African political groups. In 1922 the Tanganyika Territory of African Civil Servants Association was formed in Tanga, and in 1929 the Tanganyika African Association (TAA). Throughout the 1930's and 1940's, unions and agricultural cooperatives developed. These were not primarily political associations although their formation obviously led to an increased political awareness.

The major issues upon which attention was focused were land-use policies which were aimed in particular at soil conservation, and the eviction of Africans to make way for white settlers. The African population in 1950 was about 8 million, compared to an Asian population of 55,000 and European population of 17,000. However Europeans and Asians dominated in local government councils even in areas that were almost exclusively African. These were issues upon which the TAA focused. In 1953 Julius Nyerere became the leader of the TAA and the movement towards independence developed momentum. In July 1954 at a meeting of all political elements the Tanganyika African National Union (TANU) was created with the slogan *Uhuru na Umoja* (Freedom and Unity).

There were two major strengths of this movement as against similar movements in other parts of Africa. Firstly there was no dominating tribal group, and secondly Swahili had developed into the major language encouraged by German colonial policy and this served as an important unifying force. A further point of relevance in the run up to independence was that after WW2 Tanganyika was given UN Trustee status in place of the mandate. Both the mandatory system and the trusteeship system were very important as they meant that controversial issues could be referred to the UN Council unlike other colonial territories. In Dec 1956 Nyerere addressed the UN General Assembly's Fourth (Trusteeship) Committee. Such occasions gave Nyerere a platform to put forward the views of Tanganyikans to the outside world.

The first elections were held in two phases in Sept 1958 and Feb 1959 and TANU won a sweeping majority. These were multiracial elections but even the European and Asian candidates owed their success to TANU. The original plan of developing Tanganyika as a multiracial society was finally abandoned by the last Governor, Twining, and Tanganyika attained independence on 9 Dec 1961 with Nyerere as the first Prime Minister. The constitution was subsequently changed, Tanzania becoming a republic with Nyerere as President.

Julius Nyerere

Julius Kambarage Nyerere was born in 1922 in Butiama, E of Lake Victoria. He was the Roman Catholic son of a Zanaki chief. His father died having reportedly had 26 children by 18 wives. The name Nyerere means 'caterpillar' in the Zanaki language and was supposed to have been given to Nyerere's father because at the time of his birth (around 1860) the countryside was infested with these creatures. Nyerere attended a boarding school in Musoma and, from 1937, the Tabora Government Secondary School. He was baptized in 1943 into the Catholic Church and the same year he entered Makerere College, Uganda. After Makerere he returned to Tabora where he taught history and biology at St Mary's Catholic Boys School operated by the White Fathers. In 1949 he went to Edinburgh University and in 1952 obtained his Master of Arts. In 1953 he married Maria Gabriel Magigo who was also a Catholic of the Msinditi tribe and was to become its first woman teacher. He paid the traditional bride price of 6 head of cattle for her and they have 7 children.

Nyerere subsequently took a teaching post at the Catholic Secondary school of St Francis at Puga a few km W of Dar es Salaam and it was from here that he became involved in politics. In 1954 he became president of the Tanzania African Association and was instrumental in converting this into the political organization TANU. He was appointed a temporary member of the Tanganyika Legislative Council in 1954, and a full member of the Legislative Assembly in 1958 where he remained until his assumption of the Presidency in 1962. He resigned as President in 1985. Nyerere has become known as *Mwalimu* which means teacher and he is undoubtedly one of Africa's greatest statesmen, admired for his integrity, modest lifestyle and devotion to equality and human rights.

Post independence Tanzania

In 1964 Zanzibar and Tanganyika merged to form Tanzania. An awkward union has resulted in which Zanzibar has retained its own President, Parliament, a full range of Ministries and handles most of its own finances. The President of Zanzibar is, *ex officio*, one of the Vice-Presidents of Tanzania. Despite having a population that is less than 5% of the total, it has almost a third of the seats in the Tanzanian Assembly.

After independence there was pressure to replace Europeans with Africans in administration and the business sector. There was also considerable demand for basic education and health services. Although economic progress was significant in these early years, there was an impatience at the slow pace of development, and Nyerere made plans for a bold, radical change.

This culminated in the 1967 Arusha Declaration. It was a programme of socialist development accepted by TANU

The Uhuru Railway

The enthusiasm for building this line dates back to Cecil Rhodes who envisaged a Cape-to-Cairo railway linking all the territories then under British control. However it was not until the 1970s that the link between Zambia and Tanzania was finally completed, and there is still a gap from Gulu in Uganda to Kartoum in Sudan.

The line is important for two reasons, one political and the other economic. The line was to link landlocked Zambia with the coast of Tanzania and in doing so free Zambia from her economic dependence on what was then white-ruled Rhodesia (now Zimbabwe). Until the line was built all Zambia's exports and imports had to be carried by rail through Rhodesia to reach the ports of Mozambique. Just a year after Zambia's independence, Rhodesia's Unilateral Declaration of Independence (UDI) increased tension, and the country felt that this dependence on the hostile regimes of Southern Africa had to end. The objective of building a railway line that would enable Zambia's trade to avoid going through white-ruled Africa thus became paramount.

There was also economic reasoning behind the arguments for a rail link between the Zambian copperbelt and Tanzania. The rich mineral deposits as well as the rich agricultural land in SW Tanzania added to the economic viability. Until the line was built there was actually little contact between the two countries. The so-called "Great North Road" that joined the two was actually over 1600 km of dirt track which was frequently rendered impassable during the rainy season. There was thus little trade between the two countries. In the immediate post-independence era the establishment of links between African countries, and the commitment to African unity that this implied were also considered important political objectives.

Various requests for assistance – both financial and technical – in the building of the line were made to Britain, the US, Germany, the Soviet Union and the World Bank as well as others. However they were all reluctant to commit such a large sum of money for a single development project, and in 1965 China offered to finance and build the line. This was seen as China's most ambitious move into Africa and in 1967 the agreement between China and the governments of Zambia and Tanzania was signed. A survey was made of the route and construction of the line began 2½ years later.

The West put much emphasis at the time on the ulterior motives of China in becoming involved in development of East Africa and some saw it was an attempt to thrust communism into the heart of Africa – calling it the 'Red Railway'. The white rulers in southern Africa also felt threatened and saw it as an attempt to undermine their political and economic domination as well as providing logistical support to guerilla fighters in Rhodesia and South Africa. The Chinese themselves, however, called it the "Friendship Route", aimed at strengthening the newly independent African states against the forces of Imperialism. Rumours of CIA involvement in attempts to discredit the Chinese and their motives abounded: for example there was a picture published (said to be a forgery by the CIA) showing a poster requesting Chinese volunteers for the railway. The text of the poster said that those who helped in the construction of the line would be offered "good land" when the line was completed. This was said to be an attempt by the CIA to stir up anti-Chinese sentiments in Zambia and Tanzania.

China committed a loan of some US$166 million for the railway, and construction began in Apr 1970. One of the first buildings to be completed was the reception centre for the Chinese workers when they first arrived. Also built were a hospital, staffed by Chinese doctors, an equipment depot, repair workshops and a huge passenger station. The whole project employed about 25,000 Chinese, 50,000 Tanzanians and 15,000 Zambians and was extremely labour intensive.

The line was a great engineering feat completed in just 5 years. 300 bridges were built and 23 tunnels totalling 8 km were cut into the rock. The line was 963 km in Tanzania and 885 in Zambia making a total of 1848 km plus a further 185 km of sidings. Because of the problems of access to land-locked Zambia, and as all the equipment and rails were imported from China, construction took place from the Tanzania end and progressed S. An immediate problem was that the port at Dar es Salaam became seriously congested and found it difficult to cope with the enormous increase in traffic.

Despite the successful completion of the project, it led to little genuine warmth and understanding between the 2 African countries and China. African students have been the object of hostility in China in recent years. Apart from official duties and functions The Chinese kept themselves very much to themselves during the construction period. A reflection of this was the Chinese boast that there was 'not one baby'.

and which was then amplified in a number of pamphlets by Nyerere. The 2 main themes of this programme were egalitarianism and self-reliance and it was broadly based on the Chinese communist model. It has been said that Tanzania took the Chinese model, mistakes and all and then added a few mistakes of its own. Politicians were subject to a leadership code which required that they had no private sources of income, and no more than one house or car. Banks, plantations and all major industries were nationalized. The cornerstone of the programme was the villagization and agricultural collectivization programme known as *Ujamaa*, see below. This, and efforts in the rest of the economy, would, it was hoped, lead to the development of a just and prosperous society. Education was considered to be one of the most important aims of the programme and as a result Tanzania achieved some of the highest literacy rates in Africa. In the initial years there was success, too, in extending basic health care in the rural areas.

Ujamaa

An important element in post-independence Tanzanian philosophy was *Ujamaa*, a programme for advancement in the rural areas. This was supposed to be the voluntary movement of people into villages with a major objective being to raise output through collectivization and large-scale agricultural production. Emphasis was also on the social benefits – the provision of services such as piped water, electricity, schools and clinics. Self-reliance was the key and the villages were meant to be set up and run by the villagers themselves.

There were 3 phases of villagization in the decade from 1967. The first was voluntary movement on a locally selective basis combined with compulsory movement in Rufiji and Handeni which were areas worst affected by drought and flood. From 1970 to 1973 this was replaced by a 'frontal approach' whereby incentives were given for people to move to villages, which included financial and technical assistance. The reluctance of people to move on their own accord meant the targets were not reached and so after 1973 these methods were replaced by a willingness to use force in support of rapid villagization. The results were dramatic. In 1970 the villagized population stood at about 500,000, or less than 5% of the population. In 1974 this had grown to over 2 million – or 14% of the population. After the first year of compulsory movement Nyerere claimed that there were over 9 million people – or about 60% of the mainland population, living in villages. Force was justified on the grounds that people could not always see what was best for them and had to be shown the way. Viewed in the light of easier provision of social benefits the *Ujamaa* programme was partially successful.

However attempts to farm collectively were disastrous and agricultural output fell. The programme was vigorously resisted in the major coffee-growing areas of Kagera (W of Lake Victoria) and in Kilimanjaro region. By 1977 the *Ujamaa* programme was effectively abandoned although considerable villagization remains.

In 1973 it was decided to move the capital city from Dar es Salaam on the coast to Dodoma in the centre. The position of this city is suitable in so far as it is on communication networks and is located in the centre of the country about 320 km inland. However it is also a dry and desolate area. The major problem with the plan has been the cost of moving. A Presidential official residence, the Prime Minister's office, a National Assembly building and the head quarters of the CCM have all been established there. The cost has forced the rest of central government to remain in Dar es Salaam for the time being.

In 1975 a law was passed which gave legal supremacy to TANU as the national political party, and in 1977 TANU and the Afro-Shirazi party (which had taken control in Zanzibar after the revolution) merged to form *Chama Cha Mapinduzi* (CCM) the 'party of the Nation'.

The 1970's saw the gradual disintegration of the East Africa Community (EAC) which involved Kenya, Tanzania and Uganda in a customs union and provision of common services. Tanzania and Kenya had different ideological perspectives, and the 3 countries could not agree on the distribution of the costs and services of the EAC. Things came to a head over East African Airways. The failure of Tanzania and Uganda to remit funds to Kenya caused Kenya to 'ground' the airline (conveniently when all the planes were sitting on the tarmac in Kenya) and Tanzania reacted by closing the border with Kenya in Feb 1977. The border was only reopened in 1983 after the financial affairs of the EAC were finally settled.

In 1978 Tanzania's relations with neighbouring Uganda worsened and skirmishes on the border were followed by an announcement by Amin that Uganda had annexed the Kagera salient. This is an area of about 1,800 sq km of Tanzanian territory W of Lake Victoria. The OAU applied pressure which caused Uganda to withdraw but fighting continued. In Jan 1979 a Tanzanian force of over 20,000 invaded Uganda, Amin's army capitulated and the Tanzanians rapidly took control of the S part of the country. The invading force had withdrawn by 1981 having spent the interim period in Uganda overseeing the election of Milton Obote for the second time. A remarkable feature of his episode is that, despite being the only African country ever to win a war, this event is not celebrated in Tanzania, and no monuments have been erected.

In 1985 Nyerere decided to step down as President of Tanzania (the first President in post-independence Africa to retire voluntarily). He remained as Chairman of the party (CCM) before retiring from politics completely in 1990. Vice-President Sokoine, who had been widely thought of as Nyerere's successor, was killed in a car crash in Apr 1985. Ali Hassan Mwinyi, who was then President of Zanzibar, was nominated to be the sole candidate for President and was elected in Oct 1985.

Throughout the early 1980's Tanzania was put under pressure to accept economic reforms suggested by the World Bank and IMF. These financial institutions, as well as Western governments, aid donors and foreign investors argued that the socialist development strategy had led to a crisis involving falling incomes, decaying infrastructure, deteriorating health and educational provision, and a climate of petty corruption. For many years Tanzania resisted changes, but eventually the climate of opinion changed and in 1986, under Mwinyi, a market economy policy was adopted, and Tanzania began an economic recovery.

In 1993, Tanzania allowed political parties other than CCM to form, and there are to be multi-party elections in 1995.

Art and architecture

There are five main styles of buildings in Tanzania. The most common are traditional African dwellings constructed variously of poles, mud, straw, cattle-dung and thatch. The styles of these traditional dwellings vary from one region to another. The second style, found on the coast and in Zanzibar shows strong Arabic and Islamic influence and these buildings date from the earliest arrivals of these peoples. During the German colonial period, a substantial number of impressive public buildings were constructed with a distinctive design adapted to the tropical conditions. The British introduced mainly bungalow-style dwellings along lines developed in India. The Indian community constructed commercial and residential buildings in tenement style, but often with elaborate Eastern decorations. Finally there are the concrete office-blocks of the modern era.

Traditional African dwellings

Among the main ethnic groups with distinctive building styles are: the *Wanyaleylusa*, from the South between Mbeya and Lake Malawi with *isyenge* dwellings of bamboo walls and thatched roofs; the *Wanyamwesi* from between Mwanza and Tabora with *msonge* dwellings of thatch roofs and timber and mud walls; the *Maasai* from the N border with Kenya, W of Arusha, with *manyatta* half-sphere dwellings of a timber frame entirely covered with mud reinforced with cow-dung; the *Makua* from the coast to the S near Mtwara with dwellings of mud-covered timber walls and thatch; the *Wasarame* from around Dar es Salaam with *msonge* dwellings all of thatch; the *Ha/Rundi* of W Tanzania region inhabiting grass-thatch *msonge* dwellings; the *Wahaya* from W of Lake Victoria with *msonge* elephant grass huts; the *Wangashi* from around Songea in the S with fairly extensive dwellings in *msonge* style; the *Filsa* from W of Lake Rukwa in the S with conical *msonge* dwellings; the *Wagogo* from Tabora in central Tanzania with *tembe* dwellings which feature a dried mud-covered roof; and the *Wahele* from Winga to the S with *tembe* dwellings.

The *Swahili*, the Arabic/Bantu group from along the coastal strip have *banda* with coral walls and lime mortar made from burnt coral with mangrove pole and clay tile roofs, ornately carved doors and usually a verandah. Later dwellings have corrugated iron roofs. Typically there is a central corridor with rooms off each side on solid coral and mortar floors. A stone slab in the front, shaped like a couch, is for sitting outside in the evenings.

Arabic period

Construction was typically of coral, bound together with lime mortar. The ground floor would be solid coral and mortar, while upper floors were coral and mortar on mangrove rafters (mangrove contains a chemical which discourages termites). The building tended to have thick walls and thus be cool. Decorations often involved crenellations on towers, and carved doors. Examples would be the Fort in Zanzibar, and the Old Boma in Dar es Salaam.

German period

The German colonists constructed durable buildings, with high ceilings to keep rooms as cool as possible, invariably of 2 stories with the upper floor designed to catch any breezes through open arches. Construction was in stone often on a steel frame. Steel girders were used to support floors and verandahs. Roofs were tile or corrugated iron coated with red-oxide paint. The use of steel allowed the construction to be strong, yet not as heavy in appearence as the Arabic buildings. Crenellations, fort-like towers and Islamic arches were incorporated, giving the buildings a distinctive style. In almost all Tanzanian towns, the railway station, main hotel, hospital and administration building (Boma) will still exist and be in this style.

British period

The British were not inclined to embark on an ambitious programme of public buildings as Tanzania was a protectorate (not a colony) destined for eventual self-determination. Government buildings were single-storey bungalows with overhanging galvanized-iron roofs to provide an awning giving shade, supported by slender iron poles. Residential dwellings had clay-tiled roofs, again mostly single-storey. The odd 2-storey dwelling would have tile awnings over the windows to give shade, and to throw rainwater away from the house and prevent it spattering in through the window. Examples of government buildings are the newer wards to the rear of the old German hospital in Dar es Salaam. Also in Dar es Salaam, British colonial bungalows are dotted throughout the Oyster Bay area and 2-storey dwellings are grouped along Bagamoyo Road.

Indian achitecture

The temples and mosques of the Indian community are constructed in traditional style. The Hindu and Ismaili buildings are often several storeys high with elaborate arches and columns. The commercial and residential buildings also tend to be of several storey decorated with inscriptions to the owners and the date of construction, and with the upper storeys embellished with elaborate, arches, columns and façades. The centres of all main towns contain examples.

Modern era

Some bold attempts to introduce inter-war suburban achitecture took place, most notably the Selander Bridge Police Post in Dar es Salaam, with curved windows at the corners. Nearby *Palm Beach Hotel* is another example. Otherwise concrete construction for office buildings and large Mediterranean style residential houses with arches and tiled-roofs have been the order of the day. There are numerous examples of the latter on Msasani Peninsular, and along Bagamoyo Road between Mwenge and Kunduchi Beach.

Culture and life

Estimates for 1994 give a population of 29.3 million, made up of largely mixed Bantu groups, the largest being the Sukuma and the Nyamwezi, but there are at least 120 tribes. The official languages are Swahili and English, with the majority of the population speaking Kiswahili and Kisukuma. The country is sparsely populated. The majority of the population is concentrated on the fertile lower slopes of Mount Kilimanjaro and the shores of Lake Nyasa, where popu-

EDIBLE INSECTS

There are a number of different insects which are eaten in East Africa. The most common are locusts, grasshoppers and flying ants. Locusts are collected when they arrive in swarms (which happens much less frequently now that their populations are more under control) while grasshoppers are collected particularly by children while they look after cattle. They have their wings and spiny legs removed and are either fried in butter, roasted, or are sun-dried.

Termites (or white ants) are the other most commonly eaten insect. Some people say that it serves them right, as anyone living in Africa will quickly come to regard termites as a real nuisance. Any piece of wood that has not been treated is very quickly devoured by these insects. Support poles in a vegetable garden disappear almost overnight. They will also, given the chance, eat away an entire house – all that the termites will leave of ceilings is a thin layer of paint. At certain times of the year, in particular after a prolonged period of heavy rain, the adult form of this insect (which is the flying phase) will appear in huge numbers. They emerge from the mounds or, where there is no mound, from holes in the ground, and fly off to begin new colonies. If you are around when they fly out (they somehow synchronise their exit from the mounds so that thousands leave at the same time) you may wake up to find the ground covered in these insects and their discarded wings. You will also see everybody collecting the insects – sometimes eating them immediately or else taking them home to be lightly fried in butter. They have a rather nutty flavour. You are likely also to see birds, cats and dogs gorging themselves on this 'manna from heaven'. You may also people setting 'traps' to collect the flying ants. These involve constructing a sort of 'tent' over the hole from which the ants would appear. A small opening is left at one end and as the termites struggle to get through this opening many of them fall into a bowl that has been sunk into the ground at the threshold of the opening. Many will lose their wings in the struggle and can then easily be collected.

The queen termite is another sought-after delicacy. There is just one in each mound or colony and they are usually about 125-150 mm long. The huge sausage-like body is far too big for the head and thorax and it is incapable of moving anywhere. It is little more than a highly specialised egg-producing factory (producing an egg a minute every hour of its reproductive life). To reach a queen involves a lot of digging into the termite mound – the colony is usually at least as much below the ground as it is above – so it is unusual for someone to dig up a mound just to get a queen. If however a mound is being dug away anyway then the digger will certainly try to reach the queen.

Caterpillars are also eaten in parts of East Africa. Particularly popular are the caterpillars of the silk *Anaphe infracta* which are found in nests on the branches of the trees of which they feed. These communal nests contain large numbers of caterpillars and they can be cooked and eaten fresh or else dried and stored.

Finally, another insect which is eaten occasionally in some parts of East Africa is the 'lake fly' which is found in swampy areas around lakes. You may see huge swarms of this tiny fly as they fly around the lake shores in a cloud-like formation. Traditionally they were captured by swinging a large basket, which is on long handles, around the head. As they gather in the bottom of the basket the minuscule flies are squashed together into a solid mass. These would then be moulded into cakes and dried in the sun. This practice seems to be much less common nowadays than 50 years ago.

lation densities are as high as 250 persons per sq km, whereas the average density for 1988 was 26 persons per sq km. The urban population in 1985 was around 14%, half the regional average, with a concentration around the port of Dar es Salaam. Population growth was estimated at 3.5% a year for the period 1980-87, although the initial returns from the census suggest that population growth might have been as low as 2.8%.

East Africans are frequently divided into 'tribes'; but exactly what makes a tribe is often difficult to define. A tribe usually refers to a group of people with a common language and culture. They possess a common name and recognise themselves to be distinct from their neighbours. Sometimes the group may be fairly distinctive and easy to define – but other times the divisions are much less clear. There are some observers who believe that the concept of 'tribe' is largely an artificial one imposed from outside since the colonial period. Certainly there are some 'groups' who have only attained full identity and unity in colonial times. Putting this debate to one side, the term (or similar phrases such as 'ethnic groups') is used frequently and the people of Tanzania have been classified into such groups.

About 120 different tribal groups have been distinguished in Tanzania. They vary from groups of over a million people to tribes of just a few hundred. It is obviously impractical to look at all these groups here so only the largest and most important are examined. The largest ethnic groups are the Sukuma and the Nyamwezi although no group makes

Blessing The Year

This ceremony has been observed amongst the Rangi and Wasi peoples living in the Mbulu District near Lake Manyara in the N. Three groups of men take part in the ceremony: they are the elders and grandfathers, the adult men (from initiation upwards) and the boys (the uninitiated). No women or people from other tribes are allowed to take part. Special dress is not worn at the ceremony. The participants gather around a sacrificial tree and the ceremony involves the chanting and singing of various songs followed by the sacrificing of a lamb. One of the men then whisks or agitates a liquid in a gourd which quickly generates a large quantity of foam. When the foam overflows onto the ground it is scattered around while the man calls out "Howa! Howa!". A number of the other men repeat the process of whisking the liquid and scattering the foam. Meanwhile the sheep is skinned and the juices of the stomach contents squeezed into a half gourd which is then hung from a branch of the tree using strips of the sheep's skin. Beer is then distributed amongst the men. A young girl is brought to sit at the base of the tree with a gourd containing seeds from all the plants grown in the area and some beer. This will later be carried around the boundaries before being returned to the tree. The seeds will then be divided up between all the participants who will mix them with seeds when planting the next year's crops.

The "bound-beating" party then sets off with the half gourd containing the liquid which is scattered using twigs from the tree. The party contains 2 leaders, hornblowers and all the other participants except the elders. As the party goes around the area to be blessed they are given local beer at the houses that they pass. Large quantities of beer are consumed and the ceremony continues late into the day. The elders meanwhile roast the remains of the sheep using firewood from the sacrificial tree. They then eat the meat and drink the beer.

up more than 15% of the population. About a dozen of the largest groups make up about 50% of the population. Most of these groups are of Bantu origin (although there are some Nilotic groups as well) and about 95% of the population is Bantu-speaking – the most important Bantu language is Swahili, a language which is the mother tongue of the people of Zanzibar and Pemba as well as some coastal people. Swahili became a *lingua franca* before the colonial period in some areas and this was encouraged by both the Germans and the British. It is very widely spoken and in 1963 it became Tanzania's national language.

Sukuma

This is Tanzania's largest ethnic group and makes up between 10 and 13% of the population. The name means 'people of the north' and the group lives just to the S of Lake Victoria. The ethnic consciousness of this group is fairly recent and is not entirely pervasive. In the pre-colonial period they were organized into a large number of small chiefdoms. They practise mixed agriculture, with both cattle-herding and cultivation. This is also an important cotton growing area.

Nyamwezi

The Nyamwezi people are found to the S of the Sukuma people in N Tanzania and in many ways are similar to the Sukuma. Like the Sukuma they were formerly made up of a large number of very small chiefdoms. Some of these chiefs tried later to dominate wider areas. Their identity is fairly recent and rather fragile. They are primarily a cultivating people and have established a reputation as traders.

Makonde

These people are located in the SE part of the country and are fairly isolated, being on the Makonde Plateau. Although they are one of the 5 largest groups the Makonde have been little affected by colonial and post-colonial developments. They are renowned for being a conservative people who are determined to defend their way of life. This is facilitated by the difficulty in reaching this part of Tanzania. Even today communications with the SE are poor, particularly during the wet season. The Makonde are perhaps most famous for their beautifully-crafted woodcarvings which are sold all over Tanzania. Makonde people are also found in Mozambique.

Chagga

The Chagga (or Chaga) people are found around the S slopes of Mount Kilimanjaro and constitute the third largest group in Tanzania. They are greatly advantaged by living in a fertile and well-watered region which is ideally suited to the production of coffee. They were also one of the first groups to be affected by the Christian missionaries, in particular the Roman Catholics and Lutherans, and this meant that the provision of education in the area was ahead of many other areas. The high level of education and opportunity of cash-cropping have resulted in a comparatively high level of income, and also a relatively high level of involvement in political activity. One example of the form that this has taken is through cooperative action in the production and marketing of coffee.

Chagga customs and beliefs The Chagga believe that the god that they called Ruwa was greater than all the other gods that they worshiped. They believed all men had their origin in him and that as he did not trouble them with petty demands unlike some other gods he must love men. He is believed to live in a place in the skies which they called *nginenyi* which means blue skies. Sacrifices would be made to Ruwa when someone was ill or when there was a famine or epidemic. Usually prayers would be said and then a goat would be slaughtered. The goat should be a male of uniform colour without any spots, and it should not have had its tail docked. Sacrifices would also be offered to the spirits of the dead. When a person dies it is believed that they would live in the new world but in a different form. The spirits of the dead would be able to return to the world to demand what is due to them from their relatives. Their physical presence would not be noticed but they would be seen in dreams or through the noises made by animals.

Haya

The Haya people are different from most other ethnic groups in Tanzania. They are located in the far NW of Tanzania, to the W of the shores of Lake Victoria. Culturally and linguistically they are more closely related to the interlacustrine Bantu who are found to the N and W of the Haya. Like the interlacustrine Bantu they are organized into a few centralized states. Although the Haya have common traditions, social system, culture, and language as well as territorial identity, they are divided into several chiefdoms which suggests that in this case political unity is not an essential part of tribal identity. The Haya are cultivators growing coffee and plantains and live in densely populated villages. In a similar way to the Chagga the Haya have had high levels of education and this, combined with the production of coffee, has had a clearly beneficial effect on the economy of the area.

Haya pregnancy and childbirth What follows is a description of some of the traditions which were originally recorded in the late 1950's by a Dr Moller who was the District Medical Officer in the area at the time. There is little doubt that some aspects will have changed since then, particularly with the increase of births in clinics and hospitals.

A Haya woman is usually married at about 17 or 18 years old and once married would be kept in seclusion until the birth of her first child. She is known during this period as *omu-gule*, and is not allowed to leave the house during the day. She is kept in a special part of the house and is under the watchful eye of her mother-in-law.

Once a woman discovers that she is pregnant the first person that she must tell is her mother-in-law or, if she is not available, another senior member of her husband's family. Only then can she inform her mother and her husband. There are a number of taboos imposed during pregnancy which include that the mother must not walk through any entrance backwards or the labour will be difficult, and she must chew all her food very carefully and eat very slowly. This is because it is thought that the child may be hurt by the food falling on it, and if the mother eats too quickly the child, who is also eating, may choke. There are various food taboos that apply and the mother is also given a variety of herbal medicines throughout her pregnancy.

When labour begins a midwife is sent for. These are usually elderly women who have learnt their trade from their mothers and will in turn pass it on to their daughters. As labour progresses the midwife will check that no clothing on or belonging to the mother has a knot in it as it is thought that this will adversely affect the labour. The woman is allowed to drink during labour, but not to eat. When the waters break the woman is made to lie down. Herbal drugs are sometimes given to try to speed up the labour. It was believed by a doctor who observed numerous labours that many of these drugs were actually harmful and did little good to the mother or child.

The placenta is sometimes called the 'brother' or 'dead brother' of the child born. This may lead to women saying that they had two children, when in fact only one was born and the other was the placenta. The placenta is treated like a corpse and is disposed of in the same way. It is wrapped in bark cloth and is buried inside or near a hut. There are a number of taboos relating to the placenta and its disposal and the violation of these taboos was thought to be punished by various skin diseases.

The cord is tied with a piece of string made from a kind of tough grass, and traditionally it was cut using a sharpened slice of reed. There is a belief that any blood that is lost during delivery can be used for witchcraft and this will cause barrenness of the woman from whom the blood originated.

Finally it is believed that the man who first has intercourse with a woman is the father of her first child. The traditional belief is that the first intercourse did cause pregnancy but it 'broke off' and the child was 'hiding in the back' to be born later. This is called a long pregnancy or *bisisi* and the child is known as a 'bisisi-child'. Thus if a couple marry but fail to produce children and later separate, the first child born to the woman belongs to the first husband – even if the child is born many years later. This means that any man who can prove that he has had the first intercourse with a woman can justly claim the first child of that woman as his. This is of considerable legal, social and economic importance to this district. Also from the period of the first birth, until the cord has dropped, the woman returns to her 'virginal status' – thus any man who has intercourse with her during this period can claim the next child of the woman as his. For this reason a newly-delivered woman is guarded very carefully during this period by her husband's family. To make things even more complicated, it seems that 'real' intercourse is not

Last Of The Cannibals

In 1891, the Polish writer Henryte Sienkiewicz (later to win a Nobel Prize for Literature in 1905) as part of a safari through Africa went on a hunting expedition from Bagamoyo to the Mission at Mandara in Kilimanjaro region. En route they passed though the territory of the Wadoe on the S bank of the Pangani River.

Sienkiewicz had been advised by the Holy Ghost Fathers Mission in Bagamoyo before departure that the King, Muremi-Pira, then about 70, from time to time, and in conditions of the utmost secrecy would purchase a prisoner from whom he would take a *filet au sauce naturelle*. This practice was frowned-upon by the German community, and the chief was continually apprehensive that he would be called to account by the Bagamoyo authorities. Since he preferred cutlet *homo sapiens* to beef, the restrictions, apart from the occasional treat, had reduced him to a vegetarian diet. The Holy Ghost Fathers always had a fairly good indication as to when a lapse occurred as a cow, by way of a guilt offering, would arrive at the Mission.

The Wadoe had been a pastoral community in regular conflict with their neighbours which had not been unpleasing to the previous Arab administration since the enhanced availability of captives from both sides served to increase the supply of slaves in Zanzibar and lower their price. The problem of casualties, and captives surplus to the slavers' requirements was solved in a fairly simple manner by eating them.

Sienkiewicz and his companions felt reasonably secure during their visit as the Wadoe believed that if they ate a white their country would disappear. One disconcerting custom, however, was the king's practice of serving guests with a mead made from local honey, garnished with dead caterpillars, in a human skull.

Traditional Alcoholic Beverages

A variety of grains is used in the making of the traditional beer in Tanzania known in Swahili as *pombe*. The variety of grain and procedure followed vary in different parts of the country.

In many parts, including Dar es Salaam, millet is used. It is allowed to germinate for 3 days before being sun dried – it is then called *kimea*. The *kimea* is ground and mixed together with ungerminated flour before being added to hot water and left to stand for a while before being boiled. The liquid is then left to cool and mixed with a suspension of *kimea* and cold water. Fermentation begins and more flour may be added. The whole mixture is then shaken up and roughly filtered. The *pombe* is left overnight and the next day is ready to drink. The whole process takes several days and is a skilled job often undertaken by women. The stage at which yeast is added varies – indeed in some cases no yeast is added at all and instead the sprouted millet provides wild yeasts. The alcoholic strength of pombe is 9-11% proof – double the strength of European beers.

A stronger drink than *pombe* is *tembo* which is made from part of the coconut palm. However its preparation and consumption has dropped over the years. At the turn of the century everywhere that could grow the palms did and very large quantities of *tembo* were drunk. The flower head of the palm is used. The top is cut off and the juice within it allowed to collect in a gourd overnight. The next morning a further section of the flower head is sliced off and the juice again allowed to collect. Collections are made about 3 times during the day until the whole of the flower head has been used. This liquid which has been collected ferments quickly and spontaneously. The alcoholic content of *tembo* is higher than that of *pombe* and increases with time before it goes sour. The strength is 14-16% proof. Once it has gone sour the liquid can be used as a sort of vinegar.

Tembo is not the strongest of the locally made "traditional" drinks in Tanzania – a spirit called *moshi* which is also known as *brandi* can be up to 90% proof. It is made using a still which traditionally would have been constructed of gourds. Nowadays however it is more likely that an old petrol tin (*debe*) will be used. The exact method varies, but it is based on a brew of *pombe* or *tembo* which is successively distilled.

necessarily essential – sometimes 'symbolic' intercourse is all that is needed.

Hehe

The Hehe people live in the central S region of Tanzania around Iringa. They have a strong sense of being Hehe, and have their own more or less distinctive social system and culture with a unifying political system. However within this group there are differences in the way of life and social systems between those who live in the drier E parts of the region and those who live in the wetter uplands to the W. These are caused by environmental factors as well as the effects of distance. Despite this, one observer has suggested that there is a greater unity and identity amongst the Hehe than there is with any other group of people.

Maasai

The Maasai inhabit the N border area with Kenya, but are found as far S as Morogoro and Tabora. They are a spectacular group of tall, slender cattle-herders, living off milk, blood and meat. Young men leave to become *moran* before returning to begin family life. As *moran* they carry spears, wear distinctive red garments and have elaborately decorated faces, bodies and hair. The women have shaven heads and often wear many coils of beads on their necks and shoulders.

Shirazi

The Shirazi is the name given to people who are a mixture of Africans and people who are said to have come at a very early time from the Shiraz area of Iran. They are divided into 3 'tribes' called the Hadimu, Tumbatu and Pemba. The Africans are descendants of mainlanders who came to the islands of Zanzibar and Pemba often as slaves although later on of their own accord. Decendants of the Shirazis have intermixed with other Swahili people and have become more African in race, speech and culture.

Swahili

This is the general term given to the coastal people who have a Muslim-orientated culture. They are the descendants of generations of mixing of slaves, migrant labourers and Afro-Arabs.

Other African groups

The **Hi** people are a very small group of click-speakers. They are hunter-gatherers and live on the SW shores of Lake Eyasi which is found in the central N part of Tanzania. Other click speakers that are found in Tanzania include the **Hadzapi** and the **Sandawe**. The Hadzapi live in the same area as the Hi and the groups are believed to be closely related. The Sandawe live in the interior central region of Tanzania to the N of Dodoma. The **Dorobo** are a small group of hunter-gatherers who are found throughout Maasailand and are also found in Kenya.

Non-Africans

This group makes up under 1% of the population of Tanzania and comprises Europeans, Asians and Arabs. In the mid 1970's it was estimated that there were 1,500 European citizens (compared to 23,000 in 1961 at the time of independence, and 17,000 in 1967), and about 40,000 Asians (compared to 75,000 in 1967). A recent figure for the number of Arabs is not known although there were about 30,000 in 1967 living on the mainland. Until the 1964 revolution Arabs were the dominant group in Zanzibar although they constituted only about 20% of the population.

Modern Tanzania

Politics

Since independence in 1961, Tanzania has had single party rule, under Julius Nyerere until 1985 when power was transferred to Ali Hassan Mwinyi. There has been negligible internal unrest since the revolution in Zanzibar in 1964, closely followed by a supressed army mutiny on the mainland. The invasion of Uganda in 1979, and a subsequent period of peace-keeping occupation, although costly, had minimal disrupting effect on the economy.

Tanzania is committed to multi-party elections in 1995. Twelve or so opposition parties have been formed, of which perhaps the strongest is CHADEMA, led by a former finance minister, Edwin Mtei, a passionate advocate of the market economy. At present the current ruling party (CCM) looks secure, containing as it does most of the political experience and expertise in Tanzania.

Overall, Tanzania's stability has remained excellent. The government has remained secure, despite an economic policy that has changed from socialism to capitalism. The only cause for concern is the growing pressure for separation from the predominantly Islamic islands of Zanzibar.

Economics

Economic strategy underwent a profound change in 1967 when financial and business enterprises were taken into public ownership and a major reorganization of the agricultural sector was introduced involving collective production and re-locating the population into villages. By 1977, the collectivization of agriculture had virtually been abandoned. In 1986 Tanzania signed an agreement with the IMF which heralded the beginnings of a reversal of economic strategy to more encouragement for the private sector and reliance on market forces, rather than on planning and central control.

Economic and social structure

GDP in 1991 was estimated at US$2,223 million, and this makes the economy smaller than average size in Africa. GNP per head in 1991 was US$100, and this placed Tanzania among the poorer group of low-income countries.

Agriculture contributed 61% of GDP in 1991, and this was almost twice the average dependence on this sector in Africa. The industrial sector contributed 5% of GDP, of which 4% of GDP was manufacturing. The average in Africa was for the industrial sector to contribute 28% of GDP. The services sector was responsible for 34% of GDP, and this was below the Africa average of 38%. On the demand side, private consumption was the equivalent of 96% of GDP in 1987, well above the Africa average of 73%. Government consumption was 16%, about the allocation of resources to this sector that is typical of Africa. Gross domestic investment was 22% of GDP, while saving was -11%, with the level of investment being achieved by virtue of a net inflow of resources, almost all aid, equivalent to 33% of GDP.

Exports were equivalent to 20% of GDP, and imports 53%. The percentage of GDP generated by exports is about the average for Africa, while the dependence on imports is twice as great.

Coffee was the main merchandise export, comprising 31% of the total, with cotton next at 13%. Machinery was 19% of imports, with fuel 14%, manufactures 12%, foodstuffs 9% and metals 8%.

The adult literacy rate in 1980 was estimated at 79%, well above the Africa average of 39%. Primary enrolments were 63% in 1990, and this is slightly below the Africa average of 76%. The secondary enrolment rate was 4% and this is well below the average Africa rate of 15%, and one of the lowest secondary enrolment rates in the world. The higher education enrolment was less than half of 1%, and again one of the lowest rates anywhere.

Life expectancy in 1991 was 51 years, and this is slightly above the Africa average of 50. In 1990, there was one doctor for every 25,000 persons, and this was worse than Africa average of one doctor for every 24,000 persons. Average daily calorie supply per person was 2,316 in 1990, and this was above the Africa average.

Overall, Tanzania is a low-income country, with heavy dependence on agriculture, a very small industrial sector, and a below average size for its service sector. Private consumption is a large proportion of GDP, and a significant proportion of this, as well as of investment, is sustained by net aid inflows. Exports are low and reliance on imports high. Educational provision is uneven, with high literacy rates coexisting with poor secondary and tertiary enrolment rates. Health provision is poor as a result of Tanzania's low-income status.

Economic performance

GDP grew at 2.9% a year in the period 1980-91, and this was better than the average for Africa. However, population growth estimated at 3.0% implied GDP per head falling at -0.1%, a slower rate of decline than in Africa generally.

The agriculture sector expanded at 4.4% a year in the period 1980-91, and this more than kept pace with the growth in population. However the industrial sector contracted at -2.4% a year, twice the rate of contraction experienced on average in Africa, while manufacturing declined at -3.5% a year. The services sector grew at 2.0% a year.

Export volumes declined at -1.9% a year in the 1980-91 period. Import volumes expanded by 2.8% a year, sustained by substantial aid inflows, whereas for Africa as a whole, import volumes declined by -6.9% a year.

The average price level has expanded by 25.7% a year in the 1980-91 period, and this is rather worse than the annual inflation average in Africa in the same period.

Overall, Tanzania experienced poor economic performance in the 1980's with GDP per head falling and only in the agricultural sector has output kept pace with population growth. Export performance has been particularly poor, with volumes falling and fairly rapid inflation.

Recent economic developments

In June of 1986, the Tanzanian government reached agreement with the IMF, after resisting IMF terms since 1979. The main measures involved a substantial devaluation of the currency, rises in producer prices for key export crops, and a budget which aimed to keep government spending constant in real terms. The agreement released US$400 million in frozen aid commitments and US$130m in new aid, and in Aug 1986 Tanzania requested a stand-by facility from the IMF of US$64 million. These changes, together with the revelation that the government was to register individual land-holdings, marked a decisive movement away from planning and government intervention in the economy, which had been the main feature of Tanzania's economic strategy since 1967.

As part of the reform programme, the government has ended the monopoly of the National Milling Corporation (NMC) in the purchase of domestic foodstuffs. The emergence of private traders forced the NMC in 1987 to raise its purchase prices by 50% for rice, 30% for maize and 25% for wheat to remain competitive. There is now strong pressure from farmers to wind up the other crop marketing boards, particularly those dealing with coffee, cotton, tea and sugar. Several key hotels are to be run by international corporations, and other hotels and tourist facilities have been made into private companies. Lonrho has indicated its willingness to invest in Tanzania, and is reported to be extending its tea holdings, and to be involved in brewing and tractor production.

Recent economic performance has shown an encouraging response to the reform programme, with economic growth estimated at 3.8% in 1986, the first time that output has kept pace with population growth since 1980 and this performance being sustained through to 1993. Inflation is reported to be running at 30% annually, which is about the level experienced throughout the 1980's, and given the substantial adjustments to the exchange rate, and rises in producer prices, it is a creditable achievement to have prevented an acceleration. Export volumes have shown some improvement, and the response to the increased producer prices for coffee and tea will become apparent over the next 5 years, as there is a lag between new plantings and the first crops. However cotton, which is an annual crop, reached record output levels with 390,000 bales as compared with 168,000 in 1985/6, a 132% increase, and realised US$55 million in sales. There is still a substantial balance of trade deficit, with exports in 1989 estimated at US$380 million and merchandise imports at US$1,200 million. The trade gap is covered by aid flows.

The exchange rate has continued to depreciate. It stood at TSh17.50=US$1 in mid 1985 and by 1994 had fallen to TSh508.48=US$1.

The current aid programme concentrates heavily on rehabilitation of infrastructure. There is a massive US$700 million scheme to improve roads coordinated by the World Bank. Other projects include an US$8 million programme to upgrade electricity suppliesalsofundedbytheWorldBank, and schemes to upgrade port facilities in Dar es Salaam financed by Sweden and Norway. Railway rehabilitation is being undertaken by various donors,

Comparative Economic & Social Data

	Tanzania	East Africa	Africa	Industrial Countries
Population & Land				
Population, mid year, millions, 1994	29.6	12.2	10.2	40.0
Urban Population, %, 1991	34	30.5	30	75
Population Growth Rate, % per year, 1980-91	3.0	3.1	3.1	0.8
Land Area, thou. sq km	945	486	486	1,628
Population Density, persons per sq km, 1988	31.3	24.2	20.4	24.3
Economy: Production & Income				
GDP, US$ millions, 1991	2,223	2,650	3,561	550,099
GNP per head, $US, 1991	100	250	389	12,960
Economy: Supply Structure				
Agriculture, % of GDP, 1991	61	43	35	3
Industry, % of GDP, 1991	5	15	27	35
Services, % of GDP, 1991	34	42	38	61
Economy: Demand Structure				
Private Consumption, % of GDP, 1991	96	77	73	62
Gross Domestic Investment, % of GDP, 1991	22	16	16	21
Government Consumption, % of GDP, 1991168	16	14	17	
Exports, % of GDP, 1991	20	16	23	17
Imports, % of GDP, 1991	53	24	26	17
Economy: Performance				
GDP growth, % per year, 1980-91	2.9	1.6	-0.6	2.5
GDP per head growth, % per year, 1980-91	-0.1	-1.7	-3.7	1.7
Agriculture growth, % per year, 1980-91	4.4	1.1	0.0	2.5
Industry growth, % per year, 1980-91	-2.4	1.1	-1.0	2.5
Services growth, % per year, 1980-91	2.0	2.5	-0.5	2.6
Exports growth, % per year, 1980-91	-1.9	0.7	-1.9	3.3
Imports growth, % per year, 1980-91	-2.8	0.2	-6.9	4.3
Economy: Other				
Inflation Rate, % per year, 1980-91	25.7	23.6	16.7	5.3
Aid, net inflow, % of GDP, 1991	39.2	11.5	6.3	-
Debt Service, % of Exports, 1991	24.6	18	20.6	-
Education				
Primary, % of 6-11 group, 1990	63	62	76	102
Secondary, % of 12-17 group, 1989	4	15	22	93
Higher, % of 20-24 group, 1990	..	1.2	1.9	39
Adult Literacy Rate, %, 1980	79	41	39	99
Health & nutrition				
Life Expectancy, years, 1991	51	50	50	76
Calorie Supply, daily per head, 1990	2,316	2,111	2,096	3,357
Population per doctor, 1990	24,880	35,986	24,185	550

Notes: 'Africa' excludes South Africa. Dates are for the country in question, and do not always correspond with the Regional, African and Industrial averages.

and the Petro-Canada International Assistance Corporation is engaged in a US$27 million oil exploration programme funded by the World Bank.

Economic outlook

Assuming that Tanzania maintains its record of political stability, and perseveres with a steady programme of liberalising economic reforms, general prospects are good.

DAR ES SALAAM

CONTENTS

MAPS

Basics

SOCIAL INDICATORS *Population* 1.4 million (1988); *literacy* 52% (1985); *life expectancy* 54 (1990); *birth rate* 51:1000; *death rate* 13:1000; *fertility rate* 7.1 per female (1990). *Average annual income per head* US$590 (1990); *inflation* 20% (1990). *Religion*: *Muslim* 43%; *Christian* 38%; *Other* 19%.

MAIN LANGUAGES Swahili, English.

DISTANCE of city centre to airport 15 km.

Dar es Salaam is the capital of Tanzania and the seat of government, although there are plans to move the capital to Dodoma, 480 km to the West. The city is located at sea level on the Indian Ocean coast covering an area of 90 sq km. The hottest months are Dec to the end of Mar with long rains Mar to May and short rains in Nov and Dec. The best season is May to Oct, although there is sun all the year round, even during the rains, which are short and heavy.

Dar es Salaam is by some measure the largest city in Tanzania, and has grown rapidly since independence in 1961, roughly trebling in size. Almost all administrative, political and business activity is concentrated in the city although some government bodies and the main parliamentary sittings are in Dodoma. The city dates from 1857 and was successively under the control of Zanzibar, Germany and Britain before self-determination, and these groups have all left their mark. The first impression of the city on the journey in from the airport is of very shabby buildings and a dilapidated infrastructure. There is a marked contrast between the conditions of ordinary people (walking long distances, crowded on buses and makeshift transport, living in ramshackle dwellings, operating small businesses

CLIMATE DAR ES SALAAM

	Jan	Feb	Mar	Apr	May	Jun	Jul	Aug	Sep	Oct	Nov	Dec
Max°C	32	32	32	31	30	29	29	29	30	31	31	32
Min°C	24	23	23	22	21	19	18	18	18	20	22	23
Rain mm	70	63	121	279	200	37	33	25	29	49	81	90
Sun hrs/day	8	9	7	5	6	8	8	8	8	8	8	9
Humidity %	75	74	75	76	70	62	60	61	63	66	71	75

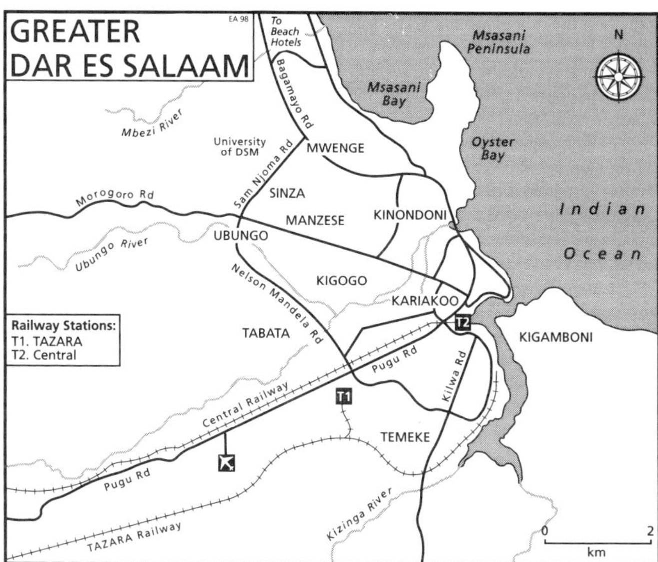

from temporary shelters) on the one hand, and the bureaucratic, business and international community which enjoys much higher standards. On closer aquaintance with Dar es Salaam the visitor is invariably surprised by the wealth of historical interest that has survived, appreciates the splendid coastal location, warms to the friendliness and relaxed manner of the inhabitants, and learns to seek out the special pleasures the city has to offer, which are not always apparent to the casual observer. There is a saying in Dar es Salaam that 'the city has sun, climate, location – everything, in fact, except luck'.

History

Zanzibar period 1862-1886

The name Dar es Salaam means 'Haven of Peace' and was chosen by the founder of the city, Seyyid Majid, Sultan of Zanzibar. The harbour is sheltered, with a narrow inlet channel protecting the water from the Indian Ocean. An early visitor, Frederic Elton in 1873 remarked that 'the climate is healthy, the air clear – the site a beautiful one and the surrounding country green and well-wooded.'

Despite the natural advantages it was not chosen as a habour earlier due to the difficulties of approaching though the narrow inlet during the monsoon season and there were other sites, protected by the coral reef, along the Indian Ocean coast.

Majid decided to construct the city in 1862 as the result of a desire to have a port and settlement on the mainland which would act as a focus for trade and caravans operating to the S. Bagamoyo, see page 264, was already well established, but local interests there were inclined to oppose direction from Zanzibar, and the new city was a way of ensuring control from the outset.

Construction began in 1865 and the name was chosen in 1866. Streets were laid out, based around what is now Sokoine Drive runnning along the shoreline to the N of the inner harbour. Water was secured by the sinking of stone wells, and the largest building was the Sultan's palace. An engraving of 1869 shows the palace to have been a substantial stone, 2-storey building, with the upper-storey having sloping walls and a crenellated parapet, sited close to the shore on the present-day site of Malindi Wharf. In appearance it was similar in style to the fort which survives in Zanzibar, see page 339. To the SW, along the shore, was a mosque and to the NW a group of buildings, some of 2-storeys with flat roofs and some with pitched thatched roofs. Most of these buildings were used in conjuction with trading activities and some of them would have been warehouses. One building which survives is the a double-storeyed structure now known as the Old Boma, on the corner of Morogoro Road and Sokoine Drive. The sultan used it as an official residence for guests, and in 1867 a Western-style banquet was given for the British, French, German and American consuls to launch the new city. Craftsmen and slaves were brought from Zanzibar for construction work. Coral for the masonry was cut from the reef and nearby islands. A steam tug was ordered from Germany to assist with the tricky harbour entrance and to speed up movements in the wind-sheltered inner waters. Economic life centred on agricultural cultivation (particularly coconut plantations), traders who dealt with the local Zaramo people as well as with the long-distance caravan traffic.

Dar es Salaam suffered its first stroke of ill-luck when Majid died suddenly in 1870, after a fall in his new palace, and he was succeeded as Sultan by his half-brother, Seyyid Barghash. Barghash did not share Majid's enthusiam for the new settlement, and indeed Majid's death was taken to indicate that carrying on with the project would bring ill-fortune. The court remained in Zanzibar. Bagamoyo and Kilwa predominated as mainland trading centres. The Palace and other buildings were abandonned, and the fabric rapidly fell into decay. Nevertheless the foundation of a Zaramo settlement and Indian commercial involvement had been established.

Despite the neglect, Barghash maintained control over Dar es Salaam through an agent (*akida*) and later a governor (*wali*) and Arab and Baluchi troops. An Indian customs officer collected duties for use of the harbour and the Sultan's coconut plantations were maintained. Some commercial momentum had been established, and the Zaramo traded gum-copal, rubber, coconuts, rice and fish for cloth, iron-ware and beads. The population expanded to around 5,000 by 1887, and comprised a cosmopolitan mixture of the Sultan's officials, soldiers, planters, traders, and ship-owners, as well as Arabs, Swahilis and Zaramos, Indian Muslims, Hindus and the odd European.

German period 1887-1916

In 1887 the German East African Company under Hauptmann Leue took up residence in Dar es Salaam. They occupied the residence of the Sultan's governor whom they succeeded in getting recalled to Zanzibar, took over the collection of customs dues, and, in return for a payment to the Zaramo, obtained a concession on the land. The Zaramo, Swahili and Arabs opposed this Euopean takeover, and this culminated in the Arab revolt of 1888-9 which involved most of the coastal region as well as Dar es Salaam. The city came under sporadic attack and the buildings of the Berlin Mission, a Lutheran denomination located on a site close to the present Kivokoni ferry, were destroyed. When the revolt was crushed, and the German government took over responsibility from the German East Africa Company in 1991, Dar es Salaam was selected as the main centre for administration and commercial activities.

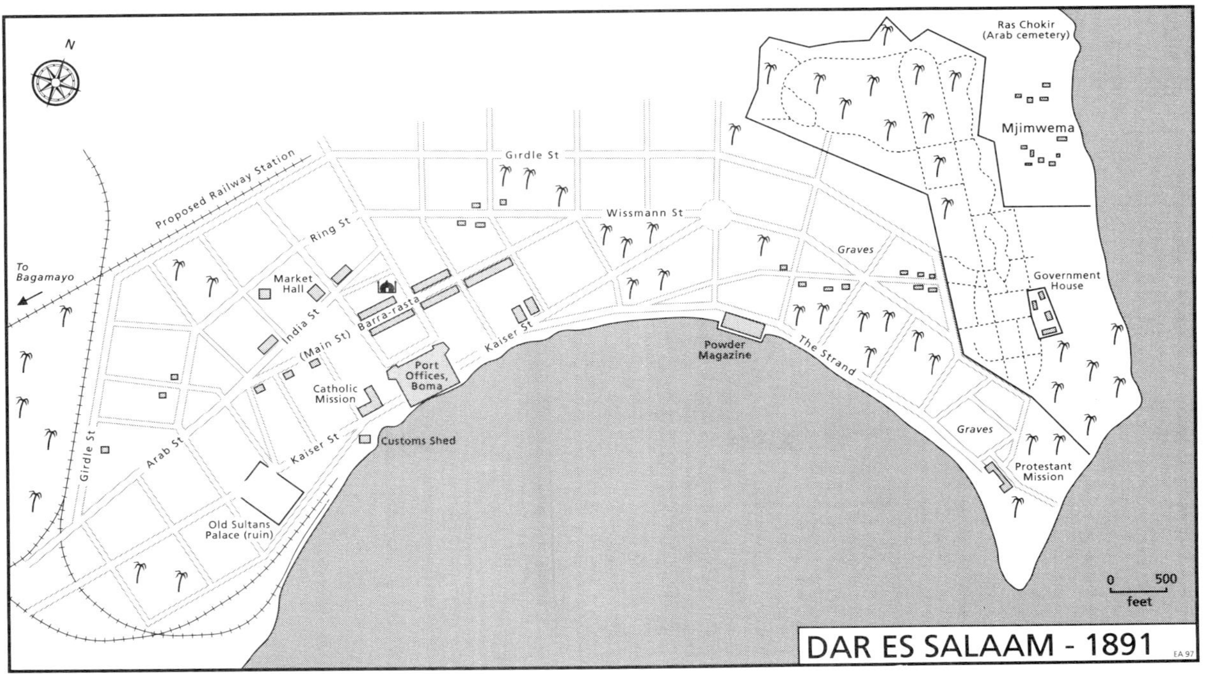
N
Ras Chokir (Arab cemetery)
Mjimwema
Proposed Railway Station
Girdle St
Wissmann St
Ring St
To Bagamayo
Market Hall
Graves
Government House
India St
Barra-rasta
(Main St)
Kaiser St
Powder Magazine
The Strand
Port Offices, Boma
Catholic Mission
Customs Shed
Graves
Girdle St
Arab St
Kaiser St
Protestant Mission
Old Sultans Palace (ruin)
0 500
feet
DAR ES SALAAM - 1891
EA 97

German development involved the construction of many substantial buildings, and most of these survive today. In the quarter of a century to 1916, several fine buildings were laid out on Wilhelms Ufer (now Kivukoni Front), and these included administrative offices as well as a club and a casino. Landing steps to warehouses, and a hospital, were constructed on the site of the present Malindi Wharf and behind them the railway station. Just to the S of Kwasani Creek was the dockyard where the present deepwater docks are situated. A second hospital was built at the E end of Unter den Akazien and Becker Strasse, now Samora Avenue. The post office is on what is now Sokoine Drive at the junction with Mkwepu Street. A governor's residence provided the basis for the current State House. The principal hotels were the *Kaiserhof* which was demolished to build the *New Africa Hotel*, and the *Burger Hotel* razed to make way for the present Telecoms building. The Roman Catholic Cathedral is behind the customs jetty on Sokoine Drive and the Lutheran Cathedral is where Kivokoni Front forks away from Sokoine Drive.

The area behind the N harbour shore was laid out with fine acacia-lined streets and residential two-storey buildings with pitched corrugated iron roofs and first floor verandahs, and most of these survive. Behind the E waterfront were shop and office buildings, many of which are still standing, and can be recognised by their distinctive architectural style, see page 226.

British period 1916-1961

In the 45 years that the British administered Tanganyika, public construction was kept to a minimum on economy grounds, and business was carried on in the old German buildings. The governor's residence was damaged by naval gunfire in 1915, and was remodelled to form the present State House. In the 1920's, the Gymkhana Club was laid out on its present site behind Ocean Road, and Mnazi Moja ('Coconut Grove') established as a park. The Selander Bridge causeway was constructed, and this opened up the Oyster Bay area to residential construction for the European community. The Yacht Club was built on the harbour shore (it is now the customs post) and behind it the Dar es Salaam Club (now the Hotel and Tourism Training Centre), both close to the present *Kilimanjaro Hotel*.

As was to be expected, road names were changed, as well as those of the most prominent buildings. Thus Wilhelms Ufer became Azania Front, Unter den Akazien became Acacia Avenue, Kaiser Strasse became City Drive. Other streets were named after explorers Speke and Burton, and there was a Windsor Street. One departure from the relentless Anglicization of the city was the change of Bismarck Strasse to Versailles Street – perhaps surprising until it is recalled that it was the Treaty of Versailles in 1918 which allocated the former German East Africa to the British. The *Kaiserhof Hotel* became the *New Africa*, the *New Burgher Hotel* became the *Prince of Wales Hotel*.

The settling by the various groups living in the city in distinctive areas was consolidated during the British period. Europeans lived in Oyster Bay to the N of the city centre in large Mediterranean-style houses with arches, verandahs and gardens surrounded by solid security walls and fences. The Asians lived either in tenement-style blocks in the city centre or in the Upanga area in between the city and Oyster Bay where they constructed houses and bungalows with small gardens. African families built Swahili style houses, see page 225, initially in the Kariakoo area to the W of the city. Others were accommodated in government bachelor quarters provided for railway, post office and other government employees. As population increased settlement spread out to Mikocheni and along Morogoro Road, and Mteni to the South. An industrial area developed along the Pugu Road, which was convenient for the port and was served by branch lines from the central railway line which heads SW.

Independence 1961 to present

For the early years of independence Dar es Salaam managed to sustain its enviable reputation of being a gloriously located city with a fine harbour, generous parklands with tree-lined avenues particularly in the botanical gardens and Gymkhana area, and a tidy central area of shops and services.

New developments saw the construction of high-rise government buildings, most notably the Telecoms building on the present Samora Avenue, the *New Africa Hotel* for which the old Kaiserhof building was razed, and the *Kilimanjaro Hotel* on a site next to the Dar es Salaam Club on Kivukoni Front.

With the Arusha Declaration of 1967, see page 221, many building were nationalized and somewhat haphazardly occupied. The new tenants of the houses, shops and commercial buildings were thus inclined to undertake minimal repairs and maintenance. In many case it was unclear who actuially owned a building. The fabric of the city went into steady decline, and it is a testament to the sturdy construction of the buildings from the German period that so many of them survive. Roads fell into disrepair and the harbour became littered with rusting hulks.

The new government changed the names of streets and buildings, to reflect a change away from the colonial period. Thus Acacia became Independence Avenue, the *Prince of Wales Hotel* became the *Splendid*. Later names were chosen to pay tribute to African leaders with Independence Avenue changed to Samora, and Pugu Road became Nkrumah Street. President Nyerere decided that no streets or public buildings could be named after living Tanzanians, and so it was only after his death that City Drive was named after Prime Minister Robert Sokoine.

Old Dar es Salaam was saved by two factors. Firstly the economic decline which began in the 1970's, see page 233, meant that there were limited resources for new modern blocks for which some of old colonial buildings would have had to make way. Secondly, the government in 1973 decided to move the capital to Dodoma. This didn't stop new government construction entirely, but it undoubtedly saved many historic buildings.

In the early 1980's, Dar es Salaam reached a low point, not dissimilar from the one reached almost exactly a century earlier with the death of Sultan Majid. In 1992 things began to improve. The colonial buildings have been classified as of historical interest and are to be preserved. Japanese aid has allowed a comprehensive restoration of the road system. Several historic buildings, most notably the Old Boma on Sokoine Drive, the German hospital on Ocean Road, the Ministry of Health building on Luthuli Road and the British Council headquarters on Samora Avenue have been restored, or are undergoing restoration. Civic pride is returning. The Askari Monument has been cleaned up and the flower-beds replanted, the Cenotaph Plaza relaid, pavements and walkways repaired and the restoration of the Botanical Gardens has begun.

Places of interest

A walking tour (about half a day) of the historic parts of old Dar es Salaam might start at the **Askari Monument** at the junction of Samora Avenue and Maktaba Street. Originally on this site was a statue to Major Herman von Wissmann, the German explorer and soldier, who

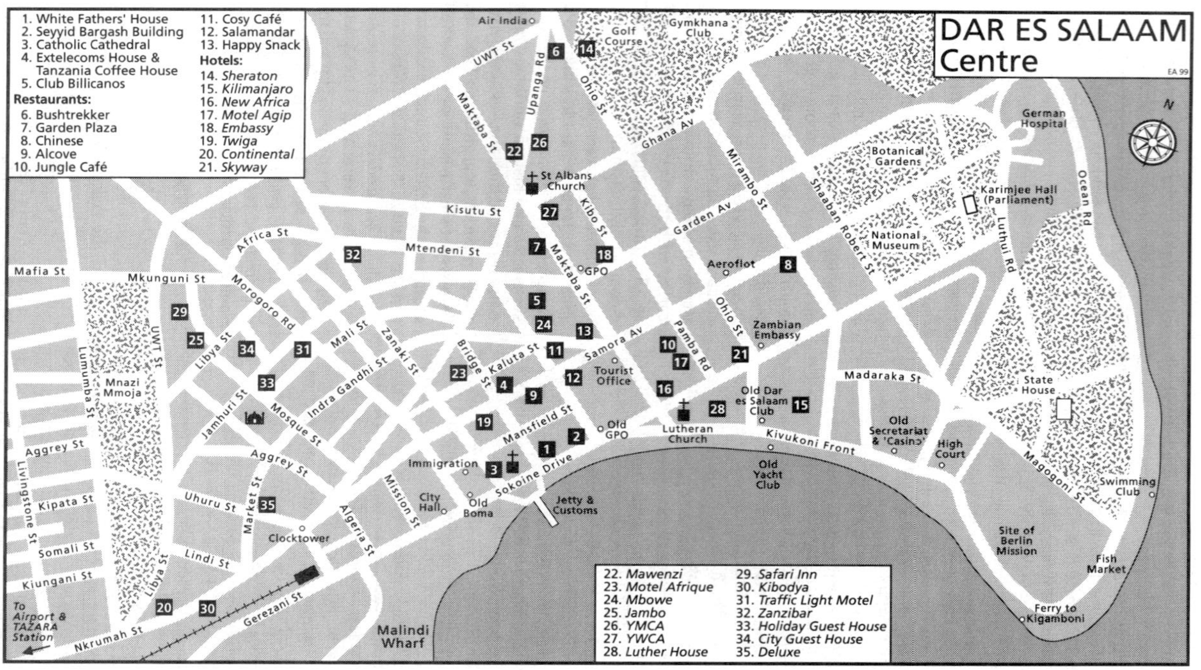
DAR ES SALAAM
Centre
EA 99
N
1. White Fathers' House
2. Seyyid Bargash Building
3. Catholic Cathedral
4. Extelecoms House & Tanzania Coffee House
5. Club Billicanos
Restaurants:
6. Bushtrekker
7. Garden Plaza
8. Chinese
9. Alcove
10. Jungle Café
11. Cosy Café
12. Salamandar
13. Happy Snack
Hotels:
14. Sheraton
15. Kilimanjaro
16. New Africa
17. Motel Agip
18. Embassy
19. Twiga
20. Continental
21. Skyway
22. Mawenzi
23. Motel Afrique
24. Mbowe
25. Jambo
26. YMCA
27. YWCA
28. Luther House
29. Safari Inn
30. Kibodya
31. Traffic Light Motel
32. Zanzibar
33. Holiday Guest House
34. City Guest House
35. Deluxe
Air India
UWT St
Upanga Rd
Maktaba St
Ohio St
Golf Course
Gymkhana Club
Ghana Av
St Albans Church
Kisutu St
Kibo St
Garden Av
Mirambo St
Shaaban Robert St
Botanical Gardens
National Museum
Karimjee Hall (Parliament)
German Hospital
Ocean Rd
Luthui Rd
Africa St
Mtendeni St
GPO
Aerofliot
Mafia St
Mkunguni St
Morogoro Rd
Zambian Embassy
Mali St
Zanaki St
Samora Av
Pamba Rd
Bridge St
Kaluta St
Tourist Office
Madaraka St
State House
Lumumba St
Mnazi Mmoja
Indra Gandhi St
Old Dar es Salaam Club
Jamhuri St
Mosque St
Mansfield St
Old GPO
Lutheran Church
Old Secretariat & 'Casino'
High Court
Kivukoni Front
Aggrey St
Immigration
Sokoine Drive
Old Yacht Club
Magogoni St
Swimming Club
Livingstone St
Kipata St
Uhuru St
Market St
Mission St
City Hall
Old Boma
Jetty & Customs
Clocktower
Algeria St
Site of Berlin Mission
Somali St
Lindi St
Libya St
Fish Market
Kiungani St
Ferry to Kigamboni
To Airport & TAZARA Station
Nkrumah St
Gerezani St
Malindi Wharf

suppressed the coastal Arab Revolt of 1888-9, see page 265, and went on to become governor of German East Africa in 1895-6. This first statue erected in 1911 depicted a pith-helmeted Wissmann, one hand on hip, the other on his sword, gazing out over the harbour with an African soldier at the base of the plinth draping a German flag over a reclining lion. It was demolished in 1916 when the British occupied Dar es Salaam, as were statues to Bismarck and Carl Peters. The present bronze statue, in memory of all those who died in WW1, but principaly dedicated to the Africa troops and porters, was unveiled in 1927. The statue was cast by Morris Bronze Founders of Westminster, London, and the sculptor was James Alexander Stevenson (1881-1937), who signed himself 'Myrander'. There are two bronze bas-reliefs on the sides of the plinth by the same sculptor, and the wording, in English and Swahili, is from Rudyard Kipling.

Proceeding W towards the harbour, on the left is the *New Africa Hotel* on the site where the old *Kaiserhof Hotel* stood. Across Sokoine Drive, on the left is the **Lutheran Cathedal** with its distinctive red-tiled spire and tiled canopies over the windows to provide shade. Construction began in 1898. Opposite is the **Cenotaph**, again commemorating the 1914-18 war, which was unveiled in 1927, and restored in 1992.

Turning left along Kivokoni Front, there is a fine view through the palm trees across the harbour. Just past Ohio Street, on the shore side, is the **Old Yacht Club**. Prior to the removal of the Club to its present site on the W side of Msasani Peninsular in 1967, small boats bobbing at anchor in the bay were a feature of the harbour. The Old Yacht Club buildings now house the harbour police headquarters. In the German period there were several warehouses along this part of the shore.

Opposite the Old Yacht Club is the site of the German Club for civilians which was expanded to form the **Dar es Salaam Club** in the British period and is now the Hotel and Tourism Training Centre. It has a spacious terrace and a handsome bar. On the first floor are rooms that were used for accommodation, with verandahs facing inward and outside stone staircases. It is possible to use the bar, and to have a lunch prepared and served by the trainees.

Passing the *Kilimanjaro Hotel*, on the corner of Mirambo Street is the first of an impressive series of German government buildings. The first two, one now the High Court, and the other the present Magistrates Court on the corner of Luthuli Road, were for senior officials. These had offices on the ground floor and spacious, high-ceilinged accommodation with verandahs, on the first floor, see architecture page 226). In between is the old **Secretariat**, which housed the governor's offices. The first floor is supported by cast iron brackets which allows the verandah to overhang. The verandah has been enclosed to provide more office space. On the other corner of Luthuli Road is the German Officers' Mess, where some gambling evidently took place as it became known as the **Casino**. These buildings are exceptional, and it is a tribute to the high quality construction of the German period that they have survived, with virtually no maintenance for the past 30 years. Construction was completed in 1893, and they have just passed their centenary.

On the shore side, just by the entrance to Luthuli Road was a landing pier in German times. Later, when a passenger pier was constructed opposite St Joseph's Cathedral, some landing steps replaced it, and these can still be seen. Further along Kivukoni Front, beyond the newer high-rise buildings is a group of single storey government offices constructed in the British period

On the high ground past these offices

is the site of the first European building in Dar es Salaam, the Berlin Mission. It was constructed in 1887, and was a fairly functional single storey rectangular building. Extensively damaged in the 1888-9 uprising it was rebuilt in 2-storeys with a corrugated-iron roof and an open gap between it and the walls which allowed ventilation. It was demolished in 1959 to make way for a hotel, which, in the event, was not constructed.

The E part of the city resembles an eagle's head (it is said the Masasani Peninsular is one of the eagle's wings). At the tip of the eagle's beak was a pier, just where the fishing village stands today, constructed in the British period for the use of the governor. This was just a little further round the promontory from the present ramp for the ferry which goes over to Kigamboni. Past Magogini Street is the Swimming Club, constructed in the British period and now mostly used by the Asian community.

Following Ocean Road, on the left is the present **State House**, with a drive coming down to gates. This was the original German governor's residence. It had tall, Islamic-style arches on the ground floor rather similar to those in the building today, but the upper storey was a verandah with a parapet and the roof was supported on cast-iron columns. The building was bombarded by British warships in 1914 and extensively damaged. In 1922 it was rebuilt and the present scalloped upper storey arches added as well as the tower with the crenellated parapet.

The **German Hospital** is further along Ocean Road with its distinctive

PORTERS

From the days of the earliest explorers in the 19th century until railways and roads were built, the use of porters was vital to the opening up of East Africa. Anyone planning an expedition inland, whether an explorer, missionary, or trader, relied on porters (*wapagazi*) as the sole means of transport. Indeed the success of a trip into the interior depended largely on the health, strength and reliability of the porters. The use of draught animals was rendered impossible by the prevalence of the tsetse fly.

Porters came from many different tribes but broadly speaking there were 2 main groups. The first are the Wanyamwezi/Wasukuma who are usually bracketed together as their language and culture are very similar, and the second group was the Zanzibari/Swahili porters. 'Zanzibari' porters were usually men who had travelled to the coast on an expedition and were then travelling back, while 'Swahili' porters were usually Muslim men of the coastal strip.

The Wanyamwezi/Wasukuma were generally considered to be the better porters and for many years were the mainstay of the caravan trade. They were said to be an ingenious people and were very musical, singing songs as they walked. They carried their loads on one shoulder (unlike the Zanzibari/Swahili who carried them on their heads) and it is said that when they arrived at a place for the night they made great efforts to make themselves comfortable. The Wanyamwezi/Wasukuma built themselves shelters and collected grass for matting, while the Zanzibari/Swahili porters were supposed to be much less bothered about their own comfort at the end of the day's walking, which some observers have put down to laziness.

These were not the only groups who undertook porterage and others included men from around Rabai near Mombasa in Kenya. They were ex-slaves who found porterage a lucrative form of employment. However they were said to be the worst of all the porters – they had little sense of obligation to fulfil a contract, they would accept wages in advance, but they regularly absconded and were said to complain thoughout the journey.

Porters from Uganda were supposed to be some of the best – they could carry heavier loads and endure longer marches more cheerfully than the other groups.

The loads that porters would carry varied a great deal. Around 1875 there were known examples of an single elephant's tusk weighing 55 kg being carried by one man – but this was very exceptional and usually it would be shared between 2 people. From the late 19th century until around the time of WW1 the loads weighed between 23 and 30 kg, although they would usually increase when a good food area was being passed through in order to be able to increase food rations. In WW1 the load in the King's African Rifles was limited to 20 kg/man, while in the German forces loads were around 27 kg. On top of these weights the porter also had to carry all his own possessions and rations.

When the time came for choosing the porters it was probably the selection of the head porter that was most important to the success of the expedition. He had to oversee the porters and to be able to maintain the morale of the caravan at times of difficulty. If one of the porters was ill, it was up to the head porter to carry the extra load. He would often lead the singing and give a marching time to the porters. The other porters would be selected, followed by a negotiation of terms. A medical examination would take place so that only the most suitable men would be chosen. The men were usually given about 2 months wages in advance depending on the length of the trip.

The routine that most caravans seemed to follow was fairly similar. Before first light a bell would be rung or a bugle blown to wake up the camp. Sometimes a medical examination was carried out to deal with minor ailments and the porters would then collect up their loads – without having had anything to eat or drink. Their employer would usually have a cup of tea while his tent was packed away and then word went around to move on. As the men marched they would often sing, led by the head porter or else would chat among themselves. About 2 hours after dawn the leader of the expedition would have a light breakfast, but the porters themselves would continue on the journey. It seems incredible that they had the stamina to march for many hours without any sort of sustenance, while carrying a huge load – but that does seem to have been the general practice. The caravan would usually stop at around 10.00, as near to water as possible, having covered about 25 km at a rate of about 5 km an hour, before the main heat of the day. They would then set up camp for the night and the porters would at last get something to eat.

There is absolutely no doubt that the trade routes would not have been functionable without the porters and their importance cannot be underestimated. Employers of porters have almost invariably spoken in appreciative terms of them, and most were treated reasonably well. The impact of the porterage on the porters villages was also important – the absence of able-bodied men during the harvest would have been partially offset by their wages and goods that they would have bought. Also the passing of a large caravan through an area would have increased the demand for food supplies and thus stimulated domestic markets. The necessity for foot safaris did not vanish until the introduction of the railway and the motor vehicle.

domed towers topped by a clusters of iron spikes. It is an uneasy mixture of the grand (the towers) and the utilitarian (the corrugated-iron roofing). It was completed in 1897 and was added-to during the British period with single storey, bungalow-style wards to the rear.

Turning left past the baobab tree down Chimera Road and taking the left fork, Luthuli Road leads to the junction with Samora Avenue. Here stood the statue of Bismarck, a replica of the celebrated Regas bust. The area either side of this boulevard, one of the glories of Dar es Salaam in the German era, was laid out as an extensive park. The flamboyant trees and *oreodoxa* (Royal Palms) still border the avenues.

The first Director of Agriculture, Professor Stuhlmann began laying out the **Botanic Gardens** in 1893. Initially there was also a vetinerary station which was moved when the construction of the hospital began. The building to house the Agriculture Department as well as the Meteorological Station and the Government Geographer lies just to the South-West and was completed in 1903. It has recently been restored. By that time the gardens were well-established, Stuhlmann using his position as Chief Secretary from 1900-1903 to channel resources to their development. Stuhlmann went on to be Director of the Amani Agricultural Research Station, (see page 297). The gardens became the home of the Dar es Salaam Horticultural Society which still has a building on the site. Recently the Gardens have undergone some rehabilitation with most of the exhibits now labelled.

To the left of the gardens is **Karimjee Hall**, built during the British era and which served as the home of the Legislative Council prior to independence. It then became the home of the National Assembly, the Bunge. In the same area is the original **National Museum** a single-storey stone building with a red-tiled roof and arched windows constructed as the King George V Memorial Museum in 1940, changing its name in 1963. A larger, modern building was constructed later to house exhibits, and the old building used as offices.

Turning left down Shaaban Robert Street, on the other side of Sokoine Drive, in a crescent behind the Speaker's Office is the first school built in Dar es Salaam (1899) by the German government. It was predominantly for Africans, but also had a few Indian pupils, all children of state-employed officials (*akidas*). Walking W down Sokoine Drive we return to the *New Africa Hotel*.

A second half-day walking tour would begin at the *New Africa Hotel* and proceed W along Sokoine Street past the National Bank of Commerce building on the right. On the corner with Mkwepa Street is the German **Post Office** completed in 1893. Athough the façade has been remodelled to give it a more modern appearance, the structure is basically unchanged. It was a pleasing 2-storey red-tiled building with a verandah on the first floor and a small tower with a pitched roof behind the main entrance which made for a more interesting roof-line. The windows were arched, and there was an impressive set of steps up to the main entrance. Just inside the entrance is a plaque to the memory of members of the Signals Corp who lost their lives in WW1 in East Africa. There are some 200 names listed with particularly heavy representation from South Africa and India whose loyalty to the British Empire drew them into the conflict.

On the opposite corner to the Post Office is the site of the old customs headquarters, the **Seyyid Barghash** building constructed around 1869. The building on the corner with Bridge Street is the White Fathers' House, which incorporates a small section inside the interior courtyard which was constructed in the 1860's in the Zanzibar period.

Continuing along Sokoine drive to the W, the next building is the **Roman Catholic Cathedral**. Construction began in 1897, and took 5 years to complete. Next to the Cathedral was Akida's Court.

On the corner of Morogoro Road is the earliest surviving building, the **Old Boma** dating from 1867. On the opposite corner is the **City Hall**, a very handsome building with an impressive façade and elaborate decoration. Further along, on the corner of Algeria Street is a 3-storey commercial building with pillars and a verandah at first-floor level. The first 2 floors are from the Zanzibar period, with the third storey and the verandah being added later.

On the corner of Uhruru Street is the **Railway Station,** a double-storey building with arches and a pitched-tile roof, the construction of which began in 1897. Between the station and the shore was the site of the palace of Sultan Majid and of the hospital for Africans constructed in 1895 by Sewa Haji, see page 240, but which was demolished in 1959.

Turning right in front of the railway station leads to the **Clock Tower**, a post-war concrete construction which was erected to celebrate the elevation of Dar es Salaam to city status in 1961. A right turn at the clock tower leads along Samora Avenue and back to the Askari Monument. There are a number of buildings of stone construction that were erected by the local community, by Goan businessmen and by German commercial interests. The German buildings can be recognised by the 2-storey style with a verandah at first-floor level, and by the use of pillars to support the first floor. Notable among these is the building that houses the former ILO office of the United Nations on the first floor, with the ground floor given over to shops and the Salamandar Cafe, on the corner of Mkwepu Street.

Other notable buildings in the City area include the present *Mbowe Hotel* on the cornor of Mkwepu and Makunganya Street, which was the *Palace Hotel*, and which dates from about 1920. On Mosque Street is the **Darkhana Jama'at-Khana** of the Ismaili community, 3-storeys high with a 6-storey tower on the corner topped by a clock, a pitched roof and a weather-vane. It is in an ornate style with arches and decorated columns, and was constructed in 1930.

There are several other mosques, two (**Ibaddhi Mosque** and **Memon Mosque**) on Mosque Street itself, one on Kitumbini Street (the **Sunni mosque** with an impressive dome), and there are 2 mosques on UWT Street, the **Ahmadiyya mosque** being near the junction with Pugo Road and the other other close by. On Kitsu Street, there are 2 Hindu temples, and on Upanga Road is a grand Ismaili building which is decorated with coloured lights during festival periods.

St Albans Church on the corner of Upanga Road and Maktaba Street was constructed in the interwar period. The **Greek Orthodox Church**, further along Upanga Street, was constructed in the 1940's. **St Peter's Catholic Church**, off the Bagamoyo Road, was constructed in 1962, and is in modern style with delicate concrete colums and arches.

The area to the NW of India Street, on either side of Morogoro Road was an Asian section of the city in the colonial period, and to a large extent remains so. The typical building would be several storeys high, the ground floor being given over to business premises with the upper storeys being used for residential accommodation. The façades of these buildings are typically ornate, often with the name of the proprietor and the date of construction prominently displayed. Two superb examples on Morogoro Road, near Africa Street, are the premises of M Jessa. One was a cigarette and tobacco factory and the other a rice mill.

Further to the W is the open Mnazi Mmoja (coconut grove) with the **Uhuru**

Monument (dedicated to the freedom that came with independence). On the far side of the space is **Kariakoo**, laid out in a grid pattern and predominently an African area. It become known as Kariakoo during the latter part of WW1 when African porters (the carrier corps, from which the current name is derived) were billeted there after the British took over the City in 1916. The houses are in Swahili Style, see page 225. The market in the centre and the shark market on the junction of Msimbazi and Tandamuti Streets are well worth a visit.

At the point of the eagle's beak, where the ferry leaves for Kivukoni is the **Msizima Fish Market**. Fresh fish can be purchased here and fishing boats, mostly lateen-sailed *ngalawas* are beached on the shore. There are some boat-builders on the site and it is interesting to observe the construction techniques which rely entirely on hand-tools.

Further along Ocean Road, past State House, are the grounds of the **Gymkhana Club**, which extend down to the shore. There were various cemeteries on the shore side of the golf course, European between the hospital and Ghana Avenue, and a Hindu Crematorium beyond.

At the intersection of Ocean Road and Ufukoni Road on the shore side is a rocky promontory which was the site of European residential dwellings constructed in the interwar period by the British. These are either side of Labon Drive (previously Seaview Road). Continuing along Ocean Road is Selander Bridge, a causeway over the Msimbazi Creek, a small river edged by marsh which circles back to the S behind the main part of the city. Beyond Selander Bridge, on the ocean side is **Oyster Bay**, which became the main European residential area in the colonial era, and today is the location of many diplomatic missions. There are many spacious dwellings, particularly along Kenyatta Drive which looks across there. The area in front of the *Oyster Bay Hotel* is a favourite place for parking and socialising in the evenings and on weekends, particularly by the Asian community. Ice cream sellers and barbeque kiosks have sprung up in the last few years on the shore.

The ferry leaves at regular intervals during the day, crossing the mouth of the harbour to Kigamboni. The ferry takes vehicles, and this is the best way to reach this area as the approach from the land side circling the harbour inlets is a journey of about 40 km over poor roads. Kigamboni is the site of Kivukoni College which provided training for CCM party members, but which is now being turned into a school and a social science academy. Just before the college, which faces across the harbour to Kivukoni Front is the Lutheran Church and a free-standing bell. On the shore, on the Indian Ocean side, can be seen several small enterprises making lime by burning cairns of coral. The beaches on Kigamboni are the best close to the city, but they have not been developed as the ferry has been out of commission for lengthy periods in the past. A couple of unserviceable ferries can be seen beached on the main harbour shore.

Further along Bagamoyo Road, turning left at Mwenge, and then right at the petrol station leads to the **University of Dar es Salaam**. The university began life as a College in 1961 in a building on Lumumba Street in the city, granting London University degrees. Initially it had only a law faculty as at the time law was not offered Makerere in Uganda or at Nairobi in Kenya. In 1964 the college moved to its present site on a hill some 10 km W of the city. It become an independent university in 1970. The location is very attractive, and there are fine views across to Dar es Salaam from Observation Hill. Nkrumah Hall is a fine example of modern architecture and the ravine, crossed by a bridge, which runs from the faculty building to

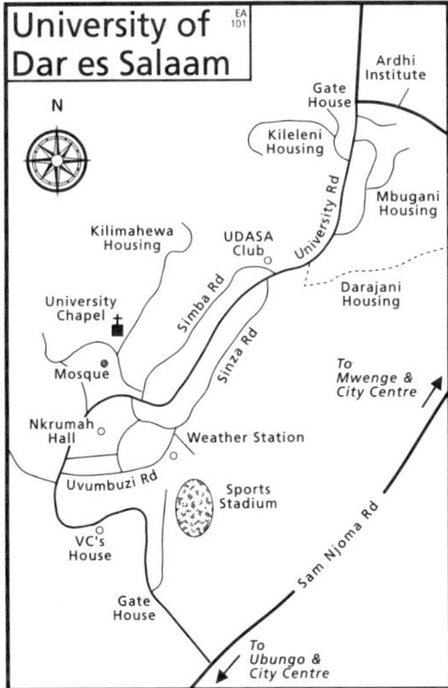

the post office and residential buildings, through trees, is particularly attractive. In the 1980's the fabric of the university buildings deteriorated considerably. In 1992, however, a rehabilitation programme started, and some of the former pride in the institution, buildings and site has begun to be restored.

Other places of interest

The Makumbusho Village Museum, open daily 0900-1900. This is situated along Bagamoyo Road, about 9 km from the centre of Dar es Salaam, on the right-hand side of the road. There is a large sign indicating the entrance. It can be reached by taxi – about TSh1,500 (US$4) – and it is advisable to ask the taxi to wait for you to return. A *dala-dala*, destination Mwenge, can be taken from Maktaba Street, just opposite the post office for TSh30 (US$0.10) and there are frequent returning *dala-dala* on this route. Entrance US$1, Tanzanians, all children free. Still photos US$2.50, video or cine US$10. The museum is well worth a visit, giving a compact view of the main traditional dwelling styles of Tanzania, examples of artists and craftsmen at work, and, on Sat and Sun afternoons, there is a team of traditional dancers performing to drum music.

There are constructions from 13 groups with examples of dwelling huts, cattle pens, meeting huts and, in one case, an iron-smelting kiln. Among the artists and craftsmen resident is Issa Bahari, a Swahili from the coastal area who does ebony signs (US$7.50), and these are better value than in town. Issa will also carve a sign to your design, and it will take 3 days.

In one of the rooms of the Swahili banda is Helman Msole, a Fiba from SW Tanzania with very striking paintings of village scenes and historical scenes on canvas (US$40 to US$80). Hand-painted postcards are US$2.50. Helman will paint a canvas from his collection (recorded on photos) in 2 days. Blassy Kisanga, a Chagga from Kilimangaro, depicts scenes with brown and black banana leaves on wooden panels (US$12.50 to US$40) and postcards (US$1.50). Petre Paulo Mayige, from Tabora makes clay figures of village scenes and *bao* games for US$7.50-US$40. Finally, Nyram Hsagula, a Swahili does the rather garish *tinga tinga* paintings on hardboad, as decorations on tins and bowls (US$2 to US$25). The art items are much a matter of taste – the clay figures and the paintings of Helman Msole are not readily available elsewhere, and most visitors regard these as unusually good.

On Sat and Sun 1600-1800 a local dance troupe performs. It is a pity there is no guidance as to where the dances originate. The troupe is recruited from all over Tanzania and they end with a display of tumbling and acrobatics that is popular with children.There is a café, and an unusual compound, the Makumbusho Social Club, to which the public is welcome, with a number of small corrugated iron partly open-sided huts,

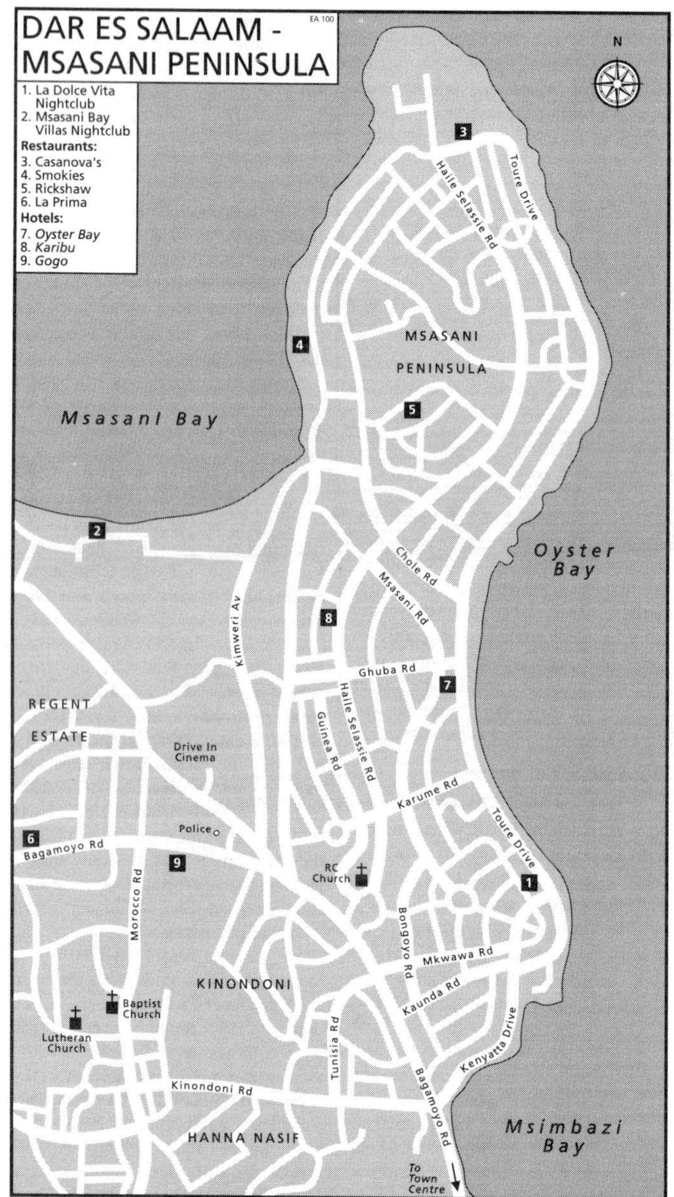
DAR ES SALAAM -
MSASANI PENINSULA
EA 100
1. La Dolce Vita Nightclub
2. Msasani Bay Villas Nightclub
Restaurants:
3. Casanova's
4. Smokies
5. Rickshaw
6. La Prima
Hotels:
7. Oyster Bay
8. Karibu
9. Gogo
N
Haile Selassie Rd
Toure Drive
MSASANI
PENINSULA
Msasani Bay
Oyster Bay
Chole Rd
Msasani Rd
Kimweri Av
Ghuba Rd
REGENT
ESTATE
Guinea Rd
Haile Selassie Rd
Drive In Cinema
Karume Rd
Toure Drive
Police
Bagamoyo Rd
RC Church
Morocco Rd
Bongoyo Rd
Mkwawa Rd
KINONDONI
Kaunda Rd
Baptist Church
Lutheran Church
Tunisia Rd
Kenyatta Drive
Kinondoni Rd
Bagamoyo Rd
HANNA NASIF
Msimbazi Bay
To Town Centre

each named after one of Tanzania's game parks.

The **National Museum**, located on Shabaan Robert Street, has collections of historical and archeological items. The old photographs are particularly interesting. Traditional craft items are on display. Fossils from Olduvai Gorge are also kept there. Open 0930-1800. Entrance US$0.10 for residents; US$0.50 for non-residents; students free.

Nyumba ya Sanaa is an art gallery with displays of paintings in various styles as well as carvings and batiks. It is located by the roundabout on the intersection of Upanga and Ohio Streets.

Karibu Art Gallery on Bagamoyo Road (beyond the Mwenge turn-off to the university) has a good selection of carvings, paintings, pottery, jewelry and musical instruments. On Sun there are traditional dance exhibitions.

Beaches

The shore close to Dar es Salaam is not particularly good for swimming. The best beaches are at Kunduchi, some 25 km N of the city. A bus leaves from outside the *New Africa Hotel* in the City centre in the mornings and afternoons, and returns in the evening. *Silver Sands Hotel* and *Rungwe Oceanic Hotel* have fairly simple facilities. *Kunduchi Beach Hotel*, though a bit dilapidated, has an excellent beach, a swimming pool, and offers a variety of excursions to nearby islands and windsurfing. Snorkelling is variable as sometimes the water is not clear, especially during the rainy seasons. A band plays during the afternoons on Sun. *Bahari Beach Hotel* is strikingly constructed from coral with thatched roofing for the main buildings and groups of rooms in similar style, and also has bands on Sun and public holidays. These hotels make a small charge for using their beaches for the day, around US$1-2.

Local information

● Where to stay

Price guide:
A+ Over US$100 a night;
A US$40-100; **B** US$20-40; **C** US$10-20; **D** US$5-10; **E** Under US$5.

Hotels in Dar es Salaam are poor as far as luxury and middle grade accommodation is concerned and not particularly good value. Many deluxe travellers choose to stay at *Bahari Beach* some 25 km N of Dar es Salaam. Two luxury hotels, a Sheraton and a Hilton are planned, and competition should serve to upgrade the general standard. The lower end of the market, however, is good value, although it is always a sensible procedure to check the room and the bathroom facilities and inquire what is provided for breakfast. Ask about phone facilities as often the switchboard does not work. Check on the security of any parked vehicle. In the upmarket hotels, at present, you are required to pay in foreign exchange. In the middle range it is often possible to pay in Tsh, and this is an advantage if money is changed at the favourable bureau rate. Hotels will often change money at an unfavourable 'official' rate. Even if staying at an upmarket hotel it is advisable to pay for everything (except the room rate) with TSh exchanged at a bureau.

A *Kilimanjaro*, PO Box 9574, Kivukoni Front, T 21281-9, Tlx 41021, F 39462. A little shabby but comfortable. The only pleasant pool in the city. A/c. Three restaurants one of which, the Summit, affords a glorious view over the harbour, particularly charming at night. 24 hr Forex Bureau. Bar and Pool Bar. Hairdresser, bookshops, curios, chemist, travel agents, business services. Creditcards accepted. **A** *Oyster Bay*, PO Box 2261, Sekou Toure Drive, T 68631. 5 km from city centre. Beach location, although the beach is poor. A/c. Good restaurant with excellent seafood. Shopping mall under construction. Bar. Bamboo gardens disco was the best in town, but has been closed for a while due to construction. No pool. **A** *Karibu*, Haile Selassie Rd, T 67760/1. Oyster Bay area. Well run. Good restaurant with Indian food a speciality. A/c Swimming pool. **A** *New Africa*, PO Box 9314, Maktaba St, T 29611/9, Tlx 81049. Comfortable but gloomy. No pool. A/c. Two restaurants. Patio Bar. Bookshop. **A** *Motel Agip*, PO Box 529, Pamba Rd, T 23511, Tlx 41276. Recently refurbished in marble and mahogany style. No pool. A/c. Good restaurant and snack bar, 1st floor bar. **A** ***Embassy***, PO Box 3152, 24 Garden Ave, T 30006. Well run and comfortable. Small pool on 1st floor with barbeque and bar. A/c. Grill, restaurant, bar, hairdressers, chemist, travel agents.

B ***Twiga*** PO Box 3199, Samora Ave, T 22561. Gloomy atmosphere. Some rooms a/c. Two restaurants (one rooftop), bar. **B** ***Continental***, Mkrumah St. Some rooms a/c. Patio bar, restaurant, shop. **B** ***Skyway***, PO Box 21248, Sokoine Drive, T 27061. Some rooms a/c. Basic restaurant and rather rough bar. **B** ***Mawenzi***,, PO Box 332, Maktaba St, T 29922/46561. Reasonably comfortable. Some rooms a/c. Pleasant patio bar, rather gloomy restaurant. **B** ***Palm Beach***, Upanga Rd, T 28892. Rather run-down, with creaky a/c, cold-water showers. Shared bathrooms. Between-the-wars style. A little away from the centre of town. Airy and cool bar and restaurant. Popular beer garden with barbeque. **B** ***Etienne's***, PO Box 2981, Ocean Rd, T 2093. Comfortable with relaxed atmosphere. Some rooms a/c. Restaurant, bar. Garden bar with barbeque. **B** ***Motel Afrique***, PO Box 9482, Zanaki St. **B** ***Starlight***, PO Box 3199, UWT St, T 23845. Recently refurbished. Well run and good value, a/c. Nr Mnazi Moja. **B** ***Gogo***, PO Box 2114. Bagamoyo Rd, T 36006. Mx 41801. About 4 km from centre. A/c. Well run. Good restaurant. Patio bar. **B** ***Mbowe***, PO Box 15261, Indira Gandhi St, T 20501/20188. Bar. Run-down colonial establishment. Central. Some rooms out of service due to roof repairs.

C ***Jambo Inn***, PO Box 5588, Libya St, T 35359/35531. Some a/c. Well run establishment. Central. Restaurant serves Indian food and is one of the best in Dar es Salaam. **C** ***YMCA***, PO Box 767, Maktaba St, T 26726. Central. No fans and can be hot. Care required over belongings.

D ***YWCA***, PO Box 2086, Upanga Rd, T 22439. Women and couples accommodated. Central. Well recommended. Good eating place. **D** ***Luther House Hostel***, PO Box 389, Sokoine Drive, T 32154. Excellent value, central and in considerable demand. Is necessary to book as it is invariably full. **D** ***Safari Inn***, PO Box 21113, Banda St, T 21113. Central. Fairly simple, but sound. **D** ***Kobodya***, PO Box 1019 Nkrumah St, T 32937/31470. Central. Straightforward. **D** ***Mount Msambara***, PO Box 22770, Kango St, T 37422/3. Kariakoo area. **D** ***Salvation Army***, PO Box 1273, Kilwa Rd, T 51467. Situated about 3 km along Kilwa Rd to the S of the port area. Well run. Good value. Swimming pool. **D** ***Traffic Light Motel***, PO Box 79, Maragwo Rd, T 23438. Central, good value, well run. **D** ***Deluxe Inn***, PO Box 2583, Uhwu St, T 20873/25534. **D** ***Keys***, PO Box 5330, Uhwu St, T 20462. Nr Mnazi Moja. **D** ***Marana Guest House***, PO Box 15062, Uhwu St, T 21014. Nr Mnazi Moja.

E ***Zanzibar Guest House***, PO Box 20125, Zanaki St, T 21197. Central. **E** ***Holiday Guest House***, PO Box 2975, Jamhuri St, T 20675. Central. **E** ***City Guest House***, PO Box 1326, Chaga St, T 22967/24071. **E** ***Malapa Inn***, Wmumba St. Central. **E** ***Ismail***, Wmumba St. Central. **E** ***Double Two***, PO Box 22102, Nyati St, T 36027. Central. **E** ***New Happy***, PO Box 15042, Lumumba St, T 34038. Kariakoo area. **E** ***Al Noor***, PO Box 3874, Uhuru St, T 37082. Kariakoo area.

● Beach hotels

The beaches are poor nr the city centre, with shallow water and rocky shorelines. Although they are an hour's journey (25 km) from Dar es Salaam along poor roads many visitors choose to stay at one of the beach hotels to the N or S of the city. There is a regular bus shuttle service between the city and the beach hotels to the N leaving from the *New Africa Hotel* on Maktaba Street. Please note that it is unsafe to walk along the beach between the N hotels.

A+ ***Ras Kutani Beach Resort***. Bookings through Rickshaw Travel, PO Box 1889, T 291125/35097, F 29125/34556, Tlx 41162. Across Kivukoni Ferry and S of Dar es Salaam. Charming thatched banda accommodation. Good beach with lagoon. Watersports. **A** ***Bahari Beach***, PO Box 9312, Kunduchi, T 47101. Accommodation in thatched rondavels. A/c. Large bar lounge. Restaurant area under high thatched roofing. Pool bar. Swimming pool. Band on Sun and public holidays. Sandy beach. Garden surroundings. Gift shop. Tour agency. The most attractive and best run of the beach hotels.

B ***Kunduchi Beach***, PO Box 9313 Kunduchi, T 47621/3. Somewhat run-down modern style accommodation, but good value. Islamic style architecture for main service areas. Bar, pool bar, restaurant. Swimming pool. Charming beach palms and flowers. Band on Sun and public holidays. Watersport facilities and trips to off-shore islands. Close to fishing village. (Hotel restaurant will prepare fresh fish bought there for half menu price.) **B** *Silver Sands*, PO Box 901 Kunduchi, T 47231. Owned by University of Dar es Salaam who house some staff there. Rather run down chalet-style accommodation but reasonable value. Restaurant, bar.

C *Rungwe Oceanic*, PO Box 35639, Kunduchi, T 47185. Good value. Bar and restaurant. Popular with budget travellers. Has camping facilities.

● Places to eat

Price guide:
♦♦♦♦ over US$10; ♦♦♦ US$5-10;
♦♦ US$2-5; ♦ under US$2.

Variety is improving all the time in Dar es Salaam, with more tourists and new places opening. Particularly recommended are ***Casanova's***, ***Smokies***, ***Summit*** for atmosphere, ***Simba Grill*** for its buffet, dining and dancing, ***Karibu*** for Indian food, ***Rickshaw*** for Chinese, ***Jungle Café*** for pizzas, ***Night of Istanbul*** for Mediterranean, ***Barbeque House*** and ***Happy Snacks*** for inexpensive and delicious tandoori grills. If you go by taxi to venues in outer areas (*Casanova, Smokies, Rickshaw*) it is worthwhile asking the driver to wait.

♦♦♦♦***Motel Agip Restaurant***, first floor of *Motel Agip*, Pamba St, T 46551. Good standard Italian cuisine. Decor rather gloomy. ♦♦♦♦***Bushtrekker***. Corner Of UWT and Upanga St. First floor with views across Gymkhana Club grounds. International cuisine, pleasant atmosphere. Good buffet at week-ends. ♦♦♦♦***Oyster Bay***. *Oyster Bay Hotel*, Sekou Toure Drive (15 mins from centre in taxi), T 68631. First floor restaurant with views overlooking Oyster Bay. Extensive menu and excellent quality. Sea food platter is especially recommended and of daunting dimensions. ♦♦♦♦***Casanova's***, Masaki St, Msasani Peninsular (30 mins from centre in taxi). Delightful atmosphere, good Italian cuisine. Currently one of the smartest Dar es Salaam restaurants. ♦♦♦♦***Smokies***, off Chole Rd, Msasani Peninsular (30 mins from centre in taxi). Roof top, open air restaurant with views across Msasani Bay. Buffet. Crowded at week-ends. Superior wine list. ♦♦♦♦***Karibu***, ground floor of *Karibu Hotel*, Haile Selassie, Oyster Bay (20 mins from centre by taxi). Good quality Indian cuisine. ♦♦♦♦***La Prima***, Bagamoyo Rd (Outer central). French cuisine. Good standard with cabaret and dancing. ♦♦♦♦***Rickshaw***, off Chole Rd, Msasani Peninsular (30 mins from centre by taxi). Good quality Chinese cuisine in pleasant surroundings.

♦♦♦***Garden Plaza***, T 23520. International Menu. ♦♦♦***Chinese Restaurant***, basement of NIC Building, Samora Ave. Good standard of cuisine. ♦♦♦***Summit***, T 21281. Top floor of *Kilimanjaro Hotel*, Kivukoni Front. International menu. Good value special menu, which runs out quickly. Fine views across harbour especially at night. ♦♦♦***Simba Grill***, T 21281. First floor of *Kilmanjaro Hotel*, Kivukoni Front. Excellent buffet and dancing at week-ends. ♦♦♦***New Africa***, Azikwe St, T 46546. Uncomplicated international food. ♦♦♦***Night of Istanbul***, UWT St and Zanaki St. Middle-Eastern cuisine of good standard plus international menu. It is possible to eat outside on the terrace. African wines from Zimbabwe, of drinkable quality available. ♦♦♦***Alcove***, Samora Ave. Reasonable Indian food, also some Chinese. Usually busy at week-ends. ♦♦♦***Embassy Grill***, T 30006. Second floor of *Embassy Hotel* on Garden Ave. (Central). Steaks recommended. ♦♦♦***Jungle Café***. Ground floor of *Agip Hotel*, Pamba St (central). Bright café atmosphere. Good pizzas. Espresso and capuccino coffee

♦♦***Twiga***, first floor of *Twiga Hotel*, Samora Ave, T 46578. Somewhat gloomy. International food. ♦♦***Bruncherie***, Ground floor of *Kilimajaro Hotel*, Kivukoni Front, T 21281. Simple grills. Steaks generally good value. Open till midnight. Rather shabby decor. ♦♦***Palm Beach***, *Palm Beach Hotel*, Upanga Rd, T 28892. Rather uninspired menu of British food. Set menu is good value, but runs out early. Pleasant verandah atmosphere. ♦♦***Etienne's***, *Etienne's Hotel*, Ocean Rd,. T 20293. Uncomplicated menu. ♦♦***Shari's Dar Bar***, UWT St. Simple charcoal grills, tandoori chicken, salad, fries. Good value. ♦♦***Shalamar***, Mansfield St (central). Sound Indian cuisine. ♦♦***Supreme***, Pugu Rd (outer central). Vegetarian. Reasonable quality, but unbearably grim decor. ♦♦***Barbeque House***, Vijimweni St, off Upanga Rd (outer central). Specialises in good quality tandoori grills. ♦♦***Cosy Café***, corner of Makunganya St and Mkwepu St (central). Simple menu. Comfortable surroundings. ♦♦***Salamanda***, corner of Samara and Mkwepu (central). Once Dar es Salaam's smartest venue. Closed in evening. Pleasant ground floor area opening onto street. Snacks and simple grills at lunchtinme. ♦♦***Gogo***, ground floor of *Gogo Hotel*, Bagamoyo Rd (15 minutes from centre by taxi). Simple but good menu.

♦*Happy Snacks*. Corner of Makinganya St and Simu St (central). Street café. Exceptional tandoori charcoal grilled chicken, fries and chapatis. Ice cold fresh juices from chest freezer. ♦*Tanzania Coffee Board*, coffee shop on ground floor of Telecoms building on Samora Ave (central). Lunchtimes and early evening only. Outside patio. Rather drab. Snacks. Disappointingly only serves instant coffee.

● Bars

All the bars in Dar es Salaam are associated with hotels. Range of local beers is limited to 2 local lagers, Safari and Pilsner, until a reported 6 new small breweries come on stream. Variety of beers available has expanded in recent years as import restrictions have relaxed and a variety of Kenyan, South African and European beers are available. Specially recommended are the beer gardens at ***Palm Beach***, ***Etiennes*** and ***Oyster Bay*** for tropical atmosphere; ***Agip*** and the ***Zebra*** for a quiet central meeting place and ***Skyways*** for local colour.

Zebra Bar, *Kilimanjaro Hotel*, Kirukoni Front. Central. Large lounge. Quiet. ***Skyways***, corner of Sokaine and Ohio St. Busy and lively. Crowded with expatriate engineers, construction workers and girls. Intriguing sign on the wall – WYBMADIITY – ask the staff what it means. ***Palm Beach***, Upanga Rd. Very popular beer gardens. Coloured fairy lights. ***Etiennes***, Ocean Rd. Pleasant beer garden. Rather drab bar inside hotel. ***New Africa***, Azikiwe St. Secluded bar on ground floor. ***Oyster Bay***, Sekou Toure Drive. Pleasant well appointed bar to rear of hotel overlooking Bamboo Gardens. ***Agip***, Pamba St. First floor bar. Secluded pleasant atmosphere. ***Embassy***, Garden Ave. First floor bar. Rather dull. ***Gogo***, Bagamoyo Rd. Outside patio bar with thatched bandas ***Mawenzi***, Maktaba St. Verandah bar along side of hotel.

● Airlines

International **Aeroflot**, PO Box 2758, Eminaz Mansions, Samora Av, T 46005. **Air France**, PO Box 2661, Upanga Rd, T 36653/4 37378/9. **Air India**, PO Box 1709, UWT St, T 46803. **Air Tanzania**, PO Box 543, ATC Building, Ohio St, T 46643/4/5. **Air Zaire**, PO Box 2564, IPS Building, Samora Av, T 20836/25988. **Alitalia**, PO Box 9281, AMI Building, Samora Av, T 23621/24318. **British Airways**, PO Box 2439, Coronation House, Samora Av, T 20322. **Egypt Air**, PO Box 1350, Matsalmat Building, Samora Av, T 46806. **Ethiopian Airlines**, PO Box 3187, TDFL Building, Ohio St, T 24174/24185. **Gulf Air**, PO Box 9794, T 37856/46808. **Kenya Airways**, PO Box, Tangayika Motors Building, Upanga Rd, T 46812. **KLM**, PO Box 3804, T 21497/46810. **Lufthansa**, PO Box 1993, Upanga Rd, T 22270/26436/46813. **PIA**, PO Box 928, IPS Building, Samora Ave, T 26944. **SAS**, Upanga Rd, PO Box 1114, T 22015/22013. **Swiss Air**, PO Box 2109, Luther House Sokoine Dr, T 46816/34068/24054. **Zambia Airways**, PO Box 21276, IPS Building, Samora Av, T 46662.

Domestic and charter **Dar Air Charters**, PO Box 18104, Old Terminal 1, Pugu Rd, T 42332. **Dar Aviation** C/O Coastal Travel, PO Box 3052, Upanga Rd, T 37479/37480 **Tanzanian Air Services**, PO Box 364, Azikiwe St, T 30232.

● Banks

Two private sector banks have opened for business, **Standard Chartered** and **Meridian**, located in the Plaza on Sokoine Drive close to the Askari Monument. The state-owned banks are notoriously slow and inefficient – it can take 2 hrs to cash a traveller's cheque. There are branches of the **National Bank of Commerce** on Samora Ave next to the *Twiga Hotel*; and on the corner of Sokoine Drive and Azikiwe St. Hours are 0830-1230 on weekdays and 0830-1200 on Sat.

Foreign exchange bureaux are to be found in almost every street in the city. Hours are usually 0900-1700 Mon-Fri and 0900-1300 on Sat. 24 hr bureaux are at the airport terminal along Pugu Rd and in the foyer of the *Kilimanjaro Hotel*. Although these bureaux offer convenience, they offer an unfavourable rate. Rates vary between bureaux and it is worth shopping around.

American Express **Rickshaw Travel**, PO Box 1889, UWT St between junctions with Ohio St and Maktaba St, T 29125/35097, F 29125/35456. Tlx 41162. Will issue travellers cheques to card-holders.

● Embassies (E), High Commissions (HC) and Consulates (C)

You can usually be sure that diplomatic missions will be open in the mornings between 0900 and 1200. Some have afternoon opening, and some do not open every day. Even when a mission is officially closed, the staff will usually be helpful if something has to be done in an emergency. **Albania (E)**, PO Box 1034, Msese Rd, T 34945; **Algeria (E)**, PO Box 2963, Upanga Rd, T 20846. **Angola (E)**, PO Box 20793, IPS Building, Samora Av, T 46188.

Argentina (E), Msasani Peninsula, T 41628/4313. **Australia (HC)**, PO Box 2996, NIC Investment House, Samora Av, T 20244/6. **Austria (C)**, PO Box 312, Samora Av, T 46251. **Belgium (E)**, PO Box 9654, T 46198/20244/5. **Brazil (E)**, PO Box 9654, IPS Building Samora Av, T 46191/35356. **Bulgaria (E)**, PO Box 9260, Malik Rd, T 23787. **Burundi (E)**, PO Box 2752, T 29281/2, 38608. **Canada**, PO Box 1022, Pan Africa Building, Samora Av, T 46001/3 46000. **China (E)**, PO Box 1649, Kajificheni Cl, T 67212/67586. **Cuba (E)**, PO Box 9282, Lugalo Rd, T 46315/6. **CIS (former USSR) (E)**, PO Box 1905, Kenyatta Dr, T 66005/6 46368/9. **Cyprus (C)**, PO Box 529, *Motel Agip*, Sokoine Dr, T 46941/21975. **Czechoslovakia (E)**, PO Box 3054, Jubilee Mansion, Upanga Rd, T 46971/23360. **Denmark (E)**, PO Box 9171, Bank House, Samora Av, T 46318/9/46320/22. **Egypt (E)**, PO Box 1668, Garden Av, T 32158/9. **Finland (E)**, PO Box 2466, NIC Investment House, Samora Av, T 46324/6. **France (E)**, PO Box 2349, Bagamoyo Rd, T 34961/3/ 66021/3. **Germany (E)**, PO Box 2083, NIC Investment House, Samora Av, T 23286/8. **Greece (C)**, PO Box 766, Upanga Rd, T 25638/22931. **India (HC)**, PO Box 2684, NIC Investment House, Samora Av, T 46341/2/33754. **Indonesia (E)**, PO Box 572, Upanga Rd, T 46347/8. **Iran (E)**, PO Box 5802, Upanga Rd, T 34622/3. **Ireland (E)**, PO Box 9612, TDFL Building, Ohio St, T 46492/3. **Italy (E)**, PO Box 2106, Lugalo Rd, T 46352/4. **Japan**, PO Box 2677, Upanga Rd, T 46356/8/9. **Kenya (HC)**, PO Box 5231, NIC Investment House, Samora Av, T 31502/37337. **Korea (E)**, PO Box 2690, United Nations Rd, T 46830/1. **Libya (E)**, PO Box 9413, Mtitu St, T 31666/35063. **Madagascar (E)**, PO Box 5254, Malik Rd, T 29442. **Malawi (HC)**, PO Box 7616, IPS Building, Samora Av, T 46673. **Mozambique (E)**, PO Box 9370, Garden Av, T 46973/4. **Netherlands (E)**, PO Box 9534, ATC Building Ohio St, T 46391/3. **Nigeria (HC)**, PO Box 9214, Bagamoyo Rd, T 66000/1. **Norway (E)**, PO Box 9012, T 46495/8. **Pakistan (HC)**, 2925, Malik Rd, T 27971/2. Poland (E), PO Box 2188, Upanga Rd, T 46294/25777. **Romania (E)**, PO Box 590, Ocean Rd, T 46295/27055. **Rwanda (E)**, PO Box 2918, Upanga Rd, T 46502. Spain (E), PO Box 842, IPS Building, Samora Av, T 66018. Sweden (E), PO Box 9274, Extelcomms House, Samora Av, T 46512/4/8. **Switzerland (E)**, PO Box 2454, Kenyatta Dr, T 66008/66629. **Syria (E)**, PO Box 2442, Alykhan Rd, T 20568/37568. **Uganda (HC)**, PO Box 6237, IPS Building, Samora Av, T 46256. **UK (HC)**, PO Box 9200, Hifadhi House, Azikiwe St, T 46302/5. **USA (E)**, PO Box 123, Laibon Rd, T 66010/86014/5. **Yemen (E)**, PO Box 349, United Nations Rd, T 46834/21722. **Yugoslavia (E)**, PO Box 2838, Upanga Rd, T 46378. **Zaire (E)**, PO Box 975, Malik Rd, T 46380/1 31672. **Zambia (HC)**, PO Box 2525, Ohio St, T 46383. **Zimbabwe**, PO Box 20762, Longido St, T 46259.

● Entertainment

Cinema Europeans and visitors seldom visit the cinema, which is a pity as the general audience reaction makes for an exciting experience. Programmes are not announced in the *Daily News*, but the *Express*, *Family Mirror* and the Swahili *Uhuru* all carry details.

There are 6 cinemas, showing mostly Indian, martial arts or adventure films. Entrance about US$1. The most popular are the ***Empire***, Maktaba St opposite the Post Office; the ***Empress*** on Samora Ave; the ***New Chox*** on Nkrumah St; the ***Odeon*** on Zaramo St; the ***Starlight*** on Kisutu St. The ***Drive-Inn-Cinema*** is on Old Bagamoyo Rd, just before Morocco Rd.

The ***British Council*** on Ohio St has fairly regular film shows on Wed. The ***Goethe Institute*** on the corner of Maktaba St and Samora Ave, and the ***Alliance Française*** on Maktaba St opposite the *New Africa Hotel* show films from time to time. Announcements in *Daily News*.

Fashion shows Popular occasions, often for charity, held at Diamond Jubilee Hall, *Embassy Hotel* Pool. Often accompanied by pop music impersonaters. Anouncements in *Daily News*.

Gambling ***Las Vegas Casino***, corner of Upanga Rd and Ufukoni Rd. US$4 entrance, converted to chips. Roulette and Vingt et Un. ***Club Billicanos***, Simu St, is applying for a gambling licence, as is a hotel under construction on Msasani Peninsula.

Music Special visits by popular African bands and artists and Indian groups occur regularly and are presented at Diamond Jubilee Hall, Bahama Mama's, Club Billicanos, *Gogo Hotel* and Bamboo Gardens, Simba Grill. Announcements in *Daily News*.

Zaita is mainly Zairean, the ***Tanzanites*** are from the Arusha area, ***BICO Stars*** are from Dar es Salaam. ***Shikamoo*** is a famous band of the 1960's with an exceptional saxophonist and lead guitarist. They play regularly at *Bahama Mama's* and at various social clubs such as Langata in Kinondoni, Kawe along the Old

Bagamoyo Rd and Mwenge off the Bagamoyo Rd just before Sam Njoma Rd. There are some music announcements in the *Daily News*, but a more comprehensive listing is in the Swahili *Uhuru* – get a local informant to translate.

Classical Music Concerts by touring artists, are presented by the British Council, the Goethe Institute, the Alliance Française and occasionally other embassies. Announcements in *Daily News*.

Theatre ***Little Theatre***, Haile Selassie Rd, off Bagamoyo Rd. Presents productions on an occasional basis, perhaps 2-3 times a year. Usually musicals. Very popular, particularly the Christmas Pantomime. Announcements in the *Daily News*. ***The British Council***, Ohio St. occasionally presents productions. Announcements in the *Daily News*. ***Diamond Jubilee Hall***, Maliki Rd, Upanga. Occasional visits by companies from India performing a bill of variety acts. Anouncements in *Daily News*.

● Hospitals and medical services

Hospitals The main hospital is *Mihumbili Hospital* located off United National Rd. *Oyster Bay Hospital* is an efficient and accessible small private medical centre (follow the signs along Haile Selassie Rd). *Kilimanjaro Hotel* will recommend a physician in an emergency. The *Aga Khan Hospital* is located on Ocean Rd at the junction with Ufukoni Rd. *Ocean Road Hospital* is on Ocean Rd at junction with Chimara Rd. All these hospitals are well equipped and staffed.

Pharmacies are located in all shopping centres. There is a good chemist in the *Kilimanjaro Hotel* foyer and one in the Namanga Shopping Centre along Bagamoyo Rd. Small **dispensaries** are located in the main residential areas. They are often short of drugs and short-staffed.

● Libraries

The ***British Council*** on the corner of Ohia St and Samora has an excellent library, with reference, lending, newspapers and magazines. It is well worth joining the lending section if you are in Dar es Salaam for any length of time. The ***US Information Service*** on Samora Ave nr the Empress Cinema has good reference facilities. The ***National Central Library*** is on UWT St nr the Maktaba St intersection. The library at the University of Dar es Salaam currently charges US$50 to use it, even for reference purposes.

● Night life

Most nightlife gets under way late – things tend not to warm up until the bars close at around 2300. Many venues open (and close) at short notice. Check the local Daily News. Specially recommended are the ***Bamboo Gardens*** for tropical atmosphere, ***The Simba Grill*** for good music and entertainment and ***Margot's*** for local colour.

Kilmanjaro Pool, Kivukoni Front. (US$2-4). Live bands on Sun by the pool. Becomes crowded during Christmas, Easter and Summer vacations. ***Bamboo Gardens***, *Oyster Bay Hotel*, Sekou Toure Drive. Open air. (US$2-4). Usually disco on Wed, Thurs, Sun with live bands on Fri and Sat. Has been closed in recent months while building work goes on at the hotel. Excellent atmosphere when busy, with a live band such as the Tanzanites or Zaita, coloured fairy lights against the backdrop of a giant baobab tree and surrounded by tropical foliage. ***La Dolce Vita***, Sekou Toure Drive. (US$2-4). Open air. Pleasant atmosphere with thatched roofing. The smart place with *Bamboo Gardens* closed. ***Margot's*** (or *Visions*), Bridge St. (US$1-2). Disco every night. Situated on the first floor of the old *Airlines Hotel* building. Formal name is 'Visions', but is known to most locals as 'Margot's' after the exotic French proprietess who started the establishment. No frills, good value. ***Club Billicanos***, Simu St. (US$5-10). Discos most nights. Ocasional live band or cabaret entertainment. Strobe lighting, smoke machines, revolving glitter balls. Expensive, but popular at weekends, though often quiet during the week. ***Continental***, Nkrumah Rd. (US$2-$4). Discos Fri and Sat. Popular with locals. ***Tazara Hostel***, Kilimani Rd, off Bagamoyo Rd. (US$4). Bands at weekends. ***Msasani Bay Villa***, off Kimnei Ave in Msasani Village. Discos at weekends. ***Simba Grill***, *Kilmanjaro Hotel*, Kirukoni Front. (US$4). You need not dine, but is essentially a dining and dancing venue with a live band and usually some cabaret, through to 0100. ***La Prima***, Bagamoyo Rd. New venue. Dining, dancing and cabaret. ***Bahama Mama's***, Morogaro Rd. (US$2-3). 15 kms from town centre. Large open air venue. Shikamoo, a legendary jazz and rumba band from the 1960's have reformed and play there regularly on Fri.

● Police station

Main police station is on Gerazani St nr the railway station. Also stations on Upanga Rd on the City side of Selander Bridge; on Bagamoyo Rd at the junction with Old Bagamoyo Rd.

Post offices

Main post office on Maktaba St. Other offices on Sokoine Drive, nr Cenotaph; behind the bus stand on Morogoro Rd and Libya St. Post offices are generally crowded. Sharooq's shop in the *Kilimanjaro Hotel* foyer will sell stamps. **DHL** office is on Upanga Rd nr Selander Bridge.

Religion

Roman Catholic Cathedral is on Sokoine Drive opposite the Customs jetty; the **Lutheran Church** is at the junction of Kivukoni Front and Sokoine Drive; **St Alban's Church** is at junction of Maktaba St and Upanga Rd; the **Greek Church** is on Upanga Rd.

Mosques are located on Zanaki St; there are 3 on Mosque St (one is Ismaili); 2 on UWT St at the Pugu Rd end; on UWT St nr Morogoro Rd; on Kitumbini St; on Ghandi St; on Upanga Rd (Ismaili); off Chole Rd on Msasani Peninsular.

Temples: There are 2 on Kisuki St which runs off India St nr the Mawenzi roundabout on Maktaba St.

Sport (participant)

Fishing Marine fishing can be arranged through *Kunduchi Beach Hotel*, PO Box 9313, T 47621/3, 25 km N of Dar es Salaam.

Hash House Harriers meet regularly in Dar on Sat afternoons. Details from British Council, Ohio St or British High Commission, corner of Samora Ave and Azikiwe St.

Golf, tennis, squash at *Gymkhana Club* on Ghana Ave. This is a membership club, but visitors can usually be accommodated. *Upanga Sports Club* on Upanga Rd just past the Greek Church also has squash facilities. An

IT WAS MAGIC, BRIAN

In 1993, Simba, Tanzania's most prominent football club, qualified for the African Club Championships. They had a marvellous run, putting out teams from Burundi, Angola and Algeria to meet Stella Artois of Côte d'Ivoire in the final. The first leg was away in Abidjan, and Simba held Stella to a goalless draw. Hopes were high. Surely Simba would now win the second leg at home in Dar es Salaam and lift the cup – a first triumph for Tanzania in any international competition.

The press warned that Simba's only problem would be over-confidence. It's the usual practice for each team to have a resident witch-doctor to put bad magic on the opposition players (not that much different, really, from European football where players observe absurd superstitious rituals and managers wear lucky suits). Both Simba and Stella would expect to have spells put on them, but all-in-all, things would cancel out, and the teams would be able to get on with the football.

Stella, however, pulled a master-stroke. Amid much publicity their players and officials arrived a week before the game and booked into a beach hotel N of Dar es Salaam for acclimatisation and final preparations. Simba's medicine man began a suitable course of treatment. Alas, this was a decoy team. The real players were bussed in secretly from Nairobi the night before the game.

The National Stadium was packed. The President and most of the Ministers were there, having left early from a graduation ceremony at the University of Dar es Salaam. Simba began brightly. Early in the first half, a cross from the left was met by an unmarked Simba striker at the far post. All of the National Stadium was on its feet (well, most were of necessity already on them – they were joined by the VIPs in the stand) as the ball was headed toward the top corner. The Stella goalkeeper appeared from nowhere, got the mearest finger-tip to the ball, deflected it onto a post, and it stayed out. The stadium went very quiet (except, that is, for a handful of fans from Simba's great rivals, Yanga, who suddenly sensed the game might turn out better than they ever dared hope). A few minutes later Stella scored against a listless Simba, and added another in the second half. Simba were *kutapika kama kasuka* and Stella *sur la lune*. The press blamed over-confidence. But all of Tanzania knew better.

informal group meets for tennis at the University of Dar es Salaam courts on the campus 15 km to the N of the city at 1700 every day.

Gym *The Fitness Centre*, off Chole Rd on Msasani Peninsula has a gym with weights and also runs aerobics and yoga classes.

Sailing The *Yacht Club* is located on Chole Rd on Msasani Peninsula. It is a membership club.

Swimming can be had at the ***Kilimanjaro Hotel*** (entrance US$2), the ***Karibu Hotel*** (US$4), the ***Embassy Hotel***, ***University of Dar es Salaam*** (but currently closed), and ***Salvation Army Hostel*** on Kilwa Rd. In the sea, the best location is at the ***Swimming Club*** on Ocean Rd nr Magogoni St. Otherwise the best sea beaches are some distance to the N and S of the city.

Sport (spectator)

Athletics Meetings at National Stadium. Details in *Daily News*.

Cricket is almost entirely a pursuit of the Asian community. There are regular games at the Gymkhana Club, off Ghana Ave and at Jangwani Playing Fields off Morogoro Rd at weekends. Announcements in *Daily News*.

Golf, tennis, squash Tournaments each year at the Gymkhana Club, off Ghana Ave. Announcements in *Daily News*.

Soccer The main African pursuit, and is followed by everyone from the President and the Cabinet down. Matches are exciting occasions with radios throughout the city tuned to the commentary. Terrace entrance is around US$1 (more for important matches). It is worth paying extra to sit in the stand. Details of games announced in *Daily News*. There are 2 main venues, the ***National Stadium*** on Mandela Rd to the S of the city and ***Karume Stadium*** just beyond the Kariakoo area, off Uhuru St. There are 2 divisions of the National league, and Dar es Salaam has 2 representatives, **Simba** and **Young Africans** (often called *Yanga*), and there is intense rivalry between them, see box, page 259). Simba, the best known Tanzanian club, have their origins in Kariakoo and are sometimes referred to as the 'Msimbazi Street Boys' – they have a club bar in Msimbazi St. Initially formed in the 1920's as 'Eagles of the Night', they changed their name to 'Sunderland FC' in the 1950's. After independence all teams had to choose African names and they became Simba. The national team **Tiafa Stars** play regularly at the National Stadium, mostly against other African teams.

Shopping

There are no department stores in Dar es Salaam. The new Shopping Mall at *Oyster Bay Hotel* has high quality goods that are imported and expensive. Otherwise shops are located along Samora Ave (electrical goods, local clothing, footware) and on Libya St (clothing and footwear). Supermarkets with a wide variety of imported foods and wines are on Samora Ave between Pamba Ave and Azikawe St on the corner of Kaluta St and Bridge St, in the *Oyster Bay Hotel* Shopping Mall. A popular location for purchase of fruit and vegetables is the market on Kinondoni Rd. Fresh fish and seafood can be bought at the market on Ocean Rd just past the ferry to Kivukoni.

Books can be bought secondhand at the stalls on Samora Ave and on Pamba St (off Samora). There is a small bookshop in the foyer of the *New Africa Hotel*, the ***Tanzanian Bookshop*** is on Makunganya St, leading from the Askari Monument, but both there have only limited selections. The shop in the foyer of the *Kilimanjaro Hotel* has a good selection of postcards, and will also sell stamps.

Curios and crafts **Lalji Ramji** has a counter in the *Kilimanjaro Hotel* foyer and he is there 1100-1600 daily to sell old stamps and coins. These are coins from the German period. A one Heller copper coin can be purchased for US$2. Copper coins from the British period can be obtained in a 1 cent, 5 cents and 10 cents set of 3 for US$1.50. They have holes in the centre so they could be carried on a loop of string. There are also silver (US$4) and nickel (US$1.25) 1 shilling coins. They have a lion on one side in front of an unrecognisable East African mountain. The silver coins can be made into earrings. There are some reproduction postcards from the German period showing the Governer's residence and the post-office, and Mr Ramji has a collection of antique postcards for sale, a sample of which he will bring in on request. Mr Ramji's grandfather came from India in 1880, and it looks unlikely that the business or the supply of antique items survive him.

There is also a good curio shop on Mkwepu St between Samora Ave and City Drive. This shop is particularly good for antique brass and copper items. Excellent quality modern wood products can be obtained from ***Domus*** on India St. Other curio shops are ***Silver Curios*** on Asikiwe St opposite the *New Africa Hotel*, and there are 2 curio shops in the *Kilimanjaro Hotel*.

Traditional crafts particularly wooden carvings are sold along Samora Ave to the S of the Askari Monument. Good value crafts can be purchased from stalls along Bagamoyo Rd nr the intersection with Haile Selassie, and at Mwege, along Sam Njoma Rd close to the intersection with Bagamoyo Rd. You are expected to bargain at the roadside stalls.

Flowers can be bought along Samora Ave and in the *Kilimanjaro Hotel* foyer. Plants, containers and makrame holders are available along Bagamoyo Rd nr the Haile Selassie intersection.

Hairdressers European Unisex hairdressing at *Kilimanjaro Hotel* and at *Embassy Hotel*. Also at Namanga Shopping Centre. Small African style hairdressers are to be found in all non-European residential areas.

● Telecommunications

Service on local calls can be varied. The Dar exchange is being up-graded, and whole areas of town can be impossible to reach. Public phones are virtually non-existent and for casual calls you will need to go through a hotel. International outgoing calls can be much easier. Hotels will usually charge up to 3 times the actual cost. Telecoms on Bridge St and Samora Ave has private booths, will arrange calls quickly and cheaply, and is open 24 hrs. Faxes can be frustrating, and telexes are widely used.

● Tourist Office

This is on Azikiwe St, opposite the *New Africa Hotel*, T 2485. It has become very demoralized, and invariably has no maps or guides. They will make reservations in the state-owned hotels and lodges. Tourism has recently come under new management and this is expected to improve services.

● Tour operators and travel agents

A variety of companies offer tours to the game parks, the islands (Zanzibar, Pemba, Mafia) and to locations of historical interest (Kilwa, Bagamoyo). It is well worth shopping around as prices (and degrees of luxury) vary. Among the most experienced companies are: *AMI Travel Bureau, Coastal Travel, Hippo Tours & Safaris, Kearsley Travel and Tours, Rickshaw Travel, Savannah Tours, Sykes, Takims Safaris, Valji & Alibhai*.

Across Tanzania Safaris, PO Box 21996, Makunganya St, T 219961/23121. *Africa Expeditions*, PO Box 1857, Mindu St, T 34574/38985. *All African Travel Agents*, PO Box 1947, T 20886. *AMI Travel Bureau*, PO Box 9041, AMI Building, Samora Av, T 27781/2. *Azania Tours and Travel*, PO Box 3707, UWT St, T 36959. *Bahari Enterprises & Safaris*, PO Box 15384, T 63422/9. *Bushtrekker Safaris*, PO Box 5350, *Bahari Beach Hotel*, T 31957/32671, Tlx 41178. *Coastal Travel*, PO Box 3052, Upanga Rd, T 37479/37480. *East African Holidays*, PO Box 2895, Samora Av, T 25989. *Flag Tours and Safaris*, PO Box 16046, T 37075. *Four Ways Travel Service*, PO Box 2926, Samora Av, T 22378. *Glide Safaris*, PO Box 4427. *Gogo Safaris*, PO Box 21114, Bagamoyo Rd, T 68410/67785. *Hippo Tours & Safaris*, PO Box 1658, Mkwepu St, T 36860. *Hit Holidays*, PO Box 1287, Azikiwe St, T 22093. *Holiday Africa Tours & Safaris*, PO Box 2132, Africa St, T 30700. *Hotel Tours & Management*, PO Box 5350, T 31957/32671. *Iramba Tours*, PO Box 21856, T 44482. *J M Tourist*, PO Box 21703, T 22433, Tlx 41207. *Kearsley Travel and Tours*, PO Box 801, Kearsley House, Indira Gandhi St, T 2067/8/9, F 35012/29085, Tlx 41014/41615. *Leisure Tours & Safaris*, PO Box 6100, T 32251. *Mill Tours & Safaris*, PO Box 19604, T 22114. *Molenveld Travel Bureau*, PO Box 456, Samora Av, T 22017. *Multi Tours and Travel*, PO Box 6940, Zanaki St, T 38288/37889/334465. *Panorama Tours*, PO Box 7534, Bakwat Building, cnr of Morogoro Rd and UWT St, T 27951. *Parklands Tours*, PO Box 19630, T 68586. *Parkway Tours and Safaris*, PO Box 6945, East Africa Publishing House, Samora Av, T 36731. *Pwani Tours & Safaris*, PO Box 50007, Cnr Kaluta St and Morogoro Rd, T 22433/32261. *Rickshaw Travel (American Express Agents)*, PO Box 1889, UWT St, T 29125/35097, F 29125/35456, Tlx 41162. *Safari Tours*, PO Box 9442, THB Building Samora Av, T 28422/28737/28765. *Savannah Tours*, *Kilinanjaro Hotel*, T 25237/25753, Tlx 41652. *Searock International*, PO Box 3030, T 32703/33589. *Selous Safaris*, PO Box 1192, T 34535, F 28486, Tlx 81016. *State Travel Service*, PO Box 5023, Bank House, Samora Av, T 29291/8 23113, F 29295, Tlx 41508. *Sunshine Safari Tours*, PO Box 5575, T 22700. *Sykes*, PO Box 1947, Indira Ghandi St, T 21899/26024/26078, F 29330, Tlx 41046. *Takims Safaris*, PO Box 20350, Jamhuri St, T 25691/2/3, F 46130. *Tankar*, PO Box 5286, T 3109. *Tourcare Tanzania*, PO Box 22878, T 42496. *Trans Africa Guides*, PO Box 853, T 30192. *Vacational*, PO Box 6649, T 34350/21015, F 34160, Tlx 81012. *Valji & Alibhai*, PO Box 786, Bridge St, T 20522/26537, F 46401, Tlx 81052. *Walji's Travel Bureau*, PO Box 434, cnr Zanaki St and

Indira Ghandi St, T 46261/25628.

Hunting Safari agents *Cordial Tours*, PO Box 1679, Jamhuri St, T 35264. *Gerald Posanisi Safaris*, PO Box 45640, T 47435.

● Transport

Local Car hire can be arranged through most travel agents (see below) Specialist companies are **Bugoni Super Auto Garage**, PO Box 25087, T 63708. **Evergreen Cabs**, PO Box 1476, T 29237/29246, Tlx 41180. **Kara Motors**, PO Box 64, T 33549. **White Cabs**, PO Box 2107, Zanaki St, T 23078/30454/33450, Tlx 41181. **Yellow Cabs**, Upanga Rd, PO Box 6100, T 35981.

Dala dala (privately run buses, minibuses, pick-ups and lorries converted to carry passengers) are uncomfortable, hot and cheap at around US$0.20 for any length of journey. The front of the vehicle usually has a sign stating the destination. They leave the start of the route when full, and as that means packed, it is sometimes difficult to get on at intermediate stops, and virtually impossible to get a seat. It is, however, an extremely efficient system providing you can handle the congestion and having to stand. Fellow passengers are unfailingly helpful and will advise on connections. The main terminals in town are at the Railway Station (Stesheni) and the Post Office (Posta) on Maktaba St.

Taxis are readily available in the town centre, cost around US$1-2/km, and are battered but serviceable. Always negotiate the fare before setting off. If you are visiting a non-central location, for example Oyster Bay or Msasani Peninsula, and there is no taxi stand at the destination, always ask the driver to wait.

Air As the main city, Dar es Salaam is the main terminus for international travel and for the domestic transport network (see page 397). International and domestic flights depart from Dar es Salaam International Airport, along Pugu Rd, 13 km from the city centre. *Dala dala* and minibuses run regularly, but are crowded and can be a problem with luggage. There is a shuttle bus service from *New Africa Hotel* on Maktaba St and the fare is about US$2. Taxis to the airport from the centre should cost about US$10.

Air Tanzania Corporation (ATC) This is the state-owned carrier. Often there are delays of several hours for a flight and a whole day needs to be allocated to a leg of air travel. ATC generally has daily flights scheduled to Zanzibar and Arusha and once or twice a week to Bukoba, Kigoma, Mwanza, Tabora, Dodoma, Mtwara, Mafia, Kilwa and Pemba. ATC has suffered from severe operating difficulties, and flights are cancelled and the schedules changed all the time. The line is rather unkindly dubbed 'Air Total Chaos' by local folk. The only sensible procedure is to call in at the ATC office on Ohio St and Garden Ave and check what is currently available. Flights are cheaper for residents, and not particularly expensive for tourists. A single flight to Zanzibar is about US$25, about US$100 to Arusha and US$200 to Mwanza, but bear in mind that fares are subject to frequent alteration. There are plans for ATC to be sold to South African Airways, who are reported eager to take over ATC's international routes, but are less keen on running the domestic network.

Other domestic air services are fairly unstable. Air transport has recently been opened up to private operators, several of whom have started services only to close them when it was apparent that the immediate market was unviable. The best advice is to explore the private carriers through one of the Dar es Salaam travel agents (see above). **ZATA** generally has 2 daily flights each way to Zanzibar and cost of a single is US$38. **Aviators Services**, T 6386 (Arusha) has 3 flights a week to Arusha, 1100 Mon, Wed, Sat; and the cost of a single is US$126. Three or 4 flights a week to Mafia, 1100 Tues, Wed, Fri, Sun, single US$42.

Train The **Central Railway Station** is located off Sokoine Drive at the wharf end of the city. This station serves the line that runs through the central zone to Kigoma on Lake Tanganyika and Mtwara on Lake Victoria and the line that goes N to Tanga and Moshi. The continuation of the line from Moshi to Taveta, Voi, and the Kenyan rail network has been closed since the break up of the East African Community in 1977. However, there are new initiatives to revive co-operation between Kenya, Tanzania and Uganda, and a declaration of intent to this effect was signed by the 3 heads of state in December 1993. The rail link from Kenya to Uganda has been restored, and the possibility of reopening the Moshi-Voi link is being explored.

The **Tazara Railway Station** is located at the junction of Mandela Rd and Pugu Rd, and is about 5 km from the city centre. It is well served by *dala dala* and a taxi from the centre costs about US$4. This line runs SW to Iringa and Mbeya and on to Tunduma at the Zambia border. It is a broader gauge than the Central and Northern Line.

Trains leave on the Central Line for **Mwanza** and **Kigoma** on Tue, Wed Fri and Sat at 1800. (Kigoma 1st class US$25, 2nd US$5, 3rd US$2).

On the Northern Line to **Tanga** and **Moshi**, trains leave on Tue, Thu and Sat at 1600 (Moshi 1st class US$12, 2nd US$5.50, 3rd US$2). Journey time to Moshi or Tanga about 1 day.

On the **Tazara** line, trains depart at 1645 on Tues, and at 1230 on Mon and Fri. The Tues train is scheduled to be slightly faster and costs a bit more (Mbeya 1st class US$18, 2nd US$10, 3rd US$6). The journey to Mbeya takes about 2 days.

Road There are 3 main bus stations for up-country travel. Iringa, Mbeya, Songea, Tanga, Mombasa: bus station on UWT St at the intersection with Uhuru St on the City side of the Mnazi Moja open space.

Arusha, Moshi, Namanga, Nairobi: bus station on Morogoro Rd at junction with Libya Rd.

Bagamoyo, Morogoro, Dodoma, Mwanza, Kilwa: bus station in Kariakooo on Msimbazi St (taxi from centre about US$3).

If you are making a long journey you can book a seat at kiosks run by the bus companies at the bus stations. Larger buses give a considerably more comfortable ride and are to be recommended on safety grounds as well. If you are taking a shorter journey (Morogoro or Bagamoyo, say), the bus will leave when full. You can join an almost full bus, and leaving immediately for an uncomfortable journey, either standing or on a makeshift gangway seat. Or you can secure a comfortable seat and wait till the bus fills, which can take 1-2 hrs for a less busy route such as that to Bagamoyo. On the larger and more travelled routes (Arusha, Mbeya) there is now a choice of 'luxury': 'semi-luxury' and 'ordinary'. **Arusha**: fare is around US$20 luxury, US$16 semi luxury and US$12 ordinary and takes about 9 hrs. The road has improved considerably. **Bagamoyo**: fare is US$1 and takes up to 3 hrs. The road is very poor. **Dodoma**: fare is about US$6 and takes about 6 hrs. Train is really the only feasible option on the Dodoma to Tabora and Kigoma route. **Mbeya**: fare is around US$15 luxury, US$10 semi-luxury and US$7 ordinary and journey takes about 12 hrs. **Tanga**: fare is roughly US$6 and takes about 5 hrs. **Mtwara**: fare is about US$10 and takes up to 24 hrs.

Sea Boats to Zanzibar, Tanga, Mafia Island, Lindi, Mtwara leave from the jetty on Sokoine Drive opposite St. Joseph's Cathedral. Dhows sailing and motorised, leave from the wharf just to the S of the boat jetty. The sea services to Mombasa have been suspended, but could resume at any time. ***Sea Express***, PO Box 5829, T 27669/27822, Tlx 81042. Has 5 departures Mon to Fri for Zanzibar at 0800, 1000, 1200, 1415, 1615; 4 departures on Sat at 0815, 0900, 1200, 1615; 3 departures on Sun, 0900, 1200 and 1615. The fare is US$10 one way and takes 75 minutes. ***Canadian Spirit*** runs once a week to Mafia and Mtwara (1st class to Mtwara US$15, 2nd US$10, takes 24 hrs). ***Tanzania Coastal Shipping Company***, PO Box 9461, T 25192 is a cargo service that takes some passengers and serves Tanga, Mombasa, Mafia, Kilwa, Lindi and Mtwara. Sailings are irregular, slow and cheap. Mtwara costs US$5 and takes 36 hrs. ***Dhows*** are irregular, slow and cheap. A motorised dhow will take 12 hrs to Mafia, and sail-powered up to 24 hrs. Cost US$3 to US$6. You sit or sleep on the cargo and need to take your own food.

NORTH COAST: BAGAMOYO AND TANGA

CONTENTS

MAPS

Bagamoyo is one of the most fascinating towns in East Africa, with a host of historical associations. Access is only really feasible by road, and although the surface has been repaired for the part of the distance, the major part is rough. It is quite possible to make a day trip from Dar es Salaam, although an overnight stay is perhaps best. Tanga was an important port in the period up to independence when sisal was Tanzania's main crop, and the main growing area was between Kilimanjaro and the coast. The Usambara Hills are a very attractive, and Lushoto and Amani can be visited either on the way to Tanga, or when travelling to Kilimanjaro and Arusha.

Bagamoyo

History

The coastal area opposite Zanzibar was first settled by fishermen and cultivators. Towards the end of the 18th century, 12 or so Muslim diwans arrived to settle, build dwellings and establish their families and retinues of slaves. These diwans were all related to Shomvi la Magimba from Oman. They prospered through levying taxes whenever a cow was slaughtered, or a shark or other large fish caught, as well as on all salt produced at Nunge, about 3 km N of Bagamoyo.

The town was threatened by Kamba around 1800, and an uneasy alliance of the Shomvi, the Zaramo and the Doe, was formed to hold them off. In return for their support against the Kamba, the Shomvi agreed to pay a tribute to the Zaramo of a third of the revenues from their commercial activities, mostly the sale of slaves and ivory.

In 1868, the diwans granted land to the Holy Ghost Fathers to establish a mission. The Zaramo challenged the right of the diwans to make this concession but, following intervention by the French Consul, Zanzibar (firstly under Sultan Majid, and, after 1870, under Sultan Barghash), put pressure on the Zaramo to accept the settlement.

Bagamoyo's location as a mainland port close to Zanzibar led to its development as a centre for caravans and an expansion of commerce in slaves and ivory soon followed. There was also growing trade in sun-dried fish, gum copal (a residue that accumulates from the *msandarusi* tree in the soil near its roots), and the salt from Nunge. Copra (from coconuts) was also important, and was used to make soap. A boat-building centre was established which supplied craft to other coastal settlements.

In 1880 the population of the town was around 5,000 but this was augmented by a substantial transient population in residence after completing a caravan or undertaking preparations prior to departure. The numbers of those temporarily in town could be considerable. In 1889, after the slave trade

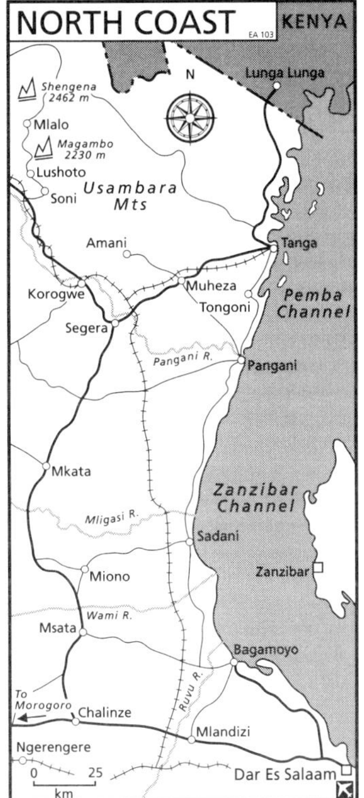

had been suppressed reducing the numbers passing through significantly, it was still recorded that 1,305 caravans left for the interior, involving 41,144 people.

The social composition of the town was varied. There were the initial Muslim Shomvi and the local Zaramo and Doe. Among the earliest arrivals were Hindus from India, involving themselves in administration, coconut plantations and boat-building. Muslim Baluchis, a people based in Mombasa and Zanzibar, and following for the most part the profession of mercenary soldiers, also settled and were involved in trade, financing caravans and landowning. Other Muslim sects were represented, among them the Ismailis who settled in 1840 and by 1870 numbered 137. A handful of Sunni Muslims from Zanzibar established shops in Bagamoyo, some Parsees set up as merchants, and a small group of Catholic Goans was engaged in tailoring and retailing.

Caravans from the interior brought with them Nyamwezi, Sukuma and Manyema porters. They might remain in town for 6 months or so before joining an outgoing caravan, and they resided for the most part in an insalubrious shanty settlement known as *Kampi Mbaya* ('bad camp') which was just off the main caravan route out of town close to the caravanserai. Some remained to take up life as fishermen or working the Nunge salt deposits.

In 1888 the German East Africa Company signed a treaty with the Sultan of Zanzibar, Seyyid Khalifa, which allowed the company to collect customs duties along the coast. The Germans rapidly made their presence felt by ordering the Sultan's representative (the Liwali) to lower the Sultan's flag, and on being refused, axed down the flag-pole.

Later in the year a dispute between a member of the company and a townsman culminated in the latter being shot. The Usagara trading house of the company was beseiged by irate townspeople, 200 troops landed from the *SS Moewe*, and over 100 local people were killed.

Further resentment was incurred when the Germans set about registering land and property, demanding proof of ownership. As this was impossible for most residents there was widespread fear that property would be confiscated.

One of the diwans, Bomboma, organized local support. They enlisted the help of Bushiri bin Salim al-Harthi who had earlier led Arabs against the Germans in Tabora. Bushiri had initial success. Sections of Bagamoyo were burned

Mangroves

Up and down the coast of East Africa you will come across stretches of mangrove forests. Ecologically these can be described as evergreen saline swamp forests and their main constituents are the mangroves Rhizophora, Ceriops and Bruguiera. These are all described as viviparous, that is the seeds germinate or sprout when the fruits are still attached to the parent plant. Mangrove forests support a wide range of other plants and animals including a huge range of birds, insects and fish.

Economically mangrove forests are an important source of building poles, known on the coast as *boriti*, which were once exported in large quantities to the Arabian Gulf.Their main property is that they are resistant to termite attack, see box, page 227. Mangrove bark is also used as a tanning material and charcoal can be obtained from mangrove wood. As with so many natural resources in East Africa care needs to be taken in the use of mangrove forests. Their over-exploitation could lead to the delicate balance that is found in the forests being upset, with serious consequences for these coastal regions.

and Bushiri formed up in Nzole about 6.5 km SW of the town ready for an assault. The German government now felt compelled to help the company and Herman von Wissman, was appointed to lead an infantry force comprising Sundanese and Zulu troops. Admiral Denhardt, commanding the German naval forces played for time by initiating negotiations with Bushiri whose demands included being made Governor of the region from Dar es Salaam up to Pangani, payment of 4,000 rupees (about US$10,000 in present-day values) a month, and the right to keep troops.

By May 1889 Wissman had consolidated his forces and built a series of fortified block houses. He attacked Nzole and Bushiri fled. The alliance of the diwans and Bushiri weakened, and in Jun the Germans retook Saadani and in Jul, Pangani. Bushiri was captured and executed at Pangani in Dec. Bomboma, and another of the diwans leading the resistance, Marera, were also executed, and other diwans were deposed and replaced by collaborators who had assisted the Germans.

It was now clear that the German government intended to extend their presence and in Oct 1890, rights to the coast were formally purchased from the Sultan of Zanzibar for 4 million marks.

In early 1891 German East Africa become a formal colony, but in Apr it was decided to establish Dar es Salaam as the capital. Commercial activity in Baganoyo revived, and in the last decade of the century rebuilding began with the construction of new stone buildings including a customs house and the Boma which served as an administrative centre.

The caravan trade resumed and there was a further influx of Indians together with the arrival of Greeks who established a European hotel. Wm O'Swald the Hamburg trading company arrived and Hansing established vanilla plantations at Kitopeni and Hurgira. An important Koran school was established in the town.

Despite these developments Bagamoyo was destined for steady decline as its harbour was unsuitable for deep draught steamships and no branch of the railway was built to serve the port. The ending of the German rule further reduced commercial presence in the town, and the present century has seen Bagamoyo decline steadily, lacking even a sealed road to link it to Dar es Salaam.

Places of Interest

Old Bagamoyo At the S approach to the town, on the road from Koale is the **Old Fort,** (sometimes referred to as the Old Prison). It is the oldest surviving building in Bagamoyo having been started by Abdallah S. Marhabi around 1860 and extended and strengthened by Sultan Baghash after 1870 and then by the German colonialists. It was used as a police post until 1992. Initially one of its functions was to hold slaves until they could be shipped to Zanzibar. It is said there is an underground passage through which the slaves were herded to dhows on the shore, although this passge is not apparent today. It is currently being restored and the plan is that it will provide teaching rooms for the nearby Nyumba ya Sanaa (Art College) The caretaker will allow you to wander round, and it is clear that the work will result in a particularly handsome building. The construction is whitewashed, 3-storeys high, with buttresses and battlements and an enclosed courtyard.

On the path to *Badeco Beach Hotel,*

Lay Down My Heart

I'm weary for travelling has taken its toll
Lay down my heart and calm my soul
Happy haven, Bagamoyo

While far away, in my heart I saw
A shimmering pearl on a jade-green shore
Coast of palms, Bagamoyo

Laden with spices and ivory
Dhows sail in on the sparkling sea
Bustling harbour, Bagamoyo

There the women are pretty and fine
All year round they drink palm wine
Garden of love, Bagamoyo

Under the stars hear the laughter ring
From lovely girls as they dance and sing
Velvet nights, Bagamoyo

My spirits lift as the drum beats roll
Lay down my heart and calm my soul
At last I'm home, Bagamoyo

On the long journey from the interior, travelling East to the Indian Ocean, caravan porters looked forward to their arrival at Bagamoyo, a place of cool sea breezes, greenery and high-living. As they marched, the porters sang to keep up their spirits. The verses above, originally in Swahili, were recorded in 1990, by Hauptmann Leue a German colonial administrator.

The name of the town is said to be derived from *Bwaga-moyo* which would be translated as 'lay down my heart'. A two-edged interpretation has arisen. The first is that like the caravan porters the weary traveller from the interier could 'lay down his heart' at Bagamoyo, resting and recuperating. More poignantly, the second interpretation is that as they were to be transported overseas, the last part of Africa the slaves would ever see was Bagamoyo. It was there they should 'lay down their hearts'.

off to the right is the **German Cemetery** with some 20 graves dating from 1889/90, and most are of Germans killed during the uprising led by Bushiri in those years. (see page 265). A German deed of freedom for a slave is reproduced on a tree. The cemetery is well tended, surrounded by a coral wall. In the ground of the *Badeco Beach Hotel* is the site of the tree reputedly used by the German administration for executions. The site is marked by a plaque.

Continuing along India Street on the left is an old 2-storey building **Liku House** with an awning supported by slender iron columns and a central double door. This served as the first administrative headquarters for the German from 1888 until the Boma was completed in 1897. Emin Pasha stayed there in 1889 (see box, page 270).

The **Boma** is an impressive 2-storey building topped by crenellations, constructed in a U-Shape. There are pointed arches on the first floor and rounded arches on the ground floor. This was the German administration centre from 1897, and it currently serves as the headquarters for the District Commissioner. The building is undergoing some restoration, and it is possible to look round. On the inland side of the building is a well constructed by Sewa Haji, see box, page 271.

On the shore side is a semi-circular levelled area on which was a monument erected by the Germans with brass commemorative plaques. With the fall of Bagamoyo to the British, the monument was razed and replaced with the present erection which commemorates the departure of Barton and Speke to Lake Tanganyika from nearby Kaole in 1857. The old German plaques have been reset in the walls which support the levelled area, on the shore-side. To the left is an Arabic 2-storey building fronted by 6 columns, a fretted verandah and curved arch windows, said to be the **Old Bagamoyo Tea House**, and is thought to be the oldest building in the town, constructed by Abdallah Marbahi in 1860. In front of the Boma is the **Uhura Monument**, celebrating Tanzania's independence in 1961, and a bandstand.

Continuing N along India Street there is a particularly fine residential house on the right with columns and arched windows, just before Customs Road. This leads down to the **Customs House**, built in 1895 by Sewa Haji and rented to the Germans. It is a double storey building with an open verandah on the first floor, buttresses, arched windows, and lime-washed. It looks onto a walled courtyard and is currently undergoing restoration. Opposite the Customs House are the ruins of the **Usagara Company Store** built in 1888 with the first arrival of a German commercial presence. The unusual construction had stone plinths on which were mounted cast-iron supports for the timber floor, raised to keep the stores dry. The cast-iron supports have cups surrounding them in which kerosene was poured to prevent rats climbing up to eat the stored grain. At one end of the building is a tower, held up by a tree growing up through it.

Halfway down Customs Road is the covered **Fish Market** with stone tables for gutting fish. When not used for this purpose they are marked out with chalk draughts boards for informal games with bottle-tops. At the top of Customs Road, just before the intersection with India Street is the **Post Office**, with a fine carved door and a blue-painted upstairs verandah. Further N along India Street are a series of Arabic buildings, one of which, the first on the right after the square to the left, is being restored as a hotel.

Continuing N, on the right, is the **Jama'at Khana**, the Ismaili mosque, which dates from 1880, double-storeyed with a verandah and carved doors. On the right beyond the mosque is the hospital, now part of Muhimbili Teaching

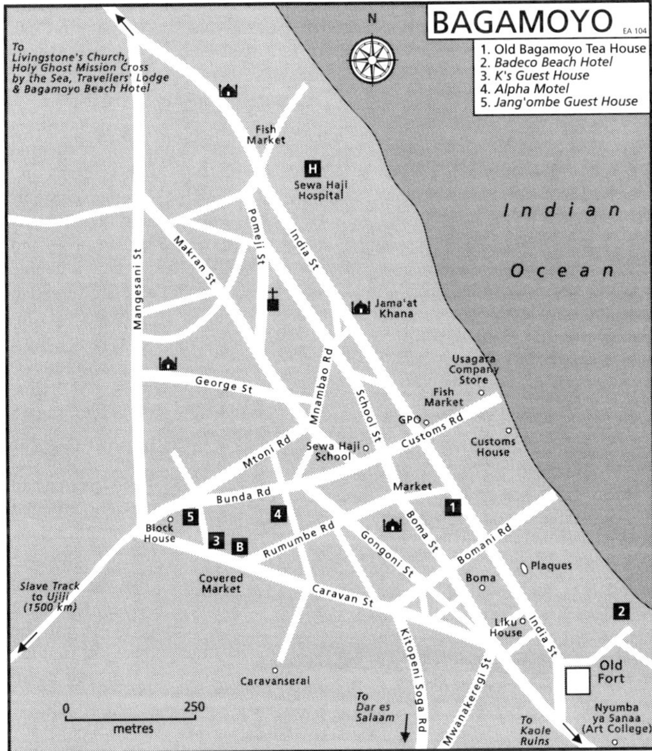

Hospital in Dar es Salaam, which is based on the original Sewa Haji Hospital, constructed in 1895. On the death of Sewa Haji in 1896, the hospital was run by the Holy Ghost Mission, and then from 1912 by the Germans. The present hospital has some handsome old buildings and some more modern blocks. It has a rather charming air, with goats lolling on the covered walkways between the wards.

At the N end of the town on the right is substantial **Mosque** and Muslim school with curved steps up to the carved door over which is a delicate fretted grill. The building is fronted by 6 columns and there is a verandah to the rear.

Other buildings of interest in Bagamoyo Town include the **Sewa Haji School**, see box, page 271, a three-storey construction with filigree iron-work and constructed in 1896.

Close to the intersection of Sunda Road and Mongesani Street at the Western approach to the town is the white **Block House**, constructed in 1889 by Herman Wissman during the Bushiri uprising (see page 265). There is a mangrove pole and coral stone roof and an outside ladder which enabled troops to man the roof behind the battlements. The walls have loopholes through which troops could fire, standing on low internal walls, which doubled as seating, to

The Bagamoyo Banquet Of Emin Pasha

Emin Pasha was born to a Jewish family in Germany and his original name was Schnitzer. At various times he presented himself as Turkish and Egyptian, and considered becoming either Belgian or British. 'Pasha' is a Turkish title given to the governor of a province. He had a Turkish wife, left behind in Prussia and he took an Ethiopian mistress with whom he had a daughter. All who met him were impressed with his charm, generosity, his scholarly interest in natural history and his devotion to his daughter. General Gordon recruited him in Egypt and appointed him Governor of Equatoria in Southern Sudan. When Gordon was killed in the fall of Khartoum in 1885, Emin Pasha was stranded. The plight of the gallant defender of the Empire captured the imagination of the British public and a public subscription was got up to finance a rescue expedition led by HM Stanley. Far from being beleagured and starving, an exhausted Stanley found Emin Pasha and his Egyptian forces living comfortably with harems and slaves. An attack by the Sudanese however caused them to flee. The Pasha's troops had melted away by the time Stanley, together with a decimated force and the Pasha in tow, reached the coast at Bagamoyo in Dec 1889.

The Germans laid on a great reception and there were 34 at the banquet on the first floor of Liku House. Roasts, fresh seafood and champagne were served. A naval band played below the balcony. In the street the returning porters celebrated their return with an orgy. Emin Pasha circulated, captivating the guests with his charm. Suddenly there was an uproar from outside. The guests rushed to the balcony to see revellers surrounding the figure of Emin Pasha, covered in blood. He'd tumbled from the balcony.

It took 6 weeks in the Sewa Haji Hospital for the Pasha to pull through. When he had recovered, a telegram from the Kaiser persuaded him to set off into the interior again to negotiate treaties with native leaders to extend Germany's power.

Three years later, in 1892, at his camp in present-day Zaire not far from Kisingani, struggling with failing eyesight to catalogue his collection of insects, plants and flowers, he was surrounded by Arab slavers who slit his throat.

give them the height to fire down on their adversaries. Behind the block house is a disused well.

The **slave track** to the interior departed from this point – a 1,500 km trail which terminated at Ujij on Lake Tanganyika. Off Caravan Street is the **Caravanserai**, a courtyard with single-storey buildings at the front and a square, 2-storey building with a verandah at the centre (the corner of which is collapsing). It was here that preparations were made for the fitting out of caravans to the interior.

Nyumba ya Sanaa This is a school for the arts where music, drama, dance and painting are taught. Most students are Tanzanian, but there are several from Europe, America and the Far East. The main buildings are located along the road to Koale to the S of Bagamoyo. They are recently constructed, with help from Norway, and are very impressive. The main building has a Greek-style open amphitheatre, with proscenium stage covered by a 15m high thatched canopy. The amphitheatre stage backs onto a second theatre area, which is roofed and enclosed. Attached to the stage are workshops and offices. Students can be observed in the area round the dormitories practising their skills.

Livingstone's Church This is a simple construction with a tin roof, curved arch windows and wooden benches. Its formal name is the Anglican Church of the Holy Cross. Above the entrance is the sign 'Through this door Dr. David Livingstone passed' referring to the fact that his body was kept in the church prior to it being returned to England.

Cross by the Sea A monument in green marble surmounted by a cross is located on the path leading to the sea from Livingstone's Church. It marks the spot where, in 1868, Father Antoine Horner of the French Holy Ghost Fathers crossed from Zanzibar (where they had operated a Mission since 1860) and stepped ashore to establish the first Christian Church on the mainland.

Holy Ghost Mission Opposite the path to the Cross by the Sea is **Mango Tree Drive** which was established in 1871 as the approach to the Mission. There is a statue of the Sacred Heart, erected in 1887 in front of the **Fathers' House**. The Fathers' House is a 3-storey stucture with an awning over a verandah on the top floor and arches on the other 2 floors. It was begun in 1873 and the third storey finally added in 1903. In 1969 the building was taken over by MANTEP as a training centre for educational management.

Behind the Fathers' House is the **First Church**, construction of which started in 1872. It comprises a stone tower topped with arches with a cross at the centre and crosses on the pediments at each corner. The main building is a simple rectangular structure with a tin roof, unusually situated behind and to the side of the tower so that the tower sits at one corner.

It was here on 24 February 1874, that the body of David Livingstone was deposited by the missionary's African followers, Sisi and Chuma, who had carried their master 1,500 km from Ujiji.

SEWA HAJI – BAGAMOYO PHILANTHROPIST

Sewa Haji's father came from the Hindu Kutch, in what is now Pakistan, to Zanzibar, setting up general stores in Zanzibar and Bagamoyo in the 1860's. Sewa Haji was born in 1851, one of 4 children, and when 2 of his brothers died in 1869, he found himself, at the age of 18, in charge of the 2 family firms, Haji Karji and Ratansi Mayi and Co.

The firms supplied caravans operating out of Bagamoyo with cloth, beads, copper wire, brass vessels, gun-powder and shot, and purchased ivory, rhino horns and hippo teeth from them on their return. Equipment and supplies would be provided on credit, financing part of the caravan. The firm also acted as an agent in recruiting porters. Sewa Haji accumulated substantial land holdings around Bagamoyo, including the Old Fort which he sold to the Germans in 1894, while renting them the Post Office and the Customs House. In 1892 Sewa Haji donated 20,000 hectares to the Holy Ghost Mission in Bagamoyo. The same year he donated the 3-storey building in the centre of town for a multiracial (African and Asian) school, an exceptionally enlightened move at the time. He established hospitals in Zanzibar, at Bagamoyo (the original building forms part of the present hospital) and in Dar es Salaam (near the present Malindi Wharf, it was demolished in 1951).

Sewa Haji died and was buried in Zanzibar, in 1894, at the age of 46. He had accumulated very consideraable wealth through his shrewd business dealings. Most of his land and houses in Bagamoyo were bequeathed to the German government on the understanding that the income be used to support lepers and the hospitals.

Speke, Burton, Grant, Stanley, Peters, Emin Pasha and Weissmann all visited the church.

Following the path to the right of the First Church is a cemetery where the early missionaries are buried. Further down this path is a small shrine built by freed slaves in 1876 with the sign 'Salamnus Maria', picked out in flowers.

A great baobab tree, planted in 1868, stands to the side of the the first church. At the base can be seen the links of the chain where Mme de Chevalier, a mission nurse, tethered her donkey.

The **New Church**, constructed of coral blocks, started in 1910 and completed in 1914, stands in front of the First Church. A small iron cross commemorates the centenary, in 1968, of the Holy Ghost Mission in Bagamoyo.

The **Mission Museum** is housed in the **Sisters' Building**. The displays present a history of Bagamoyo and there are relics and photographs from the slave period. One intriguing exhibit is the uniform presented by HA Schmit in 1965, that he wore during the East African Campaign under von Lettow, see page 216. Adjacent to the Mission Museum is a craft workshop with *Ufundi* ('craftsmen') picked out in flowers.

One of the main activities of the Holy Ghost Mission was to purchase slaves and present them with their freedom. A certificate of freedom was provided by the German authorities. These freed slaves had originally been captured hundreds of kilometres away in the hinterland, and the Mission undertook to rehabilitate them in **Freedom Village** located just to the N of the main Mission buildings

Kaole Ruins These are located 5 km S of Bagamoyo. The route is the road past Nyumba ya Sanaa (Bagamoyo Art College). It is quite possible to walk, but it is advisable to take a guide for security. At present there are no taxis in Bagamoyo.

The ruins are on the coastal side of the present day village of Koale. The site consists of the ruins of 2 mosques and a series of about 30 tombs, set among palm trees. Some of the tombs have stones pillars up to 5m in height.

The older of the 2 mosques (A on the site plan) dates from some time between the 3rd and 4th centuries and is thought to mark one of the earliest contacts of Islam with Africa, before the main settlement took place. The remains of a vaulted roof constructed from coral with lime mortar can be seen which formed the *mbirika* at the entrance. Here ceremonial ablutions took place, taking water from the nearby well. There is some buttressing with steps which allowed the muezzin access to the roof to call the faithful to prayer. The recess (*kibula*) on the E side, nearest to Mecca has faint traces of an inscription on the vaulting.

The stone pillars that mark some of the tombs were each surmounted by a stone 'turban' and the remains of some of these can be seen on the ground. Delicate porcelain bowls with light green glaze were set in the side of the pillars and the indentations can be seen. The bowls have been removed for safe-keeping and are in the National Museum in Dar es Salaam. These bowls have been identified as celadon made in China in the 14th century and are the main indication of the likely age of the structure. Some of the tombs have frames of dressed coral and weathered obituary inscriptions. Bodies would have been laid on the right side, with the face toward Mecca.

Mosque 'B' is of later construction and has been partially restored. It is similar to the triple-domed mosque at Kilwa Kisiwani, see page 288, in style, and it is thought that the builder may well have been the same.

The community that gave rise to these ruins would have been established during the Muslim period AD 622-1400. The first Muslim colonies were estab-

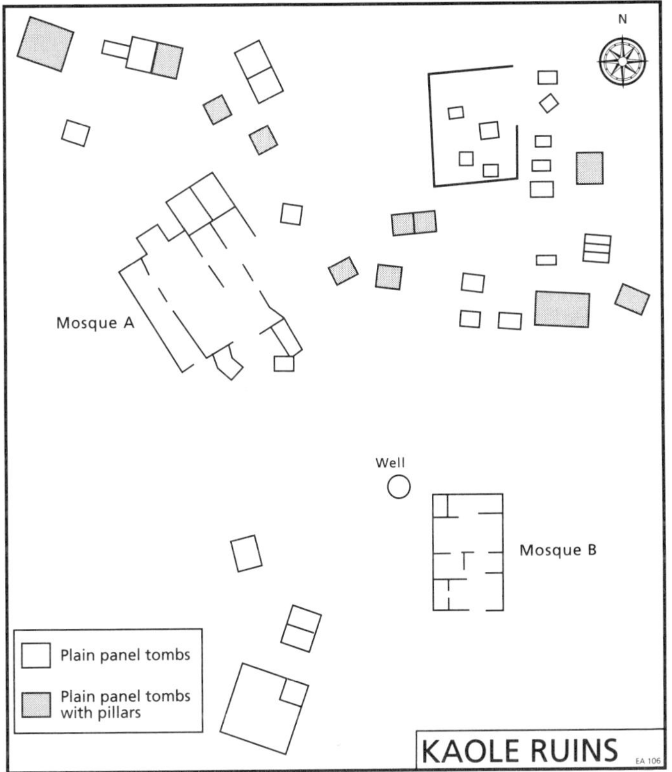

lished from AD 740 by sea-borne migrations from the Persian Gulf down the East African coast as far as Sofala, the area round the Zambezi River. The settlement at Koale would have traded mangrove poles, see page 266, sandalwood, ebony and ivory. It is suggested that Koale might have had several hundred inhabitants. Their dwellings would have used timber in their construction and thus would have been less durable than the all-stone mosques and tombs. Being on more fertile soil inland, as the dwellings collapsed they rapidly became overgrown. The settlement went into gradual decline as the shore became more densely packed with mangroves, making its use by dhows difficult, and commercial activity shifted to Bagamoyo.

Sadani Game Reserve This is located on the coast about 50 km N of Bagamoyo. However it is really inaccessible without hired transport. The best route is to turn off the Chalinze to Tanga Road for Miono. The track can be impassable in the rainy seasons. There is a very run-down rest house in Sadani Village. The main track in the reserve runs S from Sadani Village to where there is a ferry across the Wami River. This ferry cannot take vehicles. The track continues to Ngiapanda which is about 10 km W of

Bagamoyo. This latter may be a possible route for trekkers. The reserve has elephant, leopard, lion, giraffe, buffalo and zebra.

Local information

● Where to stay

Several new developments are in the process of construction. Bagamoyo is in a glorious location, with a splendid, curved, palm-fringed beach. There are only a few beach hotel rooms in town, and it is advisable to book. The currently available hotels are all good value. There are 2 hotels under construction due to be completed in 1994. One is to the N of ***Bagamoyo Beach Resort*** on the shore. The second is in the centre of town, fronting the shore, and is an imaginative restoration of an old Arab House, and it should be rather special when completed. Inquire through ***Coastal Travel***, PO Box 3052, Upanga Rd. T 37479/37480.

C *Bagamoyo Beach Resort* (sometimes referred to as the 'Gogo'), T 83 Bagamoyo or 31235 Dar es Salaam. At the N end of town – continue along India St. A/c. Hot water showers. Most of the 22 rooms are comfortable but the style is a little uninspired with tin roofs and concrete walls. There are a few traditional-style rooms with thatched roofs, but they do not face over the ocean. Simple restaurant. Pleasant open-air bar overlooking beach with thatched roof. Plans for water sports, but none at present.

D *Badeco Beach Hotel*, PO Box 261. T 18 Bagamoyo. Glorious location right on the beach at S end of town. Small, with 15 rooms, 9 self-contained. Some currently under construction. Thatched bandas along shore, garden planted with bouganvillea. Small restaurant, but with excellent and imaginative seafood menu. **D** *Travellers' Lodge*, PO Box 275 (no phone, but bookings can be made through Mr Hesse at *Badeco Beach Hotel*, T 18 Bagamoyo). At N end of town on India St. 4 small bungalows and 4 rooms. Pleasant traditional thatched style. Excellent bar.

E *K's Guest House*, PO Box 15, T 15 Bagamoyo. In town centre opposite covered market on Caravan St. **E** *Alpha Motel*, PO Box 85, T 56 Bagamoyo. In town, on Rumumba Rd, nr covered market. Pleasant shaded outside bar. **E** *Jang'ombe Guest House*, PO Box 268, Mangesani Rd, nr intersection with Mtoni Rd.

● Places to eat

Hotels are the main places. There are some snack bars nr the covered market on Caravan St. ♦♦***Badeco***. Excellent seafood, charming small restaurant. ♦♦***Bagamoyo Beach***. Simple food.

● Bars

Only in hotels and the best are ***Travellers Lodge***, ***Badeco Beach*** and ***Bagamoyo Beach***, all of which overlook the beach.

● Entertainment

At weekends there are entertainments provided by the ***Nyumba ya Sanaa*** (Bagamoyo Art College) and they include music, dance and drama. They are well attended and the atmosphere excellent. You need to ask at the college for times and programmes.

● Foreign exchange bureaux

There are none at present in Bagamoyo. *Badeco Beach Hotel* will change money in emergency. National Bank of Commerce is located off Rd to Dar es Salaam to S of town (follow the sign).

● Sport (participant)

Marine fishing can be arranged through ***Badeco Beach Hotel*** and they have plans to introduce a range of water sports.

● Sport (spectator)

Football matches at ground on road to Kaole, S of town.

● Shopping

There are some small general and pharmacy stores on School St. The covered market on Caravan St is excellent for fruit, vegetables, meat and dried fish. Fresh fish at fish market on Customs Rd. There is a curio stall wih crafts on sale at the ***Badeco Beach Hotel***. Sea shells can be bought by the Customs House.

● Religion

Churches: Holy Ghost Roman Catholic Mission N of town; small church on Pomji St in town. **Mosques**: India St N end of town; small mosque on George St, off Mangesani St.

● Useful addresses

Hospital: Bagamoyo District. T 8 Bagamoyo. Located on India St. **Post Office**: Customs Rd. **Police Station**: at intersection of Caravan St and Boma St at S end of town.

● Transport

Local Not a single taxi at present. All destinations in Bagamoyo are walkable. It is a good idea to hire someone (US$0.50) to carry any bags and being with a local person provides security.

Road is the only feasible mode at present. There are plans for a boat from Dar es Salaam which will avoid use of the poor road. There is sometimes a weekend shuttle from Dar es Salaam on the *Twiga* - check at the Msanani slipway. Buses leave from the bus stand opposite the covered market on Caravan St. To Dar es Salaam costs US$1 and takes 2 to 3 hrs.

Tanga

History

The African groups in the Tanga area, excluding those in the coastal belt, number six. The Pare who now inhabit the Pare Hills came originally from the Taveta area of Kenya in the 18th century. The Zigua inhabited the area to the S of Tanga and have a reputation for aggression and Bwana Hei attacked and defeated the force of the sultan of Zanzibar in 1882. The Nguu clan to the W occupy the Nguu hills and the Ruvu clan inhabit the Pangani islands. The Shambaa are around the Lushuto area and are closely allied with the Bondei who occupy the area between Tanga and Pangani. Both these groups have tended to be pushed inland by Swahili and Digo settlement at the coast. The Digo originated in Kenya but were forced S by expansion of their neighbours to inhabit the coastal strip between Tanga and the Kenyan border, forcing out the Bondei in their turn. The Segeju inhabit part of the coast between Tanga and Kenya. They originated in Kenya from a war party that was cut off by flooding of the Umba River which meets the sea at the border. They thus decided to settle in Digo country. In a rather touching display of male solidarity they decided to avoid any falling out over who should possess the only female in the party by killing her. As a result they have been forced to intermarry with the Digo and the Shirazi.

The coastal people are termed Swahili and are descendants of Africans and Arabs following Islam. Among the Arab immigrants are the Shirazi who are said to be originally from around Shirazi in Persia (now Iran) who came to the East African coast via Muscat in the 10th century. The Shirazis had a hierarchy of rule from the diwan, centred on Pangani, through Jumbes to Akidas. Tributes were extracted from most domestic events such as marriages and deaths. The role of the Akida was to organize the young men and they acted as headmen for caravans to the interior. With the gradual decline of the caravan trade, being an Akida in the area became little more than a sinecure entered into by paying fees to a Jumbe and extracting taxes from the populace.

European period Carl Peters and the German East Africa Company arrived in 1885 and in 1888 leased a 16-km wide strip from the sultan of Zanzibar along the entire coast of what is now Tanzania, from the Ruvuma River to the Umba River. The Germans appointed agents (calling them Akidas), though they were often not of the same tribe as the people they administered, to collect taxes and enforce law and order.

With the advent of European settlement and trade, Somalis arrived, trading in cattle but seldom intermarrying. Islanders from the Comoros also settled, but were generally difficult to distinguish in both appearance and speech from the Swahili.

Agriculture in the Usambara area expanded, see page 297, and with the construction of the railway to Moshi Tanga became a flourishing port. Tanga was the site of a substantial reversal for the British during WW1, see page 216. Allied troops, including 8,000 Indian soldiers found it difficult to disembark through the mangrove swamps and were repulsed by the well-organized German defence and some hostile swarms of bees that spread panic among the attackers. Over 800 were killed and 500 wounded, and the British

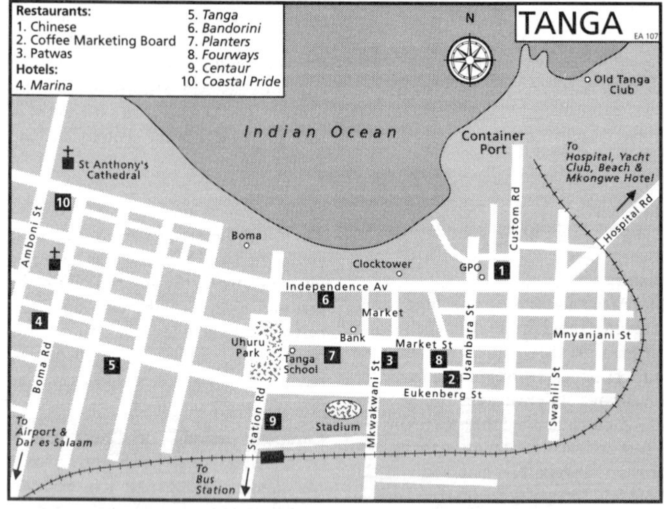

abandoned substantial quantities of arms and supplies on their withdrawal.

German settlers dwindled after this and were steadily replaced by Greek plantation owners. Tanga's prosperity declined with the collapse in sisal prices in the late 1950's and the large estates were nationalized in 1967. Some have now been privatized, and sisal has made a modest recovery.

Places of interest

Old Tanga The open space in the centre of town is Uhuru Park. It was originally Selous Square, named after the celebrated naturalist and hunter, see box, page 384. At the junction of the square with Eukenberg Street are the German buildings of **Tanga School**, see box, page 277, the first educational establishment for Africans.

On Marbot Street to the East of Uhuru Park is **Planters Hotel**. This once grand wooden building is now rather run-down, but is reputed to have seen wild times as Greek sisal plantation owners came into town for marathon gambling sessions at which whole estates sometimes changed hands.

Proceeding N across Independence Avenue leads to the Tanga Library, and to the W is the **Old Boma**, a substantial structure in typical style. Further to the W, in a location leading down to the shore is **St Anthony's Cathedral**, a school and various mission buildings.

Following Independence Avenue back towards the East is the **Clock Tower** and the old **Post Office**, the latter dating from the German period. Crossing over the railway line along Hospital Road to Ocean Drive to the S is Karimjee School and off to the left is the old Tanga Club of the British period.

Further E is the **Old Hospital**, another handsome German building, with newer hospital buildings beside.

The **Railway Station** is on Ring St. There are 2 railway offices nearby, and this group dates from the German era.

Amboni Caves These are natural limestone caves formed during the Jurassic Age some 150 million years ago, when reptiles were dominant on land. There are 10 caves, extending over a wide area, lying mostly underground, accessed through openings in the gorges of the

TANZANIA'S FIRST SCHOOL

Tanga school was established in 1892. It was initially run by the German Colonial Society, and the government took over responsibility in 1895. Paul Blank was the first headmaster, retiring in 1910. The German language, reading, and writing were taught in one large room and 3 different groups were taught, 7am to 8am adult 'coloured', 8am to 10am children, 4pm to 5.30pm houseboys.

In 1897 there were 86 enrolments, and the pupils began boarding, sleeping in bunk beds and cooking their own food. In 1899 the present buildings were started, with the pupils doing most of the construction, bringing coral from the beach for the walls. The school was now reorganised into a primary section with 4 years of schooling, a section training teachers, and a craft section. The best pupils were selected to go on to teacher training, and on graduating an assistant teacher started at 1 rupee a month (about US$3 in present-day values), rising yearly by a rupee to 5 rupees. On promotion to senior teacher the salary was 12 rupees with an extra 5 rupees if the teacher was in the band.

The craft element of the school expanded, covering carpentry, printing, book-binding, tailoring, blacksmithing, bricklaying, and masonry. In 1905 a secondary school was built, and the trade school became separate in 1907. By 1911, the staff comprised 4 Europeans, 3 craft instructors and 41 African teachers, and had begun to admit Indians.

Discipline, as typical of the period, was strict. Corporal punishment was common. On one occasion, when pupils complained of being forced to attend school against their will, they were punished for insolence with a week in chains.

The school closed with the outbreak of war in 1914. The British took over the band when they captured Tanga, and the school was reopened in 1920.

Mkilumizi River and the Sisi River. They form the most extensive cave system in East Africa, and there are chambers up to 13m high with stalactites and stalagmites. The location is of religious significance to local people, and offerings are made to ensure fertility in one of the shrines. A guide will escort you round the caves, illuminating the chamber with a burning torch.

The caves are 8 km to the N of Tanga on the road to Lunga Lunga at the Kenyan border. A taxi to the caves from town will cost about US$5 (ask the driver to wait). Alternatively you can take a bus or a dala dala for US$0.50. These are not frequent however.

Galamos Sulphur Springs These were discovered by a local Greek sisal planter, Christos Galamos. They are hot and sulphurous, and are said to relieve arthritis and cure skin ailments. A small spa was erected, but it has now fallen into disrepair. It is still possible to bathe in the springs, however. The springs are located close to Amboni Caves, see above, off the Tanga to Mombara Road.

Tongoni Ruins These ruins date from the Shirazi period and the Tongoni settlement was started at the end of the 10th century. The community would have been similar to that at Koale (see page 272), but almost certainly larger and predating it. It was to the W of the site of the ruins and only the traces of 2 wells remain. There are 40 tombs, some with pillars, and the remains of a substantial mosque. The mosque is of the type found along the N part of the East African coast. There is a central *musalla* (prayer room) with arches leading to aisles (*ribati*) at each side. The mosque is constructed of particularly finely dressed, close-grained coral, especially on the lintel of the *kiblah*, the side

The Legend Of The Shirazi Migration

Ali ben Sultan Hasan of Shiraz had a dream in AD 975 in which a rat with jaws of iron devoured the foundations of his house. He took this as a sign that his community was to be destroyed. The court in Shiraz ridiculed the notion but his immediate family and some other followers resolved to migrate. They set out in 7 dhows from the nearby port of Bushehr and sailed through the mouth of the Persian Gulf, into the Indian Ocean. There they were caught in a great storm and separated, making landfalls at 7 different points on the East African coast where they established settlements. Among these were Tongoni and Kilwa.

of the building which faces toward Mecca. The roofs were coral on mangrove rafters, and the deterioration of the rafters is responsible for their collapse.

There are depressions in the pillars where there were porcelain bowls, all apparently removed during the German period. It is said that Tongoni was founded by Ali ben Sultan Hasan at much about the same time as he established the settlement at Kilwa, see page 286. There are Persian inscriptions at Tongoni which would seem to establish a link with Shiraz.

The Tongoni ruins are 20 km S of Tanga on the road to Pangani about 1 km away. Buses or *dala dala* from Tanga cost about US$0.50 and will take up to 1 hr. A taxi will cost about US$12.

Excursions

By boat to nearby islands and Pangani can be arranged through *Banderini Hotel*.

Local information

● Where to stay

In town the ***Bandorini Hotel*** is recommended for value and efficient operation; the ***Baobab Beach Hotel*** for its location; the ***Planters Hotel*** and ***Tanga Hotel*** for their colonial atmosphere.

B ***Mkonge***, PO Box 1544, T 40711/44541, located about 1 km from the centre to the E along Hospital Rd which leads into Ocean Drive. It is set in what was designed as Amboni Park on grounds by the sea. It is based on Beach Memorial Hall which became the club for the sisal growers. It is sometimes known as the *Sisal (Mkonge) Hotel*, and there is a mosaic of a sisal plant on the floor of the foyer. It is rather run down. A/c. Bar. Restaurant. Disco at weekends. Swimming pool currently out of service. **B** ***Inn by the Sea***, PO Box 2188, T 3380/446213, located close to Mkonge on Ocean Drive.

C ***Baobab Beach***, PO Box 180, T 40162, F 40162, Tlx 45132. About 8 km from the centre going S to Pangani. A bus or *dala dala* can be taken to the turn-off, and the hotel is 3 km further toward the beach. A taxi will US$6. An outdoor bar. Reasonable restaurant. A/c. Water sports. The beach is a little disappointing. **C** ***Marina***, PO Box 835, T 44362. On junction of Boma Rd and Eukenberg St. Fairly new. Bar. Restaurant. A/c.

D ***Tanga***, PO Box 602, T 45857. On Eukenberg Rd at W end. Colonial-style. Rather dilapidated. Bar. Reasonable restaurant. Fans. **D** ***Bandorini***, located on Independence Ave nr the Old Boma. Small but very comfortable. Excellent value. Fans. **D** ***Planters***, T 2041. On Market St just E of Uhuru Park. Historic hotel from colonial era. Dilipidated. Extensive verandah overlooking street. Bar. Restaurant. Cold water only. **D** ***Fourways***, located at intersection of Market St and Guinea St. Recently constructed bar. Restaurant. **D** ***Centaur*** on Railway Rd S of Uhuru Park. Recently constructed. Bar. Restaurant. **D** ***Coastal Pride*** on corner of Independence Ave and Boma Rd. Fairly simple. Fans.

● Places to eat

♦♦***Chinese Restaurant*** on corner of Customs Rd and Independence Ave. As well as Chinese it serves international food. It is possible to eat outside in the garden. ♦♦***Planters Hotel***. Simple menu but reasonable value. ♦♦***Patwas Restaurant*** off Market St just S of market. Well-run, with a good Asian menu. ♦***Coffee Marketing Board*** on corner of Usambara Rd and Eukeberg Rd. Snacks and coffee (alas, instant). ♦***Market Restaurant***, Market St, behind market. Simple and cheap.

● **Bars**

The verandah at the ***Planters Hotel*** is recommended for atmosphere. The ***Yacht Club*** along Ocean Drive is a focus for the expatriate population.

● **Bank**

National Bank of Commerce is on Market St nr *Planters Hotel*.

● **Entertainment**

There are **discos** at the weekend at the *Mkonge Hotel*. Tanga has 4 **cinemas**, one in Ngamiani, the Swahili district about 1 km on the left along the Pangani Rd; one off Pangani Rd behind the station; one off Market St, nr Swahili St; and one off Usambara St and Market St. Do not have high expectations that they will be operating. *Marina Hotel* on Boma Rd shows **videos** in the bar.

● **Sport (participant)**

The **Golf Club** is along the main road running beside the railway as it heads W. **Sailing** at the Yacht Club on Ocean Drive. **Tennis** and **squash** at the Aga Khan Club which is behind the Aga Khan School off Swahili St, S of the railway line. Also at the Tanga Club off Ocean Drive. **Swimming** at Bathing Club on Ocean Drive before the Yacht Club, and at *Mkonge Hotel*, although the pool there is currently out of service. **Windsurfing** at *Baobab Beach Hotel*, 8 km S of Tanga.

● **Sport (spectator)**

The **soccer** stadium is on the intersection of Eukenberg St and Mlwakwani St. You will need to consult the *Daily News*, or a local enthusiast, for fixtures. **Cricket** at Aga Khan Club which is behind the Aga Khan School off Swahili St, S of the railway line.

● **Religion**

Churches: St Anthony's Cathedral W of the Old Boma; there is a Roman Catholic Church in Ngamiani. **Mosques**: the main mosque is off Independence Ave nr Uhuru Park, and there are 3 other mosques in Ngamiani. **Temple**: there is a temple off Ring St, nr Guinea St.

● **Useful addresses**

Library: Tanga library off Independence Ave nr the Old Boma. **Hospital**: on Ocean Drive to E of town centre. **Post Office**: on Independence Ave nr Msambara St. **Police Station**: off Independence Ave nr Tanga library.

● **Transport**

Local Taxis, buses and *dala dala* can be obtained in Uhuru Park. However, all of Tanga is walkable, although taxis are advisable after dark.

Train For **Dar es Salaam**, trains depart at 1930 on Mon, Wed, Fri, the trip takes 13 hrs, US$9 1st class; US$4 2nd; US$1.50 3rd. For **Moshi** trains leave at 1930 on Tue, Thu and Sat, take about 13 hrs, linking with the train from Dar to Moshi at Korogwe, US$9 1st; US$4 2nd; US$1.50 3rd.

Road Bus and *dala dala* leave from the bus stand for **Dar es Salaam** from 0800, the trip takes 4 to 6 hrs and a regular bus costs US$3 and a luxury one US$4. For **Moshi** the bus takes 4 to 6 hrs and costs US$4. To **Lunga Lunga** at the border with Kenya costs US$1, is slow as the road is poor and can take between 1 and 3 hrs. To **Pangani** buses take 1 to 3 hrs and cost US$1.

Sea Tanzanian Coastal Shipping line, a cargo service, runs boats up and down the coast which take passengers. However, they are irregular, slow, and you need to ask at the port. Other shipping companies (*Virgin Butterfly; Canadian Spirit; Sea Horse*) have operated services calling at Tanga at various times. Again, you will need to ask at the port. **Dhows** operate from Tanga. You will need to ask if any are sailing at the port. Routes to and from Tanga are not sailed that frequently.

Pangani

The town, on the N side of the river of the same name, has marvellous beaches and is a fine location for a quiet beach vacation. There are some fine old Arab houses, but these are in poor repair.

History

During the 19th century Pangani, situated at the mouth of the river, was a prosporous port. The community was ruled by an Arab Liwali, 5 Shirazi Jumbes and a network of Akidas. Indian traders financed parties under Akidas to collect ivory and rhinoceros horn in the interior, and there was some trading in slaves. The town prospered as the ivory and trade in slaves flourished. It was at Pangani that Bushiri, leader of the Arab revolt of 1888/89 was finally captured and executed, see page 265.

The mouth of the Pangani River is

crossed by a sand bar. This provided shelter for dhows, and prevented them being pursued by steam vessels when the slave trade was being suppressed after 1873. However it also meant that deeper draft vessels could not use the port, and traffic drifted steadily to the newer facilities at Tanga, subsequently accelerated by the rail line linking Tanga to Dar es Salaam and Moshi.

In 1930 the population was around 1,500, but the substantial houses on the N side of the river built, largely by slave labour, have fallen into disrepair. The economy of the town shifted to reliance on the sisal plantations, the Pangani being served by shallow draft steamers, but sisal declined drastically in price with the advent of synthetic fibres from the mid 1950's on. There are still many coco-palms and some fishing.

Places of interest

It is possible to hire a boat, through *Pamdeco Hotel*, to travel up the river, costing around US$4/hr, and it will take up to 10 people. There are crocodiles on the river and many birds.

Three islands can be visited and there is fishing and snorkelling, although the quality of the latter can be disappointing in the rainy seasons when the water is not clear. The islands are Marve Mdogo, Mwamba Marve and Mazivi. Boats can be arranged through *Pamdeco Hotel*. The fish factory has a boat that can be hired at US$7/hr.

Local information

● Where to stay

E *Pamdeco Beach*, located at the E end of the main street. Very simple. You need to give notice of meals required well in advance. Bar. **E** *Riverside Inn*, on the river between the bus stand and the ferry. Simple and cheap. **E** *Paradise Guest House*, nr bus stand. **E** *Udo Guest House*, close to ferry.

● Transport

Road is the only feasible transport, and then the only regular bus services are from Tanga. However there are several buses each day. They take between 1 to 3 hrs, depending on the season and cost US$1. There is a ferry to the S bank of the river, but no buses from the other side.

SOUTH COAST: MAFIA, KILWA, LINDI & MTWARA

CONTENTS

MAPS

The south coast receives few visitors due to its inaccessibility. However if you have the patience, or can go by plane, you will be well rewarded. Off the coast is the island of Mafia, which is a proposed marine park. It is an idyllic setting and a paradise for scuba divers and snorkellers. Further S is the town of Kilwa, with the small island of Kilwa Kisiwani just off the mainland. This is the location of the Kilwa ruins and although very remote the ruins make the trip worth the trouble. Further S still are the towns of Lindi and Mtwara. These are best known for being in the area where Makonde carvings are made. However they receive very few visitors due to their isolation.

Mafia Island

There are a number of attractions to Mafia Island which include historical remains, the deep sea fishing, and diving. The population of Mafia are mainly fishermen; the other industries are coconut palms and cashewnut trees. The plantations are those left over from those established by the Omanis. The coconut industry is particularly important and the largest coconut factory in East Africa is found on Mafia at Ngombeni Plantation. It produces copra (dried kernels), oil, coir yarn and cattle cake. However the poor soil has meant that the island has never been able to support a very large population.

History

The name Mafia is derived from an Arab word *morfieyeh* which means a group, and refers to the archipelago. There is evidence of foreign settlers on Mafia from as early as the 9th century. From the 12th to the 14th century it was an important settlement and the remains of a 13th century mosque have been found at Ras Kismani. By the 16th century when the Portuguese arrived it had lost much of its importance and was part of the territory ruled by the king of Kilwa. There is little left of the site of the settlement of the 12th to 14th century although old coins and pieces of pottery are still found occasionally particularly to the S of Kilindoni where the sea is eating away at the ruins. On the nearby island of Juani can be found extensive ruins of the town of Kua. The town dates back to the 18th century and the 5 mosques go back even further to the 14th century. In 1829 the town was sacked by Wasakalava cannibals from Madagascar who invaded, destroyed the town and dined on the inhabitants.

Evidence of Chinese visitors to the

Mafia Island group comes in the form of Chinese coins dating back to the 8th and 9th centuries which suggest that the Chinese were then trading with these islands.

It is thought that the Shirazi people from Persia may have settled on the islands of Juani and Jibondo for strategic reasons. In AD 975 Ali ben Sultan Hasan, see box, page 278, founded the sultanate of Kilwa and it is said that one of his sons, Bashat, settled in Mafia. The Shirazi, under Bashat, found the native Mwera people were settled on the islands – they also inhabited a large stretch of mainland and other islands of the coast. It is thought that the Mwera intermarried with the Shirazi. It was around this time that Islam reached Kilwa and no doubt then spread to these islands. There are believed to be some remains dating from the Shirazi period, including that of a mosque, on Jibondo Island. The Shirazi's influence was at its greatest from the 11th to the 13th centuries and from their headquarters at Kilwa they dominated the coast. Their main income was from gold from inland, and they also commanded huge customs duties on all goods that passed through Kilwa.

The town of Kisimani Mafia is thought to have been founded during the period of Shirazi and Arab domination. There were some suggestions that Kua also dated from this period but it is now believed that most of these remains are more recent, with just a few dating back further. Kisimani Mafia lies on the W tip of Mafia overlooking the delta. Kua is located on Juani, a much smaller and less hospitable island – very hot with a poor water supply. It is thought possible that some Shirazis from Kisimani Mafia were driven out of the town by Arabs and founded Kua where they would be left alone. The ruins of Kisimani are being eaten away by the sea; the larger part of the town has already been engulfed. However one observer has suggested that the size of the town has been exaggerated and the story that much of the town lies under the sea derives from the rather curious coral reef and ridge in this sea which could have been mistaken for the remains of a town.

The Portuguese arrived at the end of the 15th century. At this time the island was under the control of Kilwa. In Apr 1498 Vasco da Gama sighted the island of Mafia as he sailed on his first journey towards Mombasa. Portugal's influence spread quickly and during the 16th century a number of visits were made to Mafia and revenues were collected. However it was a period when expeditions were fitful – they would be launched to collect revenue and were then followed by years of neglect. In 1635 a Portuguese commandant,subordinate to the Governor of Mozambique, was stationed here and a small fort was erected on the E side of the island with a garrison about 10 to 15 men. This fort is thought to have been at Kirongwe although no trace of it has been found.

The islands of Chole and Juani had to make payments to passing Portuguese ships in the form of coconut fibre and gum copal. The population of the islands was believed to have been concentrated on the island of Jibono and at Kua on Juani as at some stage (the date is not known) the town of Kisimani had been destroyed. The islands seem to have been used as a port of call for repairs to ships as well as a kind of safe haven when there were troubles on the mainland as, for example, in 1570 when Kilwa was invaded by the Zimba people and about 1,000 Arabs are thought to have been killed and eaten.

At the beginning of the 17th century the grip of the Portuguese was loosening and by 1697 Portugal had lost control of her East African posts, except for Mozambique. This was followed by a difficult period for the inhabitants of the islands with pirates active in the seas around Mafia. The next major event in Mafia's history was an invasion from Madagascar by war canoes. The exact date that this occurred is not known although it is thought to have been during the time of Sultan Said, between 1810 and 1835. According to tradition, the Wasakalava came from Madagascar in 80 canoes each with 4 men. They sacked Kua and all those who did not escape were killed or carried off as slaves. At this time Kua was the chief town on Mafia and the population was believed to have been large. The news of the raid was sent to Zanzibar and an expedition was sent by the sultan to chase the invaders. The sultan's troops found the raiders on a small island nearby and they were taken as prisoners back to Mafia. Kua however was never rebuilt and instead Chole Island, which had until then been home only to a slave population, became the seat of the sultan's government.

The influence of the Omani Arabs grew although it is not known exactly when the Arabs settled on the Mafia islands. It was not until 1840 after the sultan moved their headquarters from Muscat to Zanzibar that his control over the coast reached its zenith. By 1846 he had established garrisons up and down the coast and there is little doubt that his influence on the Mafia group was considerable. Trade grew enormously and Mafia took part in this with gum copal trees being planted in large numbers. The islands were ruled by a series of governors called Liwalis appointed by the sultan of Zanzibar and after the sacking of Kua the government was moved to Chole. Chole Island is less than 1 sq km and many of the influential Arabs built houses on the island so that about half the island was covered. It has been noticed that at least one of these Liwalis had a eye for orderly town planning for many of the streets ran parallel to one another. This was unusual for Arab towns on the East African coast and comparisons with the narrow and windy streets of other towns show that this was clearly a conspicuous exception.

From the beginning of the 19th century traders from all over the world had been plying these coastal waters. 'Americani' cloth proved itself to be perhaps the most popular of all the traded goods amongst the resident population. The trading of goods and of slaves was soon to be followed by the interest of European politics. However it was not until the end of the century that this affected territorial rights. Under the Treaty of 1890, Mafia, Zanzibar and Pemba were initially allotted to the British sphere. However it was later agreed that Mafia

The Legend Of Ras Kismani

The town of Ras Kismani was originally settled by the Wasakalava from Madagascar. The townspeople built a large ship, and when it was completed they invited the local people of Kua to a feast. During the celebrations, the Wasakalava seized several children and laid them on the sand in the path of the ship as it was launched.

The Kua people planned revenge at their leisure. Seven or eight years later they invited the Wasakalava of Ras Kismani to attend a wedding at Kua. The celebrations were in a special room beneath a house. Gradually the hosts left, one by one, until only an old man was left to entertain the guests. As he did so, the door was quietly bricked up, and the bodies remain to this day. A message was sent to the head man at Ras Kismani that the account was now squared. Within a month, Ras Kismani was engulfed by the sea.

should go to Germany in exchange for Germany renouncing her claims on Stephenson Road which was between Lake Nyasa and Tanganyika. The island was therefore included in the purchase of the coastal strip from Sultan Seyyid Ali and the German flag was raised in 1890.

The Germans established a headquarters at Chole and in 1892 a resident officer was posted here together with a detachment of Sudanese troops. A large 2-storey boma was constructed with various other buildings such as a gaol. The site seemed ideal with good anchorage for dhows, but with the opening of a regular coastal steamship service a deeper harbour was needed and the headquarters were moved to Kilindoni in 1913.

During WW1 it became clear that Mafia represented an extremely useful base from which attacks could be launched. In particular the British needed a base from which to attack the *SS Königsberg* which was wrecking havoc on her fleet up and down the East African coast. In Jan 1915 a British expeditionary force under Colonel Ward landed on the island at Kisimani and the islands were captured with little resistance. A garrison of about 200 troops remained on the island.

The *Königsberg* had been damaged and gone into the mouth of the River Rufiji for repairs. This delta, with its many creeks and maze of streams proved the perfect hiding place. It was important to the British find and destroy it before any further damage could be done. In 1915 a British war plane was assembled on Mafia and took off from there. It spotted the ship, and boats went into the delta to destroy it. It was the first example of aerial reconnassance being used in warfare. A description by a local man of the intense activity of the British fleet at the time was that the search lights 'turned night into day'. The hulk of the crippled boat could be seen until 1979 when it finally sank into the mud out of sight.

For a short period the islands were under military rule, and were later administered under Zanzibar. In 1922 the islands were handed over by the government of Zanzibar to become part of the Tanganyika Territory under the United Nations Mandate.

Places of interest

Ruins at Kua Kua is on Juani Island to the S of Mafia Island. The remains are located on the W side of the island of Juani. The ruins cover a large area of about 14 ha. In 1955, when the site was cleared of bush, one observer stated that$he believed that these ruins were 'potentially the Pompeii of East Africa'.

The remains however need much work on them for them to be brought up to anything like this standard. There are several houses, one of which was clearly double-storeyed. Beneath the stairs leading to the upper level is a small room in which slaves could be confined for punishment. Under the building is the *haman* (bathroom), with a vaulted ceiling of curved coral blocks. A soil pipe runs from the remains of an upper room to a pit below. Two mosques and a series of tombs, some with pillars are nearby. The evidence suggests that the town did not have a protecting wall and that the inhabitants were mainly involved in agricultural pursuits on the island rather than in sea-trading.

Kua was famous for the supposed curative properties of milk obtained there. There is a cave on the island formed by the action of the sea. The water streaming out of the cave as the tide turns is reputed to cure *baridi yabis* ('cold stiffness' – rheumatism) and other ailments. The cure is not effective, however, unless the hereditary custodian of the cave is paid a fee and the spirits of the cave appeased by an offering of honey, dates or sugar. Local fishermen will take you to Kua for US$1.

Activities

Deep sea diving Many people will come here to experience some of the best deep sea diving in Tanzania. There is something here for everyone from the most experienced diver to those who want to snorkel in the shallower pools. The coral gardens off Mafia are marvellous – wonderfully vivid fish, shells, sponges, sea cucumber and spectacular coral reefs. Two of the most beautiful reefs are the Okuto and Tutia reefs around Juani and Jibondo Islands a short distance from Chole Bay. About 1 km off Mafia's coastline there is a 200m deep contour along the seabed of the Indian ocean. This depth contributes to

The Mermaids Of The Rufiji Delta

Around the island of Mafia and the Rufiji Delta lives an animal called the dugong (known in Swahili as the *nguva*) and it is this sea living creature that is believed to have given rise to the story of mermaids. The animal is now threatened with extinction but not many years ago they were reasonably common in these waters. One observer reported seeing 7 being landed in the time that he was stationed at Mafia – a period of under 2 years.

Looking at a specimen of these animals it may be wondered how the story of a beautiful half-woman, half-fish came into being. The animals have a large tail measuring up to 1m across and in total they measure up to 3m long. They are rather walrus or seal-like although their heads are larger – not at all like that of a beautiful woman. However these animals do display a certain human posture when feeding their young. The female supports the young with her flippers, and treading water she raises her head and teats above the water. Also the tail is very mermaid-like particularly when they dive down into the water and it can be seen most clearly.

The dugongs live in the sea grass that is found in deltas such as the Rufiji and its habitat is restricted to places where it can browse without fear from sharks and other predators. It is entirely herbivorous and defenceless, and not being an agile swimmer, is extremely vulnerable. Sadly this vulnerability has been the dugong's downfall for its population has suffered at the hands of hunters and its survival is now threatened. The nearest relative to the dugong is the freshwater manatee.

the wide variety of sea life. Mafia Lodge will provide equipment, but the quality is variable and you may prefer to bring your own.

There is a proposal that Mafia should become a marine park. This has been under discussion for some time now and implementation is imminent. The aim would be to create a series of zones around the island providing areas with differing levels of protection, whilst not ruining local fishermen's livelihoods. The preliminary scientific study for this is currently being carried out by Frontier Tanzania manned almost entirely by volunteers in collaboration with the University of Dar es Salaam. The World Fund for Nature has also become involved and if the model is successful it will be used in other marine parks around the country.

Fishing This is at its best from Sept-Mar when the currents and the NE monsoon (*kaskazi*) mean that there is an enormous variety of fish. When the S monsoon (*kusi*) blows during the rest of the year fishing can be rather sparse. Some of the 'big game' fish that can be caught in the area include marlin, shark, kingfish, barracuda and red snapper. There is a fishing club where there are records kept of some of the record catches. Mafia Island, and some of the uninhabited islands around, are also a breeding site of the green turtle. Sadly you would be very lucky to see these as they are now close to extinction as a result of man's activities – being killed both as adults for their meat and as eggs. Another threatened species is the dugong which lives in sea grass such as that found between Mafia and the Rufiji delta, giving rise to the legend of the mermaid, see box, page 285. This strange beast is protected by law, but hunting continues.

Local information

● Where to stay

B *Mafia Island Lodge*, PO Box 2, Mafia, or PO Box 2485, Dar es Salaam, T 23491, Tlx 41061. 30 rooms. A/c. Bar. Restaurant. Water sports. Lovely setting overlooking Chole Bay. Currently being refurbisheded. **D** *Lizu*. Restaurant. Bar. Simple and tidy. Fans. Disco at weekends. Can be rather noisy when the disco operates.

● Transport

Air **Air Tanzania**, PO Box 543, ATC Building Ohio St, Dar es Salaam, T 46644/5 46643, Tlx 42137, is scheduled to fly into Mafia once a week taking 45 mins. However, the flight is often cancelled – check at the Ohio St office. **Aviators Services**, T 6386 Arusha or C/O Scantan Tours, PO Box 1054, T 8170, fly from Dar es Salaam to Mafia at 1100 on Tue, Wed, Fri, Sun, and return the same day at 1200. The fare is US$40 one way.

The airport is about 20 km from *Mafia Lodge* and a Lodge vehicle will collect you – they charge US$10 if you are not staying at the Lodge. There are no taxis on the island – indeed there are few vehicles of any sort.

Sea The crossing from Dar es Salaam to Mafia can be rough, and sea-sickness pills are strongly recommended. **Tanzania Coastal Shipping Line**, PO Box 9461, Dar es Salaam, T 26192, Tlx 41532, operate a service of sorts, but is infrequent and unreliable. **Canadian Spirit** stops at Mafia Island once a week on its way to Mtwara from Dar es Salaam. Scheduled to leave Mafia on Thu for Mtwara, and on Fri for Dar es Salaam, although these schedules change. Fare to Mafia is about US$10 1st class and US$7 2nd, and takes about 6 hrs. **Dhows** can be taken from the dhow harbour in Dar es Salaam. They depart irregularly but there are usually 2-3 a week. A motorised dhow takes 12 hrs, and a sailing dhow up to 24 hrs. Passengers sit and sleep on the cargo. You need to take your own food and drink. Costs US$3 to US$6.

Kilwa

Kilwa is a group of 3 settlements, and it is of exceptional historical interest. Kilwa grew up as a gold trade terminus and when its fortunes faded some magnificent ruins were left behind. These are said to be some of the most spectacular on the East African coast. The town is divided between Kilwa Kisiwani (Kilwa on the Island), 2 km offshore; Kilwa Kivinje (Kilwa of the Casuarina Trees) on the mainland; and Kilwa Masoko (Kilwa of the Market) which was

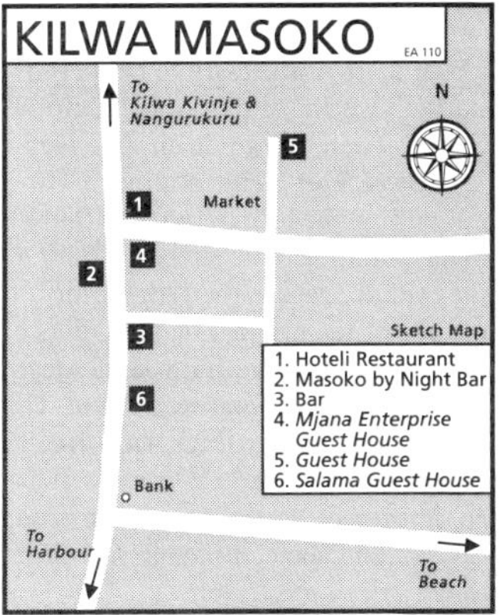

built as an administrative centre on a peninsula, and which is the site of the main present-day town.

History

Kilwa Kisiwani contains the ruins of a 13th century city of the Shirazi civilization which are well preserved and documented. The town was founded at the end of the 10th century by Shirazis, see box, page 278, and flourished with the core of commercial activity based on the trade of gold from Sofala (in present-day Mozambique). It grew to be the largest town on the S coast and prospered to the extent that Kilwa could maintain an independent status with its own sultan and its own coinage.

The large stone town that grew up thrived and the architecture was striking. The largest pre-European building in Equatorial Africa was located here – the Husuni Kubwa. However Kilwa's fortunes were reversed in the 14th century. Vasco da Gama was said to have been impressed by the buildings of Kilwa and in 1505 a large Portuguese fleet arrived and took the town by force. Their aim was to take control of the Sofala gold trade and they did this by erecting a garrison and establishing a trading post in the town from where they set up a gold trade link with the interior. Without the gold trade the Shirazi merchants were left with little to keep the wealth growing and the town quickly went into decline. Having taken over the

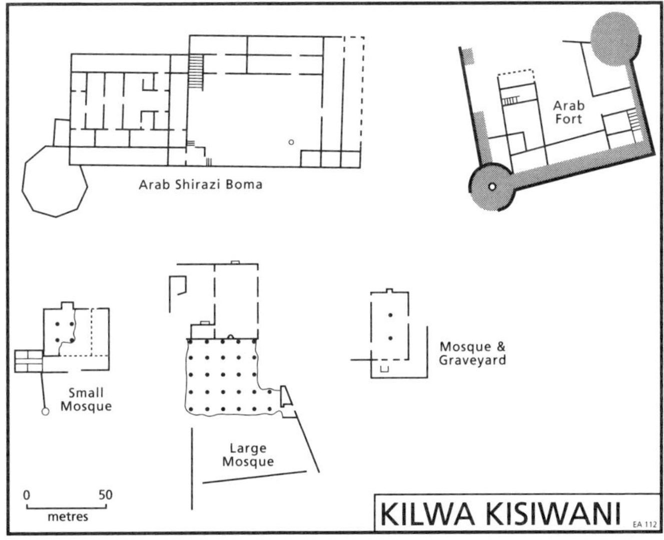

gold trade, and thus triggered off the decline of the town, the Portuguese decided there was little point in staying in Kilwa, an outpost which was expensive to maintain. They therefore withdrew from Kilwa and continued the gold trade from further afield.

Deprived of the main source of income, the town continued to decline. In 1589 disaster struck when a tribe from nearby called the Zimba attacked the town, killing and eating many of the inhabitants. In the 17th century, with the arrival of the Oman Arabs, Kilwa began to revive and many of the buildings were taken over by the sultans as palaces. The slave trade, see page 213, made a significant impact on this area and Kilwa Kivinje on the mainland flourished from the caravan route from the interior which terminated at the port.

Places of interest

Kilwa Kisiwani This demands at least half a day. Small dhows in the harbour at Kilwa Masoko will take you across the 2 km channel for US$5. The Cultural Centre will organize a half day boat trip for US$10, and the boat will take up to 6 people. It is necessary to get permission to visit the site from the Cultural Centre. There is a guide on the island.

Gereza Fort The original Gereza was built in the 14th century but the one that is standing there today was built by the Omani Arabs in the 19th century on the site of the original on the orders of the imam of Muscat. It is a large square building built of coral set in lime. The walls are incredibly thick with circular towers at the NE and SW corners. It has an impressive entrance of fine wood carving and some, although not all, of the inscription is legible.

Great Mosque (Fri Mosque) This mosque is said to have been built in the 12th century and is probably the largest of this period on the E coast. It was excavated between 1958 and 1960 and parts of it have been reconstructed. The oldest parts that remain are outer sections of the side walls and the N wall. The façade of the *mihrab* (the aspect that points towards Mecca) is dated from around 1300. The domed chamber was supposed to have been the sultan's prayer room. The water tanks and the

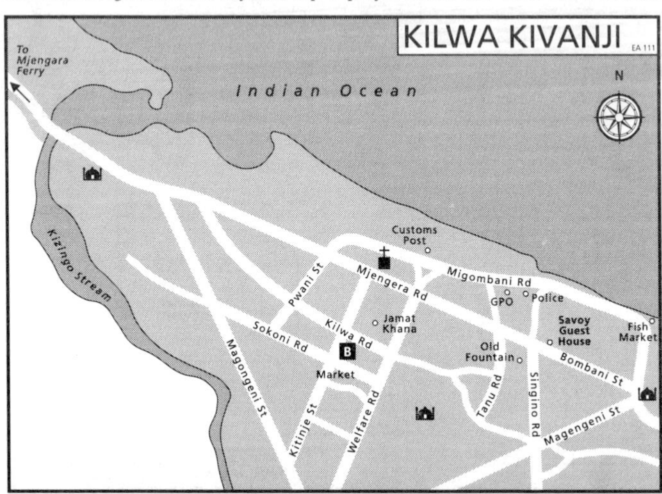

slabs of stone were for rubbing clean the soles of the feet before entering the mosque.

Great House A large one-storey building is said to have been the residence of the Sultan and the remains of one of the sultans are said to reside in one of the 4 graves found within its walls. The building is an illustration of the highly developed state of building and architectural skills in this period with examples of courtyards, reception rooms, an amphitheatre which is unique to this part of the world, latrines, kitchens and cylindrical clay ovens.

Small Domed Mosque This is without a doubt the best preserved of all the buildings in Kilwa. It is an ornamental building with beautiful domes located about 150m SW of the Great House. The long narrow room on its E side is thought to once have been a Koran school.

House of Portico Little remains of this once large building. There are portico steps on 3 of its sides from where it gets its name and its doorway has a decorated stone frame.

Makutini Palace (Palace of Great Walls) This large fortified building is believed to date from the 15th century. It is to the W of the Small Domed Mosque and is shaped in roughly a triangle. Its longest wall that ran along the coast is in ruins. Within the complex is the grave of one of the sultans.

Jangwani Mosque The ruins of this stone building are concealed under a series of mounds to the SE of the Makutini Palace. This mosque was unique for having ablution water jars set into the walls just inside the main entrance.

Malindi Mosque This Mosque to the E of the Gereza Fort was said to have been built and used by migrants from Malindi on the Kenya coast.

Husuni Kubwa This building is said to be the largest pre-European building in Equatorial Africa. It is located between 1-2 km to the E of the main collection of ruins on top of a steep cliff. It is certainly an exceptional building with over 100 rooms and a large conical dome that reaches about 30m above the ground.

Husuni Ndogo This is a smaller version of Husuni Kubwa and they are separated by a small gully. It is said to have been built in the 15th century with walls 1m thick and towers in the corners.

Excursion to Kilwa Kivinje

This is 29 km N of Kilwa Masoko and can be reached by *dala dala*, heading for Manguruturu, costing about US$1. There are half-a-dozen or so each day.

There is a handsome old boma on the shore which dates from the German period as does the covered market. Several fine houses stand along the main street, but are rather dilapidated. There is an old mosque in the centre, and to the E of the town is a cemetery with tombs and pillars.

• **Where to stay E** *Savoy Guest House*, located nr the Old Boma in Kilwa Kivinje. Fans. Simple and adequate.

Songomonanara and islands

There is a group of islands to the S of Kilwa Kiswani. It is necessary to hire a motorised dhow in Kilwa Masoko to get there, and it will cost US$20 for up to 6 people.

The ruined buildings at Songomonanara are exceptional. The settlement is surrounded by the remains of a wall. The main mosque is distinguished by stonework in a herringbone pattern and there is a double row of unusually high arches at one end.

The Sultan's Palace is extensive, with high walls, and it was evidently at least 2-storeys high. The doorways, faced with slender stonework, are particularly fine.

The building to the E of the palace has a room with a vaulted roof and porcelain bowls are set in the stonework. There are 3 other smaller mosques, 2 of which abut the surrounding wall. Some of the other ruins leave little to be distinguished, although rectangular windows and door

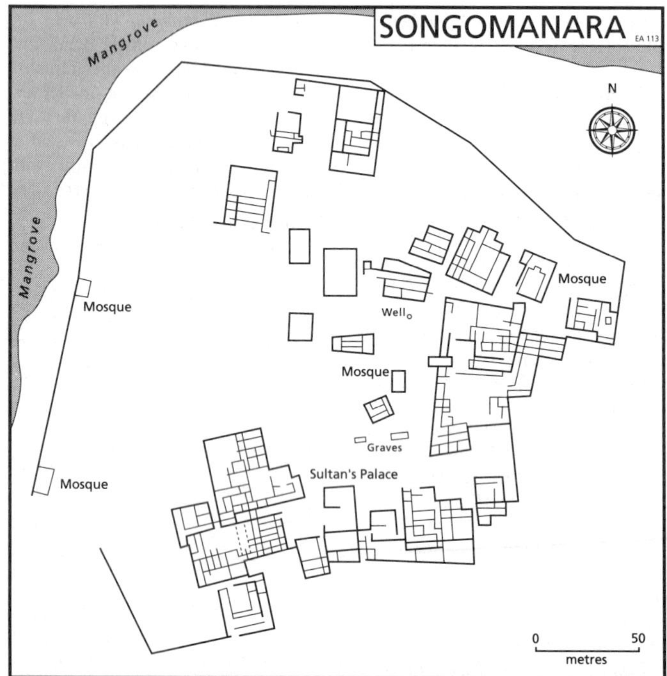

frames are a feature of the group. Fragments of porcelain and earthenware abound, and some relics have been identified as Egyptian dating from the 14th and 15th centuries.

About 3 km S of Songo Mnara is **Sanje Majoma Island** also containing the ruins of a number of once beautiful houses, complete with courtyards and stone arches. **Sanje ya Kati** is another nearby island which was once settled by the Shanga people who are now extinct. In the 13th century they were considered a force to be reckoned with and they resisted foreign control.

Local information

● Where to stay and eat

E *Mjana Guest House*, located on right of road which leads from main Mangurukivu Rd to the market. Fans. Only single rooms. Clean and tidy. **E** *Salama Guest House*, on road from Milwa Kirinje and Mangurukuru. Fans. Double rooms available. Restaurant. Bar. ♦*Masoko by Night*. Charcoal grilled chicken (kuku) and beef (mishkaki).

● Transport

Air **Air Tanzania**, PO Box 543, Ohio St, Dar es Salaam, T 46643 44111, Tlx 42137, has had a flight once a week to Kilwa Masoko, but it appears to have been discontinued. The fare is around US$100 one-way, US$40 for residents. A charter is a possibility, particularly if you are a party, see Air Charter operators in Dar es Salaam section, page 256.

Road Buses direct to Kilwa from **Dar es Salaam** leave from Kariakoo, Msimbazi St at 0500, take 13 hrs and cost US$6 Confirm exact departure time and book a ticket the day before you travel. Return from Kilwa at 0500 daily. Buses depart for **Mtwara** and **Lindi** from the Kisutu bus stand on Morogoro Rd in Dar es Salaam. They leave at 0400 and cost US$6.

There is a simple guest house in Nangurukuru if you arrive late. It is necessary to disembark at Nangurukuru and take a *dala dala* to Kilwa Masoko – you might have to wait up to an hour for one to arrive and fill up.

Sea This stretch of ocean can be rough – travel sickness tablets are recommended. **Tanzania Coastal Shipping Line**, PO Box 9461, T 25192, Tlx 41532, and **Shipping Corporation of Zanzibar**, PO Box 80, Zanzibar, T 30300 30749, Tlx 57215, run irregular freighters taking passengers. Enquire at port in Dar es Salaam or Zanzibar. **Canadian Spirit** from Dar es Salaam has sailings, at one time regularly once a week to Mtwara (connect to Kilwa by bus), and costs US$15 1st Class and US$10 2nd Class. Trip takes 24 hrs. Confirm departure times and days at port in Dar es Salaam.

It is possible to get a **dhow** from Dar es Salaam, but it is a matter of going to the dhow anchorage every day and asking about departure. You may need to go via Mafia. A motorised dhow will take 24 hrs and a sailing dhow 48 hrs. Costs US$6 to US$12. Sleep on the cargo and take your own food and drink.

Lindi

This is a town of around 40,000 inhibitants. Poor communications, and the collapse of the Ground Nut Scheme (see page 220), one site for which was at nearby Nachingwea have hampered development. Initial settlement was by Shirazi migrants, see page 278. It was a destination for slave caravans from the interior in the 19th century, being the

main seaport for Lake Nyasa. The Germans chose Lindi as the administrative headquarters of the S district, and a custom house and store for the German East African Company were constructed close to the fort which dates from the Arab period. These, and other buildings of the colonial period, are now very dilapidated.

The beach is excellent and it is possible to take a ferry across the bay to the village on the far side. You can stay here very cheaply.

● **Where to stay E** *South Honour Guest House*, Amani St, 3 blocks back from the ferry. Fans. Nets. Simple, with agreeable staff. **E** *Town Guest House*, junction of Eilat St and Makonde St, 5 blocks in from the shore. Fans. Nets. Clean and simple. **E** *City Guest House*, corner of Msonobar St and Amani St, 3 blocks in from the ferry. Fans. Rather basic. **E** *Coast Guest House*, about 500m N of ferry on beach. Fans. **E** *Lindi Beach Hotel*, just S of ferry on beach. Fans. Rather run down.

● **Restaurants & bars** All of the hotels have restaurants, and there are snack bars round the bus station. Fresh fruit can be purchased at the market on Jamhuri St. ♦♦*National Bank of Commerce (NBC) Club*, pleasant location on beach. Charges entrance fee for non-members (US$0.50). Fairly simple meals. ♦*Paris Restaurant*, Mobet Ave one block toward the beach from the market. Simple grills and chips. ♦*K's Cold Drinks*, Eilat Rd, 3 blocks in from the beach. Cheap meals.

● **Transport Air** Air Tanzania, PO Box 543, Ohio St, Dar es Salaam, T 46643/44111, Tlx 42137, has had a flight once a week which has touched down at Lindi, but it appears to have been discontinued. The fare is around US$100 one-way, US$40 for residents. A charter is a possibility, particularly if you are a party – see Air Charter operators in Dar es Salaam section, see page 256. Alternatively fly to Mtwara and connect by road.

Road Really the only feasible way unless you have time to wait for boats, or wish to charter a plane. Buses leaves from Kisutu bus stand on Morongoro Rd in **Dar es Salaam** at 0500, take 18 hrs and cost US$8. Bus to Dar es Salaam leaves at 0500 from bus stand on Makongaro Rd. To **Mtwara** buses run fairly frequently and cost US$1. A bus for **Newala** arrives at midday, takes about 6 hrs and costs US$2. To travel to **Masasi** you need to make a connection with the bus from Lindi at Mingoyo – it will be crowded, they will squeeze you on, you have to stand, and it costs US$4.

Sea Tanzania Coastal Shipping Line, PO Box 9461, T 25192, Tlx 41532, and **Shipping Corporation of Zanzibar**, PO Box 80, Zanzibar, T 30300 30749, Tlx 57215 run irregular freighters taking passengers. Enquire at port in Dar es Salaam or Zanzibar. **Canadian Spirit** from Dar es Salaam has sailings, at one time regularly once a week to Mtwara (connect to Lindi by bus), and costs US$15 1st Class and US$10 2nd Class. Trip takes 24 hrs. Confirm departure times and days at port in Dar es Salaam. It is possible to get a **dhow** from Dar es Salaam, but it is a matter of going to the dhow anchorage every day and asking about departure. You may need to go via Mafia. A motorised dhow will take 24 hrs and a sailing dhow 48 hrs. Costs US$6 to US$12. Sleep on the cargo and take your own food and drink.

Mtwara

Mtwara is a sizeable town of around 80,000. It was largely by-passed by the Shirazi settlers. German administration was centred on Lindi, and Mtwara came to prominence during the British period. Mtwara has been a centre for agricultural processing, and there is a factory for shelling and canning the cashew nuts that are grown extensively in the SE. The town itself is set a little way from the shore. There are some good beaches, but they are about 2 km from the town centre. Even the better priced hotels are good value for a beach vacation.

● **Where to stay B** *Mtwara Beach*, located on beach 2 km out of town to the N. Restaurant. Bar. Recently renovated.

D *Shangari Club Beach*, location 2 km N of town. Good restaurant. Bar.

E *Tanzania Cashew Marketing Board (TCMB) Club*, close to beach, 2 km N of town. Originally the Cashew Association of Tanganyika (CATA) Club for the growers in the colonial period and still known as the CATA Club. Restaurant. Bar. Fans. Nets. Good value and a comfortable atmosphere. **E** *National Bank of Commerce (NCB) Club*, on corner of Tanu Rd

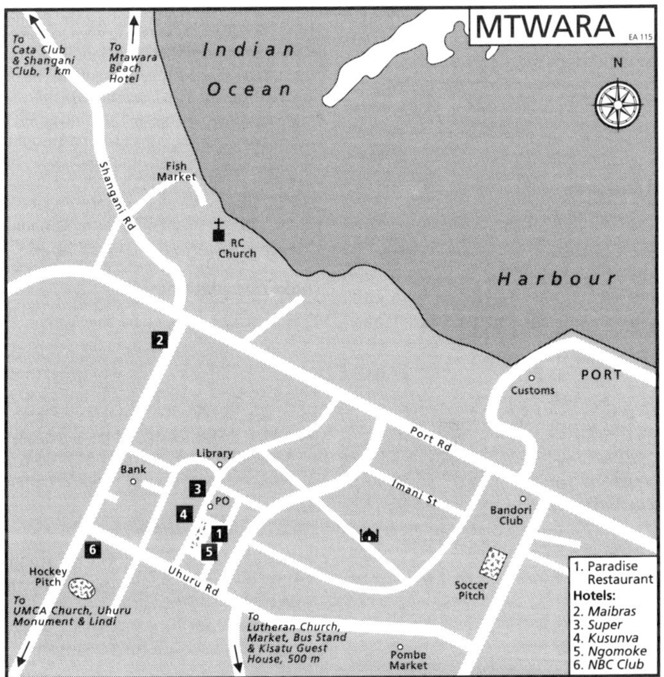

and Uhuru Rd in town centre. Restaurant. Bar. Fans. Nets. Good value, used by travelling government officials and often full. Pleasant beer garden. **E** *Kisutu Guest House*, located 1 km S of town centre, nr market and bus station. Fans. Nets. Simple. **E** *Maibras Guest House*, about 500m N of town on the way to the beach. Rather basic. **E** *Ngomeke Guest House*, in centre of town on Bazaa St. Fairly simple. **E** *Kusunva Guest House*, town centre just off Aga Khan Park. Simple fare. **E** *Super Guest House*, town centre opposite post office. Rather basic.

• **Restaurants and bars** ♦♦*Shangani Club* on the the beach is recommended. ♦♦*Mtwara Beach Hotel*, on beach, is reasonable. ♦*Paradise*, in town centre just off Aga Khan Park is cheap and good value.

• **Transport Air** **Air Tanzania**, PO Box 543, Ohio St, Dar es Salaam, T 46643 44111, Tlx 42137, has had a flight once a week. The fare is around US$100 one-way, US$40 for residents. A charter is a possibility, particularly if you are a party – see Air Charter operators in Dar es Salaam section, page 256.

Road From **Dar es Salaam** buses leave from Kisutu bus stand on Morogoro Rd at 0500, take pretty much 24 hrs and cost US$8. Buses leave for Dar at 0500 from the bus stand on Market St. Book ticket day before and confirm departure time. Buses to **Masasi** leave fairly frequently, cost US$4. Regular buses to **Lindi** which cost US$1.

Sea This stretch of ocean can be rough – travel sickness tablets are recommended. **Tanzania Coastal Shipping Line**, PO Box 9461, T 25192, Tlx 41532, and **Shipping Corporation of Zanzibar**, PO Box 80, Zanzibar, T 30300/30749, Tlx 57215 run irregular freighters taking passengers. Enquire at port in Dar es Salaam or Zanzibar. **Canadian Spirit** from Dar es Salaam has sailings, at one time regularly once a week, and costs US$15 1st Class and US$10 2nd Class. Trip takes 24 hrs. Confirm departure times and days at port in Dar es

Salaam. It is possible to get a **dhow** from Dar es Salaam, but it is a matter of going to the dhow anchorage every day and asking about departure. You may need to go via Mafia. A motorised dhow will take 24 hrs and a sailing dhow 48 hrs. Costs US$6 to US$12. Sleep on the cargo and take your own food and drink.

Mikindani

This is a small village 11 km to the W of Mtwara on the Mtwara to Lindi road. The beaches are excellent. There are several fine 2-storey town houses in Arab style with elaborate fretwork balconies. There is an old slave market and a fort dating from the German period. Mikindani was the port from which Livingstone departed on his final journey to the interior in 1867, see page 215. *Dala dala* from Mtwara to Lindi will take you for US$0.50. A taxi will cost US$15 for the return trip. A new hotel is due to have started operation at Mitengo Beach, and is expected to be in the B price range.

Makonde plateau

This area is occupied by the Makonde

Lip Plugs

About 40 years ago it was fairly common to see elderly women wearing lip plugs amongst the people of S Tanzania. Lip plugs were worn by a variety of ethnic groups and principally amongst tribes that had originated from what is now Mozambique. The tribes that wore the lip plug most commonly included the Makonde, Mwera, Mukua, Mawiha and Metu.

The procedure that was necessary for the wearing of a lip plug began when a girl was just 5 or 6. One of the older women in the tribe would pierce the girl's upper lip using a thorn and would then thread a blade of grass into it. Three days later another blade of grass would be inserted this time a little larger. This would be repeated about 3 times until a millet stalk about the thickness of the little finger would be inserted. A week later a second thicker stalk would be inserted and would be left in place for about a month. By this time the lip would have healed and from then on a series of lip plugs would be inserted each just a little wider in diameter than the last so that the upper lip would gradually be stretched. The first 3 plugs usually have a circumference of about 50 mm. The first plug was worn for about 2 months and the second for about 4 months. When the third plug was inserted a number of markings would be cut into the girl's face – usually about 3 vertical lines each side of the eyes. When the girl reached puberty a plug of about 125 mm in circumference would be used and kept in place until the birth of her second child when it would be replaced by a larger one. In Makonde plugs of about 100 mm in diameter were fairly common.

The plugs were mostly made of ebony. They would be hollowed out and often were highly polished. The plugs would be prepared by the older men of the tribe. The wearer of the plug could not remove it at any time in public – in fact it would only have been taken out to be washed. There was also the much rarer practice of having a lip plug in the lower lip. The practice of wearing a lip plug caused problems as the pressure of the plug displaced and distorted the teeth.

The origin of the lip plug is not clear and there are a number of different suggestions. One is that they were introduced to stop the women being taken away as slaves in the slave-raiding days. However others suggest that lip plugs were in use long before the slave trade and they were originally used as an ornament. No special rights were associated with the wearing of a plug and there was no religious significance attached to them.

people. They have 3 claims to distinction. The first is the exceptional ebony carvings with groups of exaggerated figures, the traditional work related to fertility, and good fortune. The second is their spectacular *sindimba* dancing with the participants on stilts and wearing masks. The third is that Makonde women are celebrated throughout Tanzania for their sexual expertise. The best place to experience the atmosphere of the Makonde is to visit **Newala**. The road passes through dense woodland as it climbs up to the plateau from the coast.

• **Transport** You need to stay at least one night in Newala as there is only one bus a day to and from **Mtwara**. It leaves Newala at 0500 and Mtwara at noon. It costs US$6 one way. There are several small lodging houses in Newala. There is a daily bus from Masasi at 1200, leaving from Newala at 0500.

The other main Mokonde town is **Masasi**, surrounded by granite hills some 140 km from Lindi and 190 km from Mtwara. The **E** *Masasi Hotel* on the road to Lindi from the town centre, has nets and fans, bar and restaurant. ♦*Top Spot*. Restaurant is nr the *Masasi Hotel* and has a beer garden.

• **Transport** From **Mtwara** there is a direct daily bus costing US$4. From **Lindi** you will need to connect with this bus at Mingoyo. From **Newala** there is a bus leaving at 0500, and from Msasi at around 1200. It takes 2 to 3 hrs and costs about US$2. Access to and from the W is limited. There are buses, but not every day to **Tunduru** (and thence Songea), they cost US$6, take 12 hrs and leave at 0500. The road can be impassable in the rainy season, Jan to Mar.

NORTH: KILIMANJARO, MOSHI, ARUSHA

Contents

Maps

Most tourists that come to Tanzania are likely to see at least part of the northern circuit. There is so much packed into what is, by African standards, a small area. Here you will find the Serengeti National Park, Mount Kilimanjaro National Park, the Ngorongoro Crater Conservation Area and Olduvai Gorge. Each of the national parks is dealt with separately in the National Park section. The major towns in this area are Arusha and Moshi, but the small towns of Lushoto and Amani are very attractive and well recommended. The road through the well-cultivated Usambara and Pare Mountains is spectacular, and there is good hiking in the hills.

Korogwe

Korogwe is a small town that you pass through on the way from Tanga or Dar es Salaam N to Moshi. It is little more than a junction and there is very little here that visitors would stop for. There are a few shops, a market and a hospital.

• **Where to stay D** *Korogwe Travellers Inn*, on the main Rd. Bar. Restaurant. Fans. Quite reasonable. **E** *Savari Guest House*, nr bus

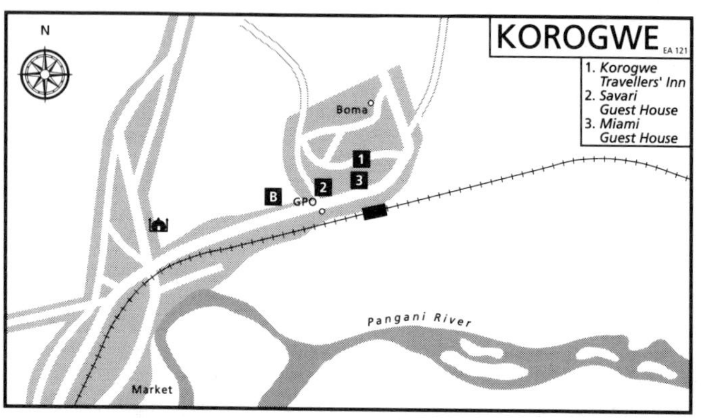

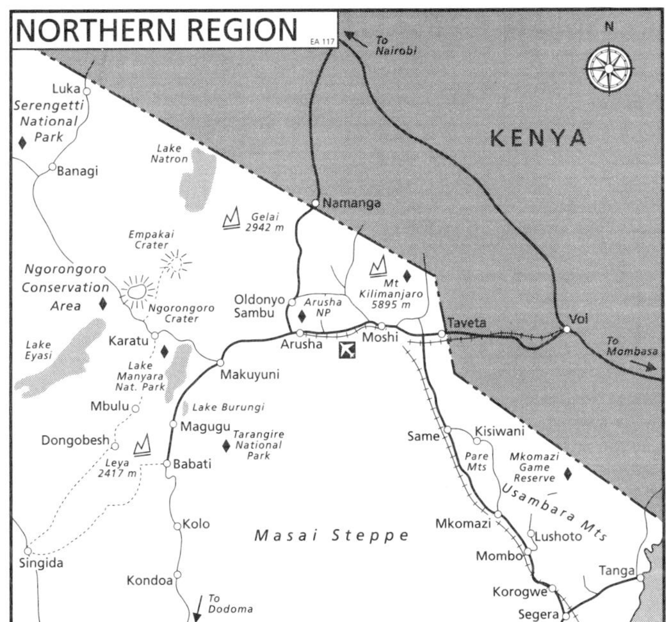

stand. Fans. nets. Simple fare. **E** *Miami Guest House*, central. Fans. Nets. Basic.

• **Transport Train** On the Northern line linking Dar es Salaam, Tanga and Moshi (see these towns for train details). **Road** Frequent buses pass through from Dar es Salaam, Tanga and Moshi (see these towns for details).

Amani

Delightful small town based on the Agricultural Institute and Botanical Garden established by the Germans in the heart of mountain vegetation.

In 1898, at Amani in the cool Usambara hills, the Germans established an agricultural reseach institute that was the envy of Africa. With the twin benefits of the N railway from Tanga to Moshi and the Amani Institute, the Usambara area flourished under settler farming. By 1914 40,000 ha were under sisal, 80,000 ha under rubber, 14,000 ha under cotton as well as extensive areas of tobacco, sugar, wheat and maize.

One of the great lessons of farming in Africa is that crops have to be carefully adapted to local conditions. Amani tested soils, experimented with insecticides and developed new varieties. After 1914, Amani turned its hand to the war effort, developing a local quinine for use against malaria from cinchona bark and manufacturing chocolate, tooth-powder, soap and castor oil.

Today Amani is a medical research centre run by the Tanzanian government. Bird life and small animals such as monkeys abound. It is excellent hiking country.

• **Where to stay E** *Rest House*, this is run by the medical centre. Charming colonial atmosphere and really excellent value.

• **Transport** You will need to make a connection at Muheza on the road linking Tanga to the Dar es Salaam to Moshi highway. There is a bus which leaves Muheza at around 1400 each day for the 25 km trip to Amani which takes about an hour and costs US$0.50. In the mornings the bus leaves Amani when full, usually around 0800.

Mombo

Small town on the Dar es Salaam to Moshi highway. Little of interest – its main activity is the provision services for travellers.

• **Where to stay** **E** *Usambara Inn*. Restaurant and beer garden. Fans.

Soni

This is on the road from Mombo to Lushoto, and is close to the capital of the Shambaa people at Vugu. The Shambaa were well organized militarily, and supported Bushiri in the 1888/9 Arab revolt (see page 265) There is a pretty waterfall, and Soni is a good staging-post for hiking in the Usambaras.

• **Where to stay** **E** *Soni Falls*, about 1 km from village. Restaurant. Bar. Comfortable and good value. **E** ***Msufino Lodgings***, located in village. Resaurant. Bar. Simple but adequate.

• **Transport** Regular buses run from Mombo to Lushoto.

Lushoto

Lushoto is located about 1½ hrs off the main Korogwe-Moshi road. The road up to Lushoto is spectacular as it twists and turns through the mountains.

Lushoto was the town chosen by early German settlers for vacation residences, when it was called Wilhemstal. It is reminiscent of Indian hill stations. The cool fresh air (it is 1,500m above sea level) and lush, green surroundings were greatly appealing and it was once thought that it might develop into the capital of the colonial administration. The Germans planned the site as their version of the ideal colonial town. Many of the surrounding farms and government buildings are originally German. Other reminders of the German connection are the horse-riding arenas, a golf course and the red tiles on the roofs of the buildings. Set in a valley in the Usambara (sometimes known as Asamabara) Mountains it can get quite cold from Jun to Sept so come prepared with warm clothes.

Places of interest

This area is very much a place to enjoy the views and countryside. It is fertile and verdant, cultivated with maize, bananas etc, and there are plenty of tracks to walk along. One such walk takes about 45 mins from Lushoto and ending at the 'Viewpoint' where the view of the hills and the Maasai Plain below really is breathtaking. Take the road out of town towards Irante and head for the Children's Home. Ask around and you'll be shown the track. Lushoto is one of only 2 places in the world where you will find the Usambara Violet (its other habitat is

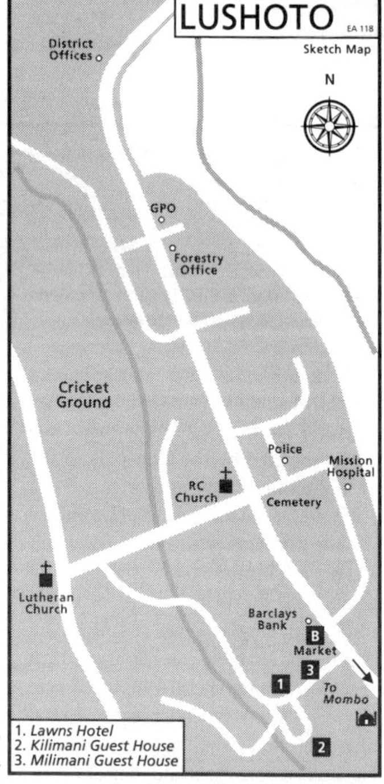

in Mexico). There are lots of different churches and missions in Lushoto which are worth visiting. Missions were established by the Protestant Mission Society; Holy Ghost; Liepzig Mission; Seventh Day Adventists; African Protestant Union. The town holds a fine market (close to the bus station) which is very colourful and lively. There is good fishing in the mountain streams, one of which runs through the centre of the town.

Local information

● **Where to stay**

D *The Lawns Hotel*, old colonial-type hotel. Wonderful views, verandah. Restaurant and bar.

E *Kilimani Guest House*, basic but friendly. Bar and restaurant. **E** *Milimani Guest House*, nr bus station. Restaurant. Bar. Simple but adequate.

● **Places to eat**

♦*Green Valley Restaurant* is very close to the market and bus station and serves reasonable, cheap food.

● **Useful addresses**

The **bank** and **post office** are both on the main street. There is a **municipal office** is beyond the Post Office on the left where it is possible to get a visa extended.

● **Transport**

Lushoto is located off the main Korogwe-Moshi road. Bus from **Mombo** which takes about one and a half hours and costs US$1. You can also get a direct bus from **Tanga**, but it is slow, taking up to 6 hrs, and costs US$2.

Mlalo

Located about 25 km N of Lushoto. Unusual village of 2-storey dwellings with fretted balconies. The Usambaras provide a spectacular backdrop.

● **Where to stay** **E** *Lonido Guest House*. Central, nr bus stand. Rather basic. Oil lamplights. **E** *Afilex Hotel*. Central. Simple but adequate.

● **Transport** One bus a day to and from Lushoto. Leaves Mlalo around 0700 when full, and returns at midday. Takes 2 hrs and costs US$.50.

Moshi

Moshi, at 890m above sea level, is set at the base of Mount Kilimanjaro. Moshi is located about 600 km from Dar es Salaam, 90 km from Arusha and is under

A Chagga Story About Mount Kilimanjaro

The Chagga people who live on the lower slopes of Mount Kilimanjaro have a large number of stories about the mountain. This one is commonly told and relates a quarrel between the 2 sisters, Kibo and Mawenzi which are the names of the 2 peaks of the mountain.

There were 2 sisters who lived in different huts and each cooked and ate her own meals in her own hut. Kibo was the more careful of the 2 sisters and always had a store of food in case of a rainy day. Mawenzi however was much more extravagant and often finished her food before the next harvest. To fill the gap she decided that at meal times she would put out her fire deliberately and go to Kibo to ask for fresh fire embers to restart her fire. She knew that when she went to Kibo her sister would always ask her to share her meals. Sure enough, whenever Mawenzi went over to Kibo to ask for embers, Kibo offered her food. However one day she went too far and 3 times in a row she asked for fire embers saying that her fire had gone out again. Each time she was offered food until finally on the third visit Kibo grew angry and hit Mawenzi across her back with a big ladle. It is this that explains the rugged appearance of the Mawenzi peak. There is also a moral – that too much spoon-feeding is a bad thing. After this incident Mawenzi decided that she had better look after herself better and she never allowed her fire to go out again.

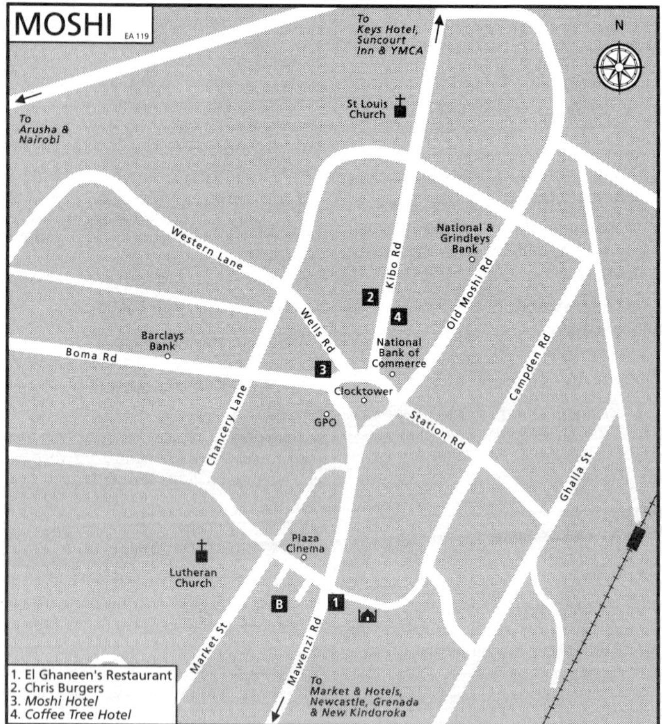

200 km from Nairobi. This is the end of the railway line and rail is the most popular approach after air. The population of the town is about 100,000.

Moshi is the first staging post on the way to climb the Mount Kilimanjaro, (see section on National Parks, page 365) and it is a pleasant place to spend a few days organising your trip. The 2 peaks of this shimmering snow-capped mountain can be seen from all over the town and it dominates the skyline except when the cloud descends and hides it from view. It is a fertile area (the soil is volcanic) and there are lots of melt-water streams fed by the snow. This is where Arabica coffee, the higher quality of the 2 coffee types, is grown by the Chagga. This has helped the Chagga to become one of the wealthiest of the Tanzanian groups and also contributed toward their early politicization. Moshi was the site of the signing of the Moshi Declaration after the war with Uganda in Feb 1979.

Places of interest

Many visitors do not stay long in Moshi, but go on to Marangu, the village at the entrance to Kilimanjaro National Park and arrange the trip up the mountain from there. There are however some things that are worth visiting in Moshi itself. These include the **Mwariko Art Gallery** on Mufutu St which exhibits local arts and crafts and the **Mweka Wildlife Museum**. This is a part of the College of Wildlife Management which is the major centre for training in conservation and wildlife management in Africa. About 100 km out of Moshi on the road towards Dar es Salaam is the **Nyumba ya Mungu** (House of God) dam on the Pangani River. This is a pleasant place to stop for a picnic.

Local information

● Where to stay

B *Keys*, PO Box 933, T 2250. Just to the N of the town centre. Restaurant and Bar. Special rate for residents. **B** *Moshi*, PO Box 1819, Moshi, T 3701, Tlx 42318. Town centre. Restaurant and bar. Rather run-down, government owned.

C *Coffee Tree Hostel*, PO Box 184, Moshi, T 2787. Town centre (2 floors of a large office block). Good views of Kilimanjaro. **C** *YMCA*, PO Box 85, T 52362. Clean. No hot water. Shared bathroom facilities. Gymnasium, shop, travel office. **C** *Motel Silva*, on Kiadha St, S of

Cultivation On The Slopes Of Mount Kilimanjaro

Mount Kilimanjaro rises high above the East African plateau and for this reason is considerably better watered than the land surrounding it. In particular the lower SE slopes of the mountain on the Tanzania side are very fertile with 2 rainy seasons in Mar-May and Nov-Dec. The SE slopes receive the most rain while the NW slopes also have 2 rainy seasons but at different times from the SE. The SW and NE sides are drier.

Rain is brought in on the rain-bearing winds that come from over the Indian Ocean, and the higher the land, the more rain that falls. On the tropical grassland savannah at the base of the mountain the rainfall is approx 380-510 mm, while half way up the mountain at the forest zone the rainfall is about 1500 mm. Above about 3000m the temperatures fall to below zero and vegetation ceases.

The Chagga people who live on the slopes of Kilimanjaro take advantage of these differences in rainfall. They cultivate between about 900 and 1400m and in some places up to 2440m. On the lower slopes just above the tropical grassland savannah they cultivate annual crops such as millet, maize and beans, while higher up, on what is called the *kihamba* land they plant coffee and bananas and keep livestock. This obviously means a lot of work, especially as inheritance can lead to a farmer owning several scatttered plots.

A variety of bananas are grown. There are some that are savoury, are known as *matoke* and are cooked by steaming for a few hours. Others are used for making traditional beer. A banana garden takes 3 years to establish, but once it has been established it needs relatively little time spent on it. The stems and leaves of a banana tree are also used as fodder for cattle, and for mulch for coffee trees.

Coffee is the main cash crop in the area. The volcanic soils of Mount Kilimanjaro are ideally suited to coffee cultivation. There are 2 types of coffee grown in East Africa – Robusta and Arabica – which each have different climatic requirements. Arabica is the type that is grown on the slopes of Mount Kilimanjaro as it requires high altitude. It is the superior of the 2 coffees and attracts better prices. Coffee cultivation demands considerable attention; the plants spend their first year in a shaded nursery before they are transplanted into the fields. They need careful pruning to ensure good yields – this is particularly important for Arabica. Care must also be taken to keep the coffee well weeded.

On a man's death his land is traditionally divided up between his sons. As in many other parts of East Africa, this tradition, combined with the high birth rate, has meant that the average size of holding is divided into 3 or 4 plots when it is inherited. Many farms are now under 2 ha and often smaller.

market. No hot water. Rooms with balconies. Good restaurant. **C** ***Newcastle***, PO Box 2000, T 3203. Close to the market, on Mawenzi St. New. Hot water. **C** ***New Kindoroka***, central, close to market. Restaurant. Bar. Well run.

E ***Rombo Cottage***, T 2112. Off road to Manrangu. Hot water, own bathroom. Bar and restaurant. Good value and atmosphere. **E** ***Suncourt Inn***, off the road to Marangu. Restaurant. Bar. Reasonable.

Camping There is camping nr the ***Golden Shower Restaurant***, which is 2 km from Moshi on the road to Marangu. It is also possible to camp at the ***Keys Hotel***.

● **Places to eat**

All of the hotel restaurants will serve non-residents. ♦♦***El Ghaneens's***, between the bus station and the mosque. Indian food. ♦♦***Golden Shower***, 2 km from Moshi on the road to Marangu. Has a good atmosphere. ♦***Chrisburger***, close to the clock tower.

● **Useful addresses**

Bank and the **post office** can be found in the centre of town nrthe clock tower. **Hospital**: Moshi is home to what is said to be the best hospital in Tanzania – the Kilimanjaro Christian Medical Centre (KCMC) which is located a few km out of town. **Immigration office** where you can renew your visa is also nr the clock tower in Kibo House. **Telephone**: International calls can be made from the post office.

● **Travel and tour operators**

Trans-Kibo Travels Ltd, PO Box 558, T 4734, 2923 which is located in the YMCA, organizes climbs of Kilimanjaro, see also National Park Section, page 365. ***Elmslies Tours***, PO Box 29, Old Moshi Rd, T 2701/4742. ***Mauly Tours & Safaris***, PO Box 1315, Rombo Av, T 2787. ***Zara Travel Agency***, PO Box 1990, T 4240. ***Fortes Safaris***, PO Box 422, Lumumba St, T 41764. ***Fourways Travel***, PO Box 990, Station Rd, T 2620.

● **Transport**

Air There is an airport halfway between Moshi and Arusha. This is Kilimanjaro International. It is served by both international flights as well as by Air Tanzania. Air Tanzania flies to Dar es Salaam and back twice a day but booking in advance is essential. Some people say its worth avoiding the hassle of Air Tanzania altogether and getting one of the international flights (such as Air France, Ethiopian Airlines and KLM) which stop off at Kilimanjaro. The Air Tanzania office is next to the *Moshi Hotel* by the clock tower and from here a shuttle bus leaves 2 hrs before the scheduled flight departure and costs US$3.

Train There are 3 trains to Moshi from **Dar es Salaam** per week leaving Dar on Tue Thu and Sat at 1600. On the way back they go on Mon Wed and Fri at the same time. The journey takes up to 18 hrs and fares are US$12 1st class, US$6 2nd, US$2 3rd. Booking in advance for anything but third class is advised

Road There are daily buses to and from **Dar es Salaam**. They leave Dar es Salaam from the Morogoro Rd bus station. Fare is around US$20 luxury, US$16 semi-luxury and US$12 ordinary and takes about 9 hrs. The road has improved considerably. For **Tanga** the bus takes 4 to 6 hrs and costs US$4. To **Marangu** there are lots of *dala dala* (US$1) or you can share a taxi (US$15).

Marangu

This is the closest village to Kilimanjaro National Park, the entrance to which is 8 km away. It is more expensive than Moshi, and budget travellers are advised to plan an assault on the mountain from the latter.

● **Where to stay** **A** ***Kibo***, PO Box 137 Moshi, T 52503. About 1 km from village. Old German building. Restaurant. Bar. Gardens. Well organized, but up-market. Kilimanjaro climbs can be organized from here. **A** ***Marangu***, PO Box 40, Moshi, T 900, then request Marangu 11. On road to Moshi, about 5 km from Marangu.

B ***Babylon***, about 500m from Marangu, past post office. Comfortable but not good value.

● **Camping** ***Kibo Hotel*** charges US$6, and with use of hotel facilities is good value. ***Babylon Hotel***, rather less good value at US$10.

● **Transport** Regular *dala dala* to and from Moshi (US$1). Taxi US$15.

Arusha

Arusha is a pleasant town set at an altitude of 1,380m above sea level. The drive up to Arusha passes through the semi-arid grass plains gradually becoming greener, more cultivated and more heavily populated. Mount Meru appears on the right with its fertile cultivated slopes. Arusha is 50 km from the

Kilimanjaro International Airport, 95 km from Moshi, 680 km from Dar es Salaam and 272 km from Nairobi. It is probably the busiest Tanzanian town after Dar es Salaam and has a population of around 150,000.

The town is at the base of Mount Meru and is a wonderfully fertile area producing coffee, wheat, sisal and maize. In 1900 the town was just a small German military garrison but it has expanded and flourished. It was once the headquarters of the now defunct East African Community. Many of the wide roads are lined with flame trees, jacaranda and bougainvillaea and if you are lucky enough to be here when they are in bloom it is a fantastic sight.

It was here that the Arusha Declaration was signed which marked the beginning of Tanzania's commitment to socialism. Arusha is the starting place for safaris in the N part of Tanzania – the Serengeti, Ngorongoro, Manyara, Olduvai Gorge, and Arusha National Parks. The huge Arusha International Conference Centre (AICC) here is a legacy of the role that Arusha played as capital of the East African Community. It is made up of 3 main blocks – the Kilimanjaro, Ngorongoro and Serengeti blocks. It has all the facilities that would be expected of an international conference centre including a hall with a seating capacity of 800, an interpretation system, meeting rooms for groups of varying sizes. The centre also has within it a bank, post office, foreign exchange bureau and cafeteria as well as various tour operators and travel agents.

Places of interest

The **National Museum** is at the top end of Boma Road. It is not very impressive. One display of interest is the tracing of the evolution of man based on the findings at Olduvai Gorge (see page 360). The **Arusha Declaration Monument** is set on a roundabout past the police station on the Makongoro Road. The Declaration of 1967 outlined Tanzania's economic and political policies. There is a small museum here dedicated to the Declaration outlining the history of Tanzania's political and economic development.

Local information

● Where to stay

Price guide:
A+ Over US$100 a night;
A US$40-100; **B** US$20-40; **C** US$10-20; **D** US$5-10; **E** Under US$5.

The best hotels in the Arusha area are out of town. They have fine gardens, good standards and charming atmosphere in the foothills of Mount Meru. They are recommended above similar priced hotels in Arusha or its outskirts. They really require that you have your own transport.

Mountain Hotels A *Mountain Village Lodge*, PO Box 376, T 2699, F 4869. Out of town, 15 km along Moshi Rd. German settler farmhouse houses main buildings. Thatched bomas. Excellent gardens, splendid location. Very good restaurant. **A** *Mount Meru Game Lodge*, PO Box 659, T 7179. About 20 km off Moshi Rd nr Usa River. High standard establishment in splendid garden setting. Very good restaurant. **B** *Lake Dulati Mountain Lodge*, PO Box 602, Arusha. Located 11 km from Arusha about 1½ km off the Moshi Rd. **B** *Dik Dik*, PO Box 1499, T 8110. About 20 km of Moshi Rd nr Usa River. Swimming pool. Good restaurant. Pleasant grounds. Well run establishment and good value. **B** *Tanzanite*, PO Box 3063, T Usa River 32. About 11 km along road to Moshi, nr Usa River. Swimming pool. Tennis. Restaurant. Good value.

Town hotels A+ *Novotel Mount Meru*, PO Box 877, T 2711/17. Full facilities including swimming pool, set in pleasant gardens. **A** *New Arusha*, PO Box 88, T 4241, Tlx 42125. Town centre, nr clock tower. Two bars and beer garden, restaurant and fast food restaurant, bookshop and craft shop. Swimming pool. Rather run-down. **A** *Equator*, PO Box 3002, T 3127, Tlx 4215. Town centre, Boma Rd. Restaurant, bar and beer garden. Disco at weekends. **A** *New Safari*, PO Box 303, T 8545/7, Tlx 42055. Central, on Boma Rd. Restaurant and outdoor bar. Weekend disco.

B *Impala*, PO Box 7302, T 8448/51, 7197/7394, Tlx 42132. Close to conference centre. Arranges tours and safaris through Classic

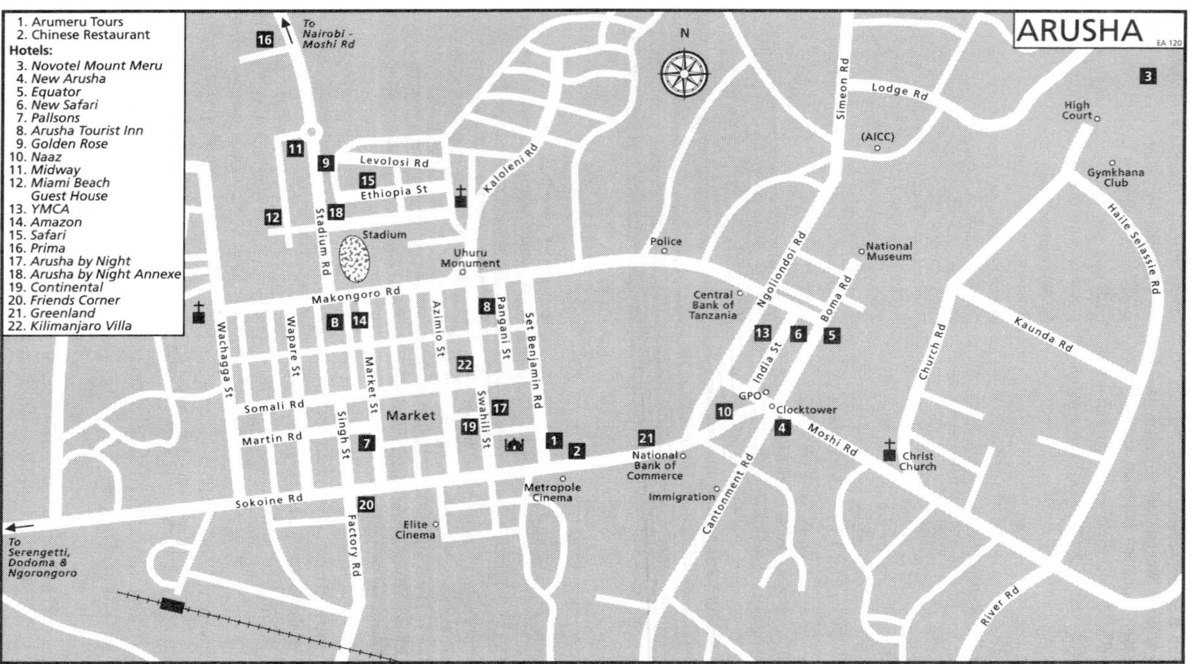
ARUSHA
EA 120
1. Arumeru Tours
2. Chinese Restaurant
Hotels:
3. Novotel Mount Meru
4. New Arusha
5. Equator
6. New Safari
7. Pallsons
8. Arusha Tourist Inn
9. Golden Rose
10. Naaz
11. Midway
12. Miami Beach Guest House
13. YMCA
14. Amazon
15. Safari
16. Prima
17. Arusha by Night
18. Arusha by Night Annexe
19. Continental
20. Friends Corner
21. Greenland
22. Kilimanjaro Villa
To Nairobi - Moshi Rd
N
Simeon Rd
Lodge Rd
High Court
(AICC)
Gymkhana Club
Haile Selassie Rd
Levolosi Rd
Ethiopia St
Kaloleni Rd
Stadium
Stadium Rd
Uhuru Monument
Police
National Museum
Central Bank of Tanzania
Ngoliondoi Rd
Boma Rd
Makongoro Rd
Azimio St
Pangani St
Set Benjamin Rd
Wachagga St
Wapare St
Market St
India St
Kaunda Rd
Church Rd
GPO
Clocktower
Somali Rd
Market
Swahili St
Martin Rd
Singh St
Moshi Rd
Christ Church
National Bank of Commerce
Metropole Cinema
Immigration
Cantonment Rd
Sokoine Rd
Elite Cinema
Factory Rd
To Serengetti, Dodoma & Ngorongoro
River Rd

Tours. **B** ***Seventy Seven***, PO Box 187, T 3800, Tlx 42055. Off Moshi Rd, about 2 km from centre. Pleasant bar and restaurant. Prefabricated rooms. Efficient but a bit utilitarian. Substantial discount for residents. **B** ***Pallson's***, PO Box 773, T 2485, F 7263. Off Sokoine Rd, nr market. Restaurant. Comfortable. **B** ***Arusha Tourist Inn***, PO Box 1530, Pangani St, T 8863. Fans. Hot water. Restaurant. Reasonable value.

C ***Golden Rose***, PO Box 361 Arusha, T 8860 Stadium Rd. Self contained. Hot water, telephones, balconies. Bar and restaurant. **C** ***Naaz***, PO Box 1060, T 2087. Central, nr clock tower on Sokoine Rd. Restaurant. Hot water. Good value.

D ***Jambo***, PO Box 1101 Town Centre. **D** ***Midway***, nr Stadium on Stadium Rd. Restaurant. Good value. **D** ***Miami Beach Guest House***, off Stadium Rd. Reasonable. **D** ***YMCA***, PO Box 118, India St. Centre. No hot water. Shared bathrooms. **D** ***Amazon Tourist***, Market St. Rather basic.

E ***Safari Guest House***, Ethiopia St, N of Stadium. Simple fare. **E** ***Prima Guest House***, Stadium Rd toward Moshi and Nairobi Rd. Rather basic. **E** ***Arusha by Night***, PO Box 360, Swahili St, T 2836. Basic, but good value. Discos every night and can be noisy. **E** ***Arusha by Night Annexe***, PO Box 360, on corner of Stadium Rd and Makongaro Rd, T 6894. Basic, good value. **E** ***Continental***, Swahili St. Very basic, but cheap. **E** ***Friends Corner***, cnr of Sokoine Rd and Factory Rd. Simple but reasonably good value. **E** ***Greenlands***, Sokoine St, E end. Rather basic. **E** ***Kilimanjaro Villa*** Swahili St. Very simple.

Camping ***Kinyoro Campsite***, 1 km along Old Moshi Rd. ***Maasai Camp***, 3 km along road to Moshi. Hot water. Restaurant. US$3. ***Lake Duluti camping ground***, about 11 km from town toward Moshi. Restaurant. US$3.

● Places to eat

> **Price guide:**
> ♦♦♦♦ over US$10; ♦♦♦ US$5-10;
> ♦♦ US$2-5; ♦ under US$2.

♦♦♦♦***Mount Meru Hotel***. International menu. Very pleasant coffee shop. ♦♦♦♦***Hotel Seventy Seven***. Comfortable atmosphere. Live band plays for diners most nights. ♦♦♦***Hotel Equator***. Good restaurant with a varied menu. ♦♦♦***Safari Grill***, next to the *New Safari Hotel*. Good standard. ♦♦♦***Chinese Restaurant***, on the Sokoine Rd nr the bridge. Extensive menu and the food is well prepared. ♦♦***Golden Rose Hotel***. Good standard and sound value. ♦♦***New Safari Ho-***

tel Garden Bar Recommended for traditional meat barbecues. ♦♦***Meenar Restaurant***, on Ngoliondoi Rd. Indian food. ♦***Ark Grill***, on Swahili St. Friendly place serving European food. ♦***Naura Yard Bar*** which is on Sokoine Rd nr the bridge. Simple but sound. ♦***Silver City Bar***. Attached to the YMCA. Good value.

● Entertainment

Bars and discos There are a number of popular bars including the ***Naura Yard Bar*** next to the Chinese Restaurant on Sokoine Rd nr the bridge. On Sun this holds a free, very loud, disco. Another popular spot is the ***Silver City Bar*** attached to the YMCA. The bar at the ***Hotel Equator*** has live bands at the weekend which are verypopular. There is another very good and popular disco held at the ***New Safari Hotel*** each weekend called the ***Cave Disco***. If you want to dance during the week there are nightly discos at the ***Hotel Arusha by Night***.

Cinemas The ***Metropole Cinema*** is on Sokoine Rd (formerly Uhuru Rd). The ***Elite Cinema*** is off Sokoine Rd, S of the market. Both these cinemas show mostly Asian films, martial arts and adventure movies.

● Shopping

There is a **bookshop** at the New Arusha Hotel which sells international newspapers and magazines as well as books. There are some good **craft shops** on Ngoliondoi Rd and nr the clock tower with some very good examples of carvings. They are probably cheaper here than elsewhere. The **market** is behind the bus station along Market St and Somali Rd and there are lots of shops along Sokoine Rd.

● Sport

Mount Meru Marathon is held yearly in Arusha and attracts competitors from all around the world. **Golf**: a 9 hole golf course is available at the ***Gymkhana Club*** which is out towards the High Court. Temporary membership is available. **Swimming** is available at the pool at the *Novotel Mount Meru*. This is open to non-residents for a temporary membership fee. There is **horseback riding** at Usa River about 15 km out of Arusha as well as at Lake Duluti which is 11 km out of Arusha on the Moshi road.

● Tour and travel agents

There are a number of tour operators based in Arusha who organize safaris to the different National Parks in the North. There are some in the International Conference Centre as well as others along India St, Sokoine Rd and Boma Rd. The ***National Parks of Tanzania Headquarters*** is on the 6th floor of the Kilimanjaro wing of the Arusha International Conference Centre, PO Box 3134, Arusha, T 3471/2. Telex 42130. It has a park guides as well as the National Parks Quarterly Reports. **Horse riding safaris** are becoming increasingly popular and can be arranged from Arusha. Most of these begin from Usa River whichis 22 km from Arusha on the Moshi road. These are discussed in more detail in the National Parks Section. ***Tanzania Game Trails*** arranges such safaris. Among the most experienced are ***Abercrombie and Kent*** and ***Ker and Downey Safaris***.

Abercrombie and Kent, PO Box 427, T 7803, F 7003, Tlx 42005. ***Adventure Tours and Safaris***, PO Box 1014, T 6015. ***African Gametrackers***, PO Box 535, T 2913/7791. ***AICC Tours***, PO Box 3801, T 3181 (ext 23). ***Arumeru Tours and Safaris***, PO Box 730, T 7637/2780. ***Blue Bird Tours***, PO Box 1054, T 3934. ***Bobby Tours***, PO Box 716, T 3490. ***Chasse d'Afrique***, PO Box 384, T 2241. ***Classic Tours and Safaris***, PO Box 7302, T 7197. ***Dorobo Tours and Safaris***, PO Box 2534, T 3699. ***Eagle Tours and Safaris***, PO Box 343, T 2909. ***Executive Travel Services***, PO Box 7462, T 2472/3181, Tlx 42136. ***Flamingo Tours***, PO Box 2660, T 6976/6152, Tlx 42003. ***Fly-Catcher Safaris***, PO Box 591, T 3622. ***George Dove Safaris***, PO Box 284, T 3090 3625. ***Jas Tours and Safaris***, PO Box 76, T 7381. ***Jeff's Tours and Safaris***, PO Box 1469, T 6980/7541. ***K and S Enterprises***, PO Box 1318, T 6465. ***Ker and Downey Safaris***, PO Box 2782, T 7755/7700, Tlx 42013. ***Kingfisher Safaris***, PO Box 701, T 2123. ***King Safari Club***, PO Box 7201, T 3958. ***Laitolya Tours and Safaris***, PO Box 7319, T 2422/2984. ***Let's Go Marve Holidays***, PO Box 2660, T 3613. ***Lions Safaris International***, PO Box 999, T 6422. ***New Victoria Tours***, PO Box 644, T 2735. ***Northern Tours***, PO Box 7452. ***Overseas Adventure Travel – East Africa***, PO Box 6074, T 6694. ***Ranger Safaris***, PO Box 9, T 3074/3023, Tlx 42063. ***Sable Safaris***, PO Box 7145, T 6711. ***Scan-Tan Tours***, PO Box 1054, T 6978. ***Sengo Safaris***, PO Box 180, T 6982. ***Serengetti Select Safaris***, PO Box 1177, T 6186. ***Shallom Tours and Safaris***, PO Box 217, T 3181. ***Simba Safaris***, PO Box 1207, T 3509 3600, Tlx 42095. ***State Travel Service***, PO Box 1369, T 3300/3113/3152, Tlx 42138. ***Star Tours***, PO Box 1099, T 2553. ***Sunny Safaris***, PO Box 7267, T 7145/8184, F 8094. ***Tanzania Game Trails***, PO Box 535, Tlx 42075. ***Tanzania Guides***, PO Box 2031, T 3625. ***Tanzania Wildlife Corporation***,

PO Box 1144, T 3501. ***Tanzanite Wildlife Tours***, PO Box 1277, T 2239. ***Tarangire***, PO Box 1182, T 3090/3625. ***Tareto***, PO Box 17586, T 31713. ***Tarimo Tours***, PO Box 6125, T 3181. ***Tarus Tours and Safaris***, PO Box 1254, T 2388. ***Tracks Travel***, PO Box 142, T 3145. ***Transafrican Safaris***, PO Box 468, T 6305. ***Tropical Tours***, PO Box 727. ***Universal Tours***, PO Box 1264. ***UTC***, PO Box 2211, T 42110, F 6475, Tlx 42110. ***Wapa Tours and Safaris***, PO Box 6165, T 3181. ***Wildersun Safaris and Tours***, PO Box 930, T 6471/3880. ***Wildtrack Safaris***, PO Box 1059, T 3547. ***W J Travel Service***, PO Box 88, T 6444.

Hunting Safaris *Bushmen Company*, PO Box 235, T 6210. *King Tours and Hunting Safaris*, PO Box 7000, T 3688.

● Useful addresses

Banks The Central Bank of Tanzania has a branch on Makongoro Rd nr the roundabout with Ngoliondoi Rd. The National Bank of Commerce is on Sokoine Rd down towards the bridge. **Hospitals** The Mount Meru Hospital is opposite the AICC on Ngoliondi Rd. The **Immigration Office** is on Sinoni Rd. The main **Post Office** is by the clock tower opposite the *New Arusha Hotel*. **Telephone** International telephone calls can be made from the *New Safari Hotel*. The **Tourist Office** is on Boma Rd (T 3842) but it is not overly helpful unless you are making a booking for a TTC hotel or lodge.

● Travel

Air Kilimanjaro International Airport is halfway between Arusha and Moshi. It is served by international flights as well as by Air Tanzania. Air Tanzania flies to Dar es Salaam and back twice a day but booking in advance is essential. Some people say its worth avoiding the hassle of Air Tanzania altogether and getting one of the international flights (such as Air France, Ethiopian Airlines and KLM) which stop off at Kilimanjaro. ***Aviators Services***, T 6386 has 3 flights a week to Dar es Salaam, 1400 Mon, Wed, and Sat, and the cost one-way is US$126. The ***Air Tanzania Office*** is on the Boma Rd. ***Air France*** and ***Ethiopian Airlines*** also have offices on Boma Rd. To get to the airport you can get the STS shuttle bus which costs US$3 and leaves about 2 hrs before flight departure. It stops at the Air Tanzania office, *Mount Meru Hotel* and *Hotel Seventy Seven*. Taxi to the airport is about US$20.

Train Trains terminate at Moshi (see page 302 for times and fares), although track does continue to Arusha. The Arusha-Moshi stretch is easy to travel by road.

Road The bus station is located in Zaramo St just to the N of the market. There are regular buses and *dala dala* to and from **Moshi**. Trip costs US$1 and takes 1½ hr. You can also get a shared taxi for which you can expect to pay at least US$35. **Dar es Salaam**: fare is around US$20 luxury, US$16 semi luxury and US$12 ordinary and takes about 9 hrs. The road has improved considerably. **Tanga**: daily buses (Tanga African Motor Transport), US$7 (luxury) and US$4 (ordinary). You can also get buses from here up to **Mwanza** on the Kajoi Bus Service. This goes every other day, takes 24 hrs and costs US$16. If you take a service which goes through the Serengeti, there will be an extra charge of US$30 in park fees. Otherwise it is possible to get to Mwanza via Singida and Shinyanga, although you may need to change buses, and the trip will take the best part of 2 days. **Nairobi**: *Dala dala* only take 4 or 5 hrs from here, depart, regularly through the day, and the border crossing is efficient. A regular bus leaves every morning to go through to Nairobi, it calls at *Mount Meru Hotel* and *Hotel Seventy Seven* and costs around US$8.

LAKE VICTORIA AND ENVIRONS

Contents

Maps

This area is fairly cut off and transport links are poor. The road to Mwanza is in a poor state and the towns along the lake are most easily reached by the ferry. The problems of accessibility were made worse by the closure of the border with Kenya from 1977 to 1983. However now that this has reopened there is more through traffic. Mwanza is a busy town, and there is much activity in exporting fish from Lake Victoria. Bukoba, on the W side of the lake is in a very attractive setting. Haya men from this region are tall, and Haya women have a reputation for great beauty.

Musoma

This small port with a population of about 65,000 is set on the E shores of Lake Victoria close to the border with Kenya. It is a bustling and friendly town with many visitors who are on their way to or from Kenya. It is also close to the Serengeti National Park and so should

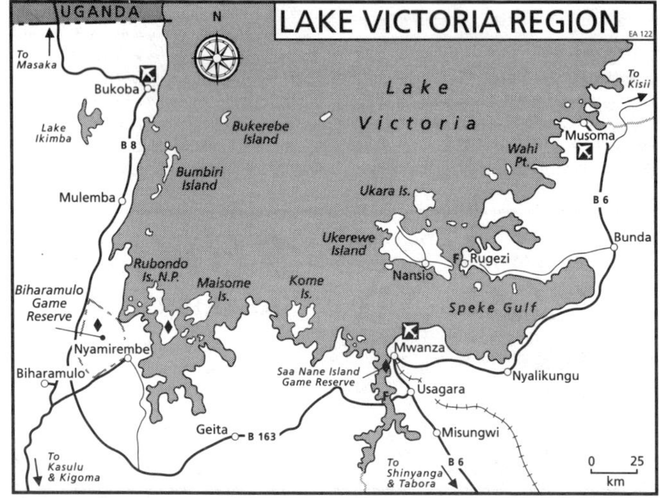

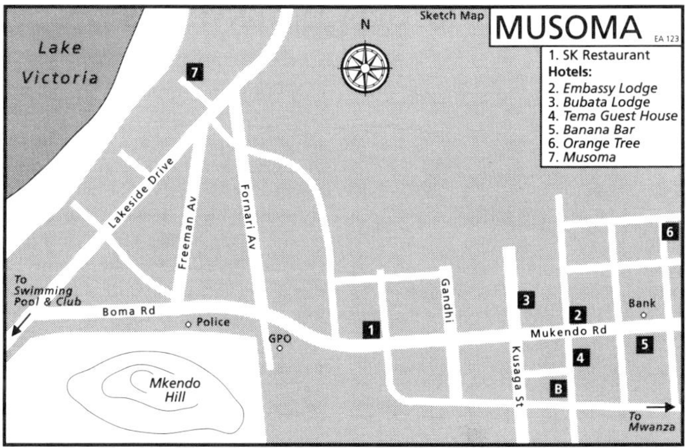

be one of the centres for safaris to the park. However because of the border closure and its inaccessibility it has not developed as such (See Section on National Parks, page 364). It has a coastal climate of hot days and cool nights.

• **Where to stay D** *Musoma Railway*, PO Box 282, T 176. Restaurant. Half-an-hour's walk out of town, on the lake shore.

E *Silver Sands Inn*, on Lake shore. Comfortable and good value. **E** *Sengerema Guest House*. Town Centre. **E** *Embassy Lodge*. Town Centre. **E** *Musabura Guest House*. Town Centre.

E *Mennonite Centre*. Some way from the ferry terminal. Clean. **E** *Bubata Lodge*. On Mukendo St in town centre. Fair. **E** *Tema Guest House*. Town centre. **E** *Banana Bar Lodge*. Central, on Mukendo St, opposite National Commercial Bank. **E** *Orange Tree*. Central.

• **Places to eat** ♦♦*Orange Tree Hotel*. Reasonable. ♦♦*SK Restaurant* Indian cuisine. Good value.

• **Transport Air** *Air Tanzania* flights go to Mwanza, see page 312, twice a week, although schedules are subject to cancellations and alterations. Link to Musoma by road.

Train To Mwanza by road and then train linking to Tabora, Kigoma and Dar es Salaam, see Mwanza, page 312.

Road **Mwanza**: the road is reasonable, and there are regular buses leaving from the bus station, which is behind Kusaga St in the centre. The trip takes up to 6 hrs, and costs US$4. **Arusha**: buses go through the Serengeti and across the top of Lake Manyara Park. The roads through the park are poor, the bus takes around 18 hrs and costs around US$15, plus if you are European, a US$30 Serengeti National Park fee. The buses do not run every day. Road travellers from **Dar es Salaam** say that the quickest road route is to Arusha, then across the border at Namanga to Nairobi, then Nakuru, Kericho, Kisii or Nakuru to Kisumu and back across the border. The roads are good all the way except for the stretch from the border to Musoma. Check if you need a visa to enter Kenya.

Lake The ferry for Kisumu to Mwanza used to stop at Musoma, but this is not now the case.

Mwanza

This is the largest Tanzanian port on Lake Victoria and with a population of 225,000 it is Tanzania's second largest town. It lies on a peninsula that juts into the lake. It is surrounded by rocky hills and the land is dominated by granite outcrops some of which are very impressive and look as if they are about to topple. As the railway terminus and major lake port, Mwanza is a bustling and lively town. The produce from the lake region is gathered here and is then trans-

Bark Cloth

Bark cloth is a product of the Lake Victoria region. It has been used in the past as a material for making ceremonial clothes and more recently you see it for sale to tourists as table mats etc.

The preparation of the cloth is a long and complex process and making good quality bark cloth is a very real skill. The process begins with the scraping down of the outer bark. It is then slit from top to bottom and a cut made around the top and bottom of the tree trunk. Using a ladder the bark is gradually removed beginning at the bottom and working upwards. It is removed from the entire circumference of the tree trunk so that the piece of bark should be fairly large. It is then rolled up and taken back to the house of the cutter. The next step in the process is to scorch the side of the bark that was closest to the tree. This "melts" the sap and helps in the softening and stretching processes. The bark is scorched by laying the bark on the ground and placing dry banana leaves on it. These are set on fire and are very quickly taken off the bark so that it is not burnt too much. The bark is then rolled up in fresh banana leaves to prevent it from drying out and is left overnight.

The next day the process of pounding the bark begins. This is done in 2 stages using a special beater with ridges on it. As the bark is beaten it gradually gets thinner and wider. The process of stretching the bark is next and is usually undertaken by 2 or 3 people. The bark is alternatively beaten and stretched until it is stretched out and fixed with stones and left in the sun to dry. By this stage it is a thin and totally malleable piece of cloth. If it is good quality the bark cloth will be large and of a uniform thickness, however it is common for several pieces to be sewn together and for there to be the odd thin patch.

ported to the coast by the railway. The lake is dotted with islands of varying sizes from the smallest specks, unmarked on maps, to Ukerewe which is heavily populated with the Wa-Kerewe. Fishing is a major commercial activity is this area, although coffee, tea and cotton are also important.

Places of interest

Saa Nane Island This wildlife sanctuary is not far from Mwanza in the lake and has on it hippo, zebra, and wildebeest as well as various caged animals. It is a pleasant place to spend an afternoon with the rocky outcrops appearing out of the grassy landscape. You can get a boat out from Mwanza, leaving the jetty 1 km S of the centre off Station Rd about 5 times a day. There is an admission charge of US$0.50

Bujora Sukuma Village Museum This is located 15-20 km from Mwanza on the Musoma road. It can be reached by taking a local bus from the bus station near the market in Mwanza to Kisessa and from there walking the remaining 1 km. The exhibits are of the traditions and culture of the Sukuma who make up the largest tribe in Tanzania. They include a traditional house, shrines, and traditional instruments including a drum collection. It was originally set up by missionaries from Quebec. There are regular traditional dances held there which include the impressive Sukuma snake dance or *Bugobogobo*, most weeks, usually on a Sat.

Another place to visit whilst in Mwanza is the **Rubondo National Park** (See section on National Parks, page 390.)

Ukerewe, Kome and Maisome Islands These 3 islands are scenically very pretty, but there is little to attract the tourists. Ukerewe Island to the N of Mwanza can be reached by ferry, taking about 3 hrs, leaving Mwanza at 0900 and Nansio, the main town on Ukerewe at 1330. It is also possible to go by road, E round the lake to Bunda and then W along the N shore of Speke Gulf, crossing by ferry to Ukerewe Island. There are no regular buses on the last leg of this route and it is necessary to hitch. There are some small hotels and a series of cheap restaurants.

Kome and Maisome Islands are served by the ferries to Myamirembe which leave Mwanza on Mon (0800), and Thu (2100). Kome takes about 3 hrs to reach and Maisome about 7 hrs. Ferries return from Nyamirembe on Tue (0800) and Fri (1900).

Botanical Gardens These are located on the road to Mwanza Airport to the N of the city centre by the lake shore. They are rather neglected, but it is a pleasant place to visit and the location is attractive.

Local information

● Where to stay

B *New Mwanza*, PO Box 25, T 40620, Tlx 46284. Central, on Post St. Restaurant. Bar. A/c. Pleasant and convenient. **B** *Tilapia*, on lake 1 km to S of town centre, on Station Rd nr ferry to Saa Nane Island. Chalet style accommodation. Pleasant and comfortable.

D *Lake*, PO Box 910, T 2062. Off Station Rd close to stadium. Restaurant. Outdoor bar. Fans. Nets. Good value. **D** *Delux*, PO Box 1471,

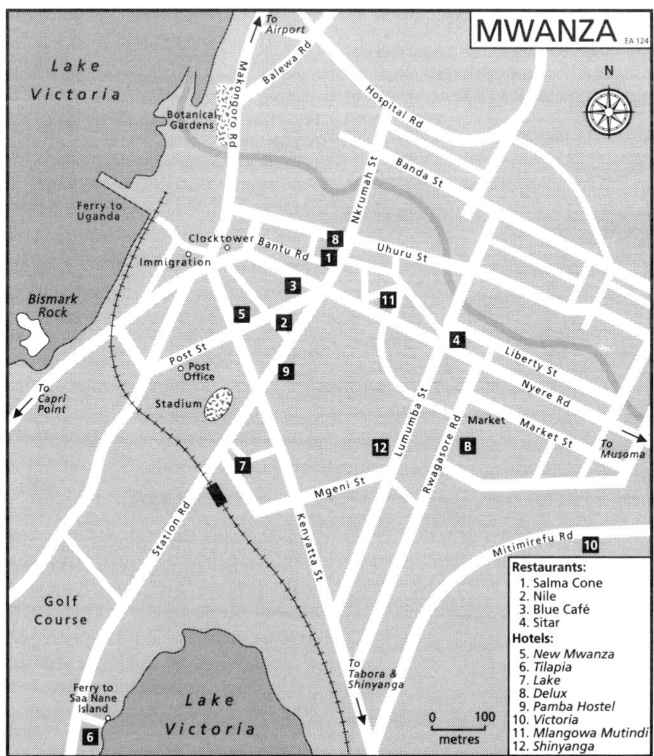

T 2411. Town centre, on corner of Uhuru St and Nkrumah St. Restaurant and lively bars. Popular. **E** ***Pamba Hostel***, on Station Rd nr roundabout. Shared facilities. Restaurant. Bar. **E** ***Victoria***, on Mitimirefu Rd. Shabby but cheap. **E** ***Mlangowa Guest House***. Central. Good value. **E** ***Shinyanga***. Lumumba St. Just off centre. Rather run down.

● Places to eat

♦♦***Lake Hotel***. Varied menu. Reasonable value. ♦♦***Delux Hotel***. Indian food. Good value. ♦♦***Sitar***, cnr of Liberty St and Lumumba St. Indian food. ♦♦***Kidepo Grill***, in *New Mwanza Hotel*. Live music at weekends and occasionally other nights.

♦***Blue Café***, on corner of Post St and Nyerere Rd is simple but good value. ♦***Nile Café***, off Post St nr Myerere Rd. Straightforward food. ♦***Salma Cone***, crn of Barti St and Nkrumah St. Serves coffee, snacks and ice cream.

● Useful addresses

The **immigration office** is on the road leading off from the clock tower towards the lake. The **hospital** is located on a hill about 1 km out of town and was built in the 1970's with Russian support. The **post office** is on Post St.

● Transport

Air There is an airport at Mwanza served by *Air Tanzania* (Dar es Salaam: PO Box 543, T 46643/4/5. ATC Building, Ohio St). There should be at least one flight every week. However it is not uncommon to turn up at the airport with a valid and confirmed ticket and be turned away due to overbooking. Fare is around US$100, but half that for residents.

Train The railway line, built in the 1920's during the British administration was completed in 1928. It forms the extension of the Central Line and was considered vital for the development of the NW area. Trains go from Dar es Salaam to Mwanza (1227 km) 4 times a week on Tue, Wed, Fri and Sun leaving at about 1800; and from Mwanza to Dar on the same days at 1900. The fares are US$25, US$11 and US$4 for 1st, 2nd and 3rd class respectively. Theoretically the journey takes 36 hrs but it can take longer. There is poor coordination on travel from Mwanza to Kigoma, and it is only possible to book as far as Tabora and then it is necessary to rebook the Tabora-Kigoma leg.

Road To **Arusha** buses go through the Serengeti and across the top of Lake Manyara Park. The roads through the park are poor, the bus takes around 18 hrs and costs around US$15, plus if you are European, a US$30 Serengeti National Park fee. The buses do not run every day. Road travellers from **Dar es Salaam** say that the quickest road route is to Arusha, then across the border at Namanga to Nairobi, then Nakuru, Kericho, Kisii (or Nakuru to Kisumu) and back across the border and S through Musoma. The roads are good all the way except for the stretch from the border to Musoma. Check if you need a visa to enter Kenya. There is at least one bus a day to Kisumu in Kenya, leaving at around 0700.

Lake This is easily the most reliable and comfortable way to travel on to **Bukoba**. The boats, though old, have recently been refitted. There is a ferry each day, (but not Wed from Mwanza, not Thu from Bukoba) leaving at 2100. and arriving next morning at around 0800. Fares are US$9, US$6 and US$3. First class provides a berth in a 4 person cabin, second in a 6 person cabin. Earplugs can be a boon. **Nyamirembe** is served by 2 ferries a week, from Mwanza at 0800 on Mon and 2100 on Thur and from Nyamirembe at 0800 on Tue and 1900 on Fri. The journey takes 10 hrs. Its ferries call at **Kome** and **Miasome Islands** and cost US$5 (2nd class) and US$3 (3rd). **Ukerewe Island** has a daily ferry, leaving Mwanza at 0900 and returning around 1300. The trip is 3 hrs, and costs US$1.50. To **Kampala** (Port Bell) there is a weekly service, leaving Mwanza at 1500 on Sun and Port Bell at 1500 on Mon. Journey takes 14 hrs and costs US$20 (1st); US$15 (2nd); US$8 (3rd). There are berths for 1st and 2nd class. There is a port fee of US$5 on leaving Tanzania. There were ferries to and from **Kisumu** in Kenya until the border closed in 1977. Although it reopened in 1983, the ferries have not returned. However there have recently been co-operation initiatives between Kenya and Tanzania, and hopes are high that the ferry will resume

Bukoba

Bukoba, set in a bay between lush hills is Tanzania's second largest lake port, with a population of 30,000. However it receives few visitors. It was founded in 1890 by Emin Pasha. It is a lovely part of Tanzania – green and fertile and with a very relaxed way of life. The major food crop here (as in much of the area around the lake) is matoke. This is the green banana which you will see grown everywhere. It is peeled, wrapped in banana leaves and cooked very slowly by steaming. The major commercial crop is coffee which has contributed significantly to the wealth of the area. There is a coffee factory near the jetty. Unfortunately the world price has fallen in recent years with notable effects on the people of this district. There are quite a few aid projects in this area so a number of expatriate aid workers live here. Huge deposits of nickel and cobalt have been discovered in the area, and there are plans to exploit these.

The Haya people have high educational standards, and, together with the Chagga from around Kilimanjaro, are strongly represented in academic life, government service and business. This feature of Tanzania has been attributed to climate. Both Kilimanjaro and Kagera (West Lake) are at high altitude and are cool, thus proving to be attractive locations for early missionaries from Europe. Both Catholic and Protestant mission activities were particularly strong, and competition between the 2 groups led to superior educational facilities being offered to converts.

Places of interest

Near the lake shore is a group of buildings from the German period – the regional administrative offices, magistrates courts and the prison. Across the road from the *Lake Hotel* is a German cemetery. Further W is the area with European housing, and beyond the aerodrome runway is Nyamukazi Fishing village. Proceeding inland along Independence Road, on the right there is the former British Club where there was a cricket pitch and tennis courts.

The centre of town has many Asian style buildings, now very shabby. To the W of the town centre on School Road are

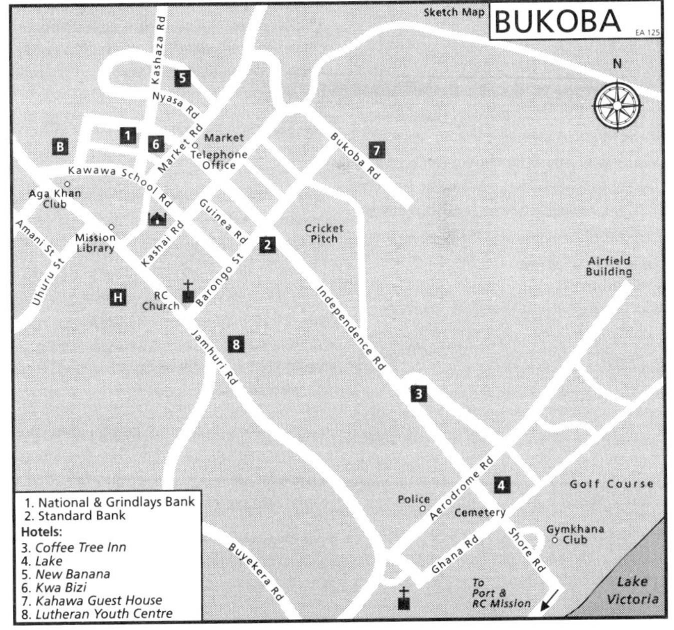

THE HEN AND THE HAWK: A BUKOBA FABLE

Once upon a time there was a hen and a hawk who were friends and lived together in the same hut. One day, during a great famine the hen went off in search of food. She was successful for she met a man who had some bananas. As she was carrying her load home she met the hawk who asked her how she had got the bananas. The hen, standing on one leg, replied that she had paid for them with her foot. The hen told the hawk that he must also buy some food with his foot.

The hawk agreed that this was indeed fair and went off in search of some food. He met a man and offered his leg in return for some food. The man agreed, cut off the hawk's leg and then gave him a some food. The hawk had great difficulty walking home with only one leg, trying to balance the load.

When the hawk eventually reached home he saw the hen standing on 2 legs. He was extremely angry with the hen, saying that although the hen was supposed to be his friend she had cheated him. The hawk told the hen that he could not forgive her and would kill her. The hen replied that he would never succeed in killing her for she would run away. Sure enough the hen ran away and lived with man, while the hawk and all his descendants remain determined to kill the hen and its offspring. This is why the hawk will always try to kill any hen that it sees.

2 mosques and the Aga Khan Sports Club. On Jamhuri St is the rather fine Mission Library.

Coffee has long been the economic mainstay of the region and there is a coffee factory at the E end of the Kashaj Road, past the school. There is a second factory on the lake shore by the wharf, S of the administative centre, and it is usually possible to be shown round. Continuing S in from the wharf is the Bunena Roman Catholic Mission buildings with a spire, gardens and a cemetery.

Local information

● Where to stay

D *Coffee Tree Inn*, PO Box 412. Town Centre. **D** *Lake*, PO Box 66, T 176. Beautiful building and setting on the Lake shore. **D** *New Banana*. East of the Market. Restaurant. Central and well run. **E** *Kwa Bizi*, on the cnr of Nyara Rd and Kashaza. Rather simple. **E** *Kahawa Guest House*. On Bukoba Rd. Cheap and reasonable. **E** *Evangelical Lutheran Church Youth Centre* (*Nyumba wa Vijana*). Dormitory accommodation. **E** *Bunena Mission*. About 5 km from town centre along Shore Rd. Dormitory accommodation.

● Places to eat

♦♦*Lake Hotel*. Reasonable if a bit uninspired ♦♦*Coffee Tree Hotel*. Adequate. ♦♦*New Banana*. Food a bit above average.

● Travel

Air Bukoba is served by *Air Tanzania* (Dar es Salaam: PO Box 543, T 46643/4/5. ATC Building, Ohio St) but the usual problems apply of unreliability and overbooking. The fare is roughly US$250 one-way to Dar es Salaam.

Road There are buses going N to Uganda and S to Mwanza and Kigoma. They are very irregular, and almost all access to Bukoba is by ferry.

Sea This is easily the most reliable and comfortable way to travel to **Mwanza**. The boats, though old, have recently been refitted. There is a ferry each day, (but not Wed from Mwanza, not Thu from Bukoba) leaving at 2100 and arriving next morning at around 0800. Fares are US$9, US$6 and US$3. 1st class provides a berth in a 4 person cabin, 2nd in a 6 person cabin. Earplugs can be a boon.

CENTRAL: MOROGORO, DODOMA, TABORA, KIGOMA

Contents

Maps

The central route to Kigoma in the far W passes through a number of different landscapes and vegetational zones. The distance between the towns is large and much of this route is sparsely populated. The major towns which you pass through are Morogoro, Dodoma, and finally Tabora before reaching Kigoma. The central railway line is the focus of this route, and it follows the old slave and caravan trail from the coast to Lake Tanganyika. The road is good only as far as Dodoma, just over a third of the distance to Kigoma.

Morogoro

Morogoro lies at an altitude 500m above sea level and is based at the foot of the Uluguru Mountains which reach a height of 2138m. The mountains provide a spectacular backdrop to the town, and the peaks are often obscured by

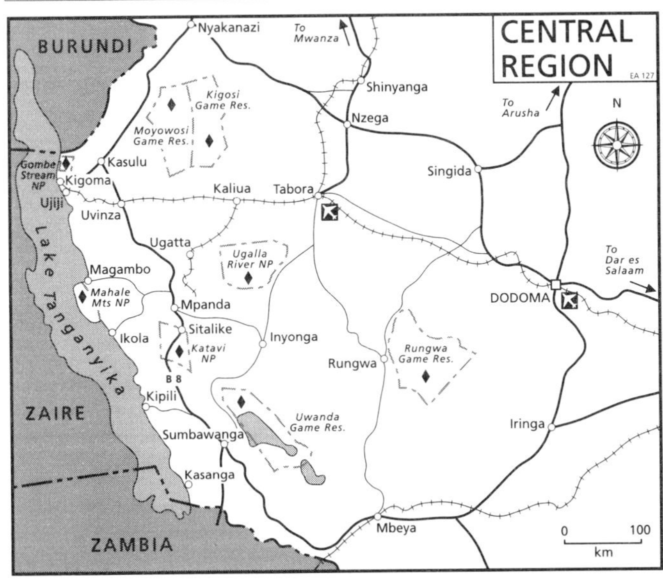

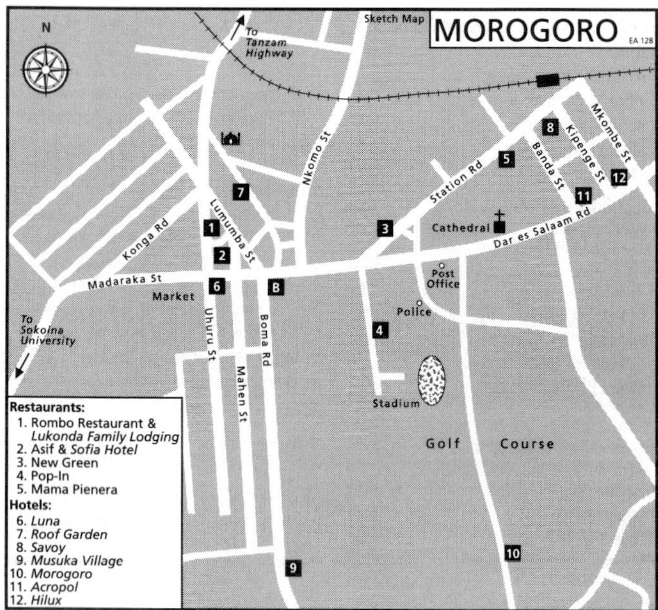

dramatic, swirling mists. It was here that Smuts was confident he would confront and destroy the forces of von Lettow in WW1 – only to be bitterly disappointed, see page 216.

Morogoro has been particularly unlucky in that the 2 main enterprises which were expected to provide substantial employment in the area, the Groundnut Plantation at Kongwa on the route to Dodoma, see page 319, and the Morogoro Shoe Factory (state-owned) have been failures.

The countryside is green and fertile, and large sisal plantations predominate. The town is an important agricultural marketing centre with a population of 120,000, and fruit and vegetables from here are transported the 195 km to Dar es Salaam. The market is probably the largest in the country; it is busy, bustling and worth visiting to soak up the atmosphere. You may well stop here en route to Mikumi National Park which is 100 km further down the road – few visitors seem to stay. It was en route to Morogoro that Edward Sokoine, the Prime Minister, widely expected to be Nyerere's successor, was killed in a road accident in Apr 1984. The Agricultural University in Morogoro has been named after him.

Places of interest

The old German **Boma** is situated to the S of the town in the foothills of the Uluguru Mountains, along Boma Road. The Railway Station is a German building, as are the main buildings of the *Savoy Hotel*, though not particularly distinguished.

At the top of Kingalu Road there is a rock garden, laid out around a mountain stream. It is very pretty, and there is a café.

Further along Boma Road, well into the Ulungurus is **Morningside**. It is a small villa with an ornate frontage and verandah, looking out over the hills. It is almost 10 km from the centre of Morogoro, and it is necessary for Europeans to obtain permission to visit from the District Commissioner's Office on Dar es Salaam Road just opposite the *Acropolis Hotel*.

Local information

● Where to stay

B *Morogoro*, PO Box 1144, T 3270. 1 km from town. Comfortable accommodataion in chalet-style rooms. Main buildings were previously thatched, but now the roofing has been replaced with currugated iron sheeting. Restaurant, bar, swimming pool (currently not in service), conference centre.

C *Savoy*, PO Box 35, T 3245. Just opposite the Railway Station. This was the former *Banhof Hotel* constructed in the German Period. It is now rather shabby and run by the government. **C** *Hilux*. Along Dar es Salaam Rd going out of town on the left. Comfortable. Pleasant outside beer garden at the back. Restaurant. Bar.

D *Acropol*, PO Box 78, Dar es Salaam Rd. Bar, restaurant. Family-run. **D** *Masuka Village*, PO Box 1144, T 3270. Along Boma Rd. New hotel with accommodation in bandas. **D** *Sofia*. Just off Madataka St. Good value. Comfortable. Small pleasant restaurant and bar.

E *Luna*, cnr of Madaralea and Uhuru. Reasonable value.

● Places to eat

♦♦*Morogoro Hotel*. Has reasonable restaurant if perhaps a bit uninspired. ♦♦*Mama Pienera*, on Station Rd. Comfortable establishment. Straightforward menu. ♦*New Green*, on Station Rd. Serves some Indian dishes. ♦*Asif Restaurant*, on Uhuru N of Mandaraka. Indian food. ♦*Sofia Hotel*, uncomplicated but sound. Cosy atmosphere.

● Entertainment

There are 2 **cinemas** – Shan and Sapna. A film here is an experience. There is also a **disco** or live band each Sat at the *Morogoro Hotel*, and a disco at the *Luna Hotel*. The *Hilux Hotel* shows **videos** in the garden bar.

● Transport

Air Morogoro has an airstrip, but there are no regular flights.

Train Tanzanian Railway Corporation (PO Box 468, Dar es Salaam, T 26241, Tlx 41308). Unfortunately the train leaves **Dar es Salaam** (4 times a week) in the evening and reaches Morogoro in the middle of the night. This obviously discourages some visitors and means there is no opportunity to see the beautiful Uluguru Mountains. Trains leave from Dar es

Harvest Dance Of The Turu

The Turu are found in central Tanzania and each year put on a dance which is one of the most colourful and elaborate of all dances in East Africa. The dance is held to celebrate the gathering of the harvest and usually lasts about 3 weeks. The men and youths paint their faces and bodies and wear elaborate headdresses. The women play only a minor role in the dance and they do not dress themselves especially for it, wearing only their normal clothes.

It is only the men and youths who actually partake in the dancing. They gather into small groups and there is competition between the groups for the best dancing. A group of about a dozen individuals stand shoulder-to-shoulder facing in the same direction. To begin with there is comparatively little movement – just a slow and rhythmic rising on their toes and contortions of the body. They all hold bows or staves which they strike together in unison. The dance gradually builds up in intensity. At various stages of the dance groups of women and girls (about the same number as the corresponding group of men and youths) line up opposite the men and youths for a few minutes. However they do not stay long before they retire to the sidelines to be spectators throughout the rest of the dance. At intervals leaders of the groups separate themselves from the group and dance alone nearby. These leaders are usually more elaborately dressed and decorated and their dances will usually be of greater intensity that those of the groups.

Salaam on Tue, Wed, Fri and Sat at 1800 (1st class US$6, 2nd US$4, 3rd US$1).

Road The 196 km road to Morogoro from Dar es Salaam is tarmac. There are numerous buses making the trip, and the fare is around US$3. Buses leave from several locations – by the *Sofia Hotel* just of Madaraka St, from the bus stand on the corner of Boma and Madaraka, and on the road out of town toward Dar es Salaam. There is a good choice of buses, and it is safest (the road is busy and notorious for accidents) and most comfortable to opt for a large coach rather than a minibus.

Dodoma

Dodoma, the new capital of Tanzania, has a population of about 100,000. It is a dry, windy, and some say desolate place to choose for a capital, lying at an altitude 1,133m above sea level which gives it warm days and cool nights. It is located 512 km W of Dar es Salaam.

Dodoma itself was formerly a small settlement of the semi-pastoral Gogo people. Caravan traders passed through the plateau and it developed into a small trading centre. It owes its growth to the Central Railway as the Germans hoped to take advantage of Dodoma as a trading and commercial centre. During WW1 Dodoma was important as a supply base and transit point. In the years after the war, 2 famines struck the area and an outbreak of rinderpest followed. The British administration were less keen than the Germans to develop Dodoma as the administrative centre, for its only real advantages were its central position and location on the railway line. From 1932 Cape to London flights touched down here and Dodoma received all Dar es Salaam's mail which was then transferred by rail.

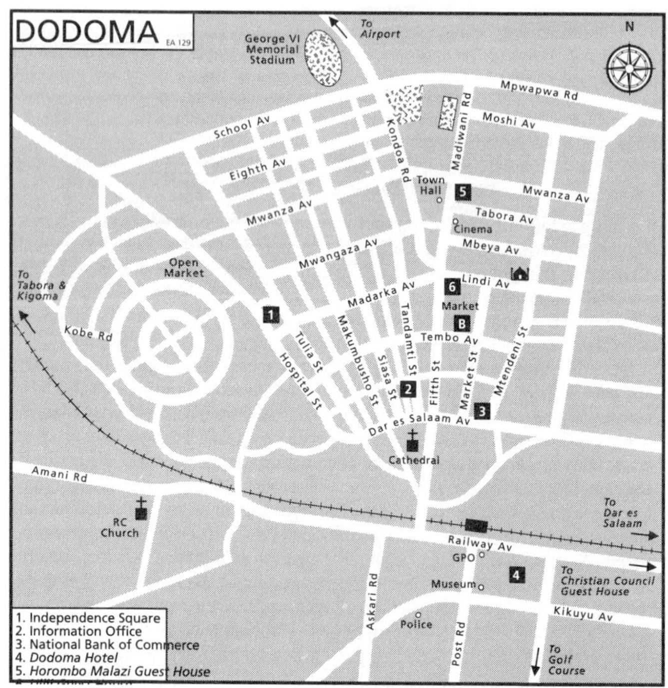

Dodoma, in the very centre of the country, has been designated the new capital and some of the Tanzanian government ministries are in the process of moving. As this process continues parts of Dodoma look rather like a giant building site. Besides this, and being the CCM party political headquarters, the most notable things about Dodoma are probably that it is the only wine-producing area in the country. Few tourists stay long here, although being the administrative centre the city is becoming fairly important for foreign businesses.

There is a ranch of 33,500 ha at nearby Kongwa which produces beef and high quality breeding cattle. It was originally a site for the ill-fated Groundnut Scheme, see page 220. A cattle crossbreed was developed here, known as Mpwapwa Sahiwal. However it has not been an enormous success and has been registered as an endangered species.

Places of interest

The Kondoa Irangi Rock Paintings

These are the nearest attraction to Dodoma and are said to be some of the finest rock paintings in the world. They can be reached 85 km down the Great North Road to Arusha set in the Great Rift Valley. They are a fine example of ancient art and a further reminder of the existence of ancient man in this part of Africa. The rock shelters were used in the later Stone Age by the Bushmanoid tribes who were mainly hunters. Many of the shelters have fantastic views over the plains for miles around. The paintings vary in quality, size, style and colour. At Kolo where interesting paintings are most accessible, guides may be hired. Other sites worth a visit are Kinyasi, Pahl, Swera and Tumbelo.

Local information

● Where to stay

B *Dodoma*, PO Box 239, T 20451. Double self-contained rooms. Old German Hotel, now extended, close to the Railway Station. Bar.

C *Dodoma Inn*, PO Box 411, Dodoma, T 23204/21012.

E *Christian Council of Tanzania Guest House*, T 21258. Past railway station going out of town. Canteen, cold showers, mosquito nets. Good value. **E** *Horombo Malazi Guest House*. Central and simple. **E** *Ujiji Guest House*. Nr the bus station.

● Places to eat

All hotels serve meals to non-residents. It might have been expected that the transfer of the seat of government would have seen the emergence of some reasonable restaurants. This doesn't appear to have been the case. Tanzanian's do not eat out extensively, and the diplomatic community has remained in Dar es Salaam.

● Transport

Air There is an airport at Dodoma and theoretically there are regular flights by *Air Tanza-*

The Miombo Woodland Of Tanzania

A type of woodland called miombo is found in large parts of the south, central and western part of Tanzania. One of the major towns in the heart of miombo country is Tabora. At a glance these areas appear to be ideally suited for agricultural and other development. However this area is infected with the tsetse fly which is a serious hinderance to settlement and so parts of it are very thinly populated, see page 376.

If you are visiting miombo country around the rains it is a very colourful sight – all shades of reds, pinks and browns – and plenty of shade. However in the dry season all the leaves fall off and bush fires are common. There is little shade and the slate grey of the barks of the trees seems to shimmer in the heat. One of the most successful economic activities in areas of miombo is the cultivation of tobacco. This has been introduced in the Urambo area and is ideal as tsetse fly make it unsuitable for livestock.

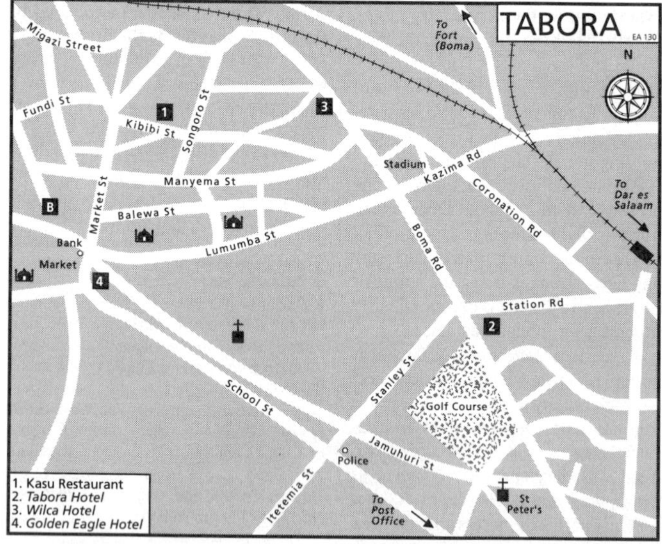

nia (Dar es Salaam: PO Box 543, T 46643/4/5. ATC Building, Ohio St) However cancellations, delays and rescheduling are a real problem. Fare is about US$80 one-way. Now that the National Assembly meets at Dodoma, the flights are often full with VIPs.

Train The Kigoma and Mwanza trains stop at Dodoma. They depart from Dar es Salaam 4 times a week. From **Kigoma** on Tues, Thurs, Fri and Sun at 7 pm, and from **Mwanza** on Tue, Wed, Fri and Sun at 6pm. Fares are US$10, US$5, and US$2 for 1st, 2nd and 3rd class respectively.

Road Buses go to **Arusha** daily theoretically taking 13 hrs. However it can take half as much again as the road is poor. They can fill up so it's advisable to book a seat a day in advance. Costs US$8. The road to **Dar es Salaam** is surfaced all the way and buses go daily, and cost about US$5.

Tabora

The railway continues along the old caravan trading route reaching Tabora. This town was founded in 1820 by Arab slave traders. It developed as a trading centre where local leaders bartered ivory and humans in exchange for guns, beads and cloth. The town has a population of 100,000. It is here that the railway splits in 2, on to Kigomo, or N to Mwanza. For this reason people often stay just a night or 2 in order to change trains.

Places of interest

Tabora is dominated by the **Fort** (or Boma) on a hill overlooking the town built by the Germans at the turn of the century. This is SE of the town centre along Boma Road

Kwihara Museum This is probably one of the major attractions of Tabora. It is located about 10 km outside the town and is dedicated to Dr Livingstone. The museum is in the house that Livingstone occupied for about 10 months before setting off on the final leg of the journey in 1872 that was to be his last. He died less than a year latter at Chitambo, Zambia. The museum, although run down, is interesting and contains various letters, maps, pictures etc associated with Livingstone as well as other early missionaries and explorers.

Local information

● Where to stay

B *Rafiki*, PO Box 310, T 2482. Town Centre. **C** *Tabora* (*Railway Hotel*), PO Box 147, T 2172. Town Centre. Hot water, bar, restaurant. **D** *Wilca*, Boma Rd Comfortable and well-run. **D** *Golden Eagle*, Songeya Rd. Central. Reasonable value. **E** *The Moravian Guest House*. Friendly and pleasant. **E** *YMCA*. Hostel accommodation, spartan.

● Places to eat

♦♦*Wilca*. Simple menu but food is well prepared. ♦*Kasu Restaurant*. Manyara St. Indian food. Good value.

● Transport

Air There is an airport at Tabora and theoretically there are regular flights by *Air Tanzania* (Dar es Salaam: PO Box 543, T 466434/5. ATC Building, Ohio St). However cancellations, delays and rescheduling are a real problem. Fare is about US$150 one-way.

Train The Kigoma and Mwanza trains stop at Tabora. They depart from **Dar es Salaam** 4 times a week – for **Kigoma** on Tues, Thu, Fri and Sun at 7 pm, and for **Mwanza** on Tue, Wed, Fri and Sun at 6.pm. Fares from Dar are US$16, US$8, US$3 for 1st, 2nd and 3rd class respectively.

Road There are daily buses to Mwanza, but the roads are poor. Buses to Dodoma are scheduled daily, but a more reliable route is via Ngeza and Singida. There is a twice-weekly bus to Mbeya, taking roughly 24 hrs over very poor roads. The road from Tabora W to Kigoma is not feasible in the wet months.

Kigoma

Population of 80,000. Altitude 800m above sea level. Kigoma is a small sleepy town on the edge of Lake Tanganyika 1,254 km W of Dar es Salaam. It has one main road that is tree-lined. Most people come here on their way to Burundi or Zambia across the lake on the steamer MV Liemba or else on their way to **Gombe Stream National Park**, see Section on National Parks, see page 387. The **Railway Station**, the terminal point of the line from Dar es Salaam, has been marked by the German colonialists by a very imposing building.

The graveyard at Kigoma

At the graveyard at the top of the hill at Kigoma there are 3 gravestones dating back to the late 19th century. The oldest is that of Rev J. B. Thompson who died at Ujiji on 22 Sept 1878; the second is that of Rev A. W. Dodgshun who also died at Ujiji on 3 Apr 1879; and the third is that of Michel Alexandre de Baize who died on the 12 Dec of the same year, also in Ujiji. The first 2 graves are those of 2 members of the London Missionary Society (LMS) while the third, not actually a missionary, was sent on behalf of the French Government. The LMS, following a donation of £5,000 from a Robert Arthington of Leeds, sent an expedition of 4 ministers and 2 laymen to establish a mission on the shores of Lake Tanganyika. The leader of the party was a Rev Roger Price. Dodgshun and Thompson were 2 of the other ministers.

Thompson had had 7 years experience as a missionary in Matabaleland, while Dodgshun was a young man who had only recently left training. Based on his experiences in South Africa, Price decided to try to use bullocks to carry some of the equipment on their journey inland. However this was impossible as none of the animals survived due to the tsetse fly which was rampant in the area. Price then decided to return to the coast to try and persuade the missionary authorities to establish a whole string of mission stations along the road that headed into the interior, instead of heading straight for the lake.

The expedition that continued onto the Lake divided into 2 with Thompson taking the forward party, and Dodgshun following on behind. The advance party reached Ujiji on 23 Aug 1878, and Thompson who had been seriously ill during the early part of the journey, again fell ill. He had never really recovered and on 22 Sept 1878 he died. Meanwhile Dodgshun was having many problems and did not reach Ujiji until 27 Mar 1879, by which time he was very

unwell. He died just one week later.

Michel Alexandre de Baize (known as Abbe De Baize) had gone out to Africa under the auspices of the French government. He was a young man, with no experience of Africa or of exploration. He had been generously equipped with a large sum of money by the French government and had a huge array of supplies and equipment. His provisions included such weird and wonderful things as rockets, fireworks, coats of armour and a barrel organ. He planned to travel across Africa from E to W and set off from Bagamoyo with a small army of about 800 men. However, all sorts of troubles beset him. He was attacked at night, many of his porters deserted which meant that much of his equipment had to be abandoned and many of his supplies were stolen (often by the deserting porters). When he reached Ujiji he apparently became upset that the White Fathers failed to come out to greet him. He is said to have paraded Ujiji firing his revolver. He received assistance from the LMS before setting off for the N shores of Lake Tanganyika. During that stretch of the journey he offended a local chief and set fire to a number of huts and had to be rescued by the LMS at Ugaha. He then fell ill and the LMS again came to his aid. When he was well enough he returned to Ujiji where he again fell ill. He died on 12 Dec 1879.

The LMS finally abandoned their station at Ujiji in 1884. Whilst here, it is well worth making a trip to Ujiji which is 10 km S of Kigoma, see page 325. The major industry here is fishing. This is mostly done by night with pressurized paraffin lamps used to attract the fish. The sight of hundreds of flickering lamps bobbing up and down and reflected in the lake waters is really quite a spectacle.

Local information

● Where to stay

C *Aqua*, on lake shore. Comfortable and new. **D** *Railway*, T 64. Overlooking the lake, beautiful views. Holds a disco on Sat. **E** *Mwanga Guest House*, PO Box 57, T 88. Town Centre. **F** *Kigoma*. Town Centre. Spacious rooms, good value. Serves reasonable food and has a noisy bar. **F** *Lake View*. Town Centre. **F** *Mapinduzi*. Basic. Doubles only.

● Places to eat

♦♦*Lake View*. Simple but good value meals. ♦♦*Kigoma Hotel*. Adequate, if a little uninspired. ♦*Ally's*. Along Ujiji Rd going E. Good value.

● Useful addresses

Banks National Commercial Bank is next to the market. **Consulates** The Burundi Consulate is just off the main street and the Zaire Consulate is next door to the police station. **Hospital** There is a Hospital a km or so down the road towards Ujiji. The **post office** is about 500m to the N of the main roundabout past the Caltex station. **Research centre** The Mahale Mountains Wildlife Research Centre has an office in Kigoma where you can ask about transport to the park and accommodation availability there.

● Transport

Air Flights to Kigoma from Dar es Salaam are costly at over US$200 one-way. Theoretically there are regular weekly flights by *Air Tanzania* (Dar es Salaam: PO Box 543, T 46643/4/5. ATC Building, Ohio St) However cancellations, delays and rescheduling are a real problem. Air Tanzania run a minibus from their office by the roundabout to the airport.

Train The train goes to **Dar es Salaam** 4 times

MV LIEMBA

The *MV Liemba* was the flag ship of the German flotilla on Lake Tanganyika in WW1 and like the German sea fleet was scuttled by the Germans. It was first raised by the Belgians, and then, with more success by the British and is still in working order going up and down the lake.

In 1910, having made rapid progress with the Central Railway line, the Germans began to consider further consolidation of their presence in Central Africa. A ship was ordered in 1913 from the shipbuilders Jos L Meyer at Papenburg on Ems at a cost of 406,000 marks (which was equal to £20,000 at the then current rate of exchange). The cost of transporting the ship and reconstructing it in Tanganyika was a further £16,000.

The first steamer was the *Gotzen* and in 1913 a second ship was ordered from the same company, called the *Rechenberg*. In Nov 1913 the first ship was completed and it then had to be taken apart, packed up and sent in 3 consignments to Dar es Salaam. From here it was taken by railway to Kigoma where it was put back together again. It was held up in Dar es Salaam for some months while the railway to Kigoma was completed. However in 1914 all the pieces of the *Gotzen* arrived in Kigoma and it was fitted back together. The first trial runs took place in Jun 1915 and average speeds of around 8 knots were reached.

The steamer was the flagship of the German flotilla on Lake Tanganyika and was used during WW1 as armed transport, particularly to carry troops down the lake from Kigoma to Kasanga (which was then known as Bismarkburg). The *Gotzen* was the largest ship on the lake at this time and could carry about 900 men in a quarter of the time that it took the dhows to do the same job. In Jun 1916 the *Gotzen* was attacked by Belgian aeroplanes but was not too seriously damaged. In Jul of the same year, when the railway to Kigoma was captured, the Germans decided to scuttle the *Gotzen*. She was filled with cement and sunk off the mouth of the Malagarasi River.

After the war, when the Belgians were in charge of the lake province, they raised the *Gotzen* and towed her to moorings at Kigoma harbour. It was not successful and she sank again in deep water. In Mar 1921 the British took over at Kigoma from the Belgians and the decision was made to attempt once more to raise the vessel. Initially the cost of salvage was estimated at £7,500 but in fact the operation took much longer, and cost much more than had been thought. The final bill for raising, refitting and reconditioning the steamer came to about £50,000. This included the money that the Belgians had spent in their attempt and compared with the German cost of building, transporting and reconstructing the steamer in the first place which came to £36,000.

The ship was to be renamed and various suggestions were put forward. Some examples of suggestions included Livingstone because of his connections with Kigoma, or Kagura which is the name by which Livingstone was known across much of S Africa and which means 'man with a little dog'. The decision that was finally made was to name the steamer *Liemba* as this was the name by which Lake Tanganyika had originally been known by the people living around it. The vessel was rechristened on 16 May 1927 and in trials held in May the average speed that was maintained was 8.5 knots – not too bad for a ship that had spent from 26 Jul 1916 to 16 Mar 1924 at the bottom of the lake.

a week leaving Kigoma on Tues, Thurs, Fri and Sun at about 7pm. The journey is a total of 1,254 km and it takes about 36 hrs although it may be worth getting off at Morogoro and doing the last stretch by road, saving a few hours. Fares to Dar es Salaam US$26 1st class, US$18 2nd, US$3 3rd. Book ahead if at all possible.

Road There are local buses to Kasulu and Ujiji, but no long distance services.

Lake The ferry on Lake Tanganyika is the *MV Liemba*, see page 323. It has a weekly service. It arrives in Kigoma from Bujumbura (Burundi) on Tues morning and leaves at 4pm on Wed for Mpulungu (Zambia), arriving there on Fri morning. It stops at lots of small ports on the way. The return to Kigoma is at 1600 on Fri, arriving Sun morning in Kigoma. The departure

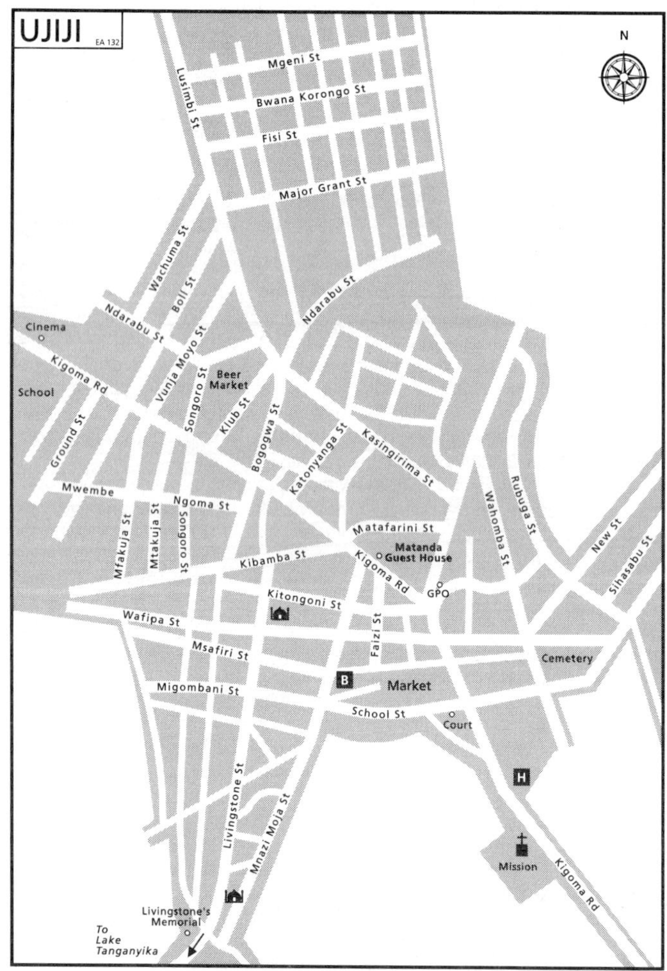

for Bujumbura is at 1600 on Sun, arriving Mon morning. Departure from Bujumbura at 1600 Mon, to arrive at Kigoma on Tues morning. Fares are to Bujumbura US$7, US$5, US$2.50 and to Mpulungu US$16, US$12, US$5.0 for 1st, 2nd and 3rd class respectively. 3rd class are benches or deck space, 2nd class cabins are small, hot and stuffy with 4 bunks. 1st class cabins have 2 bunks, a window, fan. Meals and drinks are available on the ferry and are paid for in Tanzanian shillings.

Gombe Stream National Park, see page 387, can only be reached by lake taxis (small boats with an outboard motor) which are hired at Kigoma (ask around for the best price). The journey takes about 3 hrs.

Ujiji

This village 10 km S of Kigoma is a small market village with a thriving boat building industry. It used to be the terminus for the old caravan route from the coast. The Arab influence brought inland by the caravans is clear to see. The houses are typical of the coastal Swahili architecture and the population is mainly Muslim. It is however most famous for being the location where the words 'Dr Livingstone, I presume' were spoken by Henry Stanley. The site where this is thought to have occured is marked by a plaque, between the town and the shore, on Livingstone Street. There are also 2 mango trees that are supposed to have been grafted from the one under which they met.

The **post office** on Kigoma Rd is a substantial structure dating from the German period. Further S on Kigoma Road, past the hospital, is the **White Fathers' Mission**.

- **Where to stay and eat** E *Matanda Guest House* is plain and cheap. There are several other small guest houses and eating places on Kigoma Rd between Livingstone St and the Post Office.

- **Transport** Regular buses to and from Kigoma. In Kigoma, buses leave from outside the railway station.

SOUTH WEST: IRINGA AND MBEYA

Contents

Maps

The SW has much to offer in the form of huge untouched areas of great beauty and wildlife and has only recently been 'discovered' by many tourists. The parks in the south west are increasingly popular particularly with those who want to avoid the tourist trails. The area's isolation is as much a part of its attraction as a problem. The major towns in the SW are Iringa and Mbeya. Road communications are good, and Mbeya is on the TAZARA railway.

Beyond the Mikumi National Park the road climbs into the Kitonga Hills which are part of the Udzungwa Mountains. It is quite a journey, with sharp bends, and dense forest all around. Part of the road runs alongside the Ruaha River gorge. Eventually the road levels out to the plateau on which Iringa is sited.

The southern highlands of Tanzania form one of the largest blocks of highland within East Africa. They mostly have a high rainfall and because of their altitude are cool. Like the rest of S Tanzania (and unlike the highlands to the N) they have one long wet season and one long dry season. As with most highlands areas in East Africa they are associated with the Rift Valley System and there has been much volcanic activity in the area over the years. It is probably their inaccessibility that is the most notable feature about the southern highlands. Until the construction of the TAZARA railway Mbeya was 650 km from the nearest railway and this meant that development of the area was slow. However the high rainfall and rich soil have meant that this area is agriculturally productive in both food crops and some coffee and tea which are the major cash crops in the area.

Iringa

With a population of 90,000 Iringa is a fair-sized town. At an altitude of 1,635m Iringa is 502 km from Dar es Salaam on the main Tanzania-Zambia road beyond the Mukumi National Park. A fertile area, it is an important farming centre and maize, vegetables, fruits and tobacco are grown here. The town itself, set on a plateau, commands a fantastic view over the surrounding countryside. The pleasant climate attracted settlers to the area and German architecture can still be seen in the town. The streets are lined with trees, all planted when Tanzania was German East Africa. The area is of some historical interest for near Ibinga, at Kalenga is where Chief Mkwawa fought off the Germans in an uprising of 1894. He was finally defeated in 1898, but refusing to be captured by the Germans he committed suicide. His head was severed from his body and sent back to Germany. It was finally returned to Tanzania in 1954 and is on display at

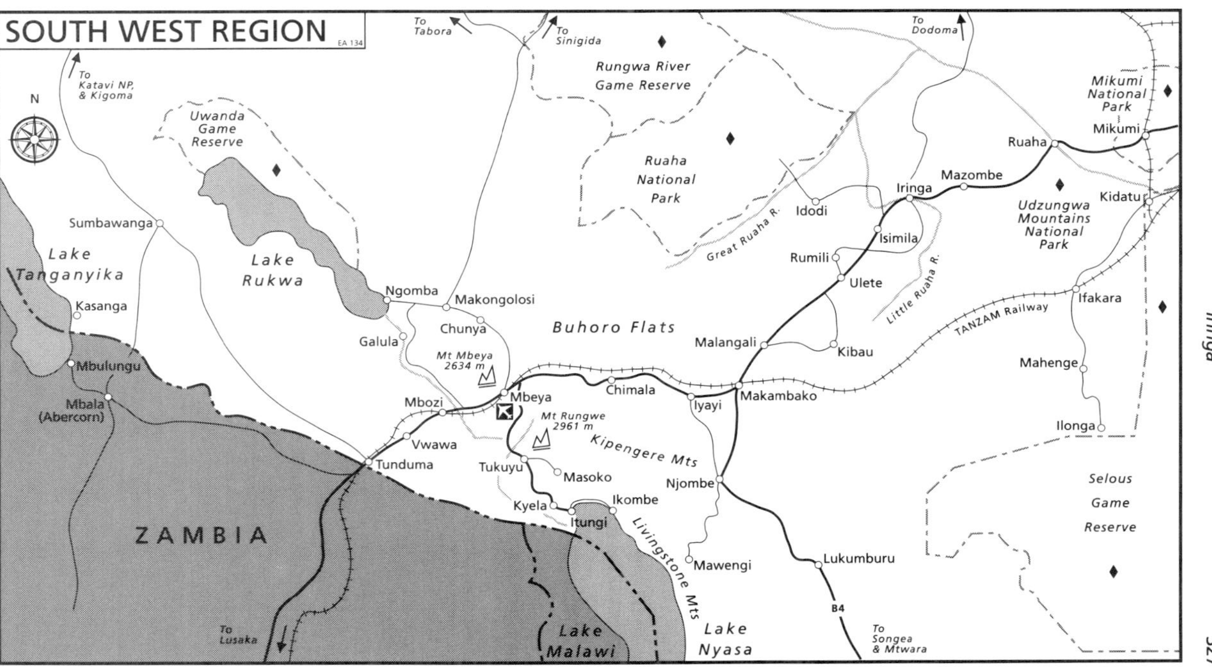
SOUTH WEST REGION
EA 134
To Tabora
To Sinigida
To Dodoma
To Katavi NP, & Kigoma
N
Rungwa River Game Reserve
Mikumi National Park
Uwanda Game Reserve
Ruaha National Park
Mikumi
Ruaha
Mazombe
Iringa
Kidatu
Idodi
Udzungwa Mountains National Park
Sumbawanga
Isimila
Great Ruaha R.
Lake Tanganyika
Lake Rukwa
Rumili
Ulete
Little Ruaha R.
Ngomba
Makongolosi
Ifakara
Kasanga
TANZAM Railway
Chunya
Buhoro Flats
Galula
Malangali
Kibau
Mahenge
Mt Mbeya 2634 m
Mbulungu
Mbeya
Chimala
Iyayi
Makambako
Mbala (Abercorn)
Mbozi
Mt Rungwe 2961 m
Ilonga
Vwawa
Kipengere Mts
Tunduma
Tukuyu
Masoko
Njombe
Selous Game Reserve
Kyela
Ikombe
Itungi
Livingstone Mts
ZAMBIA
Mawengi
Lukumburu
B4
To Lusaka
Lake Malawi
Lake Nyasa
To Songea & Mtwara

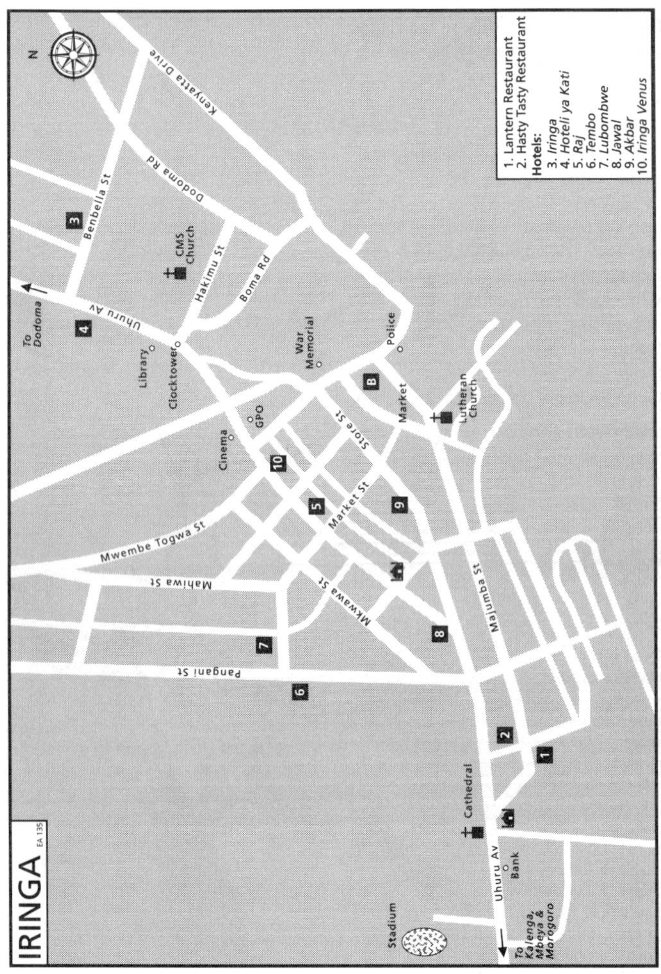

the small museum at **Kalenga**. This town is within easy reach of Ruaha National Park, see section on National Parks, page 381.

The road from Iringa to Mbeya goes through mixed woodland and savannah as well as cultivated land. Gradually it opens up to more open savannah. There are various roads that you can take off the main road that will lead you into the Usangu Plains. About 25 km from Mbeya on the right hand side of the road is the Mwambalisi River which is fairly spectacular during the rainy season. At about 37 km from Mbeya is the Mlowo River and one of its waterfalls can be seen.

The old **Boma**, the **Town Hall**, the

Hospital and **Post Office** in the centre of town are an impressive legacy of German colonial architecture.

Places of interest

Isimila Stone Age Site This is considered to be one of the finest stone age sites in East Africa. The site was once a shallow lake, now dried up. The tools found there are believed to date from 60,000 years ago. Also amongst the finds were animal bones, including those of 2 now extinct species: a hippopotamus (*H Gorgops*) and a giraffe (*Sivatherium*). A small museum was built on the site in 1969 and displays some of the tools, fossils and bones found during excavations.

Isimila Gully This is upstream from the stone age site and is a spectacular natural phenomenon. Erosion over the millenia has left several standing pillars which tower above you.

Isimila can be reached by buses going to Mbeya, and is about 20 km from town. There is then a wall to the site of about 2 km. A taxi from Iringa will cost US$20.

Local information

● **Where to stay**

C *Iringa* (*Railway Hotel*), Box 48, T 2039. Town centre. Comfortable colonial hotel, built by the Germans in anticiapation of the arrival of a railway line which never materialized.

D *Isimila*, Box 216, T 2605. Uhuru Ave.

E *Hoteli ya Kati*. On Uhuru Ave, past library. Run down, but nice garden. **E** *Raj*, Uhuru St close to Uheme St. Modest but comfortable. **E** *Tembo*, Pangani St. Small but reasonable. **E** *Lubombwe*. Just off Pangani St. Fairly simple. **E** *Jawal*. Store St. Central. Basic. **E** *Akbar*. Store St. Simple. Basic. **E** *Iringa Venus*. Central. Simple but reasonable value.

● **Places to eat**

♦♦*Lantern Restaurant*. Pleasant location. Sound cuisine. ♦♦*Raj Hotel*. Recommended. International and Indian food. ♦♦*Iringa Hotel*. Solid fare and reasonable value. ♦*Hoteli Ya Kati*. Good value. ♦*Hasty Tasty*, on Majumbu St. Good value.

● **Transport**

Road This really the only feasible mode. Buses from Dar es Salaam leave from the Mnazi Moja bus stand. They take about 12 hrs and cost US$6. To Mbeya costs US$3 and takes 3 hrs.

Mbeya

Population 160,00, altitude 1,737m. Set in the lush and fertile part of Tanzania, against the Mbeya Range, this town has a most scenic setting. The town was founded in the late 1920's when the gold mines at Lupa became active, and continued to grow after they shut down in 1956. It has developed into a bustling town and is an ideal base from which to explore the Southern Highlands. It is only 114 km from the Zambian border and is the last main station on the Tazara railway before the border and is a popular overnight stop. Because of this location it is an important trading centre. However being 875 km from Dar es Salaam it has been rather isolated until the construction of the railway and the sealed road.

Places of interest

Chunyu is an old gold-mining and tobacco market town 65 km to the N. It is rather inaccessible without your own transport. There are some small guest houses and some faded buildings from its more prosperous era in the interwar period.

Mbozi Meteorite is a 15 tonne mass, one of the world's largest, SW of Mbeya, along the road to Zambia, with the turnoff just after Mbowa. It is a good 10 km from the highway.

Walking This is walking country and you will be able to get some really fantastic views of the surrounding countryside. The mountain to the N of the town is **Kaluwe** (otherwise known as Loleza Peak) and rises to 2656m. It can be reached in about 2 hrs and is well worth it if you have a spare afternoon. Go about 150m from the roundabout towards the water works, turning left down a gravel track before you reach them. You will pass a quarry and a few houses before getting to the path that climbs up the mountain where you will undoubtedly find the views well worth the fairly steep climb. In the wet season the highland flowers are also impressive.

Mbeya Peak, rising to 2809m, is the highest peak in the range and looms above the town. There are 2 possible routes – one a harder climb than the other. The first is down a track about 13 km down the Chunya Road. From the end of this track the climb will take about 1 hr. The second, and more difficult climb, is only recommended for those prepared for a steep climb and, in parts, a real scramble. This begins from the coffee farm at Luiji. There is very charming accommodation here at C *Utengele Country Resort*. At the top you can catch your breath and admire the view for miles around.

Another worthwhile, but energetic trek is **Pungulume** (2230m) at the W end of the range. It is approached from the road at its base near Njerenji. Alternatively follow the ridge from Mbeye Peak. This particular trek should be avoided in the wet season.

Probably one of the best viewpoints in the area is known as **World's End**. From here you will see the Usangu Flats and the Rift Valley Escarpment; the view is really quite fantastic. To get to it go about 20 km down the Chunya Road to a forest camp and take the track off to the right.

Local information

● Where to stay

C *Mbeya Peak*, PO Box 822. Town centre. **C** *Mkwezulu*, PO Box 995. Town centre. **C** *Mount Livingstone*, PO Box 1401, T 3331, Tlx 51175. **C** *Rift Valley*, PO Box 1631, T 3756, Tlx 51256. Town centre **C** *Tembo Tourist Resort*, 25 km on the road to Tunduma. **C** *Mbeya Railway*, PO Box 80. Town centre. Managed by the Tanzanian Railways Corporation, comfortable, clean and with hot water, but has seen better days.

E *Moravian Youth Hostel*. Clean and friendly.

F *Karibuni Guest House*, T 3035. Modest but pleasant.

● Places to eat

♦♦*Mbeya Railway Hotel* Good value. ♦♦*Rift Valley Hotel*. Good standard of cuisine and

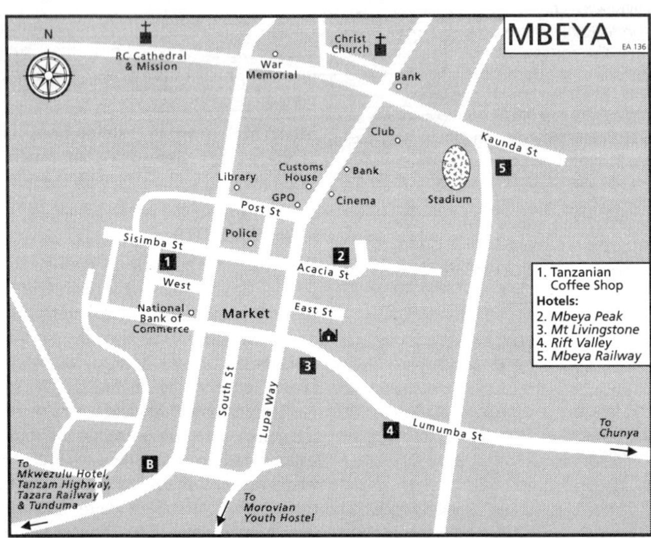

varied menu. ♦*Moravian Guest House*. Serves good value cheap food. Also good value is the dinner at ♦*Tanzania Coffee Shop*. Nr the market.

● Useful addresses

Bank National Bank of Commerce, close to Market Square. **Post office**, nr the Library.

● Transport

Air There are once-weekly flights scheduled into Mbeya, by *Air Tanzania* (Dar es Salaam), PO Box 543, T 46643/4/5. ATC Building, Ohio St). However, flights are currently erratic. Fare is about US$150 one-way. Being so close to the Mbeya Range makes for a fairly spectacular, if dramatic, landing.

Train Trains are often full and booking in advance is essential through the Tanzanian-Zambia Railway Authority, (Dar es Salaam: PO Box 2434, T 64191, Tlx 41466.) Trains depart at 1645 on Tue, and at 1230 on Mon and Fri. The Tue train is scheduled to be slightly faster and costs a bit more (1st class US$18, 2nd US$10, 3rd US$6). The journey takes about 2 days. The TAZARA rail station is outside the town on the Tanzam highway – the main road linking Dar es Salaam to Zambia.

Road Buses are very regular to **Dar es Salaam**. Fare is around US$15 luxury, US$10 semi-luxury and US$7 ordinary and journey takes about 12 hrs. The road goes through the Mikumi National Park (see section on National Parks, page 379. There are 2 buses a week to Tabora: the road is poor, they take about 24 hrs and cost around US$8. There are frequent small buses to the border at **Tunduma**, or to Kyele close to Lake Nyasa, both taking about 2 hrs and costing US$1.50.

Tukuyu

This is a small town about 40 km S of Mbeya, on the road to Lake Nyasa. It was an administrative centre for the Germans and there is a group of colonial buildings to the SE of the town.

It is a good centre for trekking. It is necessary to engage a guide, and the *Langiboss Hotel* can arrange one. Among the local attractions are **Mount Rungwe** accessed from Isangole 10 km N of Tukuyu, which will take a full day to climb; **Masoko Crater Lake** 15 km to the SW; **Kapalogwe Falls** about 10 km to the S; **Ngozi Crater Lake** about 20 km N of Tukuyu in the Poroto Mountains; **Kiwira Natural Bridge** 10 km to the N.

● **Where to stay D** *Langiboss*. About 1 km from the town centre on the road to Masoko. Modest but well run.

● **Transport** There are regular buses running from Mbeya to Kyela.

Kyele

This is the access town for the ferries that leave from Itungi to the small ports down Lake Nyasa to Mbamton Bay. There are several small guest houses. There is no regular accommodation at Itungi.

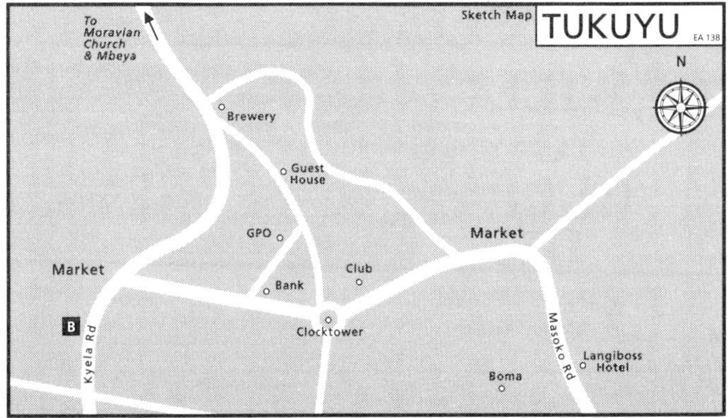

• **Ferries** The boats are run by *Tanzania Railways Corporation (TRC)* and the office is 1 km out of town toward Itungi which is 10 km further on. Ferries depart Itungi, Mon and Fri at 0700 and the main stops are at Lumbira, Lupingu and Manda before reaching **Mamba Bay** at midnight. It leaves Mamba at soon after midnight and arrives back at Itungi at 1700. The fare is US$4 to Mamba. A bus leaves the TRC office for Itungi at around 0500.

Makema Beach

This is a pleasant resort at the N of Lake Byara. There is a regular bus from Kyela each day, the distance is 35 km, and it costs US$0.50. **E** *Lutheran Mission* has good value accommodation in bandas and is well recommended. It is possible to camp.

Mamba Bay

This is mainly a transit point for travellers en route for Songea. As the ferry arrives at midnight, you will probably need to stay at the **E** *New Mbamba Guest House*.

Njombe

This is on the route from Songea to the Mbeya-Iringa highway. There are frequent buses between Mbeya and Songea which pass through Njombe. Accommodation at **E** *Milimani Hotel*, close to centre, or **E** *Shamboi Guest House*. Nr bus stand.

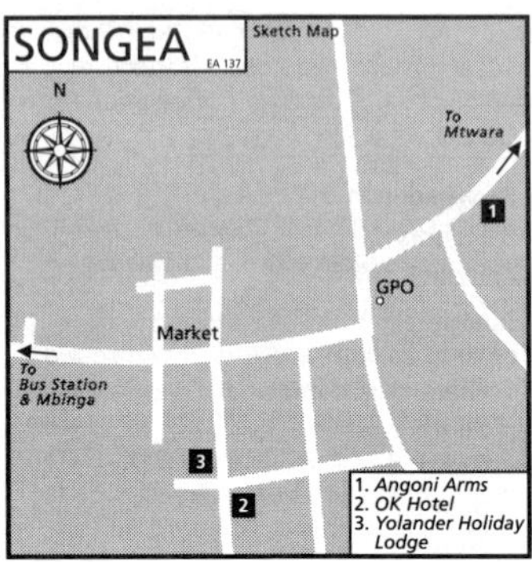

Songea

This town was comparatively isolated until the construction of the sealed road from the Iringa-Mbeya highway.

• **Where to stay** **E** *Angoni*. Located to the E of the centre, past the post office on the road to Mtwara. **E** *OK Hotel*. To the S of the market. **E** *Yolander Holiday Lodge*. Located S of market.

• **Transport** Buses go to **Mbamba Bay** via Mbinga. You should allocate a whole day to the 180 km journey. In the wet seasons, Dec to Apr, the unsealed road can be very slow. There are regular buses between **Mbeya** and **Songea** via Njombe. The road is sound, and the buses, leaving in the morning at 0700 take about 10 hrs to cover the 400 km and the fare is around US$6.

ZANZIBAR AND PEMBA

CONTENTS

MAPS

ZANZIBAR

The very name Zanzibar conjures up exotic and romantic images. There are 2 main islands making up Zanzibar, Unguja and Pemba. Zanzibar Town is on Unguja Island, but Unguja Island is popularly refered to as Zanzibar. The town is steeped in history, is full of atmosphere and immensely attractive. There are excellent beaches on the E coast. The island is about 96 km long and is separated from the mainland by a channel 35 km wide. The main rains are from Mar to May, and the best time to visit is from Jun to Oct.

Zanzibar is perhaps most famous for once being the home of the slave trade, and being an important trading post for spices and cloves. Zanzibar was once the world's most important supplier of cloves but it has now been overtaken by producers in the Far East. Cloves do remain the most important export of the island, while tourism is now the largest source of foreign currency. On the W part of the island there are clove plantations with trees 10-20m tall.

The island has been a stopping-off point for traders going up and down the coast for many years and as a result has seen many different travellers including Greeks, Egyptians, Persians and Chinese. European explorers and missionaries also visited the island and it was used as a starting point for their travels inland. The legacy of these early visitors is shown in the people, architecture and culture.

Since 1964, when the rule of the Sultans ended, Zanzibar has neglected its heritage. In a union with the mainland, Zanzibar sought to progress by socialist policies and a modernising philosophy. The relics of this period are to be seen in the brutal concrete blocks constructed to the E of Creek Road in Zanzibar Town. Fortunately the glorious old Stone Town escaped unscathed, and with a change of heart toward the past, is now being restored.

History

The origin of the name Zanzibar is disputed. The Omani Arabs believe it came from Zayn Zal Barr which means 'Fair is the Island'. The alternative origin is in two parts – the early inhabitants of the island were from the mainland and were given the name *Zenj*, a Persian word which is a corruption of *Zangh* meaning negro. The word *bar* which means coast was added to this to give negro coast.

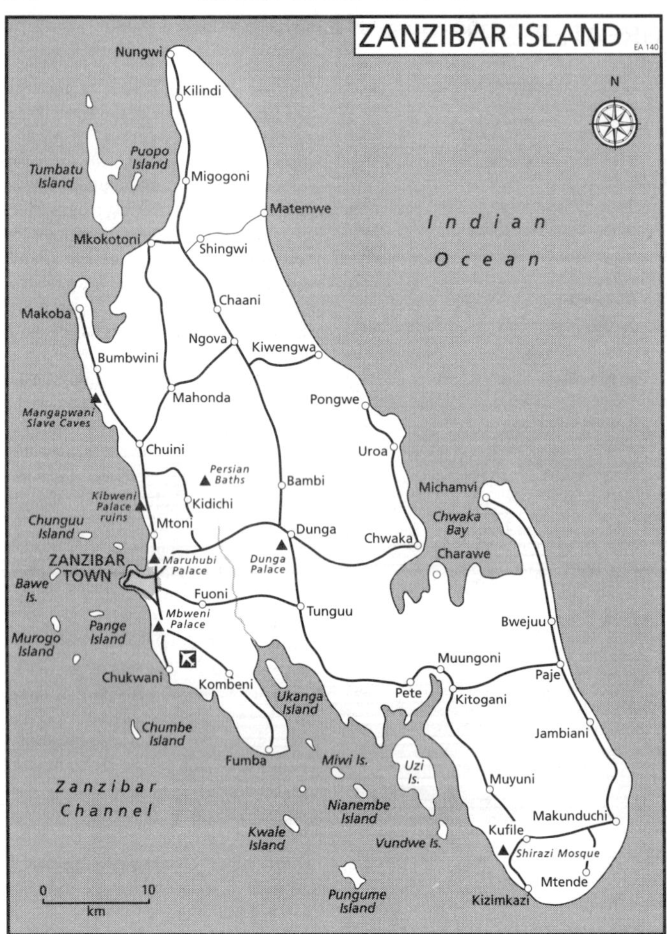

The earliest visitors were Arab traders who brought with them Islam which has remained the dominant religion on the island. They are believed to have arrived in the 8th century. The earliest building that remains is the mosque at Kazimkazi which dates from about 1100.

By the 17th century Zanzibar had developed into a prosperous town and was considered to be so important a trading post that Sultan Seyyid Said moved his capital from Muscat in Oman to Zanzibar. He built palaces for himself and his family and his presence caused trade to boom, particularly after treaties with Britain and France. The slave trade gradually developed and when demand for slaves peaked, Zanzibar was an important trading centre for slaves. Many

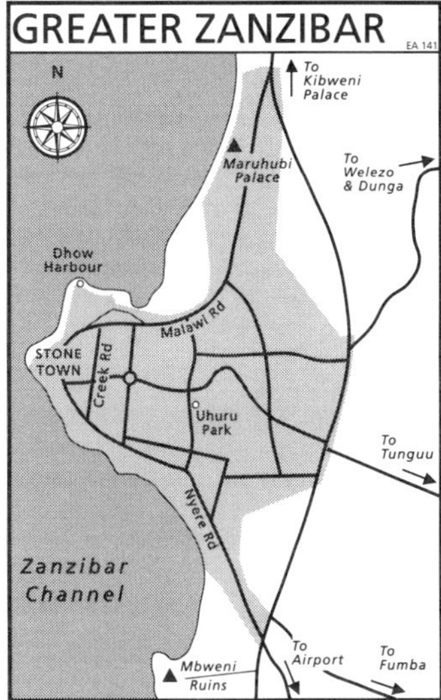

of the slaves were exported whilst others were bought by plantation owners to work on the clove and other plantations in Zanzibar and on the mainland.

With the arrival of European missionaries, campaigns for the abolition of the slave trade began and in 1873 the slave trade was formally abolished. The demand however continued and by the 1880's the internal demand had overtaken the external demand in importance and the trade continued illegally in Zanzibar into the 20th century. Underground tunnels and caves, which can be see at Mangapwani, see page 346, were used to hide the slaves until they could be shipped out in secret at night.

Colonial Zanzibar

Zanzibar became a British protectorate under the Sultan in 1890 and the British rapidly assumed almost complete control. By 1963 the Arab population was about 50,000 (out of a total population estimated at 300,000). At this time the African population was divided into Shirazis who were longterm residents and the mainlanders who were either descendants of slaves or more recent immigrants.

In the mid 1950's the Arab population decided that their survival depended on them taking up the leadership of Zanzibarian Nationalist Movement. By being well organized, gaining the support of many Shirazis and with the mainlanders split, the Zanzibar and Pemba Peoples Party (ZPPP) and the Arab Sultanate Nationalist Party (ASP) formed the government when independence was granted in 1963. The Afro-Shirazi Party had formed in 1957 and although it gained popularity rapidly, it failed to win power.

Independence and Union

Following elections in 1961 there were riots when an estimated 70 Arabs were killed and there could be little doubt of the strength of feelings running in the communities. In Jan 1964 a Ugandan-born adventurer crossed at night from the mainland in a small boat with 3 others. They were armed with rifles. On hearing some shooting, the young Sultan panicked, thinking a full-scale invasion was underway, drove to the airport and fled to Britain. He continues to live in Plymouth on the south coast of the UK.

This event sparked a violent revolution in which an estimated 5,000 Arabs were massacred, a similar number exiled and the rest dispossessed. A revolutionary council led by Abeid Amaan Karume and formed by the ASP replaced the sultan. In 1964 Zanzibar, Pemba and Tanganyika merged to form the United Republic of Tanzania with Karume as Zanzibar's president. It was not until 1977 that the 2 parties, TANU and ASP merged to form the present-day Chama cha Mapinduzi (CCM).

A Zanzibar Excursion From Kenya

Zanzibar is easily accessible from Kenya and is highly recommended as an extension to your Kenyan holiday. However it is important to remember that it is very different from the relaxed Kenyan atmosphere. 90% of the population are Muslim and the contrast with the friendly Kenyans is marked. Allow perhaps five nights: it is worth staying in Stone Town for perhaps two of these and the remainder of your time on the East coast. Spice Tours are excellent but only if the spices are in season. Don't worry if you find it all very different and strange: relax and enjoy this wonderful island.

Arrival

For many travellers who arrive from Mombasa, Zanzibar can seem a little daunting which can quickly tarnish the island's romantic picture. For a start, there is a degree of bureaucracy at both Mombasa and Zanzibar airports which involves queueing apparently pointlessly in several lengthy lines – this can be hot and irratating. Having the correct documentation and particularly a current Yellow Fever certificate will help. If you don't have one, you will not be allowed on the plane until it has been obtained (this will certainly cost money one way or another).

Money

Make sure that you take a lot of hard currency in small denomination notes. It is easy to forget that Zanzibar is an international destination and you will have to pay the full departure tax BOTH ways. In 1994, there was a small bank in the airport immediately before you exit the baggage retrieval area. It does NOT accept travellers cheques or Kenyan shillings but will change US dollars, Pounds sterling, Deustche Marks and some other hard currencies. Rates are not very good so change a small amount in order to have sufficient funds to get a taxi or bus into town. US$20 or equivalent should suffice.

Despite official denials, many hotels still insist on being paid in US dollars. Very few will accept travellers cheques and even fewer credit cards. Often they will want paying in advance. If you run short of hard currency, go to the Bank of Tanzania behind the fort. This is the only bank where you can change travellers cheques for hard currency. Again it will not change Kenyan shillings. Officially you will only be able to change 50% into dollars, the remainder will be given to you in Tanzanian shillings.

There is no problem in paying for restaurants or tours in local currency. There are many bureaux which open long hours and give good rates – the one at the *Hotel International* near the market is recommended.

Hotels

If your hotel is in Stone Town (and this is highly recommended), don't be surprised when the vehicle stops amidst run down buildings. This will be the closest the vehicle is able to go before the narrow alleys begin. A walk of 5-10 minutes with your luggage is common especially if you are staying near the centre (eg *Spice Inn*). Make sure that the taxi driver actually takes you to the hotel but don't assume that he will carry your luggage. With this in mind, take as little luggage as possible. Telecommunications from Kenya are not always reliable. Don't be surprised if the hotel has not heard of you – keep insisting that they find a room. Finally, don't expect to be able to sleep in, there are many mosques in Stone Town: the morning call to pray invariably starts well before dawn.

Orientation

The bewildering maze of streets can be disorientating (they are dusty and dirty) and when coupled with the very Arab nature of the town can even feel a little threatening. Only bicycles, scooters and hand carts are able to use the narrow alleys. You must constantly make way for those with wheels – listen out for the tinkling of bells and the 'quack-quack' of horns. It is important to follow Muslim dress code to avoid offence. Avoid open-toed footwear as you never know what you may find in your path.

However, this feeling quickly passes. Stone Town actually covers quite a small area and once accustomed to the 'feel', you will be able to walk around more confidently and enjoy the atmosphere as well as the architecture and lovely doors. Remember it is quite safe, even at night. The streets are very poorly lit in places so you may find a torch useful. Try to avoid the really dark ones. You will fairly quickly find a guide to help you back to your hotel if you do become lost (a small tip will be expected). Do not be afraid to ask at your hotel reception for help either – they usually have someone on hand.

Further information can be found in the Tanzania information for visitors section on page 394.

Zanzibar Town

Even with a map it is suprisingly easy to get lost as the narrow winding alleys and overhanging balconies mean it is difficult to mantain a sense of direction. Alternatively hire a guide who will show you all the sights. A local artist John da Silva (T 32123) gives walking tours that are particularly attractive if you are interested in the architecture of the island. As you wander around the streets you will notice that the ground floor of many of the buildings is taken up by shops and businesses, whilst above are the homes of the Zanzibaris. Exploring on foot during the day or night is quite safe and will give you a real feel of this wonderful town and its people.

The area to the W of Creek Road is known as the old **Stone Town** and a tour will take at least a day. It is such a fascinating place that it is easy to spend a week wandering the narrow streets and still find new places of charm and interest. A good place to start the trip is from the **Central Market** located on Creek Road. This was opened in 1904 and remains a bustling, colourful and aromatic place. Here you will see Zanzibarian life carrying on as it has done for so many years – lively, busy and noisy. Outside are long, neat rows of bicycles carefully locked and guarded by their minder while people are buying and selling inside the market. Fruit, vegetable, meat and fish are all for sale here as well a household implements, many of them locally made, clothing and footwear. **NB** The chicken, fish and meat areas are not for the squeamish.

Nearby, also on Creek Road, is the **Anglican Church of Christ** which was built in 1887 to commemorate the end of the slave trade. It is built on the actual site of the slave market. Inside are impressive marble pillars and stained glass windows. Other points of interest are the small wooden crucifix said to have been made from the wood of the tree under which Livingstone died in Chilambo in Zambia. If you can, try to go up the staircase of the church to the top of the tower from where you will get an excellent view of the town. It is sadly run down and needs all the funds it can get. Next door, under the St Monica restaurant, you can visit the underground slave pens. Also on Creek Road is the **City Hall** which is a wonderfully ornate

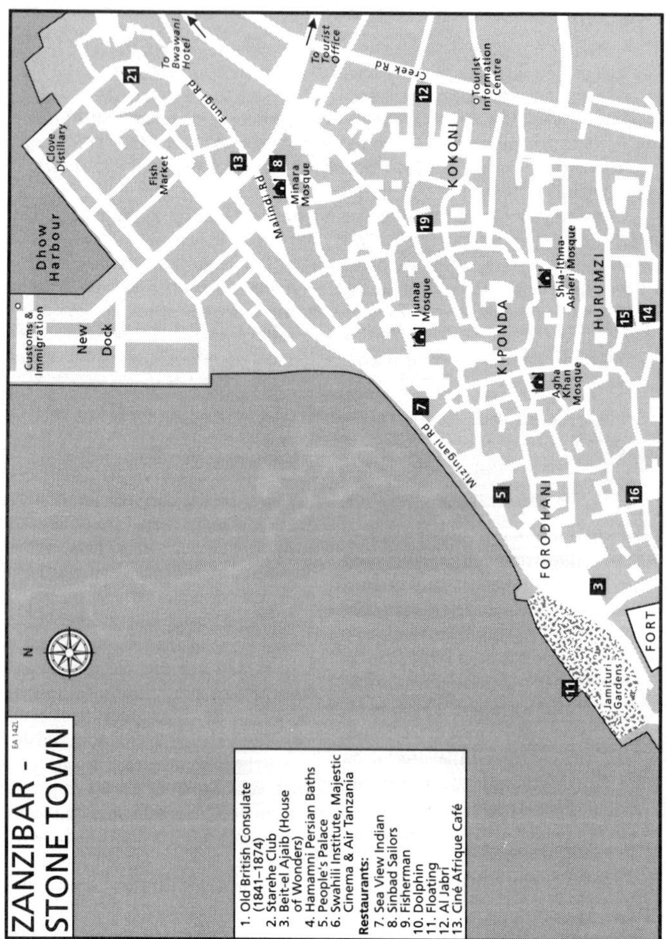

building currently undergoing renovation.

Mathews House is located close to *Africa House Hotel*, just to the S of Ras Shangani at the W tip of the town, and before WW1 was the residence of the German Consulate, with characteristic overhanging balconies. The **Africa House Hotel** was once the British Club. Also in this area is **Tippu Tip's House** which has a splendid carved wooden door and black and white marble steps.

At the W tip of the town is the building known now as **Mambo Msiige** which was once owned by a slave trader. It is said that he used to bury slaves alive within the walls of the building in accordance with an ancient custom. Since then the building has been used as the headquarters of the Universities Mis-

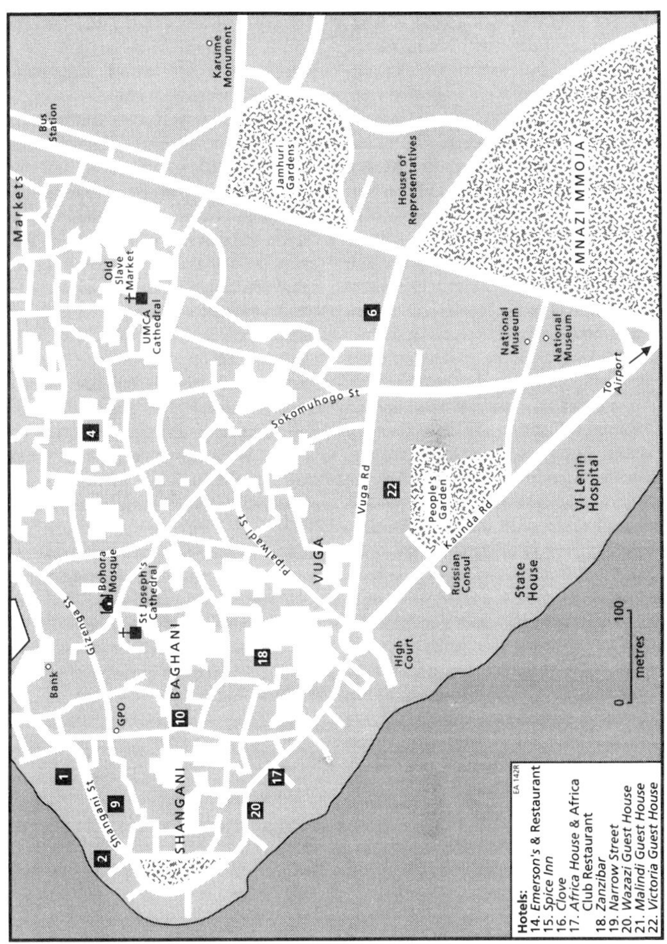

sion to Central Africa and later as the British Consulate.

The **Fort** is located in the W of the town next to the House of Wonders. This huge structure was built in 1700 by the Portuguese. There is little to see inside it apart from a small display of crafts although the interior is currently being renovated.

Beit-el-Ajaib (House of Wonders) is Zanzibar's tallest building and is located close to the fort opposite the Jamituri Gardens. It was built in 1883 by Sultan Barghash and served as his palace. It has fine examples of door carving. At the entrance are 2 Portuguese canons which date from about the 16th century. It is a 4-storey building and is surrounded by verandahs. In 1896 in an attempt to persuade the Sultan to abdicate, the palace was subjected to bombardment by the British navy. Inside the floors are of marble and there are various decorations which were imported from Europe, there are also exhibits from the struggle for independence. The building served as the local headquarters of Tanzania's political party CCM, but there are now plans to open it to the public.

On Mizingani Road there is the **Beit al-Sahel (People's Palace**) which is located to the N of the House of Wonders. It was here that the sultans and their families lived from the 1880's until their rule was finally overturned by the revolution of 1964. This has now been opened as a museum. There are three floors of exhibits and it is well worth a visit. There is a wide variety of furniture including the Sultan's huge bed. Lookout for the formica wardrobe with handles missing – obviously very fashionable at the time. Good views from the top floor. Open Tues-Sat 1000-1800, entrance US$5. The palace has grounds which are can sometimes be viewed, containing the tombs of Sultan Seyyid Said and his 2 sons Khaled and Barghash. Also along this road is the **Na Sur Nurmohamed Dispensary** a very ornate building which was donated to the community by a prominent Ismailian Indian Sir Tharia Topan. It is currently undergoing renovations funded by the Agha Khan Cultural trust.

Further up Mizingani Road is the **Dhow Harbour** which is another lively and bustling place especially in the morning when it is at its busiest when the dhows arrive and unload their catches, and buyers bargain and haggle over the prices.

Livingstone House is located on Malawi Road. It used to be the offices of the Zanzibar Tourist Corporation. Currently it appears to be closed, but it is possible to look around inside if you speak to the caretaker. In 1886 it was used by Livingstone as a base whilst he was staying on the island before what was to be his last journey into the interior. It was from Zanzibar that he arranged his trip inland, organizing porters, supplies and guide.

The **Hamamni Persian Baths**, in the centre of Stone Town, were built by Sultan Barghash for use as public baths and have been declared a protected monument. If you want to have a look inside them ask for the caretaker, Hakim Wambi, who keeps the key and he will let you in and show you around. As there is no water there any more you have to use your imagination as to what it was like in the old days. Hakim also runs the Zanzibar Orphans Trust from the building opposite the baths. Hw ill show you around – donations are gratefully received.

The **Museum** is located in 2 buildings and although fairly run down and shabby has some interesting exhibits relating to Zanzibar's history. It was built in 1925 and has relics and exhibits from the Sultans, the slave traders and European explorers and missionaries. Livingstone's medicine chest is here and the story of the German battleship the *Königsberg*, sunk during WW1 in the Rufiji Delta, is told. There are also displays of local arts and crafts. It is located near the junction of Creek Road with Nyerere and Kuanda Roads at the S end of the town. If you are 'out of season', it has a most interesting exhibit on clove production. There are giant tortoise in the grounds of the Natural History museum next door. The entrance fee is US$1 for both buildings.

Tours

In order to maximise your time in Zanzibar it is worth considering going on a tour. This applies especially if you have not the time to stay on the East coast and transport can be a problem. Most companies offer a number:

- **City Tour** Half day: includes the major sites of the Stone Town – market, national museum, cathedral, Beit al-Sahel and Hamamni baths. Cost US$15.

FREDDIE MERCURY

In 1946 Farokh Bulsara was born in Zanzibar to parents who were Parsees – followers of the Zoroastrian faith. The Zoroastrian Fire Temple in Zanzibar is located on Vuga Road to the E of Zanzibar Stone Town. His father worked as a civil servant for the British colonial government on the islands. The Parsees had a great affinity with the British, and Mr Bulsara senior was a cricket enthusiast, spending much of his leisure time at the ground at Mnazi Moja. The family lived in a house in the square behind the present Post Office. When he was 9, Farokh was sent to boarding school in India, and he never subsequently returned to the place of his birth.

In 1970, while studying graphics at Ealing College, he joined up with some students at London University's Imperial College of Science and Technology. He changed his name to Freddie Mercury and they formed the group Queen.

The influence of his Zanzibar background is expressed in the lyric of Queen's best-known song *Bohemian Rhapsody* with '*Bismillah* will you let him go'. *Bismillah* means 'the word of God' in the Islamic faith, and it has become a rallying cry for Muslim groups pressing for Zanzibar to break away from Tanzania.

Freddie Mercury died in 1992, his body being cremated at a Zoroastrian funeral ceremony in London.

- **Spice Tour** About 4 hours: pleasant stops at various villages to taste the freshly picked local fruits and herbs, see spice and copra production. The highly decorated persian baths at the Kidichi are often included. You may be offered a swim on the West coast - the water is usually cloudy and useless for snorkelling. **NB:** This tour is highly recommended during the harvest - out of season you may get weary of looking at leaves that look very similar. Cost: US$20.

- **East Coast** Full day: the tour may include a visit to the Jozani Forest where the rare red collubus monkey is found (recommended). Cost: US$35 (US$15 if you only go to Joazani).

- **North Coast** Full day: this can be combined with the spice tour and usually ends at the beach at Nungwi. The Mangapwani slave caves are sometimes also included. Cost: US$35.

Your hotel will be able to arrange the above for you but it may be better to contact one of the specialist companies, see page 343. See below for further details of excursions outside of Zanzibar Town, page 344.

Local information

- **Where to stay**

Price guide:
A+ Over US$100 a night;
A US$40-100; **B** US$20-40; **C** US$10-20; **D** US$5-10; **E** Under US$5.

All non-residents are expected to pay for hotel accommodation in US dollars even for somewhere very cheap. However the relaxation of currency controls and the introduction of foreign exchange bureaux may mean that local currency is becoming more generally accepted, but see box, page 336. The main exception is *Bwawani Hotel*, which is government-owned. The explosion of interest in Zanzibar has resulted in many houses being turned into hotels and guest houses. Nevertheless it has been the case that the town has been full in Jun, Jul and Aug, and the overspill has been accommodated in tents on the beach. It is advisable to book.

A *Bwawani* is the most expensive hotel in Zanzibar old town, PO Box 670, T 30200, located overlooking the Funguni Creek. Its a dull and characterless modern concrete building, now in poor repair with shabby decorations and fittings. A/c, swimming pool (currently out of service), tennis courts, restaurant, bar and disco on Sat. **A** *Emersons*, PO Box 4044, T 32153/30609. Located fairly centrally on Mkunazini Rd (but quite hard to find: look for a small brass plaque), this old house has recently been restored by an American after whom it is named. There are 8 rooms which vary in size and price and whether they have a bathroom attached. They are beautifully decorated and are named by colour. There is a small dining area on the roof with wonderful views, and the food is superb. However, you need to book meals 24 hrs in advance. *Fadimans Café* is on the ground floor.

B ***International***, PO Box 3784, T 33006, F 300525. Part of the *Narrow Street Hotel* Group, comfortable, restaurant, bureau de change, approached through the market which adds to the atmosphere. **B** ***Spice Inn***, PO Box 1090, T 30728/30729/28826. Used to be very popular, exudes atmosphere. The rooms vary so ask to take a look before you decide. Price includes breakfast. Some rooms with a/c available, shared or private bathroom.

C ***Clove***, PO Box 1117, located on Hurumzi St, T 31785. Self contained with fridge and fan. Hot water. **C** ***High Hill***, T 30000/32550. Located on Nyerere Rd and is rather out of the way and difficult to get to. Modern, a/c rooms available, price includes breakfast. Hot water.

D ***Africa House***, T 30708. Located on Kaunda Rd. This used to be the British Club in the pre-independence days. A comfortable, rambling traditional building, it has had problems with its water supply. It has a good bar overtaking the sea and the staff are friendly. Private or shared bathrooms, a/c also available. **D** ***Zanzibar***, PO Box 392, T 30708. This is located close to the *Africa House Hotel* and is good value. It is a fine example of Zanzibari architecture and has a wonderful atmosphere. **D** ***Narrow Street Annexe II***, PO Box 3784, T 326020, F 30052. Located on Koroni St, off Creek Rd. Despite the rather unprepossessing exterior the rooms themselves are quite pleasant and all have baths attached. Restaurant. Friendly staff. **D** ***Wazazi Guest House***. Rather basic.

E ***Malindi Guest House***, T 054 30165. Located on Malindi St at Funguni Bazaar – excellant value and a wonderful atmosphere. Central courtyard with plants, plenty of space to relax, clean and prices include breakfast. **E** ***Victoria Guest House***, T 32861. Located on Victoria Rd – good value, friendly staff.

● Places to eat

There are a number of moderate standard

> **Price guide:**
> ♦♦♦♦ over US$10; ♦♦♦ US$5-10;
> ♦♦ US$2-5; ♦ under US$2.

eating places in Zanzibar and you will not usually need to reserve tables. Many of them have good fresh seafood. The only first rate resturant is ♦♦♦♦***Emerson's***, T 32153/30609, where you can eat in wonderful surroundings in the rooftop retaurant. If you are not staying there you need to book a day ahead as space on the roof is limited. Among the others, the ♦♦***Sea View Indian Restaurant (Tomane Palace)*** has a splendid location which overlooks the harbour. You can eat inside or out and there is a wide range of food on the menu. However service is slow, and if you want to sit on the balcony you would be advised to book ahead. Kitchen reported as "filthy". ♦♦♦***La Lampara***, good Italian. The ♦♦***Africa House Club*** has a mediocre restaurant and cold beer. The ♦♦***Narrow Street Hotel*** on Koroni St has good food (but not to everyone's taste). If you want a seafood meal its best to order in advance. The ♦♦***Fisherman Restaurant***, T 33101, located on Shangani St has good food and is fairly good value. Slightly cheaper is the ♦♦***Dolphin Restaurant*** which is popular and sells mainly seafood plus some other dishes (dull). Other places include the ♦♦***Floating Restaurant*** on the dock in front of the old Fort which is sound value and a good place to watch the children summersaulting from the seawall into the water; the ♦♦***Zee bar and Zee pizza***, oven spice shop, very good. Other good value places include the café at the ♦***Ciné Afrique*** and ***Cit Chat***, near Cathedral. Finally there are a large number of vendors selling a variety of foods in the ♦***Jamituri Gardens*** between the fort and the sea. Here you can get corn on the cob, cassava and curries all very cheaply. Fun to wander around even if you don't feel hungry.

● Banks

The chaotic **People's Bank of Zanzibar** (the only place to change money into dollars) is located close to the fort as is the **Tanzania Commercial Bank**. However it should now not be necessary to use the banks for changing money – they will normally give an inferior rate compared with the foreign exchange bureaux. There is a foreign exchange bureau opposite the Tourist Bureau at N end of Creek road.

● Entertainment

The most popular bar in the town is that at the

Id-ul-Fitr Festival

At the end of Ramadan there is a festival called Id-ul-Fitr. It lasts about 4 days and is a time of general celebration. If you are in Zanzibar at this time go down to Makunduchi which is in the SE part of the island where there is a carnival atmosphere.

Africa House Hotel which looks out across the ocean. The beers are usually cold and plentiful although rather expensive and it is a good place to meet people. Get there early if you want to watch the sun set: seats are quickly taken. Other bars include the ***Wazazi Bar*** next door to the *Africa House Hotel*. It is cheap, popular, and there is music (sometimes live) and it stays open fairly late. Finally the ***Starehe Bar*** located on Shangani St overlooks the harbour and tends to be less crowded that the *Africa House Hotel*. It sometimes holds discos. There is a disco next to the ***Fisherman's Restaurant*** on Shangani St. The ***Bwawani Hotel*** has popular disco's on Sat.

● Hospital and medical services

There is a state hospital (V I Lenin) on Kaunda Road. Also private Clinic – *Mkunazini Hospital*, near to the market. British trained doctor. Pay fee to register, wait tom see doctor then pay for any prescription necessary. Pay again when go to collect medicine: this may be at the clinic or in a nearby drug-store. An interesting way to pass a few hours if not too ill.

● Post office

The post office is located in the W of the town close to St Joseph's Cathedral.

● Shopping

The Market Place off Creek road sells mainly fresh fruit and vegetables. However the shops nearby sell kikios and kangas, wooden chests and other souvenirs. The ***Rashid A Nograni Curio Shop*** and the ***Chanda Curio Shop*** sell carvings, wooden boxes, brass and copper coffeepots and jewelry. Zanzibar is a good place to buy film (mostly Konica) and tends to be cheaper than Kenya.

● Travels agencies and tours

Mitu, contactable at the café next door to the Ciné Afrique early in the mornings or in the evenings. Get a group of 4 together, and Mitu an elderly Indian (or one of the people he has trained) will take you on one his own guided tours. They are good value. However they have become very popular and you may find yourself in a large group. Advance bookings in Dar es Salaam: Coastal Travels Ltd, PO Box 3052 Upanga Rd, Dar es Salaam, T 1 37279 37480, F 36585.

Chemah Bros Tours, PO Box 1865, Shangani Rd, T 31751. ***Classic Tours***, c/o Emerson's House, T 83629. ***Dolphin Tours***, PO Box 138, New Mukanazini Rd, T 33386. ***Jasfa Tours***, PO Box 4203, Shangani Rd, T 30468, F 32387. Good reputation and will confirm flights, organize hotel bookings etc. ***Orient Expeditions***, T 30813. ***Ras Tours & Safaris***, T 31078. ***Sama Tours***, PO Box 2276, Changa Bazaar St, T 33543. ***Sun and Fun Safari Tours***, PO Box 666, Shangani Rd, T 32132. ***Triple M Tours Africa House Club***, T 30708/30709. ***Zanea Tours***, PO Box 620, Shangani Rd, T 30413. ***Zanzibar Safari Tours***, PO Box 4042, Kenyatta Rd, T 31463. ***Zanzibar Tourist Corporation***, Creek Rd, PO Box 216, T 32344. Incompetent.

Tourist office

There is a **Tanzania Friendship Tourist Bureau** located on Creek Rd, at the N end. Sells map of island but otherwise not terribly helpful.

Transport

Air *Air Tanzania* (PO Box 773, T 30297) is scheduled to have 2 flights daily in each direction between **Dar es Salaam** and Zanzibar which costs US$43 and takes about 20 minutes. The Air Tanzania office is on Vuga St and closes for lunch (1230-1400). You can also fly to Zanzibar from **Mombasa** on *Kenya Airways* for US$35 (plus US$20 airport tax). The Kenya Airways office is on Creek St. As always book in advance as this is a popular route.

ZATA, Zanzibar Airport, T 33569 32001; or C/O Jasfa, PO Box 4203, T 30468, F 32387; or Pemba 2016, has 2 flights most days between Zanizibar and **Dar es Salaam**. Depart Zanzibar 0930 and 1600 (1700 on Wed and Sat) Depart Dar es Salaam 1300 (not Mon, Thu, Sat) and 1730 (1815 Wed and Sat). The fair is US$41 one-way. ZATA also has 2 flights most days to **Pemba**. Depart Zanzibar 0730 (not Sun) and 1400 (Wed, Fri, Sun only). Depart Pemba 0830 (not Sun), 1615 (Wed and Sun only) 1500 Fri. Fare US$46 one-way.

There are buses between the airport and the town for a US$0.50. Alternatively you can get a taxi for about US$10.

Sea *Sea Express Services*, PO Box 4096, T 32619/33002, which runs 2 Russian built hydrofoils from **Dar es Salaam**. It costs US$20 one way (US$30 first class) and takes 1-2 hrs. It can sometimes be quite a rough journey, and sea-sickness tablets are a sensible precaution. The offices are located on Malawi Rd nr the harbour, and at Malindi dock in Dar es Salaam (T 20712). If possible book in advance although you may be lucky if you get there early. You will have to pay in foreign currency. *Flying Horse*, PO Box 4087, T 32312, has 2 trips each day to and from **Dar es Salaam**. Prices are US$30, US$20, US$10 for 1st, 2nd and 3rd class.

Dhows A cheaper alternative from **Dar es Salaam** is by motorized dhow (nicknamed *yongo* which is Swahili for milipede). These goes each way most days leaving early in the morning (about 0600) costing about US$3 and taking up to 8 hrs. It is hot and there is no food or water on board so take your own. To get back to Dar es Salaam book from the Malindi Sports Club opposite Sinbad Sailors Restaurant one day in advance. This si strictly speaking illegal as there have been some restrictions on non-Tanzanians travelling by dhow. You can also get a dhow to **Pemba** and **Mombasa**. For Pemba book at the Malindi Sports Club. For Mombasa they go once or twice a week. Ask for details at the Institute of Marine Science on Mizingani Rd. It costs about US$3 and takes about 6 hrs to Pemba, to Mombasa US$10 and takes about 24 hrs.

The *Zanzibar Shipping Corporation* runs a weekly service between Dar es Salaam, Pemba and Zanzibar. The Zanzibar booking office is at the wharf, and the fare is about US$2-3.

Getting around the island

You can hire **minivans** which seat 8 passengers through one of the tour agencies. It will cost about US$40 for the van. At the S end of Jamituri Gardens it is possible to hire **4WDs** that are parked there for US$30 a day. Pickup vans with wooden benches in the back are the cheapest way of getting around the island. It will cost about US$2 per person to the E coast and is a hot, dusty and not very comfortable journey. You can hire **bicycles** (there is a shop close to the Tourist Bureau on Creek Rd) for US$5 a day and there is a US$50 deposit. **Motorbikes** can be hired for US$20 a day from behind the tax office close to Jamituri Gardens. **Buses** to the E coast go from the bus station on Creek Rd opposite the Market. To Chwaka takes 1½ hrs, to Jambiani takes 3 hrs, and to Bwejuu takes 4½ hrs.

Beyond Zanzibar Town

Changuu Island

Also known as Prison Island, this island was once owned by an Arab who used it for 'rebellious' slaves. Some years later in 1893 it was sold to General Mathews, a Briton who converted it into a prison. However it has never actually been used as such and was later converted to serve as a quarantine station for East Africa in colonial times. The prison is still relatively intact and a few remains of the hospital can be seen including the rusting boilers of the laundry. There is good snorkelling, wind surfing and sailing from the beautiful little beach. Jelly fish can sometimes spoil bathing and snorkelling however. The island is also home to giant tortoises which are supposed to

Clove Production

It has been estimated that there are about 6 million clove trees on the islands of Zanzibar and Pemba and they cover about one tenth of the land area. The plantations are found mainly in the W and NW of the islands where the soil is deeper and the landscape hillier. To the E the soil is less deep and fertile and it known as 'Coral landscape'.

Cloves were at one time only grown in the Far East and they were greatly prized. On his first trip back from the East, Vasco da Gama took a cargo back to Portugal and they were later introduced by the French to Mauritius and then to Zanzibar by Sayyid Said who was the first Arab sultan. At this time all the work was done by slaves who enabled the plantations to be established and clove production to become so important to the economy of the islands. When the slaves were released and labour was no longer free, some of the plantations found it impossible to survive although production did continue and Zanzibar remained at the head of the world production of cloves.

Cloves are actually the unopened buds of the clove tree. They grow in clusters and must be picked when the buds are full but before they actually open. They are collected in the sprays and the buds are then picked off before being spread on the ground to dry out. They are spread out on mats made from woven coconut palm fronds for about 5 days, turned over regularly so that they dry evenly – the quicker they dry the better quality the product.

There may be many clove trees on Zanzibar now – but there were even more in the past. In 1872 a great hurricane passed over the island destroying many of the trees and it was after this that Pemba took over from Zanzibar as the largest producer. Zanzibar however has retained the role of chief seller and exporter of cloves so the Pemba cloves first go to Zanzibar before being sold on.

have been brought over from Aldabra (an atoll off the Seychelles) around the turn of the century.

• **Where to stay** C *Changuu Island Resort*, PO Box 216, T 32344, Tlx 57144. Simple and reasonable with cold beers. Also has facilites for snorkelling, wind surfing and sailing. Plans are afoot for a huge holiday complex to be built by Lonrho.

• **Transport** You can get there through one of the tour agencies. Or a boat will take you across to the island for about US$5. There is a US$1 entrance fee. Day trips can be arranged from *Africa House Hotel*. Alternatively ask around on the beach in front of the Sea View Indian Restaurant.

South West

Kiungani, Mbweni and Chukwani

This route will take you past Kiungani where there was once hostel built in 1864 by Bishop Tozer for released slave boys. A little further on are the ruins of **Mbweni Settlement** which was also established for rescued slaves. This was built in 1871 by the Universities Mission to Central Africa. In 1882 a church was built in the same place for the use of the released slaves. There is a fine carved door and a tower.

Also at Mbweni is **Kirk House** which was built by Seyyid Barghash in 1872. Kirk came to Zanzibar as part of Livingstone's expedition to the Zambezi as the Medical Officer. He played an important role in the fight to end the slave trade and in 1873 was appointed His Majesty's Agent and Consul General in Zanzibar. He was also a botanist, introducing a number of plants to the island including cinnamon, vanilla, mahogany and eucalyptus.

Further S as Chukwani are the

Mbweni Palace Ruins. This was once a holiday resort of Sultan Seyyid Barghash and it had a wonderful position overlooking the sea. However it has been totally neglected and as a result is slowly crumbling away. The main palace has completely disappeared, although some of the other buildings do remain and may be toured. The ruins are located to the S of the town off the airport road.

Central East

Dunga, Uroa and Chwaka
This route takes you across the centre of the island. Just over 20 km down the road are the Dunga Palace ruins which were built by Chief Mwinyi Mkuu Ahmed bin Mohamed Hassan. Unfortunately there is little left of the palace today besides a few arches and bits of wall, and the area has been taken over by a plantation. At the end of this route you will reach Chwaka Bay – see section on the East Coast, page 347. Also on the E coast to the N of Chwaka is Uroa another beach resort.

South East

Bwejuu, Makunduchi, Kizimkazi
There is a small nature reserve, **Jozani Forest**, located about 40 km to the SE of Zanzibar town which is home to the last few remaining red Colubus monkeys.

The road continues S to the village of Kitongani. From here you can take a road across to the coastal village of Paje on the E coast about 50 km from Zanzibar town. Also on this coast is the resort of **Bwejuu** (see Coastal section, page 347. There are a series of other villages on the coast as you head S before you reach **Kizimkazi** the southernmost village. There is little of significance in this small fishing village besides the mosque. However this was once the site of a town built by King Kizi and his mason Kazi from whom the name Kizimkazi originates.

Shirazi Dimbani Mosque ruins Found near Kizimkazi in the S of the island this mosque contains the oldest inscription found in East Africa – from AD 1107. The mosque has been given a tin roof and is still used. However its significance should not be underestimated for it may well mark the beginnings of the Muslim religion in East Africa. It was built by Sheikh Abu bin Mussa Lon Mohammed and archeologists believe that it exists on the site of an even older mosque.

North

Maruhubi Palace ruins These are located about 3 km to the N of the town. They were built in 1882 by Sultan Barghash for his harem of many (said to be 99) women. The palace was almost completely destroyed by a fire in 1899. All that remains are the pillars and aqueducts which brought water to the palace from the nearby springs. The site is very overgrown, and marble from the baths has long since been stolen.

Persian Baths at Kidichi Built on the highest point of Zanzibar Island by Sultan Seyyid Said in 1850, they were for his wife who was Persian, and are decorated in a ornamental stucco work that is in the Persian style.

Mangapwani slave caves Located about 20 km N of the town, these were used to hide slaves in the times when the slave trade was illegal but in fact continued unofficially. One particular trader, Mohammed bin Nasser, built an underground chamber at Alwi which was used as well as the naturally formed cave. The cave itself is said to have been discovered when a young slave boy lost a goat that he was looking after. He followed its bleats which led it to the cave containing a freshwater stream. The discovery of the cave, (although it was used to hide slaves and thus helped the slave trade continue illegally) was actually a blessing in disguise, as the freshwater stream was a boom to the confined slaves. You may well see women carrying water from this very same stream today. If you want to get there independently the caves can be reached by taking the bus from Creek Rd opposite the market.

Mvuleni ruins These are in the N of the island and are the remains of the Portuguese attempt to colonize Zanzibar. At the N tip of the island is Nungwi, located about 56 km from Zanzibar town.

Spice and fruit plantations These are usually included in tours of the island (in fact many of the tours are called Spice Tours). You will be invited to taste all the different herbs, spices and fruits that the island produces. Most hotels can put you in touch with a spice tour organizer.

East Coast

The E part of the island is fairly difficult to get to which is, of course, part of its attraction. Here you will see the fishermen go out in their dhows, while the women sit in the shade and plait coconut fibre which they then make into everything from fishing nets to beds. In principle you still have to pay for accommodation in foreign currency and book at the tourist office in Zanzibar but these regulations are being relaxed.

Communications with the E coast are poor. For the most part is is necessary to book through an agent in Zanzibar or in Dar es Salaam – or take a chance on getting a room when you arrive. This is particularly risky from Jun to Sept. However, the number of places offering accommodation will have increased significantly by 1995. At the end of 1993, it was reported that licence applications had been made for a further 200 hotels in Zanzibar.

Chwaka

This is located 32 km from Zanzibar town and is a popular beach. It was also popular as a holiday resort with slave traders and their families in the 19th century. The beach is lovely and the fishing is said to be good. **D** *Bungalows* (two). Run by the Tourist Office at Chakwa. **D** *Kichipwi Guest House*. Book through Ali Khamis, PO Box 25, Zanzibar.

Uroa

Located 10 km to the N of Chwaka. **A+** *Uroa Bay Hotel*, C/o Coastal Travels, PO Box 3052, Upanga Rd, Dar es Salaam. T 37279/37480, F 36585. Italian-run establishment. High standard. Swimming Pool. Tennis courts. Water sports. **A** *Tamarind*, located between Uroa and Chwaka. European-run. No pool. Pleasant restaurant and open-air bar.

Paje

Small village on the E coast mainly relying on fishing. **D** *Amani Guest House*. Modest but good value. **D** *Ufukwe Guest House*. Simple but adequate.

Bwejuu

This is often considered to be the best of the E beaches. **C** *Palm Beach Inn*. This is simple and basic. Some bungalows have been added. There is no running water or electricity just buckets and paraffin lamps, for many adding to the charm. The food is fresh and good and the staff friendly. If you want to drink while you are there, take your own alcohol. **C** *Bwejuu Beach Hotel*. Another simple place and popular with budget travellers. All rooms and bathrooms are shared. There is a bar here and beers are usually cold. **D** *Dere Guest House*. Simple facilities, and good straight-forward food. Hires out snorkelling equipment.

Jambiani

C *Jambiani Beach Hotel*, run by the very friendly and helpful Mr Abu. Bookings through, PO Box 229, Zanzibar. **D** *Gomani Guest House*. Uncomplicated but comfortable. **D** *Horizontal Inn*, owned by local Zanzibaris. Simple and good value.

PEMBA

The island of Pemba is located 40 km to the N of Zanzibar and is about 70 km long and 23 km wide. It has not, so far, been developed as a holiday spot and so is much less touristy. There is however an airport on the island and

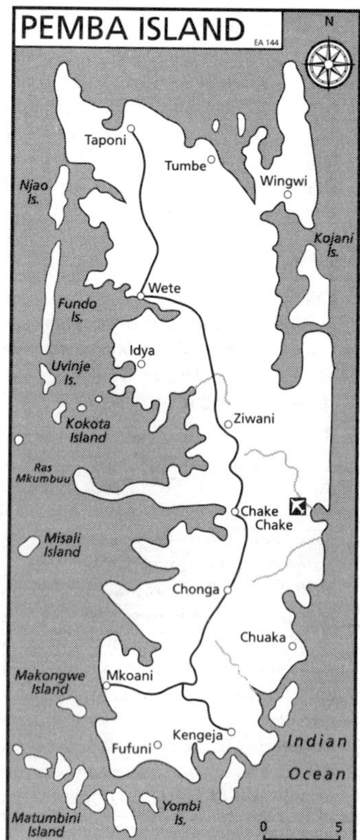

there are plenty of attractions. There have been plans to build a resort geared towards scuba diving but so far this has not materialized. There are some important ruins here although the island is perhaps most famous for its clove production. The island is much hillier that Zanzibar and the higher rainfall ensures that the vegetation flourishes

The major income on the island is from cloves – the clove production of this island is actually about 3 times that of Zanzibar – and it is the mainstay of the island's economy. Also, unlike Zanzibar production is largely by individual small scale farmers who own anything from 10 to 50 trees each. Most of the trees have been in the family for generations and date back many years. They were first introduced to the island at the beginning of the 19th century by the Moluccas. The production is very much a family affair especially during the harvest when everyone of the island joins in the picking. Harvest occurs about every 5 months and everything is geared toward it and even the schools close. The cloves are then laid out in the sun to dry and the distinctive fragrance fills the air.

Chake Chake

This is Pemba's main town located on the W coast of the island. The town sits on a hill overlooking a creek and is fairly small. A new sports stadium has also recently been built. The market and bus stand are both located in the centre of town close to the mosque.

• **Where to stay** There is currently only one place to stay in town and that is **B** ***Hoteli ya Chake Chake***, T 2189/2069. It is government owned and rooms must be paid for in hard currency. All rooms have bathrooms and a fan – it is a clean and friendly place. The hotel has a restaurant with a fairly limited menu, and a bar.

• **Useful addresses Airline office** The *Air Tanzania* office is also located in Chake Chake, Tel 2162. **Bank** People's Bank of Zanzibar is the only bank on the island to change travellers cheques. It is expected that from early 1995 there will be foreign exchange bureaux established. **Hospital** A new hospital has recently been completed. **Tourist information** There is a tourist information office, T 2121, but it has no maps and little information.

• **Transport** The airport, T 2357, serving the island is located about 5 km out of town. There are buses or *dala dala* between Chake Chake, Wete and Mkoani. Also from Wete to Tumbe and Michiweni in the N of the Island. It is possible to hire vehicles at around US$35 a day by asking at the hotels. Similarly with bicycles at US$2 a day.

Places of interest

Nanzim Fort located in Chake Chake is now used as a hospital.

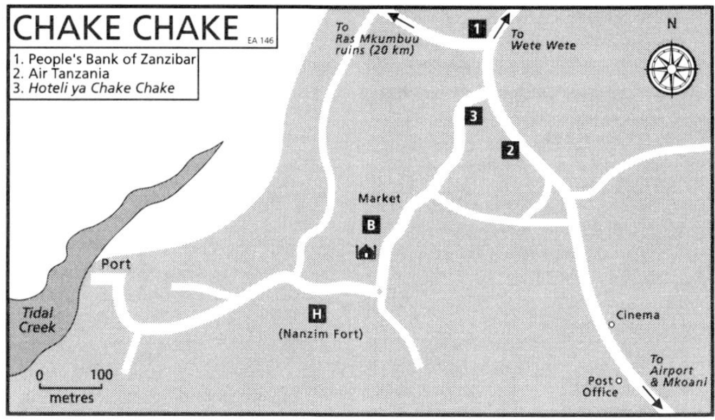

Ruins at Ras Mkumbuu About 20 km W of Chake Chake, these are probably Pemba's most important ruins and are believed to date back about 1200 years, the site of a settlement originating in the Shairazi period, see page 278. The ruins include stone houses and pillar tombs and the remains of a 14th century mosque. Access is best by boat, which can be hired informally at the shore. Zanzibar Tourist Corporation Office at the *Hoteli ya Chake Chake* has a boat for hire at about US$40 for the day. From Ras Mkumbuu it is possible to go on to **Mesali Island** where the marine life on the reef is excellent for snorkelling.

Ruins at Pujini About 10 km SE of Chake Chake, this settlement is thought to date back to the 15th century. It is believed to have been built by a particularly unpleasant character, nicknamed Mkame Ndume which means 'a milker of men' because he worked his subjects so hard. The memory remains and local people believe that the ruins are haunted. The settlement and the palace of Mkame Ndume were destroyed by the Portuguese when they arrived on the island in about 1520. It is best to visit by hiring a bicycle (ask at the hotel).

Tumbe is at the N end of Pemba and is a busy fishing village. Local fishermen contract to provide catches for firms which chill the fish and export it from the mainland. Tumbe can be reached by bus from Chake Chake.

Bull fighting

This is a legacy from the time of the Portuguese. Pemba is the only place in Tanzania (indeed in East Africa) where this has been practised. Although there are reports that it continues, it is irregular and informally organized.

Wete

This town is located on the NW coast of Pemba and serves as a port for the clove trade. There is very little to the town – it is half of a hill and overlooks the port.

• **Where to stay and eat** **B** *Hoteli ya Wete*, T 4301. Government-owned. It has a restaurant and bar.

D *Sharooq Guest House*, is located just nr the market and bus stand and is good value.

Other places to eat besides the hotel include ♦*Pop-In Restaurant* and ♦*New 4-Ways Restaurant*, which are both located opposite the hotel. There are also a couple of restaurants down towards the docks. They are very limited.

• **Useful addresses** **Bank** There is a People's Bank of Zanzibar on the main road but you cannot change travellers cheques here. Also on the main road is the **post office** and the **police station**. The market and matatu stand are located in the centre of town.

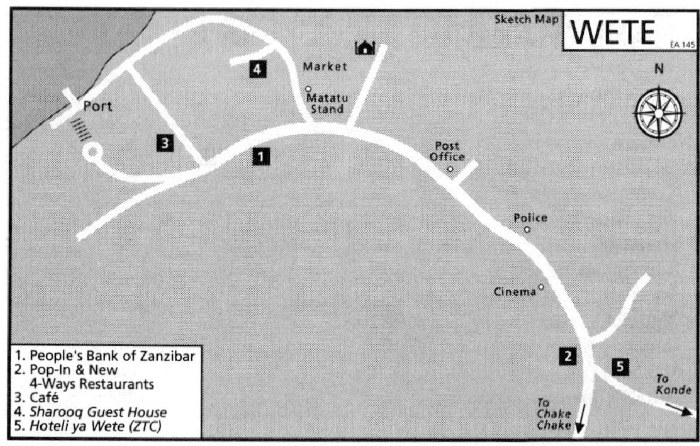

Mkoani

This town is located to the S of the island and is the principal port. If you come to Pemba from Zanzibar by boat this is where you will arrive. The hotel is **B** *Hoteli ya Mkoani* and is identical in facilities and price to the other 2 government run hotels on the island.

Local information

● Transport

Local There is one main road in Pemba running from Msuka in the N to Mkoani on the S which is served by public transport. Although the vehicles themselves are not the most comfortable they do provide a fairly good service. From Chake Chake the No 6 goes to Wete and the No 3 to Mkoani. From Chake Chake to Wete takes about 45 mins and costs US$0.30. Besides this, it is very difficult to get around.

Air There are *Air Tanzania* flights to Pemba from Zanzibar and Tanga about 3 times a week. The flights are usually fairly empty – bookings can be made at the Air Tanzania office in Chake Chake. The airport departure tax is about US$1 but you do not have to change money on arrival. Public transport to and from the airport only operates when there is a flight due. ***ZATA***, Zanzibar Airport, T 33569/32001; or C/o Jasfa, PO Box 4203, T 30468, F 32387; or Pemba 2016. This also has 2 flights most days to between **Zanzibar** and Pemba. Depart Zanzibar 0730 (not Sun) and 1400 (Wed, Fri, Sun only). Depart Pemba 0830 (not Sun), 1615 (Wed and Sun only) 1500 Fri. Fare US$46 one-way. ZATA also flies to **Tanga** twice a week on Wed and Sun, leaving Pemba at 1445 and Tanga at 1530. The fare is US$42 one-way.

Sea From Zanzibar, **dhows** arrive at Mkoani and from Tanga they arrive at Wete. Bookings from Zanzibar (which is easier and more reliable) can be made at the Malindi Sports Club in Zanzibar and the trip takes 6-8 hrs, and costs around US$3. You can also get a dhow to **Mombasa**. Departures are from Wete, cost about US$7 and take about 12 hrs for a motorised dhow, and 24 hrs for a sailing vessel.

NATIONAL PARKS AND GAME RESERVES

Contents

Maps

There are a large number of national parks and game reserves in Tanzania. Some are well known, have excellent facilities and receive many visitors, while there are some that rarely see tourists and have no facilities for them. The differences between national parks and game reserves is vitally important to the local people. In national parks the animals have the parks to themselves. In game reserves however the local people, in particular pastoralists such as the Maasai, are allowed rights of grazing. Game reserves are often found adjoining national parks and have usually been created as a result of local pressure to return some of the seasonal grazing lands to pastoralists.

Background information

It is essential to tour the parks by vehicle. In fact, walking is prohibited in all parks except Selous, Gombe Stream and Mahale Mountain National Parks, and Gombe Stream and Mahale Mountains are the only parks that can really be enjoyed without a vehicle. You will either have to go with an organized tour (the least expensive option), hire or have your own a vehicle. It is a waste not to take a guide – the cost is modest, and without one, you will miss a lot of game, and not go to the promising locations for viewing.

Arrangements can be made through tour operators who will generally offer a variety of tours of differing durations, luxury and expense. Lists of operators are given below, see page 352. If you are making your plans from either Dar es Salaam or Arusha, there are lists of operators with offices in these locations, see page 261 for Dar es Salaam, and page 306 for Arusha.

Hunting safaris are very specialized and expensive operations, and hunting is strictly controlled to ensure conservation. It is possible to hunt all the big game with the exception of rhinoceros, as well as most of the minor species and birds. A hunting safari is usually for a minimum of 7 days. A list of specialist hunting operators is given below, see page 353.

Fees

The fees for the parks have to be paid in hard currency unless you are a resident of Tanzania in which case you pay in local currency. The fees for each 24 hr period are as follows (with fees for Tanzanian residents in brackets):

Adult entry	US$15 (TSh100)
Child entry	US$5 (TSh30)
Vehicle entry	
(up to 2000 kg)	US$30 (TSh300)
(over 2000 kg)	US$150 (TSh7500)
Guide	US$10 (TSh100)

These are the fees for all the National Parks except Gombe National Park which charges US$50 (TSh500).

Rules of the National Parks

The rules of the national parks are really just commonsense and are aimed at visitor safety and conservation. The Parks are open from 0600-1900 and at other times driving in the parks is not permitted. Walking is prohibited in all parks except Selous, Gombe Stream and Mahale Mountain National Parks, so you must stay in your vehicle at all times. Do not drive off the main track. This causes damage to the vegetation and is strictly banned. Do not ask your driver to do this in order to get closer to game. Blowing your horn is prohibited, as is playing radios or tape recorders. The speed limit is 50 kph but you will probably want to go much slower most of the time as at 50 kph you will miss a lot of game. Chasing the animals is strictly prohibited, as is feeding the animals – this includes animals that gather around the lodges. Take all litter home with you, and be careful when discarding cigarette butts as the fire risk is high particularly during the dry season.

Tour operators

Until 1989 only Tanzanian registered tour operators were allowed to operate in Tanzania. That has now changed and overseas-based companies have established themselves in Tanzania. There are a large number of safari companies and organized safaris are the most common way of seeing the parks. Safaris to Serengeti National Park, Ngorongoro Conservation Area, Lake Manyara National Park, Tarangire National Park and Arusha National Park are best arranged from Arusha if you have not arranged it before you arrive in Tanzania. For trips to Mikumi National Park, Ruaha National Park and Selous arrangements are best made in Dar es Salaam, while trips to Gombe Stream National Park and Mahale Mountain National Park should be arranged from Kigoma.

More extensive lists of tour and travel companies are given in the sections for Dar es Salaam (see page 261) and Arusha (see page 306). The lists here are of experienced operators.

● Hotel and Lodge Safaris

Abercrombie & Kent, PO Box 427, Arusha, T 7803, F 7003, Tlx 42005. ***Bushtrekker Safaris***, PO Box 3173, Arusha, T 3727. or PO Box 5350, Dar es Salaam, T 31957/32671. ***Equatorial Safaris*** , PO Box 2156, Arusha, T 2617, F 2617, Tlx 42103. Located in Serengeti Block, AICC (Conference Centre). ***Hoopoe Safaris***, PO Box 2047, Arusha, T 7541, Tlx 42103. Located India St, Arusha. ***Ker and Downey Safaris***, PO Box 2782, Arusha, T 7755 7700, Tlx 42013. ***Selous Safaris***, PO Box 1192, Dar es Salaaam, T 34535, F 28486, Tlx 81016. ***Let's***

Go Travel, PO Box 12799, Arusha. Located in Goliondoi Rd, Arusha. *Simba Safaris*, PO Box 1207, Arusha, T 3509 3600. Located between Ngoliondoi Rd and India St, Arusha. *Takims Holidays Tours and Safaris*, PO Box 6023, Arusha, T 3174 7500. Located Room 421, Ngorongoro Wing, AICC, Arusha. Or PO Box 20350, Dar es Salaam, T 25691 30037. Located Jamhuri St. *Tanzania Safari Tours / Rufiji River Camp*, PO Box 20058, Dar es Salaam, T 64177/63546. Located on Pugu Rd, Dar es Salaam. *United Touring Company*, PO Box 2211, Arusha, T 7931, F 6475, Tlx 42100. Located on corner of Sokoine St and Ngoliondoi Rd, Arusha. *Valji & Alibhai*, PO Box 786, Dar es Salaam, T 20522/26537, F 46401, Tlx 81052. Located on Bridge St. *Wildersun Safaris and Tours*, PO Box 930, Arusha, T 3880 6471, Tlx 42021. Located on Sokoine Rd, Arusha.

● **Camping safaris**

Sengo Safaris, PO Box 207, Arusha, T 3181 ext 1518/1519/1520. Located Room 153-3, Ngorongoro Wing, AICC, Arusha. *Dove Safaris*, PO Box 284, Arusha, T 3090/3625. Located Sokoine Rd, nr clock tower, Arusha. *Arumeru Tours and Safaris*, PO Box 730, Arusha, T 2780. Located Seth Benjamin Rd, Arusha.

● **Hunting Safaris**

Bushmen Company, PO Box 235, Arusha, T 6210. *Cordial Tours* PO Box 1679, Jamhuri St, Dar es Salaam, T 35264. *Gerald Posanisi Safaris*, PO Box 45640, Dar es Salaam, T 47435. *King Tours and Hunting Safaris*, PO Box 7000, Arusha, T 3688. *Tanzania Wildlife Corporation*, PO Box 1144, Arusha, T 3501/2, Tlx 42080.

Costs

Safaris vary in cost and length. On the whole you get what you pay for. Obviously the longer you spend actually in the Parks, rather than just driving to and from them, the better. To see Ngorongoro Crater and Lake Manyara you will need, absolute minimum, 3 days and 2 nights. To see these two plus Serengeti you will need 4 days and 3 nights, and if you add Tarangire to these three you will need 6 days and 5 nights.

The costs will also vary enormously depending on where you stay and how many of you there are in a group. For a **tented camp or lodge safari** the cost will average out at about US$100-140 per person per day. This assumes that there is a group of at least 6 of you. If you want to go in a smaller group you can expect to pay substantially more, and if you are alone and not prepared to share a room/tent then you will have to pay a 'single supplement'. You will have to pay in hard currency and the price will include accommodation, park fees, food and transport.

For a **camping safari** you can expect to pay about US$60-80 per person per day including park entrance fees, cost of vehicle and driver, camping fees and costs of food. This assumes you get a group of at least 5 together.

Hunting safaris are extremely expensive and require considerable preparation

Car rental

Car rental is not as well organized in Tanzania as it is in Kenya. There are fewer companies from which to hire vehicles (although this is changing) and it is expensive. Also many of the vehicles are poorly maintained and you may find it difficult to hire a car without a driver. More common is hiring a car with a driver. The hire charge for this will depend on where you get the vehicle from. Dar es Salaam is usually cheaper with a Land Rover or VW kombie costing US$20 plus US$1/km plus US$5 for the driver. A Nissan minibus will cost about US$25 plus US$1/km. (Both have a minimum mileage of 100 km per day.) In Arusha a Land Rover will cost about US$40 plus US$1/km. You will have to pay the entrance fees for the car and the driver and although it will work out expensive this method does allow for greater flexibility than an organized safari.

Facilities

Hotels and lodges These vary and may be either typical hotels with rooms and facilities in one building or individual bandas or rondavels (small huts) with a central dining area. Most have been built with great care and blend very well into the environment.

Tented camps A luxury tented camp is really the best of both worlds. They are usually built with a central dining area. Each tent will have a grass roof to keep it cool inside, proper beds, and verandah and they will often have a small bathroom at the back with solar heated hot water. But at the same time you will have the feeling of being in the heart of Africa and at night you will hear animals surprisingly close by.

Camp sites There are camp sites in most national parks. These are both normal which cost US$10 (TSh100 for residents) per person per night and 'special' camp sites which cost US$40 (TSh200) per person per night. Both cost US$5 (TSh40) for children per night. You will almost always need to be totally self sufficient with all your own equipment. The campsites usually provide running water and firewood. Some campsites have attached to them a few bandas or huts run by the park. The extent to which you will have to be self sufficient varies from park to park.

The Northern Circuit

The Northern Circuit is an extremely popular route as it includes the best known of the national parks in Tanzania. It is an incredible resource and the country is obviously very keen that full advantage of it should be taken. It is therefore seeing rapid and increasing tourist development and while it is not yet as developed as some of the Kenyan parks, nor are there as many visitors, this can be expected to change in the future.

Popular routes take in Lake Manyara National Park, Ngorongoro Crater Conservation Area (with the Olduvai Gorge) and the Serengeti National Park.

Poaching

This is a serious problem in Tanzania. An example of the devastation that the poacher has wrought on Tanzania's wildlife can be seen by examining the estimated national elephant population which fell from around 200,000 in 1977 to 89,000 in 1987 – a fall of some 55% in just 10 years. These figures give rise to the fully justified concern for the future survival of some of these species. It is important that the ivory trade is discouraged and every tourist can help in this by not buying any ivory of any description. This rule should extend beyond ivory to other living creatures. For example there was a time when on a trip to the coast you would be sure to see a great many extremely beautiful shells along the reef. As a result of the tourist trade you are now less likely to see them in the sea and more likely to see them being sold to tourists on the road side. Many people collect the brightly coloured star fish found on the reefs. However these quickly die and fade once they are out of the water. Their population has undoubtedly been affected as a result of tourists collecting them. If you want these species to survive do not buy or collect any such souvenirs.

If you want to become involved in any conservation activities in Tanzania there are a number of societies and organizations you can contact. These include the **Tanzania Wildlife Protection Fund**, PO Box 1994, Dar es Salaam; **The Wildlife Conservation Society of Tanzania**, PO Box 70919, Dar es Salaam; **African Wildlife Foundation**, PO Box 48177, Nairobi, Kenya or 1717 Massachusetts Avenue NW, Washington DC, 20036, USA; **Frontier Tanzania**, PO Box 9473, Dar es Salaam or Studio 210, Thames House, 566 Cable St, London, E1 9HB, England.

However there are a number of other major attractions and these are worthy of a visit to Tanzania for their sakes alone. In particular keen climbers and walkers visit the area to climb Mount Kilimanjaro and Mount Meru in Arusha National Park. The Tarangire National Park, as a dry season retreat for many animals, is a superb game viewing opportunity and is also located in the N of the country.

Lake Manyara National Park

Approach

Many visitors go to Lake Manyara National Park on a safari circuit which will include Ngorongoro and Serengeti. The park is located 130 km W of Arusha and is reached via the Arusha-Serengeti road. The drive from Arusha takes about 2½ hrs, the road is fairly good and is an enjoyable journey. The entrance to the Lake Manyara National Park is off the left of the Great North Road at Makuyuni. From here there is a track that goes past the lake and through the village of Mto wa Mbu to the park entrance at the foot of the Great Rift Escarpment. Lake Manyara National Park is small enough to be ideal for a day visit. The main road is good enough for most vehicles; although some of the tracks may be closed during the wet season. Taking a guide with you is recommended as they will be much better at spotting the game – in particular the lions – than you.

The village of **Mto wa Mbu** (meaning Mosquito Creek) is a small busy market town selling fruit and vegetable produced by the fertile surrounding farms. You will also be surrounded by people trying to sell you arts and crafts. However they seem to be more expensive here than in Arusha. At the gate of the national park is a small museum displaying some of the bird and rodent life found in the park.

Background

The word 'Manyara' is derived from *emanyara* the name of a plant used by the Maasai used in the building of their kraals. The plant's Latin name is *Euphorbia tirucalli*. Lake Manyara National Park was established in 1960. It is set in the Great Rift Valley and covers an area of 325 sq km, of which 229 sq km are the lake. However within this small area there is a diversity of habitats including open grasslands with rocky outcrops, forests and swamps as well as the lake itself. The best times to visit are Dec to Feb and May to Jul.

Formation

The lake is believed to have been formed about 2 or 3 million years ago when, after the formation of the Rift Valley, streams poured over the valley wall. In the depression below, the water accumulated and so the lake was formed. It has shrunk significantly and was probably at its largest about 250,000 years ago.

Wildlife

The major attraction to the Lake Manyara National Park are the tree-climbing

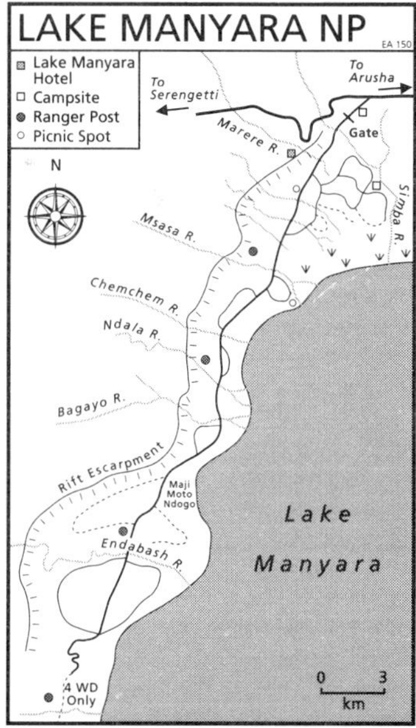

lions. Unfortunately there is no guarantee that you will see them. However there are other things to see – elephants, hippo, plain animals as well as a huge variety of bird life, both resident and migratory. At certain times of the year Lake Manayara is home to thousands of flamingoes which form a shimmering pink around the lake shore. As with all the other parks poaching is a problem and it affects elephants in particular. It was a shock when the census of 1987 found that their population had halved to under 200 in the last decade.

Routes

The road from the park gate goes through the ground water forest before crossing the Marere River Bridge. This forest, as its name suggests, is fed not by rainfall, but by ground water from the high water table fed by seepage from the volcanic rock of the rift wall. The first animals you will see on entering the Park will undoubtedly be baboons. About 500m after this bridge the road forks. To the left the track leads to a plain known as *Mahali pa Nyati* (Place of the Buffalo) which has a herd of mainly old bulls cast out from their former herds. There are also zebra and impala in this area. This is also the track to take to the Hippo Pool. The pool is formed by the Simba River on its way to the lake and is home to hippos, flamingoes and many other water birds. Some of these tracks may be impassable in the wet season and you may have to turn round and go back the way you came.

Back on the main track the forest thins out to bush and the road crosses the Mchanga River (Sand River) and Msasa River. Shortly after this latter bridge there is a turning off to the left which leads down to the lake shore where there is a peaceful picnic spot. Soon after this bridge the surroundings changes to one of Acacia woodland. This is where the famous tree climbing lions are found so drive through very slowly, look out for a tail dangling down through the branches.

Continue down the main road crossing the River Chemchem and on to the Ndala River. Here you will probably see elephants although their numbers have been reduced severely in recent years as a result of poaching. As the park is small they tend to stray across into the surrounding farmland where great damage is done to crops. Outside the park boundaries there is little to stop them being killed. During the dry season the elephants may be seen digging in the dry river bed for water. At the peak of the wet season the river may flood and the road is sometimes impassable as a result. Beyond the Ndala River the track runs closer to the Rift Valley Escarpment wall which rises steeply to the right of the road. On this slope are many different trees from those on the plain and as a result they provide a different habitat for various animals. The most noticeable are the very impressive baobabs with their huge trunks.

The first of the 2 sets of hot springs in the park are located at about where the track runs along the wall of the escarpment. These are the smaller of the 2 and so are called simply *Maji Moto Ndogo* (small hot water). The temperature is about 40°C, heated to this temperature as it circulates to great depths in fractures that run through the rock that were formed during the formation of the Rift Valley. The second set of hot springs is located further down the track over the Endabash River. These, known as Maji Moto, are both larger and hotter, reaching a temperature of 60°C. You are supposed to be able to cook an egg here in about 30 mins. The main track ends at Maji Moto and you have to turn round and go back the same way. In total the track is between 35 and 40 km long.

● Where to stay

Hotels A *Lake Manyara*, PO Box 3100, Arusha, T 3300 3113. 212 rooms. Swimming pool and shop. Located 10 km from the park gate, 300m above the park on the escarpment overlooking the lake and park – wonderful views. **E** *Kudu Guest House*. Basic but friendly, includes breakfast and dinner. Located in Mto wa Mbu. **E** *Starehe Bar and Hotel*. Located about 100m down a left turning off the road from Mto wa Mbu to Ngorongoro. Clean and friendly. Cold water only. Good food.

Bandas 10 bandas located just before park entrance. Booking through Tanzania National Parks Headquarters, PO Box 3134, Arusha or Chief Park Warden, Lake Manyara National Park, PO Box 12, Mto wa Mbu.

Youth Hostel Located at the park headquarters. Booking through Tanzania National Parks Headquarters, PO Box 3134, Arusha or Chief Park Warden, Lake Manyara National Park, PO Box 12, Mto wa Mbu. Sleeps 48 people. Facilities are basic.

Camping Two camp sites located at the entrance to the park. Both have water, toilets and showers. Mosquito nets are essential. Bring sufficient food and drinking water. The camp site in the park is expensive and facilities are minimal.

Ngorongoro

Approach

The Ngorongoro Conservation Area is 190 km W of Arusha, 60 km from Lake Manyara and 145 km from Serengeti and is reached via the Arusha-Serengeti road. The drive from Arusha takes about 4 hrs and is a splendid journey. You will go across the bottom of the Rift Valley and pass the entrance to the Lake Manyara National Park on the left of the Great North Road at the foot of the Great Rift Escarpment. Just beyond the entrance to the park the road climbs very steeply up the escarpment and at the top the turning to the Lake Manyara Hotel is off to the left. From here the country is hilly and fertile and you will climb up to the Mbulu Plateau which is farmed with wheat, maize and coffee. 25 km from Manyara at Karatu (known as Safari Junction), is the turning off to Gibbs Farm, which is 5 km off the main road. You turn right towards the Park entrance and on the approach to Ladaore Gate as the altitude increases the temperature starts to fall. Your first view of the crater comes at Heroes Point (2286m). The road continues to climb through the forest to the crater rim to the lodge.

Background

The Ngorongoro Conservation Area was established in 1959 and covers an area of 8,288 sq km. In 1951 it was included as part of the Serengeti National Park and contained the headquarters of the park. However in order to accommodate the grazing needs of the Maasai people it was decided to reclassify it as a conservation area. In 1978 it was declared a World Heritage Site in recognition of its beauty and importance. The crater has an area of 265 sq km and measures between 16 and 19 km across. The rim reaches 2,286m above sea level and the crater floor is 610m below it. The best times to visit it are Dec to Feb and Jun to Jul. During the long rains season (Apr to May) the roads can be almost impassable and so access to the crater floor may be restricted.

The name 'Ngorongoro' comes from a Maasai word *Ilkorongoro* which was the name given to the age group of Maasai warriors who defeated the previous occupants of the area, the Datong, around 1800. The sound of the battle bells that the Maasai wore during the battle, that was supposed to have terrified their enemies into submission, was 'koh-rohng-roh' and it is from this that Ngorongoro comes. The Maasai refer to the Ngorongoro Southern Highlands as 'O'lhoirobi' which means the cold highlands; while the Germans also referred to the climate calling these the 'winter highlands'.

Ngorongoro has been called the 'Garden of Eden' and 'Paradise on Earth'. Obviously for this reason it has attracted a large number of tourists which has affected it a great deal. When you come here be prepared for the fact that many other people have the same idea. If you are expecting to have a pride of lions to

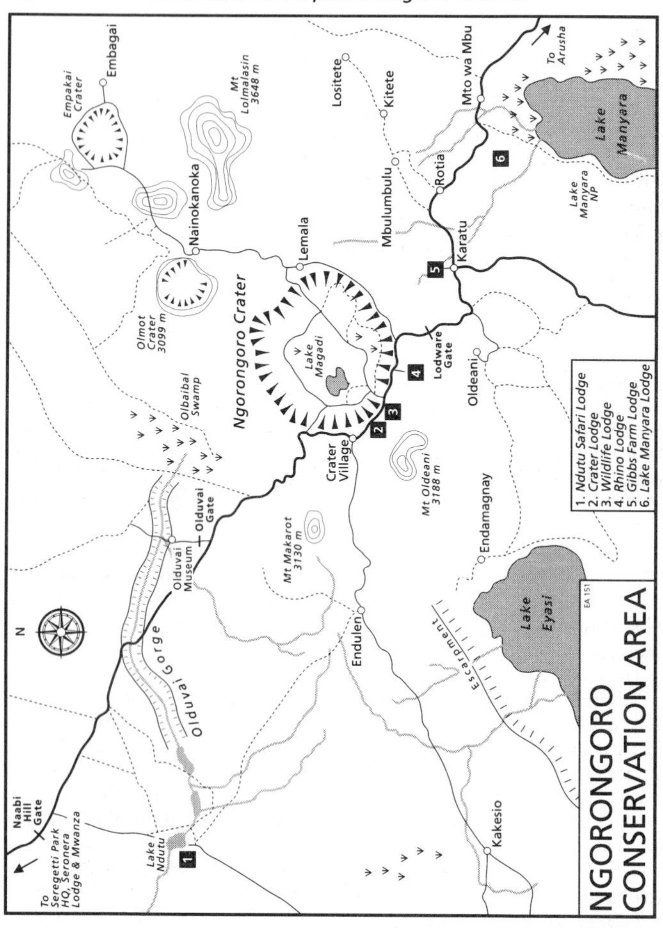

yourself think again – it is more likely that there will be a mob of minibuses surrounding it. Some people find this a huge disappointment and feel there is an almost zoo-like atmosphere to the crater. However you can expect to see almost all of the big game; there are an estimated 30,000 animals living in the crater. As this is a conservation area rather than a national park you will also see some of the local Maasai people grazing their cattle here. Poaching has affected the animal population and in particular the rhino population is believed to be under 15.

Formation

Ngorongoro is believed to date from about 2.5 million years ago – relatively modern for this area. It was once a huge active volcano and was probably as large as Kilimanjaro. After its large major eruption, as the lava subsided its cone collapsed inwards leaving the caldera. Minor volcanic activity continued and the small cones that resulted can be seen in the crater floor. To the NE of Ngorongoro crater are 2 smaller craters Olmot and Empakal. From the crater on a clear day you should be able to see 6 mountains of over 3,000m.

Route

In the crater itself for most of the year only 4WD vehicles are allowed. Sometimes in the dry season other vehicles will be allowed but do not rely on this. Whether you have your own vehicle or hire one there you will have to take a park ranger with you which costs US$15 per day. 4WD Land Rovers can be hired in the village where you pick up the ranger, which is cheaper than hiring through the lodges.

Where the road gets to the rim of the crater you will see 2 memorials to Professor Bernhard Grzimek and his son Michael. They were the makers of the film *'Serengeti Shall Not Die'* and they spent their lives working for the preservation of the wildlife of Tanzania. They conducted surveys and censuses of the animals in the Serengeti and Ngorongoro Parks and were heavily involved in the fight against poachers. Tragically Michael was killed in an aeroplane accident over the Ngorongoro Crater in 1959 and his father returned to Germany where he set up the Frankfurt Zoological Society. He died in 1987 requesting in his will that he should be buried beside his son in Tanzania. Their memorials remain as a reminder of all the work they did to protect this part of Africa.

Access to the crater is by way of 2 steep roads which are both one way. You enter by the Windly Gap road and leave by the Lerai road. The Windly Gap branches off the Serengeti road to the right and descends the NE wall of the crater to the floor of the crater 610m below. The road is narrow, steep and twists and turns as it enters the crater which is rather like a huge amphitheatre.

Encounters with animals are frequent and there is a wide variety of game in the crater. These include lion, elephant and rhino as well as buffalo, Thompson's gazelle, wildebeest and zebra. You are also likely to see ostrich and Lake Magadi, the soda lake at the floor of the crater, is home to thousands of flamingoes.

Lerai Forest is a good place for a picnic lunch. Beware of dive-bombing kites while eating your lunch as they try to snatch it from you.

● Where to stay and eat

A *Gibb's Farm* (Ngorongoro Safari Lodge), PO Box 1501, Karuta, T Karuta 25, Tlx 42041. (Bookings can be made through Abercrombie and Kent, Sokoine Rd, PO Box 427, Arusha, T 7803/3181). Managed by Abercrombie and Kent. Discount between Easter and end of Jun. On the outer slopes of the crater located at the edge of a forest facing the Mbulu Hills to the SE. **A** ***Ngorongoro Crater Lodge***, PO Box 751, Arusha, T 7803, Tlx 42762. (Bookings can be made through Abercrombie and Kent, Sokoine Rd, PO Box 427, Arusha, T 7803 3181). Managed by Abercrombie and Kent. Discount between Easter and end of Jun. Old lodge built on rim of the crater in 1937. Individual cottages. Good views. Lovely old bar with roaring log fire. **A** ***Ngorongoro Wildlife Lodge***, PO Box 3100, Arusha, T 3842, Tlx 42037. Modern building on the rim of the crater with wonderful views. 75 rooms, heated. Excellent meals and friendly bar with log fire. **C** ***Ngorongoro Rhino Lodge***, PO Box 776, Arusha, T 3466. On the rim of the crater. Lovely site but does not have the views of some of the other lodges. Can sometimes camp here if you have your own tent. **D** *Simba Camp Site*, located about 2 km from Crater Village. Facilities include hot water, showers, toilets and firewood. **E** ***Usiwara Guest House*** (Drivers Lodge). Located in Crater Village nr the post office. Basic, will need sleeping bag. Can get food here.

Ushirika Co-op Restaurant also does cheap simple food. You can usually buy food in the village but the stock is limited so you would be advised to bring supplies with you.

Road

If you do not have your own transport you will be able to get a bus from Arusha to Karatu. From there you will have to try and hitch which may be difficult.

Olduvai Gorge

Approach

This lies within the Ngorongoro Conservation Area to the NW of the crater. The site is located about 10 to 15 minutes off the main road between Serengeti and Ngorongoro.

Background

Olduvai Gorge has become famous for being the site of a number of archaeological finds and has been called the 'cradle of mankind'. The name Olduvai comes from the Maasai word *oldupai* which is the name for the type of wild sisal that grows in the gorge.

Archaeological finds

Olduvai Gorge aroused interest in the archeologcal world as early as 1911. This was when a German, Prof Katurinkle, whilst looking for butterflies in the gorge, found some fossil bones. These caused great interest in Europe and in 1913 an expedition led by Prof Hans Reck was arranged. They stayed at Olduvai for 3 months and made a number of fossil finds. At a later expedition in 1933 Prof Reck was accompanied by 2 English archeologists Dr Leakey and his future wife Mary.

The Leakeys continued their work and in Jul 1959 discovered 400 fragments of the skull *Australopithecus-Zinjanthropus Boisei* – the 'nutcracker man' who lived in the lower Pleistocene Age around 1,750,000 BC. A year later the skull and bones of a young *Homo Habilis* were found. The Leakey's assert that around 1.8 to 2 million years ago there existed in Tanzania 2 types of man, *Australopithecus-Zinjanthropus Boisei* and *Homo Habilis*. The other two, *Australopithecus Africanus* and *Arobustus*, had died out. *Homo Habilis* with the larger brain, gave rise to modern man. *Habilis* was a small ape-like creature and, although thought to be the first of modern man's ancestors, is quite distinct from modern man. Tools, such as those used by *Homo Erectus* (dating from 1-1½ million years ago), have also been found at Olduvai as well as at Isimila near Iringa. Other exciting finds in the area are the footprints found in 1979 of man, woman and child at Laetoli (this is a site near Oldovai) made by 'creatures' that walked upright. Dating back 3.5 million years they pushed back the beginnings of the human race further than ever before. In 1986 a further discovery at Olduvai by a team of American and Tanzanian archaeologists increased the archaeological significance of the site. This find was of the remains of an adult female dating back 1.8 million years. In total the fossil remains of about 35 humans have been found in the area at different levels.

Prehistoric animal remains were also found in the area and about 150 species of mammals have been identified. These include the enormous Polorovis with a horn span of 2m, the Deinotheruium which was a huge elephant-like creature with tusks that curved downwards and the Hipparion, a three-toed horse-like creature.

At the site there is a small museum which is open until 3 pm. It may, however, be closed during the wet season, Apr to end Jun. It holds displays of copies of some of the finds as well as pictures of what life was like for Olduvai's earliest inhabitants. You can go down into the gorge to see the sites and there will usually be an archeologist to show you around.

● Where to stay

There is nowhere to stay on the actual site so you will have to make this a day trip. The nearest place to stay is **B** ***Ndutu Safari Lodge***, PO Box 1182, Arusha, T 3625. Sleeps 70. Bar and restaurant. Beautiful setting overlooking Lake Ndutu. Located about 90 km from the Ngorongoro Crater nr S boundary of Serengeti National Park.

Serengeti National Park

Approach

The Serengeti is usually approached

from Arusha along a fairly good road. From Arusha you will pass the entrance to Lake Manyara National Park and through the Ngorongoro Conservation Area. Shortly before the park boundary there is the turning off to Olduvai Gorge. Seronera, the village in the heart of the Serengeti is 335 km from Arusha. Approaching from Mwanza or Musoma on the lake shore take the road E and you will enter the Serengeti through the Ndaraka Gate in the W.

Background

Serengeti is probably the most famous of Tanzania's national parks. The name is derived from the Maasai word 'siringet' meaning 'extended area'. It was established in 1951 and at 14,763 sq km is Tanzania's second largest national park (after Selous). It rises from 920-1,850m above sea level and its landscape varies from the long and short grass plains in the S, the central Savannah, the more hilly wooded areas in the N and the extensive woodland in the Western corridor. The Maswa Game Reserve adjoins the W border of the Serengeti National Park. The main rainy season is from Nov to May.

Serengeti is perhaps most well known for the annual migration which takes place across the great savannah plains. This is a phenomenal sight: thousands and thousands of animals, particularly wildebeest, as far as the eye can see.

Wildlife

During the rainy season the wildebeest, whose population has been estimated at around 1.5 million, are found in the E section of the Serengeti and also the Maasai Mara in Kenya to the N. When the dry season begins at the end of Jun so the annual migration commences as the animals move in search of pasture. They concentrate on the remaining green patches, forming huge herds. It is also around this time that the rutting season starts and territories are established by the males who then attempt to attract females into their areas. Once mating has occurred, the herds merge together again and the migration W begins. The migrating animals do not all follow the same route. About half go W, often going outside the park boundaries and then swing NE. The other half go directly N. The 2 groups meet up in the Maasai Mara in Kenya. To get to the W section of the Serengeti and the Maasai Mara, where they will find pasture in the dry season, the wildebeest must cross a number of large rivers and this proves too much for many of them. Many of the weaker and older animals will die during the migration. Needless to say predators follow the wildebeest on their great trek and easy pickings are to be found. They return to the E at the end of the dry season (Nov) and calving begins at the start of the wet.

Other animals for which Serengeti is famous include lions some of which migrate with the wildebeest while others remain in the central plains (the population was estimated at 3,000 in 1978) and cheetah (500). However, because this park is so vast, they are in fact spread fairly thinly on the ground. The elephant population in Serengeti has been decimated by poaching and is estimated to have fallen from around 2,500 in 1976 to under 500 in 1986.

Routes

If you are approaching the Serengeti from the SE you will first reach the Short Grass Plains. The flat monotonous landscape is broken by the Gol Mountains which are seen to the right and by kopjes. The grass here remains short during both the wet and dry seasons. There is no permanent water supply in this region as a result of the nature of the soil. However during the rains water collects in hollows and depressions until it dries up at the end of the wet season. It is then that the animals begin to move on.

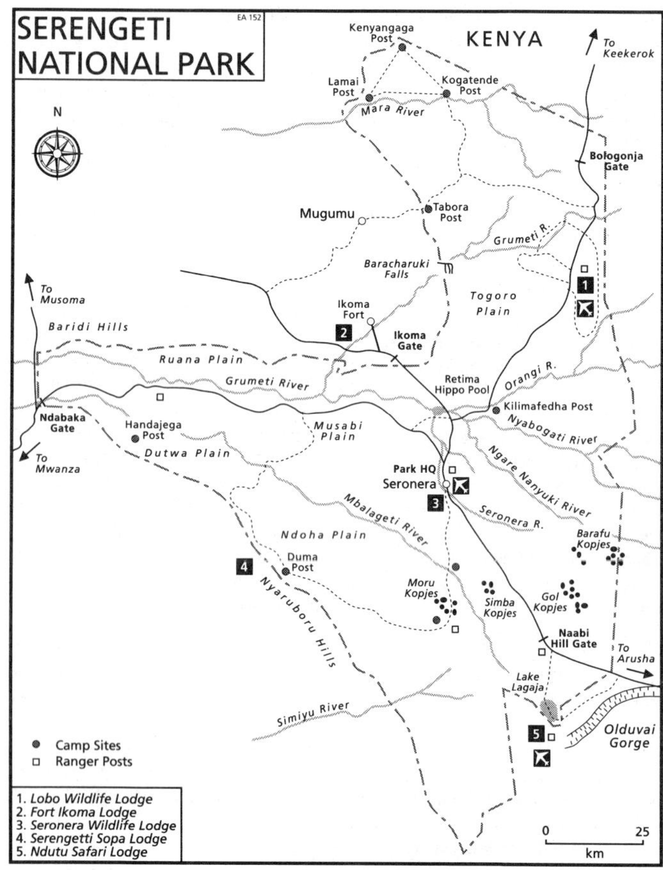

Naabi Hill Gate marks the end of the Short Grass and beginning of the Long Grass Plains. Dotted across the plains are kopjes. These interesting geological formations are made up of ancient granite which has been left behind as the surrounding soil structures have been broken down by centuries of erosion and weathering. They play an important role in the ecology of the plains providing habitats for many different animals from rock hyraxs (a small rodent-like creature whose closest relation is actually the elephant) to cheetahs.

A number of kopjes that you might visit include the Moru kopjes in the S of the park to the left of the main road heading N. You may be lucky enough to see the Verreaux Eagle which sometimes nests here. These have a cave with Maasai paintings on the wall and a rock called Gong Rock after the sound it makes when struck with a stone. There are also the Simba Kopjes located on the left of the road before reaching Seronera, which, as their name suggests are often

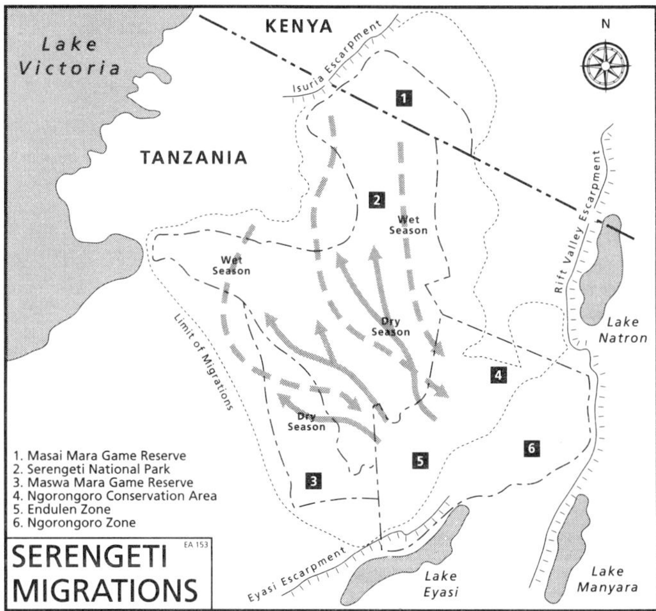

SERENGETI MIGRATIONS

a hide out of lions.

Passing through the Long Grass Plains in the wet season from around Dec to May is an incredible experience. All around, stretching into the distance, are huge numbers of wildebeest, Thompson's gazelle, zebra etc.

The village of **Seronera** is in the middle of the park set in the Seronera Valley. It is reached by a gravel road which is in fairly good condition. In the approach to Seronera the number of trees increases – particularly the thorny Acacia trees. The valley itself is home to a large number of animals and is a popular viewing area. You can expect to see buffalo, impala, lion, hippo and elephant. If you are really lucky you might see leopard; however they are few and far between, are nocturnal and spend most of the day in trees, so the chances of seeing them are fairly remote.

About 5 km N of Seronera the track splits. To the right it goes up to Banagi and Lobo beyond, and to the left to the so-called Western Corridor, about 20 km N of Banagi Hill which is home to both browsers and grazers. At its base is the Retina Hippo Pool which is located about 6 km off the main track at Banagi. Banagi was the site of the original Game Department Headquarters before it became a national park. North of here the land is mainly rolling plains of both grassland and woodland with a few hilly areas and rocky outcrops.

In the NE section of the park is Lobo. Wildlife remain in this area throughout the year including during the dry season. Lobo is the site of the Lobo Lodge, 75 km from Seronera. Further N the Mara flows with forest on each of its banks. This is one of the rivers that claims so many wildebeest lives every year during the migration. You will see both hippo and crocodile along the river banks.

If you take the left hand track where the road splits N of Seronera you will follow the Western Corridor. (This is also the route to take if you are heading for Mwanza.) The best time to follow this track is in the dry season (Jun to Oct) when the road is at its best and the migrating animals have reached this area. Part of the road follows the Grumeti River which you will see on your right. On the banks of this river you will also see huge crocodiles basking in the sun. The Musabi and Ndoha Plains to the NW and W of Seronera respectively can be seen if you have a 4WD. The latter plain is the breeding area of topi and large herds of up to 2000 will often be seen here.

● Where to stay

The Park Headquarters are at Seronera and there are airstrips at Seronera and Lobo. **A** ***Seronera Wildlife Lodge***, PO Box 3100, Arusha, T 3842, Tlx 42037. Book through Tanzanian Tourist Corporation in Dar es Salaam (see page 261) or Arusha. (see page 307). 50% discount from Easter to 30th Jun. 75 rooms. Fantastic building built on and around a kopje with wonderful views of the plains around. Restaurant. Shop. Bar and viewing platform at the top of the kopje – beware the monkeys. **A** ***Lobo Wildlife Lodge***, PO Box 3100, Arusha, T 3842, Tlx 42037. Book through the Tanzanian Tourist Corporation in Dar es Salaam (see page 261) or Arusha. (see page 307). 50% discount from Easter to 30th Jun. 75 rooms. Located NE of the Seronera village. Swimming pool, shop. Also built overlooking the plains. Good restaurant and bar. **B** ***Ndutu Safari Lodge***, PO Box 1182, Arusha, T 3625. Accommodates about 25 in rooms and about 40 in tented camp. Located about 90 km from the Ngorongoro Crater nr S boundary of Serengeti National Park. Wonderful view of Lake Lagaja and the plain beyond.

● Camping

Be prepared to be totally self-sufficient and bring food with you as there is little available in the village. **C** ***Special camp sites*** at Seronera, Lobo, Ndutu, Nabi Hill, Hembe Hill. **D** ***Public camp sites*** at Lobo, Nabi Hill and Kirawira. **D** ***Camp sites*** at Seronera close to the Seronera Wildlife Lodge.

Kilimanjaro National Park

Approach

There are a number of approaches to Mount Kilimanjaro. The easiest is to fly to Kilimanjaro International Airport and on the approach you will get a fantastic view of the mountain (provided it is not covered by cloud). The park entrance is about 90 km from the airport which takes about 1½ hr. Alternative routes are to go to Moshi by train or road and from there to Marangu. Marangu is the village at the park entrance at the base of the mountain. It is located 11 km N of Himo which is a village 27 km E of Moshi on the road to the Kenya border. It is also cheap and easy to get to Kilimanjaro from Kenya by taking a matatu from Nairobi to the border (about 4 hrs) and from there another matatu to Marangu Gate.

Formation

Kilimanjaro was formed about a million years ago by a series of volcanic movements along the Great Rift Valley. Until these movements the area was a flat plain lying at about 600-900m above sea level. About 750,000 years ago volcanic activity forced 3 points above about 4,800m – Shira, Kibo and Mawenzi. Some 250,000 years later Shira became inactive and it collapsed into itself forming the crater. Kibo and Mawenzi continued their volcanic activity and it was their lava flow that forms the 11 km saddle between the 2 peaks. When Mawenzi died out its NE wall collapsed in a huge explosion creating a massive gorge. The last major eruptions occurred about 200 years ago and Kibo now lies dormant but not extinct. Although Kibo appears to be a snow clad dome it does in fact contain a caldera of 2.5 km across and 180m deep at the deepest point in the S. Within the depression is an inner ash cone which rises to within 60m of the summit height and is evidence of former volcanic activity. On the S slopes the glaciers reach down to about 4,200m whilst on the N slopes they only descend a little below the summit. Kilimanjaro has well defined altitudinal vegetation zones. From the base to the summit these go: plateau, semi-arid scrub; cultivated, well-watered southern slopes; dense cloud forest; open moorland; alpine desert; and moss and lichen communities.

Background

Some people will come to Tanzania just to climb Kilimanjaro, the highest mountain in Africa. The national park was established in 1973 and covers an area of 756 sq km. The altitude rises from 1,829m at the Marangu Gate to 5,895m at Kibo Peak. Although it can be climbed throughout the year it is worth avoiding the 2 rainy seasons (late Mar to mid-Jun and Oct to beginning of Dec) when the routes become slippery. Probably the best time to visit is Jan to Feb and Sept to Oct when there is usually no cloud.

When, in 1848, the first reports by the German missionary Johannes Rebmann of a snow-capped mountain on the equator arrived in Europe, the idea was ridiculed by the Royal Geographical Society of Britain. In 1889 the report was confirmed by the German geographer Hans Meyer and the Austrian Alpine mountaineer Ludwig Purtscheller who climbed Kibo and managed to reach the snows on Kilimanjaro's summit. Mawenzi was first climbed by the German Fritz Klute in 1912.

The mountain was originally located in a part of British East Africa (now Kenya). However the mountain was given by Queen Victoria of England as a gift to her cousin, and so the border was moved and the mountain included within German Tanganyika.

Climbing Mount Kilimanjaro

Officially anyone aged over 12 may attempt the climb. The youngest person to climb the mountain was an 11 year old, while the oldest was 74. However it is not that easy and estimates of the number of people that attempt the climb and do not make it to the top vary from 50-80%. The important things to remember are to come prepared and take it slowly – if you have the chance spend an extra day half way up which will give you the chance to acclimatize.

Being well equipped will also increase your chances of succeeding in reaching the summit. In particular be sure you have a warm sleeping bag, insulating mat, thermal underwear, gloves, wool hat, sun glasses or snow goggles, sun cream, large water bottle and first aid kit. If you are going on any route apart from Marangu you are advised to take a tent and stove. Although organized climbs will provide food, some people recommend that you should take your own freeze-dried food and cook it yourself. This will decrease the likelihood of getting diarrhoea and thus having to turn back.

Altitude sickness is often a problem while climbing Kilimanjaro. If you know you are susceptible to this you are advised not to attempt the climb. Symptoms include bad headache, nausea, vomiting and severe fatigue. It can be avoided by ascending slowly and if at all possible spending an extra day half way up to acclimatize. It can be cured by descending to a lower altitude. There is a drug called Diamox which helps if taken before the ascent. Other more serious conditions include acute pulmonary oedema and cerebral oedema. In the former, the sufferer becomes breathless, turns blue in the face and coughs up frothy material. The latter is even more serious – symptoms are intense headache, hallucinations, confusion and disorientation and staggering gait. This is caused by the accumulation of fluid on the brain and can cause death or serious brain damage. If either of these conditions are suspected the sufferer should immediately be taken down to a lower altitude to receive medical care. It is however normal to feel breathless and fatigued at high altitudes and these are not precursors to the more serious conditions.

Marangu is the usual route for tourists and only experienced climbers

The Meaning Of Kilimanjaro

Since the earliest explorers to East Africa, people have been intrigued by the name Kilimanjaro and its meaning. There is in fact no simple explanation. The Chagga people do not actually have a name for the whole mountain – they have names for the 2 peaks – Kibo and Mawenzi. Kibo (or kipoo which is the correct term in Kichagga) means 'spotted' and refers to the rock which can be seen standing out against the snow on this peak, and Mawenzi (or Kimawenze) means "having a broken top" and again describes its appearance.

The question of the origin of the name Kilimanjaro for the mountain as a whole has been much discussed and a number of theories put forward. Most of these break the word down into 2 elements: kilima and njaro. In Swahili the word for mountain is actually *mlima* while *kilima* means hill – so it is possible that an early European visitor incorrectly used kilima because of the analogy to the 2 Kichagga words Kibo and Kimawenzi.

The explorers Krapf said that the Swahili of the coast knew it as Kilimanjaro 'mountain of greatness' but he does not explain how he came to this conclusion. He also suggests it could also mean 'mountain of caravans' (*kilima* = mountain, *jaro* = caravans) but while *kilima* is a Swahili word, *jaro* is a Chagga word. Other observers have suggested that *njaro* has at some time meant 'whiteness' and therefore this was the 'mountain of whiteness'. Alternatively *njaro* could be the name of an evil spirit, or a demon which causes colds. The first known European to climb Mount Kilimanjaro does make reference to the spirit, mentioning 'Njaro, the guardian spirit of the mountain' and this seems quite a plausible explanation. There are many stories in Chagga folklore about spirits who live on the mountain. Most of them tend to be kind and have good intentions although there is one who was supposed to destroy anyone who climbed up beyond a certain point. However there is apparently no evidence of a spirit called Njaro, either by the Chagga or by the coastal peoples.

Another explanation involves the Maasai word *njore* for springs or water. The suggestion is that the mountain was known as Mountain of Water because it was from there that all the rivers in the area rose. The problems with this theory are that it does not explain the use of the Swahili word for 'hill' rather than 'mountain', and also it assumes that a Swahili word has been put together with a Maasai word.

The final explanation is from a Kichagga term *kilelema* which means 'which has become difficult or impossible' or 'which has defeated'. Njaro can be derived from the Kichagga words *njaare* a bird, or else *jyaro* a caravan. The suggestion is that attempts to climb the mountain were a failure and thus the mountain became known as kilemanjaare, kilemajyaro or kilelemanjaare meaning which defeats or is impossible for the bird or the caravan. The theory has the advantage of being made up of all Kichagga parts. It seems possible either that this was the name given to the mountain by the Chagga themselves, or else people passing through the area, who heard the Chagga say kilemanjaare or kilemajyaro meaning that the mountain was impossible to climb associated with their own kilima and so the name caught on and was standardised to Kilimanjaro.

should use the other routes. A guide is compulsory on all the routes. However if you are going on one of the other routes although you must take a guide with you, be sure to have a good map and compass as he may not know the route. Do not be tempted to go it alone to avoid paying the park and guide fees – above the tree line the path is not always clear and you will be in big trouble is you are caught. It is also well worth hiring porters – they are not too expensive and will increase your enjoyment enormously.

Costs

Climbing Mount Kilimanjaro is a fairly costly experience. But everyone who does it agrees that it is well worth it. Park fees US$15 per day plus US$10 entrance fee which, assuming you take 5 days will take you to US$85 immediately. Hut fees on Marangu are US$15 per night (whether you use the huts or not). Porters and guides are US$2-3 per day. On to this you must add getting to the start of the trail, food, hiring equipment and tips for the guide and porters. The cheapest you will probably manage to do it will be around US$200, but it will more likely be closer to US$500. Organized climbs do not usually work out much more expensive than doing it yourself and are considerably less hassle.

Anyone planning to climb the mountain is advised to buy the *Map and Guide* by Mark Savage. This is difficult to obtain in Tanzania but you can get it in Kenya or before you leave from England (32 Seamill Park Crescent, Worthing, BN11 2PN, UK). Another guide particularly useful if you want to climb the mountain (rather than walk up like the rest of us) is the *Guide to Mount Kenya and Kilimanjaro* edited by Iain Allan and published by the Mountain Club of Kenya.

Tour operators

There is one tour operator at Moshi (*Trans-Kibo Travel* PO Box 558, Moshi, T 4734 2923. Located inside the YMCA) and two at Marangu, the village at the gates of the National Park, contactable through *Kibo Hotel* or *Marangu Hotel* (see page 302)

Routes

There are a number of different trails. The most popular is the Marangu trail.

Marangu trail This is probably the least scenic of the routes but being the gentlest climb and having a village at the start and accommodation on the way means that it is the most popular.

The national park gate (1,830m) is about 8 km from the *Kibo Hotel*. This is as far as vehicles are allowed. From here to the first nights stop at Mandara Hut (2,700m) is a walk of about 4 hrs. It is through shambas growing coffee as well as some fantastic rainforest and is an enjoyable walk although it can be quite muddy. On the walk you can admire the moss and lichens, the vines and flowers including orchids. The Mandara Hut, near the Maundi Crater, is actually a group of huts which can sleep about 200

An Unusual Way Up Mount Kilimanjaro

On the 11 Mar 1962, 3 French parachutists, Jean-Claude Dubois, Bernard Couture and Jean-Claude Camus, landed on the crater of Mount Kilimanjaro and broke the world record for the highest parachute landing drop. They had had some problems finding a plane that would fly high enough, and organising a ground rescue team, but the jump itself went off without incident and they landed less than 50m from the targetted landing zone. Two of the 3 were doctors, and they studied the repercussions on the human body of an abrupt change in altitude. Having landed in the crater at around midday, they descended immediately and reached the *Marangu Hotel* at one o'clock in the morning.

people. Mattresses, lamps and stoves are provided but nothing else. This complex was built by the Norwegians as part of an aid programme. There is piped water, flushing toilets and firewood available. There is a dining area in the main cabin.

The second day will start off as a steep walk through the last of the rainforest and out into tussock grassland, giant heather and then on to the moorlands. There are occasional clearings through which you will get great views of Mawenzi and Moshi far below. You will also probably see some of the amazing vegetation that is found on Kilimanjaro including the giant lobelia, Kilimanjaro 'everlasting flowers' and other weird 'alpine' plants. The walk to Horombo Hut (3,720m) is about 14 km with an altitude gain of about 1000m and will take you anything between 5 and 7 hrs. This hut is again actually a collection of huts that can accommodate up to 200 people. There is plenty of water but firewood is scarce. Some people spend an extra day to help get acclimatized and if you are doing this there are a number of short walks in the area. It is a very good idea to spend this extra day – but obviously the extra cost puts off a lot of people.

On the next day of walking you will climb to the Kibo Hut which is 13 km from Horombo and is at 4,703m. As you climb, the vegetation thins to grass and heather and eventually to bare scree. You will feel the air thinning and will probably start to suffer from some altitude sickness on this day of walking. The route takes about 6 to 7 hrs up the valley behind the huts, past 'Last Water' and onto 'The Saddle.' This is the wide fairly flat U-shaped desert between the 2 peaks of Mawenzi and Kibo and from here you will get some fantastic views of the mountain. After Zebra Rocks and at the beginning of the saddle the track forks. To the right about 3 hrs from Horombo Hut is Mawenzi Hut and to the left across the saddle is Kibo Hut. Kibo Hut is where the porters stay and from here on you will just take with you the absolute bare essentials. Kibo Huts sleep about 120 people. There is no vegetation in the area and no water unless there has been snow recently so it has to be carried up from Last Water. Some people decide to try and get as much sleep as possible before the 2 am start, while others decide not to sleep at all. You are unlikely to sleep very well because of the altitude and the temperatures anyway.

On the final day of the climb, in order to be at the summit at sunrise, and before the cloud comes down, you will have to get up at about 0200. One advantage of beginning at this time is that if you saw what you were about to attempt you would probably give up before you had even begun. You can expect to feel pretty awful during this final 5 hr ascent and many climbers are physically sick. You may find that this climb is extremely slippery and hard going. As the sun rises you will reach Gillman's Point (5,680m) – it is a wonderful sight and makes the climb well worth it. From here you have to decide whether you want to keep going another couple of hours to get to Kibo Peak (5,896m). The walk around the crater rim to Kibo Peak is only an extra 200m but at this altitude it is a strenuous 200m. At the peak there is a fair amount of litter left by previous climbers. You will return to Horombo Hut the same day and the next day return to Marangu where you will be presented with a certificate.

Umbwe trail This climb is short and steep but is a wonderfully scenic route to take and as a result is becoming increasingly popular. However it is not recommended for inexperienced climbers. To get to the start of the trail take the turning off the Arusha road about 2 km down on the right. From there it's 14 km down the Lyamungu road, turn right towards Mango and soon after crossing the Sere River you will get to Umbwe village. Ask at the mission school to leave your vehicle here.

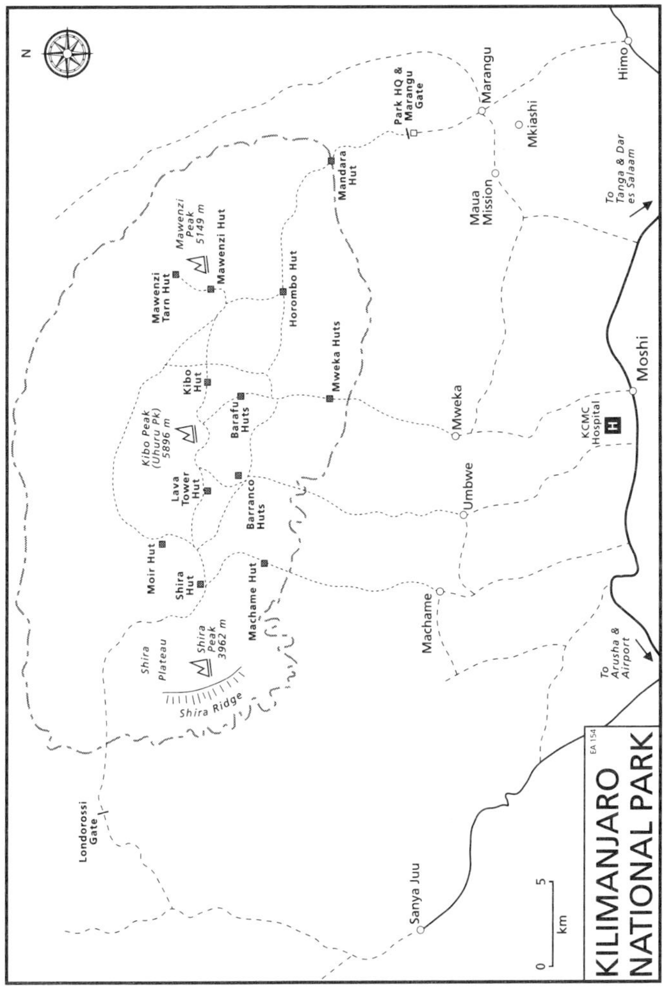

From the mission the track continues for about 3 km up towards the forest to Kifuni village. From there it's another 6 km before you get to the start of the trail proper. There is a sign here and the trail branches to the left and climbs quite steeply through the forest along the ridge that is between the Lonzo River to the W and Umbwe River to the E. You will reach the first shelter which is a cave (2,940m) about 6 to 8 hrs from Umbwe. This is Bivouac I which is an all weather rock shelter formed from the rock overhangs. It will shelter about 6 or 7 people. There is firewood nearby and a spring about 15m below under a rock face.

If you made an early start and are fit you can continue on to Bivouac II. From the cave, continue up, past the moorland and along the ridge. It is a steep walk with deep valleys on each side of the ridge and this walk is magnificent with the strange 'Old Man's Beard' – a type of moss – covering most of the vegetation. The second set of caves is Bivouac II (3,800m) about 3-4 hrs from Bivouac I. There are 2 caves – one about 5 minutes further down the track which will both sleep 3 or 4 people. There is a spring down the ravine about 15 mins to the W.

From the second set of caves the path continues up less steeply up the ridge beyond the tree line before reaching Barranco Hut (3,900m). Barranco Hut is about 5 hrs away from the first caves. The path is well marked. The hut is a metal cabin which sleeps 6 to 8 people. About 200m beyond the hut is a rock overhang which can be used if the hut is full. There is water available about 250m to the E and firewood available in the area.

Just before reaching the hut the path splits in 2. To the left, climb the W lateral ridge to the Arrow Glacier Hut (now defunct) towards the new Lava Tower Hut (4,600m) about 4 hrs away. Up this path the vegetation thins before disappearing completely on reaching the scree slopes. Having spent the night here you will want to leave very early for the final ascent. Head torches are imperative and if there is no moon the walk can be quite difficult. Climb up between Arrow Glacier (which may have disappeared completely if you are there towards the end of the dry season) and Little Breach Glacier until you get to a few small cliffs. At this stage turn to the right heading for the lowest part of the crater rim that you can see. This part of the walk is on scree and snow and parts of it are quite a scramble. Having reached the crater floor cross the Furtwangler Glacier snout to a steep gully that reaches the summit plateau about another 500m W of Kibo Peak.

If you take the path to the right from Barranco Hut (E) you will cross one small stream and then another larger one as you contour the mountain to join the Mweka Trail. The path then climbs steeply through a gap in the W Breach. From here you can turn left to join the routes over the S glaciers. Alternatively continue along the marked path across screes, ridges and a valley until you reach the Karangu Campsite which is about a further 2-3 hrs on from the top of the breach. A further couple of hours up the Karangu valley will come out at the Mweka-Barafu Hut path (part of the Mweka Trail). If you go left down along this you will get to the Barafu Hut after about 1-1½ hr. If you go straight on for about 3 hrs you will join the Marangu Trail just above the Horombo Hut.

Machame trail This trail is considered by some to be the most attractive of the routes up Kilimanjaro. It is located between Umbwe Trail and Shira Trail and joins the latter route at Shira Hut. The turn-off to the trail is to the W of Umbwe off the main Arusha-Moshi road. Take this road N towards Machame village, and leave your vehicle at the school or hotel there. From the village to the first huts takes about 9 hrs so be sure to start early.

Take the track through the shambas and the forest to the park entrance (about 4 km) from where you will see a clear track that climbs gently through the forest and along a ridge that is between the Weru Weru and Makoa streams. It is about 7 km to the edge of the forest, and then 4-5 hrs up to the Machame Huts (3,000m). The 2 Machame Huts, on the edge of the forest, will sleep about 7 people each. There is plenty of water down in the valley below the huts and firewood available close by.

From the Machame Huts go across the valley, over a stream, then up a steep ridge for about 3 or 4 hrs. The path then goes W and drops into the rivergorgebefore climbingmoregradually up the other side and onto the moorland of the Shira Plateau to join the Shira Plateau Trail near the Shira Hut (3,800m). This takes about 5 hrs in total. From the Shira Plateau you will get some magnificent views of Kibo Peak and the Western Breach. The Shira Hut (3,800m) sleeps about 6 people and is used by people on the Shira Plateau Trail as well as those on the Machame Trail. There is plenty of water available to the N and firewood nearby. From here there are a number of choices. You can go on to the Barranco Hut (5-6 hrs, 3,900m) or the Lava Tower Hut (4 hrs, 4,600m). The path to Arrow Glacier Hut is well marked. It goes E from Shira Hut until it reaches a junction where the North Circuit Route leads off to the left. The path continues E crossing a wide valley before turning SE towards the Lava Tower. Shortly before the tower a route goes off to the right to Barranco Hut and the South Circuit Route. To the left the path goes to Arrow Glacier Hut and the Western Breach.

Shira Plateau trail This route needs a 4WD vehicle and so for this reason is little used. However if you do have access to such a vehicle and are acclimatized you can get to the Arrow Glacier Hut in one day.

The drive is a complex one and you may need to stop and ask the way frequently. Pass through West Kilimanjaro, drive for 5 km and turn right. At 13 km you will pass a small trading centre on the left. At 16 km you will cross a stream followed by a hard left. At 21 km you will enter a coniferous forest which will soon become a natural forest. The plateau rim is reached at 39 km. Here the track continues upwards gently and crosses the plateau to the roadhead at 55 km. From here you will have to walk. It is about 1½ hr to Shira Hut (3,800m). From here you continue E and join the to join the Umbwe Trail to the Lava Tower Hut. The walk is fairly gentle and has magnificent views.

Mweka trail This trail is the most direct route up the mountain. It is the steepest and the fastest. It begins at Mweka village, 13 km N of Moshi, where you can leave your vehicle at the College of Wildlife Management with permission.

The trail follows an old logging road which you can drive up in good weather, through the shambas and the forest, for about 5 km. It is a slippery track which deteriorates into a rough path after about 2 hrs. From here it is approx a further 6 km up a ridge to the Mweka Huts (3,100m) which are about 500m beyond the tree line in the giant heather zone. In total the first day's walk takes about 6-8 hrs. There are 2 huts here which each sleep about 8 people. Water is available nearby from a stream in a small valley below the huts 5 mins to the SE and there is plenty of firewood.

From the Mweka Huts follow the ridge E of the Msoo river through heathlands, tussock open grassland and then onto the alpine desert to the Barafu Hut (4,400m) about 6-8 hrs. These metal shelters sleep about 12 people. There is no water or firewood available so you will need to bring it up from Mweka Hut.

From the Barafu Huts the final ascent on a ridge between Rebmann and Ratzel glaciers takes about 6 hrs up to the rim of the crater between Stella and Hans Meyer Points. From here it is a further hour to Uhuru Peak. At the lower levels the path is clearly marked, but becomes obscured further up. It is steep being the most direct non-technical route (although specialized climbing equipment is not needed) so be prepared for a scramble.

Loitkitok trail This approach from Kenya is closed to the public and is not recommended. However you may be able to obtain special permission from the park's department to climb it. See the warden who is based in Marangu. You may have problems getting porters to go up this route.

This, and the Shira Plateau Trail, both come in from the N unlike the other trails. From the Outward Bound School take the path towards the border road and on reaching it turn left down it. Cross over the bridge over the Kikelewa River and go a further 150m. Here you will see a rough track leading through the plantations. Take this track, you will recross the Kikelewa and continue up through the forest, and on to the heather and moorlands until you reach the caves. It is a total of approx 5-6 hrs to the caves.

From these caves follow the path which heads towards a point just to the right of the lowest point on the Saddle. You will pass 'Bread Rock' after about 1½ hr. The track then divides, to the right is the Outward Bound Hut which you will almost certainly find locked. The path continues upwards to the Saddle towards the Kibo Huts – a climb of about 3-4 hrs. To the left the another path crosses towards the Mawenzi Hut.

● **Where to stay**

A *Kibo*, PO Box 102, Marangu, T 4. Old German hotel. Cool and comfortable. Fine gardens. Evelyn Waugh stayed here in 1959 and was delighted with the place. **A** *Marangu*, PO Box 40, Marangu, T 11. 7 km from park gates. Self contained cottages with bathrooms and hot water. Well established. **C** *Kilimanjaro National Park Hostel*, PO Box 96, Marangu, T 50. Located at entrance to park. Bunk beds and bedding supplied. You will need to bring your own food.

Arusha National Park

Arusha National Park is situated about 25 km E of Arusha and 58 km from Moshi. The road is a good one and the turning off the main road, about 35 km from Kilimanjaro International Airport, is at Usa River and is clearly signposted. There are 2 lodges at Usa River. From the airport the landscape changes from the flat dry and dusty Sanya Plain which gradually becomes greener, more fertile and more cultivated. Take the turning (on the right if you are heading towards Arusha) and follow the gravel road for about 10 km until you reach the Ngordoto Gate. This is coffee country and you will see the farms on each side of the road. On reaching the Park entrance this changes to dense forest. At the entrance a small museum provides information for the visitor on the bird, animal and plant life of the park.

Background

The Arusha National Park, which contains within its boundaries Mount Meru, was established in 1960. The park has actually changed its name a number of times from Ngurdoto Crater National Park to Mount Meru National Park and finally to Arusha National Park. It covers an area of 137 sq km and rises from 1,524m at the Momella Lakes (also spelt Momela) to 4,572m at the peak of Mount Meru. Although it is only small because of this gradation there is a variety of landscapes, a variety of ecosystems and therefore a wide variety of flora and fauna. Within the park are the Ngurdoto Crater and the Momella Lakes. The best time to visit is from Oct to Feb.

Formation

Mount Meru is believed to have been formed at around the time of the great earth movements that created the rift valley, about 20 million years ago. The crater was formed about 250,000 years ago when a massive explosion blew away the E side of the volcano. A subsidiary vent produced the volcano of Ngurdoto which built up over thousands of years. In a way similar to Ngorongoro, when the cone collapsed the caldera was left as it is today. Ngurdoto is now extinct, while Meru is only dormant, having last erupted about 100 years ago. The lava flow from this eruption can be seen on the NW side of the mountain. It was at around this time in 1872 that the first European, Count Teleki, a Hungarian,

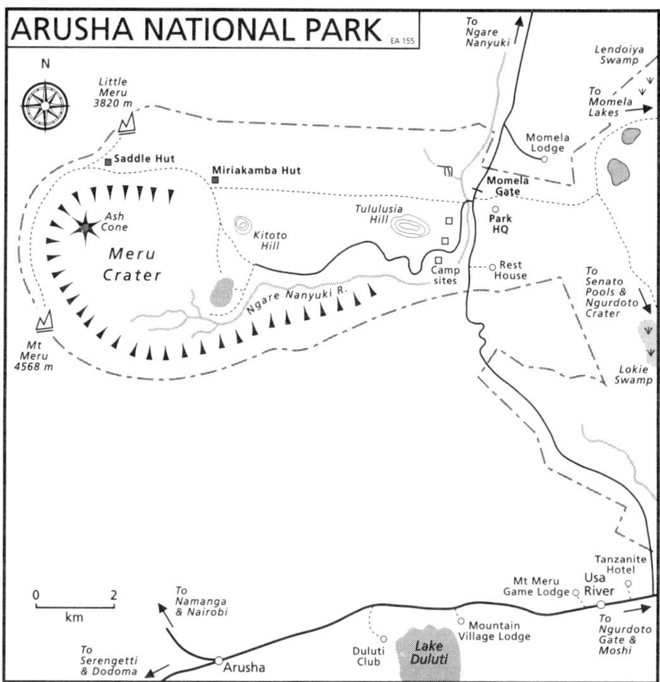

saw the mountain.

Wildlife

Arusha National Park contains many animals including giraffe, elephant, hippo, buffalo, rhino (if you are lucky), colobus monkey, bush buck, red forest duiker, reed buck, waterbuck and wart hog. In fact Arusha is supposed to contain the highest density of giraffes in the world. There are no lions in the park although you may see leopard.

Routes

Within the park there are over 50 km of tracks. However no road has been built into the Ngurdoto Crater in order to protect and preserve it. From the Ngurdoto Gate a road leads off towards the Ngurdoto Crater. The road climbs up through the forest until it reaches the rim. At the top you can go left or right, either going around the crater clockwise or anti-clockwise. The track does not go all the way round the rim of the crater so you will have to turn round and retrace your tracks back to the main road. You will be able to look down into the animals in the crater below but will not be able to drive down. The crater is about 3 km in diameter and there a number of viewing points around the rim from which you can look down to the bottom of the crater. These include Leitong Point (the highest at 1850m), Glades Point, Rock Point, Leopard Hill, Rhino Crest and Mikindani Point. From this latter point you will be able to view Mount Kilimanjaro in the distance.

From the gate if you take the left track you will reach the Momella Lakes. This track goes past the Ngongongare Springs, Lokie Swamp, the Senato Pools and the 2 lakes Jembamba and Longil. At the peak of the dry season they may dry up but otherwise they are a good place to watch the animals and in particular the bird life. At various spots there are observation hides. At Lake Longil there is a camping and picnic site in a lovely setting.

From here the track continues through the forest which gradually thins out and through the more open vegetation you will be able to see Mount Meru. The Hyena Camp (Kambi ya Fisi) is reached where you will probably see a pack of spotted hyenas. Beyond this there is a small track leading off the main track to Bomo la Mengi which is a lovely place from which to view the lakes. Unless the cloud is down you will also be able to see Kilimanjaro from here. The main track continues past 2 more lakes – Lake El Kekhotoito and Lake Kusare before reaching the Momella Lakes.

The Momella Lakes are shallow alkaline lakes fed by underground streams. Because they have different mineral contents and different algae their colours are also different. They contain few fish but the algae attracts lots of bird life. What you see will vary with the time of year. Flamingoes tend to move in huge flocks around the lakes of East Africa and are a fairly common sight at Momella Lakes. Between Oct and Apr the lakes are also home to the migrating waterfowl which are spending the European winter in these warmer climes.

The track goes around the lakes reaching the Small Momella Lake first. This lake often has a group of hippos wallowing in it. Follow the road anti-clockwise and you will pass Lake Rishetani which is a fantastic emerald green colour. Along this route you will be able to stop off at the various observation sites. The next lake that you will get to is the Great Momella Lake which has a huge variety of bird life and is a lovely spot. The last 2 lakes are Tulusia and Lekandiro where you may see animals grazing.

Mount Meru

The other major attraction of Arusha National Park is Mount Meru (4565m) the second highest mountain in Tanzania. The mountain lies to W of the Ngare Nanyuki road in the W half of the Park. There is a road that leads up the mountain from Momella, passing through an open space called Kitoto from where there are good views of the mountain, to about 2439m and from there you must walk. The road up Mount Meru requires a 4WD vehicle and even this may have problems in the wet season.

The climb takes 2-3 days depending on how pushed you are for time and whether you have a vehicle or not (and also on how fit you are). On the ascent you will pass through the changing vegetation. The first change is to lower montane forest at about 2000m, then to higher montane forest. Although you will not need to hire porters, you will have to take a guide/ranger with you. These can be hired for US$10 per day from the Park headquarters in Momella as can porters if you decide you want them. Booking a guide and accommodation in advance is recommended: The *Warden, Arusha National Park,* PO Box 3134, Arusha.

Be prepared for a steep climb, and take plenty of warm clothes as the temperatures fall dramatically at night. During the wet season be sure to have a good pair of walking boots. You will also need to provide all your own food. The road climbs up the mountain up to the heath zone at about 2439m from where you can climb to the peak. Follow the track from the roadhead until you reach the first hut. Alternatively if you do not have transport you can walk from the park headquarters to Miriakamba Hut which takes about 3 hrs. The first mountain huts sleeps about 48 people, while the second, Saddle Hut, sleeps about 24 people. Both huts provide firewood. It is 3 hr walk between the 2 huts and having reached Saddle Hut you can spend the

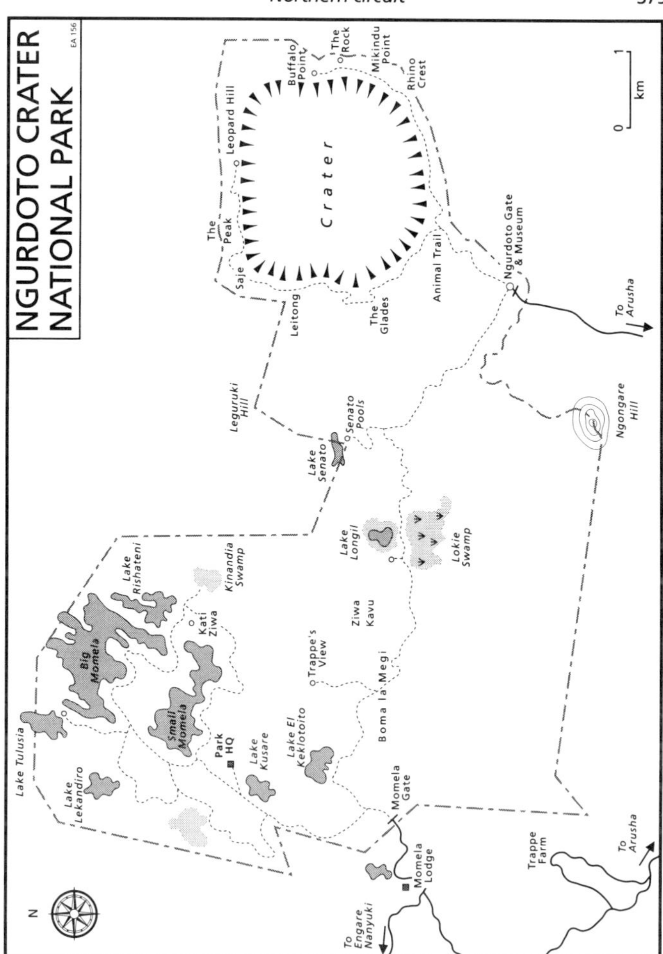

afternoon climbing Little Meru (3820m) which takes about 1½ hr. From Saddle Hut climb up to the rim of the mountain and around to the summit (4572m) before returning to the Momella park headquarters.

● Where to stay

A *Momella Game Lodge*, PO Box 418, Arusha, T 3798/3038. Accommodates 40 people. Located just outside the park nr the Momella Gate. Wonderful views. **A** ***Mount Meru Game Lodge***, PO Box 427, Arusha, T 7803, Tlx 42005. Located along turn-off from Usa River, 22 km from Arusha. Small, well-run, excellent cuisine. Fine gardens and charming atmosphere. **B** ***Ngaresero Mountain Lodge***, PO Box 425, Arusha, T Usa 38. Located 16 km from Arusha at Tengeru in the Mount Meru foothills. **B** ***Tanzanite***, PO Box 3068, Arusha, T Usa 32, Tlx 42038. Located along turn-off from Usa River 22 km from Arusha. Swimming pool. Tennis. Good

TSETSE FLY

The tsetse fly is a little larger than the house fly and is found over much of East Africa including Tanzania. Its presence is a serious threat to human habitation because it is a carrier of 2 diseases. The first is a human disease known as 'sleeping sickness' and the second is a disease which affects cattle that is called trypanosomiasis known as *nagana* amongst the people of Tanzania. This disease can be deadly to cattle while leaving man uninfected or can affect both man and cattle. In the former areas people can live and can cultivate the land but cannot keep cattle, whilst in the latter areas the presence of the tsetse fly has meant that large areas of Tanzania are uninhabitable by human beings and are left to the wild animals. Interestingly the tsetse fly does not affect wild animals. When it was realised that humans would never be able to live in these areas, but that wild animals could, large areas were designated to be game reserves in the early colonial era.

There are 8 different species of tsetse fly found in Tanzania of which 4 are most important. The different species are each suited to a different type of environment and vegetation. Unfortunately there is a species of fly for almost all conditions in East Africa. Areas where there are no tsetse include land over about 1830m, and areas with under 400 mm of rainfall. Tanzania is probably the worst affected of all the countries of East Africa.

Since the colonial period great efforts have been made to control the movement of tsetse fly. This was done by moving people out of certain areas and clearing the bush. A belt of 5 km wide is cleared of bush and people moved into this belt in a dense settlement. This belt provides a barrier which the tsetse cannot move across. Spraying has also been used. However a lapse in the efforts is all that is needed for the fly to return to areas that have been cleared.

value. **C *Rest House***. Sleeps 5. Located nr the Momella Gate. Bookings through the Warden, Arusha National Park, PO Box 3134, Arusha. **D *Camp sites***. There are 3 sites in the park. All have water and toilets and provide firewood. Book through The ***Park Warden, Arusha National Park,***, PO Box 3134, Arusha.

Tarangire National Park

Approach

Tarangire National Park is reached on the main Arusha-Dodoma road. From Arusha the road leaves the bustling town and enters the heavily cultivated countryside. You will pass maize, coffee and banana plantations. A few acacia trees start to appear and you will probably see groups of Maasai grazing their herds along the road. About 85 km from Arusha at Makuyuni the main road up to the Serengeti and Ngorongoro branches off to the right. Continue along the Great North Road towards Tarangire which is signposted – it is about 120 km from Arusha.

Background

The Tarangire National Park, established in 1970, covers an area of 2,600 sq km and lies at 1,110m above sea level. Its name is from the Tarangire River which flows through the park throughout the year. The best time to visit is from Jul to Sept when, being the dry season, the animals gather in large numbers along the river. Although you may not see as many animals here as in other places, Tarangire is a wonderful national park. There were fewer people here than in Ngorongoro and that is very much part of the attraction.

One of the most noticeable things on entering the park are the baobab trees which rise up from the grass. With their massive trunks they are instantly recognisable. As the park includes within its boundaries a number of hills, as well as river and swamp, there is a variety of vegetation zones and habitats. The river rises in the Kondoa Highlands which are located and flows throughout the length of the park. It continues to flow during the dry season and so is a vital watering point for the animals of the park as well as those from surrounding areas.

Wildlife

The Tarangire National Park forms a 'dry season retreat' for much of the wildlife of the southern Maasailand. The ecosystem in this area involves more than just Tarangire National Park. Also included in the ecosystem are the Lake Manyara National Park to the N and a number of 'Game Controlled Areas'. The largest of these are the Lake Natron Game Controlled Area further N and the Simanjiro Plains Game Controlled Area towards Arusha. The Mto wa Mbu Game Controlled Area, the Lolkisale Game Controlled Area, and Mkungunero Game Controlled Area are also included in the ecosystem. The key to the ecosystem is the river and the main animal movements begin from the river at the beginning of the short rains around Oct and Nov. The animals that move N during the wet season include wildebeest, zebra, Thompson's gazelles, buffalo, eland and hartebeest. The elephant population in this park was estimated at around 6,000 in 1987. At the height of the rainy season the animals are spread out over an area of over 20,000 sq km. When the wet season ends the animals begin their migration back S and spend the dry season (Jul-Oct) concentrated around the River Tarangire until the rains begin again.

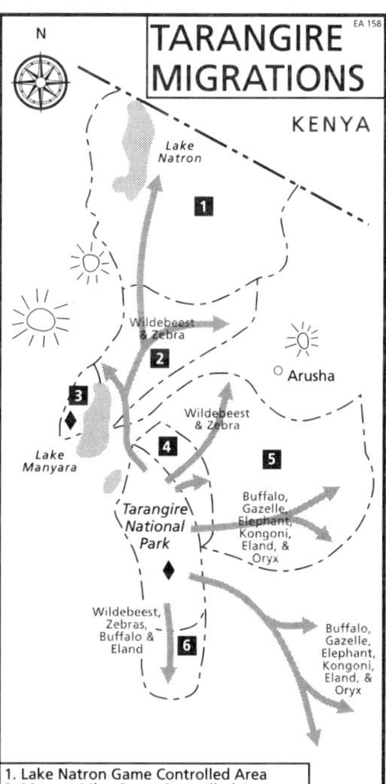

The number of species of birds recorded in Tarangire National Park has been estimated at approx 300. These include migrants which fly S to spend Oct to Apr away from the winter of the N hemisphere.

Part of the reason that this area was put over to national park status is that being a tsetse fly infested area it is not suitable for stock rearing, see box, page 376.

Routes

The park is large enough for it not to feel crowded even when there are quite a few visitors. There are a number of routes or circuits that you can follow that take you to the major attractions.

Lake Burungi Circuit This track covers about 80 km. It begins at the Engelhard Bridge and following the circuit clockwise, goes along the river bank. Continue along through the Acacia trees until about 3 km before the Kuro Range Post where you will see a turning off to the right. Down this track you will pass through a section of Combretum-Dalergia woodland as you head towards the W boundary of the park. The route continues around and the vegetation turns back to parkland with acacia trees and then back to Combretum as the road turns right and reaches a full circle at the Englehard Bridge. If you are very lucky you may see leopard and rhino in this area.

Lemiyon area This circuit covers the N area of the park bound on each side by the E and W boundaries of the park and to the S by the River. This is where you will see the fascinating baobab trees with the large silvery trunks and gourd like fruits. These huge trunks enable the trees to survive throughout a number of rain failures and they are characteristic of this type of landscape. Also here are the acacia trees which are the food of giraffe.

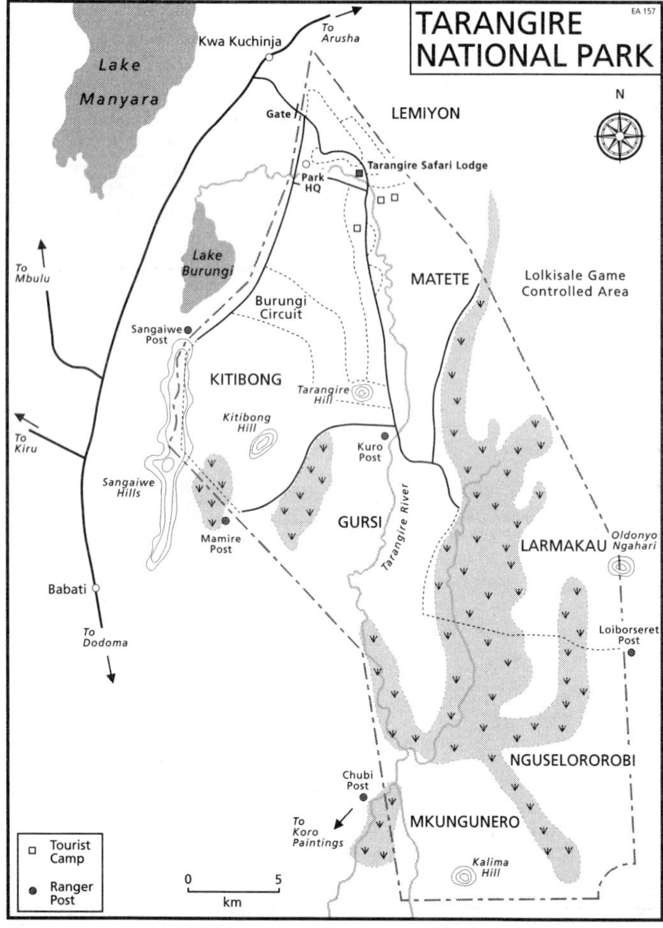

Other animals that you expect to see are wildebeest, zebra, gazelles and elephant.

Kitibong Hill circuit This track covers the W section of the park and is centred on Kitibong Hill. It includes acacia parkland in the E and Combretum-Dalbergia woodland in the W, the Gursi floodplains to the S and the foothills of Sangaiwe Hill which are along the W boundary of the Park. This area is home to a variety of plain animals including buffalo and elephant.

The Gursi and Lamarkau circuit The area is in the S of the park. The grasslands found here are home to many plain grazing species. You are also likely to see ostrich here. During the wet season a large swamp forms in what is known as Larmakau – a corruption of the Maasai word '*o'llakau*' which means hippo. And sure enough you will, in the wet season, be able to see hippo in this area.

Without a 4WD vehicle you will not be able to see much of the southernmost section of the park and during the wet season it will probably be impassable to all vehicles. There are 2 areas in the S – Nguselororobi to the E and Mkungunero in the SW corner. The former of these is mainly swamp, with some plains and woodland and if you are lucky you might see cheetah here. Mkungunero has a number of freshwater pools which serve to attract many different species.

● **Where to stay**

B *Tarangire Safari Lodge*, PO Box 2703, Arusha, T 7182, Tlx 42126. Sleeps 70. Luxury tented camp with hot water, showers, toilets etc. Good restaurant and bar. Swimming pool. Overlooking the river – wonderful setting. **C** *Six special camp sites*. Water and firewood are provided. **D** *Two public camp sites*.

Mkomazi Game Reserve

This national park of 3,600 sq km lies about 100 km N of Tanga and is adjoined to Kenya's Tsavo National Park. There are no hotel facilities in this Park, although there are some in the form of the **E** *Elephant Motel* located in the nearest town Same. **Same** is a small town on the Moshi road at the foot of the Usambara Mountains. This is the road that leads to **Lushoto** a lovely town in the hills. There is a campsite located at Ibeye which is within the Reserve, if you are prepared to be self sufficient.

Central and Southern Parks

Mikumi National Park

Approach

This park is located in central Tanzania about 300 km W of Dar es Salaam. From Morogoro the main Tanzania-Zambia road continues W. The road travels through well populated cultivated land for about 100 km before reaching the boundary of Mikumi National Park. It only takes about 4 hrs from Dar es Salaam on a good road and so is popular with weekend visitors. The national park is on both sides of the road so be sure to drive with care. The S boundary adjoins Selous National Park.

Background

Mikumi National Park, established in 1964, covers an area of 3,230 sq km and is set at 549m above sea level. The park lies in a horseshoe of towering mountains – the Uluguru range which rises to 2,750m. The park lies between the villages of Doma and Mikumi from which it takes its name. 'Mikumi' is the Kiswahili name for the Borassus palm, a type of palm tree that is found in the area. The best time to visit is from Sept-Dec.

Wildlife

There is a lot of wildlife to be seen in this park including elephant, buffalo, giraffe, lion, leopard, zebra and many sorts of antelope.

Routes

From the park gate the road leads to the floodplain of the Mkata River which is particularly important for the wildlife. To the N the floodplain remains swampy throughout the year, whilst in the S water channels drain to the Mkata River. Here you will see amongst other animals elephant, buffalo and hippo.

About 15 km NW of the park gate there are some hippo pools where there are almost always a number of hippos wallowing in the mud.

Other areas worth visiting are the Choga Wale area and Mwanambogo area. The latter of these can only be reached in the dry season. The track is to the E of the flood plain and heads N towards the Mwanambogo Dam. The Kisingura Circuit is another popular drive as is the Kikoboga area where you are likely to see elephant particularly during Dec and Jan.

The road that goes along the river is a good one to take for viewing. It passes through a patch of woodland and some swampy areas before coming onto the grasslands of the Chamgore. Chamgore means 'place of the python' and here there are 2 waterholes which are always ideal for spotting game.

Hill Drive leads up the foothills of the Uluguru Mountains and from here you will get wonderful views all around. The vegetation is miomba woodland and the ebony tree grows here.

To get to the S part of the park take the track which branches off opposite the Park entrance which heads towards an area called Ikoya. Here you will see sausage trees (*Kigelia africana*) with their distinctive pods hanging down. This is also where you may see leopard.

● Where to stay

There is an airstrip near the park headquarters for light aircraft. **B** ***Mikumi Wildlife Lodge***, PO Box 2485, Dar es Salaam, T 23491. Located down a left turning off the main road about half way across the park. Discount of 50% between Easter and end of Jun. Built of local materials around a waterhole. Restaurant, bar, swimming pool (but currently out of service), shop, garage and petrol station. Rather run-down and shabby. **C** ***Mikumi Wildlife Tented Camp***, T Dar es Salaam 68631. Located about 300m off the main road to the right about

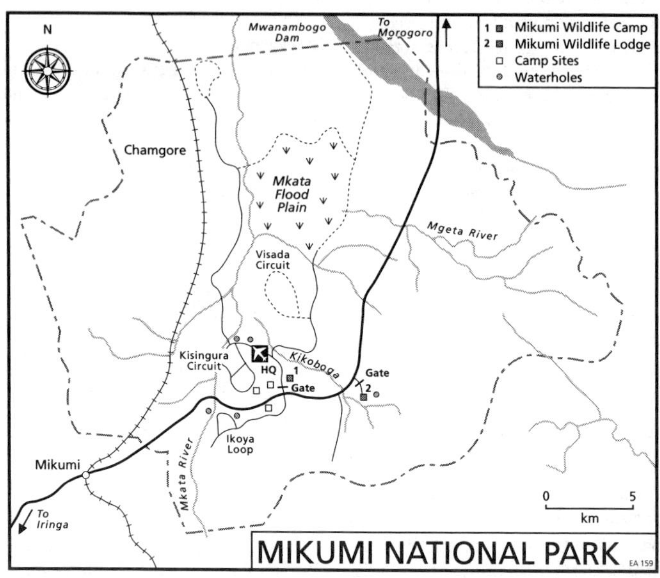

⅔ rds of the way across the park, nr the park headquarters. Very comfortable. Accommodates about 10 people. Bar and restaurant. Booking through *Oyster Bay Hotel*, PO Box 1907, Dar es Salaam. **D** ***Youth Hostel***, located at park headquarters. Bookings through Chief Park Warden, Mikumi National Park,, PO Box 62, Morogoro. Sleeps 48 people. Basic. **D** ***Camp site***. Located about 4 km from park entrance gate. Water and firewood usually available, otherwise very basic.

Ruaha National Park and Rungwa Game Reserve

Approach

Ruaha National Park is located 130 km W of Iringa and from Iringa it is a drive of about 4 hrs. Initially the road passes through densely populated countryside until the population gradually thins out. The vegetation becomes miomba woodland and about 60 km from Iringa the turning off to the right to the park is indicated. It is another 50 km down this road to the park boundary and from there about 10 km to Ibuguziwa where you cross the Ruaha River and pay the Park entrance fees. About 1 km beyond the river there is a junction. To the right the track goes to Msembe and the park headquarters and to the left to Ruaha River camp.

Background

Ruaha National Park was classified a national park in 1964 having been a part of Rungwa Game Reserve until then. It covers an area of 12,950 sq km and ranges from 750m to 1,900m above sea level. The Park gets its name from the River which forms part of its boundary. The name *Ruaha* is from the word *Luvaha* which means great in the Hehe language and the river certainly is this. It is vital to the economy of the country for it supplies much of Tanzania with electricity through hydro-electric power from the dam at Kidatu. Further downstream the Ruaha joins with the Ulanga to make the Rufiji River. Visiting is only possible during the dry season. In the wet the tracks are mostly impassable and when the grass is long, game viewing is almost impossible so the best time to visit is from Jul-Dec. The park's inaccessibility means that not many people visit it although the Ruaha River camp is very popular.

Wildlife

There is a wide variety of wildlife in this park including elephant, ostrich, greater and lesser kudu, gazelle, and other antelope and, in the river, hippo and crocodile. There are over 400 recorded species of bird in the park. It is a huge park and is largely underdeveloped and inaccessible. Unfortunately poaching in this park is a serious problem and the animal population has suffered enormously from this. In particular rhinos which were once found here are probably now extinct. Also the elephant population has fallen tremendously from over 22,000 in 1977 to under 4,000 in 1987. This is probably the most dramatic decline in all the national parks of Tanzania. However efforts are being made to improve the situation and the Friends of Ruaha Society (PO Box 60 Mufindi, or, PO Box 786 Dar es Salaam) is the motivating force behind this. They, together with the park's wardens have improved the roads and sign-posting and thus the game drives have improved. They have also increased the anti-poaching patrolling.

Routes

There are 4 major vegetation zones within this park. The river valleys; the open grassland; the miomba woodland; and undulating countryside where baobabs dominate.

Around Msembe is bush country with acacia and baobab trees, and elephants are often found here. Along the river, particularly during the dry season, many animals congregate. You can expect to see elephants, giraffe, baboons, wart hogs, buffalo, zebra, all sorts of antelope and if you are lucky leopard and cheetah. In the river itself are both

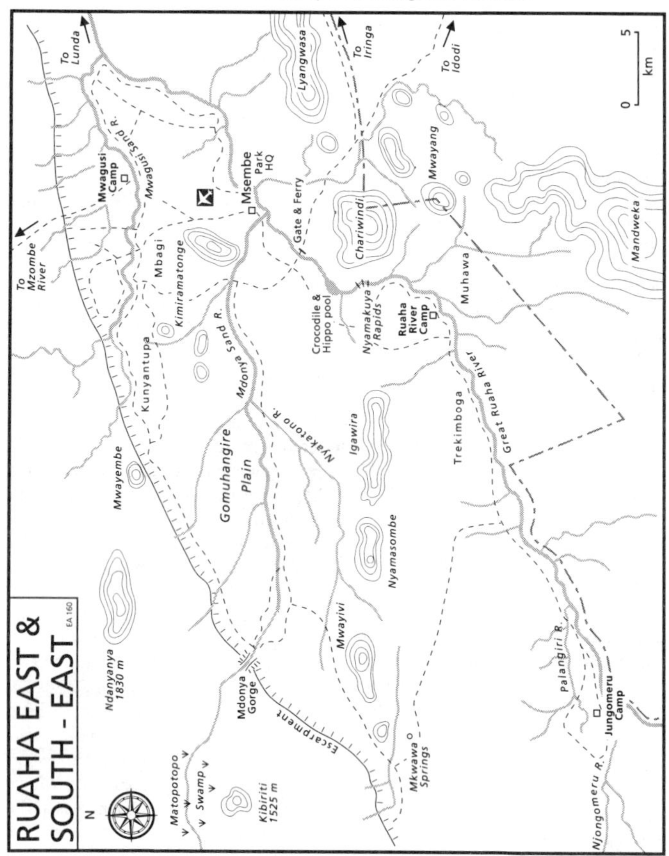

hippo and crocodile.

The Mwagusi Sand River joins the Ruaha about 10 km from Msembe. If you cross this river and follow the track you will get to Mwayembe Hill and the escarpment where there is a salt lick often frequented by elephant and buffalo.

The Mdonya Sand River joins the Ruaha between the ferry and the park headquarters. From the ferry a drive SW will take you past the Nyamakuyu Rapids and Trekimboga to where the Jongomero joins the Ruaha about 40 km upriver. This is a good place to see hippo and crocodile.

● Where to stay

The park headquarters are located at Msembe which is 112 km from Iringa and 615 km from Dar es Salaam. It is halfway from Dar es Salaam to the Zambia border town of Tunduma. There is an airstrip at the Park headquarters for light aircraft.

B *Ruaha River Camp* (C/o Foxtreks, PO Box 84, Mufindi; or Valji & Alibhai, PO Box 786, Dar es Salaam, T 20522 26537, F 46401, Tlx 81052). Price includes full board. Bandas or tented camp accommodation. Located 10 km S of Msembe on and around a kopje overlooking the Ruaha River. Restaurant and bar. Vehicle hire available. Wonderful setting, excellent value, you will undoubtedly enjoy your stay here. **D** ***Rondavels and campsite***, located at the park headquarters. Bookings through Chief Warden, Ruaha National Park, PO Box 369, Iringa. Other campsites around the park.

Udzungwa Mountains National Park

This has recently been been classified as a national park, previously it was a national forest reserve.

This is a forest area and covers an area of approx 1,000 sq km lying between 300 and 2,800m. This great altitudinal range makes for a great diversity of vegetation and thus habitats for many different species. These include the Iringa Colobus monkey and the Sanje mangabey, as well as elephant, buffalo, lion and leopard.

As yet there are no facilities here but it is close enough to Mikumi National Park for those facilities to be used. The best time to visit is from Sept-Dec.

Selous Game Reserve

Background

This enormous reserve in S Tanzania, first established in 1922, is the largest park in Africa and the second largest in the world, covering an area of 55,000 sq km. This makes it about twice the size of Denmark. It is relatively untouched by man and being here gives you a feeling of being somewhere where little has changed for hundreds of years. The park is named after a Captain Frederick Selous who was killed in action in Jan 1917 whilst scouting in the area. The best time to visit is from Jul-Oct. The camps and lodges are closed at the peak of the wet season from Apr-Jun when the rains render many of the roads impassable.

History

This park has an interesting history. In the days of the slave trade the caravan routes passed through the park. It is said that the occasional mango groves that can be seen grew from the mango stones discarded by the caravans on their way to the coast. In the early 20th century during German colonial rule some of this area was designated into game reserves but in those days big game hunting was the most significant activity. In 1910 Kaiser Wilhelm gave part of the reserve to his Kaiserin as an anniversary gift. This is how the nickname 'Shamba la Bibi' meaning 'The Woman's Field'

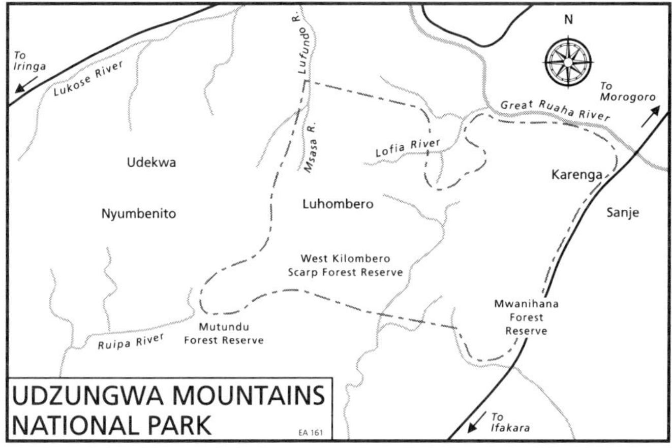

came to be. During WW1 the area was the location of confrontation as described in William Boyd's *An Ice Cream War*.

Wildlife

There are supposed to be over a million animals in this park and it is probably best known for its large numbers of elephant. However poaching is an enormous problem and the numbers have been reduced substantially in recent years. A very disturbing report that came out in 1988 estimated that the elephant population had fallen by 80% in Selous in just 10 years from 1977

Frederick C Selous, Greatest Of The White Hunters

Born in 1852 in London, the young Selous went to Rugby school. An early expedition saw Selous trek to a lake 25 km from Rugby, strip-off, swim through the icy water to a small island and shin up a tree to collect 8 blue heron's eggs. On returning to school he was rewarded by being made to copy out 63 lines of Virgil for each egg. Inspired by the writings of Livingstone, Selous determined to visit Africa. After toying with the idea of becoming a doctor, he travelled to South Africa in 1871, and rapidly established himself as a supreme tracker and hunter.

Hunting was tough. The rifles were heavy muzzle-loaders, and powder was carried loose in one pocket, ignition caps in another and a supply of 4oz lead bullets in a pouch. It was not uncommon for a hunter to be knocked out of the saddle by the gun's recoil and accidents were common.

Selous killed numerous game in his early years, partly for trophies in the case of lion and rhinoceros, for ivory in the case of elephants, and anything else as meat for his party. Later he was to become more restrained, virtually giving up trophy hunting. His skills were based on absorbing the skills of African hunters and trackers, and in 1881 he published the first of a series of highly successful books on his methods and exploits, *A Hunter's Wanderings in Africa*. In 1887 he began a career of paid work leading safaris for wealthy clients, which culminated in a huge expedition organised for President Roosevelt in 1909. A young British diplomat in South Africa, H. Rider Haggard, based his character Allan Quatermain on Selous and his adventures in his novel *King Solomon's Mines*, published in 1895.

During one visit to England, Selous took delivery of a new.450 rifle at his hotel an hour before he was due to catch the boat train from Waterloo to return to Africa. There was no time to test the sights and alignment on a rifle range, so Selous ordered a cab to stand-by, flung open his bedroom window, squeezed off 5 shots at a chimney stack, checked that the grouping was satisfactory with his binoculars, swiftly packed the rifle and skipped down to the cab, forcing his way through a throng in the lobby, pausing only to remark that he had heard some shots on his floor, and the manager had better look into it.

By 1914, Selous, now married, had retired to Surrey and busied himself with running his own natural history museum. At the outbreak of war, despite being 63, he was determined to serve in East Africa, where he felt his skills would be useful. He joined the legion of Frontiersmen, a colourful outfit which included French Legionnaires, a Honduran general, a handful of Texan cowboys, Russian émigrés, some music hall acrobats and a light-house keeper.

In Jan 1917, scouting in the campaign against General von Lettow Vorbeck, see page 216, he was killed by a German sniper at Behobeho on the Rufiji River. Behobeho Camp is now part of the Selous Game Reserve. In 1985, the Rugby School Natural History Society was renamed the Selous Society.

(census estimated population at 22,852) to 1987 (population estimated at 3,673). Rhino have also been seriously affected and their population in Selous is estimated to have fallen from 2,500 in 1976 to less than 50 in 1986. Other animals you may see include lions, buffalo, hippo, crocodile. Part of the reason for the lack of human habitation in this area is that it is infested with the tsetse. For this reason using insect repellent on any exposed areas of your body is a good idea. Although sleeping sickness is said to be rare, the flies do have a nasty bite.

Routes

Much of this enormous park is without tracks and in the wet season is completely inaccessible. The best explored area is to the N where the lodges and camps are located. Central to the park is the Great Rufiji River. This river and its associated water system has the largest catchment area of any river in East Africa, and is probably the most significant feature of the park. It rises from the S and becomes the Rufiji where the Luwegu and Mbarangandu join together. Other rivers join it and further N it swings E before it is forced through Stiegler's Gorge. At its delta, opposite Mafia Island, millions of tonnes of silt are deposited every year during the wet season. During this season it swells to

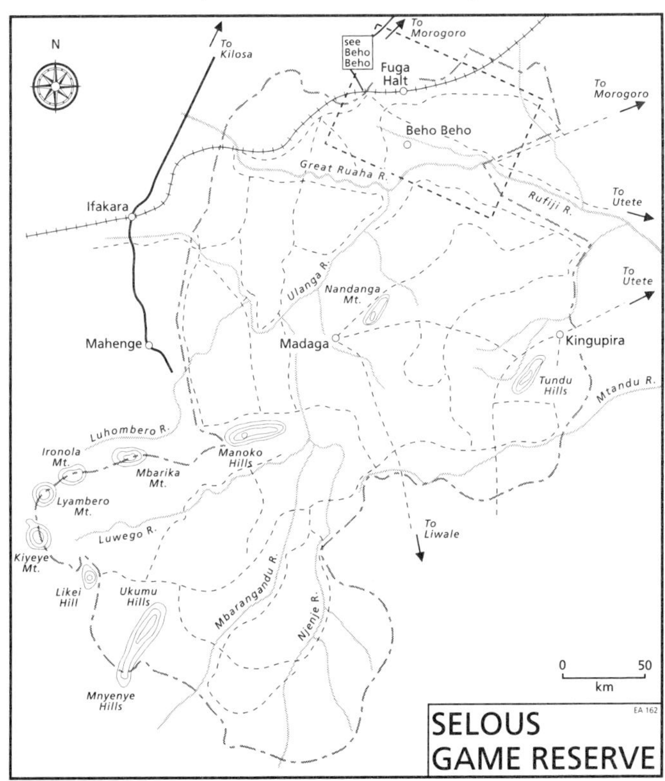

such an extent that is renders much of the park inaccessible. During the dry season it subsides and the sand banks are revealed.

Stiegler's Gorge is found in the N of the reserve at the junction of the Rufiji and Ruaha rivers. It is a bottleneck as the water from this huge catchment area is forced through the narrow gorge. The gorge is named after a German explorer who was killed here by an elephant in 1907. The gorge is about 100m wide and the same deep and if you have a head for heights there is a cable car which spans it. There was a plan to build a hydro-electric dam here. This project was to be undertaken by the Rufiji Basin Development Authority (RUBADA) with Norwegian funds. However it has been put on hold and the Stiegler Gorge Safari Camp is made up of what were to be the housing facilities of the expatriate workers on the project.

Beyond the gorge the river widens out again and splits to form a number of lakes – Tagalala, Manze, Nzerakera, Siwando, and Mzizima. This swampy area is home to many animals who congregate there especially when water is scarce during the dry season. In particular elephant, buffalo and of course hippo gather here, sometimes in large numbers.

Other attractions in the park include the hot springs known simply as Maji Moto (hot water in Kiswahili). These are located on the E slopes of Kipalala Hill and the water flows down into Lake Tagalala. You get to them by walking (with a ranger at all times) up the ravine. The water is heated deep in the earth by thermal activity and emits the strong smell of sulphur. The highest springs are the hottest whilst further down they cool down enough for you to be able to swim in them.

Tours

Apart from seeing Selous by road, the other popular ways are by foot and by boat. This is one of only 2 national parks where you are allowed to walk. All 4 camps can arrange a walking safari. You will normally set off early in order to avoid the worst of the midday sun when most of the animals retire for a siesta. You must be accompanied by a ranger.

Rufiji and Mbuyu Safari Camps can both arrange boat trips up the River Rufiji. Boat trips are a wonderful way of seeing this park which could almost have been designed for them.

The S part of the park is characterized by a feeling of great emptiness. The Lewegu, Mbarangandu and Njenji Rivers flow through the area, much of which is heavily forested. There are a series of steep cliffs in the S formed by geological faults.

● Where to stay

The Park Headquarters are located at Matambwe. **A** *Mbuyu Safari Camp*, bookings through Bushtrekker Safaris, PO Box 5350, Dar es Salaam, T 31957 32671. Named after the large baobab tree that the camp is sited around. Accommodates about 30 people. Located on a high bank overlooking the River Rufiji. Luxury tented camp, all tents with hot water and shower. Lovely setting. Restaurant and bar. Fishing equipment, boats and Land Rovers for hire. Walking safaris can be arranged from here. **A** *Rufiji River Camp*, bookings through Tanzania Safari Tours Ltd, PO Box 20058, Dar es Salaam, T 64177/63546. Located overlooking the Rufiji River. Accommodates about 20. Tented camp with hot water and communal showers. No electricity so a real feeling of being in the 'bush'. Restaurant and bar. Fishing equipment, boats and Land Rovers for hire. **A** *Selous Safari Camp*, on the Behobeho River. Individual huts with hot water and shower. View overlooking the lakes. Restaurant and bar. **A** *Stiegler's Gorge Safari Camp*, bookings through Gorge Tours and Safaris, PO Box 348, 30 India St, Dar es Salaam, T 21012. Individual huts with hot water and shower. Restaurant and bar. Located close to watering hole. Wonderful views.

● Safari companies

Because of the problem of accessibility most people go to Selous on organized safaris. Companies to contact include: ***Selous Safaris***, 788 Bath St, Cranford, Middlesex, TW5 9UL, UK, T 081 897-9991. ***Ecosafaris***, 146 Gloucester St, London SW7, UK, T 071 370-5032. ***Abercrombie and Kent***, Sloane Square House, Holbein Place, London SW1W 8NS, UK, T 071 730-9600.

● Transport

Air There are a number of approaches to the park. The most convenient is certainly by air and there are airstrips at all the camps. The flight takes about 45 mins from Dar es Salaam.

Train Take the TAZARA railway as far as Fuga. From here, with prior arrangement, the lodges will collect you. This will be expensive unless you get a group together to share the costs.

Road If you have your own vehicle take the Dar es Salaam-Kibiti-Mkongo road. The road is tarmac to Kibiti (250 km from Dar es Salaam) which is also the last place you will be able to get petrol. It will take about 7-8 hrs by road from Dar es Salaam. The other road you can take is the Dar es Salaam-Morogoro-Matombo-Kisaki road which will take you into the N section of the park to Stiegler's Gorge Camp. This road should only be attempted in the dry season and will require a 4WD vehicle.

Western Game Parks

Gombe Stream National Park

Approach

Gombe Stream National Park is about 16 km from Kigoma and can only be reached by boat from there. You can get a boat fairly easily, they normally leave around 1000 and the trip takes about 3 hrs and costs about US$3. They return to Kigoma at around 1700. They do not run on Sun. The boats continue to Banda, on the border of Burundi, so you can approach the Park from both ways. The main purpose of the Park is research rather than tourism and the facilities there are minimal. Entry to the park costs US$50 per person for each 24 hr period.

Background

The major attraction of the park are the chimpanzees that were made famous by Jane Goodall. In 1960 she set up the area as a chimpanzee research station. She wrote a book on the findings of her research called *In the Shadow of Man*. Her work was later filmed by Hugo van Lawick the wildlife photographer. This attracted much publicity to the Reserve and in 1968 the Gombe Stream National Park was established. It covers an area of 52 sq km making it the smallest park in Tanzania. It is made up of a narrow, mountainous strip of land about 16 km long and 5 km wide that borders Lake Tanganyika. The mountains, which rise steeply from the lake at a height of about 681m to over 1,500m, are intersected by steep valleys which have streams running in them and are covered in thick gallery forest. The park headquarters is located at Kasekela. The park can be visited all the year around. One point worth noting is that, being so closely related to humans, chimpanzees get many of the same diseases. You will not be allowed to visit Gombe if you have a cold or any other infectious illnesses.

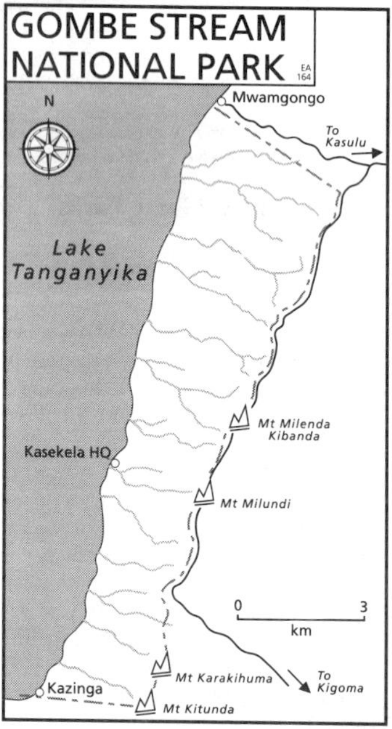

Wildlife

There are approx 200 chimpanzees in the park divided into 3 family troupes. They each mark their territory fiercely. One of the groups often goes down to the research station so you can observe them from there. Alternatively there are a number of observation points around the park and the wardens usually know where to go to see them.

Routes

It is compulsory to take a guide with you into the forest. From the guest house there is a trail leading up to the research station about 2 km away and a lovely waterfall a bit further on. If there are no chimps at the station itself you will have to ask one of the guides to take you into the forest to try and track them down. Another route you can take (which does not require a guide) is along the lake shore.

● Where to stay

There is a ***hostel*** that sleeps about 15 people. It is advisable to book ahead in Kigoma. Beds and mattresses are provided but all cooking equipment and food should be brought with you from Kigoma. Camping is allowed with permission, in fact the park is becoming so popular that it is a good idea to have your own tent and stove.

Mahale Mountains National Park

Approach

There is no main road to the park although there is a track of sorts. The easiest way to get to the park is by boat from Kigoma. There are no roads in the park so you will have to walk. It is very remote and difficult to get to and for this reason is visited by few tourists.

Background

This is another chimpanzee sanctuary

that, in 1985, was established as a national park covers an area of 1,577 sq km, and lies at an altitude of over 1,800m. The highest peak reaches 2,460m and the prevailing winds from over the lake when forced up to this level condense and ensure a high rainfall. The best time to visit is from May-Sept during the drier months.

Vegetation and wildlife

The park is largely made up of montane forests and grasslands and some alpine bamboo. The E side of the mountains is drier, being in the rain shadow, and the vegetation there is the drier miomba woodland which is that found over much of W Tanzania and E Zaire. The wildlife found in this park is more similar to that found in Western Africa than Eastern. It includes chimpanzee, porcupine, colobus monkeys (both red and the Angolan black and white). The range and numbers of animals found here has increased since the ujaama villagization programme of the 1970's. Indeed animals such as leopard and lion have reappeared in the area. The park is probably best known for its chimpanzee population and they have been the focus of much research by scientists from around the world. There are an estimated 1000 in the Park divided into 20 family troupes of about 50 each.

● Where to stay

E *Guest House* at Kasiha village. Facilities are minimal. Bring all food requirements from Kigoma.

● Camping

Allowed in designated areas. If possible take your own equipment although you may be able to hire it. Check at the MMWRC (Mahale Mountains Wildlife Research Centre) in Kigoma for current availability of accommodation and transport.

● Transport

Lake To get to the Park, take the lake steamer (*MV Liemba* or *MV Mwongozo*) from Kigoma, see page 325. You get to Lagosa (also known as Mugambo) after about 6 hrs at about 0300 and will have to get a small boat to take you to the shore. From Lagosa you will have to hire another boat to take you the 3-hr journey to Kasoge. As you are relying on the lake steamer you will have to stay until the next ferry comes, which is usually about a week although it is not very reliable.

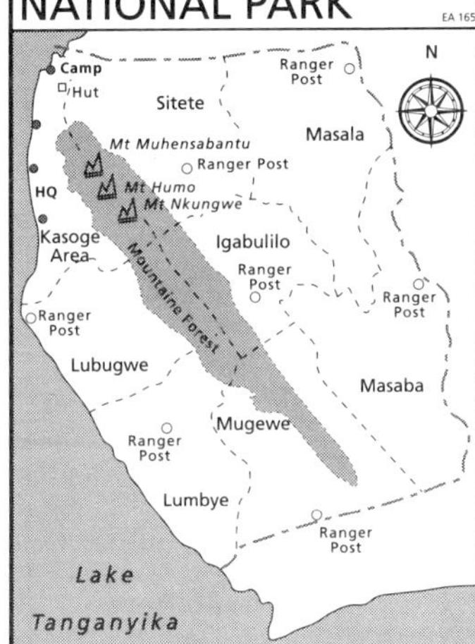

Ugalla Game Reserve

The Ugalla River Game Reserve, located to the W of Tabora, is approx 5,000 sq km. Its inaccessibility and lack of facilities mean that it receives few visitors. If you do manage to get there, and are prepared to be totally self sufficient, there is a wide variety of game.

Katavi National Park

Katavi National Park is located in the W of Tanzania, close to Lake Tanganyika. It is 40 km SE of Mpanda town astride the main Mpanda-Sumbawanga road. It was upgraded to a national park in 1974 and covers an area of 2,253 sq km. Travelling from Tunduma (the border town of Tanzania and Zambia) to Kigoma the road passes through the Park. The best times to visit are Jul-Oct. However, like the Ugalla River Game Reserve its isolation and lack of facilities has meant that it receives few visitors.

The Park is made of mioba woodland, acacia parkland as well as some grassland plains. There is also a large swampy area around the Katuma River which joins the 2 lakes in the park – Lake Katavi and Lake Chada. Wildlife that you may see in the park includes hippo, crocodile, zebra, elephant, buffalo, all sorts of antelope as well as lion and, if you are lucky, leopard.

The nearest hotels and other facilities are at Mpande which is 40 km away. If you have your own camping equipment you can use the sites in the Park.

Lake Victoria

Rubondo Island National Park

Rubondo National Park is an island located NW of Mwanza. It has an area of about 240 sq km which includes the main island and a number of smaller ones. The best time to visit is Nov-Feb.

There are a number of different vegetation types on the island which provide differing habitats for a variety of animals. With a high water table the island is able to support dense forest. Other vegetation includes more open woodland, savannah grassland, and swamps. There is little 'big game' on the island although some has been introduced including giraffe, elephant and rhino. Other animals include crocodile, hippo, bushbuck, sitatunga (a swamp-dwelling antelope only found here and in Selous), vervet monkeys and mongeese. The park is said to be an ornithologists paradise. Birds you are likely to spot include fish eagle, martial eagle, sacred ibis, saddle billed stork, kingfishers, water fowl, cuckoos, bee eaters and sunbirds. There are animal hides from where you can view the wildlife.

There are camping facilities on the island but they are very basic so you are advised to take all your own equipment. All food supplies must be taken with you.

The park headquarters are located at Kageye. There is an airstrip here suitable for light aircraft. No vehicles are allowed on the island although there is a lorry that can be hired to drive visitors

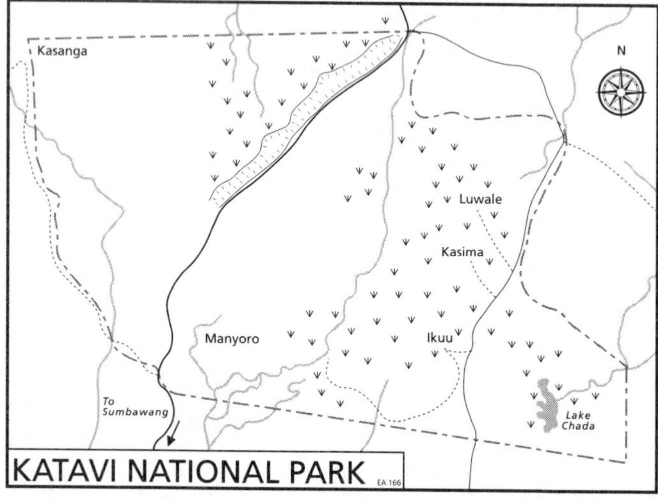

around. Boats and camping should to booked in advance: The Park Warden, Rubondo Island National Park, PO Box 11, Geita, or send a message through the National Parks radios, or through the Schumann's Garage in Mwanza.

Approach

The island can be reached by a number of different ways. The quickest and easiest way is to fly in. Other cheaper ways are by hiring a boat directly from Mwanza. Alternatively you can drive the 6 or 7 hrs to Nkome (300 km via Sengerema-Gieta-Nzera) from where it is a 2 hr boat journey or you can drive the 10 hrs to Mnganza (via Sengerema-Gieta-Chato) from where the boat journey is about ½ hr.

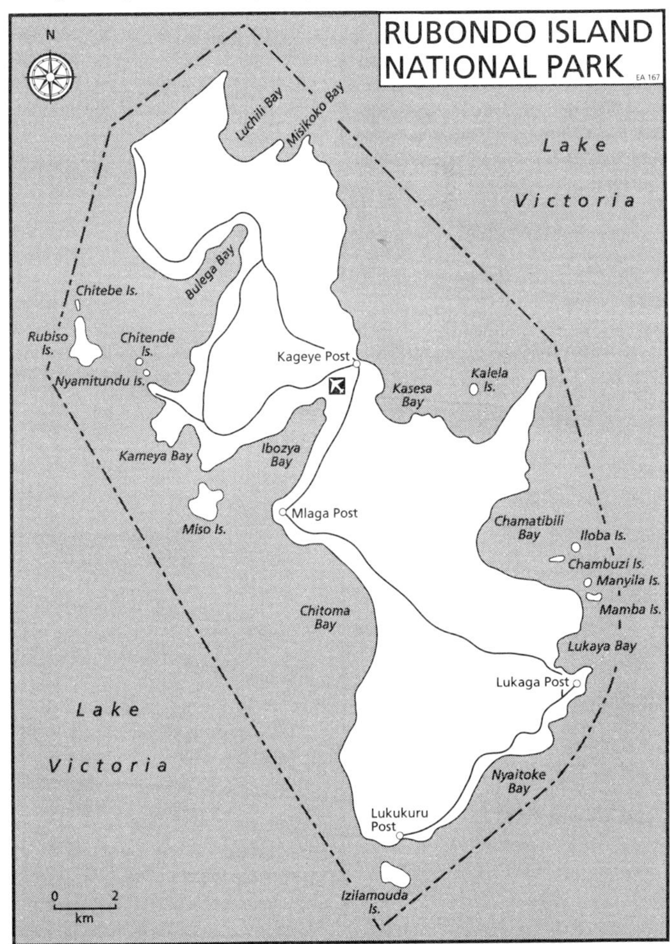

Biharamulo Game Reserve

Adjacent to Rubondo Island National Park on the mainland is the Biharamulo Game Reserve which covers an area of 1,300 sq km. This is located to the S of Bukoba on the main Mwanza to Bukoba road but as this is a bit of a dead end it receives very few visitors.

Saa Nane Island

This wildlife sanctuary is situated in Lake Victoria just off Mwanza. It can be visited as a day trip from Mwanza. It is mainly savannah grassland broken by rocky outcrops. The animals here include zebra, wildebeest, hippo as well as some caged chimpanzees, lions and leopards which seems rather unnecessary.

The Coast

Marine Parks of Tanzania

The National Parks Department of Tanzania has been planning to set up some marine parks since the 1960's. The first to go ahead will probably be Mafia Island. This has been the site of detailed scientific study on the part of Frontier Tanzania, a non-profit making organization based in London, manned almost entirely by volunteers. It is proposed that a series of zones should be established to enable multi-use of this area by local fishermen as well as tourists in a manner to ensure the conservation of the coral gardens and many sea-living species found around the island. In a joint venture with Frontier Tanzania (also known as the Society of Environmental Exploration) and the University of Dar es Salaam, the scientific research for the proposal is being undertaken and these zones are being created. The World Wildlife Fund has also become involved in the implementation of the proposal. It is hoped that careful planning will ensure that the local people are on the side of the park authorities. If this method is successful it will be used as a

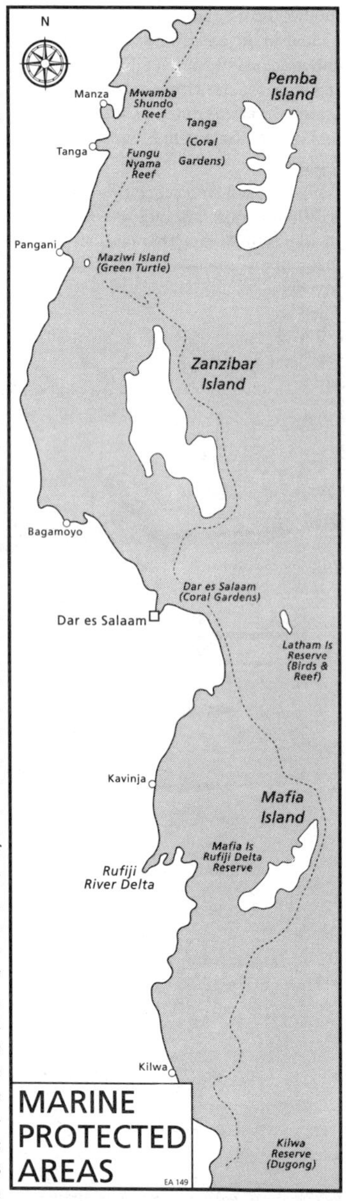

model for other marine parks in the country. Currently the major threat to the area is in the form of dynamite fishing which is the method used by large scale fishermen from the cities to the N and mining for coral which is used as a building material, in particular as a source of lime.

Other possible sites of marine parks include Tanga Coral Gardens which are made up of 3 reefs – Mwamba Wamba, Mwamba Shundo and Fungu Nyama. They are located between 10 and 15 km out to sea. Around Dar es Salaam there are coral gardens near the islands of Mbudya and Sinda which may be developed into a marine park. At Latham Island a reserve has been established, being a site of nesting sea birds and the rare green turtle. Around Kilwa, in the S is another likely site for a marine park, being one of the few places where the dugong is found.

Other Game Reserves

There are a number of other game reserves in Tanzania. These include **Saadani** which is 300 sq km and is located on the coast. **Kigosi**, 4,000 sq km, is found in Singida Province; **Moyowosi**, 6,000 sq km, in Kigoma Province; and **Uwanda**, 5,000 sq km, located in Rukwa Region. **Burigi**, 2,200 sq km, and **Ibanda**, 200 sq km, are located in Kagera Province. **Rumanyika Orugundu Game Reserve** covers an area of 800 sq km and lies in the Kishanda Valley also in Kagera Province, accommodates buffalo, elephant, eland as well as other antelope. **Umba Game Reserve**, 1,500 sq km, is found in Tanga Province. However none of these reserves have been developed and they do not contain any facilities.

INFORMATION FOR VISITORS

Contents

Before you go

Entry requirements

● Visas

Visas are required by all visitors except citizens of the Commonwealth, Republic of Ireland, Sweden, Norway, Denmark, Finland, Romania. Citizens of neighbouring countries do not normally require visas. For other nationalities, visas can be obtained from Tanzanian Embassies, require 2 passports, cost US$40 (although this varies according to nationality) and are issued in 24 hrs. An entry stamp is valid for non-visa visitors and is valid for 1-3 months.

Resident status for persons permanently employed in Tanzania can be arranged after arrival. Your employer will need to vouch for you, and the process can take several weeks. Resident status does, however, confer certain privileges (lower rates on air-flights, in hotels, game parks) as well as possible tax advantages.

● Vaccinations

You require a valid yellow fever vaccination certificate.

● Tanzanian Representation Overseas

Angola, CP 1333 Luanda, T 335205; **Belgium**, 363 Ave Louise, 1050 Brussels, T 6476479; **Burundi**, Patrice Lumumba Av, BP 1653, Bujumbura, T 24634; **Canada**, 50 Range Rd, Ottawa, Ontario KIN 8J4, T (613) 2321500; **China**, 53 San Li Tun Dongliujie, Beijing, T 521408; **Egypt**, 9 Abde Hamid Loufty St, Dokki, Cairo, T 7041556; **France**, 70 Boulevard Pereire Nord, 75017 Paris, T 47762177; **Germany**, Theatreplatz 26, 5300 Bonn 2, T (0228) 353477; **Guinea** BP 179 Donka, Conakry, T 461332; **India**, 27 Golf Links, New Delhi 110-003, T 694351/2; **Italy**, Via Giambattista Visco 9-00196, Rome, T (06) 3610898; **Japan**, 21-9 Kamiyoga, 4 Chome Setagaya-ku, Tokyo 158, T (03) 4254531/3; **Kenya**, PO Box 47790, Nairobi, T 331056; **Mozambique**, Ujamaa House, Avenida Marites Da Machava 852, PO Box 4515, Maputo, T 744025; **Netherlands**, Amaliststraat No 1 251JC, The Hague, T (070) 653800/1; **Nigeria**, 8 Agor Odiyan St, Victoria Island, PO Box 6417, Lagos, T 613594; **Russia**, Pyatnitskaya, Ulitsa 33, Moscow, T 2318146; **Rwanda**, Rue de Commerce, BP 669, Kigali, T 6074; **Saudi Arabia**, PO Box 94320, Riyadh 11693, T (45) 42859; **Sudan**, PO Box 6080, Khartoum, T 78407/9; **Sweden**, Oxtorgsgatan 2-4, PO Box 7255, 103-89 Stockholm, T (08) 244870; **Switzerland**, 47 Ave Blanc, 1202 Geneva, T 318929; **Uganda**, 6 Kagera Rd, PO Box 5750, Kampala, T 256272; **UK**, 43 Hertford St, London W17 8DE, T (071) 4998951; **USA**, 2139 R St NW, Washington DC 20008, T (202) 9396128, and, 205 East 42nd St, 13th Floor, New York, NY 10017, T (212) 9729160; **Zaire**, 142 Boulevard du 30 Juin, BP 1612, Kinshasha, T 32117; **Zambia**, Ujamaa House, Plot No 5200, United Nations Av, PO Box 31219, Lusaka, T 211422 211665; **Zimbabwe**, Ujamaa House, 23 Baines Av, PO Box 4841, Harare, T 721870.

● Overseas Representation in Tanzania
See under Dar es Salaam, **page 256** and Kigoma, **page 322**.

● Tourist information
Tanzania Tourist Corporation has offices in Dar and Arusha but it is an ineffective organization concerned only marketing its own state-run hotels, transport services, and the national parks. it is now being wound up and a new body is revamping information services but it remains to be seen how effective it will be.

The National Parks office in the Arusha International Conference Centre is a good source of information and has such booklets on the individual parks as are currently in print.

Travel and Tour Agents These are listed under the place of their location: Arusha, **page 306**; Dar es Salaam, **page 261**; Zanzibar **page 343**. For the UK **page 387**. Special interest safari operators, **page 352**. Specialist hunting tour operators **page 353**.

When to go

● Best time to visit
Mar, Apr and May can be months of heavy rain making travel on unsealed roads difficult. Even in these months, however, there is an average of 4-6 hrs of sunshine each day.

Health

● Staying healthy
See page 21 for detailed specialist advice. Malaria is the most serious risk. Take the tablets, use vapour tablets on heated electrical pads, ask to have your hotel room sprayed each evening. Cover your arms and legs at night and put repellent on your hands and face. If you observe mosquitoes in your hotel room, sleep under a net treated with insecticide.

It is not unusual to have a stomach upset on your first visit. Avoid drinking tap water and peel all fruit.

● Water
It is unwise to drink water, even when provided in a flask in a hotel. Stick to soft drinks, boil water in a travelling jug, or use water purifying tablets.

Money

● Currency
Currently in circulation are TSh50, 100, 200, 500, and 1000. notes. Coins are TSh5, 10 and 20 but are little used.

The currency has suffered from extensive depreciation since 1983. Depreciation has been rapid since 1986, but has slowed down now that the main adjustments have been made. The rate is currently set by the market with only limited government intervention. In current conditions, the exchange rate will probably continue to depreciate at around 15% a year. In early 1995, if the present level of international support for Tanzanian continues, it can be expected to be around TSh530 = US$1 (it was TSh9 =$1 in 1983).

It is advisable to bring some foreign currency in small denomination notes and to keep at least one US$20 bill for when you leave. An endless source of annoyance is for a traveller to offer a US$20 travellers' cheque to pay the airport departure tax, only to be told to go to the bureau and obtain dollars. Because of commisssion, the cheque will realise less than the US$20 required.

Foreign exchange bureaux The government has authorised Bureau de Change to set rates for buying foreign currency from the public. They will also sell foreign currency up to US$3,000 for *bona fide* travellers (you need to produce an international airline ticket).

Foreign exchange payments In the state-owned and other large private hotels, rates are calculated directly in dollars, and must be paid in foreign currency. Airline fares, game park entrance fees and other odd payments to the government (such as the US$20 airport international departure tax) must be paid in foreign currency. There is pressure from the IMF and World Bank for Tanzania to end this requirement, so don't be surprised to find it is no longer the case at the time of your visit. At smaller hotels (our B grade possibly, and certainly below) you can pay in local currency. You should pay all hotel bills other than the room rate (such as meals, drinks) in local currency – the rate used to convert the bill into dollars is usually markedly inferior to the Bureau rate.

Black market There is now no temptation to deal on the black market. The genuine street rate is no different from the bureau rate. You will be approached in the main towns, however, with offers of very high rates of exchange. The purpose is to trap you into circumstances where a swindle can be perpetrated. This will most likely take the form of an exchange in a back alley, hurriedly completed on the spurious grounds that the police are coming, only for you to find later that the Tanzanian currency is only a fraction of the sum agreed.

A more sophisticated ploy is to offer a generous rate for US$100, and to hand over the Tanzanian notes for you to count. When you produce the US$100 bill, the contact will express dismay. He says he has raised the Tanzanian shillings from several sources (the contact, in the old days of the thriving black market, always operated as a front for the real financier), and wants smaller denomination dollar notes to pay them off. He will suggest you hold on to the Tanzanian shillings while he goes off to try to break the US$100 bill. In a short while he returns. Alas he explains, he can't do it at the moment, but if you return later, he will have raised enough Tanzanian shillings from one source for the US$100. He hands you back the US$100, and you return the Tanzanian shillings. You are naturally a bit annoyed at the inconvenience. But not as annoyed as when you next try to change the US$100, only to find it is a high-class forgery (but clearly so from the quality of the printing and paper when you look at it closely), printed in Taiwan. Foreign exchange bureaux all have forgery detection machines.

● Credit cards

These are now accepted by large hotels, airlines, major tour operators and travel agencies. Otherwise you need cash. Travellers cheques will not be taken by small hotels, restaurants and so on. It is wise to have a selection of small denomination dollar bills for any unforeseen needs.

● Cost of living

In first rate hotels expect to spend US$150 a day. Careful tourists can live reasonably comfortably on US$60 a day and budget travellers can get by on US$20.

Getting there

● Air

The majority of travellers arrive in Tanzania through Dar es Salaam Airport. There are also direct international flights to Arusha (Kilimanjaro Airport) and to Zanzibar. These carriers will usually make the final leg of the journey from an airport in their own country, but will arrange connecting flights from the other main European cities.

From **Europe** to **Dar es Salaam**, British Airways has 3 flights a week. Airlines with regular flights once a week are Aeroflot, Air France, Egypt Air, Ethiopian Airlines, Gulf Air, KLM, Lufthansa, Swissair. Air Tanzania has suspended its service to London. To **Kilimanjaro** (Arusha/Moshi), flights by Air France, Egypt Air and KLM touch down on the way to Dar es Salaam. To **Zanzibar**, Gulf Air has a direct flight.

From other part of **Africa**, there are regular flights by Air Botswana, Air Tanzania, Air Zimbabwe, Kenya Airways, Royal Swazi, Zambia Airways, South African Airways. Air France connects from **Comoros**.

Specialist agents will arrange economical fares from Europe, typically for fixed arrival and departure dates, and for stays of a week or longer. Fares depend on the season. High season is generally Jul-end Mar (expect to pay around US$900 return from Europe with a prestige carrier, depending on country of departure), with the low season for Apr, May, Jun at around US$750. You may do significantly better by shopping around. Gulf Air have occasionally offered heavily discounted fares of around US$400 return. It is not generally cheaper to arrange a return to Nairobi and a connecting return flight to Dar es Salaam. The connecting flights are not reliable, and delay in Nairobi erode any cost advantage. For budget travellers, a return to Nairobi and a road connection to Dar es Salaam can result in a savings of perhaps US$100.

For specialist agencies offering discounted fares, **see page 12**.

● Train

Rail services link Dar es Salaam, **see page 262** and Zambia. From Kapri Mposhi in Zambia the journey takes 36 hrs, there are 2 trains a week and the fare is US$22, US$15, US$7 for 1st, 2nd and 3rd class. Trains used to run across the border to Kenya from Moshi. These were ended with the break-up of the East Africa Community in 1977, but there are discussions on resuming the service.

● Road

The main road crossing is at Namanga, **see page 312**, on the road between Arusha and Nairobi. This is reasonably quick and efficient and there are through buses and good roads all the way. Other crossings are at Lunga Lunga, **see page 279**, between Mombassa and Dar es Salaam. The road on the Tanzanian side is less good, but there are overnight through buses between the 2 cities. There are also crossings at Taveta, between Moshi and Voi; at Isebania, between Kisuma, and Musoma, see page 309; and across the border from Maasai Mara Park into the Serengetti. From Uganda there is crossing at Mutakulu, p 314, between Bukoba and Masaka but there are no regular buses to the border on either side.

From **Burundi** there is no feasible road access. From **Rwanda** there is a good bus link to the border at Rusomo. There is a bus leaving very early each day from Ngara on the Tanzania side and arriving at Mwanza in the evening.

From **Mozambique** there appears to be no feasible road access.

From **Zambia** there are buses to the border at Nakonde, see page 331. You have to walk between the border posts (or use a bicycle-taxi) to Tunduma where there are buses to Mbeya.

Sea

From Kenya there have been boats from Mombasa to Tanga, Zanzibar and Dar es Salaam. Although these have not been operating for a while, resumption of the service is expected. The cost was about the same as the air fare from Mombasa (US$45).

It is possible to take a dhow from Mombasa, see page 263. However you must expect to wait around for a week or more for one to depart. It will take 1 or 2 days depending on the weather. Expect to pay about US$15, bring all your own food, and you will sit and sleep on the cargo.

Lake

From Burundi there is a lake ferry to Kigoma from Bujumbura, every Mon. From Mpulungu (Malawi) there is a weekly ferry to Kigoma on Fri, see page 324, for further details. From Uganda there is a ferry from Port Bell, Kampala, see page 312, to Mwanza on Mon.

Customs

There is now no requirement to change currency on entry. A litre of spirits or wine and 200 cigarettes are duty free. There will be no duty on any equipment for your own use (such as a laptop computer). Narcotics, pornography and firearms are prohibited. Duty is payable on fax machines, TVs, video recorders and other household electrical items.

When you arrive

Airport information

Dar es Salaam airport lies 15 km W of the city. There are foreign exchange bureaux, but limited hotel bookings or car hire facilities. Visitors are advised to proceed directly to a hotel where these things can be arranged. Flight information is virtually impossible to obtain by telephone at the airport. Contact airline direct.

Airline offices Offices of these airlines in Tanzania are listed under Dar es Salaam p 256, and Arusha p 307.

Departure Tax

This is payable on leaving and is US$20 or £15, payable in foreign currency. A travellers cheque will need to be changed into dollars.

Transport to town

Bus: there are official buses which cost around US$3 and go to the *New Africa Hotel* in the town centre. There are private buses (*dala dala*) which cost about US$1 but are very crowded, leaving when full. **Taxi**: a taxi to town will cost US$10-15 depending on your destination.

Conduct

Respect is accorded to elderly people, usually by the greeting *Shikamoo, mzee* to a man and *Shikamoo, mama* to a woman.

At work in offices men will wear slacks, shoes and open neck shirts. If you are visiting a senior official it is safest to wear a tie and a jacket and a suit is desirable. In the evening at social functions there is no particular dress code although hosts will feel insulted if you arive for dinner in shorts, sandals or bare feet. Long hair on men makes local people uneasy. Visiting mosques requires removing shoes and modest dress.

Electricity

220 volts (50 cycles). However the system is notorious for power surges. Computers are particularly vulnerable and laptops which operate from a charged battery are wise for the traveller. Offices will invariably run desk-tops through a voltage regulator. New socket installations are square 3-pin. However, do not be surprised to encounter old round 3-pin (large), 3-pin round (small) and 2-pin (small) in old hotels. An adaptor is essential.

Hours of business

Most offices will start at 0800, lunch between 1200-1300, finish business at 1700, Mon to Fri; 0900-1200 on Sat, although the introduction of competition from the private sector will probably lead to longer banking hours.

● **Official time**
3 hrs ahead of GMT.

● **Safety**
Tanzania is a particularly safe country. There is minimal violent crime and the overwhelming majority of people are trustworthy. The following are sensible precautions to observe.

It is unwise to venture into unpopulated areas after dark particularly alone – always take a taxi. There are notices displayed to the effect that muggers operate on the beaches between the hotels N of Dar es Salaam and this is certainly the case. Stay within the beach areas controlled by the security guards. There are warning signs in Bagamoyo, but you are quite safe if a local person, even a child, accompanies you (they would identify any assailant).

Things left lying around may well get stolen. Always lock your hotel door (a noisy air-conditioner can made it easy for a sneak thief). Do not wear expensive jewellry, or watches and beware of having a camera or necklaces snatched in a crowd. Leave your passport,

GECKOS

You are bound to see these interesting little creatures on even a short visit. They are the small lizard-like creatures up to 180 mm long, that live in houses behind picture frames and curtains etc. They should not be killed. Not only are they totally harmless to humans but they are in fact very useful as they eat many other less pleasant insects. House geckos usually appear from their hiding places at nightfall and go off in search of food in the form of anything from flies, moths and cockroaches to spiders and centipedes. You will see them running across walls and ceilings with ease – they have suction cups on their feet which enable them to stick to almost any surface. On a white wall they appear pale and almost translucent for they are like chameleons in that they change colour to suit their background. They thrive in houses but in fact they live almost anywhere and are found all across Africa. There are actually a number of different species of gecko, some of which are very hard to tell apart, but the house gecko is the one that you are most likely to come across. The gecko's name in Swahili is *mjusi kafiri*.

They lay eggs, usually in pairs, which, are soft and sticky and are spherical. They stick to a crevice of the wall, rock or tree on and the egg shell very quickly sets hard. The eggs are brittle but they are very firmly attached to the wall. In colour they are opaque or bluish white and are up to 10 mm in diameter. When the eggs hatch the young gecko emerges, measuring about 65 mm long, of which about half is the tail and the rest the head and body. As it grows the gecko's tail grows faster than the body, so for most of the animal's life the tail is longer than the rest. It is said that if the gecko is lined up in the right direction, with the light behind it, you can see through its ear openings all the way through its head. To see this you need a very still gecko.

The house gecko has a number of enemies including birds and snakes as well as small children who seem to get some kind of a pleasure from seeing the tails of these creatures wriggling around without a body. Tail dropping is the gecko's most important defense mechanism and is used whenever they feel under threat. The tail falls off (or is pulled off by the hunter) but continues to wriggle and so provide a distraction so that the gecko can run off and hide. It will quickly grow another – in fact you may well see a gecko with a half-grown tail. One interesting phenomena about tail regeneration is when the original tail only partly breaks off a new one starts to develop at the point of injury. This results in a fork-tailed gecko.

spare cash, airline ticket and credit cards in the hotel safe unless you will be needing them. It is particularly risky to have all these items in a snatchable waistbelt traveller's bag.

Tricksters These are not common in Tanzania, but always be cautious when approached by a stranger with a sponsorship form.

Beggars It is difficult to have a rational policy towards beggars. It is best not to give to street children – they are often encouraged to skip school or forced to beg by their parents. It is quite unnecessary to pay to have your car 'watched'. See Introduction and hints, page 13.

● Tipping

Large hotels will add a service sharge. In smaller places tipping is optional. In restaurants most vistors will tip about 10% of the bill.

Where to stay

Hotel Classifications

- **A+** Over US$100 a night. International standards and decor, air conditioning, self contained rooms, swimming pool, restaurants, bars, business services.
- **A** US$40-100. First class standards, air-conditioning, attached bathrooms, restaurants and bars, swimming pool.
- **B** US$20-40. Tourist class, comfortable with air conditioning or fans, attached barthrooms, restaurant, bar, public rooms.
- **C** US$10-20. Budget, fans, shared bathroom facilities.
- **D** US$5-10. Guest house, no fan, shared bathroom, cold water.
- **E** Under US$5. Basic guest house, simple bed, no soap or towels, no wardrobe, shared bathroom facilities, erratic cold water supply, no fans or mosquito nets.

● Hotels

Places to stay have been polarised between those used by well-heeled tourists, and are expensive, at around US$100 a day, self contained with air-conditioning, hot water and swimming pools, and those used by local people (and budget travellers) at under US$5 a day, which may comprise a simple bed, shared toilet and washing facilities, irregular water supply. The expensive establishments were run by the monopoly Tanzania Tourist Corporation and the others by the private sector. More private hotels are opening and the competition is giving travellers better choice. There are now some acceptable places to stay (except, alas, in the parks) with fans or air conditioning, hot water and self contained at around US$20 a day.

Some of the small beach hotels are in splendid locations and despite having only simple facilities are excellent value.

In the parks camping in either a tented camp or a campsite is often more atmospheric and certainly cheaper than staying in one of the lodges.

Food

● Restaurants

Cuisine in Tanzania is not one of the country's main attractions. There is a legacy of uninspired British catering (soups, steaks, grilled chicken, chips, boiled vegetables, puddings, instant coffee). Asian eating places can be better, but are seldom of a high standard. There are a few Chinese and Italian restaurants. Some of the best food is simple charcoal grills outside in beer gardens.

● Street snacks

A variety of items can be purchased from street venders who prepare and cook over charcoal, which adds considerably to the flavour, at temporary roadside shelters (kiosks). Street cuisine is pretty safe despite hygiene methods being fairly basic. Most of the items are cooked or peeled which deals with the health hazard. Grapes require careful washing or peeling.

Savoury items include chips, omelettes, barbequed beef on skewers (*mishkaki*), roast maize (corn), hard-boiled eggs and roast casserole (look like white, peeled turnips) with red chili-pepper garnish. Fruits variously in season

Eating Classifications

- ♦♦♦♦ Over US$10 for a meal. A 3-course meal in a restaurant with pleasant decor. Beers, wines and spirits available.
- ♦♦♦ US$5-10 for a meal. Two courses, not including alcohol, reasonable surroundings.
- ♦♦ US$2-5 for a meal, probably only a single course, surroundings spartan but adequate.
- ♦ Under US$2. Single course, often makeshift surroundings such as a steet kiosk with simple benches and tables.

include oranges (peeled and halved), grapes, pineapples, bananas, mangoes (slices scored and turned inside-out), paw-paw (*papaya*). In the evenings, particularly, but all day at markets, bus and railways stations there are traditional swahili coffee vendors with large portable conical brass coffee pots with charcoal braziers underneath. The coffee is ground (not instant), is sold black in small porcelain cups fished out of a portable wash-bowl, and is excellent. They also sell peanut crisp bars and sugary cakes made from molasses. These items are very cheap – a skewer of meat is US$0.25, an orange (US$0.05), a cup of coffee (US$0.05). They are all worth trying, and when travelling, are indispensable.

Drink

● Beer

Local beer bottle (lager) are very sound and cheap (US$1 a litre). There is a wide variety of imported lagers from Kenya and South Africa particularly, but also from Europe at around 3 times the price of local lagers.

● Wine

Imported wines are good value at US$6 a bottle upwards for European and South African labels. Wines from Zimbabwe are quite pleasant. Tanzanian wines produced by the White Fathers at Dodoma, 'Bowani Wine', are reputed to be excellent. Wines made by the National Milling Corporation are undrinkable.

● Soft drinks

Soft drinks are mainly limited to cokes, orange, lemon, pineapple, tonic and club soda. No diet sodas available. Fresh juices are very rare. Coffee is invariably instant. When fresh ground it is the local Arabica variety with a distinctive, acidic flavour.

● Weights and measures

Officially metric, but expect to pay for fruit and vegetables by the item.

Getting around

● Air

Air Tanzania Corporation (ATC) has a schedule of domestic flights. However ATC has run into financial difficulties and some routes do not operate.

Dar es Salaam-Zanzibar is well served with daily flights scheduled from ATC (US$43) 2 flights a day from ZATA (US$35). **Zanzibar-Pemba** has a daily flight from ZATA and 2 flights on Wed and Fri (US$40). **Pemba-Tanga** has 2 flights a week by Jasfa (US$35). **Arusha-Dar** has 3 flights a week by Aviators Services (US$120). **Dar-Mafia**. Three flights a week by Aviators Services (US$40).

Fares vary between US$50 a 100 km on short-hauls to US$15 a 100 km on the longer trips.

● Train

Train services are reasonably reliable. There are services to the N between Dar es Salaam, Moshi and Tanga 3 times a week. Four trains a week between Dar es Salaam, Kigoma and Mtwara. Five trains a week run between Dar es Salaam, Mbeya and the Zambian border Tunduma.

● Road

There is now an efficient network of privately run buses across the country. On the main routes (Arusha, Morogaro) there is a choice of 'luxury', 'semi-luxury' and 'regular'. Fares are very reasonable – roughly US$2/100 km. On good sealed roads they cover 50 km/hour. On unsealed or poorly maintained roads they will average only 20 km/hour.

On the main routes it is possible to book ahead at a kiosk at the bus stand and this is wise rather than turning up at the departure time on the off-chance. It is sensible to avoid being placed on a make-shift gangway seat with only a small seat back, or sitting over the wheel arch where it's impossible to stretch your legs.

● Lake ferries

The ferries are reliable and pleasant. Between Dar es Salaam and Zanzibar there are several sailings each day, with a choice of hydrofoil or steam ship. On **Lake Victoria**, the main sailings are between Mwanza and Bukoba, though small islands and some other lakeside towns are served. On **Lake Tanganyika** boats go from Kigoma to various small ports south. On **Lake Nyasa**, there is a boat going from the north part of Ztunga to Mbamba, the last Tanzanian port on the east shore.

The cost of travel varies between US$40/100 km for 1st class hydrofoil travel to US$2/100 km for 3rd class on a steamer.

● Car Hire

Car hire is expensive and is difficult to justify for in-town travel in view of the availability, cheapness and willingness-to-wait of local taxis. Drivers with a hired car are normally more trouble than they are worth in town.

Other local transport

Dala dala Local private buses and passenger vehicles constructed from small trucks (called *dala dala*, it is said, because they charged a dollar, although this seems a high sum) are for the adventurous. Tanzania banned these vehicles until recently, and road transport was a state monopoly. However, inability to provide enough buses (Dar es Salaam required 250 minimum, and was down to 60 in 1989) led to unseemly fights to get on, huge queues, and many commuters were resigned to walking up to 20 km a day. State corporations and private firms tended to provide their own buses for staff. Liberalization of transport is an enormous improvement but although the *dala dala* are steadily expanding, they get very crowded and there is usually a fight to get on. A modifed truck vehicle will carry 50, of which 30 will stand and you really need to hang on as it sways around. *Dala dala* are cheap, US$0.10 for any length of journey, and are frequent on main routes into and out of town. Fellow travellers will be very helpful in directing you to the correct *dala dala* if you ask (most have a sign indicating their route and destination on the front), will advise on connections, fight on your behalf to try to get you a seat and get you off at your destination.

Taxis Hotels and town-centre locations are well served by taxis, very run-down but serviceable. It is wise to sit in the back if there are no front seat belts. Hotel staff, even at the smallest locations, will rustle-up a taxi even when there is not one waiting outside. If you visit an out-of-town centre location, it is wise to ask the taxi to wait – it will normally be happy to do so for benefit of the return fare. Up to 1 km should cost US$1. A trip to the outskirts of Dar es Salaam such as the University (13 km) would be US$7.50. There is a bargaining element: none of the cabs have meters, and you should establish the fare (*bei gani*? – how much?) before you set off.

Communications

Language

Facility in English is poor. Even well-educated, professional Tanzanians, although perfectly able to make themselves understood, write and express themselves awkwardly. A few phrases of Swahili are invaluable in dealing with local people.

Postal services

Postal system is reliable. Airmail takes about 2 weeks to destinations in Europe and North America. Buy stamps at the hotel or at a postcard shop. The post offices are crowded and queueing is not observed.

DHL has offices in the major cities. Packages to Europe take 2 working days, to North America, 3 days.

Telephone Services

Poor. However the system is being up-graded at present. Local calls often more dificult than international. If you have an important appointment to make or flight to confirm, send a driver or go in person.

In Dar es Salaam there is an efficient international service from Telecoms, off Samora Ave. Connections are quick and about a third the price of a call through a hotel.

Entertainment

Cinemas

Found in most large towns, they will show mostly Indian, King Fu and Western films of the action variety.

Music

Most musical entertainment is in hotels where traditional dance programmes are staged for tourists, and there are live bands and discos. Hotels and social halls often stage fashion and musical shows where local entertainers impersonate Western pop stars. These events are all well-publicised in the local press.

Newspapers

Tanzania has one English daily, *Daily News*, and a Swahili daily, *Uhuru* but are difficult to obtain outside Dar es Salaam. They are both government-owned and very local in their coverage. The Kenyan daily, *The Nation*, is available in Arusha, Mwanza and Dar es Salaam from midday, and is a high quality source of regional and international news. There are a number of independent weeklies. The *Business Times* gives excellent coverage of commercial matters, *Family Circle* has served as a vehicle for criticism of the government, as does *The Express.* The Tanzanian press is worth sampling for the bizarre and curious local stories that appear (eg 'Vicar Kicks Worshippers Who Insist on Kneeling' – *Daily News* Dec 1992) as well as being the main vehicle for entertainment and sporting announcements.

● Radio

There are 2 stations, both government operated. Radio Tanzania on 1442 KHZ MW broadcasts in Swahili. The External Service at 1204 MW has programmes in English. News bulletins tend to contain a lot of local coverage. Programmes of African music are good, and the discussion programmes tend to be fairly serious, on health, development, education etc. In 1994 a new private station, Radio One, began broadcasting, mostly music and in Swahali.

● Sporting events

In large towns the main activities will be soccer matches. Fixtures tend to be arranged, or postponed, at short notice and details should be checked in the daily press. There are also cricket matches over weekends (predominantly a pursuit of the Asian community), golf, tennis and squash tournaments are held at clubs but open to the public. Occasional sailing regattas are held at the yacht clubs in Dar es Salaam and Tanga. Hash House Harriers (a paperchase running and social event) meet every Sat afternoon in Dar es Salaam (details of the location of the meet can be obtained in the British Council offices on Samora Ave). Track and field meetings are staged, the Mount Meru marathon is an annual event in Jun, and there are boxing tournaments. For details see local press.

● Television

In 1994 ITV began to transmit with a mixture of locally produced Swahili items and international programmes. Zanzibar has had television since the early 1970s, and the larger hotels will have a TV in one of the public rooms. It only operates in the evening, it is difficult to find a programme schedule, and a lot of videos are shown – it is said that if you hand a recent tape into the TV station they will put it out that evening. There is a flourishing video market with hire shops in all towns, though the quality is poor as most tapes are pirated.

Holidays and festivals

1 Jan	New Year's Day
12 Jan	Zanzibar Revolution Day (Zanzibar only)
5 Feb	CCM Foundation Day
26 Apr	Union Day
1 May	Mayday Workers Day
9 Dec	Independence Day
25 Dec	Christmas Day

Good Fri, Easter Mon, Id-ul-Fitr (end of Ramadan), Id-ul-Haji (Festival of Sacrifice), Islamic New Year, Prophet Mohammad's Birthday are other holidays which vary from year to year.

The Christian holidays will not be observed by all Muslims and vice-versa.

Further reading

● History

Millar, C *Battle for the Bunge.* Superbly readable account of WW1 in German East Africa. Hibbert, C (1982) *Africa explored: Europeans in the Dark Continent,* London: Penguin. Fascinating detail on the early visitors and their motivations. Packenham, T (1991) *The Scramble for Africa,* London: Weidenfeld and Nicholson. The events that laid the foundations for the modern history of Tanzania.

Swahili Slang

It will not take you long to notice that many Swahili words sound remarkably similar to English words. Indeed Swahili, which is by origin a Bantu language, has been greatly influenced by Arabic and more recently the language has been further enriched by borrowings from other languages including English. There are also examples where 2 words are in common usage, each with the same meaning but with different origins. For example 'week' – *juma* or *wiki* – derived from Arabic and English respectively; 'handkerchief' – *anakachifi* or *leso* – derived from English and Portuguese respectively; and 'report' – *ripoti* or *taarifa* – from English and Arabic respectively.

Some words that have been adopted are very obvious and, for example, modern transport has produced a large number of words which need no explaining – for example *basi* (bus), *treni* (train), *stesheni* (station), *teksi* (taxi), *petroli, tanki, breki*. A rich man is *mbenzi* – he would be expected to drive a Mercedes. A traffic bollard is a *kiplefti.*

Other adoptions may not seem immediately obvious – for example 'electricity' is sometimes called *elekrii* but more commonly *stimu* is used. This is because when the word was originally coined nearly all the electricity generating stations were run by steam engines. In the same way the word for steamship, *meli*, probably derives from the fact that when the word was first used almost all the ships that were around would have carried mail. The dockyards are *kuli* which is from the dockyard workers who were known as coolies.

WW2 also produced a number of words which were adopted into the Swahili language, many of them relating to animals. For example a submarine was *papa* which is the word for shark, a tank was *faru* which means rhino, an aeroplane is *ndege ulaya* which means white-man's bird.

Swahili, like all other languages, also has a large collection of slang words. For example the period shortly before pay day when all the previous month's money has been spent is known as *mwambo* which is derived from the word *wamba*, to stretch tight. This implies that the user is financially stretched. Coins have also been given a variety of nicknames. Examples include *ng'aru* which derives from the word to shine, *ku-ngaa*. During the colonial era the shilling, which had a picture of the king's head on it, was known as *Usi wa Kinga* meaning the king's face. Five and 10 cents pieces which used to have a hole in the centre were nicknamed *sikio la Mkwavi* meaning 'the ear of the Mkwavi'. The Kwavi people are a pastoral tribe who pierce their ear lobes and often used to hang coins from them as decoration.

A slang phrase for bribery that has come into common usage is *kuzunguka mbuyu* which literally translated means to go behind a baobab tree, the implication being that behind the baobab tree, which is an exceptionally wide tree, no-one will see the transaction that takes place. The slang term for liquor is *mtindi* which actually means skimmed milk – it was probably used to conceal what was really being drunk. The term for drunk that is frequently used is *kupiga mtindi* which translates to mean 'to beat up the liquor' and is used in the same way that we would use 'to go on a binge'. Someone who is drunk may be described as *amevaa miwani* which literally translated means 'he is wearing spectacles' but is used to suggest that he can't see well as a result of the alcohol – we might say he was seeing double. Another similar phrase is *yuko topu* which translates to 'he is full right up to the top'.

Clothes have also attracted various nicknames. For example *americani*, the name given to the cheap cloth that was imported from America during the colonial era and became very popular. Drainpipe trousers were known as *suruwali ya uchinjo* which means cut off trousers – because being so narrow they look as if part of them is missing. Many of the names given to items of clothing are derived from English words, such as *tai* (tie), *kala* (collar), and *soksi* (socks). The phrase used by off-duty policemen to describe their clothes also needs little explanation: *kuvaa kisivilyan* which means 'to wear civilian clothes', while a fashionable haircut is known as *fashun*.

There are many other examples of slang words and words from other languages that have been adopted into Swahili – too many to list here, but you will undoubtedly come across some of them. What is interesting is that they are adopted into the language and quickly become an integral part of it. Swahili, perhaps more than many languages, has been enriched by the absorption of words and phrases from other languages from all over the world – it is a living organism of great vitality.

● Natural History

Grzimek, B (1959) *Serengeti Shall Not Die*, London: Collins. Classic account of the unique character of this world famous park. Douglas-Hamilton, I (1978) *Among the Elephants,* London: Penguin. Interesting perspective on elephant conservation in Lake Manyara. Goodall, J (1971) *In the Shadow of Man,* London: Collins. Gives something of the flavour of what is involved in making a life's work of studying a particular species.

● Field guides

Dorst, J and Dandelot, PA (1970) *Field Guide to the Larger Mammals of Africa*, London: Collins. Williams, J and Arlott, NA (1980) *Field guide to the Birds of East Africa*, London: Collins. Larcassam, R (1971) *Hand guide to the Butterflies of East Africa*, London: Collins. Blundell, MA (1987) *Field Guide to the Wild Flowers of East Africa*, London: Collins. Hedges, NR (1983) *Reptiles and Amphibians of East Africa*, Narobi: Kenya Literature Bureau.

● Travellers' tales

Waugh, E (1960) *A tourist in Africa*, London: Chapman and Hall. A trip through Tanzania just prior to independence. Dahl, R (1986) *Going Solo*, London: Penguin. Impressions of a young man sent out to work in the colonies.

● Fiction

Boyd, W *An Ice Cream War.* Neatly observed, humorous and in parts sensitive tale set against WW1 campaign in East Africa. Boyd, W *Brazzaville Beach.* Although written as a West African story, clearly based on Jane Goodall and the chimps of Gombe Stream.

● Other Guides

Brriggs, P (1993) *Guide to Tanzania*, Bradt: Chalfont St Peter. Very good for budget travellers and those planning hikes and treks. Else, D. *Guide to Zanzibar* Bradt: Chalfont St Peter. Comprehensive, modern guide to the Islands. Good items of background information. Spectrum (1992) *Guide to Tanzania.* Nairobi: Camerapix. Quite glorious photographs which serve to capture the special flavour of Tanzania and Zanzibar.

UGANDA

Contents

Introduction

Uganda is a land-locked country on the northern shore of Lake Victoria in the centre of Africa. The equator runs through the country. The North is arid except where the Albert Nile runs through it. The rest of the country is extremely fertile. There are some fine parks and wildlife; attractive countryside with tremendous mountain ranges, lakes, rivers and waterfalls; and a rich cultural background among the people.

Uganda's history, however, has been scarred by a descent into chaos and anarchy for a period from the early 1970s until 1986. Untold numbers died; skilled people of both African and Asian origin fled overseas; residents of towns sought refuge in the countryside eking out a bare survival existence. Institutions of excellence, such as the famous Makerere University, collapsed; buildings, roads, factories and farms were destroyed, or fell into disrepair.

In the last 8 years, Uganda has made a remarkable recovery. Peace has returned to the main parts of the country, although there are still some bands marauding in in the N. Many Asians and skilled Africans have returned, and the economy has begun to allow improved living standards. Many of the features that were so attractive to visitors before 1970 are there to be enjoyed again and Uganda offers tremendous value in wildlife viewing.

Exchange Rate 1994 Ush 930 = US$1

Environment

Geography

Uganda, in the East African region, is a medium-sized landlocked state bordered by Sudan, Kenya, Tanzania, Rwanda and Zaïre. It forms part of the central African plateau, dropping to the White Nile Basin in the N. Lake Kionga and Lake Albert lie in the Rift Valley and much of the territory to the S is swampy marsh. To the E is savannah and the western part of the country forms the margins of the Congo forests. Generally the S is agricultural and the N is pastoral.

There are hydro-electric schemes on the Owen Falls Dam. Mineral resources include copper, tin, bismuth, wolfram, colombo-tanalite, phosphates, limestone, gold and beryl (a gemstone).

Climate

Temperature varies little; there is an equatorial climate modified by altitude. Rainfall, greatest in the mountains and the Lake Victoria region, reaches an annual average of up to 200cm. Elsewhere it averages 125cm but the dry NE and parts of the S receive up to 75cm. The dry season varies between one month in the centre and W, to the months of Jun, Jul and Aug in the S. There are 2 dry seasons in the N and NE in Oct and Dec to Mar, making 2 harvests possible.

People

The largest group in Uganda are the Baganda, with 16% of the total. Other main groups are the Soga with 8%; the Nkole with 8%; the Teso with 8%; the Kiga with 7%; the Lango with 6%; the Gisu with 5%; the Acholi with 4% and the Alur with 4%. In all, there are 14 groups with more than 1% of the population. Prior to their expulsion in 1972 the Asians comprised about 2% of the total.

History

Before the arrival of the British there were as many as 30 different ethnic groups in the area that now forms modern Uganda, each with its own language, culture and social organisation.

The political organisation of these different states ranged from those with a highly developed centralized system of government, through small chiefdoms, to areas with no obvious system of government. Buganda, Toro, Bunyoro and Nkore, were of the first type, and all had a highly developed centralized system of government with a monarch in place. Around 1830 Toro broke away from Bunyoro when Prince Kaboyo rebelled against his father. For some time Bunyoro was the strongest and most powerful of the 4, but from the second half of the 18th century they were overtaken by Buganda. In Nkore the system was rather different as the minority pastoral Bahima ruled over the majority agriculturalist Bairu.

Other areas had no obvious system of government and interpersonal relations were controlled by fear of spirits and the supernatural.

The first foreigners to arrive in the area now called Uganda, were Arab traders in the 1840s. From about 1850 the first Europeans began to arrive. John Speke reached Buganda in 1956 and was the first European to locate the source of the Nile.

The late 19th century was a period of instability in much of Uganda, and there were wars on a surprisingly large scale. In 1888 the British East Africa Company was given the royal charter and their control over the area was consolidated by a treaty with the Kabaka of Buganda (the central and most prominent kingdom of what was to become Uganda) in 1891. However the Company found administering the territory too much for it to manage, and in 1894 the British Government took over responsibility and Buganda was declared a Protectorate. Similar status was given to Bunyoro, Toro and Ankole in 1896. During the following years the boundaries of the country were finalised, with a section of Uganda being transferred to Kenya as late as 1912.

The Buganda Agreement of 1900

The so-called 'Buganda Question' goes back to the signing in 1900 of the Uganda Agreement (at this time, and until about 1906 the British referred to the District of Buganda as Uganda, or as the Kingdom of Uganda) which proved to be a watershed in the history of Buganda and, indeed, the whole of Uganda. It formalised the association between the British and the Buganda that had developed since Speke's arrival in 1862.

One of the most important aspects of the Agreement was that it secured a remarkably privileged position for Buganda in comparison with its neighbours. The constitutional relationship between the Protectorate Government and the Government of the Kingdom of Buganda was set out at some length, and it emphasized Buganda's political identity while assuring it a greater measure of internal autonomy than the other dis-

tricts enjoyed. Some of the other districts had their own agreemenets, but none were as comprehensive or as favourable as that accorded the Bugands.

The Agreement led to important changes in land tenure. It won over the majority of the chiefs by giving them land grants known as *mailo*, and in doing so it recognized that land was a marketable commodity. The land not given to the Kabaka and chiefs became +Crown land to be used for the benefit of the Kingdom. The Agreement thus created a landed class. It also gave, for the first time, recognition to the notion of indirect rule through the chiefs who were granted *mailo* land. The colonialists needed allies local allies to help them administer with the minimum expenditure of resources, and to produce an economic surplus that could pay for the administration. In time the interests of the chiefs and the Government became more closely interwoven. The chiefs collected regular salaries and promoted government policies, and in the public's mind they began to be associated with the Protectorate administration.

The benefit of the Agreement was in addition to the natural advantages that Buganda already had with fertile soils, regular rainfall, and a location on the shore of Lake Victoria which ensured good transport links. Missionary activity in the area, stimulated by competion between the Protestant and Catholics led to a greater concentration of hospitals, schools and other educational facilities. Britain encouraged the production of cotton, the major cash crop in the S, while parts of the remaining areas were discouraged from growing cash crops and were instead developed as a labour reserve. This served to accentuate further the differences between Buganda and the rest of the Protectorate, with the S producing cash crops and the N providing migrant labour. In keeping with this division, the N also provided soldiers to the army throughout the colonial period. Buganda's farmers benefited greatly from high coffee prices after the war and in the early 1950's industrial and commercial development were concentrated in the S generally and in Buganda with its locational and educational advantages, in particular.

The period of British rule in Uganda saw dramatic changes in the politics and economy of the country. Most of the wars and disputes were brought under control and the peace which grew up became known as Pax Britanica. The country was divided into Districts which were headed by a District Commissioner, and the Districts into Counties (*saza*), Sub-counties (*gombolola*), Parishes (*miruka*) and Sub-Parishes (*bukungu* or *batongole*). A system of indirect rule was developed, with local people used at all these levels. In cases where a system of government was already in place the incumbents were used, but where this was absent other Ugandans – usually Baganda – were brought in. This meant that in many parts of Uganda in the early years of British Administration the British controlled large areas of Uganda through appointed Baganda chiefs.

While the S of the country developed into an agriculturally productive area producing, in particular cotton and coffee, the N and SW developed mainly as a labour pool. Migration into the southern and central region became crucial to maintaining the high production in these areas. There was also a great deal of migration from outside Uganda to the central region. This was mainly from what was then known as Ruanda Urundi (later to be Rwanda and Burundi) but was also from Tanganikya and the Congo. Migration was not just to government jobs on large scale, such as the building of the railway and the army, but also to work for individual cotton and coffee farmers in Buganda. There were some large-scale European-owned farms and plantations in Uganda, but they were never as extensive as in Kenya and it was always planned that Uganda should be developed primarily for Africans. Thus, during the Depression of the late 1920s and early 1930s, the Uganda Colonial Government was not prepared to give the Europeans financial support to get them through the difficult times. Many went bust and left the country. A number of the plantations were later bought up by Asians and were developed into the sugar plantations that can be seen on the road from the Kenya border to Kampala.

The Christian missions arrived in Uganda early and their impact was enormous. Islam was also introduced into Uganda but never made the same impact. The first schools and hospitals were all mission-run and the Catholic and Protestants tried desperately to win the most converts, and the key was to provide superior education. The 2 Christian faiths divided the country up between their different groups so that, for example the White Fathers went to Southern Uganda, the Mill Hill Fathers to Eastern Uganda and the Verona Fathers to the North. The Church Mission Society (CMS) are to be found across most of the country and their influence was very great.

In recent times, countries under colonial rule have achieved independence when a growing nationalist movement has been successful both in mobilizing a large section of the population and in extracting concessions from the colonial power. In Uganda however, it has been said that it was not nationalism that produced independence but instead it was the imminence of independence that produced nationalist parties. It was taken for granted that independence would be granted at some stage and instead concern was concentrated on the position and role that Buganda would take in an independent country. The Baganda did not wish for their role to be diminished after independence. By the same token, the rest of the country had no wish to be dominated by the Baganda.

The Kabaka Crisis of 1953-55

The issue of Baganda separatism came to a head when Sir Andrew Cohen was appointed governor in 1952, and was determined to push Uganda as quickly as possible along the road to self-government. A vital principle underlying his policies was that Uganda must develop as a unitary state in which no part of the country should dominate any other. Thus a strong central Government was required, in which all districts, including Buganda, would be represented on an equal footing. This challenged the privileged position that the Buganda had enjoyed since 1900.

The crisis of 1953-55 was sparked off by a chance remark in London by Sir Oliver Lyttleton, the Colonial Secretary, about the possibility of introducing a federal system in East Africa embracing the 3 British territories of Kenya, Uganda and Tanganyika. This was very unpopular with all Ugandans as it was feared the federation would be dominated by the Europeans in Kenya. In a wider union the Baganda were even more apprehensive that they would be able to safeguard their privileged position. Cohen responded to Lyttleton's remarks by giving public reassurances in the Legislative Council that there would be no imposition of a federation against public wishes. The Kabaka, Mutesa II, accepted these reassurances but took the opportunity to ask for the affairs of Buganda to be transferred from the Colonial Office to the Foreign Office, which would be a clear indication that Baganda was not merely just another colony, but had a more privileged position being a protected state whose monarch had invited British protection. He also asked for a timetable for Independence to be drawn up.

The Kabaka then went a step further and rejected the policy of a unitary state and asked for the separation of Buganda from the rest of the country. Cohen demanded assurances in line with the 1900 Agreement that the Kabaka would not publicly oppose the government's policies for Uganda's development. However the Kabaka refuse, pleading that he first needed to consult the *Lukiko*, the Buganda council of elders. On 30th Nov 1953 Cohen signed a declaration withdrawing Britain's recognition from Mutesa as Native ruler in Buganda, deported the Kabaka by air to Britain and declared a State of Emergency. Troops were deployed around Kampala but there was no outbreak of violence.

Following the Kabaka Crisis discussions got underway to attempt to resolve the situation which led to the Namirembe Conference of Jul-Sep 1954. In Oct 1955 the Kabaka returned to Uganda and signed the Buganda Agreement of 1955 – the outcome of the Conference. The Agreement declared that Buganda should continue to be an integral part of the Protectorate of Uganda, and recommended that the *Lukiko* should agree to elected Baganda participation in the Legislative Council, a step which, fearful of being submerged, it had consistently rejected. The Kabaka in theory returned as a constitutional monarch stripped of political power, but in reality the crisis had served to unite the various clans of the Baganda firmly behind the Kabaka, and thereby increased his political influence.

The crisis had a number of major effects. Firstly the question of federation with the rest of East Africa was ruled out. Secondly, the Buganda continued to have a special position and virtual internal self-government. Thirdly, the Kabaka's personal power and popularity increased. Fourthly a statement in the House of Commons was made that Uganda would be developed primarily as an African country, with proper safeguards for minorities. Fifthly, non-Baganda members of the Legislative Council adopted an increasingly nationalist attitude and began to question the special treatment accorded to the Buganda, sowing the seed of confrontation. And finally, now that independence in Uganda was clearly just a matter of time the major question turned to who would hold the power after independence, and what would Buganda's and the Kabaka's role be in Uganda – would they remain the first among equals?

From the mid-1950's the first political parties were formed. They were the Democratic Party (DP), led by Benedicto Kiwanuka, with particular support amongst Catholics. They wanted a unitary state after independence and wanted to limit the powers of the Baganda – so initially the party did not find much support in Buganda. The Uganda National Congress (UNC) was more nationally-based and wanted greater African control of the economy in a federal independent state. In 1958 a splinter group broke off from the UNC and formed the Uganda People's Congress (UPC), led by Milton Obote. A political party called Kabaka Yekka (KY) – 'The King Alone' – also formed,representing the interests of the Baganda.

The immediate run-up to independence was one of non-cooperation by the Baganda who feared losing their political identity as part of a unitary state and became increasingly hostile towards the Protectorate Government. They refused to proceed with elections for Buganda's Legislative Councillors until Buganda's role in a future central government and the role of the Kabaka had been decided. On the 31st Dec 1960 the Baganda declared themselves independent however this was a meaningless gesture as they did not have the power to make independence a reality.

In 1961 an inquiry was set up to look into the question of the relationship of the various parts of Uganda with the centre. It recognized that Buganda enjoyed what was virtually a federal relationship with the rest of the Protectorate, and recommended that this should continue. Uganda should therefore become a single democratic state with a strong central government, with which Buganda would have a federal relationship.

In 1961 the first elections were held – the 2 main parties being UPC and DP. The Baganda boycotted the election so that only 3% of the Buganda electorate voted, allowing the DP to make a clean sweep in Buganda. Overall UPC won a majority of votes but DP's success in Buganda gave them the majority of the seats. Obote, as leader of the UPC opposition, and the Kabaka were both anxious to eject the DP from power in the 1962 elections, and so Obote agreed to support Buganda's demands – particularly for indirect elections to the National Assembly – in return for Buganda's return to the centre and acceptance of a single central government. Thus Buganda took her place in London at the Constitutional Conference in Sep 1961.

Independence: Obote I

At this conference the structure of the future government was agreed to and the date of full independence was set for 9 Oct 1962. Buganda obtained virtually everything that she asked for. She would be in a federal relationship with the centre, and the constitution would define all matters concerning the Kabakaship and her traditional institutions. This opened the way for the Baganda to participate once again in central government which they did through the Kabaka Yekka party, formed in 1961. They formed an alliance with the UPC and the Feb 1962 elections in Buganda were really a fight between KY and DP, and KY won 65 of the 68 seats. The KY victory determined the composition of the new government formed after the national pre-independence elections in Apr 1962. Obote's UPC won a comfortable victory over DP outside Buganda, and within it the KY-UPC alliance ensured a majority of seats for the alliance. In May 1962 Obote was sworn in as Prime Minister of the UPC-KY government and the Kabaka's role was that of constitutional monarch. On Oct 9 1962, the day Uganda became an independent nation, Obote spoke of the joy felt by all in Uganda at the achievement of Uganda's independence, and particularly as this had been reached in peace and goodwill. He went on to speak of the need for a unity of purpose, mutual understanding and respect, and a resolve to place our country above tribe, party and self.

The coalition was however between UPC and KY was fragile and by 1964 enough KY and DP members had crossed the floor to join the UPC so that the alliance was no longer necessary and Obote dismissed KY from the government.

In Feb 1966 Obote suspended the constitution, deposed the president and transferred all executive powers to himself. Shortly afterwards an interim constitution was imposed that the parliament had neither read or debated, which withdrew regional autonomy, and introduced an executive presidency – which Obote assumed, thus becoming Head of State with absolute power. This became known as the pigeon-hole constitution because MPs were told to vote on it before they were allowed to read it – it was placed in their pigeon holes for them to read afterwards. When the Baganda demanded the restoration of their autonomy, troops led by second-in-command of the army, Col Idi Amin, seized the Kabaka's palace. The Kabaka fled to Britain, where he died in exile in a Bermondsey council flat – a sad end for a man who had spent much of his time at Cambridge travelling down to the engineering works in Derby to supervise the carving of ivory from elephants he had shot, to make the switches on the dashboard of his Rolls Royce.

Amin

The late 1960's saw the beginning of the years of repression for which Uganda was later to became notorious. Detentions and armed repression became increasingly common. A "Move to the Left" was introduced which redistributed resources by way of nationalization and increased central power. However, Obote, who had used the army to prop up his own regime, was to be ousted by that same army under the command of Amin. The takeover occurred in Jan 1971 while Obote was out of the country at a Commonwealth Conference. Amin declared himself the new head of state and promised that there would be a return to civilian government within 5 years. This however was not to be. It is worth remembering that Amin was initially greeted with widespread support amongst the Ugandan population, particularly the Baganda, as well as in the Western world.

Not long into his regime, however, Amin suspended all political activity and most civil rights. The National Assembly was dissolved and Amin ruled the country by capricious decree. In Aug 1972 Amin announced the expulsion of all non-citizen Asians. The directive was later expanded to all Asians, although under great pressure Amin backtracked on this latter point. However in the atmosphere that had by then been established, all but a handful of the 75,000 Asians left the country. Most went to Britain, while many others went to Canada and the States. Britain cut off diplomatic relations and imposed a trade embargo. By the end of the year most other Western countries had followed suit. The businesses that had been owned by Asians were Africanised, that is, given to various cronies of Amin. The expulsion of Asians and policy of Africanisation was popular with the majority of the Ugandan population. Many had resented the success of Asian businesses and this seemed to be the time to make things fairer. However many businesses collapsed and the sudden and dramatic loss of technical skills brought many other entreprises to a standstill. Amin attempted to gain the popularity of the Baganda by returning the body of the Kabaka for burial in the Kisubi tombs outside Kampala. The administration under Amin was propped up by military aid from the Soviet Union and Libya. Meanwhile the infrastructure – water supply, schools, hospitals, roads – collapsed, and many former cash-crop producers returned to subsistence production in an effort to survive. Unexplained disappearances increased, particularly among the Acholi and Langi people. There was was conflict within the army.

In 1978, in an attempt to detract attention from the internal turmoil, Amin launched an attack on Tanzania. The Kagera Salient in SW Uganda has, since the drawing of international boundaries, been rather an problematic area. Just to the W of Lake Victoria the international boundary is a straight line following the 10 latitude. However the Kagera River forms a loop to the S of this. There is, therefore, an area of land which is part of Tanzania, but because of the river, has more contact with Uganda. One of the most important agreements that the Organisation of African Unity (OAU) reached soon after its formation was that, however unfair or illogical, the international boundaries drawn by the colonial powers, they should not be disputed. Amin's claim to the Kagera salient was clearly in breach of this. Amin's undisciplined troops were no match for the Tanzanian army and 1979 war led to massive destruction, as the army fled N pillaging and destroying as it went. Amin fled and went into exile, first in Libya, and later in Saudi Arabia.

Following the war the Tanzanian army remained in Uganda to maintain the peace. Meanwhile on the political front the Tanzanians arranged the Moshi Conference in Mar 1979. At this conference Dr Lule (who had formerly been Vice Chancellor of Makerere) was chosen to be the leader of the National Consultative Committee of the Uganda National Liberation Front which together with a military commission undertook the interim rule of Uganda. In Apr, Lule was sworn in as president. He was not, however, to last long and in Jun, was voted out of office by the 30 strong National Consultative Committee. In his place was put Binaisa, the former Attorney General. His length of office was to be only a year and in May 1980 the UNLF's military commission took over. This was headed by Paulo Mwanga and was supported by Museveni as vice-chairman. Elections were set for Dec 1980 and was contested by 4 political parties. The major 2 were UPC (headed by Obote) and DP (headed by Paul Ssemogerere), a newer party the Uganda Patriotic Movement (UPM), headed by Museveni, and the Conservative Party which was largely a Buganda-based party derived from Kabaka Yekka.

Obote II

This election for which Uganda had such high hopes would usher in a new era, is widely believed to have been fixed – crowds had gathered in the streets of Kampala as the first results came out and word was that the DP had won. However Mwanga announced that no further results of the election could be released before they had been approved by him. Needless to say, when the results finally did come out – announcing a UPC victory – there was widespread belief that the results had been falsified. The truth of the election result will probably never be known – but in the end the UPC had a majority of 20 seats, Obote was proclaimed President with Mwanga as Vice-President. The election of the new government did not, however, bring peace and stability to the country. The ideology that the UPC put forward was such as to attract World Bank and IMF sponsored economic reconstruction, but rebuilding the country was not to be easy. On the security side the situation in many parts of the country deteriorated still further.

The disatisfaction that had resulted from the doubts over the elections had led to a number of groups going into the bush from where they carried out a guerilla war. These included the National Resistance Army (NRA) led by Museveni who were based largely in the southern part of the country. The NRA was the most organised and it grew from a small collection of fighters into a powerful army. The atrocities perpetrated by the government in what became known as the Luwero Triangle, an area to the N of Kampala were an attempt to rid the NRA of civilian supporters. Large numbers of these people displaced by these atrocities joined up with the NRA, including children orphaned by the civil war.

Meanwhile there was also trouble within the UNLA – it was an ethnic division within the army, which was largely made up of Acholi and Langi, that was to lead to another change in leadership. This was led by the 2 Okello's (Tito and Basilio – not related) and occured in Jul 1985. Obote fled to Kenya and from there to Zambia and Tito Okello took over as president. The NRA did not join Okello but remained fighting and within a few months had taken over Fort Portal and Kasese in the W of the country. By the end of the year the NRA was within a few miles of Kampala. There were efforts at negotiation at a conference held in Nairobi and in late Dec a peace treaty was signed. However, just 3 weeks after the signing, Museveni's troops advanced on Kampala.

Museveni

Okello's troops fled N, Museveni was sworn in as the President and formed a broad-based government with ministries being filled by members of all the main political factions. However, in the N fighting continued. By the late 1980's under an amnesty offered to the rebels, almost 30,000 of them surrendered.

Museveni, however, has not been without his critics. An Amnesty International report published in late 1991 accused the NRA of torturing and summarily executing prisoners during the operations against the rebels in the N. The criticism most commonly aimed at Museveni, particularly by the Western donors, is his apparent avoidance of democratic elections. When he first came to power political parties were suspended and it was announced that there would be no elections for 3 years. In Oct 1989 the NRM extended the government's term of office to a further 5 years from Jan 1990, when their mandate was due to run out. Museveni argued that the time was not ready for political parties and that a new consitution had to be drawn up before elections could take place. In Mar 1990 the ban on political party activities was extended for a further 5 years.

Museveni has allowed the Kabaka (King) of Buganda to return to the country and to be crowned in an highly publicised ceremony in 1993. This was obviously immensely popular with the Baganda, although the government insists that his role will be purely cultural and ceremonial without any political function. Whether the Baganda will settle for this remains to be seen. The Asian community have been encouraged to return, and the property they relinquished on their departure has been restored. The Asians have been cautious, but they are once again filling positions in retailing, distribution and provision of skilled services.

Modern Uganda

Politics

Since independence in 1963, Uganda had 9 years of civilian government before a military coup in 1971 led to 8 years of capricious and chaotic rule by General Amin. Amin was overthrown by Tanzanian intervention, but despite the return of Obote, political institutions were weak, and the economy suffered from disruption by lawless groups. In 1985 there was a military coup followed by a takeover in 1986 by the National Resistance Army of Museveni.

Although Museveni has remained in power for 8 years, and brought political stability and economic recovery to the country, Uganda's appalling record makes him wary of a return to a multiparty political system. No new political structures appear to have emerged, and the parties waiting in the wings are based on the old groupings that fought the initial pre-independence election. Given that they failed on 2 occasions before, Museveni has little confidence that they would succeed now. In addition there is the restoraton of the Kabaka and the possible re-emergence of pressure for separation Buganda. If boxed completely into a corner by the international community (and Uganda is the only country in the region not committed to a multiparty system) it is thought Museveni will launch his own party incorporating key figures from other political groupings.

Museveni has continued to argue that multi-party democracy is not suited to Uganda which needs instead what he calls 'no party democracy' with representatives of the main factions involved in government. During 1993 the constituent assembly sat to discuss and amend the new constitution and in Apr 1994 elections were held on non-party lines.

Economics

Economic strategy has fluctuated with Obote initially pledged to pursue a socialist development path, followed by the chaos of the Amin years which included the expulsion of the skilled Asian community. The restored Obote regime relied on market forces, but lack of security prevented any substantial progress. Museveni spent a while considering development options, but now appears to have committed the government to an IMF supported market-oriented strategy.

Economic and social structure

The uplands in the E and W form the most densely populated areas, whereas the W has low population densities. The average density of population was 79 persons per square km in 1994, and this is high by African standards. Urbanisation, at 11%, as a result of the turmoil of recent years, is well below the African average. Many urban dwellers returned to the countryside to engage in subsistence production, and have been reluctant to return. Population growth at 2.5 % a year for 1980-91 has been slightly lower than is the norm in Africa, but is beginning to increase now that more stable conditions are returning.

GDP in 1991 was estimated at US$ 2,527m, making it roughly average for East Africa in terms of economic size. GNP per head was estimated at US$170,

BANANAS

There are a huge number of different banana species – there are sweet ones, those that are cooked and those used for making beer.

Matoke (green banana) is the main item of the Baganda diet. There are actually 14 varieties of matoke alone. These include *Muvubo, Musakala, Nakitembe, Kisubi, Ssiira, Nnambi* and *Manwoge*.

The sweet bananas eaten as fruit are known as *Ndizi* (the small ones) and *Bbogoya* (larger). Other varieties include *Gonja* which is eaten cooked – either baked, roasted or fried and which can be dried and stored. The main types used for making beer are *Kisubi, Mbidde and Kabula*.

and this places Uganda at the bottom end of the low-income group of countries. Agriculture provides the bulk of GDP, contributing 51% in 1991, and this is a higher dependence on this sector than is typical elsewhere in Africa. The industry sector provides only 12% of GDP, the services sector contributed 37% of GDP, and the contributions of industry and services are very low compared with other African countries.

On the demand side, private consumption was equivalent to 93% of GDP in 1991, and the low level of income means a high proportion of GDP needs to be allocated to consumption needs. Government consumption was 8% of GDP, investment was 12%, and these 3 categories are well below the African norm.

Exports are equivalent to 7% of GDP, and imports are 20%, the gap is covered by the net inflow of aid. Exports are predominantly coffee, providing 98% of the total with some of cotton and tea also sold overseas. Imports are mostly machinery (46%) and manufactures (38%), with fuel comprising 9% of the total.

The adult literacy rate was estimated at 52% in 1990, and this is above the African average. In 1989, enrolment in primary education was 76%, and in secondary education it was 15%, and at that time this was a rather better provision than on average elsewhere in Africa. The enrolment rate in tertiary education was 1%, and this is below the African average which is close to 2%.

Life expectancy in 1991 was 46, close to the African average of 51. In 1986, there were 21,830 persons per doctor and 2,050 persons per nurse, comparable with the average for the rest of Africa, and this is a considerable achievement given that many skilled professionals have migrated or been expelled since 1970. Average calorie supply, at 2,153 per person per day, is above the African average.

Overall, Uganda is a low-income country with an economy of about average size for the region. The turmoil of the past 2 decades has led to a reliance on agriculture for subsistence, which in turn has caused consumption to be emphasised at the expense of investment. Uganda takes limited advantage of the opportunities offered by trade. Educational and health provision are good considering the disruptions and migration of professionals which the country has experienced.

Ecomomic performance

GDP grew by 2.8% a year from 1980-90, and when population growth is taken into account, GDP per head rose by 0.3% a year. Agriculture, grew by 2.5% a year, a little slower than the rate of population increase. The industrial sector, boosted by the return of some skilled Asians has recovered well to grow at 5.5%, while the service sector, growing at 3.3% a year is also expanding faster than population.

Export volumes increased by 2.3% a year, over the past decade, and this compares favourably with the rest of Africa. Import volumes were able to grow faster than exports, at 3.6% a year, as a result of increases in aid inflows.

The inflation rate for 1980-90 was 107% a year, the highest in Africa, reaching 224% during 1987, and has been a real cause for concern. Salaries have not risen at the same rate, thus encouraging corruption and poor work performance, particularly in the public sector. Encouraged by Uganda's return to stability, the international community has increased its aid flows, and at close to 20%

COMPARATIVE ECONOMIC AND SOCIAL DATA

	Uganda	East Africa	Africa	Industrial Countries
POPULATION & LAND				
Population, mid year, millions, 1994	18.6	12.2	10.2	40.0
Urban population, %, 1991	11	30.5	30	75
Population growth rate, % per year, 1980-91	2.5	3.1	3.1	0.8
Land area, thou. sq. km.	236	486	486	1,628
Population density, persons per sq km., 1988	78.8	24.2	20.4	24.3
ECONOMY: PRODUCTION & INCOME				
GDP, US$ millions, 1991	2,527	2,650	3,561	550,099
GNP per head, US$, 1991	170	250	389	12,960
ECONOMY: SUPPLY STRUCTURE				
Agriculture, % of GDP, 1991	51	43	35	3
Industry, % of GDP, 1991	12	15	27	35
Services, % of GDP, 1991	37	42	38	61
ECONOMY: DEMAND STRUCTURE				
Private Consumption, % of GDP, 1991	93	77	73	62
Gross Domestic Investment, % of GDP, 1991	12	16	16	21
Government Consumption, % of GDP, 1991	8	15	14	17
Exports, % of GDP, 1991	7	16	23	17
Imports, % of GDP, 1991	20	24	26	17
ECONOMY: PERFORMANCE				
GDP growth, % per year, 1980-90	2.8	1.6	-0.6	2.5
GDP per head growth, % per year, 1980-90	0.3	-1.7	-3.7	1.7
Agriculture growth, % per year, 1980-90	2.5	1.1	0.0	2.5
Industry growth, % per year, 1980-90	5.5	1.1	-1.0	2.5
Services growth, % per year, 1980-90	3.3	2.5	-0.5	2.6
Exports growth, % per year, 1980-91	2.3	0.7	-1.9	3.3
Imports growth, % per year, 1980-91	3.6	0.2	-6.9	4.3
ECONOMY: OTHER				
Inflation Rate, % per year, 1980-90	107.0	23.6	16.7	5.3
Aid, net inflow, % of GDP, 1991	19.5	11.5	6.3	-
Debt Service, % of Exports, 1991	70.0	18	20.6	-
EDUCATION				
Primary, % of 6-11 group, 1989	76	62	76	102
Secondary, % of 12-17 group, 1989	15	15	22	93
Tertiary, % of 20-24 group, 1989	1	1.2	1.9	39
Adult Literacy Rate, %, 1990	52	41	39	99
HEALTH & NUTRITION				
Life Expectancy, years, 1991	46	50	50	76
Calorie Supply, daily per head, 1989	2,3153	2,111	2,096	3,357
Population per doctor, 1980	17,360	35,986	24,185	550

Notes: 'Africa' excludes South Africa. Dates are for the country in question, and do not always correspond with the Regional, African and Industrial averages.

of GDP, these are well above the African average. Uganda has increased its international borrowing, but has not been able to improve its export performance at the same rate, and debt service is now a high proportion of export revenues.

Overall, Uganda has had creditable expansion of GDP in the 1980s, with a small rise in GDP per head. Agricultural output is still slow to expand, industrial output is recovering well, as are services. Export expansion is still rather slow. Price stability has been the worst in Africa.

Recent economic developments

In May of 1987 President Museveni appeared to end the period of indecision over Uganda's economic strategy when agreement was reached on a programme which would see the IMF supplying US$76m and the World Bank US$100m in balance of payments support. The currency was exchanged with a substantial devaluation and a conversion tax, producer prices for export crops and import prices were raised. There have been large rises in domestic prices, but the government indicated that there would be no return to control of prices. Some of the properties returned to their former Asian owners were repossessed by the government after concern that the ownership claims were not valid, and this move is expected to discourage participation by Asian entrepreneurs. Administration and production continued to be hampered by shortages of skilled personnel.

The currency exchange introduced in May of 1987, together with a conversion tax of 80%, involved a substantial devaluation of the currency. The exchange rate for the new currency was initially set at USh 60 = US$1. Further devaluation of the currency has seen the rate depreciate to USh 370 = US$1 in 1994.

With improving security, and the resolution of Uganda's economic strategy, there has been an increase in aid commitments and substantial promises of new funds, mostly in infrastructure, health and education.

Economic outlook

Future prospects depend on maintaining political stability and internal security. The longer Uganda is able to maintain the current favourable conditions, the greater confidence will be and international business will be encouraged to expand investment. As things stand, Uganda can expect to enjoy slowly rising living standards, and this modest pace of improvement will accelerate if tourism and mining can be restored to the levels of the 1960s.

KAMPALA

Contents

Maps

The population of Kampala, the capital of Uganda, has increased in recent years to about 800,000. It is a compact city and the spread of suburbs is really a fairly recent phenomenon. The city centre is located about 7 km to the N of Port Bell on the shore of Lake Victoria and the average height above sea level is 1,230m. It is a friendly city and in the last few years security has improved dramatically so that a nightlife is beginning again. Accommodation in the city is rather limited, and relatively expensive. The city was always known for its greenery, but in recent times much of this has been lost. Makerere University, at one time the intellectual centre of East Africa but now sadly faded, is located in the city outskirts.

History

Early Days

The name Kampala came from a Bantu word Mpala meaning a type of antelope which, it is said, the Buganda chiefs used to keep on the slope of a hill near Mengo Palace. The name Hill of the Mpala was given specifically to the hill on which Captain Fredrick Lord Lugard, a British Administrator, established his fort in Dec 1890. At the Fort, which was also an administrative post, Lugard hoisted the Imperial British East African Company flag in 1890, which in 1893 was replaced by the Union Jack. The Fort at Kampala Hill as it became known (now known as Old Kampala Hill) attracted several hundred people and a small township developed.

As time went on traders erected shops at the base of the hill, and by 1900, the confines of the Fort had become too small for administrative purposes and it was decided that the Colonial Offices and government residences that were in Kampala (at this time most offices were at Entebbe) should be moved to Nakesero Hill. The shops and other commercial premises followed.

Kampala grew and the town spread over the surrounding hills – until it became known, like Rome, to be built on 7 hills. These historical hills are Rubaga, Namirembe (Mengo), Makerere, Kololo, Kibuli, Kampala (Old Kampala) and Mulago. On top of 3 of these hills, Rubaga, Namirembe and Kibuli, places of worship were built – Catholic, Protestant and Muslim respectively.

In 1906 Kampala was declared a township, and the railway joining Kampala with the coast reached Kampala in 1915. In 1949 it was raised to municipality status, in 1962 it became a city and in Oct of the same year, it was declared the capital. The city has continued to grow and now covers 23 hills over an area of nearly 200 sq km.

Independence and after

Like the rest of Uganda Kampala has suffered enormously in recent years. Prior to these years Kampala had developed into a green city – it was spacious and well laid out and had developed into the cultural and educational centre of Eastern Africa. During the Amin period the most dramatic changes to Kampala came with the expulsion of the Asian

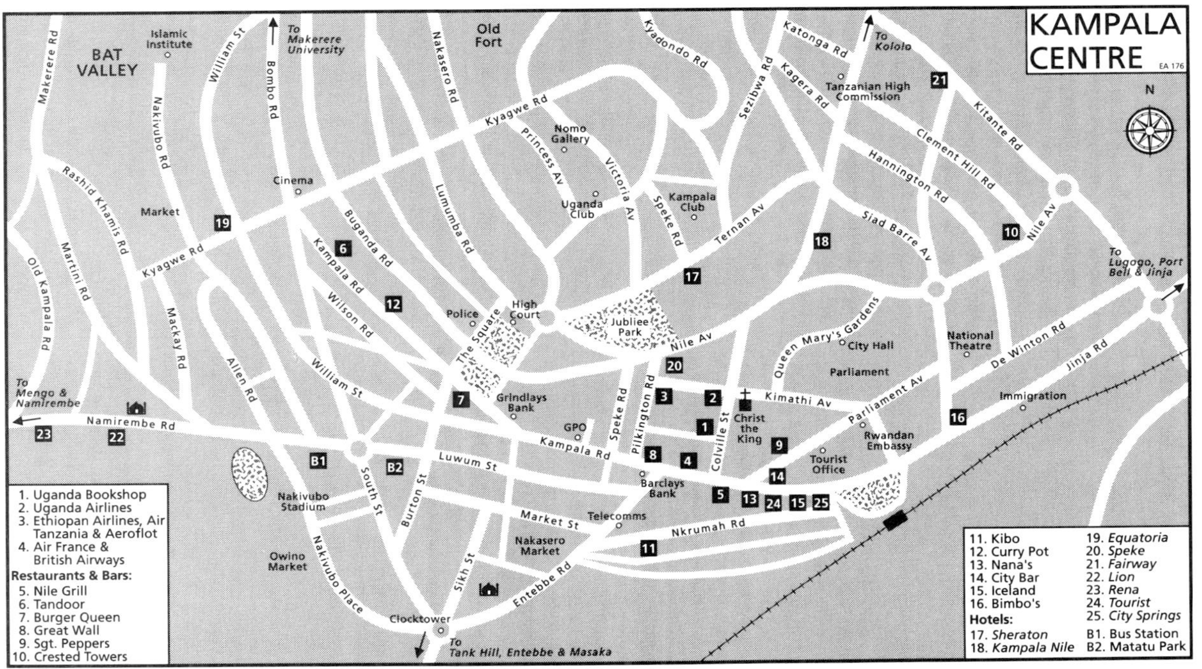
KAMPALA CENTRE
EA 176
N
To Makerere University
To Kololo
To Lugogo, Port Bell & Jinja
To Mengo & Namirembe
To Tank Hill, Entebbe & Masaka
BAT VALLEY
Islamic Institute
Old Fort
Makerere Rd
William St
Bombo Rd
Nakasero Rd
Kyadondo Rd
Katonga Rd
Kagera Rd
Sezibwa Rd
Tanzanian High Commission
Kitante Rd
Clement Hill Rd
Hannington Rd
Kyagwe Rd
Nomo Gallery
Princess Av
Victoria Av
Nakivubo Rd
Rashid Khamis Rd
Cinema
Market
Lumumba Rd
Uganda Club
Speke Rd
Kampala Club
Ternan Av
Siad Barre Av
Nile Av
Buganda Rd
Kampala Rd
Old Kampala Rd
Martini Rd
Mackay Rd
Wilson Rd
Police
The Square
High Court
Jubilee Park
Queen Mary's Gardens
City Hall
National Theatre
De Winton Rd
Jinja Rd
Parliament
Allen Rd
William St
Grindlays Bank
Pilkington Rd
Kimathi Av
Christ the King
Parliament Av
Immigration
Namirembe Rd
GPO
Colville St
Rwandan Embassy
Tourist Office
Luwum St
South St
Burton St
Barclays Bank
Nakivubo Stadium
Market St
Telecomms
Nkrumah Rd
Nakasero Market
Owino Market
Nakivubo Place
Sikh St
Entebbe Rd
Clocktower
1. Uganda Bookshop
2. Uganda Airlines
3. Ethiopan Airlines, Air Tanzania & Aeroflot
4. Air France & British Airways
Restaurants & Bars:
5. Nile Grill
6. Tandoor
7. Burger Queen
8. Great Wall
9. Sgt. Peppers
10. Crested Towers
11. Kibo
12. Curry Pot
13. Nana's
14. City Bar
15. Iceland
16. Bimbo's
Hotels:
17. Sheraton
18. Kampala Nile
19. Equatoria
20. Speke
21. Fairway
22. Lion
23. Rena
24. Tourist
25. City Springs
B1. Bus Station
B2. Matatu Park

community. Until then trade was almost entirely in the hands of Asians and because of this large areas of the town itself were Asian-owned. Apart from their residences – which were concentrated around Old Kampala – their businesses were also handed over to officials in the Amin administration and these premises were allowed to gradually fall apart. By the early to mid-1980's there were many business premises and blocks of flats that had not been touched for over a decade and were very delapidated.

With the return of stability to the country Kampala has also gradually been recovering. One of the most obvious of these changes is the sight of premises that have been refurbished from top to bottom. Many of these are in fact Asian properties which have been returned to their original owners as part of Museveni's attempts to attract investment to the country. Other buildings have also been renovated and the roads repaired, and Kampala is gradually smartening itself up. Having said that, there are still parts of the city that remain in a very poor state of repair.

Visitors to Kampala often comment on the greeness of the city and the number of trees. Much of this has been lost in the last 5 to 10 years. This is due to 2 factors. Firstly there has been a massive building boom since 1986 in Kampala, and this has led to previously empty areas being divided up and built on. One example of this is Kitante Valley (which runs from the golf course to the museum) which a few years ago was public land, on which pupils at Kitante School used to go cross country running. It has now been built up almost entirely. Secondly the bricks used for building are made locally and they are made by being baked in furnaces which are fuelled by woodfuel. As you drive into Kampala you may notice these furnaces dotted all over the countryside – trying to keep up with the tremendous demand for bricks – and in the process decimating Kampala's trees.

Places of interest

Kisubi Tombs

These are situated a few km out of town on Nabulagala Hill off the Kampala-Hoima Road. They are the site of the tombs of the Kings known as the Kabakas of Buganda. The site contains the tombs of Muteesa I (1856-1884), Mwanga II (1884-1897), Sir Daudi Chwa (1897-1939), and Edward Muteesa II (1939-1966). Mwanga II was exiled to the Seychelles in 1899, died there in 1903 and his body was returned to Uganda and buried at Kisubi in 1910. The last of the Kabaka's, Muteesa II was removed from his position soon after independence during the Obote I regime and died 3 years later in 1969 in London. His body was returned to Uganda in 1971 and buried at Kisubi in an attempt by Amin to appease the Baganda. During Museveni's rule Muteesa II's son has been allowed to return to Uganda and in Jul 1993 he was crowned as the Kabaka at Budo.

The tombs are open from 0900 to 1800 throughout the week and there is a small charge, and for this you will get a very knowledgeable guide. The largest building, which is the tomb house, is called *Muzibu-Azaala-Mpanga*. It is a large thatched round house which although it can be said to reflect traditional Ganda architecture is actually a modern structure built during the colonial period by a British company of architects. You can have a look at the plans for the building in the small shop. There is a guidebook for sale in the shop, as well as a variety of souvenirs.

There is a 2-doored house, *Bujjabukula* which you pass through as you enter the main enclosure, as well as the drum house *Ndoga-Obukaba*. There are also a number of smaller buildings of similar design around the outside, within the inner enclosure. Originally there was an outer fence that enclosed the whole of the area – over 6 km in length as well as the inner wall – but only the inner wall remains.

Just outside the main tomb to the right is a small cannon which was presented to the Kabaka Muteesa I as a gift by Speke and Grant in 1862. Visitors remove their shoes, enter to sit in the cool, dark interior on mats. There are pictures of the different Kabakas and some of their belongings – including a large number of spears and a stuffed

The Coronation Of The Kabaka

This event eventually took place at the end of July 1993. There had been a number of delays from when it was first announced that the son of Edward Muteesa II could return to Uganda and be crowned. An amendment had to be made to the constitution and it was made clear that the new Kabaka would not have any political powers but merely would be a cultural leader. The occasion also gave rise to much discussion as to the future of the other four kingdoms in Uganda – the people of at least one of these kingdoms (the Ankole) did not want their king to return.

Finally it was declared that the coronation could go ahead and suddenly the Baganda found they had a huge amount to organize before the great day. There were invitations to be sent out, a hill-top to clear, large grass thatched constructions to be built, a road to be surfaced, not to mention all the traditional rituals that the *Sabataka* (the one who was to be King) had to perform before he could be pronounced the Kabaka. These included the tuning of the drums and a series of visits to culturally important sites around Buganda.

In the weeks before the coronation day hoards of volunteers gathered at the site at Namugongo near the famous Kings College, Budo, and set about clearing the hill-top. Groups of women sat around cleaning and preparing the reeds used for the construction of walls of the buildings. They were dressed in the Ugandan *busuti*, many made from bark cloth. The atmosphere was one of great anticipation, and they frequently broke into song.

Eventually the great day arrived. Events began at day break with a mock cane fight in which the *Sabataka* had to prove his worthiness to become the Kabaka. Thousands of people began to arrive in traditional dress and gathered on the hill top. It is a wonderful site, with fantastic views of Buganda all around, and as the sun rose, the mist gradually cleared.

Foreign dignitaries took their places in the shade of a pavilion. President Museveni and his wife were the last of the guests to arrive and the president was greeted extremely warmly as the Baganda thanked him for returning their King to them. The ceremony was split into two parts – the first being the traditional one under a tree, and the second, in view of many more people, was the religious ceremony when prayers were said. The *Sabataka* was carried into the enclosure where the coronation was to take place and took his seat on a barkcloth-covered throne underneath the traditional tree. As part of the ritual he prodded a cow (in the past he would have killed it) and as the ceremony progressed he was dressed in layers of barkcloth covered by animal skins.

Just after the actual crowning dark clouds started to gather and the wind suddenly rose. There had been no rain in the area for a few weeks and now it looked as if there was to be a thunderstorm, which would forebode ill. But after just a few spots of rain the clouds cleared and the sun came out – as the Bagandans said: God is being kind to us.

leopard. The main hut is divided into 2 by a barkcloth curtain behind which are the actual tombs. The area with the actual tombs is called *Kibira,* and is closed to visitors. Each of the graves has a corresponding platform just outside the *Kibira*.

The descendants of the wives of the Kabaka's live in huts around the main tomb and look after it – they are usually sitting inside making mats – and you are expected to leave a tip for them in the bowls provided. The duty that they perform is called *Ejisanja* – looking after the house and making mats.

The Kabaka's Lake

Located close to the Kabaka's capital this lake was constructed from about 1885 to 1888 by Kabaka Mwanga. The original plan was to link it up with Lake Victoria but this was not to be as Mwanga was deposed. The lake got into a fairly terrible state and by 1993 was very stagnant. However, before the coronation many Baganda got together and cleared out the debris. The Kabaka-to-be reopened the lake and unveiled a statue to Mwanga.

Namugongo Shrine

The Namugongo Martyrs Shrine is located about 12 km out of Kampala off the Jinja Road. This is the site were 22 Ugandan Christian converts were burnt to death on the orders of Kabaka Mwanga in 1886. On the visit of Pope Paul VI to Uganda in 1969 the victims were canonized and since then the shrine has been an important site for Ugandan Christians. On the site there are 2 churches – one built by the Roman Catholic Church, and the other by the Church of Uganda. The steel structure, built in traditional style, has artistic work on its interiors depicting scenes from this important episode in Uganda's religious history and, in the centre, preserved in glass, are some of the remains of one of the martyrs, Kaloli-Lwanga. Nearby is an artificial lake that is believed to have been formed from a well that belonged to one of the Kabaka's soldiers who was staying in the area. There is a public holiday every year on Jun 3rd in remembrance of the martyrs.

Kampala Museum

Located out of the town centre on the Kira Road, open 0900 to 1700, and there is a small entrance fee. Most of the displays have been renovated and the rest are in the process of being restored. Many of the items were looted during 1970-86 and a big effort is being made to return the museum to its former standard. Displays include a number of items from archaeological sites from around the country; a collection of musical instruments including many drums and a large and impressive canoe. Every so often the museum holds live traditional music afternoons.

Nommo Gallery

This small building is Uganda's National Art Gallery where art work by local artists as well from other parts of East Africa are displayed. Exhibitions are advertised in the local press, but there is invariably something on display. There is also a shop attached with both artworks and crafts available. It was once a private house and is set in spacious grounds. It is located in Kololo on Victoria Avenue – there is a signpost opposite the main *Sheraton* entrance gate and is open from 0900 to 1700 on weekdays, and from 0900 to 1500 on weekends.

National Theatre

The National Theatre is located on Dewinton Street at the end of Parliament Avenue. It was built in the 1950s and first opened in 1959. There is something presented most weekends – dances, drama and music. There is a notice board outside that announces the events planned. The British Council

The Uganda Museum

The possibility of establishing a museum in Kampala was first put forward in 1907 when the grand sum of £200 was allocated for the purpose. The Officer in Charge of the Botanical, Forestry and Scientific Department, Mr Dawe, was informed that the collection of items for display should begin immediately or the money would lapse. Circulars were sent out to a number of private individuals as well as to Colonial Officials asking for exhibits.

Within a matter of months a considerable number of items had been collected and until a permanent building was built they were housed at Coronation House in Kampala. The original museum was built on the site of the Old Fort in Kampala and when the contents outgrew their home it was moved to the larger site currently in use. Sadly many of the specimens collected in the earlier period of the museum's history no longer survive.

shows films here once a month, and the Alliance Française holds French classes here. Occasionally there are visiting musicians from around the world – they are usually advertised in main daily paper *New Vision* and on posters around town.

Parliament Buildings

The Parliament Buildings complex is located on Parliament Avenue (the road that has undergone the most name changes in Kampala – it has been Obote Avenue twice and this is the third time it has been Parliament Avenue) and is the seat of the Uganda Government. The archway at the entrance is the symbol of Uganda's independence and on it there are often perched what must be one of the world's ugliest birds – the marabou stork. If you look at the pillars from behind you will notice that there are quite a few gun shot holes – only the ones at the front have been filled in. On the metal gates at the entrance there are the emblems of the original districts of Uganda. Inside, at the entrance to the main Chambers (which is far as visitors can go) there are engravings representing the different modes of life in all the districts.

Makerere University

This is the oldest University in East Africa and for many years had a fine international reputation. However, it has suffered greatly in the past 2 decades and is now struggling to return to its former high standards. Despite the rather shabby look at present, the original impressive appearance is unmistakable. The main campus contains the administrative buildings, the academic faculties, the library, 7 halls of residence, the Guesthouse, staff residences as well as recreational facilities include the Student Guild and a swimming pool. Within the Faculty of Fine Art there is a gallery which holds exhibitions of students works and is open from 1000 to 1800 Mon to Sat.

Sikh and Hindu Temples

In the town centre close to the matatu park are 2 temples – one Hindu and the other Sikh. One of these was used as a school for some years but has now returned to its original use.

Kibuli Mosque

On Kibuli Hill is the mosque, which as a result of recent cutting down of trees is now visible from Kampala town centre. Prayers are held here 5 times a day.

Bana'i Temple On Gayaza Rd, Kikaya Hill. 6km from city centre. Only temple of this faith in Africa. Excellent views of city.

Namirembe Cathedral

This brick red Anglican Cathedral, with its impressive dome is visible from much of Kampala and is located at the top of Mengo. Particularly interesting is the graveyard which includes the graves of both the Cooks (who established Mengo Hospital) and the remains of Bishop Hannington – who was murdered in 1885 (see box, page 436). The congregation is called to the service by the beating of drums instead of by bells and is you are staying at *Namirembe Guesthouse* you will certainly hear them.

Rubaga Cathedral

This is the Catholic Cathedral and was restored in preparation for the visit of the Pope to Uganda. It is a huge building and has an illuminated cross outside. Inside the Cathedral are the remains of the first African Catholic Bishop and the first African Archbishop of Kampala Diocese, Joseph Kiwanuka.

Bahai Temple

The Bahai Temple is situated about 4km out of Kampala on Kikaya hill off the Gayaza Road. It is the only Temple of the Bahai religion that is found in Africa. This religion believes that each religious manifestation forms a successive chapter in one great and continuous revelation of God. People of all faiths are therefore welcome to visit this temple for prayer and meditation at any time. There are services held here on Sundays at 1030. A wonderful view of the Temple can be seen from the end of Kira Road in Kampala, just beyond the Museum to the left. From the temple itself there are excellent views of Kampala and the surrounding countryside.

Excursions from Kampala

Pleasant day-trips, either in your own vehicle or by public transport, can be made to **Entebbe** (see page 433), **Jinja** (see page 434) and the **Mpanga Forest Reserve** (see page 454).

Local information

● Where to stay

Price guide:
A+ Over US$100; **A** US$40-100;
B US$20-40; **C** US$10-20; **D** US$5-10; **E** Under US$5.

A+ ***Sheraton***, PO Box 7041, Ternan Avenue, T 244590/7, F 256696. Located in the town centre the *Sheraton* has been totally renovated. It is set in well maintained gardens – which used to be part of a public park but were quietly absorbed and fenced in by the hotel. It has a squash court and a swimming pool which is only open to residents and to those who pay the annual fee of US$350. There are conference facilities for up to 450 people. There is the outdoor Lion Bar which does snacks and a buffet – it is fairly pricey but the food is good. In the foyer there is a coffee bar which has CNN and BBC World Service Television. Most Sundays there is a band playing in Leopards' Gardens. The Rhino Pub has draught lager, a pool table and darts.

A ***Kampala Nile Hotel***, PO Box 7057, Nile Avenue, T 235900/9, F 259130. Recently refurbished. Swimming pool, bars and restaurants. **A** ***Equatoria***, Junction of Bombo Road and Kyagwe Road. This is a newly refurbished, Indian-owned hotel. It has 2 restaurants including the excellent ***Chop Sticks*** with Chinese cuisine.

B ***Speke***, Speke Ave. One of the oldest hotels in town and has recently been renovated. It is very attractive, but the staff are very casual. **B** ***Fairway***, PO Box 4595, 1/2 Kafu Road, T 259570/5. Located opposite the Golf Course close to the Kampala Club this is an attractive hotel with nice grounds. It is also one of the more friendly hotels in Kampala.

C ***Colline***, PO Box 7, T 290212. Located in Mukono about 20 km to the E of Kampala. Signposted on the left of the road. There is traditional music and drumming most Sundays afternoons. **C** ***Diplomat***, Tank Hill. Out of the hustle and noise of the city centre. **C** ***Reste Corner***, PO Box 9153, Tank Hill, T 267685. Fairly modern. **C** ***Antler's Inn***, Bat Valley, opposite *Uganda Crafts*. Nicer than it looks from the outside. It caters mainly for businessmen, and if you are planning to be in town for a fairly long time you can usually negotiate for a reduction in the price. The staff are very helpful and friendly and it is good value. Restaurant that does breakfast only.

D *Lion*, PO Box 6751, Namirembe Rd, T 243490. Clean and comfortable. Hot water. Good value. **D** *Makerere University Guest House*, University campus. Biggest problem with it is the noise from the Student Guild which has loud music until late at night. Rooms facing away from the Guild are quieter. Food is available (both European and African). Breakfast is included. **D** *Rena*, Namirembe Rd. On the way up to the Cathedral. Shared bathrooms. Bar and restaurant. Very good value. **D** *Silver Spring*, on the Port Bell road. There are either small cottages, or cheaper bandas which are particularly popular. There is a swimming pool which is free to guests, a gym and sauna. There is a restaurant and bar. Excellent value. **D** *Namirembe Guest House*, Mengo, close to Mengo hospital, and just below the Cathedral. There are is a range of rooms – singles, triples and dormitories – in the original building and in the new extension. The extension has hot water showers and is generally nicer, but more expensive. Some dormitory accommodation. **D** *College Inn*, Wandegaya, close to the university campus. It is a friendly place and is clean although rather basic.

E *Tourist Motel*, Kampala Road, Jinja Road end. Central. Not bad value for its location although the rooms are nothing special. Basic meals available. **E** *St John Bugolobi Guest House*, on the Port Bell road. Popular with travellers. Clean and friendly. Good value. **E** *YMCA*, Bat Valley. Popular with campers and backpackers and is probably the cheapest place in town. It is however very basic – you have the choice of the floor (with a mattress if they haven't run out) or camping outside. The main problem it suffers from is that during the day it acts as a school – so you have to pack up and move out by 0700. If you have a tent you can camp in the grounds, although being on the main road you have little privacy at all and security is poor. Having said all this the staff are friendly and for years it has been the best place to meet other travellers. **E** *Natete Hostel*, PO Box 3690, Natate. The newest (1993) and probably the best of all the budget accommodation in Kampala. It is run by a friendly Australian who is working on a sustainable agriculture project. There is the choice of double rooms, dormitory, floor space or camping space. Cooking facilities are available and there is a good notice board. The only slight disadvatage being its location which is a little way out of Kampala. To get to Natete take a matatu from the centre of town.

● Camping

See *YMCA* and *Natete Hostel* above.

● Places to eat

Price guide:
♦♦♦♦Over US$10; ♦♦♦US$5-10; ♦♦US$2-5; ♦Under US$2

♦♦♦♦***The Lion Restaurant***, at the *Sheraton* does a buffet lunch which is popular. Also at the *Sheraton* there are other restaurants and snack bars – they are rather expensive but the quality of the food is excellent.

♦♦♦♦***Sitar's***, Bat Valley. Indian restaurant is generally considered to be the best in town. The menu is extensive, the food is excellent and there is a nice atmosphere.

♦♦♦***Nile Grill***, Uganda House, Kampala Road. This popular drinking spot also does some food. Useful meeting place. There are regularly live bands in the evenings when it is packed to overflowing. ♦♦♦***Tandoor Restaurant***, Kampala Road (the Bombo Road end). Formerly the Odeon Cinema. Downstairs is ***Fido Dido***, which serves ice-cream and snacks. Very clean and modern. Excellent ice-cream. ♦♦♦***Burger Queen***, Kampala Road opposite City Square, upstairs. There are seats inside as well as outside on the cool balcony. International and African food with a good selection of hamburgers, steaks and fish. Try fish fingers – rather different to the Birds Eye variety. Good standard and value. ♦♦♦***China Great Wall***, Kampala Road near the Diamond Trust building. Chinese cuisine. Generous portions and good standard. ♦♦♦***Sergeant Peppers***, off Parliament Avenue, close to British High Commission. Pizzas. ♦♦♦***Fasika***, Kabalagala. Located in the village at the bottom of Tank Hill, just off the Gaba Road in Kabalagala. Serves traditional Ethiopian food and on Wed and Sat there is a buffet. It is the best way of sampling Ethiopian food as you get a chance to try a bit of everything.

♦♦***Nectarine Bar and Restaurant Crested Towers***, Siad Barre Avenue – this has become a fashionable hang out in recent years. It has rather an odd atmosphere however, and is more of a bar than restaurant. ♦♦***Kibo Restaurant***, Nkrumah Road, opposite UCB Building. Fish and chips and other basics. ♦♦***Curry Pot***, Kampala Rd, Bat Valley end. It has a rather limited menu but the food is alright. ♦♦***Nana's***, Kampala Rd, close to the *Nile Grill* in the

The Canoe Regatta At Munyonyo

The landing site at Munyonyo has a history dating from the late 19th century and from the time of Kabaka Muteesa I. It was used by Kabakas from Muteesa onwards and canoe races were first introduced during the reign of Daudi Chwa – however, it was not until 1986 that the modern races were reinstated.

In 1871 Kabaka Muteesa I fell in love with the place and a hunting lodge was built for him there. Here he could indulge in some of his favourite pastimes – canoeing on the lake and hunting for hippos. After embracing the Moslem faith, Muteesa I used his lodge at Munyonyo during the month of Ramadan as a retreat. He ordered the construction of two canoes which he named *Waswa* and *Mbaliga*. These were used by later Kabakas after Muteesa's death in 1884.

Following Muteesa's death his seventeen-year-old son, Mwanga Basammula, became Kabaka. He also used the lodge at Munyonyo – especially when his palace at Mengo was undergoing repairs following a fire.

Kabaka Daudi Chwa also used Munyonyo for a place for relaxation, and he was the first of the Kabakas to hold an organized canoe race. In turn his son, Muteesa II, also spent time at the lakeside, buying a yacht which he named *Nguwu*. This was kept at Munyonyo until the political unrest of the mid-1960s between the Baganda and the Obote Government which resulted in the Kabaka's exile. The yacht was taken by government troops to Luzira where it remains.

In 1986, when peace began to return to Uganda, a group of Baganda royalists got together and organized a canoe race to mark the centenary of the Uganda Martyrs. One year later it was repeated in the presence of Prince Ronnie Mutebi. Since then it has become an annual event and in 1993 it was brought forward to July so that it could be part of the coronation celebrations.

Munyonyo is a small landing site on Lake Victoria which is located down the Gaba Road. Normally a *matatu* goes as far as the turning off the main road and then there is a walk to the shore, but on the day of the regatta you will have no problems getting public transport all the way. Food and drink are available – mainly roasted meat and roasted maize. On the day of the races a festive mood descends on the area and thousands of Baganda arrive for a day out. The men are dressed up in the traditional white *kanzus*, the women in brightly coloured *busutis*, many wearing hats to show which clan they support. In past years the teams all represented clans of the Baganda. However, at the 1993 race there was a change to the rules and the teams represented clubs rather than clans. This meant that a European team was able to enter, proving extremely popular with the crowd as they were thoroughly beaten in every race.

Once the guests of honour have arrived and taken their places the teams set off. There are a number of races. In the first the teams race to the nearby island and back. The major race of the day is also the longest and that is all the way around the nearby island. During much of the race the teams are out of sight and dancers and musicians entertain the crowds. It is also possible, on payment of a small fee, to go for a trip in one of the motor canoes that follow the racing canoes during the contest. As the boats turn the corner of the island the attention of the crowd returns to the race as the onlookers strain their eyes to see who is leading. As they come closer the cheering begins, and if the race looks likely to be close the crowds go wild. Part of the tactics involves trying ram other competitors. It is altogether an exciting and entertaining day out.

Uganda House complex. Although not as popular as the Nile it is just as pleasant with seats outside. The service is good and it serves good fruit juices and snacks. *******Bimbo Ice Cream Parlour***, Siad Barre Ave. Ice cream is variable.

Airlines

International Air Tanzania, Airline House, 1 Kimathi Avenue, T 234631/134673. **British Airways**, Kampala Road, T 256695/257414. **EgyptAir Metroploe**, 8/10 Entebbe Road, T 241276/233960. **Ethiopian Airlines**, Airline House, 1 Kimathi Avenue, T 254796/7. **Kenya Airways**, Airline House, 1 Kimathi Avenue, T 256506/259721. **Sabena**, *Sheraton Hotel* Arcade, T 259880/234200. **Uganda Airlines**, Airline House, 1 Kimathi Ave, T 232990. **Zambia Airlines**, 1 Kimathi Avenue, T 244082/ 244067.

Air services: domestic and charter Anyone hoping to see Uganda, particularly the N, who is short of time and wants some comfort is likely to use one of the charter airlines. ***Bel Air Ltd***, Spear House, T 242733/243800. ***Speedbird Aviation Services***, PO Box 10101, Kampala, T 231290/231729, 1st Floor, *Sheraton Hotel* Arcade or *National Insurance Building*. Airport Office, T Entebbe 042 20689.

Banks

Barclays, PO Box 2971, Kampala Rd, T 232597. **Grindlays**, PO Box 485, Kampala Road, T 230074/231151. **Standard Chartered Bank**, PO Box 7111, Speke Road, T 258211.

Embassies (E), High Commissions (HC) and Consulates (C)

Belgium (E), NIC Building, Pilkington Rd. **Burundi** (E), Nehru Ave, Nakasero. **Denmark** (E), T 256783/256687/250938/250926. **France** (E), PO Box 7218, Embassy House, 9/11 Parliament Avenue, T 24210/242176. **Germany** (E), PO Box 7294, 24/26 Kololo Hill Drive, T 241721/231334. **Italy** (E), PO Box 4646, 11 Laurdel Road, Nakasero, T 241786/256416. **Kenya** (HC), PO Box 5220, 60 Kira Road, T 231861/233146. **Norway** (E), Barclays Bank Building, Kampala Rd. **Rwanda** (E), 2 Nakaima Rd. **Switzerland** (C), PO Box 4187, T 67305/41574. **Tanzania** (HC), PO Box 5750, 6 Kagera Road, T 256755. **UK** (HC), PO Box 7070, 10/12 Parliament Avenue, T 257054/257303. **USA** (E), PO Box 7007, British High Commission Building, 10/12 Parliament Avenue, T 259791/2/3. **Zaire** (E), 20 Philip Rd.

The following countries handle diplomatic affairs for Uganda from their Nairobi Embassies or High Commissions (see page 65): **Australia, Austria, Canada, Japan, Greece, Zimbabwe, Zambia**.

Entertainment

Bars *Slow Boat*, next to the *China Great Wall* and a comfortable bar. ***Kabalagala***. This is one of the areas on the outskirts of Kampala that established themselves as night spots when it was not safe to drive across town. Originally there were mainly shops with just a couple of bars which served warm beers – now it is lively with bars, restaurants, and well-stocked shops. The bars have chairs outside on the pavement and include the ***Tex Bar*** (one of the oldest) and the ***Afrianex***. ***Half London***, Gaba Road beyond the turning for Tank Hill. Thriving and popular place for eating and drinking. There is often a live band here and it can be too noisy to talk. However there is a good atmosphere and the service is fairly good. There is food available – steak, fish, chips and excellent pizzas.

Music See the *New Vision* for announcements of where the local bands are playing. Particularly popular are ***Afrigo*** and the ***Waka Waka Band***, *Nile Grill*, Kampala Rd. One of the most popular places in town, particularly for the wealthier section of the Kampala community. On Thursdays to Fridays there is usually a live band and singers. Members of the audience will often get up on the stage and join them.

Nightspots *Ange Noir*, 2nd Street, Industrial Area. Currently the hottest nightspot in town. They have recently introduced a dress code – dress smartly and no flip flops. They also have a large notice at the entrance saying No firearms allowed and its not a joke. At time of writing they have different music on each night of the week – for example Sat is disco, Sun is African – but in practice by the end of the evening there is little difference. This is the only club in Kampala that has fluorescent lights, nets on the ceiling, even a smoke machine. ***Tropicana***, Jinja Road opposite the station, this has a reputation for being a particularly popular spot for young single men looking for company. ***The Crocodile***, *Sheraton Hotel*. Open weekends. Occasionally has bands. ***Little Flowers***, Bat Valley Part of the Uganda Crafts /UNICEF/ and Sitar restaurant complex. Not as popular as it used to be, but still blasts its music across Bat Valley. ***Starlight***, close to Nakasero Market on the Kampala Road side.

From the outside it looks very unimpressive and a bit of a dive. Inside the bar and dance floor are actually outdoors, in a sort of courtyard – it is very popular with local people. Foreigners and travellers here are relatively rare, although it is very friendly.

● Foreign exchange bureaux

The relaxation of the foreign exchange regulations has meant that there are a large number of foreign exchange bureau all over town. These offer a quick and efficient service 5 days a week, and on Sat mornings. The rates around town may vary by a few shillings but not by an enormous amount. Banks also change money – but it takes longer, and they are only open in the mornings.

● Hospitals and medical services.

There are several hospitals but the quality of care varies. ***Nsambya***, PO Box 7161, T 268016, a private Catholic Mission hospital was undoubtedly the best through the difficult years although the difference is now reduced. ***Mulago***, adjoining Makerere University, PO Box 7161, T 268016. Has had an enormous amount of foreign aid invested in it and although the infrastructure is much improved (there is running water etc), and there are doctors available. Many of the staff suffer from apathy (not really surprising considering the wages that they get paid) and it is necessary to pay to get the necessary attention. You will also have to buy almost all the necessary drugs at local pharmacies.

● Post Office

The main Post Office is situated in the centre of town on Kampala Road and is open from 0830 to 1700.

● Shopping and bookshops

Bookshops *Uganda Bookshop* Colville St just past the Blacklines building, off Kampala Road. It is one of the best bookshops in town but even here the stock is fairly limited. Other bookshops around Kampala tend to mainly sell stationery and text books.

General shopping *Minimarket*, Kampala Rd Located in the new shopping centre opposite City Square on this supermarket is run by a European and caters largely for the expatriate community. Prices are high and most of the goods are imported. ***Hot Loaf Bakery***, Kampala Rd, next door to the *Nile Grill*. Actual bakery is out on the Jinja Road. Apart from many different breads it sells lovely pastries, pizzas and croissants. ***Beaton's Cookies***, Kampala Rd, just round the corner from *Hot Loaf*, in the same shopping complex. Small shop which specializes in cookies. Expensive by Ugandan standards – but very good. ***Nakasero Market***, Town centre. The largest and best fruit and vegetable market in the town centre. The prices are slightly high because this is mainly catering for expatriates. It is divided into 2, and all around the edge are small shops. In the lower market (built in 1929) there are stalls with a wonderful range of unusual spices. As you approach the market you will be inundated with offers from boys to carry your bag. ***Owino Market***, by the Nakivubo Stadium sells everything from pots, pans, sheets, bags, clothes. As with all similar markets you should be prepared to bargain. There is also a large second-hand clothes section and if you pick carefully you will be able to find very good quality. Do not be surprised if you find designer labels from the West going very cheap here. Any repairs or alterations can be done for you while you wait. ***Shauri Yako Market***, by the Nakivubo Stadium is particularly good for second-hand clothes from Europe. Don't be put off by the idea of buying second-hand here – the quality is usually very good and you will always pick up a bargain.

Handicrafts *Uganda Crafts* This is the largest craft shop in Uganda and has a wide range of products from all over East Africa. The goods are made by the disabled. There is a Uganda Crafts Village on the Entebbe Road. Prices are fixed and the quality generally fairly good.

● Sport (participant)

Climbing and Trekking Mountain Club of Uganda. John Woodall (Chairman) Room 5.21, Ministry of Finance, T 241772 or Deo Lubega (Secretary) Room 1A8 Blacklines House, T 254240.

Golf Located on Kitante Rd opposite the *Fairway Hotel*. Uganda Golf Course has 18 holes. Club Secretary, PO Box 624, Kampala, T 257345.

● Sport (spectator)

Canoe Racing Annual event, the date of which has varied (most recently in Jul). At Munyonyo on Lake Victoria (see box, page 426).

Cricket Lugogo, on the Jinja Road. Regular games between local clubs. Europeans, Indians and Africans all participate.

Football The most popular sport in Uganda. Matches at the Nakivubo War Memorial Stadium near the taxi park. As well as international matches for the Africa Cup, there are also league matches. Supporters are extremely loyal. Even if you are not a great football fan you will find the occasion fun.

Kololo Indoor Stadium Near Lugogo on Jinja Road. Tennis, cricket and hockey.

● Telecommunications

International telephone calls can be made from the card phones outside the post office and you can ask your caller to return your call to one of the phones inside the post office. This system works very well and efficiently – the numbers to receive calls on are 232805, 257527, and 257218. Buy your card and make the call and then be sure to go and tell the operator (at the counter round the corner on the right at the far end) your name and that you are expecting a call.

● Tourist office

The Ministry of Tourism, Wildlife and Antiquities, PO Box 4241, 1 Parliament Ave, T 232971/2, F 241247. Here the staff and friendly but have little in the way of maps and information to give out. They often have one copy of various information sheets – but none for sale. If you are desperate it is possible to get photocopies. *Uganda National Parks*, PO Box 3530, Kira Rd, just beyond the Museum, T 530158, F 530159. Permits to see the gorillas from here.

● Tour operators and travel agents

Abercroombie & Kent, PO Box 7799, F 259181. *Afrique Voyages*, PO Box 10895, T 251366, F 242437. *Air Masters*, PO Box 5649, T 250267, F 255288. *African Pearl Safaris*, PO Box 4562, Embassy House, Parliament Avenue, T 233566, F 235770. Run by an Australian. Does trips to the gorillas as well as to most other parts of Uganda. *Belex Tours*, PO Box 10542, T 244590, F 234252. *Blackline Tours*, PO Box 6968, Blacklines House, Dewinton Rd, T 255520, F 254240. *Crimux Tours*, PO Box 4458, T 258266. *Delmira*, PO Box 9098, T 235494, F 231927. *Express Transport*, PO Box 353, T 259029. *Hippo Tours*, PO Box 16183, T230727. *Flyway*, PO Box 6263, T 233207. *Hot Ice*, PO Box 151, Kampala, T 242733, F 244779. Run by a British family who have lived in East

Nakivubo Stadium

At the end of the First World War a certain amount of money remained in what was known as the Gifts and Comforts Fund. This had been raised by public subscription for the purpose of sending comforts to African soldiers serving in the war zone. The Government of Uganda, who administered the fund, decided that the money should be used for a memorial to those who had died during the war. Many schemes were considered by the Committee and finally it was decided that a sports ground should be built and dedicated to the war dead.

The Government allocated a piece of land between Makerere and Mulago and a football ground was quickly and inexpensively constructed, with the help of prison labour. However, it did not take long for the Government to realise that this piece of land was totally inadequate for the intended purposes and future development on this piece of land would be difficult. It was decided to sell the land to Makerere College and the memorial authorities were given nearly 12 acres of land in the Nakivubo Channel.

The work began again. The land was ideal in that it was central and flat, but it was little more than a marsh. Much of it was under papyrus and very rough. The prison authorities were unable to provide labour this time and workers proved difficult to procure. It was decided therefore to send recruiters to West Nile district and they brought back nearly 200 labourers. Deep drains were cut and levelling was completed. The old Nakersero-Mengo had to be moved and a new one on the W side constructed. Finally the ground was ready for football and on the 10th April 1926 the ground was officially opened by the then Governor of the Protectorate, with a match between the Uganda Kobs and a team selected by the Uganda Football Association.

Africa for many years. Very experienced and versatile. ***Jet Tours***, PO Box 5710, T 245158, F 235292. ***Jumbo Tours***, PO Box 11420, T 255317. ***KEB Creative Tours***, PO Box 87663, T 250839. ***Luxury Tours***, PO Box 10842, T 256815. ***Nile Safaris***, PO Box 12135, Farmers House, Parliament Ave, T 245092, F 245093, Tlx 61283. Tours ranging from 1 day to 19 days. ***Pearl Africa Travel***, PO Box 1102, T 232730. ***Rwenzori Mountain Tours and Travel***, PO Box 10549, Impala House, T 321290, F241754. ***Safari Seekers***, PO Box 7493, T 235165, F 245597. ***SM Tours and Travel Ltd***, PO Box 5184, 54 Kampala Road, T 254738, F 258785. ***Spear Touring Safaris***, PO Box 5914, T 232395, F 257239. ***Speedbird***, PO Box 10101, Kampala, 1st Floor, *Sheraton Hotel* Arcade or National Insurance Building, T 234669, F 234252. ***Sunshine Tours***, PO Box 5011, Kampala Rd, Georgiadis Chambers, T 243255, F 231927. ***Uganda Incoming Tours***, PO Box 2633, T 230910. ***Uganda Voyages Ltd***, PO Box 10805 3, Parliament Ave, T 242437/251366/251367, F 242437. ***Vacational Tours***, PO Box 10460, T 236211 F 236211. ***Value Tours***, PO Box 8316, T 250072. ***VIP Tours***, PO Box 4443, T234658.

● Transport

Local Unless you are staying outside the centre of town you probably will not need to use public transport much as most places are within easy walking distance.

Bus Cheaper than matatus but are less regular, have fewer routes and are extremely crowded. They have the advantage of going across town so on some routes you do not have to change buses. They stop around City Square and are usually marked with where they are going.

Matatu Matatus are minibuses running along the main routes and leaving the terminus when full. They are the cheapest way of travelling between the centre and the suburbs. At the matatu park very few of the vehicles are marked, and there is no system of route numbering, but the matatus all have regular stations in the park. Keep an eye on your belongings and put any jewellery or smart watches out of sight – particularly in the evenings. Most matatus stop running at about 10 in the evening; some run later, although they usually charge more. The fare to most places in town is US$0.30; to Entebbe it is US$1.

Taxis If you have a lot of luggage or miss the last matatu you can get a private hire – this may be a matatu or a taxi. You will have to bargain the fare – from Kampala city centre to one of the suburbs will cost around US$3.

Air The main international airport is at Entebbe 37 km from Kampala. Many of the larger airlines are starting to use Entebbe after many years of absence – including British Airways which flies in twice a week.

There are plenty of matatus shuttling up and down to Entebbe town – getting to and from the airport itself is not so easy. Having arrived at the airport you can of course take a taxi all the way to Kampala although there is a tendency to overcharge new arrivals. If you are trying to save your money the best thing to do is try to persuade the taxi to take you to Entebbe town and from there take a matatu which will only cost you US$1. However, not surprisingly the taxi drivers may refuse to do this in the hope you will go with them all the way to Kampala. British Airways run a bus starting from the *Sheraton Hotel*. Check at their office on Kampala road.

Train Kampala is linked by the Uganda Railway Service to **Malaba** on the border with Kenya in the E and with **Kasese** at the foothills of the Rwenzoris in the W. The line up to the N is also functioning. The final part of the line from Lira to **Pakwach** was opened in the middle of 1993 after being closed for 8 years due to security problems. It currently goes once a week to Pakwach although this may increase if there is the demand.

Road The most common approach to Kampala from Kenya is by road. If you have your own transport then you can choose whether to cross the border at **Busia** or **Malaba**. At the time of going to press there is little difference between the routes although this does vary. For example at one time a regulation insisted that all lorries went through Malaba which meant that for a while it took several hrs to get through the border. The regulation no longer applies.

If you are planning on using public transport you can go all the way from **Nairobi** on an overnight bus. There is now one company, Akamba, that goes direct – meaning it is no longer necessary to change buses at the border. The Akamba office is on Lagos street in Nairobi and they have a number of buses that go each day at 0700 getting in at about 1000 the next morning. The Kampala Office is on Dewinton Street near the National Theatre. They return to Nairobi at 1500 – book a day ahead to be sure to get a seat. The bus stops at about 0200in the morning at Kericho – but there is little to eat there – and gets in to Nairobi at about 0530 the next morning.

Lake There is a weekly steamer service between Port Bell on the shores of Lake Victoria 10 kms from Kampala, and **Mwanza** in Tanzania. There is also a twice weekly steamer service to the **Sese** Islands.

ENTEBBE

Entebbe is the home of Uganda's international airport. Entebbe became famous in 1976 when an Air France plane from Israel was hijacked and was forced to land there. The Jewish passengers were held hostage as demands were made for the release of certain prisoners in Israeli jails. All but one of the prisoners were rescued when Israeli paratroopers stormed the airport building. The raid actually took place in an old part of the airport which is no longer used.

Entebbe is situated on the shores of Lake Victoria, about 30 km from Kampala, and until 1962 was the administrative capital of the country. On the drive down to Entebbe you will pass a signpost of the **Kajansi Fish Farm** which used to be home to a number of huge crocodiles. It is a very good birdwatching spot.

At the turn of the nineteenth century the colonialists built their administrative centre at Entebbe and some government offices are still located here, including the Ministry of Works, Ministry of Agriculture and Ministry of Health. State House, the official residence of the Head of State is also located in Entebbe.

Colonial Entebbe

Walking along the crisscross of lanes between the main road and the lake shore there are a number of beautiful old buildings. Most of these were built when Entebbe was the capital of the Uganda Protectorate – they have painted red roofs and wide verandahs and are used mainly as Government departments and ministries. Particularly attractive, and recently repainted is the Ministry of Agriculture building which dates from the 1920's.

Botanical Gardens

The Botanical Gardens were established around the turn of the century by the Protectorate Government and the first curator was a Mr Whyte. There was originally a natural forest and the gardens were used as a research ground for the introduction of various exotic fruits and ornamental plants to Uganda. There are species in the gardens from all over the world and they include plants like cocoa trees, and rubber plants that were introduced to see how well they would thrive in Uganda's climate and soils.

Throughout all the troubles the Gardens were relatively well maintained and have survived quite well. However, some of the trees have died natural deaths and have not been replaced. Many of the trees still have their metal labels on them, and there is a small patch of virgin forest down close to the lake shore. Walking through this (there are well maintained paths) you will experience lots of different noises and smells, and it is worth remembering that large areas of Uganda were once forested like this patch. For people spending longer in Uganda, there is also a very good plant nursery.

Mugala's Chair

The word *entebbe* means chair and there is a legend attached to this name. Mugala was the head of the Mamba (or lungfish) Clan. Apparently Mugala used to command his domain from a royal enclosure not far from the present Entebbe Airport, seated in a chair carved out of the rock. Eventually the seat was submerged by the Lake but the area continued to be known as Entebbe.

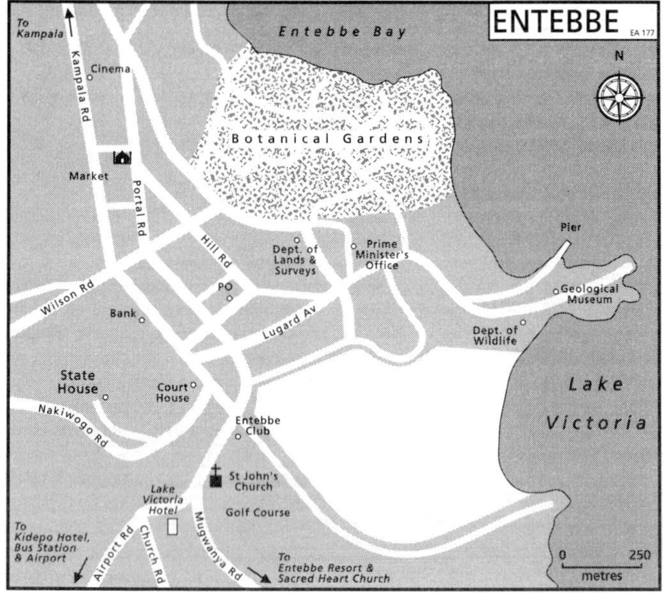

To get there, take a matatu from the matatu park in Kampala – they go every few minutes and take about 45 minutes, costing US$1. Stay on until the turning off to the right to Entebbe town which is just after a Shell petrol station. Walk down the main road (which heads towards the *Lake Victoria Hotel* and the airport) for about a hundred yards when you will see a murrum road forking off to your left. Follow this until you see the sign for the Botanical Gardens on your left.

Entebbe Wildlife Education Centre
At Entebbe is the zoo which was originally established as an animal orphanage and gradually developed into zoo with a wide range of species. Up until fairly recently it was a fairly miserable sight, and a place to avoid. However it has just been renamed the Entebbe Wildlife Education Centre and attempts are being made to improve the conditions. Large amounts of aid money are being spent on the rehabilitation. The master plan has been designed by experts from the New York Zoological Society and it will incorporate an educational centre as well as dormitories for visiting school children and other visitors. The proposals for the Centre itself include replicating some of the country's ecological zones, such as savannah, wetlands and tropical forest. The main features will be a forested reserve for primates and an island surrounded by moats for chimpanzees.

Kigungu Landing
Located about 5 km off the Airport Road is the place where the first Catholic Missionaries to Uganda, Rev Fr Simon Lourdel and Brother Amans of the Society of White Fathers, landed on 17th Feb 1879. There is a small brick church marking the spot and a memorial plaque. There is a small fishing village here nearby.

EAST AFRICAN
WILDLIFE GUIDE

A SHORT GUIDE TO THE FAUNA AND FLORA OF EAST AFRICA

MARGARET CARSWELL

ILLUSTRATED BY JOAN CALLAGHAN-ROCHE

"None of the books I read gave any idea of the beauty of
the country or the still remaining quantity of game"

Ernest Hemingway

CONTENTS

Please refer to the main text of the *Handbook* for descriptions and maps of the Game Reserves and Wildlife Parks.

MAMMALS

The 'big nine'

It is a reasonable assumption that anyone interested enough in wildlife to be travelling on safari in Africa is also able to identify the more well known and spectacular African animals. For example an **Elephant** *(Loxodonta africana)* or a **Lion** *(Panthera leo)* can hardly be confused with anything else, so there is not the need to describe them in great detail. It is indeed fortunate that many of the large and spectacular animals are also on the whole fairly common, so you will have a very good chance of seeing them on even a fairly short safari. They are often known as the Big Five. Unfortunately, no one agrees on quite which species constitute the Big Five! The term was originally coined by hunters who wanted to take home trophies of their safari. Thus it was, that in hunting parlance, the Big Five were **Elephant**, **Black Rhino**, **Buffalo**, **Lion** and **Leopard**. Nowadays the **Hippopotamus** is usually considered one of the Big Five for those who shoot with their cameras, whereas the **Buffalo** is far less of a 'trophy'. Equally photogenic and worthy to be included are the **Zebra**, **Giraffe** and **Cheetah**.

The major game areas where you might expect to see these larger and more spectacular animals, are shown in the table. But whether they are the Big Five or the Big Nine these are the animals that most people come to Africa to see, and, with the exception of the **Leopard** and **Black Rhino**, you have an excellent chance of seeing all of them. They are all unmistakable and when seeing them for the first time in the wild you will find that they are amazingly familiar and recognisable. The only two that could possibly be confused are the **Leopard** and the **Cheetah**. The **Leopard** *(Panthera pardus)* is less likely to be seen as it is more nocturnal and more secretive in its habits compared with the Cheetah. It frequently rests during the heat of the day on the lower branches of trees and as you drive round the parks, your best bet is to look for the animal's tail, which hangs down below the branches, and can be quite easily spotted while the rest of the animal remains well concealed. If you are lucky you will see one with its kill, which it may have hauled up into the lower branches. This is by no means impossible to see, so keep your eyes open.

Cheetahs *(Acinonyx jubatus)* are often seen in family groups walking across the plains or resting in the shade. They are *slimmer and longer legged* than Leopards, with a characteristic *sway back*. The *black 'tear' mark on the face* is usually obvious through binoculars. If all else fails you can identify Cheetahs by the accompanying mini buses! Leopards are far less tolerant of man. One point to bear in mind is that **Lion** cubs have spotted coats which gradually fade as they get older. Their parents are unmistakable.

Elephants are awe-inspiring by their very size and it is wonderful to watch a herd at a water-hole. Although they have suffered terribly from the activities of poachers in recent decades they are still readily seen in many of the game areas, and you will not be disappointed by the sight of them. There is one curiosity you will notice: the elephants in Tsavo National Park in Kenya, are reddish in colour, unlike the more familiar grey seen in other areas. This is because of their habit of taking dust baths and the red soil of Tsavo stains their skin, giving it this unusual appearance.

The other animals which have suffered very badly in recent times are the two **Rhinos.** The **White Rhino** *(Diceros simus)* is now probably extinct in much of its former range in eastern Africa though it flourishes in the southern part of the continent, and has been reintroduced into Meru National Park in Kenya. The

The big nine

Rhino: Now You See Them...

Two species of rhino are found in Africa, the **White Rhino** and the **Black Rhino**. These names have no bearing on the colour of the animals as they are both a rather nondescript dark grey. In some guide books the White Rhino is described as being paler in colour than the Black Rhino, but this by no means obvious in the field. The name White Rhino is derived from the Dutch word '*weit*' which means wide and refers to the shape of the animal's mouth. The White Rhino has a large square muzzle and this reflects the fact that it is a grazer and feeds by cropping grass. The Black Rhino, on the other hand, is a browser, usually feeding on shrubs and bushes. It achieves this by using its long, prehensile upper lip which is well adapted to the purpose. The horn of the rhino is not a true horn, but is made of a material called keratin, which is essentially the same as hair. If you see rhino with their young you will notice that the White Rhino tends to herd its young in front of it, whereas the Black Rhino usually leads its young from the front.

Originally in East Africa, the Black Rhino was found only to the east of the Nile, whereas the White Rhino was to be found only to the west of that river. However in 1961 some White Rhinos were introduced into Murchison Falls National Park in Uganda from their home in West Nile Province. This was an attempt to establish a breeding population and at one time it was possible to see them there. Unfortunately this fragile population did not survive the many civil wars that raged in Uganda in the 1970s and 80s. Concurrently the original population in West Nile in Uganda was also poached to extinction. The White Rhino is now severely endangered in E Africa, and a small population has been introduced into Meru National Park in the hope of reversing this trend. The Black Rhino is also severely endangered due to poaching, and work continues to rescue both these species from extinction.

Black Rhino *(Diceros bicornis)* has also diminished dreadfully in numbers in recent years. Whereas previously you could be sure of seeing this rhino in many of East Africa's Game Parks, now you can only be fairly sure of seeing it in the Ngorongoro Crater. It does exist elsewhere, for example in the Masai Mara, where, due to a determined effort by conservationists, its numbers are slowly increasing, but your chances of seeing it are not great. The two rhinos may be distinguished by the shape of their mouth. The White Rhino has a square muzzle, whereas the Black Rhino has a long upper lip. This difference is in fact quite easy to see. The remaining two species of the Big Nine are still common and easily seen. The **Buffalo** *(Syncerus caffer)*, considered by hunters to be the most dangerous of the big game, occurs in many areas, sometimes in substantial herds. From the safety of a minibus the Buffalo does not feel dangerous, even in fairly large numbers. The danger lies in the unpredictable behaviour of the lone bull. These animals, cut off from the herd, become bad-tempered and easily provoked. Particularly at risk are women on their way to cut fire wood or collect water, who will sometimes disturb such an animal as it rests in the shade. Severe injury or even death can result from these encounters.

The **Hippo** *(Hippopotamus amphibius)* is another animal which appears harmless, even comic, from a safe vantage point. During the day it rests in the water and you can get excellent views and interesting photographs, particularly if there are displaying males active in the area. These Hippos will 'yawn' at each other and two animals will sometimes

The big nine

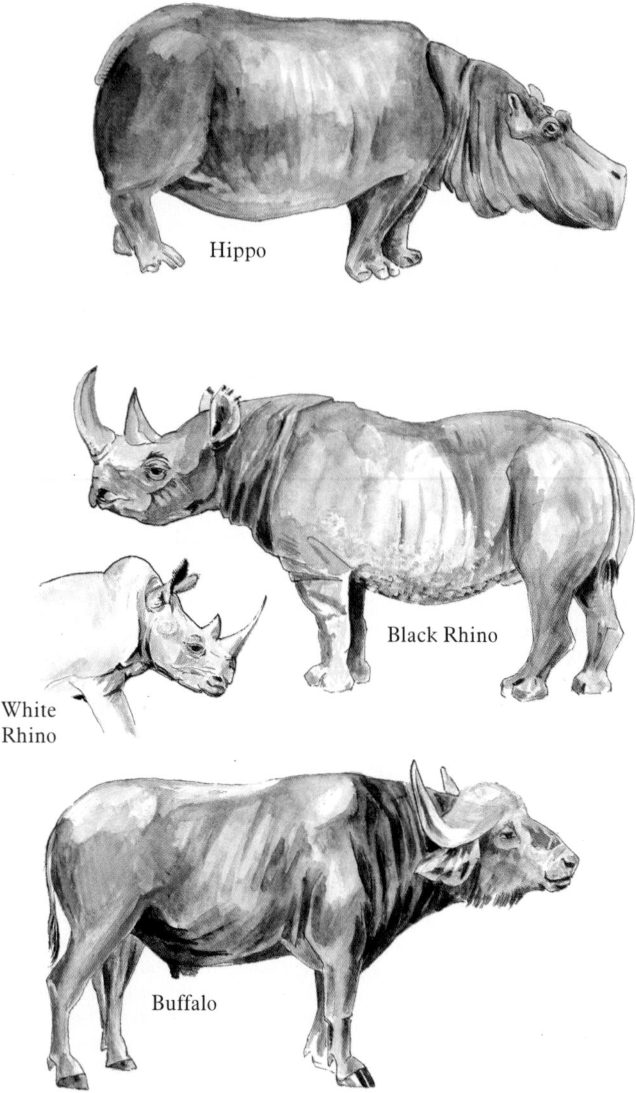
Hippo
Black Rhino
White Rhino
Buffalo

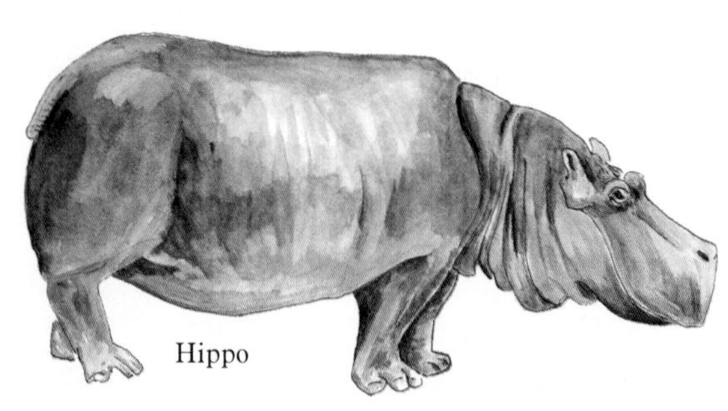

spar. At night the Hippo leaves the water and ranges very far afield to graze. A single adult animal needs up to 60 kilos of grass every day, and to manage this obviously has to forage far. The nearby banks of the water-hole with a resident Hippo population will be very bare and denuded of grass. Should you meet a Hippo on land by day or night keep well away. If you get between it and its escape route to the water, it may well attack.

In many ways the most stunning of the Big Nine is the **Giraffe**. It may not be as magnificent as a full grown Lion, nor as awe-inspiring as an Elephant, but its elegance is unsurpassed. To see a small party of Giraffe galloping across the plains is seeing Africa as it has been for hundreds of years. Although the Giraffe itself is unmistakeable and easily identified, it is interesting to note that there is, in fact, a variety of types which differ from each other. The authorities, though, are not always agreed on the exact division into species and races, as there seems to be much overlap of the types. Extending from about the Tana River northwards and eastwards into Somalia and Ethiopia is the area of the almost chestnut coloured **Reticulated Giraffe** *(Giraffa reticulata)* which is sometimes considered a separate species. This is the most handsome of the various forms, its *reddish brown coat being broken up by a network of pale, narrow lines,* like the outlines of crazy paving stones. To the south of the Reticulated Giraffe occurs the **Common Giraffe** *(Giraffa camelopardalis)* which has two forms, or races: one is the **Masai Giraffe** which occurs in south-west Kenya and down into Tanzania southwards. This has a *yellowish-buff coat* with the characteristic *patchwork of brownish markings with very jagged edges*. In most animals there are only *two horns*, though occasionally animals are seen with *three horns*. The other form of the Common Giraffe is known as **Rothschild's Giraffe** and this is a western form extending west and north of the Masai Giraffe into Uganda as far west as the Nile. It is usually rather *paler and heavier* looking than the Masai Giraffe and can have as many as *five horns,* though more commonly *three*. Near Lake Baringo and in Uganda this giraffe is often unusually dark and sometimes even melanistic individuals are found. You should note that in the giraffe both male and female animals have horns, though in the female they may be smaller.

In times gone by the giraffe was found in what is now central Sahara. There are rock paintings in the region which clearly show this. Nowadays, it is confined to eastern and southern Africa having been driven out of much of northern Africa by increasing aridity, and from west Africa by shooting.

The lolloping gait of the giraffe is very distinctive and it produces this effect by the way it moves its legs at the gallop. A horse will move its diagonally opposite legs together when galloping, but the giraffe moves both hind legs together and both fore legs together. It achieves this by swinging both hind legs forward and outside the fore legs.

The giraffe is not dumb and voiceless as many people believe, but can produce a low groaning noise and a variety of snorts.

The **Zebra** is another easily recognised animal. It forms herds, often large ones, sometimes with antelope. As with giraffe, there is more than one sort of zebra in eastern Africa and again, the relationship between the types is complex, but they can be considered as two main types: Grevy's Zebra (*Equus grevyi*) and the **Common** or **Burchell's Zebra** *(Equus burchelli)*. **Grevy's Zebra** is the larger of the two and has much *narrower stripes* which are arranged in such a way as to meet in a sort of *star-shaped arrangement at the top of the hind leg.* **Burchell's Zebra** on the other hand has *broad stripes* which cross the *top*

The big nine

Reticulated Giraffe
Masai Giraffe
Elephant
Rothschild's Giraffe

of the hind leg in unbroken oblique lines. The ranges of the two animals overlap to a certain extent and they can be seen in mixed herds in some northern areas. Generally though, Grevy's Zebra prefers the more arid areas and seems less dependent on water. It occurs mainly north of the equator, whereas Burchell's ranges to the south.

The larger antelopes

The first animals that you will see on safari will almost certainly be antelope. These are seen on the plains. So what antelope are you likely to see? Although there are many different species, it is not difficult to distinguish between them. For identification purposes they can be divided into the larger ones which stand about 120cms or more at the shoulder, and the smaller ones about 90cms or less.

The tables show the game areas where the various species of antelope occur.

Antelope are not 'deer', which do not occur in Africa, except in parts of the very north. There are many differences between the two groups. For example, deer have antlers, which are solid bony, branching outgrowths from the skull, which are shed annually. Antelope, on the other hand have horns, which are hollow, unbranched sheaths made of modified skin, rather like finger nails and toe nails. If a horn is lost it is not replaced, and they are not shed seasonally.

The largest of all the antelopes is the **Eland** *(Taurotragus oryx)* which stands 175-183cms at the shoulder. It is very *cattle-like* in appearance, with a noticeable *dewlap and shortish spiral horns,* present in both sexes. The general colour varies from greyish to fawn, sometimes with a rufous (reddish brown) tinge, with narrow white stripes on the sides of the body. It occurs, usually in small herds in a wide variety of grassy habitats.

Not quite as big, but still reaching 140-153cms at the shoulder, is the **Greater Kudu** *(Tragelaphus strepsiceros)* which prefers fairly thick bush, sometimes in quite dry areas. Although nearly as tall as the Eland it is a much more slender and elegant animal altogether. Its general colour also varies from greyish to fawn and it has several white stripes running down the sides of the body. Only the male has horns, which are *very long and spreading, with only two or three twists along the length of the horn.* A noticeable and distinctive feature is a *thick fringe of hair which runs from the chin down the neck.* Greater Kudu usually live in family groups of not more than half a dozen individuals, but occasionally larger herds of up to about thirty can be seen. Its smaller relative, the **Lesser Kudu** *(Strepsiceros imberis),* has similar horns, but stands only 99-102cms high. It lacks the throat fringe of the bigger animal, but has *two conspicuous white patches on the underside of the neck.* It inhabits dense scrub and acacia thickets in semi-arid country, usually in pairs, sometimes with their young.

The **Roan Antelope** *(Hippoptragus equinus)* and **Sable Antelope** *(Hippotragus niger)* are similar in general shape, though the Roan is somewhat bigger, being 140-145cms at the shoulder, compared to the 127-137cms of the Sable. In both species, both sexes carry ringed horns which curve backwards, and these are particularly long in the Sable. Both animals have a horse-like mane. The Sable is usually *glossy black with white markings on the face and a white belly.* The female is often a reddish brown in colour. The Roan can vary from dark rufous to a reddish fawn and also has white markings on the face. The black males of the Sable are easily identified, but the brownish individuals can be mistaken for the Roan. Look for the *tufts of hair at the tips of the rather long ears* of the Roan (absent in the Sable). The Sable is found in well wooded areas: the best place to see it is in the Shimba Hills National Reserve

The larger antelopes

near Mombasa in Kenya. The Roan has been introduced here, so it is possible to see both animals in this Reserve. The Roan generally is more widespread and is found in open grassland. Both the Roan and the Sable live in herds.

Another large antelope with a black and white face is the **Oryx** *(Oryx beisa)*. This occurs in two distinct races, the **Beisa Oryx** which is found north and west of the Tana River, and the **Fringe-eared Oryx** which occurs south and east of this river. Both these animals stand 122cms at the shoulder and vary in colour from greyish (most Beisa Oryx) to sandy (most Fringe-eared Oryx), with a *black line down the spine and a black stripe between the coloured body and the white underparts*, rather like that on found on the much smaller Thomson's Gazelle. They both also have *very long straight* (not curving) *horns*, present in both sexes, which make identification of this animal quite easy. The two races may be distinguished by the *long dark fringe of hair on the tips of the ears* in the Fringe-eared Oryx, absent in the Beisa Oryx. The Beisa Oryx is found in herds in arid and semi desert country and the Fringe-eared Oryx, also in herds, in similar habitat, but also sometimes in less dry areas.

The two **Waterbuck** are very similar, both being about 122-137cms at the shoulder, with *shaggy grey-brown coats*. These shaggy coats are very distinctive. The males have long, gently curving horns which are heavily ringed. The two species can be distinguished by the white mark on the buttocks. In the **Common Waterbuck** *(Kobus ellipsiprymnus)* this forms a *clear half ring on the rump and round the tail*, whereas in the **Defassa Waterbuck** *(Kobus defassa)* this ring is filled in, forming a *solid white area*. Both animals occur in small herds, in grassy areas, often near water. Solitary animals are also often seen. They are fairly common and widespread.

The **Wildebeest** or **Gnu** *(Connochaetes taurinus)* is well-known to many people from published photographs of the spectacular annual migration through Serengeti National Park. It is a big animal about 132cms high at the shoulder, looking rather like an American bison in the distance, especially when you see the huge herds straggling across the plains. The impression is strengthened by its *buffalo-like horns* (in both sexes) and *humped appearance*. The general colour is greyish with a few darker stripes down the side. It has a noticeable *beard and long mane*.

The four remaining large antelope are fairly similar, but, as there is not a lot of overlap in their ranges, it is not too difficult to identify them. Check the table as well as the descriptions before you make an identification. Three of these four are **Hartebeest** of various sorts and the fourth is called the **Topi**. All four antelope have *long, narrow horse-like* faces and rather comical expressions. The shoulders are much higher than the rump giving them a *very sloped back appearance*, especially in the three hartebeest. Again all four have short, curved horns carried by both sexes. In the three hartebeest the *horns arise from a bony protuberance on the top of the head* and curve outwards as well as backwards. One of the hartebeests, **Jackson's Hartebeest** *(Alcelaphus buselaphus)* standing about 132 cms, is similar in colour to the **Topi** *(Damaliscus korrigum)*, which is a little bit smaller at about 122-127cms, and is a *very rich dark rufous* in colour. But the Topi has *dark patches on the tops of the legs*, a coat with a *rich satiny sheen* to it, and more 'ordinary' looking lyre-shaped horns. Of the other two hartebeest, **Coke's Hartebeest** is much the same size as the Topi at about 122 cms. It is also known as the **Kongoni**, is usually considered to be a race of Jackson's Hartebeest, but is a very different colour being a more *drab pale brown with a paler rump*.

Lichtenstein's Hartebeest *(Alcephalus*

The larger antelopes

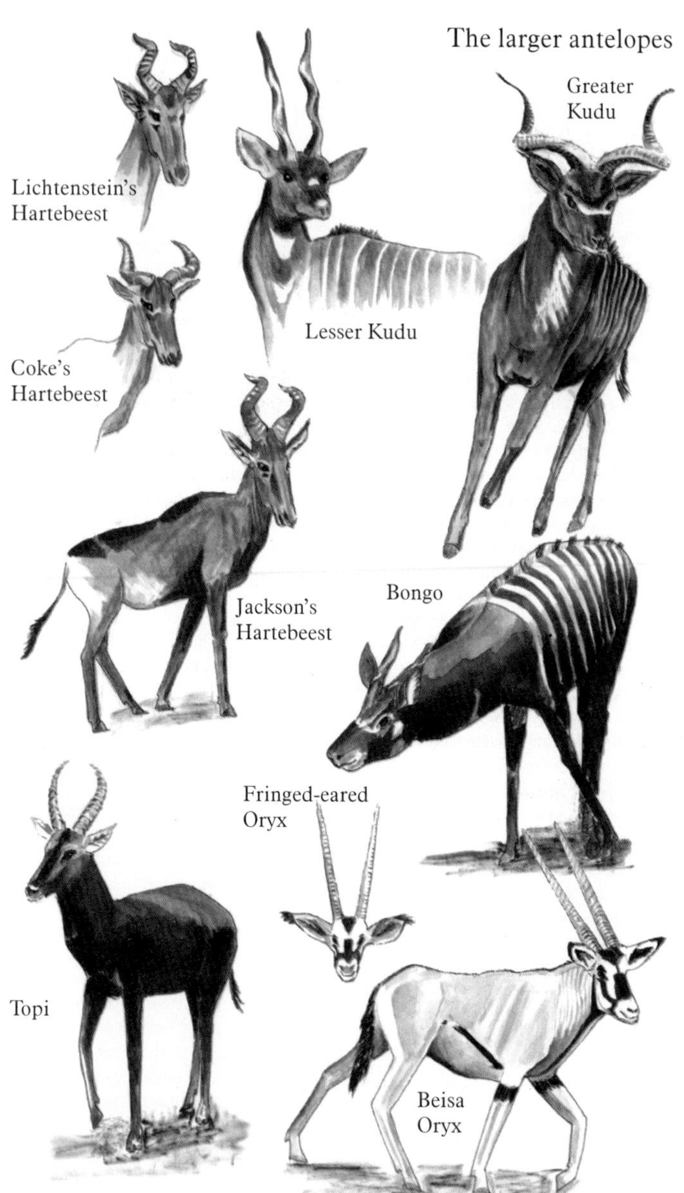

Naming The Animals: A Beest Called Fred?

Several birds and animals in Africa are named after people who were, no doubt, famous in their day, but are now largely forgotten. These names mirror an era of African history when Europeans were exploring and travelling in Africa, and writing home to describe the wonders that were to be found in that continent. Most of African wildlife was not known to science in those days, and classifying and naming species became a preoccupation of these early writers.

Many of the early explorers and travellers are among those honoured in this way. Thomson's Gazelle and Grant's Gazelle are named after two early European travellers in Africa. Joseph Thomson (1858-95) was a young Scot who travelled widely in Masai land. He and his companion Chuma, who is better known for having carried the body of David Livingstone to the coast in 1873, undertook many expeditions together in this part of Africa. James Grant (1827-92), another Scottish explorer, is particularly known for his travels in what is now Uganda. Kirk's Dikdik is named for Sir John Kirk a doctor and botanist, who started his African travels as a member of one of David Livingstone's expeditions in 1858 and later became British consul in Zanzibar. Jackson's Hartebeest is named for Sir Frederick Jackson (1860-1938) an amateur naturalist, who became Governor of Uganda and who is particularly known for his work on the birds of the area.

lichtensteinii), standing about 127-132cms at the shoulder, is also fawn in general colouration, but usually has a *rufous wash over the back*. Also look out for *dark marks on the front of the legs*, and often, a dark patch on the side near the shoulder. All four of these antelope are found in herds, in the case of Topi quite large herds. Sometimes they mix with other plain dwellers such as zebra. The hartebeest has the habit of posting sentinels, which are solitary animals who stand on the top of anthills keeping a watch out for predators.

Finally, mention must be made of a rare antelope which is fairly frequently seen in the Aberdare National Park in Kenya. This is the **Bongo** *(Boocercus eurycerus)*, a large and handsome forest antelope, which comes often to the saltlick at the Ark Lodge. If you are lucky enough to see it you will not mistake it for anything else. It stands 112-127cms at the shoulder and is *bright chestnut* in colour with *white stripes running down the side.* Both sexes have curved horns.

The smaller antelopes

The remaining common antelopes are a good deal smaller than those described above. The largest is the **Impala** *(Aepyceros melampus)* which is 92-107cms at the shoulder and a *bright rufous* in colour with a white abdomen. From behind, the *white rump, with black lines on each side* is characteristic. Only the male carries the *long lyre shaped horns*. Just above the heels of the hind legs is a *tuft of thick black bristles,* which are surprisingly easy to see as the animal runs. This is unique to the Impala. Also easy to see is the *black mark on the side of abdomen, just in front of the back leg.*

The **Uganda Kob** *(Adenota kob)*, which is about 92cms at the shoulder, is superficially rather like the Impala as it is also usually a bright rufous in colour. In Ethiopia the upperparts of the males tend to become darker with age and can be almost black in general colour whilst the ears are white. Here it is called the **White-eared Kob**. In all forms it may be distinguished by the *white ring around the eyes and white mark on the throat,* and the *black marks on the front of the fore legs.* Only

The smaller antelopes

the males carry horns, which are beautifully proportioned and *lyre-shaped*. Both Kob and Impala live in herds in grassy areas, but occasionally you may see solitary males. The Uganda Kob is most likely to be seen in western Uganda, whereas the Impala is most common in Kenya and Tanzania.

Two slightly smaller antelope are **Grant's Gazelle** *(Gazella granti)*, about 81-99cms at the shoulder, and **Thomson's Gazelle** *(Gazella thomsonii)*, about 64-69cms at the shoulder. They are superficially similar. Grant's, the larger of the two, has longer horns, but this is only a good field characteristic when the two animals are seen together. The general colour of both varies from a bright rufous to a sandy rufous. In both species the curved horns are carried by both sexes. Thomson's Gazelle can usually be distinguished from Grant's Gazelle by the broad black band along the side between the rufous upperparts and white abdomen, but not invariably, as some forms of Grant's also have this dark lateral stripe. If in doubt look for the *white area on the buttocks* which *extends above the tail on to the rump in Grant's, but does not extend above the tail in Thomson's*. This is the surest way to distinguish them. The underparts are white. Thomson's Gazelle or 'Tommies', as they are called, are among the most numerous animals that inhabit the plains of Kenya and Tanzania. You will see large herds of these graceful animals often in association with other game. Grant's Gazelle occurs on rather dry grass plains, in various forms, from Ethiopia and Somalia to Tanzania.

The **Bohor Reedbuck** *(Redunca redunca)* and the **Oribi** *(Ourebia ourebi)* are not really very similar, but they do both have a curious and *conspicuous patch of bare skin just below each ear*. The horns (carried only by males) are quite different being *sharply hooked forwards at the tip* in the **Bohor Reedbuck**, but straight in the **Oribi** and this is enough to distinguish them. There is a slight difference in size, the Bohor Reedbuck being about 71-76cms at the shoulder, and the Oribi only about 61cms. The Oribi is much more slender and delicate looking than the Bohor Reedbuck, with a proportionally longer neck. Both animals are a reddish fawn, but the Oribi tends to be duller or more sandy in appearance. Both Oribi and Bohor Reedbuck are usually seen in pairs in bushed grassland, never far from water.

The last two of the common smaller antelopes are the **Bushbuck** *(Tragelaphus scriptus)* which is about 76-92cms at the shoulder, and the tiny **Kirk's Dikdik** *(Rhynchotragus kirkii)* only 36-41cms. Both are easily identified. The Bushbuck's colour varies from chestnut (probably the most common) to a darkish brown and in Ethiopia to almost black. The coat has a *shaggy appearance and a variable pattern of white spots and stripes* on the side and back. There are in addition *two white crescent shaped marks* on the front of the neck. The horns, present in the male only, are short, almost straight and slightly spiral. The animal has a curious *high rump which gives it a characteristic crouching appearance*. The white underside of the tail is noticeable when it is running. The Bushbuck tends to occur in areas of thick bush especially near water. They lie up during the day in thickets, but are often seen bounding away when disturbed. They are usually seen either in pairs or singly. Kirk's Dikdik is so *small* it can hardly be mistaken for any other antelope. In colour it is a greyish brown, often washed with rufous. The legs are noticeably thin and stick-like, giving the animal a very fragile appearance. The *snout is slightly elongated*, and there is a conspicuous *tuft of hair on the top of the head*. Only the male carries the very small straight horns.

Other mammals

Other mammals

Although the antelope are undoubtedly the most numerous animals to be seen on the plains, there are others worth keeping an eye open for. Some of these are scavengers which thrive on the kills of other animals. They include the dog-like **Jackals**, of which there are three main species, all being similar in size, that is about 86-96cms in length and 41-46cms at the shoulder. The **Black-backed Jackal** *(Canis mesomelas)*, which is the most common ranges throughout the area. It is a rather foxy reddish fawn in colour with a noticeable *black area on its back*. This black part is *sprinkled with a silvery white* which can make the back look silver in some lights. In general colour the **Side-striped Jackal** *(Canis adustus)* is greyish fawn and it has a rather variable and sometimes *ill-defined stripe* along the side. It is most likely to be seen around Lake Victoria and in Tanzania. In parts of Ethiopia and Somalia, the **Common Jackal** *(Canis aureus)* occurs, often around villages and other habitation. In colour it is a reddish yellow with some black on the back. It can be seen by day or night.

The other well known plains scavenger is the **Spotted Hyaena** *(Crocuta crocuta)*. It is a fairly large animal, being about 69-91cms at the shoulder, and its *high shoulders and low back* give it a characteristic appearance. It is brownish with dark spots and has a *large head*. Usually it occurs singly or in pairs, but occasionally in small packs.

A favourite and common plains animal is the comical **Warthog** *(Phacochoerus aethiopicus)*. This is unmistakeable being almost *hairless* and grey in general colour with a *very large head with tusks and wart-like growths on the face*. They are often seen in family parties. The adults will run at speed with their *tails held straight up in the air*, and followed by the young.

In suitable rocky areas, such as kopjes, look out for an animal that looks a bit like a large grey-brown guinea pig. This is the **Rock Hyrax** *(Heterohyrax brucei)*, an engaging and fairly common animal that lives in communities in rocky places.

The most common and frequently seen of the monkey group are the **Baboons.** The most widespread species is the **Olive Baboon** *(Papio anubis)*, which occurs almost throughout the area. This is a large (127-142cms), heavily built animal, olive brown or greyish in colour. Adult males have a *well-developed mane*. In the eastern part of Kenya and Tanzania, including the coast, the Olive Baboon is replaced by the **Yellow Baboon** *(Papio cynocephalus)* 116-137cms, which is a smaller and lighter animal than the Olive Baboon, with *longer legs* and almost no mane in the adult males. The tail in both species looks as if it is broken and hangs down in a loop. In parts of Ethiopia and Somalia the **Hamadryas** *(Papio hamadryas)* occurs. This looks very different from the other two species, the male being mainly ashy grey in colour with a massive *cape-like mane*. The *face and buttocks are bright pink*, and the tail does not appear broken. Females lack the mane and are brownish in colour. Baboons are basically terrestrial animals, although they can climb very well. In the wild they are often found in acacia grassland, often associated with rocks, and are sociable animals living in groups called troops. Females are very often seen with young clinging to them. In parts of East Africa they have become very used to the presence of man and can be a nuisance to campers. They will readily climb all over your vehicle hoping for a handout. Be careful as they have a very nasty bite!

The smaller monkey that makes a nuisance of itself is the **Vervet** or **Green Monkey** *(Cercopithicus mitis)*, which abounds at camp sites and often lodges. This has various forms, the commonest

Other mammals

and most widespread having a *black face framed with white across the forehead and cheeks*. Its general colour is greyish tinged with a varying amount of yellow. *The feet, hands and tip of the tail are black*. In western Uganda and eastern Zaire it has longer white whiskers and a whitish tip to its tail. In Ethiopia and Somalia the whiskers are even longer and fluffy in appearance.

The **Chimpanzee** *(Pan troglodytes)* and the **Gorilla** *(Gorilla gorilla)* are not animals you will see casually in passing: you have to go and look for them. They occur only in the forests in the west of the region in Uganda, Rwanda and Zaire. In addition there are some Chimpanzee in western Tanzania.

At dusk in Africa you will notice many bats appearing. The most spectacular of them is the **Straw-coloured Fruit Bat** *(Eidolon helvum)* which has a wing span of 76cms. If you are in Kampala in the evening you cannot fail to see it. Until quite recently a large colony existed in what is still called Bat Valley near the University. Unfortunately harassment has driven the bats away from here, but they still roost in smaller, scattered colonies within the city limits. At dusk they can be seen streaming out over the city towards their feeding grounds. This is a very beautiful sight and one which you will always remember.

THE BIG NINE

	Lion	Leopard	Cheetah	Elephant	Buffalo	Black rhino	Zebra	Giraffe	Hippo
KENYA									
Aberdare		•		•	•				
Amboseli	•	•	•	•	•		B	M	•
Marsabit	•	•	•	•	•		G	R	
Masai Mara	•	•	•	•	•	•	B	M	•
Meru	•	•	•	•	•		BG	R	•
Mt Kenya		•		•	•		B		
Nairobi	•	•	•		•		B	M	•
Lake Nakuru					•		B	Roth	•
Samburu/Shaba	•	•	•	•	•		BG	R	•
Shimba	•	•		•	•				
Tsavo	•	•	•	•	•		BG	M	•
TANZANIA									
Arusha		•		•	•		B	M	•
Katavi	•	•		•	•		B		•
Kilimanjaro		•		•	•				
Lake Manyara	•	•		•	•		B	M	•
Mikumi/Selous	•	•	•	•	•		B	M	•
Ngorongoro Crater	•	•	•	•	•	•	B	M	•
Ruaha/Rungwa	•	•	•	•	•		B	M	•
Serengeti	•	•	•	•	•		B	M	•
Tarangire	•	•	•	•	•		B	M	
UGANDA									
Kidepo Valley	•	•	•	•	•		B	Roth	
Lake Mburo	•	•			•		B		•
Murchison Falls	•	•		•	•			Roth	•
Queen Elizabeth	•	•		•	•				•
ETHIOPIA	•	•	•	•	•		BG	R	•
SOMALIA	•	•	•	•	•		BG	R	•
ZAIRE	•	•	•	•	•		B		•

B = Burchell's Zebra
G = Grevy's Zebra
M = Masai Giraffe
R = Reticulated Giraffe
Roth = Rothschild's Giraffe

The Larger Antelopes

	Hartebeest	Gnu	Topi	Waterbuck	Roan	Sable	Oryx	Kudu	Eland
KENYA									
Aberdare				C					•
Amboseli	K	•		C				I	•
Marsabit							B	GI	
Masai Mara	K	•	•	D	•				•
Meru	K			C			B	I	•
Nairobi	K	•		CD					•
Lake Nakuru				D					•
Samburu/Shaba				C			B	I	•
Tsavo	K			C			F	I	•
TANZANIA									
Katavi			•	D	•				•
Lake Manyara	K			C					
Mikumi/Selous	L	•		C		•		G	•
Ngorongoro Crater	K	•		C					•
Ruaha/Rungwa	L			C	•	•		GI	•
Serengeti	K	•	•	CD	•		F	I	•
Tarangire	K	•		C			F	I	•
UGANDA									
Kidepo Valley	J			D	•			GI	•
Lake Mburo			•	D	•				•
Murchison Falls	J			D					
Queen Elizabeth			•	D					
ETHIOPIA			•	D			B	G	
SOMALIA			•	C			B	GI	

K = Kongoni (Coke's Hartebeest)
J = Jackson's Hartebeest
L = Lichtenstein's Hartebeest
C = Common Waterbuck
D = Defassa Waterbuck

B = Beisa Oryx
F = Fringe-eared Oryx
G = Greater Kudu
I = Lesser Kudu

The Smaller Antelopes

	Oribi	Kob	Reedbuck	Impala	Thomson's Gazelle	Grant's Gazelle	Bushbuck	Dikdik
KENYA								
Aberdare			•	•			•	
Amboseli			•	•	•	•	•	•
Marsabit						•	•	
Masai Mara	•		•	•	•	•	•	•
Meru	•		•	•		•	•	•
Nairobi			•	•	•	•	•	•
Lake Nakuru			•	•	•	•	•	•
Samburu/Shaba				•		•	•	•
Tsavo			•	•		•	•	•
TANZANIA								
Lake Manyara			•	•			•	•
Mikumi/Selous			•	•			•	
Ngorongoro Crater			•	•	•	•	•	
Ruaha/Rungwa			•	•		•	•	•
Serengeti	•		•	•	•	•	•	•
Tarangire			•	•		•	•	•
UGANDA								
Kidepo Valley	•		•			•	•	•
Lake Mburo	•	•	•	•			•	
Murchison Falls	•	•	•				•	
Queen Elizabeth		•	•				•	
ETHIOPIA	•	•	•		•	•	•	
SOMALIA	•					•	•	•

BIRDS

The eastern part of Africa is one of the richest bird areas in the world. The total number of species is in excess of 1300, and it is possible, and not too difficult to see 100 different species in a day. You will find that a pair of binoculars is really essential, and even a simple pair will make a lot of difference. Most people find a lot of pleasure in putting names to things. The birds described here are the common ones. With a little careful observation, you will soon find that you can identify them even though faced with such a varied number of totally strange and exotic looking species. Almost everyone looking at a totally unknown avifauna will turn first to pictures for identification. Therefore, the birds are not described in great detail where a glance at the picture will identify it for you. Rather, this short guide concentrates on emphasising the diagnostic points, and also on other characteristics which will help. To make it easier, the birds have been grouped according to the habitat in which you are most likely to see them. Remember that birds, on the whole, are creatures of habit, with likes and dislikes about habitat. For example, you will not see a Jacana far from water, nor will the Red-cheeked Cordon-bleu venture into the forest. So consider habitat before you make your final identification. Lastly, remember common birds are common and rare birds are rare.

Urban birds

The first birds that you will notice on arrival in any big city will almost certainly be the large numbers soaring overhead. Early in the morning the numbers are few, but as the temperature warms up, more and more are seen circling high above the buildings. Many of these will be **Hooded Vultures** *(Neophron monachus)* 66cms and **Black Kites** *(Milvus migrans)* 55cms. They are both rather nondescript brownish birds which are superficially similar. They are, however, easily distinguished by the shape and length of the tail. The tail of the Hooded Vulture is *short and slightly rounded* at the end, whereas the Black Kite (which incidentally is not black, but brown) has a *long, narrow tail* which looks either *forked when the tail is closed or slightly concave* at the end when spread. The end of the tail never looks rounded. In flight the Kite looks very buoyant and uses its tail a lot, twisting it from side to side. Also soaring overhead in some cities (notably Kampala) you will see the **Marabou Stork** *(Leptoptilos crumeniferus)* 152cms. Although this bird is a stork, it behaves like a vulture in that it lives by scavenging. Overhead its *large size, long and noticeable bill and trailing legs* make it easily identified.

The commonest crow in towns and cities is the **Pied Crow** *(Corvus albus)* 46cms. This is a very handsome black bird with a *white lower breast* which joins up with a *white collar* round the back of the neck. In towns along the coast you will see another member of the crow family, the **Indian House Crow** *(Corvus splendens)* 38cms. This is not indigenous to Africa, but was introduced and is spreading along the coast. It is a slender, shiny *black* bird with a *grey neck*. In gardens and parks there are a number of smaller birds to look out for. The **Dark-capped** or **Common Bulbul** *(Pycnonotus barbatus)* 18cms, can be heard all day with its cheerful call of "Come quick, doctor, quick". It is a brownish bird with a *darker brown head and a slight crest*. Below, the brown is paler fading to white on the belly, and under the tail it is *bright yellow*.

There are a large number of **Weaver** birds to be seen, but identifying them is not always easy. Most of them are *yellow and black* in colour, and many of them live in large noisy colonies. Have a close look at their intricately woven nests if you get

Urban birds

Hooded Vulture in flight
Black Kite in flight
Indian House Crow
Black Kite
Hooded Vulture
Pied Crow
Scarlet-chested Sunbird
Common Bulbul
African Thrush
Olive Thrush
Black-headed Weaver
Marabou
Marabou in flight

the chance. The commonest one is probably the **Black-headed Weaver** *(Ploceus cucullatus)* 18cms, which often builds its colonies in bamboo clumps. The male has a mainly *black head and throat,* but the *back of the head is chestnut.* The underparts are *bright yellow*, and the back and wings mottled black and greenish yellow. When the bird is perched, and seen from behind, the markings on the back form a *V-shape*.

Also in parks and gardens, and especially among flowers, you will see members of another large and confusing bird family: the **Sunbirds**. These are even more confusing than the Weavers, but you will probably be able to identify the males of the commoner ones. Like female weavers, female sunbirds are difficult even for the experts to identify. The thickset and sturdy looking **Scarlet-chested Sunbird** *(Nectarinia senegalensis)* 15cms, often perches on overhead wires so allowing you to get a good look at it. The male is a *dark velvety* brown in colour with a *scarlet chest.* The *top of the head* and *the throat are an iridescent green.* The *tail is short.*

There are two common thrushes often seen in parks and gardens. They look rather similar, but they do not occur in the same areas. The **Olive Thrush** *(Turdus olivaceous)* 23cms is the common thrush of the highlands, where it is often seen in gardens. The very similar garden thrush of lower areas, especially in Uganda, is the **African Thrush** *(Turdus pelios)* 23cms. Both birds are basically brown, but the Olive Thrush is a much richer looking bird with a *rufous belly and a bright orange bill.* The African Thrush has a *wash of rufous on the side* and is duller looking altogether.

Because the above birds are described as occurring in towns and cities it does not mean that you will not see them elsewhere. They can all be seen in natural habitats as well, though the Indian House Crow is particularly associated with man, and the Hooded Vulture is not common in the Game Parks.

Birds of open plains

Along with the spectacular game, it is here that you will see many of the magnificent African birds. In particular, there are two large birds which you will see stalking across the grasslands. These are the **Ostrich** *(Struthio camelus)* 2 metres, and the **Secretary Bird** *(Sagittarius serpentarius)* 101cms. The Secretary Bird is so called because the long plumes of its crest are supposed to resemble the old time secretaries who carried their quill pens tucked behind their ears. This bird is often seen in pairs as it hunts for snakes, which form its main food source. The Ostrich is sometimes seen singly, but also in family groups. There are other large terrestrial birds to look out for, and one of them the **Kori Bustard** *(Otis kori)* 80cms, like the Secretary Bird, quarters the plains looking for snakes. It is quite a different shape however, and can be distinguished by the *thick looking grey neck.* This effect is caused by the loose feathers of its neck. It is particularly common in Serengeti National Park and in the Mara.

The other large ground bird that you are likely to see on the open plains is the **Ground Hornbill** *(Bucorvus cafer)* 107cms. When seen from afar, this looks for all the world like a turkey. Close up, it is very distinctive and cannot really be mistaken for anything else. They are very often in pairs and the *male has bare red skin around the eye and on the throat.* In the *female this skin is red and blue*.

Soaring overhead on the plains you will see vultures and birds of prey. The commonest vulture in game areas is the **African White-backed Vulture** *(Gyps africanus)* 81cms. This is a *largish, brown bird with a white lower back,* and it has, of course, the characteristic *bare head* of its family. Because they are commonly seen circling overhead, the white rump is sometimes difficult to see. So look out for the other diagnostic characteristic - *the broad white band on the leading edge of the*

Birds of open plains

undersurface of the wing. The **Bateleur** *(Terathopius ecaudatus)* 61cms, is a magnificent and strange looking eagle. It is rarely seen perched, but is quite commonly seen soaring very high overhead. Its *tail is so short* that it sometimes appears tailless. This, its buoyant flight and the *black and white pattern of its underparts* make it easy to identify.

Where there is game, look out for the Oxpeckers. The commonest one is the **Red-billed Oxpecker** *(Buphagus erythrorhynchus)* 18cms. These birds are actually members of the starling family although their behaviour is not like that of other starlings. They associate with game animals and cattle and spend their time *clinging to, and climbing all over the animals* while they hunt for ticks, which form their main food. They can be positively identified by this behaviour, as it is unique. There are other birds which associate with animals in a different way. For example the **Cattle Egret** *(Bubulcus ibis)* 51cms, follows herds and feeds on the grasshoppers and other insects disturbed by the passing of the animals. Occasionally too, the Cattle Egret will perch on the back of a large animal, but this is quite different from the behaviour of Oxpeckers. Cattle Egrets are *long legged and long billed white* birds which are most often seen in small flocks. In the breeding season they develop *long buff feathers on the head, chest and back.*

Birds of dry, open woodland

There is no hard division between open plain and dry, open woodland and the two habitats merge into each other. This means that the bird lists for these two areas are to a certain extent interchangeable. But between them, the two habitats form a vast area of Africa and most of the Game Parks come into these categories. As well as being quintessentially African, this dry open woodland with acacia thorn trees is an extremely rewarding area for bird watching. It supports an enormous variety of species and it is relatively easy to see them. This contrasts with the other rich habitat, the rain forest, which can be extremely frustrating for bird watchers.

The Guinea Fowls live in flocks and if you surprise a group on the road they will disappear into the bush in a panic, running at great speed. There is more than one sort of Guinea Fowl, but they are rather similar, being a slaty grey with white spots. The **Vulturine Guinea Fowl** *(Acryllium vulturinum)* 59cms, is a most handsome bird with *long blue, white and black feathers covering its neck and upper body.* The rather small head is bare, hence the bird's name. The **Helmeted Guinea Fowl** *(Numida meleagris)* 55cms, is rather less handsome, but with its *dark slaty and white spotted* plumage and the bony "*helmet*" on its head it is nonetheless a striking bird.

The tops of the thorn trees are used as observation perches by a number of different species. Especially noticeable is the **Red-billed Hornbill** *(Tockus erythrorhynchus)* 45cms, which has *blackish-brown back, with a white stripe down between the wings.* The wings themselves are *spotted with white*. The underparts are white and the bill is *long, curved and mainly red.* As the bird flies into a tree the impression is of a black and white bird with a long red bill and a long tail. Another striking bird which perches on tree tops is the **White-bellied Go-away Bird** *(Corythaixoides leucogaster)* 51cms. This gets its strange name from its call which can roughly be represented by "Go-away, go-away". It is a basically *grey* bird with a *very upright stance.* The top of the head carries a *long and conspicuous crest*. The *belly is white* and the long tail has a black tip. It is usually seen in small family parties.

There is a strange looking, brightly coloured bird called **d'Arnaud's Barbet** *(Trachyphonus darnaudii)* 15cms which is quite common in the dry bush country.

Birds of dry open woodland

The impression you get is of a *very spotted bird, dark with pale spots above, and pale with dark spots below.* It has rather a long dark tail which again is heavily spotted. Its *call and behaviour* is very distinctive. A pair will sit facing each other with their tails raised over their backs and wagging from side to side, and bob at each other in a duet. All the while they utter a four note call over and over again. "Do-do dee-dok". They look just like a pair of clockwork toys. Another brightly coloured bird is the **Lilac-breasted Roller** *(Coracias caudata)* 41cms, which is very easy to see as it perches on telegraph poles or wires, or on bare branches. The brilliant blue on its wings, head and underparts is very eye catching. Its *throat and breast are a deep lilac* and its tail has two elongated streamers. It is quite common in open bush country. Also often seen sitting on bare branches is the **Drongo** *(Dicrurus adsimilis)* 24cms, but this is an all black bird. It is easily identified by its *forked tail,* which is *'fish-tailed'* at the end. It is usually solitary.

There are two common birds which in the field look rather similar, although they are not related at all. These are the **White-crowned Shrike** *(Eurocephalus rueppelli)* 23cms, and the **White-headed Buffalo Weaver** *(Dinemellia dinemelli)* 23cms. They both occur in small flocks in dry acacia country and are both thickset, rather chunky birds which appear basically dark brown and white. To distinguish between them look at the *rump* which is *red* in the White-headed Buffalo Weaver, but *white* in the White-crowned Shrike. This is usually easy to see as they fly away from you.

There are many different species of starling to be seen in eastern Africa, and most of them are beautifully coloured. Two of the most spectacular are the **Golden-breasted Starling** *(Cosmopsarus regius)* 32cms, and the **Superb Starling** *(Spreo superbus)* 18cms. Both are common, but the Superb Starling is the more widespread and is seen near habitation as well as in thorn bush country. Tsavo East is probably the best place to see the Golden-breasted Starling. Look out for the *long tail* of the Golden-breasted Starling, and the *white under tail and white breast band* of the Superb Starling. Both these starlings are usually seen hopping about on the ground. Another long-tailed bird quite commonly seen in bush country is the **Long-tailed Fiscal** *(Lanius cabanisi)* 30cms (12 inches). Unlike the Golden-breasted Starling, however, it is a black and white bird which is usually seen perched on wires or bare branches. It can be identified by its *very long all black tail* and *mainly black upperparts*, which are *grey on the lower back and rump.*

Finally look out for four birds which though small are very noticeable. The **Red-cheeked Cordon-bleu** *(Uraeginthus benegalus)* 13cms, is a lovely little *blue bird* with a brown back and *bright red cheek patches.* They are seen in pairs or family parties, and the females and young are somewhat duller in colour than the males. They are quite tame and you often see them round the game lodges, particularly in Kenya and parts of Uganda and Tanzania.

In the less dry grasslands you can see the beautiful red and black Bishop birds. There are two species both of which are quite brilliant in their colouring. The brightest is the **Red Bishop** *(Euplectes orix)* 13cms, which has *brown wings and tail,* and noticeable scarlet feathers on its rump. The almost equally brilliant **Black-winged Bishop** *(Euplectes hordeaceus)* 14cms, may be distinguished from the Red Bishop by its *black wings and tail* and rather less obvious red rump. Both species occur in long grass and cultivation, often, but not invariably, near water.

Birds of more moist areas

Birds of more moist areas

Although so much of eastern Africa consists of grass plains, in the west of the area there are moist wooded grass lands which support a very different variety of bird species. The tall and elegant **Crowned Crane** *(Balearica pavonina)* 100cms, is quite common near Lake Victoria, though it also occurs in much of the rest of the area as well. It cannot really be mistaken for anything else when seen on the ground. In flight the *legs trail behind* and the *neck is extended*, but the *head droops down* from the vertical. Overhead, flocks fly in loose V-shaped formation. The curious **Hamerkop** *(Scopus umbretta)* 58cms, is another unmistakable bird. It is a rather dull brown in colour and has a stout, moderately long bill. Its most distinctive feature is the *large crest which projects straight backwards* and is, rather fancifully, said to look like a hammer. It is a solitary bird usually seen on the ground near water, sometimes even roadside puddles. It nests in trees, and builds an enormous nest, which is so large and strong that it can easily support the weight of a man.

A rather dull looking ground bird which is common is the **Hadada Ibis** *(Hagedashia hagedash)* 76cms. This is a *greyish olive* bird with a *long down curved bill* and a *green wash on the wings.* It is almost invariably seen in pairs and flies off with its characteristic loud call "Ha-da-da, Ha-da-da". It is one of Africa's most familiar birds, and walks about on lawns and open spaces. The **Black-and-white Casqued Hornbill** *(Bycanistes subcylindricus)* 70cms, is yet another loud and conspicuous bird, but it is always seen in trees and is particularly common in moist woodland in the west. The rather similar **Silvery-cheeked Hornbill** *(Bycanistes brevis)* 70cms, replaces it to the east, though their habitat requirements are broadly similar. Both are basically black and white birds, but the wings of the Silvery-cheeked Hornbill are *wholly black,* whereas the Black-and-white Casqued Hornbill has a *large white patch on the black wings*. Look also at the casque on top of the bill, which is carried by both species. This casque is *all pale* in the Silvery-cheeked, but, as its name would suggest, *black and white* in the other bird.

The moist forests and woodlands around Lake Victoria which are the home of the Black-and-white Casqued Hornbill, are also home to the **Grey Parrot** *(Psitticus erithacus)* 30cms. This bird is usually seen in flocks and is best distinguished both in flight and at rest, by its bright red tail. The **Paradise Flycatcher** *(Terpsiphone viridis)* male 33cms, female 20cms, is very easily identified by its *very long tail and bright chestnut* plumage. The head is black and bears a crest. The tail of the female is much shorter, but otherwise the sexes are similar. It is seen in wooded areas, including gardens and is usually in pairs. In certain parts, notably eastern Kenya. its plumage is often white, but it still has the black head. Sometimes birds are seen with partly white and partly chestnut plumage. Another long tailed bird, but this time a brown one is the **Speckled Mousebird** *(Colius striatus)* 36cms. They are usually seen in small flocks and follow each other from bush to bush. The mainly brown plumage has a speckled appearance and the *tail is long and graduated.* It has a *red rather parrot-shaped bill* and a *crest.*

Water and waterside birds

The inland waters of Africa form a very important habitat for both resident and migratory species. A lot can be seen from the shore, but it is especially fruitful to go out in a boat, when you will get quite close to, among others, the large and magnificent herons which occur here. The king of them all is the aptly named **Goliath Heron** *(Ardea goliath)* 144cms, which is usually seen singly on mud banks and shores, both inland and on the coast. Its *very large size* is enough to dis-

Water and waterside birds

tinguish it, but the smaller **Purple Heron** *(Ardea purpurea)* 80cms, which frequents similar habitat and is also widespread, may be mistaken for it at a distance. If in doubt, the colour on the top of the head *(rufous in the Goliath and black in the Purple)* will clinch it, also the Purple is much more slender with a slender bill.

The Flamingos are known to most people and will be readily identified. However, there are two different species which very often occur together. The **Greater Flamingo** *(Phoenicopterus ruber)* 142cms, is the larger and paler bird and has a *pink bill* with a black tip. The **Lesser Flamingo** *(Phoenicopterus minor)* 101cms, is deeper pink all over and has a *deep carmine bill* with a black tip. They both occur in large numbers in the soda lakes of western Kenya, but are also seen elsewhere occasionally. The magnificent **Fish Eagle** *(Haliaeetus vocifer)* 76cms, has a very distinctive colour pattern. It often perches on the tops of trees, where its *dazzling white head and chest* are easily seen. In flight this white and the white tail contrast with the black wings. It has a wild yelping call which is usually uttered in flight. Try and watch the bird as it calls: it throws back its head over its back in a most unusual way.

There are several different kingfishers to be seen, but the most numerous is the black and white **Pied Kingfisher** *(Ceryle rudis)* 25cms. This is easily recognised as it is the only *black and white* kingfisher. It is common all round the large lakes and also turns up at quite small bodies of water. It hovers over the water before plunging in to capture its prey.

In quiet backwaters with lily pads and other floating vegetation you will see the **African Jacana** *(Actophilornis africana)* 25cms. This is a mainly *chestnut* bird almost invariably seen *walking on floating leaves*. Its toes are greatly elongated to allow it to do this. When flying away from you the legs dangle right down which is very distinctive. Do not confuse this with the **Black Crake** *(Limnocorax flavirostra)* 20cms, which also frequents the quieter backwaters. This is an all *slaty black* bird with *bright pink legs*. It is rather shy and disappears into the vegetation at your approach. But if you wait quietly it will reappear.

REPTILES AND AMPHIBIANS

Reptiles and amphibians abound in Africa, but most of them are not often seen. There are some, however, which you are virtually certain of spotting and one such is the Crocodile. The **Crocodile** *(Crocodilus niloticus)* is readily recognised. It is particularly common on the Nile in Uganda, but also occurs elsewhere in the region. The only place where you might expect to find it, but where it does not occur, is in Lakes Edward and George, although it is plentiful in the other large nearby lake - Lake Albert.

The largest lizard by far is the **Monitor** *(Varanus niloticus)* which can be up to 2 metres in length, about half this being tail It is a greyish brown in colour, with lighter markings. It stands fairly high on its legs and constantly flickers its tongue. It appears for all the world like a small dragon. It is fairly common and you have a good chance of seeing one, especially near water.

You will notice around your lodge or camp site several lizards with bright blue or bright orange heads. These are the **Blue-bodied Agama** *(Agama atricollis)* and **Orange-bodied Agama** *(Agama agama)*. They are some 15 to 20cms long and only the males have the brightly coloured head. They run along walls and rocks and are frequently seen doing press-ups. They make lovely photographs, but are not easy to approach. The Blue-bodied is the commoner and more widespread of the two.

Inside the house, especially in the evening you will probably see the common **House Gecko** *(Hemidactylus brookii)*. This is a rather drab looking, but entertaining lizard which spends most of the day hiding behind pictures, but in the evening comes out to hunt moths and other insects. It is not usually more than about 13-14cms long, has big eyes, a fat tail and big feet with sticky pads (not suckers) which enable it to run across walls and ceilings. Its body is brownish and is curiously transparent. Geckos are rather aggressive towards each other and when two males fight they make a loud squeaking noise. Another smaller gecko, called the **Dwarf Gecko** *(Lygodactylus picturatus)*, is darker in colour, only 6-7cms long and much more slender than the House Gecko. All geckos are quite harmless.

Look out for the well known and colourful Chameleons. There is more than one species, but the commonest is probably the **Green Chameleon** *(Chamaeleo gracilis)* which is fairly widespread.

Unless you go to a snake farm you are unlikely to see many snakes. Mostly you just catch a glimpse of them as they wriggle rapidly across the road in front of your vehicle. Seen like that they are difficult to identify, but the beautiful **Black Cobra** *(Naja melanoleuca)* is fairly distinctive and is quite common in the forested areas from Zaire, Rwanda, and Burundi to coastal Kenya and Tanzania, as well as western Ethiopia. It is often seen on forest roads. It can be nearly 2 metres in length. The yellowish underparts, which contrast with the shiny black of the back and sides, can quite easily be seen as the snake lifts itself up to look at you as you pass. This raising up and spreading of its hood can give the impression that it is aggressive, but in fact it is only inquisitive. Like all cobras it is very poisonous.

As you sip your evening sundowner, and if there are ponds or swamps nearby, you are likely to hear the melodious tinkling of **Tree Frogs** *(Hylidae)*, which, like the gecko, have adhesive pads on their feet which enable them to climb. There are many different sorts of tree frog. They are all small amphibians which are not often seen, but occasionally one can be found half way up a door post or window frame which it has mistaken for a tree. In colour they are usually bright greens or yellows, often with pretty markings.

BENI RAPIDS: NO GO FOR CROCS

Strange though it may seem there are no crocodiles in the two western Uganda lakes of Edward and George, nor in the Kazinga Channel which connects the two lakes. Fossil evidence shows that in the distant past Nile type fauna, for example crocodiles and the Nile Perch, did occur in these lakes. But in the comparatively recent past, in geological terms, a violent volcanic eruption covered the whole area of Lakes Edward and George with a thick blanket of volcanic ash, rather like a much bigger version of what happened at Pompeii. This killed off all the wildlife in these lakes. At the same time, the southern half of the Semliki River, which now flows northwards from Lake Edward to Lake Albert mainly within Zaire, was raised up resulting in the spectacular rapids near Beni. When, in time, the Nile fauna from Lake Albert began recolonising the area these rapids prevented the passage of animals up the Semliki River to Lake Edward and Lake George. Today, below these rapids the Nile crocodile and Nile perch are plentiful. Also important to the spread of crocodiles is the fact that the Semliki River flows through very dense forest and thus is in heavy shade. The crocodile will not venture into dense shade but needs sunlight. Hence this provides yet another barrier to its spread upstream.

Crocodile

Reptiles and Amphibians

FRESHWATER FISH

The fish in this area are many and those who enjoy fishing can be sure of plenty of opportunity to practice their sport.

The king of the fresh water fish is without doubt the massive **Nile Perch** *(Lates albertianus)*. This huge predator originally came from the Nile below Murchison Falls, but was introduced into Lake Kyoga and the Nile above the Falls in 1955 and 1956. It has now spread to Lake Victoria itself, which has proved to be very much a mixed blessing. Weights of 20 to 40 kilos are common and there are several records of over 100 kilos. The best place to catch them is in Murchison Falls Park in Uganda, although you can have luck on Lake Victoria. In eastern Zaire, where they are present in Lake Albert, they are known as 'Le Capitan'. Also caught commonly in fresh waters is the **Tilapia** *(Tilapia nilotica)*, a much smaller, rather bony fish which makes good eating. Unlike the Nile Perch this much smaller fish is herbivorous, and is now being farmed in fish ponds, where it is fed largely on the green leaves of the cassava plant.

Tilapia

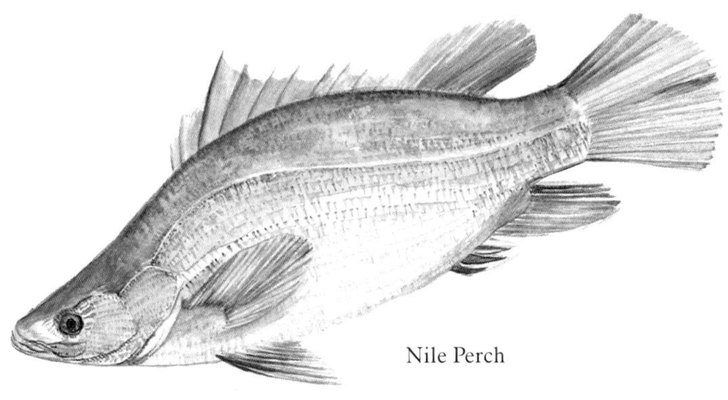

Nile Perch

THE BEACH, THE REEF AND BEACHCOMBING

To most visitors the east African beaches mean the reef. The fish and coral that you can observe here are indeed wonderful, and you do not have to dive to see them. This section concentrates on the many interesting creatures you can see by paddling and snorkelling on your own. You do not need to be a strong swimmer to do this, nor do you need expensive equipment.

Many of the fish that you will see do not have universally recognised English names, but one that does is the very common **Scorpion** or **Lion Fish** *(Pterois)*, which is probably the most spectacular fish you will see without going out in a boat. Wherever there is live coral you are likely to see it, and sometimes it gets trapped in the deeper pools of the dead reef by the retreating tide. It can be up to 26cms long and is easily recognised by its peculiar fins and zebra-like stripes. Although it has poisonous dorsal spines it will not attack if you leave it alone.

While most visitors naturally want to spend time snorkelling on the live reef and watching the brilliant fish and many coloured living corals, do not by pass the smaller, humbler creatures which frequent dead as well as living coral. These can be seen on most of the beaches, but one of the best places is Tiwi beach at Twiga Lodge. Here a vast area of dead coral is partly exposed at low tide and you can safely paddle there, which is especially good for children. Be sure to wear shoes though, because there are many sea urchins. These sea urchins *(Echinoidea)* are usually found further out towards the edge of the reef, but can be found anywhere. There are two forms the more common **Short-needled Sea Urchin** and the much less common **Long-needled** variety. Their spines are very sharp and treading on them is extremely painful. You can take home a souvenir of these creatures in the form of a **Sea Urchin skeleton** which you may find lying on the sand. These are fragile and beautiful spheres which can be up to the size of a small tangerine. They are sandy coloured with lines and dots running down the sides. Look out also for the common **Brittle Stars** *(Ophiuroidea)* which frequent sandy hollows. They vary considerably in size, but are usually 10cms across. They are so called because the arms break off very readily, but they will grow again. These are not sea urchins, though they are related, and can safely be picked up for a closer look, but handle them carefully.

Other living creatures which you can see crawling along in the shallows include the **Sea Slug** *(Nudibranchia)* and the **Snake Eel** *(Ophichthidae)*. Both are quite common in sandy places. The Sea Slug is blackish brown and shaped a bit like the familiar garden slug, though much bigger. It often has grains of sand sticking to it. This is not a beautiful creature. Don't be put off by the name of the Snake Eel, it is quite harmless. It looks a bit like a snake and has alternating light and dark bands on its body. What are beautiful, without doubt, are the **Starfish**, *(Asteroidea)* which are best seen by going out in a boat, but you will see some nearer in shore. *Please don't collect them.* The colours fade in a week or so, and they are far better left to themselves.

Small pieces of broken off coral can also be found on the reef. These you can safely collect, without doing any harm to the reef. In particular there is the **Mushroom Coral** *(Fungia)* which looks like the underside of a mushroom and can be up to 20cms across, though it is usually less than that and the **Star Coral** *(Goniastraea)*. The flat **Sand Dollar** *(Echinoidea)* can also be found lying on the sand. It is rather fragile and is the skeleton of a creature related to sea urchins.

Two rather hard objects which may

The beach, the reef and beachcombing

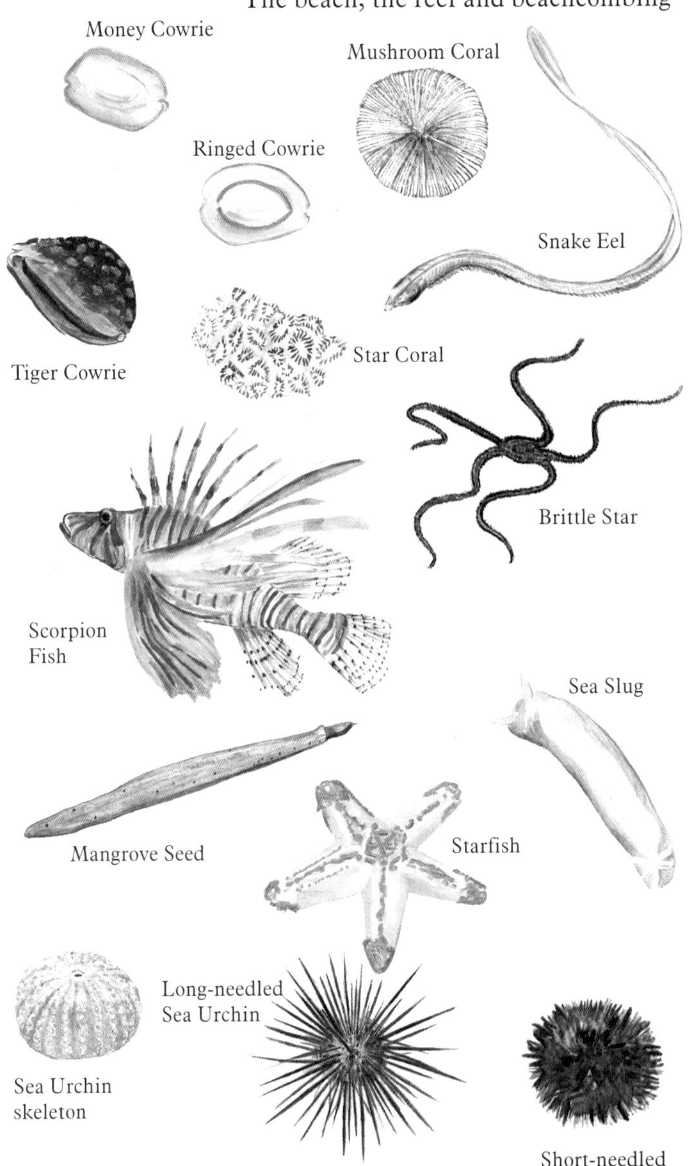

Dangers Of The Reef Watch Your Step

The reef and sea shore are very safe places, but there are a few things you should look out for. The Scorpion Fish has already been mentioned, but as long as you just look there is no danger. Stingrays are quite common too and lie buried in the sand: if you were to tread on you could get quite a nasty wound. The most famous hazard of the reef is the dreaded Stonefish which looks exactly like a piece of old coral, and whose dorsal spines can inject a very painful venom. A sort of mythology has grown up around them but you are unlikely to see one, and even less likely to tread on one. You are much more likely to step on a Sea Urchin, which can be very painful. There are two poisonous *shells*: odd but true. They are both cones, the Geography Cone and the Textile Cone. You quite often see dead ones washed up on the shore, but live ones keep buried in the sand. Should you see a live one, treat it with respect. Moray Eels are common on the reef, and though their bite is painful, it is not poisonous.

puzzle you are the seed of the **Mangrove** tree and small pieces of **pumice** which are still being washed up on this shore line, probably from the great explosion of Krakatoa in 1883.

The commonest shells are without doubt the **cowries**. Many dead ones can be found on the beach. *Please do not take live ones.* The two commonest cowries the **Ringed Cowrie** *(Cypraea annulus)* and the **Money Cowrie** *(Cypraea moneta)* are illustrated. Of these the Ringed is especially plentiful and is a pretty grey and white shell with a golden ring. The Money Cowrie was once used as money in Africa and varies in colour from greenish grey to pink according to its age. The big and beautiful **Tiger Cowrie** *(Cypraea tigris)* is also seen occasionally. This can be up to 8cms in length. There is quite a lot of variation in colouring, but it is basically a very shiny shell with many dark round spots on, much more like a leopard than a tiger. There are many more varied and beautiful sea creatures to be seen on the coast. The best way of doing this, especially if time is short, is to go to one of the Marine Parks, where you can go out in a glass bottomed boat with a guide.

In addition to the creatures which you will find in the sea, there are animals and plants which are to be seen a few yards in shore. The trees for example are varied and many. The well known **Coconut Palms** *(Cocos nucifera)* are almost everywhere, both in commercial plantations and growing singly. Unlike the coconut with its familiar straight trunk, the trunk of the **Doum Palm** *(Hyphaene thebaica)* has branches. This palm grows well on abandoned cultivation. The young palm looks like a fan of palm leaves sticking up out of the soil. The **Screw Pine** *(Pandanus kirkii)*, whose fruits you will pick up on the beach, is common and notice-

Pumice

Sand Dollar

able. It grows just above the high water mark, and has remarkable roots.

Another very common tree is the feathery **Casaurina** which has no common English name, but is generally known by its scientific name. It has small spiky cones, which drop off and cover the ground under the tree, making it rather unpleasant if you are bare-footed.

Look out for the rounded, sturdy trees of the **Cashew Nut Tree** *(Anancardium occidentale)*. This has bright green, shiny, rounded leaves and casts a very dense shade. It is, of course, cultivated and forms an important cash crop. The nuts grow on what are called cashew apples.

Another tree which was introduced for its commercial value is the strange looking **Kapok Tree** *(Ceiba pentandra)*. It is a very tall tree up to about 25 metres whose branches grow straight out horizontally, almost at right angles to the trunk. The seed pods produce the fluffy, white kapok which is used to stuff mattresses and pillows.

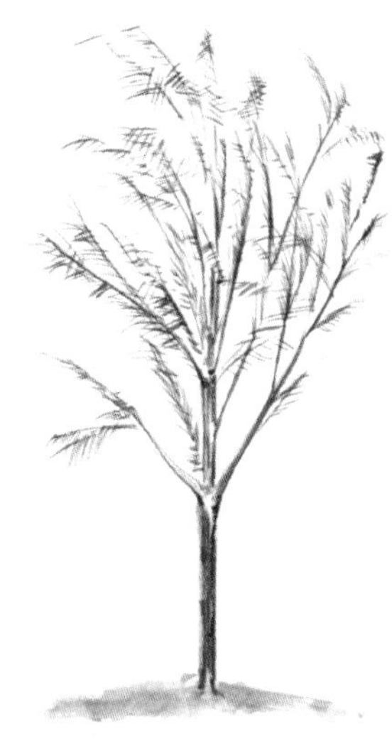

Casaurina

Cashew Nut Tree

The beach, the reef and beachcombing

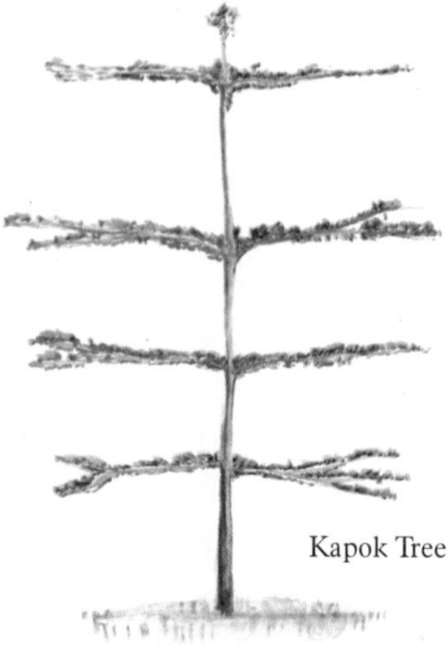

Kapok Tree

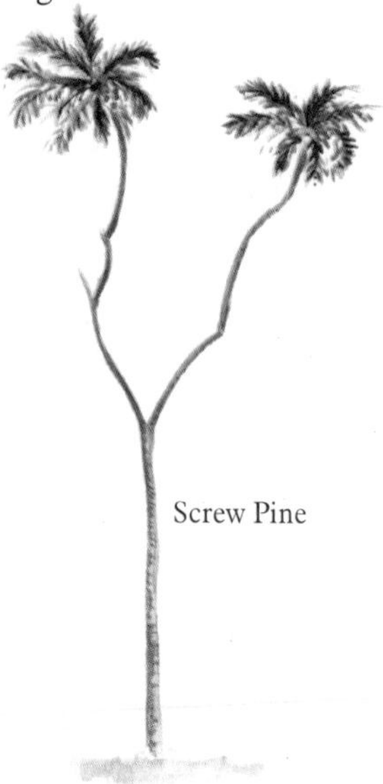

Screw Pine

Coconut Palm

Doum Palm

INSECTS

There are probably 100,000 different species of insect in Africa, and certainly some not yet known to science. Even the casual visitor to Africa, who never leaves the urban areas and sees only the city streets and insides of houses, and whose only glimpse of animal life is urban dogs and cats, cannot fail to notice the insect life. Inside houses you will see tiny, brown ants, especially in the kitchen. These are the so called **Sugar Ants** *(Camponotus maculatus)* which are seen following predetermined paths across the window sill and down the wall before disappearing into a tiny hole or crack in the plaster. They are harmless, but a bit of a nuisance in the kitchen. A good deal more unpleasant are the **cockroaches** which do not usually appear until after dark. The commonest household cockroach is known as the **American Cockroach** *(Periplaneta americana)*. It is about 30mm in length, and a dark shiny reddish brown in colour, with long antennae which are constantly waved about. Another smaller darker cockroach also occurs and is called the **German Cockroach** *(Blattella germanica)*. The 'wild' cockroach which occurs in Africa, lives in the bark of trees and under fallen logs. Cockroaches are usually seen scuttling about the floor or up walls and furniture. They rarely fly, but when they do it is peculiarly disconcerting. Cockroaches do not bite or sting and their role in the spread of disease is debated, but nevertheless, they are associated in most people's mind with dirt.

On safari keep your eyes open for insects, and don't be tempted into ignoring everything less obviously impressive than a full grown lion. Long before you see a lion you will see the termite mounds or termataria so conspicuous a feature of many parts of eastern Africa. Termite mounds, ant hills as they are also called, when freshly built are the colour of the underlying soil and, therefore, often reddish. They can be 2 metres high or more, and old established ones acquire a covering of herbs and bushes and often small trees. The **Termites** *(Termitidae)* which live within these ant hills are commonly, though incorrectly, known as **White Ants**.

Stick Insects *(Phasmatodea)* and the **Praying Mantis** *(Mantodea)* are fairly common, but not easy to see. Both of them are masters of cryptic coloration, which means that they resemble their background in the most amazing ways. The incredibly thin, brown body of the stick insect, with its long legs, exactly resembles a piece of dry twig or grass. Similarly, some species of praying mantis grow the most extraordinary appendages on their bodies to mimic flowers and bark. The reproductive habits of some of these insects is rather strange, as it seems that male stick insects are very rare indeed, and, the female praying mantis devours her partner after mating. Neither praying mantises nor stick insects sting or bite, but both can hurt the fingers by the sharp spines on their legs. A praying mantis, so-called because it holds its front legs together in an attitude of praying, is an attractive insect with an alert and seemingly intelligent way of moving its head from side to side.

Locusts *(Acrididae)* are probably the most famous members of the grasshopper group to be found in Africa. You are not likely to see a classical swarm of the Desert Locust, but you may see the occasional members of the group, which are recognisable as very large grasshoppers, which, when they fly, reveal colourful wings. There are two important species of locust in Africa. The **Desert Locust** *(Schistocera gregaria)* which is the one mentioned in the Bible and which occurs mainly in northern Africa including Ethiopia, Somalia and

Insects

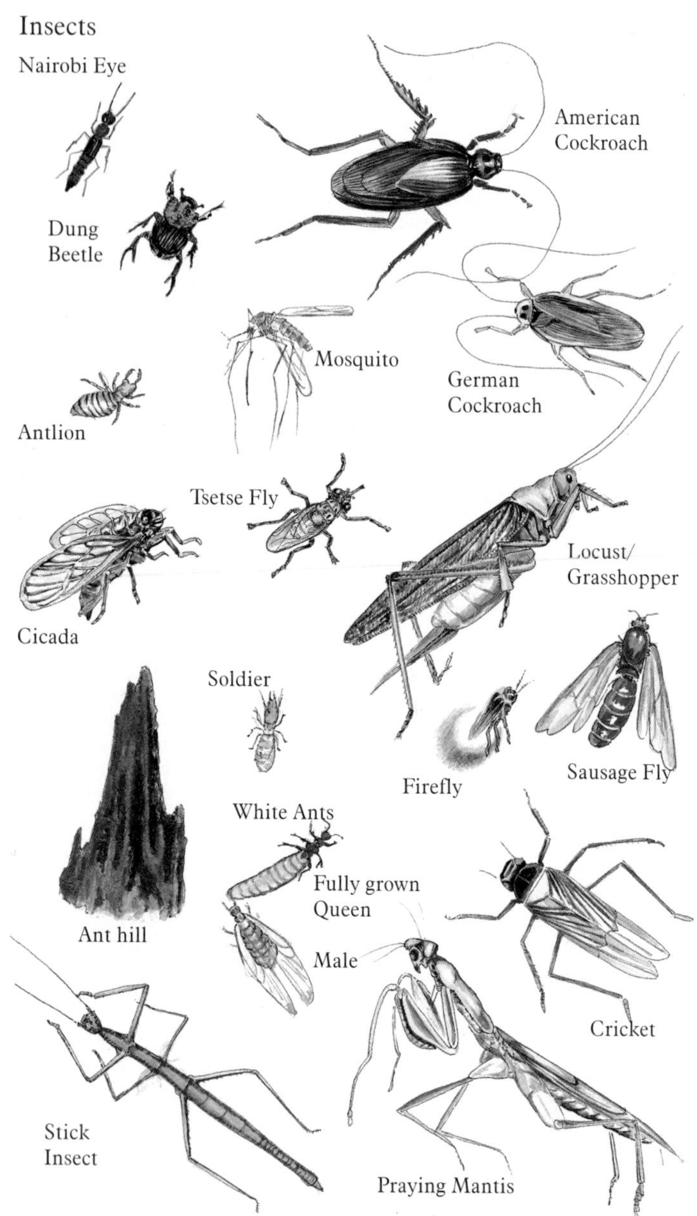
Nairobi Eye
American Cockroach
Dung Beetle
Mosquito
German Cockroach
Antlion
Tsetse Fly
Locust/ Grasshopper
Cicada
Soldier
Sausage Fly
Firefly
White Ants
Fully grown Queen
Male
Ant hill
Cricket
Stick Insect
Praying Mantis

Termite City: 100 Million Years Underground

Termites have existed in a similar form for 100 million years, and are by far the most ancient organised community in the world. They pre-date other communally living creatures, such as man, by many millions of years. There are many different species of termite, but all species have certain features in common. They live within the sometimes huge mounds known properly as termataria and commonly as ant hills. Most termites are blind and never venture out nor see the sun. Almost nothing is known about the organisation within these communities. The workers look after the young, the queen produces the eggs and the soldiers defend the community from their arch-enemy the ants. This much is known, but how are decisions made, how is food gathering organised, and which creature, if any, has control over the others? They appear to live in a very totalitarian world, and cannot survive as individuals. If you break open a mound you will see the termites inside running around in apparent disarray. The workers will rush down the tiny corridors and tunnels to get away from the dangers of the outside world. On the other hand the soldiers will appear with their formidable jaws wide open, ready to defend the colony. Meanwhile the workers will very quickly repair the hole to seal off the colony. But who issues the orders, who organises it? The workers collect vegetable matter from the outside world to take into the colony as food. Anything with cellulose, dead wood, leaves and even paper is gathered. If you leave a piece of paper out on the grass where these insects are foraging, the next morning you will find it full of holes. Should you disturb foraging workers with their attendant soldiers, you may not see them, but you will hear a strange rustling noise which is produced by hundreds of insects tapping the ground to warn of danger. The noise will end as quickly as it started, but stamp on the ground again and you will trigger the response once more. The termites' appetite for dead wood is what makes them a nuisance in eastern Africa. Older houses can be riddled with them, and silently and unknown to the human occupants they eat they way through the wooden beams leaving only the paint behind. It is not uncommon to poke your finger through the paint of a door post to find that the post has almost vanished, leaving the paint like an empty skin.

northern Kenya, and the **Red Locust** *(Nomadacris septemfasciata)* which is found in southern Uganda and western Tanzania. While swarming, locusts fall prey to many birds such as Marabous, White Storks and various birds of prey which follow the swarms for the abundant food source they provide.

Another member of the grasshopper family very common in Uganda at certain times of the year, is the **Nsenene** or Edible Grasshopper. This is a mainly green or brown grasshopper about 6-8cms long. It swarms at certain times of the year, and being attracted to lights can be seen in hundreds, sometimes thousands around the lights of Kampala after dark. It is much prized as a delicacy and small boys risk death and injury from passing cars by running across the roads in attempts to catch the insects. They are eaten either raw or cooked and taste slightly sweet.

Out-of-doors in Africa you will frequently hear the persistent high pitched whine of the **Cicada** *(Cicadidae)*. There are several species of cicada and they spend their time clinging to the bark of trees where their camouflage is so perfect that even guided by their song you will find them difficult to see. They are particularly irritating in that as soon as you get near enough to spot them they

THE CICADA: IT'S NOT A CRICKET

Cicadas have a very interesting life cycle. The African species have not been studied in quite such depth as have the American ones, but it is likely that they have similar life histories. The so-called periodical cicada lays its eggs in the bark of a tree. On hatching, the nymph drops to the ground and immediately burrows beneath the surface. It then spends its entire life tunnelling through the soil going from tree root to tree root. It feeds on these roots by sucking the sap from them. This nymph stage lasts in the African species probably two or three years. In some American species it lasts up to 17 years. When it is ready the nymph tunnels out of the soil and climbs up the bark of the nearest tree. At this stage you can see them. They are about 2.5cm long and look like some monster from outer space with hard bodies and longish legs. They always emerge after dark and interestingly enough they will climb up the side of the tree away from any light. During the course of the night the hard skin splits down the back and a white soft floppy looking insect with crumpled wings emerges which gradually hardens and darkens into the familiar cicada. While they cling helplessly to their cast off 'skins' they are very vulnerable to ants. Eventually they fly off leaving the empty colourless skins still hanging on to the bark. You can see these quite often on trees.

become silent and immediately invisible. They sing by day, especially in the heat of the day when their song is a quintessential part of the African noon, and also at nightfall.

Another noisy insect is the **Cricket** *(Gryllidae)*. There are many species found in Africa, and many are nocturnal. If one gets into your room at night you will not get any sleep until you have captured it and put it out. Catch it in an upturned glass, then slide something like a post-card under the glass and shake it outside.

If you look on the dry ground under the eaves and overhangs of houses you will notice small smooth conical pits an inch or so wide and deep. These are seen in fine or sandy soil which remains dry all the time. These pits are made by the **Antlion** *(Myrmeleontidae)*, a strange little creature which is the larval form of a dragonfly-like insect. Take a piece of grass and very gently scratch the side of the pit so that grains of sand tumble down into the bottom. If you do it right you will provoke the antlion, who lives in the pit, to attack. It builds these pits as traps for ants which tumble into the pit, and, because of the soft soil, are unable to climb out, so fall to the bottom. The antlion promptly emerges and with its ferocious jaws, grabs the ant. Have a look at one of them. They are a brownish nondescript little insect perhaps 5-10mm long, with the most enormous jaws for the size of the animal. When you let it go it will burrow into the soil at great speed going backwards. These quaint little creatures seem very different from the adult insect, which is rather like a dragonfly to look at, with large gauzy wings.

Ants seem to get everywhere in Africa and there are many different sorts. Everyone has heard of the so called **Driver Ants** *(Dorylinae)*. They are more commonly known as **Safari Ants** or **Siafu** in this part of Africa. These are the ants of legend which supposedly can engulf whole households and devour every living thing. In reality it is not quite like that. For a start the column of ants moves quite slowly so most animals have plenty of time to get out of the way. Secondly the marching columns are not as big as the ones in story books. Still it is quite a sight to see these ants on the move. If you are unlucky enough to tread into the middle

Queens And Gardeners: How To Start An Ant Hill

The queen is a large soft bodied creature, white or yellowish white in colour and about the size of your little finger, which you will never see unless you dig out an ant hill. Her role is to lay eggs on demand which she does with great efficiency. The young of the next generation, the 'princes' and 'princesses', leave the colony altogether when the weather is favourable. If you are present at this time you will not miss it. The insects, about 5-10 mm long and quite fat-bodied, appear mainly at night and the next morning you will find them everywhere. They start off with wings and fly varying distances before falling to the ground. There they shrug off their wings and the females give off a pheromone to attract the males. The male will land behind the female and keep in contact with her and follow her about in tandem. Soon others join on behind, until you get small lines of perhaps half a dozen or more white ants scurrying around in single file. The object of this behaviour is for the female and attending male to burrow into the ground where they will, in due course found a new colony. Unfortunately, the whole world is against them. While they are in flight birds will catch them in hundreds, and on the ground everything from man to frogs to geckos will relish them. Some couples, however, manage to run this gauntlet to start the next generation.

There is a species of white ant which is actually a gardener. Inside the ant hill they construct thin shelves of mud on which they cultivate a certain type of fungus, which is needed as a food for the young termites. The workers collect this fungus from above ground. Only a specific type of fungus will do, and 'weeds' are carefully removed. In their fungus gardens they do not allow the fungus to grow as it does normally above ground, but tend it in some way so that it produces small white spherical growths, which are fed to the developing termites. The gardeners manage their garden skilfully so that a regular supply of food is available for the needs of the colony.

of a column, you will know all about it. Their bite is ferocious! The adult breeding male of these ants is called a **Sausage Fly**. It is about 3.5cm long and is a brown, slightly hairy looking insect which bumbles around the lights at night. Although it flies, it seems to spend a lot of its time crashing into objects in the room and falling to the floor where it wriggles about helplessly until it takes off again, only to crash into something else. It is difficult to associate its comic incompetence with the ruthless efficiency of the Safari Ants.

Perhaps the most photographed insects in Africa are the **Dung Beetles** *(Scarabaeidae)*. Pictures of them rolling their balls of dung across the grasslands are often shown in natural history films. They collect the dung into balls, which the female then lays her eggs in and the young feed on. They are related to the sacred scarab beetle, which was worshiped by the ancient Egyptians.

The **Mosquito** and the **Tsetse Fly** are two well-known insects in Africa. Not all mosquitos are malarial, but only those belonging to the *Anopheline* group. These can be distinguished from the harmless *Culex* mosquitos by the way they stand before biting. The malarial ones hold their body at an angle of 45° to the surface, whereas the body of the harmless ones is parallel to the surface. Only the female bites and she can be recognised by her thread-like antennae. The male has feathery antennae, and feeds only on the nectar of flowers. There is more than one species of **Tsetse Fly** *(Glossina)*. They have a bite like a red hot needle and carry various diseases of animals, as well as sleeping sickness in humans. It is about 8mm long and holds its wings overlapping one on top of the other like the closed blades of a pair of scissors.

Mention must be made of a rather unpleasant insect. This is a *Staphylinid* beetle really called a rove beetle, but commonly known as **Nairobi Eye**, after the painful condition it inflicts if you crush it. It is a small, thin, red and black insect which on casual inspection does not appear to have wings. It has a way of wriggling its abdomen about. Typically, the insect alights on your neck, and you instinctively put up your hand to brush it away. In doing this you will crush the insect: its body juices are intensely irritating and cause very painful blistering of the skin. Should you then rub your eyes before washing your hands it will be extremely painful.

The **butterflies** of Africa are so numerous that it is not possible to do more than mention them here. Most of them can only be identified with certainty in the hand. This, of course, means catching and killing them, which is really not a good idea. Probably the most beautiful are the **Swallowtails** or *Papilionidae* which can be recognised on the wing as a group by the noticeable "tail" on the hind wing. Africa's largest butterfly *Papilio antimachus*, which has a wing span up to 20-23cms, belongs to this group. It is a forest dwelling butterfly which, sadly, is quite rare. One other butterfly is easily identified on the wing, not by its appearance, but by its behaviour. This is a member of the Whites or *Pieridae* family which at certain times of the year migrates in large numbers. You cannot fail to notice the **African Migrant** as large numbers of them are seen, all flying determinedly in the same direction.

Lastly, look out for the beautiful **Firefly** *(Lampyridae)*. The sight of dozens and dozens of these lovely insects flitting through the trees after dark is one of the sights of Africa you will never forget. They are rather local in their distribution, but are worth looking out for especially, but by no means only, in the higher areas.

TREES

Visitors to Africa often comment on the numbers of flowering trees seen in all the major cities. Trees such as the Jacaranda and Flamboyant are very beautiful when in full flower. The **Jacaranda** *(Jacaranda mimosifolia)* is not in itself a beautiful tree being very straggly and rather tall, but when it bears its masses of beautiful mauvish blue tubular-shaped flowers it is very striking. You can recognise it when it is not in flower by the large divided leaves, each division of which carries very many small leaflets arranged along a central axis. The **Flamboyant Tree** *(Delonix rex)* has similar leaves. When not in flower it can be distinguished from the Jacaranda by its very different, and much more attractive, shape. It does not grow as tall, only up to about 7.5 metres and is spreading and more compact in shape. This makes it an ideal tree to sit under on a hot day. When you see it in flower, you know why it is called the Flamboyant Tree. It is covered in a mass of mainly scarlet flowers. Some of the flowers have yellow tips giving the tree a golden appearance. Both Jacaranda and Flamboyant trees are often planted in towns. Another tree with brilliant red flowers, and one which is often confused with the Flamboyant, is the indigenous **Flame Tree** *(Spathodea nilotica)*. The two trees really look very different, except for the flowers. The Flame Tree is very tall, up to 18 metres with a straight smooth trunk, and in the wild is found on the forest edge. Particularly fine specimens can be seen in western Kenya. The rather shiny leaves are also divided, but into largish lobes, rather than the tiny leaflets of the Flamboyant Tree. The flowers are almost tulip shaped and bright scarlet in colour.

Other trees seen in towns and gardens include the **Bottle Brush** *(Callistemon)*, a rather small and slender tree whose branches are thin and tend to droop downwards at the ends. Its flower is shaped just like a bottle brush and is usually red, though white ones occur. The leaf is long and narrow.

Yet another tree with scarlet flowers is the indigenous **Coral Tree** *(Erythrina)* which grows in rather scrubby land. This has a gnarled appearance with a rough corky bark, often armed with blunt spines. The leaves are rather leathery and divided into three sturdy leaflets. The scarlet flowers appear before the leaves. The seeds are interesting in that they are the familiar red and black 'lucky beans'. Often planted in or near towns and settlements you will see the **Gum** or **Eucalyptus Tree**. It was planted to drain swamps and also to provide firewood. This is readily recognised by its height, its characteristic long, thin leaves and the colourful peeling bark.

In the plains the most characteristic tree is no doubt the **Thorn Tree** *(Acacia)*. There is more than one sort of Thorn Tree, and though they vary a lot in size and shape, they all have very divided, almost feathery leaves and long sharp thorns. Some have a noticeable yellow bark, and many are characteristically flat topped. Two other very noticeable trees are the **Baobab** *(Adansonia digitata)* and the **Candelabra Tree** *(Euphorbia candelabrum)*. The Baobab cannot be mistaken for anything else. It grows particularly on the coast and also inland for some miles. The trunk of a fully grown specimen is enormous in girth and the usually leafless branches stick out of the top of the tree for all the world as if they were roots and the tree was planted upside down. The Candelabra Tree is often mistaken for a large cactus, as it has succulent branches with ridges or 'wings' running up them.. It is widespread in grasslands. These three trees are all indigenous to east Africa.

The **Sausage Tree** *(Kigelia aethiopica)*,

Trees

which grows on the African grasslands is a rather ordinary looking tree which has extraordinary looking fruit. The name given to it is understandable when you see the long sausage shaped fruit hanging down. These fruit can be nearly one metre in length and 15 cms wide. They hang down on long thin stalks, giving the tree a remarkable appearance.

Two fruits that you will certainly enjoy are the **Mango** *(Mangerifera indica)* and the **Paw-paw** *(Carica papaya)*, and both the trees are widely grown. The Mango Tree has very dense dark shiny foliage and grows in a round shape. It is a good shade tree, too. The Paw-Paw on the other hand has enormous hand-shaped leaves, which are almost invariably tattered in appearance. The trunk is thin and the leaves come off at the top. Only the female tree bears the fruit, which hang down close to the trunk just below the leaves.

It is a curious fact that many of the familiar trees and shrubs, which are thought of as quintessentially African, are actually not indigenous at all, but were introduced into Africa by the early European settlers, many of whom were fanatical gardeners. For example the Jacaranda comes from Brazil, and the Flamboyant from Madagascar. The Frangipani was introduced from Mexico, both the Gum and the Bottle Brush are Australian in origin, the Mango and the Hibiscus come from Asia and the Pawpaw and the Purple Wreath from the Americas. If you are interested in trees, both indigenous and introduced you should make a point of visiting the Botanical Gardens in Entebbe. This is a beautiful spot on the shores of Lake Victoria where the trees are well tended and are labelled.

Bottle Brush

Flame Tree

Trees

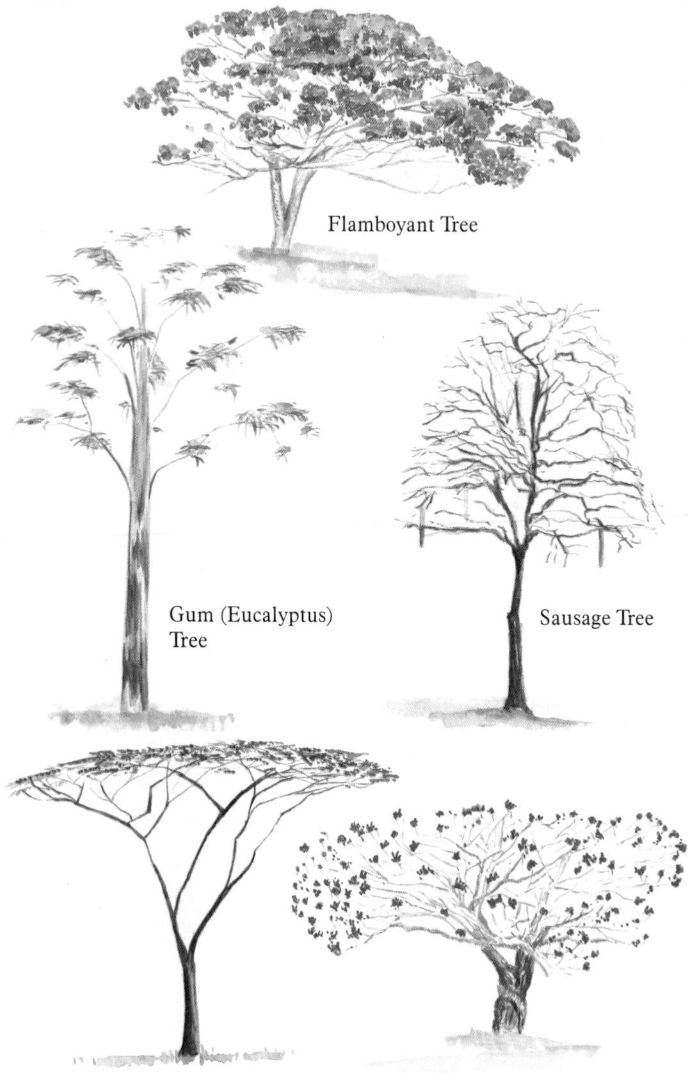
Flamboyant Tree
Gum (Eucalyptus) Tree
Sausage Tree
Thorn Tree
Coral Tree

FLOWERS AND FLOWERING SHRUBS

Flowers and flowering shrubs surround you in east Africa. They are planted in towns and cities and you will see them in the countryside too. One of the most colourful and widely planted in city flower beds is the **Canna Lily** *(Canna indica)* with large leaves which are either green or bronze, and lots of large bright red or yellow flowers. It can be more than 1 metre high.

Flowering shrubs include the well-known **Frangipani** *(Plumeria rubra)*, which often has a sweet scent. This is a shrub with fat rather stubby branches and long leaves. The flowers are about 3 cms across and usually pink or white in colour and of a waxy appearance. If you cut the bark the sticky sap which oozes out, can be very irritating to the skin. The **Hibiscus** is another bushy shrub, which, like many other plants, is always known by its scientific name. This is cultivated in many forms, but is basically a trumpet shaped flower as much as 7 or 8 cms across, which has a very long "tongue" growing out from the middle of the trumpet. The colours vary from scarlet to orange, yellow and white. The leaves are more or less heart shaped or oval with jagged edges.

One of the commonest cultivated flowering shrubs is the **Bougainvillea**. This is a dense bush, or sometimes a climber, with oval leaves and rather long thorns. The flowers often cover the whole bush and can be a wide variety of colours including pinkish-purple, orange, yellow and white. If you look carefully at one of the flowers you will see that the brightly coloured part is not formed by the petals, which are quite small and undistinguished, but by the large bracts, which, at first glance may be mistaken for petals. Look out too for the **Purple Wreath** *(Petrea)* which is a semi-climber often used as a hedge. It has strange papery leaves, and the masses of small purple-blue flowers grow densely in long spikes. A plant which is both beautiful and interesting is a form of morning glory

Lantana

Canna Lily

Flowers and flowering shrubs

sometimes called the **Moon Flower** *(Ipomoea).* The Moon Flower is a creeper with large trumpet-shaped white flowers, very like a large version of the bindweed or convululus of Europe. The interesting thing about it is that it opens only after dark, and opens so quickly that you can watch it happening. This is a never-failing source of pleasure.

All the plants mentioned above are mainly to be seen in gardens and city parks, but there are also many interesting or beautiful flowering plants which grow wild. One of these, which is interesting, rather than beautiful is the **Touch-me-not** or **Sensitive Plant** *(Mimosa pudica).* The Touch-me-not is a prickly, woody, low growing plant only a few inches high which grows in poor soil. The leaves are like that of the mimosa and the interesting thing is that when you touch them they immediately fold up. As in the movement of the moonflower, you can see this happening. A very common flowering shrub in grassland and scrub is **Lantana**, which comes in various forms. It is rather straggly and has rough, toothed, oval leaves which grow in pairs up the square and prickly stem. The flowers grow together in a flattened head, the ones near the middle of the head being usually yellowish, while those at the rim are pink, pale purple or orange. The fruit is a black shiny berry.

In the mountains of east Africa you will find many strange plants. They are the familiar types such as **Heather** *(Ericaceae)*, **Groundsel** *(Senecio)* and **Red-hot Poker** *(Kniphofia)*, but the strange thing about them is that they are giant sized.

Lastly mention must be made of a plant which is very common in all swamps, but does not have very distinguished looking flowers. This is the **Papyrus** *(Cyperus papyrus)*. Its feathery topped stalks form huge swamps, especially in the region of the large lakes such as Lake Victoria.

Bougainvillea

Moon Flower

CROPS

Eastern Africa is very much an agricultural part of the world, and many different crops are grown here. Some of them will be very familiar to visitors from Europe and America, but others are quite different. Subsistence level farming is still widespread, and most settlements have their small fields of crops planted nearby for the use of the inhabitants. These vary according to the part of the country. In the west of the area, in Uganda, you will see small **banana** plantations surrounding almost every house. The very large, darkish green, shiny leaves are unlike any other, and the tree often has a tattered appearance. This banana is not the familiar sweet yellow one favoured in Europe, but a large green one which does not turn yellow and is more correctly called a **plantain,** known locally as **matooke.** Matooke is eaten as a staple rather in the way we eat potatoes. It is peeled and cooked by steaming. This is done by wrapping the raw plantain in its own leaves and steaming it, usually over an open fire out of doors, for several hours. It then becomes soft and a little like mashed potatoes in consistency. This matooke is quite local in its distribution being favoured by the Baganda and their neighbours around the shores of Lake Victoria.

Other crops are more widespread. In particular, **maize** (sweet corn) is eaten in many parts and as **posho**, is the staple food in large areas of Tanzania and Kenya. Mostly, but not exclusively, in the drier parts of the region **cassava** is grown. This is a rather straggly bush some 2 metres high. The leaves are dark green and divided into thin fingers. The part that is eaten is the root. Cassava is traditionally a famine, or reserve crop, because the root can stay in the ground for long periods without spoiling and be harvested when needed - a sort of living larder. In colonial times planting of cassava was compulsory as an insurance against famine. The plant is doubly useful as the leaves can be used to feed the Tilapia which are raised in fish farms. Cassava is better known in Europe as Tapioca.

Tea, coffee and sugar cane are all grown here in the wetter parts, and there are places where you can see all three growing near each other, for example on the road from the Kenyan border to Kampala. If a herd of cows happens to be passing, you have all you need for a tea or coffee break! **Tea**, though, is mainly a highland crop, and the large tea gardens, with their flat topped, shiny leafed bushes can be seen in western Kenya and western Uganda. The tea gardens are almost all run by large, sometimes international companies. If left to itself tea will grow to a tree 10 metres tall. **Sugar Cane** is a large grass-like crop standing nearly as high as a man, and is grown in many areas, but not the very dry parts. **Coffee** comes in two forms, **robusta** which used to grow wild in Uganda, and the more highly prized **arabica** which is native to Ethiopia, and is now grown in the highland regions. In East Africa coffee growing is a family enterprise and families grow and tend their own plots or plantations. They sell the coffee beans to the Government and it is East Africa's most important cash crop. When the flowers are in bloom, which is mainly in January and February, the sweet smell is quite overpowering and unforgettable. The unripe coffee berries, or cherries, can be seen as green, and later red, berries clustering along the length of the stems. These three crops are, of course, cash crops and need processing, but a stick of sugar cane is often chewed, especially by children, as a sweet.

Sisal which is grown in the hotter, drier

Crops

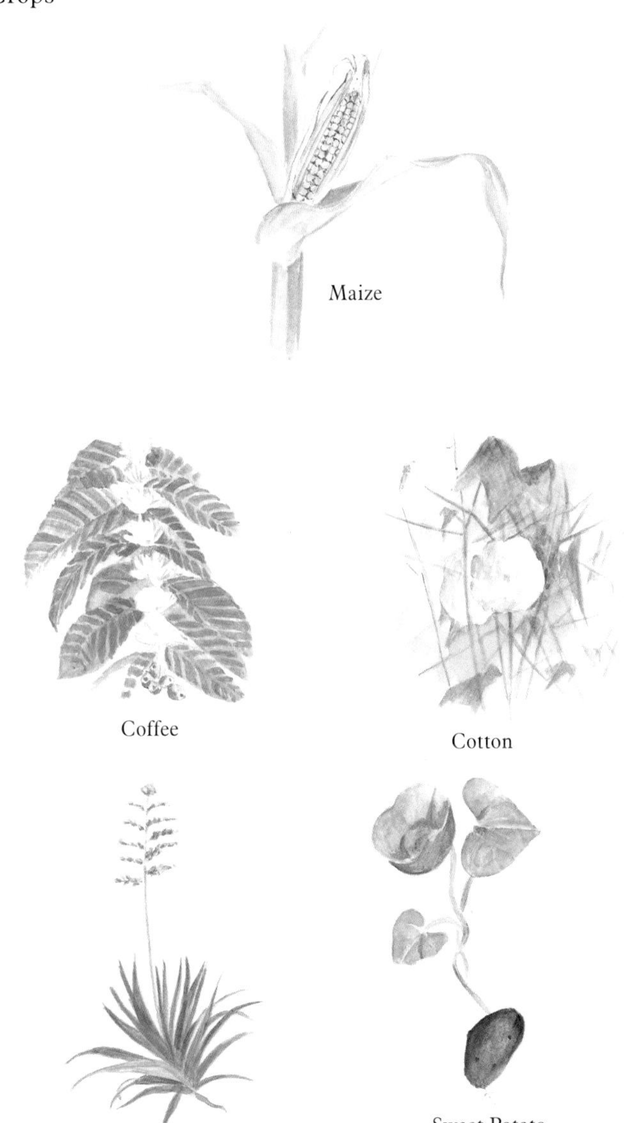

Maize

Coffee

Cotton

Sisal

Sweet Potato

Crops

Sugar Cane

Ground Nut

Tea

Banana

Cassava

Carnation

Pyrethrum

areas of Kenya and Tanzania is another cash crop. It is planted in straight rows in large plantations, and looks rather like the familiar yucca seen growing in pots in Europe. The leaves are straight and have a very spiky tip. From the middle of the leaves grows a very tall stem on the top of which is the flower. The fibre, extracted from the leaves, was a very important cash crop for the making of rope and string, but the advent of synthetic fibres has affected the market. But you still see it especially in eastern Kenya. Another cash crop subject to the whims of fashion is **cotton**. At one time it was the prime earner of foreign exchange, but now has been superseded by coffee. You can see it by the road side in the rather drier areas growing in rather nondescript knee high bushes. When the cotton is ready for picking the fluffy white bolls are unmistakeable. It is processed in factories called ginneries.

Ground nuts are an inconspicuous crop which tends to lie close to the ground. The plant above ground has a clover shaped leaf. The nuts themselves are clustered on the roots and out of sight. Another low growing crop is the **sweet potato**. This is invariably grown on mounds of soil scraped up with the local hoe or *jembe*. The plant is a straggly one with large flat leaves and a very pretty pale purple trumpet-shaped flower.

There are two flowers which are grown in parts of Kenya which are a fairly recent cash crop. One of these is **pyrethrum**, which you will see in small plots near houses, especially in the highlands around Nairobi. This is a daisy-like flower and it is harvested to make the natural insect killer, pyrethrum. The other flower which is being grown in the cooler parts of the region, especially near Hell's Gate in Kenya, is the **carnation.** This is grown for export and the square fields with the bright green foliage and almost constant irrigation, are conspicuous against the drier natural vegetation.

More about crops

It may surprise you to know that apart from coffee and perhaps cotton, none of these crops is indigenous to Africa. The plantain probably originated in Asia, as did tea. Sugar cane is from the South Pacific. Cassava, sweet potato, ground nuts and maize are all from the Americas. They were all introduced by early settlers, mostly towards the end of the nineteenth century or the early part of this century.

FIELD NOTES

FIELD NOTES

How The Leopard Got His Spots

'Well, make up your mind', said the Ethiopian, 'because I'd hate to go hunting without you, but I must if you insist on looking like a sunflower against a tarred fence.'

'I'll take spots, then,' said the Leopard; 'but don't make 'em too vulgar-big. I wouldn't look like Giraffe—not for ever so.'

'I'll make 'em with the tips of my fingers,' said the Ethiopian. 'There's plenty of black left on my skin still. Stand over!'

Then the Ethiopian put his five fingers close together (there was plenty of black left on his new skin still) and pressed them all over the Leopard, and wherever the five fingers touched they left five little black marks, all close together. You can see them on any leopard's skin you like, Best Beloved. Sometimes the fingers slipped and the marks got a little blurred; but if you look closely at any Leopard now you will see that there are always five spots—off five fat black finger-tips.

'Now you *are* a beauty!' said the Ethiopian. 'You can lie out on the bare ground and look like a heap of pebbles. You can lie on the naked rocks and look like a piece of pudding-stone. You can lie out on a leafy branch and look like sunshine sifting through the leaves; and you can lie right across the centre of a path and look like nothing in particular. Think of that and purr!'

Just So Stories, Rudyard Kipling

INDEX

A

B

C

D

E

F

G

H

I

J

K

L

M

N

O

P

R

S

T

U

V

W

Y

Z

Kasenyi Fishing Village

This fishing village is located 6 km off the Entebbe-Kampala road. Both traditional and more modern techniques are used today – often the traditional canoes are used with an outboard motor attached. Nile perch and tilapia are amongst a number of species caught. You will be able to see fishermen mending their nets and boats and it is possible to arrange a trip to some of the nearby islands.

Local information

● Where to stay

A+ *Lake Victoria*, PO Box 15, Circular Road, T 20644/20645/21078, F 20404. Newly refurbished hotel is often described as the best in Uganda. The facilities are excellent and include a swimming pool and the nearby golf course. Swimming for non-residents at US$7. Snacks and drinks available and hot showers. If you are flying out of Entebbe on the early morning British Airways flight you can get a discount to stay here and you will be provided with transport to the airport the next morning. Ask for details at the British Airways office in Kampala.

B *Entebbe Resort*, left after the *Entebbe Club* and go through the golf course towards the lake. Banda accommodation. There is a beach although as with all of Lake Victoria remember that swimming here you risk contracting bilharzia.

E *Kidepo*, beyond the *Lake Victoria Hotel* on the airport road. It is rather basic and not particularly good value, but is convenient if you cannot get to Kampala, or have an early flight.

● Camping

At Entebbe Resort.

● Places to eat

Apart from the hotels themselves the best place to eat is the *Entebbe Club*, it is pleasant with tables outside and serves up a fairly limited menu – including fish and chips and such like. This was the club for old colonial officials – being close to the other crucial institution of a colonial town – the golf club.

● Shopping

Crafts On the road down to Entebbe there are a number of stalls selling everything from pottery, mats, baskets and a huge range of fruit and vegetables. Prices are not as cheap as you would expect – the sellers obviously are used to people buying on their way to and from the airport. They include brightly coloured woven baskets which are made by Nubian women. Generations of Nubians have lived close to Entebbe – but they have maintained their cultural identity.

Maps The Department of Surveys and Mapping has its office in Entebbe – turn left opposite the playground, walk down the road and it is on the left. The staff are very helpful and will do their best to dig out the maps that you want. Get a receipt if you do buy anything, as there are reports of much of the money disappearing into the wrong hands. Many however are out of stock although the department is in the process of re-printing many of the old series.

● Transport

Road Minibus from the matatu park in **Kampala**. They go every few minutes and take about 45 minutes, costing US$1.

EAST FROM JINJA TO TORORO & MOUNT ELGON

Contents

Maps

Compared to the West of Uganda the East part receives relatively few visitors apart from those passing through on the way to and from Kenya. Some visitors however do stop off at Jinja and interest in climbing Mount Elgon from the Uganda side is once again increasing.

Jinja

The town of Jinja is located on the road to Kenya 80 km from Kampala and 143 km to the Kenyan border. It is perhaps best known for being the source of the Nile and is located at the head of Napoleon Gulf, on the northern end of Lake Victoria, the second largest freshwater lake in the world (after Lake Superior). During the bad times in Uganda, Jinja, like most other towns in the country, fell into disrepair. However there was one important exception to this – through the enthusiasm of one individual in the Jinja Parks Department the gardens, roundabouts and verges were kept immaculately – the flower beds were always planted and weeded and the lawns mowed. In recent years Jinja, has recovered impressively, the roads are being repaired and the town centre rehabilitated. As you walk through the town you will see the old colonial and Asian bungalows in their spacious gardens. Many of these are extremely overcrowded and dilapidated, while others have recently been renovated.

Places of interest

Source of the Nile The source of the Nile was actually at the site of the Rippon Falls. These were submerged during the construction of the Owen Falls Dam, however ripples can still be seen from the picnic area. It is lovely to sit on the lawn in the shade listening to the birds and watching the swirling river below. The islets and rocks recorded by Speke (see box below) have disappeared with the building of the Owen Falls Dam. There is a plaque marking the spot from which the Nile begins its journey through Uganda, Sudan and Egypt.

To get to the Source of the Nile you can either walk or take a bicycle taxi from the town centre – you will have no problems finding someone to take you. If you are walking, go along Bell Avenue

Speke And The Source Of The Nile

Speke was the first European to see source of the Nile in 1862, from the other side of the inlet to the present picnic area. He recorded the moment thus:

"Most beautiful was the scene, nothing could surpass it! It was the very perfection of the kind of effect aimed at in a highly-kept park; with a magnificent stream from 600 to 700 yards wide, dotted with islets and rocks, the former occupied by fishermens' huts, the latter by terns and crocodiles basking in the sun, flowing between fine high grassy banks, with rich trees and plantains in the background. The expedition had now performed its functions; old Father Nile without any doubt rises in the Victoria Nyanza."

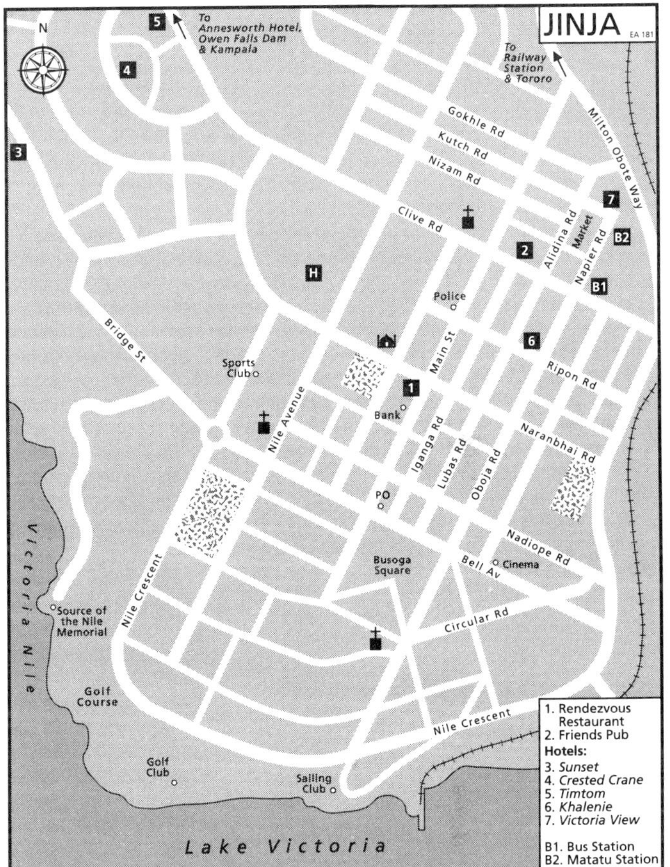

out beyond the Sports Club and then turn left along Cliff Road.

Owen Falls Dam The Owen Falls Dam was built in 1954 and it supplies most of Uganda, and a good part of Kenya, with electricity. During the turmoil of the Amin period a group of dedicated engineers managed to keep the generators going almost without interuption. The falls themselves were hidden during the construction of the dam, but the dam and the new falls that it creates are impressive in themselves. The main road from Kampala to the E crosses the dam, so if you are travelling by bus or in a matatu try and get a seat on the appropriate side (left if you are heading E) in order to get a good view. Because of the dam's strategic and economic importance and its perceived vulnerability you are not allowed to take photographs.

Bujagali Falls Downstream from the Owen Falls Dam are the Bujagali Falls. These can be reached by crossing the

Bishop Hannington

Coming from Kampala, a little beyond Jinja on the right, is a place called Buluba (meaning the place of Luba, once chief of the area) which is the site of some historical interest in the history of religion in Uganda. For it was here that Bishop Hannington, who in 1884 was consecrated as the first Bishop of the Diocese of Eastern Equatorial Africa, met his death. Hannington kept a detailed diary during his journeys and it is through these, and the stories from the survivors, that we know what happened.

James Hannington had first visited East Africa in 1882 as the leader of a party of reinforcements for the Victoria Nyanza Mission in Uganda. However, he had suffered severely from dysentery and had been forced to return to Britain. However, after being made bishop he began to plan his return to Africa almost immediately. At this time the route into Uganda that was used was from Zanzibar, through what is now Tanzania, to the S of Lake Victoria. However, in 1883 a new route had been used, through Kenya, via Busoga, to the N of the Lake. This route through Maasai country was more direct and had less harsh climatic conditions.

However, in Oct 1884 the Kabaka of Buganda, King Mutesa I, died and was succeeded by his son Mwanga. The missionaries in Uganda now found themselves in a position that had changed from one of tolerance to one of suspicion. Hannington arrived on the East African coast in Jan 1885 and made plans to use the Maasai route. The missionaries in Buganda, on hearing of his plans, wrote to tell him that the current political situation in Buganda was such that entering by what was considered to be the back door, through Busoga, was extremely dangerous. However, the warning arrived about two weeks after Hannington set off.

Hannington's only real mistake was that he did not stick to his plans as set out in a letter to the missionaries in Buganda. He told them that he would go overland as far as Kavirondo on Lake Victoria where the mission boat should meet him and he would enter Buganda by boat. This would mean he would avoid entering Uganda through Busoga, which was what was so sensitive. Mwanga had been told that those entering Buganda from the East (that is, Busoga) would destroy the Kingdom of Buganda. Indeed the mission boat did go to the northeast of the Lake in early Oct, but hearing nothing of the Bishop it left after two days. The missionaries based in Buganda assured Mwanga that the Bishop would not enter through Busoga, so when he did so, it appeared as a calculated deceit.

On the 21st of Oct Hannington reached the headquarters of Luba, the chief of the area of Busoga. He was imprisoned, and on the orders of messengers from Buganda, speared to death and his porters massacred.

In March 1890 a small boy who had been with Hannington but who had survived the massacre, arrived in the camp of Jackson, another missionary, who was on his way to Uganda. He had with him Hannington's skull (although the lower jaw bone was missing) which was identified by his gold teeth, the soles of his boots, a rubber hot water bottle and the lid of an Army and Navy canteen. There was also another smaller skull, which was believed to be that of Pinto who was the Goan cook who had accompanied Hannington. The remains eventually found their way to Kampala and on 31st Dec 1892 they were buried on Namirembe Hill.

Owen Falls Dam (if you are coming from Kampala) and turning northwards at the Kyabazinga roundabout. It is a truly beautiful, and not fully appreciated, area with about one kilometre of raging water. There is a legend that says that a man called Mr Bujagali sometimes sits on the river on a bark cloth mat.

Local information

● Where to stay

C *Sunset*. This hotel has a wonderful location overlooking the Owen Falls Dam and is set in lovely gardens. It is rarely full and it is possible to negotiate the price down. **C** *Crested Crane*, PO Box 444, 4-4 Hannington Square, T 21513/4/5. This sprawling one-storey building is run by *Uganda Hotels* and has clearly seen better days. It is rather lacking in character and distinctly shabby round the edges.

D *Annesworth*, PO Box 1253, 3 Nalufenya Crescent, T 20086. Located not far from the *Crested Crane Hotel* and is one of the old Asian buildings. **D** *Tim Tom*, Clive Road roughly opposite the *YMCA*. Also converted from an old Asian built building. Not bad value. **D** *Triangle*, same area as the *Annesworth* and *Tim Tom*. Reasonably comfortable.

E *Victoria View Inn*, close to the market in the town centre and is good value. It is clean and friendly. **E** *Kahlenje*, Ripon Road, centre of town. Clean and friendly. Good value.

● Places to eat

There are a few in town worth trying besides those attached to hotels. ♦♦*Rendezvous*, Main Street. Simple menu, but reasonable value. ♦♦*Friend's Pub*, Clive Road near the market. Fairly straightforward grills.

● Sport (participant)

There is a **Golf Club** at Jinja as well as a **Sailing Club**.

Tororo

Situated in the far E of Uganda this is close to the border with Kenya and many people pass through on the way to and from the border crossing at Malaba. Its major claim to fame is the rock named after it,which can be seen from miles around. Built during the colonial period in the late 1940's the Tororo Cement Works made an important contribution to the development of Uganda as it took away the necessity of importing cement from Kenya. It functioned well until Amin's time. As everything in Uganda began to fall apart so did the roof of the cement works – it collapsed under the weight of cement dust as no-one had bothered to sweep it.

From Jinja the road to Kenya continues first NE and then swinging E. You will pass through the town of Iganga. This is another town with wide streets bordered by shops and houses with broad verandas. The road to the border is good and you will pass through fairly typical Ugandan scenery – clusters of small huts surrounded by farmland, as well as areas of verdant bush and elephant grass with the occasional anthill sticking up. There are stretches of hills, between which are marshy swamps. There are also many mango trees in this part of Uganda and during the mango season they can be bought on the roadside. As you approach the border you can

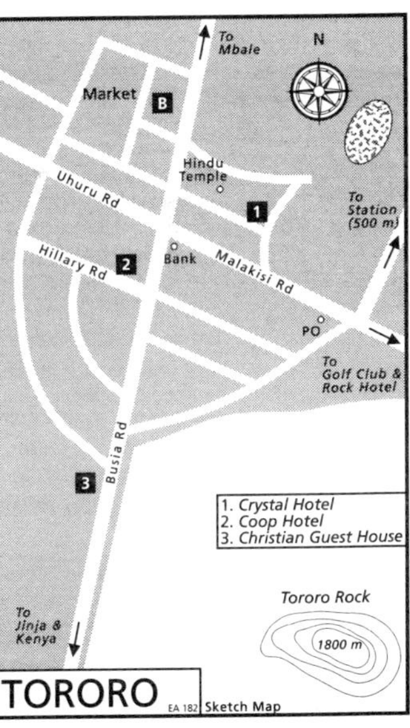

either continue straight on to Tororo for the Malaba crossing or take a right turning to Busia. There is a road block at this turning which is apparently there to stop smugglers – it seems to do little more than collect bribes. From about this point you should be able to see the Tororo rock sticking up in the distance.

Tororo Rock The Tororo rock is a volcanic plug which rises to about 1800m above sea level. It is possible to climb and the views from the top are fantastic. There are steps and ladders to help you get to the summit, and the climb takes about an hour.

Local information

● Where to stay

C *Rock*, PO Box 42, T 4458/4426. Located a few kilometres out of town beyond the golf course. Run by *Uganda Hotels* this is a pleasant enough establishment, set in gardens.

D *Crystal*, medium-sized hotel with views of Tororo Rock. Rooms are self-contained and have balconies. Simple and clean. Restaurant and bar. Good value.

E *Co-op*, one of the cheaper hotels in Tororo Not particularly good value and has water supply problems. **E** *Tororo Christian Guest House*, rather run down with water supply problems.

● Transport

Train Tororo is on the railway line and is the junction for trains heading N and those heading E into Kenya. Although few travellers do use the train it might be worth knowing that the service to the North has now resumed – the final part from Lira to Pakwach was reopened in the summer of 1993. The passenger trains at the moment only go once a week, but this may change depending on demand. To Kampala the trains go 3 times a week on Mon, Wed and Fri. As the journey takes over 9 hrs – while the bus takes only about 3 – few people use it at present.

Road Tororo is 217 km to Kampala, about 3½ hrs by matatu or bus. They go frequently – however if you are heading for Kenya there is little reason to stop over at Tororo now that Akamba Bus do a direct service from Kampala to Nairobi.

Mbale

This town in the eastern part of Uganda in the foothills of Mount Elgon, giving it a pleasant climate. Mbale shows clearly the Asian influence on towns in Uganda – in particular many of the buildings have the distinctive verandah that is seen all over East Africa. It is a bustling market town and for many years you could buy all sorts of things in Mbale smuggled in from Kenya that were unobtainable in Kampala. During the colonial years eucalyptus plantations were planted all around Mbale as an anti-mosquito measure. During the past 25 years the trees have gradually been cut down and malaria, which was once eradicated from the area, has returned. There is a large **Commonwealth War Graves Cemetery**. Mbale is also home of the **Islamic University**, one of only 2 such institutions in Africa, founded in 1988.

Mount Elgon

Near Mbala is an extinct volcano located on the border of Uganda and Kenya. It has gradual slopes up to the peaks on the crater rim which means that non-mountaineers can climb it. For information about climbing Mount Elgon (see below). The foothills around the base of Mount Elgon are also a good hiking area, and here are caves to visit as well as the Sipi Falls (see below). This area is well known for its high quality Arabica coffee and you are likely to see coffee plantations in this area. They are mostly small-scale farms using family labour.

Climbing Mount Elgon

Until very recently anyone wishing to climb Mount Elgon approached it from the Kenya side and most of the recently published mountaineering and hiking guides reflect this. However, in the last year or so efforts have been made to improve facilities on the Uganda side to enable climbers to approach it from here.

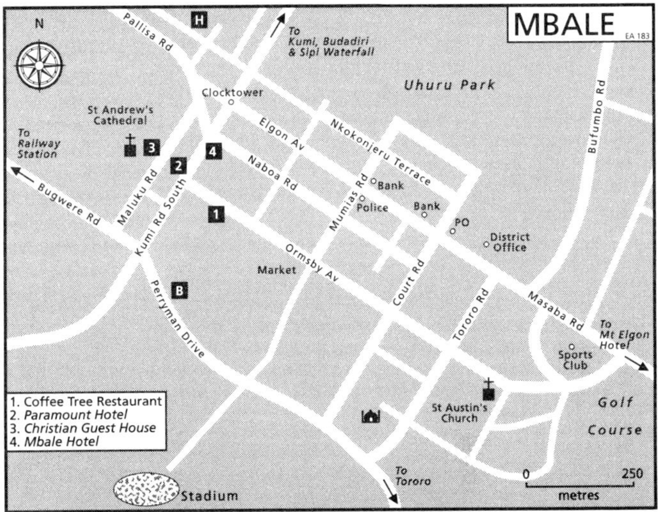

Encompassing the largest surface area of any extinct volcano in the world, Mount Elgon rises through a series of gradual slopes punctuated by steep cliffs to a height of 4,321m above sea level. Volcanic foothills, cliffs, caves, gorges and waterfalls combine with panoramic views across wide plains to create some of the most spectacular scenery in Uganda. Elgon's upper slopes are cloaked in tropical montane forest while above this lies a vast tract of Afro-Alpine moorland. This unique moorland vegetation extends over the caldera – a collapsed crater covering over 40 sq km at the top of the mountain.

Weather-wise the time to avoid is the long rains which are Apr and May. Climbers should first head for the village of Budadiri where the climb begins. The **C** *Wagagai* houses the Mount Elgon Club and they can arrange the climb for you – guides, porters food etc. The facilities on the mountain itself are currently minimal but this is set to change. It you plan to get to the top expect the climb to last 4 days at a cost of between US$50 to US$75. However, if you are less ambitious there are many different walks that you can take, that range from easy hikes to hard climbs. The Tourist office in Mbale can give you maps and make suggestions to suit your requirements.

The climb itself is straight forward and can be accomplished easily by non-mountaineers. The trail is steep in places but it is possible to reach the caldera and return to the roadhead within 3 days of setting off walking at a comfortable pace. With an extra 2 days you could also reach Jackson's Summit on the highest point, Wagagai, or visit the hot springs at the head of the Suam gorge.

The Caves of Mount Elgon

There are numerous caves on Elgon and one of the most interesting and most readily accessible is that situated within the spur on which Bulago Camp stands. Its entrance is impressive, being some thirty feet wide and 10 feet tall, and (during wet weather) is partially hidden in spray from a small waterfall which drops down of banks of ferns which almost block the mouth. Just inside the main chamber are flat ledges cut into the rock, which are believed, at one time, to have been used as sleeping berths by the Bagisu when hiding from their enemies. The size of the main chamber is approximately 60 feet by 150 feet in depth, with a height over 15 feet.

According to native legend the tunnel at the far end of the cave to the left leads to another much larger cavern. This is supposed to be full of water to a considerable depth. Whether this is true or not is not known – but certainly water can be seen trickling from the tunnel.

The main cavern has no stalactites or stalagmites, nor any rock paintings. There are instead a number of garnet-like stones, embedded in a nest of a fine scintillating material resembling spiders' webs. The floor of the cave is flat and soft and is littered with the

Bugisu Circumcision

The Bugisu have a strong belief in their rites – and the ceremony of circumcision is very much an important part of the life cycle. All men must undergo circumcision and it is believed that men who die before they have been circumcised will be circumcised before they are buried in order to complete their life on earth.

Circumcision takes place every other year and is performed on young men aged between 14 and 25. The circumcision season is said to be marked by the appearance of a strange bird whose singing marks the beginning of the preparations. The elders gather under the clan tree – which is said to be older than the memory of man itself. They then begin training the candidates for the rituals, which last three days.

On the first day the young man is smeared with sorghum paste all over the body. He wears the traditional dress of animal skins and a head dress, puts three heavy bangles on each leg and then visits his relatives, singing and dancing. The songs he sings are mainly praising his forefathers and the gods. Every so often he stops and leaps high in the air.

On the second day his hair is cut and he is allowed to bathe – the last opportunity before the ceremony proper begins. This symbolizes the death of the past and of what he has been, and a new beginning. The white sorghum paste is again smeared on his body. The singing and dancing continues and this evening is one of great celebration amongst the people of the village.

On the morning of the circumcision the young man wakes at first light and is again smeared with sorghum paste. He then sets off to visit his maternal uncles who give him gifts of cows or goats which are part of the bride price paid by his father. As the day progresses and the sun gets overhead the man returns home where he is taken down to the river by the men who wash him thoroughly from the waist to the knees. He is then brought at a slow pace to the ground which is traditionally used for these ceremonies. On the ground is a Y-shaped stick which he picks up and holds behind his head. The circumcision itself is fairly quickly over and a whistle is blown to announce that the candidate has been successful. Occasionally it happens than a man will try to run away – but this is looked upon with great shame as the epitome of disgrace and cowardice.

Traditionally once a man has been circumcised he can sit in on tribal meetings and participate in decision-making, and he is now allowed to marry. Only once you have been through what is known as the pain of the knife can you be called a man, and it is said that, just like birth and death, it can only be done once in one's life-time.

droppings of bats. Looking out towards the entrance of the cave, especially when the sun is shining through the waterfall, giving off rainbows, is a lovely sight.

Other well known caves on Mount Elgon include one opposite Sipi Camp. However this bears no comparison either in size or interest to the one described above.

Sipi Falls

These are situated in the lower slopes of Mount Elgon close to the village of Sipi and are a drive of about 1½ hrs from Mbale. The waterfall and the surrounding area are very pretty and a pleasant place to spend a few days unwinding. There is a small cottage here with just 2 rooms – it was orginally built as a holiday house for the Governor and colonial officials during the colonial period. Each room only has one bed – but you are allowed to squeeze as many people in as you want for a fixed rate (US$3). There is also a communal sitting room and you can camp in the garden if you have your own tent. There is a kitchen if you have your own food – otherwise order it in advance and it will be cooked for you.

Nkokenjeru

Not far from Mbale is a large rock called Nkokenjeru which means the White Rock. On this, Idi Amin planned to build to huge international hotel and conference centre. The building began with the construction of the road – almost a motorway – up to the top of the rock. That was as far as it got and the complex itself was never begun. There are wonderful views from and it is sometimes possible to see peregrine falcons which live on the rock.

Imbalu dances

If you happen to be in this area during even years you may manage to see some of the local festivities of the Imbalu people, as well as the mass circumcision ceremonies of the Bugisu and Sebei people. The festivities reach a climax during Dec and involve singing, dancing, drumming and general merrymaking. See box, page 440.

Local information

● Where to stay

C *Mount Elgon*, PO Box 670, T 3612. Located a little way out of town. Run by *Uganda Hotels* it has recently been done up and is a comfortable place to stay. Set in peaceful gardens.

E *Paramount*, a pleasant clean hotel with a bar and restaurant, this is not bad value. **E** *Christian Guest House*, this has a range of rooms and is good value. It is clean and friendly and has a restaurant attached. **E** *Mbale*, rather run down. Basic but cheap.

● Places to eat

♦♦♦*Mount Elgon*. The best place to eat in Mbale, if you don't mind a ½-hr walk. The food is very good and the setting makes the walk and cost worth while. ♦♦*Coffee Tree Bar and Restaurant*, Town centre. Good value.

● Tourist Office

There is a tourist office in Mbale, located not far from the *Mount Elgon Hotel*, which provides information about climbing Mount Elgon. There are maps as well as up to date advice, and anyone planning to climb the mountain is advised to visit the office.

● Transport

Train Mbale is on the railway that goes from Tororo up to Pakwach in the NW of the country. This railway line has recently been reopened (see page 438).

Road Mbale is 272 km from Kampala, about a 4 hr drive via Tororo on a good road. It is an 1½ hr from Busia on the Kenyan border.

NORTH TO SOROTI AND GULU

The North of Uganda can be divided into the Northwest, North and Northeast. The Northwest covers what is known as West Nile – that is, anything beyond Murchinson Falls and includes Pakwach, Nebbi, Arua and Moyo. The North includes Lira, Gulu and Kitgum. The main towns in the Northeast are Soroti, Karamoja, Moroto and Kotido.

The northeast of Uganda, bordering on Sudan to the N and Kenya to the E is one of beautiful scenery ranging from mountains to vast, flat, empty plains. It is a magnificent part of Uganda and so totally different to the southern part of the country. For information about **Kidepo National Park**, see section on National Parks, page 477.

The inaccessibility of the N of Uganda, as well as the relative insecurity of the area compared to the rest of Uganda discourages visitors. Although security in the N has improved dramatically in the last 5 years, this part of Uganda does still suffer from being one of the most heavily armed. There is a high proportion of male adults carrying guns and raids by bandits are not uncommon. However the situation can change rapidly. All the main churches have missions in the N and their representatives in Kampala are a reliable source of information on the current situation. For example at certain times it is considered prudent to only drive in convoy. Don't let this put you off completely – but be aware of the situation.

Soroti

Although not that far N, there is something about Soroti which gives it a northerly feeling. It is a hot and airless town with a frontier atmosphere. It is the site of the **Soroti Flying School**, set up to train pilots for the whole East African region.

The drive from Soroti to Moroto is really quite something. The acacia thorn bush goes on. Every so often you will see a herd of scrawny goats being looked after by a couple of young boys, or perhaps some cattle with some Karamajong guarding them. Most of the time it is very hot and dusty but at certain times of the year there are the most fantastic thunderstorms. On this road as you pass from Teso into Karamoja you go between 2 hills called **Akisim** and **Napak**. They are quite impressive as they can be seen for some miles around as they stand up above the plains. They mark the boundary into Karamoja.

Nyero Rock Paintings These are located in Kumi district and consist of 3 painted shelters close to each other. Paintings are in red and white pigment and are mainly of geometric shapes. They are believed to be between 300 and 500 years old.

Other attractions in the area include **Moru Apeso Rock** viewing and climbing and the **River Awoja** where there is a camp site.

• **Where to stay** **C** *Soroti*, PO Box 397, Serere Rd. T 269. Run by *Uganda Hotels*.

• **Transport** **Air** There are no scheduled flights to Soroti at the moment, but it is possible to charter a light aircraft from Kampala. **Train** Soroti is on the same railway line as Mbale which goes up to West Nile (see page 438). **Road** Soroti is a drive of about 5 hrs from Kampala – a distance of about 385 km. It is 128 km from Lira, 113 km from Mbale and about 200 km from Moroto.

Moroto

In the NE of the country lie the vast open spaces of Karamoja. Here rocky mountains interrupt the plains making it an arid land of great scenic beauty. Mount Moroto, which reaches a height of about 3,400m above sea

THE KARAMAJONG

The Karamajong are one of the tribes inhabiting the more southerly part of the district of Karamoja, which is situated in the northeast corner of Uganda.

The marriage system is polygamous, the number of wives being limited solely by financial circumstances. No boy is allowed to marry until he has been admitted by the elders to the status of manhood. Up to this time a boy must pluck out all his pubic hair. When the time comes (there are usually a group presented at the same time) his father gives him a bull which the boy kills and shares with his male relatives. He smears himself with the dung from the entrails and gives his mother the head, neck, hump, stomach and ribs. His hair is cut by an adult male friend leaving a tuft at the back to which a short string is attached. Traditionally when the hair grows back he moulds it into two buns, one on top of the head and one at the back, with coloured clay.

When a youth has obtained manhood he may seek a wife. It is usual that he will already have at least one lover (although a girl is only supposed to have one) and if his father approves, a lover may be taken as his wife.

When a woman is about to give birth she is assisted by her female relatives. The umbilical cord is tied with fibre and cut near to the body. If the baby is a boy the cord is cut with the arrow used for bleeding cattle but if it is a girl a knife is used. The cord is buried in the cattle enclosure.

When someone dies the body is wrapped up in a hide and buried in a goat enclosure. If that person is a pauper without friends the body would simply be thrown outside the kraal and left to the wild animals.

When a husband dies the widow passes into the possession of his principal brother. He will bring a sheep to her door which he will then kill and they will smear themselves with dung from its entrails. From this time onwards she belongs to him. If there is no brother then she will pass to the son of a co-wife.

level offers challenging climbing to the enthusiast. It is the traditional area of the pastoralist Karamojong people (see box above).

Labwor and **Nangeya** hills to the northwest of Moroto are noted for their giant inselbergs, volcanic plugs that remain after the erosion of the cones. **Matheniko**, **Pain Upe**, and **Bakora** are all game reserves in the area around Moroto, stretching from N of Mount Elgon up to Kotido.

• **Where to stay C** *Mount Moroto*, PO Box 54, T 97. Run by *Uganda Hotels*.

• **Transport Air** The easiest way to reach Moroto is undoubtedly by air. Charter flights go fairly regularly from Entebbe. **Road** Kampala to Moroto is a distance of some 840 km so is not for the feeble-hearted.

Lira

Situated 352 km from Kampala in the N. Lira Spinning Mill is the main economic activity in town.

• **Where to stay D** *Lira*, PO Box 350, T Lira 24.

• **Transport** Matatus from *Gulu* – not particularly frequent.

Gulu

Gulu is the largest town in northern Uganda and is located on the northern edge of the the Murchinson Falls National Park and many people pass through it on the way to either the Murchinson Falls or to Kidepo National Park.

Bakers Fort If you have the time while you are passing through Gulu you might want to go to see Bakers Fort which is located at Patiko, about 30 km N of Gulu. This was founded by Sir Samuel Baker in 1872 when he was Governor of Equatorial Province. It was built as a base from which to crush the slave trade and was later occupied by Gordon and Emin Pasha (see page 270). There are said to be rock paintings at Samuel Baker's camp.

The handicrafts made in the area around Gulu are worth having a look at. they range from baskets to earthworks, as well as iron workings.

• **Where to stay** **C** *Acholi Inn*, PO Box 239, Gulu T Gulu 108. Run by *Uganda Hotels* and offering fairly good services. **E** ***Church of Uganda Guesthouse***, Simple but sound. **E** ***Luxor Lodge***, opposite the lorry park. Fairly basic.

• **Transport Air** There is an airstrip at Gulu which is used by small aircraft. There are no scheduled flights to Gulu but there are charter flights from Entebbe. **Train** The northern railway line in Uganda did, until recently end at Gulu. Trains go from Tororo, via Kumi and Lira to Gulu. After an 8 year suspension, due to insecurity, the line N of Gulu has been reopened to Pakwack which is the end of the line. Initially the train will go once a week, although this may increase if the demand is there. Gulu-Pakwach takes about 4 hrs, the railway crosses the Nile just before it gets into Pakwach. **Road** Gulu is a distance of 328 km from Kampala and is accessible via **Lira** from the E and **Masindi** from the W.

Arua

Small town in northwest, located close to border with Zaire about 500 km from Kampala.

• **Where to stay and Bars** **C** *White Rhino*, PO Box 359, T Arua 157, ***The Grid***. Local drinking spot frequented by aid workers.

• **Transport** Difficult. There is the occasional bus and matatu from Gulu via Pakwach. Otherwise it may be possible to arrange a ride with an aid vehicle.

WEST TO FORT PORTAL AND KASESE

Contents

Maps

The West of Uganda can be reached directly from Kampala by taking the Mubende-Fort Portal road, or the Kasese train, and this route is covered here. However many travellers opt to take the Southwest road to Mbarara (covered) in the Southwest section, and then North either via the Queen Elizabeth National Park or direct to Fort Portal.

Mubende

Mubende town is a small pleasant town which few tourists visit. It is about half-way between Kampala and Fort Portal and if you are particularly interested in archaeology you may want to stay here on the way to the Bigo site.

Bigo Earthworks consist of a series of trenches and mounds, not far from Mubende, on the Mubende-Masaka road. It is something of a mystery as to who constructed them and why. The main outer trench forms an oval enclosure measuring some 5km around the perimeter, its flanks resting on the Katonga and Kachinga rivers. Within the massive enclosure is a subsidiary complex of earthworks with an entrenched inner stronghold in which there are 2 artificial mounds about 3m high which were probably look-out posts. From the top of these mounds – they are likely to have been taller at the time of construction – a clear view would have been had of the surrounding countryside.

The remains 2 forts of considerably smaller dimensions can be found at **Kasonko**, 5km NE of Bigo and at **Kagago**, 3km NW. They consist of a rampart and a ditch sunk into the slopes of small hills and do not have inner fortifications. It is believed that the constructors of Bigo also built these low flanking strong points as part of an all-round defensive system.

To get to Bigo turn off the Masaka-Mubende road at Makole. Follow this bad road for about 10 miles which is as far as you can go by vehicle. From here it is a walk for about 5km through the bush.

• **Where to stay** E *Nakaima*, pleasant and good value, although not very friendly. There is a restaurant here, which does the usual range of food.

Bushenyi

Bushenyi is the district centre and there is a hospital, a few shops, a couple of cheap guest houses and 2 petrol stations.

The road from Bushenyi to Kasese is excellent, courtesy of one of the western governments. At first the road goes up and down through forested hills, before it reaches the escarpment down to the Rift Valley. As you descend you will be able to see ahead of you Lakes George and Edward. From the cooler heights you descend into the hotter, dustier floor of the Rift Valley which the road crosses, passing through the Queen Elizabeth National Park (see National Parks, page 466). The vegetation around is mainly acacia bush and the grass is sprinkled with the occasional ant hill. A causeway crosses the Kazinga Channel – a natural channel that joins the 2 lakes. A bit further on you cross from the southern to the northern hemisphere – on each side of the road there is a large round wheel marking the Equator. The countryside around is mixed bush and some cultivation, including what was, for many years, Uganda's most important cash crop, cotton.

Kasese

This is the terminal of the western railway in Uganda and you might visit it on the way to a trip up the Rwenzori's, to Kibale Forest or to the Queen Elizabeth National Park (64 km away). For information about climbing the Rwenzori Mountains, see page 483; for Queen Elizabeth National Park, see page 466.

Kilembe Copper Mines Located 13km to the W of Kasese are the mines which were once an important foreign exchange earner for Uganda. They later closed down although there were rumours of them being re-opened by the Japanese. It is possible to hire a bicycle and cycle to the mines. It is a long hard slog up (especially as the bikes are nothing special) but wonderful on the way down. Contact the manager of the *Saad Hotel* (see below) for bicycle rent.

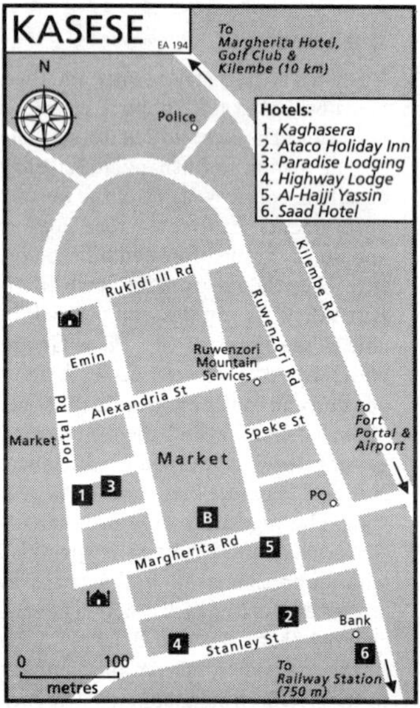

Kibale Forest To the N of Kasese and S of Fort Portal is Kibale Forest which forms a unique habitat for animals, birds and plants. Kibale lies at an altitude of about 1,230m above sea level. The forest provides a rich habitat for more than 250 species of animals and over 300 of birds. The animal species include 11 primate species including black and white colobus monkeys and chimpanzees.

Guided forest walks are available from knowledgeable staff, and the centre has become a major centre of research for scientists from around the world. The forest has a camp site at Kamyanchu which is about 35 km S of Fort Portal. It is on an elevated grassland located within the forest itself and has a beautiful view of the Rwenzori Mountains. Interesting features outside the forest include a number of crater lakes, one of which has a fascinating natural lava formation making a bridge under which water flows. Kibale forest is divided into 7 zones for management purposes: research, natural reserve, civic-cultural, recreation, harvest, community and protection (see national parks, page 479).

Local information

● Where to stay

C *Margherita*, PO Box 90, T 4015. Best hotel in Kasese and is set in beautiful surroundings. It is located with the Rwenzori Mountains on one side and a golf course on the other. There is something magnificent about the vegetation in this area – especially when the trees are in flower. It is situated about 3 km down the road to Kilembe to the W of town and so unless you have your own transport is not very accessible. It is one of the *Uganda Hotels* Corporation chain and although it has seen better days the setting makes it all worth while. There is a good restaurant.

D *Saad*, clean and friendly and the manager

is helpful. The rooms are doubles with their own facilities, and there are also beds in a dormitory. The restaurant is good (although there is no alcohol served on the premises because the owner is Muslim). Bicycles for hire. Videos screened.

E *Kaghasera*, double rooms with own bathrooms. Fairly basic and simple. Not bad value. **E** *Ataco Holiday Inn*, all rooms have shared bathrooms. Restaurant and bar. Straightforward and basic. **E** *Paradise Bar and Lodgings*, rather basic with shared bathrooms. **E** *Highway Bar and Lodge*, shared bathrooms. Not especially friendly.

● **Camping**
Is possible in the grounds of the *Margherita Hotel* at no charge although they expect you to eat and drink at the hotel.

● **Places to eat**
The most popular places in town are the ♦♦*Margherita* (if you have a car or don't mind the walk) or else ♦♦*Saad's Hotel*. ♦♦*Al-Hajji Yassin*, close to bus park. Local food: matoke and beans; rice and beans.

● **Shopping**
There are quite a few shops situated close to the market where you can buy food suitable for hiking – such as dried soups imported from Kenya.

● **Tour Agent**
Rwenzori Mountain Services, Box 33 Kasese, T 493 259175.

● **Transport**
Air Charter flights go to Kasese airport, although as they are more often than not taking tourists they are more likely to go direct to the Mweya Lodge landing site.

Train Uganda Railways runs an overnight service from Kampala to Kasese. There is a first class service with sleeping berths leaving Kampala on Mon, Wed and Fri at 1500 and arriving at 0600 the next day. Few travellers seem to use this route and it is not entirely reliable.

Road Kasese is 418 km from **Kampala** via Mubende and Fort Portal. The more common route used, because the road is better, is via Mbarara.

Bigodi

The nearest village to the forest, 6 km from Kanyanchu River Camp Site. To get from Bigodi to Kanyanchu you can hire bicycles from the lodges below. They will also organise tours of the Bigodi swamp, where there is a variety of birdlife and monkeys.

● **C** *Omucuso Lodge*, just outside Bigodi. Has about 10 bedrooms and serves excellent food – rather better than the usual menu. **C** *Safari Lodge*, new and fairly popular.

Fort Portal

Heading to Fort Portal, from Kasese, a distance of about 75 km, is another beautiful drive. The road climbs out of the dry plain in which Kasese sits and gradually enters the hilly greenness that surrounds Fort Portal.

Located a little over 300 km to the W of Kampala and 70km N of Kasese at 5,000 ft above sea level, Fort Portal is situated at the foothills of the Rwenzori Mountains known as the Mountains of the Moon. Small, quiet and refreshing it is one of Uganda's most pleasant towns.

Fort Portal is now the regional headquarters for Kabarole, Kasese and Bundibugyo districts. The town currently has a population of about 400,000 people. The town enjoys an excellent climate, almost temperate in nature with moderate sunshine and heavy downpours during the rainy season. The main rains are from Mar to May and from Sep to Nov – although there are no real dry seasons. The annual temperatures are about 25-28° C. The climate is mainly influenced by the surrounding environment – particularly the hills and mountains. The River Mpanga meanders through the municipality, its source being the tributaries from the Rwenzoris. It is this river that is the main source of water for the town.

From the town there is a beautiful view of the **Rwenzori Mountains**. They are snowpeaked – although cloud often covers the peaks themselves. The Rwenzori Mountains were recently turned into a fully fledged national park and the animals found in the park include

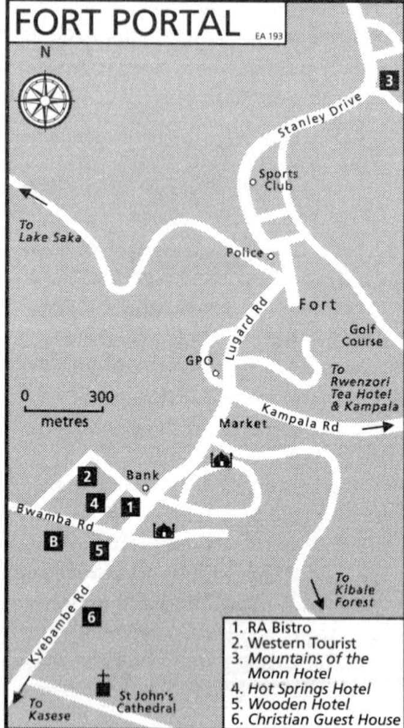

elephants, leopards, many sorts of monkeys and a huge range of birdlife (see National Parks, page 466).

The countryside surrounding Fort Portal is tea country and in the old days this was an important export for Uganda. During the colonial period many of the plantations were run by Europeans on land leased (rarely owned) from the Government. Labour migrated from other parts of Uganda, particularly the southwest to work on the estates usually for 6 months after which they would return home. Many migrants made this same journey year after year. In recent decades, however, many of the plantations have fallen into disrepair – if a tea tree is not picked over a long period of time it is difficult to revive it into a useable state. However efforts have been made on some of the plantations – but the years of neglect are obvious if you compare them to plantations around, for example, Kericho in Kenya.

Some people base themselves at Fort Portal while organising a trek up the Rwenzori's but, in fact, although not so pleasant, Kasese is more convenient for this as it is closer to the starting point at Ibanda. You might also pass through on the way to the **Murchinson Falls National Park** or to **Bundibugyo** in Semliki Forest to see the hot springs and the pygmies. Another place of interest is the **Bunyuruguru Crater** Lake which is situated between Kibale Forest and the main Kasese-Fort Portal road.

History of Fort Portal

Fort Portal was founded in 1893 under the name of Fort Gerry, and was later renamed Fort Portal after Sir Gerald Portal a British explorer who mounted an expedition to the area in 1900. Gerald Portal was the British Consul General of Zanzibar who arrived in Uganda in late 1892 and died of malaria while in Uganda. He was instrumental in the signing of agreements with the leaders of the Kingdoms of Uganda that led to the formalising of Protectorate status for the country. Fort Portal is in the centre of the Toro Kingdom and the town started as a base from where the British colonial power protected the then Omukama (or King) of Toro. In 1876 Toro was captured by the Banyoro king, Kabalega, but the British expelled him in 1891 and replaced him with a new Toro king, Kasagama. In later years Catholic and Protestant missionaries followed the colonial administration in order to establish churches, schools and hospitals. By 1900 the town was expanding rapidly. The development of the town was helped by the booming trade in food and cash produce. In the 1930's Europeans and Indians came and started large tea estates, and shops and residential premises were built. The growth of the town was also helped by the establishment in 1952 of the railway line from Mombasa as far as Kasese for the transportation of copper for the mines at Kilembe. A cement factory was set up at Hima along the Fort Portal-Kasese road. As with the other Kingdoms in Uganda, Toro was abolished in 1966 during Obote's first term of office. However, it was restored by Museveni in 1993.

Places of interest

Toro Palace Ruins Close to Fort Portal, on one of the highest hills around the town, is the site of the former palace of the King of Toro (Omukama). It was built in the 1960's for the then Omukama, Rukidi III (son of Kasagama, the British installed King) but was destroyed when the Kingdoms were abolished and is now only a ruin. It is not a particularly attractive site but there are good views of the Rwenzoris from the hill on which it stands.

Fort Ruins The Fort after which the town is named, is now the site of the town's golf course, where it is now little more than a collection of rocks. It is said that one of these rocks contains the footmarks of General Gerald Portal's men.

Karimbi Tombs These are also the Karambi tombs, or burial ground for the former Toro royal family, where both Kasagama and Rukidi III are buried. Located about 5 km along the Fort Portal-Kasese Road.

Nearby attractions

There are a number of tourist attractions accessible from Fort Portal and if there are a group of you then you might be able to organise a day trip. *Kabarole Tours*, and *Semliki Safaris* both based in Fort Portal are very friendly and helpful and will be able to help you arrange any of these trips.

Bundibugyo is located the other side of the Rwenzori Mountains from Fort Portal and the 2 main attractions there are the **hot springs** and the **pygmy tribes** who live in the forests nearby. The journey to Bundibugyo through the mountains is spectacular.

Lake Saka This small crater lake is located about 8km out of Fort Portal and can be visited quite easily. Take the road that goes towards the *Mountains of the Moon Hotel* and go beyond the market and post office, until you reach a turning to the left down Saka road roughly opposite the golf course. Follow this road which leads to the lake.

Bunyuruguru Crater Lake Field This is a collection of crater lakes located about 30km to the S of Fort Portal between the main Fort Portal-Kasese road and Kibale Forest. There are plans to establish a camp site close to the lakes which will make visiting easier – but at the moment a day trip is all that is really feasible. However without your own transport this is not all that easy as there is not very much traffic going along the road to the lakes. They are situated between Kasenda and Rwaihamba villages which are 10km apart. On Mons and Thursdays, when there is a market at the latter village there are a few vehicles to Rwaihamba from where you will have to walk. *Kabarole Tours* can arrange transport.

Sempaya Hot Springs Heated underground and come to the surface at temperatures close to boiling. They are located about 45km to the southwest of Fort Portal just off the main road. There is a **campsite**, close to the springs run by *Semliki Safaris* – but it is new and facilities are rather limited, but it is a nice location.

Pygmies

In the Semliki River Valley is Ntandi village and near to this is the Semliki Forest which is home to the pygmies. There is one matatu a day that leaves Fort Portal early in the morning for Ntandi. The pygmies themselves can be visited. However many visitors are disappointed. Not surprisingly the pygmies have been quick to learn their novelty value and demand huge sums of money from tourists. Disconcertingly, they appear to spend the largest proportion of this money on drink and drugs, often staggering around unaware of what is going on. It is difficult to find anyone who has visited the pygmies and considers it a worthwhile part of their trip to Uganda.

Semliki Forest Located in Bundibugyo District. There is at present no accommodation in Semliki although some is being developed, and should be available in 1995. The forest is at the southern end of the Semliki Valley, flanked on the E by the Rwenzori Mountains. It is a low lying forest and ecologically it is part of the great Zaire **Ituri Forest** separated from it by the Semliki River. It contains many species of animals and birds that are not found elsewhere in East Africa. Larger mammals such as elephant, leopard and buffalo, exist in the forest but although evidence of their presence can be observed, the animals themselves are rarely seen. A large number of smaller mammals are found in the forest including a black and white colobus, chimpanzees, brazza monkey, African palm civet, giant forest squirrel, black mangabey and many others. The bird life at Semliki is phenomenal with about 400 species recorded.

Itwara Forest Located to the southeast of Fort Portal this is another forest with a large number of small mammals as well as a great range of bird life. Primates that are found include chimpanzees, black and white colobus, blue monkey, red-tailed monkey, and red colobus. Also found are the African palm civet, the giant forest squirrel and the scaly-tailed flying squirrel.

Local information

● Where to stay

D *Mountains of the Moon*, about 2.5 km from the town centre this is a lovely, rather run-down old colonial hotel. It is set in beautiful grounds. There is a restaurant which does good steak and chips.

E *Rwenzori Tea*, about 6 km out of town on the Kampala road and is another old colonial hotel. Somehow it seems to be a rather bleak, set in the middle of the tea plantations. Part of it was done up some years ago, but much of the building is still rather run down. **E** *Hot Springs*, this is a simple good value budget hotel. There is good food available and it is popular. **E** *Wooden*, situated in the middle of town. Popular with travellers. Bar and restaurant. **E** *Christian*, one of the best of the cheap hotels, this is clean and simple. It is popular with Peace Corps and is a friendly place. Food is available.

● Places to eat

♦♦*Mountains of the Moon*, a bit out of town, but nice setting and varied international menu; ♦♦*RA Bistro*, reasonable standard; ♦*Western Tourist*, good value.

● Sport

Golf The town has a 36-hole course which is open to members and those from affiliated clubs. Temporary membership is also available. Other facilities that are available include **table tennis**, **tennis** and **squash**. The course is a 20-minute walk from the Mountains of the *Moon Hotel*.

● Travel and tour companies

Kabarole Tours and *Semliki Safaris* specialise in arranging excursions to places of interest around fort Portal.

● Useful addresses

Public library at Fort Portal has an excellent selection of books.

Places of Worship Every sort of religion is represented at Fort Portal – there are several mosques and churches of Anglican, Roman Catholic, Pentecostal, Seventh Day Adventist, and Church of Uganda denominations.

● Transport

Air The nearest airport is Kasese – this is for small airplanes only and there are no longer any scheduled flights, only charters.

Train The railway line goes as far as Kasese from where you have to travel the last 50km by road to Fort Portal.

Road Fort Portal is accessible by road, by 2 alternative routes from **Kampala**. The first is through Mubende district and is 320 km long but is only partly paved; the other is through Masaka, Mbarara, Bushenyi and Kasese and is 430 (Somewhere else said 507 km) km. There are frequent matatus to and from **Kasese** taking about 2 hrs.

Fort Portal to Hoima

Heading for Hoima and Masindi from Fort Portal be prepared for a bad road – this road is not used much and in parts

The Spirit Of Ndahura

Situated not far from Kibale and Kisomroro is a hot spring call Rwagimba, which, literally translated, means that which pushes or jets out. The hot waters from the spring run into two rock pools which lie, one below the other, within a few yards of the ice-cold waters of the Ruimi river.

The spring is widely known for the healing powers of its hot sulphurous waters, which are used both for washing and drinking, particularly by those suffering from skin diseases. The healing powers of the spring are supposed to be under the spiritual sway of Ndahura, who was a Muchwezi warrior whose career ended disastrously in defeat and small pox. His name became so closely connected with small pox that it was actually known as Ndahura's disease.

The spring is jointly owned by two clans – the Bachwamba and the Basambu, and its keeper is always a Muchwamba man married to a Musambu woman. Although the man is the keeper he cannot exercise full powers, for it is the woman who is the actual priestess of the spring. It is in her that, from time to time, when she becomes possessed, the spirit of Ndahura becomes immanent. The spirit of Ndahura is not normally regarded as being immanent in the spring itself but in the shrine which is maintained near to the keeper's house, where small offerings of food and beer are made. The spirit of Ndahura only becomes immanent in the spring when the waters are troubled. This seems to occur fairly rarely and in the rest of the time people seem happy to use the spring to bathe in and to help reduce aches and pains.

is both very steep and almost impassable. However, if you have the time and a good 4-wheel drive you will be rewarded with going though one of the most lovely parts of Uganda. The first part of the journey is through low cultivated hills. But as you proceed N it changes to a mountainous, partly-forested area and every so often the road reaches a spot where you can look around for miles. It really is fantastically beautiful. The forest is interspersed with patches of cultivation, but this is one of the poorer parts of Uganda being so cut off.

Hoima

The most direct route to Hoima from Kampala is on a poor road via **Kiboga** but the journey is an interesting one and runs through the bush. After about 30 miles the tar road becomes murrum and gradually deteriorates. The landscape is hilly with a scattering of huge boulders amongst the farmland. The town of Kiboga is about 120 km from Kampala and is strung out along the road, it is rather shabby and run down.

Soon after leaving Kiboga the road begins a gradual descent into the plain beyond which Hoima, the capital of Bunyoro, is located. The plain is punctuated by the occasional bare hill, and Hoima itself is spread across 2 such hills. Hoima can be seen from quite a distance, the town is surrounded by eucalyptus trees planted as an anti-malarial measure during the colonial era. On entering the town you pass through the instantly recognisable old colonial part of town – the bungalows surrounded by wide verandahs, set in large gardens, and the fading government offices. The town centre sits overlooking a deep valley with a number of buildings, including one of the town's churches on the opposite side.

Nearby attractions

Katasiha Fort This is located about 3km along the Butiaba road which leads N out of town towards Lake Albert. The fort was established in 1894 by Col.

Colville when he was trying to subdue Kabalega, the King (Omukama) of Bunyoro. All that survives of the fort are a rampart and a ditch.

Mparo Tombs These are situated 4 km along the Masindi road which is to the northeast of Hoima. They are the tombs of the former Omukamas of Bunyoro – Kabalega and his son Tito Wimyi who died in 1923 and 1971 respectively. The building is similar is the Kasubi tombs in Kampala although not as grand. As with those tombs it is guarded by an old woman who will allow you to go in and take a look around. Be sure to remove your shoes before entering and leave a small donation. Inside there are some of Kabalega's belongings. He was the Omukama who fought against the British at the end of the last century, until he was captured in 1894.

Local information

● Where to stay

E *Nsamo Inn*, new, clean and comfortable. Good value. **E** *Kwebiiha Hostel*, fairly simple. **E** *Hoima Inn*, basic accommodation. **E** *Red Cross Hostel*, clean, though a touch spartan.

● Places to eat

♦♦*Nsamo Inn*, reasonable restaurant, with fairly simple food. ♦*Ebony Bar and Reataurant*, straightforward local food, mostly grills.

● Transport

Road The town of Hoima is located about 200 km from **Kampala** via Kiboga, a drive of about 3 hrs. Unfortunately because the road is not good there is little traffic on this road. There are alternatives – it can be reached via **Masindi** – it is about 70km from Masindi – making a total of about 270 km from Kampala, or from **Fort Portal**. If you are doing the latter on public transport you will probably have to change vehicles at least once, usually at Kagadi.

Masindi

Many people pass through Masindi on the way to the Murchison Falls National Park. Apart from the Park there are a few things near to Masindi which you may also want to do. For information about Murchinson Falls National Park (also known as Kabalega NP) see section on National Parks, page 474.

Masindi can either be reached via Hoima (see above), or else by taking the more direct road. The latter leaves Kampala heading N (starting at the Wandegeya roundabout near Makerere University) and passes through Bombo and Luwero, before swinging westwards, taking about 5 hrs from Kampala. About 30 km out of Kampala you will go through the town of **Bombo** – very much an army town. You pass row upon row of barracks. It began as an army town at the beginning of this century with the Sudanese Volunteers in the King's African Rifles – they were always known as the Nubians. The area became known as the Luwero Triangle and was very severely affected during the Obote II regime when army atrocities resulted in the killing of many thousands of people. Houses were looted and then burnt to the ground, along with the surrounding shambas. It did not take long for the vegetation to grow up again and the sight of the remains of a house with bush growing through it is not unusual. As a result of the events in the area Luwero has received considerable attention from aid workers and foreign governments.

Kihande Palace A couple of km out of town is the palace of the Omukama, the former king of Bunyoro. This is situated on Kihande Hill but is no longer in use as a palace. The Bunyoro kingdom and its kingship was one of those abolished in 1967 during the Obote I regime.

Bundongo Forest

This wildlife area, about 30km W of Masindi on the Butiaba road, lies between Masindi and Lake Albert, and is renowned for the presence of chimpanzees and therefore receives a fair number of visitors. Before the opening up of Kibale Forest for viewing chimpanzees, Budongo was considered to be the most

> ### THE PRINCE OF WALES HUNTING LODGE
>
> Between the road and the escarpment on the way down to Lake Albert there was once a hunting lodge which was built for Edward, Duke of Windsor, when he was the Prince of Wales in the 1930s. Gradually, during the 1960s and 1970s, it fell into disrepair and brick by brick was removed by the local people so that little of it now remains.

accessible of Uganda's forests where chimpanzees could be viewed. More recently however most visitors go to Kibale and the researchers are less willing to take people to see the chimps here. There are however plans to set up a tourism project that will enable tourists to visit the chimps here. Other animals found in the forest include the scaly-tailed flying squirrel, the giant forest squirrel, the tree pangolin and the black and white colobus monkey. Budongo Forest also has an extremely rich bird life with an estimated 90 bird species. These include the cuckoo falcon, crowned hawk eagle, great blue turaco, the great honey guide and the dwarf kingfisher.

There is a daily bus which will drop you off at the turning for Nyabyeya Forestry College from where it is a short walk. On the way back you should be waiting at the turn off early in the morning as there are few matatus after about 0900.

There is a guesthouse at the Forestry College which has rooms and camping available. It is cheap but you will need to bring your own food.

Masindi Port

This is different from Masindi itself, and is about 40 km to the E. It is located on Victoria Nile at the western end of Lake Kyoga which extends across much of central Uganda. In the days when steamers on the Nile were an important form of transport the 2 sets of falls in the Murchinson Falls National Park were major obstacles to travelling up the Nile. Coming from Lake Victoria, the steamers went up Victoria Nile and into Lake Kyoga. Passengers and goods then disembarked at Masindi Port and travelled overland to Butiaba on Lake Albert. From here they continued their journey N. Masindi Port has now declined in importance, and is mainly a market town.

Lake Albert Excursions to Lake Albert can be made from Masindi. Head for the town of **Butiaba Port** on Lake Albert – a distance of about 70 km. The drive on the escarpment to the Rift Valley is an experience in itself. Once you get to Butiaba ask the local fishermen and you should be able to hire a boat for the day.

Local information

● Where to stay

C *Masindi*, PO Box 11, Butiaba Road, T Masindi 23. About a kilometre out of town. Because it is never anywhere near full you can usually negotiate the price. Run by the *Uganda Hotels*. **E** *Soft Lodge*. There are 2 *Soft Lodges* in Masindi which offer moderate accommodation and are clean and friendly. **E** *Codia Lodge*, fairly simple. Restaurant. **E** *Emmest Guest House*, basic and unpretentious.

● Sports (participant)

Tennis Courts available for temporary membership.

● Sports (spectator)

Football There is a sports stadium in Masindi and matches are held there on a regular basis.

● Transport

Road Masindi is a drive of about 3½ hrs from **Kampala**, a distance of about 200 km. There are regular buses and matatus.

SOUTH WEST TO KABALE AND KISORO

Contents

Maps

The southwest runs from Kampala to Kabale and Kisoro, and includes as well the Sese Islands. The main tourist attractions in this area are the Impenetrable Forest with the mountain gorillas, the Sese Islands, Lake Mburo National Park and the less frequently visited Lake Nabugabo and Mpanga Forest Reserve.

The road leading out of Kampala through Masaka and on the southwest of the country is one of the best in Uganda. You will pass through some swamps and small patches of forest and the surrounding countryside seems fertile and well watered. About 40km out of Kampala you will reach the village of **Mpigi** and if you are hoping to buy any traditional music instruments (particularly drums) this is the place to do so. You will see drum makers and their stalls on the side of the road. Near to here is the Mpanga Forest Reserve which you might want to visit either on the way S or else it makes an easy day trip from Kampala.

Mpanga Forest Reserve

This is not a well known tourist location, it is a small (450 ha) patch of the type of forest that once was found almost all over the northern section of the Lake fringe, but which has now been mostly destroyed. This has been partly as a result of extending cultivation into forested areas; but is also the result of the policies (see box, page 376) of the colonial period that were aimed at reducing the incidence of sleeping sickness (*trypanomiasis*). The area was preserved during the colonial period partly for research purposes and so remains as a small reminder of what was once all around.

The forest has a number of clearly marked foot paths and you are unlikely to get lost. However, a guide will help you get more out of your visit. There are a variety of monkeys living in the forest and there is a wide range of bird life.

There are no facilities for overnight stays at Mpanga Forest, although if you have your own tent you could probably camp. There is certainly a lovely site in a clearing in the forest but apparently you are supposed to get written permission from the Forestry Department in Kampala in order to camp actually in the forest although this may not be strictly necessary any longer. If you are stuck there are a few basic hotels in Mpigi village.

To get to the forest on public transport take a matatu that goes through Mpigi (any of the Masaka matatus will do) and once you have passed the turning for Mpigi village itself continue for about 3 km. Here the road dips and goes through the southern part of the forest, where you should ask to be let off. To the right, just beyond the dip, is a turnoff down an unmarked track which goes to the forest station. Follow this for about 500m keeping to the right when the path forks and you will reach the forest station. Here you must meet the ranger to let him know that you are planning to visit the forest – entrance however is free. He should be able to give you some information sheets about the forest and arrange for a guide if you want one.

Masaka

About 75 km from Kampala you will cross the Equator which is marked. Further along the road, about 150 km from Kampala, is **Kinoni** which is one of the best places to buy papyrus mats. Another 20 km further on is **Kyazanga** where you can buy snacks of roasted meat, sodas and roasted bananas (*gonja*). Masaka is about 2 hrs from Kampala.

Masaka was entensively damaged during the Tanzanian invasion of 1979, and much of the destruction has not been repaired. Further through the town you will see the road to Tanzania which was the route along which the Tanzanian troops advanced.

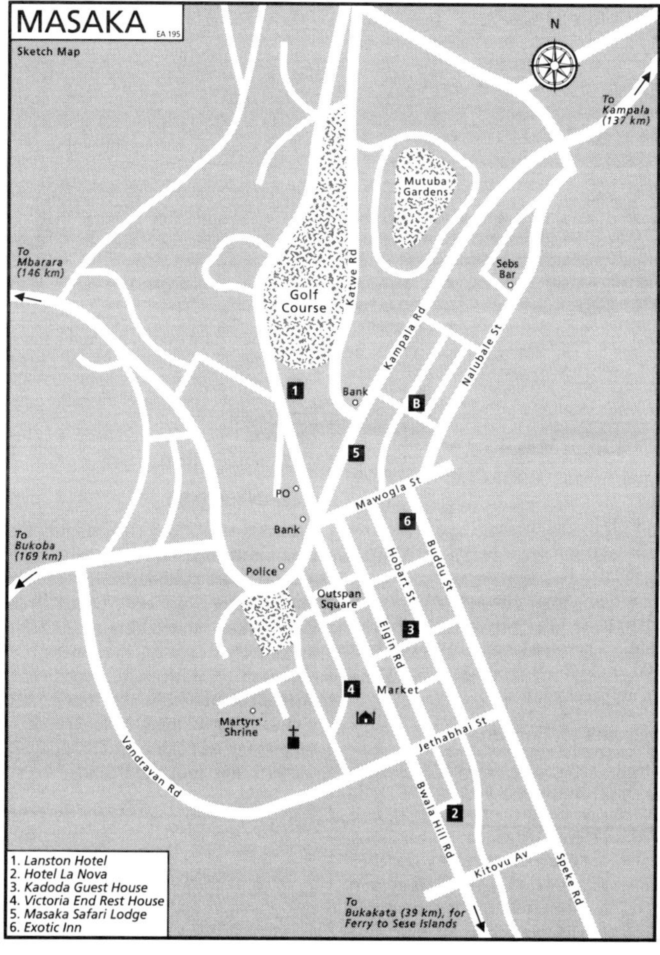

Local information

● **Where to stay**

D *Lanston*, this is about 500m from the bus station and is probably the best place to stay in Masaka. It is clean with hot water and is friendly and well run. **D** *La Nova*, not particularly good value. It is a fair step from the bus station and is often full.

E *Kadoda Guest House*, this is a centrally located, clean and simple, and is a pleasant place to stay. **E** *Victoria End Rest House*, town centre. A rather basic hotel. There is a range of rooms. **E** *Masaka Safari Lodge*, Main street, close to the bus station. Clean and comfortable.

● **Places to eat**

♦♦*Lanston*, good value and reasonable standard. ♦*Exotic Inn*, simple fare. ♦*Elgon Inn and Restaurant*, fairly cheap and basic.

● **Transport**

Road There are frequent matatus and buses to Masaka from **Kampala**. Get to either one of the 2 bus stations in Kampala early in the morning as most leave soon after daybreak. Alternatively go to the matatu station as they continue later in the day. Masaka is a distance of 128 km from Kampala. Masaka is also where you change to pick up matatus to Bukakata for the Ssese Islands and for the overland journey to Mutukula on the Tanzanian border.

West from Masaka

After leaving Masaka and heading W the countryside gradually gets drier and more hilly and the density of population falls as you move into Ankole which is populated by pastoralists.

About half way between Masaka and Mbarara is the trading centre of Lyantonde. There is a turning to the right and 100 km to the N is **Ntusi** where there is an archaeological site.

Masaka to Tanzania

From Masaka you can head for Tanzania – this is not nearly as pleasant as the alternative route using the Port Bell-Mwanza ferry (see page 493) – but as that only goes once a week many travellers prefer to go by road. The road is not very good and this route is not used very much, although traffic is increasing. There are matatus from Masaka which go as far as Kyotera and from there you will have to get a lift to the border, crossing at Mutukula, with one of the trucks going across – this is not usually a problem. The road takes you through the district of Rakai which has become infamous for being devastated by the AIDS epidemic. Evidence of it can be seen in the number of abandoned homesteads and shambas.

If you get to the border shortly before dark you may want to stay at the small guesthouse which is on the Uganda side of the border – there is nothing on the Tanzania side until you get to Bukoba. For crossing the border you will need to have patience as you go through the rather long drawn out process. The road on the Tanzania side is worse than the Uganda road but there are 4-wheel drive vehicles operating on the route. They go when full.

In the far S of Uganda, on the Tanzania border there was once a hotel. It was on an island in the Kagera river at a place called **Kitagatoa** and was reached by a pulley system across the river. The place was run by a very eccentric English woman called Toni.

Lake Nabugabo

This is a small oval lake, slightly less than 5 miles in length and about 3 miles wide. It is located about 2 miles from the western shore of Lake Victoria, from which it is separated by rough undulating country. Because of the mineral content of the lake it is said that bilharzia does not occur here and this has made it popular for swimming. It is a very peaceful place to relax for a couple of days in the friendly Church of Uganda resort.

● **Where to stay** There is a guesthouse at Lake Nabugabo which is run by the Church of Uganda (who also run the *Namirembe guesthouse* in Kampala.) There are a range of bandas to rent which are clean and comfortable. There are 2 family bandas and 2 doubles (both have a sitting room and their own shower

Crocodiles In Lake Nabugabo

During the colonial period Lake Nabugabo was a popular holiday resort in Uganda for expatriates. One of the reasons why swimming here was preferred over swimming in Lake Victoria was that there was supposed to be an absence of crocodiles. One report of a crocodile seen in 1932 was dismissed, but when a dog was snatched while swimming in the lake in 1946, a meticulous search was made. So much for no crocodiles – in a period of about 3 months a total of 10 crocodiles were seen and shot in the lake. These included a particularly huge male which was 4.5m long, with an enormous girth, 167 cm round the body, 140 cm round the neck and 125 cm round the base of the tail. This was estimated to be at least 30 years old.

The lake was cleared of crocodiles with the aim of making it safe for swimmers. However, exceptionally heavy rains later that year flooded the land between the two lakes and crocodiles reappeared. It is doubtful whether there are currently crocodiles in Lake Nabugabo – but you might want to check with local residents before you dive in.

– as well as a dormitory). Food is available at the restaurant if you order it in advance – but no alcohol is served on the premises. It is occasionally full at weekends. Check with the *Namirembe Guesthouse*, Mengo close to Mengo hospital, just below the Cathedral, in Kampala. **Camping** is permitted but bring equipment.

- **Transport Road** Lake Nabugabo is located about 16km from Masaka, a few kilometres off the Masaka-Bukukata road. Getting to get to it by public transport from Masaka is easiest if you happen to be in Masaka on a Mon, Wed or Fri. This is because this is the day when a bus goes to Butukula for the Sese Islands. It leaves at about 1400 from the main Masaka bus station, and goes past the turning to Lake Nabugabo which is clearly signposted. Alternatively take a matatu from Masaka to Nyondo (2km from Masaka) and change there to get onto the Bukutula road – you will probably end up getting a shared taxi. From the main road the lake is about 4 km but traffic along here is scarce and it is probably quicker to walk than wait for a lift. The easiest alternative of all is, of course, to arrange a special hire from Masaka all the way – it will only cost you US$10-15 depending on your bargaining powers, and good value if you are in a group. The resort can be reached by road from Kampala in a few hrs which makes it a popular weekend destination for Kampala residents.

Sese Islands

This collection of islands is situated in the northwestern part of Lake Victoria and are an increasingly popular tourist destination. There are 84 islands in the group, and they are very attractive. Apart from being a birdwatcher's and botanist's paradise, the islands are particularly suited to those keen on walking. Being cut off, the islands have retained an easy-going atmosphere – a wonderful place, with friendly people.

There are forests to walk around and plenty of paths to follow – you will see monkeys, hippos, crocodiles as well as many species of birds. The islands are hilly and in the uncultivated parts, are still forested. The most important crops on the island are cassava, bananas, sweet potatoes and coffee.

The main island is **Buggala Island** which is about 34 km long and whose main towns are Kakangala and Luku. It has a bus and matatus which link the main towns. The second largest island is **Bukasa Island** and other islands which are easy to visit are **Bubeke** and **Bufumira**.

Buggala Island

The island has about 50km of road on it

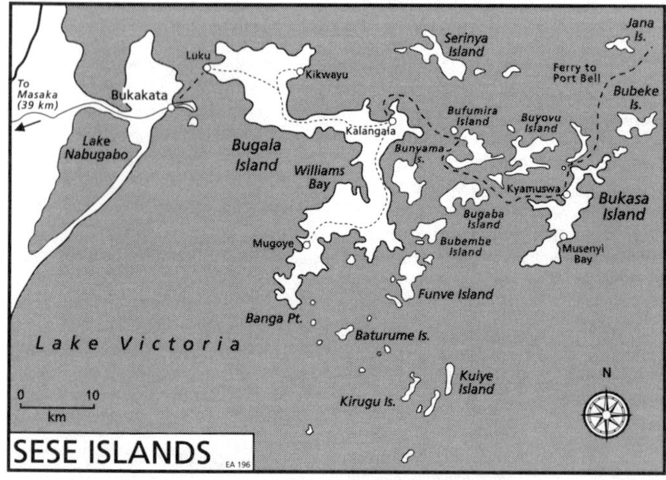

and really the best thing to do is simply to set off and explore – either by foot or by bicycle (which can be hired from Andronica's at Kalengala). All around are wonderful views of the lake and all the other islands – some forested, others cultivated and others a mixture of both. The forests do contain a certain amount of wildlife – although nothing spectacular. There are various species of monkey and a profusion of birdlife. A popular trip is to Mutambala Beach which is off the Kalengala-Luku road – some people do swim despite the risk of bilharzia.

Other Islands

Although most people stick to Buggala Islands there is no reason why you should not venture further afield. Provided you are flexible and not in any hurry you can explore the other islands at your leisure. Bukasa is a particularly attractive island – it has a smaller population, is more forested and has a wider range of wildlife. There are 2 beautiful beaches on the island as well as a waterfall. For further information on how to reach these ask at the Agnes' Guest House. Bufumira Island can be visited from Kalangal for the day, as can many of the uninhabited islands. Either talk to one of the fishermen or arrange it through *Andronica's Lodge*.

Local information

● Where to stay

There are no hotels in the upper price brackets and if you come to the Seses you should expect to stay in fairly basic accommodation. There are only a few lodges on the islands – all other accommodation is with families. If you ask around someone will be able to put you up, and you will undoubtedly be made to feel most welcome.

Kalangala D *Malaanga Safari Lodge*, (also known as *PTA Andronica Lodge*) PO Box 1165, Kalangala, Masaka, T Kalangala 26. Run by the very friendly Mr Andronico Semakula, (known to everyone as Mzee Andronico) and his daughter this lodge provides food and lodging. It is the sort of place that some people love and others hate. You will certainly meet other travellers here, but this is a place that has not had to face much competition and so standards have been allowed to slip – reports of wildlife in the mattresses may prompt you to ask around elsewhere for other accommodation. There is also a small library and bicycles are available for hire. There is food available at the lodge – but there are much cheaper, and equally good, places nearby. Mzee Andronico is a bit of a character – he is a retired teacher and likes to exercise his business skills so you may have to negotiate over the price of the room. He is full of stories and will be able to tell you all about the island. **E** ***Church of Uganda Hostel and Campsite***. This has opened recently and is close to *Andronica's*. It is clean, friendly and cheaper than *Andronica's*. **Camping** at *Church of Uganda Hostel*.

Luku E ***Luku Guest House***, Buggala Island. Run by Mr Kalwangi this is another small and simple lodge. It is useful for people who arrive from Bukakata and is located about a kilometre from the pier. Food is available and it is possible to camp. **E** ***Sikopian Lodge*** (*Scorpian Lodge*). This is a new hotel with 3 doubles and 5 singles, as well as camping space available. Serves food and has bicycles available for rent. Cold water only and no electricity. **Camping** At both *Luku Guest House* and *Sikopian Lodge*.

Bukasa E ***Agnes' Guest House***, located on the second largest island this has a beautiful location overlooking the lake. It is a friendly place – there are both rooms and space for camping. A limited range of food is available.

● Camping

Apart from the places mentioned you can theoretically camp anywhere on the islands – although obviously you should ask if you are going to be anywhere near people's houses. It is meant to be very safe here – but it goes without saying that you should keep your valuables with you at all times and don't flaunt your wealth.

● Transport

Local To get between the islands ask one of the **fishermen** and agree a price. There are **matatus** on the island of Baggala. Other than that the best way to see the islands is to walk around them.

There are several ways of reaching the Seses. You can either go on the steamer *MV Barbus* from Port Bell; the ferry via Masaka; or finally via the village of Kisenyi by ferry or small boat. Which ever way you get to the Sese Islands you may well find yourself arriving as it is getting dark. The first thing to do is a formality – you are required to inform the police post of your arrival on the island.

Ferry The alternative is to go from Masaka by the Bubakata Ferry, which goes to **Luka** and has the advantage that the journey is shorter. Again the timetable has changed recently – the ferry used to go daily – but now goes 3 times a week on Mon, Wed and Fri. Uganda Transport Company runs a bus from Kampala, leaving early in the morning, which goes via Masaka and on to the ferry terminal at Bukakata. Here it takes the ferry to Buggala Island and then drives the last 20 miles to **Kalangala**. The return journey is run on Tue, Thu and Sat, leaving at 0600 in the morning.

Small Boat From Masaka take a matatu to Nyondo from where you should get a share taxi to Butukula to catch the ferry to the town of Luku in the northwest of **Buggala**. Besides

Water Hyacinth

The attractive water hyacinth plant is posing a serious threat to the ecology of Lake Victoria. This fast-growing plant is rapidly choking the shores of the Lake and in the past 5 years the spread of the plant has been phenomenal. Murchinson Bay, which is the part of the Lake that can be seen from some of the hills surrounding Kampala, has been severely affected and huge islands of the weed can be seen floating in the Lake.

The plant, which reproduces very fast, covers the water surface completely, starves the water of oxygen with a serious impact on all other species, both plant and animal. It also makes navigation through the water very difficult.

Efforts are being made to find a solution to the problem. Pulling up the weed appears to be ineffective as the smallest piece of root left behind will regrow rapidly. Other suggestions that have been made include the introduction of a beetle from West Africa that will eat the water hyacinth. Extensive tests are being undertaken to ensure that the beetles will not then eat everything else in sight.

People who rely on fish as the major component of their diet, such as those living on the Sese's, are reported to have had to invest in stronger and more expensive fishing nets as a result of the hyacinth.

the ferry are are smaller boats that shuttle between the 2 on which you should be able to negotiate a ride with. Once in Luku, if you are heading for Kalengala, you may have to wait a while as there is not much traffic along here. There are a couple of places to stay in Luku so it is not really a problem if you arrive late.

Steamer The *MV Barbus* steamer, operated by Uganda Railways was brought back into operation in 1988. It originally left from Port Bell 3 times a week for Lutoboka on **Buggala** on Tue, Thu and Sat at 0830 in the morning, although this has been reduced to twice a week missing out the Thu voyage. The timetable is not altogether reliable – so check in advance of when you want to travel. The return journey from Buggala leaves very early in the morning before the sun rises (about 0400) on Wed and Sun. When you are returning it is probably easier to be at the port when the ferry comes in so that you can get onboard straight away and spend what remains of the night on the boat. The journey takes about 9 hrs (although it can be longer). There is little available on board in the way of snacks so you would do well to take plenty of food and drinking water. The ferry stops at the island of **Kome** for about 1 hr and you can buy lunch. It also passes and stops at other islands including Bubeke, Bukasa and Bufumira.

Mbarara

Mbarara is an important trading centre and is a crossroads for travellers heading towards the Rwenzori Mountains and Kabale in the southwest. The town of Mbarara also suffered over the past 20 years but not to the same extent as Masaka. Just before you enter the town centre you will see in the middle of a roundabout a statue of an Ankole steer with its impressive horns. The town is home to one of Uganda's Universities.

The town is the centre of the Kingdom of Ankole. The Kingdom was, like the other kingdoms of Uganda, broken up soon after independence but as part of Museveni's policies all the Kingdoms were offered the chance to have their kings back – on the understanding that they were to be cultural figures only without any political role. The palace of the Omugabe (King) of Ankole is located in Mbarara on a hill on the outskirts of town. The buildings have been taken over by the army and huts have sprung up all around the main buildings, as accommodation for the wives and families of the soldiers. Although you will probably not be able to walk around the building (which is in poor repair) you can drive past it. There is the one main building and a few secondary ones. To the right of the main structure is the building which used to house the royal drums. A few miles to the W of Mbarara is the Nkokonjeru which is the burial place of the last 2 Omugabe of Ankole, Kahaya II and Gasyonga II.

About 45 km from Mbarara is **Lake Mburo National Park**, and about 70 km away is the **Kitagata Hot Springs**.

Local information

● Where to stay

D *Lake View*, located on the western outskirts

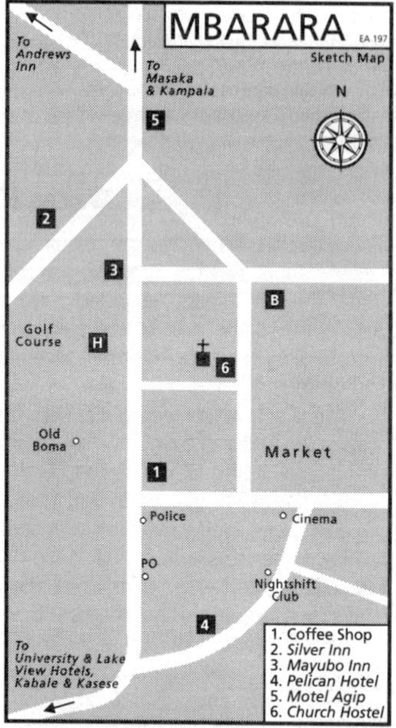

Ankole Cattle

These are the very large horned cattle that are famous throughout the country. Large horns are considered to be very beautiful and they are highly prized possessions. You will even see some cattle whose horns are so large that they are unable to raise their heads, or their heads are constantly leaning to one side.

of town and as its name suggests it overlooks a lake. The lake is said to be the King of Ankole's lake and nearby on top of a hill you will be able to see his palace. The hotel is very modern and has good facilities. **D** *Agip Motel*, on the main road from Kampala on the lefthand side as you approach from Kampala. It is modern and comfortable and has a bar which is popular with local business men.

E *University Inn*, double rooms with bathrooms. Set in very pleasant gardens. The water supply is not terribly reliable but the surrounding make it worth staying here. Restaurant. **E** *Pelican*, centre of town. Good value. Rooms clean and comfortable. **E** *Andrews Inn*, situated about 1 km off to the right just before you reach Mbarara. Unless you have your own vehicle it is rather out of the way. There is a range of rooms. **E** *Bunhorro*, located up to the right of the main road near the church. Cheap and simple food available. **E** *Church Of Uganda Hostel*, next to the bus station. Dormitory accommodation. **E** *Silver Inn*, located off the main road to the right just after the *Motel Agip*. The rooms are basic but clean. Restaurant and bar. Good value. **E** *Sabena Club*, located about 3 km out of town, down a turnoff roughly opposite the *Lake View Hotel*. There is food available.

● **Camping**

At the *Sabena Club* and *Katatumba Hotel*, below.

● **Outside Mbarara**

A-E *Katatumba Hotel*, PO Box 1177, Mbarara, T Mbarara 20152/20090, F Mbarara 21300. Luxurious resort-style hotel and has a fine variety of facilities – sauna, tennis courts, horse-riding, satellite television and camel-riding. There is a range of accommodation available – there are self contained rooms in bands **A** to **C**, then there are economy rooms (**D-E**) If you have equipment you can camp for US$4. There is an excellent restaurant and bar. Run by the same people as the *Hotel Diplomate* on Tank Hill in Kampala.

B *Pan Africa*, PO Box 1169, Mbarara Resort-style hotel. Located 40 km from Mbarara on the road to Kabale. The staff are friendly and they will try very hard to persuade to do one of their many activities. These include guides around coffee farms, banana plantations, a trip to the Hot Springs at Kitagata.

● **Transport**

Air There is a small airport at Mbarara but there are no scheduled flights any longer – only charter.

Road Mbarara is located nearly 300 km from **Kampala** and about 150 km from Kabale. The road is excellent – one of the best in the country. There are buses to and from Kampala every day. They leave from both the UTC bus station and the private bus station from 0600. Returning to Kampala there are also early morning buses or else you might also be able to get onto the bus that has come from Kabale, although this is sometimes full by the time it reaches Mbarara. There are of course also matatus although many people choose to avoid them as they drive particularly fast on this road. There are also buses from Mbarara to **Kasese** and **Fort Portal**, a distance of about 180 km on a newly improved road.

Kabale

The road from Mbarara to Kabale is good – you pass through the pastoral areas – a mix of dry plains and some more undulating countryside. Shortly before you reach Kabale the terrain changes and becomes more hilly and greener. Before long the scenery becomes increasingly dramatic with very steep slopes. If you are driving through this area very early in the morning the valleys are all filled with mist.

Kabale is located in the southwestern corner of Uganda, an area which is characterised by great diversity of topography, landscape and vegetation. Parts of this area are densely forested while the

RINDERPEST

The first recorded outbreak of Rinderpest in East Africa occurred in 1889 in what was then Somaliland. It is generally believed that the disease followed the introduction of cattle from India and Aden for use by the Italian army during the first expedition to Abyssinia. Once established, Rinderpest spread like wildfire over the whole of East Africa reaching Lake Tanzania by 1890.

The devastation resulting from the disease was terrible. Lugard was in Africa at this time and tells of the misery and suffering that the pastoral tribes, such as the Maasai and the Bahima, endured as a result of this disease. Many were made destitute with mortality rates generally over 90% In some areas, not a single animal survived. It is believed that many people also perished along with their animals – often of malnutrition. Many species of game were also exterminated – buffalo, eland, wart hog and wild pig were particularly badly affected.

rest is extremely heavily populated and intensively cultivated. You will see some hillsides that have been terraced to increase the cultivable area. This was undertaken during the colonial era.

The old part of the town is located up the hill – here you will find the government offices – many dating back to the early colonial period, the hospital, the church and the White Horse Inn. The other essential part of colonial life – the golf course – is also on the hill. It is all very spaciously laid out with well kept flower beds and mowed lawns in between. The newer part of the town is spread out along the main road, down in what used to be a swampy valley – it is wide with the buildings set back from the road.

The area around Kabale is ideal for hikers – it is often described as the Little Switzerland of Africa. There are tracks and paths through the hills and local guides.

Places of interest

Lake Bunyonyi A popular day trip which you can either walk to or else hire a bike. If you are cycling then be prepared for a long hard slog up and a wonderful run down. Once you get to Lake Bunyonyi you will almost certainly be offered a canoe trip across to Bwama island in the lake. You can expect to pay US$1-2 per person to be rowed across. On the island there is a centre for the disabled (originally it was a leper sttlement) run by the Church Missionary Society. The centre makes craft items for sale to tourists.and there is a shop on the island. If you want to stay overnight at the island there is a cheap rest house and food available.

Hot Springs These are some 10km to the S of Kabale. You can either hire a bike or walk, although you may need a guide to find it. Before you set off check that there are no problems – being so close to the Rwanda border this is a senstive area.

Kisizi Waterfalls This 90 foot waterfall near to the village of Kisizi about 30km from Kabale can be visited by matatu from Kabale. They leave about once an hr and take 2 hrs.

Gorillas Kabale is the town that you will pass through, and probably stay a night or 2, if you are planning a visit to the gorillas – whether in Uganda and Zaire. (For Uganda see National Parks Section, page 487 and for Zaire, see page 571). Be warned if you want to see them in Uganda you must book your day and buy your tracking permit in Kampala – there are no facilities to make the booking in Kabale and many people who turn up there are disappointed. If you have been told in Kampala that there are no spaces but have decided to risk it and see if

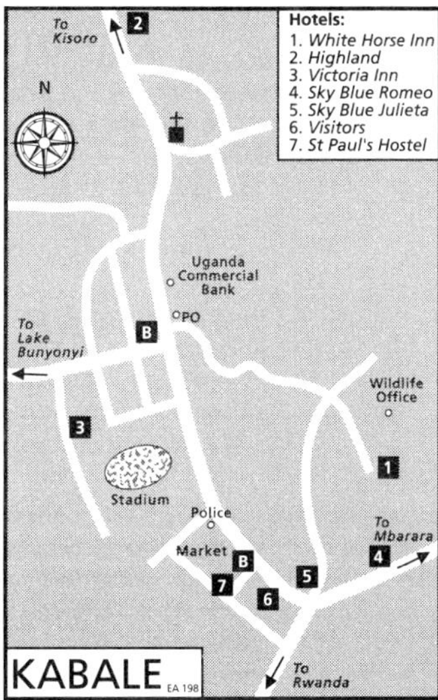

anyone has cancelled it is worth hanging around Kabale for a couple of days and talking to people on the way back. They will be able to tell you if there is a huge backlog of people on the waiting list at Buhoma and whether it is worth you going straight there or waiting in Kabale for a few days. (a National Park permit is for 3 days only).

Local information

● Where to stay

C *White Horse Inn*, PO Box 11, Lwamafa Road, T 20, Kabale. This is the best hotel in Kabale and is one of the *Uganda Hotels* Corporation chain. It has recently been done up – there is a pleasant lounge, bar and restaurant. It is set in wonderful gardens.

D *Highlands*, a little way out of town. It is so is not very well located for people without their own transport. It has running water although there is only bucket hot water. Good value. **D** *Victoria Inn*, PO Box 741, Kabale, T 0486 22154/22134. Located in the southwestern part of town the Victoria Inn has about 20 very clean rooms all with their own bathrooms with running water. There is hot water available in buckets, and an electricity generator. Restaurant and bar.

E *Skyblue Romeo*. There are 2 *Skyblues* in Kabale. This is the first that is seen on the approach to town from the E. A new building on the right hand side of the road. It has a range of rooms (all named after animals and birds) including rooms with own facilities. There is a balcony, a bar and snacks are available. **E** *Skyblue Julieta*, opposite the matatu stop. All rooms have common facilities. Running water is intermittent but plenty of buckets of hot and cold water are provided. Well organised. The Skyblues are run by a very helpful manager called Elisa who will give you all sorts of useful advice. **E** *Visitors*, next door to the matatu stop and they usually send someone to meet all the buses. It is very friendly and is slightly cheaper than the Skyblue. The rooms are a bit shabbier but there is a lovely verandah. Meals good. **E** ***St Paul's Training Centre and Hostel***, take the left turning off the main road beyond the market and it is located a little way down on the right. It is signposted. Cheapest of all the places in Kabale. There are basic meals available.

● Places to eat

There are no separate restaurants, but all the hotels provide meals. The ♦♦♦*White Horse* is the most expensive, and reasonable. Popular are ♦♦*Visitors* and the central ♦♦*Skyblue Julieta* and the food is good value. The ♦♦*Highlands* does very acceptable food.

● Transport

Road Kabale is a distance of about 400 km from **Kampala**. There are daily buses direct in both directions. They leave Kampala (from both the UTC bus station and the private bus station) around 0600 and arrive in Kabale sometime early in the afternoon. The bus costs US$5 for UTC and US$6 for the private buses. If you miss the bus you may want to get a matatu. There is actually little to be gained by doing this – the time of departure is not fixed and you wait until it is full. They usually leave about mid-morning and take about an hr less than the buses – but do so by driving like maniacs. They are uncomfortable and cost nearly twice the price of the buses. Return departs at 0600. You can either go down to the bus station itself or else wait outside the central Skyblue Julieta, ready (preferably with a torch) to wave and whistle to be picked up. It is a lovely journey as the sun rises as you leave Kabale.

If you are heading for **Kasese** or **Fort Portal** take the bus as far as Mbarara and change there.

There are 2 possible routes to **Rwanda**. The first is the border post of **Gatuna** (also known as Katuna) which is the more direct route. Alternatively you can go via Kisoro to **Ruhengeri** which is the longer, about 3 hrs, but a more scenic route. Matatus to **Kisoro** go occasionally throughout the day. This is a wonderful journey and some say that this is the most beautiful part of Uganda.

Kisoro

Kisoro is in the extreme southwestern corner of Uganda about 490 km from Kampala, and just over 70 km from Kabale. At the moment the town is suffering rather from the lack of traffic through to Rwanda. The **Mufumbiro Mountains** are located in this corner of the country – made up of 3 extinct volcanoes: Muhabura (4,125m), Mgahinga (3,474m) and Sabyinyo (3,674m). These are located on the border of Uganda, Zaire and Rwanda and are known as the Virunga Range. Anyone planning to visit the Zairian gorillas will come to Kisoro, and once the Mgahinga National Park is fully developed this will also be an added attraction. (See National Parks page 488). Near to Kisoro to the N is **Lake Mutanda**. Ask around for a guide to take you there or else head back up the Kabale road for about 2 kms and the turnoff is on your left.

Gorillas in Zaire

Visiting the gorillas in Zaire is possible although some of the tour operators are anxious about the political situation. This changes almost from week to week and obviously you will have to talk to local people to establish the current situation.

The basic difference with Uganda is that the Zairian gorillas are much more used to humans – many people would say that they are over-habituated. It is one thing to get close to these animals so that you get a good view, but it is another to feel that you are really in little more than a zoo. In Uganda you truly feel that these are wild animals – and you are entering their world, leaving a genuine feeling of awe for the gorillas. Rules and regulations, which are largely ignored in Zaire, are made solely to increase the chance of the long term survival of the gorillas. Those involved in gorilla-tourism in Uganda are trying to learn from the mistakes made in Zaire, and to a lesser extent in Rwanda, and not repeat them.

To get to Zaire you will need to get a lift in a truck to the border via Kisoro – ask around at the matatu station and someone should be able to put you in touch with someone heading in that direction. Alternatively take a matatu to Kisoro (there should be a few each day, as well as a bus once a day) and ask around for a lift for the remaining 9 km to the border. At the border you will be met by a guide who will offer to take you to the huts and from there to see the gorillas. If you refuse him you will probably end up walking about 8 hrs as you will not know the short cuts – with a guide it should take you about 2 hrs. This is where the tipping begins and it is from here that the costs of seeing the gorillas are so difficult to estimate. Basically, although the permit to see the gorillas is cheaper in Zaire than in Uganda and transport to them is cheaper, there are many more hidden costs involved in a trip to Zaire. You will need to take into account the extra cost of visas for entering Zaire and then reentering Uganda, tips to the border officials, tips to the guides, and so on. It is also more costly in that once you reach the huts that you stay in for the night, everything, including accommodation, food and drinks are all expensive.

Local information

● Where to stay

D *Travellers Rest*. This is a well known hotel amongst gorilla experts for it was once known as the unofficial gorilla headquarters. This was because in the mid-1950's the game warden, Walter Baumgartel, was also the owner of the Travellers Rest. He was one of the first people to take an interest in gorillas and their protection. Amongst the scientists who stayed here are Diane Fossey (see page 520) and George Schaller and it became a centre for scientists from around the world. Baumgartel left Uganda in the late 1960's and the hotel was later taken over by the *Uganda Hotels* Corporation. Although rather run down it has plenty of charm and is a most agreeable place to stay. It is now owned by a local Ugandan, and it is to be hoped its atmosphere will be retained.

E ***Mubano***, all rooms have bathrooms. There are doubles and triples only. There is an excellent restaurant attached. **E** ***Centenary***, the cheapest in Kisoro this is very basic. Singles and doubles are available, but the facilities are fairly minimal.

● Transport

Road There are matatus to **Kabele** occasionally throughout the day. There are matatus to the Rwanda border to cross to **Ruhengeri**, taking about 3 hrs, a more scenic route and it is said that this is the most beautiful part of Uganda.

NATIONAL PARKS

CONTENTS

MAPS

The National Parks covered in this section are the Queen Elizabeth National Park, Murchison Falls, Kidepo, Lake Mburo, Kibale Forest, Rwenzori Mountains, Bwindi Impenetrable Forest and Mgahinga Gorilla National Park. Apart from the 8 parks covered in this section, there are another 7 designated (their locations are marked on the country map, see page 407). However, they do not have any facilities and are, at present, unpromising to visit.

For up-to-date information on the parks, and to buy a gorilla tracking permit you should visit the Uganda *National Parks Headquarters*. This has recently moved location and can now be found a little way out of town – take a matatu from the matatu park down Kira road past the museum. This is a dual-carriageway and the turning is off on the right. If you get to the Police Station on the left then you have gone too far.

Queen Elizabeth (Rwenzori) National Park

The Queen Elizabeth National Park lies across the equator in the SW of Uganda. It is bordered to the SW by Lake Edward and to the NE by Lake George. The 2 lakes are joined together by the 33km long Kazinga Channel. The park covers an area of 1978 sq km, mainly flat and gently undulating terrain which rises from the Lakes 910m to 1390m above sea level at the crater area to the N of the Kazinga Channel. To the NE are the Rwenzori Mountains, often known as the Mountains of the Moon, which rise to over 5000m. On a clear day it is possible to see the Rwenzoris.

There are 2 centres for touring the Park, from Mweya Lodge in the N, and *Ishasha River Camp* in the S. After covering the general history and ecology of the park, accommodation, travel details and viewing routes are first presented for the northern (*Mweya Lodge*) sector, and then for the southern (*Ishasha River Camp*) sector.

Prehistory

In the early 1930's Sir Vivian Fuchs discovered fossils from the Early Pleistocene period along the Kazinga Channel,

NATIONAL PARK BYLAWS

- Camping and camp fires permitted at official sites only.
- Off-road driving prohibited
- Driving between 1915 and 0630 is forbidden.
- Blowing of motor horns is prohibited.
- A speed limit of 40 km/h should be observed.
- Carrying of arms or ammunition is forbidden.
- Dogs are not allowed in the Park.
- Littering in the Parks is an offence.

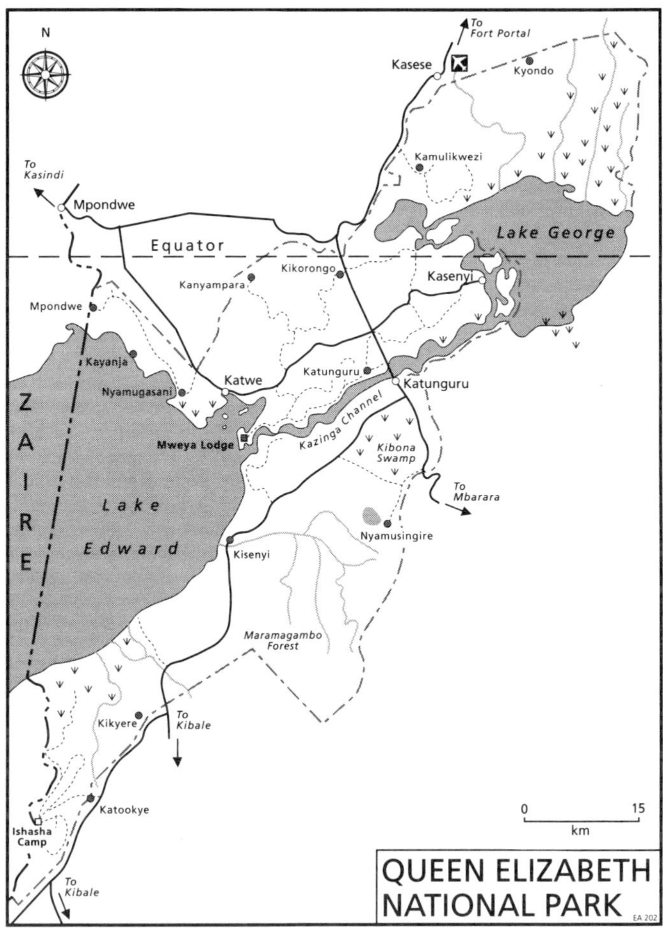

but it was not until some years later that prehistoric material was found. From the finds and work in Queen Elizabeth National Park it is possible to indicate a little of the prehistory of this area. The fossils that have been found are water snails and other molluscs, crocodiles (which do not occur in Lakes George or Edward), hippos (including the pygmy variety), members of the pig family and various fish including Nile Perch.

No tools belonging to the Early Pleistocene have been found in the fossiliferous ironstone bands, which are readily seen outcropping along the Kazinga Channel. Elsewhere in Africa this was an important period in human evolution and in East Africa ape-men of the Australopithecine family were beginning to make recognisable stone tools and became effective hunters rather than scavengers. Over a large area of the Queen Elizabeth National Park, and possibly as far N as Murchinson Falls, transient lakes existed in the comparatively shallow trough of the Rift Valley. It seems that these early palaeolithic hunters would have lived around these lakes hunting their prey whose bones are often found in the ironstone bands.

Following the faulting in the middle Pleistocene, the Rift Valley became more pronounced and the lakes more permanent. Stone tools found in the deposits from the period have been handaxes of quartz and quartzite and pebble tools, which are water worn pebbles flaked to give a sharp cutting edge.

At Mweya on the peninsula of land leading to the present Lodge, stone tools have been found in gravels which date from a slightly later period. The material found in a 1958 excavation consisted of all the types of tools of a fully developed Acheulean hand-axe culture – hand axes, cleavers, round stone balls and waste flakes. Similar tools have been found on the S bank of the Kazinga Channel.

The stone balls were thought to be wrapped in skin and attached to thongs and used to throw at animals. Hunting was probably conducted by making drives using wooden spears. The handaxe was a standard tool, an all-purpose cutting and scrapping implement. The cleaver (or straight-edged hand-axe) was used for skinning or chopping whilst the waste flakes, resulting from the making of the tools would have been used to scrape skin, and sharpen spears. The tools were made quickly and had a short life. The constant search for food would account for the widespread nature of the stone tools as well as their profusion – it is likely that many temporary camps around the lakes and water holes were established.

Judging from the profusion of waste flakes of quartz dating from the Late Stone Age, right along the Kazinga Channel, the Queen Elizabeth National Park continued to be an area eminently suitable for hunting, fishing and fowling until recent times. It is not known when agriculture was introduced although this was probably some time before the end of the first millennium AD, from which time the area became progressively pastoral. It is unlikely that a large population was ever supported. Surface collections of pottery indicate that the Kazinga Channel and lake shore regions, where fishing supplemented agriculture, were always more populous than the drier plains. The present depopulation of the Park is largely a result of the ravages of rinderpest and smallpox in the 1890s and then the arrival of tsetse at the beginning of this century. In 1910 the seriousness of the animal trypanosomiasis and human sleeping-sickness led the officials to move the inhabitants to areas free of the tsetse fly.

Modern History

In 1925 the Lake George Game Reserve was declared and was followed in 1930 by the Lake Edward Game Reserve. These were later enlarged to include the crater areas and the area S of the Kazinga Channel. The Kibale Forest Corridor Game Reserve, to the N of Lake George, was also established to provide a corridor for elephants to pass to and from Kibale Forest. The park was renamed the Kazinga National Park and was gazetted in 1952. In 1954 it was renamed again following the visit by Queen Elizabeth II. The park headquarters were established in Mweya and in 1960 the Nuffield Unit of Tropical Animal Ecology, later renamed the Institute of Ecology, was also developed there.

Ecology

The Park lies in the area of Africa where 2 types of vegetation meet – the rainforest which stretches out to the W for thousands of km to the shores of the Atlantic, and the Eastern and Southern

Africa grassland. The Park, like much of Uganda, gets 2 rainy seasons each year – from Mar-May and from Sep to Nov. However there is often rain during the rest of the year and prolonged droughts are unusual. The temperature varies from a minimum of 18°C to a maximum of 28°C.

Animals that occur in the Queen Elizabeth National Park include hippos, lions (well-known for being tree-climbers), elephants, buffalo, Uganda kob, waterbuck, bushbuck and topi. Smaller animals that occur (although are not neccesarily seen easily) include wart hog, hyenas, mongoose, red-tailed monkey, black and white colobus monkey, baboon, vervet monkey, and chimpanzees. Giant forest hogs occur in the Park – you are particularly likely to see them onthe escarpment on the way up to Mweya, just outside the Maramagambo Forest. They look rather like large shaggy wart hogs for which they can be easily mistaken. The Park is famous for its wide range of bird life – an estimated 540 species have been recorded. In marshy and waterside areas larger species such as cormorants, goliath herons, egrets, spoonbills, and sacred ibis can be seen. Others include fisheagles and pied kingfishers.

Northern Sector (Mweya Lodge)

This is the most visited part of the park, partly because access from Kampala is better, and because there is a wider choice of accommodation.

Routes

Launch Trip on the Kazinga Channel The journey takes about 2 hrs and you can expect to see plenty of hippos and a wide range of birdlife. For information ask at the information desk at Mweya Lodge. The launch goes twice a day and costs US$60 for up to 10 people – and for parties of more than that, is US$6 each. You should not have too much difficulty in getting a group together. You can also organize game drives through Mweya Lodge if you do not have your own transport.

Channel Track and North of the Kazinga Channel This area is perhaps the most popular for game drives and there is a network of roads that enable you to choose a length of drive that suits you. If you plan your route there is no need to double back on yourself. Generally the roads are passable although after heavy rain patches of thick sticky mud may make some routes difficult. Hippo trails cross the road every so often – it has been observed that individual hippos tend to use the same route every night when they go inland to feed. If you do come across any hippos on land be sure to give them a wide berth and do not come between them and the water. There are hyenas, buffalos, Uganda kob, and down by the Channel Nile monitor lizards. The most elusive of animals, the leopard, lives in this area – but they are extremely difficult to spot.

Crater Area There are 7 Crater Lakes in this area, although only 4 of these are accessible on the existing roads. These are Katwe, Kikorongo, Munyanyange and Nyamanuka. They are all alkaline although to differing degrees. The name Nyamanuka literally translated means animal smell and is so-named because there is a strong smell of sulphur whih is emitted from the water. Lake Katwe is known throughout Uganda for being an area of salt production (see box, page 471) and has been producing high quality salt for many years.

Take the track opposite the Main Gate at Kabatoro to the Baboon Cliffs and follow it through the rolling grasslands. The road is generally good although after rain there may be some muddy patches suitable only for 4-wheel drive vehicles. The grasslands are burned regularly as dominant plants are all fire-loving species whose growth is encouraged with regular burnings. There is no permanent fresh water in this area so, apart from during the rainy season, you are unlikely to see many animals. During the rainy season however there are often herds of both buffalo and elepant. There are always plenty of birds (particularly grassland birds) and the area is particularly popular with ornithologist.

The track to Baboon Cliffs is worth taking for the views alone. The road continues upwards, and thorn trees (*Acacia gerrardii*) become more common. About 12 km from Kabatoro the track ends at Baboon cliffs and here you get a splendid view of the park and surrounding coutryside. The crater of Kyemango is below and in the distance Lake George can be seen. To the N are the Rwenzoris and on a clear day you will be able to see the snow caps.

Lake George and Lake Kikorongo To follow this route take the right turning just after the main gate at Kabatoro and drive towards and then across the main Kasese road. The track continues towards Lake George and the fishing village of Kasenyi through open grassland. About 10 km from the main road look to your left and you should be able to see a Uganda Kob lek (see box, page 470).

Just before you reach Kasenyi you will see the small crater lake of Bunyampaka which is also used for salt panning on a small scale. You can take the track around the rim of the crater lake from Kasenyi that will also lead you to the Channel. Alternatively you can return along the main track and after 6km turn right. This leads you to the village of Hamukungu, turn left and you will pass through a large swamp and then pass the crater lake of Kikorong before reaching the main Kasese road. On this latter route you may see elephant and in the swamp there is the possibility of seeing the shoebill, while there are sometimes flamingoes in the Kikorongo Crater Lake.

UGANDA KOB

This is probably the most numerous mammal in the Queen Elizabeth National Park with an estimated population of about 17,000. They prefer low-lying, open country without too much bush. Female kob and their young form loose herds of about 50, and during the dry season they join up with males and with other groups to form herds of up to 1,000 in areas where green grass is still available. Uganda kob once found in southern Sudan, throughout Uganda, into western Kenya and down into northern Tanzania. They are now limited to western Uganda and eastern Zaire.

Male Uganda kobs mate with females in what is known as a breeding territory. Other antelopes breed in a similar way, but kobs have a more refined system that involves them using permanent grounds known as leks. Within a lek, there are a cluster of small, usually roughly circular, breeding territories. The males will defend their territory by ritualized displays and by fighting when necessary. They defend their territory for a fairly short time, usually a few days, before they have to wander off to find food and water, or if they are chased away by another male. The females range freely within the lek and appear to favour males that hold territories in the centre of the lek. For this reason there is most activity within the central area of the lek, with these males constantly being challenged by other males. When a male loses his territory he will go off to join other males in a bachelor group and will later try to regain his territory.

The leks can be recognised by the flattened grass that is the result of being trampled on over many years. They are usually located in open grassland near to water. During a prolonged dry season leks are usually abandoned and the herds join together in search of food and water.

Lake Katwe and Pelican Point To get to Lake Katwe take the left turning just after the Main Gate and head for the now abandoned village of Kabatoro. About 5 km from this is Katwe town and on your right are the crater lakes of Katwe and Munyanyange. These provide Katwe inhabitants with their main sources of income, by salt panning and fishing. They are outside the Park boundaries so it is possible to leave your car. You should be able to visit the salt works at Lake Katwe

LAKE KATWE SALT

The salt industry at Katwe is hundreds of years old and over many years has provided the local inhabitants with an important source of income. About 25 km from Butiaba on the eastern shores of Lake Albert is the village of Kibiro where salt is produced in a process that appears to have changed little in over 7 centuries. The only change is that the containers used, formerly pottery, are now metal.

There is archaeological evidence of production going back 700-800 years. The first written reports of production came from Speke in 1863 and Grant in 1864 who described it as perfectly pure in colour and taste. Emin Pasha (see page 270) was the first to give a first-hand description of the production methods used.

The basis of the salt production are the hot springs which are found here at the base of the Western Escarpment. One unusual aspect is that both the production and marketing of salt is solely by women. The salt gardens are owned by women and ownership is by female inheritance. It is not possible to buy a salt garden, although recently it has become possible to hire one.

The main method of salt collection is by evaporation andthe rate of production depends on the weather. First,what is called a salt garden is prepared. This can be of any size and shape, and the area is cleared of grass. In the second stage dry soil is scattered over the wet exposed surface.

The loose soil is left to dry and as it does so it draws salty moisture from below and the moisture evaporates by the heat of the sun. This process increases, the salt content of the scattered soil at the end of the day is scraped together and heaped up so that if it rains all the salt will not be lost. The spreading and drying process continues for a few days depending on the weather, and as the salt content of the scattered soil increases, the colour changes to a greyish brown.

Once a sufficiently high concentration is reached the third stage begins. This is a process whereby the soil impregnated with salt is leached with water so that all the salt dissolves into the water. To do this the loose soil is put in a container with holes in the bottom and water is poured through it and collected in a second container held underneath the first. The liquid collected is dark brown and has a very high salt content.

This liquid is then taken indoors to special salt-boiling buildings for the final stage of boiling the solution to evaporate the water. Firewood is used and its supply is one of the major restrictions on the amount of salt that can be produced. As the brine boils the water evaporates and after an hour or two the salt starts to form. By the final stages the salt is white and porridge-like and is poured onto a mud platform where it immediately solidifies. As more salt is ladled on, a salt cone grows until it is about 3 to 4 kg. The number of cones that a saltworker will be able to take to market will depend on how much firewood she could gather and how much brine she could prepare. These in turn depend on the size of the female labour force working on her gardens.

UGA_BX19

on payment of a small fee. You may be able to get a guide to show you around and explain the methods by which salt is evaporated and purified. As Lake Munyanyange is an alkaline lake it is sometimes the home of lesser flamingoes in varying numbers. It is possible to walk around the rim of the lake.

The road continues beyond Katwe. It is not in very good condition and if there has been recent rain then you would be advised to avoid this route unless you have a 4-wheel drive. From the track you will be able to see the Nyamagasani Delta and the Kihabule Forest before you reach Pelican Point.

South of Kazinga Channel Take the main road and cross the Kazinga Channel. About 5 km S of the crossing turn right along the Ishasha road and follow it S. This route is mainly through grasslands, and about 8 km after the turning there is a kob lek on your left (see box, page 470).

Lake Nyamusingiri and Maramagambo Forest This is one of the longer trips taking a full day and requires a 4-wheel drive. Go back to the main Kasese road and turn E towards the Kichwamba escarpment. Cross the Katunguru bridge and continue along the road for about 12 km before turning right and starting to climb up the escarpment. The road takes you through both grasslands and acacia woodland, to your right you should be able to see the Kibona swamp, while ahead of you is the Maramagambo forest.

Lake Kasanduka and the start of the Maramagambo forest is reached about 9 km along this track, and a further 3 km is Lake Nyamusingiri. There are trails into the forest although you are advised to take a rancher who knows the forest. Chimpanzees do live in the forest but are not habituated so you are unlikely to see them. Other primates that you may see are black and white colobus and red-tailed monkeys.

Chambura River Gorge The Chambura Gorge marks the boundary between the Queen Elizabeth National Park and the Chambura Game Reserve. The Gorge was formed by a river which flows off the Kichwamba escarpment and into the Kazinga Channel at Katunguru. The Gorge is 10 km long and supports thick forest which is home to many different forest-living species. These include chimpanzees, but so far visits to these chimpanzees by tourists are not organized at present, although one tour operator *Hot Ice* (see page 429) has plans to begin chimpanzee viewing trips. On each side of the Gorge is savannah, and the view from the edge is spectacular. You can walk along the top of the Gorge and look down onto the forest. This gives a wonderful view of the tops of the trees and any birds or animals that may be feeding off them.

The easiest way to get to the Gorge is to take a park ranger with you who will be able to advise you on up-to-date conditions locally. One possible route is to take the road from Katunguru for about 8km towards the escarpment. There is a turning off to the left shortly before the road begins to climb the escarpment and from here it is about 2 km to the edge of the Gorge. Once you get to the Gorge it is possible to climb down the 2 to 3 hundredm into it. This is a bit of a scramble as it is fairly steep. You pass from dry grasslands at the top, to thick forest and the river at the bottom. Mweya Lodge should be able to organise a trip to Chambura River Gorge between a group of you.

Park information

● Where to stay

C *Mweya Lodge*, PO Box 22, Kasese. T Kasese 0493 4266. Managed by *Uganda Hotels*, PO Box 7173, Kampala, T Kampala 234296. Located on the Mweya Peninsula on a bluff overlooking Katwe Bay. The original lodge was built in the mid-1950's but in 1967 was replaced with the present building. It has 75 beds, a good restaurant and a terrace with wonderful views overlooking the water. There is a small shop here and you can change money. The lodge is rarely full although as it is a popular destination for Kampala residents at weekends. **C** *Chambura River Gorge Camp* run by (*Hot Ice* see page 429)

E *Institute of Ecology*, next to *Mweya Lodge*. There are singles and doubles available, all with shared facilities. There is no bed linen provided so it is pretty basic but is clean and comfortable. Meals available. **E** *Student Hostel*, 1 km from the Ecology Institute and is the cheapest place to stay. However it is very basic and not especially good value.

● **Camping**

There are also a number of camp sites near Mweya Lodge. The first is on the S side of the peninsula overlooking the Kazinga Channel. This is the most convenient if you want to use some of the Lodge's facilities. The other 2 are located off the Channel Track – the first is 4 km from the Lodge and the second is 6 km. Each of the camp sites has a pit latrine, water and firewood provided. It is also possible to camp at a Student Hostel, but you need to bring all equipment and food.

● **Transport**

Air Services can be chartered from Kampala to the Airstrip at Mweya Lodge or alternatively to Kasese, which is 64 km from the Park.

Road From **Kasese** take pickup matatu going in the direction of Katwe on the N shore of Lake Edward – they go every day in the morning. Ask to be dropped off on the main road at the turning for the Park entrance which is a hundred yards down a track. From the gate it is about 6km to Mweya – you can either try and hitch and this is not as difficult as it sounds or you can ask the people at the gate to radio for a vehicle to be sent to pick you up. This latter option will cost you about US$10-15 split between however many there are in your group.

If you are driving to Mweya Lodge, it is 435 km from **Kampala**, via Mbarara, a journey which takes about 6 hrs. The Kazinga channel is crossed on a iron bridge and then onto the small village of Katunguru. From Katunguru there are 2 different routes. You can either continue on the main road towards Kasese turning left after 5 km and then a further 15 km to the Main Gate at Kabatoro passing Lake Nyamanuka. From the Main Gate it is 8 km to the Lodge. Alternatively you can turn left immediately after Katunguru and follow the road to the Katunguru Gate from where it is 20 km to the Lodge along the Channel Track.

Southern Sector (Ishasha River Camp)

Mainly open partly-wooded grasslands and more heavily populated with animals, the southern part of the Park is quite beautiful. It is less accessible, than the northern part (and offers only spartan accommodation) and so receives substantially fewer visitors. **Ishasha River Camp** is located in the far southwestern corner of the Park, close to the Zairean border. The Park Sub-headquarters are at Ishasha which is over 120 km S of Mweya.

Park Information

● **Where to stay at Ishasha River Camp**

At **Ishasha** the only accommodation available are simple **bandas** with beds for up to 6 people and campsites. These were built during the colonial period and seem to have had little done to them since. For **camping** there are 2 sites which are very pleasant – both are located on the banks of the river in the riverine forest and have firewood and pit latrines provided but little else. There is no food available so you must come fully self-sufficient.

● **Transport to and from Ishasha Camp**

From **Mweya Lodge** take the main Kasese-Mbarara road S and turn off (right) at Katunguru. Although this is a route used by commercial traffic it has not had any maintenance for many years and its condition deteriorates sharply during the rains and may become impassable. About 100 km after joining the road at Katunguru you will see a turning to the right with a sign to the Katookye gate. From the entrance gate to the camp is a further 7 km.

An alternative route from **Mweya Lodge** is much longer in terms of distance via Ishaka to Rukungiri. It is not a very well signposted route – Ishaka is on the main Kasese-Bushenyi-Mbarara road about 6km before Bushenyi. This is the route if you are coming from **Kampala** via Mbarara. From Ishaka take the road S to Rwashamaire and then W to Rukungiri. If you are travelling independently there are matatus from Ishaka to Rukungiri. From Rukungiri head for Ishasha village and a few km before you

Elephants In The Queen Elizabeth National Park

A recent report suggested that the herd of about 200 elephants that shuttles between the Queen Elizabeth National Park and neighbouring Parc Virunga in Zaire now stay longer in Uganda. The habits of this herd are said to have become an index of the level of security in the 2 neighbouring countries. The study also suggested that the age composition of the herd reflected the years of poaching and other forms of disturbance, with a third of the population under 5 years of age and an unusually large proportion of orphans. It was also found that there were hardly any bull elephants over 45 years old, and tuskless elephants dominated, due to selective killing by poachers.

reach it the road joins the main road from Katunguru. Turn up this road and follow it for 7km to the entrance gate. If you do not have your own vehicle you will have to get off at this junction and walk it or try to hitch a lift to the entrance gate. Once at the gate it is another 7km to the camp – at a cost of about US$12 you can get a Park vehicle to come and collect you.

Routes

South Kigezi Route The route covers a distance of about 14 km and begins at the bandas. Close to the bandas is a large hippo wallow which apart from being home to hippos is also a watering point for various antelope and buffalo. The birdlife here is also fairly extensive – there are herons, storks and ibises.

In the woodland in this southern area there are the famous tree-climbing lions. They are rarer now before and it has been suggested that their habit of climbing trees is less common. In this area you may also see topi. These are splendid animals with beautiful coats. They are also found in Lake Mburu National Park in Uganda, and only a few other National Parks in Kenya and Tanzania.

North Kigezi Route A rarely visited part of the park. There are plans to rehabilitate the roads. It is an area of grassland with patches of woodland. There are elephants in this area – these are the ones that move between Uganda and Zaire (see box, page 474), although they are very shy.

Murchison Falls National Park (Kabalega Falls NP)

The Murchison Falls National Park is the largest National Park in Uganda and covers an area of nearly 4,000 sq km and offers some of the most spectacular scenery in Uganda. Until about 20 years ago the waters of the Nile were forced through a narrow gap in the rocks to fall through a series of foaming, roaring cascades down a drop of about 50m, creating one of the world's most spectacular waterfalls. However, in 1961, a year of particularly heavy rains and floods in Uganda, the waterfall broke through another gap in the rocks so that there are now 2 breaches.

Prehistory

The area around Chobe in the eastern part of the Murchinson Falls National Park has been a popular habitat for man from early times for a number of reasons. Firstly it has good animal and vegetable resources; it also had a good agricultural potential; and later iron-ore suitable for primitive smelting technology was present in the area.

The earliest artifacts found in the area of Chobe date from the middle stone age, when the banks of the Nile were peopled with small groups of hunters and gatherers, who may also have done some fishing. Some rough pebble tools, large flakes, some picks and a hand-axe have been found dating from this period, when it is believed that the

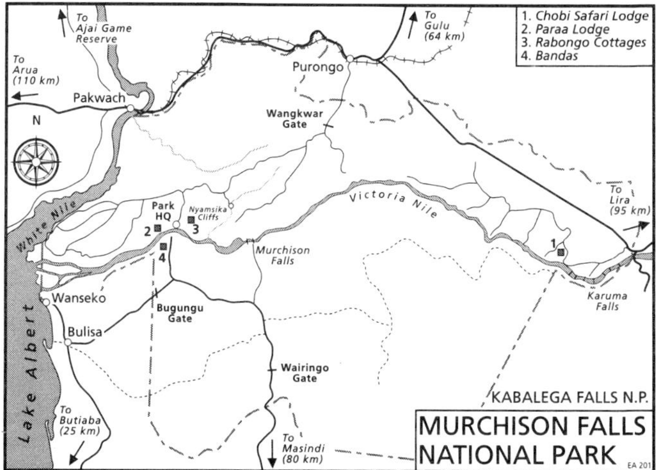

Nile was flowing at a higher level than at present.

Throughout the Middle and Late Stone Age agriculture and the domestication of animals were not known to the river bank dwellers – they continued to eke out an existence based on hunting and gathering. However over the years the manufacture of stone tools became more sophisticated and some new types of tool appeared for the first time. The abundance of flakes and chippings in places along the eroded banks of the river suggests that these may have been places where tools were made rather than actual settlements.

Along the banks pottery fragments, iron-ware and iron slag has been collected dating back as far as 2000 years. The bulk of the finds, however, are much more recent, and dating from the last 200 years. The settlers who are thought to have first introduced iron technology to this part of Africa left behind a very distinctive type of pottery known as dimple-based ware. This is characterised by bevelled rims and incised cross-hatched or grooved decoration, and is to be found over much of the Lake Victoria basin. Related pottery types occur over most of the sub-continent; but the most northerly occurrence of this archaeological complex yet discovered is at Chobe.

Most of the pottery fragments found in recent years carry decorative motifs identical to those used by the people surrounding the National Park today. They consist of concentric circles, raised bosses and zigzag chevrons applied to the wet clay with a carved wooden roulette or a knotted cord.

Launch Trip

Everyone who visits Murchison Falls National Park is recommended go on this trip. It is operated by Uganda National Parks from Paraa to the Falls themselves. The cost is US$80 for up to 20 people – so if you can gather a group together it is not too expensive. There is also the US$20 National Park entrance fee on top of this. During the ride you can expect to see crocodiles and hippos. Other game that are found at Murchinson Falls include elephants, buffalo, giraffes and a range of antelopes. You can arrange for the boat to stop at the base of the Falls while you walk up the foot-

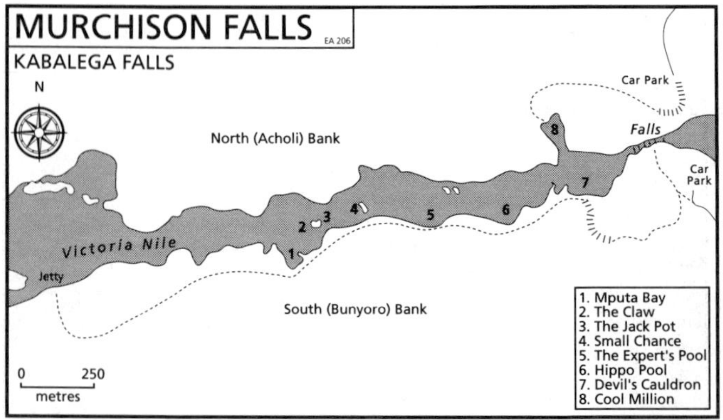

path to the top, which gives an excellent the views of the Falls.

Park information

Where to stay

There used to be 2 high standard lodges in Murchinson Falls National Park – *Chobe Safari Lodge* and *Paraa Safari Lodge*. They were both virtually destroyed during the troubles and have been closed for some years. However there is talk of reopening ***Chobi Safari Lodge***, which is situated on the northern bank of the Nile. ***Paraa Lodge***, which is located in the western part of the National Park was looted, bombed and burnt down, it was then rebuilt in 1987, only to be looted again a few months later. It has now been taken over by *Windsor Hotels* and is being rebuilt and should open fairly soon.

C ***Rabongo Cottages***. The only high standard accommodation currently available at Murchison Falls. Run by *Hot Ice* (see page 429).

D ***Bandas***. More basic accommodation is available S of the river, built in about 1988. There are simple bandas which are kept very clean and have mosquito nets and bedding provided. The bandas can be booked through the Uganda National Parks (PO Box 3530, T 256534, Kampala). If you ask in advance meals can be made for you, or else if you bring your own food you can borrow a charcoal stove.

Camping

Is also possible here.

Transport

Air There is an airstrip at Paraa and charter flights do fly here from Entebbe. Alternatively you could fly to Masindi and continue by road from there.

Train The railway from Tororo to Pakwach on the W bank of the Nile, has recently been reopened. The service is not regular at present.

Road (own vehicle) Murchison Falls can be reached by road from Kampala via Masindi. From Masindi there are 2 routes to Paraa but one is in much better condition than the other. From Masindi take the road to Butiaba on the shores of Lake Albert and from there head N, through the village of Bulisa to the park entrance. It is a very attractive drive looking across the Rift Valley towards the Lake and across to Zaire on the other side. The alternative route is more direct and goes through the park and forest – but it is only suitable for reliable 4-wheel drive vehicles. Alternatively if you are heading for Chobe (not very likely until the lodge re-opens) take the road from Kampala towards Gulu. At Kigumba turn right to Karuma and from here it is a further 15 km to Chobe.

Road (Public Transport) Getting to Murchinson Falls National Park by public transport involves a number of changes. From Hoima or Masindi you want to head for Bulisa which is N of Butiaba and about 30 km from the Park entrance gate. It is a small town where you will probably have to stay the night. There is a simple lodge **E** ***Bulisa Corner Guest House***. From Bulisa you can either try and hitch or failing that can hire a bicycle from the Bulisa Corner Guest House. It is 27 km to Paraa and is mostly flat.

Kidepo National Park

Kidepo is one of the most spectacular National Parks in Uganda but being the most isolated it is also one of the hardest to visit. However while it may not have the animals of many of the National parks, it is one of the few remaining places in the world where you get a real feeling of wilderness.

Kidepo National park is located in the far NE of Uganda on the border of Sudan and close to the border with Kenya. It is about 840 km from Kampala, and is an area of about 1334 sq km with an altitude that ranges between 1350m and 2750m. The Napore Nyangea Mountain Range is located to the W of the camp and the Natera hills to the E. In the distance to the N you will be able to see the peak of Mount Lotukei. The vegetation is typical savannah with some acacia woodland.

One problem which Kidepo National Park suffers from more than the other National Parks in Uganda is that of water supply. This is a problem that the plants and animals of the area have adapted themselves to well. Low rainfall in the form of a long and severe dry season of almost 6 months is characteristic of Karamoja as a whole. The effect of this regime is best appreciated between Oct and Mar when the National Park is progressively baked, bleached and burnt by sun and often fire. Every scrap of moisture, except that which manages to survive in a few waterholes and dams, turns to dust under the scorching breath of the tireless NE wind. Unattractive that this might sound it is in fact perhaps the best time to visit for these conditions are good for game-viewing. Animals are more tied to the available water sources, and there tends to be a concentration of animals around Apoka, the Park headquarters at the height of the dry season. This is the time when animals tend to leave Kidepo Valley, which dries out very rapidly once the rains have ceased, and head for the comparatively lush savannas and woodlands of Narus valley where there is enough water to see them through until the rain breaks again in Mar or Apr. Once the rains begin the animals drift back to the

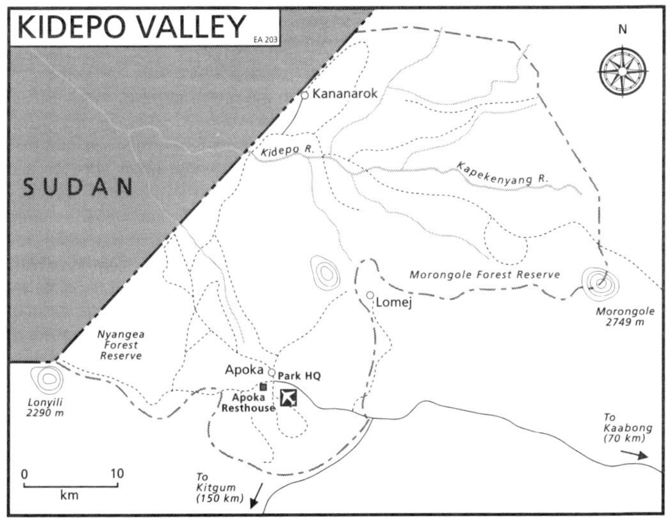

Karamojong Phrases

The Karamojong language is one of the Nilotic languages. The vocabulary is fairly limited with only about 180 words. Here are some that you might find useful:

General greeting	*Imaata!*	No	*Mam*
Did you sleep well?	*Iperi ejok a?*	Please and thank you	*Alakata*
Yes	*Aye*	Where is the office?	*Aye ayai apis?*

Kidepo Valley, and from Apr-Oct, when the grass is shorter this is probably the best viewing area.

The Kidepo river is a sand river, which only flows visibly for a few days of the year. However, below the sand, at depths that vary from a few cm to a few m, there is water. How deep it is depends on how far into the dry season it is. The animals of the Park dig holes to reach the water. This also explains why on the banks of an apparently dry river the vegetation is often more green and lush than elsewhere in the Park.

Game in Kidepo suffered badly during the recent turmoil and lawlessness. The animals include lion, buffalo, elephant, zebra and a wide range of antelope.

Museum

The National Park has a museum which is open to visitors. There are some pieces of skeletons as well as some insect specimens. There are also some photographs of some of the rangers involved in earlier efforts at conservation.

Park information

● Where to stay

C *Apoka Resthouse*. The Lodge at Kidepo has survived surprisingly well. There are 32 beds and bedding and mosquito nets are provided. There is some food although it is advisable to take with you fresh fruit and vegetables with you and the staff will cook it for you. The same applies to drinks and if you want them cold it may also be advisable to take paraffin for the fridge. With a bit of organisation it is possible to have a very comfortable stay here.

● Camping

There are four sites close to *Apoka Lodge*.

Air You can charter a light aircraft from Kampala which will take about 2-3 hrs, and will cost somewhere in the region of US$1,000 per person for a 2-day and one night all inclusive stay. Contact Bel Air (see page 427).

Road The drive up to Kidepo should not be undertaken lightly and before you contemplate a trip you should speak to people who can give you up to date information, such as Bel Air (see page 427). This part of the world is heavily armed and when you arrive there you will notice the high percentage of Karamojong men who carry guns. There have been periods when, because of the bandits it has not been safe to travel in this area and it may therefore be advisable to drive up in a convoy.

Lake Mburo National Park

Lake Mburo National Park is one of the newest of Uganda's National Parks. For for many years there has been a great deal of dispute between the use of this area by man as against game. This began during the colonial period when the area was declared to be a hunting ground for the Ankole royalty. After independence it became a game reserve and in the early 1980s was finally gazeeted as a National Park. However, to establish the Park it was necessary to resettle large numbers of people and their herds of cattle, and this is still a fairly controversial issue.

It is the only Park in Uganda to contain an entire lake and it is probably the most easily accessible from Kampala. The Park is a landscape of open plains, acacia grasslands and marshes. Around the lake itself is thicker riverine woodland while much of the rest of the park is acacia woodland.

Animals that occur in Lake Mburo National Park include impalas, zebras, topi, oribi, land, klispringer, buffalos, waterbucks, reedbucks and warthogs. Baboons and vervets are commonly seen and the Lake contains hippos and crocodiles, while buffaloes can often be found in the marshes. Leopards are present but they are rare. Interesting birds include crested crane (Uganda's national emblem), saddlebill storks and Abyssinian ground hornbills. There is also a wide range of water birds.

One of the great advantages of Lake Mburo National Park is that you can walk around the park (rather than having to drive in a vehicle) as long as you are accompanied by a ranger. In addition to this you can also walk between the camp and the lake without a ranger – a distance of about a kilometre. A game drive in the Park vehicle can be arranged, and it is posible to hire a canoe to go onto the lake for about US$8 per group – the canoe takes 6 people.

Park information

● Where to stay

D *Rwonyo Rest Camp*, there are double and single bandas as well as one 4 bed family banda, which are simple but comfortable. Bedding and mosquito nets are provided, and showers are shared. Meals are available and are cheap and simple.

● Camping

There are 4 sites in the Park where the facilities are basic – the one on the lakeshore is the most popular.

● Transport

Road (own vehicle) The Park is located 230 km (about 4 hrs) from Kampala along the Mbarara Road. Take the main road through Masaka and the turning is marked 13 km past the Lyantonde trading centre. If you are coming in the other direction, from Mbarara, a turning to the park at Sango, about 25 km from Mbarara, is probably better. From Mbarara the Park headquarters are about 47 km, a journey which will take about an 1½ hr. Unless there has been recent rain the road is not too bad although at certain times of the year 4-wheel drive is recommended.

Road (public transport) There are a number of possibilities. You can arrange a special hire from Mbarara for about US$35. There is a National Parks vehicle which goes between Mbarara and the Park on most weekdays – obviously this not very reliable. If you know what day you will be going you can arrange it through the Uganda National Parks Office in Kampala – they have a radio contact with the Park. If there is not a vehicle going they can arrange to meet you at Sango for about US$20. If you get to Sango early you can walk-it is about 20 km and is fairly flat but be sure to take plenty of water. From the Park entrance to the rest camp is further 4km and you may have to wait until someone is ready to escort you. Coming from Kampala is easiest as at the weekends as the park is fairly popular with Kampala residents and lifts are possible.

Kibale Forest National Park

Kibale Forest, which covers an area of about 560 sq km, was, until recently a Forest Reserve but has now been taken over by the Uganda National Parks. There is now an emphasis on conservation, sustainable utilisation and non-consumptive uses of the forest. The viewing of chimpanzees in their natural environment is the main tourist attraction.

Nature trails into the forest have been created and quite apart from the chimps the walks in the forest are wonderful. Tracking to the habituated chimp troops is conducted by trained guides who will also be able to tell you about the forest. The group of chimps in the Kanyanchu community is believed to be the largest group in Kibale Forest, numbering about 45. Individuals are named and include Miika, a strong and authorative male; Mutaganya a female; Nkojo a male identified by a scar; Nkazi a female with a swelling on her chin; Kaara with a stiff digit on its right hand. The forest is believed to contain the highest concentration of primate species in East Africa – these include chimpanzees, black and white colobus monkeys, red colobus monkeys, blue monkeys and baboons. Other animals that are found in the forest include elephants, buffaloes, bush pigs, and duickers. However many of these are very shy and you will be lucky to see them. There is also a huge range of bird life and an estimated 140 species of butterfly.

More trails are being constructed and efforts are being made to restrict the number of people that go along these in any one day. Plans are also underfoot to have a number of new campsites in the park – all will be within the grassland part of the park. An information centre and exhibition hall will also be established.

The emblem of Kibale Forest is a black and white colobus monkey designed by Lysa Leland, a researcher and photographer who with her husband Tom Struhsaker, worked in Kibale for many years, long before its popularity took off.

Forest walks

There are organised excursions to the chimps twice a day leaving from Kanyunchi at 0700 and 1500 which cost US$5 per person – the earlier walk is meant to be better as you have a better chance of seeing the chimps. Tourists are not allowed to walk in the forest unaccompanied and you must take a guide – but you will find their knowledge will greatly increase your enjoyment of the walk.

• **E** *Kanyanchu River Campsite*, situated about 35 km from Fort Portal. It is simple and is not geared for the tourist looking for luxury. There are 5 covered camping sites – which are invaluable during very wet weather as well as an open camping site. It is a wonderful setting, surrounded by thick forest and the design of the site has been well thought out. There are long drops, washing facilities, drinking water and firewood available but there is no food so bring anything you need. Tents and paraffin lamps are available for rent.

• **Transport Road (own vehicle)** The Kanyanchu River Camp is located 35 km E of Fort Portal. If you are coming direct from Kampala on the Kampala-Mubende-Fort Portal Road and have a 4-wheel drive you can take the right turning through the Katonga Game Reserve. Coming from Fort Portal, Bigodi and the Kanyanchu River Camp are located off the Fort Portal-Kamwenge-Mbarara road.

Road (public transport) Travellers without their own vehicles can get one of the matatus from Fortal Portal that leave about 3 times a day in the morning and take about 2 hrs. In the other direction they leave Kamwenge very early, before sunrise, and take about 2 hrs. Returning to Fort Portal you have to catch the pickup at about 0700- after this time you will have to try to hitch, which is difficult along this road. If you are using the road on a Tue there is a market at Rukunyu (a village between Bigodi and Kamwenge) so there is more traffic.

Rwenzori Mountains National Park

".. you may be familiar with the Alps and the Caucasus, the Himalayas, and the Rockies, but if you have not explored Rwenzori, you still have something wonderful to see."

DW Freshfield (Explorer, 1906).

The Rwenzoris (Ruwenzoris) lie along the border of Uganda and Zaire, rising to a height of about 5600m above sea level. The range is about 100km in length and is about 50 km wide. It was formed from a block which was tilted and thrust up during the development of the Rift Valley. These beautiful, often mist-shrouded, mountains are non-volcanic and offer mountaineers and walkers a superb country and wonderful views.

The Rwenzoris are also known as the Mountains of the Moon – they were first described as such by Ptolomy because they were believed to be the *Lunae Montes* predicted by the ancient Greeks to be the source of the Nile.

A number of the mountain peaks are named after early explorers to Uganda and some of those in the centre of the range have permanent snow cover – these include Mounts Stanley (5,109m), Speke (4,889m), Baker (4,843m), Gessi (4,797m), Emin (4,791m) and Luigi di Savoia (4,626m). On Mount Stanley are the twin summits of Alexandra (5,044m) and Margherita (5,109m). There is some divergence on the actual heights of these peaks, and other sources mark them as being significantly higher.

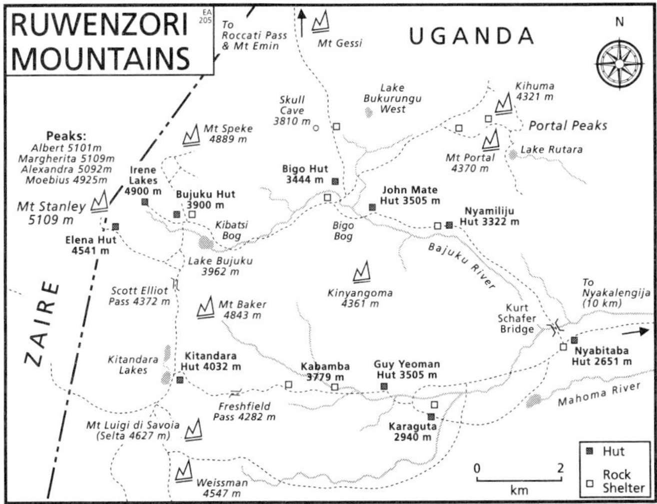

Geology

Rwenzoris are young mountains at less than 10 million years old. Until that time, the area was part a huge plain that extended to the Atlantic coast to the W and rivers flowed to the W. A series of movements of the earth's crust resulted in major rifting and in the Rwenzori area an uplifting of the underlying rock. The Rwenzoris are made up of quartzite and gneiss.

Although not the highest, the Rwenzori range is certainly the largest and most important group of snow mountains in Africa. Mt Kilimanjaro (5,968m) and Mt Kenya (5,225m) are both higher, but are single volcanic peaks. Rwenzori, whose highest point is the Margherita peak of Mount Stanley (5,109m) is a massif composed of 6 separated mountains all of which carry permanent snow and glaciers. The general axis of the range is North-South and the snow peaks, divided by lower snow-free passes, lie roughly along this axis along the middle of the range. The mountain range is about 120 km long and 50 km wide. Unlike all the other great mountains of central Africa, Rwenzori is not of volcanic origin but is the result of an upthrust associated with the formation of the western Rift Valley, in which it stands.

There are 6 separated glaciated groups and the glaciers are the equatorial type. That is they are more truly ice-caps than ice-rivers; movement is very slight as can be seen from the clearness of the streams and the absence of large moraines (accumulations of debris carried downby the glaciers). There have been times of much greater glaciation in earlier eras on the Rwenzori's, reaching thousands of feet below the current levels, and many of the valleys are characteristically shaped by ice erosion. The existing glaciers are in retreat.

Vegetation and wildlife

One of the most delightful aspects of the Rwenzoris is the diversity of plants and trees. Cultivation rarely extends above about 2,000m around the base of the mountain, and in many places it is considerably lower. Ascending, the climber passes from the foothills where most of the vegetation is elephant grass up to

Exploration Of The Rwenzori Mountains

It is now generally accepted that Ptolemy (c AD 150), when writing of the Mountains of the Moon, the legendary source of the Nile, was referring to the Rwenzori massif. Interestingly Speke, on his discovery of the Virunga volcanoes in 1861, did at the time associate them with Ptolemy's Moon Mountains.

It was in 1864 that the first European saw the Rwenzoris – this was when Baker observed, to the S of Lake Albert, a huge mountain mass which he named The Blue Mountains.

In 1876 Stanley looked across at the Rwenzoris from the escarpment above Lake George but, like other explorers before him, had failed to appreciate the importance of this natural feature. It was another 12 years before the ice caps were first seen and it was Sir Henry Stanley who was the first to proclaim the existence of the Rwenzoris as snow mountains. In his book Darkest Africa he claims to have made the discovery himself, but in fact 2 members of his expedition had seen the snows a month before him. They were Surgeon Parke and Mountenoy-Jephson who saw the snows on 20th Apr 1888. The following year, another member of the expedition, Lieut. Stairs, ascended the mountains up to a height of over 3,050m.

It is to Stanley that we owe the name Rwenzori (sometimes also spelt Ruwenzori). The word means the place from where the rain comes. The word was transcribed by Stanley as Runzori; hence Rwenzori. No name appears to have been given to the mountains by the local residents and their custom was to name the rivers running off the mountains rather than the actual peaks.

In the summer of 1891 Emin Pasha's companion Dr F. Stuhlmann climbed up the Butagu valley to a height of 4,062m and had the first close glimpse of the snow. A few years later in 1894-95 G. F. Scott Elliott, a naturalist, also made a number of expeditions which were of significant botanical importance. In 1900 an expedition by C. S. Moore proved the presence of glaciers; and shortly afterwards Sir Harry Johnston reached the Mobuku glacier at a height of 4,520m. The first purely non-scientific climb, and the first by a woman, was in 1903 by the Rev. A. B. and Mrs Fisher. The twin peaks of Mount Stanley, Alexandra (5,044m) and Margherita (5,105m), were climbed for the first time in June 1906 by an expedition led by the Duke of Abruzzi. This expedition produced important scientific results and an excellent topographical survey of the range was completed with information on the areas of the glaciers. It was this expedition that named most of the main peaks, the Duke naming one (the smallest), Luigi de Savioa, after himself.

about 1,800m. From there is the montane or true forest which is a mixture of trees, bracken and tree ferns. This zone, which extends to about 2,500m it is possible to see orchids. Higher still is the the bamboo zone which contines up to about 3,000m. The vegetation here also includes tree heather and, in moister patches, giant lobelias. The next, and fairly extensive zone is the heather forest, which extends from about 3,000m up to about 3,800m. The humid climate at this altitude causes vigorous development of mosses and lichens which cover the ground and the trunks of living and fallen trees. At this level, on the better drained slopes are tree groundsels and shrubby trees while the wetter parts are distinctly boggy. This zone also has brambles, orchids and ferns – all of which form a tangle which make passage through them difficult. The highest vegetative zone, extending from about 3,800m to the snowline, is alpine. From here most of the common herbaceous plants disappear leaving tree heaths, giant lobelias and senecios. Reeds grow in the marshes and shrubby bushes with everlasting flowers (*Belichrysums*) are abundant. The rocks are covered with a loosely adhering carpet of moss. Above about 3,000m there is little sign of life except hyrax and other small rodents. Birds are also fairly sparse.

People

The Bakonjo live on the Rwenzoris, a Bantu tribe who speak Lukonjo which is believed to be one of the earliest forms of Bantu speech. They are a short and sturdy people and frequently find work as guides and porters as many are excellent climbers. Apart from when they are acting as guides and porters, they rarely actually go high up into the mountain range believing that a god called Kitasamba lives in the upper reaches of the mountains. You may see small grass huts with offerings to Kitasamba in them on your ascent.

Climbing the Rwenzoris

The Rwenzoris are suitable for almost all climbers and walkers who are reasonably fit. There are hiking routes in the foothills for those with no climbing experience – all that is needed is a little stamina and waterproof clothing. More demanding is the ascent of Mount Speke which is a simple glacier requiring limited mountain experience. Most difficult are some of the routes on Mts Stanley and Baker, and only those with experience in rock, snow and ice climbing should attempt these.

The Rwenzoris have a reputation for being wet – and with good reason. The best time of the year to visit them are from the end of Dec to Feb and from mid-Jun to mid-Aug. The rest of the year there is often a lot of rain and apart from making the walk or climb slippery, the views are not so good with mist sometimes shrouding the mountain, in particular the peaks, and blocking off the views.

The situation as regards climbing the Rwenzoris is changing almost constantly. Up to date information is best gathered from other travellers who have reently completed the climb. In the middle of 1993 the *Rwenzori Mountains Services (RMS)*, PO Box 33, Kasese, who maintain the huts and trails, sharply raised their prices. Safari companies such as *Semliki Safaris* (Fort Portal), who have a site at Ntandi, have responded by setting up their own campsites along the route, competing directly with the RMS. The total price that you can expect to pay, very roughly, for a 6-day hike will be in the region of US$100 per person – this includes all fees, porters, guides, equipment hire and food. Most equipment that you may need can be hired from the RMS and food bought in Kasese. It is wet for much of the year and cold at night – so come well prepared with waterproofs and plenty of warm clothing. Pack everything inside your rucksack in plastic bags.

It is obligatory to take porters and a guide. Porters carry loads of 22 kgs excluding their own blankets and supplies. The headman does not carry a load although is expected to relieve a tired member of the party. Guides are also necessary. It is important to get absolutely clear what the charges are going to be – they depend on the number of days taken up on the trip and the stages covered.

You should take all the food that you will need. A stove is certainly worth taking – apart from the environmental impact of cutting wood for cooking, the wood is almost without fail wet and difficult to light.

For more serious climbers who intend to climb the peaks be sure that your guide is experienced. The best written work is Osmaston and Pasteur's *Guide to the Rwenzoris* although it is rather out of date as far as the huts go, the actual description of climbs and so on, has not changed. This is not available in Uganda but can be obtained from *Stanfords Map and Travel Bookshop* (Longacre, Covent Garden, London WC2E 9LP, England). The other good guide with a detailed map is Wielochowski's *Rwenzori Map and Guide* which is available from the author (32 Seamill Park Crescent, Worthing BN11 2NP, England), and also in some bookshops in Nairobi.

You should allow about 10 days for the trip and the most popular route (the Circuit) should take you 6 to 7 days. This is described below. This is obviously just one suggestion – you can break the route up with more frequent stops – for example Day 1 to Nyabitaba; Day 2 to Nyamileju; Day 3 to Bigo Hut; Day 4 to Lake Bajuku; Day 5 to Kitandara; Day 6 to Buy Yeoman and Day 7 back to Nyakalengija.

The Circuit

Day 1 Begin by heading for Nyakalengija (1,600m) 3 miles from Ibanda and 22km from from Kasese, where the trail begins and from there take the path to the Nyabitaba Hut (2,651m)- about 10 km. If you have made arrangements through the RMS they should be able to arrange transport to their office at Nyakalengija where you will pay your fees etc. You can also park vehicles here fairly safely, and camp if you want to start the walk early the next day. From Nyakalengija head through a coffee plantation and a field and on into some elephant grass. The path gradually deteriorates as you enter the bush and the cultivation disappears and is replaced by elephant grass and nettles. There is the Mubuku River on your right (which has trout – introduced by the British). You descend to the edge of the river and then climb up and into the forest. Cross 2 streams and continue for several km before crossing the Mahoma River. The final ascent is up a moraine ridge to Nyabitaba – before you get to the hut itself there is a small rock shelter. There is a large rock shelter a little beyond the hut – which many people use in preference to the hut, alternatively, you can camp in the clearing by the hut. The Nyabitaba Hut is a 2-roomed hut built in 1987 which sleeps up to 12 people. There is a water supply at the hut.

Day 2 Nyabitaba (2,651m) to John Mate Camp (3,500m). This is the most difficult day of the circuit, and will take you at least 7 hrs. You follow the ridge through the forest and then fork down steeply to the left to the Mabuka River. This you cross using the Kurt Schafer Bridge which was built in 1989 after the old one collapsed. From here you climb up again on the other side – the path gradually gets harder becoming a slippery scramble – and continue on to the bamboo forest. The walk through the bamboo forest is relatively easy but before reaching Nyamiliju there is a long hard climb upwards. It is here that you will start to go through the heather and groundsel towards Nyamiliju – in fact Nyamiliju actually means place of beards – a name that refers to the moss and lichen that hangs from the trees. There is an old hut at Nyamiliju (3,322m) which is a round uniport with a wooden floor. It is not much used any longer as most people prefer to push on to John Mate Hut. But if you wish to go slower, it is there, and has a good water supply. There is also a nearby rock shelter which some people prefer to use but there is no room for tents here. If you are lucky, and it is clear, you should be able to see Mt Stanley and Mt Speke as well as the glaciers, and Nyamiliju can make a good lunchtime stop. From Nyaniliju it is a further 2 hrs to John Mate Hut (3,505m) climbing up through the giant heather and groundsel forest. The trail is much less clear – start by crossing the stream just below the rock shelter and carry on towards the river, although don't actually cross it. Continue from the heather forest until it opens out a bit, and up 2 fairly steep moraines before you reach the camp. The hut is modern and in good condition. It is close to the Bajuku River from where you can collect water.

Day 3 John Mate (3,505m) to Lake Bujuku (3962m). On the third day you go through the muddy bog of Bigo, past the Bigo Hut and on to the Bujuku Hut. Begin by crossing the river and then head for the left-hand edge of the valley skirting around the bog. You will find it almost impossible to avoid getting muddy. Bigo Hut (3,444m) sleeps 12 and is in fairly good condition and there is flowing water nearby. There is also a rock shelter here, which the porters tend to use.

From Bigo Hut you can choose a number of different routes. You can go N to Roccati pass which runs between Mts Gessi and Emin; or NE to Bukunguru pass between Gessi and the Portal Peaks; or SW to Lake Bujuku. The latter route is the most popular for Circuit users and is the one described below.

From Bigo (3444m) to Lake Bujuku (3,962m) you cross the Kibnatsi Bog to what is known as the Cooking Pot Cave and from there to the Lake Bujuku hut with its beautiful setting. Begin by following the route which swings southwestwards with Mt Stanley on your right (W) and Baker on your left (E). The path starts off rather steep but levels off as you round the southern spur. You will shortly reach the Kibatsi bog which will take you 2 to 3 hrs to cross and from the bog there is another steep climb. Here you reach Cooking Pot Cave, where the track splits into 2. Take the right (northwest) route to the huts. The left fork leads to the Scott Elliot pass and you will return here tomorrow to continue the Circuit. The Lake Bujuku Hut is actually 2 huts which sleep up to 14 people and are in fair condition. There is water available close by. It is one of the loveliest settings of all the huts on the routes, with Mount Stanley and an incredible ice cave in the Peke glacier on Mount Speke clearly visible.

Lake Bujuku Hut is the base for those planning to climb Mount Speke (4,889m). Serious climbers hoping to reach the highest point on the range, Margherita Peak on Mount Stanley (5,109m) should base themselves at Elana Hut (4,541m). This is located about 2km off the circuit and is about 3 or 4 hrs from Bujuku or Kitandara huts.

Day 4 Lake Bujuku (3,962m) to Kitandara (4,032m). This walk is a fairly light one, taking about half a day, and you climb to the highest point on the circuit at the Scott Elliot Pass. Begin by returning to the Cooking Pot Cave and from there take the southerly path that leads to the Scott Elliot Pass (4,372m). The track takes you through groundsel to a scree slope. At the head of this is a rock buttress – the pass is to the right. There is a cleft in the rocks to the left and from here the descent continues with the vertical cliffs of Mount Baker on your side. Before reaching Lake Kitandara the path rises then descends again. The 2 huts at Lake Kitandara are also in a wonderful setting – next to one of the 2 lakes and close to the foot of Elena glacier.

Day 5 Lake Kitandara Hut (4,032m) to the Kamamba Rock Shelter (3,779m) or to Guy Yeoman's Hut. If you go on to Guy Yeoman's hut this is a walk of about 5 hrs. The day begins with a steep climb to the Freshfield Pass (4,282m), followed by a descent down to a rock overhang called Bujongolo. This is where the first expedition to explore the mountains in 1906 based themselves. A little further on is a second, and larger rock shelter called Kabamba located close to a waterfall, where you can spend the night. Alternatively you can continue onto the Guy Yeoman Hut (3,505m) which is one of the newer sites.

Day 6 Guy Yeoman (3,505m) to Nyabitaba Hut (2,651m), or on to Nyakalengija (1600m). Continue your descent via Kichuchu where there is another rock shelter. From Kichuchu the descent continues through bog and bamboo forest and then across the Mubuku River. Having forded the river, follow the path along a ridge and down to the Nyabitaba Hut (2,651m). Alternatively you can go via Lake Muhoma where there is a hut, if you want to spend an extra night. From Nyabitaba Hut you then have to retrace your steps hack to Nyakalengija, about another 3 hr hike.

● **Transport**

Air Chartered flights go to **Kasese** from where you can complete the journey by road.

Train You can take the train to **Kasese** which goes Mon, Wed and Fri from Kampala (see page 447), and then by road.

Road The Rwenzoris are approached from **Ibanda** in Mubuku Valley. Ibanda can be reached from Kampala via Mbarara and Kasese from where it is a further 18 km.

Alternatively from Kampala to Fort Portal and then 75 km on the Fort Portal-Kasese road before turning off for Ibanda. Coming from Kasese, about 10 km along the main Kasese-Fort Portal road, there is a turning off to Ibanda. Take this for about 12 km – it is a fairly good gravel road. On reaching Ibanda you will see a sign-post for the Rwenzori Mountaineering Service on the right hand side of the road and this is where you will need to go to organise guides, porters etc.

Bwindi National Park (Impenetrable Forest)

Bwindi Impenetrable National Park covers an area of 321 sq km and is located in S Western Uganda on the edge of the Western Rift Valley. It lies along the

Bwindi Gorilla Visit

Early in the morning, the day we were to go gorilla-tracking, I awoke to a dawn chorus of birds and monkeys echoing across the forest valley to our camp. Opening my tent I watched as the mist lifted from the trees and the forest came to life. After struggling to get our fire going we had a quick breakfast and then set off. We were introduced to our Ugandan guide for the day who explained some of the rules of the park such as no smoking, eating or drinking once we reached the gorillas. More disconcertingly, he then went on to explain what to do in the event of a silver-back charging us. Above all, we were told, we must stay still, crouch down and keep our heads down. We should at all times follow his instructions while he and the 2 trackers would speak in gorilla language to reassure the boss of the group that we were friends not foes.

The first part of the walk was the easiest, being along a sunlit path decorated by scores of dancing butterflies. About 45 minutes into the forest we turned off this and the hard walking began. From here it was about 2½ hrs up and down the steep valley sides – ascending, we pulled ourselves up with the help of nearby trees and on the way down slid most of the way on our backsides. We traversed 3 valleys before we reached the place where the gorillas had spent the previous night. This spot is marked by the nests of branches and leaves that the gorillas make for themselves and huge piles of dung. From here the trackers hacked through the thick bush following the trail of the gorillas. Occasionally the pungent sweetness of jasmine descended. Everywhere cicadas hummed, punctuated occasionally by the haunting shrieks of chimps. We tried to spot them in the trees around – but in vain. Suddenly the trackers stopped – we are very close, they told us, so this was the last chance for a drink and a snack.

Uganda-Zaire border in Kabale and Rukungiri districts. Bwindi Forest was first gazetted to the status of a forest reserve in 1932 and in 1961 as an animal sanctuary. From 1961 it was under the joint management of the Forest and the Game Departments, until 1991 when it became a National Park and was taken over by Uganda National Parks.

The forest has had a number of names in the past including Bwindi, and Kayonza. In the local language Bwindi means a Place of Darkness, a result of the thick vegetation. The other popular name for the forest is the Impenetrable Forest – a perfect description.

Mountain Gorillas

There are only 3 countries in which it is possible to visit mountain gorillas (*Gorilla beringei*) namely Uganda, Rwanda and Zaire. With the war in Rwanda continuing in 1994, visiting the gorillas there has been rendered impossible but see page 519 for information on gorillas. Currently Zaire is the main competitor to Uganda and has been running gorilla tours for a number of years (see page 464 and 571). Since Apr 1993 it has been possible to visit the gorillas in Bwindi National Park.

It has been estimated that there are only about 630 remaining specimens of the Mountain Gorilla in the world – and about half of these are thought to be in Uganda. The vast majority of these are in Bwindi although there are a few at Mgahinga National Park, which is part of the Virunga volcano range which extends across Rwanda, Uganda and Zaire. The development of gorilla tourism and habituation of the gorillas is proceeding with great care in order to avoid dangers such as the gorillas catch-

After this rest we walked on – the atmosphere changed as we realised we were so close. About 15 minutes later we suddenly heard a loud grunt – it sounded very close and my heart missed a beat but, peering through the bush, I could see nothing. The grunting continued – I would have sworn it was less than a metre away but the bush was so thick that still I could see nothing. Our guide started to reply to the gorilla making a deep coughing noise and we slowly crept around keeping a fair distance away from the source of the grunting. Peering into deep green vegetation, I could see nothing. Suddenly I caught sight of an enormous hand reaching up from ground level to pluck a green shoot. At the end of the arm was the face of a female sitting with her young close by. She was staring at us but was remarkably unconcerned at our presence as she continued to eat her meal. As we watched our eyes were drawn upwards to the sounds of 2 infants playing in the trees – they were absolutely delightful as they clambered up the branches and pushed each other down again. We still hadn't seen the silverback, but knew where he was, as he was the source of the deep grunts. Slowly he emerged from the bushes, familiar from films and photographs, but in the flesh he was quite awe-inspiring. Everything about him was bigger than I'd imagined and as he moved through the undergrowth it collapsed around him.

We stayed with the family group for about an hour before returning to our camp, thoroughly delighted with the experience. The route back was more direct but a downpour slowed our progress. I had always been led to believe that in a rainforest the tree canopy overhead prevents most of the rain reaching the forest floor – but it soon became clear this was not so. I put on a raincoat but within minutes the warm and heavy rain had soaked through it. As we left the forest the rain stopped almost immediately, and we returned dripping to the camp for a cup of hot coffee.

Grace Carswell 1993

ing human diseases.

There are 2 ways of seeing the gorillas. The first is to go it alone organising transport, permits and camping equipment. etc. yourself. The alternative is much easier but for many is prohibitively expensive: that is to pay a tour operator to organise the whole trip including transport, accommodation and permits. These can be arranged in the USA, in Europe, in Kenya or else in Kampala (see Tour Operators listed in Kampala section page 429). At the present *African Pearl Safaris* is the only operator that has accommodation at Buhoma, in the form of a small lodge, located just outside the Park entrance opposite the campsite. It is spotlessly clean and very friendly.

Independent gorilla excursions

If you are planning to go it alone the first thing to do is to book your tracking permit. This is the difficult bit, for at present only one group is fully habituated and so only 5 people per day can see the gorillas. Obviously the demand is greater than this and the permits sell out weeks in advance. The permit will cost a non-resident foreigner US$120. They are available from the *National Parks Headquarters*, PO Box 3530, 31 Kanjokya St, Kampala, T 256534/258351. If you have not booked, or find there are no spaces you can go to Bwindi and hope that someone fails to turn up. At the moment it seems that most people who turn up and wait at the campsite do eventually get on a tour.

You can go on half-day guided tours of the forest for US$5 – there is a waterfall nearby which you can visit which makes a nice walk. The forest has been estimated to have at least 120 species of mammals of which 10 are primates. There are chimpanzees, black and white colobus, red-tailed monkeys and vervets. Other species include giant forest hog, and bushbucks although these are both rare and shy animals. There are an estimated 20 elephants which have survived in the forest – their population has been brought near to extinction over the past 20 years. The forest maintains a huge range of birdlife – over 330 species. The plant and insect life is also phenomenal – there are about 150 tree species as well as a wide range of ferns, orchids, mosses and lichens.

Park information

● **Where to stay**

The nearest accommodation is at Kabale (see page 463)

● **Transport**

Road (public transport) Buses leave between 0600 and 0700 every morning from **Kampala** take 6 hrs and cost US$6, Matatus leave when full – usually mid-morning – from Kampala, take about 5 hrs and cost US$11. From **Kabale** it is a journey of 3 hrs to the campsite at Buhoma – but transport links are difficult. Because you have to start tracking at 0830 in the morning it is strongly advised that you get to Buhoma the night before. If you are late you lose your booking and do not get any money back.

To get to the campsite you have a number of choices. You can either hire a pickup, or go as far as possible on public transport and walk part of the journey. *M/S Tour Operators*, PO Box 640, 147/149 Kabale Rd, Kabale, T Kabale 22700. Can also arrange transport.

The cheapest alternative is to take a public pickup as far as possible and then walk the rest of the way. The campsite is at Buhoma, and the pickups go part of the way, leaving from the Kabale matatu stand at about 0800. The nearest village is Butagota from where it is a 14 km hike. Using public transport you shouldn't pay more than US$4 one way.

If you are relying on public transport and want to be sure not to miss your allocated day, you should allow at least one spare day. There is plenty to do around the forest itself, and your park entrance fee lasts 4 days.

Mgahinga Gorilla National Park

This, the smallest National Park in Uganda at just 36 sq km, was established in 1991. It is found in the far SW of the country in Kisoro District. It makes up the northeastern part of the Virunga Volcano range which extends into Zaire and Rwanda.

The protection of gorillas on the Ugandan side of the Virunga volcanoes began in the mid-1950's when a game warden, Walter Baumgartel, took an interest in them. Baumgartel left Uganda in the late 1960's and in the years that followed there was much encroachment into the forest particularly along the lower slopes of Mount Muhavura, Gahinga and Sabinyo. Poaching was also a threat and many of the gorillas retreated into better protected areas in the neighbouring countries. It has been estimated that the gorilla population of the Mgahinga National Park declined by about 50 percent between 1960 and the early 1980s and is currently believed to be 45.

It was not until 1989 that gorillas began to receive some protection under the Gorilla Game Reserve Conservation Project which began to operate along the Virunga Volcanoes on the Uganda side. This became the Mgahinga Gorilla National Park Project in 1991. However at the moment there are no plans to introduce gorilla tourism to this Park, and if the troubles in Rwanda continue then this park is unlikely to receive many visitors.

Other animals that are found in Mgahinga include a small number of elephants, buffaloes, giant forest hogs, the rare golden monkey, and the rare blue monkey. The golden monkey is only found in the Virunga Volcano range and 2 other forests in central Africa. The monkey gets its name from the colour of its fur, which unfortunately puts it under threat from poachers. The project leader has adopted and tamed a young elephant which you will see around the camp.

The summit of Mount Muhavura forms the highest point of the park at 4,127m and has a small crater lake which tourists may want to visit. The vegetation in the Park includes montane, alpine and subalpine flora at each of the different levels up the volcano as vegetation varies with altitude. The lowest vegetation zone of the mountain is mainly bamboo and this is the area where the gorillas are likely to be found. The alpine zone is dominated by the impressive giant senecios and giant lobelias which are found at an altitude of between 3,600 and 4,200m. It is possible to climb to the peaks of Gahinga and Muhavura if you are reasonably fit. This can be organised at the Mgahinga National Park office in Kisoro, where they collect entrance fees, etc. If you do not feel fit enough for this there are other shorter walks that can be arranged, including a visit to a the Garama Cave. In addition to the Park entrance fee (US$20 per person) you will be charged for a trip to the peaks (US$15 per person) and shorter walks within the park (US$5 per person). All such walks must be accompanied by a ranger which costs US$10 (or US$5 for half a day) for the group.

Park information

● Where to stay

E *Camping* Site at the park entrance with water and firewood but nothing else.

● Transport

See travel to Kisoro, page 464.

INFORMATION FOR VISITORS

CONTENTS

Before you go

Entry requirements

● Visas

Visas are **not** required by citizens of the following:

All *EU* countries (Belgium, Denmark, France, Germany, Greece, Ireland, Italy, Luxembourg, Netherlands, Portugal, Spain, United Kingdom).

All *PTA* countries (Burundi, Comoros, Djibouti, Eritrea, Ethiopia, Kenya, Lesotho, Madagascar, Malawi, Mauritius, Mozambique, Namibia, Rwanda, Seychelles, Somalia, Sudan, Swaziland, Tanzania, Zambia, Zimbabwe).

Antigua and Barbuda, Australia, Bahamas, Bahrain, Barbados, Belize, Botswana, Canada, Fiji, Finland, Gambia, Grenada, Hong Kong, Israel, Jamaica, Japan, Kuwait, Libya, Malaysia, Malta, New Zealand, Norway, Oman, Pakistan, Saudi Arabia, Sierra Leone, Singapore, Solomon Islands, South Korea, St Lucia, St Vincent, Sweden, Switzerland, Taiwan, Tonga, Tuvalu, United Arab Emirates, United States of America, Vanuatu.

Citizens of all other countries require visas, except if in transit and remaining in the airport.

A visa application must include a valid passport; a completed application form; 2 passport-size photographs; the appropriate fee (US$15, single entry, valid 3 months from date of issue; US$30, multiple entry, valid 6 months from date of issue); letter of invitation or introduction if travelling on business; a registered, stamped, self-addressed envelope if applying by post. Visa applications are processed in one working day. Visas are issued by the Ugandan representatives listed below).

Journalists are required to notify, in advance, and obtain accreditation and clearance from the Director of Information, Ministry of Informationa and Broadcasting, PO Box 7142, Kampala T 254410/232734/235764 F 256888 Tlx 61188.

● Vaccinations

A certificate indicating vaccination against Yellow Fever is required.

● Ugandan Representation Overseas

(*,denotes office does not issue visas) **Australia***, Canberra; **Belgium**, Brussels; **Canada**, 231 Coburg St, Ottawa T 789 7797, F 232 6689; **China**, Beijing; **Cuba**, Havana; **Denmark***, Copenhagen; **Egypt**, Cairo; **Ethiopia**, PO Box 5644. Addis Ababa*, T 513088, F514355, Tlx, 21143; **France***, 13 Ave Raymond Poincaré, 7116 Paris, T 274680, F 559394; **Germany**, Dürerstrasse 44, 5300 Bonn 2, T 228 355027, F 228 351692; **India**, New Delhi; **Italy***, via G Pisanelli1, Rome 00196, T 3605211, F 3225220, F 330970; **Japan***, Tokyo; **Kenya**, PO Box 60853, Phoenix House, Kenyatta Ave, Nairobi, T 330801; **Nigeria**, Abuja; **Rwanda***, Ave de la Paix, Kigali. BP 656, T 76495; **Saudi Arabia**, Riyadh; **Sudan***, Khartoum; **Tanzania**, Dar es Salaam; **United Kingdom**, Uganda House, Trafalgar Sq, London WC2 5DX, T 071 839 5783, F 071 8398925; **USA**, 5909 16th St NW, Washington

DC20011, T 726 0416, F 726 1727, also New York; **Russia**, Moscow; **Zaire***, Kinshasha; **Zambia***, Lusaka.

● Overseas Representation in Uganda

See Kampala page 427.

● Tourist information

See Kampala page 429 for the main tourist office. Ugandan Embassies and High Commissions around the world have a tourism attaché who will advise (see above).

Mountain Clubs of Uganda, PO Box 4692, Kampala. *Safari Uganda Asscociation*, PO Box 3530, Kampala T 233566, F 235770. *Uganda Tourist Association*, PO Box 7452, T 245092 F 41245092. *Uganda Tourist Board*, PO Box 7211, Kampala, T 232971/2, F 241247. *Widlife Clubs of Uganda*, PO Box 4596, T 256354.

● Travel and tour agents

For those based in Uganda, see Kampala page 429; Kasese page 447; Fort Portal page 450.

United Kingdom *One World Tours*, 80 Stuart Rd, London SW19 8DH, T 081 946 6295, F 081 946 1985. Specialise in tourism that supports conservation and traditional life. *African Adventures*, 55 Huddlestone Rd, London NW2, T 081 451 2446. *Nile Safaris*, Meadow Cottage, Watlington, Oxford OX9 5HR, T 0491 612033, F 0491 613356. Organise a variety of tours covering the main attractions from 1 day to 19 days.

When to go

● Best time to visit

The heavy rainy season is Mar to May, and there are lighter rains in Nov and Dec. It is probably best to try to avoid Mar to May. Generally there is some sunshine each day even in the rainy seasons.

Health

● Staying healthy

It is not uncommon for travellers, particularly those visiting the country for the first time, to have some form of stomach upset. Plenty of fluids are advised, and a rehydration preparation such as *Dioralyte* can be invaluable.

Still pools and lakes present a risk of bilharzia, and it is wise to ask local advice before taking a swim.

Uganda has a high prevalence of AIDS.

● Malaria

Malaria is a serious risk, and the appropriate prevention tablets, sleeping under a treated net and the use of insect repellents after dark are essential.

● Water

It is not safe to drink local water. It should be boiled or treated with sterilisation tablets. The local soft drinks and bottled water are quite safe.

● Further Health information

For more details see the Health Section page 21.

Money

The Ugandan shilling floats against other currencies, and the exchange rate can be expected to depreciate steadily as prices have been rising faster in Uganda than in the rest of the world. In 1994, the exchange rate was Ush 930 = US$1.

Banks Money can be exchanged in banks or in the foreign exchange bureaux that have recently been established. The bureaux tend to offer better rates than the banks and to stay open longer hrs. Money can be changed in the large hotels 24 hrs a day. There is now no effective black market, and persons approaching visitors in the street and offering implausibly favourable rates of exchange are invariably engaged in some exercise designed to cheat the traveller.

US dollars are the best form of cash to carry. It is helpful to have some US currency in small denomination notes to avoid changing too much at an unfavourable rate when that is the only option, and for last minute transactions when leaving.

● Cost of living

It is possible to stay in the better hotels, eat well and travel in reasonable comfort for US$30 a day. On a strict budget, it is possible to stay, travel and eat for US$10 a day.

● Credit cards

Credit cards are accepted by the large hotels, airlines, main car hire fims, tour and travel agents. American Express is the most widely accepted card, with Visa, Diners and Mastercard also taken by some establishments.

Getting there

● Air

Direct flights are only available from 5 cities in Europe and 5 in Africa. There are no direct flights from America. For all other points of departure, connecting flights are necessary. An economical way to access Uganda is to obtain a cheap excursion flight to Nairobi and then to travel overland or take a local connecting flight from Kenua Airways. Otherwise Aeroflot tend to be able to offer the most competitive fare, but it will mean flying through Moscow.

Europe Sabena Brussels, Belgium. **British Airways** London, United Kingdom. **Aeroflot** Moscow, Russia. **Air France** Paris, France. **Lufthansa** Frankfurt, Germany.

Africa Ethiopian Airlines Addis Ababa, Ethiopia. **EgyptAir** Cairo, Egypt. **Air Zambia** Lusaka, Zambia. **Sudan Airways** Khartoum, Sudan. **Kenya Airways** Nairobi, Kenya.

The national carrier is **Uganda Airlines**. They are anticipating starting scheduled services to other African counties, covering:

Nairobi and Mombasa, **Kenya**. Dar es Salaam, **Tanzania**. Harare, **Zimbabwe**. Kigali, **Rwanda**. Johannesburg, **South Africa**.

Specialist Agencies for discounted fares, see page 12

● Train

From **Nairobi** there is also a train to **Malaba** on the Ugandan border 3 times a week. This takes over 17 hrs – it leaves Nairobi at 1500 on Fri and Sat, arriving early the next day, and leaves Malaba for **Nairobi** at Sat and Sun at 1600. A one-way ticket costs US$20 for 1st, US$10 for 2nd and US$5 for 3rd.

There are through trains running once a week between **Nariobi** and **Kampala**. Departs Nairobi on Tue at 1000. Naivasha 1323. Nakuru 1510. Eldorest 2145. Webuye 2356. Bungoma 0043. Malaba 0155. Tororo 0305. Inganga 0518. Jinja 0615. Kawolo 0724. arrives Kampala 0850.

Departs Kampala on Wed at 1600. Kawolo 1731. Jinja 1842. Iganga 1932. Tororo 2230. Malaba 2305. Bungoma 0011. Webuye 0057. Eldoret 0355. Nakuru 0940. Naivasha 1123. arrives Nairobi 1425.

● Road

Kenya There are buses that run from Nairobi to Kampala, crossing at **Malaba** and **Tororo**, taking about 15 hrs and costing around US$15. There is a variety of standards of service. It is possible to do the journey in stages in minibuses or peugeot taxis, but buses are more comfortable and safer.

There are also a border crossings at **Busia**, but no through buses, but convenient for Kisumu; and at **Suam** to the N of Mt Elgon.

Tanzania The route is S from Masaka to Bukoba. The road is not very good and this crossing is not used very much, although traffic is increasing. There are matatus from Masaka which go as far as Kyotera and from there you will have to get a lift to the border, crossing at **Mutukula**, with one of the trucks going across – this is not usually a problem. If you get to the border shortly before dark you may want to stay at the small guesthouse which is on the Uganda side of the border – there is nothing on the Tanzania side until you get to Bukoba. For crossing the border you will need to have patience as you go through the rather long drawn out process. The road on the Tanzania side is worse than the Uganda road but there are 4-wheel drive vehicles operating on the route. They go when full.

Rwanda In normal times, there are frequent daily minibuses between Kabale in Uganda and the **Katuna** border post the trip taking an hr. There are frequent minibuses to Kigali from Katuna until mid afternoon and they take about 2 hrs. Check locally.

The other crossing is from Kisoro in Uganda to Ruhengeri in Rwanda via **Cyanika**, This route is not as busy and it may be harder to get a ride from here. There is an hr time difference between Uganda and Rwanda, Uganda being an hr ahead.

Zaire The most reliable crossing is **Kisoro** to Rutshuru. Minibuses from Kisoro to the border, about 10 km and costing US$0.50, and on the Zaire side a motor-taxi (motorbike) to Rutshuru.

Alternatively Kasese to Beni via **Kasindi** There is infrequent public transport along this route. Some minibuses from Kasese to the border at Kasindi. The leg from Kasindi to Beni can be awkward, some minibuses, but a motor-taxi (motorbike) is probably the best possibility. There are small hotels on both the Uganda and Zaire side of the border in case you are stuck there late at night.

Finally, it is possible to cross the border from Kasese to Rutshuru the border post being at **Ishasha**. There are infrequent minibuses on this route and hitching is possible.

The crossing to the N of Lake Albert, at **Arua**, although possible, is extremely difficult to access and security is less certain.

Sudan The current impossible political situation in Southern Sudan rules out the routes from Juba to Gulu, which in normal times allow crossings at **Moyo** and **Nimule** to the W and

E of the Nile respectively.

Vehicle entry If you are driving into Uganda, you must be registered in your home country, with registration plates, log book, and insurance against third party risks. A thirty day licence will cost between US$20 (2,000 kg vehicle) and US$100 (10,000 kg).

Lake Ferry

Tanzania Weekly service from **Mwanza** to Kampala (Port Bell) leaving at 1500. on Sun. Services departs Port Bell 1500 on Mon. Journey takes 14 hrs and costs US$20 (first); US$15 (second); US$8 (third). There are berths for first and second class. There is a port fee of US$5 on leaving Tanzania.

Customs

Duty Free Cigarettes & tobacco 250gms; wines & spirits 1 lire; toilet water & perfume 0.5 litre (perfume 0.25 litre max). Equipment for personal use. **Pets** require permit in advance from Ministry of Agriculture, Animal Industry and Fisheries, PO Box 102, Entebbe, T 20981/9. **Game Trophies** Permit required from Chief Game Warden, The Ministry of Tourism, Wildlife and Antiquities, PO Box 4241, 1 Parliament Ave, T 232971/2, F 242247.

When you arrive

Airport information

Uganda's international airport is at Entebbe, 30 km from the capital, Kampala. There is a departure tax of US$20 on leaving Uganda by air.

Transport to town A taxi to Entebbe costing US$3 and then a matatu (minibus) to Kampala US$1. Taxi from airport to Kampala US$20. British Airways run a bus starting from the *Sheraton Hotel*. Check at their office on Kampala road.

Conduct

As in much of Africa, it is considered a courtesy and a mark of respect to dress neatly and smartly. If you have an appointment with a senior government official or member of the business community men should wear a collar and tie or safari suit; women be conservatively dressed with a medium length skirt.

Electricity

220 volts. You will encounter a variety of sockets, particularly in the older hotels, and an adaptor is advisable.

Hours of business

Business and offices Mon-Fri 0800-1245 and 1400-1700. **Banks** Mon to Fri 0830 to 1400. **Post Offices** Mon to Fri 0830 to 1700. **Shops** Generally from 0800 to 1700 or 1800 Mon-Sat.

Offical time

3 hrs ahead of GMT

Safety

Apart from the N of the country, where special precautions are advised, Uganda now has a good record for safety and security. It is sensible to take taxis at night outside the centre of towns; not to walk about in dark or deserted areas; and to be careful about belongings in crowded areas.

Where to stay

Hotels

The most luxurious hotels used by business travellers and up-market tourists have prices set in dollar terms, and are similar in cost and value to those in Kenya. On the other hand, devaluation of the Ugandan currency has made most other accommodation, particularly that used used by ordinary Ugandans, good value. There is plenty of budget accommodation at less than US$5 a night, and reasonably comfortable lodgings can be had for between US$10 and US$20. Accommodation in the parks is good value and generally the best lodges are not above US$20-US$30 a night.

Hotel Classifications

A+ Over US$100 a night. International standards and decor, air conditioning, self-contained rooms, swimming pool, restaurants, bars, business services.

A US$40-100. First class standards, air-conditioning, attached bathrooms, restaurants and bars, swimming pool.

B US$20-40. Tourist class, comfortable with air conditioning or fans, attached bathrooms, restaurant, bar, public rooms.

C US$10-20. Budget, fans, shared bathroom facilities.

D US$5-10. Guest house, no fan, shared bathroom, cold water.

E Under US$5. Basic guest house, simple bed, no soap or towels, no wardrobe, shared bathroom facilities, erratic cold water supply, no fans or mosquito nets.

Food and drink

● Food

Simple meals are good value, but the range and variety of food is limited. Local food includes *ugali*, which is maize ground and boiled to form a stiff dough: and *matoke*, which is boiled plaintains (cooking bananas). Indian additions to the menu include *chapatati*, a flat bread, and *pilau* which is a rice and meat together with a vegetable curry.

● Drink

Imported wines, spirits and beers are widely available. Uganda produces a range of soft drinks and beers that are are quite acceptable and good value compared with the imported alternatives.

EATING CLASSIFICATIONS

- ♦♦♦♦ Over US$10 for a meal. A 3-course meal in a restaurant with pleasant decor. Beers, wines and spirits available.
- ♦♦♦ US$5-10 for a meal. Two courses, not including alcohol, reasonable surroundings.
- ♦♦ US$2-5 for a meal, probably only a single course, surroundings spartan but adequate.
- ♦ Under US$2. Single course, often makeshift surroundings such as a street kiosk with simple benches and tables.

Getting around

● Air

There are currently no scheduled internal flights. It is possible to charter light aircraft to fly to airstrips around the country (see Kampala page 427). These are located in **East** Tororo and Moroto; **North** Soroti, Lira, Gulu, Chobe, Paraa (for Murchison Falls National Park), Pakuba, Katarum (for Kidepo National Park); **West** Masindi (for Queen Elizabeth National Park), Kasese; **South West** Mbarara.

● Train

The rail system is gradually being improved, and new sections opend up. There are now through trains from Nairobi to Kampala, though the regularity of the service needs to be checked. The line continues on to Kasese in the W. There is a branch that runs N through Soroti and Gulu to Pakwach, and the final section of this line has now been restored.

The railway in East Africa was designed mainly for freight, and has to contend with some very hilly terrain. Consequently the guage is narrow to allow for tight turns and the trains move relatively slowly, and rock a fair bit when travelling at maximum speed. Road is invariably quicker.

There are 3 classes: First has 2-berth compartments with beds that fold up in the day, washbasins and fans; Second has 4 berths, fans and washbasins; Third has seating. There are dining cars on each train, serving fairly simple meals and drinks.

● Road

There are good roads on the main routes, and travel is comfortable and swift.

Buses are are safer, slower and cheaper than other modes. Bus travel is roughly US$0.02 per km.

Matatus are minibuses; or pick-up trucks converted to carry passengers; or cars or station wagons carrying passengers. They are privately owned, and operate on the basis of departing from the terminus when full. Minibuses are fine for short journeys, a Peugeot station wagan is more comfortable and safer for a longer journey. Costs are roughly US$0.04 per km.

Taxis Generally available in large towns. Always advisable to agree the fare before departure.

● Lake ferries

There are steamers and ferries that sail between ports on the shore of Lake Victoria and the Sese Islands.

Communications

● Language

Official language is English, and it is widely spoken, although for most Ugandans it is their second language. Swahili is also spoken, but not as widely as in Kenya and Tanzania.

● Postal services

Services are reliable and letters take about 10 days airmail from Europe. There is a Post Restante service in Kampala (Post Restante, GPO, Kampala Rd, Kampala).

● Telephone services

International calls can be made from the GPO office on Kampala Rd in Kampala.

Entertainment

Newspapers
The main newspaper is *New Vision*, published in English. Although it is government-owned it has considerable editorial freedom. It contains good listings of up-coming events in Uganda.

Radio
Radio broadcasts mainly in English, but some in Swahili and Luganda.

Sporting events
There are regular football and cricket matches in the main towns.

Television
There is a colour television service run by the government and broadcasting for about 6 hrs every evening, mostly in English.

Holidays and festivals

1 Jan	New Year's Day
26 Jan	NRM Day
Apr	Good Fri
Apr	Easter Mon
1 May	International Labour Day
9 Oct	Independence Day
25 Dec	Christmas Day
26 Dec	Boxing Day

Further reading

General
Hansen, B. and Twaddle, M. (eds) 1988. *Uganda Now*. London: James Currey. An excellent series of essays on the political, economic and social problems that have plagued Uganda since independence.

History
Miller, C. *Lunatic Express* Weaves the history of East Africa round the story of the building of the Uganda Railway, from Mombasa to Kampala. Well researched, engagingly written, and with a fine eye for the bizarre and amusing. Moorehead, A. 1960. *The White Nile*. London: Hamish Hamilton. Highly readable account of exploration to find the source of the Nile.

Natural History
Blundell, M.A. 1987. *Field Guide to the Wild Flowers of East Africa*. London: Collins. Dorst, J. and Dandelot, P.A. 1970. *Field Guide to the larger Mammals of Africa*. London: Collins. Hedges, N.R. 1983. *Reptiles and Amphibians of East Africa*. Narobi: Kenya Literature Bureau. Larcassam, R. 1971. *Handguide to the Butterflies of East Africa*. London: Collins. Williams, J. and Arlott, N.A. 1980. *Field Guide to the Birds of East Africa*. London: Collins.

RWANDA

Introduction

Until the recent violent disturbances, Rwanda impressed as a small country without any valuable mineral resources, that had succeeded in providing excellent infrastructure and a viable agricultural system from an apparently unpromising terrain. The roads are superb with stone-faced culverts and drainage channels; the hillsides are marvels of neat terracing to grow coffee and tea; and the houses, unlike anywhere else in the region, are substantial and roofed with Mediterranean-style clay tiles.

The missions are an important part of life, particularly outside the larger towns. They provide guest house accommodation, run schools and clinics, teach crafts and skills and manufacture traditional items. They are the centres of most local communities. No doubt they will have an important part to play in trying to reunite this bitterly divided country.

The violent disturbances and the flight of refugees in 1994 have put Rwanda off limits to travellers. It is clearly only wise to plan any kind of trip to Rwanda when order has been fully restored. In the meantime, we continue to offer the traveller a glimpse of the country prior to April 1994. Although much will have have been destroyed, much will remain and we hope to be able to report on an improving situation in our next edition.

Contents

Maps

Environment

Rwanda is a land of contrasts offering many different types of activities. Most people know about the mountain gorillas in the Parc National des Volcans in the North of the country, but Rwanda has much more to offer. Its Parc National de l' Akagera on the Burundi border has herds of zebra, impala and buffalo as well as giraffe, elephants, lions, and other animals who live on the wide savannahs of East Africa. On the other side of the country, close to East Zaire is the Nyungwe Forest Reserve, home to more than 270 species of trees, 50 species of mammal, 275 species of birds as well as an astonishing variety of orchids and butterflies. Its climate is temperate due to the high altitude of most of the country with an average temperature of 30°C.

Geography

Rwanda is a landlocked country lying in Central Africa bordered by Uganda to the N, Tanzania to the East, Burundi to the South and Zaire to the West. Measuring only 26,338 sq km, Rwanda is one of Africa's smallest nations, but with a population of approx 8 million (308 people per sq km), Rwanda is the most densely populated country on the mainland.

The physical environment of the country is both diverse and spectacular due to numerous upheavals which have affected the earth's crust in this part of central and east Africa. This forms the Rift Valley which runs from the Red Sea down to Mozambique and has created a landscape of mountains and valleys which gave Rwanda the name of the 'land of a thousand hills'.

To the W runs the Rift Valley floor containing lakes Kivu and Tanganyika which are connected by the Ruzizi river valley. The landscape surrounding the lakes is mountainous, rising to about 3,000m to the N, slope down in the middle and rise up again to more than 2,700m in the S which is covered with the protected virgin forest of Nyungwe. This mountain range is known as the Zaire-Nile crest.

In the N the land is made up of the Birunga volcanoes which form a chain spreading between Rwanda, Uganda and Zaire. In this chain of mountains the Rwandan authorities have established a national park for the protection of mountain gorillas.

Rwanda – A Tragedy In The Making

The colonial period began at the end of the nineteenth century, Germans ruled in Rwanda from 1890 until 1916 when their garrisons were surrendered to the Belgian forces during WW1. At the Treaty of Versailles, Rwanda and Burundi were mandated to the Belgians by the League of Nations. From then until independence in 1962, the power and privileges of the minority Tutsi increased as the Belgians found it convenient to rule indirectly through the *mwami* and his princes. Tutsi were trained to run the bureaucracy and had a monopoly of the education system, operated by the Catholic missionaries.

During this time, the conditions of the Hutu peasantry deteriorated, leading to demands for radical reform. In 1959, following the death of Mwami Matara III, a ruthless clan of Tutsi seized power, killing Hutu leaders. This proved to be a serious miscalculation and led to a massive Hutu uprising when about 100,000 Tutsi were killed, many others fleeing the country. Faced with carnage on this scale, the Belgian colonial authorities were forced to introduce political reforms. A referendum in 1961 decided to abolish the monarchy and to establish a republic. Since independence in 1962, the majority Hutu have been in power in an uneasy alliance, and many Tutsi fled the country to live in neighbouring Tanzania, Uganda and Zaire. The alliance between the majority Hutu and minority Tutsi has not been an easy one, often erupting into violence. The most recent resurgence was in 1990 when a small band of Tutsi invaded NW Rwanda from Uganda where they had been living in exile.

During 1989 economic and political conditions in Rwanda deteriorated sharply. The combined effects of soil degradation, population increases and crop disease reduced harvests, resulting in the need for emergency food aid for over 600,000 people. The collapse of world coffee prices, Rwanda's main export, combined with a low output, meant serious budgetary problems. These economic factors coincided with a series of political scandals in which several government

The East and centre of Rwanda are far less mountainous, the majority of this part of the country is on a plateau at an altitude between 1,500 and 2,000m, the area is characterised by smaller hills with innumerable valleys which peter off towards the E which is a region of lakes and swamps. To the S the country is surrounded by marshland.

Only about two-fifths of the land can be cropped due to the difficulty of the terrain and poor soil quality over much of the country. This problem coupled with the high population density of the country has led Rwandans to practise innovative techniques to make farming the steep slopes possible. Schemes are underway to clear some of the swampland in the E so they can be cultivated.

Climate

The climate is tropical with 4 discernible seasons. There are 2 annual rainy periods, the big rains running from mid-Feb to the beginning of Jun and the small rains which occur from mid-Sep to mid-Dec. Rainfall is particularly heavy in the N over the Birunga volcanoes which are covered by rainforest. The summit of Kalisimbi (4,507m), the highest of these volcanoes, is often covered with snow. Rainfall is not even throughout the country; generally it is drier in the E. The ideal time for tourism is from Jun to the beginning of Sep.

Temperatures in the country are moderated by high altitude. The average temperature during the day is 30°C, though there can be a daily range of as ministers and members of the president's family were accused of corruption, illegal currency dealings and nepotism. At this time, there had been many discussions of the position of Rwandan refugees in Uganda who wished to return to their homeland. This atmosphere of political unrest and economic hardship erupted on 1 Oct 1990 when an estimated 10,000 Tutsi exiles crossed from Uganda to NW Rwanda.

Internationally the invading Front Patristique Rwandais (FPR) presented itself as a democratic and multi-ethnic movement seeking to depose a corrupt and incompetent regime. Belgium was asked to intervene to secure a ceasefire and accelerate political reform. Full freedom of the press was established in Apr 1992, and a new constitution was drawn up. On 4 Aug 1993 a peace accord was formally signed by both sides and a new transitional government was installed. The FPR joined the political mainstream, and preparations were made for multi-party general elections. When returning from further talks with the FPR in Tanzania in Apr 1994, the plane carrying the delegations from both Rwanda and Burundi was shot down, and the president killed.

The country plunged into chaos as Hutu sought retaliation against the Tutsi, and the FPR advanced to the capital, Kigali. In the wake of the violence, hundreds of thousands fled to Zaire and Tanzania. Aid agencies were quickly overwhelmed as disease and lack of facilities killed many. Graphic reporting and television pictures provoked world-wide concern and public opinion in the west stung governments to act unilaterally or under the guise of UN humanitarian relief. Diplomatic efforts to try to stablize the situation continued but with limited success.

On capturing Kigali in August 1994, the FPR attempted to form a broadly-based government and tempt (with the encouragement of the Aid agencies) a return to Rwanda of the refugees. Most preferred the squalor and uncertainty of the camps to the perceived threat of further violence if they returned to their homes.

much as 14°C. Kigali, the capital has an average temperature of 19°C. Towards the S, where the land relief is less high, temperatures are far higher and are more similar to equatorial heat.

Flora and fauna

The diverse geography and climate of Rwanda have resulted in rich and varied plant and animal life. There are a number of national parks throughout the country: Gishwati nr Gisenyi on Lake Kivu in the NW, and Nyungwe in the SW are both 'natural forests' housing a wide variety of orchids and more than 250 species of trees. A number of primates live in these areas including the mountain gorilla, chimpanzees, and colobus. Other animals in the forests are servals, leopards, small antelopes and duikers.

In the E part of Rwanda, the environment is more similar to the savanna of Kenya or Tanzania. Small bushes of acacia break the monotony of wide grassy plains of zebras, topis and buffalo with some herds of elephants. The marshy regions of Mutara-Mubari, Buganza and Gisaka in the S are typified by forests of papyrus and reeds.

History

Rwanda was settled initially by the Twa pygmies. From around 1000 AD the agriculture-based Hutu people moved into the region and from the 15th century the cattle-raising Tutsi came into the area, dominating both the Hutu and the Twa. The Tutsi introduced a feudal land system and a landlord-peasant relationship with the Hutu even though the Hutu made up about 89% of the population. This system was overseen by a king (*mwami*) whose authority was absolute, with the power to allocate land or evict people. Military organisation was the sole preserve of the Tutsi. The system was reinforced through ceremonial and religous practices.

The agricultural Hutu intensively farmed land eventually beginning to denude the hills of trees. The consequent erosion, lack of fuel and reduced agricultural productivity led to competition for land. At various times this has led to food shortages and many Hutu emigrating to other areas of East Africa in search of land. In the 20th century alone, there have been 6 famines in the region. Eventually this situation led to competition for land with the Tutsi pastoralists and consequent conflicts.

Culture and life

People

The population of Rwanda is approx 7,200,000. The majority of the population are Hutu (84%), with the Tutsi making up 15% and the Twa only 1% of the population. The Hutu are regarded as being short, dark-skinned and round-faced. The Tutsi are thought of as tall, with lighter complexions and angular-faced. The Twa are considered very short and stocky, with dark skins. However, as in neighbouring Burundi, although there are many Rwandans that can be recognised as belonging to one or other of the main groups on the basis of their features, it is quite impossible to classify many others by their physical appearance.

The official languages of the country are Kinyarwanda and French (spoken by approx 8% of the population), though some people speak Swahili. The predominant religion is Catholic, with about 25% following traditional religions.

The majority of Rwandans live in rural areas over 95% of the population. As a result, the urban areas remain small, and there are few towns. The country dwellers are not grouped in villages. The majority of Rwandans live on their farms separated from other families by fields. This preference of Rwandans to live in rural rather than urban areas, coupled with a government policy which prohibits people living in towns unless they were born there or have proof of employment opportunities, has placed pressure on scarce land resources. The result has been some encroachment into the country's national parks which cover more than 10% of the area of the country. Recently reclamation of swampland in the S and E of the country

The Fable Of Tutsi, Hutu and Twa

The mythical king of Rwanda, Gihanga, had 3 sons, Tutsi, Hutu, and Twa. He gave each son a jar of milk, and instructed them to keep the milk safe until the next day.

However, during the night, Twa became thirsty and drank his milk. Hutu fell asleep, knocked over his jar and the milk was spilt. Only Tutsi succeeded in keeping his milk safe until the morning

The king decided that Twa, who had clearly disobeyed, should be punished by never being allowed to own cattle, and from time to time he should suffer starvation. Hutu, who had been careless, would only be allowed to own cattle if he worked for Tutsi. The worthy Tutsi was to be rewarded by possessing all the cattle, and being allowed to rule the the others, for only he could be trusted with the jar of milk, which was Rwanda.

Secretion Secrets

In traditional society in Rwanda bodily fluids are seen as having great powers and to be key elements in medicine and procreation.

Saliva is traditionally thought to have healing properties. The treatment for a skin disease is often to spit on the affected part. Saliva is thought to come from the brain, and mad people are said to have dry mouths.

Male semen is considered to be a pure form of blood, originating in the brain, and passing down the spine and into the penis. Taking milk and weak sorghum beer will produce good semen. Stronger alcohol such as banana beer, bottled lager and whisky dehydrate the body, hinder semen production and delay ejaculation.

During intercourse copious vaginal secretions are highly desirable as they will increase the likelihood of an orgasm for the woman, and this in turn will improve the chances of conception. To encourage wetness during intercourse, a woman will often not eat after midday, but drink lots of fluid. Young girls stretch the lips of their vaginas as it is believed big labia will assist vaginal secretion.

has increased land available for agriculture.

Although Catholicism is the predominant religion in the country, other traditional religions are still practised, though rarely openly because of the opposition of Christianity to such customs. Among these is *kuragura* (divination). The belief is that each human enters the world of the ancestors after death. Once dead, the visible body (*umubiri*) disappears and liberates the spirit (*umuzimu*) which continues to intervene in the world of the living, for good or evil, depending on whether the deceased had respected traditions or transgressed taboos. People seek the help of a diviner to interpret the ancestors' messages.

Traditional music and dance plays a strong part in Rwandan culture. Two traditional groups are the *Intore* dancers and the *Tambourinaires*. The *Intore* dancers were attached to the court of the former monarchs. They were not considered artists but were warriors, and they formed a small militia attached to the king (*mwami*). In essence, the dances are war exercises. The *Tambourinaires* were also attached to the royal court acting as drummers. Drums were emblems of the mwami's power as well as musical instruments. It was said that inside the drum was the 'heart', a sacred and secret object known only to the mwami and the priest.

Art and crafts

Traditional crafts include baskets and mats woven from raffia, banana leaves or sisal. Banana leaves can be used to make particularly sturdy items, recognisable from the light and dark brown coiled construction, and include cribs, furniture, bookcases, trunks, and hanging baskets. Banana leaves are also used to make collages for pictures and postcards. Sisal is also used for woven seats and backs of furniture.

Leather and skins are used for rugs, hats, wallets, hand bags, drums and belts, and is generally of high quality both in design and fabrication.

Wood carving includes small figures of traditional figures and of animal, particularly high quality friezes of village life, small jars with lids and attractive raised relief designs, board games, kitchen utensils, combs, pipes, stools and furniture. Musical instruments have decorated wooden sounding boards for strings and vibrating flattened metal rods.

Gourds have traditional designs

etched on their surfaces. They are also made into musical instruments.

It is thought that Rwanda developed iron-working in the 7th century BC, possibly as the result of migrations from the Cushite empire to the N W. Traditional metal-work is expressed in spears and knives with decorated wooden shafts. These skills are used to produce metal kitchen utensils, farm implements and building tools.

Earthenware is very high quality. The Twa make symmetrical traditional pots without the use of potters wheels. Finally, there is pottery with abstract fired glaze design as well as with hand-painted foliage decoration.

Modern Rwanda

Politics

President Habyarimana, a Hutu and formerly a Major-General in the army, was in power 1973-94 at the head of the Mouvement Revolutionnaire National pour le Developpement (MRND). Until Jun 1992 MRND was the only political party. In 1990 a small group of Rwandan refugees, led by Major General Fred Rwigema, invaded N Rwanda calling for political change. Rwegima was killed in the subsequent fighting. Nevertheless, the incursion by the FPR, made up mainly of exiled Tutsi, succeeded in bringing the injustices of the existing system and the need for reforms to the attention of the international community.

Since that time about 15 political parties have been officially recognised including the FPR. On 4 Aug 1993 a peace accord was officially signed by President Habyarimana and Col Alex Kanyarengwe of the FPR in Arusha, Tanzania. A new transitional government had been installed, and multi-party general elections were expected to be conducted by mid-1995. This has all been thrown into disarray with the shooting-down of the plane returning from further talks in Tanzania, and the death of Habyarimana in Apr 1994 and the mass exodus that followed. After capturing Kigali in Aug 1994, the FPR have been attempting to form a broadly based government. For further information on the background to the current crisis, see box page 498.

Economics

In 1994 the population is estimated to be 8.0 million, with the highest population density on mainland Africa of 308 persons per square kilometre. The population is growing at 3.0% a year. Only 8% of the population live in towns.

GDP in 1991 was estimated at US$1,579 million, which places Rwanda among the medium-sized African economies. GNP per head in 1991 was US$270 per head, placing Rwanda in the low-income category.

Agriculture generates 37% of GDP, industry 23%, of which 16% was manufacturing, and services generated 40%. All this represents a slightly larger industry sector and a slightly smaller agricultural sector than might be expected for a small, low-income African economy.

On the expenditure shares of income, private consumption comprises 83% of GDP, government consumption 12%, and domestic savings 5%. Gross domestic investment is 17% of GDP, and the gap between this and domestic savings, equivalent to 12% of GDP, was covered by net inflow of resources from overseas. These figures imply a larger commitment to consumption, and lower savings than the average in Africa.

Exports of goods and services are 12% of GDP, and imports 23% of GDP. This is a rather lower dependence on international trade than is usual in Africa. 82% of merchandise exports are coffee, and 11% tea. Merchandise imports are 26% machinery 19% fuel, 15% raw materials, 11% manufactures, and 11% foodstuffs.

The adult literacy rate was 50% in 1981, and this is good by African standards, where the average is closer to 40%. The primary school enrolment rate was 67% in 1986, with a 3% enrolment rate for secondary education, but negligible tertiary enrolments. Although primary enrolments are comparable with Africa generally, the secondary and tertiary enrolments are significantly lower.

Life expectancy is about the Africa average at 49 years. There were 34,680 persons per doctor and 3,650 persons per nurse in 1983, and these provision rates are below the African average. Average daily calorie supply at 1,830 in 1986 was 14% below the Africa average.

Overall, Rwanda is of medium economic size and has low-income levels. It has a larger industrial sector than might be expected. This reflects a greater degree of self-sufficiency than is common elsewhere in Africa, and export and import dependence are consequently low as well. Secondary and tertiary educational provision are poor as are nutrition and health services.

Economic performance

GDP grew by 2.4% from 1980-87, above the regional and African averages of 1.6% and 0.6% respectively. Nevertheless, this implied falling GDP per head at -0.7% a year. Despite a policy of aiming for self-sufficiency in food production, the agricultural sector grew by only 1.1%, the same as the regional average, and slower than the rate of population expansion. Industrial growth reached 4.8% while the regional average was only 1.1%. The service sector grew by 3.9% compared with a regional growth rate of 0.7%. Export volumes expanded by 2.5% a year, 1980-87, better than elsewhere in Africa, where export volumes declined. Import volumes increased by 5.4% while in the region on average they only increased by 0.2%. The inflation rate was 4.5% which compares favourably with the regional and African rates of 23.6% and 16.7% respectively.

Overall, bearing in mind the fast-growing population, little unused land and a poorly developed infrastructure, Rwanda has not performed too badly, although GDP per head has declined in the 1980's. Industrial sector growth and price stability have been above average.

Recent economic developments

Unlike most of Africa, economic policy in Rwanda has not undergone a change in favour of state withdrawal from marketing and manufacturing, or a liberalisation of tariffs, price controls and exchange rates. The main emphasis has been on food self-sufficiency in the face of the rapid rate of population growth at 3.5% a year, and government spending has emphasised infrastructure to aid agriculture. Economic progress has been negligible in the 1980's, with GDP exhibiting substantial year-to-year fluctuations as a result of the impact of weather on agricultural output and of international prices on export earnings.

Rwanda's exports peaked at US$203 million in 1979, since which time they have declined to a reported US$90 million in 1989. Increased aid has enabled Rwanda to increase its levels of imports, and these have risen from US$196m in 1980 to US$380 million in 1989.

Rwanda is estimated to have US$780 million of outstanding external debt, little of this being with commercial lenders. As a result of the long repayment periods on most of Rwanda's debt and the low interest charges, Rwanda's debt servicing is running at a manageable 8.6% of merchandise export revenues.

Rwanda has an exchange rate which has fluctuated. Although Rwanda has had a modest rate of domestic inflation since 1970, there is little doubt that the Rwanda franc is overvalued by the maintenance of the fixed exchange rate policy, and any continuing balance of payments problems which lead to requests for IMF credit will involve pressure for depreciation and a more flexible system.

Rwanda has typically run a budget deficit of around -2.0% of GDP, and this has contributed substantially to the good record of price stability. Infrastructure has featured heavily in aid commitments to Rwanda, with France committing US$4.4 million to telecommunications, and Japan US$2.5 million to roads. A major water development is to receive US$15 million from the World Bank, US$16 million from France, US$11.1mn from the African Develop-

Comparative Economic And Social Data

	Burundi	East Africa	Africa	Industrial countries
Population and land				
Population, mid year, millions, 1994	8.0	12.2	10.2	40.0
Urban Population, %, 1991	8	30.5	30	75
Population Growth Rate, % per year, 1980-91	3.0	3.1	3.1	0.8
Land Area, thou. sq. kilom.	26	486	486	1,628
Population Density, persons per sq km, 1994	308	24.2	20.4	24.3
Economy: production and income				
GDP, US$millions, 1991	1,579	2,650	3,561	550,099
GNP per head, US$, 1991	270	250	389	12,960
Economy: supply structure				
Agriculture, % of GDP, 1986	40	43	35	3
Industry, % of GDP, 1986	23	15	27	35
Services, % of GDP, 1986	37	42	38	61
Economy: demand structure				
Private Consumption, % of GDP, 1986	71	77	73	62
Gross Domestic Investment, % of GDP, 1986	19	16	16	21
Government Consumption, % of GDP, 1986	20	15	14	17
Exports, % of GDP, 1986	12	16	23	17
Imports, % of GDP, 1986	22	24	26	17
Economy: performance				
GDP growth, % per year, 1980-86	1.8	1.6	-0.6	2.5
GDP per head growth, % per year, 1980-86	-1.5	-1.7	-3.7	1.7
Agriculture growth, % per year, 1980-86	0.9	1.1	0.0	2.5
Industry growth, % per year, 1980-86	4.8	1.1	-1.0	2.5
Services growth, % per year, 1980-86	1.1	2.5	-0.5	2.6
Exports growth, % per year, 1980-86	1.3	0.7	-1.9	3.3
Imports growth, % per year, 1980-86	6.5	0.2	-6.9	4.3
Economy: other				
Inflation Rate, % per year, 1980-86	5.6	23.6	16.7	5.3
Aid, net inflow, % of GDP, 1986	11.5	11.5	6.3	-
Debt service, % of Exports, 1984	7.6	18	20.6	-
Budget surplus (+), Deficit (-), 1979	-1.7	-3.0	-2.8	-5.1
Education				
Primary, % of 6-11 group, 1985	64	62	76	102
Secondary, % of 12-17 group, 1985	2	15	22	93
Higher, % of 20-24 group, 1985	..	1.2	1.9	39
Adult literacy rate, %, 1981	50	41	39	99
Health and nutrition				
Life expectancy, years, 1986	48	50	50	76
Calorie supply, daily per head, 1985	1,935	2,111	2,096	3,357
Population per doctor, 1980	32,150	35,986	24,185	550

Notes: 'Africa' excludes South Africa. Dates are for the country in question, and do not always correspond with the Regional, African and Industrial averages.

ment Bank, US$7 million from Austria, US$7.5 million from the Arab Bank for Economic Development in Africa, and US$8.3 million from Switzerland.

Economic outlook

Even in circumstances of political stability, Rwanda's economic prospects are poor. The long-term outlook for tea and coffee, on which Rwanda depends for most of its export earnings is only modest. In these circumstances it will be extremely difficult for Rwanda to expand the economy at the rate at which population is increasing. The most likely outlook is that living standards would continue a slow fall.

In the wave of violence following the assassination of President Habyarimanay, Rwanda has developed into a crisis zone requiring international emergency assistance. Even if the disturbances can be promptly contained, the long term economic outlook will have been severely impaired.

KIGALI

Kigali was developed by the Germans in 1907 as the administrative centre of their Rwandan territory. They chose to build on Mount Kigali because of its central location and because it was far away from Nyanza, S of Gitarama which was the traditional administrative centre of Rwanda and the court of the Tutsi kings. The purpose was to develop a major post from which to conduct German trade in central Africa. Until then, the German military government had allowed the Tutsi kings to continue to rule, limiting themselves to sending an occasional expedition to Rwanda from their headquarters in Dar-es-Salaam to reestablish order when internal problems developed.

In those early days, Kigali's location was unsalubrious. Malaria was rife due to the number of anopheles, the mosquito which carries malaria, which bred on the numerous streams, and humidity was high. The situation today is very different. Kigali is a small, attractive city of broad avenues shaded by jacaranda and eucalyptus. The temperate weather and abundant rainfall means vegetation is lush and the city is surrounded by gardens and greenery. Most hotel gardens are filled with tropical flora; palm trees, porcelain roses, banana trees, hibiscus and bougainvillea. Even the banks and other commercial buildings are situated behind bushes of bougainvillea and hibiscus.

From its beginnings at the foot of Mount Kigali, the city has stretched into the neighbouring hills of Nyamirambo, Kimihurura, Kacyiru and Kanombe. As a result, views from many parts of the city are spectacular. On clear nights it is said you can see the great volcanoes to the N of Rwanda more than one hundred kilometres away.

Kigali is small with 370,000 inhabitants. Nyarugenge Hill is the city centre and the location of government administrative buildings, commercial businesses and banks. It is, however, fairly cosmopolitan due to the large number of expatriates and because the United Nations Food & Agriculture Organisation and the European Community have bases there. Apart from European expatriates, there are a number of people from the Far East particularly China who are involved in aid projects. The only disadvantage to Kigali is that unless you know people here, it is difficult to enjoy much of a social life. There are relatively few restaurants and bars and many of these are expensive.

Places of interest

The small size of Kigali makes everything within easy walking distance. The **Franco-Rwanda Cultural Centre** is by the large traffic roundabout at the entrance to the Avenue de la Republique. The Centre regularly presents films and concerts in the afternoons and evenings. The Kigali **Grand Market** (*isoko*) is open all day and is a large fruit and vegetable market offering both tropical and more familiar produce. There are a number of open-air terraced restaurants in this part of town.

South from Nyarungenge Hill down Nyamirambo Hill and then up the other side is the **Muslim Quarter** where in former times Arab traders from the Indian Ocean coast settled. The area is bustling day and night and has many craftsmen's stalls in the streets. The **Mosque** and **Islamic Cultural Centre** are based here.

A pleasant place to visit in the evening is **Lando's**, a hotel and restaurant complex which is popular with Rwandans and travellers alike. There is an excellent restaurant on the upper level

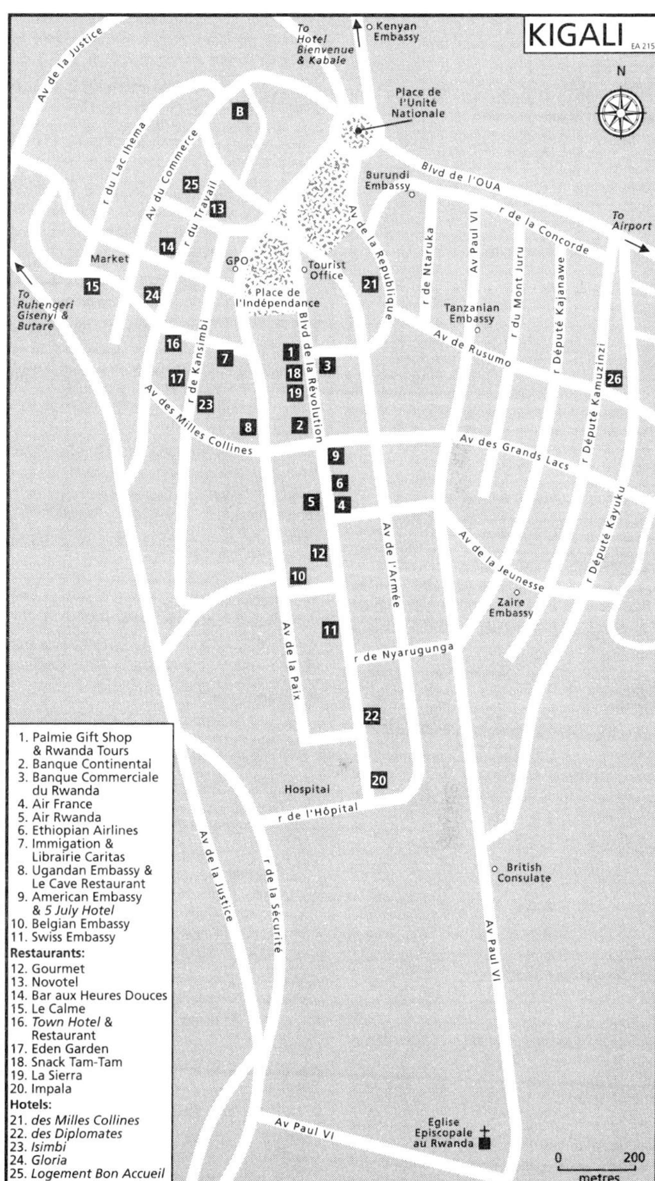
KIGALI
EA 215
N
To Hotel Bienvenue & Kabale
Kenyan Embassy
Place de l'Unité Nationale
Av de la Justice
Blvd de l'OUA
Burundi Embassy
r de la Concorde
To Airport
r du Lac Ihema
Av du Commerce
r du Travail
Market
GPO
Tourist Office
Place de l'Indépendance
Av de la République
r de Ntaruka
Av Paul VI
r du Mont Juru
r Député Kajanawe
Tanzanian Embassy
Av de Rusumo
r Député Kamuzinzi
To Ruhengeri Gisenyi & Butare
r de Kansimbi
Blvd de la Révolution
Av des Milles Collines
Av des Grands Lacs
r Député Kayuku
Av de la Jeunesse
Av de l'Armée
Zaire Embassy
Av de la Paix
r de Nyarugunga
Hospital
r de l'Hôpital
r de la Sécurité
British Consulate
Eglise Episcopale au Rwanda
0 200 metres
1. Palmie Gift Shop & Rwanda Tours
2. Banque Continental
3. Banque Commerciale du Rwanda
4. Air France
5. Air Rwanda
6. Ethiopian Airlines
7. Immigation & Librairie Caritas
8. Ugandan Embassy & Le Cave Restaurant
9. American Embassy & 5 July Hotel
10. Belgian Embassy
11. Swiss Embassy
Restaurants:
12. Gourmet
13. Novotel
14. Bar aux Heures Douces
15. Le Calme
16. Town Hotel & Restaurant
17. Eden Garden
18. Snack Tam-Tam
19. La Sierra
20. Impala
Hotels:
21. des Milles Collines
22. des Diplomates
23. Isimbi
24. Gloria
25. Logement Bon Accueil
26. Auberge d'Accueil

and a snack brasserie below. Lando's is also the home of the best of the night-clubs in town. There are a number of good quality restaurants, though they are relatively expensive, offering a range of cuisines such as Chinese food at the Amahoro sports complex, Greek at the Restaurant Hellenique, French at La Taverne and Italian at Le Petit Kigali.

Local information

● Where to stay

Price guide:
A+ Over US$100; **A** US$40-100; **B** US$20-40; **C** US$10-20; **D** US$5-10; **E** Under US$5.

Kigali tends to be expensive and there are very few hotels or hostels catering for the budget traveller. The cheaper places tend to get full quickly.

A ***Hotel des Milles Collines***, BP 1322, 1 ave de la Republique, T 76530/6, F 76441. 112 rooms, bar, restaurant, swimming pool, shops. Very central. Good standard. **A** ***Meridien Umubano***, Blvd de l'Umuganda, BP 874, T 82176/7/8 83362/3/4, F 83361, Tlx 22561. 100 rooms, a bar and a popular French restaurant, swimming pool, tennis, shops, conference room and miniature golf. **A** ***Village Urugwiro***, Blvd de l'Umuganda, BP 1169, T 84459, F 76512, Tlx 22542, to the NE of the city centre. 66 rooms including 22 apartments, bar-restaurant and swimming pool. **A** ***Chez Lando***, BP 1519, T 82050, F 84380, 32 rooms, bar, restaurants, swimming pool, discotheque. **A** ***Rebero l'Horizon***, BP 52, T 75736/73615. Bar, Restaurant, Disco, Swimming pools.

B ***des Diplomates***, BP 269, T 75111, F 72734), 43 Blvd de la Revolution. 40 rooms, bar, restaurant, tennis (professional available at US$5/hr), boutiques, reception room. Fairly central and good value. **B** ***Bienvenue***, Boulevard de Nyabugogo, BP 1090, T 74608/73615, just to the N of the city centre. **B** ***Kiyovu***, 6 ave de Kiyovu, BP 1331, T 75106, F 76512, Tlx 22542. 40 rooms, bar-restaurant and barbeque. **B** ***Panafrique***, BP 82, T 75056. Small, with 10 rooms, bar and restaurant. **B** ***5 July***, Blvd de la Revolution. Just S of US Embassy. Colonial-style hotel set in excellent gardens. Was closed in 1994, but looks one of the nicer and more stylish places to stay.

C ***Isimbi***, BP 163, T 75109) rue du Karasimbi. New hotel. Bar, Restaurant. Well run and comfortable. Popular, often full. **C** ***Gloria Hotel***, BP 974, T 72268, on the corner of rue du Travail and ave du Commerce has rooms with attached bathrooms. Was closed in 1994 due to failure of water supply. **C** ***Town***, ave du Commerce, BP 1515, T 76690. This place has a good restaurant and hot showers, 12 rooms. **C** ***La Vedette***, BP 850, T 73575. Small. Bar Restaurant.

D ***Bellevue***, just off ave du Commerce, next to *Town Hotel*. Simple, friendly and secure. **D** ***Logement Bon Accueil***, rue du Travail, nr the bus station. It is basic but clean with single and double rooms with attached shower cubicles Good value **D** ***Auberge d'Accueil***, at the Eglise Presbyterienne au Rwanda, 2 rue Depute Kayuku, close to the bus station, T 73640. This is the most popular hostel for budget travellers. Friendly and good value. Single rooms and dormitory accommodation. Private rooms have a wash basin and clean sheets are provided. No hot water. There is a canteen which serves breakfast as well as soft drinks and beers. Closes at 2200 but will admit guests later if arranged. **D** ***Guest House***, Eglise Episcopale au Rwanda, 32 ave Paul VI, T 76340. Reasonable with clean rooms. Dormitory style accommodation costs. About a 30 minute walk from the city centre. Breakfast is available. No hot water.

● Places to eat

Price guide:
♦♦♦♦Over US$10; ♦♦♦US$5-10; ♦♦US$2-5; ♦Under US$2.

All of the A and B class hotels offer good quality food.

♦♦♦***Eden Garden***, rue de Karisimbi. Western-style food. ♦♦♦***La Sierra***, Blvd de la Revoluution. Indian, Chinese and Continental cuisine. ♦♦♦***La Cave***, ave de la Paix close to the Ugandan Embassy. Staple European foods like pizza, spagetti, steaks. Serves breakfasts. ♦♦♦***Snack Tam-Tam***, Blvd de la Revolution. Pleasant atmosphere. ♦♦♦***Restaurant Impala***, Bld de la Revolution, next to the *Hotel des Diplomates*. Brochettes, a type of kebab, are a lunchtime speciality.

♦♦***Le Gourmet***, Blvd de la Revolution. Close to Chinese Embassy. Pleasant atmosphere in nice location. Good value. Open 0800-1700. ♦♦***Town Hotel Restaurant***, offers some of the cheapest and best food in Kigali at prices around US$5. Another place worth remembering is ****Restaurant Bar aux Heures Douces**. Down a small lane off rue du Travail, which has an excellent value set menu. The beer is cheap, and there is a good lively atmosphere. ****Restaurant Café Flora**, ave de la Justice. 5 minute walk from the centre of town. There is a set menu and a la carte dishes.

***Motel Le Calme** Near the market. ***Restaurant Novotel**, rue Prefecture nr the bus station. ***Restaurant Umaganura**, Blvd de l'OAU opposite the end of rue Depute Kayuku nr the *Auberge d'Accueil*. The food is basic, but the atmosphere is friendly.

● Bars

There is little in the name of entertainment in the price range of the budget traveller apart from bars in Kigali. Luckily there are quite a few to choose from as most of the restaurants and eateries mentioned above have bars, as do the larger international hotels.

● Airline offices

International airlines flying into Rwanda are: ***Aeroflot***, ***Air Burundi***, ***Air France***, ***Air Tanzania***, ***Air Zaire***, ***Ethiopian Airlines***, ***Kenya Airways*** and ***Sabena***. ***Air France***, BP 411, T 5556, C/O Enterpise Degreef, 64 rue du Commerce; ***Air Rwanda***, BP 808, T 73793) Blvd de la Revolution. Also at Airport, T 85472; ***Ethiopian Airways***, Blvd de la Revolution, just S of US Embassy; ***Kenya Airways***, Blvd de la Revolution, close to Rwanda Tours; ***Sabena***, BP 1322, T 75290/76530, F 76441, *Hotel des Milles Collines*, 1 ave de la Republique, BP.

● Banks and money changers

Bank of Kigali, ave de la Republique. Banque Commerciale du Rwanda, at Corner of Blvd de la Revolution and ave de la Republique. **National Bank of Rwanda**, rue du Mont Kabuye. **BACAR Continental African Bank**, Blvd de la Revolution. Banks are open from Mon-Fri from 0700-1200 and 1400-1800 and Sat from 0800-1200.

● Embassies

Belgium, rue Nyarugence BP 81, T 75554; **Burundi**, rue de Ntaruka, BP 714, T 73465; **Canada**, rue Akagera, BP 1177, T 73210; **China**, ave Depute Kayuku, BP 1345, T 75415; **France**, 40 ave Depute Kamunzinzi, BP 53, T 75225; **Germany**, 8 rue de Bugaramab, BP 355, T 75222; **Kenya**, Blvd de Nyabugogo, next to the *Panafrique Hotel*, BP 1215, T 74771. Open Mon-Fri 0830-1630; **Russia**, ave de l'Armee, BP 40, T 75286; **Tanzania**, ave Paul VI, BP 669, T 76074. Open Mon-Fri, 0900-1400; **Uganda**, 3rd floor, ave de la Paix, nr the corner of ave des Collines. BP 656, T 76495. Open Mon-Fri 0800-1500; **UK**, 55 ave Paul VI, T 75905; **USA**, Blvd de la Revolution BP 28, T 75601; **Zaire**, 504 rue Longue BP 169, T 75289.

● Entertainment

Cinema There is a cinema on the Blvd de la Revolution opposite the Banque Commerciale du Rwanda. Sometimes the Centre Culturel Francais puts films on in the afternoons or evenings.

Nightlife *Eden Garden* rue de Karisimbi. Disco under restaurant. Very central and lively. Lots of local colour. ***Rebero l'Horizon Hotel*** and ***Chez Lando*** also have discos. You will be expected to be reasonably dressed for these and they are more expensive.

● Hospitals and medical services

Hospitals There is a hospital towards the Muslim area of town on rue de l'Hôpital

Pharmacy *Peuple*, T 74009.

● Libraries

Librairie Caritas, ave du Commerce. Has a good selection of books and fairly recent magazines, mostly from France.

● Police

Ave de la Justice.

● Post Office

Ave de la Paix nr the intersecton with rue de Karisimbi. The opening hrs are Mon-Fri from 0730-1800 and Sat from 0830-1300. The poste restante service is well organised and reliable.

● Shopping

Most of the larger hotels have boutiques selling everything from tourist curios and crafts to clothes, pharmaceuticals, films. You should remember that anything which needs to be imported is likely to be expensive, roughly 3 times the price in its country of origin.

Curios and crafts *Palmie Gift Shop* on ave de la Republique has a good selection. ***Bijou du Rwanda*** at *Hotel Milles Collines* has high quality silvered steel jewellry and leather goods. ***Antiques et Bijou*** on ave des Milles Collines, just opposite the Belgian School, has an excellent selection of antique items, not readily available elsewhere in Kigali.

● Sport (participant)

There are **tennis** courts at the *Hotel Meridien*

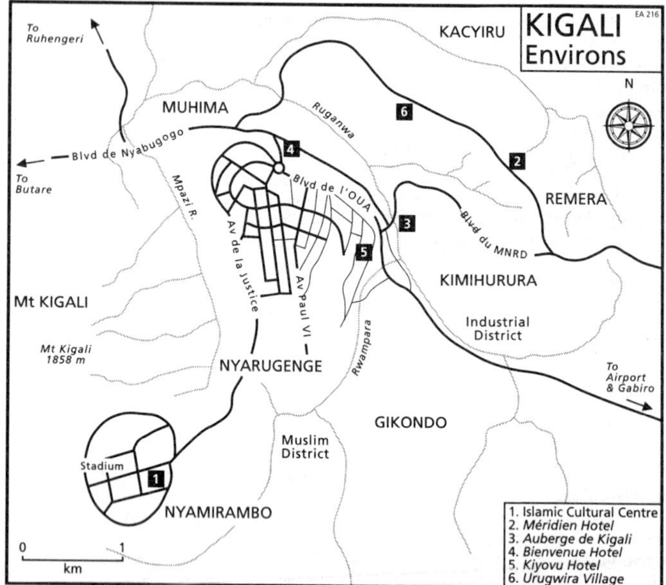

and Hotel des Diplomates (professional available at US$5/hr), **swimming** at *Hotels Meridien, Mille Collines, Rebero l'Horizon, Village Urugwiro, chez Lando*. **Golf** at the *Hotel Meridien*. The **Kigali Hash** (a social running club) meets each Sat in the capital. For details ask at the Canadian Embassy in rue Akagera, T 73210). Runs are generally through the delightful hillside country around Kigali.

● Sport (spectator)

The National Stadium in Rewera presents football, volleyball and athletics.

● Telecommunications

The telephone service is based at the Post Office on ave de la Paix nr the intersection with rue de Karisimbi. It is possible to make direct international calls from here though they are expensive. It is also possible to make phone calls from the major hotels, though they are likely to charge 3 times the rate from the Post Office.

● Tourist Information

Office Rwandaise du Tourisme et des Parcs Nationaux (ORTPN), BP 905, Kigali, T 76514, is on the edge of a traffic roundabout at the entrance to the grand Boulevard de la Revolution. Open 7 days a week including public holidays from 0700-2100. Reservations to see the gorillas at Volcanoes National park or for sightseeing safaries to Akagera National Park and Nyungwe Forest are all made here. Information and a good selection of tourist documents on Rwanda including maps, brochures, books and even videocassettes are available.

● Tour operators and travel agents

Abercrombie and Kent, ave du Commerce, BP 1 545, T 73284. ***Andrew's***, **rue du Lac Rwero, BP 556, T 72355.** ***Metro-Paul Tours***, Metro Café, ave du Commerce, 1st Flr block to W of bus stand, BP 1507, T 72283/77640. Enterprising small company run by a Rwanda/Belgium partnership. Offers tours to Kibuye; Gitesi (source of Nile); and to local craft and manufacture establishments. Very competitive prices. ***Rex Rwanda Explorations***, ave du Commerce, BP 514, T 73284. ***Rwanda Tours***, BP 449, T 75037, F 73626/85893, Tlx 22541. Very experienced operator, arranging gorilla trekking in Rwanda and Zaire; chimpanzee trekking in Zaire; game drives; birdwaching safaris; walking tours in Nungwe Reserve. ***Rwanda Travel Service***, 43 Blvd de la Revolution, BP 140, T 72210, F 72734. ***Rwanda***

Vision, BP 280, T 76061, F 7361/375691. *Transintra Rwanda*, **BP 338, T 75884.** *Umbano Tours Agency*, 160, T 82176/76790. *Le Zebre*, BP 210, ave de la Paix, T 73589.

● Transport

Local Car hire Europcar based *Hotel Mille Collines*, 1 ave de la Republique, T 72893; or *Hotel Meridien*, Blvd de l'Umuganda 76530, T 82178.

Air Air Rwanda flies from Kigali to **Gisenyi** in the N twice a week and to **Kamembe** nr Cyangugu in the S, 6 times a week. The airport is at Kanombe about 12 km from the city centre. Taxi to the airport is around US$12.

Road Buses and minibuses run to all parts of Rwanda each day. The roads (except for the stretches from Gitarama to Kabuye and from Cyangugu and Gisenyi to Kabuye) are superb. Road travel is a pleasure given the spectacular nature of the scenery. The bus station is at the end of rue du Travail.

NORTH: RUHENGERI AND GISENYI

The route to the N is to Ruhengeri, the second largest town in Rwanda. Ruhengeri is the town from which to access Volcanoes Park and make visits to the mountain gorillas. West from Ruengeri is Gisenyi, a well-developed resort on the shores of Lake Kivu. The roads to these 2 main towns are excellent.

Ruhengeri

Most people come to Ruhengeri (population 33,000) as a stopping-off point before embarking on the climb up the Birunga volcanoes to see the mountain gorillas. As a result there are a number of hotels and eating places catering for tourists. This small town is also home to 2 army barracks and a hospital. The town is situated in a beautiful location with magnificent views of the volcanoes to the N and the W.

The most popular trip from Ruhengeri is to the **Parc National des Volcans**, see page 518. There are other possible excursions around the town for instance, visits to **Lake Bulera** and **Lake Ruhondo** are worth noting. Once these 2 lakes were one but they were separated by the flow of lava from the Muhabura volcano. This volcano is no longer active. In the middle of these lakes, which are more than 1,800m above sea level, are a number of small islands covered in dense vegetation. Legend has it that they were placed there as stepping stones for King Ruganzu when he came hunting. Local people say King Ruganzu's footprints and those of his dogs are preserved in the rocks nr **Nyamugali**. Nearby are the **Rusumo Falls** which tumble from a small marshy river onto a rocky setting. There is another set of falls with the same name falls on the Rwanda/Tanzania border.

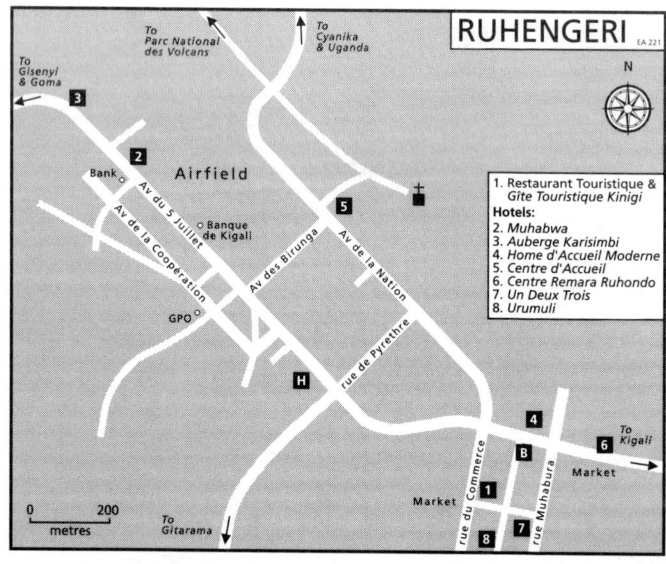

Local information

Where to stay

B *Muhabura*, ave du 5 Juillet, BP 118, T 46296. 14 rooms, bar, restaurant, swimming pool, shop. This is a rather overpriced hotel offering single, double, and triple rooms with attached bathrooms. Restaurant. Bar. **C** *Gite Touristique Kinigi*, BP 12, T 46685, F 76512, Tlx 22542. Bungalow accommodation. Bar. Restaurant. **C** *Auberge Karasimbi*, ave du 5 Juillet. Past *Hotel Muhabura* on road to Gisenyi.

D *Home d'Accueil Moderne*, ave du 5 Juillet. Modern. Opposite bus stand. Parish mission guest house. **D** *Centre d'Accueil*, ave de la Nutrition. 10 minute walk from the centre of town. Rooms are clean. No hot water. Dormitory accommodation, single and double rooms. **D** *Centre Remara Ruhondo*. Parish mission guest house. Quite large. On road to Kigali. **D** *Un Deux Trois*, near market. Small and simple. **D** *Urumuli*, near markets. 5 rooms. Reasonable and comfortable.

Places to eat

♦♦♦*Restaurant Touristique*, rue du Commerce. Excellent food. A la carte and 4 course set menu costs. ♦♦*Centre d'Accueil*, ave de la Nutrition. Stews, rice, vegetables. Simple and sound. ♦♦*Restaurant Amahoro*, on the main street. Basic African menu. ♦♦*Hotel Urumuli*, off rue du Marche. Outdoor area.

Banks and money changers

Open Mon-Fri from 0745 to 1100 and 1400-1500.

Post Office

The post office is open Mon-Fri from 0800-1200. It is also open from Mon-Thu from 1400-1800 and on Sat from 0800-1300.

Transport

Local Taxi motors (motorcycle, passenger on pillion, luggage balanced on handle-bars) readily available. Best way of getting up to the Parc National des Volcans if you intend to see the gorillas. Hitching can be hazardous. It is also possible to hire bicycles from the local market.

Road Good sealed road from **Kigali**. Minibuses take about 2 hrs. There are also regular minibuses to and from **Muhavura** on the Rwanda-Uganda border (sealed road, about 1 hr) and to and from **Gisenyi** on the Rwanda-Zaire border (sealed road, about 2 hrs).

Gisenyi

Gisenyi was founded in 1894 as an army post for the German colonial forces. When the Belgians succeeded the Germans in Rwanda at the end of WWI, they developed this site into a riviera with villas and hotels lying on the fine sand beaches of Lake Kivu. Lake Kivu is a small lake set in spectacular mountain scenery with the Birunga volcanic chain to the N. Gisenyi is at an altitude of 1,400 metres and therefore enjoys both good mountain air and the equatorial heat tempered by lake breeze. Its climate is similar to that in the Mediterranean. Mary Hemingway remarked in 1953 that she she had never seen a more beautiful lake.

Gisenyi is Rwanda's primary resort town for rich Rwandans and expatriates. High standard hotels have been built on the lakefront offering holiday makers wind-surfing and water-skiing as well as tennis courts, swimming pools and botanical gardens. Gisenyi is a useful springboard for the Volcanoes National Park and the mountain gorillas, as there is a good sealed road directly into the park.

Local information

Where to stay

A *Izuba-Meridien*, BP 252, T 40381/2/3 F 40129, Tlx 22561. At the left hand end of ave de la Cooperation. 72 rooms, bar-restaurant, pool, tennis, disco, boutiques, wind surfing. **B** *Palm Beach*, ave de la Cooperation, BP 282, T 40304. Located on the lake shore. 9 rooms (no singles) with a bar-restaurant. **B** *Edelweiss*, ave de l'Independence, BP 82, T 40282, is probably the best in this category of hotels offering a homely and clean environment. Alpine style chalet. Well run.13 double rooms each with a private toilet and hot shower. Bar-restaurant attached. **B** *Regina*, ave de la Cooperation, T 40263. Well located on the lake shore. **B** *Mont Muhe*, BP 12, Rambura. Small. Bar Restaurant.

D *Centre d'Accueil*, Mission Presbyterienne, rue du Marche, T 40522, close to the market and the bus station. Single and double rooms. Some dormitory accommodation. Shared bathrooms. Popular with budget travellers.

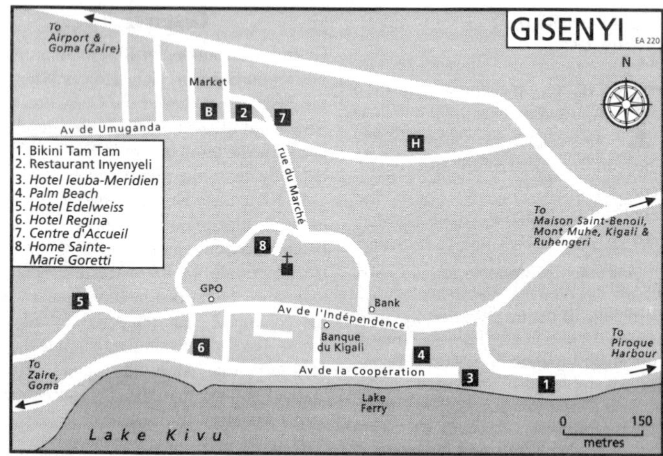

D *Home Sainte-Marie Goretti*, Parish Mission guest house. **D** *Maison Saint Benoit*. Located at Kigufi. Parish mission guest house.

● Places to eat

♦♦♦♦The hotels along the beach front offer high standard food. ♦♦♦*Bikini Tam-Tam Bar and Restaurant* on the beach on rue Kanarampaka. Good value. ♦♦*Restaurant Inyenyeli*. Opposite the *Centre d'Accueil* on rue du Marche. Varied menu. Good value. ♦There are a number of simple restaurants on the main road in the African part of town offering *matoke* (cooked bananas), rice, beans and stew.

● Bars

The bar at ***Hotel Edelweiss*** is good value and the views are spectacular. If you are looking for a more lively atmosphere, try the bar next to the ***Restaurant Inyenyeli***, and ***Gusenyi Club Loisirs***.

● Banks and money changers

Banks tend to give less good rates than in Kigali. *Hotel Ibuzi-Meridien* will change money 24 hrs, but at a rather unfavourable rate. There are a number of money changers in the market but they will not purchase travellers' cheques.

● Entertainment

Nightlife *Gusenyi Club Loisirs*. Entry US$5. Bands on Sat nights. Disco other nights.

● Shopping

Curios and crafts There are a number of craft stalls on ave de l'Independence at the back of the *Hotel Palm* Beach.

● Transport

Air There are twice weekly flights from Kigali to Gisenyi, and a once weekly flight from Kamembe near Cyangugu, both on ***Air Rwanda***. The agents are the *Hotel Edelweiss*, ave de l'Independence, BP 82, T 40282.

Road Road to Gisenyi from **Kigali** is first class, and minibuses leave regularly from the main bus stand in the capital. A minibus runs from **Ruhengeri** to Gisenyi. The journey takes about 2 hrs through upland forest. There are beautiful views as you descend to the town centre looking over Lake Kivu.

Lake There is a small modern motor ferry which covers the route from Cyangugu to Kirambo, Kibuye and Gisenyi. It leaves Cyangugu on Mon and Thu and Gisenyi on Wed and Sat all at 0600. The full trip takes about 6 hrs.

SOUTH: BUTARE AND CYANGUGU

To the S of Kigali the main route runs S W to Gitarama, a small cross-roads town of little interest. The road from Gitarama W to Kibuye is poor, although the town itself is a delightful small resort on the shore of Lake Kivu. The route directly S from Gitarama leads to Butare, the location of the University, and the splendid National Museum. From Butare the route W passes through the spectacular Nyungwe Forest to Cyangugu, the gateway to Bukavu and Eastern Zaire.

Kibuye

Kibuye is a small town (5,500 inhabitants) on Lake Kivu with an excellent beach and good water sports facilities. It is situated about halfway between the better known lakeside towns of Kisenyi and Cyangugu. The approach to the town is beautiful, the mountain road runs along an inlet set into the hills. The scenery around Kibuye itself is splendid. There are little islands with steep shores covered in vegetation.

It is not yet as developed as its N counterpart of Gisenyi, though a guest house has already been built to cater for holiday-makers. The road from Gitarama is not sealed, and this has discouraged visitors.

There are a number of excursions within easy reach of Kibuye in the region of Budaha. There is a small waterfall in **Rubengera** off the Gitarama road called **Ntaruk**. The **Mukura Forest Reserve** is a short drive away. South of Kibuye slightly inland is **Mount Karongi** (2,584m) which can be climbed, and has spectacular views of the surrounding countryside.

Local information

● Where to stay

A *Guest House Kibuye*, BP 55, T 68181, F 76512, Tlx 22542. On the lakeside 9 bungalows, bar, restaurant, swimming pool, tennis, disco and boutique. The views from here are wonderful, and it is a nice place to have a drink at its outside bar, which is open to non-residents. **A** *Vacation Village*. Currently under construction. Was expected to be operational in 1994, but current disturbances will probably delay opening.

D *Centre Bethania*, BP 9, T 68235. Guest house of Presbyterian Church. Restaurant.

E *Home St Jean*, 2 km from town toward Kigali. Good value hostel offering dormitory-style accommodation as well as some single and double rooms.

● Places to eat

♦♦*Home St Jean*. Good, simple meals at reasonable prices.

♦*Restaurant Moderne*. Eastern side of town. Simple African-style food. Bar. ♦*Restaurant Nouveauté*. Close to *Restaurant Moderne*. Good value.

● Sport (participant)

Water sports are a popular pastime here including wind surfing, water skiing, boat trips and fishing. These can all be arranged through *Guest House Kibuye*.

● Transport

Road The road to Kibuye goes from **Gitarama** and is not sealed. The journey can take about 4 hrs. The section from Gitarama to **Kigali** is excellent. Minibuses run regularly between these towns, but it is wise to allocate a full day to travelling from Kigali to Kibuye.

Lake The ferry sails up and down the lake between from Cyangugu and Gisenyi, stopping at Kibuye. It departs from **Cyangugu** on Mon and Thu at 0600, and sails from Kibuye around 0900 for **Gisenyi**. It departs from **Gisenyi** on Wed and Sat at 0600, and leaves Kibuye for **Cyangugu** at around 0900.

Butare

Butare was developed during the Belgian colonial period. It was initially known as Astrida in honor of the Belgian queen who died in 1935. At independence there was a choice whether Butare or Kigali (then only a small town of 6,000 inhabitants) would become the capital. Kigali was favoured because of its more central location. Today Butare's architecture reflects the days of its former splendour and it has become the spiritual and intellectual centre of Rwanda. It is the home of Rwanda's higher education institutions; the University, the National Pedagogical Institute, the National Institute of Scientific Research, the School of Agriculture and other institutions which make Butare a bustling young town.

Places of interest

The **National Museum** is based in Butare and is probably the best museum in East Africa. Built in 1989, the building is an imaginative design of brick, glass and wood but borrowing from traditional Rwandan architectural forms and craftsmanship. It is made of sun-dried clay bricks using traditional colors of ochre, beige and tea rose. It was developed with Belgian funding to commemorate 25 years of independence and is full of ethnological and archaeological displays. There is a particularly interesting display on daily life, covering agriculture, livestock care, hunting, fishing, diet and transport. The museum is open Tue to Sat from 0900-1130 and 1430-1630; Sun and public holidays from 0900-1200 and 1400-1700. Closed on Mon. Entry costs about US$1.50, less if you have a student card. It is N of the centre, past the bus station.

The **Catholic Cathedral** has 3 naves, is built entirely of brick, and is the largest and most handsome in Rwanda. The **Franco-Rwandan Cultural Centre** presents concerts, films and exhibitions.

Local information

● Where to stay

A *Faucon*, BP 40, T 30391, 10 rooms, bar and restaurant. **A** *Ibis*, BP 103, T 30335, 15 rooms. Bar, restaurant and shop. Pleasant terrace bar which serves drinks and snacks.

C *International*, nr market. This has double rooms. Comfortable. Hot water. **C** *Weekend*, nr the market. Single and double rooms. Clean and friendly.

D *Chez Nous*, central, nr the market. Small and comfortable. **D** *Procure de Butare*, 2 km from bus station. Ask directions. Singles, doubles and triple rooms. Comfortable and clean.

● Places to eat

♦♦*Procure du Butare*. Good value. Three course set meal. ♦*Jacaranda Restaurant*. Three course set menu. ♦*Restaurant Chez Nous*. Near the market. Local food.

● Entertainment

The Grand University Auditorium, Palais du MRND and Butare School all have cultural events from time to time. Announcements are posted in town.

● Shopping

There are a number of bookshops along the main high street.

Crafts and curios There are several craft centres not far from Butare such as *Gihindamuyaga* (10 km) and *Gishamvu* (12 km) which are cheaper than the crafts sold in the 2 top range hotels in town. Minibuses from the bus station go to both villages.

● Sport (spectator)

Football is played regularly at the Huye Stadium.

● Transport

Local Motor taxis (motorcycles) are reaily available.

Road Minibuses go to and from **Kigali**, taking about 3 hrs on a good sealed road. There are also minibuses to **Gitarama** and to **Kamembe** and **Cyangugu**. There are less frequent minibuses to the Burundi border, taking about an hour. All these routes out of Butare are sealed, and in excellent repair.

Cyangugu

Cyangugu (population 12,000) is at the S end of Lake Kivu. The border separates Cyangugu from the town of Bukavu in Zaire. There is a lot of cross-border traffic with may people living in Bukavu and working, studying or going to school in Cyangugu, and vice versa. The town is slowly opening up to visitors. At present it is an unpretentious lakeside town with a thriving traditional market, and a stopping-off point for travellers going to and from Zaire.

East of the town lies the **Nyungwe Forest Reserve**, designated as a protected area. It is a sanctuary to numerous interesting plants and animals like chimpanzees, colobus and cercocebus monkeys. Guides, all of whom are members of the ORTPN (Tourism Office of Rwanda and its National Parks), can be hired at the entrance to the forest.

Local information

● Where to stay

B *Hotel du Lac*, BP 191, T 37171/3. Located just by the border post at the side of the stream that runs into Lake Kivu. 24 rooms. Comfortable. Bar. Pleasant restaurant. Swimming pool (although currently out of use). Very close to the crossing post to Zaire, next to the stream which marks the border, Government-owned, but due for privatisation. **B** *Hotel des Chutes*, BP 132, T 37405, 10 rooms, bar, restaurant and disco. Fine location on the side of the steep road that runs from Cyangugu to the border. Good value.

C *Inyenyeli*, BP 38, T 37365. 20 rooms. Bar Restaurant. **C** *Vacation Village of Ituze*, BP 191, T 37101, F 76512, Tlx 22542. 17 rooms, bar and restaurant. **C** *Mission St Francois*. Located just opposite the *Hotel du Lac*, just by the border post. Well-run and friendly hostel offering single, double and triple rooms at reasonable prices.

● Places to eat

♦♦♦*Hotel du Lac*. Quite reasonable food in a pleasant restaurant. Rather casual service. ♦♦*Mission St Francois*. Good value meals. ♦*Plenty* of small eating places on the main road nr where the minibuses depart.

● Shopping

Curios and crafts Along the coastal road leading from Cyangugu N toward Kibuye is the village of **Kirambo** where there is a traditional market. On sale are many interesting craft objects such as woven mats, baskets, wooden bowls.

● Transport

Air *Air Rwanda* flies from Kigali to Kamembe nr Cyangugu 6 times a week. There are also one flight a week connecting Gisenyi and Kamembe near Cyangugu. Office C/O Garage Ruzimeca, T 407).

Road Minibuses run between Cyangugu and **Kigali**, via **Butare**, each day. This road is excellent, and there is spectacular section as it passes through the Nyungwe rainforest.

Lake A small ferry connects Cyangugu to Kibuye and Gisenyi in the N. It leaves Cyangugu sailing N for Kibuye and Gisenyi on Mon and Thu at 0600. Sailing S from Gisenyi (depart 0600) and Kibuye (departs 0900) on Wed and Sat. The trip between Cyangugu and Gisenyi takes about 6 hrs.

Parc National des Volcans

The Parc National des Volcans is situated along a chain of 7 volcanoes known as the Birunga (Virunga in Zaire), one of them more than 4,500m high. The scenery is spectacular from the start of the journey in Ruhengeri up to the reception centre of the park, **Kinigi**. The chain of volcanoes marks the frontier between Rwanda, Zaire and Uganda and spills over the borders into all 3 countries. Covered in forests, the volcanoes in Rwanda are dormant, their craters filled by water making small lakes. Some on the Zaire side are still active. Five volcanoes can be seen from the reception area. **Sabyinyo** ('father of teeth') is the oldest and bristles with 5 jagged peaks. **Gahinga** ('mountain of cultivation') is the smallest. **Muhabura** ('the one who shows the way') is a young volcano.

To the W are 2 more large volcanoes which were the home of the zoologist Dian Fossey who lived and studied the mountain gorillas at a primate research center between Mount **Bisoke** and Mount **Karisimbi**, which at 4,507m, is the highest summit of the chain.

The idea of setting up a natural preserve for the mountain gorilla started, paradoxically, with a big game hunter called Carl Akeley in 1925. Disappointed about coming away from his safari in the mountains empty handed, he worried about the scarcity of mountain gorillas and decided that their slaughter must stop. As a friend of the Belgian king, Albert 1, he was able to obtain the right to set aside the first national park in Africa on the Zairian side of the Virunga chain of volcanoes. In 1929 the park was extended over the Rwandan border. At its inception it was known as Albert Park, changing to Parc National des Volcans at Independence.

The Rwandan government with the support of the World Wildlife Fund have taken steps to ensure the protection of the gorillas from trophy hunters and collectors for zoos as well as from farmers who encroach upon the park. Dian Fossey's efforts to stamp out poaching,

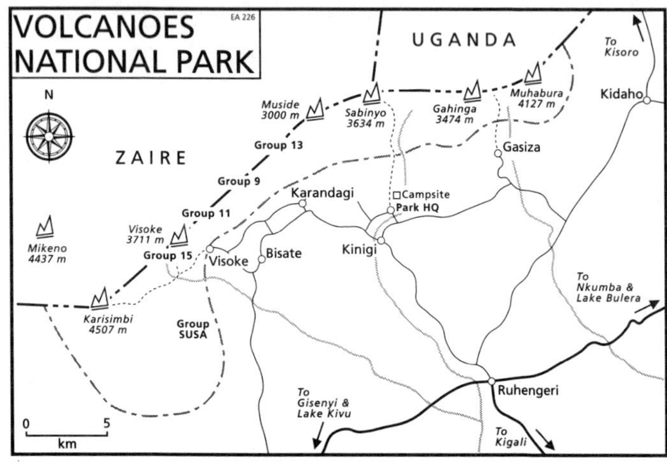

narrated in her book *Gorillas in the Mist*, and later the film of the same name, has helped publicise the problems, and been important in ensuring the continued existence of the gorilla, see box, page 520. Unfortunately, it is not just poaching which threatens the gorillas. A project supported by the European countries in 1969, to grow pyrethrum (used to make a natural insecticide) absorbed more than 8,900 ha of the park.

Gorilla tourism, where people are charged to visit the park, was introduced in 1979 to help pay for protecting gorillas as well as for educational campaigns to persuade Rwandans to conserve the park and protect its flora and fauna. A maximum of 20 tourists are allowed in to see the gorillas each day, escorted by trained guides.

Visiting the gorillas

A visit to see the gorillas is quite strenuous. The terrain is hilly, very muddy from the frequent ranfalls, and is covered in dense vegetation. Each group of gorillas has a territory of about 6 km from side to side. It can take hrs locating a group as they are constantly on the move. The gorillas are used to tourists and tolerate their presence although visitors are not allowed to get closer than 5 metres, not to use flashes for photographs, to talk in whispers and to limit the length of the visit. If a gorilla becomes threatening it is advisable not to run away, or act aggressively in return,

A Day In The Life Of A Gorilla

Gorillas get up at about 0600. However, if it is cloudy (and it mostly is in the Birunga Mountains) they sleep in. They are slow starters, and it takes them a while to get going on the main business of the day, which is food. There are over a hundred edible plants in the mountains, but they are fussy eaters, and turn up their somewhat flattened noses at all but twenty-nine. Some of their preferred delicacies, such as stinging nettles, are not that popular with other mountain creatures. They don't drink and rely on the plants for fluid intake. In fact they don't much care for water at all, and will never cross rivers or streams.

Gorillas are fairly sociable and like to hang out in a gang of around a dozen, but it might be as few as a couple, or as many as thirty. The boss is a silverback, an adult male whose coat has gone grey across the back. He will weigh around 180 kilos (400 pounds, over 28 stones), with the females half his size. The other males are allowed to stay in the group only at the indulgence of the silverback.

Around 0800, the whole entourage is usually on the move, trailing behind the silverback as he browses leisurely from plant to plant, covering a kilometre in about 7 hrs.

At 1000 they knock off for a break, doze a bit, and the kids romp around. Communication is through a range of sounds, gestures, and facial expressions. The females sometimes squabble among themselves. The silverback is intimidating enough when roused to ensure that the gorillas have no enemies among the mountain creatures. When aggravated, the silverback starts hooting, draws himself up to his full height, beats his chest loudly, roars, screams, bares his teeth and charges. He winds down after this exertion by beating the ground with his fists.

After about 4 hrs of relaxation they get under way again, pressing on a bit more in the afternoon, finally calling it a day at about1700. They mooch around for about an hour until the silverback decides to hit the sack, breaking off a few leafy fronds which he flattens to make a bed. The rest get themselves organised in the same way, some making nests in the trees. Lights out at around 1800.

Nyirmachabelli
Dian Fossey And The Gorillas

Dian Fossey was born in San Francisco, USA, in 1932. Her parents divorced when she was 3, and she did not see her father again for another thirty years. Her mother remarried, but Dian never got on with her step-father. Tall, 6 foot one in height by the age of fourteen, she spent a lot of her leisure time horse-riding. She never felt she had a particularly happy childhood.

Poor grades in her early years at the University of California meant missing out on veterinary science, her first choice, and she graduated as an occupational therapist, specialising in working with handicapped children. In 1955 she started her first job at the Kosair Crippled Children's Hospital in Louisville, Kentucky.

In 1963, a friend took a holiday in Rhodesia (now Zimbabwe) and Dian was enthralled by the photographs she brought back. She borrowed US$8,000 and set off for Kenya, hired a safari guide, crossed into the Congo (now Zaire), climbed Mount Mikeno in Albert National Park (now Volcanoes National Park) and saw some of the 300 or so rare mountain gorillas that live there. Back in Louisville she wrote up an account of her visit for the local *Courier Journal*. Louis Leakey) was shown the article by Dian when he was in Louisville on one of his fund-raising lecture tours. He promised to raise money to send Dian to make a long-term study of the gorillas. There was one condition. As it was in a remote area, she had to have her appendix out before she went. Leakey got the cash from *National Geographic*, in Dec 1966 she left for Africa, and the legend of Dian Fossey began.

Primate study involves finding the subjects, getting them used to your presence ('habituating') and taking meticulous notes on what they are doing. In the early months it was not much fun up the mountain. It was cold, rained almost every

but to appear submissive.

There are 4 gorilla groups in the mountains that have been habituated for visiting. For the 2 smaller gorillas groups, known as Group 9 (7 gorillas) and Group 11 (11 gorillas), there is a limit of 6 visitors a day. For the 2 larger groups, Group 13 (16 gorillas) and SUSA (30 gorillas), the limit is 8 visitors a day. The SUSA group involves starting out at 0530. Visits to the other groups start at 0800.

Many visitors go with a tour company, such as Rwanda Tours, see page 510, who take responsibility for all the arrangements.

However, it is possible to go more cheaply if you go independently. Reservations to visit the park are compulsory and can be made at the ORTPN (Office Rwandais du Tourisme et des Parc Nationaux) in Kigali. A visit costs about US$126 per person, (US$95 for 15-18 year olds or students with proof of age or status) including the cost of a compulsory guide, and park entry. Porters are available at a cost of US$2 for the day. You will also need to stay 2 nights in Ruhengeri as well as taking food with you for the visit.

Numbers are restricted, which means there are often waiting lists to make visits, especially during the European summer vacation period, Jun to Sep. However, cancellations are not infrequent and it is often possible to join a group if you arrive at the park headquarters before 0800. Children under 15 are not allowed.

Once a reservation has been made in Kigali, it is necessary to arrive at the park headquarters between 0700 and 0800 with the permit. The gorilla tour is scheduled to start at 0900. It is best to day making the tracks through the thick vegetation into heavy mud, and the accommodation was a small tent. In the course of the next thirteen years, Dian Fossey was interned by Congolese soldiers, who, she claimed, repeatedly raped her; expelled from her original site on the Congo side of the Virungas and forced to relocate at Karisoke on the Rwandan side; had a brief fling with a married photographer; had a 3-year affair with another married photographer; and had 2 abortions for fear that motherhood would interfere with her work. Several thousand hrs of gorilla contact were logged, culminating in Dian eventually being touched by a gorilla, leading later to her fondling and hugging them. She registered for a Doctorate at Cambridge University, and became a world-recognised authority on primate research.

Never easy to get along with, Dian fell out with many who came to study at Karisoke. She ate alone in the evenings, smoked heavily, and by 1974 was drinking a case of whisky a week. Her bitter enemies were the poachers who killed gorillas to sell their skulls. Only a shoot-to-kill policy, she thought, would deter them. As it was, several poachers did get shot, though not fatally. Into the bargain Dian killed the cattle of poachers, whipped the poachers' genitals with stinging nettles, smeared them with gorilla dung, spat on them, and made mock preparations for executions. In May 1978 she was fined US$600 by a Rwandan court for torturing a poacher.

In 1979, Dian Fossey took a break from Karisoke to be visiting Professor at Cornell University and to write her book, *Gorillas in the Mist*. She returned to Karisoke in 1983. On 26 Dec 1985, an intruder forced an entry into her cabin and killed her with a machete blow to the head.

Dian Fossey is buried among the gorilla graves on the mountain at Karisoke. The headstone is engraved **NYIRMACHABELLI** – 'woman who lives alone in the mountains'.

take a motor taxi (motorcycle ride) from Ruhengeri. Alternatively, it is possible to camp for the night outside the park. Light clothing, some waterproof cover against rain, and stout footwear are advisable.

If you intend to visit the SUSA group, it is necessary to pay the park entry fee and show your permit the day before the visit. You will then need to be at the Gashinya entry point by 0530. There is a minibus from Ruhengeri to Busoyo which is a 7 km walk from Gashinya. A better alternative is to take a motor taxi from Ruhengeri.

Other activities

Apart from sightseeing tours to meet the gorillas, it is possible to organise other treks in the volcanoes. Entrance to the Park is US$16 ($8 for 15-18s or students; US$4 for members of a school party), and the valid for 4 days. The treks are through magnificent tropical vegetation. They can take from a few hrs to a number of days and hiring a guide is compulsory. It is forbidden to cut trees, or damage the vegetation and fires are only permitted in designated camping areas.

Among the more popular treks are: **Visoke** (3,711m), return trip take 6-7 hrs from Parking Bisoke. **Lake Ngezi** (3,000m), return trip takes 3-4 hrs from Parking Bisoke and is one of the easier treks. At the right time of day, it is possible to see a number of different animals coming to the lake to drink. **Karisimbi** (4,507m), return trip takes 2 days. This is the tallest of the volcanoes. At about 3,800m there is a platform topped with extinct volcanic chimneys, each of which has formed a pool. The view from the top looks out over Rwanda, S Zaire and Uganda to the N.

The summit is sometimes snow-covered, so warm clothes and a good sleeping bag are important as the overnight hut is at 3,660m. **Sabinyo** (3,634m), return trip takes 5-6 hrs from the park headquarters at Kinigi. **Gahinga** and **Muhabara** (3,474m and 4,127m), return trips take 2 days from Gasiza.

• **Where to stay and eat** D *Chalet accommodation.* About 100m from the park headquarters. There are 4 chalets, each with 5 beds and a fireplace. Clean sheets are provided, but you will have to buy fuelwood. The communal bathrooms. Bar. Basic restaurant.

• **Camping** Near the chalet site. Use of facilities at chalets. Own tent required.

• **Transport** There is no public transport from Ruhingeri the Park so your options are either to walk, hitch or take a motor taxi (motorcycle ride) unless you have your own transport. It is possible to get a minibus part of the way to the Gashinya park entrance if you are visiting the SUSA gorillas.

Parc National de l'Akagera

Located on the E of Rwanda by the Tanzania border, this is a wildlife park with 3 distinctive environments. Open savannah dotted with acacia trees is broken up by a chain of low mountains running the length of the park with a huge swampy area running along the Tanzanian border. The park is large, covering 285,000 ha and is one of the least visited but one of the most interesting of the wildlife parks of East Africa.

The diversity of the environment means that there is a huge variety of animals. Elephants, hippopotami, giraffes, rhinoceros, baboons, buffalo, zebra, impala, roan antelope, warthogs, lions, leopards, hyenas, and crocodiles all can be found here.

An interesting way of exploring the park is to combine a sightseeing safari in a 4WD vehicle with a mini cruise on Lake Ihema. A motorboat can take a maximum of 12 people and they are able to glide over the open channels of floating 'praries' covered with Nile grass and water lilies.

Lake Ihema the largest lake, to the S of the park and **Lake Hago** in the centre can both be explored by hiring a boat. There are a number of interesting aquatic birds like the red and black gonolek or the white-shouldered warblers as well as the more common waders such as the ibis, herons, and cormorants. There are also many animals which live in this marshy area of the park including the sitatunga, a large antelope which is particularly well suited to the marshy conditions with very long hooves which can spread out preventing it from sinking. These exceptionally timid animals hide in the reeds leaving just the tips of their muzzles above the water.

The main attractions of the park are the big herds of zebras, antelopes (impalas and topis) and buffalo which roam the wide open spaces of the **Kirara plain**. Impalas are very common, living in groups of 20 or so females, protected by a male. Less common types of antelope are the eland, waterbuck and ourebies as well as their predators, lions and leopards. The elephants are the descendants of about 20 which were introduced here in 1975 from other parts of the country. The giraffes were donated by the Kenyan government.

Various types of monkeys include doguera baboons and several species of cercopithecids (silver monkeys), though these are more numerous in the Nyungwe Forest, see page 524.

Park information

Entry fees are US$20 per person plus US$10 for a car or US$12 for a 4WD vehicle. The best entry points to the park are Gabiro Hotel in the N or Akagera Hotel in the S. It is not necessary to hire a guide to take you round the park, though they can be useful if you are particularly keen to see the more elusive animals. You can buy park maps at ORTPN (Office Rwandais du Tourisme et des Parc Nationaux) in Kigali, see page 510. It is possible to persuade the hotels in the park to sell you petrol.

It is unwise to swim in the lakes in the park, not only because of the crocodiles but also because of the risk of contracting bilharzia, see page 29.

• **Where to stay** **A** *Hotel Akagera*, BP 1322, Kigali, T 67250. Inside the park nr Lake Ihema. 67 rooms, bar, restaurant, swimming pool, boutiques, tennis, boat rentals for the lake. **A** *House de Gabiro*, BP 1322, Kigali, T 65047. At the N entrance to the park. 60 rooms, bar, restaurant, swimming pool, boutiques. **B** *Ranch Mpanga*, T 73234. On Lakes Cyambwe and Rwampanga, S of the park. 42 rooms. **D** *Gite du Lac Mihindi*. Simple shelter accommodation close to the lake.

• **Camping** *Plage Hippo*, halfway up the park close to the Tanzanian border. Bar restaurant, tennis, water sports. There are also campsites attached to the hotels and designated camp sites at various points around the park. There are no facilities at the designated sites, but usually some staff are around which make them a bit safer.

• **Places to eat** The restaurants in the hotels

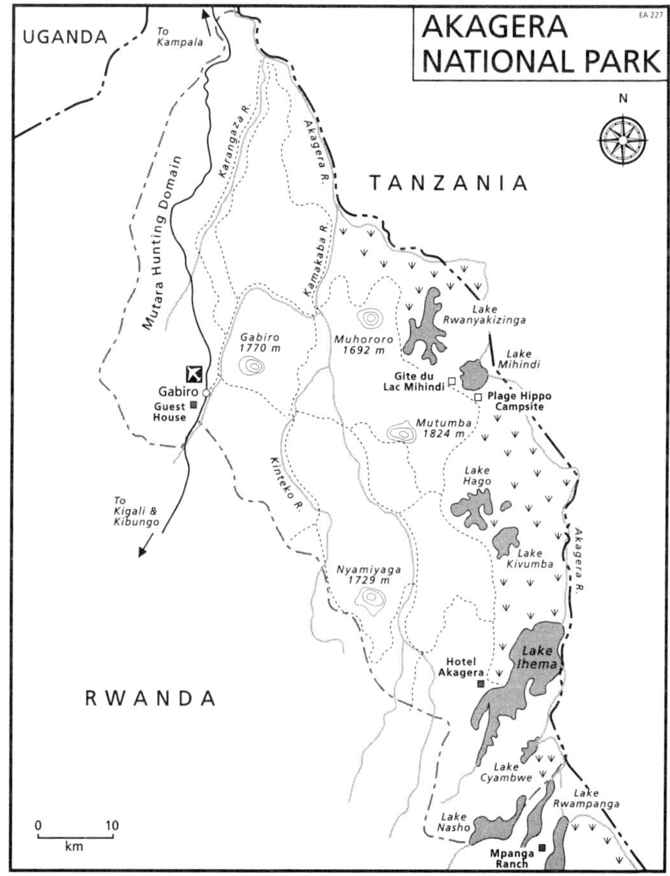

The Origin Of Death

Legend has it that when time began in ancient Rwanda there were 4 brothers, Lightning, the King, Imaana (a spirit), and Death. Three of the brothers received gifts from the Creator. But Death was frustrated. He wanted blood, but his brothers thwarted him by preventing him having any access to beings that would bleed.

Death complained to the Creator, who said Death could have anything relinquished by his brothers. However, Death went further than this, and began to take liberties with the possessions of his brothers. The brothers decided to kill Death, and they chased him to a field where he took refuge in the folds of the dress of an old woman working there. Lightning wished to kill the old women to get at Death. But Imaana prevented him, saying it was wrong to kill the old woman, and that Death would have to emerge sometime and then they would be able to slay him. But Death was content to stay in the folds of the old woman's dress, where he had access to a being with blood at last. In due course, the old woman transmitted death to her children, and they, in their turn, took it to every corner of the the earth.

in the park are all quite expensive as everything needs to be brought in. An alternative is bring all your own food and drink with you.

• **Transport** You will need to organise your own transport to go into the park or go on an organised safari. If you go independently, travel arrangements to the park need to be booked in Kigali. You can hire a car or arrange a safari trip at *Rwanda Travel Service*, T 2210, *Hotel des Diplomates*, 45 Blvd de la Revolution, *Umubano Tours Agency*, T 2176), BP 1160 and *Agence Solliard*, T 5660) 2 ave de la Republique.

Mutara Hunting Reserve

The Mutara hunting reserve is adjacent to the Akagera National Park. Strictly controlled hunting is authorised for a specific period of the year. In order to use the reserve it is necessary to have a valid arms licence from your own country. The season for big game hunting is from 1 Nov to 31 Mar. Quotas are set for hunters: one single animal of a species may be shot with a maximum of 4 animals. You will need to obtain a licence to kill animals from the Office du Tourisme Rwandais et des Parcs Nationaux in Kigali. Apart from the cost of the licence, there is a slaughter tax to be paid on each animal, and a guide must be hired. Hunting from a vehicle is not permitted.

Hunting is an expensive and specialised activity. Safari companies able to make all the arrangements on your behalf are: *Andrews*, rue du Lac Rwero, T 72355, Kigali; *Umubano Tours*, BP 1160, T 82176, Kigali; *Le Zebre* ave de la Paix, T 73589, Kigali.

• **Where to stay A** *Guest House de Gario*, T 65047. 60 rooms, bar, restaurant, swimming pool, boutiques.

Nyungwe Forest Reserve

This natural forest covering 970 sq km of land by the Burundi border is the biggest and one of the last virgin forests at high altitude in Africa. It has been protected by the Rwandan authorities since 1988 in conjunction with the US Peace Corps, and The New York Zoological Society in order to study the ecology of the forest, promote ecologically sound tourism and persuade people of its value. The forest rises in tiers from 1,700m to 3,000m offering splendid views out to Lake Kivu or to the volcanoes of the Birunga, in the far distance, to the N.

Conserving the forest is becoming an increasingly difficult task as the country's ever increasing population searches for new land to cultivate and timber for construction or fuel. In order to try to reduce the pressure on the land for timber, the Rwandan authorities have developed a managed section to the N of the forest where trees are cut for timber and replaced with rapid growing species like pines, cypresses or acacias.

Conducted tours to see groups of black and white colobus monkeys, in packs numbering up to 300, are the main attraction of the forest. There is a wide variety of other species such as chimpanzees, cercocebus, golden monkeys and silver monkeys and Hoest's monkey. Besides monkeys, the forest is home to several types of antelopes, leopards, servals and porcupines as well as the occasional elephant. There are also over 250 different species of birds in the forest. For botanists there are numerous varieties of wild orchids.

Entrance to the forest is free. Walking is the best method of seeing it, with stout

walking boots and a waterproof windbreaker. Nyungwe Forest Conservation Project, BP 363, T 37193 Cyangugu, for further information.

• **Where to stay** The nearest hotels are in **Butare** (see page 516) or **Cyangugu** (page 517). Butare is 90 km and Cyangugu 55 km from the Nyungwe Forest, both on excellent paved roads.

• **Camping** *Uwinka HQ* Toilet facilities. Wood and charcoal is for sale here but it is necessary to bring everything else: tent, sleeping bag, cooking equipment, food and water and warm clothes. There is also a camp site at *Karamba* about 14 km towards Cyangugu from Uwinka.

• **Places to eat** There is nowhere in the forest to get food or drink, and you need to bring everything with you.

• **Travel around the forest** By car Roads are sealed making driving through the forest possible without a 4WD.

On foot Hiking is permitted through the forest and unguided walks are possible along marked paths. There are 6 trails ranging from 1 km to 9 km. Guided tours leave from the **Uwinka Information Centre** 3 times every day at 0900, 1100 and 1400. The tour costs about US$6.50 and takes an hour. Rwanda Tours, see page 510, also organise walking excursions.

• **Transport** The Nyungwe Forest lies between Butare and Cyangugu. Minibuses leave from **Kigali** going through Butare to the forest throughout the day. The Uwinka headquarters are just past the 90 km post marked by a board of a black and white colobus monkey. The journey from Kigali takes about 4 hrs. From **Cyangugu** take a minibus towards Butare and get off at Uwinka. The journey takes about an hour.

INFORMATION FOR VISITORS

Contents

WARNING: The violence which has affected Rwanda for much of 1994 continues to make the country unsafe to visit. For the latest situation, you are strongly advised to contact your embasssy before your departure.

Before you go

Entry requirements

● **Visas**

Visas are required by everyone except German nationals. It is best to apply for them in East Africa to avoid red tape. Visas are valid for one month, cost about US$10 and require 2 photographs. It generally takes 24 hrs for the visa to be issued. It is useful to note that you have to give the exact date you intend to enter Rwanda on your visa, as it is only valid from that date. It is sensible to apply for a multiple-entry visa (no extra cost) because you may need to passing through the country between Burundi and Zaire and transit visas cost US$10 for 12 hrs.

It is possible to extend your visa in Kigali, at the immigration office on rue du Commerce next to the Air France office. This costs US$17. It is also possible to extend a transit visa in Kigali (for 7 days) though this costs US$40.

You will not be required to show how much money you are carrying, nor are you required to have a letter of introduction from your embassy and onward ticket.

● **Vaccinations**

A cholera vaccination certificate is compulsory for entry or exit by air, and some officials ask for one from those entering overland. You will also need proof of inoculation against yellow fever. It is best to get the shot at least 8 to 10 days before departure in case of any possible reaction to the vaccine. It is wise to take precautions against malaria in Rwanda, though generally, because of the altitude, mosquitoes are not a problem, see Health Notes see page 27.

● **Rwandan representation overseas**

There are Rwandan embassies in Brussels (Belgium), Ottawa (Canada), Cairo (Egypt), Addis Ababa (Ethiopia), Paris (France), Bonn (Germany), Abidjan (Ivory Coast), Tokyo (Japan) and Washington DC (USA).

Visas for travel to Rwanda can be obtained from the following embassies in East Africa: **Burundi**, 24 ave Zaire, Bujumbura, T 26865, next to the Zaire Embassy. Office hrs are Mon-Fri 0800-1600 and Sat from 0800-1130. **Kenya**, 12th floor, International House, Mama Ngina St, Nairobi, T 334 341. Office hrs are Mon-Fri 0830-1230 and 1400-1700. There is also a consulate in Mombasa. **Tanzania**, 32 Upanga Rd, Dar es Salaam, T 20115. Visas cost US$20. Office hrs are Mon-Fri 0800-1430 and Sat 0800-1200. **Uganda**, 2nd Floor, Baumann House, Parliament ave, Kampala, T 241 105. Opening hrs are Mon-Fri 0830-1230 and 1430-1700. Visa applications are accepted in the morning only. The cost is US$2.20 for a one week visa, US$4.30 for one month and

US$8.60 for 2 to 6 months all payable in local currency. **Zaire** There are no Rwandan consulates in E Zaire though it appears that Rwandan transit visas are available at the border for RFr 1600. It is possible to get a visa from Kinshasa. It is also possible to get a tourist visa from the Belgian Consultate in Goma for about US$17, though this takes 2 weeks to issue and you have to leave your passport with them. Regulations change constantly, so do not rely on this possibility.

● Overseas representation in Rwanda

See entries under Kigali, see page 509.

● Tourist information

Maps of Rwanda from Office Rwandaise du Tourisme et des Parcs Nationaux (ORTPN) in Kigali, see page 510. A more detailed and readable map on a scale of 1:250,000 is available from Service de Cartographie du Rwanda-Mirenamica, 15 ave des Grands Lacs, Kigali, T 5771/6757.

Film is expensive and choice is limited. If you intend to photograph the gorillas it is useful to remember that the forest where they live is often very dark, so normal film will produce disappointing results.

Do not take photographs of any government or military buildings such as banks, post offices, bridges, the border posts, barracks, prisons etc. Your film will be confiscated and possibly your camera too.

When to go

● Best time to visit

Rwanda is most pleasant in its 2 dry seasons, Jun to early Sep and mid-Dec to mid-Feb.

Health

● Staying healthy

(See Health Information, page 21.) It is wise to take anti-malaria medication. It is best not to drink the water unless it is boiled or you use sterilisation tablets.

HIV/AIDS is a serious problem in Rwanda, and though attempts have been made to ensure a safe blood supply, there is a risk from a transfusion outside Kigali. If you need injections, take your own disposable syringes.

There are certain parts of Lake Kivu where it is can be dangerous to swim as volcanic gases are released from the bottom and, in the absence of wind, can to collect on the surface of the lake and cause asphyxia. Check local advice.

Bilharzia can be a risk on the shores of Lake Kivu and other lakes in the country where there is a lot of reedy vegetation, or in slow moving rivers.

Money

● Banks

Are open from Mon-Fri from 0700-1200 and 1400-1800 and on Sat from 0800-1200.

● Credit cards

These are generally only accepted in the larger (and more expensive) hotels in Kigali and Gisenyi. The most useful cards are American Express, Diners Club and Visa.

Can be used at the major hotels, travel agents, airlines and car hire. The most useful cards are Diners, American Express and Visa.

● Currency

The unit of currency in Rwanda is the Rwandan france (RFr) which is divided into 100 centimes.

Bank commissions are high at about US$3-5 per transaction to exchange traveller's cheques, thus it is wise to carry cash to Rwanda. Bank rates are generally below black market rates. Banks are open from Mon-Fri from 0700-1200 and 1400-0600 and on Sat from 0800-1200. If you are only carrying travellers' cheques you could have problems exchanging them into cash outside these hrs. Some traders may exchange them in Kigali, though it is unlikely in other parts of the country. The large hotels will normally change money 24 hrs, but at an unfavourable rate.

You are likely to find many people willing to exchange US dollars or other hard currencies for cash in the country. You will find quite a few people around the petrol station on the main street in Gisenyi. The Kigali street market has many individuals willing to exchange your cash or traveller's cheques for Rwandan currency. You may be able to change your money on the minibus into Kigali.

Getting there

You can only enter Rwanda by air or by road as there is no railway service, and though there are river ferries operating on both the Rwandan and the Zaire sides of Lake Kivu, they only connect towns on their own sides of the lake.

● Air

International airlines flying into Rwanda are: Aeroflot, Air Burundi, Air France, Air Tanzania,

AirZaire, Ethiopian Airlines, Kenya Airways and Sabena. As there are no charter flights to Rwanda, travel by air is expensive. The cheapest route to Rwanda is an excursion ticket to Kenya and a connecting flight to Rwanda.

Tour operators A few specialised tour operators offer package trips to Rwanda which can save time and money such as: ***Nouvelles Frontieres***, 87 Boulevard de Grenelle, 75738 Paris, France, T 42 73 10 64. ***Explorator***, 16 Place de la Madeleine, 75008 Paris, T 42 66 66 24). ***Uniclam Voyages***, 63, rue Monsieur-le-Prince, 75006 Paris, T 43 29 12 36). ***Terres d'Aventures***, 16 rue Saint-Victor, 75005 Paris, T 43 29 94 50). For other agencies specialising in discount fares see page 12.

NB: Air tickets bought in Rwanda for international flights tend to be very expensive.

● Road

Burundi There are 2 main routes between Rwanda and Burundi, at **Kayanza** leading to Butare, and **Bugarama** in the far SW corner of Rwanda leading to Cyangugu. There are daily minibuses from Bujumbura, the capital of Burundi, to Kayanza and from there you can get a minibus to the border. There is little delay crossing the border There is an infrequent minibus service from the Rwandan side of the border to Butare.

Crossing at Bugarama, there is no shortages of minibuses along the first part of this route, from Bujumbura to Rugombo. From Rugombo to the border is about 20 km, and minibuses are less frequent. There are bicycle taxis for transport between the border posts.

Tanzania To get into Rwanda from Tanzania you can take a bus from Mwanza leaving at 0400 to Ngara, and get off at Lusahanga. Lusahanga is an overnight truck stop and it is easy to get a lift over the Tanzania/Rwanda border and into the country. The first town in Rwanda is Rusumo where there is a daily bus into Kigali.

Uganda There are 2 main crossing points at **Katuna** or **Cyanika**. There are frequent daily minibuses between Kabale in Uganda and the Katuna border post the trip taking an hour. There are frequent minibuses to Kigali from Katuna until mid afternoon and they take about 2 hrs.

The other crossing is from Kisoro in Uganda to Ruhengeri in Rwanda via Cyanika. This route is not as busy and it may be harder to get a ride from here. There is an hour time difference between Uganda and Rwanda, Uganda being an hour ahead.

Zaire The 2 main crossing points are between Goma and **Gisenyi** at the N end of Lake Kivu and Bukavu and **Cyangugu** at the S end of the lake. These borders are open between 0600 and 1800 for non-Africans, and from 0600 and 2400 for Africans. There are 2 border points between Goma and Gisenyi both along the Poids Lourds crossing. If you cross at the main road N of Gisenyi you will need to take a taxi or walk (approx 2 km) to the border, and then take a taxi into Gisenyi (about 2 km). The other route is along the sealed road by the lake shore. Minibuses are available to take you from the border to Gisenyi.

If you are crossing from the S end of Lake Kivu into Rwanda, you will need to either take a taxi or walk (approx 3 km) from Bukavu to the border. The 2 border posts are only 50m apart. Take a motor taxi (motorcycle ride) to the Cyangugu bus stand.

When you arrive

● Airline Offices

These are listed under Kigali, see page 509.

● Hours of business

Administrative offices open from Mon-Fri from 0700-1200 and 1400-1700 and on Sat from 0700-1200.

● Official time

Rwanda time is GMT plus 2 hrs

● Shops

Open Mon-Sat from 0700-1800. Boutiques in urban areas are often open until 2200 at night. Traditional markets stay open all day.

Where to stay

● Hotels

There are a number of class A hotels in the country particularly in Kigali, in the national parks and at Gisenyi by Lake Kivu. These hotels offer bar and restaurant facilities as well as a swimming pool, tennis courts, boutiques

● Hostels

These provide dormitory-style accommodation for about US$5 without food. Single and double rooms are sometimes available. The conditions are likely to be spartan but clean. Because of the dearth of cheap and reasonable accommodation, the mission hostels are often full, particularly at weekends. Usually they close at 2200.

HOTEL CLASSIFICATIONS

- **A+** Over US$100 a night. International standards and decor, air conditioning, self contained rooms, swimming pool, restaurants, bars, business services.
- **A** US$40-100. First class standards, air-conditioning, attached bathrooms, restaurants and bars, swimming pool.
- **B** US$20-40. Tourist class, comfortable with air conditioning or fans, attached barthrooms, restaurant, bar, public rooms.
- **C** US$10-20. Budget, fans, shared bathroom facilities.
- **D** US$5-10. Guest house, no fan, shared bathroom, cold water.
- **E** Under US$5. Basic guest house, simple bed, no soap or towels, no wardrobe, shared bathroom facilities, erratic cold water supply, no fans or mosquito nets.

● Camping

Casual camping outside official sites is officially forbidden in Rwanda, but if you are off the beaten track, you are unlikely to be challenged. Camping is a useful option for the budget traveller in the national parks where the cost of hotels is prohibitive. It is best to bring your own tent as they are not always for hire, and renting them is expensive. Toilets and shower facilities are generally, but not always, available at camp sites. It is wise not to leave valuables in the tent unguarded, and sleep with them under your pillow.

Food and drink

● Food

Food varies enormously around the country. In the international hotels or good restaurants in Kigali or Gisenyi high standard French cuisine is offered, albeit expensive. In the food stalls and smaller restaurants a wide range of food is offered at similar prices to other parts of East Africa. Meat is always considerably more expensive than vegetable meals. Fish along some of the lakes, particularly Lake Kivu, is good. Local specialities such are *capitaine* or *isambaza*. Some of the specialities of Rwandan cuisine are dishes such as *sombe* with *isambaza* – Lake Kivu sardines with pounded manioc leaves, or *umutsima*, bananas, pumpkin, cabbage and spinach dish.

● Drink

Locally produced beers (Primus, Mutzig and Guinness) are considerably cheaper than the imported beers, and are of good standard. One of the main national drinks is banana wine which is available throughout the country and is produced by OVIBAR (Office de Valorisation Industrielle de la Banane). A local beer made from sorghum is made in the rural areas.

EATING CLASSIFICATIONS

- **♦♦♦♦** Over US$10 for a meal. A 3-course meal in a restaurant with pleasant decor. Beers, wines and spirits available.
- **♦♦♦** US$5-10 for a meal. Two courses, not including alcohol, reasonable surroundings.
- **♦♦** US$2-5 for a meal, probably only a single course, surroundings spartan but adequate.
- **♦** Under US$2. Single course, often makeshift surroundings such as a steet kiosk with simple benches and tables.

Getting around

● Air

Air Rwanda flies from Kigali to Gisenyi in the N twice a week and Kamembe nr Cyangugu in the S, 6 times a week. There are also flights connecting Gisenyi and Kamembe. Offices Kigali, Butare, Gisenyi, and Kamembe.

● Road

The roads in Rwanda are, on the whole, superb and the only unsurfaced roads in the country are those to Kibuye on the shore of Lake Kivu. There are well-maintained minibuses serving all main routes in the country. Destinations are displayed in the front window of the bus and fares are fixed. Bus travel tends to be between dawn and 1500. There are also a number of government buses which are cheaper than minibuses but they take longer and do not run on all routes.

● Lake Ferry

There is a small modern motor ferry which covers the route from Cyangugu to Kibuye and Gisenyi. It leaves Cyangugu, going N, on Mon and Thu at 0600, Kibuye at 0900 and arrives at Gisenyi around 1200. On Wed and Sat it departs from Gisenye, sailing S, at 0600, Kibuye at 0900, and arrives at Cyangugu at 1200.

● Car hire

Europcar offices in the *Meridien Hotel*, Kigali

and *Hotel des Milles Collines*, Kigali. TAT *Hotel des Milles Collines*, Kigali.

Other local transport

Taxis are avaliable at the main hotels and at the bus stands. **Taxi-motors** are are motorcycles with the passenger on the pillion and luggage balanced in front of the driver. **Bicycles** can be rented in the main towns.

Communications

Language

The official languages of the country are Kinyarwanda which is spoken everywhere and French.

Postal services

Post can be sent from the major hotels as well as post offices. Stamps can usually be bought at the large hotels.

Telephone services

The telephone service has been fully automatic since 1988. This means you can make your own domestic or international calls from the major hotels or from the post office in Kigali. Overseas telephone calls are expensive, and roughly triple the post office price if made from a large hotel.

Entertainment

The US Embassy, Blvd de la Revolution, T 75601, provides an information service for special events.

Cinema

There is one cinema in Kigali at Blvd de la Revolution opposite the Banque Commerciale du Rwanda. The Centre Culturel Francais often puts on films in the afternoons and evenings.

Music and dance

In Kigali or Nyanza, there are regular performances by **Intore**, the National Ballet of traditional dancers accompanied by local drummers.

Radio

There are 2 radio stations. **Radiodiffusion de la Republique Rwandaise** is a state-controlled radio station and broadcasts daily in Kinyarwanda, Swahili, French and English. There is also the **Deutsche Welle Relay Station Africa** which broadcasts daily in German, English, French, Hausa, Swahili, Portuguese and Amharic.

Sport (participant)

Tennis, **golf** and **swimming** are available in the large hotels. Running Kigali Hash, see page 510. Big game hunting is allowed in the Hunting Domain of Mutara NW of Akagera National Park, **see page 524**.

Television

As of 1994 there was no television service, though one is planned.

Holidays and festivals

1 Jan	New Year's Day
28 Jan	Democracy Day
Mar/Apr	Good Friday; Easter Mon
1 May	Labour Day
May	Ascension; Whit Mon
1 Jul	National Day
5 Jul	Peace and National Unity Day
1 Aug	Harvest Festival
15 Aug	Assumption
8 Sep	Culture Day
25 Sep	Kamarampaka Day
1 Nov	All Saints' Day
25 Dec	Christmas Day

Many shops and offices close between 1-5 Jul.

Further reading

Wildlife

Fossey, D (1983) *Gorillas in the Mist*, Boston: Houghton Mifflin. A rather selective account of the work in Rwanda on the gorilla project. Hayes, HTP (1991) *The Dark Romance of Dian Fossey*, London: Chatto & Windus. A fairly revealing account of the life of the legend.

People

Taylor, CC (1992) *Milk, Honey and Money: Changing Concepts in Rwandan Healing*, Washington and London: Smithsonian Institution Press. Anthropological study of traditional Rwandan society.

Guide

Klotchkoff, J-C (1990) *Rwanda Today*, Paris: Les Editions du Jaguar. Guide, notable for some marvellous photographs which really capture the special atmosphere of Rwanda.

BURUNDI

CONTENTS

MAPS

INTRODUCTION

Burundi is a small landlocked country between Central and Eastern Africa. Tourism is relatively undeveloped and consequently facilities for either the affluent holidaymaker or the budget traveller are limited. Tourism is further hampered by the recent outbreaks of violence in the country and the situation in nearby Rwanda. At the time of writing Burundi is calm and the capital, Bujumbura, is safe to visit, but there is anxiety that the violence in Rwanda will spill over. In normal times the country has a quite a bit to offer anyone who does visit it, particularly nature lovers.

Environment

Geography

The Republic of Burundi is small, only 27,834 sq km bordered by Zaire, Tanzania and Rwanda. Most of this tiny country is rolling plateau, 1500-2000m above sea level with a rich volcanic soil suitable for many different types of agriculture. A W backbone of mountains runs N into Rwanda and drops down into Lake Tanganyika, the N tip of which provides the only natural exit for an otherwise landlocked transportation system. To the E the land rises sharply to levels of around 1,800m above sea level in a range of mountains which stretches N into the much higher volcanoes mountains of Rwanda. The majority of the rest of the country is made up of a plateaux about 1,400-1,600m above sea level.

Climate

Burundi's climate is variable. The lower land around Lake Tanganyika is hot and humid with temperatures of around 30 degrees centigrade and the average temperature on the SW lake shore is 23 degrees. In the more mountainous regions of the country, the temperature falls to around 20 degrees. The rainy season lasts from Oct to Dec and from late Jan to May. Average rainfall throughout the country is 1200 millimetres per annum.

History

In common with its N neighbour, Rwanda, Burundi's territory today roughly corresponds with that of an ancient precolonial kingdom centred on the old capital of Gitega. The land was originally settled by the Twa. In about 1000 AD the Hutu arrived and finally

the Tutsi pastoralists moved in from Ethiopia and Uganda in the mid 16th century. The Tutsi gradually subjugated the Hutu and Twa in a feudal system headed by a king *(Mwami)* and princes *(Ganwa)*. Under this system the Hutu worked for the Tutsi and exchanged land in return for cattle, the symbol of wealth and status in Burundi. Unlike Rwanda, the relationship between the Tutsi and Hutu was stable, and intermarriage was common. However, this situation soon changed after European colonial intervention.

Struggles for power between the Tutsi lineages allowed German military rule to be imposed in the 1890's. The Germans governed both the Rwanda and Burundi territories from their headquarters in Dar-es-Salaam in Tanganyika. After WWI, Burundi ceased to be politically linked with Tanganyika, and became a Belgian administered Trusteeship Territory, mandated by the League of Nations and loosely connected to the Congo. Belgium retained this mandate under the United Nations after WW2.

The Belgian administration exploited the Tutsi elite's rule of Burundi, granting the *Mwami* and *Ganwa* wide ranging powers. The most significant aspect of this was the ability to determine access to education. This increased the inequality between the Tutsi and Hutu and increased tribal friction. The establishment of lucrative coffee plantations and the resulting accumulation of wealth among the Tutsi elite further exacerbated these tensions.

During the 1950's a nationalist organisation led by Prince Louis Rwagasore, a Tutsi, called the the Union Pour le Progres National (UPRONA) aimed to unite all groups and interests in the country. UPRONA won 58 of the 64 seats in the new national assembly during the first democratic elections in Jan 1962, but Rwagasore was assassinated later that year by a European. The absence of his unifying influence led to the emergence of open conflict between the Hutu and Tutsi in the country. Since then, Burundi's history has been stormy. From 1962-65 the country was ruled by the *Mwami*, Mwambutsa'IV who sought to ensure a proper balance of ethnic interests in government. However, tensions were common, resulting in the Hutu prime minister being assassinated in 1965 and Mwambutsa appointing a Tutsi prince in his place. Incensed by this, a faction of the Hutu attempted a coup but were unsuccessful.

The suppression of the Hutu-led coup was extremely violent resulting in virtually the entire Hutu political elite being massacred as well as thousands of other Hutus throughout the country. In 1966, Colonel Michel Micombero, a mixed Hutu-Tutsi, seized power and the monarchy was abolished. The government was ruled by a military junta representing a minority within the Tutsi, a leadership drawn from the S province of Tutsi-Hima.

Systematic exclusion of the Hutu from positions of responsibility in the state resulted in another abortive Hutu-led coup in Apr 1972. This occasioned a massive repression of Hutu, partly spontaneous, partly a planned genocide of all educated Hutu, by military and para-military forces. Most deaths occurred in May 1972, the total death toll mounting to around 200,000. Some 120,000 Hutu fled to neighbouring countries.

In Jul 1974 a new constitution was passed, stressing national unity and banning appeals, or reference, to ethnic differences. On 1 Nov 1976 Lieutenant Colonel Bagaza, a Tutsi, seized power in a bloodless coup as a result of the then president, Colonel Micombero dismissing all cabinet members. Bagaza attempted to encourage national reconciliation by introducing agrarian reforms whereby Tutsi overlords were compelled to hand over much of their land to the Hutu peasants who farmed it, and many refugees were encouraged to return. Moreover, feudal systems were abolished. A new constitution was established in 1981 trying to increase democratic participation in government and the first elections were held in 1982. Bagaza, the sole candidate for the presidency, was re-elected.

From 1984-1987 there was a sharp deterioration in the government's record on human rights, particularly with regard to religious freedom. Many church members were imprisoned ostensibly for criticising government restrictions on religious activities, and torture of prisoners was reported. In 1987 Bagaza was deposed by an army-led coup whilst he was out of the country. Major Buyoya, a Tutsi, was sworn in as the new president heading the Military Committee for National Salvation (CMSN).

The new regime did not differ much from Bagaza's except in allowing greater religious freedom. It still depended on the support of a small Tutsi elite. The Hutu still had a justified claim for fuller participation in public life.

In 1988 tribal tensions erupted in the N of the country when groups of Hutu slaughtered hundreds of Tutsi. The Tutsi-dominated army was called in and the subsequent massacre of Hutu was similar to the massacre of 1972. The death toll was said to be in the region of 20,000, with more than 60,000 fleeing the region. Following this, Buyoya announced changes to the existing political system the most significant being that the council was now to be made up of equal numbers of Tutsi and Hutu representatives.

After the 1988 disturbances there were several attempted coups by hardline Tutsi activists. By Jan 1992 discontent had escalated resulting in a renewal of violence. Many people were killed, up to 3,000 by government security forces and tens of thousands have fled the area. Most of the troubles are based in the N W corner of the country.

In 1993, democratic elections led to the installation of Melchoir Ndadaye, as president, the first full Hutu to hold the post. Ndadaye's party, the Front for Democracy, formed the government. In Oct of that year Ndadaye, was assassinated by a group of Tutsi army officers. After an inconclusive period Cyprien Ntaryamira, a Hutu, and formerly Minister of Agriculture under Ndadaye was appointed President by the government in Feb 1994. In Apr the plane carrying Ntaryamira was shot down returning from talks in Tanzania, the President killed, and the country plunged into chaos.

Culture and life

The population of the country is estimated at 5.9 million and with a population density of 212 per sq km, Burundi is one of the most populated countries in Africa. The majority of its people are Hutu (85%) with a Tutsi minority (15%) and a few pygmoid Twa, similar to the ethnic make-up in its neighbour, Rwanda. The Hutu are characterised as being darker, round-faced and short in stature. The Tutsi have elongated faces, lighter skins and are tall and slim. Although there are many Burundians that can be recognised as belonging to one or other of the 2 main groups on the basis of their features, it is quite impossible to classify many others by their physical appearance.

As only the fertile, volcanic soils away from the arid and hot floor and margins of the rift valley can be cultivated, land pressure is severe. This has resulted in many Burundi migrating to neighbouring countries though this is becoming harder and harder as Tanzania, Rwanda and Zaire close their borders to migrants.

There is a divide between the culture of the predominantly cultivating Hutu and the pastoralist Tutsi. The government has made efforts to try to preserve local traditions which have been so important in influencing the music, dance, art and way of life of the people, and to set up institutions to display them. The Musee Vivant in Bujumbura and the National Museum in Gitega emphasise aspects unique to Burundi such as the *rugo*.

The rugo

The *rugo* is the traditional hut of the Tutsi. It is divided into sections and set in an enclosure. There is an entrance courtyard, leading into a central courtyard, at the end of which is the main dwelling hut. Behind the main dwelling is a rear courtyard. The entrance courtyard has a hut off it for guests, and another for the cattle herders as well as a manger holding grass for the cattle. The central courtyard will be where the cattle are herded for the night, and there is a rubbing post for them so they won't knock down the fencing instead. In the rear courtyard are 2 huts, one for children, and one for women. There are also enclosures for traditional religious ceremonies, grain stores and an enclosure for bathing. As the majority of Burundi people still live in rural areas working as farmers, the *rugo* is an important part of people's existence.

Crafts

The Twa have a reputation as potters, and examples of their work are to be seen in the museums in Bujumbura and Gitega and in the display of crafts for sale at the Tourist Office in Bujumbura.

Craft items that are particularly distinctive include large carved wooden figures; decorated shields; earthenware gourds; arrays of spears; lightshades woven from banana leaves and from bamboo slivers; and musical instruments, particularly those with flattened metal rods vibrating against a sounding board. Some of the larger carved wooden figures are very striking.

Modern Burundi

Politics

Since 1990 the political situation in Burundi has been turbulent. Following the visit of Pope John Paul II to the country in Sep 1990, international attention has focused on the government, UPRONA and its reaction to a draft charter which had been drawn up by members of a cross-section of people, representing all interest groups in the country, on national unity in the country between the Hutu and the Tutsi. This was to be the beginning of moves towards democracy in the country and multi-partyism. The charter was accepted by an electoral margin of 90%. By mid-1991 both Buyoya, the president and the prime minister Adrien Sibomana expressed hopes that a new constitution providing for a more democratic form of government would be approved by referendum in early 1992.

By Sep 1991, Buyoya presented the recommendations of the constitutional commission on the issue of national democracy. Among the recommendations were: the establishment of a parliamentary system to operate in conjunction with a presidential system, the introduction of proportional representation, freedom of the press, a declaration of human rights and a system of controlled multipartyism. This meant political groups could seek legal recognition so long as they fulfilled certain requirements such as commitment to the charter on national unity.

In Feb 1992, the government announced that a referendum was to be held in Mar to ascertain what support there was for the recommendations of the constitutional reform commission. It was said that if there was electoral endorsement of its recommendations, elections and a presidential poll would follow in 1993. The recommendations received the support of more than 90% of the voters.

By Apr 1992, 15 of the 25 ministerial posts in the government had been taken from Tutsis, and Hutus were appointed in their place. New legislation was developed relating to the creation of new political parties regardless of ethnic or regional origin, gender and religion and by Oct later that year, 8 political parties had received legal recognition. Later in Nov the National Electoral Preparatory Commission (NEPC) was set up by the president which was to be responsible for orchestrating the process of democratisation. The 33 member Commission was made up of members of all the political parties as well as members of the administrative, judicial, religious and military establishments.

In Feb 1993, President Buyoya announced that presidential and legislative elections would take place in Jun that year and that elections for local government officials would be held in Nov. The presidential poll was won by Melchior Ndadaye, a Hutu, of the Front pour la Democratie au Burundi – (FRODEBU) with 65% of the vote. FRODEBU also did well in the legislative elections with 71% of the votes and 65 of the 81 seats in the new legislature. Buyoya, the president and head of the party in power, UPRONA, received

32.5% of the votes and his party received 21% of the votes in the legislative elections. In Jul 1993 Ndadaye took his seat as president of Burundi, the first Hutu to head the country. The prime minister, Sylvie Kinigi, was a Tutsi.

With the assassination of Ndadaye in Oct 1993, and of his successor in Apr 1994, the progress that had been made toward a pluralist society has been dashed. The actions of a handful of Tutsi extremists has yet again started the cycle of ethnic violence and retaliation. It needs to be stressed that the Tutsi are by no means a united group, with various factions competing for political power.

Comparative Economic and Social Data

	Burundi	East Africa	Africa	Industrial countries
Population and land				
Population, mid year, millions, 1994	5.9	12.2	10.2	40.0
Urban Population, %, 1991	6	30.5	30	75
Population Growth Rate, % per year, 1980-86	2.7	3.1	3.1	0.8
Land Area, thou. sq. kilom.	28	486	486	1,628
Population Density, persons per sq km, 1994	165	24.2	20.4	24.3
Economy: production and income				
GDP, US$millions, 1986	1,090	2,650	3,561	550,099
GNP per head, US$, 1986	240	250	389	12,960
Economy: supply structure				
Agriculture, % of GDP, 1986	58	43	35	3
Industry, % of GDP, 1986	17	15	27	35
Services, % of GDP, 1986	25	42	38	61
Economy: demand structure				
Private Consumption, % of GDP, 1986	79	77	73	62
Gross Domestic Investment, % of GDP, 1986	17	16	16	21
Government Consumption, % of GDP, 1986	12	15	14	17
Exports, % of GDP, 1986	12	16	23	17
Imports, % of GDP, 1986	20	24	26	17
Economy: performance				
GDP growth, % per year, 1980-86	2.3	1.6	-0.6	2.5
GDP per head growth, % per year, 1980-86	-0.4	-1.7	-3.7	1.7
Agriculture growth, % per year, 1980-86	1.3	1.1	0.0	2.5
Industry growth, % per year, 1980-86	4.9	1.1	-1.0	2.5
Services growth, % per year, 1980-86	3.2	2.5	-0.5	2.6
Exports growth, % per year, 1980-86	11.6	0.7	-1.9	3.3
Imports growth, % per year, 1980-86	3.6	0.2	-6.9	4.3
Economy: other				
Inflation Rate, % per year, 1980-86	6.4	23.6	16.7	5.3
Aid, net inflow, % of GDP, 1986	15.7	11.5	6.3	-
Debt Service, % of Exports, 1984	19	18	20.6	-
Budget Surplus (+), Deficit (-), 1979	-0.9	-3.0	-2.8	-5.1
Education				
Primary, % of 6-11 group, 1985	53	62	76	102
Secondary, % of 12-17 group, 1985	4	15	22	93
Higher, % of 20-24 group, 1985	1	1.2	1.9	39
Adult Literacy Rate, %, 1980	25	41	39	99
Health and nutrition				
Life Expectancy, years, 1986	48	50	50	76
Calorie Supply, daily per head, 1985	2,233	2,111	2,096	3,357
Population per doctor, 1980	40,020	35,986	24,185	550

Notes: 'Africa' excludes South Africa. Dates are for the country in question, and do not always correspond with the Regional, African and Industrial Country averages.

The only positive features of the current situation is that they are the desperate actions of what is quite clearly a dying cause. The Tutsi die-hards cannot turn back the tide of change toward multiparty democracy that is sweeping across Africa, stoutly supported by an outside world that is no longer split into capitalist and communist ideological blocs. There will doubtless be a period of turmoil in Burundi following recent events, but stability will eventually return. This process will be hastened if the international community takes an active role in peace-keeping and in taking a tough line in making financial support conditional on multiparty democracy in a pluralistic setting.

Economics

GDP, estimated at US$1,035 million in 1991 is under half the regional average, and there are only 3 smaller economies in the region, Comoros, Djibouti and Seychelles. Income per head was estimated at US$210, which is about the regional average, and which places Burundi in the low-income category.

Agriculture generates 57% of GDP, and only Uganda in the region which has seen a reversion to subsistence production in the face of political instability, has greater reliance on farming. Industry accounts for 14% of GDP, close to the East African average, and services account for 27%. The small size of the service sector, which on average in East Africa provides 42% of GDP, is a reflection of low levels of income per head, and of the low degree of urbanisation.

Private consumption was about average for the region, taking about 76% of GDP while government consumption of 17% was 2% higher than average. Investment of 20% was reasonably high compared to regional and African averages of 16%. Exports generate 9% of GDP in 1987 and this is well below the regional average of 16%. Only Rwanda in the region has lower export dependence. Imports make up 21% of expenditure, which is just below the regional average.

Exports are mostly coffee, with 68% of earnings in 1987. There is a little cotton and tea, which represent 4% and 6% respectively. Imports are mostly industrial goods, with chemicals, manufactures and machinery making up 62% of the total. 14% of imports by value are fuels and 7% is food.

Debt service took up 38.5% of export earnings in 1987, and this is well above the regional average.

In 1981, 25% of the adult population were literate, and this is well below the East African average of 41%. In 1986, 59% of the relevant age group were in primary education, which is similar to the regional average. There was a 4% enrolment in secondary education, a sixth of the regional average, and only Rwanda and Tanzania had lower enrolments at this level. 1% were in higher education, and this is in line with the average for the region.

Life expectancy in 1987 was 49, almost the same as the East African average. Nutritional levels were on average better than elsewhere in the region, with the minimum calorie requirement just being met. Provision of doctors is slightly better than the regional average with one practitioner for every 21,000 people, though only Ethiopia, Rwanda and Uganda have a worse ratio.

Overall, Burundi's economic structure is one of a densely populated, small, low-income country, with a predominantly rural population relying heavily on agriculture to provide income, and on coffee to provide foreign exchange for manufactured goods. Educational and health provisions are poor, and reflect the low average standard of living.

Economic Performance

Burundi's GDP grew at 2.6% a year over the period 1980-87, and this was a growth rate over 60% faster than the average for the region. GDP per head fell at 0.2% a year over this period, and this was similar to the rest of the region.

From 1980-87 the agriculture sector showed a rate of growth of 1.7% a year, which is below the rate of increase of population. The industrial sector grew at 4.9% a year, and this was the fastest rate in mainland East Africa, though better growth was recorded in Mauritius and the Seychelles. The services sector grew at 3.5% and this was faster than the regional average.

Export volumes increased at an impressive 8.3% a year, and this compared well with the region. Imports expanded at 2.4% a year, and this was above the East African average. Aid inflows in 1987 were 15.3% of GDP, and this was above the level for the region. Aid contributed substantially to the level of investment achieved.

The budget deficit was 0.9% of GDP in 1983, and this was a third the size of the budget deficit on average in the region. Inflation averaged only 7.5% a year in the period 1980-87, and this was lower by about 2 thirds than was experienced in the region.

Overall, Burundi's economic performance has been good, with substantial aid inflows enabling high investment levels, a steady expansion of all sectors, and improving living standards. Budgetary policy has been cautious, and rate of inflation modest, with falls to under 5% inflation in some recent years.

Recent economic developments

Burundi received a US$25 mn stand-by loan and a US$24 mn structural adjustment loan from the IMF in Aug 1986. In addition there were funds from the IDA US$15 mn and from the World Bank's Special Facility for Sub-Saharan Africa US$17 mn in support of a structural adjustment programme. The programme involves a 28% increase in coffee producer prices, a reduction in public sector spending, reduction in tariffs and rises in interest rates. The Burundi franc has been allowed to depreciate steadily since 1982, when it was held fixed at BF90 = US$1. In 1994 it stood at BF250= US$1, and this represents an annual depreciation averaging about 10% a year. 1986 saw boom conditions in the economy with the increase in coffee prices, which, for part of the year, saw a doubling of prices. Coffee performance has been good, with a 20% increase in production in 1985, and a further improvement of 17% in 1987 with the high prices discouraging inter-cropping and leading to intensified harvesting.

Oil has been discovered under Lake Tanganyika, and Amoco of the US is conducting test drilling. The current low price of oil may prevent immediate exploitation as costs of lifting will be high.

Government expenditure emphasises infrastructural development, and major projects in hand include extending and up-grading the road network, installing new hydro-electric capacity and extending electrification.

Economic outlook

Burundi's economic prospects depend on the continued inflow of aid, the world price of coffee, and the ability of the regime to estabilish stability. Burundi can expect, by virtue of her low level of income per head, and the willingness of the government to undertake the structural reforms instigated by the IMF and World Bank adjustment programmes, to continue to receive substantial donor support, provided there is a determined effort to resolve the political conflicts. Over the longer-term, Burundi faces serious problems posed by land shortage exacerbated by the likelihood of faster rates of population growth. Prospects will depend heavily on the success of the structural adjustment programme in diversifying exports away from dependence on coffee, and continuing the expansion of the industrial sector.

BUJUMBURA

Bujumbura is on the NE corner of Lake Tanganyika, and has a population of 215,300. The central part of Bujumbura was at one time a picturesque area of grandiose public buildings built in the colonial era, set in wide boulevards with views across Lake Tanganyika onto the mountain ranges in Zaire opposite. It has now become rather dilapidated. The residences built up in the hills behind the town have glorious vistas. The beach on the shore of Lake Tanganyika is sandy, fringed with palms and very pleasant. The outer regions of the city are typical of African suburbs elsewhere, dusty, overcrowded shanty towns. Certain parts outside the centre are unsafe, even during the day, and it is wise to take a taxi except in the very centre of town.

Places of interest

There are 2 museums and a reptile park in the city all within a block of each other on the Ave du 13 Octobre leading down to the Cercle Nautique on the lake front. **Musée Vivant** is a reconstructed village of traditional Tutsi dwellings, the *rugo*, (see page 535). There are displays of traditional crafts and customs such as basket and pottery making and drumming as well as a photographic display. The museum is open daily from 0900-1200 and 1430-1700 except on Mondays when it is closed all day.

Musée de Geologie du Burundi is opposite the reptile park. It has a good collection of fossils. It is currently being rehabilitated, entry is free and it is open on weekdays from 0700-1200 and from 1400-1730.

Parc des Reptiles is adjacent to the Musee Vivant. This exhibits live reptiles and is open on Saturdays from 1400-1600 or by appointment at other times. Cobras, tree snakes, mambas, crocodiles and tortoises. Entrance US$2.

There is a **chimpanzee orphanage**, the Jane Goodall Institute, T 228430, located just N of the city. Two researchers run the establishment, and they will explain the work they are doing. There are usually about 15 chimps in residence.

Just outside town on the Zaire border is the **Rusizi Reserve**, see page 547.

Local information

● Where to stay

Price guide:
A+ Over US$100; **A** US$40-100;
B US$20-40; **C** US$10-20; **D** US$5-10; **E** Under US$5.

There are few cheap hotels in Bujumbura and if you do find one in normal times, it is likely to be full at weekends or if you arrive late in the day. **A** ***Novotel***, Chaussée du Peuple Murundi, BP 1015, T 22600, Tlx 600644. Best run and most comfortable hotel in town. a/c. Telephones. TV, including CNN. Swimming pool. Pleasant gardens. **A** ***Source du Nil***, Ave du Stade, BP 2072, T 2522, Tlx 5030 A little on the gloomy side. a/c Telephones. Swimming pool. **A** *Club du Lac*, BP 2784, T 2510, Tlx 5106. Off Chaussée d'Uvira on the lake side. Accommodation in thatched chalets. Pleasant restaurant adjoining the swimming pool You will have to pay to use the beach here if you are not a resident, but there is a nightclub.

B *Tanganyika*, Ave del la Plage, BP 109, T 24433. Pleasant location. Rather old-fashioned in style. **B** ***Doyen***, Chaussée du Peuple Murundi. Just N of *Novotel*. Some rooms a/c, others fans. Some rooms with own bathrooms.

C *Burundi Palace*, Blvd d'Uprona, BP 225, T 22910 . Opposite *Novotel*. The best value in the centre of town. Some rooms with a/c. Telephones. Rather grand art deco style, now a little run down. No restaurant. **C** ***New Tourist***, Ave des Paysanne, BP 153, T 23794. Just off the SW corner of the Place de l'Independence. Central Fans. Reasonable value. The rooms are a little gloomy. Restaurant adjoins, and is of good standard. **C** ***Le Residence***, Blvd d'Independence, T 23886. A bit gloomy. **C *Hotel de l'Amitie***, Ave de Amitie, T 26195. Very central.

Cheap hotels Many of the cheapest hotels are in the suburb of Mbwize to the NW of the city. This is a local African area. **D *Hotel Restaurant le Village*** (*Hotel Central*), Place d'Independence, T 26058. Well located in the centre of town and very good value. **D *Panama***, 5th Ave, Mbwize. Basic , but acceptable. **D *Au Chateau Fort***, 5th Ave, Mbwize. Reasonably secure. **D *Au Bon Accueil***, 6th Ave, BP 1657, T 22178. Well run. Pleasant veranda. Bar and restaurant.

There are some other budget hotels in Mbwize **E *New Bwiza***, T 23095; **E *Ecotisse***; **E *Au Coin de Paris***; **E *Au Chateau Fort***. E ***Vigizu Mission***, T 32059, nr the University Hospital in Kamenge and some distance from the centre of Bujumbura to the NW, along Blvd du 28 Novembre. The facilities (a 2-bed caravan and a 2-man tent) are free. It is straightforward to get a minibus from the main bus stand to Kamenge.

Camping If you have a tent, it is possible to pitch it at ***Cercle Nautique***, the yacht club on the lake shore about 15 mins to the SW of the city centre. Be cautious, as this can be unsafe if you are walking, and a taxi is advised. ***Royal Beach***, close to Club du Lac, off Chaussée d'Uvira on the lake side. Bar and restaurant. Also some bungalows.

● Places to eat

> **Price guide:**
> ***♦♦♦♦Over US$10; ♦♦♦US$5-10;♦♦US$2-5; ♦Under US$2.***

Food in Bujumbura is surprisingly varied and good. Many of the restaurants are run by the Greek community. As well as formal dining areas, several hotels and restaurants have snack menu cafes, often outside. These include ***Novotel, Source du Nil, Restaurant Hellenique, Club du Lac, Hotel Le Residence***.

♦♦♦♦***Chez Laurent***, Ave du Stade, BP 2901, T 25176. Open 1200-1400 and 1900-2300. The best restaurant in Bujumbura. ♦♦♦♦***Chez Vaya***. Located in Kiriri, in the hills to W of city, T 228231. International cuisine. Marvellous views. The proprietor will arrange to collect you from the centre of town if you telephone. ♦♦♦♦***Olympique***, Blvd de l'Uprona, T 226792. Mainly greek cuisine, but also pizzas and steaks. ♦♦♦♦***Le Kundava***. At *Novotel Hotel*, T 22600. French cuisine. Very comfortable atmosphere. It is possible to dine under a pergola adjoining the swimming pool. Also good café-bar overlooking pool and gardens. Fresh baguettes. ♦♦♦♦***Ikayaga***. At *Hotel Source du Nil*, T 25222. Comfortable decor, open for dinner. ♦♦♦♦***Restaurant Resha***, T 25222. 60 km S of Bujumbura. Run by *Hotel Source du Nil*. Very attractive location on the shore of Lake Tanganyika. Sandy beach. Barbeque style. Very popular at weekends. ♦♦♦♦***Foresta***, Blvd De l'Uprona International cuisine. ♦♦♦♦***Restaurant Hellenique***, Ave du Zaire, BP 572, T 22267. Open 1900-2300. Closed Thu. Greek food. Pleasant decor. It is possible to eat outside. Good value and very popular. Snack menu in the garden café. ♦♦♦♦***Restaurant Pizza Oasis***. On the corner of Ave Victoire and Blvd de l'Uprona. Pleasant decor. It is open Mon-Sat 1200-1400 and from 1900-2200. The brick pizza oven in the corner of the restaurant has glowing charcoal piled inside, and the pizzas are excellent. ♦♦♦♦***Club du Lac***. Off Chaussee d'Uvira on the lake side, T 25010. Open every day. 1200-2200. International cuisine. Also snack-bar by the pool. ♦♦♦♦***Cercle Nautique***, Ave du 13 Octobre, T 2559. Good view over the lake. The restaurant is rather formal. Open 1900-2300 Sat 1200-2300 Sun 100-2300. Closed Tue. Also snack menu served in the café on the terrace. ♦♦♦♦***L'Auberge Basque***, Ave du Plage, T 227569. Continental and Spanish cuisine. 1630-2200. Closed Mon.

♦♦♦***Le Sitar*** (previously *Cremaillère*), Blvd de la Liberté, BP 557, T 22295. French and Indian cuisine. ♦♦♦***Shama Chinese Palace*** (previously *La Jardiniere*), Blvd Mwezi, T 24807. South of city centre. Mainly Chinese, but also serves Indian and French food.

♦♦♦***Le Rugo***. At *Hotel Source du Nil*, T 25222. Open for breakfast and lunch. Coffee shop style, adjoining the swimming pool. ♦♦♦***Restaurant Grands Lacs***. *New Tourist Hotel*, Ave des Paysanne, T 23794. Good standard, and good value. Fine view over the lake to Zaire. ♦♦♦***Restaurant Tanganyika***, Ave de Plage, T 24443. International cuisine. 1700-2300. Comfortable atmosphere. Good value. ♦♦♦***Le Restaurant Jean Cabiotis***, Blvd d'Uprona. Terrace restaurant facing *Novotel*. Good reputation and excellent location. This was closed in late 1993 during the political disturbances, but is expected to reopen when things return to normal. ♦♦♦***Le Rendez-Vous***. Blvd d'Up-

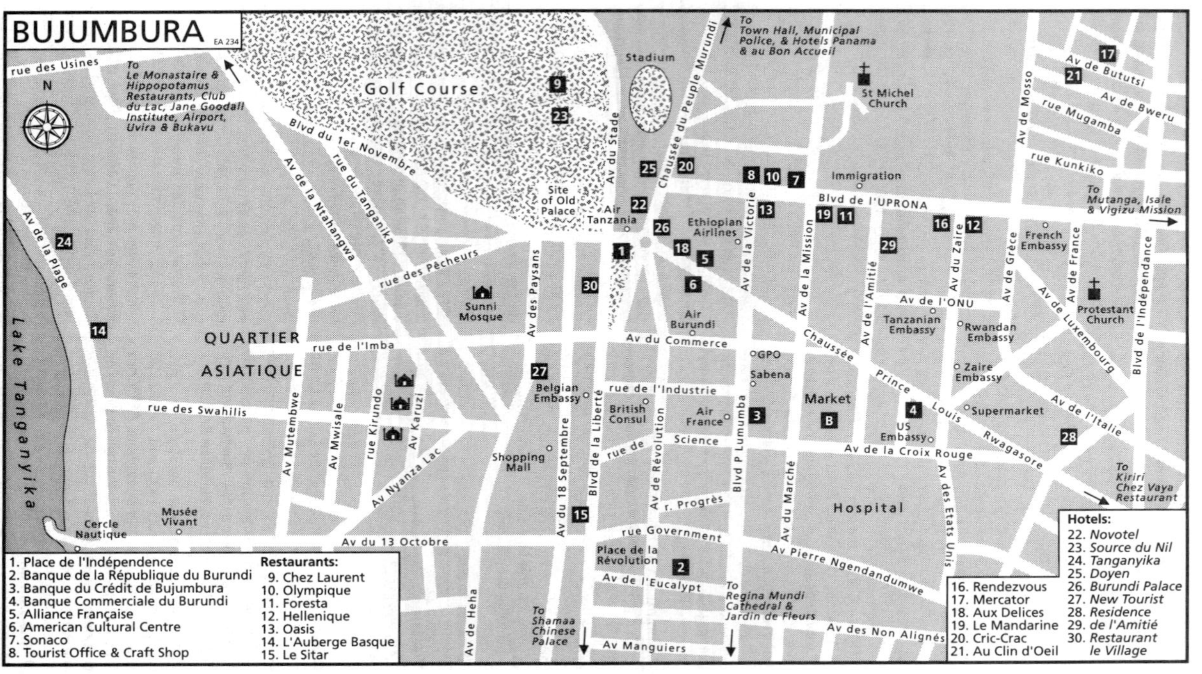
BUJUMBURA
EA 234
N
To Le Monastaire & Hippopotamus Restaurants, Club du Lac, Jane Goodall Institute, Airport, Uvira & Bukavu
Golf Course
Stadium
To Town Hall, Municipal Police, & Hotels Panama & au Bon Accueil
St Michel Church
Immigration
To Mutanga, Isale & Vigizu Mission
Site of Old Palace
Air Tanzania
Ethiopian Airlines
French Embassy
Protestant Church
Sunni Mosque
Air Burundi
Tanzanian Embassy
Rwandan Embassy
QUARTIER ASIATIQUE
GPO
Sabena
Zaire Embassy
Belgian Embassy
British Consul
Air France
Market
Supermarket
US Embassy
Shopping Mall
Hospital
To Kiriri Chez Vaya Restaurant
Lake Tanganyika
Cercle Nautique
Musée Vivant
Place de la Révolution
To Shamaa Chinese Palace
To Regina Mundi Cathedral & Jardin de Fleurs
rue des Usines
Blvd du 1er Novembre
Av de la Ntahangwa
rue du Tanganika
rue des Pêcheurs
Av de la Plage
Av du Stade
Chaussée du Peuple Murundi
Blvd de l'UPRONA
Av de Mosso
Av de Bututsi
Av de Bweru
rue Mugamba
rue Kunkiko
Av des Paysans
Av de la Victorie
Av de la Mission
Av de l'Amitié
Av du Zaire
Av de Grèce
Av de France
Blvd de l'Indépendance
Av de l'ONU
Av de Luxembourg
Chaussée Prince Louis Rwagasore
Av de l'Italie
rue de l'Imba
Av du Commerce
rue de l'Industrie
rue des Swahilis
Av Mutembwe
Av Mwisale
rue Kirundo
Av Karuzi
Av Nyanza Lac
Av du 18 Septembre
Blvd de la Liberté
rue de Science
Av de Révolution
Blvd P Lumumba
Av du Marché
Av de la Croix Rouge
Av des Etats Unis
r. Progrès
rue Government
Av du 13 Octobre
Av Pierre Ngendandumwe
Av de l'Eucalypt
Av de Heha
Av Manguiers
Av des Non Alignés
1. Place de l'Indépendence
2. Banque de la République du Burundi
3. Banque du Crédit de Bujumbura
4. Banque Commerciale du Burundi
5. Alliance Française
6. American Cultural Centre
7. Sonaco
8. Tourist Office & Craft Shop
Restaurants:
9. Chez Laurent
10. Olympique
11. Foresta
12. Hellenique
13. Oasis
14. L'Auberge Basque
15. Le Sitar
16. Rendezvous
17. Mercator
18. Aux Delices
19. Le Mandarine
20. Cric-Crac
21. Au Clin d'Oeil
Hotels:
22. Novotel
23. Source du Nil
24. Tanganyika
25. Doyen
26. Burundi Palace
27. New Tourist
28. Residence
29. de l'Amitié
30. Restaurant le Village

rona, T 24300. Open at lunchtime and 1900-2300. Closed Thu. French and Chinese menu. Small but lively. Good reputation for Chinese food. Snack menu in the garden café. ♦♦♦*La Grande Muraille*, Chaussée Prince Louis Rwagasore, T 23612. Chinese and international food. ♦♦♦*L'Horizon*, Blvd Ntare Rushati. South of the city centre, past the Cathedral. ♦♦♦*Hippopotamus*, Chaussée d'Uvira, T 23016. 1200-1430 and 1830-2100. Closed Mon. Restaurant on the beach N of the city centre. Dancing in the evening. This was closed in late 1993 during the political disturbances, but is expected to reopen when things return to normal. ♦♦♦*Mercator*, Ave Batutsi. West of Eglise St Michel in residential area, T 25075. 1700-2230. International menu. Fine garden.

♦♦*Aux Delices*, Chaussée Prince Louis Rwagasore. Coffee, snacks and ice cream. ♦♦*Café Polar*, on Chaussée Prince Rwagasore. Snacks, coffee and ice cream. ♦♦*Le Residence*, Blvd d'Independence, T 23886. 0700-2100. Café in the garden of the Hotel. ♦♦*Le Palladium*, Ave de Plage, BP 1136, T 26690. 1200-1400 and 1700-2300 Sun opens at 0900. Closed Mon. Set in a pleasant garden. ♦♦*Le Mandarine*, Blvd d'Uprona. 1200-1400 and 1700-2300. Closed Tue. Light meals and snacks. ♦♦*Cric-crac*, Chaussée du Peuple Murindi. Snack bar. ♦♦*Le Monastaire*, Chaussée d'Uvira. Cafe on the lake shore N of the centre. ♦♦*Au Clin d'Oeil* (chez Pipon Mobali), Ave Batutsi. W of Eglise St Michel, in residential area. Open every day 1700-2300. Rather charming. Barbeque style.

♦*Restaurant des Jeunes*, Mbwize. Behind the FINA petrol station. African food. ♦*Nusura Restaurant*, 7th Ave, Mbwize. Rice, stews, plantains.

● Bars

As well as at the main hotels, there are pleasant bars at *La Fontaine*, Ave Ngozi, nr Cathedral to the S of the city centre. 1200-1400 and 1700-2300. Closed Mon; *Cercle Hippique* (Riding Club) Blvd du Port, T 22970 1700-2100 Closed Mon; *Cercle Nautique* (Yacht Club) Ave du 13 Octobre, T 2559 Good view over the lake. 1900-2300 Sat 1200-2300 Sun 1100-2300. Closed Tue.

● Airline offices

Air Burundi, 40 Ave du Commerce, BP 2460, T 24456; *Air France*, T 26310) has an office on Blvd Lumumba and a branch office in the *Novotel hotel*. The *Air Tanzania* office is also in the centre of town on Place de l'Independence. Ethiopian Airways The *Sabena* office is on Blvd Lumumba nr the corner of Ave de la Croix Rouge. Other airline bookings can be made through travel agents.

● Banks and money changers

The central bank is the **Banque de la Republique du Burundi**, BP 705, T 25142. Commercial banks are: **Banque Burundaise pour le Commerce et l'Investissement SARL**, Blvd du 1 Novembre, BP 2320, T 2 23328; **Banque Commercial du Burundi SARL**, 84 Chaussée Prince Louis-Rwagasore, BP 990, T 2 22317; **Banque de Credit de Bujumbura SARL**, Ave Patrice Emery Lumumba, BP 300, T 2 22091; **Caisse d'Epargne du Burundi**, 40 Chaussée Prince Louis-Rwagasore, BP 615, T 2 25462. **Banking hours**: Mon-Fri 0800-1130.

● Embassies and Consulates

Algeria, Ave Ruhuhuma, BP 976, T 26346, Tlx 5098; **Belgium**, Blvd de la Libertie, BP 1920, T 26176, Tlx 5033; **Canada** (Consulate), C/O Siruco, Blvd du 1er Novembre BP5 T22816; **China**, 675 Ave du Lycée, BP 2550, T 24307, Tlx 5137; **Cuba** (Chancellery), Ave de Ngozi BP 2228, T 26476; **Denmark** (Consulate), BP 2880, T 26099, Tlx 5089; **Egypt**, 31 Ave Nzero, BP 1820, T 22031, Tlx 5040; **France**, 60 Blvd de l'Uprona, BP 1790, T 26464, Tlx 5044; **Germany**, 22 Ave 18 Septembre, BP 480, T 26412, Tlx 5068; **Greece** (Consulate), Immeuble Sogerbu, T 2242; **Italy** (Consulate), Ave du 18 Sep, T 26054; **Korea**, 55 Blvd de l'Uprona, BP 524, T 22881; **Luxembourg** (Consulate), T 22381; **Netherlands** (Consulate), Blvd de l'Uprona, BP 152, T 23558, Tlx 5062; **Romania**, rue Pierre Ngendandumwe, BP 2770, T 24135; **Russia**, 75 Blvd de l'Uprona, BP 1034, T 26098, Tlx 5164; **Rwanda**, 24 ave du Zaire, BP 400, T 23140; **Sweden** (Consulate), C/O Old East, BP 330, T 24005, Tlx 5064; **Tanzania**, 8 Ave de l'Onu, BP 1653, T 24630, Tlx 5032; **Uganda**, 7 Place de l'Independence, T 22086; **UK** (Consulate), Rue d'Industrie. T23711; **USA**, Ave des Etats-Unis, BP 1720, T 23454; **Vatican**, Ave des Travailleurs, BP 1068, T 22326; **Zaire**, 24 Ave du Zaire, BP 872, T 22306.

● Entertainment

Cinema *The American Cultural Centre*, Chaussée Prince Rwagasore, T 23312 screens video news from the US on weekdays at 1715. The *Alliance Française*, T 22351 runs a similar service and is across the road. *Cine Burundi*,

Place de l'Independence all films start at 2030. ***Cine Odeon*** Chaussée du Peuple Murundi. ***Cameo Cinema***, Ave des Paysans. Mostly W films. Programmes begin 2050.

Night Life There are a number of nightclubs by the lake side, N of the city, close to the *Hotel Club du Lac*. The best are said to be ***Le Monocle***, Club du Lac, T 25010. Open 2200-0400. Closed Mon. Over 21s only; ***Star Light***, T 23540, 2100 to dawn, closed Mon; ***Black and White Vision***, T 22280, 2100 to dawn, closed Sun and ***Bamboo***, closed Mon, starts at 2330. It is wise to take a taxi to and from these places as it is not safe to walk.

Also ***Keur Samba***, *Hotel Source du Nil*, T 25222), 2100 to dawn, but closed during recent disturbances; ***Black and White City***, Odeon Palace, Chaussée du Peuple du Murundi, T 25201. Open 2100 to dawn. Closed Sun. ***Get-up***, Chaussée du Peuple du Murundi, T 22468. 2100 to dawn. Closed Mon.

Other entertainment The **Islamic Cultural Centre**, built using Libyan money supplied by Colonel Gadaffi, is a striking building. There are sometimes performances of dance, drumming and singing. It is in the centre of town just W of Independence Square.

● Hospitals and medical services

Hospitals **Hôpital Prince Regent Charles** on Av de l'Hopital off Chaussée du Peuple Murundi, T 26160. There is also a clinic, **Clinique Prince Louis Rwagasore** at the Av Prince Ngendandumwe, T 23881.

● Libraries

There are a number of libraries in town. Both the American and French cultural centres have libraries which are open Mon-Fri from 1400-2000 and there is the University library at Ave de l'Universite at the corner of Blvd du 28 Novembre.

● Police station

This is on Chaussée du Peuple Murundi towards the N in the suburb of Mbwize, just opposite the Hôpital Prince Regent Charles.

● Post offices

The main post office is in the city centre on the corner of Blvd Lumumba and Ave du Commerce. Hours are Mon-Fri 0800-1200 and 1400-1600 and Sat from 0800-1100. **DHL**, ATS-DHL Worldwide Express, 26 Ave du 18 Septembre, BP 761, T 26696, Tlx 5130.

● Religion

There are a number of churches in Bujumbura catering for all denominations; **Catholics** can go to the Church of St Michel off Blvd de l'Uprona, or to Cathedrale Regina Mundi slightly further from the centre of town off Blvd Niare Rushatsi to the S of the city. **Protestants** are served by the Temple Protestant off Blvd de l'Independence. There are also a number of other small churches around town. **Mosques**: The Grande Mosque is on Rue d'Imbo at the site of the Islamic Cultural Centre. On Ave Karuzi are Shia and Sunni mosques and an Ismaili mosque on Rue des Swahili. There are 2 other mosques, one in the district of Buyenzi and one in Mbwize.

● Shopping

Hairdressing, Photographic supplies, Pharmacies There are several estabishments providing these services on Chaussée Prince Louis Rwagasore.

Curios and crafts *Office National du Tourisme*, Blvd De l'Uprona, T 25084 (good variety of craft items); ***Sow et Jaou***, Chaussée du Peuple Murundi, opposite *Novotel*; ***Libraire Saint-Paul***, Blvd de l'Independence; ***Boutique Josephine***, *Novotel Hotel* (rather expensive, and not a particularly wide variety); ***Marche Central***, Ave de la Croix Rouge (several kiosks, good value); ***Le Bougainvilliers*** 30 Ave de l'Industrie, BP 2914 T24992.

● Sport (participant)

Swimming at *Novotel* which does not always admit non-residents. A public pool at the *Entente Sportive* is just further N of *Novotel*. *Club du Lac* has a pool, and it is possible for non-residents to spend the day there. Also *Hotel Source du Nil*; *Campus Kiriri*, W outskirts of city. **Yachting** and **water ski-ing** at *Cercle Nautique* (the Yacht Club – this is a members club, but visitors are accommodated), *Hotel Source du Nil*, and *Club du Lac*. **Squash** *Cercle Nautique*; *Hotel Source du Nil*. **Basketball** and **Judo** at *Entente Sportive*, Ave du Stade, T 24056. **Horse-riding**, at *Cercle Hippique* (Riding Club), Blvd du Port, T 22970, or through *Hotel Source du Nil*. **Golf** at *Golf Club* on Blvd du 1er Novembre, or through *Hotel Source du Nil*. **Tennis** at *Novotel*; *Hotel Source du Nil*; *Club du Lac*. **Gym** *Salle Omnisport de Buyenzi*, Ave Rwinda; *Campus Kiriri*, W outskirts of city; *Campus Kamenge*, Blvd du 28 Novembre, T 3135; *Terrain du Stade*, Blvd de l'Independence; *Cercle Hellenique* (Greek Club), Ave du Zaire. **Dance** (Afro-jazz) *Centre Culturel Francais*, Chaussée Prince Louis Rwagasore, T 4001. **Yoga** *Lycee Vugizo*, Ave du Lycee. Western outskirts of city. BP 1108, T 26614

Sport (spectator)

There are soccer matches at the **National Stadium** on Chaussee du Peuple Murundi, at the Stadium on Blvd d'Independence and at **Nyakabiga Stadium** on Ave del la Jeunesse. Notices of games are posted up around town.

Telecommunications

Service is in the main post office and opening hrs are the same for both.

Tourist information

Office National du Tourisme, BP 902 Bujumbura, T 22202, is responsible for the promotion and supervision of the tourism sector. Most information is published in French only.

Tour operators and travel agents

Eden Travel, Galerie Alexandre, Place de l'Independance, BP 1075, T 221616, F 224733. Organises safaris to Kahuzi Biega National Park in Zaire for gorilla tracking, stays in Zaire, cruising on the Lake Kivu; visits to the other Burundi Parks and to see the celebrated Tambourinnaires; safaris to Gombe Stream National Park in Tanzania for chimpanzee tracking. ***Nile Travel Agency***, 7 Place de l'In-

Jungle-Boy John

In Apr 1976 a South African newspaper carried a startling story. A group of soldiers on patrol in the jungle, near Nyanza Lac in the S of Burundi, disturbed a a pack of monkeys. As they scampered for the trees, one of the monkeys seemed slower and more awkward than the rest. The other monkeys stopped from time to time to help him. Amazed, the soldiers saw it was in fact a small, naked human boy, screeching with alarm as he clambered clumsily through the branches.

The soldiers caught the boy and took him first to Bujumbura and then to a Catholic orphanage in Gitega. There he was observed to scurry on all fours, make wild chattering noises, and to have a coat of fine black hair – the classic hall-marks of *homo ferus,* a child brought up in the wild. As he had spent so much time in the wilderness, the priests named him John, after John the Baptist.

Two American academics from Boston, Harlan Lane, a psychologist, and Richard Pillard, a psychiatrist, were beside themselves with excitement when they read the South African newspaper clipping. The only previous authentic feral child was Victor, who had been discovered running wild in the forests of Aveyron in Southern France in 1799. Harlan Lane had made a special study of the case. Experience with this child had profoundly influenced subsequent generations of specialists in child psychology. John presented an extraordinary scientific opportunity. In a blaze of publicity, loaded with research grants, and weighed down with medical and photographic equipment, Lane and Pillard were on a jet to Burundi within 2 weeks.

They found John in the orphanage – a sign outside announced 'John, Monkey Boy, Donation 50F'. His body-hair had disappeared since he had been in captivity (this had also happened with Victor), and he had now been taught to walk upright. The scientists subjected the child to a battery of tests, X-rays and blood samples. They flew him to Nairobi to have have his brain-wave patterns recorded on an electroencephelograph.

Background enquiries revealed that the orphanage thought John had previously been known as Balthazar. They had a record of his father's name and district. Research turned up a baptism entry and together with the orphanage and hospital registers, it showed conclusively that John could never have been a feral child. Lane and Pillard reasoned that he was unable to speak, uttered chattering noises and beat his forehead obsessively with his hand because he was autistic.

The academics went home. John remained at the orphanage. The monkey-boy sign was taken down.

dependence. BP 1402, T 22321. *Ami Burundi*, Place de l'Independence. BP 750, T 23975 F3153, Tlx 5055. *Transintra*, Blvd Patrice Lumumba BP 1306, T 23083, Tlx 2920. *Intercontact Services*, Place d'Independence. BP 982, T 26666, Tlx 5126.

● **Transport**

Local Bujumbura is a small city, so it is easy to get around the centre on foot. The main bus stand is located in the centre of town in front of the new market.

Car hire From **Garage des Grands Lacs**, Chaussée Prince Louis Rwagasore, T 25045; or through **Office National du Tourisme**, Blvd d'Uprona, BP 902, T 22202; ***Novotel Hotel***, Chaussée du Peuple Murundi, BP 1015, T 22600, Tlx 600644. **Intercontact Services**, Place d'Independence. BP 982, T 26666, Tlx 5126.Air The international airport to Burundi is just outside Bujumbura served by Aeroflot, Air Burundi, Air France, Air Tanzania, Air Zaire, Cameroon Airlines, Ethiopian Airlines, Kenya Airways and Sabena. **Taxis** to the airport cost US$12.

Road There are roads into Bujumbura from all the principal towns in Burundi; Rutana in the S, Gitega in the centre, Kayanza in the N and Karuzi in the NE. On all routes public transport is available, and minibuses depart from the main bus stand nr the new market.

Lake The ferry on Lake Tanganyika is the *MV Liemba*. It has a weekly service. Departure from Bujumbura is at 1600 Mon, to arrive at Kigoma in Tanzania on Tues morning. It leaves Kigoma at 1600 on Wed for Mpulungu (Zambia) arriving there on Fri morning. It stops at lots of small ports on the way. The return to Kigoma is at 1600 on Fri, arriving Sun morning in Kigoma. The departure for Bujumbura is at 1600 on Sun, arriving Mon morning.

Fares from Kigoma to Bujumbura are US$7, US$5, US$2.50 and from Kigoma on to Mpulungu US$16, US$12, US$5 for first, second and third class respectively. Third class are benches or deck space, second class cabins are small, hot and stuffy with 4 bunks. First class cabins have 2 bunks, a window, fan. Meals and drinks area available on the ferry and are paid for in Tanzanian shillings.

Gitega

Gitega is the second largest town in Burundi and is home to the National Museum. Before the colonial era, Gitega was the capital of the territory which now makes up Burundi. It is a pleasant town with a cool climate and some interesting walks in the area.

Places of interest

The **National Museum**, though small, has a good display of local cultural exhibits. Entrance is free. The main administrative building dates from the German colonial period. There are occasional performance of the *Tambourinnaires*, a colourful singing and dancing group. If they are not playing here, they usually perform at **Gishola** which is about 10 km away on the last Sun in every month. There is also a local beer market where traditional alcoholic beverages are available.

● **Where to stay D** *Mission Catholique* has a guest house. It is possible to camp in the grounds.

● **Transport** Minibuses leave regularly from the main bus stand in Bujumbura when full. The road is sealed and the journey takes 2-3 hrs.

Kayanza

Kayanza is the first town you come to if crossing from Butare in Rwanda to Burundi. It has a market on Mon, Wed and Sat. Kayanza is the nearest town with hotel facilities to the **National Park of Kibira**, see page 547.

● **Accommodation E** *Auberge de Kayanza*. Located in the centre of town. Simple but adequate.

● **Transport** To get here from Bujumbura takes about 2 hrs and there are regular minibuses which make this trip. If you are coming from Rwanda, there are minibuses, which go when full, from the Burundi border to Kayanza.

NATIONAL PARKS AND NATURE RESERVES

Information on the parks and reserves of Burundi is sparse, and facilities for people wishing to see them are limited. There are so few current visitors that there is no transport direct to any of the parks. One alternative is to take a minibuses to the town nearest the park, walk or hitch the rest of the way, or hire a local vehicle and driver. The other is to go on a tour organised by *Eden Travel*, see page 545.

Kibira National Park

This is at the top of the Zaire-Nile apex. It is the largest virgin forest in Burundi, 40,000 ha of forest sheltering chimpanzees, baboons, black colobes and a host of other species of monkeys. Access to the park is through the tea plantations of Teza and Rweguro. Guides are available at the park entrance if you wish, or you can explore it on your own along the 180 km of paths and tracks.

Ruvubu National Park

The National Park of Ruvubu runs along the Ruvubu river in the NE of the country. The nearest towns are Karuzi to the W and Cankuzo to the E. This land used to be farmed but is now the largest national park in the country. Mountains close in the area and make for many spectacular views. There is a campsite on the edge of the park.

Rusizi Nature Reserve

This is just outside Bujumbura on the Zaire border. The River Rusizi Delta runs through this 500 ha nature reserve and is banked by tall palm trees. The environment is particularly well suited to hippopotami and crocodiles, and many types of antelope graze in the surrounding grasslands. Bird-life is particularly abundant, attracted by the river and marshlands.

Bururi Nature Reserve

The reserve at Bururi is an area of tropical rainforest which has been set aside and houses about 117 species of birds and 25 different mammals. You are able to walk around this reserve along a number of tracks and lanes. Minibus transport is available from Gitega to Bururi town which is in the middle of the reserve. There are waterfalls at Mutara, about 25 km away nr Lake Tanganyika.

Karera Falls and Faille des Allemands

These are both in the S part of the country near Rutana. There are minibuses from Gitega to Rutana. From Rutana it is a 10 km walk down a dirt road to Muishanga, and the waterfall is 2 km further on. It is possible to camp at the falls, or there is a hut you can use. From here to the gorge is a 4-hr walk upstream from the Karera Falls. It is possible to camp alongside the gorge.

INFORMATION FOR VISITORS

Contents

Before you go

Entry requirements

● Visas

Everyone entering Burundi needs a visa. Visas can be obtained for a maximum of 3 months. It is necessary to nominate a day on which you will be entering the country and how long you intend to stay. The visa costs about US$10 for any length of stay, so it is worth asking for the full 3 months to be safe. There is no extra charge for getting a multiple-entry visa. Visas need to be obtained before reaching Burundi, although you can get a 3-day transit visa at the border.

Visa extensions may be obtained in Bujumbura at a cost of US$7 per month, and take 24 hrs to issue.

● Vaccinations

There is no formal requirement for vaccinations to enter Burundi though it is advised to protect against yellow fever, malaria and cholera.

● Burundi representation overseas

You will be able to get a visa in any country with a Burundi Embassy. Outside East Africa these are: Addis Ababa (Ethiopia), Algiers (Algeria), Cairo (Egypt), Tripoli (Libya), Beijing (People's Republic of China), Bonn (Germany), Brussels (Belgium), Bucharest (Romania), Geneva (Switzerland), Moscow (Russia), Washington DC (USA), Ottawa (Canada) and Paris (France).

In East Africa, you will be able to get a visa in: **Kenya**, 14th Floor, Development House, Moi Ave, Nairobi, T 728 340). Applications can be made on Mon or Wed and collected on Tuesdays or Thu at 1600. The embassy opening hrs are Mon-Thu 0830-1230 and 1400-1700. You will need to produce 2 photographs. **Tanzania** at the consulate in Kigoma or at the Embassy in Dar es Salaam on Lugala Rd next to the Italian Embassy. You will need to produce 2 photographs and the visa is issued 24 hrs later. The opening hrs in Kigoma are Mon-Fri 0800-1500 and in Dar es Salaam from Mon-Fri from 0800-1400. **Zaire** at the consulate in Bukavu (SINELAC Building, 184 Ave du President Mobutu). You will need 2 photographs and it takes 24 hrs. The opening hrs are Mon-Fri from 0730-1200 and 1430-1700.

NB: Although there are Burundi embassies in both Uganda and Rwanda, they only issue visas to nationals of these countries.

● Overseas representation in Burundi

All neighbouring countries, the main European and North American countries, the former USSR and China all have embassies in Bujumbura. For list see page 543.

● Tourist Information

The Tourist Information Office is in Bujumbura, see page 545.

● Travel and tour agents

These are based in Bujumbura. Two useful ones are: the ***Nile Travel Agency***, 7 Place de l'Independance, T 22321 and ***Ami Burundi***, also on Place de l'Independance, T 23975.

When to go

● Best time to visit
Jun to Sep. The weather in Burundi is quite variable but the heavy rains are from Feb to Mar.

Health

● Staying healthy
As with other parts of East Africa, the main risk is from malaria. It is also wise to protect yourself against both cholera and yellow fever (see Health notes, page 22).

If you intend to go swimming in Lake Tanganyika, avoid parts where there is reedy vegetation and still water as these generally house the snail which passes on bilharzia.

Money

● Credit cards
These are accepted in the major international hotels, but it is unlikely they will be accepted elsewhere. The most popular cards are American Express, Visa and Diners Card.

● Cost of living
Burundi, like Rwanda, is not a paticularly cheap place to stay as it is not really geared for the budget traveller, particularly in Bujumbura. Food, drink and transport costs are reasonable, similar to other parts of East Africa.

● Currency
The unit of currency in Burundi is the Burundi Franc. Exchange rates are:

The exchange rate fluctuates widely as it is no longer fixed to a hard currency, and it has gone through a series of devaluations since 1983. Black market rates tend to be 33% higher than bank rates.

Commission rates for changing traveller's cheques can be high. The best rate is at the Banque de la Republique du Burundi who only charge BFr 3 commission. Outside banking hrs travellers' cheques can be changed at the Novotel Hotel.

US dollars attract a better rate in Burundi than travellers' cheques and can be exchanged relatively easily in most places. For currencies other than US dollars, you are better off at the bank. Money changing is also big business at the border posts.

Getting there

● Air
There are a number of airlines which fly to Burundi. Aeroflot, Air Burundi, Air France, Air Tanzania, Air Zaire, Cameroon Airlines, Ethiopian Airlines, Kenya Airways and Sabena. Flights from Europe are expensive as there are as yet no package deals or charter flights catering for tourists. The airport is about 11 km outside Bujumbura. For specialised agencies offering discounted fares, see page 545.

● Road
The main overland routes into Burundi are from Rwanda or Zaire.

Rwanda There are 2 routes depending on whether you are coming from Kigali (the capital of Rwanda) or Cyangugu (on Lake Kivu). From **Kigali** take a minibus to Butare. Take a minibus from Butare to the border, these are infrequent. From the Burundi border take a minibus to Kayanza, they only go on Tue, Fri and Sun which are market days in Kayanza. At any other time you will have to walk or hitch. It is possible to hire a lift on a motor cycle, or sit on the carrier of a bicycle while another bicycle carries your luggage. From Kayanza there are frequent minibuses to Bujumbura and the journey takes 2 hrs. Crossing the border at this point is relatively quick as there is very little traffic. There are a number of moneychangers who will change Rwandan francs into Burundi francs. From **Cyangugu**, take a minibus to the border village of Bugarama. From here hire a lift on a motor cycle for the 8 km to the Burundi border post at Luhwa and for the next 12 km to Rugombo in Burundi as there is no public transport. At the border there are bicycles that will ferry you and your luggage between the posts. From Rugombo you will be able to get a minibus to Bujumbura and this part of the journey takes under 2 hrs.

Zaire There are also 2 possible routes. One is from Bukavu to Bujumbura via Cyangugu as outlined above. This is the preferable route as the road through Rwanda is better than the one though Zaire, although it involves an extra border crossing into Rwanda, and you will need a multiple entry visa or a transit visa for Rwanda. From Bukavu to Bujumbura via Uvira is the easier route if you don't have a visa for Rwanda. There are minibuses to Uvira from where you will need to take a taxi to the border. These operate on a shared basis until mid afternoon and the journey takes about 15 minutes. From the Zaire border post to the Burundi post is about 1 km and there are bicycles to give you and your luggage a lift. Generally you will have to get a taxi from the Burundi border post to Bujumbura though sometimes there are minibuses. It is about a 15 minute ride.

● Lake ferry

It is possible to enter Burundi from Tanzania via 2 routes at different points. There is a direct routes from Kigoma on the river ferry (see Bujumbura Transport, page 546) or the more picturesque route from Kigoma via Nyanza Lac and Gombe Stream National Park, the chimpanzee sanctuary in Tanzania.

Via Gombe Stream National Park There is a lake taxi (a small boat with an outboard motor) between Kigoma and Kagunga on the Tanzanian border with Burundi which takes you to the chimpanzee sanctuary. However, the trip is not cheap as the entrance fee to the park is US$50. The lake taxi leaves from Kalalangabo (about 3 km outside Kigoma). The trip down to Kagunga via Nyanza takes about half a day. The boats do not run on Sun and there is no regular timetable. A lake taxi with some cover to give shade is more comfortable. The taxis tend to get very full. From the border, there is a 2 km walk or a motor cycle or bicycle ride to the Burundi border post. From here there is a minibus to Nyanza Lac. From Nyanza Lac there are a number of minibuses to Bujumbura.

When you arrive

● Conduct

A note of caution Be careful when taking photographs that you have the permission of any people around you as people can be sensitive on this issue. Also, as in many other parts of East Africa, it is not a good idea to take photographs of any government buildings, military posts, post offices, police stations, border posts etc.

● Hours of business

Official hrs of business are from 0800-1200 and from 1400-1700. Government Offices 0700-1200 and 1400-1700, but closing at 1200 on Mon and Sat. Banking hrs are 0800-1130, Mon-Fri. Local markets are open all day.

● Official time

Burundi is 2 hrs ahead of GMT.

● Religion

More than 60% of the population are Christians, the majority of whom are Roman Catholics. Fewer than 40% of the population adhere to traditional beliefs, which includes the worship of the God 'Imana'. About 1% of the population are Muslims.

● Safety

In periods of political stability travelling around the country and visiting the sights seems to be safe. There are areas of Bujumbura, the capital, which it is not safe to walk in, see page 540, as muggings have occurred.

● Tricksters

These are only likely to be a problem when trying to change money on the street. To guard against it, make sure you know the official exchange rate before entering into negotiations.

Where to stay

There are few hotels in Burundi, and if things return to normal, it can be difficult to find a room. If in doubt is wise to book ahead, although this is not easy to do with some of the less expensive hotels.

Food and drink

● Food

The standard of food in Burundi is generally good in comparison with other parts of East Africa, and with a surprising variety of types.

Hotel Classifications

A+	Over US$100 a night. International standards and decor, air conditioning, self contained rooms, swimming pool, restaurants, bars, business services.
A	US$40-100. First class standards, air-conditioning, attached bathrooms, restaurants and bars, swimming pool.
B	US$20-40. Tourist class, comfortable with air conditioning or fans, attached barthrooms, restaurant, bar, public rooms.
C	US$10-20. Budget, fans, shared bathroom facilities.
D	US$5-10. Guest house, no fan, shared bathroom, cold water.
E	Under US$5. Basic guest house, simple bed, no soap or towels, no wardrobe, shared bathroom facilities, erratic cold water supply, no fans or mosquito nets.

Eating Classifications

♦♦♦♦ Over US$10 for a meal. A 3-course meal in a restaurant with pleasant decor. Beers, wines and spirits available.

♦♦♦ US$5-10 for a meal. Two courses, not including alcohol, reasonable surroundings.

♦♦ US$2-5 for a meal, probably only a single course, surroundings spartan but adequate.

♦ Under US$2. Single course, often makeshift surroundings such as a steet kiosk with simple benches and tables.

Bujumbura is particularly well served.

Drink

There are no restrictions on alcohol and a wide variety of imported beers, wines and spirits are available. There is a local brewery which produces lagers (*Primus* and *Amstel*) under licence from Belgium.

Getting around

Air

There are no regular internal flights.

Road

The road network in Burundi is very dense with a total of 6,285 km of roads. The government has spent much money rehabilitating the road network and as a result many of the frequently-used routes are good. Minibus services are fairly frequent, good value and not too crowded. Destinations are displayed in the front window of the bus and they depart when full. Services taper off in mid-afternoon. There is a government bus service in the area around Bujumbura.

Car hire

It is possible to hire a cars in Bujumbura, see page 546.

Communications

Language

The official languages are Kirundi and French. Some Kiswahili is spoken. Hardly anyone speaks English.

Postal services

The postal service is reasonably efficient from Burundi. Post offices are open from Mon-Fri from 0800-1200 and from 1400-1600, and on Sat from 0800-1100. There is a poste restante service.

Telephone services

You will be able to make international calls from the post office in Bujumbura or at any of the main hotels. Connection takes only a few minutes but international calls are extremely expensive, particularly from hotels.

Entertainment

Radio and television

There is one station which is government controlled and which transmits both the radio and television broadcasts in Kirundi, Swahili, French and English. Television transmission began in the country in 1985. The local station concentrates on news items and cultural performances by local artists. *Radiodiffusion et Television Nationale du Burundi*, BP 1900, Bujumbura, T 2 23742.

Newspapers

There are 3 locally produced papers. *Burundi Chretien* a Roman Catholic weekly paper in French, *Le Renouveau du Burundi* a daily paper published by UPRONA the Tutsi-dominated political party, which is also published in French, and *Ubumwe* a weekly paper in Kirundi.

Burundi Hyperbole

Exaggeration is a common style of expression in Burundi. If it is said 'there are no crops', it probably means the harvest has been disappointing. To hear that 'the roads are impassable' might indicate only that there are some hold-ups. On further examination 'my family are all dead and I am left alone' might reveal that a man's eldest son has died.

Of course, this is a style found in western cultures as well, to create emphasis. But it is usually it is clear from the context when this is being done. In Burundi you often have to question more closely to get an accurate picture of what is going on.

Holidays and festivals

1 Jan New Year's Day
Apr Good Friday, Easter Sunday
1 May Ascension Day
1 Jul
5 Aug
18 Sep
3 Oct
1 Nov
25 Dec Christmas Day

Further reading

Lane, H and Pillard, R (1978) *The Wild Boy of Burundi,* Random House: New York. An account of the expedition by 2 American academics to investigate the case of the small Burundi boy reported to have been found living among monkeys in the forest.

ZAIRE

CONTENTS

MAPS

INTRODUCTION

Eastern Zaire refers to a narrow strip of land running from Lake Tanganyika to Lake Mobutu Sese Seko (Lake Albert) in Kivu Province. It is included in a book about East Africa because it is more accessible from the East than from West or Central Africa, and because it includes part of the same mountain range as Burundi, Rwanda and Uganda – the western wall of the Rift Valley. The countryside in this part of Zaire is magnificent, said to be the most impressive in Zaire, and there are many different types of wildlife, some unique to the area. However, travelling in this part of the world can be extremely frustrating as there is erratic public transport, bribery is a way of life, and border crossing can be slow.

NB The current crisis in Rwanda, with the mass exodus to the refugee camps in Goma, has meant that travelling in East Zaire is not recommended at present. Consult your embassy before attempting any journey for whatever purpose.

Environment

Geography

This is a land of contrasts, huge volcanoes and great lakes. Many of the volcanoes are still active and have erupted in the last decade, others along the borders of Zaire, Uganda and Rwanda are the last remaining habitats of the mountain gorilla. The varied terrain has created environments for a huge variety of vegetation and animals making this a scenic and very attractive area.

Climate

Kivu District is temperate as most of the land is at high elevation. The average yearly temperature is about 20°C with low humidity. However, rainfall is fairly heavy all year round though usually only in short bursts. There is less rainfall from mid-May to mid-Sep and mid-Dec to mid-Mar. However, the demarcation in to rainy and dry seasons seems to have become less clear in recent years.

History

In pre-colonial times, this area was the domain of pygmies who lived in the great forests existing as hunter-gatherers. The area was first visited by the Portuguese in 1482 and became a source of slaves from the seventeeth to the nineteenth centuries. In 1885 Leopold II of Belgium established a series of trading posts along the River Congo. The flourishing rubber trade induced Belgium to make it a colony in 1908 and from then the mineral deposits of the SE area began to be exploited. Parts of E Zaire were developed into coffee plantations. Several towns were built along Lake Kivu such as Bukavu and Goma, and together

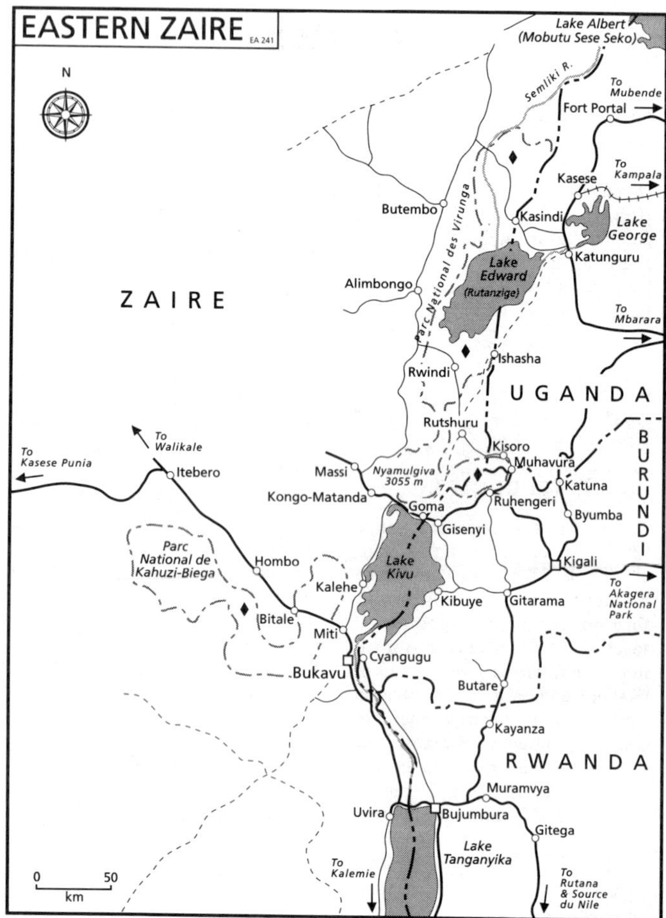

with many mountain retreats, became vacation centres for the colonial administrators.

Independence was granted in 1960, but preparation was inadequate and the nationalist Prime Minister Patrice Lumumba and President Joseph Kasavubu were immediately faced with an army mutiny and the threat of secession by the mineral rich province of Katanga (now called Shaba) and South Kasai. United Nations forces intervened and, following the assassination of Lumumba, a new government was formed under Cyrille Adoula. By 1963 the UN forces and the army, led by Col. Joseph-Desiré Mobutu, had defeated both rebel groups. A new federal constitution was adopted and in 1964 Moïse Tshombe, leader of the Katanga rebellion, was invited to become Prime Minister. Further rebellions in Kwilu and Katanga were

Children's Games In Zaire

Nikiendi

Game played by boys, on all fours, but face upwards, as the 'hunters'. One boy, not on all fours, is the 'antelope'. There is an agreed area to which the game is restricted, within which the 'hunters' chase the 'antelope'. The 'hunter' who finally captures the 'antelope' by gripping him between his legs, becomes the new 'antelope'.

Dibulunga

Players sit round in a circle, with their legs stretched out toward the centre. A ball made of bound dry grass is placed on the legs of one of the players. By lifting his right knee he attempts to tip the ball onto the legs of the player on his left, and so on, round the circle. Any player that misses, and allows the ball to roll away, has to perform a forfeit by dancing in the centre of the ring.

Titi kia lukusa

The players stand in a circle, each loosely grasping the wrist of the player to his right, and having his left wrist held by the player on the other side. One of the players then raises his right leg and passes it back over his right arm. He then passes his left leg over his right arm. He is now facing out of the circle with his arms crossed behind his back. He now passes his left hand over his head to face back into the circle. Each player does this in turn, going anticlockwise round the circle. Amusement comes from the players on each side making the manoevure difficult for the player in the centre by pulling on his arms, or lifting them up, making the player fall, or get stuck.

Vit a mbuta

Two teams line up, about 10m apart, each with a good supply of croton fruit (about the size of a walnut). Each player builds himself a 'house' of three fruit placed together on the ground, with a fourth on top. Each team then throws fruit to knock the top fruit off the 'houses' of the opposition. The first side to destroy all the other side's houses is the winner, and is allowed to pelt the losers with fruit.

crushed. In Apr 1964 there was an uprising in southern Kivu and northern Katanga pressing for the secession of mineral-rich Katanga province (now Shaba). The rebels established their own capital at Stanleyville (now Kisangani), but were defeated in early 1965.

The elections were won by Tshombe's coalition, but the grouping collapsed following deadlock and executive power was passed to President Mobutu in 1965. In 1966 President Mobutu formed his own political organisation, Mouvement Populaire de la Révolution (MPR), and power began to concentrate in the Presidency. Union Minière, the main mining company, was nationalised in 1967. At the same time a referendum established Presidential government. Further elections endorsed Mobutu and in 1972 he took the title of Mobutu Sese Seko and inaugurated a programme of authenticity, which involved name changes and alterations to modes of dress. In Shaba (formerly Katanga) there were uprisings in 1977 and 1978 which were suppressed with French and Moroccan help.

Mobutu has progressively concentrated control of the country in the Office of the President. The 21 provinces which made up Zaire were consolidated into 8. Provincial institutions were abolished leaving only provincial governors, who were directly responsible to

THE CARAVAN

Feathery bush and tufted grass, and silver mists of morn,
And smouldering fires when we pass the camping place at dawn
And silent beasts that prowl at night, and slink and crouch and creep
Round and about the firelight when all the world's asleep

The ragged, jagged screen of trees, the belt of bush between
The spacious upland where the breeze peeps out across the scene
The shrouded streams that wind away in shadow at high noon
The tiny tasselled clouds that play about a silver moon

We love each whisper of the wind, each rumour of the road,
Each frowsy goatskin slung behind, and every knotted load
Each red-brown village framed in smoke among the feathered maize
Even the belt of scrub that cloaks the glory of the ways.

Cullen Gouldsbury *From the Outposts* (1923)

Mobutu. Consequently, local governors who had been virtually autonomous from 1960-1965 now had very limited power over their regions. Inevitably this has had some serious consequences on the running of Kivu province, exacerbated by it being over 2,600 km from the capital, Kinshasa. Infrastructure in the region is very poor, salaries are not paid and bribery and corruption have become the means of surviving among administrative officials.

Culture and life

Zaire's ethnic make-up is extremely diverse. Its population of about 42 million is divided into some 200 tribes with about 250 different dialects. The official language is French, but over 400 Bantu and Sudanese dialects are spoken; most people communicate in one of 4 major languages: more than 50% in Kikongo, 20% Kiteke, with the rest Mbosi and Lingala. About half the population have traditional beliefs with 30% Roman Catholics and 13% Protestant.

Eastern Zaire is one of the few regions with significant numbers of Twa (pygmies) which are the original inhabitants of this part of the world, extending into Rwanda and Burundi. They continue their traditional way of life as hunter-gatherers within the forest.

Modern Zaire

Politics

Zaire is a one party state under President Mobutu who came into power in 1965. Since that time, Mobutu has banned party politics in the country and greatly reduced the power of regional administrators and made them directly responsible to the office of the president. In order to gain and maintain political stability in the country, labour organisations were deprived of their right to strike, the claims of existing political groups to official recognition were ignored and senior politicians were dismissed or arrested for ostensibly plotting against the president. In 1970 the constitution was amended so that the government, the legislature and the judiciary all became institutions of the MPR. In 1977 thousands of solidiers who had fled Zaire invaded from Angola. Mobutu, with assistance from France and Morocco, put down the 'First Shaba War' and announced a presidential election to be held in 1977. He was re-elected (unopposed) and amended the legislative council to allow for holding inquiries into ministers' activities and public services. In May 1978, the 'Second Shaba War' broke out, and again the French helped Mobutu to crush it.

In 1982 a second political party was established in Zaire, the Union pour la Democratie et le Progrès Social (UDPS), formed in connection with members of the national legislative council who had been imprisoned by Mobutu and politicians who had been dismissed from office. Members of it have frequently been arrested and tried for 'insulting the head of state'. In 1986 Amnesty International published a report condemning Zaire for human rights abuses (not for the first time) and criticising the treatment of members of the UDPS. The report resulted in limited changes in Zaire, but by 1989 disturbances broke out in Kinshasa due to the arrest of key members of the UDPS. Since then political unrest is common and various international humanitarian organisations have voiced their concerns of the government's method of rule.

Mobutu announced that full multiparty politics would be established in Zaire in 1991. A conference was to be held to draft a new constitution but this was postponed until mid 1992. Since this time, many of Mobutu's powers have been reduced or withdrawn. A transitional government was chosen by the conference with new powers over the military and legislature. Mobutu failed in his attempt to declare the new government dissolved. However, he successfully managed to make it impotent. The current situation is confused, with Mobutu clinging to office, and the Transitional Government, headed by Ettienne Tshisekedi, operating alongside the Government of National Salvation, under prime Minister Faustin Birindwa. The stability of the country deteriorated during early 1993 and tribal warfare re-emerged in Shaba and north-east Kivu provinces. In most parts of Eastern Zaire, government has collapsed and mission stations have taken on the role of providing health, education, and havens of order and sanity.

Economics

The survey of the economy below relates to all of Zaire. It needs to be borne in mind that the Eastern part of the country is probably marginally more prosperous than other areas outside Kinshasa and the mining province of Shaba, these latter 2 being the most developed areas of the country.

Economic and social structure

Estimates for 1994 suggest a population of 42.3 mn. With an area of 2.3 mn sq km, the density of population is 18.5 persons per sq km, lower than the density in Africa generally. The density varies from 100 per sq km in Bas Zaïre to between 1 and 3 per sq km in the S. Urbanisation is high at 40% in 1994. The rate of population growth was 3.% per year over the period 1980-90, about average for Africa.

In 1990 Zaïre had a GDP of US$7,540 mn, making it, by virtue of its population size and mineral wealth, one of the larger African economies. GNP per capita at US$220, however, one of the lowest in Africa, makes Zaire a low-income country. Zaïre's rural population is particularly poor with most of the wealth being in the hands of a urban élite in the capital and the mining zone in the S.

The agricultural sector is proportionately smaller than in most other countries in Central Africa, generating only 30% of GDP. Industry, which includes the important mining sector, accounted for a further 33% (against a regional average of 15%), while the service sector generated the other 26% (below the regional average of 42%). Private consumption was 75% of GDP, with government consumption 10%. The

THE GAZELLE AND THE GREEDY LEOPARD

One day the Gazelle and the Leopard went in search of palm-nuts. As they were passing down one of the paths they saw a tree with some fine bunches of nuts. The leopard said, 'Friend Gazelle, wait here while I climb the tree and cut down the nuts'.

With his strong, sharp claws the Leopard soon ascended the tree and found three bunches of delicious, ripe nuts. But instead of cutting them and throwing them down, he sat on a frond and began to eat them.

By and by the Gazelle shouted out, 'Throw me some of the nuts'. But the Leopard replied, 'While I am eating palm-nuts, I cannot hear anything'.

The gazelle waited a little time and then called out again 'Please throw me down some of the nuts, for I have hoofs, and cannot climb a tree like you." But the Leopard ate on greedily, and took no notice of his friend's request.

The Gazelle went and gathered some firewood and grass, and made a large fire at the bottom of the palm tree. In a short while the Leopard called out, 'Friend Gazelle, put out your fire; the heat and smoke are choking me.' The Gazelle, however, answered him saying, 'When I am warming myself by the fire, I cannot hear anything'; and he threw on some more wood and grass. The Leopard, choking, lost his grip on the tree and fell to the ground, dead. The Gazelle returned to the town and took all the Leopard's possessions.

The fable of the Gazelle and the Greeedy Leopard is one of the traditional stories told in Zaire, as entertainment in the village by the fire. Usually the narrator will pretend to imitate the voice and manner of the animals in the story, to add to the dramatic effect. The stories are invariably moral tales with a weak, timid or defenceless creature (a sparrow or a gazelle) pitted against a stronger, selfish, bullying animal (an elephant, a crocodile or leopard). Some cleverness of the under-dog allows it to triumph, usually with some ironic twist (as in the story above, with the Gazelle, in turn, pretending not to hear).

level of investment is low compared with the rest of Africa, at 13%, of which 10% is contributed by domestic saving. Exports were equal to 37% of GDP with imports 24%. The main exports are copper 42%, coffee 13% and diamonds 9%, while main imports were machinery 40%, food produce 29% and fuels 24%.

The adult literacy rate was estimated at 72% in 1990, quite a bit better than in the region and in Africa generally. It was estimated in 1990 that 60% of primary-age children were in school with 24% of secondary-age children being educated. Of the 20-24 year age group, 2% were in higher education. These figures make Zaïre's educational provision well above average.

Life expectancy of 53 years is a little above the African average. There were around 13,400 people per doctor and Zaïre would appear to have better health provision than the region, though many rural areas have limited health services. Average daily calorie supply per head in 1987 was just above the Africa norm.

Overall, Zaïre has a large economy in the African context but with very low average income. The agriculture and services sectors are small, and the industry sector, which includes mining, is large. Investment levels are low. There is about average trade dependency. Educational and health provisions appear good, although there is considerably better provision in the urban areas than in the rural.

Economic performance

GDP grew by 1.8% a year over the period

1980-90, compared with a regional average of 1.6%, though this is still above the figure of 0.6 % for the whole of Africa. GDP per head declined at -1.4% a year.

The 2.5% growth in the agricultural sector for this period is well above the regional rate of 1.1%. The industrial sector, which is largely dependent on mining, shows growth at 3.6%, above the regional average of 1.1%. Services grew by 1.6% a year in Zaïre while the region as a whole showed growth of 2.5%.

It is in the trade sector that performance has been paricularly poor, with export volumes falling by -11.2% a year, import volumes declining by -4.0%.

Inflation in Zaïre was 61% a year, 1980-90, well above the regional and African averages of 24 % and 16% respectively.

Overall, Zaïre has managed to achieve expansion of GDP in the 1980s, but there has still been declining GDP per head, with agriculture and industry performing better than the services sector. Export volumes have fallen steadily, although imports have shown a smaller decline. The inflation rate has been one of the highest in Africa.

Recent economic developments

Zaïre began a programme of economic reform in 1983 which involved a float of the currency, the ending of price controls, reductions in government spending, the ending of state monopolies and the winding-up of some state-owned enterprises. There has been some faltering in this programme, and the IMF and World Bank have pressed for more rapid withdrawal from public sector involvement in manufacturing, mining and marketing. In Oct 1986 the President indicated that debt servicing would be limited to 20% of overall government spending or 10% of export earnings. This led to the withholding of World Bank lending, but this was restored by mid 1987 when further agreements with the IMF introduced plans to reduce projected public sector spending, increase tax revenues and petrol prices, and continue reforms of public sector enterprises. In Aug 1987, 9 state-owned enterprises covering trading, housing, management training, savings, fishing, livestock, construction and steel, were dissolved. Zaïre has now revised its debt servicing proposals, and with re-schedulings these will be kept to 30% of government spending.

There have been some signs of improvement in economic performance since 1983. Economic growth has been positive, but below the rate of population growth. Rehabilitation of Zaïre's mining sector is expected to be a long process, and will depend on improvements to the transport network, and are not expected to be completed before the end of 1990. There have been encouraging increases in diamonds marketed through official channels with the ending of the government monopoly in 1982 and the depreciation of the currency has discouraged smuggling.

Inflation performance has been variable, with annual rates of price increase in the 1980s between 20% and 75%. From 1983 to 1985, the inflation rate fell, from 77% to 24%, but then rose again to 47% in 1986. Inflation in the current climate of crises is very high, with the government printing money to meet its expenditures, but collecting virtually no taxes. In 1992 inflation was over 4,000%.

A combination of falling prices for Zaïre's main mineral exports and poor production performance have resulted in falling export earnings, though copper prices have started to improve again recently. However, Gécamines has invested over US$700 mn for repair and modernisation of capital equipment and in 1989 the World

Bank granted them US$20 mn for a technical assistance programme.

Zaire's external debt was estimated at US$8.9 bn in 1990, of which 28% is with commercial banks. The currency has steadily depreciated in the 1980s, first by devaluations, and then after 1983 by a floating exchange rate. This has seen the exchange rate for Zaïre depreciate from Z 2.8 = US$1 in 1980 to Z 119.6 = US$1 in Aug 1987 and further devaluations brought it down to Z 435 = US$1 by the end of 1989. The current economic crisis saw the value of the currency depreciate

Comparative Economic And Social Data

	Burundi	East Africa	Africa	Industrial countries
Population and land				
Population, mid year, millions, 1994	42.3	12.2	10.2	40.0
Urban Population, %, 1990	40	30.5	30	75
Population Growth Rate, % per year, 1980-91	3.2	3.1	3.1	0.8
Land Area, thou. sq. kilom.	2,345	486	486	1,628
Population Density, persons per sq km, 1994	18.5	24.2	20.4	24.3
Economy: production and income				
GDP, US$millions, 1990	7,540	2,650	3,561	550,099
GNP per head, US$, 199	220	250	389	12,960
Economy: supply structure				
Agriculture, % of GDP, 1990	30	43	35	3
Industry, % of GDP, 1990	33	15	27	35
Services, % of GDP, 1990	26	42	38	61
Economy: demand structure				
Private Consumption, % of GDP, 1989	75	77	73	62
Gross Domestic Investment, % of GDP, 1989	13	16	16	21
Government Consumption, % of GDP, 1989	10	15	14	17
Exports, % of GDP, 1989	27	16	23	17
Imports, % of GDP, 1989	24	24	26	17
Economy: performance				
GDP growth, % per year, 1980-90	1.8	1.6	-0.6	2.5
GDP per head growth, % per year, 1980-90	-1.4	-1.7	-3.7	1.7
Agriculture growth, % per year, 1980-90	2.5	1.1	0.0	2.5
Industry growth, % per year, 1980-90	2.3	1.1	-1.0	2.5
Services growth, % per year, 1980-90	1.6	2.5	-0.5	2.6
Exports growth, % per year, 1980-90	-11.2	0.7	-1.9	3.3
Imports growth, % per year, 1980-90	-4.0	0.2	-6.9	4.3
Economy: other				
Inflation Rate, % per year, 1980-90	60.9	23.6	16.7	5.3
Aid, net inflow, % of GDP, 1990	11.9	11.5	6.3	-
Debt service, % of Exports, 1990	15.4	18	20.6	-
Budget surplus (+), Deficit (-), 1990	1.9	-3.0	-2.8	-5.1
Education				
Primary, % of 6-11 group, 1989	60	62	76	102
Secondary, % of 12-17 group, 1990	24	15	22	93
Higher, % of 20-24 group, 1990	2	1.2	1.9	39
Adult literacy rate, %, 1990	72	41	39	99
Health and nutrition				
Life expectancy, years, 1989	53	50	50	76
Calorie supply, daily per head, 1989	2,130	2,111	2,096	3,357
Population per doctor, 1987	13,540	35,986	24,185	550

Notes: 'Africa' excludes South Africa. Dates are for the country in question, and do not always correspond with the Regional, African and Industrial averages.

to Z 1,990,000 = US$1 in 1994, and this has prompted a replacement of the currency with New Zaires at the rate in 1994 of NZ 120.5 = US$1.

The IMF committed US$230 mn in structural adjustment lending in mid-1987, and the World Bank US$149 mn. Belgium has committed US$ 24.1 mn of programme aid and Japan US$ 15.9 mn. There are numerous aid projects, covering sugar rehabilitation, hydro-electricity, mining, railway upgrading, an inland waterways scheme, harbours, roads, education, farming, rural manufacturing, and small industry schemes, rural development and electrification.

Foreign investment has included a US$20 mn commitment by Belgium's Petrofund for oil exploration, and a joint venture by Romania in a US$17 mn manganese project.

Economic outlook

Zaire has enormous long-term economic potential, with its mineral wealth, some oil deposits, and fertile agricultural land. Foreign investors have become involved on the basis that they can establish safe enclaves, but their operations in the minerals sector have had very little impact on the living standards of ordinary people. There is little prospect of generally improving economic circumstances until political stability improves and sound government returns.

GOMA

For much of the summer of 1994, the world's attention has been focused on Goma as the tragedy in Rwanda unfolded. Because of its proximity to the Rwandan border, hundreds of thousands of refugees have been allowed to enter Zaire. The camps at Goma have quickly become disease ridden and many have died. Aid agencies and foreign governments have been unable to stem the flow of refugees or, despite valiant efforts, alleviate the suffering for the majority. For more background information, see box page 498.

Before the refugee crisis, Goma was a pleasant cosmopolitan town (population 100,000) at the foot of Nyiragongo volcano in the Virunga Massif on Lake Kivu, close to the Rwanda border. It is 1,500m above sea level in the heart of Zaire's most important region for tourism. It is also the commercial centre for East Zaire and a popular place for government officials. Consequently, the airport at Goma has been upgraded to take international flights and services for tourists and budget travellers are well developed. Now the airport has been used for an almost unprecedented airlift of supplies for the refugees. The administrative centre for Virunga National Park is in the town. The architecture in the centre is colonial, but the outskirts are unusual, made up of wooden huts painted black with brightly coloured doors and windows.

WARNING Because of the current crisis in Rwanda, Goma must be regarded as off limits for travellers and tourists. Check with your embassy before attempting to enter this area.

Places of interest

Nyragongo and Nyamulagira Volcanos
Nyragongo at 3,470m was last active in 1977, Nyamulagira is 3,056m and was last active in 1981. For both a guide is obligatory and it is best to plan to take about 2 days to climb each. You will need to provide your own camping equipment though there is a hut on the Nyrangongo excursion. The **Lac Vert**, a few km from the centre of Goma on the way to Bukavu is idyllic. It is green because of the reflection of the green slopes surrounding the lake. The **Mokoto Lakes** further on towards Bukavu are 4 lakes again in beautiful surroundings. **Mont Goma** to the western part of the city has good views of the city, the lake and the volcanic mountains. Also of interest is the **market** which is beyond Avenue President Mobutu to the N along a dirt road in a residential area of Goma where there are woven baskets and other curios. Goma is not far from the **Parc National des Virunga** on the Rwanda/Zaire border which is home to mountain gorillas. The lake shore in Goma is poor for swimming, and the nearest good beaches are at **Gisenyi** in Rwanda, just across the border.

Local information

● Where to stay

A *Hotel des Grands Lacs*, PO Box 253, Avenue President Mobutu. Restaurant. Bar. Own bathrooms.

B *Masques*, PO Box 530. In the centre of town, near Point Rond de la Poste. Garden. Swimming pool, Patio bar. Restaurant. Good value. **B** *Karibu*, PO Box 266. On the NW edge of the city on the lake about 4 km from the centre. Swimming pool, tennis courts, restaurant and bar. All rooms have bath and toilet facilities.

C *Rif*, PO Box 576, Rue Mont Goma, near the centre of town. Restaurant and bar. Own bathrooms. Good value. **C** *Mont Goma*, PO Box 320. Near the Rond Point de la Poste. All rooms with wc/bath. Bar. **C** *Jambo* Centre of town. Well run and pleasant.

D *Lumumba*, just N of post office. Best value in this price range. **D** *Cookboki*, just W of market. Good restaurant. Shared bathrooms.

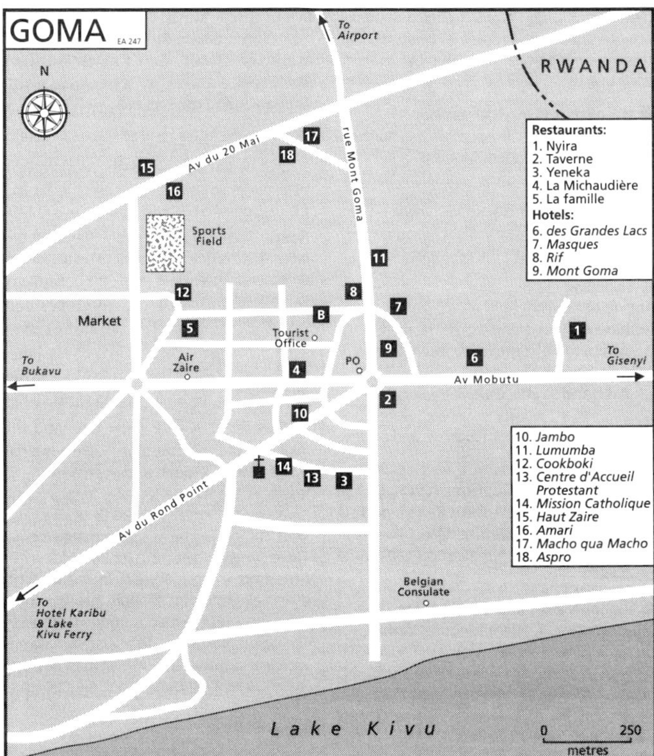

D *Centre d'Accueil Protestant*, Avenue Bougainvillea, just off Ave du Rond Point. Single rooms with shower and wc. No admission after 2200. **D** *Mission Catholique*, Ave du Rond Point. Clean, quiet and secure.

E *Haute Zaire*, N of market. Best in this price range. **E** *Amari*, Ave du 20 Mai. Reasonable value. **E** *Macho kwa Macho*, near market in town centre. Very basic. **E** *Chambres Aspro*, just off Ave du 20 Mai. Facilities spartan.

● Places to eat

♦♦♦♦*La Nyira*, Ave President Mobutu. Good standard. Provides selection of magazines (in French).

♦♦♦*Karibu*, on the NW edge of the city on the lake about 4 km from the centre. Music in the evenings. Very pleasant atmosphere. Take taxi or motor-taxi.

♦♦*Taverne Restaurant*, Rond Point de la Post is also good. ♦♦*Restaurant Yeneka*, Centre d'Accueil Protestant, just W of market. Solid fare, sound value. ♦♦*La Michaudiere*, Ave Mobutu. Grills.

♦*Restaurant La Famille* Close to market. Unpretentious.

♦*Hotel Cooboki* Local food, but good standard.

● Bars

Many of the restaurants listed above have good bars including *La Michaudiere*, and *La Nyira*, on Ave Mobutu. *Karibu* and *des Grands Lacs* have popular and comfortable bars.

● Banks

Banque Commerciale Zairoise, and *Banque de Kinshasa*, both are on the Avenue President Mobutu. ***Des Grands Lacs*** will change traveller's cheques and cash 24 hours, though the rate is not particularly favourable, the service is quick.

● Hospitals and medical services
The Zairian-African Hospital at the northern end of Avenue President Mobutu.

● Post offices
The main post office is at Rond Point de la Poste (roundabout) on Ave President Mobutu which runs straight through the centre of Goma.

● Shopping
The road leading to the airport has many boutiques and souvenir shops. The market has a wide range of clothing, household goods; mild bartering is expected.

Arts and crafts ***Galerie***, Ave de l'Aeroport. Excellent quality jewellery, wood-carvings. ***Caritas***, Rond Point. Baskets and pottery.

● Tourist office
Office National du Tourisme (ONT), BP 730 Just near Rond Point. ***Institut Zairois pour la Conservation de la Nature (IZNC)***, Ave President Mobutu for information on seeing the gorillas.

● Tour operators and travel agents
Agetraf, Ave President Mobutu. ***Amiza***, PO Box 372 , Ave President Mobutu, T 514. ***Kivu Voyage Liwali***, Point Rond. ***Zaire Safari***, PO Box 530, *Masques Hotel*. In the centre of town, near Point Rond de la Poste. ***Zaire Gorilla Safari***, PO Box 530, *Masques Hotel*. In the centre of town, near Point Rond de la Poste.

● Transport
Local This is a small town, easy to get around by foot. There are taxis and motor-taxis (motor-bikes).

Car hire is possible from travel agents ***Kivu Voyage Liwaili***, ***Zaire Safari***, and ***Agetraf***.

Air **Goma-Bukavu**: several times daily on TMC, VAC and Scibe Airlift; **Goma-Butembo**: 4 times weekly on TMC and VAC; **Goma-Beni**: direct daily except Sat on TMC, VAC and Scibe Airlift; **Goma-Bunia**: direct once a week on Scibe Airlift; **Goma-Butembo-Bunia**: twice a week on TMC; **Goma-Kalemie-Lubumbashi**: twice a week on Scibe Airlift; **Goma-Bunia-Kinangani**: once a week on Scibe Airlift.

To book onto the flights, Air VAC and Scibe Airlift have an office next to the *Masques Hotel* near the main roundabout, and the Air Zaire office is on Ave Mobutu.

Road There is limited public transport, and what there is does not operate on any regular timetable. There is a road from **Goma to Bukavu** known as the *Route de la Beauté*, this is generally negotiable all year round though the surface is terrible, full of potholes, making the journey exhausting and time consuming (up to 24 hours). There is a daily minibus from the *Hotel Rif* which leaves at about 0700. You will need to buy your ticket the day before (from behind the post office). There is a daily bus between **Goma and Rutshuru** which leaves in the early afternoon from Boutique Lavao on the Rutshuru road (N of Ave du 20 Mai). The journey takes approximately 3 hours. There is meant to be a bus running to and from **Butembo** 4 times a week from the Centre d'Accueil Protestant though they do not always run, and the road is in very poor shape. The journey takes over 10 hours. Hitching rides with trucks (you will be expected to pay) from Ave President Mobutu is not difficult and is safe.

Lake There is a ship the ***Vedette*** to Bukavu on the southern end of Lake Kivu, 2 round trips a week, leaving early in the morning, days of departure vary (US$11 one way). The journey takes 6 hours. There is also the ***Karisimbi*** a cargo ship which makes one round trip a week (US$8 one way), and a delivery boat for the Bukavu brewery the ***Mulamba*** which makes one round trip a week and takes some passengers (US$12 first class, US$6 second). All ferries should be booked a day in advance, tickets are for sale from the port. You will need to show your passport to buy tickets.

SOUTH TO BUKAVU AND UVIRA

The road along the western shore of Lake Kivu from Goma to Bukavu is a splendid journey, running through the Kahuzai Beiga National Park. The highway is part of the extended *Route de la Beauté* which runs up to Beni. Uvira is significant for its position on one of the routes to Bujumbura. South of Uvira there is little of interest to the traveller accessing the region from the E.

Bukavu

This is the capital city of Kivu region, and is at the southern end of Lake Kivu at 1,500m above sea level. It has a population of 185,000, and is built on several promontories extending into the lake, and on the slopes of the hillside, surrounded by tea plantations, cinchona groves (used to produce quinine) as well as woodland of pine and eucalyptus. The city itself is an attractive place to stop off en route to the Kahuzi-Biega National Park which is 30 km away. The countryside surrounding the town is beautiful. More English is spoken here than in most other parts of Eastern Zaire primarily because of the American Peace Corps training centre based here.

Places of interest

Daily markets in the districts of Nyamugo and Tshimbunda are very African, offering produce for everyday use. Apart from this, the views of the lake are wonderful.

Local information

● Where to stay

B *Residence*, PO Box 406, Ave President Mobutu, T 2941. Bar. Restaurant. Rooms with bath/wc. Colonial style, a little faded.

C *Riviera*, Avenue du Lac. This is on the main peninsula, facing W over the lake. Restaurant. Bar. Nightclub. Rooms have bath and toilet facilities. Splendid location.

D *Nambo*, Route d'Uvira, southern end, about 2 km from town centre. **D** *Jolis Logis*, Ave des Martyre de la Revolution. Garden. Outside bar. Good value. Own bathroom. **D** *Belle-Vue*, Ave President Mobutu, T 2266. Small, clean. **D** *Canadien*, Ave President Mobutu, southwest of cathedral. Comfortable, well run. **D** *Lolango I*, Ave President Mobutu, N end, on peninsula. Some rooms with bathrooms. **D** *Lolango II*, Ave President Mobutu, less well located than its sister hotel, but near centre. Some rooms with bathroom. **D** *Fregate*, Ave President Mobutu Pleasant garden. and rooms have en suite bath/wc. Colonial-style. **D** *Metropole*, Ave President Mobutu. This is small but comfortable. Good value. Pleasant garden café.

E *Taifa*, Ave des Martyrses de la Revolution. Lively bar. Cold water only. **E** *De la Victoire*, just off Ave des Martyres de la Revolution. Cheap but basic. **E** *Moderne*, Ave des Martyres de la Revolution. Very cheap, very basic. **E** *Mu-ungu*, Ave des Martyres de la Revolution. Southern end. **E** *Mondial*, Ave des Martyres de la Revolution. Southern end. **E** *Ngeza Guest House*, Ave des Martyres de la Revolution. Southern extremity.

● Camping

At the *Cercle Sportif* on the lake shore, though it is not that cheap. Excellent location at tip of main peninsula.

● Places to eat

Restaurants are attached to all hotels, there are many small places serving local food in town. ♦♦♦♦*Restaurant Bodega*, *Hotel Residence*, Ave President Mobutu. International food, prepared to a good standard. ♦♦♦♦*Restaurant Hotel Riviera*, Ave du Lac. Marvellous location. Varied menu.

♦♦♦*Cafe Negrita*, Ave President Mobutu. Good standard.

♦♦*Café Hotel Metropole*, Ave President Mobutu. Pleasant outdoor café. ♦♦*Patisserie du Kivu*, on Ave President Mobutu. Continental style.

♦*Restaurant Docteur Wa Tumbo*, near market on Place du 24 Novembre.

● Bars and night life

Riviera has a nightclub. *Taifa* has a lively bar and nightclub. There are many places along Ave des Martyres de la Revolution. Many have African music and stay open late.

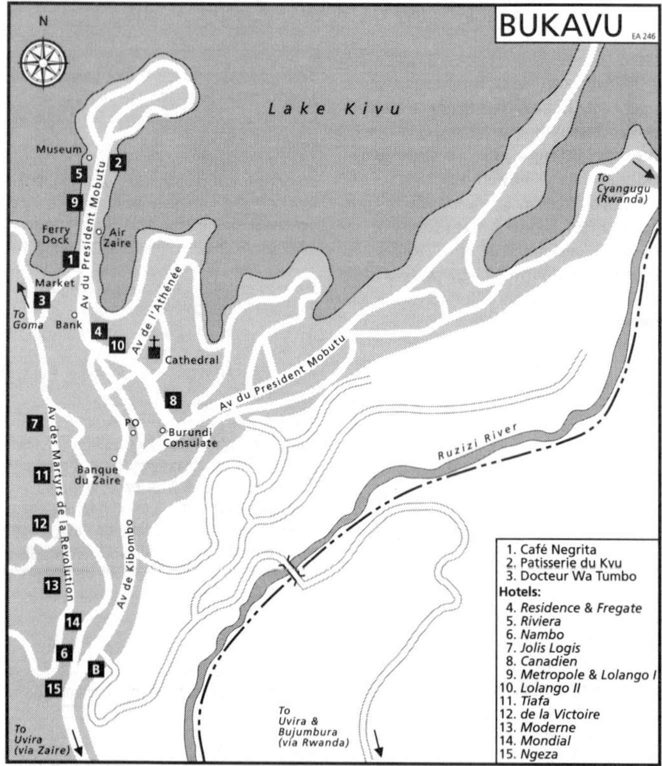

● Banks

Union Zairoise de Banques and **Banque Commercial Zairoise** both on Ave President Mobutu. The best place to change travellers' cheques is the Banque Commercial Zairoise.

● Curios

There are a number of good craft shops, and you will be approached by many hawkers on Ave President Mobutu. Local masks, drums and wood carvings a speciality.

● Embassies, high commissions and consulates

The **Belgian** Consulate is on Ave de Kibembo N from the Banque de Zaire. The **Burundi** Consulate is on the top floor of the SINELAC Building at 184 Ave du President Mobutu. It is open Mon-Fri from 0730-1200 and 1430-1700.

● Entertainment

Centre Culturel Français on Ave President Mobutu sometimes has films. There is the *Cercle Sportif* on the peninsula where you will be able to bathe on the beach, rent boats, water ski or play tennis or table tennis.

● Post offices

Ave de Kibombo open Mon-Fri from 0730-1230 and 1300-1630 and on Sat from 0730-1200.

● Telecommunications

Next to the post office on Ave de Kibombo, open 24 hours a day every day of the week including public holidays.

● Tourist office

Institut Zairois pour la Conservation de la Nature at 185 Ave du President Mobutu is where you will need to book a visit to the gorillas. It is open from Mon-Fri 0830-1500 and on Sat from 0830-1200. A visit to the gorillas costs US$100 payable in dollars or travellers cheques.

● Tour operators and travel agents
Amiza (PO Box 2836 T 2877/78) and *Agetraf*, both on Ave President Mobutu, deal with plane reservations, car hire and excursions.

● Transport
Air Goma-Bukavu several times daily on TMC, VAC and Scibe Airlift. Their offices are next to the *Hotel Lolango* and VAC has an office in the *Hotel Residence*.

Road There is are minibuses between **Bukavu and Goma** from the Place du 24 Novembre, though it is more pleasant to take the ferry. Minibuses to **Uvira** from the Place Major Vangu which take 4 hours and leave when it is full. **Bukavu to Cyangugu** in Rwanda leave regularly from Place Major Vangu heading down to the Rwanda-Burundi border at Bugarama – if you have a visa for Rwanda this is a better way to reach Bujumbura than via Uvira. **Parc National de Kahuzi-Biega**, catch a minibus heading for Miti from Place du 24 Novembre. If you are hitching, the main truck stop is by the Mare Maman Mobutu close to the Place Major Vangu.

Lake Boats to and from Goma (see page 564)

Uvira

This is a small town with little of interest except that it is the nearest point of entry to Zaire from Burundi. It is quite nicely located, on Lake Tanganyika, with mountains behind. There is a **Catholic Mission** behind the main thoroughfare which runs along the shore. If you are travelling from Bujumbura to Bukavu, and you do not wish to go via Rwanda, either because you haven't got a visa, or because of the security situation there, it is worth going via Uvira. Otherwise, the road N, and the transport links, despite the extra border crossing, are better through Burundi, to Cyangugu and then across to Bukavu. In principle there should be boats going S down the lake on the Zaire side, but none appeared to be running regularly in 1994.

• Where to stay **D** *la Cote*, shore side of main street, Ave Bas Zaire. Reasonably well run with an open-air bar in the centre of the courtyard, a restaurant. Fans. Some rooms a/c. Good value. **E** *Babyo*, rather run-down and grubby on the shore side of main street, Ave Bas Zaire. No bar or restaurant.

• Transport Road There are fairly regular minibuses to **Bukavu** going N, leaving from the main street, Ave Bas Zaire. The journey takes about 4 hours and costs US$3. To the S, transport is much more problematical. Minibuses do go, but on a very irregular basis, passing through a series of small fishing villages, and then cutting inland before reaching **Kalemie**, 300 km distant, which is on the railway. To **Bujumbura**, there are taxis (US$5) to the Zaire border post, you can walk or get a lift on a bicycle (US$0.50) to the Burundi post, from where there are minibuses into Bujumbura (US$1.50). **Lake** Boats are very irregular, and could involve a wait of many days. The port, Kulundu, is about 2 km S of the main town. If you are checking out boats it is advisable, for safety, to take a taxi or a motor-taxi (motorcycle) or hire a local guide to go with you.

NORTH TO BUNIA

The road from Goma N to Bunia is known as the Route de la Beauté. It is a tremendous scenic attraction, with the traveller passing through mountains covered with rich vegetation, with glimpses of the mountain lakes, and plentiful wildlife and bird species to be seen, particularly through the Virungu National Park (see page 572).

Masisi

NW of Goma, aboout 30 km distant, is the small village of Sake, and the **Mokoto Lakes**, an area with 4 mountain waters of great scenic beauty, are close by. A further 30 km on, in the direction of Lubuto is Masisi. There are several farms at this high altitude (2,000m) location, with dairy operations and producing a variety of temperate zone fruit and vegetables, which will provide tours for visitors. *Ferme de Rushengo* makes a point of welcoming travellers, *Ferme de Bunyole* has a cheese factory that can be toured.

• **Where to stay D** *Ferme de Lushebere*, run by the Catholic mission also has a cheese factory, and has some simple but comfortable accommodation. **C** ***Auberge de Monts***, C/O BP 429 Goma; or via a Goma travel agent, see page 564). Further up in the mountains from Masisi, but is a delightful place, Swiss chalet-style, open fires, horse-riding, a good base for mountain treking. It can be reached in about 3 hours from Goma. It is difficult to reach if you do not have a vehicle, and the best tactics are to fix your stay, with travel included, through the Goma agents. It is popular, so it is wise to book.

Rutshuru

Rutshuru, 75 km from Goma, is a convenient place from which to start your visit to the mountain gorillas in the **Parc National des Virunga** (see page 572). You are also likely to come to Rutshuru if you are crossing to or from Uganda via Kisoro. Just S of the town is the **Rutshuru Waterfall**, a popular scenic site, with the falls surrounded by vegetation.

• **Where to stay and eat D** *Gremafu* To N of town. Bar. Restaurant. Rather charming atmosphere. **E** *The Lodging House* On main road. Very simple. **E** *Catholic Mission Guest House* Restaurant. Simple clean and good value.

• **Camping** available in grounds of Catholic Mission Guest House.

• **Transport Road** There is a daily bus to *Goma* taking about 2 hours which costs US$4. Bus to ***Butembo*** takes 12 hours and costs US$8. There is also a route to Ishasha and on to Kabele in Uganda (see page 568)

Rwindi

The small town of Rwindi is 55 km from Rutshuru on the road to Butembo. The entrance to Park National des Virunga is on this section. The road through the park leads to **Vitshumbi**, a rather charming fishing village at the southern end of Lake Edward. From Vitshumbi there is a road to Ishasha, the crossing point into Uganda. On the road to Vitshumbi are the **Maji ya Moto** hot sulphur springs. A *Hotel de la Rwindi* is in the park, just past Maji yo Moto springs. It has a pool, bar and restaurant, and rooms have own bathrooms.

• **Transport** See Goma, page 564, or Rutshuru (above).

Kayna-Bayonga

The small town of Kayna-Bayonga is 2 km from Rwindi. It is at an altitude of over 2,000m, on a very hilly site, and from the **Catholic Church** it is possible to see all the surrounding area. A small kiosk at the southern end of town sells crafts. **E** *Hotel Italie*, on the main road, and has a bar and restaurant. Oil lamps.

• **Transport** See Goma, page 564, or Rutshuru (above).

Butembo

Butembo is a large town (population 100,000) about halfway between Goma and Bunia. It is set in beautiful countryside and has a good market.

Local information

● Where to stay

D *Ambiance* Well run with good facilities and a pleasing atmosphere. Bar. Restaurant.

E *Logement Apollo II*, simple facilities. **E** *Semuliki Restaurant. Fairly basic, but reasonable value.*

● Places to eat

♦♦*Semuliki* Restaurant serves reasonable standard food.

♦*Restaurant Cafeteria* Near the market. Good value.

● Transport

Road Buses to **Goma** take about 10 hrs and cost about US$10. Trucks leave from the southern end of the main street in Butembo. There are frequent minibuses travelling between **Beni** and Butembo, the journey takes about 4 hrs and costs US$2.

Beni

Beni is a small town at the crossroads of routes going N to S, and E to Uganda. It is the most convenient starting point for climbing the **Rwenzori Mountains** from the Zaire side. If you are making an excursion to the mountains, this is the place to aquire fresh provisions. North of Beni is Mt Hoyo, with a waterfall, grottoes and pygmy villages.

Local information

● Where to stay

C *Virunga* Fairly comfortable. Good facilities. **C** *Busa Beni* Just S of Rond Point. **C** *Isale* Just off road to N, past Rond Point. Comfortable and good value.

D *Sina Makosa* Reasonable value.

E *Jumbo* Fairly simple. Oil lamps. **E** *Walaba* Oil lamps. Restaurant. Self-catering if required. **E** *Basmie* Restaurant. Good value. **E** *Majestic*. Central. Fairly basic.

● Places to eat

♦♦♦♦*Busa Beni* Good quality. International food.

♦♦*Lualaba* Solid fare, mostly local. Good value. ♦♦*Restaurant du Rond Point* Central. Simple dishes, well prepared.

♦*Somalia Restaurant* Just E of Rond Point. Sound local food.

● Transport

Road There is plenty of public transport between Beni and **Butembo**, (2 hrs, US$2) and on to **Goma** (14 hrs, US$10). Bus and truck park on Komanda Rd for transport N to to **Komanda**, takes about 6 hrs and costs US$7.

Komanda

Small town 125 km N of Beni, on the road to Bunia. About 125 km W of Komanda, just beyond Mambasa is **Epulu**, there is a reserve for okapis, a species endemic to Zaire, and similar to the giraffe. **E** Hotel LL, small, simple, but reasonable.

● Transport see Beni above, and Bunia, below.

Mt Hoyo

This site is about 25 km S of Komanda. It is administered by the parc National de Virunga. A 7 day permit costs US$5, and a photography permit is US$0.50, administered through the lodge at the site, Auberge de Mount Hoyo. The mountain itself is 1,450m high, and can be climbed, although you will need a guide. The waterfall is the *Steps of Venus* (Chutes des Venus). The grottoes are cave systems, three in all, one of which emerges at the base of the waterfall. The pygmies will, for a small fee that it is wise to fix at the outset, entertain with dances, allow you to tour the village, let you take photographs of them, and show you examples of their crafts.

● Where to stay **C** *Auberge de Mount Hoyo*. Situated at 1,200m, constructed in chalet-style, has a restaurant, and is reasonably comfortable.

● Camping, with use of showers and toilets, at the Auberge de Mount Hoyo.

● Travel see Beni above, and Bunia, below.

Bunia

A town of reasonable size. It has an airstrip and a bank. It is the northern end of the *Route de la Beauté*. A small, pleasant and lively fishing village is **Tshoma**, near Kasenyi, about 10 km E of Bunia on the shore of Lake Mobuto Seso Seko (Lake Albert). Much of the fishing is done at night for *dagaa* (small freshwater sardines), using pressure oil-lamps hung over the back of the boat to attract the shoals. One of the implications of this nocturnal work is that bars and food kiosks stay open all night. Unfortunately the lake is infected with bilharzia.

Local information

● Where to stay

(all fairly central, on the main thoroughfare): **D** ***Semliki***, restaurant; **D** ***Ituri***, tolerable; **D** ***Chez Tout Bunia***, restaurant, reasonable value.

E ***Rubi***, simple but sound; **E** ***Palace***, restaurant. Good value; **E** ***Butembo II***, restaurant. Well run.

● Transport

From **Goma** to Bunia, if you manage to get a bus going all the way, takes 24 hours and costs US$20. It is likely that you will find it easier to manage in 2 stages, with an overnight stop at either Beni or Butembo. For sightseers, there is little point in travelling along the ***Route de la Beauté*** in darkness. To **Komanda**, the nearest town to the S takes 3 hrs, and costs US$3.

NATIONAL PARKS AND RESERVES

Kahuzi-Biega National Park

The Kahuzi-Biega National Park is about 30 km from Bukavu and covers about 600,000 ha. Its name comes from the 2 highest peaks in the park, Kahuzi at 3,308m and Biega at 2,790m. The region of thick mountainous forest was created into a national park in 1970 to protect the eastern lowland gorilla which is an endangered species. It was expanded in 1975.

The vegetation of the park varies. Bamboo forests make up a third of the park lying between 2,400 and 2,600 m. Above this the area is savanna covered with heather. As a result of the varied vegetation, many different animals and birds live in the park including chimpanzees, many other species of monkeys, elephants, buffalo, antelope, leopard and mongoose. The dry season is from Jun to Aug and average yearly temperatures are around 16 degrees centigrade.

There are many different excursions worth making into the park. Climbing **Mount Kahuzi** (3310m) takes about three hours through rich Alpine flora. The weather is variable, so it is wise to take a raincoat and sturdy climbing shoes. The departure point is Poste Patrol Kahuzi which is along the sealed road from the entrance at Tshivanga. Guides are compulsory. You will need to bring everything you may need.

A 10 km hike takes you to the top of **Mont Bugulumiza** which has splendid views reaching out to the Virunga National Park on a clear day. It is also possible to drive up Mont Bulgulumiza.

The main reason people come to the park is to see the gorillas. There are 2 groups of gorillas who have become used to people, and are therefore approachable, including the large male silverbacks.

Practical information for seeing the gorillas

The gorillas can be visited every day of the year including bank holidays. Excursions to see the gorillas are limited to 8 people per day per gorilla family in order not to upset their behaviour patterns. It is necessary to make reservations at the IZCN offices in Goma or Bukavu and they do get fairly full during peak season, particularly as tour groups from the neighbouring countries of Uganda and Rwanda often come here. However, it has been known for people to get on the tour just by turning up at the Station Tshivanga an hour before departure time for visiting the gorillas.

The tour leaves at 0900 and the visit ends at 1300. You can only enter the park with a tour guide and the group usually has 2 other people to help clear a path through the undergrowth to look for the gorillas. It can take over 2 hours for the guide to track down the gorillas through difficult terrain, so you will need to be in a reasonable state of fitness. Depending on how long it has taken to track down the gorillas, you usually can spend about an hour with them. Good clothes to wear are sturdy boots, long trousers and shirts with long sleeve and a rainproof jacket as well as gloves.

It costs US$100 (only US dollars are accepted), half price for children though no children under 15 are permitted. The ticket entitles you to a 7 day visit in the park, though only one trip to the gorillas. You will be able to take photographs, but not with a flash. The locations of the gorillas can be shaded and dark, and if you intend to take photographs, get the fastest film you can.

For your safety, you are advised to always follow the guide and stay with the group. If approached by one of the gorillas do not retreat, and follow the guide's instructions. Never try to touch one of the young gorillas. Avoid making sudden movements. You will not be able to eat or smoke during the observation. There is a risk to the gorillas of infection from humans (which is one of the reasons children under 15 are excluded), and you will not be allowed to visit if you have an illness, however slight.

Departure point for the guided tour is from Tshivanga.

Park information

Where to stay

The station at Tshivanga in the park has a simple **E** *Tshivanga Lodge* which can sleep up to 12 people and has bathroom facilities. Camping is possible with your own tent.

Places to eat

You will need to bring all provisions with you.

Organised safaris

Orchids Safari Club, Zaire-based, but with offices in Rwanda and Belgium (22 Ave Kahuzi Beiga, Bukavu, Zaire; PO Box 357 Cyangugu, Rwanda T & F 37569; 13 Ave Porte de Hal, 1069 Brussels, Belgium, T 5390592/5388457, F 5370303 Tlx 25110). Has three establishments that can serve as bases for visits to Kahuzi Biega Park: a very attractive villa on the edge of Lake Kivu; a cottage at Mbayo; and a campsite on the Luhoho River at Irangi. The Irangi sites is very close to the edge of the park. Very experienced in the local situation in Zaire. *Eden Travel* Burundi-based (Galerie Alexandre, Place de l'Independance BP 1075 T 221616 F 224733. Organises safaris to Kahuzi Biega National Park in Zaire for gorilla tracking, stays in Zaire, cruising on Lake Kivu. *Rwanda Tours* Rwanda-based (BP 449 Kigali T 75037 F 73626/85893 Tlx 22541). Very experienced operator, arranging gorilla trekking in Rwanda and Zaire; chimpanzee trekking in Zaire. *Yare Safaris* Kenya-based (PO Box 63006 Nariobi offers a 25 day safari from Nairobi which visits the gorillas of Kahuzi-Biega, Nyiragongo Volcano, Goma, Lake Kivu, Rutshuru Falls, the Parc National des Volcans in Rwanda, the Serengeti National Park in Tanzania and the Maasai Mara in Kenya. You will need to pay the entry fee to each of the national parks and the tour costs about US$550 including food.

Transport

There is a minibus leaving **Bukavu** at 0600 from the Place du 24 Novembre to Miti. From there you will need to hitch or walk to Tshivanga which is about 7 km. It is best to travel the day before your visit in the park to make sure you are there on time. A taxi from Miti costs US$15.

Virunga National Park

This is the oldest and most famous of the national parks in Zaire, first opening in 1929. It stretches along the border with Uganda and Rwanda. It was established for the protection of mountain gorillas though it has expanded since then and now covers a total area of 800,000 ha. Virunga National Park is the most developed park for tourism. Not only gorillas live here but also buffalo, various species of antelope, hippopotami, elephants, lions, leopards and warthogs.

A number of tours are offered: a 26 km tour along Kibirizi to view buffalo, antelopes, hippos, warthogs and occasionally lions. A 31 km trip along the Rwindi River to see, as well as the occasional elephant, the waterfowl in the Lake Edward bay. The Rutshuru track (48 km) has impressive landscape and you are more likely to see lions here as well as large herds of hippos.

There are also gorilla visits at **Djomba** and **Bukima**. Cost per person is US$100. The Volcanoes **Nyiragongo** and **Nyamulgira** can be climbed (the fee is US$30); as can **Mt Rwenzori** (fee of US$50). All these excursions will need to be arranged through the tourist office in Goma (see page 564).

Entry to the park

This is from the pavilion at the *Hotel de la Rwindi*. The office is open from 0700 to 2100. Admission is US$50 for adults and half price for children unless you are just passing through on transport between Rutshuru and Kayna-Bayonga when you do not have to pay. The price includes an obligatory guide and lasts for 7 days and enables you to go into any part of the park. You need to apply for a photography permit if you intend to use a camera.

INFORMATION FOR VISITORS

Contents

Before you go

Entry requirements

● Visas

All nationalities need a visa which can be frustratingly hard to obtain. If you are applying for one in East Africa, the Kampala and Nairobi offices are said to be the easiest to obtain a visa from. You will need to fill in 4 forms to be submitted together with 4 passport photographs, a travel document, International Vaccination Document (Yellow Fever), and a medical certificate to state that the applicant has no contagious diseases. There are a host of different types of visas you can apply for, all with different costs: a transit visa with one entry (US$15); transit with multiple entry US$25); one month with one entry (US$25); one month with multiple entries (US$30); 2 months with one entry (US$40); 2 months with multiple entries (US$50); three months with one entry (US$60); three months with multiple entry (US$75).

If you are applying for a stay of more than one month, a police character reference will need to be submitted with your application. Visas normally take a week to be issued. If you are applying outside your own country, you will need a letter of introduction from your own embassy (many countries charge for this letter).

Visa extensions can be obtained in Bukavu for up to three months.

In practice it is often possible to get a visa quickly and without all the specified documentation. Zairean officials have not received their salaries for some time now, and they appear to get by on the fees raised in each embassy or consulate. If you indicate that you are prepared to pay over the odds, or that you will get the visa in another place, this can often get you the visa on the spot.

● Vaccinations

A yellow fever certificate is obligatory.

● Zairean representation overseas

East Africa **Burundi**, PO Box 872, Ave Zaire T 23584. **Ethiopia**, PO Box 2723, Makanisa Rd T 710111 Tlx 21043. **Kenya**, PO Box 48106, T 229771/2, Electricity House, Harambee Ave, Nairobi. Open Mon-Fri from 0900-1200. **Rwanda**, 504 Rue Longue, Kigali, T 5026/5327. **Tanzania**, PO Box 21638. Embassy on Malik Road near the junction with United Nations Road in Dar es Salaam, T 23452. Open Mon, Wed and Fri from 1100-1400. Consulate in Kigoma on Lake Tanganyika whose office hours are Mon-Fri from 0900-1200; **Uganda**, PO Box 4972, 20 Philip Road, Kololo District, Kampala, T 23377/232021, Tlx 61284. Embassy hours are Mon-Fri from 0800-1500.

Other Africa Abidjan (Cote d'Ivoire); Algiers (Algeria); Bangui (Central African Republic); Brazzaville (Congo); Cairo (Egypt); Conakry (Guinea); Cotonou (Benin); Dakar (Senegal); Khaartoum (Uganda); Lagos (Nigeria); Libreville (Gabon); Lome (Togo); Lusaka (Zambia); Maputo (Mozambique); Monrovia (Liberia); N'Djamena (Chad); New Delhi (India); Nouakchott (Mauritania); Rabat (Morocco); Tunis (Tunisia); Yaounde (Cameroon); Harare (Zimbabwe); Luanda (Angola).

Europe Bonn (Germany); London (UK); Madrid (Spain); Paris (France); Rome and Vatican City (Italy); Athens (Greece); Belgrade (Yugoslavia); Berne and Geneva (Switzerland); Lisbon (Portugal); Moscow (Russia); Brussels (Belgium); Bucharest (Romania); Tel Aviv (Israel); Warsaw (Poland); Vienna (Austria); The Hague (Netherlands).

Americas Ottawa (Canada); New York and Washington DC (USA); Brasilia (Brazil); Havana (Cuba).

Asia Tokyo (Japan); Beijing (China); New Delhi (India).

● Overseas representation in East Zaire

Burundi Top floor, 184 Ave du President Mobutu (the SINELAC building), Bukavu. The consulate is open Mon-Fri from 0730 till 1200 and 1430-1700.

● Tourist information

Office National du Tourisme, 2A Ave des Orangers, Kinshasa. (PO Box 9502 T 30070)

When to go

● Best time to visit

The drier months are from Jun to Sep, particularly Jul. Travelling during the rainy season becomes extremely difficult at other times, and animals search for cover in the forests making them hard to see.

Health

● Staying healthy

A yellow fever vaccinnation is obligatory. It is also recommended to have vaccinations against cholera, tetanus, and typhus. Protection should be taken against malaria. See general Health section, page 574.

Money

● Credit Cards

These are not generally accepted, but are taken by some airlines and travel agents.

● Cost of living

As in other parts of East Africa, services for tourists tend to be expensive so costs for up-market hotels, restaurants, and excursions are all quite expensive compared with services consumed by local people such as minibus transport, kiosk food, and basic hotels. Any imported item (say photographic film) will cost three times as much as in its country of origin.

● Currency

The unit of currency is the New Zaire. However, the rate of exchange has been depreciating rapidly, and this must be expected to continue. Currency declaration forms were abolished in 1986.

There was a currency replacement to the New Zaire in 1993, and traders in Bukavu showed some reluctance in accepting the new notes. It is best to carry US dollars.

There is little different between the bank rate and the black market rate in Zaire, though changing cash on the street is far easier and less time consuming than in the banks. The best bets for changing money are Asian or European shop keepers.

Travellers's cheques are not always accepted by banks in East Zaire.

Travelling with US dollars is imperative as you need them to enter all the national parks, and you need to carry a good range of smaller denomination notes. They are also useful to pay for hotels etc.

Getting there

● Air

There are scheduled services from other parts of Zaire and East Africa, by Zairean airlines, although they are often cancelled. The flights into Goma are the most regular and reliable. Flights serving Eastern Zaire**: Goma** from Kinshasa and Kisangani. **Bukavu** from Bjumbura; **Kalemie** from Lubambashi.

Air Rwanda flies from Kigali to Gisenyi (close to Goma) twice a week and Kamembe near Cyangugu (close to Bukavu) in the S, 6 times a week. **Air Zaire**, PO Box 8552, Ave du Port Kinshasa, T 24986, Tlx 21313. **Scibe Airlift**, PO Box 614, Kinshasha, T 22276 Tlx 21003. **Zairean Airlines**, PO Box 2111, Blvd du 30 Juin, Kinshasa T 24624, Tlx 21525.

● Road

It is possible to get to East Zaire overland from Burundi, Rwanda and Uganda. Be sure to have all relevant documents on you and be prepared for petty bribery unless you are resigned to spend a long time crossing borders.

Burundi There are 2 main routes. **Bujumbura** to **Bukavu** via **Cyangugu** take a minibus from Bujumbura to Rugombo then you will need to make your own way for the next 12 km via Rugombo to the Burundi border post at Luhwa and the next 8 km to the border village of Bugarama. These legs are best handled by getting a motor-taxi (motorbike). There is a minibus from there to Cyangugu and it is just a short crossing from Cyangugu to Bukavu in Zaire. This route takes you via Rwanda, so you will either need a transit visa or a multiple entry visa for Rwanda. Another route (less easy) is from **Bujumbura** to **Uvira**.

Rwanda You can get into Zaire between **Gisenyi** and **Goma** across the Poids Lourds crossing – minibuses run along the border road. From the border to Goma is only a couple of km by taxi or motor-taxi (motorbike). This is said to be the easiest way of entering the country from East Africa. A second route is via **Cyangugu** to **Bukavu** as described above under Burundi.

Uganda Kisoro to **Rutshuru**. This is the most reliable crossing. Minibuses from Kisoro to the border, about 10 km and costing US$0.50, and on the Zaire side a motor-taxi (motorbike) to Rutshuru. **Kasese** to **Beni** via **Kasindi**. There is infrequent public transport along this route. some minibuses from Kasese to the border at Kasindi. The leg from Kasindi to Beni can be awkward, some minibuses, but a motor-taxi (motorbike) is probably the best possibility. There are small hotels on both the Uganda and Zaire side of the border in case you are stuck there late at night.

Kasese to **Rutshuru**. It is also possible to cross the border on this route, the border post being at **Ishasha.** There are infrequent minibuses on this route and hitching is possible.

● Customs
Be prepared for your luggage to be checked, and have all papers required for Zaire in order. Also, you may be asked to buy a photography permit for each camera you have (usually US$3 each), though this does not appear to be a legal requirement so much as a method of customs officials supplementing their meagre income.

When you arrive

● Airline offices
Air Zaire, PO Box 8552, Ave du Port Kinshasa, T 24986, Tlx 21313. **Scibe Airlift**, PO Box 614, Kinshasha, T 22276, Tlx 21003. **Zairean Airlines**, PO Box 2111, Blvd du 30 Juin, Kinshasa, T 24624 Tlx 21525.

● Hours of business
For shops, business hours are generally Mon-Fri from 0900-1200 and 1500-1800. For administrative offices and banks, hours are normally Mon-Fri from 0800-1430. Post offices are generally open Mon-Fri from 0730-1200 and 1300-1630 and on Sat from 0730-1200.

● Official time
1 hour later than GMT

● Photography
It is best to be cautious with taking photographs in the country and task permission. It is prohibited to take pictures of military establishments or public buildings such as airports, harbours, bridges, train stations, administrative buildings, and post offices. Film in Zaire is expensive and is only available in Bukavu and Goma, so it is best to take all you need with you.

● Religion
About 50% of the population follow traditional beliefs, 30% are Roman Catholics and 13% Protestant.

Where to stay

● Hotels
There is plenty of accommodation in Kivu District, and prices are very reasonable. Few places have air-conditioning, but it is not essential in the relatively cool climate of the mountains and lakes. The cheapest and best run accommodation is invariably provided by mission hostels.

Hotel Classifications

A+	Over US$100 a night. International standards and decor, air conditioning, self contained rooms, swimming pool, restaurants, bars, business services.
A	US$40-100. First class standards, air-conditioning, attached bathrooms, restaurants and bars, swimming pool.
B	US$20-40. Tourist class, comfortable with air conditioning or fans, attached barthrooms, restaurant, bar, public rooms.
C	US$10-20. Budget, fans, shared bathroom facilities.
D	US$5-10. Guest house, no fan, shared bathroom, cold water.
E	Under US$5. Basic guest house, simple bed, no soap or towels, no wardrobe, shared bathroom facilities, erratic cold water supply, no fans or mosquito nets.

Food and drink

● Food
This country is ideally suited for agriculture so

fresh food is abundant and cheap. You will be able to get international food, and some specialised cuisine at some of the more expensive places in Goma or Bukavu. In smaller places, there are only usually African style meals of grills, rice, stews.

Eating Classifications

- ♦♦♦♦ Over US$10 for a meal. A 3-course meal in a restaurant with pleasant decor. Beers, wines and spirits available.
- ♦♦♦ US$5-10 for a meal. Two courses, not including alcohol, reasonable surroundings.
- ♦♦ US$2-5 for a meal, probably only a single course, surroundings spartan but adequate.
- ♦ Under US$2. Single course, often makeshift surroundings such as a street kiosk with simple benches and tables.

● Drink

There are no restrictions on alcohol and a wide variety of imported beers, wines and spirits are available in Goma and Bukavu; beer only in the other towns. There is a local brewery in Bukavu which produces lagers (*Primus* and *Amstel*) under licence from Belgium.

Getting around

The most convenient (but least interesting) way of getting about is to go on an arranged tour. Hiring a car is expensive. Hitching (paying for the ride) is often quite productive. Public transport, via minibuses, can be a bit erratic, and can involve some lengthy waits. Air travel is unreliable. Lake travel, where possible, is very pleasant, and reasonably reliable.

● Air

There are three small companies offering charter flights, these are VAC and TMK Commuter. These are often booked up in peak season (Jun – Sep) so it is best to reserve one well in advance. There is also the airline Scibe Airlift. Flight connections in Kivu district are:

Goma-Bukavu several times daily on TMC, VAC and Scibe Airlift; **Goma-Butembo** 4 times weekly on TMC and VAC; **Goma-Beni** direct daily except Sat on TMC, VAC and Scibe Airlift; **Goma-Bunia** direct once a week on Scibe Airlift; **Goma-Butembo-Bunia**, twice a week on TMC; **Goma-Kalemie-Lubumbashi** twice a week on Scibe Airlift; **Goma-Bunia-Kisangani** once a week on Scibe Airlift; **Butembo-Beni** twice a week on VAC; **Beni-Bunia** once a week on VAC; **TMC and VAC** via travel agents in Bukavu (page 567) and Goma (page 564), and in other towns the office at the airstrip.

● Train

There is no train service in Kivu district. The nearest terminal is at Kalemie halfway down Lake Tangangika, which links to Lumumbashi. Unfortunately the road links to Uvira and the rest of Eastern Zaire are poor.

● Road

Patience is the key to travelling around Eastern Zaire by road. In the rainy season it could be days before you will be able to get from one point to another and in the dry season, although roads may be more passable you are still not guaranteed a lift. Most the roads are in a poor state. If you are on a budget, do not be afraid to ask for lifts, offering to pay for the ride. Many drivers are happy to supplement their income by taking hitchers.

● Lake ferries

There are three boats on Lake Kivu travelling from Goma to Bukavu (see page 564).

● Car hire

Hiring a car is expensive costing between US$70-US$100 per day depending on whether you pay a flat rate per km or a daily rate. However, most rental cars are actually minibuses which can take about 7 people, so the cost can be shared with other travellers. It is also possible to hire a driver for the day which is often a good idea as they know the area and are able to handle almost any situation which may arise, and will ensure you do not run into any safety problems. This is particularly relevant if you are travelling in the rainy season when cars frequently get stuck in the mud. See Car Hire under Goma, page 564 and Tour and Travel Agents under Bukavu, page 567.

Taxis are generally available. Almost anyone with a motorbike can be approached to hire a lift (motor-taxi), similarly anyone who is driving a vehicle.

Communications

● Language

French is the official language in Zaire though 4 main languages (French, Lingala, Kikongo and Swahili) are spoken and about 250 dialects throughout the country. Kiswahili is widely spoken in Eastern Zaire. Lingala is also used, particularly by military personnel.

● Postal Services

Letters overseas take approximately 10 days to arrive, postcards take longer. It is not advised to send anything valuable in the post, as post often goes astray.

● Telephone services

Telephone calls can be made direct to Belgium, Spain, US, UK, France, Germany, Greece and Switzerland. They are very expensive, particularly if made from a hotel, and are calculated for a minimum of three minutes. 18% tax is added to the cost of the call.

Entertainment

● Music

Zairean bands are famous throughout the world among those appreciating modern popular music, and they are particularly well regarded in East Africa. Bukavu, Goma and Beni all have bands playing every night. Most bars will play recorded Zairean music until well into the night.

● Newspapers

There are 4 daily papers; *L'Analyste, Elima, Mjumbe, Salongo*, none of which are published in English, and none of which are readily available in Eastern Zaire.

● Radio

There are 2 radio stations: *La Voix du Zaire*, which is state-controlled and broadcasts in French, Swahili, Lingala, Tshiluba, Kikongo. There is a regional station based at Bukavu. The other station is *Radio Candip* which broadcasts educational programmes in French, Lingala, Swahili and 6 local dialects.

● Television

This is not widely available in the country, in 1990 there were only said to be 40,000 television receivers in use. Television is controlled through Zaire Television based in Kinshasa which broadcasts for 5 hours daily on weekdays and 10 hours daily at weekends. This service is not available in Eastern Zaire.

Holidays and festivals

Jan 1	New Year's Day
4	Veterans' Day
May 1	Labour Day
20	Festival for the party
Jun 24	Fishermen's Festival
30	Independence Day
Aug 1	Parents' Day
14	Memorial Day
Oct 14	President's birthday
27	Festival of the 3 Z's (when names in Zaire were Africanised)
Nov 17	Festival of the National Army
24	Day of the Second Republic
Dec 25	Christmas Day

ETHIOPIA

Contents

Maps

Introduction

Ethiopia is a large country both in terms of population and geographical area. Its main distinction is that it has experienced no protracted period of colonial rule, although the country was occupied by the Italians for six years from 1935. It has recently emerged from a disastrous period under a military regime, 1974-1991, which followed the fall of Haile Selassie. Visitors were prevented from going to many parts of the country, the north was off-limits because of the fighting there, and permits, issued by an infuriatingly obstructive and inefficient bureaucracy, were required for travel outside the capital. Happily this is now all in the past, but the legacy is that tourist facilities have been neglected. The exciting aspect is that Ethiopia outside Addis Ababa has been virtually unvisited for two decades. Travellers seeing the countryside, people, culture, wildlife and historical sites for the first time are astonished by the richness and diversity.

Ethiopia has a unique atmosphere. The people have a distinctive appearance, partly like their neighbours in the Middle East and partly like the rest of Africa. However they are a strongly Christian people, and the influence of the church is considerable. Ethiopia has its own written language, Amharic, and traditions in literature, dress, dance and music that have flourished in the relative isolation provided by their mountainous territory.

Major attractions are the ancient cities of Gondar, Axum, and Harar, and these have all retained the atmosphere of their historical backgrounds. There are some extraordinary churches hewn from rock in Lalibela. This circuit is becoming popular with visitors and there are daily flights between the cities.

Ethiopia has some fine wildlife, and all the major animals except for rhinoceros are present in the selection of relatively small but delightful parks scattered across the country. The birds are a particular attraction.

The capital city, Addis Ababa, is friendly, and attractively located on a hilly site. It has a strong diplomatic community and the UN Economic Commission for Africa, and the Organisation of African Unity have their headquarters there.

Ethiopia covers an area of 1,251,282 sq km and is bounded to the W by Sudan, to the S by Kenya and to the E and SE by Somalia and Djibouti. Eritrea, which gained formal independence from

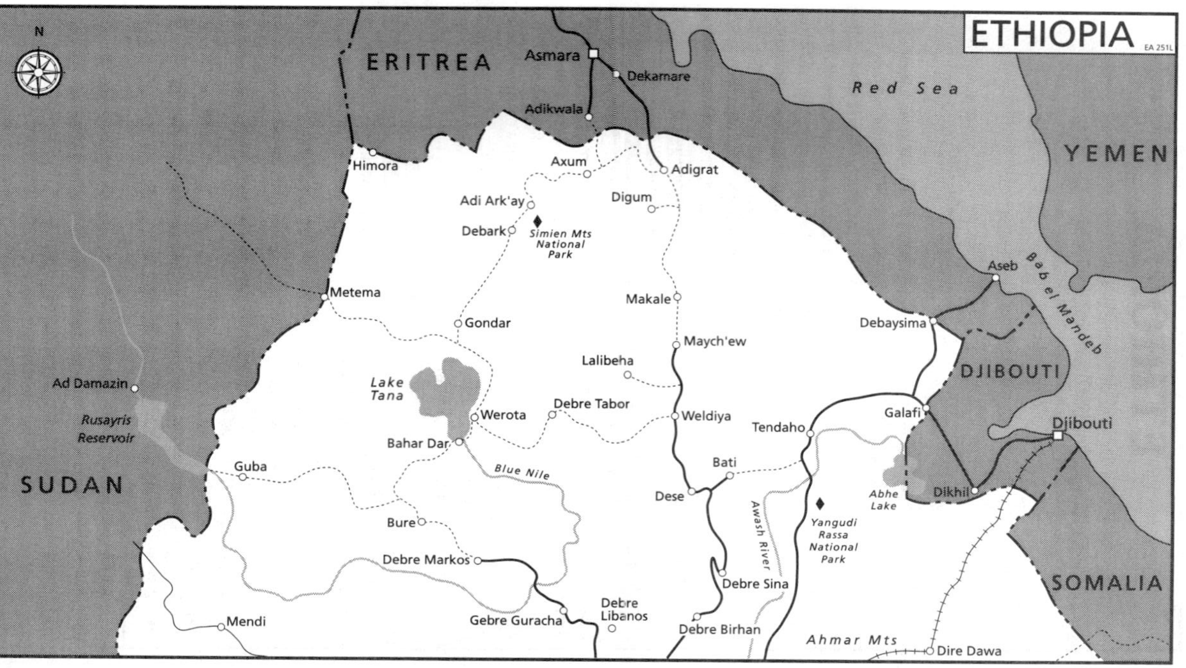
ETHIOPIA
EA 251L
N
ERITREA
YEMEN
DJIBOUTI
SOMALIA
SUDAN
Red Sea
Bab el Mandeb
Asmara
Dekamare
Adikwala
Himora
Axum
Adigrat
Adi Ark'ay
Digum
Debark
Simien Mts National Park
Metema
Makale
Aseb
Debaysima
Gondar
Maych'ew
Lalibeha
Ad Damazin
Lake Tana
Debre Tabor
Weldiya
Werota
Galafi
Djibouti
Tendaho
Rusayris Reservoir
Bahar Dar
Guba
Blue Nile
Bati
Dese
Dikhil
Abhe Lake
Awash River
Yangudi Rassa National Park
Bure
Debre Markos
Debre Sina
Debre Libanos
Gebre Guracha
Debre Birhan
Mendi
Ahmar Mts
Dire Dawa

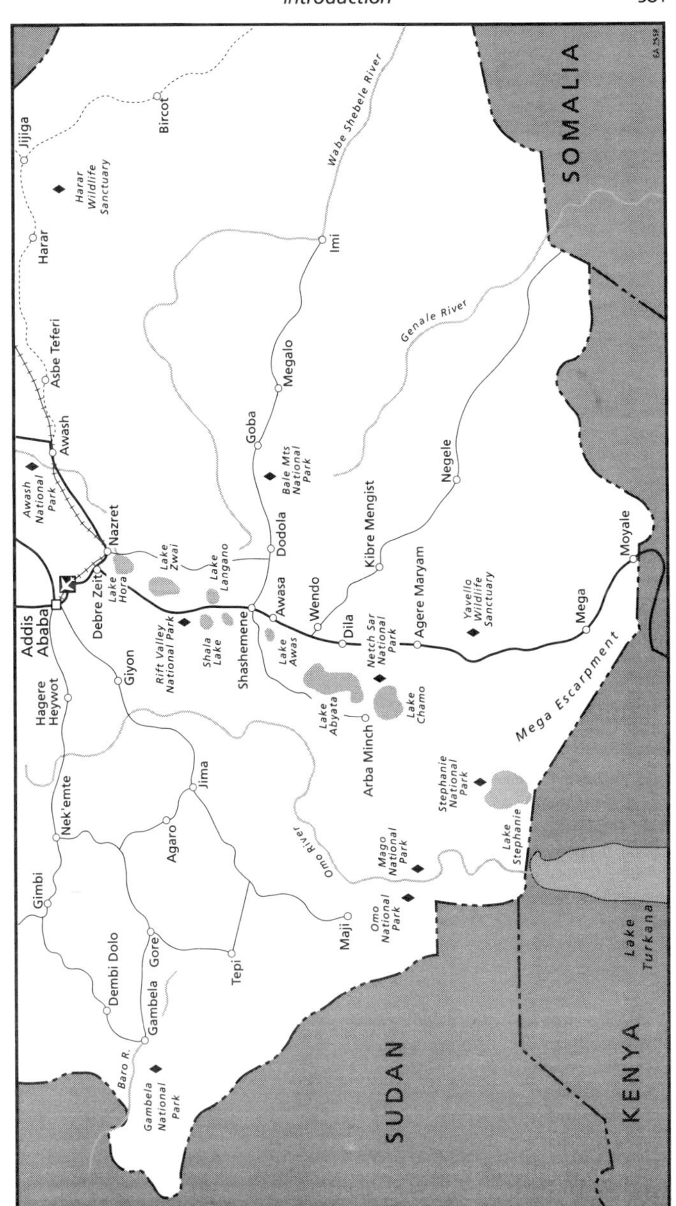
SOMALIA
SUDAN
KENYA
Addis Ababa
Debre Zeit
Nazret
Awash
Asbe Teferi
Harar
Jijiga
Bircot
Harar Wildlife Sanctuary
Awash National Park
Lake Hora
Lake Zwai
Lake Langano
Shala Lake
Rift Valley National Park
Lake Awas
Lake Abyata
Lake Chamo
Netch Sar National Park
Shashemene
Awasa
Wendo
Dila
Agere Maryam
Yavello Wildlife Sanctuary
Mega
Moyale
Mega Escarpment
Kibre Mengist
Negele
Genale River
Dodola
Bale Mts National Park
Goba
Megalo
Imi
Wabe Shebele River
Giyon
Hagere Heywot
Jima
Agaro
Nek'emte
Gimbi
Dembi Dolo
Gore
Gambela
Baro R.
Gambela National Park
Tepi
Maji
Omo River
Arba Minch
Omo National Park
Mago National Park
Stephanie National Park
Lake Stephanie
Lake Turkana

Ethiopia in May 1993 lies to the N, and Ethiopia is now land-locked. The country is divided into 12 self-governing regions and 2 chartered cities – Addis Ababa and Harar.

The names of places and people are spelt in a variety of ways reflecting periods of French, Italian and British influence in translating the Amaharic characters into a European equivalent. The phonetic sound of a word is sometimes the clearest guide.

Exchange rate in Aug 1994 US$1 = Birr 5.45

Environment

Geography

Elevations range from 4,000m above sea level to 100m below, the highest point in the country being Ras Dashan in the Semien mountain range, which rises to a height of 4,620m NE of Lake Tana. The southern part of Ethiopia is bisected by the East African Rift Valley, 40-60 km wide, the valley floor scattered with lakes. North of Addis, the western wall of the valley runs parallel to the Red Sea coast, creating a wide plain between the escarpment and the coastline. Further N, this plain narrows until the foothills of the escarpment run right down to the sea. To the W of the rift system, the gently dipping plateau runs down into Sudan, drained by the tributaries of the Nile which have scarred deep canyons in the land. This part of the country is seriously denuded of top-soil, much of it having washed away to collect on the flood-plains of Egypt.

The eastern wall of the rift valley runs due E from Addis, forming a steep escarpment which rises abruptly to over 1000m, commanding wide views over the Afar plains to the N.

The dominant feature of the country's topography is the high Central Plateau, generally between 2,000-3,000 m, and it is here that the majority of the population is concentrated. This plateau is bisected by a number of river systems, the most significant of which is the Blue Nile (*Abbas*). The most fertile part of Ethiopia lies to the extreme S. Agricultural potential here is rich, and parts of the Sidamo Highlands, with rolling grassland and wooded hills completely contradict received images of Ethiopia as unrelentingly dry and arid.

The vegetation of the plateau is dominated by mountain grassland and settled agriculture. Population pressure has forced farmers into areas which are very marginal in rainfall and soil quality, particularly along the eastern escarpment, and this has exacerbated the drought and famine conditions which have characterised parts of Ethiopia since 1973. Coniferous forests have now largely disappeared from the highlands, although in the S, lower elevations and higher temperatures have produced broad-leaved forests which, largely due to their inaccessibility, have not yet been subjected to extensive commercial exploitation.

The lowlands, depending on the amount of rainfall, are characterised by dry zone vegetation, ranging from limited areas of desert to thorn scrub and savannah.

Climate

Ethiopia's climate is determined by altitude and proximity to the Indian Ocean. Considerable variations in temperature are reflected in the traditional climate zone divisions: *dega*, the temperate plateau, *kolla*, hot lowlands, and the intermediate frost free zone of the *woina dega*. Average annual temperatures vary over these zones from 16° to 26°C.

Rainfall varies considerably. In most parts of the central highlands the average is well over 1000 mm per year, while the drier lowlands receive less than 500 mm. There are 2 principal seasons; rainy from Jun to Oct and relatively dry for the rest of the year, although some regions experience short Apr rains as well (the *belg*). The country is extremely vulnerable to drought conditions, particularly in the low lying pastoral areas and along the eastern escarpment, where there is widespread dependence on the *belg* rains.

History

Cradle of mankind

Fossil remains discovered at a site on the Lower Awash river in NE Ethiopia in 1974 have been identified as the earliest example of an upright walking hominid. Dated at 3.5 million years old, these remains constitute our oldest known ancestors, and many now consider this region of Ethiopia to be the true cradle of mankind.

The early history of Ethiopia begins with the glorious but still only partly understood Axumite Kingdom, which grew up around Axum in the N highlands in the third century BC and endured until the 10th century AD. The achivements of this early civilisation are recorded today in the ruins of the old Axumite cities and towns, reservoirs, dams, temples and stone stele (pillars) on which are recorded fragments of the history of the empire and dynasty. Legend records that Cush, son of Ham and grandson of Noah, came to Ethiopia from Mesopotamia (now Iraq). Other stories claim that Menelik I, the child born to the union of King Solomon and the Queen of Sheba (see box), settled in Axum, bringing with him the Ark of the Covenant from the Temple in Jerusulem and establishing a dynasty which ruled – with only brief interruptions – until the fall of Haile Selassie in 1974.

Ethiopia's historical importance stemmed partly from its favourable location and terrain. Lying on the edge of the Graeco-Roman world it was linked to both by the Red Sea and the Nile. Kinship, trade and culture also tied it strongly to the Persian Empire. Axumite commerce was based largely on the export of gold and ivory and trade links reached as far as Ceylon, although the strongest links were with Egypt and Greece.

Christianity reached Axum in the fourth century AD, during the reign of the Conqueror King Ezana. He was converted by a young Syrian named Frumentius who was shipwrecked off Adulis and who subsequently became the first Bishop of Axum. Early coins from Ezana's reign show the traditionally worshipped symbols of the sun and moon, while later coins bear the sign of the cross.

The Axumite empire reached its zenith in the sixth century when King Kaleb crossed the Red Sea to conquer parts of S Arabia. However, the rise of Islam in the seventh century drove the Axumites back onto home territory and as Islam asserted itself in East Africa, the Ethiopian Christians became increasingly isolated.

Middle Ages

The Axumite Kingdom, denied the trade routes which were its lifeblood, declined during the 10th century, after which the balance of political and religious power shifted S to Lasta and the new Zagwe dynasty. Its most important ruler was King Lalibela, renowned for the rock-hewen churches which he built at the capital which was later to bear his name.

The Zagwe were in turn overthrown in the late 12th century by Yekuno Amlak, who claimed descent from the rulers of Axum and thus restored the Solomonic dynasty. This was a period of rule by chiefs and warlords who collected taxes and made war on each other, but who would submit themselves to the king of their province and through him to the King of Kings.

In 1531, as the Ottoman empire began to expand, General Ibn Ibrahim, or Gragn (the left handed), led a Muslim army into the Ethiopian Highlands.

Emperor Labna Dengal appealed to Portugal for military assistance, which duly arrived in the form of Christopher de Gama (son of the explorer Vasco) and 400 men, and defeat was avoided. Subsequently, in 1571, the Pope sent a Jesuit mission to Ethiopia in an attempt to introduce Roman Catholicism, but little headway was made and the Jesuits were banished in the mid 17th century.

The monarchy of Gondar, which had become an important political and commercial centre in the early 17th century lost its authority in the 18th century when the feudal lords became independent of central control. A hundred years of near anarchy ensued, giving way eventually to major attempts at reunification in the second half of the 19th century, moves which were given greater urgency as first France and England and then Italy began to cast covetous eyes on

King Solomon, The Queen Of Sheba And The Lion Of Judah Dynasty

On the last day of the visit of the Queen of Sheba to King Solomon in Jerusalem, the King prepared a grand banquet. There were 10 courses of carefully prepared and well-spiced dishes. As they finished the last course, the King asked if the Queen would spend the night in his room. She consented, but took his invitation literally, making it a condition that Solomon did not force his attentions upon her against her will. Taken aback, Solomon sought to save his dignity by demanding that the Queen, in her turn, should repect both his person and his property. An agreement was struck, and they settled for the night in separate beds, a vessel of water between them. A little peeved, the King made do with a maid from the Queen's entourage, and the son she subsequently bore became the first King in the Zagne dynasty in Ethiopia.

During the night, the Queen became thirsty, and drank some water from the vessel between the beds. This allowed Solomon, somewhat ungallantly, to claim that the Queen had broken the agreement, and that she must now replace the maid in his bed. The child of this union was Menelik I, the first Ethiopian King of the line that was to stretch down the centuries.

During the course of this modestly productive night, Solomon had a disturbing dream. He saw a glittering sun rise over Israel and then shift to shine on Axum. A second sun arose, illuminating all the world but casting its rays with special brilliance on Italy and Ethiopia.

The first sun is interpreted as the Ark of the Covenant, taken by Menelik I from the Temple in Jerusalem to St Mary's Church in Axum, where it is concealed in a secret chamber.

The second sun represented the teachings of Christ. In 330 AD a Syrian ship sailing up the Red Sea was boarded, and all but 2 boys from the crew were slain. The 2 were taken to the Imperial court at Axum where one, Frumentius, so impressed with his wisdom that a few years later he ruled for a while in place of Ezana, the young Regent. When Ezana became Emperor, Frumentius went to Alexandria where he was consecrated as the first Bishop of Axum. On his return to Ethiopia, he spread the word of Christ throughout the land.

This legend is recorded from oral sources in the fourteenth century in *Kebra Nagast*, the Ethiopian Book of the Glory of the Kings. The work was commissioned by St Tekla Haimanot, who pursued holy devotions for 27 years in a cave at Debre Libanos.

Ethiopia. The main work of unification was left to Menelik II, an enterprising, vigorous and imaginative young king from Shoa, who guided Ethiopia through the maelstrom of Europe's Scramble for Africa. Menelik reigned as king of Shoa from 1865-1889 and as Emperor of Ethiopia from that year until his death in 1913.

By fraudulent misrepresentation of the Treaty of Wuchale, which Italy concluded with Menelik, Italy laid claim to Ethiopia as its protectorate – a claim supported by Britain and France as they shared out the rest of eastern Africa between themselves. However, at the Battle of Adwa, on Mar 1, 1896, Menelik's forces routed the Italians, thus preserving Ethiopia's independence throughout the colonial era. Menelik established most of Ethiopia's present frontiers. He also founded Addis Ababa and was a great moderniser, setting up schools and banks, a railway and a postal system.

Italy still continued continued to have designs on Ethiopia, and although it became a member of the League of Nations after WW1, this did not prevent Mussolini from overrunning the country in 1936. Italian forces remained in occupation for 5 years, despite pleas to the international community from the young emperor, Haile Selassie. Italy was forced out of Ethiopia by guerrilla and Allied forces during WW2 and the country resumed its status as an independent nation. However, unrest continued in the N. After 11 years of British administration, Eritrea was federated to Ethiopia in 1952, but when, in 1962 the federation was dissolved and the province was annexed by Haile Selassie, guerrilla warfare broke out. Eritrea had not been part of Ethiopia for several hundred years, and the subsequent struggle for independence was to dominate Ethiopian history until the early 1990's.

Haile Selassie

Haile Selassie had established himself as a national hero during the campaigns against the Italians and had become a respected African statesman. He concentrated on international affairs, securing Addis Ababa as the headquarters of the organisation for African Unity (OAU) and the UN Economic Commission for Africa. A close ally of the US, he ensured that Ethiopia was a major recipient of US aid in the 1950's and 1960's. However, Haile Selassie governed Ethiopia like a medieval fiefdom, unable to understand or respond to the growing agrarian crisis, inequitable distribution of land and general lack of development. The continuing cost of revolt in Eritrea and drought and famine in Wollo 1972-74, with the death of 200,000 people, contrasted starkly with the accumulation of wealth by the nobility and the church. This caused a mass outbreak of resentment and on Sep 12 1974, against a background of strikes, student demonstrations and army mutiny, Haile Selassie was deposed. The monarchy was abolished the following year. The former emperor died in his palace, under armed guard, several months later. Haile Selassie's son, Crown Prince Asfa Wossen, lives in exile in London.

Civil war and revolution

The imperial regime was replaced by a provisional military administrative council, known as the Dergue, which saw itself as the vanguard of the Ethiopian Revolution. It began to implement a programme of socialist, revolutionary reforms – nationalising companies, implementing literacy campaigns and setting up over 30,000 locally elected associations. After 2 years of infighting within the Dergue, Lt-col Mengistu Haile Miriam emerged at the head of the dictatorship – executing his rivals within the regime and launching an urban terror campaign against the

Ethiopian People's Revolutionary Party, which argued for the immediate creation of civilian government and supported the Eritrean struggle. Tens of thousands were killed or tortured as Mengistu wiped out the opposition and imposed his own vision of Marxism-Leninism.

Military disarray in Addis prompted the Eritreans to step up their campaign, and in 1977 Somalia began encroaching into S Eastern Ethiopia. The Dergue may well have collapsed at this time but for the intervention of the USSR and Cuba who re-equiped and trained the Ethiopian army. With this new weaponry and some 16,000 Cuban troops the army went back on the offensive, repulsing Somalia from occupied Ogaden and rolling back the gains which the rival Eritrean People's Liberation Front (EPLF, predominantly Christian) and the Eritrean Liberation Front (ELF, predominantly Muslim) had made in Eritrea. The EPLF dug in around the remote N town of Nacfa and over several years continued to inflict heavy losses on the Ethiopian army. In 1982 the EPLF, in alliance with the Tirayan People's Liberation Front (TPLF), drove the ELF into Sudan where they disarmed and fragmented.

Mengistu was never able to achieve widespread support, largely due to his failure to solve the nationality problem, of which the stuggle in Eritrea was the most obvious symptom. The revolution had raised expectations of regional autonomy among various nationalities such as the Oromos in the S and the Tigrayans in the N. The Oromo Liberation Front (OLF), advocating self-determination for Oromia and respect for its language and culture, gained support during the early 1980's from the rural base in the region which had benefited from reforms implemented in 1975. But the most serious threat came from the TPLF established in 1975 to struggle for Tigrayan self-determination, receiving arms and training from the EPLF.

Mengistu's political and military responses to the nationalist movements were inadequate and the country was further weakened by the catastrophic famine of 1984-85. The international community's response to the disaster was slow, partly because of Ethiopia's close links with the Soviet Union and when help did arrive, conflict ensured that many of the worst-hit rebel areas, especially in Tigray, were denied relief. The government's own relief measures consisted largely of an unpopular resettlement programme, in which 600,000 people were moved into the S and W of the country. At the same time the TPLF moved 200,000 Tigrayans into the Sudan.

The military situation deteriorated for Mengistu after 1988. While the EPLF continued to make gains in Eritrea, the TPLF now controlled all of Tigray and began to push S to Addis under the flag of the Ethiopian People's Revolutionary Democratic Front (EPRDF). Disillusionment grew in the army and Mengistu's refusal to seek a political solution was increasingly seen as a liability. By Feb 1990 the EPLF had captured the Red Sea port of Massawa, cutting off supply lines to the Ethiopian Army in Eritrea, and Mengistu was forced to make concessions. He abandoned Ethiopian socialism, invited opposition groups to participate in a unity party and built free market principals into economic planning. But this was insufficient and problems began to mount. The fall in the world price of coffee added to economic hardships, and with the collapse of the East European regimes, Ethiopia lost most of its overseas alliances. As the opposition forces closed in on Addis Ababa in Feb 1991, Mengistu fled to Zimbabwe. On May 28 the EPRDF entered the capital and subsequently established an interim government.

Wax And Gold

In fashioning a gold figure, the first step is to make a wax model, which is then covered in with wet clay. A small hole in the clay allows the wax to run out when the clay is fired. Molten gold is poured through the hole into the cast, and when it sets, the mould is broken to reveal the figure.

In Ethiopian poetry, and in verses sung by minstrels, at the initial level there is a story, pleasing in itself. But this is an allegory for something more valuable and profound. Puns and double meanings are features of this structure.

The imagery for the 2 levels of meaning is *sammena wark*, wax and gold.

Arts and crafts

Jewellery is particularly fine, forged mostly from silver in a characteristic style, sometimes with amber decoration. Bracelets, necklaces, rings and pendants are all made.

Weaving traditional cloth, mostly from cotton, but sometimes from wool. Decoration is often by delicate embroidery, or in the rural areas by sewing on cowrie shells.

Leatherwork, hides and skins. Sheepskin capes are a speciality. It is possible to obtain some exotic skins such as leopard. Traditional curing of leather involves sun-drying the skin and then treating it with clotted milk and linseed oil.

Pottery is made without use of a wheel by coiling ribbons of clay. Decoration is sometimes effected by smoking the clay, and polishing with a stone after open-pit firing.

Horn and ivory are carved and polished to make drinking vessels, boxes and ornaments. Horn is fashioned into vessels by heating it until it is malleable.

Basketwork includes both woven items, and pieces made by coiling bundles of fibres. As well as containers, basketry techniques can be used to make brushes, brooms and umbrellas.

Woodcarving products are furniture, particularly 3-legged stools and coffee tables. Vases, ashtrays and candle-sticks and musical instuments are also made.

It is often possible to watch craftsmen at work in cooperatives. Contact the Handicrafts and Small-scale Industries Development Agency nr the Wabe Shebelle Hotel, T 44 88 09.

Culture and life

People

There has never been a full census carried out in Ethiopia, but the population is estimated at about 57 million, with 90 per cent working on the land. The central plateau is characterised by settled cultivation of cereals and pulses, while nomadic lifestyles persist at the desert margins.

There are over 80 languages and dialects. In Tigray region, around Axum, the Semitic language Tigrinya is spoken, while the heartland of Ethiopia is the home of Amharic, the official language. To the S and E are the Cushtic speaking peoples, the Oromos, Afars and Somalis. Ethiopia's Nilotic peoples, the Nuer and the Anuak are found to the far S and W. The Falasha, living around Gondar, are linked to Ethiopia's early ties to Judaic Palestine, and thousands of Falasha were airlifted out of the country by Israel during the 1984-85 famine. Amharas and Tigrays are predominantly Orthodox Christian while Oromos, the largest ethnic group in the country, are more mixed, with communities following Christian, Muslim and traditional religions.

PROVERBS OF ETHIOPIA

To lie about a far country is easy
When you eat crow, call it pigeon
One stone is enough against fifty clay pots
You cannot build a house for last winter
A good man earns more than his wages
Even if you know many things, do not argue with the judge
The fool and a rich man can say what they please
Small boys and smoke disappear mysteriously
When a wise man is foolish it is a big matter
One who proposes an exchange knows which is the better
After the hyena passes, the dog barks
A hearty eater is not in love
Who hits the father, hits the son
Do not try to taste honey if you see it on a thorn

Modern Ethiopia

Politics

With the overthrow of the Dergue regime, the EPRDF drew up a national charter which allowed for the creation of an 87 seat council of representatives, representing some 32 political organisations and with the EPRDF occupying 32 of the seats. New internal boundaries were created, reflecting ethnicity and political power. Large powerful and concentrated groups (Tigray and Oromo) appeared to gain fertile areas and relinquish desert while weaker and dispersed groups (Amhara and Gurage) lost good land.

The intention is to allow Ethiopia's main ethnic groups to have self-determination within a federal structure comprising twelve regions and 2 chartered cities. The EPRDF has found it difficult to maintain cohesion as there are now over 100 political groups based mostly on ethnic affiliations. The OLF and some other minor groups decided not to particiapate in the elections in 1992, and also withdrew from the government. An attempt by the OLF to revive guerrilla resistance was quickly crushed by the EPRDF.

The EPRDF dominated the 1992 elections, winning 890 out of 978 seats in Addis Ababa, and 81 out of 84 in the regions. Elections were postponed in 2 areas, it is said because the EPRDF had not got itself well enough organised.

By 1991, the EPLF had established a provisional government in Eritrea. In the process, more than 100,000 non-Eritreans were deported to Tigray. A referendum in Apr 1993 endorsed separation from Ethiopia, Eritrea became an independent state and joined the UN.

Economics

Overall, Ethiopia is a large country in terms of population but with low urbanisation, poor medical and food provision, and very low income per head. It takes only limited advantage of the opportunities offered by world markets, and its economy is heavily dependent on agriculture.

Economic and social structure

Estimates for 1994 indicate a population of 57.2 million, and Ethiopia is the most populous country in Africa after Nigeria and Egypt. Population density is well above average for East Africa at 46.8 persons per square kilometre, but densities fall dramatically in the desert and mountains. Urbanisation at 13% is a little below average for the region. Population grew at 3.1% a year for the period 1980-1991, slightly above the regional average of 2.9%, but the effect of recent drought and famines will limit this, with estimates of up to a million deaths and consequent effects on fertility.

GDP in 1991 was US$5,982m, and it is the second largest economy in the region after Kenya. GNP per head was estimated at US$120, and this made Ethiopia the third poorest country in the world. Agriculture is the mainstay of the economy, providing 47% of GDP in 1987, with industry providing 13% and services 40%. This supply structure is fairly representative of the East African region which has negligible mineral resources and relies on agriculture for export revenue.

On the demand side, private consumption was equivalent to 78% of GDP in 1991, gross domestic investment was 10% and government consumption was 21%. The high commitment to private consumption is a reflection of the low income levels generated and the low allocation to investment results from the need to meet immediate consumption needs as a priority in the short run.

Exports generated 8% of GDP in 1991, and this indicates that the economy is rather less open than the average in East Africa. Coffee is the main export, and provides 44% of export earnings, with hides and skins providing 13%. Imports comprise 18% of total expenditure and again this is a lower dependence than in the region or in Africa generally. The gap between imports and exports is filled by foreign assistance from a variety of sources including the World Bank, the EEC, Libya and China.

Literacy among adults was estimated at 66% in 1990, and is a marked better than the 15% literacy level recorded in 1980. The improvement has come about by concerted adult literacy campaigns mounted by the government after the fall of Haile Selassie. 38% of the relevant age group are in primary education, which is well under the regional average of 62%. 15% of the 12-17 age group were in secondary education, and this is more in line with averages elsewhere in Africa, as is the 1% in higher education. The inferior primary enrolments are reflections of the low income generated in the rural areas which contain most of the population.

Life expectancy in 1991 was 48 years, lower than the regional average of 52, food supply was 1,708 calories per person per day, and this is well below the 2,100 a day average in the rest of Africa. Medical provision at one doctor for every 32,650 inhabitants in 1990 was about average for East Africa.

Economic performance

GDP has grown at 0.9% in the period 1980-91, and this is below the East Africa performance of 1.6% for the same period. With population growing at 3.1% a year, GDP per head contracted at -2.2% annually. The performance in the major sectors in the eighties was varied. Agriculture grew at 0.3% a year, and was badly affected by drought and political instability. On the other hand, the industry sector grew at 1.8% and the services sector at 3.1%, and these 2 sectoral performances were better than the average elsewhere in the region and in Africa.

Export volumes grew at 1.9% a year 1980-91. Recent years have shown better growth – earlier stagnation was the result of policies which sought to reduce external dependence and a dogged refusal to depreciate the exchange rate in order to encourage exports. Import volumes grew at 3.3% a year in the same period as a result of the response of the international community to the stress experienced by the population under the impact of drought and armed conflicts.

Inflation figures for 1980-91 show a modest annual rate of price increase of 2.4%, and this is the best record of price stability in East Africa. Development effort in respect of the ratio of gross domestic investment to GDP was low in that this ratio was 10% in 1991. At this level, there is grave danger of delapidation of the country's infrastructure and capital stock, making high growth rates in the future even more difficult to attain.

Overall, Ethiopia has had a poor economic performance in the 1980's with GDP per head falling, and agriculture

Comparative Economic And Social Data

	Ethiopia	East Africa	Africa	Industrial countries
Population and land				
Population, mid year, millions, 1994	57.2	12.2	10.2	40.0
Urban population, %, 1991	13	15	30	75
Population growth rate, % per year, 1980-91	3.1	3.1	3.1	0.8
Land area, thou. sq. kilom.	1,222	486	486	1,628
Population density, persons per sq km. 1994	46.8	24.2	20.4	24.3
Economy: production and income				
GDP, US$ millions, 1991	5,982	2,650	3,561	550,099
GNP per head, US$, 1991	120	250	389	12,960
Economy: supply structure				
Agriculture, % of GDP, 1991	47	43	35	3
Industry, % of GDP, 1991	13	15	27	35
Services, % of GDP, 1991	40	42	38	61
Economy: demand structure				
Private consumption, % of GDP, 1991	78	77	73	62
Gross domestic investment, % of GDP, 1991	10	16	16	21
Government Consumption, % of GDP, 1991	21	15	14	17
Exports, % of GDP, 1991	8	16	23	17
Imports, % of GDP, 1991	18	24	26	17
Economy: performance				
GDP growth, % per year, 1980-91	0.9	1.6	-0.6	2.5
GDP per head growth, % per year, 1980-91	-2.1	-1.7	-3.7	1.7
Agriculture growth, % per year, 1980-91	0.3	1.1	0.0	2.5
Industry growth, % per year, 1980-91	1.8	1.1	-1.0	2.5
Services growth, % per year, 1980-91	3.1	2.5	-0.5	2.6
Exports growth, % per year, 1980-91	1.9	0.7	-1.9	3.3
Imports growth, % per year, 1980-91	3.3	0.2	-6.9	4.3
Economy: other				
Inflation rate, % per year, 1980-91	2.4	23.6	16.7	5.3
Aid, net inflow, % of GDP, 1991	16.5	11.5	6.3	-
Debt service, % of Exports, 1991	18.6	18	20.6	-
Education				
Primary, % of 6-11 group, 1990	38	62	76	102
Secondary, % of 12-17 group, 1990	15	15	22	93
Higher, % of 20-24 group, 1990	1	1.2	1.9	39
Adult literacy rate, %, 1990	66	41	39	99
Health and nutrition				
Life expectancy, years, 1991	48	50	50	76
Calorie supply, daily per head, 1991	1,708	2,111	2,096	3,357
Population per doctor, 1990	32,650	35,986	24,185	550

Notes: 'Africa' excludes South Africa. Dates are for the country in question, and do not always correspond with the Regional, African and Industrial averages.

the sector most badly affected. Export volumes have fallen, investment ratios have been low, but prices have been fairly stable.

Recent economic developments

In the face of evidence of a downward spiral in the economy, the later period of the Mengistu regime saw some belated efforts at economic reform. Private traders were allowed in the agricultural sector and prices to small farmers rose.

After 1991 the new EPRDF government, supported by the IMF and the World Bank, committed itself to a more thorough-going reform in its Economic Relief and Rehabilitation Programme (ERRP). Prices have been decontrolled, private traders allowed in most markets, and moves have been made to privatise state-owned enterprises. The currency was devalued in Oct 1992 and foreign currency auctions were used to set the exchange rate. These reforms appear to have been a significant factor in in the modest economic recovery of the past 3 years. However, the mainstay of the economy, the agricultural sector, is still very vulnerable to the pararies of the weather. Despite favourable harvests in 1991 and 1992, food aid needs were still considerable, and poor harvests in 1993/4 now threatened Ethiopia's food security once again.

Economic outlook

The economy can be expected to show continuing recovery, although agricultural output it will remain heavily dependent on the weather. There are considerable deposits of minerals in Ethiopia, all of which are only partially exploited. Foreign investment in the mining sector would be a big boost to the economy, but the international mining houses will need to be sure that Ethiopia's political future is stable, and that the government is going to persevere with the economic reforms before they commit themselves.

ADDIS ABABA

Addis Ababa (the name means 'new flower') is of fairly recent origin – Menelik II founded the city in 1887. Situated in the foothills of the Entoto mountains and standing 2,400m above sea level (the third highest capital in the world), the city has a population of about 2 million. Before moving to the present site of Addis Ababa, Menelik had established temporary capitals at 6 different locations – reflecting the shortage of fuelwood at each of these sites. Addis itself was in danger of being abandoned until the introduction of fast-growing eucalyptus trees from Australia provided the city with a regular source of fuel.

The city is now large and sprawling, displaying little evidence of planning. Bounded by mountains to the N, Addis is spreading S, and industrial and residential suburbs are expanding rapidly.

Addis Ababa is an important administrative centre not only for Ethiopia but for the whole of Africa. The headquarters of the UN Economic Commission for Africa was established here in 1958. In 1963 the city hosted the African Heads of State Conference at which the charter of the organisation of African Unity (OAU) was signed by 30 independent African nations, and Addis Ababa was subsequently chosen as the site of the OAU's secretariat.

Places of interest

Africa Hall is on Mekelik II Avenue – an imposing symbol of African independence and optimism, perhaps now looking a little jaded. It houses the headquarters of the UN Economic Commission for Africa. The huge stained glass windows depict the suffering of the people of Africa. Just to the W of the Africa Hall are the **Filwoha Springs** (now a murky pool) which prompted Queen Taytu to persuade her husband to establish his new capital at Addis Ababa. The thermal waters are now diverted to an adjacent bathing complex. Also next to the Africa Hall lies the huge **Abiot (Revolution) Square** – a natural amphitheatre where rallies were held every Sep to mark the 1974 revolution. Portraits of Marx, Engels, Lenin and Comrade Mengistu used to adorn the square.

At the other (N) end of Churchill Road, the city's main commercial boulevard, behind the dominant city hall, lies the **St George Cathedral** (Giorgis Cathederal). Built in 1896 in the traditional octagonal shape to commemorate Ethiopia's victory over the Italians at the Battle of Adwa, the cathedral houses the work of Afewerk Tekle, the renowned Ethiopian artist responsible for the stained glass windows of the Africa Hall. Nearby are the **Menelik Mausoleum** and the **Trinity Cathederal**, built in 1911 and 1941 to serve as the tombs of emperors and princes. The Trinity

St Yared

As a young man in sixth century Ethiopia, Yared was full of doubt regarding his own talents. He felt musical composition to be quite beyond him.

One day, as he sat despondently below a tree, he saw a caterpillar struggling to climb up it. Three times it fell, but on the fourth attempt it reached one of the branches and began to spin a cocoon. Inspired, Yared buckled down to his studies and went on to compose almost all of Ethiopia's religious music.

A painting of St Yared is to be seen in St Georges Cathedral in Addis Ababa.

Cathederal was built to commemorate Ethiopia's liberation from 5 years of Italian occupation. Haile Selassie's **Grand Palace** is just to the E of Churchill Ave at the end of Colsen St. The Emperor had a second residence, Juilee Palace, on Menelik Ave, just N of the *Ghion Hotel*.

North of the cathederal lies **Addis Ababa University**. The **National Museum** is part of the campus and contains, among other items, the female fossil skeleton 'Lucy' found in NE Ethiopia and thought to be 3.5 million years old.

The **Merkato** covers a vast area of western Addis Ababa. It is one of the largest markets in Africa and offers a dazzling array of colours, aromas, costumes, produce and jewelry.

Entoto, the mountain range which rises to the N of Addis, is easily accessible from the city. This is where Menelik started his first capital, and the **Church of Entoto Mariam** where he was crowned can still be visited. Reaching the top of the Entonto plateau stunning views unfold away to the N and the Blue Nile Gorge. At the top of the hill is the **Church of Entonto Raguel** which was previously at the centre of the old capital of Entoto.

Local information

Price guides:
A+ Over US$100;
A US$40-100; **B** US$20-40; **C** US$10-20;
D US$5-10; **E** Under US$5.

● Where to stay

A *Addis Ababa Hilton*, very central on Menelik Ave, T 15 84 00, Tlx 21104. Luxury accommodation with comprehensive business and recreation facilities. A/c. Swimming pool (warm water from thermal spring). Tennis. Restaurants. Bars. Jacuzzi, sauna, massage. Bookshop. Gift shop. Tours office. Pharmacy. Pleasant gardens.

B *Ghion*, very central on Menelik Ave, close to Revolution Square, T 44 31 70, Tlx 21112. Bungalows and appartments. Swimming pool (Olympic size, natural hot-spring water). Function rooms. Tours office. Gift shop. Restaurants. Bars. Extensive gardens. The Saba Rooms have ceiling paintings of the Queen of Sheba legend. **B** *Ethiopia*, Yohannes Ave, nr Churchill Rd, T 44 74 00, Tlx 21072. Located in business and commercial district. Restaurant. Coffee bar. Souvenir shop. Function rooms. **B** *Wabe Shabelle*, Ras Abebe Aragay St, T 44 71 87/90. **B** *Africa*, Dejazmach Wolde Mikael St, T 44 73 85. Bar. Restaurants. Mosaic of Ethiopian folklore on wall of one function room. **B** *Harambee*, Taitu St, T 15 40 00/15 43 27/15 42 26/15 44 57, Tlx 21072. Souvenir shop. Magala Lounge is decorated in the style of the old city of Harar. **B** *Ras*, Churchill Rd, T 44 70 60, Tlx 21485. Just N of railway station. Very popular, one of the oldest hotels in Addis. Restaurants. Bar. Gardens. **B** *National*, Menelik Ave, T 15 51 66, Tlx 21112. Some scope for self-catering in rooms with kitchenettes. Bar. Restaurant. **B** *Nile*, Ras Mekonin Ave. **B** *Guenet*, Beyene Merid St. Older style. **B** *Aros*, Belai Zeleke St.

C *Tourist*, nr Grand Palace and Trinity Cathederal. Popular. Restaurant. **C** *Awaris*, nr Piazza. Restaurant. **C** *Taitu*, nr Piazza.

● Places to eat

Price guide:
♦♦♦♦Over US$10; ♦♦♦US$5-10; ♦♦US$2-5;
♦Under US$2

♦♦♦♦***Abiata Restaurant***, *Wabe Shabelle Hotel*, Ras Abebe Aragay St, T 44 71 87/90. International cuisine. ♦♦♦♦***Addis Ababa Restaurant***, Weatherall St. Traditional Ethiopian food, in a circular dining room (*tukul*). Once the home of Queen Zauditu. An excellent variety of *wat*, see page 618, is on offer and food is eaten the local way – without knives and forks. ♦♦♦♦***Addis Tsegenet***, *Wabe Shabelle Hotel*, Ras Abebe Aragay St, T 44 71 87/90. Roof-top location, on 11th floor, splendid views. ♦♦♦♦***Casino Restaurant***, *Ghion Hotel*, Menelik Ave, T 44 31 70, Tlx 21112. International cuisine. ♦♦♦♦***China Bar***, off Ras Mekonin Ave. Wide variety of Chinese dishes. Well decorated in Oriental style. ♦♦♦♦***Finfine Hotel***, Atse Yohanness Ave, nr the *Hilton Hotel*. Ethiopian cuisine. Leather stools and mats in one dining area. Previously the home of a *Ras* (nobleman) who used Greek craftsmen to decorate and carve the wooden interior. ♦♦♦♦***Ghion Restaurant***, *Ghion Hotel*, Menelik Ave, T 44 31 70, Tlx 21112. International cuisine. ♦♦♦♦***Harrar Grill***, *Addis Ababa Hilton*,

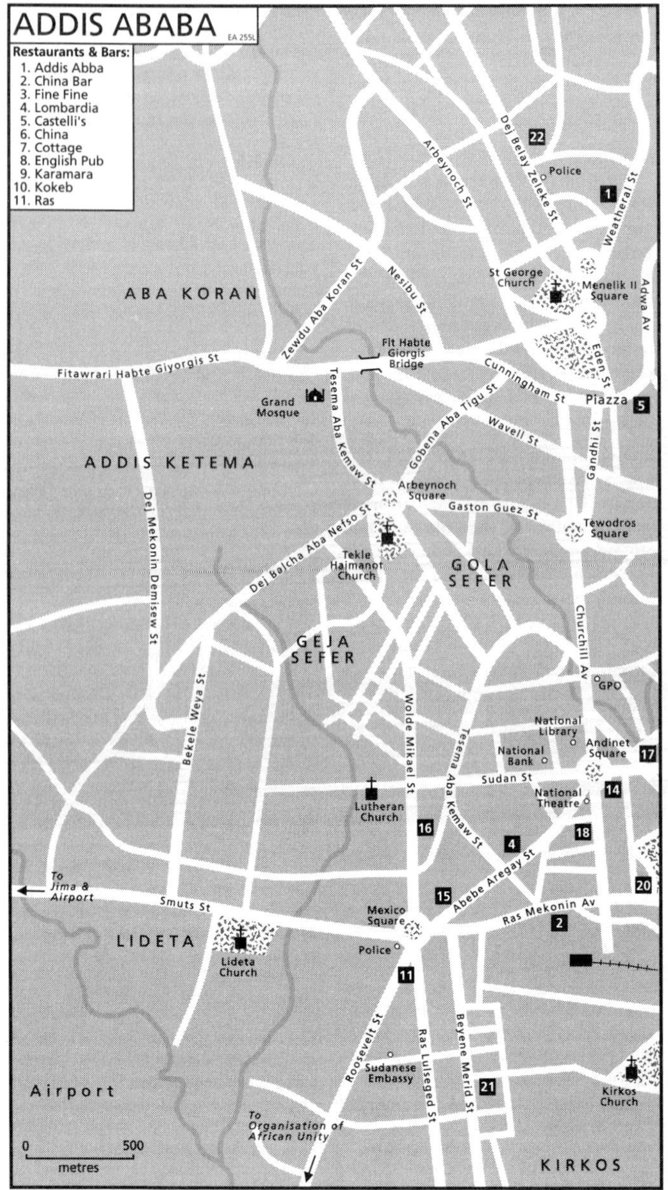
ADDIS ABABA
EA 255L
Restaurants & Bars:
1. Addis Abba
2. China Bar
3. Fine Fine
4. Lombardia
5. Castelli's
6. China
7. Cottage
8. English Pub
9. Karamara
10. Kokeb
11. Ras
ABA KORAN
ADDIS KETEMA
GOLA SEFER
GEJA SEFER
LIDETA
KIRKOS
Airport
Dej Belay Zeleke St
Arbeynoch St
Weatheral St
Police
St George Church
Menelik II Square
Adwa Av
Nesibu St
Zewdu Aba Koran St
Fit Habte Giorgis Bridge
Fitawrari Habte Giyorgis St
Eden St
Cunningham St
Piazza
Grand Mosque
Tesema Aba Kemaw St
Gobena Aba Tigu St
Wavell St
Gandhi St
Arbeynoch Square
Gaston Guez St
Tewodros Square
Dej Balcha Aba Nefso St
Tekle Hajmanot Church
Dej Mekonin Demisew St
Churchill Av
GPO
Bekele Weya St
Wolde Mikael St
National Library
National Bank
Andinet Square
Sudan St
National Theatre
Lutheran Church
Abebe Aregay St
To Jima & Airport
Smuts St
Mexico Square
Ras Mekonin Av
Lideta Church
Police
Roosevelt St
Ras Lulseged St
Beyene Merid St
Sudanese Embassy
Kirkos Church
To Organisation of African Unity
0 500 metres
22
1
5
17
14
18
4
16
15
20
2
11
21

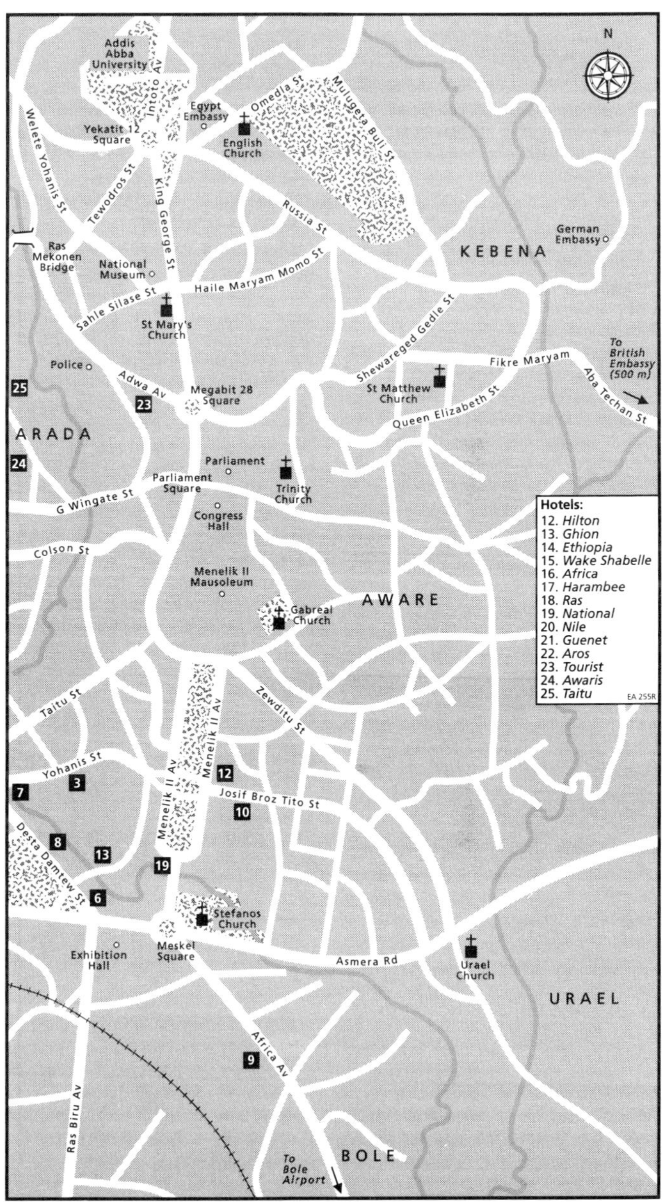
N
Addis Abba University
Intoto Av
Egypt Embassy
Omedla St
Mulugeta Buli St
Yekatit 12 Square
English Church
Welete Yohanis St
Tewodros St
King George St
Russia St
German Embassy
Ras Mekonen Bridge
National Museum
KEBENA
Haile Maryam Momo St
Sahle Silase St
St Mary's Church
Shewareged Gedle St
Police
Fikre Maryam
To British Embassy (500 m)
Aba Techan St
25
Adwa Av
23
Megabit 28 Square
St Matthew Church
Queen Elizabeth St
ARADA
24
Parliament
Parliament Square
Trinity Church
G Wingate St
Congress Hall
Colson St
Menelik II Mausoleum
Gabreal Church
AWARE
Hotels:
12. Hilton
13. Ghion
14. Ethiopia
15. Wake Shabelle
16. Africa
17. Harambee
18. Ras
19. National
20. Nile
21. Guenet
22. Aros
23. Tourist
24. Awaris
25. Taitu
EA 255R
Taitu St
Zewditu St
Menelik II Av
Yohanis St
3
12
7
Josif Broz Tito St
10
Desta Damtew St
8
13
19
6
Stefanos Church
Exhibition Hall
Meskel Square
Asmera Rd
Urael Church
URAEL
Africa Av
9
Ras Biru Av
BOLE
To Bole Airport

Menelik Ave, T 15 84 00. Tlx 21104. French cuisine. ♦♦♦♦***Jacaranda***, *Addis Ababa Hilton*, Menelik Ave, T 15 84 00. Tlx 21104. Italian and Mexican food. Overlooks pool and gardens. ♦♦♦♦***Lombardia***, on Ras Abebe Aregay Ave, T 15 07 91, Italian food. ♦♦♦♦***Ras Hotel***, Churchill Rd, T 44 70 60, Tlx 21485. Second floor restaurant with international cuisine. Buffet on Sat. Live band on Fri and Sat. ♦♦♦♦***Unity House***, *Ghion Hotel*, Menelik Ave, T 44 31 70, Tlx 21112. Stands in gardens with bar and terrace. *Flambé* nights on Fri and Sat.

♦♦♦***Africa Hotel***, Dejazmach Wolde Mikael St, T 44 73 85. Basement of hotel has a restaurant in traditional style, with thatched roof, serving Ethiopian food. There is also a restaurant with international cuisine. ♦♦♦***Castelli's***, T 11 10 58. In Piazza area close to Ethiopian Airways. Local paintings of 18th and 19th Century. ♦♦♦***China Bar & Restaurant***, Desta Damtew Ave. ♦♦♦***Cottage Restaurant & Pub***, nr the *Harambee Hotel* on Desta Demtew Ave offers Swiss food, and Swiss chalet-style decor. ♦♦♦***English Pub***, off Desta Demtew Ave International food. Darts. ♦♦♦***Ethiopia Restaurant***, *Ethiopia Hotel*, Atse Yohannes Ave, nr Churchill Rd, T 44 74 00. *Flambé* night with live band on Sat. Buffet with Ethiopian dishes on Thu. ♦♦♦***Fanfan Tavern***, *Harambee Hotel*, Tito St, T 15 40 00/15 43 27/15 42 26/15 44 57, Tlx 21072. Second floor barbeque grill. Traditional *masho* bead lamps. Murals on walls. ♦♦♦***Garden Snack Bars***, *Wabe Shabelle Hotel*, Ras Abebe Aragay St, T 44 71 87/90. Three traditional circular *tukuls*, one serving traditional Ethiopian food. ♦♦♦***Gazebo***, *Addis Ababa Hilton*, T 15 84 00. Tlx 21104. Café beside the pool. Barbeques and snacks. ♦♦♦***Harar Restaurant***, *Harambee Hotel*, Tito St, T 15 40 00/15 43 27/15 42 26/15 44 57, Tlx 21072. Decorated in style of old city of Harar. International cuisine. ♦♦♦***International Hotel***, Menelik Ave, T 15 51 66. Tlx 21112. Ground floor restaurant overlooking gardens to the rear. International cuisine. ♦♦♦***Kaffa House***, *Addis Ababa Hilton*, Menelik Ave, T 15 84 00. Tlx 21104. Coffee shop with reasonably extensive menu. ♦♦♦***Karamara Restaurant***, on Africa Ave, between Revolution Square and Bole Rd. Rondavel style. Entertainment from strolling singers and musicians. Ethiopian cuisine. ♦♦♦***La Tavern Grill***, off Debre Zeit Rd, T 16 21 79. International food. Good for children, with playground in the garden. *Al Fresco* barbeques on Sat. ♦♦♦*Lalibela*, Ras Desta Ave, T 15 87 34. International cuisine. Elaborate decor based on the rock-hewn churches of Lalibela. ♦♦♦***Oroscope Pizzeria***, off Churchill Rd. Serves international food as well as pizza. ♦♦♦***Pizzeria Ristorante de Goiton***, nr the Piazza and *Awaris Hotel* is good, friendly and reasonably priced. ♦♦♦***Shala Bar***, *Wabe Shabelle Hotel*, Ras Abebe Aragay St, T 44 71 87/90. American food. ♦♦♦***Villa Verde***, off Churchill Rd. Italian cuisine.

♦♦***Enrico*** Off Churchill Rd. Coffee, pastries, ice cream. ♦♦***Four Corners Armenian Restaurant***, Desta Damtew Ave, nr Revolution Square. Good value. ♦♦***Hong Kong Chinese Restaurant***, Churchill Rd, nr St Saviour Cathedral. ♦♦***Kokeb Restaurant***, Menelik II Ave. Near Africa Hall. Display of jewellery and horse-riding equipment. On 10th floor of apartment block. International and Ethiopian food. Good views from terrace. ♦♦***Kunama***, Africa Hotel, Dejazmach Wolde Mikael St, T 44 73 85. Terrace snack bar. ♦♦***Kyriazis Patisserie***, Piazza area, nr Ethiopian Airways. ♦♦***Peacock Restaurant***, Bole Rd. Convenience food. ♦♦***Pool Café***, *Ghion Hotel*, Menelik Ave, T 44 31 70, Tlx 21112. Barbeques and pizzas. Draught beer. ♦♦***Post Rendez Vous***, off Churchill Rd, nr Postal museum. Coffee bar with outside terrace. ♦♦***Ras Restaurant***, Mexico Square, T 44 41 82. International and Ethiopian food. Modern decor. Good value. ♦♦***Rendez Vous***, Abiot Square, off Ras Mekonin Ave. Barbeques on central grill. ♦♦*Sangam*, Bole Rd. Indian cuisine. ♦♦***Tukul***, *Ghion Hotel*, Menelik Ave, T 44 31 70, Tlx 21112. Snack bar.

● Snack bars

Cheap snack bars are clustered around the Piazza and offer local food. ♦***Kili Snack***; ♦***Star Café***; ♦***Port Bar***.

● Airline offices

Aeroflot, PO Box 7018, T 15 73; **Air Djibouti, T 15 73 22; Air France, T 15 90 44; Air Tanzania Corporation, T 15 75 33; Alitalia**, PO Box 3240, T 15 46 40 ; **Alyemda**, PO Box 40461, T 44 10 49; **Ethiopian Airlines** has 3 offices in City centre. Near National Theatre on Churchill Ave, T 44 70 00; *Addis Ababa Hilton*, Menelik Ave, T 15 84 00, Tlx 21104; and in Piazza at southern end of Eden St; **Interflug**, PO Box 4640, T 15 70 94; **Kenya Airways**, PO Box 3381, T 44 30 18; **Lufthansa**, PO Box 2484, T 15 59 61; **Yemenia**, PO Box 1079, T 44 50 76.

Banks

Commercial Bank of Ethiopia, at airport. *National Bank of Ethiopia*, Churchill Rd. *Commercial Bank of Ethiopia*, Churchill Rd.

Embassies

Algeria, PO Box 5740, T 7113000, F 712586, Tlx 21302; **Argentina, Tlx 21172; Austria**, PO Box 1219, T 712144, Tlx 21060; **Bulgaria**, PO Box 987, T 612971, Tlx 21450; **Burundi**, PO Box 3641, T 651300, Tlx 21069; **Cameroon**, Bole Rd, PO Box 1026, Tlx 21121; **Canada**, African Solidarity Insurance Building, 6th Floor, Churchill Ave, PO Box 1130, T 511100, F 512818, Tlx 21053; **Chad**, F 612050, Tlx 21419; **China**, PO Box 5643, Tlx 21145; Congo, PO Box 5571, T 154331, Tlx 21406; **Cote d'Ivoire**, PO Box 3668, T 711213, Tlx 21061; **Cuba**, Jimma Rd, PO Box 5623, T 202010, Tlx 21306; **Czech Republic**, PO Box 3108, T 516132, F 513471, Tlx 21021; **Djibouti**, PO Box 1022, T 613200, F 612504, Tlx 21317; **Egypt**, PO Box 1611, T 113077, Tlx 21254; **Equatorial Guinea**, PO Box 246; **Finland**, Tedla Dest Building, Bole Rd, PO Box 1017, T 513900, Tlx 21259; **France**, PO Box 1464, T 550066, F 551793, Tlx 21040; **Gabon**, PO Box 1256, F 181075, Tlx 21208; **Germany**, PO Box 660, T 550433, F 551311, Tlx 21015; **Ghana**, PO Box 3173, T 711402, F 712511; **Greece**, PO Box 1168, T 449712; **Guinea**, PO Box 1190, T 449712; **Holy See**, PO Box 588, T 712100, Tlx 21815; **Hungary**, Abattoirs Rd, PO Box 1213, T 651850, Tlx 21176; **India**, PO Box 528, F 552521, T 552100, Tlx 21148; **Indonesia**, Mekanisa Rd, PO Box 1004, T 202104, Tlx 21264; **Iran**, Jimma Rd, PO Box 1144, T 200369, Tlx 21118; **Israel**, PO Box 1075; **Italy**, PO Box 1105, T 551565, F 550218, Tlx 21342; **Jamaica**, National House Africa Ave, PO Box 5633, T 613656, Tlx 21137; **Japan**, Finfine Building, Revolution Sq, PO Box 5650, T 511088, F 511350, Tlx 21108; **Kenya**, Fikre Mariam Rd, PO Box 3301, T 610303, Tlx 21103; **Korea Democratic People's Republic**, PO Box 2378; **Korea Republic**, Jimma Rd, PO Box 2047, T 444490, Tlx 21140; **Liberia**, PO Box 3116, T 513655, Tlx 21083; **Libya**, PO Box 5728, Tlx 21214; **Malawi**, PO Box 2316, T 712440, F 710494, Tlx 21087; **Mexico**, Tsige Mariam Building, Churchill Rd, PO Box 2962, T 443456, Tlx 21141; **Netherlands**, PO Box 1241, T 711100, F 711577, Tlx 21049; **Niger**, Debrezenit Rd, PO Box 5791, T 651175, Tlx 21284; **Nigeria**, PO Box 1019, T 120644, Tlx 21028; **Poland**, Bole Rd, PO Box 1123, T 610197, Tlx 21185; **Romania**, Africa Ave, PO Box 2478, T 181191, Tlx 21168; **Russia**, PO Box 1500, T 552061, F 613795, Tlx 21534; **Rwanda**, PO Box 5618, T 610300, F 610411, Tlx 21199; **Saudi Arabia**, PO Box 1104, T 448010, Tlx 21194; **Senegal**, Africa Ave, PO Box 2581, T 611376, Tlx 21027; **Sierra Leone**, PO Box 5619, T 710033, Tlx 21144; **Slovakia**, PO Box 3108, T 516152, F 513471, Tlx 21021; **Spain**, Entoto St, PO Box 2312, T 550222, Tlx 21107; **Sudan**, PO Box 1110, Tlx 21293; **Sweden**, PO Box 1029, T 516699, Tlx 21039; **Switzerland**, Jimma Rd, PO Box 1106, T 711107, F 712177, Tlx 21123; **Tanzania**, PO Box 1077, T 44064, Tlx 21268; **Tunisia**, PO Box 10069; **Turkey**, PO Box 1506, T 612321, Tlx 21257; **Uganda**, PO Box 5644. T 513088, F 514355, Tlx 21143; **UK**, Fikre Miriam St, PO Box 858, T 612354, F 610588, Tlx 21299; **USA**, Entoto St, PO Box 1014, T 550666, F 551166, Tlx 21282; **Venezuela**, Debre Ziet Rd, PO Box 5584, T 654790, Tlx 21102; **Vietnam**, PO Box 1288; **Yemen**, PO Box 664, T 21346; **Yugoslavia**, PO Box 1342, T 517804. Tlx 21233; **Zaire**, Makinisa Rd, PO Box 2723, T 20485, Tlx 21043; **Zambia**, PO Box 1090, T 711302, Tlx 21065; **Zimbabwe**, PO Box 5624, T 183872, Tlx 21351.

Entertainment

Casino *Ghion Hotel*, Menelik Ave, T 44 31 70, Tlx 21112. Chemin de Fer, Blackjack, Roulette.

Cinema Mainly American, Indian and Arabic films. *Ambassador Theatre*, nr National Theatre and *Harambee Hotel* on Atse Yohannes Ave. *Cinema Ethiopia*, nr Piazza. *Addis Katama* in Merkato. *Agar Fikhr* (Patriotic Association), close to Piazza. Shows films on an occasional basis. *National Theatre* on Churchill Rd, and *City Hall*, at the N end of Churchill Rd also show films from time to time. See *Ethiopian Herald* for programmes.

Nightclubs *Disco Dahlac Paradise*, next to the Ambassador Theatre on Churchill Rd. *Ghion Nightclub*, T 44 31 70, Tlx 21112. Very central on Menelik Ave, close to Revolution Square. Live music. Features Roha, a celebrated Ethiopian band. *Ras Hotel*, Churchill Rd, T 44 70 60, Tlx 21485. Just N of railway station. Regular discos. *Shala Bar*, *Wabe Shabelle Hotel*, Ras Abebe Aragay St, T 44 71 87/90. From 2200. Live band. Fri and Sat only.

Theatre Traditional dance, music and classical western plays (Shakespeare is very popular, and has been translated into Amharic) at the ***National Theatre*** on Churchill Rd nr the Ethiopia Hotel, and at ***City Hall***, at the N end of Churchill Rd. National Theatre has regular traditional dance and music 1600-1800 on Thu. ***Agar Fikhr*** (Patriotic Association), close to Piazza. Traditional dance and music 1600 Tue. See *Ethiopian Herald* for programmes.

● Hospitals and medical services

Hospitals *Black Lion Hospital* on Churchill Rd behind Tiglachin monument. Modern. Good casualty department. ***Ethio-Swedish Clinic***, T 44 99 33.

Pharmacies City Council runs a number of inexpensive public pharmacies. There is one next to the National Tour Operation head office, nr *Ghion Hotel* off Meneloik Ave. Also pharmacy in *Hilton Hotel*.

● Newspapers

Foreign newspapers (*International Herald Tribune, Times, Washington Post*) available at airport, *Hilton* and British Council Library.

● Post Office

Main Post Office on Churchill Ave nr Adua Square. Open 0800-1600.

● Shopping

The high quality shopping area is along *Churchill Ave*. The main hotels all have a variety of shops. The area for bargains is *Merkato*, the main market of the city to the W (it is about 1 km from Churchill Ave, access is easy by taxi). Merkato has food, household items, imported goods and traditionally-made craftwork. There are some covered sections, the Adrash market halls, which contain the imported goods and the traditional items. The other local shopping area is the *Piazza*, at the N end of Churchill Rd, to the W. The jewelry, gold and silverware is mainly concentrated here, as well as flower shops, ceramics and leather goods.

Curios and crafts The *Hilton Hotel* and the *Ghion Hotel* both have shops selling traditionally made and antique items. The ***Ethiopian Tourist Trading Corporation*** (ETTC) has shops at Bole Airport, and in the Tourist Commission building in Abiot Sq off Ras Mekonin Ave. *Churchill Rd* has many small shops and stalls selling these items. ***Ethiopian Crafts and Antiques***, close to the Ras Hotel on Churchill Rd has a good selection of high quality craftwork. There are also craft items in *Merkato*, the large market to the W of the City centre, and jewelry and leather goods in the *Piazza*, off the N end of Churchill Ave. ***Addis Ababa City Gold*** and the ***Silversmith Cooperative Society*** are particularly good sources for jewelry in the Piazza.

Hairdressers Salons at *Hilton* and *Filwoha hotels*

● Sport (participant)

Bowling at Emboy Mesk in Debre Zeit Rd. Also *Guenet Hotel*. **Gym** at Arat Kilo to the N of the city, going NE from the Piazza along Adwa Ave. **Canoeing**, archery at Jan Meda. NE of the City centre off Mulugetsa St. Call the race track at Jan Meda (T 11 25 40) for information. **Horse Riding** at a site nr the Victory Department Store along the old Airport Rd. **Swimming** at *Ghion Hotel* (Olympic-size pool) and at *Hilton Hotel*. **Tennis** at *Ghion Hotel*, *Hilton Hotel*, *Guenet Hotel*, *Taitu Hotel*.

● Sport (spectator)

Horse racing at Jan Meda, T 11 25 40. NE of the City centre off Mulugetsa St. **Soccer** at Addis Ababa Stadium on Ras Desta Damtew Ave. There are games on most Thu evenings and on Sat and Sun. See *Ethiopian Herald* for programmes.

● Tourist information

National Tour Operation (NTO). Near *Ghion Hotel* on Ras Mekonin Ave, PO Box 5709, T 15 29 55. Branch in *Addis Ababa Hilton*, T 15 84 00. Tlx 21104. Menelik Ave.

● Tour operators and travel agents

The travel business has opened up dramatically since the collapse of the Mengistu regime. In addition to the state-owned National Tour Operation, there are many private tour and travel agencies offering their services. ***Alfa Travels***, PO Box 4263, T 511177. ***Al-Tad Travels***, PO Box 1223, T 513755, F 515244, Tlx 21981. ***Distance Travel Agency***, PO Box 70186, T 151715, F 515963. ***Eastern Travel and Tourist Agency***, PO Box 1136, T 511574, F 511468. ***East West Travel Agency***, PO Box 2020, T 204 245/46, F 513977. ***Ethio-Adam International Tour and Travel***, PO Box 3543, T 518003, F 510947. ***Forship Travel Agency***, PO Box 30754, T 552159, Tlx 21634. ***Four Season Travel Agency***, PO Box 2856, T 613121, F 613616 ***Galaxi Travel Services***, PO Box 8309, T 510875, F 511236. ***Gebre Admasu Travel***, PO Box 7611, T 513890, F 513890. ***Globe Travels***, PO Box 5603, T 510437, Tlx 21305. ***Host Ethiopia Travel***, PO Box 5944, T 157878, Tlx 21274. ***Itco Tourist and Travel Agency***, PO Box 1048,

T 516311, F 512382, Tlx 21131. ***Kaleb Travel Agency***, PO Box 3541, T 515704, F 513977. ***Lalibela Travel Agency***, PO Box 2590, T 514403. ***Luxor Travel Agency***, PO Box 30714, T 515730, F 517422. ***Nile Touring Co.***, PO Box 4090, T 518238, F 518238. ***No 9 Travel Agency***, PO Box 26847, T 112226, F 551233. ***Peers Tours and Travel Agency***, PO Box 3545, T 515140, F 513177. ***Prime Tours***, PO Box 8542, T 515529, F 515099. ***Safeway Travel and Tours***, PO Box 8449, T 511600, F 511800. ***Selam International Travel and Tourist Agency***, PO Box 30208, T 117444, F 513950. ***Sheba Travel Agency***, PO Box 3422, T 513032. ***Skyline Travel Agency***, PO Box 50146, T 756656, F 754688. ***Solast travel Agency***, PO Box 26847, T 513423, F 551233. ***Telul Travel Agency***, PO Box 5576, T 514342, F 512826. ***Union of Nations Travel Agency***, PO Box 5261, T 519550, F 519550. ***Yumo International Agency***, PO Box 5698, T 518878, F 513451.

● **Transport**

Local Bus: red and yellow *ambasa* (lion) buses operate within the city, stopping at every red and yellow marking. There is a flat fare per person for a one-way trip. Minibuses (*wi yi yit*) are also available, running on set routes, leaving the bus stand when full. The main bus terminal is at Merkato

Taxi: cream coloured NTO (National Tour Operator) taxis operate at Bole International Airport and outside all the major hotels. Also, a private taxi service operates in smaller blue and white cars along set routes, often on a vehicle-sharing basis.

Air The national carrier ***Ethiopian Airways*** connects with many European destinations and with 23 African cities. In addition there are direct flights by ***Alitalia, Aeroflot, Alyemda, Lufthansa, Interflug, Yemenia***, and ***Kenya Airways***.

Bole International Airport is 5 km from the city centre. Taxis to and from the airport are run by the National Tour Operation. On a shared basis the fare is about US$8. A minibus ride is about US$1.

Road Buses to and from the regions are frequent. The main bus terminal is at Merkato, while a second bus station nr the railway station has frequent services to nearby destinations such as Debre Zeit and Awasa.

Train A 782 km railway connects Addis with Djibouti on the Red Sea. The trains from Addis Ababa leave daily at around 0700 and 1930, arriving in Djibouti approximately 24 hrs later. The main stop is at Debre Dawa, a bit over half way. Booking is at the railway station at the southern end of Churchill Rd. It is necessary to make a reservation as the train is often full. The fare to Djibouti is US$60 1st class (a sleeper on the overnight train); US$30 2nd class; US$16 3rd class. Djibouti-Ethiopian Railroad Company, T 44 72 50.

Around Addis Ababa

Debre Zeit and Crater Lakes

An hour's journey S of Addis brings you to Debre Zeit, a busy commercial centre tangled under a canopy of bougainvillea, flame trees and jacarandas. The town is encircled by 5 crater lakes, characteristic of the East African Rift Valley. The principal lake, Hora, is used for water sports and is home to a stunning array of bird life. The most dramatic lake, Bishoftu, is a short walk off the main highway – a sheer wall plunging down to the dark green surface. **B** *Hora Ras Hotel*, perched on the rim of the crater beside Lake Hora, provides excellent views.

Mount Zaquella

This is an excursion off the main highway from Debre Zeit rises 600m above the plain. An ancient monastery stands on the crater rim looking down at the lake. It is a stiff 2½ hr climb to the top, but majestic views looking S and E down the rift valley, the valley lakes glinting away in the distance, are the reward. A little way beyond Debre Zeit, past the small transit town of Mojo (one petrol station, 2 hotels) the road crosses the Awash river. Here the hot blue waters of thermal springs gush up from the molten interior of the rift and merge with the silty waters of the Awash. Lurking crocodiles prey on the fish here, and further downstream there's a hippo pool. On through the bustling cattle town of Nazareth to the spa town of Sodere – 2 hrs drive from Addis and a favourite week-end resort. Here, the volcanic mineral springs constantly replen-

Rock Of Truth

In the fourteenth century, a recluse, Gabre Manfus, is said to have lived for 363 years, much of that time among his friends, the creatures of the wild on Mount Zaquella. He become Ethiopia's patron saint of animals.

On the feast of Gabre Manfus, lovers travel to Mount Zaquella. High on the mountain is a split rock. As they pass through the cleft, they know that if their love is untrue, the rock will close and crush them

Scores of followers of Gabre Manfus, hermits in flowing yellow robes, continue to live on the mountain, existing on the fruits of the forest and sleeping in caves.

A painting of Gabre Manfus, surrounded by a lion, a leopard and a raven, is in St Georges Cathedral in Addis Ababa.

ish swimming pools with clear blue, warm water. Giant shade trees cast a cool canopy around the pools and baboons, hippos and crocodiles can be seen when walking along the river bank. **B** *Sodere Filwoha Resort*.

Mangasha to Ambo

The Mangasha park lies only 35 km W of Addis Ababa; a mountain forest sanctuary for birds and animals, and the climb through the forest to the beautiful crater valley of Wachacha is popular. The church of Debre Tsion at Addis Alem is worth a visit, and then on to Ambo, or Hagere Heywot, 125 km W of Addis Ababa on the same road. The spas here are good for swimming and 26 km away along a dirt track is the beautiful volcanic crater lake of Wonchi. **B** *Ras Hotel*, located at Ambo.

Blue Nile Gorge

Ninety minutes N from Addis a turning leads down to the ancient 13th century monastery of **Debre Libanos**, perched on the edge of a 700m gorge. Not long after Debre Libanos is the Blue Nile Gorge. This river begins its journey far to the N at Lake Tana, finally carving its way through a gorge that must be one of the most remarkable and breathtaking phenomena on Earth. A mile wide and almost as deep, the road winds down over 1000m, a journey of over 45 minutes in a car, and at times the road actually leaps away from the side of the gorge, supported by Italian-built stanchions. A single span bridge crosses the river at the bottom before the ascent again on the other side.

WEST TO GAMBELA

The Nilotic peoples – Anuak and Nuer – who inhabit the lowlands around Gambela are quite unique, as is the surrounding vegetation, landscape and climate. The western section of the central plateau comes to an abrupt end in the province of Lullabor, around the picturesque town of Gore, and from here the land falls away to the Nilotic lowlands.

Descending from the highlands, where it is forced between steep-sided gorges, the River Baro loses momentum as it reaches the plain, spreading out to a broad river bed. Here, the Anuak settlements are interspersed between mango and banana plantations, while further downstream the vast grassland plains begin.

Gambela

It is about 600 km by road from Addis Ababa to the inland port of Gambela. Empty docks and delapidated warehouses are now a reminder of a time when Gambela was a prosperous river terminal. The British government established dock facilities here in the late 1940's linking the town with Khartoum, 1,388 km away, via the navigable Baro river. The River Baro can only take traffic during the rainy season, the 4 months from Jun to Sep. When the port was at its peak, up to 40 ships would be in dock at any one time.

Gambela gives access to the **Gambela National Park**. The undulating plains of high Sudanese grass offer excellent opportunities for wilderness exploration. All the elements of African safari are found here, including elephants, lions, crocodiles and 100 kg Nile perch.

Beyond Gambela towards the Sudanese border, the Anuak cultivators give way to the nomadic Nuer. These pastoralists herd their long-horned cattle into huge camps when they stop for the night.

• **Where to stay and eat** C *Ethiopia*. The only tourist class hotel, it is government-owned, and somewhat drab. There is a restaurant and bar. It is now also possible to stay in local guest houses round the market area and the docks. Accommodation is a bit of a lottery in these establishments. There are many small eating places in these areas as well.

• **Transport Air**: there are 4 flights a week by *Ethiopian Airlines* from Addis Ababa (Mon, Thu, Fri, Sun), and the fare is around US$125 return. **Road**: buses leave from the bus stand on Addis Katema St, just to the W of Merkato in Addis Ababa, the fare is around US$18 one-way, and the journey takes at least about 2 days, longer in the rainy season.

EAST TO DJIBOUTI

Following the Assab highway E, 225 km from the capital is the spectacular AwashNationalPark – the oldest game reserve in Ethiopia. The headquarters of the park are found near the dramatic Awash falls. One of the most beautiful areas is the Kudu valley which takes its name from the large antelopes which inhabit it. Other game includes oryx, Soemmerrings gazelle, wild pig, the tiny dik-dik antelope, zebra, hippos and big cats such as leopard and Cheetah. Over 400 species of bird are found within the 700 km square park.

Another feature is the extensive area of hot springs found to the N of the park – an oasis surrounded by tall green shade trees amidst the dry desert scrub. The superheated water emerges into translucent turquoise pools, quickly cooling to temperatures which are ideal for swimming.

Dire Dawa

Roughly half way on the Addis Ababa – Djibouti railway is Dire Dawa. It is 517 km E of Addis and with a population of 98,000, has existed for less than a century, and the main reason for its expansion is its position on the road and railway. The climate here is warm and dry and the atmosphere is relaxed. The market place is full of camel-herding Oromos, Somalis and Afars. The caves, just outside town, contain prehistoric rock paintings.

Dire Dawa is most useful as a point from which to explore the ancient city of **Harar**, only 54 km away – a spectacular journey up the escarpment of the rift valley. The road passes lakes Adele and Alemaya, and in these rich farmlands, some of Ethiopia's finest coffee is cultivated. The local narcotic, *khat*, is also widespread here.

Local information

● Where to stay

B *Ras*, Government-owned. A/c. Swimming pool. Bar. Restaurant. Good standard. **C** *Karamara*. Bar Restaurant. Reasonably comfortable. **C** *Olympic*. Bar. Restaurant. Adequate.

There are some cheaper local guest houses round the station and market place. There are many small eating places in these areas as well.

● Useful addresses

There are 2 open air cinemas in the town.

● Transport

Air *Ethiopian Airways* flies daily to Dire Dawa. The cost is around US$100 return. If you are visiting other cities, there are special round-trip fares, see page 618.

Train The trains from Addis Ababa leave daily at around 0700 and 1930, arriving in Dire Dawa approximately 12 hrs later. Booking at the railway station at the southern end of Churchill Rd. It is necessary to make a reservation as the train is often full. The fare is US$32 1st class (a sleeper on the overnight train); US$15 2nd class; US$8 3rd class

Road Buses leave from the bus stand on Addis Katema St, just to the W of Merkato in Addis Ababa, the fare is around US$15 one-way, and the journey takes a day, longer in the rainy season.

Harar

Harar, with a population of 62,000, stands on the eastern wall of the great rift valley and is the capital of Ethiopia's largest administrative region, Hararghe. The city's lofty situation gives wonderful views of the surrounding country – the vast Danakil desert to the N, the fertile Harar mountains to the E and the cattle-rich Ogaden plains to the S.

Harar was a fiercely religious city from the early days of Islamic expansion into the Horn of Africa until 1887 when Menelik restored central rule. It was from here that Ahmed Gragn launched his attack on the Christian highlands in 1527, and Harar, with its 99 mosques is considered to be the fourth most holy city in

Islam. The crowning glory is the 16th century Grand Mosque, with its beautiful twin towers and slender minaret.

The setting is thrilling. Medieval walls tightly embrace the ancient city, its bustling and vivid market place regarded as one of the most colourful in all Ethiopia. The twisting alleys and flat roofed buildings are little changed from when the town was visited in the 19th century by the British explorer Sir Richard Burton. The French poet Rimbaud built a house here, which is still standing. The whole town is surrounded by soaring mountains and is fanned by cool, bracing air.

One of the city's peculiarities is the so-called **Hyena Men**, who make their living by collecting offal and bones to feed to the wild hyenas outside the walls. The snarling creatures come out of the darkness just after sunset to take food from their benefactor's hands. If you go to watch there is a small charge for this spectacle.

Harar is famed for its silversmiths, and there are beautiful necklaces, bracelets and chains to be found in the market. The basketry is also impressive.

Local information

● Where to stay

B *Ras*, one of the better establishments in this government-owned chain. Bar. Restaurant. Food quite good.

There are some small private guest houses, bars and eating places nr Feres Magala, the old horse market.

● Transport

A shared taxi or a seat in a minibus costs around US$2 from Dire Dawa. Dire Dawa can be reached by train road or air, see page 618.

SOUTH: RIFT VALLEY LAKES & BALE MOUNTAINS

The East African Rift Valley displays some of the most dramatic scenery in the world. The valley's passage through Ethiopia is marked by a string of lakes, seven in all, which dot the valley floor and are home to a fine array of flora and fauna.

Travelling S from Addis, past the Koka dam and on the highway to Awasa, the first lake reached is **Lake Zwai**. 26 km long and 18 km wide this is the largest of the valley lakes, dotted with islands and fringed with fig trees. Birds to be seen here include herons and storks, black headed orioles, jacanas and the handsome African fish eagle. To the N, the Mekli river flows in to replenish the lake's waters, creating a wide bay where hippos gather. B *Bekele Mola Hotel*, N of Lake Zwai.

Lake Langano

Before you reach the lake, there are the ruins of an old fortress, towering over the village of Adami Tulu. Langano itself is a very popular resort – 210 km from the capital and set against the beautiful Arsi mountains. There is a wide choice of hotel and camping accommodation and the lake is good for swimming and water sports.

• **Where to stay A** *Langano Resorts*, on shores of lake. Pleasing location. Bar. Restaurant. **B** *Bekele Mola*, on Lake Langano. **D** *Ghike Guest House*, self-catering. on the shores of nearby Lake Shala, close to the Ghike hot spring.

• **Camping** is available at *Bekele Mola Hotel* and at 2 sites on nearby Lake Shala, just S of the park HQ at Dole.

Lakes Abyata and Shala

Not far from Langano, situated in the heart of the Rift Valley Park, are lakes Abyata and Shala. Abyata is a bird paradise. A soda lake, it has vast expanses of white shoreline and its surface is a carpet of pink flamingos. Also resident are fish eagles, herons, cormorants and storks, spoonbills and ibises and numerous species of duck. During the Northern winter, the lake becomes home to thousands of migrant European birds. Shala is a pristine wilderness, surrounded by an aura of almost primeval splendour. It is also an important breeding ground for the birds and is well known for its colony of great white pelicans.

Beyond the town of **Shashamene**, there is a beautiful wooded valley of ancient indigenous trees. In the valley is a lodge at **Wendo Gunnet** with natural hot springs. Just N Shashamene is **Jamaica**, a community of Rastafarians from the Caribbean. This cult worships Haile Selassie, whose name was Ras Tafari before he became emporer. Close by is lake **Awasa**, generally considered the most beautiful of the valley lakes. A gentle chain of mountains and a low plateau surround the waters, opening to a wide bay in the S. The local fish is a speciality.

• **Where to stay B** *Wabe Shabelle*, close to Wendo Gunnet. **B** *Awasa Resort*, on lake.

Lakes Abaya and Chamo

The 2 southernmost lakes of the chain, Abaya and Chamo, are quite remote and demand a trip of several days. There is, however, rich wildlife, lush vegetation and hordes of hippos and crocodiles. One spot on the western shores of lake Chamo is referred to locally as 'crocodile market' because of the many crocodile that congregate there. **Necht Sar** National Park encompasses the eastern shores of these lakes – a sanctuary for Swaynes hartebeest, an endangered animal unique to Ethiopia.

On the bluff between the 2 lakes is the town of **Arba Minch**, a good base from which to explore the area. **B** *Bekele Mola Hotel*. This is stylish and pleasantly located, though a little delapidated. **Camping** is available at a pleasant site in the Netch Sar National Park, on the Kulfi River.

• **Transport** *Ethiopian Airlines* flies to Arba Minch on Mon, Wed, Sat and Sun. The fare is around US$100 return.

Omo National Park

Further to the SE is the remote and little visited Omo National Park. Virtually free from human habitation, except along the banks of the river Omo, this is the largest park in the country – 3,450 km square – an area of true wilderness. Zebra, oryx, elephants, buffaloe, giraffes, lions, leopards and cheetahs roam this park in huge numbers. The valley is also rich in fossils, the latest hominid remains to be discovered date back over 4 million years.

• **Transport to and from Rift Valley Air**: there are no scheduled air-flights to the S. **Road**: there are regular buses running along this route from Addis Ababa.

NORTH TO TIGRAY

The area to the N of Ethiopia contains some of the most most interesting historical sites, including the ancients cities of Gondar and Axum as well as the site of the extraordinary rock-hewn churches at Lalibela. Lake Tana has the specatacular Tissisat Falls on the Blue Nile, and between Gondar and Axum is the Simien National Park.

Bahar Dar

Travelling N about 300 km from the Blue Nile Gorge you come to the town of Bahar Dar, population 54,000, situated at the southern end of **Lake Tana** (3,700 sq km). This is the centre from which to explore the spectacular **Tissisat Falls** – the largest waterfall on the Blue Nile river – which drains the lake just to the N. The falls are 30 km S of the town and are reached on foot from a nearby village. The awsome roar of the water crashing into the mist-shrouded gorge far below is a vivid experience. Lake Tana was established by John Bruce ('Abyssinian Bruce') as one of the sources of the Nile in 1770, travelling from Massawa in present-day Eritrea.

The monastery of **Dek Stefanos** at Bahar Dar holds a priceless collection of icons and manuscripts and houses the mummified remains of a number of Ethiopian emperors. There are monasteries on many of the numerous islands which dot the southern end of the lake, most dating from the 14th century. The most accessible from Bahar Dar are **Kebran Gabriel** (still forbidden to women) and **Ura Kidanemereth** on the Zegie peninsula which is famous for its frescoes.

Local information

● Where to stay and eat

A *Tana*, on shores of lake. Good standard, pleasant location. Excellent food. **B** *Ghion*, town centre. **B** *Ras Hotel*.

● Transport

Air *Ethiopian Airways* flies daily to Bahar Dar. The cost is around US$75 return. If you are visiting other cities, there are special round-trip fares, see page 618. Taxi from airport is around US$6.

Road Route is via Bahar Dar and the whole journey is 400 km. Travel is difficult Jun-Sep when the rains are heavy. It is realistic to allow 2 days for the journey there, with a stop in Debre Markos. There are regular buses running along this route.

Gondar

At the N end of the lake, 500 km N of

A Leper In The Scales Of Justice

Balaya Sab was a cannibal, whose lifetime sustenance comprised 69 souls. One day, however, out seeking a snack, he came across a leper. Considering the item well past its sell-by date, Balaya Sab declined him as a repast, gave him some water, and carried on foraging.

When Balaya Sab died, things did not look to promising as St George stacked up the 69 two-footed take-aways in one pan of the scales of justice. But when the Virgin Mary tossed the spared leper, to whom Balaya Sab had extended the merest morsel of kindness in the form of a sup of water, into the other pan, such was the power of human kindness in the final reckoning that it outweighed the 69 sins and Balaya Sab was allowed to enter paradise.

There is a fresco of Balaya Sab in the Church of Debra Kota Mariam on Dek Island in Lake Tana.

Addis Ababa and nestling in the foothills of Simien mountains is the ancient city of Gondar, population 64,000, undoubtedly one of the most thrilling experiences that Ethiopia has to offer with its churches, castles and mountain scenery. Gondar was the capital of Ethiopia from the rise of Fasiladas (1632-1635) to the fall of Tewodros (1855-1868), a status that is reflected in the many castles and palaces which grace the city. At first site the architecture seems to reflect Moorish-European influence, and indeed, the presence of the Portuguese in the 16th centry may have influenced the design of some of the fortresses. But closer inspection reveals a continuity with the Axumite tradition. The city's main imperial precinct contains the most impressive castles. The oldest of these is the **Castle of Fasiladas**. His grandson, Iyasu the Great, who was considered one of Gondar's greatest leaders, built his own fantastic castle and decorated it with ivory, gold and precious stones.

Other than the castles there is the **Palace of Ras Beit**, built in the 18th century as a private residence of the the famous king maker, Ras Mikael Sehul – and in continuous occupation ever since. A short distance away is the impressive **Bath of Fasiladas**.

The **Church of Debre Birhan Selassie** stands on raised ground to the NE of the city. Built during the reign of Iyasu the Great, it is well preserved, its ceiling and interior walls being beautifully decorated with colourful religious paintings.

Excursions

North of Gondar are the **Simien Mountains,** designated by UNESCO as a world heritage site. The jagged peaks of this volcanic range are so young that erosion has not yet softened their outline. The highest peak in Ethiopia and the fourth highest in Africa, **Ras Deshen**, stands adjacent to the 225 km square park. In this spectacular setting are to be found the Waliba ibex, the Simien red fox, and the Gelada baboon – 3 animals unique to Ethiopia.

Local information

● Where to stay and eat

B *Goha*, c/o Ethiopian Hotels and Spaas Corporation (EHC), PO Box 1263, Addis Ababa,, T 15 27 00. Tlx 21112. Fine location on rise on the edge of town. Good standard food. **C** *Quara*, close to centre of town, in the Piazza. **D** *Ethiopia*, *Fasil*, *Fogera* (c/o EHC above), and *Terrara* (also c/o EHC above).

● Transport

Air *Ethiopian Airways* flies daily to Gondar. The cost is around US$100 return. If you are visiting other cities, there are special round-trip fares, see page 618. Airport is 17 km from town and a taxi is around US$6.

Road Route is via Bahar Dar and the whole journey is 600 km. Travel is difficult Jun-Sep when the rains are heavy. It is realistic to allow 3 days for the journey there, with stops in Bahar Dar and Debre Markos. There are regular buses running along this route.

The Legend Of Gondar

Archangel Raguel revealed to Emperor Lebna Dengel in a dream that Ethiopia would be blessed with a sacred capital, and that the name of the location would begin with the letter 'G'.

Nothing daunted, successive Emperors began worked their way doggedly down a list of places with names beginning with the designated consonant, dragging their entourage of 50,000 or so courtiers and camp-followers from site to site. Here and there they started some tentative civic construction, but never managed to establish anything that endured. Until, that is, Emperor Fasilades, hunting in the mid 17th C, stood to drink at a lake. As he raised his eyes, he saw a holy man rise up out of the waters. Fasilides was advised that he was in the paradise of Ezra and Enoch, and he was commanded to build his capital right there, at Gondor.

Axum

Further N still is the town of Axum, site of Ethiopia's oldest city. Axum dates back some 2000 years to when it was the hub of the Axumite empire. All that remains now of its past glories are the huge granite stele (pillars), some fallen and some still standing, each hollowed to create buildings several stories high. Made of single blocks of granite, the tallest stood over 33m high – the largest monolith in the world. The biggest now standing is 23m. The carving is deep and precise, showing beams and windows at each floor. It reflects a style of building still employed at Hadramaut in southern Yemen.

Also of interest is the 16th century **Church of St Mary of Zion**. Supposedly the repository of the original Ark of the Covenent (a sacred gold-covered chest from Old Testament times), St Mary's is the holiest Christian sanctuary in Ethiopia.

Other historical sites include the **Grave of King Kaleb** and the **Grave of King Gabre**, the reputed **Bath of the Queen of Sheba** and the ruins of the vast royal palace, over which the road to Gondar now passes.

Local information

● **Where to stay and eat**

C *Axum*, c/o Ethiopian Hotels and Spaas Corporation (EHC), PO Box 1263, Addis Ababa,, T 15 27 00. Tlx 21112. **C** *Yeha*, c/o EHC above.

● **Transport**

Air *Ethiopian Airways* flies daily to Axum. The cost is around US$150 return. If you are visiting other cities, there are special round-trip fares, see page 618.

Road Route is via Bahar Dar and Gondar and the whole journey is 800 km. Access is difficult Jun-Sep when the rains are heavy. It is realistic to allow at 4 days for the journey there, with stops in Debre Markos, Bahar Dar and Gondar. There are regular buses running along this route.

Lalibela

Travelling east from Axum, some 25 km to Adowa, is the beginning of an area of rock-hewn churches centred on Digum. The greatest concentration is in the **Gheralta** region. Continuing south, down the eastern flanks of the Simien mountains, you will pass through **Makale**, the regional capital of Tigray and eventually hit the extraordinary city of Lalibela, high-up, at an altitude of 2,600m. The **rock-hewn churches** here,

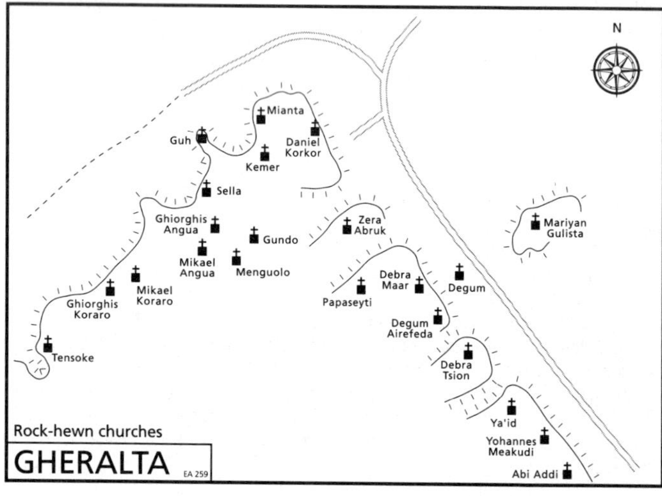

set in rugged, awe-inspiring scenery, are surely one of the unacknowledged wonders of the world.

Lalibela was built as the capital of a local king following the fall of Axum, and it became the centre of religious authority in Ethiopia. The churches were sculpted out of the rock in the 12th century, standing completely free from the surrounding stone. They are tended by priests who guard their precious artistic and religious treasures and each contains beautiful murals, crosses and manuscripts.

The town is inaccessible during the rainy season (Jun-Sep) and the best time to visit is probably during the Ethiopian Easter or at *Timket* (epiphany) in Jan, these being the most lavish holy festivals.

Local information

● Where to stay and eat

C ***Seven Olives***, c/o Ethiopian Hotels and Spas Corporation (EHC), PO Box 1263, Addis Ababa, T 15 27 00. Tlx 21112. **C** ***Roha***, c/o EHC above.

● Transport

Air *Ethiopian Airways* flies daily to Lalibela. The cost is around US$100 return. If you are visiting other cities, there are special round-trip fares, see page 618. Airport is some distance away. A government-owned bus runs into town.

Road Access is not easy overland – for a long while Laibela was in the zone affected by the fighting in Tigre. The route is via Dessie, which is 300 km to the N-E. Lalibela is a further 200 km from Dessie. Access is impossible Jun-Sep when the rains are heavy. It is realistic to allow at least 3 days for the journey there.

NATIONAL PARKS AND SANCTUARIES

The parks are well run with helpful staff who try hard to make visitors welcome. All the major African aninmals are present, with the exception of rhinoceros. Awash, Abyatta-Shala, Nechisar, Simien Mountains, Harar Elephant Sanctuary and Bale Mountains are readily accessible from Addis Ababa. Bale Mountains offers horse trekking, which is a splendid way to tour the park.

Tours are available and there is a wide variety of operators, as well as the state-owned service, see page 614. Until 1991 there were daunting restrictions on visitors, and the tourist sector is only now beginning to get back to normal.

Awash National Park

The park is located 225 km from Addis Ababa off the highway to Assab (now part of Eritrea) It stretches about 30 km from E to W and a little less from N to S. The terrain is covered with grassland and acacia woodland. The central feature is the Fantalle volcano, now dormant. A track leads part of the way up the volcano, and it is possible to climb the rest of the way to the crater edge. There are hot-springs in deep, clear, blue pools at Filwoha in the N. The area also contains unusual rock formation in the shape of blisters. The Awash River Gorge runs along the southern edge of the park and there is a waterfall near the park headquarters.

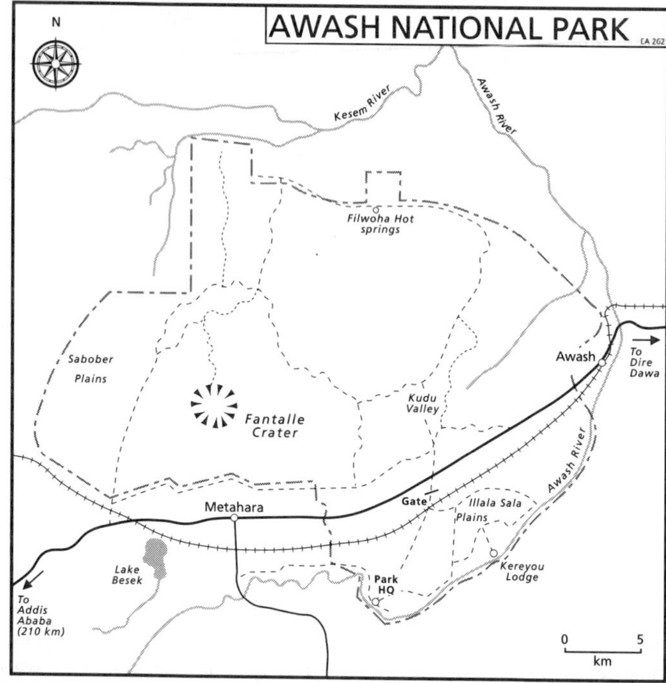

The main African wildlife of the plains are present with the exception of rhinos, giraffe and buffalo. The main species to be seen are leopard, bushbuck, hippo, Soemmerring's gazelle, oryx, caracal, colubus and green monkeys, Anubis and Hamadryas baboons, klipspringer, Grevy's Zebra, cheetah, greater and lesser kudu, ardvaarks, and bat-eared foxes. Over 400 species of bird are present.

• **Where to stay** C *Kereyou Lodge*, c/o Ethiopian Hotels and Spas Corporation (EHC), PO Box 1263, Addis Ababa,, T 15 27 00. Tlx 21112. Located on the Awash River on the southern boundary of the park. It is a group of caravans, but reasonably comfortable.

• **Camping** is available at 6 sites, a couple of which are just outside the park boundary.

• **Transport** Regular buses and minibuses from Addis Ababa along the route through Debre Zeit to Awash

Bale Mountains National Park

The Bale mountains park is 400 km S-W of Addis Ababa, to the east of the the town of Shashamene on the highway that runs S to the Kenyan border. It is about 60 km from E to W and 80 km from N to S. The terrain is juniper and heather moorlands in the foothills, with woodland in the higher reaches. There are many swift-flowing streams, and the climate is alpine. Several of the peaks are over 4,00m, the highest being Mt Tullu Deemtu at 4,377m.

The main feature of the park is that it houses 3 of the species unique to Ethiopia, the Simien red fox (also found in the Simien Mountains), Menelik's bushbuck, and the Mountain Nyala. Other wildlife includes leopards, black servals, lions, black and white colubus monkeys, olive baboons, grivet, and Sykes monkeys. There are several endemic rodents, including the giant mole rat, which burrows leaving heaps of debris on the surface. The streams contain rainbow and brown trout introduced from Kenya. The giant lobelia, growing up to 5m in height is a form of vegetation unique to the park. Over 200 bird species are to be found, including the bearded vulture.

Horses can be hired from the Park HQ at Dinsha, and there is a variety of established riding trails.

• **Where to stay** **B** *Goba Ras*, c/o Ethiopian Hotels and Spaas Corporation (EHC), PO Box 1263, Addis Ababa, T 15 27 00. Tlx 21112. Just to the E of the park. **C** ***Bekele Mola***, c/o EHC above, in Robe, 15 km N of Goba. **D** ***Swedish Guest House***. At Dinsha. Self-catering. Comfortable and popular.

• **Camping** at 2 sites nr the park HQ at Dinsha, and at a site to the S of the escarpment at Katcha on the road from Goba to Mena, which runs through the park.

• **Transport** Goba is among ***Ethiopian Airlines*** list of destinations, but not on included in the current schedules. It is understood that they will put down at the airstrip at Goba if required. There are 6 flights a week (not Thu) on this route.

Rift Valley National Park

The park is in the chain of 7 lakes which run from Debre Zeit S toward Lake Turkana in Kenya. For description of the Lakes that are not parks, see page 604.

The park is about 200 km S of Addis Ababa, and consists of 2 lakes, just to the W of Lake Langano. They are particuarly attractive stretches of water, and they are very different in character to each other. The main interest stems from the the extensive bird life that the lakes attract, with over 400 species recorded. **Senkello Swayne's Hartebeest Sanctuary** is close to the park, and is administered by the staff. It contains about 2,000 of these hartebeest, which are endemic to Ethiopia.

Lake Abyatta is the more N of the 2, and is about 20 km across. It is shallow and surrounded by grass-covered shores and acacia woodland. The water is alkaline, and among the birds attracted to feed on the algae are greater and lesser flamingoes and white pelicans, white-necked cormorants, herons, storks, spoonbills, ibises, ducks, gulls and terns. Surrounding woodland contains trogons, turacos and weaver birds. In the N hemisphere winter, the lake is host to migratory ducks and waders from Europe and Asia. There are a few mammals on the shores, including Grant's gazelle, warthog and oribi.

Lake Shala is deep, 260m at maximum, and it is surrounded by black peaks and cliffs. There are 2 lots of hot springs on the margins of the lake. One, Ghike, is close to the park HQ at Dole, and the other is further round the lake on the southern shore. The lake is particularly famous for its colony of great white pelicans, (about 15,000 pairs), ibis, Abdimi's stork, and the white-necked cormorant

• **Accommodation and transport** details are to be found under Lake Langano which is adjoining, see page 604.

Netch Sar National Park

South of Shashamene, 500 km from Addis Ababa on the Rift Valley road, this park lies on the eastern shores of Lake Abaya and Lake Chamo. There are some hot springs in the SE corner. The lakes are surrounded by heavy vegetation, and the waters contain Nile perch, tigerfish, hippos and crocodiles. In the park itself are Swayne's hartebeest (one of the species unique to Ethiopia) Guenther's diddidk, greater kudu, Burchell's zebra and olive baboons. Arba Minch is the nearest main town, and the park headquarters are nearby.

• **Accommodation and transport** details are to be found under Arba Minch, see page 604.

Simien Mountains National Park

The park is 120 km to the N of Gondar, off the road to Axum. The park was generally inaccessible up to 1991 as a result of the fighting in the N, but it is now possible to visit again.

It is a rocky massif which slopes down to grasslands. The slopes are cut by gorges, some over 1,000m deep, with fast-flowing streams. The highest peak in Ethiopia is in the park, Mount Ras Desthen at 4,620m, and it is the fourth highest mountain in Africa.

Three of Ethiopia's endemic mammals are found here, the Walia ibex, the Simien red fox, and the Gelada baboon. Also present are Hamadryas baboon, the klipsringer and the bushbuck. Birds include the lammergeyer (the 'bonebreaker', a spectacular vulture with a wingspan of 2.5m which drops the bones of animals killed by other predators onto rocks, to consume the marrow), the Auger buzzard, Verreaux's eagle, kestrel and Lanner falcon.

• **Accommodation and transport** see Axum, which is about 100 km distant, page 608, or Gondar (120 Km), page 607.

Gambela National Park

This park is 600 km W of Addis Ababa on the River Baro. It is not particularly easy to access. The terrain is undulating grassland. In the river are to be found huge Nile perch, up to 100kg, crocodiles and hippos. Other wildlife includes buffalo, giraffe, tiang, waterbuck, Roan antelope, zebra, bushbuck, Abyssinian reedbuck, warthog, hartebeest, lion and elephant.

• **Accommodation and transport** details are to be found under Gambela, the nearby town, see page 601.

Omo and Mago National Parks

These parks are located either side of the Omo river in the S-west of Ethiopia, 700 km from Addis Ababa. Access is via the highway that runs through Jimma. There is negligible human habitation in the parks, and they are particularly abundant in wildlife, including oryx, Burchell's zebra, Lelwel's hartebeest, buffalo, giraffe, waterbuck, kudu, lion, leopard and cheetah.

The are has proved a rich source of early hominid remains, and in 1982 skeletons were found which are thought to be over 4 million years old.

• **Accommodation and transport** It is possible to charter a plane to visit Omo and Mago through NTO, see page 598. **Camping** There are several sites, but negligible facilities, and all equipment and provisions need to be taken.

Yangudi Rassa National Park

About 500 km from Addis Ababa on the road to Djibouti and Assab. It was primarily established to preserve a population of Somali wild ass. There are only a few other animals in the park, mainly Grevy's zebra, greater and lesser kudu, gerenuk and cheetah.

• **Accommodation and transport** Nearest reliable accommodation is at Awash, about 200 km away, see page 611.

Stephanie National Park

This new park surrounds Lake Chew Bahir (also known as Lake Stephanie) on the southern border with Kenya. The lake is seasonal, and for much of the year is marshland. There is a rich variety of bird-life, with black-tailed godwits and spotted redshanks to be seen.

• **Accommodation and transport** Nearest reliable accommodation is at Arba Minch, 150 km away, see page 604. There are 4 flights a week by ***Ethiopian Airlines*** to Jinka, which is very close, on Tue, Wed, Sat and Sun. The fare is around US$150 return.

Harar Elephant Sanctuary

Located just S of the city of Harar, a large area devoted to a sub-species of elephant only found in Ethiopia. The park is not particularly well developed, and it is not easy to sight the elephants.

• **Accommodation and transport** see nearby Harar, page 603.

Yavello Sanctuary

South of Addis Ababa, about 600 km distant, and to the E of the road to Kenya. The area is mainly to preserve 4 endemic bird species: Stresemann's bush crow, the Sidamo lark, the white-tailed swallow and Prince Ruspoli's turaco. The sanctuary also contains lesser and greater kudu, gerenuk, Grevy's zebra, beisa oryx, dikdik and giraffe.

• **Accommodation and transport** There are some small hotels in nearby Yavello town. There are flights to Arba Minch, about 150 km distant, page 604.

INFORMATION FOR VISITORS

Contents

Before you go

Entry requirements

● **Visas**

Visas are required by all visitors (with the exception of Kenyan nationals), and should be obtained before departure through an Ethiopian Embassy, see page 614. Tourist visas are usually valid for 3 months.

A **transit** visa for 72 hrs can be granted on arrival. Can be extended for up to 7 days.

Business visas for 1 month can usually be obtained by an Ethiopian contact.

Journalists must obtain a permit from the Ministry of Information, PO Box 1020 Addis Ababa, T 11 11 24, and this can take up to 3 months to be granted.

● **Vaccinations**

A yellow fever innoculation certificate is compulsory. Vaccination against cholera is only required if the visitor is coming from an affected area, but it is wise to have the vaccination in any case.

● **Ethiopian representation overseas**

Austria, Freidrich Schmidt Platz 3/3, 1080 Vienna, Austria, T 402 84 10, F 402 94 13. **Belgium**, B-1040 Brussels, T 733 3929/4869/9818, F 732 1816. **Canada**, Suite 208, 112 Kent St, Ottawa. **China**, No 3 Xiu Shui Nan Jie, Jian Gue Nen Wai, Beijing. **Cote d'Ivoire**, Immeuble Nour Al Hayat, 4 eme Etage, PB 3712 Abidjan 01. **Egypt**, 3 Ibrim Osman St Mohandessin Cairo, T 3477805, F 3477902. **France**, 35 Ave Charles Floquet, 75007 Paris, T 47838395, Tlx 43065214. **Germany**, Brentanostrasse 1, D-5300, Bonn 1, T 233041/42/43, F 233045. **India**, 7/50 G Satya Marg, Chanakyapuri, New Delhi 11021. **Iran**, 772 North Pasdaran Ave 19547, PO Box 19575/544 Sahebgharanie, Tehran, T 283 217 / 282 312, F 289 441, Tlx 226621. **Israel**, 69 Bograshov St Tel Aviv 63429, T 525 0383, F 525 0428. **Italy**, Via Andrea Vesalio, 16-18, 00161 Rome, T 4402602 / 4403653, F 4403676, Tlx 614414. **Japan**, 1-14-15 Midorigaoka, Meguro-ku, Tokyo 152, T 718-1003/5, F 718-0978, Tlx J28402. **Korea (North)**, PO Box 55, Pyongyang. **Nigeria**, PO Box 2488 Marina, Lagos T61 31 98, F 61 50 55. **Saudi Arabia**, PO Box 459, Jeddah 21411, T 525 0383, F 525 0428. **Sweden**, Ostemalmsgatan 34, PO Box 26116, 10041 Stockholm. **Switzerland**, 56 Rue de Moillebeau, PO Box 204, 1211 Geneva 19. **United States**, 2134 Kalorama Rd NW, Washington DC 20008, T 234 2281, F 328 7950. **Zimbabwe**, PO Box 2745 Harare, T 725 823/720 259

● **Overseas representation in Ethiopia**

See under Addis Ababa, see page 597.

● **Tourist information**

Ethiopian Tourism Commission, Ras Mekonin Ave, PO Box 2183, Addis Ababa. T 44 74 70, provides information for tourists, and promotes tourism overseas. *Ethiopian Airways* offices are situated in 54 cities around the world. Invariably they have a staff member who takes responsibility for providing tourist information, and is a reliable source for information on any recent changes in visa regulations, health requirements etc.

● Travel and tour agents

National Tour Operation is the state-owned tourist organisation. Main office nr *Ghion Hotel* on Ras Mekonin Ave, PO Box 5709, T 15 29 55. Branch in *Hilton Hotel*. Has 5 regional offices, including one in Dire Dawa. It organises a sightseeing around Addis Ababa; excursions from Addis Ababa; vistis to Omo, Gambela, Bahar Dar, Gondar, Lalibela, Harar; hiking tours; hunting safaris; fishing; birdwatching.

There are many new private travel and tour firms, that have set up since 1991, see page 598.

When to go

● Best time to visit

It is best to avoid the rainy season from Jun to Sep. The hot and dry months are Apr and May.

Health

● Staying healthy

Yellow fever inoculation is compulsory. It is wise to have a cholera vaccination even though it is only compulsory if the visitor is coming from an infected area. Inoculation against typhoid and hepatitis are strongly recommended.

Anti-malaria tablets and general anti-mosquito measures, see page 26, are strongly recommended for visitors to the low-lying areas outside the capital. Addis Ababa is above the mosquito zone.

Acclimatisation to the altitude normally takes about 3 days. Visitors with heart conditions or high blood pressure should take the precaution of seeking medical advice before they arrive.

Swimming in lakes that have still water sometimes carries the risk of billharzia – it is necessary to check locally. The alkaline lakes at Debre Zeit and Langano are safe.

● Water

In Addis Ababa, tap water is safe to drink. Many people will, however, try to avoid even the smallest risk of a stomach upset by drinking only boiled, sterilised or bottled water. Tap water should not be drunk outside Addis Ababa.

● Further health information

For further advice see the section on Health, see page 21.

Money

● Currency

The currency is the Birr. 100 cents = 1 Birr. Denominations: 1, 5, 10, 25, and 50 cent coins; 1, 5, 10, 50 and 100 Birr notes.

The value of the currency was held fixed at Birr 2.07 = US$1 from 1973 to Oct 1992, and in this period there was a black market in foreign exchange. The devauation in 1992 set the exchange rate at Birr 5 = US$1. The exchange rate is now set by foreign currency autcions, and fluctuates slightly round the Birr 5 = US$1 level.

The Commercial Bank of Ethiopia (state-owned – all banks were nationalised in 1975) offers foreign exchange facilites, and is represented in all the major towns.

The larger hotels and the government-owned hotels operate *Bureau d'Exchange*, and some, such as the Hilton in Addis Ababa offer a 24-hr service.

● Credit cards

The large hotels and the main airlines (including *Ethiopian Airlines*) will accept cards. Outside Addis Ababa cards are not accepted.

Getting there

● Air

The national carrier is ***Ethiopian Airlines***. It is one of the most efficient airlines in Africa. It has offices in 54 cities around the world. In Addis Ababa, it has 3 offices in City centre: nr National Theatre on Churchill Ave, T 44 70 00; *Addis Ababa Hilton*, T 15 84 00. Tlx 21104. Menelik Ave; in Piazza at southern end of Eden St.

In the Horn of Africa region, Ethiopian Airways flies twice a week to **Djibouti** from Addis Ababa (Tue and Thu) and the fare is US$306 return. There are daily flights to **Asmara** (US$195 return). There are no flights currently to Somalia.

NB: that flights to Djiboutis and Asmara can be included in special round-trip tickets taking in destinations in Ethiopia other than Addis Ababa.

Ethiopian Airlines international flights: **Europe**: Athens, Berlin, Frankfurt, London, Moscow, and Rome. **Asia**: Beijing and Bombay. **Middle East**: Abu Dhabi, Aden, Dubai, Jeddah, Sanaa. **Africa**: Abidjan, Asmara, Cairo,

Djibouti, Harare Kinshasha, Lago and Nairobi.

Other carriers The following airlines have flights to and from their capitals and Addis Ababa. ***Aeroflot***, PO Box 7018, Addis Ababa. T 15 73. ***Alitalia***, PO Box 3240, Addis Ababa. T 15 46 40. ***Alyemda***, PO Box 40461, Addis Ababa. T 44 10 49. ***Interflug***, PO Box 4640, Addis Ababa. T 15 70 94. ***Kenya Airways***, PO Box 3381, Addis Ababa. T 44 30 18. ***Lufthansa***, PO Box 2484, Addis Ababa. T 15 59 61. ***Yemenia***, PO Box 107, Addis Ababa. T 44 50 76.

The following airlines have offices in Addis Ababa. *Air France*, T 15 90 44. *Air Tanzania Corporation*, T 15 75 33.

● Specialist agencies

Special excursion fares for fixed dates of departure and return (around US$900 return London/Addis Ababa in high season in Jul, Aug and Dec; otherwise low season US$730) can be arranged through: ***World Express***, 29 Great Pulteney St, Room 202, London W1R 3DD, T 071 437 2955/071 434 1897, F 071 734 2550.

Willesden Travel Service (WTS), 5 Walm Lane London NW2 5SJ, T 081 451 7778, F 081 451 4727; ***Ericommerce***, Robin House, 2A Iverson Rd, London NW6 2HE. T 071 372 7242, F 071 624 6716. See also general section, page 12.

● Train

A 782 km railway connects Addis with Djibouti on the Red Sea. It is primarily a freight service, but passengers are taken. The stretch of line running through the Awash National Park affords stunning views, making the what can be an uncomfortable trip more than worthwhile.

The trains from Addis Ababa leave daily at around 0700 and 1930, arriving in Djibouti approximately 24 hrs later. Booking is at the railway station at the southern end of Churchill Rd. It is necessary to make a reservation as the train is often full. The fare is US$60 1st class (a sleeper on the overnight train); US$30 2nd class; US$16 3rd class. Djibouti-Ethiopian Railroad Company, T 44 72 50, Addis Ababa.

● Road

In principle it should now be possible for non-Africans to enter Ethiopia overland. The main routes are from Kenya, crossing at Moyale; from Malakal in Sudan to Gambela; from Eritrea on the routes from Asmara to Adua, and Assab to Dessie; from Djibouti to Dire Dawa; and from Hargeisa in Somalia to Jijiga.

The routes from Sudan and Somalia are not really feasible as a result of restictions and turmoil in these 2 countries. The route from Kenya is becoming easier, and there is no problem in crossing from Eritrea and Djibouti.

● Sea

Since Eritrea became Independent in 1993, Ethiopia has become land-locked. Access by sea is through Massawa and Assab in Eritrea, or through the port at Djibouti.

● River

In the period when the rains make the River Baro navigable (Jun-Sep) it should be possible to enter by boat from Khartoum to Gambela. The current political situation in the S of Sudan make this a proposition to be explored only by the intrepid.

● Customs

Under the Mengistu regime, there were comprehensive restrictions. These are now in the process of being relaxed, and some of the limitations listed below may no longer apply. **Ethiopian Customs Office**, PO Box 4838 Addis Ababa, T 15 31 00.

Duty free allowance of 100 cigarettes, 50 cigars, 250 gms tobacco, 1 litre spirits, equipment for personal use. All duty-free goods must be declared. Souvenirs for export are limited to a value of around US$250 per person. Any specialised film, recording or video equipment requires a special permit form Ministry for Informantion and National Guidance (PO Box 1020 Addis Ababa), T 12 10 11).

Export of any antiquities requires a permit from the Antiquities Department of the National Museum (PO Box 76 Addis Ababa, T 11 71 50).

Sporting firearms require a permit from Wildlife Conservation Department (PO Box 386 Addis Ababa, T 44 44 17).

Export of any wildlife items requires a permit from Wildlife Conservation Department (PO Box 386 Addis Ababa, T 44 44 17).

Export and import of books, cassettes and records may require a permit from the Censorship Department (PO Box 1364 Addis Ababa, T 11 57 04).

When you arrive

● Airport information

The main airport is Bole International Airport, some 5 km SE of the city. There is a departure tax of US$10.

Transport to town A taxi from Bole Airport to town is around US$8. A minibus is around US$1.

● Business contacts

Addis Ababa Chamber of Commerce, PO Box 2458 Addis Ababa, T 44 82 40. **Ministry of Foreign Trade**, PO Box 2559 Addis Ababa, T 15 10 66.

● Calendar

Ethiopia uses the Julian calendar, named after Julius Caeser, which is 7 years and 8 months behind the Gregorian (European) calendar – a result of differences of opinion over Christ's exact date of birth. The Julian calendar consists of 12 months of 30 days and a 13th month of 5 or 6 days.

● Conduct

It is customary for men to wear suits for business occasions, particulary when visiting government offices. Women would normally be expected to dress neatly on such occasions – it is regarded as a mark of respect for the persons you are meeting as much as anything else.

Visitors are invariably offered a cup of tea or coffee, and it is a friendly gesture to accept.

When entering a church or mosque, it is necessary for shoes to be removed. Women are not normally allowed to enter mosques unless there is a special prayer room for women.

When photographing local people, religious ceremonies or festivals, it is courteous to ask permission first.

● Electricity

220 volts, 50 cycles AC. A variety of sockets are to be found around the country, and an adaptor is desirable.

● Hours of business

0800-1200 and 1300-1600.

● Safety

Ethiopia is a very safe country, and it is possible to walk around with confidence in the cities and towns even after dark. It is wise to keep a close eye on belongings.

Although there are no restrictions on photographing tourist sites, military installations, airports, bridges, civil engineering works, government buildings, military personnel and political gatherings should not be photographed.

Photographs of museums, art works, churches and mosques will often require permission.

● Time

Three hrs later than GMT. Local people use a 12 hr clock, which starts at 0600. Thus 0800 is 'hour 2 of the day'. At 1800 the night clock begins. Thus 0400 is 'hour ten of the night'.

● Weights and measures

Metric weights and measures are in use in the main towns and cities. In country areas, customs vary.

Where to stay

● Hotels

Until the demise of Mengistu, tourists were officially only allowed to stay in the large hotels owned by the state. and run by ***Ethiopian Hotels and Spas Corporation (EHC)***. These hotels were grouped into 5 regional chains, each with a flagship hotel in Addis Ababa. The ***Ghion Hotels*** cover the N and the historic towns of Godor and Axum. The ***Ras Hotels*** are in the E and include Dire Dawa and Harar. ***Ethiopia Hotels*** cover the W and in the S are the ***Wabi Shabelle Hotels***. The ***Filwoha Hotels*** specialise in resorts and spas, with no regional concentration. The ***Hilton Hotel*** in Addis Ababa is the one major hotel that has remained independent.

There has been pressure to privatise these hotel chains, and in principle the government is in agreement with this policy, but as yet there has been little actual implementation.

Apart from the EHC hotels, there are smaller establishment all over the country which serve the needs of ordinary Ethiopians.

Hotel Classifications

A+ Over US$100 a night. International standards and decor, air conditioning, self contained rooms, swimming pool, restaurants, bars, business services.

A US$40-100. First class standards, air-conditioning, attached bathrooms, restaurants and bars, swimming pool.

B US$20-40. Tourist class, comfortable with air conditioning or fans, attached barthrooms, restaurant, bar, public rooms.

C US$10-20. Budget, fans, shared bathroom facilities.

D US$5-10. Guest house, no fan, shared bathroom, cold water.

E Under US$5. Basic guest house, simple bed, no soap or towels, no wardrobe, shared bathroom facilities, erratic cold water supply, no fans or mosquito nets.

They are very simple, but cheap, and the proprietors are invariably very welcoming to visitors.

Food and drink

Food
Staple food in Ethiopia is *wat*, a hot sauce sometimes containing lentils, beans or meat, and *injera,* the national bread which has a spongy pancake texture and a grey colour, and is made from fermented millet.

Drink
Tella is the local beer and *tej* a local type of mead. A local liqueur is *araki*. The Ethiopian Coffee Ceremony, where the beans are roasted in an open pan, ground, and the coffee brewed, is an important social ritual. The ***Hilton Hotel*** presents a coffee ceremony each week.

There is a local mineral water *Ambo*, which is slightly sparkling.

RESTAURANT GUIDE

- ♦♦♦♦ Over US$10 for a meal. A 3-course meal in a restaurant with pleasant decor. Beers, wines and spirits available.
- ♦♦♦ US$5-10 for a meal. Two courses, not including alcohol, reasonable surroundings.
- ♦♦ US$2-5 for a meal, probably only a single course, surroundings spartan but adequate.
- ♦ Under US$2. Single course, often makeshift surroundings such as a steet kiosk with simple benches and tables.

Getting around

Air
The national carrier is ***Ethiopian Airlines***. It is one of the most efficient airlines in Africa. It has offices in 54 cities around the world. In Addis Ababa, it has 3 offices in City centre: nr National Theatre on Churchill Ave, T 44 70 00; *Addis Ababa Hilton*, T 15 84 00. Tlx 21104. Menelik Ave; in Piazza at southern end of Eden St.

There are daily flights to Bahar Dar, Gondar, Axum, Lalibela and Dire Dawa. Special round-trips at discounted fares are available. Thus the Historic Route (Bahar Dar, Gondar, Axum and Lalibela) is US$167, and these cities as well as Dire Dawa (for Harar) is US$267. Asmara and Djibouti can be included in these round trips.

Train
There are 2 trains daily in each direction along the line from Addis Ababa to Djibouti, see page 599.

Road
There are asphalt roads in Ethiopia, mostly linking Addis with the regional capitals. However, the instability of the Mengistu period has led to some of these asphalt roads being in poor repair, and in the rainy season (Jun-Sep) there will be delays. Elsewhere, roads are mostly unsealed. Bus and minibus transport is available on all main routes. As a rough guide, road transport costs around US$0.05 a Km.

Car hire
Car hire can be arranged through the ***National Tour Operation***. Main office nr *Ghion Hotel* on Ras Mekonin Ave (PO Box 5709, T 15 29 55). Branch in *Hilton Hotel*. Has 5 regional offices, including one in Dire Dawa.

Communications

Language
The official language is *Amharic*. It has its own unique alphabet, and a wide and extensive vocabulary. There are about 80 other local languages and dialects.

English is widely spoken, and is the language of instruction in secondary schools and at the University. French, Italian and Arabic are also spoken.

Postal Services
Post offices open 0800-1600. Mail is delivered only to PO box numbers.

Telephone services
Calls can be made throught the Telecommunications Head Office opposite Holy Saviour Church. Telex and telegram sevices are also available from here, and from the main Post Office on Churchill Road. Collect (reverse charge) calls can be made. Most of the larger hotels have telex and telegram facilities.

Entertainment

Cinemas
Most large towns will have cinemas, often open-air.

Newspapers
Ethiopian Herald is the English language daily. There is also an English language quarterly, *Yekatit*. *Yezareyitu* is a weekly paper in Amharic, *Al Ahem* is a weekly Arabic newspaper,

Amharic Qwerty

An alphabet of 236 characters presented a challenge in adapting the typewriter to Amaharic. The problem was solved by allocating 2 characters to each key, and a further 6 keys for the vowel suffixes. Many of these original machines can still be seen in use in offices throughout Ethiopia. The first Amaharic typewiter is on display in the National Museum in Addis Ababa.

and*Berissa* is a weekly Oromo paper.

● Radio

Radio Ethiopia has a National Service and an International (External) Service. There are broadcasts in 6 Ethiopian languages each day. Broadcasts are in Arabic 1700-1800, English 1800-1900 and French 2000-2100.

● Television

There is one television channel, which broadcasts in colour, 1900-2300 on Mon to Fri and on Sun, and 1800-2400 on Sat. About a third of the programmes are in English and 2-thirds are in local languages, mostly Amharic. The service can only be received in Addis Ababa.

Holidays and festivals

7 Jan	*Genna* (Ethiopian Christmas: birth of Christ)
19 Jan	*Timket* (Ethiopian Epiphany: baptism of Christ))
2 Mar	*Adwa Day* (Commemorates the victory by Menelik II over Italy in 1896)
6 Apr	*Patriots' Day* (Celebrates end of Italian occupation in 1941)
1 May	*International Labour Day*
May	(variable) Ethiopian Good Friday
May	(variable) *Fasika* (Ethiopian Easter Sunday)
May	(variable) *Idd al Fitr* (End of month of fasting for Ramadan)
Aug	(variable) Idd al Adha
11 Sep	*Engutatsh* (Ethiopian New year)
12 Sep	Popular Revolution Day
27 Sep	*Maskal* (Finding of the True Cross)
Nov	(variable) *Maulid* (Birth of Prophet Mohamed)

Further reading

● History

Marcus, HG (1975) *The Life and Times of Menelick II*, Oxford: Clarendon Press. A thorough account of career the extraordinary emperor who defeated the Italians and created modern Ethiopia. Haile Selassie, I (1975) *My Life and Ethiopia's Progress: the Autobiography of Emperor Haile Selassie,* Oxford: OUP. The man who ruled Ethiopia for 48 years, and whose demise brought to an end a dynasty reputedly stretching back to Solomon and Sheba.

● Travellers' Tales

Marsden-Smedley, P (1990) *A Far Country: Travels in Ethiopia,* London: Arrow Books. An account of travels undertaken by an Ethiopia enthusiast in 1988 when the restrictions imposed by the Mengistu regime on tourists were a source of considerable frustration.

● Fiction

Waugh, E (1932) *Black Mischief*, London: Chapman & Hall. Based on material gathered by Waugh when he went to Addis Ababa in 1930 to report on the coronation of Haile Selassie for *The Times* newspaper.

ERITREA

Contents

Maps

Introduction

After 20 years of war, Eritrea achieved effective independence from Ethiopia in 1991 and this was formally declared on 24 May 1993. Since then this newly-formed country has concentrated on consolidating political stability and forming reconstruction and development plans. Consequently, little has been done to encourage tourism. Having said this, the mountain scenery is beautiful, and the coast line of miles of unspoilt white sand beaches with warm water safe from sharks, the coral reefs and aquatic life at Dahlak Islands (said to be one of the best places for underwater diving in the Red Sea), and a number of historical sites of the ancient Kingdom of Axum, will all attract the more adventurous traveller.

Visitors find Eritrea a very friendly country to visit where you are made to feel at home very quickly. This atmosphere is helped by the relaxed attitude to security, and relatively few restrictions, which is surprising in a country so recently in the throes of war.

Exchange rate in August 1994 US$1= Birr 5.45

Environment

Geography

Eritrea is 121,320 sq km in area, being narrow in the S and broadening out in the N. It is situated in the Horn of Africa bordered by Sudan to the W and N and Ethiopia and Djibouti to the S. There is about 1,000 km of the country bordering onto the Red Sea opposite Saudi Arabia and Yemen. Its territory includes the Dahlak Islands which were formally used as a military base by the Ethiopians.

Eritrea comprises 4 main geographical regions. The first runs from Djibouti upwards and is little more than a long strip of desert. The central and northern part of the country – covering about 30% of the land mass – is made up of highlands and is an extension of the Ethiopian highlands, at an average height of 1,500m (Asmara, the capital, is in this area). It is in this region that most cultivation takes place. Much of the coniferous forest that used to cover the hillsides has been cleared either for fuelwood or land and as a consequence, soil erosion is becoming an increasingly severe problem. W of the highlands spreading into Sudan lies the potentially fertile lowlands which are mainly flat and the fourth region is in the far N and comprises rugged hills which give way to lowlands going down to the coastal plain to the E where only pastoralism is possible.

The war over the last 3 decades has meant little exploration for minerals has been possible. In prehistoric times there was evidence of iron ore, gold and copper ore being mined and it remains to be seen if these are still exploitable assets. Off the coast, some seepages of oil and offshore natural gas have been

recorded and exploration for these resources is currently under way.

Climate

Given the diverse geographical makeup of the country, there are a number of different types of climate throughout the country. The higher plateaux expect an average temperature of 18 degrees centigrade with an annual rainfall of around 500mm while the coast's average temperature is 30 degrees centigrade with rainfall of less than 200 mm each year. The main rainy season throughout the country is between Jun and Sep and there are short rains between Oct and Mar along the northern coastal region, though these are unpredictable.

History

Eritrea's history is a long and splendid one. During the 3rd and 4th centuries AD, it was part of the Kingdom of Axum which spread from Meroe in Sudan right across the Red Sea to Yemen. The capital of Axum was in the highlands of Tigre (now a province in Ethiopia), and the main port was at Adulis which is now called Zula in Eritrea. This kingdom was based on trade across the Red Sea and was founded by Semetic people originally from Arabia. Christianity was the predominant faith of Axum introduced through contact with traders throughout the region.

By the 6th century AD the Persian empire expanded and with it went the expansion of Islam. In 710 AD Muslims destroyed Adulis and the ancient Kingdom of Axum declined until it was reduced to a small Christian enclave. For the next few centuries, the region settled into being a remote, isolated community only reemerging by the early 16th century as Abyssinia. The Abyssinian kingdom covered the Ethiopian and Eritrean highlands ruled by kings and peopled by Christian Tigrinyans and remaining fairly isolated. The community had little or no contact with the lowlands of the region which was home to predominantly Muslim communities.

This period in Eritrea's history is highly contentious. The Ethiopians claimed Eritrea had been an integral part of historic Ethiopia but though there are some common practices and religious beliefs between Eritreans and Ethiopia, these ties do not extend throughout Ethiopia. In fact, large parts of Eritrea, it would seem, were linked to other empires. The Ottoman empire and Egypt had relations with the N and E part of the country, and various Sudanic empires to the W and N W have had their influence. In fact, the Egyptians, eager to expand their concerns in the region, moved into the lowlands of Eritrea by the 1860s though they never won control of the coastal regions.

In 1869 a group of Italian missionaries saw an opportunity for Italy to gain a foothold in Africa and 18 months later the Italian government authorised the Rubattino Shipping Company to buy the port of Assab as a fuel and trading base. The British encouraged the Italians to develop their interests in Eritrea in order to offset French ambitions in the area. By 1881 the Italian government had designated Assab as the Colonia di Assab under the rule of Italy; 4 years later they captured Massawa, and began plans for the railway into the interior.

At this time, the Abyssinians under the authoritative rule of Emperor Yohannes saw that the Egyptian control of the Eritrean lowlands was weakening and took the opportunity to move down from the highlands and defeat them. The Italians started to move inland from the coast and clashed with the Abyssinian forces led by Ras Alula, Yohannes' general, where they were soundly beaten at the Battle of Dogali in 1887. This was the first victory of an African army over a European force.

The Italians relaunched their incursion into the interior of Eritrea and this time were unopposed as the Abyssinian force was busy fighting other wars. By 1889 the Italians occupied all territory up to the River Mareb, the traditional frontier of Abyssinia where they signed the Treaty of Wichale with Menelik II (Yohannes' successor) which effectively handed Eritrea over to the Italians. In 1890, the Italians officially declared Eritrea as their colony and for the first time since the days of the Axum kingdom the area was under one ruler. The Italians continually looked to increase the size of their territory by moving across the River Mareb into Abyssinia, but were repulsed.

In 1935 the Italians under Mussolini succeeded in over-running Abyssinia and decreed that Eritrea, Italian Somaliland and Abyssinia were to be known as Italian East Africa (Africa Orientale Italiana). They introduced the rudiments of social and economic order to the country replacing the semi-feudal system which had existed under Ethiopian rule. This situation remained until the British defeat of the Italians during World War II when Eritrea came under British rule (1941) and Abyssinia was returned to Emperor Haile Selassie. The British were not sure what to do with either Eritrea or Italian Somaliland and left it to the United Nations to decide. In 1952, the UN decided that Eritrea should be federated with Abyssinia though remaining autonomous. The situation between Ethiopia and Eritrea soon became problematic as Ethiopia attempted to control Eritrea as its only access to the sea, culminating in the autocratic Emperor of Ethiopia, Haile Selassie annexing Eritrea as a province of Ethiopia in 1962.

From Nov 1962 to 1991 Eritrea fought for its independence from Ethiopia – the longest war in Africa. The first part of the struggle was characterised by in-fighting amongst the Eritreans whilst they resolved ethnic, religious and cultural differences. In the 1980s the Eritreans finally united as one people coming together in the Eritrean People's Liberation Front (EPLF).

Through most of the war, Ethiopia occupied the southern part of Eritrea. The EPLF had to settle in the inhospitable northern hills towards the Sudanese border. These hills became a safe haven for the families of soldiers and the orphans and disabled. Consequently, much of these regions around Afabet and Nakfa in Sahel province is home to makeshift homes, schools, orphanages, hospitals, factories, printers, bakeries etc in an attempt to live life an normally as possible under extraordinary conditions. Most structures were built either into the ground or in caves to avoid being bombed by Ethiopian jets. The steep narrow areas were chosen as they were the hardest for the jets to negotiate.

The Ethiopian army under Haile Mariam Mengistu (an army officer who deposed Haile Selassie in 1974) intensified the war against Eritrea, but it was easily defeated in 1991 after Mengistu fell from power.

The war has had a devastating effect on Eritrea. Around 60,000 people lost their lives, there are an estimated 50,000 children with no parents and 60,000 people who have been left handicapped. However, there is now great optimism with people pulling together to rebuild the country. The 100,000 strong army (without pay) is helping with reconstruction and Eritreans who fled the during the fighting are returning with their skills and their capital.

People

In 1984, the Ethiopian census put the population of Eritrea at 2.7 million, though years of war have affected this figure. Around 50,000 people are said to have been killed and at least 750,000 fled the country into neighbouring Sudan and Ethiopia. With a natural rate of population increase at 3% a year, this will leave the population currently at around 2.6 million, though figures are very rough.

Eritrea was a creation of the colonial era whose boundaries were drawn up in the late 19th century with little consideration for the customs and cultures of different groups of people, consequently the country has a diverse ethnic make up. There are 2 main groups, the Tigrinya making up about 50% of the population, and the Tigre who account for a further 34% of Eritreans. The 2 groups are closely associated, the language of both groups having originated from the ancient Ethiopian language of Ge'ez. The Tigrinya are mainly highland Christians who live in the high plateau of the country. They have much in common with their neighbouring highlanders in the Tigre province of Ethiopia having similar language, faith and customs. The majority of Tigrinya are agriculturalists cultivating *tef* (a local type of grain), maize, wheat, millet and barley as well as a variety of different vegetables. Some people also herd animals as a supplementary form of income.

The Tigre are lowland Muslims. They mainly live in the western lowlands, the northern hills and the coastal

Shamma

This is the dress worn widely in both Ethiopia and Eritrea by both men and women. It is made from handwoven cotten, and is very delicate in texture. Two pieces, one being about one m square, and the other 2m by 1m, make up the garment. The borders of the fabric are decorated with bright borders, sometimes with linen and silk interleaved in the weave. The larger piece is wrapped round to make a dress, with the border making up the hemline. The smaller piece is used as a scarf or to make a hood over the head.

An Unusual Gift

When contemplating matrimony, it is the practice of Danalik bandits, known as a *shifta*, to acquire an extra set of male genitals to present to their betrothed.

regions of the country. Their way of life is primarily as nomadic pastoralists. This group is made up of many different clans including the Beni Amer, the largest clan who have historial ties with the Beja of Sudan.

Eritrea's other Muslim peoples include the Danakil herdsmen who live in the desert regions in the S and who are closely associated with the Afar in Djibouti. There are also the Rashayda of Arabic origin and the Tukrir who are originally from Nigeria. The Tukrir set off from Nigeria on a pilgrimage to Mecca but came to Eritrea and decided to settle there.

Arabic is widely spoken throughout the coastal areas of the country reflecting Eritrea's long trade associations with countries across the Red Sea.

Modern Eritrea

Politics

The Eritrean Liberation Movement was founded in 1958 to liberate Eritrea from Ethiopian rule. It was succeeded by the Eritrean Liberation Front (ELF) in 1961. Clashes of ideology soon developed between its members who were from both the Christian highlands and the Muslim eastern lowland towns. A group left the ELF to set up what became known as the Eritrean People's Liberation Front (EPLF). Between 1972-1974 a civil war developed. By the early 1980s the different factions came together to form a disciplined political and military organisation.

Throughout the 1970s and 80s new recruits joined the EPLF as Ethiopian forces terrorised resistance groups. By 1978 the EPLF had retreated into the hillsides of northern Eritrea with thousands of young supporters, both male and female. From then on, the EPLF steadily pushed back Ethiopian forces, capturing military equipment in the process. As they grew in numbers and military strength, so they turned from a guerilla force into a regular army. In 1990 the EPLF had captured the strategically important port of Massawa, and they entered Asmara, now the capital of Eritrea, in 1991.

At a conference held in London in 1991 the Ethiopian People's Revolutionary Democratic Front (EPRDF), who were now in control of Ethiopia having ousted Mengistu and were sympathetic to Eritrean nationalist aspirations, accepted the EPLF as the provisional government of Eritrea. So began the long process towards independence and international legitimation of Eritrea as a separate country.

In Apr 1993 a referendum was held in which 1,102,410 Eritreans voted; 99.8% endorsed national independence and on 28 May Eritrea became the 182nd member of the UN. Thus it is now eligible to receive international aid to help reconstruct and develop its shattered economy. The Head of State is Issaias Afewerki formerly secretary-general of the EPLF. The government is in the process of establishing a constitution and with a pluralist political system. Since establishing a provisional government in 1991, Eritrea has been a stable and peaceful political entity.

Economics

As Eritrea is such a new nation, data is very sparse, and it will be a while before the necessary surveys are undertaken to give a more complete picture of economic life and performance.

Even such basic statistics as the level of population are not reliable – there were 2.7 m people enumerated in the most recent Ethiopian census in 1984,

Comparative Economic And Social Data

	Eritrea	East Africa	Africa	Industrial Countries
Population and land				
Population, mid year, millions, 1984	2.7	12.2	10.2	40.0
Urban population, %, 1984	10	31	30	75
Population growth rate, % per year, 1980-91	3.1	3.1	3.1	0.8
Land area, thou. sq. km.	121	486	486	1,628
Population density, persons per sq km., 1984	22.3	24.2	20.4	24.3
Economy: production and income				
GDP, US$ millions, 1991	324	2,650	3,561	550,099
GNP per head, $US, 1991	120	250	389	12,960
Economy: supply structure				
Agriculture, % of GDP, 1991	65	43	35	3
Industry, % of GDP, 1991	5	15	27	35
Services, % of GDP, 1991	30	42	38	61

Notes: 'Africa' excludes South Africa. Dates are for the country in question, and do not always correspond with the regional, African and industrial averages.

but it is not clear what the overall impact of war has been. Many hundreds of thousands of people fled from Ethiopia; on the other hand the natural rate of population increase has been around 3.0 % a year, and refugees have begun to return since 1991. A reasonable expectation is that the population has not changed much overall since 1984. Urbanisation is low by African standards, but this again has been affected by the war, with people fleeing the towns and reverting to subsistence production in the countryside. The population growth rate of 3.0% reflects only the natural rate – it is to be expected that the actual population growth will be boosted by the return of refugees. Population density is close to the African and regional average, but needs to be assessed in the light of much of the southern coastal strip being arid.

The economy is very small, with most activity being subsistence agriculture on small-scale family farms. Levels of income are very low, reflecting the struggle for existence that the war has brought about. Income levels are among the lowest in the world.

Almost all the labour force is involved in agriculture in one form or another, as growing food has been the key to survival. There is very little activity classified as industrial, and most manufacturing activity has been destroyed by the war.

Eritrea's future prospects are reasonably promising. Aid flows will give a firm boost to economic activity, and the rehabilitation of the transport system will be a priority. The government appears keen to encourage foreign investment, and there will be inflows of capital from Eritreans overseas. The most encouraging factor is that peace seems likely to endure, with a secure government and good relations with Ethiopia.

ASMARA

Asmara is the capital city in the centre of Eritrea set on the eastern edge of the high plateau with a population of around 300,000. As it is about 2,300 m above sea level, the temperature is comfortable, an average of 17 degrees centigrade. Rainfall is approximately 500 mm per year, and comes mostly in Jun and Jul. Prior to the Italian occupation from 1889, Asmara was a small village and the home of Ras Alula the then governor of the region. More recently it was the second largest city in Ethiopia.

There are surprisingly few signs that this city has been at war for over 20 years in that, except for the obvious neglect of buildings, there are few bullet scars or signs of bomb damage. However, Asmara was occupied by the Ethiopian Dergue and a legacy of this era is the prison at Mariam Gimbi where members of the Ethiopian army tortured EPLF sympathisers. The prison is now open to the public. Other signs of the recent turmoil in the country is the huge number of refugees in the city from other parts of the country. Also, there are hundreds of captured tanks and armoured vehicles waiting to be disposed of at Kagnew Station, a US communications centre in the time of the Empero, now a military base on the edge of town, and home to the EPLF.

Overall the atmosphere is easy-going and friendly with a slow pace of life.

Places of interest

It is easy to get around Asmara on foot. The main market is a popular place to visit with its abundance of fruit, vegetables, spices and crafts and bustling atmosphere. During the Italian occupation of Asmara, the market area was the 'native' quarter of town. The main boulevard, National Avenue which runs through the centre of Asmara is a pleasant palm-lined street with a number of open-air cafes that reflect a style of life established during the Italian period. The old **Imperial Palace** in

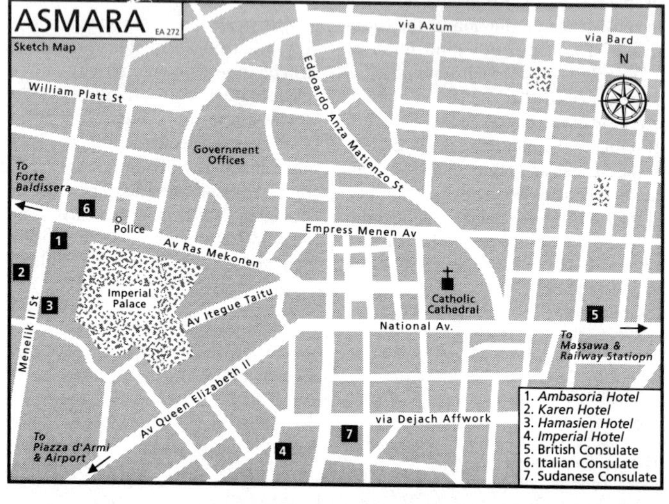

neoclassical style, is at the western end of National Avenue, and is surrounded by pleasant wooded grounds. The imposing **Catholic Cathedral**, red brick with a distinctive narrow gothic bell-tower, designed by an Italian architect Scanavini, and built in 1922, lies about half way along National Avenue. Other religious buildings are the **Kidane Mehret Orthodox Church** about a km N of National Avenue, whose dome and minaret tower over the market; and the Grand Mosque, designed by an Italian and built in 1937, at the eastern end of National Avenue.

Just a few hours' drive from Asmara there are a number of historic sites. To the S, 116 km toward **Adigrat** there is a small site of ancient Axumite ruins, part of the great Kingdom which ruled this part of the world in the 3rd and 4th centuries AD. There are also Axumite buildings at **Yeha** dating back to the 4th or 5th century BC.

Local information

● Where to stay

Price guide:
A+ Over US$100; **A** US$40-100;
B US$20-40; **C** US$10-20; **D** US$5-10;
E Under US$5

There are 5 hotels which are deemed to be of reasonable standards for visitors. There are also a number of smaller guest-houses which meet the needs of local travellers.

B *Ambasoira*, 32 Dejatch Hailu Street, T 113222. Is the best hotel in town and also the most modern. 32 Dejatch Hailu Street, T 113222. A few blocks from National Avenue. **B** *Nyala*, 67 Col Belay Haileab Street, T 113111. Is slightly further out down town and is a high-rise building.

C *Ambassador*, 36 National Avenue, is the most centrally placed and is another high rise. It is in the process of being refurbished and upgraded. **C** *Karen*, 7 Victory Street, T 110740. Is a few blocks from National Avenue opposite the Ambasoira. This hotel was built in the colonial era and its interior of decorative urns and chandeliers reflects this, though it has gone a bit to seed. **C** *Hamasien*, 30 Dejatch Hailu Street, T 110233. Is similar to *Karen* in that it also was built in the colonial era and has a certain charm though it is in need of renovation. It is next to the Ambasoira.

● Places to eat

Price guide:
♦♦♦♦*Over US$10;* ♦♦♦*US$5-10;* ♦♦US$2-5;
♦*Under US$2.*

All the above named hotels have restaurants attached serving Western style food. Most restaurants are quite cheap, meals are unlikely to cost more than US$5 for supper. ♦♦♦*San Giorgio*, National Ave. Italian cuisine. Reasonable standard.

♦♦*Asmara*, National Ave, near Post Office. Serve *injira* and other Eritrean food as well as most of the popular Italian dishes.

♦♦*Cafe Alba*, serves a good breakfast and is run by an Italian family in a street running parallel to National Avenue. It also serves pizza and Italian pastries.

♦*Cafe Royal*, National Ave. Popular street cafe with seats outside.

● Banks

The main branch of the **National Bank of Eritrea** is on National Avenue where money can be exchanged. It was established in 1992.

● Curios and crafts

Lack of tourists means there are few places specialising in curios and crafts. However, textiles, ceramics, woodwork, silverware and basketry are available in Asmara's main market. Some of Eritrea's religious artefacts are very attractive and you will see a few shops around town specialising in old and new Abyssinian Christian objects including destinctive Coptic crosses. Haile Gebrehiwat at the end of Ras Mangesha Street near the *Keren Hotel* has craftwork and curios of a high standard.

● Embassies, High Commissions and Consulates

To date, the only people to have reopened its embassy in Eritrea are **Italy**, Box 220, Villa Roma, T 117103. Near the *Ambasoira Hotel*. However, there is diplomatic representation of the **USA**, **Ethiopia** and **Sudan**, in Asmara.

● Entertainment

Some of the hotels organise evening entertainment. The Italian community have set up a club at *Casa d'Italiano*, off National Avenue which apart from being an interesting place to visit can be a useful source of advice about how to get around the country, what to visit etc. ***Caravelle*** not far from the *Nyala Hotel* has a disco on Fri nights. The ***Mocambo Club***, off National Avenue has live music each week.

● Post offices

The post office is just off the main street, National Avenue.

● Religion

The Orthodox Church is ***Kidane Mehret***, near the main market. There is a Catholic church about half way along the central boulevard, National Avenue. A number of mosques are scattered throughout the city.

● Tourist office

The government is in the process of developing a tourist office but at present the best source of information is from the Department of Protocol at the *Ambasoira Hotel*. The Department of Tourism is in the process of setting up in the Post Office square.

Another useful source of information, particulalry about conditions outside Asmara can be from the numerous Western development agencies which have set up in Asmara.

● Transport

Local Bus The main bus station is near the market and there are fairly frequent buses to Massawa, Dekamere, Adi Keyeh, Mendefara and Keren from here. Most journeys only take a few hours along reasonable roads. There are also minibuses/taxis available from the bus depot.

Car hire It is possible to rent chauffeur driven vehicles, either Fiat cars, Land Rovers or minibuses from Africa Garage at 29 Ras Wole Butul, T 111755.

Air There is a daily flight between Asmara and Addis Ababa costing about US$100 one- way. Asmara is the international airport in Eritrea, so all incoming flights arrive here.

Road There is a road from Asmara to Addis Ababa, Ethiopia but it is in bad condition and the journey can take 5 days. It is also possible to reach Asmara from Assab on the Ethiopian border in the S but again the road is not good and the journey is exhausting.

Asmara environs

Dekamere

Dekamere was once a beautiful small town to the S E of Asmara developed by the Italians in an Italian style, set in a fertile region which produced the best wine in the country. Unfortunately today it is almost destroyed as for some time it straddled the frontline of the war.

Although the town itself has little to

THE RAILWAY

The line was built by the Italians and it was the first railway to be constructed in East Africa. The work began on the 95 cm guage track from Massawa in 1887, and it reached its present point of termination, Agordat, 280 km inland, in 1928. Market towns sprung up around the various stations along the route, and it was vital to communications and the economy. It was envisaged that the line would eventually be extended W to Khartoum.

It is a very considerable engineering feat, considering the difficult terrain and the fact that it climbs to a high point of 2,128m a few km before the gentle descent into Asmara. There are 65 bridges and 30 tunnels, the longest being 320m, with most tunnels having to be bored through solid rock. The crossing at the Obel River is a fourteen arch bridge, and there are viaducts before Nesfit, and just after Devil's Doors, the highest point on the line, where the track runs along the edge of a precipice. Between Mai Atal and Damas the gradient is so steep that trains have to be split and each half hauled up separately.

At its peak in 1965 the railway carried 446,000 passengers and 200,000 tonnes of freight. There was a daily service hauled by diesel locomotives between Asmara and the coast, and trains ran on alternate days from Asmara up-country to Agordat. It ceased operation during the war, and there is some doubt as to whether it will ever be re-opened.

recommend it except as a reminder of past glories, the surrounding countryside is spectacular. The road from Dekamere through the hills of **Adi Keyeh** is particularly lovely. Along the route you can see the start of the rebuilding process underway in Eritrea with irrigation schemes in operation nurturing nurseries and market gardens. There are some small guest houses and cafés near the market. Regular buses run from the bus stand near the market in Asmara.

Keren

This is a small town 105 km W of Asmara. It has villas from the Italian period, and has a pretty aspect with bougianvillea and acacia trees. There are some stylish public buildings, and a Romanesque Catholic church. There is a strong Muslim community. Before the war Keren was noted for its silver market, which took place once a week. A critical battle between the Italians and the British took place in the nearby hills, and there are 2 war cemeteries.

There are some very basic guest houses near the market, and several quite reasonable cafes. Keren can be reached by regular buses from Asmara.

Agordat

This is 75 km further W from Keren, and is a town of 24,000 in the western lowlands. It is at the western termination of the railway from Massawa. The town can experience high temperatures, and sandstorms known as *haboob*. It is located on the River Barca, and the area is famous for its banana plantations. The main hotel, the **D** *Savoy*, near the railway station is now very run-down. There are some small guest houses and basic cafés in the railway staion area. There are regular buses from outside the railway station to Keren.

MASSAWA AND THE COAST

Massawa

Massawa consists of 2 islands and 2 peninsulas and used to be the headquarters of the Ethiopian navy. It is 105 km from Asmara, and has a population of about 20,000. It can get extremely hot, up to 40 degrees centigrade Jun to Aug, and the monsoon rains are Dec to Feb. The earliest signs of settlement here were when the Turks occupied the island port in the 16th century. By around 1850 the Egyptians took control only to be ousted by the Italians under a special arrangement in 1885. Unfortunately today there is very little to see of its rich and varied history as it was fought over by both sides during the war and was devastated by the fighting. Haile Selaissie's palace, the colonial residences, the mosque, the waterfront and all major hotels were destroyed. At one time there yacht club, and the nearby beaches and islands were popular places for weekends and vacations for the residents of Asmara. A famous craft of Massawa was the manufacture of mother-of-pearl buttons.

Massawa is now Eritrea's main port and access to the rest of the world and is being rehabilitated. The dockyard is back in operation and handling an impressive tonnage of merchandise. An arrangement between Eritrea and Ethiopia has meant Ethiopian trade still comes via Massawa. As a result of the dilapidated state of Massawa, there is little to recommend it as a tourist destination.

The road between Asmara and Massawa descends the Rift Valley escarpment, and the views are spectacular. The road is a major stock route, and before the war over 30,000 sheep and goats were driven from the highlands to the coast to be exported to Saudi Arabia. The highlands are basically Christian, and the coast is Muslim, and at Ghinda, about halfway, more camels, rather than mules, are seen, and clothing becomes darker, in

THIEF-SEEKERS

In traditional areas of Eritrea, if someone discovers he has had possessions stolen, he will hire the services of a *lieba shai*. This is a boy thief-seeker, trained for the purpose and retained by a local elder. The thief-seeker fasts for a night, takes a draught of drugged milk, and smokes a pipe containing some special herbs. This potent cocktail on an empty stomach, causes the boy to collapse, and the elder intones over the inert form until he recovers and reels away, sometimes in quite a frenzy. The elder follows, holding onto a sash round the boy's waist. Care is taken to avoid water, which will break the spell. The boy leads the elder to the stolen articles, and identifies the thief by breathing in great gasps, kneeing the culprit, and grasping him by the kneck. The thief-seeker is then given beer and bread to make him vomit and throw off the effects of the drugs.

A wrong-doer can thwart the thief-seeker by drenching himself in water, which makes him proof against the charm. Another ploy is to make as if to jump off a precipice, which the thief-seeker will copy unless the elder can manage to haul him back in time.

Sons of poor families are chosen to be thief-seekers and are trained by being drugged and set to find previously hidden goods. The powers disappear with the onset of puberty, but there are long-term effects such as 'weakness in the head', ex-thief-seekers have reputations as 'drunkards and ravers', and alcohol induces wild staring eyes, a vacant expression and physical weakness.

browns and black rather than white.

Scuba diving is said to be among the best in the Red Sea, and offshore from Dahlak Islands the coral gardens are beautiful. The Islands were once an Ethiopian military base upon which the Israelis have built an air strip.

About 15 minutes out of Massawa to the S there is a hotel-restaurant on the sea front offering swimming and sunbathing on the white sands. There are also excellent beach facilities a few km to the N of the city.

Fishing along this part of the Red Sea is said to be particularly good as it has never seriously been exploited. The area is rich in tuna, barracuda, dolphin and mero.

South of Massawa is **Danakil** which lies 116m below sea level and is one of the hottest and most inhospitable places on earth with temperatures reaching up to 50°C.

Local information

● Where to stay

Most of the better hotels were destroyed during the war and are in the process of being restored, though you should be able to find somewhere to stay near the port. It is wise checking if the room has a fan as it is desirable whatever the time of year.

● Places to eat

Most of the reasonable places to eat are along the harbour front selling simple meals of fish at reasonable prices.

● Transport

The 105 km road from Asmara to Massawa takes you through breathtaking scenery down from the hills to the Red Sea. Regular buses run from the bus depot near the market in Asmara.

Assab

Located on the coast, close to the border with Djibouti, about 1,100 km from Asmara, with a population of about 15,000. It is in the process of negotiation to become a freeport and Ethiopia's main road transport outlet to the sea. The city has an old Arab quarter on the waterfront and a more modern port with an oil refinery constructed by the Soviet Union. The town has been little affected by the war, which was waged mainly in the N. However, it became generally run-down during the Mengistu period, but is now slowly recovering. The weather is hot Jun to Sep, when temperatures of 42°C have been recorded in the shade. Although with a sea breeze, even at night the temperature does not fall below 23°C. For the rest of the year the climate is more moderate, and there are attractive beaches close to the old part of town. There is an open-air cinema in town.

Local information

● Where to stay

B *Agip Motel*, rather uninspired, but a reasonable standard and good restaurant.

C *Albergo Assab*, old colonial-style. Bar. Restaurant. Some rooms a/c.

● Transport

The distance between Asmara and Assab is considerable (1,100 km), the roads are in poor shape and transport is very meagre. The best approach to Assab is the road from Addis Ababa (750 km away), along which there are regular buses.

NATIONAL PARKS

An unfortunate casualty of the recent war was the protection of flora and fauna. However, given the diversity of environments in Eritrea and the fact it is so unspoilt, there is potential for the country to develop national parks. Prior to the war there were Reserves near Teseney in the west; just to the north east of Keren; and in the north on the border with Sudan. The information given here is based on the only park established before the split with Ethiopia.

Dahlak Marine National Park

The Dahlak islands lie between 15 and110 km from the Massawa coast scattered over an area of approximately 15,500 sq km. There are some 200 islands in all though not all are inhabited and many are barren. Although some were used as a military base by the Ethiopian army and the military base is still there, the waters provide a fascinating place to visit. The shallow waters and coral gardens house a great diversity of marine life including the barracuda and the manta ray and the less common dugong (nicknamed the sea cow). On the islands themselves you may be able to spot soot falcons, the brown booby, spoonbill, osprey and a number of other birds and gazelle graze amongst the acacias.

To visit the park, enquire at the Department of Protocol at the *Ambasoira Hotel* in Asmara or at the Department of Tourism when it begins operation in the Post Office square.

INFORMATION FOR VISITORS

Contents

Before you go

Entry requirements

● Visas

A visa is required by anyone wishing to enter Eritrea. Visas are available from Eritrean embassies around the world and they cost about US$40 in European cities and are usually obtainable within 24 hours. If there is no embassy in your country, you will be able to get one from Addis Ababa in Ethiopia.

● Vaccinations

You will need a Yellow Fever vaccination certificate.

● Representation overseas

The only embassy established so far is in Ethiopia, in Addis Ababa. There are a number of EPLF representatives around the world, and Eritrea is likely to begin setting up embassies in the future. For the present information can be obtained from Ethiopian Embassies around the world (see page 597).

● Overseas representation in Eritrea

All the diplomatic representation is in Asmara (see page 627).

● Tourist information

This can best be obtained from the Office of Protocol in Asmara, (see page 628).

● Travel and tour agents

The main carrier into Eritrea is *Ethiopian Airways*, with offices situated in 54 cities around the world. Invariably they have a staff member who takes responsibility for providing tourism information, and will cover developments in Eritrea, providing a reliable source for information on any recent changes in visa regulations, health requirements etc.

When to go

● Best time to visit

The main rainy season in the hinterland is between Jun and Sep, and it is best to try to avoid this period. The coast has rain in Dec to Feb, but the showers are short, and the rest of the day will be sunny. Oct, and the months of Mar and Apr are thought to be periods of the year for visitors.

Health

● Staying healthy

Yellow fever inoculation is compulsory. It is wise to have a cholera vaccination even though it is only compulsory if the vistior is coming from an infected area. Inoculation against typhoid and hepatitis are strongly recommended.

Anti malaria tablets and general anti-mosquito measures are strongly recommended.

Although the water is said to be safe to drink, many people will try to avoid even the smallest risk of a stomach upset by drinking only boiled, sterilised or bottled water.

For further advice see the section on Health, page 21).

Money

● Currency

The unit of currency is the Ethiopian Birr. Negotiations on future arrangements are underway between the Ethiopian and Eritrean governments with a view to Eritrea establishing its own currency. The exchange rate in 1994 was Birr 4.94 = US$1.

You will be best advised to get money exchanged in the capital, Asmara, as banking facilities in other parts of the country are hard to find. The best currency to carry is the US dollar, though the English pound, the Italian lire, German mark and Japanese yen are alright. You many have problems having any other currencies recognised.

A fairly strict eye is kept on any hard currency coming into and going out of the country as it is so desperately needed by the fledgling government. You will be expected to declare any hard currency being brought into Eritrea and have receipts for exchange at officially recognised bureaux. Having said this, there is a thriving black market with the most favoured currency being the US dollar which fetches 2 to 3 times the official rate on the street.

● Credit cards

Major cards taken by large hotels in Asmara and Ethiopian Airways. Not generally acceptable outside Asmara.

Getting there

● Air

Ethiopian Airways is increasingly routing its services via Asmara which is making air travel direct from Europe to Eritrea easier. However, if there are no direct flights, it is easiest to go to Addis Ababa and take the daily flight into Asmara from there.

● Road

It is possible to get into Eritrea from Ethiopia by road but both routes are in a bad condition and consequently the journey is long and very tiring. The 2 routes are either directly from Addis Ababa to Asmara via Adigrat taking about 5 days or from Addis Ababa to Assab and then N along the coast. There is no regular public transport operating on this route. It is also possible to enter the country from Djibouti to Assab, though the route from Assab to Asmara is particularly uncomfortable and long (1,100 km).

● Sea

There are 2 important ports in Eritrea. Massawa is currently operational, though in disrepair, and many cargo ships dock here from other countries along the Red Sea. You may be able to get dhows to Assab on the Djibouti, Ethiopian, Eritrean border in the S.

When you arrive

● Calendar

When Eritrea was part of Ethiopia it used the Julian calendar, named after Julius Caeser, which is 7 years and 8 months behind the Gregorian (European) calendar – a result of differences of opinion over Christ's exact date of birth. The Julian calender consists of 12 months of 30 days and a 13th month of 5 or 6 days.

● Conduct

It is expected that dress will be sober for formal occasions, particularly when visiting government offices – it is regarded as a mark of respect for the persons you are meeting as much as anything else.

Visitors are often offered a cup of tea or coffee, and it is considered a friendly gesture to accept.

When entering a church or mosque, it is necessary for shoes to be removed. Women are not normally allowed to enter mosques unless there is a special prayer room for women.

Photographs of museums, art works, churches and mosques will often require permission. When photographing local people, religious ceremonies or festivals, it is courteous to ask permission first, and a small fee might be requested.

● Electricity

220 volts, 50 cycles AC. A variety of sockets are to be found around the country, and an adaptor is desirable, and it is sensible to bring one with you.

● Hours of business

0800 to 1200 and 1300 to 1600.

● Official time

Three hours later than GMT. Local people use a 12 hour clock, which starts at 0600. Thus 0800 is 'hour 2 of the day'. At 1800 the night clock begins. Thus 0400 is 'hour 10 of the night'.

● Religion

The country is fairly equally divided between Muslims and orthodox Christians though there are a few Roman Catholic and Protestant communities. A small number of the population follow traditional beliefs.

● Safety

Eritrea is a very safe country, and it is possible to walk about with confidence in the cities and towns even after dark. It is sensible to keep a close eye on belongings.

Although there are no restrictions on photography, military installations, airports, bridges, civil engineering works, government buildings, and military personnel should not be photographed.

● Weights and measures

Metric weights and measures are in use in the main towns and cities. In country areas, customs vary.

Where to stay

● Accommodation

The only place you are likely to find reasonable quality accommodation is in the capital, Asmara as most facilities around the rest of the country were either destroyed during the war or have fallen into disrepair. However, you will be able to find modest places to stay in most towns.

HOTEL CLASSIFICATIONS

A+	Over US$100 a night. International standards and decor, air conditioning, self contained rooms, swimming pool, restaurants, bars, business services.
A	US$40-100. First class standards, air-conditioning, attached bathrooms, restaurants and bars, swimming pool.
B	US$20-40. Tourist class, comfortable with air conditioning or fans, attached barthrooms, restaurant, bar, public rooms.
C	US$10-20. Budget, fans, shared bathroom facilities.
D	US$5-10. Guest house, no fan, shared bathroom, cold water.
E	Under US$5. Basic guest house, simple bed, no soap or towels, no wardrobe, shared bathroom facilities, erratic cold water supply, no fans or mosquito nets.

Food and drink

Italian food has been absorbed into traditional Eritrean eating habits in the hotels and a standard menu will have pasta followed by a meat or fish course and ice cream or fruit. Traditional Eritrean food is the large pancake made of fermented batter called *injera* which is served with a variety of meat or vegetable sauces. Local cheeses, particularly those made from goats' milk, are well worth trying.

EATING CLASSIFICATIONS

♦♦♦♦	Over US$10 for a meal. A 3-course meal in a restaurant with pleasant decor. Beers, wines and spirits available.
♦♦♦	US$5-10 for a meal. Two courses, not including alcohol, reasonable surroundings.
♦♦	US$2-5 for a meal, probably only a single course, surroundings spartan but adequate.
♦	Under US$2. Single course, often makeshift surroundings such as a steet kiosk with simple benches and tables.

You will be able to find most forms of alcohol – beer, whisky, wine – though they are expensive as they have to be imported. It is well worth trying Melotti a local beer or the spirit *araki*, a colourless aniseed drink both of which are available in most bars around the country. You should also be able to find local fruit wines.

The water is supposed to be safe to drink, though this very much depends on your constitution. Local bottled spring water is available throughout the country.

Getting around

● Air

Air Eritrea operates an internal service between Assab and Asmara.

● Train

The railway between Massawa Asa,ara. Lerem amd Agordat was dismantled during the war and no money has yet been allocated to rehabilitate it.

● Road

Eritrea's transport infrastructure was severely damaged as a result of the war though the government is putting much of its financial and manpower resources into redeveloping the road system. Few roads in the country are tarmaced and they are invariably in a bad state of repair. The way N is rough and difficult from Asmara up towards Sudan through the arid hills of Afabet and Nakfa. The route being given particular attention is between Asmara and the port of Massawa.

● Car hire

It is possible to hire chauffeur driven cars from Asmara (see page 628).

Communications

● Language

Arabic and Tigrinya are both commonly spoken.

Entertainment

● Newspapers

Hadas Eritrea is published twice a week in Tigrinya and Arabic by the transitional government of Eritrea.

● Television and radio

Voice of the Broad Masses of Eritrea is a government-controlled radio station broadcasting in Arabic, Tigrinya, Afar and Kunama. *ERI-TV* was established in 1992 by the government and began broadcasting in 1993 to provide educational and technical information for the purpose of national reconstruction. Transmissions are limited to Asmara and are broadcast in Arabic and Tigrinya.

Holidays and festivals

As yet no official set of holidays and festivals has been declared. However, it seems clear that 28 May will be celebrated as Independence Day. Otherwise the following are days that will be observed by at least some section of the Eritrean community:

7 Jan	*Genna* (Ethiopian Christmas – birth of Christ)
19 Jan	*Timket* (Ethiopian Epiphany – baptism of Christ)
1 May	*International Labour Day*
May	(variable) Ethiopian Good Friday
May	((variable) *Fasika* (Ethiopian Easter Sunday)
May	(variable) *Idd al Fitr* (End of month of fasting for Ramadan)
Aug	(variable) Idd al Adha
11 Sep	*Engutatsh* (Ethiopian New year)
27 Sep	*Maskal* (Finding of the True Cross)
Nov	(variable) *Maulid* (Birth of Prophet Mohamed)

Further reading

Parkyns, M. 1868. *Life in Abyssinia* London: John Murray. An account of travels from Massawa W to Khartoum, which began in 1843, and took 6 years. Tonkin, T 1972 *Ethiopia With Love* London: Hodder and Stoughton. Contains descriptions of Massawa and Asmara during the time of Haile Selassie, with some excellent line drawings which evocatively capture the atmosphere of Eritrea.

SOMALIA

INTRODUCTION

Since 1991 a particularly horrifying civil war has been raging, resulting in anarchy, turmoil and widespread famines. When this situation changes and the country stabilises, the traveller will be able to enjoy a country with a fascinating culture dating back to stone age times and still unspoilt by commercial tourism. For the meantime, it is likely the only people to visit the country will be development and relief workers or members of the UN forces.

Somalia's diverse environment houses a variety of different types of animals, miles of unspoilt coastline with some of the best beaches in the world, and a rich historical past, that even in more tranquil times was enjoyed by very few tourists or travellers.

At some stage Somalia will again be accessible to travellers, and this guide is prepared in the spirit of cataloguing what was available before the current chaos. Much will be irrevocably lost, but it is always surprising how much remains, how much carries on working, and how much can be rapidly restored when political stability is re-established.

Exchange rate in August 1994 US$1 = SS2,602

CONTENTS

MAPS

Environment

Geography

The coastline of Somalia is stunning with long beaches of white sand, though one needs to be careful about swimming due to the danger of sharks which are a problem along most of the coast. The N of the country is mountainous with high plateaux and little vegetation; no type of agriculture is possible. The mountains gradually slope S and W to the central, largely waterless, plateau which occupies most of the country. South of Mogadishu, the capital, the land becomes greener though it is rather flat and monotonous. There are 3 ports, Mogadishu, Kismayu and Marka and other natural harbours are rare. A coral reef runs from N of Mogadishu to the Kenyan border in the S, but sharks are not unknown on the shore side of the reef.

There are only 2 perennial rivers, the Juba and the Shebelle both starting from the Ogaden region of Ethiopia. Most agricultural land lies on the banks of these 2 rivers in the S. Much of the interior is unsuitable for agriculture because of the lack of water.

Climate

Somalia experiences 4 seasons. *Jilal* starts around Jan and is the hottest time, *Gu* is the first rainy season lasting from Mar to Jun, *Hagaa* in Aug is the start of the dry season when dust clouds are everywhere and monsoon winds blow, and *Dayr* lasting from Sep to Dec is the second rainy season.

The climate throughout the country is hot and humid during the rainy seasons and for the rest of the year it is fairly pleasant, though always hot, rising to 42°C in the northern coastal towns. The mountains and plateaux of the N are particularly hot and dry. Rainfall is generally higher in the S though is still very low, 30-50cm a year. Drought is a perennial problem in this part of the world.

History

Rock paintings and cave inscriptions such as those at Gaanlibah and Gelweita near Las Khoreh have been found dating back thousands of years and bear witness to people having lived in the northern region of Somalia since the early Stone Age. The port of Mogadishu was known to the Egyptians, they called Somalia the Land of Punt, and early Greek and Arab writers called Somali people the Black Berbers. Mogadishu traded with the Phoenicians and supplied most of the frankincense and myrrh to the pre-Muslim kingdoms of the Arabia peninsula.

Many centuries later, the Somali coast was part of the Arab-controlled trans-Indian Ocean trading network, trading as far afield as Thailand and China as well as other parts of East Africa and the Middle East. Many ports along its coast including Mogadishu, the capital, and Brava formed part of a chain running the length of East Africa down to Sofala in Mozambique. The trade brought much prosperity to the region, but this was largely destroyed by the Portuguese in the early 16th century after they discovered the sea route to India via the Cape of Good Hope. There are still signs of its former glory in the architecture of Mogadishu, Berbera and Marka and the now ruined city of Zeila near the Djibouti border. Zeila was not only the capital of a powerful city-state but was also one of the acknowledged centres of Islam, which reached this part of East Africa from Saudi Arabia in the 7th century. The area lapsed into obscurity, ignored by the Europeans until the 19th century because of its lack of exploitable resources.

In the 19th century, the area came back to prominence only to be carved up to serve the commercial or political interests of rival colonial empires. The Ogaden Desert to the W was annexed by Emperor Menelik I of Ethiopia despite the fact that the nomadic tribesmen of the region were ethnically Somali. The Sultanate of Oman took control of southern Somalia as part of its empire which extended from Zanzibar off Tanzania to Pakistan. The British administered the northern part of the country opposite South Yemen in 1886 with the objective of safeguarding its trade route through the Suez Canal to Aden. Later the Italians bought the area S of Mogadishu as well as the city itself from the Omani-Zanzibari dynasty and began active occupation by the early 1900s.

The Somali people did not take to colonial rule by Europeans easily. A major rebellion led by Mohammed Abdille Hassan in the S E corner of the British Protectorate in 1899 began and did not end until his death in 1921. The combined efforts of Ethiopian, British and Italian troops using aircraft could not destroy his movement, though later it succumbed to a smallpox epidemic.

In 1940 the Italians overran Ethiopia and the Somali Protectorate and all Somalis except those in Kenya (British) and Djibouti (French) were under one administration. After the defeat of the Italians in 1941 the British took over, first with a military administration, and after 1950, with civilian control. However, in 1950, Italian Somaliland became a UN Trust Territory, and was returned to Italian administration for a 10-year period in preparation for independence. The 2 parts were reunited at independence in 1960, the British and the Italians leaving their former colonies within 5 days of each other.

The Ogaden region though officially part of Ethiopia, was inhabited almost entirely by Somali nomads. Repeated efforts were made by the United Nations in the 1950s and 60s to try to establish an acceptable boundary between Ethiopia and Somalia (rather than the provisional administrative line which had been drawn up by the British, Italians and Ethiopians in the 1940s), without success. This issue has led to much hostility between Somalia and Ethiopia which culminated in the Ogaden War in 1977.

The Ogaden war was won by Ethiopia with massive support from Cuba and USSR. This led to a guerilla campaign by the Somali National Movement (SNM) which continues and has cost the lives of about 50,000 people with 400,000 more fleeing the area.

Archaeology

There are numerous sites, very few of which have been thoroughly explored, and which are almost completely unprotected.

All over the N of the country are burial cairns (*taalo*) from which excavations have revealed bones, stone-age weapons and household items. At **Gaanlibah**, about 100 km E of Hargeisa, and at **Kal-Sheikh** in the Sheikh valley are caves with rock-paintings of animals and other figures. Close to the present town of **Elayo** are the remains of buildings from an earlier era. At **Gwelweita**, which is about 40 km from La Koray on the N coast, are stone-age remains and rock paintings. Between Las Koray and Elayo is **Karinhegane** where there are rock paintings of animals, and also some fascinating paintings of animals that are either extinct or are mythical. There are inscriptions beneath each painting, none of which has been deciphered, and it has been suggested these are 2,500 years old. About 5 km away, further into the mountains is another site, **Hilayo**, with similar paintings and inscriptions.

In the Wadi valley at **Mudun**, there are the ruins of an ancient settlement which was clearly a substantial town. There are the remains of three large mosques, and about 2 thousand tombs. At the end of the Baladi Valley, close to **Bosaso** on the N coast, is an extraordinary earthwork, 3 km in length, said to be a grave. Halfway between Skushuban and Gardo, in the **Arie** valley was once a considerable town, with very substantial, thick-walled constructions. Possibly more recent are the ruins at **Goan Bogame** in the Las Anod area. Over 2 hundred buildings can be identified, and they are similar in style to those in the Hammawein in Mogadishu. Nearby at **Gubyaley** close to a well are markings similar to those used today to denote the ownership of cattle. Also in Las Anod is **Golharfo**, about 25 km E of Hudun, where there are rock paintings of animals, weapons and household objects. It is particularly interesting as it appears to be the only site where humans are included in the paintings.

Architecture

Akal

This is the traditional dwelling of the nomadic groups and is a domed hut, sometimes known as the 'beehive hut'. It is made of a wooden frame of light, flexible sticks, lashed together and covered with mats or skins held in place by tied thongs. The mats, of palm leaves, can be tightly woven to make them waterproof. In towns the coverings may be cardboard, cloth, polythene, or flattened petrol tins. The *akal* can be erected or dismantled in about 2 hours, and this task is invariably undertaken by the women. A temporary fencing of branches will enclose the livestock and the cooking area.

Mudul

Cultivating groups dwell in the *mudal*, a more permanent structure than the *akal*. It has a circular frame for the walls made from lashed wooden staves, plastered with mud mixed with straw and dung. The roof is thatched and conical.

Arish

Somalis who live in urban areas will normally dwell in an *arish*, rectangular, with timber, mud, straw and dung walls, sometimes with windows and a pitched thatch or tin roof. The walls are often whitewashed. The **baraca** is similar to the *arish*, but the floor is stone or cement, and the walls made of timber slats, usually from old packing crates. A baraca with stone or cement walls is a **casa matoni** ('house of stone'). *Baracas* and *casa matoni* are mostly found in the coastal areas and are unusual in the interior.

Casa moro
These are Arab-style dwellings, mostly 2-storey, of stone and timber, with verandahs. Most buildings in the Hammawein and Shangani districts of Mogadishu are in this style, as well as those in the old sections of Merce, Brava and Kismayo.

European
Finally there are buildings, usually 2-storey and with a walled courtyard that were introduced in the Italian colonial period. Roofs are pitched and tiled and the appearance is predominantly Mediterranean. Modern Somali urban dwellings tend to be built in variations of this style.

Culture and life

People

The population of Somalia is around 7.8 million, and, unusually for Africa, they are all of the same ethnic group and speak the same language. This ethnic group spills over into Djibouti, Ethiopia and northern Kenya. Within this group there are a number of clans. Physically, the Somali are tall with dark skin, aquiline features and a dignified bearing.

The 6 main Somali clans all trace their ancestry to 2 brothers, Samaal and Sab, who are said to have descended from the Quraysh of Arabia who are, in turn, descendents of Muhammed. The society is highly segmented, and it has been observed that the divisions histori-

Courtship In 19th Century Somalia

A female slave cuts out the girl's clitoris and nymphae with a large knife; when the excision has been made she takes a needle and sews up the lips with a continuous series of large stitches. This barbarous guarantee of virginity and chastity is preserved until marriage.

The Somal, when they can afford it, marry between the ages of fifteen and twenty. On first entering the nuptial hut, the bridegroom draws forth his horsewhip and inflicts memorable chastisement on the fair person of his bride, with the the view of taming any lurking propensity to shrewishness. This is carrying out with a will the Arab proverb, 'the slave girl from her capture, the wife from her wedding'. The husband will take great pains to amplify his strength with a meat diet, and will strain to break through the blockage with his sword of love. Generally he is unsuccessful and he opens up the pudendum from the lower end with his finger, or failing that, with a knife. For about a week husband and wife stay in the same hut and devote themselves day and night to the act of love.

The Somalis have only one way of making love. Both parties lie on their sides, never, as is our custom, the man on the woman. The woman lies on her left side, the man on his right.

The fair sex lasts longer in Eastern Africa than in India or Arabia: at thirty, however, charms are on the wane, and when old age comes on they are no exceptions to the hideous decrepitude of the East.

As a general rule, Somali women prefer *amourettes* with strangers, following the well-known Arab proverb "The new comer filleth the eye".

There are no harlots in Somalia, but there are plenty of wives who, because of the inactivity of their husbands, prostitute their bodies without scruple. The man makes his intentions clear by nods, smiles and shameless finger gestures. If the woman smiles, Venus rejoices.

Sir Richard Burton *First Footsteps in East Africa* (1956)

cally have been more significant than common Somali ancestry. In these divisions can be seen the basis of the violent conflicts of the 1990s.

Four of these clans trace their ancestry to Samaal (and they are known collectively by this name) and they are the Dir, Darod, Isaaq and Hawiye. These clans are further segmented into lineages of twelve to fourteen generations. They are pastoralists, account for about 75% of the population, and they herd mainly camels, sheep and goats, inhabiting the the more arid regions outside the fertile area between the Juba and Shabelle rivers. Competition for pasture and water lead to conflicts between these clans. There are formal arrangements for the compensation of clans sub-groups (a *dia* payment) and close relatives (a *jiffo* payment) of people who have been killed. The *dia* and *jiffo* groupings form the basis of further subdivision in the clans. The Samaal consider themseves to be superior to all other groups in the country.

The 2 clans descending from Sab are the Digil and Rahanweyn. They comprise 20% of the popuation and are engaged in cultivating and cattle-raising in the inter-riverine area. These 2 clans are subdivided into a series of sub-clans called *gember.* Again these clans and subclans are divided into lineages of 3 to 5 generations.

In addition to the 6 clans there are 2 other groups. The *habash* are descended from the hunting and cultivating inhabitants of the area before the arrival of the Somalis, and they have been joined as a group by the descendents of former slaves. The *habash* do not intermarry with the Somalis, and are regarded by the Somalis as their inferiors.

The final group, comprising perhaps only 1% of the population are the peoples with specialised skills, such as hunters, leather-workers, blacksmiths, carpenters, barbers and circumcisers. Their ethnic origin is uncertain. The Samaal call this group the *sab* (rather confusingly – sab is a general term meaning low, or low-caste), and the Sab themselves call them *bon*. They are regarded as inferiors by the Somalis. The majority of the population live in the coastal towns, in the northern areas in the highlands and in the S near the 2 rivers. The population in the interior is mostly nomadic.

Religion

For over a thousand years, Somalis have been Muslim. This, and the fact they form a cultural, linguistic homogenous unit makes them unusual in East Africa. The official language is Somali which was not written until 1972 when a Latin orthography was chosen. As a result of the oral tradition in the country, narrative poetry is a popular art form and of exceptional quality.

A significant movement over recent times has been the revival of Somali national culture, particularly as demonstrated through its literature and poetry. Traditional dance, music and folk songs are very popular. Dances are performed to placate evil spirits and to ward against disease, crop failures, foreign invaders and other threats. There are also a number of dances to celebrate happy events such as the coming of rain, the harvest, marriages and births.

The *istun-ka* festival is a traditional ceremony and contest which takes place between 2 groups of men from the banks of the Shebelle River at Afgoi, 32km from Mogadishu. The winner gets the better part of the river's water during the dry season.

Excision and infibulation of girls still appears to be practised in traditional areas. This involves female circumcision by cutting out the clitoris (excision), and sometimes also part of the labia, and then sewing up the mouth of the vagina (infibulation), leaving only a small aperture for urination. The girl remains in this state until marriage. The practice, apart from being extremely painful as it is performed without anaesthetic, leads to risks of infection, leaves scar tissue which can make childbirth impossible without tearing, and removes the possibility of sexual pleasure. There have been occassions in recent times when communities of Somali refugees in Europe have practised excision and infibulation. Details of the practice were first related by Sir Richard Burton after his trip to Somalia in 1854 (see page 640).

Crafts

Somali craftsmen are renowned for their gold and silver jewellery, finely woven cloth, basketry and wooden carvings. Pottery is rather simple, but incense-burners have attractive fretted designs. There are water and milk containers made from calabashes with patterned exteriors and leather carrying thongs. Palm leaves are used to weave baskets, mats, and trays for winnowing grain. Wood is carved into bowls, ladles and small pieces of furniture, particularly stools. Leatherwork includes sandals, bags and belts, often decorated with sewn-on sea-shells.

Modern Somalia

Politics

Between 1960 and 1969 a series of multi-party governments ruled the new Republic of Somalia with increasing levels of corruption and inefficiency. Eventually Major-General Mohammed Siyad Barre took power in a bloodless coup in 1969 putting into place the 'Supreme Revolutionary Council' pursuing socialist policies with the emphasis on self-help schemes. A single party was formed, the Somali Revolutionary Socialist Party (SRSP).

President Barre and the People's Assembly (a new institution developed in 1979) were re-elected twice since he took office, but in the absence of any opposition. He assumed personal control of the government, steadily nationalising all major sectors including medical services, schools, banks, electricity and transport services. The state controlled all imports and exports and all land was nationalised. Prices and salaries were rigidly regulated. After 1984 constitutional amendments steadily transferred all effective power to the President.

From 1970-1977 Somalia increasingly turned to the Soviet Union and the Eastern bloc countries for aid and support, particularly after the severe drought in the mid-1970s when a massive Soviet airlift relocated some 140,000 people to farming settlements in the agricultural S, saving many thousands of lives. However, the links between Somalia and the USSR became increasingly strained during the time of the Ogaden war in 1977. Somalia wished to reunify Somali lands, but the Soviet Union wished to support Ethiopia as a more significant ally in the horn. At the same time, the US and Western countries offered financial support to Somalia to break its links with the USSR. The outcome of the Ogaden war was that Ethiopia retained its territory with the aid of Soviet Union arms and troops and Somalia expelled the 6,000 Soviet personnel in its country.

Somalia settled into an uneasy dependence on the West for aid which inevitably led to modifications in its political structure, though the political monopoly of the SRSP remained. At this time huge numbers of refugees were pouring into the country, perhaps as many as one million from the wars in Ogaden and Ethiopia. Western relief agencies responded generously to appeals from Barre for help with the refugee problem but even so, the cost of housing them placed enormous strain on the national economy. The situation became particularly difficult in 1984 when Saudi Arabia, hitherto a main importer of Somali cattle, cut off imports due to an outbreak of cattle plague, and this severely affected Somalia's already fragile economy. The diversion of resources to refugees led to an acute shortage of many essential items in the country creating widespread discontent and allegations of misappropriation of relief supplies by the government.

A further drought resulted in more large-scale refugee movements into the country and led the government to declare a state of emergency in 1987 with about 3 million people at risk of starvation all of which increased political unrest. At around this time, diplomatic relations between Somalia and Ethiopia improved resulting in Ethiopia expelling rebel Somali political parties. There then began a guerilla warfare in the N of Somalia with members of the Somali National Movement (SNM) trying to capture certain key areas such as Hargeisa, Burao and Berbera. By 1988 it was reported that about 15,000 people had been killed and that most of the buildings in Hargeisa had been destroyed.

In 1989 Said Barre's government announced a programme of political and economic reforms for the turbulent northern provinces. It also announced its intention of introducing multi-party elections. However, the economic disarray and political discontent resulted in violent disturbances in Mogadishu.

In mid 1990, the government launched a military offensive in the N against the SNM. At the same time a partial curfew was imposed in Mogadishu which was experiencing a growing breakdown in public order. Government promises of political reform had little impact on opposition leaders and their parties who were calling for Barre's resignation. By early 1991 an airlift of foreign nationals out of Mogadishu was completed as the situation deteriorated. Barre fled a month later as the country descended into a civil war between various factions divided along clan affiliations.

In May 1991 the SNM declared a Republic of Somaliland with Hargeisa as its capital in the N, its borders being approximately those of the former British protectorate. Despite attempts by various transitional governments representing the views of all the other political movements of the country, Somaliland retains its independence saying this is a 'non-negotiable and irreversible' situation. To date, Somaliland has not been recognised by any international government, but despite this lack of support from abroad, the area has established peace and is in the process of rebuilding its devastated infrastructures and services, albeit with extremely limited resources.

In 1991, fighting in the S broke out between the United Somali Congress (USC) and forces loyal to former President Barre. Barre had joined forces with the Somali Patriotic Movement (SPM) a group of mainly Ogadeni deserters from the army and the Somali National Front (SNF) a group from the Darod clan who are mainly pastoral nomads from various parts of the more fertile regions of Somalia. A series of reconciliation conferences took place between the 6 main political groups who agreed a ceasefire and confirmed Ali Mahdi, a former government minister of Somalia and one of the founders of the USC, as interim president for 2 years.

By the beginning of Sep 1991, however, fighting had broken out again in Mogadishu between supporters of General Aidid, the elected chair of the USC and supporters of Ali Mahdi. Aidid challenged the authority of Ali Mahdi on the grounds that he had contravened the reconciliation by not standing for re-election. Over the next few months fighting in Mogadishu intensified resulting in the loss of many civilian lives with Aidid's forces taking control of the city. Many people fled into neighbouring Kenya and the Red Cross believed many others were in danger of starvation. Italy's attempts to intervene were viewed with hostility as an attempt to interfere with Somalia's internal affairs.

By Jan 1992 the international community were forced into action after the failure of the UN Secretary-General to achieve a peace agreement. An arms embargo was placed on the country and by Mar a formal cease-fire was signed after which a UN team prepared the way for the distribution of emergency aid to the country, with 500 armed troops to ensure the security of aid convoys. Agencies tried to get aid to the worst affected areas in rural Somalia but faced increasing difficulties because of the state of anarchy, and were forced to employ armed guards. The UN suspended aid flights after armed bandits stole food from the airport and by Sep 1992 only a third of the UN aid designated for Somalia had arrived.

General Aidid was known to be strongly opposed to foreign armed troops entering Somalia to oversee the distribution of aid, and problems came to a head when Aidid accused the UN of bringing in arms and money for the supporters of Ali Mahdi (it was later found that a Russian aircraft used on UN flights had brought in supplies including weapons for Ali Mahdi).

There was growing criticism of the UN's humanitarian aid programme by other relief agencies. The UN was said to be slow at reacting to the desperate situation of many Somalis – it was estimated that over one million Somalis had fled to neighbouring countries and that a fifth of the remaining population (over a million) were at risk of dying from starvation within the next 6 months. Not only was it slow and bureaucratic, but up to 80% of its supplies were being looted. The UN representative in Mogadishu resigned in frustration.

On 4 Dec 1992 President Bush deployed 28,000 US troops on 'Operation Restore Hope' to the dismay of UN officials and aid workers in Somalia. The express aim was to disarm the rival factions and protect the flow of aid but the aims were ill-defined and ultimately unworkable. It was also unclear how long the US troops were to remain in Somalia. On 27 Dec the 2 main factions under Aidid and Ali Mahdi signed a reconciliation agreement where both men promised to work together to unite Somalia, but this broke down within a matter of days. The United Task Force (UNITAF) began seizing weapons and armed vehicles which resulted in a skirmish killing 2 US marines and a number of Somalis. Notwithstanding the frequent violent outbreaks, the US declared that they had been successful at restoring security allowing the free flow of relief aid throughout Somalia. The US prepared to remove its troops and leave UNITAF in charge in Mar 1993 whilst yet another reconciliation conference opened in Addis Ababa.

It was agreed that Somalia would hold elections in 2 years. In the meantime a transitional national council made up of representatives of all factions would administer the country. Each faction committed itself to disarming within 90 days, a process to be monitored by the UNITAF peace-keeping force known as UNOSOM II. The deployment of UNOSOM II failed to reduce tensions in Mogadishu and fighting between UNOSOM II forces and supporters of Aidid broke out.

In Jun 1993 the US, under the guise of UNOSOM II, attempted to capture Aidid for whom a warrant for his arrest had been issued by the UN for war crimes. The US were unsuccessful at finding Aidid and their attempts to oust him from power resulted in fierce reprisals by Aidid's supporters and were said to obscure the operation's original humanitarian mission. However, the attempt to find Aidid and disarm all factions continued, resulting in the deaths of more UN soldiers and other non-Somalis in the country. By mid-1994, however, all but 50 US troops had left Somalia and most other western countries had withdrawn, leaving security in the hands of 16,000 troops, mostly from Egypt, Indian and Pakistan.

The stalemate continues, with relief operations taking place amid the skirmishing and sporadic attempts to reach a political solution among the twelve or so groups purporting to represent Somali factions.

Economics

It must be stressed that the survey of the economy given here relates to the situation that existed before the breakdown in 1991.

Economic and social structure

Estimates put the size of population for 1990 at 7.8 mn. The population was swollen by a steady influx of refugees from the Ogaden and surrounding areas after 1977, and since 1991 there has been an outflow of refugees fleeing the current turmoil. The density of population was 12.2 per sq km in 1990, and this comparatively low density reflects the unsuitablity of much of terrain for agriculture. Generally permanent settlements are scattered, but the drought and ensuing refugees staying with their kin groups have increased the urban population to 36%, high for East Africa. Population growth was 3.1% for the period 1980-90, but famine, drought and refugee movements will have a significant, and as yet undetermined, effect on population expansion in the future.

GDP in 1990 was estimated at US$890 mn, and GNP per head was US$120, placing Somalia in the low-income group, and the people of Somalia were among the 5 poorest countries in the world.

The agriculture sector generated 65% of GDP in 1990, with industry generating 9% and services 26%. The contribution of the agriculture sector is over twice the average for low-income countries, and the industry and service sector shares are correspondingly low. On the demand side, private consumption was equivalent to 91% of GDP in 1989, with government consumption 23%, and domestic saving -14% of GDP. However, gross domestic investment was 21% of GDP, made possible by substantial financial transfers from overseas. Exports of goods and services comprised 8% of GDP in 1989, and imports were 43% of GDP. The main exports were livestock 60%, bananas 12% and hides 3%. In the import category, machinery comprised 28%, foodstuffs 20% and fuel 4%.

The adult literacy rate in 1990 was 24%. Primary school enrolment rates were 20% in 1986, while secondary enrolments were 12%, with 4% enrolment in higher education. These figures indicate good educational provision for one fifth of the population, almost all urban, and very little for the rest.

Life expectancy was 46 years in 1990, significantly below the African average of 51. There was one doctor for every 19,950 persons, and this provision is rather better than is general in Africa, although distribution of medical care is very unequal, with urban groups substantially better served. Average daily calorie supply was 1,874 in 1989, and this is about 80% of the estimated minimum requirement.

Overall, Somalia is a low-income country with heavy dependence on agriculture to generate GDP and export revenues. There is heavy reliance on overseas aid to finance imports. Educational provision is poor and unequally distributed, as is health. Nutrition, even before the problems after 1991, was a cause for acute concern.

Economic performance

GDP grew by 2.% from 1980-90, which was better than the regional average of 1.6%. Nevertheless, GDP per head fell by -0.7% a year. Despite serious drought and some exporting difficulties, the agricultural sector grew by 3.3% while the regional average was only 1.1%. Industrial growth of 1.0% was on a par with the regional average, though 0.9% growth in the service sector was below the regional average of 2.5%.

Export volumes declined rapidly by -3.3% a year 1980-90 as drought and import restrictions by Saudi Arabia, a major livestock buyer, reduced the number and quality of animals sold. Import volumes fell by -4.3% a year, compared with the regional average which increased by 0.2%.

Inflation averaged almost 50% a year for 1980-90. By comparison, the average rate of inflation in the region for 1980-90 was 23.6%, and the whole of Africa 16.7%.

COMPARATIVE ECONOMIC AND SOCIAL DATA

	Somalia	East Africa	Africa	Industrial Countries
Population & land				
Population, mid year, millions, 1990	7.8	12.2	10.2	40.0
Urban Population, %, 1990	36	30.5	30	75
Population Growth Rate, % per year, 1980-90	3.1	3.1	3.1	0.8
Land Area, thou. sq. kilom.	638	486	486	1,628
Population Density, persons per sq kilom., 1990	12.2	24.2	20.4	24.3
Economy: production and income				
GDP, US$ millions, 1990	890	2,650	3,561	550,099
GNP per head, US$, 1990	120	250	389	12,960
Economy: supply structure				
Agriculture, % of GDP, 1990	65	43	35	3
Industry, % of GDP, 1990	9	15	27	35
Services, % of GDP, 1990	26	42	38	61
Economy: demand structure				
Private Consumption, % of GDP, 1989	91	77	73	62
Gross Domestic Investment, % of GDP, 1989	21	16	16	21
Government Consumption, % of GDP, 1989	23	15	14	17
Exports, % of GDP, 1989	8	16	23	17
Imports, % of GDP, 1989	43	24	26	17
Economy: performance				
GDP growth, % per year, 1980-90	2.4	1.6	-0.6	2.5
GDP per head growth, % per year, 1980-90	-0.7	-1.7	-3.7	1.7
Agriculture growth, % per year, 1980-90	3.3	1.1	0.0	2.5
Industry growth, % per year, 1980-90	1.0	1.1	-1.0	2.5
Services growth, % per year, 1980-90	0.9	2.5	-0.5	2.6
Exports growth, % per year, 1980-90	-3.3	0.7	-1.9	3.3
Imports growth, % per year, 1980-90	-4.3	0.2	-6.9	4.3
Economy: other				
Inflation Rate, % per year, 1980-90	49.7	23.6	16.7	5.3
Aid, net inflow, % of GNP, 1990	45.9	11.5	6.3	-
Debt Service, % of Exports, 1990	5.8	18	20.6	-
Education				
Primary, % of 6-11 group, 1986	20	62	76	102
Secondary, % of 12-17 group, 1986	12	15	22	93
Higher, % of 20-24 group, 1986	4	1.2	1.9	39
Adult Literacy Rate, %, 1990	24	41	39	99
Health and nutrition				
Life Expectancy, years, 1990	46	50	50	76
Calorie Supply, daily per head, 1989	1,874	2,111	2,096	3,357
Population per doctor, 1987	19,950	35,986	24,185	550

Notes: :'Africa' excludes South Africa. Dates are for the country in question, and do not always correspond with the Regional, African and Industrial averages.

Overall, Somalia has had poor economic performance in the 1980s, when, despite increases in GDP, GDP per head fell. Agriculture performed reasonably well, but the other sectors grew more slowly than population growth, exports and imports declined and inflation has been high.

Recent economic developments

In 1980 Somalia began to introduce reforms which reversed some of the measures dating from 1975 which extended government ownership and control in the economy. The currency was devalued, though not by as much as was urged by the IMF. In 1985 the government agreed to liberalise imports and dismantle controls in agriculture and marketing. In Sep 1986, an auction system for foreign exchange was introduced, but by early 1987 there were reservations that the implementation of reforms had been slow. In Jun it was announced that the government would allow private traders in hides and skins, but would retain its monopoly over the export of these goods. In Aug it was announced that the state monopoly of banking would be ended. In Jul the IMF agreed US$70 mn of programme lending to support the reform programme. Agriculture was hit by drought when the early rains of 1987 failed. High domestic prices and shortages of petrol were considerable sources of unrest.

Somalia is estimated to have US$1,922 mn outstanding in external debt in 1990, most of it to Arab creditors The debt-service payments are clearly beyond Somalia's capacity to service.

Somalia's exchange rate remained virtually unchanged up to 1981, but steadily depreciated from the SS 6.30 = US$1 of 1981 to SS 408.1 = US$1 at the end of 1989, and to SS 2,602 = US$1 in August 1994.

Aid projects have concentrated on infrastructure and agriculture. The World Bank has loaned US$24.4 mn for ports and USUS$ 26.1m for nomad settlement and agricultural projects. The African Development Bank is allocating USUS$ 9m to agricultural extension, and the EU US$2.1 mn to hospitals. Several oil companies are engaged in oil exploration, both on-land and off-shore.

Since 1991 the conflicts have produced severe shortages of all basic commodities, and food, fuel and medical supplies are all very scarce. Estimates have suggested that 1.5 million are at risk of death from starvation, and another 4.5 are likely to suffer sever malnutrition. International activity has concentrated on the provision of food aid, but has been severly hampered by the lack of security.

Economic outlook

There can be no improvement in economic conditions until stability and security return. Some pockets, such as Somaliland in the N, will make some progress, but they are hampered by lack of the international recognition that will encourage aid flows.

MOGADISHU

Mogadishu was founded in the 10th century by Arabs from the Persian Gulf and was at the height of its importance by the 13th century when the mosque of Fakr al Din and the minaret of the Great Mosque were built. Its wealth was derived from the trade passing through the town between Persia, India and China. Unlike other East African coastal cities, Mogadishu was never conquered by the Portuguese; it continued to be ruled by its own people until it accepted the overlordship of the Sultan of Oman in the 19th century. In the mid-20th century it was occupied by the Italians, and their influence is everywhere.

Places of interest

The **Hammawein** is the old city of Mogadishu which is fascinating although now rather neglected. There is a gold and silver market in the centre, and a range of jewellery can be bought, particularly necklaces, rings, bracelets and cuff-links. A feature of the designs is often the Star of Somalia and the Croce du Sud (the Southern Cross). Gemstone traders and cutters are also to be found. It is possible to ask craftsmen to to fashion jewellery to your specification. Benadiri weavers work at their looms in a small courtyard. The area has a mosque **Fakhr-Din** dating from the 13th century.

The **Sheikh Abdul Aziz** mosque is along Lido Road toward the Anglo-American Club, close to the shore. It has a distinctive circular minaret, and is constructed in Persian style. The mosque is of unknown age, and local legend has it that it emerged by itself from the sea.

The National Museum of Somalia is in the mansion constructed for the representative of Said Bargash, a former Sultan of Zanzibar. At this time Said Bargash was also Sultan of Muscat, and the construction is in the Southern Arabian style of architecture. The building was first restored for use as a museum by the Italians in 1933, when it was known as the Garesa Museum. It fell into disrepair, and was refurbished again in 1962. It has some fine carved doors and windows, and illustrations on the floors and ceilings, and decorative plasterwork. The Egyptian forays into the Land of Punt, as Somalia was known, is recorded on 3 panels which reproduce those found at Theba in the Deir-el-Bari temple. The intitial expedition was sent by Queen Haschepsut to obtain incense, spices, ivory and skins. Wooden headrests known as *barkin* were introduced from Egypt at that time, and examples can be seen in the museum. Gravestones, funeral inscriptions and bronze coins date from the eighth century. The Persian influence, of Shirazis along the Benadir coast from the tenth century is reflected in collections of swords, daggers, pottery and marble work. Portuguese cannons are on display. The archives contain documents and photographs from the colonial period. There are also displays of Somali stamps and coins, as well as exhibitions relating to everyday life among the traditional groups. The museum is generally open from 0900-1300.

In the more modern quarters of town, places of interest include the Italian-constructed **Roman Catholic Cathedral**. There is a good market by the main bus station where you can buy Somali cloth and carved meerschaum objects.

Gezira Beach is the most popular beach among both locals and expatriates but you will need your own transport to get there. The hotel beach here is protected from sharks. The restaurant is reasonably priced and serves fish, lobster, rice and spaghetti. There are a number of coves where you will be able to be completely alone, though watch out for sharks if you go swimming.

Local information

● Where to stay

A *Croce Del Sud*, T 23201, Tlx 745. Located on Soqaamadin St on the western side of the Hammawein. A/c. Bar. Restaurants. **A** *Al Aruba*, on Soomaliya St, just to the N of the Hammawein. Swimming pool and own beach. The most recent of the main hotels. A/c. Bar. Restaurants. Disco. **A** *Juba*, on the northern side of the town centre on Jamhuuriyadda St. A/c. Bar. Restaurants

B *Makha*, on Makha Rd, to S of centre. Own bathrooms. Good standard.

C *Dalsan*, centrally located on Birimo Luulia St. Overlooks Indian Ocean.

E *Kaffa*, Makha Road, near the Kenyan Embassy. Fans. Pleasant courtyard layout and good value. **E** *Hargeisa*, on Italiya Rd, on the western edge of the centre of the city, near the Obelisk. Simple, but good value.

There are numerous small hotels, simple and reasonable in price along Makha Rd.

● Places to eat

Food in Mogadishu is varied, cheap and of a reasonable standard with seafood being a particular speciality. Lobster is a good buy here. **Note that during Ramadan restaurants are closed until sundown**. The only exceptions are *al Ruba*, and *Juba*, which serve meals during the day in this period.

♦♦♦*Anglo-American Club* on Lido Road has a western style menu though prices are high in comparison with other places in the city. ♦♦♦*Croce Del Sud* (T 23201 Tlx 745) Located on Soqaamadin St on the western side of the Hammawein. Open-air restaurant has a pleasant atmosphere. ♦♦♦*Ming Sing*, Birmo Luuliya St. Good quality Chinese food.

♦♦*Azans*, has a rooftop restaurant offering Italian and international cuisine. Live music at weekends. ♦♦*Hong Kong Chinese Restaurant*, Chinese food, as well as international menu. ♦♦*Pizzeria*, Birmo Luuliya St. Italian food and international dishes as well as pizza. ♦♦*Pakistani Restaurant*, Birmo Luuliya St. Reasonable standard Indian food.

♦*Mubarak*, Makha Road near *Hotel Kaffa* has good meals and fresh fruit juices.

● Arts and crafts

Either the *market* on Soqaamadin St or the *Anglo-American Club* has interesting objects for sale including items made of camel bone, carvings and fabrics.

● Banks

Central Bank of Somalia Corso Somalia 55, PO Box 11, T 725 and **Commercial Bank of Somalia**, Place Lagarde, PO Box 2004, T 35 12 82.

● Embassies and consulates

Algeria, PO Box 2850, T 81696. **Bulgaria**, Via Travis, PO Box 119, T 81820. **China**, PO Box 548, Via Scire Uarsama, T 20805. **Czechoslovakia**, KM4, PO Box 1167. **Egypt** PO Box 76, via Maka al-Mukarama, Km 4, T 80781. **France**, Corso Primo Luglio, PO Box 13, T 21715. **Germany**, Via Muhammad Habi, PO Box 17, T 20547. **India**, Via Mogadishu, PO Box 955, T 21262. **Iran**, Via Maka al-Mukarama, PO Box 116, T 80881. **Iraq**, Via Maka al-Mukarama, PO Box 641, T 80821. **Italy**, Via Alta Jiuba, PO Box 6, T 20544. **Kenya**, Km 4, PO Box 618, Via Mecca, T 80857. **Korea**, Via Km 5. **Kuwait**, Via Lenin, PO Box 1348. **Libya**, Mia Medina, PO Box 125. **Nigeria**, Villa Haji Fara, Via Km 5, T 81362. **Pakistan**, Via Afgoi, Corso Somalia, PO Box 339, T 80856. **Romania**, Via Lido, PO Box 651. **Saudi Arabia**, Via Benadir, PO Box 603, T 20287. **Sudan**, Via Mecca, PO Box 552. **Syria**, Via Medina, PO Box 986. **Turkey**, Via km 6, PO Box 2833, T 81975. **UK**, Hassan Geedi Abtow 7/8, PO Box 1036, T20288. **USSR**, Via Repubblica, PO Box 607. **USA**, Via Primo Luglio, Km 5, PO Box 574, T 39959. **Yemen Arab Republic**, Via Km 5, PO Box 493.

● Entertainment

It is possible to join the *Anglo-American Club* on Lido Road on a temporary basis. It is a good place to make contacts, and has a duty-free shop. A popular disco is in the basement of the *Al Aruba* (Soomaliya St, just to the N of the Hammawein) and *Azan's* which often has local bands playing European and African music.

The **Mogadishu National Theatre** puts on regular performances of Somali poetry and drama.

● Religion

Most Somalis are Sunni Muslims and there are a number of mosques throughout the city, particularly in the Hammawein, the old centre. There is a Roman Catholic Cathedral built by the Italians at Ahmed bin Idris.

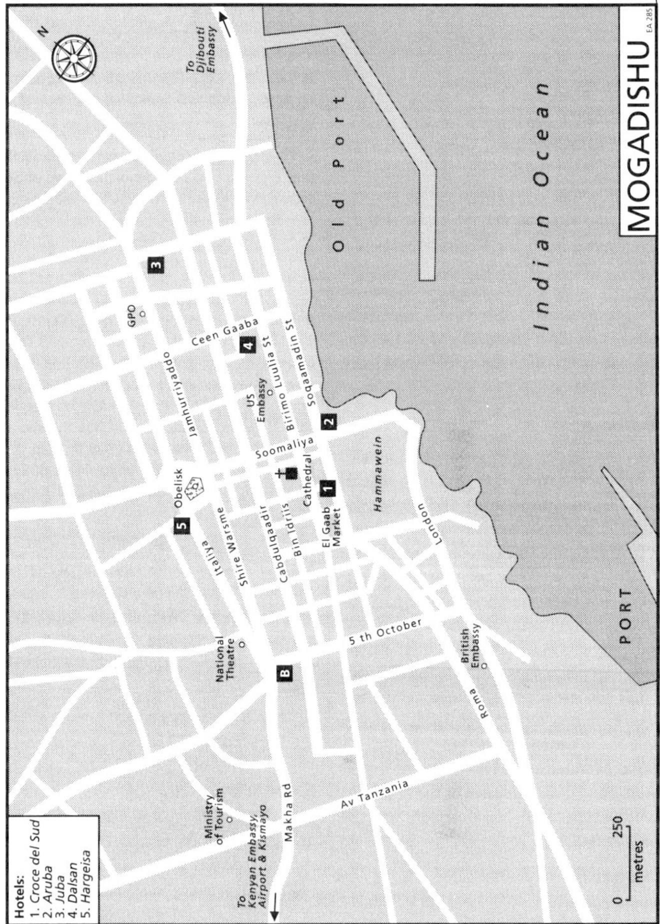

● Tourist office

The *National Agency for Tourism*, PO Box 533, T 2031. If you intend to visit towns or parks in the country, you will need to make arrangements here first.

● Transport

Taxis are plentiful, about US$2-3 for a journey in town. Minibuses are about US$0.20 a trip.

Air The international airport is 4 km outside town to the S. Taxi to airport is US$6.

Road There are a regular buses and minbuses travelling into Mogadishu from around the country. Bus stand near the market on Soqaamadin St.

Sea Dhows sometimes travel from Mombasa or Lamu to Mogadishu depending on winds and time of year.

NORTH TO DJIBOUTI

Baidoa

This town is 200 km NW of Mogadishu, en route to Dolo in Ethiopia. The full name is Isha Baidoa, and *isha* means an eye in Somali. 2 springs, which emerge from an opening shaped like an eye in the rocks, form an attractive cascade. There are vineyards, a distinctive mosque, and a busy market. There are plenty of cheap hotels in town, and minibuses run daily to Baidoa from the bus station near the market in Mogadishu on Soqaamadin St.

Berbera

Ancient seaport, now rather dilapidated, with a population of 65,000. The British used to ship fresh fruit and vegetables from here across to their base in Aden. There are some fine beaches, and in more peaceful times it has been the main holiday resort in the northern region, particularly popular during the cooler months of Jul, Aug and Jan, Feb. There are the ruins of an **Egyptian Mosque** from the Khedive era. There are the remains of the Egyptian **Old Fort** just to the S of Shaab Square, and the **Aqueduct,** 10 km long, which brought water to the Old Fort, can still be seen. Also the **Residence** of the first British Governor, is off Shaab Square, and the old **Coast Club**.

• **Where to stay** **C** *Sahel* Air conditioning in all double rooms. **E** *Saaxil* Fans. Good value. **E** *Wabera* Clean and cheap.

• **Places to eat** There are many small eating places offering sea food which, as you would expect, is very fresh. Around US$3 will buy you fish, rice and salad. There are more expensive restaurants along the seafront where an excellent spaghetti will cost around US$5. It is best to avoid the water here.

• **Transport** **Air** Somali Airlines used to run a daily flight. **Road** There is transport from Mogadishu and the journey takes about 3 days. There are a number of minibuses between Berbera and Hargeisa along a paved road. The route takes about 4 hours including a stop for lunch. **Sea** In normal times it was possible to travel by dhow to Djibouti, S to Mogadishu and on, and across to Aden.

Hargeisa

Hargeisa is the former capital of British Somaliland, with a population of 70,000, situated in the highlands of the N. It contains the **Sheikh Maddar's Tomb**, the original founder of the town. The **Hargeisa Club** overlooks the river from the S in the western end of town, and the old **Government House** is just over the bridge. The old **Post Office**, and the **Secretariat** are close by. A little further E is the **Old Hospital**, the **High Court** and the **Somali Club**. Just S of the

BURTON ON BERBERA

'The "Mother of the Poor" as the Arabs call the place, in position resembles Zeila. The town – if such a name can be given to what is now a wretched clump of dirty mat-huts – is situated on the northern edge of alluvial ground, sloping almost imperceptibly from the base of the southern hills. The rapacity of these short-sighted savages has contracted its dimensions to one-sixth of its former extent: for nearly a mile around the desert land is strewn with bits of glass and broken pottery. Their ignorance has chosen the worst position: *Mos Majorum* is the Somali code, where the father built there son builds, and there shall grandson build. To the S and E lies a saline sand flat, partially overflowered by high tides: here are the wells of bitter water, and the filth and garbage make the place truly offensive.'

Sir Richard Burton *First Footsteps in East Africa* (1856).

Hargeisa Club was the old **Italian Club,** and further to the E was the cinema, barracks and a polo ground. Hargeisa is currently the capital of the self-proclaimed Republic of Somaliland.

Local information

● Where to stay

D *Hargeisa Club* Was the old British club and has an atmosphere that harks back to that era.

E *Oriental* Not a very high standard. **E** *Daali* Simple. **E** *Maaweel*. **E** *State House* is just outside town and *camping* is available there.

● Places to eat and drink

♦♦♦*Gouleds* The food is good but expensive.
♦♦*Lake Victoria Restaurant* Charcoal grills. shish kebabs and chips as well as cold drinks on offer.
♦*Oriental* Has a quite serviceable restaurant.

LIFE IN ZEILA

In 1854, Sir Richard Burton spent twenty-six days in Zeila, gathering together provisions and transport for a journey to Harar in Abyssinia. His first sight of the town, as the dhow crossing from Aden entered the harbour, was of a 'strip of sand with a deep blue dome above and a foreground of the darkest indigo'. The buildings rose high, apparently from the bosom of the deep, a spectacle of whitwashed houses and minarets, peering above a long, low brown wall flanked by round towers.

In Zeila, Burton was entertained by the governor, al-Hajj Sharkamaky bin Ali Salih, in one of his houses. The ground floor was a warehouse with bales, boxes and scales. On the first floor was a prepared room, the walls whitewashed, the floor spread with mats and cushions, with a *kursi* or cot covered with Persian rugs and gaudy silk and satin pillows.

Burton settled into a routine of of rising at dawn and observing his neighbours from the terrace, at their devotions. At 6 a breakfast of sour graincakes and roast mutton, followed by coffee and pipes. In the morning visitors were received and business transacted. At eleven, fresh water arrived from the wells, followed by dinner of exceedingly greasy mutton stew, boiled rice, maize cakes, fish, curds and milk. Then coffee, pipes and a siesta. From 2pm there were more visitors and business until sundown at 5pm, when it was time for a walk eastwards along the shore for a game of draughts by the mosque, a bit of musket target-practice, spear-throwing or gymnastics.

After exercise the stroll continued round the walls to the southern gate where young lads playhockey with sticks and stones. Outside the gates wass a camp of Beduoins. These people werre a 'spectacle of savageness'. Their heads a shock of red-dyed hair, dripping with rancid butter, stuck with a 3-pronged comb and an ostrich feather if the wearer had 'killed his man'.

At sunset the gates were locked, a 'vain precaution when a donkey could clear half-a-dozen places in the town wall'. The strollers return home to the sound of the call to evening prayers. None of Burtons's companions attend to their devotions, excusing themselves with 'if Allah please, tomorrow'.

Supper wass similar to the midday meal, after which they repaired to the roof to enjoy the prospect of the far Tajjurah hills across the water, the 'white moonbeams sleeping on the sea'. The evening star hangs like a diamond on the still horizon, around the moon a pink zone of light mist, shading off to turquoise blue and delicate green. Behind, purpling in the night air and silvered by the radiance above, lie the wolds and mountains. 'Sweet as the harp of David, the night breeze and the music of the water come up from the sea: but the ripple and the rustling sound alternate with the hyena's laugh, the jackal's cry, and the wild dog's lengthened howl.'

● **Transport**

Air Somali Airlines used to run a daily flight, and Air Djibiouti also flew here. Now suspended.

Road From Djibouti, it is possible to hire a lift with a truck driver from Loyada (at the Djibouti Border). The journey takes about 2 days along an unpaved road. There is also transport to and from Berbera and Mogadishu (See under Berbera for details).

Zeila

On the coast close to the border with Djibouti. In the nineteenth century, Zeila in the was a more important port than Djibouti for access to Ethiopia. However, the building of the railway from Djibouti at the turn of the century heralded Zeila's decline. It has the remnants of some fine buildings, but is now mostly a transit point for vehicles travelling from Berbera and Hargeisa to Djibouti. There are some small places to stay, rather simple, and local food is available. For travel see under Berbera and Hargeisa.

SOUTH TO KENYA

Merca

The second largest town in the Benadir region after Mogadishu. Located 100 km S of the capital in an attractive coastal location and a good beach. There is some rather spartan accommodation in the town. The beach offers better prospects with some simple huts for rent. There are regular buses between Mogadishu and Kismayo which pass through.

Brava

Just off the road S from Mogadishu to Kismayo is the old Arab town of Brava. It was ransacked by the Portuguese in the twelfth century, and never recovered its former position. It serves as a port for the export of produce from the agricultural area between the Juba and Shabelle rivers, particularly bananas and citrus fruit. Fine beaches. The **E** *Kolombo* is at the entrance to the town. There are regular buses between Mogadishu and Kismayo which pass through.

Kismayo

Pleasant coastal town, with a population of 70,000, built in Arab-Portuguese style, with some fine beaches. A very attractive place to stay. It is the main centre for the National Park (see page 656) and the Reserves in the S. The vegetable **market** in town is colourful and the fish on sale is particularly cheap, although you will need to bargain. The **Old Port** has some distinguished buildings, and there is a fine **Town Square**.

Off the shore are the **Bajuni Islands**. It is possible to hire a boat at the Old Port to take you across. The islands contain ruins of early settlements, dating back to the Shirazi migrations (see page 278).

Local information

● Where to stay

C *Wamoo* Located just out of the centre, on the road to Mogadishu on the shore. This is a good quality hotel offering chalet-style accommodation set in attractive parkland with monkeys and ostriches. There is a disco here on Fri nights. **C** *Quilmawaaye* Close to centre of town. Peasant setting in a well-kept garden.

● Places to eat

♦♦*Quilmawaaye* Spaghetti and international food. Reasonable standard. ♦*Shoreline Restaurant* Charcoal grills. Good value.

● Transport

Air Somali Airlines used to run a daily flight from Mogadishu, now suspended.

Road There is a bus between Kismayo and *Mogadishu* each day. It leaves Kismayo at 0600 from the square next to the police station. There are several daily buses going from Kismayo to Liboi on the *Kenyan border*. The distance is about 200 km, and although slow, the sandy track is fairly smooth. The trip takes at least 6 hours, and costs about US$8.

Liboi

Lively transit and market town, always with a lot of cattle herders passing through. Local food available. There is cheap accommodation on both the Somali and Kenyan side, but it is very spartan. For travel see under Kismayo, above.

NATIONAL PARKS AND GAME RESERVES

Somalia's diverse environment houses a wide variety of wildlife from those which live in semi-arid surroundings to the more typical East African species. Most of the country's wildlife is found in the S around the 2 perennial rivers, the Juba and the Shabelle, where it is possible to see all the 'big nine': lion, elephant, rhino, hippos, giraffe, zebra, leopards, cheetah, and buffalo. Also greater and lesser kudu, hartebeeste, oryx, Soemmering's gazelle, Speke's gazelle, Waller's gazelle, Clark's gazelle, beira, wart-hogs, monkeys and baboons. In the drier northern regions there are oryx and wild ass.

Birds to be seen in the parks include bright bee-eaters, king-fishers, eagles, kites, and storks. Game birds are guinea fowl, yellow-necked geese, partridges, sand-grouse, rock-pigeons and bustards.

Somali has 3 game parks. The 2 best established are are Kismayo National Park and Hargeisa National Park. The Gezira National Park, close to the S-W of Mogadishu and with a fine beach, is more recent and facilities are less well developed. The 10 game reserves were undergoing improvements before the current disturbances. There are absolute game reserves at Lac Badana (where a new lodge was being constructed), Gedka-Dabley, Mogadishu and Mandere. Controlled game reserves have been established at Borama, Bush Bush (where a new lodge was being constructed) and Juba; and partial game reserves at Jowhar, Beled, Weyne and Bulo-Burti.

Fishing

This is possible in both the Juba and Shabelle rivers, and they also contain many crocodiles. The **hunting** season runs from 31 Jul to 1 Mar each year. Prior to independence, Somalia was one of the great big-game hunting areas of Africa, particularly the area round Afmadu in the Kismayo National Park. When Somalia regains stability, safaris and licences can be arranged through the Kenyan hunting safari companies (see page 68).

Kismayo National Park

This is in the SW of the country and contains a great profusion of animals with all the species you would expect to see in East Africa, including all the 'big nine', as well as some rarer ones including Soemmering gazelle, the Speke gazelle and the Somali dibtag.

Hargeisa Game Park

To the N of Hargeisa bordering the Gulf of Aden has some rare animals such as the wild ass and the klipspringer.

INFORMATION FOR VISITORS

Contents

Before you go

Entry requirements

● Visas

All visitors require visas. You cannot get a visa at the border, or at the airport, so you will need to arrange this in advance. It is not possible to get a Somali visa from the UK unless you will be working there or have an invitation from the Somali government. However, it is possible to obtain one from a number of embassies in North and East Africa including Egypt, Kenya, Djibouti and Tanzania.

● Vaccinations

Yellow fever and cholera vaccination certificates are required. If you do not have one, the authorities may insist on vaccinating you there and then. It is wise to vaccinate against smallpox though this is not a mandatory requirement. It is also advisable to protect against tetanus, typhus and typhoid though not essential. See general section on Health, page 21).

● Representation overseas

Djibouti Visas are readily obtainable from the Consulate in Djibouti (Boulevard del Republique BP 549, T 35 35 21) require 3 photographs plus a letter of introduction from your embassy, and take 24 hours to issue. They are valid for up to 3 months and are multiple entry.

Egypt Dokki Street, Cairo. You will only be able to obtain a visa if you are travelling by air and have **onward** air tickets. No overland visas are issued. They take 24 hours to issue, require 3 photographs and a letter of recommendation from your embassy.

Kenya International House, Mama Ngina Street, Nairobi. You can obtain a 3 month visa and need to supply 3 photographs and a letter of introduction. The visa takes 24 hours to issue.

Tanzania Issued by the Italian Embassy (Lugalo Rd PO Box 2106 T46352/4). A 3 month multiple entry visa is issued with the same requirements as mentioned above.

● Overseas representation in Somalia

Following the overthrow of Siad Barre in Jan 1991, all foreign embassies in Somali were closed and all diplomatic personnel left the country. Some embassies were reopened in Dec 1992 following the introduction of the US-led United Task Force, including the French, Sudanese and US embassies. It is best to check on the situation of your own embassy before leaving.

All the embassies are based in Mogadishu the capital (see page 650).

When to go

● Best time to visit

The cooler months are Jul, Aug and Jan, Feb.

Health

● Staying healthy

Malaria is a huge problem throughout the country and even if you take precautions against it, you may still contract the virus. If this happens, it is best to get to the nearest refugee aid centre rather than a Somali hospital. Until recently Somalia was virtually free from yellow fever, smallpox and sleeping sickness, but it is wise to protect against them now. Do not drink any water unless it has been boiled or sterilised (see general Health section, page 21).

Money

● Currency

The unit of currency is the Somali shilling (SS), which is nominally divided into 100 cents. However, the value of the currency has depreciated so dramatically since 1981 (when it was SS6.3 = US$1) that the cent is reduced to a historical curiosity of old coins.

In August 1994 the exchange rate was US$1 = SS2,602.

There is a black market where US dollars and Saudi rials are the most sought-after hard currencies.

When normal customs post and border checks were in operation, currency declaration forms may not automatically be issued at border crossings, it is wise to ask for one to avoid any problems changing money at banks. It has been known for people to be referred to the customs office from banks if they do not have one. You will have to purchase the form if you arrive by air, the fee is nominal. Make sure you declare all your money as you are likely to be searched thoroughly.

● Credit cards

These are only accepted by the airlines.

● Cost of living

Due to the devaluation of the Somali shilling, the country is a cheap place to visit

Getting there

● Air

Somalia was served by the following airlines: Air Djibouti, Alitalia, Aeroflot, Al Yamda, Ethiopian Airlines, Kenya Airways and Somali Airlines. There were 2 flights a week between Nairobi, Kenya and Mogadishu on Sun (Kenya Airways) and on Sun (Somali Airlines). All these services are now suspended.

● Road

The border crossings between Somalia and Ethiopia are closed due to diplomatic problems between the 2 countries. If you are coming from **Kenya**, the crossing point is Liboi (Kenya) to Kisimayo (Somalia) from which there are several daily buses. The road is just a track through scrubland. There is another route from Lugh to Garissa in Kenya via Mandera though this route is less reliable. Buses are unreliable, but it is possible to hire a lift on a truck.

Djibouti's border crossing is from Loyada (Djibouti) through Zeila to Hargeisa. The route from Berbera to Zeila is less good and less frequently travelled. Again buses are unreliable, and it is usually necessary to negotiate a lift with a truck. The road is unpaved so the journey is slow and uncomfortable but it is probably the most scenic route in the country.

● Sea

There are a number of dhows plying their trade up and down the coast from Djibouti down to Kenya. If you want to take this trip, you will need to enquire at the ports in Berbera, Mogadishu and Kismayo. The journey takes about a week from Djibouti to Mogasishu and 3 days Mogadishu to Lamu in Kenya. The dhows travel with the Trade Winds, which blow from S to N Apr to Sep, and N to S for the other 6 months.

When you arrive

● Drugs

A note of caution Qat is a feature of everyday life in Somalia. The leaves of this plant are a type of amphetamine and produces a mild stimulant. It is widely available throughout the country, but is officially illegal.

● Hours of business

Banks are open from Sat to Thu, from 0800 to 1130. Government offices are open Sat to Thur from 0800 to 1400. Offices and shops times are Sat to Thu from 0900 to 1300 and 1600 to 2000.

● Official time

3 hours later than GMT

● Photography

At the best of times, taking photographs in Somalia needs to be done with care. Prior to 1991, it was necessary to have a permit. To get a permit it was necessary to produce 3 photographs plus 2 copies of your Somali visa and pay around US$2 to the National Censorship Office on Birimo Luuliy St, near the American Embassy in Mogadishu.

● Religion

Nearly all Somalis are Sunni Muslim. There is an Italian-built Roman Catholic cathedral in the capital, Mogadishu.

Where to stay

● Hotels

Outside the 4 main towns, there are very few hotels to stay in and what there is varies in quality quite considerably. If you are unmarried, it is best to pretend you are if you intend to share a double room. If you intend to sleep out in the desert remember to take a warm sleeping bag as it gets cold at night. There is a system of Government resthouses in some of the out-of-the-way places which provide cheap dormitory-style accommodation.

Food and drink

Hotel Classifications

A+ Over US$100 a night. International standards and decor, air conditioning, self contained rooms, swimming pool, restaurants, bars, business services.

A US$40-100. First class standards, air-conditioning, attached bathrooms, restaurants and bars, swimming pool.

B US$20-40. Tourist class, comfortable with air conditioning or fans, attached barthrooms, restaurant, bar, public rooms.

C US$10-20. Budget, fans, shared bathroom facilities.

D US$5-10. Guest house, no fan, shared bathroom, cold water.

E Under US$5. Basic guest house, simple bed, no soap or towels, no wardrobe, shared bathroom facilities, erratic cold water supply, no fans or mosquito nets.

Food and drink

The food shows signs of the Italian influence with macaroni, spaghetti and rice being the staple foods in many parts of the country. Sheep and goat meat is also widely available, though more expensive. Vegetables are often not available in small local restaurants. A popular local breakfast is fried liver (sheep, goat or camel) with onions and bread. *Mofu* is the local bread which is unleavened quite like a chapati. Seafood, particularly lobsters, prawns and squid are excellent and reasonably priced.

Tea and coffee are the standard drink served throughout the country. Alcohol is available though expensive, and mostly imported. There is a locally-produced rum.

Eating Classifications

♦♦♦♦ Over US$10 for a meal. A 3-course meal in a restaurant with pleasant decor. Beers, wines and spirits available.

♦♦♦ US$5-10 for a meal. Two courses, not including alcohol, reasonable surroundings.

♦♦ US$2-5 for a meal, probably only a single course, surroundings spartan but adequate.

♦ Under US$2. Single course, often makeshift surroundings such as a street kiosk with simple benches and tables.

Getting around

● Air

There used to be 2 flights a week between Berbera in the N and Mogadishu on Somali Airlines. There were also flights to Kisimayo in the S and Hargeisa in the N leaving once a week on Tuesdays. These are now suspended.

● Road

There are surfaced roads between Mogadishu, Kisimayo and Baidoa in the S. and Hargeisa, Berbera and Burao in the N. In other parts of the country the roads are either gravel or just tracks but are usually passable except in the wet season. There is a network of buses in the S of the country but very few in the N. It is extremely difficult to travel from the N (Berbera and Hargeisa) to the S (Mogadishu).

Lifts with the relief agencies used to be advertised at UNHCR (United Nations High Commission for Refugees) in Mogadishu. The Anglo-American Club is also a good place to look for lifts, as is GTZ, the German aid agency.

● Taxi and car hire

In most of the larger cities there are taxi services, though they are quite expensive. In Mogadishu there are both regular cabs and motor scooters. Taxis can be hired by the hour, but it is wise to fix the rate beforehand. If you have an international driver's licence, you can hire a drive yourself car in Mogadishu.

Communications

● Language

Somali is the official language. English is spoken in many parts of the N and some Italian in the S.

● Telephone Services
International phone calls are quite reasonable in price and the service is efficient.

Entertainment

● Newspapers
The Country a daily paper in English; *Heegan* a weekly paper published in English; *New Era* published weekly in Italian and Arabic; *Rajo Newspaper* set up by the US-led United Task Force; *Xiddigta Oktobar* a daily paper in Somali.

● Radio
There are 4 radio stations within the country and one outside. The *Voice of Peace* was set up in 1993 based in Ethiopia to promote peace and reconstruction in Somalia. In Mogadishu there is the *Somali Broadcasting* service transmitting in Somali, English, Italian, Arabic, Swahili, Amharic, Galla and Afar, the *Radio Manta* set up in 1993 by the US-led United Task Force and *Radio Mogadishu*, the Voice of the Great Somali People set up in 1993 by General Aidid. In Hargeisa there is Radio Hargeisa serving Somaliland and it broadcasts in Somali and Amharic.

● Television
Programmes are transmitted for 2 hours a day in Somali and Arabic, extended to 3 hours on Fridays and bank holidays. Transmission is limited to within a 30 km radius of Mogadishu.

Holidays and festivals

1 Jan	New Year's Day
1 May	Labour Day
Apr	Eid al-Fitre*
26 Jun	Independence of Somaliland
1 Jul	Independence for the Somali Republic
Jul	Eid al-Arifa*
Jul	Hijra*
Aug	Ashoura*
21-22 Oct	Anniversary of the 1969 Revolution
Oct	Prophet's Birthday*

*Holidays whose dates vary as they are based on the lunar calendar.

Further reading

● History
Lewis, I M. 1965. *The Modern History of Somalia: From Nation to State.* New York: Praeger. Thorough account of Somalia's history.

● Travellers' Tales
Burton, R. 1856 *First Footsteps in East Africa* Gordon Waterfield (ed.) 1966. London: Routledge and Kegan Paul. Detailed, scholarly and beautifully written account of travel through Somalia in 1854 to visit Harar.

● Other guides
Kaplan, I. et al. 1977 *Area handbook for Somalia.* (2nd ed.) Washington DC: Government Printing Office. Sound survey of geography, history, society and economy.

DJIBOUTI

CONTENTS

MAPS

INTRODUCTION

Djibouti is a small country sandwiched between Eritrea, Ethiopia and Somalia consisting of little more than a port at the S entrance to the Red Sea. Its importance increased dramatically during both the Gulf War and the UN intervention in Somalia when it acted as a base for allied troops. The capital, Djibouti houses over half the population of the country acting as an international transit port and refuelling centre. Although some people visit the country for its desert scenery, interesting sea life and fine white sand beaches, most people are simply passing through to other countries in the area.

Exchange rate in August 1994 US$1= DFr 176.5

Environment

Geography

The country covers an area of 21,783 sq km, most of which is volcanic rock-strewn desert wastes with occasional patches of arable land and spectacular salt lakes. The physical core consists of a triangular depression which is part of the East African rift system and is made up of a complex pattern of volcanic plateau, sunken plains and lakes (most of which are salty). Much of the territory is below sea level – millions of years ago this area was ocean floor but submarine volcanic activity caused rock and lava formations to develop into what is there today. There are vast deposits of salt around the country which are mined, mainly by the Afar, and used throughout the region.

Vegetation in the country is spartan and seasonal and comprises mainly grasses, thorn trees and scattered palms. The only part of the country with continuous annual vegetation is the upper part of the basaltic range, N of the Gulf of Tadjourah where the altitude reaches more than 1,200m above sea level. The poor quality of the soil and the arid climate prevents any large scale crop production.

Climate

The climate is tropical with high temperatures and humidity during the monsoon season. Average rainfall is less than 125 mm per annum, and temperatures can reach as high as 45°C. The country is particularly parched between Jun and Aug when temperatures are at their highest, and the dusty *khamsin* blows from the desert. It is cooler between Oct and Apr with occasional light rains.

History

The area known as Djibouti was only sparsely populated by nomadic peoples, mainly the Afars and the Issas who used it as grazing land, until the French became interested in its strategic value in 1859. The initial interest by the French in the area was to counteract the British trading presence in Aden on the other side of the Babel-Mandeb Straits stimulated by the desire of both countries to control the entrance to the Red Sea. In 1862 they established themselves in Obock on the coast and drew up a treaty with Afar leaders, the Sultans of Obock and Tadjourah, to legitimise their acquisition of the coastal region in the N. In 1888 the construction of Djibouti began. Treaties in 1884, 1885 and 1896 with the Afars, the Issas and Emperor Menelik of Ethiopia eventually led to the establishment of the boundaries of French Somaliland (later to be known as Djibouti). The establishment of the boundaries was made without any consideration to the ethnic links, language, trading patterns or even traditional grazing rights of the Afar or Issa people. The problems caused by these issues continue to dominate politics.

In a treaty in 1897, the French made an agreement with Emperor Menelik which designated Djibouti as the 'official outlet of Ethiopian commerce' and led to the building of a railway from Djibouti to Addis Ababa which would act as the major trade route into Ethiopia. The railway was completed in 1915 and from this point on, the port of Djibouti and the trade route has become the mainstay of the Djibouti economy. The railway is of vital strategic and commercial importance to Ethiopia and it is for this reason that Ethiopia is hostile to the idea of a merger between Somalia and Djibouti.

The French had habitually supported the Issas in the region but the anti-colonial demonstrations, which started as early as 1949 by the Somalis and Issas, eventually meant that in the 1960's the French switched their support to the Afar, with their strong Ethiopian links, in order to counter Somali government claims to the territory. This also served to strengthen Emperor Haile Selassie in Ethiopia, who was seen as an ally. As a result of the switch of allegiance, the French placed the Afar, Ali Aref and his Afar colleagues in control of the local government council, displacing the previous Issa administration.

In 1967 a referendum was held to determine if the people of Djibouti wished to remain a colony of France. Electoral manipulation condoned by the French meant the country remained a French overseas territory with the Afar dominating local politics. The vote was achieved by arresting opposition leaders and by the massive expulsion of Somalis, many of whom went on to join the Somali Coast Liberation Front. In 1973 the Afar still dominated local politics and reaffirmed Djibouti's links with France but by the mid 1970's Issa opposition to Afar rule grew, culminating in an assasination attempt on the Afar leader, Ali Aref in 1975.

International pressure from the Arab League and the OAU, local unrest and the increasingly turbulent situation in the horn of Africa eventually led to the French withdrawing from Djibouti in 1976. An independent referendum was held in which a predominantly Issa assembly was elected headed by Hassan Gouled, leader of the Ligue Populaire Africaine pour l'Independance (LPAI).

Independence did not bring harmony to the former colony and tensions between the Afar and Issa have abounded over the last 15 years. Hostilities broke out in the late 1980's after Aden Robleh Abwalleh, a former cabinet minister was expelled from the party for opposing Hassan Gouled and the existing regime. Abwalleh fled the country and formed a new opposition party,

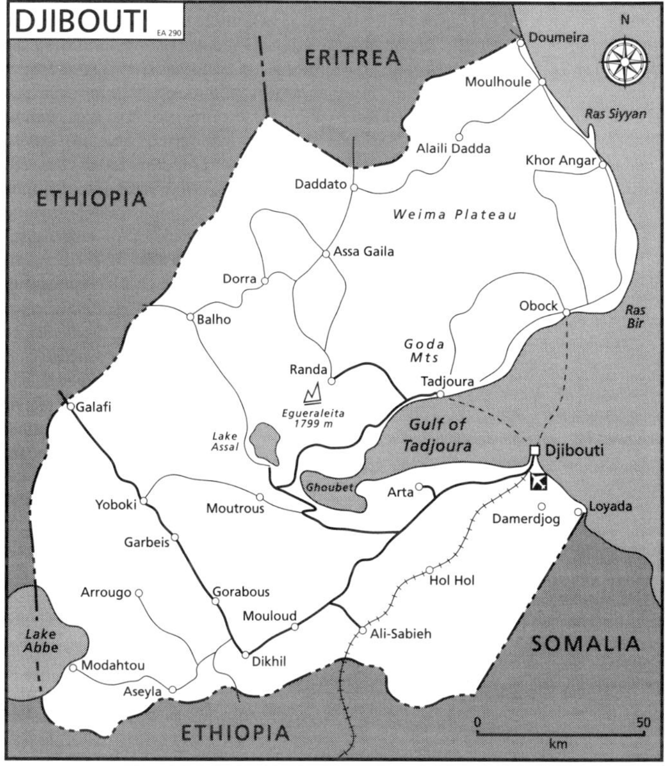

the Mouvement National Djiboutien pour l'Instauration de la Démocratie (MNDID). Inter-tribal hostilities erupted in Djibouti city in 1989 and in the Afar town of Tadjourah. Security forces subsequently arrested several hundred people, some of whom were deported. From 1990-1992 a number of opposition parties were formed to press for political reform. Among these was the Front pour la Restauration de l'Unité et de la Democratie (FRUD), an Afar-based group committed to armed conflict. FRUD suffered a set-back from a determined government assault in Jul 1993, and has now retreated to the mountains in the N.

A new constitution was drawn up in 1992 and multi-party system has been introduced. Gouled was re-elected as president of the country and many opposition leaders have been released from custody. Djibouti still has close links with France and over 3,500 French troops remain on its territory.

Culture and life

The population of the country is thought to be around 500,000 though seasonal migrations of the nomadic peoples who make up about half the population of the country make any accurate figures hard to estimate.

The indigenous population of Djibouti is evenly divided between the Issa who are of Somali origin and mainly occupy the S part of the country, and the Afar who live in the N part of the country. Both the Afar and the Issa are Muslim Cushitic-speaking peoples with a nomadic culture and close cultural affinities despite frequent rivalry. Both groups spill across the artificial boundaries of Djibouti into neighbouring Somalia and Ethiopia. There are also many refugees, about 30,000, who have fled into the country as a result of various wars in neighbouring Ethiopia, Ogaden and Somalia. Expatriates, mostly French, make up the rest of the popula-

THE WHITE TRAIN AND THE BLACK ARROW

Emperoer Menelik II, the architect of modern Ethiopia, conceived the idea of a rail line from Djibouti to Addis Ababa. A pair of European engineers formed the Compagnie Imperiale des Chemins de Fer Ethiopiens, and bolstered by the Franco-Ethiopian Treaty of 1897, French financiers backed the project. Construction started the same year.

The terrain was difficult, mostly desert and mountains, and Addis Ababa is 2.5 km higher than Djibouti. Avoiding the most obstructive features added another 150 km to the line on its way up to the Ethiopian capital. Local labour was supremely uninterested in joining the work-camps building the line, and most of the labourers and all the skilled craftsmen were imported for the job. The nomads along the route gleefully took the iron rails, pins and fittings to fashion into spears, bracelets and necklaces. They grumbled about their cattle being killed by the locomotives, so the company agreed to compensate them for every animal lost. This was the signal for the pastoralists to round up every sick, halt and lame beast in the horn of Africa and lay fodder for them on the tracks.

By 1900, the line had got to Dire Dawa, and a watering post and repair workshops were established there. The traffic was limited on this stretch, and the company went bankrupt in 1907. A new company with loans guaranteed by the French goverment was formed in 1908, and a slngle line of 1 metre gauge, 748 km long, finally reached Addis Ababa in 1917.

Two trains departed in each direction each day, and stopped at 32 stations along the line. Passengers were taken in the White Train which travelled only in the day and took 2 and a half days to make the whole journey. Freight went by the Black Arrow which took 5 days, at an average speed of under 7 kph.

Having a virtual monopoly of of transport up to the capital of the Mountain Kingdom enabled the line to charge high rates, and the company was reported to be the most profitable in the entire history of railways. This was particularly the case in the period 1936-38 when the Italians were obliged to ship vast quantities of men and munitions up to Addis Ababa in their effort to subdue the country. So stung were the Italians by the charges that they built a road from Addis to the port of Assab in Eritrea (which they controlled), and imported 400 trucks to haul freight. So good was this road that the winner of the motor-cycle race staged in 1938 to inaugurate the route won at an average speed of 85 kph. Competition from the road heralded the end of the highly profitable era for the line.

When the British captured Ethiopia from the Italians in 1941, they ran the line until 1946, when ownership was restored to the original French company. In 1959, the Ethiopian government took half ownership of the railway, by which time diesel locomotives had cut the travel time up to Addis to 24 hrs.

tion and are mainly in government employment or are members of the armed forces.

Religion Largely Muslim though there are a small number of Christians.

Modern Djibouti

Politics

Since independence, politics in Djibouti have been heavily influenced by events in the neighbouring countries of Somalia and Ethiopia reflecting the sympathies of the Issa to Somalia and Afar to Ethiopia. In 1977, just after independence, tension between the 2 groups was considerable over the Ogaden war between Ethiopia and Somalia (Somalia were trying to recapture the region which had strong ethnic links with its people), with the Issa supporting Somalian interests. President Hassan Gouled used the initial Somali successes in the Ogaden war as an opportunity to remove Afars from key posts in the administration and security forces. As a result, Ethiopia reduced its trading activities through Djibouti which had negative effects on the country's economy.

The Ethiopian victory in the Ogaden war (won with Russian and Cuban support) highlighted the importance of Djibouti's links with that country and led to President Gouled to try to reach a compromise between the interests of the Issa and the Afar. Thus, the majority of Afar prisoners were released and any Afar who had been removed from office was reinstated into the civil service and security forces. Also, efforts were made to develop the N Afar region of the territory.

A further source of political and economic discontent has been the substantial flow of refugees from the Eritrean and Ogaden conflicts in Ethiopia into Djibouti since the early 1980's. The United Nations High Commission for Refugees (UNHCR) has begun a programme to repatriate Ethiopian refugees, said to number about 35,000, but has only had limited success. This problem has been exacerbated by the number of immigrants flooding in from Somalia – by 1993 these were estimated to number 120,000. Djibouti has attempted to tighten its border controls and the checking of identity papers, but has not really succeeded in materially stemming the flow. The high influx of peoples not only places an economic burden on the country, but is also a source of insecurity as it damages the balance between the Issa and Afar.

Djibouti's geographical position, and limited natural resource base, has meant that good relations with its neighbours are essential. Since 1985, Djibouti has developed agreements with Ethiopia and Somalia for closer co-operation in transport, communication and trade. It has played an important role in developing diplomatic relations between Ethiopia and Somalia, firstly by promoting the creation of the Intergovernmental Authority on Drought and Development with a permanent secretariat in Djibouti, and secondly by bringing heads of state of the 2 countries to meet and agree to re-establish diplomatic relations and withdraw troops from their common borders.

Economics

Economic data is sparse for Djibouti, and such that there is tends to be almost a decade out of date. Nevertheless, such information as is available is presented and gives a reasonable overall picture of economic conditions in the territory.

Economic structure

Estimates for 1994 suggest a population of around half a million. It is thought that over 100,000 of these are refugees from Somalia, but it is difficult to be certain as to the exact numbers. There is a density of 21.7 persons to the square kilometre, and although this is not greatly different from elsewhere in Africa, it has to be viewed in the context of Djibouti's arid terrain. Population growth is 5.6% for the period 1960-1991, very high, and kept at this level by regular influxes of refugees from troubled neighbouring states. About half of the population live in the town of Djibouti which has a population of over 300,000.

GDP was estimated at US$327m in 1982, and only Comoros and Seychelles in East Africa have smaller economies. GNP per head in 1990 was roughly estimated at US$1,000 and this compares very favourably, with only Mauritius, Seychelles, Réunion and Mayotte and having higher average incomes per head. This places Djibouti in the lower-middle income country grouping.

The economy relies heavily on the port facilities it provides, and this is reflected in the supply-side structure of the economy with agriculture providing only 4% of GDP, industry 19% and services 75%. Only Seychelles has a comparable supply structure, with services the leading growth sector, in the East African grouping.

The demand structure of the economy for 1982, the latest year for which figures are available, indicates that private consumption represents 70% of GDP. Gross domestic investment absorbed 25% of GDP, and this is a high investment ratio, exceeded only by Comoros in East Africa, while government consumption was 38% of GDP, again high. The openness of the economy resulting from small size and specilised activities is reflected in 35% of GDP being generated by exports. Expenditure on imports is equivalent to 68% of GDP. The gap is mainly covered by foreign assistance with France the main benefactor.

The nominal figure for adult literacy in 1990 was 19%, the lowest in East Africa. Literacy has improved, although with only 44% of the relevant age group in primary schooling, educational effort is desperately low compared to other lower-middle income countries where almost every child is enrolled. Secondary enrolments are by contrast again poor for a lower-middle income country, with 15% of the relevant age group in secondary education. There are negligible enrolments in higher education. The pattern of enrolments and the low overall literacy indicate a marked contrast between the urban areas where there is good provision going through to the end of secondary education, and the rural areas where educational provision is poor.

Life expectancy in 1986 was projected at 48 years, again low for a lower-middle income country. Food supply compares well at an average of 2,400 calories a day, whereas the East African average is 2,100. The number of doctors in 1987 was one for every 4,180 persons, low for a lower-middle income country. Poor medical provision is exacerbated for the those in most need by the disparity between the urban areas and the rural parts of the country.

Overall, Djibouti has a small economy with high urbanisation, moderate population density and a rapid increase in population due to the inflow of refugees. Income levels are in the lower-middle income range. The economy depends heavily on the supply of port services, levels of government expenditure appear high, and there is a substantial deficit on the current account of the balance of payments. Educational and health provision are poor.

Economic performance

GDP is estimated to have grown at 0.8% a year in the period 1973-82, and this implies a fall in GDP per head at an annual rate of -4.8%. Indications are that falls in GDP have been experienced in recent years. The 1973-82 record for GDP per head growth is the worst in East Africa, and this is mostly due to the influx of refugees leading to such a large increase in the population, allied to stagnant demand for port services from Ethiopia.

At the sectoral level, agriculture achieved a growth rate of 5.6% in 1973-84, keeping pace with population growth. The industry sector contracted at -2.1% a year, while the service sector grew at 2.5% a year. Export volumes declined at -0.4% a year, although merchandise exports are very modest, being only US$9 million in 1982. Merchandise import volumes expanded at 5.1% a year, and this is rather more significant as merchandise imports were US$225 million in 1982.

COMPARATIVE ECONOMIC AND SOCIAL DATA

	Djibouti	East Africa	Africa	Industrial countries
Population and land				
Population, mid year, millions, 1994	0.5	12.2	10.2	40.0
Urban population, %, 1982	81	31	30	75
Population growth rate, % per year, 1960-91	5.6	3.1	3.1	0.8
Land area, thou sq km	23	486	486	1,628
Population density, persons per sq km, 1994	21.7	24.2	20.4	24.3
Economy: production & income				
GDP, US$ millions, 1982	327	2,650	3,561	550,099
GNP per head, US$, 1990	1,000	250	389	12,960
Economy: supply structure				
Agriculture, % of GDP, 1982	4	43	35	3
Industry, % of GDP, 1982	19	15	27	35
Services, % of GDP, 1982	75	42	38	61
Economy: demand structure				
Private consumption, % of GDP, 1982	70	77	73	62
Gross domestic investment, % of GDP, 1982	25	16	16	21
Government consumption, % of GDP, 1982	38	15	14	17
Exports, % of GDP, 1982	35	16	23	17
Imports, % of GDP, 1982	68	24	26	17
Economy: performance				
GDP growth, % per year, 1973-82	0.8	1.6	-0.6	2.5
GDP per head growth, % per year, 1973-82	-5.2	-1.7	-3.7	1.7
Agriculture growth, % per year, 1973-82	5.6	1.1	0.0	2.5
Industry growth, % per year, 1973-82	-2.1	1.1	-1.0	2.5
Services growth, % per year, 1973-82	2.5	2.5	-0.5	2.6
Exports growth, % per year, 1973-82	-0.4	0.7	-1.9	3.3
Imports growth, % per year, 1973-82	5.1	0.2	-6.9	4.3
Economy: other				
Inflation rate, % per year, 1973-81	12.6	23.6	16.7	5.3
Aid, net inflow, % of GDP, 1982	1.7	11.5	6.3	-
Debt service, % of Exports, 1982	13.7	18	20.6	-
Budget surplus (+), Deficit (-), 1982	0.0	-3.0	-2.8	-5.1
Education				
Primary, % of 6-11 group, 1988	44	62	76	102
Secondary, % of 12-17 group, 1989	15	15	22	93
Higher, % of 20-24 group, 1985	..	1.2	1.9	39
Adult literacy rate, %, 1990	19	41	39	99
Health and nutrition				
Life expectancy, years, 1991	48	50	50	76
Calorie supply, daily per head, 1985	2,316	2,111	2,096	3,357
Population per doctor, 1987	4,180	35,986	24,185	550

Notes: 'Africa' excludes South Africa. Dates are for the country in question, and do not always correspond with the Regional, African and Industrial averages.

Inflation 1970-81 ran at 12.6% a year. Evidence indicates that it has been even lower, at around 7.0% a year for 1980-86. This is considerably better than the East African average of 23.6% a year for the early 1980's, and has been aided by the openness of the economy.

Djibouti's growth performance has been poor, and inflow of refugees has led to sharply falling GDP per head. Sectorally, the industrial sector has performed worst, but the agriculture sector has shown a creditable rate of expansion. Growth in import volumes has been steady, and price stability has been good.

Recent Economic Developments

The completion of a new container terminal in 1984, at a cost of US$142 million, is expected to be the country's major source of revenue up to the end of the 1990's. Customs-free port facilities are offered for storage and freight in transit. Traffic with Ethiopia fell by 70% after the 1977-78 Ogaden war, and Djibouti hoped to increase trans-shipment traffic to other regional ports to compensate for this loss. However, results have been disappointing. Port up-grading has continued, and tonnage handled almost doubled in 1990 as a result of the Gulf War. France is providing US$8 million for dock modernisation and management improvement.

Parastatal organisations have accumulated arrears, with the airport US$2.8 million behind with payments to creditors on a US$22 million upgrading programme. Air Djibouti has an accumulated deficit of US$4 million.

Two geothermal drillings of a 4-well US$16.6 million drilling programme have not yielded water of high enough temperature in the Hanle Gaggade region to make them commercially viable, but later drillings in the Goubet-Lac-Assal region appear more promising. It is hoped that the wells could meet Djibouti's electricity needs, and the programme is being funded by the International Development Association of the World Bank, Italy, the African Development Bank, the OPEC Fund for International Development and the UN Development Programme.

Construction of an US$800 million petroleum refinery began in 1990, and was expected to come on-stream in 1994. This may now be delayed because of disturbances caused by FRUD's activities.

Economic outlook

It is assumed that Djibouti's stability will remain good, with continuing French support and military presence. The activities of FRUD are containable, and the government will hope support for FRUD will diminish in the new multiparty setting. Djibouti's outlook is particularly sensitive to the strength of economic recovery in Ethiopia, and there are reasons to be confident that Ethiopia will make progress in the forseeable future. The coming years should see steady economic growth, although the refugee problem will continue to hamper improvements in living standards until the Somali situation is resolved.

DJIBOUTI CITY

The city lies on a peninsula separating the Gulf of Tadjoura from the Gulf of Aden at the mouth of the Red Sea. More than half the population of the country live in Djibouti. The city is the centre of economic activity in the country as well as the administrative, political and legal centre. In recent years it has become of strategic importance to the UN and allied forces, firstly in the Gulf War and later as a base from which to go into Somalia. The city has an Arab flavour to it both in terms of its architecture and its culture. It is an expensive place to visit not geared to the needs of budget travellers.

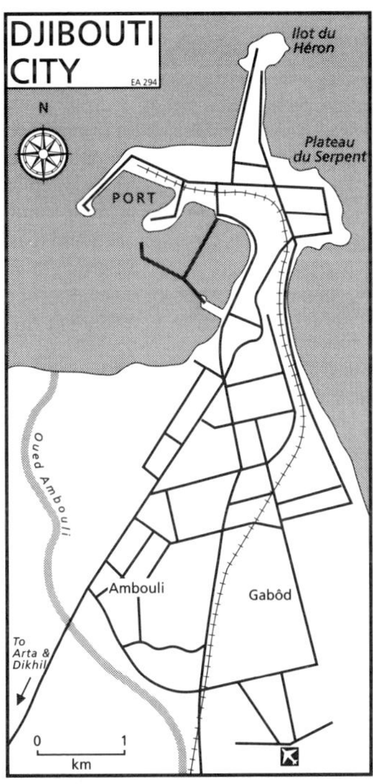

Places of interest

There is a colourful and interesting market in the centre of town near the mosque which retains elements of African, European and Arab culture. Just outside Djibouti (about 5 km) there are pleasant walks in the **Ambouli palm grove**. There are good beaches at **Dorale** (12 km) and **Khor Ambado** (15 km) though you will need a 4WD to reach the latter.

Local information

● Where to stay

There are relatively few cheap places to stay in Djibouti, and they are all situated in the African quarter of town.

A+ *Djibouti Sheraton*, PO Box 1924, T 35 04 05, F 35 58 92, Tlx 5912. A/c. Pool. Restaurant. Bars. Pleasant gardens.

A *La Siesta*, Plateau du Serpent, PO Box 508, T 35 14 92. A/c. Bars. Restaurant. **A** *Plein Ciel*, Blvd Bonheure, PO Box 1869, T 35 38 41. Pleasant location on W edge of commercial area, close to shore. A/c. Bars. Restaurant. **A** *Continental*, Place Menelik, PO Box 675, T 35 01 46. A/c Bars. Restaurant. **A** *L'Europe*, Place Menelik, PO Box 83, T 35 04 76. A/c Bars. Restaurant.

B *Djibouti Palace*, Ave General de Gaulle, PO Box 166, T 35 09 82. Eastern side of commercial centre. Overlooks railway line and bay. **B** *Relais*. Close to the airport.

C *Bienvenue*, Blvd du Bender. On the S edge of the commercial centre. **C** *Hotel de France*, Blvd de Gaulle, T 35 18 43). **C** *Doraleh*. 10 km outside the city.

● Where to eat

Restaurants in the hotels tend to be expensive, but serve good European style food. ♦♦♦♦*Restaurant Le Kintz*. French cuisine. High standard. ♦♦♦♦*Chez Mamma Elena*. High quality Italian food. ♦♦♦♦*Hanoi*. French influenced Chinese and Vietnamese cuisine.

♦♦♦*Restaurant Palmier en Zinc*. Sound French fare. ♦♦♦*Mickey Restaurant*, both serve high quality Italian food. ♦♦♦*Chez Therese*. Local Ethiopian food. ♦♦♦*Vietnam*. Chinese and Vietnamese cuisine. Friendly atmosphere.

There are a number of local restaurants serving cheap Arab and local dishes, some good ones are nr the market past the Place Mahamoud Harbi.

● Airline offices

International A number of international airlines operate to Djibouti; Air France, Air Madagascar, Yemen Airways, Al Yemda, Ethiopian Airlines, and Somali Airways. All these airlines have offices on Rue de Marseilles.

Airlines: charter There is a small private airline from which it is possible to charter a plane. Contact the Aero Club at the airport.

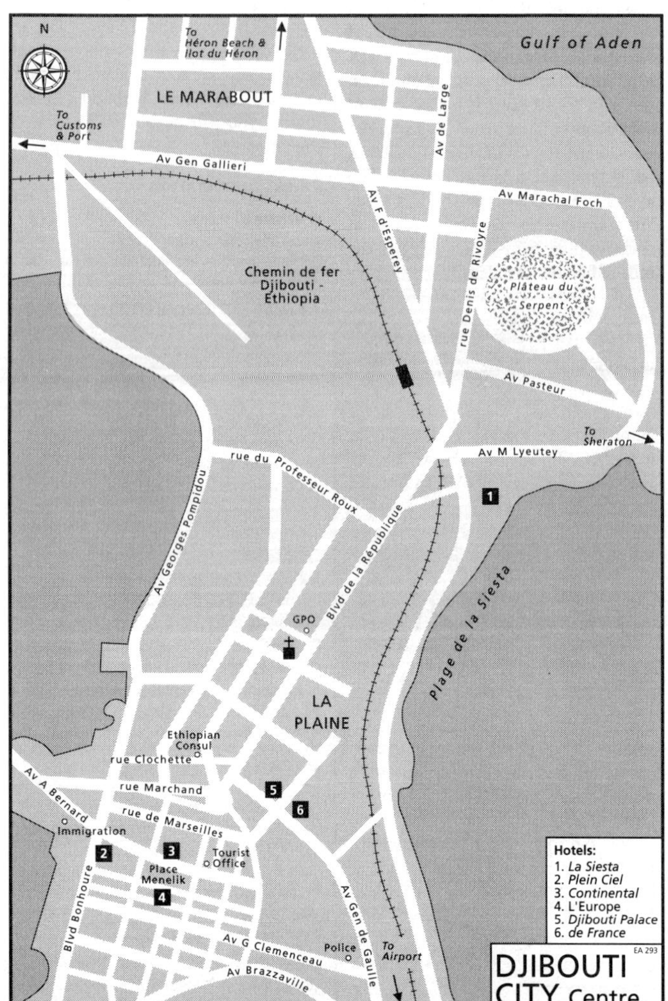

● **Banks**

There are several Bureaux de Change in the Place Menelik. The main banks are: **Banque de Djibouti et de Moyen Orient**, BP 2471; **Banque Indosuez**, Place Lagarde, PO Box 88, T 353 016; **Banque pour le Commerce et l'Industrie**, Place Lagarde, T 350 857; **British Bank of the Middle East**, Place Lagarde, T 353 291.

● **Embassies and Consulates**

* = Consulate. **Belgium***, T 35 09 60 ; **China**, T 35 22 46; **Egypt**, BP 1989, T 35 12 31; **Ethiopia**, BP 230, T 35 07 18; **France**, 45 Blvd du Marechal Foch, BP 2039, T 35 25 03/35 07 18; **Germany***, T 35 05 07; **India***, T 35 02 19; **Iraq**, BP 1983, T 35 34 69; **Italy***, T 35 11 62; **Libya**, BP 2073, T 35 33 39; **Nether-**

WAUGH IN DJIBOUTI

In 1930 the novelist Evelyn Waugh went from Djibouti to Addis Ababa by train. He was travelling to report on the coronation of Haile Selassie for *The Times* newspaper.

His first sight of the low coastline of French Somaliland, as Djibouti then was, came at dawn from the deck of the French steamship *Azay le Rideau* from Marseille. A haggard couple in evening dress were dancing to a wind-up gramophone. Sleep was impossible as the retinue of the Egyption delegation barked orders dragging around numerous tin trunks of luggage and the massive crates which contained the Egyptian gift to the Emperor, a suite of bedroom furniture.

It began to rain. Exhausted, the dancing couple slunk off to bed. Small boys hung around the deck, shivering and offering to dive for coins. Bags of coal were being hauled aboard over planks from barges. Ashore, they found the next train, in 3 day's time, was reserved in its entirety for the Duke of Gloucester. The next, in a further 3 days, was allocated to Prince Udine.

Waugh, and a traveller morbidly obsessed by the impossibility of staying healthy in the tropics, repaired to the *Hotel des Arcades*. Run by a handsome Frenchwoman it had a fading stucco façade, a few first floor bedrooms at the back facing onto a broad verandah, and hot water. In the courtyard a black monkey sat in a lemon-tree.

After lunch the rain subsided and Waugh toured the town in a one-horses cab churning through pools of steaming mud. The 'elegant and smiling boulevards' of the guidebook proved to be mere stretches of waste land between blocks of decaying buildings. A shower of stucco and bricks fell about them from one of the structures and a clutch of Indian clerks and Greek traders scampered into the street. It was an earthquake that they had not noticed due to the jolting of the cab.

The local people struck Waugh as a race of exceptional beauty, slender and tall, with delicate features and wide-set eyes. Most wore a strip of rag round the waist and a few coils of copper wire on their wrists and ankles. Heads shaven or dyed with yellow ochre. Half-a -dozen harlots besieged the cab. Naked children splashed through the mud screeching for money. Some warriors with spears spat contemptuously as they passed. At the edge of town, Waugh viewed the local dwellings which he likened to inverted birds' nests of mud, twigs, grass, rags and flattened tins with one low hole through which a man might crawl on his belly.

On returning to the hotel the travellers learned that places had been secured for them on a special train leaving that evening. Cheered up, Waugh bought a French novel with a lurid cover, some cheroots and changed some bank-notes for Marie Therese silver thalers, the massive coins minted in Vienna and the principle currency in Ethiopia. As darkness fell they chuffed and creaked slowly out of what Waugh described as 'the intolerable desolation of French Somaliland – a country of dust and boulders, utterly devoid of any sign of life'.

lands*, T 35 20 22; **Norway***, T 35 23 51; **Oman**, BP 1996, T 35 08 52; **Russia**, BP 1913, T 35 20 51; **Saudi Arabia**, BP 1921, T 35 16 45; **Somalia Blvd del Republique**, BP 549, T 35 35 21; **Sudan***, T 35 14 83; **Sweden, T 35 20 22; Yemen Arab Republic**, BP 194, T 35 29 75; **USA**, Villa Plateau du Serpent, Blvd Marechal Joffre, BP 185, T 35 39 95/35 38 49.

● Police station
Ave General de Gaulle

● Post office
Blvd de la Republique

● Religion
Almost the entire population is Muslim, consequently there are a number of mosques throughout the city. There is a Roman Catholic Church on blvd de la Republique, as well as a Greek Orthodox church and a Protestant church.

● Shopping
Curios and crafts A good place to buy souvenirs is around the Place Mahamoud Harbi though they are expensive.

● Telecommunication
Main post office on Blvd de la Republique.

● Tourist office
L'Office de Developement du Tourism, Place Menelik, BP 1938, T 35 37 90. For railway information go to Plateau-du-Serpent T35 03 53. For information on ferries to Obock and Tadjoura, Societé du Bac le Goubet, T 35 23 51.

● Tour operators and travel agents
Djibouti Tours, Blvd de Gaulle, T 35 30 22.

● Transport
Local Taxis are widely available in the city and from the airport. Tariffs increase by 50% at night.

Car hire It is possible to hire a car in Djibouti from **Hertz**, T 35 26 51 or from the airport, T 35 25 13. **Stophi**, T 35 24 94 rents out 4WD vehicles for trips into the interior of the country. It is advisable to take plenty of water and petrol on any expedition off the beaten track.

Air *Air France* has daily flights between **Paris** and Djibouti. ***Ethiopian Airways*** flies twice a week between Djibouti and **Addis Ababa** (Tue and Thu) and the fare is US$306 return. Also twice a week between Djibouti and **Asmara** (Mon and Wed). Ther are no flights currently to Somalia. ***Air Djibouti***, T 35 26 51, flies daily to **Tadjoura** and **Obock**.

As there is no bus service from the airport to the city which is 5 km S of the centre, you will need to get a taxi. There are no left luggage facilities at the airport.

Road The best roads are between Djibouti and Ethiopia especially the road towards Assab or W into Ethiopia via Dikhil. Most other roads are rough but passable throughout the year. There is a good tarmac road between Addis Ababa in Ethiopia and Djibouti.

Train A 782 km railway connects Djibouti with Addis Ababa. The trains leave daily at around 0700 and 1930, arriving in Addis approx 24 hrs later. Stops at Ali-Sabieh before the Ethiopian border and at Dire Dawa and Aouache in Ethiopia before going on to Addis Ababa. It is a long slow journey, but comfortable, with sleeping accommodation available in first class carriages.

Booking is at the railway station at the N end of Blvd de la Republique. It is necessary to make a reservation as the train is often full. The fare to Addis Ababa is US$60 1st class (a sleeper on the overnight train); US$30 2nd class; US$16 3rd class. Djibouti-Ethiopian Railroad Company, T 44 72 50.

OUTSIDE DJIBOUTI

There are a number of places which are interesting to visit around the country. **Arta** is a small summer resort used by the expatriates, situated in the mountains overlooking the Gulf of Tadjoura. It is about 40 km outside Djibouti on a sealed road. There is a good restaurant there which is part of a hotel school.

100 km SW of Djibouti is **Lake Assal**. At 153 km below sea level this dead lake is encircled by mountains and makes an interesting though somewhat eerie place to visit. The cold dead waters of the lake are surrounded by a crystal bank of salt and startlingly white gypsum. There are hot springs nearby. The road to the lake is only passable using a 4WD vehicle.

Lake Abbe near the Ethiopian border in the S W corner of the country is the home of flocks of flamingoes, ibis and pelicans. This lake has an unearthly moonlike appearance as it is surrounded with jagged needles of rock. This lake is near the town of **Dikhil**, an attractive small town perched on a rocky outcrop. The area around the town is home to many gazelle, antelope, hyenas, jackals and camels.

The mountain town of **Ali-Sabieh** makes an interesting excursion from Djibouti for those with a 4WD vehicle. This is an Issa town which has a large flourishing market. It is a major stop-over for the train between Addis Ababa and Djibouti.

The **Gulf of Tadjoura** to the N of Djibouti is a haven for those interested in aquatic life. It is possible to go skin diving, spear fishing or to do some underwater photography here as the area offers a wide variety of flora and fauna including many species of fish and different types of coral. The best time for these activities is between Sep and May when the waters of the Red Sea are at their clearest. The picturesque town of **Tadjoura** is worth a visit for its beautiful mountain setting. The **Goda Mountains** just behind the town have a wealth of rare plants and there is a fossilized forest which has been created into a national park.

INFORMATION FOR VISITORS

Contents

Before you go

Entry requirements

● Visas

All people entering Djibouti require visas except French nationals. French nationals only need a visa if intending to stay for more than 3 months. Visas are easily obtainable from Djibouti embassies around the world and are valid for 10 days. They can be renewed at the airport if necessary.

A transit visa can be obtained on arrival at the airport for nationals of Belgium, Denmark, Finland, Germany, Italy, Japan, Luxembourg, Netherlands, Norway, Sweden, UK and US. In order to get a transit visa you must have an onward ticket, if you do not, you will be forced to buy one before being granted a transit visa. The cheapest onward ticket is from Djibouti to Hargeisa in Somalia.

● Vaccinations

International certificates of vaccination against yellow fever and cholera are required. It is wise to protect against malaria.

● Djibouti representation overseas

There are very few Djibouti embassies: in Paris (France), New York (US), Cairo (Egypt), Djedda (Saudi Arabia), Addis Ababa (Ethiopia) and Mogadishu (Somalia). Visas can be obtained from French embassies in other parts of the world.

● Overseas representation in Djibouti

All embassies and consulates are based in the capital city. For list see section under Djibouti city, see page 671.

● Tourist information

Tourist Information is available from Djibouti City at **L'Office de Developpement du Tourism**, Place Menelik, BP 1938, T 35 28 00, F 35 63 22, Tlx 5938.

Travel and tour agents *Djibouti Tours*, Av General de Gaulle, T 35 30 22.

When to go

● Best time to visit

From Nov to Apr, when it is cooler with occasional showers.

● Time

3 hrs ahead of GMT

Health

● Staying healthy

Remember to protect against malaria. All water should be boiled or filtered before drinking. It may be wise to take protections against prickly heat. Clothing should be light and cotton; avoid synthetic fabrics. See general Health section, page 21.

● Water

It is quite safe to drink tap water.

Money

● Currency

The currency is the Djibouti Franc divided into 100 centimes. In 1994 the exchange rate stood at US$1 = 176.5 DFr.

Any amount of local or foreign currency may be taken into or out of the country. US dollars and French francs are widely accepted, and welcomed by the authorities. There are no money changing facilities at the airport.

● Credit cards
All major cards accepted by large hotels, restaurants and travel agents.

Getting there

If you intend to travel between Djibouti, Ethiopia or Somalia, it is best to check on access before making your travel plans.

● Air
All flights go to the capital city and flight information is on page 672.

● Train
The Djibouti-Ethiopian railway provides regular services from Addis Ababa and Dire Dawa to the capital. It is a long slow journey, but comfortable with sleeping accommodation available in first class carriages, see page 672.

● Road
There is a sealed road from Addis Ababa to Djibouti. Buses go from Djibouti to Assab in Eritrea, but it is an awkward journey through Tadjoura and Obock, and the roads are poor from Obock on. There are also road links with Somalia, with a mixture of bus and lorry transport to Hargeisa and Berbera. However, the current political situation will need to stabilise before this route becomes possible again.

● Sea
The importance of Djibouti as a port means many cargo ships dock here. In principle it should be possible to travel by boat from Marseille and Aden, although the political disturbances in Aden in 1994 rule this possibility out for the present. Djibouti has many dhows and it is possible to get to Berbera, Sudan, Karachi, Aden and the Persian Gulf this way. It is also possible to reach Djibouti by dhow from Al Mokha in North Yemen, it takes about 16 hrs and you are even able to take a car or motorcycle with you.

When you arrive

● Hours of business
Banking hrs are from Mon-Sat 0700-1200.

Where to stay

● Hotels
There are a number of first class hotels in the capital all of which are air conditioned and have restaurants, but they are expensive. There are also some cheaper hotels without a/c in the African quarter of town. In other parts of the country, accommodation for tourists or travellers is scanty.

Hotel Classifications

A+	Over US$100 a night. International standards and decor, air conditioning, self contained rooms, swimming pool, restaurants, bars, business services.
A	US$40-100. First class standards, air-conditioning, attached bathrooms, restaurants and bars, swimming pool.
B	US$20-40. Tourist class, comfortable with air conditioning or fans, attached barthrooms, restaurant, bar, public rooms.
C	US$10-20. Budget, fans, shared bathroom facilities.
D	US$5-10. Guest house, no fan, shared bathroom, cold water.
E	Under US$5. Basic guest house, simple bed, no soap or towels, no wardrobe, shared bathroom facilities, erratic cold water supply, no fans or mosquito nets.

Food and drink

There are restaurants to suit all tastes in both the capital and the main seaside resort of Arta with French, Vietnamese, Chinese and Arab cuisine. In other parts of the country simple local food (grills, stews and rice) are available.

Eating Classifications

♦♦♦♦	Over US$10 for a meal. A 3-course meal in a restaurant with pleasant decor. Beers, wines and spirits available.
♦♦♦	US$5-10 for a meal. Two courses, not including alcohol, reasonable surroundings.
♦♦	US$2-5 for a meal, probably only a single course, surroundings spartan but adequate.
♦	Under US$2. Single course, often makeshift surroundings such as a steet kiosk with simple benches and tables.

Getting around

● Air
There are domestic flights on Air Djibouti to Tadjoura and Obock each day. It is possible to charter a plane, (see details under Djibouti City, page 670).

● Train

The railway between Djibouti and Ethiopia makes stops in Djibouti at Hol Hol, Daasbiyo and Ali-Sabieh.

● Road

Public transport is limited. Hiring a car is a good option for travelling around the country by road. Over two-thirds of the roads are not surfaced, and half are only usable by lorries or 4WD vehicles. There are now roads linking the capital, Djibouti City with both the N and S of the country, and the road to the Ethiopian frontier is bitumen-surfaced.

● Car hire

It is possible to hire cars in Djibouti City (see under car hire section, page 672).

Communications

● Language

French and Arabic are the official languages, and Afar and Somali are spoken locally. Some English is spoken in the capital.

Entertainment

● Newspapers

There is only one local paper, *La Nation* which is published weekly. There are also *L'Atout*, a twice yearly paper published by the Centre National de la Promotion Culturelle et Artistique, and the *Carrefour Africain* published fortnightly by the Roman Catholic mission.

● Television and radio

Broadcasting is state controlled and operated from Djibouti City. There are programmes in French, Afar, Somali and Arabic. Radio transmission is 24 hr and television 7 hrs daily. Djibouti is also a member of the Arab Satellite Communication Organisation which transmits both radio and television programmes.

Holidays and festivals

2 Feb	New Year
Feb	Lailat al-Miraji*
1 May	Labour day
Apr	Eid al-Fitr*
27 Jun	National Day
Jul	Eid al-Adha*
15 Aug	Assumption Day
Jul	Muslim New Year*
Aug	Al-Ashura*
Oct	Prophet's Birthday*
1 Nov	All Saints Day
25 Dec	Christmas Day.

* These dates marking Muslim holidays are approximate as they depend on the lunar year.

Further reading

● General

Thompson, V and Adloff, R (1968) *Djibouti and the Horn of Africa*, London: OUP. Thorough coverage of historical, political and economic issues prior to independence.

● Travellers' Tales

Waugh, E (1931) *Remote People*, London: Duckworth. Includes Waughs's impressions of Djibouti on the way to Addis Ababa in 1930, and on the way back.

COMOROS

Contents

Maps

Introduction

Comoros is a state comprising three of the four islands in the Comores archipelago. The fourth island, Mayotte, chose to remain linked to France rather than to join the other three in becoming independent. The group of four islands are referred to as the Comores. The three islands of Comoros have officially had their names changed since independence. Thus Grande Comore is Njazidja, Moheli is Mwali and Anjouan is Nzwani. However, the old names have remained in general use.

The islands are very attractive, and as a result of their long Islamic, Portuguese and French background, have much to interest and charm the tourist. There is something for all types of visitor – it is possible to stay simply and inexpensively in glorious beach locations, and there are some luxury hotels of a high standard. The prevalence of Islam imposes no significant restrictions, and the islands are very relaxed. The Muslim influence, together with the small size of the communities, serves to make the islands quite safe. There is continual political intrigue, but this has minimal effect on outsiders.

Environment

Geography

The Comores Archipelago lie on a Northeast to Southeast diagonal between mainland Mozambique and the northern-most tip of Madagascar. The 4 islands that make up the Archipelago cover a total area of 2034 sq km (including Mayotte) and comprise: Grande Comore (1025 sq km); Moheli (211 sq km); Anjouan (424 sq km) and Mayotte (374 sq km).

It is thought the islands emerged some 8 million years ago at the end of the Miocene era during a period of volcanic activity. Today, however, only Mount Karthala (2361 m) on Grande Comore remains active with the most recent eruption occuring in 1977). Since the islands are volcanic, the bedrock is largely basaltic igneous rock, formed from molten lava which cools once exposed to the air.

Soils throughout the Comores are lateritic in nature and despite being rich in minerals have a low organic matter content which exposes them to rapid

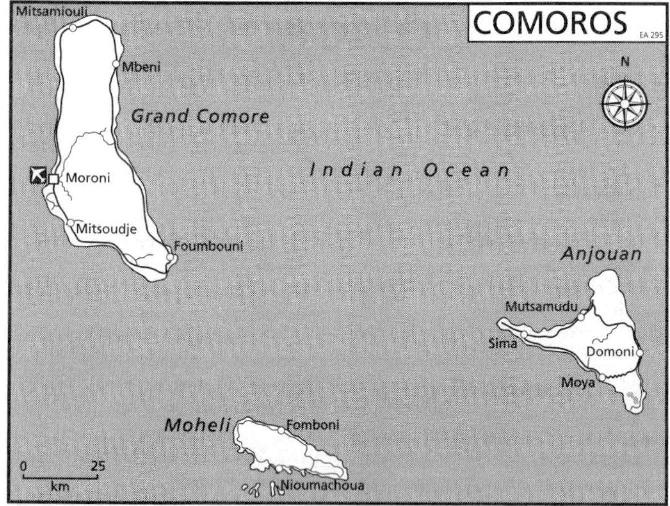

rates of erosion during the rainy season. The severity of the erosion process can be seen best after a heavy rain storm in Anjouan when topsoil is carried down rivers, flowing into the sea, turning it red. On the Island of Grande Comore the porous nature of the fissured basalt bedrock has resulted in the lack of any perennial surface watercourse. The islands' main source of drinking water comes from collected rainwater and shortages are not uncommon.

Climate

These tropical islands are exposed to a variety of weather patterns throughout the year. For much of the year the Islands are affected by the Southeast tradewinds, the *Kusi*. The *Kusi* determine the nature and extent of the dry season, which falls between May and Oct. This is probably the best time to visit since conditions are at their most pleasant, with little rain (the average is 84 mm during Oct) and temperatures around 20°-22°C.

During Nov through to Apr, as the *Kash-kazi* winds blowing from the Northwest meet the Southeast tradewinds, the wet season arrives. At this time of the year temperatures range between 24°-35°C which, coupled with high rainfall (Jan with 424 mm on average is the wettest month) and humidity (steady at 80%) can make conditions uncomfortable. From Apr to May the islands experience a cold season, the Nyombeni. During this period temperatures at the summit of Mount Karthala can fall below 0°C.

Flora and fauna

Flora

The vegetation on the islands is characteristically tropical though species change altitudinally from the coast to more mountainous areas. Tree species such as frangipani, fig, casurina (*filao*), pandanus (*vacoa*), poinciana (*flamboyant*), coconut, tamarind, clove, and ylang-ylang (used to make perfume) are found on coastal and low lying areas. With increasing altitude however these species give way to yam, maize, sweet potato, rice, tea, coffee and manioc. Above 1000m, beyond the agricultural

COELACANTH

The many fossils that remain suggest that the Coelacanth (*Latimeria*) emerged 350 million years ago, existed for 290 million years, and then became extinct. Until 1938, that is, when a specimen (*Latimeria chalumnae*) was trawled up from a depth of some 75 metres off the Eastern coast of South Africa. In 1952 another (*Malania anjouanae*) was caught off the Comores Islands by a local fisherman using a hand-line. In the next 2 years a further 5 were landed, and it became clear that their main habitat was the seas around the Comores.

Only one of the 4 types of coelacanth identified from the fossils appears to have survived. The captured fish are bigger than the fossils, more than 1.5m long and weighing over 50 kgs. Their 4 fins resemble legs, and these have some rotating movement which allows the coelacanth to crawl along the sea bed. The tail is large, and some specimens have what appears to be a a second small tail behind the main tail. A powerful set of jaws and strong teeth allow the coelacanth to feed by preying on quite large sea creatures, as witnessed by the fact that the first coelacanth caught had the remains of a 7 kg fish in its stomach.

land, there is still primary rainforest in some areas. Here native trees such as eugenia, badamia and lasodiscus can be seen whilst acacias, ebony and takamaka cover the hill sides. Ferns, lichens and orchids are to be found beneath the canopy of the rainforest .

In recent times, however, the islands have come under increasing pressure from the expansion of agricultural land which has begun to penetrate the primary rainforest, particularly in Anjouan. Reforestation projects have introduced Eucalyptus trees which not only grow quickly on recently deforested land but also provide a good source of firewood for the resident population. As a result, much of the archipelago's indigenous rainforest is now restricted to the slopes of Mount Karthala.

Fish

A great variety of tropical fish inhabit the waters around the Comores Archipelago such as tuna, wahoo, barracuda, and sharks but probably the most famous is the coelacanth fish,thought to have been extinct, see box, above.

Birds

The islands exhibit a wide variety of bird life and boast 13 species unique to the islands. These include Humblot's flycatcher (*Humblotia flavirostris*) found only on Grande Comore; the Humblot's sunbird (*Nectarinia humblotii*) found only on Grande Comore and Moheli; the Grande Comore scops owl (*Otus pauliani*) one of the rarest birds in the archipelago; and the Anjouan sunbird (*Nectarinia comorensis*).

Other birds found on the islands are visitors and include a variety of herons such as the Giant egret, the Cattle egret, the Humblot's heron, the 2 Squacco herons and the Green-backed or Striated heron. Kingfishers also exist though in smaller numbers. These include the Madagascar Malachit kingfisher, a relatively small bird, and the Malagasy kingfisher. Other occasional visitors include the flamingo and a variety of waders.

Mammals

There are 3 species of fruit bat unique to the Comores, see Box, page 680. The *Pteropus seychellensis comorensis* fruit bat is very common. The second species, *Pteropus livingstonii*, is thought to be the largest bat in the world with a wing span of approx 2m and with only 60 known to survive, probably the rarest. Finally, there is the forgotten fruit bat *Rousettus obliviousus*, so called because from 1903

Bats

Bats are mammals with web-like skin flaps between their arms and legs and their bodies, and between their elongated fingers that enable them to fly. They have fur rather than feather-covered bodies, teeth rather than beaks, and the females have mammary glands to nurse their young. The feet are formed into hooks which allow the bat to hang, upside-down, high up in trees and caves well out of the way of predators without any effort while asleep or hibernating (or even when dead). By emitting sounds and receiving their reflections, they are able to fly in the dark. Many species restrict their activities to twilight or night-time, sleeping in the day. In European cultures, bats are symbolic of darkness and evil. In the Far East, however, they represent good luck, happiness and long life.

Most bats live by catching insects, using their sonor navigation systems to detect their prey, as their eyes tend to be small and weak. A single bat will consume up to 1,000 insects in a day.

The species that are unique to Comores, Mayotte and Madagascar are *Pteropidae* that feed on fruit. They tend to have larger and stronger eyes than the insect-eaters. Some species of fruit-bat hover in front of flowers, sucking out pollen and nectar with their long tongues and elongated snouts. Vampire bats, which live by sucking the blood of mammals, are only found in Central and South America. Free-tailed bats have skin-flaps joining the hind-legs and the tail, but the tail has a section extending beyond the flap.

to 1981 it went unrecorded. This bat is largely nocturnal, lives in caves and remains mostly unobserved. Other species are *Miniopterus minor griveudi* and *Myotis goudoti anjouanensis* and the *Tadarida pumila* or freetailed bat.

A mammal unique to the Comores and Madagascar is the Lemur. On the Comores 2 members of the Lemuridae family are represented and they are the brown or fulvous lemur (*Lemur fulvus*) and the mongoose lemur (*Lemur mongoz*). The brown lemur can be found in large numbers on the Island of Anjouan and has recently been introduced onto Grande Comore. The mongoose lemur is only found on Mayotte.

Reptiles

The islands are also home to the green turtle (*Chelonia mydas*) and the hawksbill turtle (*Eretmochelys imbricata*). These turtles lay their eggs throughout the archipelago but favour the Nioumachoua islands which are just S of Moheli. Smaller animals such as lizards, chameleons, geckos and snakes can also be seen and are all features of the islands' comparatively rich ecology.

History

The name Comores is thought to have come from the Arabic *al kamar* (the moon)and therefore the islands are often referred to as the 'islands of the Moon'.

Today the islands are strongly Muslim with 99% of the population following the Islamic religion. However, the islands do have some pre-Islamic records which offer some idea of what earlier society was like. It is thought that originally the population (probably from Malay Polynesia) relied on a political system centred on chiefs, each of which controlled a village. These chiefs were known as *bedja* on Grand Comore and *fani* on Anjouan. The society had strong egalitarian characteristics and followed a matrilineal kinship system.

The arrival of Islam

Islam arrived some time between the eighth and thirteenth centuries, though recent digs by archaeologists suggest that the date might have been closer to the tenth century since this seems to coincide with an exodus by Sunni Muslims from Shiraz in Iran which had come under attack by Shi'ite Muslims. Many settled down the SE coastline of Africa, some reaching Madagascar and the Comores. But it was not until the thirteenth century, when Shiraz immigrants arrived in greater numbers, that Islam began to establish firm roots on the islands. Islamic traditions merged with a traditional Comorien base, sultanates were created and the traditional political system though still operating, lost much of its power to the sultans.

However, original social structures such as the matrilineal descent system survived. On Grande Comore for instance certain land is controlled by women and though men in the family are allowed use, it remains the property of the women. Similar systems exist on the other 3 islands. Matrilocal traditions are also followed in some areas, that is to say after marriage the husband moves into the bride's family house rather than his own. The islands therefore maintain systems from both pre-Islamic and Islamic society, a fact best illustrated by the existence of a matrilineal Islamic society, which is something of a rarity in the Islamic world.

Though the majority of the population are Muslim, some festivals are still strongly influenced by African traditions. Witch doctors (*Wagangi*) still operate offering advice to those possessed by ancestral spirits. Many agricultural festivals originate from the African continent.

The arrival of Europeans

The first Europeans to arrive on the islands were the Portuguese in 1506 after they had sacked Kilwa (now in Tanzania). The attack prompted further waves of Shiraz immigrants to the Comores. Next the French arrived in Anjouan in 1529 and were followed by the British in 1591. During the seventeenth century Anjouan became an important commercial centre and soon the area became notorious for piracy.

Piracy died out by the early 1700's, the French took Mayotte in 1841, and by 1886 France had control of the entire Archipelago. In 1912 the islands were attached to the French colony of Madagascar and as the islands' dependency on Madagascar grew, a noticeable stream of Islanders moved to Madagascar. With exception to a brief period in 1942, when the British occupied the islands, they remained French. In 1956 universal suffrage was granted but it wasn't until 22 Dec 1961 that the islands were granted self-government though defence and foreign policy continued to be controlled by France. Said Mohammed Cheik was elected president and remained so until his death in 1970. Said Ibrahim followed Chiek as president but only lasted 2 years before being forced to resign and was replaced by Ahmed Abdallah.

Independence

During the early 1970's the pressure for independence heightened and, though the majority of the population rallied behind this cause, Mayotte remained undecided. Finally on Jul 6 1975 Ahmed Abdullah, accused of supporting an anti-independence cause, resolved matters by announcing the independence of Grande Comore, Moheli and Anjouan to be known as the Republic of the Comoros, whilst Mayotte remained French.

On Aug the 3rd 1975 Abdallah was deposed by a group of French mercenaries under Bob Denard who then installed Said Ibrahim of Parti Blanc. By 1976 Said Ibrahim was replaced by the more radical Ali Soilih. Ali Soilih spared no time in introducing rapid reforms aimed at promoting decentralisation and self-sufficiency whilst attacking traditional Islamic values. As he began to lose support from traditional sources, he turned to the younger generation. France withdrew its support, ministers left and chaos ensued as Soilih became frustrated trying to implement policy with a young and inexperienced government. By 1978 the country was in crisis, Bob Denard returned to reinstated Abdallah and in the process Soilih was shot dead.

A period of personal rule by Abdallah followed, bolstered by Denard and his mercenaries, which lasted some twelve years during which time the country was expelled from the UN and OAU. However on Nov 26th 1989, apparently as a result of an argument between Denard and Abdallah, both the president and his guard were shot. Though Denard maintained his innocence in the affair, public unrest was such that he had to be flown out to South Africa, accompanied by 25 mercenaries. Said Mohamed Djohar, then president of the Supreme Court, is now president and Comoros has been readmitted into the OAU and the Indian Ocean Commission.

Arts and crafts

The islands are famous for **perfumes** which are extracted from the Ylang Ylang and used in perfumes (e.g. Channel No 5) all around the world. The best places to buy it is from the distilleries of Bambao SA on Anjouan, or at Kalfane in Moroni. **Wood carving** is another Comores speciality and is best bought from workshops in and around Domoni on Anjouan. Anjouan **dolls** are a speciality, though these are increasingly hard to come by. Other local products include traditional brightly coloured red and orange **cloth** worn by Comorien women, embroidered Muslim **hats** and **jewelry**, best bought on Moroni. You may also discover turtle shells on sale. Turtles are an endangered species and export of turtle shells is strictly prohibited.

Modern Comoros

Politics

Since gaining independence from France in 1975, there have been 3 successful coups and several other attempts to overthrow the government. In 1977, under Ali Soilih, there were radical attempts to reorganise society on a mixture of Maoist and Islamic lines. This period introduced a major change in development strategy when the regime began moves to restructure the economy into decentralised socialist units. All French property was nationalised and French officials expelled. The socialist experiment has been ended for the most part, and Comoros formally joined the Franc Zone in 1976. With the restoration of Abdallah in 1978, French aid was re-established, only to be suspended with his death.

Djohar's presidency has been precarious. The elections to the Legislative Assembly in 1989 and again in 1992 (the latter giving a narrow support to Dhojar), have been disputed. In mid 1993, following a motion of censure against the government, Dhojar dissolved the Assembly. There are now 24 registered political parties. New elections have been postponed, and opposition groups have responded with strikes and campaigns of civil disobedience. It is difficult to see how Djohar would survive if the opposition were more united. As things stand, the presence of French troops is an important factor in maintaining order.

Overall, the stability record of Comoros, although not threatening to visitors, has been very poor. The future course of government is unclear. Although economic policy has been more practical over the past 9 years, the dislocation introduced by the Soilih era has had an enduring effect in damaging confidence.

Economics

Collection of economic data has been hampered by the dislocation of the Soilih period, and the subsequent years of comparative isolation under Abdallah. Nevertheless, although many of the statistics presented relate to the 1980's, economic life has not changed dramatically in the subsequent decade, and they provide a reasonable basis for assessing economic conditions and future prospects for Comoros.

Population

Estimates for 1989 indicate a population of 453,000. The average density of population has risen from 182.5 per square kilometre in 1980 to 217 per square kilometre in 1988. Only Rwanda and Mauritius in Africa have higher densities. Anjouan averages 349 persons per sq km and is increasing. There has been some recent immigration from Mozambique.

Economic and social structure

Comoros had a population of under half a million in 1989, making it one of the smallest countries in the African region. In 1982, 12.3% of the population were estimated to live in urban areas, well below average in both the East African region and Africa generally, which is close to 30%. Population is growing at 4.1% each year, and is a reflection of reasonably good medical care reducing death rates, with little influence of urbanisation and wider opportunites for women contributing to reductions in the birth rate.

GDP in 1982 was US$99 million. Income per head was estimated at US$320, and this is above the average of US$250 for East Africa, but below the African average of US$389. The most important sector is agriculture which generates 45% of GDP, which is representative of the East African region, industry generating 18%, and services 38%. East Africa has a rather lower level of industrialisation than Africa generally, where 27% of GDP comes from industry. On the demand side, private consumption was equivalent to 66% of GDP in 1982, and this is lower than elsewhere in the region. Investment was 28% of GDP, and this represents a substantial development effort, being almost twice the 16% investment ratio in Africa generally. Government consumption was 22% of GDP, and this is 56% greater than is typical for Africa. Exports generate 22% of GDP and this is a rather higher dependence on outside earnings than in the East Africa region.

The main exports are vanilla (63%), ylang-ylang (22%) and cloves (11%). Expenditure on imports was equivalent to 40% of GDP, and was made possible by substantial aid flows which were equivalent to 16% of GDP. The main imports are rice (20%), petroleum (6%) and transport equipment (6%).

In 1980, Comoros had an adult literacy ratio of 48%, better than in East Africa, or in Africa generally. Of the relevant age-group 93% were in primary education, an achievement 50% better than in the East African region. Secondary enrolments were 50% better than the average for the East African region at 24% of the relevant age group. There were negligible enrolments in higher education.

Life expectancy was estimated at 56 years in 1986, and this is better than the regional and African average of 50. Daily calorie supply averaged 1,920, which is little below the regional and African averages. The most recent figures for availability of physicians suggests good provision of medical services at one doctor for every 15,000 inhabitants in 1973, whereas in East Africa the average was one doctor for every 35,000 and in Africa generally, one doctor for every 24,000; these latter figures being for 1981.

Overall, Comoros is a small economy with a low-income status, but among the better-off low income countries. It has a small population, but high population density. There is heavy dependence on agriculture, high investment and levels of government consumption. Aid flows allow a high proportion of total expenditure to be on imports. Educational provision is good, as is health provision.

Economic performance

GDP growth was estimated at 0.3% annually for 1973-81 by the Economic Commission for Africa, but this is affected by 2 particularly poor years in 1975 and 1976. GDP growth was below the rate of population growth, and GDP per head fell at -3.4% a year in this period. GDP is estimated to have risen by 1.7% a year, 1980-87, and this indicates a fall in GDP per head of -1.4% a year. Agricultural growth has been at 2.4% a year in the period 1973-81, but industrial output fell at -7.7% in the same period. Services grew at 5%, the only sector to have grown faster than the rate of expansion of the population. Export volumes grew by 3.5% annually 1973-81, helped by membership of the Franc Zone which maintains high prices for exports. Import volumes declined in the period by -0.6% annually, although it needs to be observed that there is substantial year-to-year variation, with the US$ value of imports halving between 1974 and 1976 and then almost tripling by 1980. The 1982 investment ratio of 28% is high, but subsequent growth between 1983 and 1985 at 3.5% a year implies poor capital productivity, perhaps reflecting a rather wasteful public sector investment programme. Inflation has been modest at 5.3% a year for the period 1980-91, and this is a result of the fiscal discipline imposed by membership of the Franc Zone.

Overall, Comoros has had relatively slow GDP growth and, until recently, falling GDP per head, although performance has been less bad than in many African countries. Industry has performed poorly, especially considering the high investment rate. Growth in export volumes has been good, and inflation performance has been significantly better than that elsewhere in Africa.

Recent economic developments

Vanilla, which provides 63% of export revenue, is subject to considerable variation in annual output. The 1982 export total of 259 tonnes was 10 times the 25 tonnes exported in 1984. Similarly with cloves which make up 11% of export revenue. 1981 saw 500 tonnes exported, but this grew to 1,200 tonnes in 1983. Ylang-ylang made up 22% of export revenue in 1985, and 29 tonnes were exported in 1984, and 60 tonnes in 1985. These factors cause substantial overall variations in export revenue, with this more than doubling in 1985 to US$16 million from the low of US$7 million in 1984. Production prices for cloves were reduced by 67% between 1983 and 1985, and this will have an effect in limiting the expansion of clove production from 1987 on, as clove trees take 4 years before new plantings produce crops.

Overall external debt totals US$285 million, and debt-service was estimated at US$9.9 million in 1987 rising to US$10.7 million in 1988. Debt service payments will comprise 50% of export earnings even in years of good export performance, and Comoros continues to depend on aid, particularly from France to meet the deficit on the current account on the balance of payments.

The International Development Association of the World Bank committed US$7.9 million in soft-loan funds to improve the educational system, and to provide vocational training. In May 1987, the OPEC Fund for International Development made a US$1m loan on soft terms to improve petroleum storage facilities. A South African Consortium is building 4 new hotels at a total cost of US$13 million.

A structural adjustment programme was agreed in 1990 with the IMF and the World Bank, which involved liberalisation of the economy, privatisation of state-owned enterprises, and retrenchment of civil servants. Despite slow progress, funding continued until the

Assembly failed to approve the 1993 budget, and the programme effectively came to a halt.

Economic outlook

The adverse impact of the unresolved political situation that has resulted from the 1989 assassination continues to impair prospects. The outlook is poor, and the forecast rates of GDP growth indicate GDP per head declining. Import volumes can be expected to rise if resolution of the political situation leads to restoration of aid flows. Provided Comoros remains a member of the Franc Zone, inflation will continue to be modest.

COMPARATIVE ECONOMIC AND SOCIAL DATA

	Comoros	East Africa	Africa	Industrial Countries
Population and land				
Population, mid year, millions, 1989	0.435	12.2	10.2	40.0
Urban population, %, 1982	12.3	30.5	30	75
Population growth rate, % per year, 1973-82	4.1	3.1	3.1	0.8
Land area, thou. sq. kilom.	2	486	486	1,628
Population density, persons per sq km, 1988	217.5	24.2	20.4	24.3
Economy: production & income				
GDP, US$millions, 1990	227	2,650	3,561	550,099
GNP per head, US$, 1990	480	250	389	12,960
Economy: supply structure				
Agriculture, % of GDP, 1982	45	43	35	3
Industry, % of GDP, 1982	18	15	27	35
Services, % of GDP, 1982	38	42	38	61
Economy: demand structure				
Private consumption, % of GDP, 1982	66	77	73	62
Gross domestic investment, % of GDP, 1982	28	16	16	21
Government consumption, % of GDP, 1982	22	15	14	17
Exports, % of GDP, 1982	22	16	23	17
Imports, % of GDP, 1982	40	24	26	17
Economy: performance				
GDP growth, % per year, 1978-81	0.3	1.6	-0.6	2.5
GDP per head growth, % per year, 1978-81	-3.8	-1.7	-3.7	1.7
Agriculture growth, % per year, 1978-81	2.4	1.1	0.0	2.5
Industry growth, % per year, 1978-81	-7.7	1.1	-1.0	2.5
Services growth, % per year, 1978-81	5.0	2.5	-0.5	2.6
Exports growth, % per year, 1978-81	3.5	0.7	-1.9	3.3
Imports growth, % per year, 1978-81	-0.6	0.2	-6.9	4.3
Economy: other				
Inflation rate, % per year, 1980-91	5.3	23.6	16.7	5.3
Aid, net inflow, % of GDP, 1983	16.6	11.5	6.3	-
Debt service, % of Exports, 1984	24.6	18	20.6	-
Budget surplus (+), Deficit (-), 1979	-1.0	-3.0	-2.8	-5.1
Education				
Primary, % of 6-11 group, 1980	93	62	76	102
Secondary, % of 12-17 group, 1980	24	15	22	93
Higher, % of 20-24 group, 1980	-	1.2	1.9	39
Adult literacy rate, %, 1980	48	41	39	99
Health and nutrition				
Life expectancy, years, 1986	56	50	50	76
Calorie Supply, daily per head, 1983	1.920	2,111	2,096	3,357
Population per doctor, 1973	15,315	35,986	24,185	550

Notes: 'Africa' excludes South Africa. Dates are for the country in question, and do not always correspond with the East African, African and Industrial Country averages.

MORONI

This is the largest town in Comoros, and has been the capital since 1961. Historically the town was politically independent, though with the arrival of Shiraz immigrants and the readjustment of the political order, Moroni became part of the new sultanate of Bamboo which had its capital in Iconi, a few km to the south. In 1798 Moroni was fortified to protect it from the threat of Sakalava aggression from Madagascar. Moroni's importance returned with the arrival of the French at the turn of the century.

Places of interest

Old Moroni gives some idea of what life was like during the Bamboo dynasty. The old town grew around the dhow harbour and comprises 2 quarters, M'Tsangani to the N and Badjanani to the S.

In Badjanani, centre of the old town, is the site of the **Mosquee du Vendredi**. The original building dates from 1427 and a further minaret was added in 1921 as part of an enlargement programme. Beside the mosque lies the **Msirimtsini Moroni Palace** which dates from the Bamboo dynasty, whilst the **Shashanyongo Palace** is just S of the square. Opposite the Mosque, past the old **Post Office**, formerly the residence of the French administrator, lie the ruins of the **Dhwahira Palace** built at the end of the 19th century for Sultan Said Ali.

Up the hill stands the **Old Market** which dates from 1921. Above this is the **Place de France** where the main post office, bank and Gouvernorat are located. The **Centre National de Documentation et de Recherche Scientifique Museum** is a short walk away, down the hill. Opening times are (Tue-Thu 0800-1300 and 1500-1800, Fri 0800-1100 and 1500-1800, Sat 0800-1200 and 1500-1700).

Local information

● Where to stay

Price guide
A+ Over US$100; **A** US$40-100;
B US$20-40; **C** US$10-20; **D** US$5-10;
E Under US$5.

A *Novotel Ylang-Ylang*, T 720240/731523 south of town centre. All rooms a/c, television, telephone. No beach. Swimming pool, tennis courts. Good restaurant.

B *Itsandra Palace*, T 730765. Splendid location. The oldest hotel in the Comores. A/c. Terrace restaurant and a small beach. Snorkelling available. **B** *La Grillade*, Route de la Corniche, T 731781. Chalets with a/c. **B** *Coelacanthe*, T 720240/731523. Chalets with a/c. Swimming pool. Restaurant. A little dilapidated. **B** *Moifaka Studio*. At Hamramba nr *Novotel*, T 731556. Rooms with own bathrooms. **B** *Tiboulen* On the corner nr *La Grillade*, T 733061. Rooms with own bathrooms. Good restaurant.

C *Karthala*, T 730765. Dates from the colonial period. Has some style but now a little run down. **C** *Pension Zilimadjou*, T 731696. Behind the Palais du Peuple at the S end of the town. Well run. **C** *Pension Kohinoor*, T 732806. On the Route de Mitsamiouli nr the Belgian Embassy. Well run. Good restaurant. Some rooms with own bathrooms.

D *Pension Karibu*, T 732117. Some cheap dormitory rooms. Shared bathrooms. Cooking facilities available. Meals on request. **D** *Pension Zam-Zam*, T 730427. On Route d'Iconi, a little out of town. Good value. **D** *Dzindani Village des Vacances*. At the Trou du Prophete nr Maloudja Beach and Mitsamiouli. Shared bathrooms. No electricity.

● Places to eat

Price guide:
♦♦♦♦Over US$10; ♦♦♦US$5-10; ♦♦US$2-5;
♦Under US$2.

Most hotels have restaurants but some of the more expensive hotels only allow residents to eat. ♦♦♦♦*Restaurant du Port*. Located nr harbour. Food must be ordered in advance. Local and continental cuisine. Good value. ♦♦♦♦*Restaurant Sahala*. Nr Place de France.

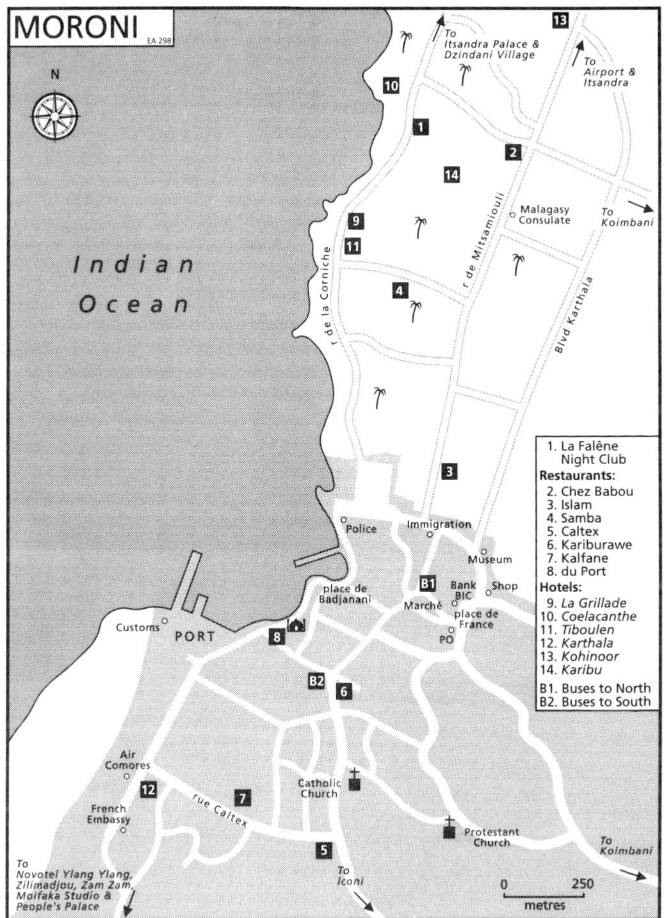

High standard. ♦♦♦♦*Chez Babou*. Just past Volo-Volo market. A little expensive, but well-prepared seafood. Indian food also served. ♦♦♦♦*Islam Restaurant*. Near Rue des Ambassadeurs. Formerly Moroni's best restaurant and still quite good.

♦♦♦*Restaurant Samba*. Rue des Ambassadeurs. ♦♦♦*Restaurant Caltex*. In Rue Caltex. Friendly and efficient.

♦♦*Restaurant Karibunawe*. In a side street nr Rond-Point Gobadjou is basic but inexpensive local haunt.

♦*Kalfane Salon de Thé*. The tea house attached to a bakery. Open in the mornings, from 0500.

● Entertainment

The *Alliance Franco Comorienne* (nr the *Coelacanth Hotel*). Shows films once a week (see notice board outside French Embassy for programs. Several *video saloons* exist next to the UniCoop.

Nightclubs are on the Route d'Iconi (*Club des Amis* and *La Derobade*) and *Maki* at

Voidjou. There is dancing at *La Falene* restaurant just before *Coelacanth Hotel*.

● Shopping

La Maison du Livre sells mainly French books, but also stocks *Time* and *Newsweek*. Stationery, maps and magazines at ***Nouveautés*** on the Place de France. Ylang-Ylang perfume can be bought at ***Ets Kalfane*** in Caltex Rd.

● Local Transport

Taxi Fare US$1-2 for trips around town.

● Travel Agents

Comortour, BP 404, *Comores Services*, BP 374.

● Transport

Air The international airport for the Comoros is at Hahaya, about 20 km north of Moroni, and there are regular international (see page 697 and local flights (see page 688). Taxi to Moroni is US$15, *taxi-brousse* US$1.50. **Sea** There are boats between the islands (see page 698). **Road** *Taxi-brousse* depart from Place de France for north of island and Chomoni on east coast; from Gobadjou for south of island.

Itsandra

5 km N of Moroni. Reached its peak as a cultural and commercial centre in the 18th century under Wabedja and some fortifications still remain today. A short walk from the main public beach (where Bob Denard landed on 12 May 1978 to depose Ali Soilih and install Abdallah as president) lie the ruins of a 15th century **Fort**. In the town itself lie the ruins of the **Gereza Palace**, a fortified structure built at the end of the 18th century during the Famnau era.

The beach at Itsandra is popular with both locals and tourists and water sports are available. Diving and wind-surfing can be arranged through the **Twamaya Nautical Club** located on the beach. **Café La Pirogue** (Chez Gerard) serves food but evening meals have to be ordered in advance. Next door, the **Gombessa Diving Centre** organises diving and excursions up Mount Karthala (although it is quite possible to make the climb independently). A little inland, **Chez Claude** serves *sim sim*, locally caught fried fish.

N'Tsoudjini

Located to the N of Itsandra and was capital of the Sultanate of Itsandra under Ntibe wa kandza during the 15th century. Today watch towers are the only significant remaining fortifications as most buildings were destroyed by Malagasy pirates in 1806. The S E corner of the town houses several tombs with *wafaku* inscriptions said to have magical significance. In the SW corner are the **Goba la Salama** (Gates of Peace). Those going on long journeys would leave through the the Gates to ensure their safe return. There are 3 main Palaces in N'Tsoudjini. To the N are the ruins of the **M'Badjini Palace**, built by Famnau for his daughter. To the W is the site of the **Dahwamhadju Palace** for the royal women, and to the W, off the main square, are the ruins of the **Singani Palace** the Sultans Palace, built in the 15th century.

N'Tsaoueni

Lying just beyond the airport, N'Tsaoueni was capital of the M'Bude Sultanate, and fortified in the 18th century. At this site Islam was first introduced into the Comores by Mohammed Athoumani. Athoumani travelled to Arabia to visit Mohammed, but the prophet died before he could reach Mecca. Athoumani returned with one of Mohammed's cousins, Caliph Kouba, who helped him spread the word of Islam. A seventh century **mosque** built by Mohammed Athoumani now houses his tomb.

Mitisamiouli

Lies to the N of N'Tsaoueni and is the second largest town on Grande Comore. It was the capital during the Inya Matsu Pirusa dynasty but little now remains of historic significance. The town has an extensive beach and it takes an hour to get there from Moroni by taxi. Accommodation in Mitsamiouli is available but tends to be expensive. The *Resto Bourdah*, N of the town, serves local dishes. A little beyond Mitsamiouli are some of the best beaches on Grande Comore but some large tourist developments along this coast line have begun to intrude into an area of natural beauty. **A** *Le Gawa*, T 738118 in this area is one of the newest of Comore's large hotels of international standard. The office of Tourisme Services Comores is situated in the hotel and can arrange tours around the island.

A little further up the coast lies **Maloudja Beach**. Accommodation **B** *Hotel Le Maloudja*, popular with tourists. Further still is **B** *The Royal Orchard Hotel*. North of these beaches is **Trou Du Prophete** (named by a captain whose *boutre* was in danger of sinking during a storm. He prayed to Allah to deliver him, and his boat subsequently moved into the calmer waters of the cove). The beach has French holiday villas and several simple shelters which can be rented cheaply.

Lac Sale is a deep sea water lake rich in sulphur and good for treating skin ailments. Taxis can be taken from Moroni

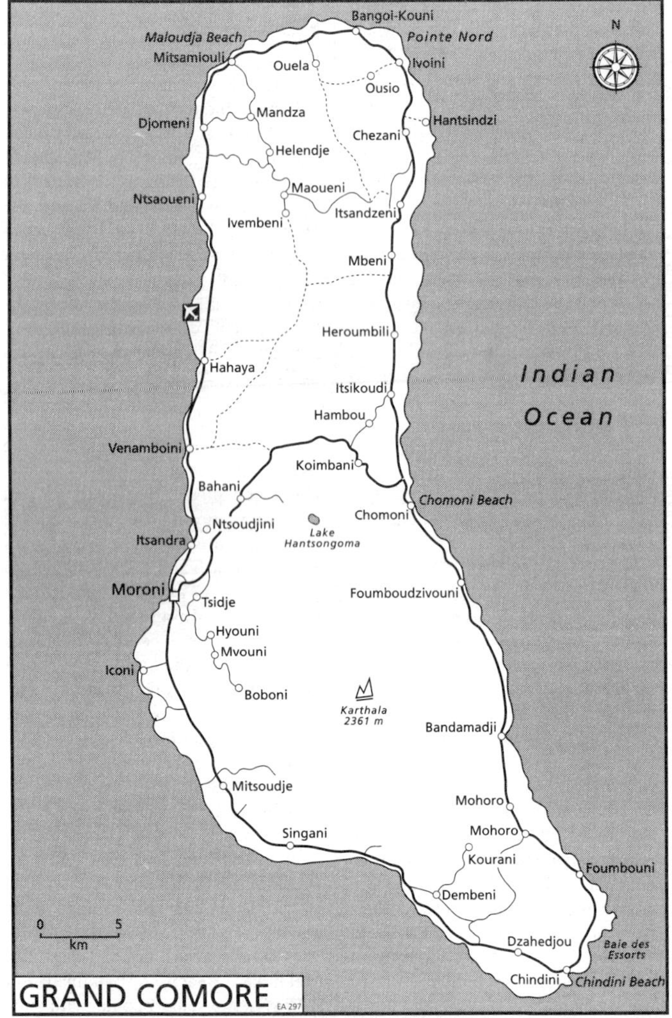

to drive to the crater. A little further away lies **Goulaivoini**, the remains of a crater, where the peninsula continues in the shape of an arc and resembles the backbone of a sleeping dragon, from which it takes its name.

East Coast

These exposed beaches are a little rougher than the sheltered W beaches. **Chomoni** beach is probably the best on this coastline, lying in a bay. **Foumbouni** is the third largest town on Grand Comore. Capital under Sultan of Badjini, the town is famous for its pottery. **Iconi** is the oldest settlement and original capital. The town suffered under attacks by Malagasy pirates during the 16th and 17th centuries. **Chindini Beach** is at the most southerly point of the island. Many marriage festivals are held here in Aug and take place at night with traditional food, music and dance.

Mount Karthala

The climb to the summit is well marked and it is possible to go on your own, although guides are available. Hikes normally begin from either Mvouni or Boboni (the shorter route). From Boboni the track climbs to La Convalescence (a 4 hr walk) where it is advisable to spend the night before carrying on the next day to the summit, a further 3 hr walk. To the N it is possible to see La Soufriere (2060m) a fuming sulphur pit. On your trek you may be lucky enough to see the Black Parrot or even the Scops Owl, although sighting this is more difficult as it is a nocturnal bird.

MOHELI (MWALI)

This island is the smallest of the Comores group, being 50 km long and 20 km wide. It has an area of 211 sq km and a population of 30,600. It is the least developed and most fertile and most economic activity is small-scale farming. The main attraction of Moheli is that it presents a view of traditional Comorien life that has been little affected by tourism, and which can be easily toured on foot.

Fomboni

This is the main town on the N coast.

Places of interest East of the Island is **Lake Dziani Boundouri**, a crater with sulphurous waters. It is also possible to walk from Miringoni to the chalet de St. Antoine. Near the village of **Djwayezi** on the Nyombeni river lies the ruins of a settlement built in the 19th century later destroyed by Malagasy pirates. There are a number of good beaches on Moheli and the best include **Miremani-Sambadjou**, **Sambia** and **Itsamia**.

- **Where to stay** **C** *Relais Singani*. Reasonable standards, but not particularly good value for money. **D** *Mledjele*. Communal bathrooms. Fairly simple.

- **Places to eat** ✦✦*L'Africaine*. Mixture of local and international cuisine. Moderate.

- **Transport** See **Getting There** and **Getting Around**, pages 697 and 698.

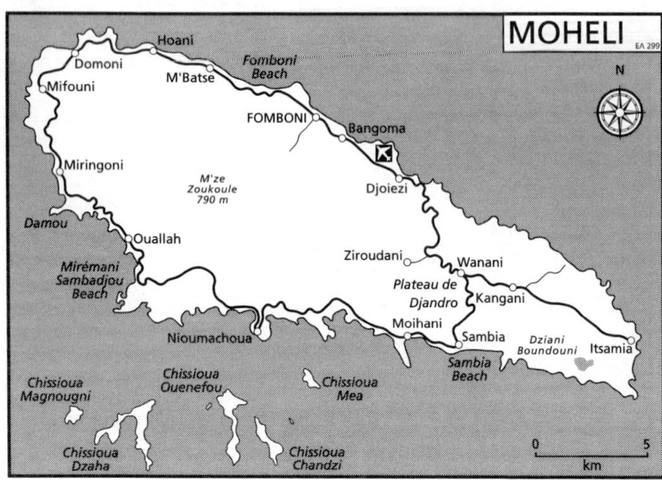

ANJOUAN (NZWANI)

This island is often referred to as the 'Pearl of the Comores'and is said to have a different atmosphere altogether from the other islands, being noted for its warm hospitality and beauty. However, with a population of 150,000 over an area of 424 sq km, there is considerable pressure on the land. Intensive cultivation in fertile regions allows exposed soils to be washed away in heavy rain. These soils flow down river turning the coastal sea red in the worst affected areas, particularly in N Anjouan near Jimilimi, and there has been an adverse impact on marine life by damaging corals.

Beaches At the S most tip of Anjouan, **Chiroroni** is regarded as the best on the island. **Hayoho** in the NE is extensive, but not easy to reach.

Mutsamuda

This town has been the capital of Anjouan since the 18th century. It is very picturesque and has both a modern section, facing the port, and old town. Over looking Mutsamuda is the **Citadel**, flanked by a number of cannons, and built in the 18th century by Sultan Abdallah I to protect the town from the notorious Malagasy pirates. The **Sultan's Palace** in the centre of town is still inhabited by his descendants. The Old Town (*Homoubou*), characterised by narrow winding streets, is dominated by the

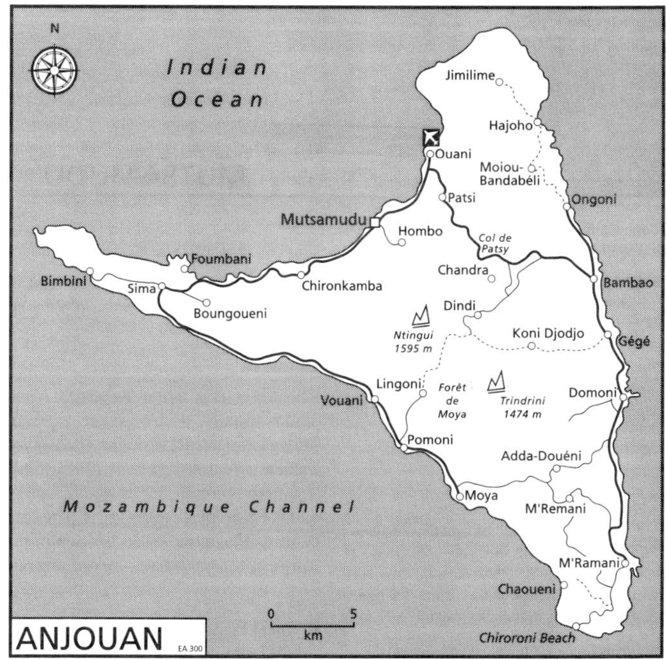

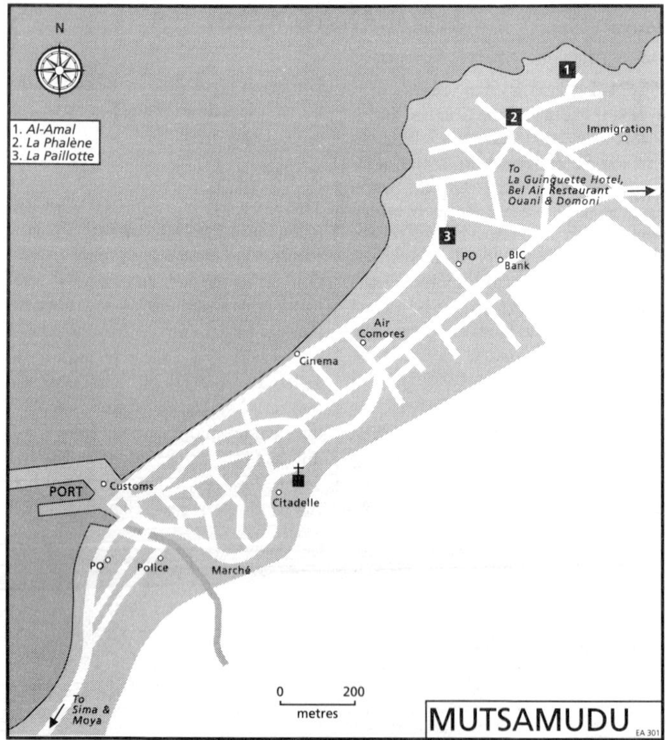

minaret of the **Mosque de Vendredi**.

● **Where to stay** **B** *Al-Amal*, T Matsamuda 365. Restaurant only moderate. A/c. Swimming pool, beach and tennis courts. Small jeeps can be hired from the hotel. **C** *La Phalene*. Shared bathrooms. Vehicles can be hired through the manager. **C** *La Guinguette*. Located towards Ouani. Rooms with own bathrooms. Fine location and nice beach. Good value. **C** *La Paillotte* Shared bathrooms. Good restaurant.

● **Places to eat** ♦♦♦*La Paillotte*. Located in Mutsamuda. Marginally the best food in town. ♦♦*Café Restaurant Bel Air*. Located at Ouami. Fairly simple. ♦♦*AL-Amal*. Open only in the evening. Good value. There are many small restaurants in the Old Town.

● **Nightlife** *La Paillotte* has music and dancing. Also *La Phalene* in the Missiri quarter.

● **Services** The post office and police post are in the Port area; the hospital is on the road to Hombo; Air Comoros is in Missiri.

Domoni

The original capital of the island, it was almost totally destroyed in 1780 by Malagasy pirates. President Abdallahs's **Palace** is situated here as is his tomb. The town is famous for its wood carvings and is a good place to buy gifts. The 15th century **Mosquee Mkiri Shirazi** in the centre of the town has a carved mihrab.

● **Where to stay** **C** *Domoni Café* Near Abdallah's Palace. Shared bathrooms.

Moya

One of Anjouans oldest settlements, lying above Chiroroni.

• **Where to stay** C *Relais Moya* chalets. Shared bathrooms. Good location on the cliff above the beach.

Sima

Another old town, archaeological digs suggest earliest settlement could have been as early as the 6th century. The town is Shirazi and has a 15th century **Mosque**.

Bambao

The town is the site of the **Palace** of Sultan Abdallah III, built in the 19th century. There is also a ylang-ylang distillery which produces perfumed oil.

• **Transport** See **Getting Around**, page 698.

INFORMATION FOR VISITORS

Contents

Before you go

Entry requirements

● Visas and Vaccinations

No visas or vaccinations are required to enter Comoros, but you must obtain a visa once you have arrived to cover the duration of your stay. The visa costs around US$40 for up to 45 days, usually takes a week to be issued, and can be obtained from the Ministere de l'Interieur in Moroni. It is essential to get a visa, otherwise you will not be allowed to leave.

● Overseas representation in Comoros

Belgium, located in Moroni, Route de Mitsamiouli, Quartier Coulée des Laves; **China**, located up the hill from the Al Kamar cinema. **France**, on Grande Comore, in Moroni nr the *Hotel Karthala* (Mon 1500-1700, Wed 0800-1100. BP 465, T 730753, Tlx 220. On Anjouan in Mutsamudu at Hombo. Visas for Mayotte cost 60 French Francs (about US$10). **Madagascar**, in Moroni route de Mitsamiouli (Mon-Fri 0800-1200). Visas for Madagascar cost about US$17, issued in 48 hrs, valid for 30 days. You will need a valid ticket and 4 photos. **South Africa**. On Moroni route de la Corniche (Mon-Fri 0800-1400). Visas for South Africa are issued while you wait but you need to have a return air ticket.

The following also have their embassy located in Moroni: **Italy**; **Mauritius**; **Seychelles**; and **USA**, just N of Itsandra.

● Tourist information (in Comoros)

Societe Comorienne de Tourism et d'Hotellerie (COMOTEL), *Itsandra Hotel*, Grand Comore, T 2365. National tourist agency.

● Tourist information (overseas)

France, *Jettours*, 22 quai Megisserie 75001 Paris. *MVM*, 16 rue Litre, 75006 Paris. *Africantours*, 23 rue de Linois, 75015 Paris. **Germany**, *Indian Ocean Tour*, Freiburger Strasse 6a, 6082 Morfelden. **Mayotte**, *Office Mahorais du Tourism et de l'Aristisanat* BP 42, Dzaoudzi 97610 Mayotte, T 40 14 48. *Office Territorial du Tourisme et de l'Information* BP 169, Mamoudzou 97600 Mayotte, T 61 16 04. **UK**, *Indian Ocean Hideaways*, International Services Ltd, Haymarket, London SW1Y 4BY. *Silk Cut Travel*, Meon House, Petersfield, Hants GU32 3JN, T 0730 265211.

● Travel and tour agents

Tourism Services Comores, *La Gaura Hotel*, Grande Comore, T 738118. Also see Moroni, page 688.

When to go

● Best time to visit

The dry season, which falls between May and Oct, is probably the best time to visit. There is little rain (the average is 84 mm during Oct) and temperatures are around (20°-22°C).

● Time

3 hrs ahead of GMT.

Health

● Risks

Malaria is the main health risk, see **Health Section** page 21.

Water

It is unwise to drink local water without boiling or using sterilising tablets.

Money

Currency

The local currency is the Comorien Franc and in 1994 the rate of exchange was KF 586 = US$1. French francs and US dollars are acceptable throughout as are American Express travellers cheques. It is wise to carry some cash in small denomination bills.

Banks

Banque Internationale des Comores (BIC) has branches in Moroni (Place de France) and Mutsamudu opening hrs 0710-1330 Mon-Thurs and Fri 0710-1130. During Ramadan banks close 1 hr earlier than usual. It is also possible to change money 24 hrs a day (though at a lower rate) at the *Novotel Ylang-Ylang* in Moroni. The bank has other branches in Domoni, Fombouni, and Mitsamiouli open most mornings but they are only small branches and can be a little erratic. There are no banks on Moheli or at Hahaya airport.

Getting there

Air

There are a number of routes available but prices fluctuate depending on the season. High season occurs between Jul and Aug and also during Christmas whilst low season falls between Oct and Apr.

There are direct flights from Paris, Marseilles, Johannesburg, Nairobi, Dar es Salaam, Antananarivo (Madagascar), Mahajanga (Madagascar) and Mauritius. Travelling from London can be cheaper to buy a return flight to Nairobi or Dar es Salaam and then an additional return from these locations to Moroni. Be prepared for delays on the leg to Moroni. Aeroflot fly to Antananarivo (Madagascar), from where there are flights to Moroni. A standard economy (IATA) ticket rather than an Apex ticket will enable you to use another airline (providing it is an IATA airline) if your original flight is cancelled.

Air Comoros is the local carrier and flies regularly to Mombasa and Dar es Salaam once a week. If you plan to visit Mayotte book well in advance.

Fares from **Dar es Salaam** or **Zanzibar** to Moroni US$178 single, US$248 return; **Mombasa** to Moroni US$216 single, US$325 return; **Nairobi** to Moroni US$222 single, US$275 return; **Majunga** (Madagascar) to Moroni or Anjouan US$105 single.

Air Madagascar and Air Mauritius operate a joint service which connects Mauritius to **Antananarivo** (Madagascar) and thence to Moroni and Nairobi. Antananarivo to Moroni on Thu, return on Fri, is US$125 single, US$175 return. Moroni to Nairobi on Thu, return on Fri, is US$265 single, US$330 return.

To **Mayotte** from Moheli US$100; from **Moroni** US$125.

Sea

By ferry from Mayotte costs US$30, by small *boutres* US$60.

It is possible to travel by boat from Mombasa and Majunga (Madagascar), although these are infrequent and are basically freight services. To find out available boats contact shipping agencies in Mombasa and Madagascar. Cruises can be arranged (they are expensive) through agents specialising on the Indian Ocean Islands. Contact *Croisiers Paquet*, 5 Boulevard Malesherbes, 75008 Paris.

When you arrive

Airport information

The international airport is Hahaya, close to Moroni on Grand Comore. Moheli and Anjouan have air-strips for flights by light aircraft between the islands.

Transport to town The taxi fare to and from the airport at Hahaya is around US$7.

Airline offices

Air Comoros: **Grand Comores**, BP 544 Aeroport, Moroni, ICONI, T 730524. **Anjouan**, BP 37 Mutsamudu, T 710174. **Moheli Fomboni**, T 720252. **Mayotte Fougoudjou**, T 601020. **Kenya (Mombasa)**, Highways Kenya Ltd, PO Box 84787, Mombasa, T 316490/2/3.

Conduct

Although Comoros is an Islamic country, it has a relaxed atmosphere, and there are no unduly restricting rules on dress or behaviour.

Electricity

Standard 220v 2 pin sockets are used. An adaptor is necessary for British and North American plugs.

Hours of business

Offices open Mon-Thu 0800-1200 and 1400-1600. Fri 0900- 1200. Shops keep roughly

HOTEL CLASSIFICATIONS

A+ Over US$100 a night. International standards and decor, a/c, self contained rooms, swimming pool, restaurants, bars, business services.

A US$40-100. First class standards. Air-conditioning, attached bathrooms. Restaurants and bars. Swimming pool.

B US$20-40. Tourist class. Comfortable with a/c or fans, attached barthrooms. Restaurant, bar, public rooms.

C US$10-20. Budget. Fans. Shared bathroom facilities.

D US$5-10. Guest house. No fan. Shared bathroom. Cold water.

E Under US$5. Basic guest house. Simple bed. No soap or towels. No wardrobe. Shared bathroom facilities. Erratic cold water supply. No fans or mosquito nets.

EATING CLASSIFICATIONS

♦♦♦♦ Over US$10 for a meal. A 3-course meal in a restaurant with pleasant decor. Beers, wines and spirits available.

♦♦♦ US$5-10 for a meal. Two courses, not including alcohol, reasonable surroundings.

♦♦ US$2-5 for a meal, probably only a single course, surroundings spartan but adequate.

♦ Under US$2. Single course, often makeshift surroundings such as a steet kiosk with simple benches and tables.

similar hrs but some take long siestas and stay open late.

● **Safety**
The combination of small communities and Islamic traditions combine to make Comoros perfectly safe for the visitor, even after dark.

Where to stay

High class accommodation is limited to Moheli in Grand Comore and some beach hotels. Small hotels by the beach are very good value. The best restaurants are located in the expensive hotels.

Drink

Despite being an Islamic country, a full range of alcoholic drinks is available, all of which are imported.

Getting around

● **Air**
Air Comoros flies regularly between the islands. Round trips which land on each of the Islands are available and there are discounts for students. Fares Moroni to Moheli US$60, to Anjouan US$75. Moheli to Anjouan US$60.

● **Boat**
A variety of boats operate between the Islands. There are traditional dhows, known locally as *boutres*, which are officially only allowed to carry 12 persons; private motorised boats; and regular ferry services. Routes cost about US$40 from Moroni to Moheli, the ferry US$20. Moroni to Anjouan by *boutres* is US$50, by ferry US$25. Moheli to Anjouan by *boutres* US$40, by ferry US$20. There is a small port tax on landing of 3 French francs (US$0.50). Travel sickness tablets are recommended for less hardy ocean-goers.

● **Car hire**
Avis and **Europcar** operate car rentals and can be arranged through travel agents in Moroni, see page 696. Your own national drivers licence will normally be valid for 3 months.

● **Other local transport**
There are no formal buses on the islands. Public transport is by *taxi brousse* (a pick-up truck with bench seats in the back) or taxi. Ask a local person to find out where the *taxi brousse* depart for your destination, and it is wise to ask the fare as well. **Taxis** Taxis can be shared or privately hired and are widely available. Most local taxi trips are around US$1-2, but be prepared to bargain.

Communications

● **Language**
The traditional language of the Comores before they became a French Protectorate was Swahili, but, with the introduction of Islam, Arabic began to make inroads. After it became a French protectorate in 1886, French became the official language although locals also speak Comorien which has close similarities to Swahili and Arabic. Each island has its own dialect and all are mutually comprehensible.

Postal services
Mail is reliable. There is a charge for collecting mail poste restante.

Telephone services
Telephoning Comoros is expensive There is no direct dialling and all calls pass via the operator.

Entertainment

Newspapers
There are 2 weekly newspapers. *Al Watany* is government-owned and published in Comoran. *L'Archipel* is independent, published in French.

Radio
Radio-Comoros (BP 250 Moroni, T 730531, Tlx 241) is a government-owned station. It broadcasts in Comoran and French, and has an international service that broadcasts in Swahili, Arabic and French.

Television
There is no television service, but video players are widely used.

Holidays and festivals

Muslim festivals are based on the lunar calendar and vary from year-to-year. **Ramadan** (Apr/May); **Id-ul-Fitr** (ends the fasting of Ramadan and is marked by a full moon in the ninth month of Lunar year); **Muharram** (start of the Islamic new year); **Leilat ul-Miradj** (Mohammed's ascension to heaven); and **Maoulid** (the anniversary of Mohammed's birth day). Independence Day falls on 6 Jul.

MAYOTTE

INTRODUCTION

Mayotte (known as Mahore locally) is surrounded by a reef and is the oldest settlement and the most developed of the islands in the Comores archipelago. The local people are known as Mahorais. The island is a collective territory of France, voting not to join with the 3 islands that comprise Comoros when the latter opted for independence in 1975. Mayotte is split into La Grande Terre (Mamoudzou) and La Petite Terre (the small islet of Pamandzi). Just off the coast of Pamandzi a causeway links the island to the rock of Dzaoudzi.

LEMURS

Lemurs are an early from of primate. Their distinguishing features are large eyes, thick fur coats, extensive bushy tails, long hind legs, and all their paws have long, finger-like claws. They live in trees, are very shy and are mostly nocturnal. Although they will eat insects, eggs and small reptiles, they are mainly vegetarian. Baby lemurs cling to their mothers for many months before they become independent.

In earlier ages, when the Madagascar was linked to the other continents, lemurs were common in Europe and North America. With the emergence of the monkey, lemurs were driven out of their traditional areas and are now found only in Madagascar and the Comores.

CONTENTS

MAPS

As a result of maintaining the link with France, most high ranking officials are French. This has led to the Mayotte having upper middle-income status. It is an attractive tropical island with high standards in accommodation and services.

Environment

Geography

The island is volcanic, although there is no longer any activitiy. It is thought the Mayotte was formed by volcanic eruption some 8 million years ago. Soils are predominantly basaltic igneous rock, formed from cooled lava. There is also some trachyte, a gritty volcanic rock. The nature of the soils results in few permanent pools or streams, and there is a problem in ensuring a regular water supply. The island is sheltered by an inner and and outer coral reef.

Climate

There is a dry season from May to Oct, a wet season from Nov to Apr, and a cold season in Apr and part of May. For more detail see Comoros, page 678.

Flora and fauna

Flora

Vegetation is tropical, with spices, palms

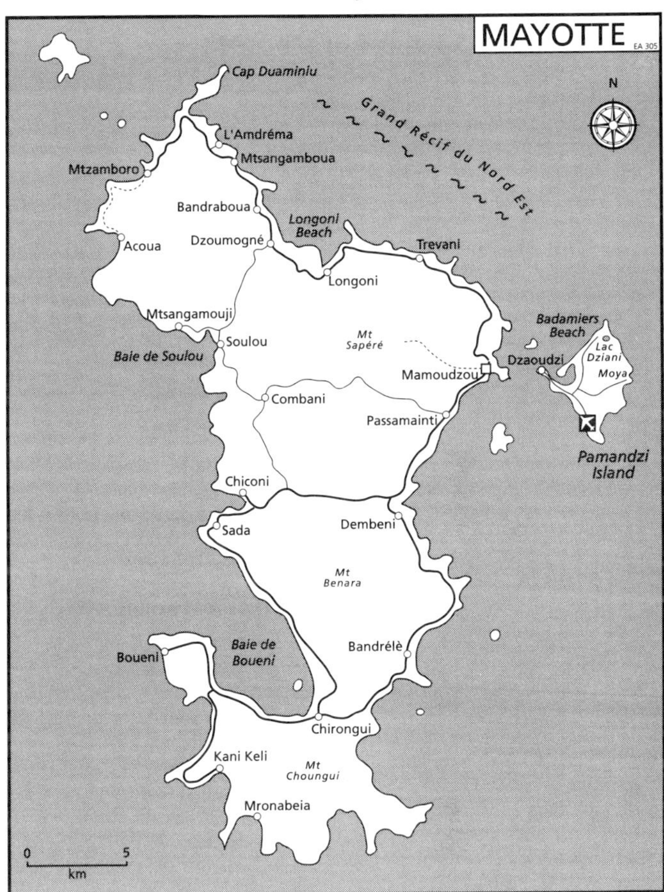

and perfumed flowering shrubs and trees. In the higher areas there is tropical rainforest with lichens, ferns and orchids. The climate allows rice, tea, coffee, maize, and yams to be grown.

Fauna

Fish, birds, mammals and reptiles are similar to Comoros, see page 678. One species of bird unique to the island, however, is the Mayotte Yellow-bellied Sunbird (*Nectarina coquereli*). A mammal unique to Mayotte is the Mongoose Lemur (*Lemur Mongon mayottensis*).

History

Prior to 1975 Mayotte was an integral part of the Comoros islands, see page 680. The original population were thought to be from Malay Polynesia. Islamic migrants arrived after the 8th century, most likely from Shiraz in present-day Iran. A hierarchy evolved with Shirazi families (*kaba'ila*) ruling society, headed by the Sultan and the Sharif (the

Calendar Of The Winds

Mahorais mark the year, and their activities, by the direction of the prevailing wind as it veers clockwise through the seasons.

The *Kashkazi* blows from the N from Nov to Mar, and these 5 months are the 'bad' season of heavy rains at least every other day, occasional destructive cyclones, and cloudy skies. The sea is rough and on land, unsealed roads a are a morass of mud. It is a time for putting in new stands of bananas and there is heavy work, clearing, planting and weeding the rice fields.

In Apr to May, the *Matulahi* blows from the E. It marks the end of the monsoons, and the harvesting of rice gets under way. It is the transition period between the grim time of the *Kashkazi* and the happier days of the *Kusi*.

The balmy S breezes of the trade winds mark the *Kusi* from Jun to Aug. It is dry, and a good time to travel and fish. The days are filled with festivals, marriages, celebrations, and socialising.

By Sep the *Myombeni* begins, and the winds have veered to blow from the W. There are odd showers, and planting begins.

religious leader) who claimed ancestry going back to the Prophet Mohammed. Below the Shirazi were free slave and indigenous Mahorais, the *wagwana*. Finally there were the slaves, *warumwa*, imported by the Shirazi from the African mainland.

The Portugese presence began in 1500, but by 1529 the French, and after 1591 the British, controlled the islands. The French regained control of Mayotte in 1841, and by 1886 the rest of the islands. These 40 years were crucial in establishing a stronger French presence in Mayotte than in the other islands. Initially France attempted to establish a sugar industry with French plantation owners and local labour. The scheme was never a success, as Mahorians showed little inclination to work as hired labourers when they could tend their own plots. There is very little sugar grown today. Self-government was achieved (as part of Comoros) in 1961, with the French retaining control of defence and external affairs.

When Comoros elected to become independent in 1975, a referendum in Mayotte was in favour of retaining links with France, and a special status, *collective territoriale*, was established. A Prefect, appointed by France is the chief executive. There is an elected General Council with 17 members. Mayotte has one seat in the National Assembly in Paris, and one seat in the Senate.

Arts and architecture

Mayotte bears the cultural imprint of the various groups that have controlled the islands. Urban dwellings of local people are strongly influenced by the Shirazi/Arabic period, and decorations and styles are Islamic. The short Portuguese occupation resulted in a few fortifications. The French are responsible for the main public buildings, such planned layout of the towns as the sites have allowed, and for the bulk of the more substantial houses.

In the villages the house usually has a man's room and a woman's room with a verandah. At the rear is a fenced compound with a cooking shelter, a grain store, a coop for chickens and a bathing enclosure. The whole complex is called a *shanzu*.

A house with a timber frame of poles lashed together with walls, roof and fencing of coconut fronds is known as a *maratsu*. Coconut fronds need to be replaced every 3 years or so, and are not regarded as particularly desirable on a long term basis for walls. Grass thatch for the roof is more expensive, but lasts longer (about 10 years) and makes for a cooler interior. Slats made from the *raphia* palm tree are used for walls in a more substantial type of house known as a *buru*, which is cool, well-ventilated and less damp than houses with solid mud walls. Mud and straw walls are the feature of *troto* houses which are sturdy and effective in resisting rain and cyclones. A cement block structure, with a corrugated-iron roof is known as a *bwe* or *parapain*.

Culture and life

A study undertaken in the late 1970's by J. H. Breslar, an anthropologist, gives a good impression of village life in Mayotte.

The man starts with a visit to the mosque at 0530, followed by the first meal of the day. The morning is taken up with tending livestock, clearing land and cultivating. Between 1300 and 1400 there is the midday meal and relaxation. The afternoon comprises some more agricultural work until about 1700, when he will bathe, visit the mosque again, play cards, and relax with other menfolk. The evening meal is taken at around 2000 and sleep at 2200. The main departure from this routine is on Fri when between 1100 and 1330 there are ablutions, readings from the Koran, and prayers at the mosque. In all, there is an average of 7 hrs of work a day over the 7 days of the week.

For a woman, water collection starts at 0530, followed by a meal and household cleaning. From 0800 she will clear land and cultivate, wash clothes, weave mats, perhaps go fishing in the shallows by using a purse seine with other women, or by spearing octopus. From 1200-1300 the midday meal is prepared and taken between 1300 and 1400. In the afternoon there is some more cultivation, food preparation and weaving, with maybe an hour of relaxation on one of the days of the week in hair-dressing with the other women. From 1800 the children are tended and the evening meal prepared. After the meal is cleared at around 2030, there will be time for bathing and some relaxation before bed at 2200. Work averages 12 hrs a day.

Modern Mayotte

Politics

Comoros has pressed its claims to sovereignty over Mayotte since 1975, and the UN and the OAU have endorsed this position. In 1984, the French govern-

The Family Economy

Mayotte's Agricultural Service surveyed the income and expenditure of typical families in 1977. A typical urban family would be a husband, wife and 5 children. The man has 8 ha of land and his wife 1 ha. Income is from the husband's carpentry (US$1,000 a year) cultivating vanilla, coconuts, rice and manioc (US$800 a year plus household food), herding ($200). Main expenses would be food ($500), clothing US$400, farm labour costs US$500, schooling US$300 and other expenditures US$300.

A rural family would comprise a husband, wife and 6 children, farming 5 ha and doing some fishing. Coconuts and coffee sales would bring in US$300 a day, and they would produce most of their own food. Sales of coconut oil by the wife would earn US$75. Expenditure would be US$100 on food (mostly rice), US$75 on clothing, household items US$50, school materials US$10, other items US$140.

Comparative Economic And Social Data

	Mayotte	East Africa	Africa	Industrial Countries
Population and land				
Population, mid year, millions, 1994	0.099	12.2	10.2	40.0
Urban population, %, 1985	39	30.5	30	75
Population growth rate, % per year, 1988-91	5.8	3.1	3.1	0.8
Land area, thou. sq. kilom.	0.37	486	486	1,628
Population density, persons per sq km, 1994	252.4	24.2	20.4	24.3
Economy: production and income				
GNP, US$US millions, 1991 (approx)	350	2,650	3,561	550,099
GNP per head, US$US, 1991 (approx)	3,500	250	389	12,960
Economy: demand structure				
Exports, % of GDP, 1991	9.1	16	23	17
Imports, % of GDP, 1991	80.1	24	26	17
Education				
Primary, % of 6-11 group, 1985	105	62	76	102
Secondary, % of 12-17 group, 1985	15	15	22	93

Notes: 'Africa' excludeS South Africa. Dates are for the country in question, and do not always correspond with the regional, African and industrial averages.

ment announced that it would take steps to integrate Mayotte within Comoros, and talks were held between the 2 governments. However, France will not cede Mayotte without a referendum supporting the move. Plans for the islanders to vote on the issue in 1984 have been postponed indefinitely.

In the meantime, Mayotte has been pressing for full overseas department status (which will mean more representation in Paris and rights to enhanced social benefits). This has so far been resisted by France, mainly on the grounds of cost. Nearby Reunion has departmental status, but is a much bigger island with a larger population at 650,000. Mayotte's population is just about 100,000. A substantial number of illegal migrants from Comoros have been attracted by the better prospects in Mayotte, and there is continual friction between these arrivals and the local people.

The reality of the situation is that Mayotte enjoys high living standards as a result of its link with France. When added to the lack of political stability and direction in Comoros, see page 682, the prospects of a referendum supporting a union are negligible, and the present arrangements are set to continue for the forseeable future.

Economics

As Mayotte is administered by France, separate economic data for the territory is meagre. It would seem clear that Mayotte is among the better-off developing territories, and the World Bank currently classifies Mayotte as being in the upper-middle income group. There are only 6 countries in Africa and the Indian Ocean in this category, the others being Botswana, Gabon, Réunion, Seychelles and South Africa.

Economic and social structure

The population of Mayotte is small at just around 100,000, and the land area is very limited at only 374 square kilometres. Thus population density is high, compared with most of Africa, although Burundi and Rwanda on the mainland have comparable densities. However, most of the small Indian Ocean territories are equally densely populated, the only exception being Madagascar. Population is increasing rapidly at 5.8% a year. Most of this is due to migration from Comoros, and the natural rate of population growth is 2.2%.

Most local economic activity is agricultural. There is minimal manufacturing, and a substantial services sector dominated by administration and tourism. Exports of merchandise are mostly ylang-ylang (80%) and vanilla (18%). Receipts from tourism are the other main source of foreign earnings. There is heavy dependence on imports for manufactured goods (48% of imports) and also for food (22%). The value of merchandise imports is over 10 times as great as the value of exports. This situation is only sustained by virtue of the fact that France assumes responsibility for the bulk of government spending, and in 1991, this accounted for 90% of all recorded expenditures.

The French presence has led to good provision of basic education, although secondary provision at 15% enrolment is well below the level in Réunion, where it is 51%. Medical provision is good, and substantially better, in terms of numbers of doctors and nurses per head of the population, than is typically the case on mainland Africa.

PETITE TERRE (Pamandzi)

This was the administrative and governmental centre. With land becoming scarce on Dzaoudzi Island (now largely occupied by the military) it has become a haven for the rich.

Places of interest

The **Prefecture**, the **Hotel Rocher** and scattered private houses are particularly fine. The other 2 towns on the islands are **L'Abattoir** and **Pamandzi** (the richer of the 2, with shops like Maison de l'Artisanat and Khodidas). At the foot of the hill between the roundabout and the cemetery lies the **Vato Mena** (Red Stone) a local sacred site. L'Abattoir is the poorest town but since it has more room to expand than the other 2 towns it is becoming a popular place to live for the wealthier. The town has more shops than Dzaoudzi and Pamandzi. North of L'Abattoir is **Badamiers** the site of an oil terminal and military camp. **Lac Dziani** (*Dziani Dzaha*), a crater lake, lies to the N and a path leads to the lake through marshy ground. Tradition has it that snakes (*massimo*) reincarnated as evil spirits inhabit the lake which is sacred. To the E lies **Moya**, a cove formed from an eroded volcanic crater. It is popular with bathers but is not a particularly good beach.

Local information

● Where to stay

A *Rocher Dzaoudzi*, T 60 14 44. Mayotte's oldest and most handsome hotel is above the ferry terminal in Dzaoudzi. All rooms with bathrooms, a/c, TV, telephones. **B** *Kelimaharava*, Blvd Amoureux, L'Abattoir. Shared bathrooms.

● Places to eat

♦♦♦♦*Resto le Fare*, Blvd des Crabes, Dzaoudzi. On the waterfront. Good standard. ♦♦♦♦*Reflet des Iles*, Dzaoudzi. Mainly a lunch venue. ♦♦♦♦*Le Lagon* (Chez Gaston), T 40 12 45. Located on road to L'Abattoir. Smart restaurant on terrace overhanging the sea. ♦♦♦♦*Moya Restaurant*, T 60 14 23. On the route out of L'Abattoir. At weekends customers play boules. Indian, Creole and French cuisine. ♦♦♦*Ylang Ylang Bar & Restaurant*, T 60 12 78. Chinese and Vietnamese food.

● Shopping

Mayotte is noted for its jewelry and good examples can be found in Khodidas in Pamandzi.

● Transport

See **Getting there**, page 708 and **Getting around** page 709.

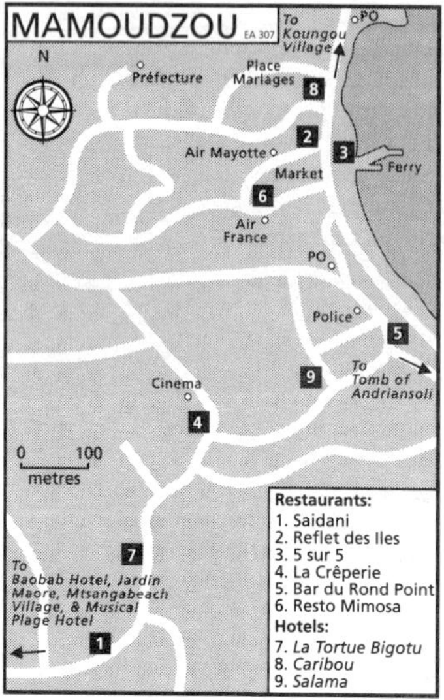

GRANDE TERRE

Mamoudzou

The main town and Prefecture, Mamoudzou has been the seat of local government since WW2. The Place du Marché is the centre of Mamoudzou and where the bank, Air France, Air Mayotte agents, the tourist office and the market are to be found. South of the port is the site of Mayotte's last palace, the **Palace of Andriantsoli.** Andriantsol's tomb also lies there. It is the site of a pilgrimage and a ceremony every year, when a female said to be possessed by Andriantsoli's spirit presides over the *tromba* (a ceremony to contact the spirits). To the E is **Mount M'Sapere** (572m) which can be climbed. Further to the N is **Longoni** the island's only deep water port. Some good beaches can be reached by boat from N Mayotte. Due E of the capital lies **Soulou** the site of a large waterfall. To the S is **Combani,** the site of plantations in the pre-war era. Between here and M'tsangachehi lies **Sada**, famous for its hats. Further S is **Choungui** (594m) and there is a route to the summit. Continuing round the coast is **Saziley** where turtles lay their eggs in season. The Service des Eaux Forêts de Mayotte has marked a hiking trail around the island for visitors. It takes 10 days to complete the circuit, staying in fairly simple accommodation. Further information can be obtained from the tourist board, see page 708. Visits can be made by small boat to the islands around Mayotte (**M'Zamboro** is the largest). If you are visiting the beach and hoping to swim it is a good idea to check the times of the tides. At the S of Mayotte Lagoon is the **L'Ilot du Sable** (*M'Sanga Tsohole*) a sand bar, and, although there is no vegetation, it is perhaps Mayotte's best beach.

Local information

● Where to stay

A *Trevani Village*, Koungou, T 60 13 83. Rooms have bathrooms, a/c. TV. Some cooking facilities. Well located. Water sports. Swimming pool. **A** *Le Tortue Bigotu*, Mamoudzou, T 61 11 32, F 61 19 52. Rooms with bathrooms. Pleasant atmosphere. Game fishing. **A** *Baobab*, T 60 11 40, F 61 18 24. Chalets with bathrooms, a/c TV. Telephones. Fishing and car hire can be arranged. **A** *Le Caribou*, T 61 14 18. Rooms with bathrooms. Popular with business people. Can arrange excursions. **A** *Jardin Maore*, N'Gouja Village, Kani Keli, T 60 14 19. Rooms with bathrooms. Pleasant location on SW coast, 40 km from Mamoudzou. Fishing available.

B *Mtsangabeach Village* M'Tsangachehi Sada, T 60 19 72, F 60 17 48. Chalets with bathrooms. Some family chalets with cooking facilities. Rustic, pleasant location on W coast 25 km from Manoudzou. Good restaurant. Diving and boat trips available. **B** *Musical Plage* Bandrele. Bar and chalets under construction on E coast, 25 km S of Mamoudzou. Named because French fishermen sing on the beach in the evenings. **B** *Salama*, rue de Commerce, Mamoudzou, T 61 07 03. Shared bathrooms. Restaurant. Good value.

● Eating

♦♦♦*Caribou Hotel*, Pizzas recommended. Bakery next door serves snacks. ♦♦♦*Restaurant Saidani*, T 60 12 23. Good views over bay but a little dilapidated. ♦♦♦*Reflet des Iles*. French cuisine. Fixed-price menu is good value. ♦♦♦*5 sur 5*. Located on harbour, nr ferry. Fixed-price menu and snacks ♦♦♦*La Crêperie*. Located on road to *Hotel Baobab*. Good standard. ♦♦*Bar du Rond-Point*. Snacks served. Good value. ♦♦*Resto Mimosa*, Place du Marché. Local food. Good value. Several brochettes in the market place also serves snacks.

● Nightlife

Golden Lagoon, Mamoudzou. Open weekends only. Local atmosphere. *Ningha*, Dzaoudzi Open every day except Mon. *Mahaba*, Mamoudzou. Open weekends only. Interesting decor with fishtanks. *Bar du Rond Point*, Mamoudzou. Fairly boisterous.

● Tourist information

Centre Mahorais d'Animation Culturelle (CMAC) T 61 11 36. Near the post office. Posts news on events.

● Transport

See **Getting Around**, page 709.

INFORMATION FOR VISITORS

Contents

Before you go

Entry requirements

● Visas

The cost of a visa is 60F (US$10) and the nearest French embassy is in Moroni in Comoros. There is a consulate in Mutsamuda in Comoros.

Members of the EU and citizens of Austria, Sweden, Switzerland, Andorra and Monaco do not require visas. If you are an American, Canadian, South African, Australian or New Zealander you will need a visa but it is advisable to check with your local French Embassy since the situation can change. New Zealand and Australian visa applications presently have to be referred to the authorities on Mayotte which can take up to 2 months to process.

● Vaccinations

These are not required.

● Mayotte Representation Overseas

This is handled by the French embassies and consulates.

● Travel and tour agents

Komba Tours, T 61 10 38, is recommended for its trips around the Lagoon but also arranges other trips round the island. It is possible to have a quick tour of the island by helicopter.

For the adventurous, microlight hire is available from the aero club (enquire at airport).

● Tourist information

Office Mahorais de Tourisme, BP 42, 97610 Dzaoudzi, situated on the Place du Marché in Mamoudzou.

When to go

● Best time to visit

The dry season, which falls between May and Oct, is probably the best time to visit. There is little rain (the average is 84 mm during Oct) and temperatures are around 20°-22°C.

Health

● Staying healthy

Malaria is the main health risk, see **Health Section**, page 21.

● Water

In the main towns and the large hotels the water supply is perfectly safe. In the rural areas, it is unwise to drink local water without boiling or using sterilising tablets.

Money

● Currency

The unit of currency on Mayotte is the French Franc. There is only one bank on the island, the Banque Française Commerciale de l'Ocean Indien (BFC) and the branches are in Dzaoudzi and Mamoudzou (Mon-Fri 0730-1130 and 1330-1530).

● Credit cards

These are accepted by large stores, the main hotels, travel agents, and by all airlines except Air Comores. If you wish to use a credit card for an Air Comores flight, book through a travel agent rather than directly with the airline.

Getting there

● By air

There are no direct flights to Mayotte from Europe, only from other Indian Ocean islands. The airport is only able to take light aircraft, but there are plans to extend the runway for long-haul flights.

The cheapest way to get to Mayotte by air is to take an excursion ticket to Nairobi or Dar es Salaam, then a flight to Moroni in Comoros, finally a flight to Mayotte.

Comoros Daily flight by *Air Comoros* US$100-125. **Réunion** is connected by a daily flight to-and-from Mayotte by *Air Austral*. The flight takes 2 hrs and 10 minutes and costs US$510 if booked in Europe. **Madagascar** is served once a week by *Air Mayotte* in conjunction with Somacram, making stops at Majunga, Antananarivo, Diego Suarez and Nosy Be. From US$105 single.

● Specialist agencies

For discounted fares from Europe, North America and Australasia, see page 14.

● By sea

The Ylang Ylang ferries passengers to Anjouan in Comoros, fare US$30 (tickets etc available from *SMART*, T 60 10 24, Place de France, Dzaoudzi. Alternatively you can travel on a dhow *(boutre)* but this is more expensive at US$60 (information on dockside).

When you arrive

● Airport information

There is an airport tax of 6F (US$0.50) on all flights.

● Airline offices

Air Austral. Represented by SARL (Issoufali) in Dzaoudzi and Mamoudzou. *Air Comoros*. Office is on the Boulevard des Crabes (Air Comoros do not accept credit cards – book through an agent if you wish to pay by card). *Air France*. Agents SARL (Issoufali) are in Dzaoudzi and Mamoudzou (accept credit cards).

● Conduct

Although Mayotte is predominantly Islamic, French administration has established a relaxed atmosphere, and there are no unduly restricting rules on dress or behaviour.

● Electricity

Standard 220v 2 pin sockets are used. An adaptor is necessary for British and North American plugs.

● Hours of business

Offices open Mon-Fri 0800-1200 and 1400-1600. Shops keep roughly similar hrs but some take long siestas and stay open late.

● Safety

The combination of efficient French administration, small communities and Islamic traditions combine to make Comoros quite safe for the visitor, even after dark.

● Time

3 hrs later than GMT.

Food and drink

A wide selection of imported wines, spirits and beers are available, with French brands particularly prominent.

Getting around

● Ferry service

The 'barge' takes passengers from Grande Terre to Petite Terre and is currently free for foot passengers. (Timetable is posted at piers).

Hotel Classifications

A+	Over US$100 a night. International standards and decor, a/c, self contained rooms, swimming pool, restaurants, bars, business services.
A	US$40-100. First class standards. Air-conditioning, attached bathrooms. Restaurants and bars. Swimming pool.
B	US$20-40. Tourist class. Comfortable with a/c or fans, attached barthrooms. Restaurant, bar, public rooms.
C	US$10-20. Budget. Fans. Shared bathroom facilities.
D	US$5-10. Guest house. No fan. Shared bathroom. Cold water.
E	Under US$5. Basic guest house. Simple bed. No soap or towels. No wardrobe. Shared bathroom facilities. Erratic cold water supply. No fans or mosquito nets.

Restaurant Classifications

♦♦♦♦	Over US$10 for a meal. A 3 course meal in a restaurant with pleasant decor. Beers, wines and spirits available.
♦♦♦♦	US$5-10 for a meal. Two courses. Comfortable surroundings.
♦♦	US$2-5 for a meal. Probably only a single course. Surroundings spartan but adequate.
♦	Under US$2. Single course. Often makeshift surroundings such as a street kiosk with simple benches and tables.

● **Car hire**

Available from *SMA*, T 61 10 29. *MAKI-LOC*, T 61 19 51. *LMV*, T 60 00 34/60 15 00.

● **Other local transport**

Most public transport is by *taxi brousse* (a pick-up truck with bench seats in the back) or taxi. Ask a local person to find out where the *taxi brousse* departs for your destination, and it is wise to ask the fare as well.

● **Taxis**

Taxis can be shared or privately hired and are widely available. Most local taxi trips are around US$2-5. Be prepared to bargain.

Communications

● **Language**

French is the main language in the towns, but is only spoken by about 15% of the population in the rural areas. Local dialects, mixtures of Arabic and Swahili, are spoken outside the towns. The main local dialect is *shimaore*.

● **Postal services**

The new Post Office in Mamoudzou lies N of the pier. The charge for collecting letters from the poste restante is 3F (US$0.50)

● **Telephone services**

The telephone network on the island is better than that found in Comoros. International dialling is available from all phones though reverse charge phone calls cannot be made. Calls to France are less expensive than to other parts of Europe (the Dialling Code to phone into Mayotte is 269 and out is 19).

Entertainment

● **Newspapers**

There is one French language weekly newspaper, *Le Journal de Mayotte*, BP 181, Mamoudzou, 97600 Mayotte, T 61 16 95, F 61 08 88.

● **Radio**

Broadcasts in French and Mahorian. Government-owned, began operation in 1977.

● **Television**

Government-owned television station has been in operation since 1986. Societe Nationale de Radio-Television Francaise d'Outre Mer (RFO) – Mayotte, BP 103, Dzaoudzi, 97610 Mayotte, T 60 10 17, F 60 18 52, Tlx 915822.

MADAGASCAR

INTRODUCTION

Madagascar, in the East African region, is the fourth largest island in the world. It lies to the East of Mozambique in the Indian Ocean. The mountainous island has a narrow eastern coastal strip, central highlands and wide western plains. The East and Northwest are hot and humid, typically tropical; the central highlands are temperate, whilst the West and South are arid. Most of the island is savanna with rain forest surviving in the remoter wet areas.

Madagascar has a unique wildlife, with many small animals, birds and plants found nowhere else. There are miles of unspoiled beaches. Charming towns with colonial buildings, the legacy of contact with Europeans that began in earnest around 1810, and a strong French influence on architecture, culture and education from 1895. Travel is generally easy, with an excellent network of air services, 2 small rail systems, and quite good roads served by frequent, and cheap, minibuses. The accommodation available does not a offer a great number of luxury hotels, but there is plenty of choice, lodgings are seldom crowded and they are excellent value.

The island is perfectly safe for travellers who take the normal sensible precautions. Malagasy people are friendly, helpful and welcoming.

Exchange rate in August 1994 MGF 3346 = US$1

CONTENTS

MAPS

Environment

Geography

Madagascar lies some 400km E of the coast of Mozambique, S of the equator. It is traversed by the Tropic of Capricorn near the southerny town of Tulear. The Island is approximately 1600km long, has a coastline that stretches for over 4,000 km and occupies a total area of nearly 590,000 sq km. Unlike the other islands located in the S-western region of the Indian ocean, such as the Seychelles, Mauritius and the Comores, Madagascar does not owe its existence to Volcanic activity but was once part of the landmass of the mainland. Madagascar is thought to have broken away from Africa some 165 million years ago reach-

MADAGASCAR
EA 315
N
Mozambique Channel
Indian Ocean
Antsiranana (Diégo-Suarez)
Mgne d'Ambre NP
Nosy Be
Ambilobe
Vohimarina (Vohémar)
Hell Ville
Marivorahona 2236 m
Ambanja
Nosy Berafia
Ambondrara 2262 m
Sambava
Bealanana
Analalava
Antsohihy
Andapa
Antalaha
Port Bergé
Maroantsetra
Mahajanga (Majunga)
Befandriana
Mampikony
Mananara NP
Mandritsara
Tanjona Masoala
Mananara
Mitsinjo
Marovoay
Soalala
Manompana
Miarinarivo
Andilamena
Ile St Marie
Besalampy
Maevatanana
Fenoarivo
Lake Alaotra
Ambatondrazaka
Toamasina (Tamatave)
Ankazobe
Tsitondroina 1626 m
Mantady NP
Maintirano
Antananarivo
Ambila
Tsiroanomandidy
Moramanga
Vatomandry
Antsalova
Tsiafajarona 2643 m
Ambatolampy
Miandrivazo
Antsirabe
Belo Tsiribihina
Itongafeno 2367 m
Fandriana
Morondava
Nosy Varika
Atofinandrahana
Manajary
Ifanadiana
Fianarantsoa
Ranomafana NP
Morombe
Beroroha
Ambalavao
Manakara
Lake Ihotry
Isalo NP
Ihosy
Ankazoabo
Ranohira
Pic Boby 2658 m
Farafangana
Sakaraha
Ifaty
Vangaindrano
Toliara (Tuléar)
Betroka
Bezaha
Betioky
Trafanaamby 1957 m
St Luce
Ampanihy
Amboasary
Tolanaro (Fort-Dauphin)
Beloha
Ambovombe
0 75 150
km

ing its present position approximately 120 million years ago.

Madagascar can be divided into 3 quite distinct geographical zones: to the W low lying plains and plateaus; to the E a narrow alluvial coastal plain; and the central highlands, largely dominated by large granitic massifs. The western plain is predominantly sedimentary in origin though there are some isolated volcanic formations. Slow moving rivers have created fertile alluvial flood plains which provide much of Madagascar's productive agricultural land. The region is dominated by savannah grassland and scattered deciduous trees but also houses the Bongo Lava, a highly eroded scarp zone that marks the western tip of the central highlands. In the Southwest, the Mahafaly Plateau provides the visitor with an example of limestone karst, whilst the Islao National Park contains eroded sandstone. The eastern half of Madagascar is largely dominated by a large alluvial plain running from Ft Dauphin in the S to Baie d'Antongil in the N E. Along this coastal alluvial strip lie numerous lagoons and inland waterways. Inland the landscape changes giving way to abrupt escarpments and areas of tropical forest before eventually reaching the highland plateaus that dominate central Madagascar. Probably the most noticeable topographical features to dominate Madagascar are the large granitic massifs that extend across the central highlands. In the far N stands the Montagne d'Ambre and the Tsaratanana Massif which includes Maromokotro point (2,876m), the highest point on the island.

Climate

Madagascar experiences a largely tropical climate. However, the tradewinds which blow across from Mozambique warmed by sea currents influence climatic patterns as they reach Madagscar and in so doing contribute to regional climatic disparities. The hot, wet season generally runs from Nov to Apr and the cool dry season from May to Oct. Regional disparities in altitude and latitude as well as the effects of the trade winds influence the length of these seasons. On the East Coast the dry season only lasts a few weeks and rainfall varies from 4,000 mm a year in Maroantsetra to 1520 mm a year in Fort Dauphin. The S E trades, having passed over the West Coast, move northwards and deposit rain along the N western tip of Madagascar. Cyclones frequently hit Madagascar's eastern coast and are most likely to occur between Dec and Mar.

In the Highlands, the South E prevailing winds have lost most of their moisture before they arrive and variations in altitude determine temperature and rainfall. For most of the year skies remain clear (7 months a year without rain, on average) and frosts are common on higher ground (especially around Antsirabe-Faratsiho where the lowest temperature recorded is -8°C). In Oct there are a few days of rainfall but the main rainy season does not arrive until end of Nov, lasting through to Apr.

Western Madagascar experiences a 7-8 month dry season. Rainfall totals in the area range between 1,520 mm a year (Majunga) to 360 mm (Tulear). Rainfall decreases from N to S, while the hottest temperatures are found in the valley between Bonga Lava and Bemaraha Plateau. The driest area lies in the S W where rainfall totals of 50 mm have been recorded.

North W Madagascar is exposed to the N W monsoon and residue from the S E trades which curve northwards after having crossed over the western coast. Home to both the island of Nosy Be and the Tsaratanana massif the area has rainfall averaging 2,030 mm a year.

Natural History

The ancestors of Madagascar's unusual assortment of animals and plants prob-

Traveller's Trees

These spectacular trees, *Ravenella adagascariensis*, look like giant fans with the fronds splaying out from opposite sides of the bole (rather than from all round it). The tree is very useful, with the main stem of each frond isused to make doors, and the bark provides flooring. The leaves are used for thatching roofs, and to make plates for food.

Rainwater falling on the leaves runs down to collect at the base of the stem. Tilting the leaf spills the water out, and small children have fun drenching each other in this way. In dry spells when these small reservoirs are empty, it is still possible to get drinkable water by cutting the base of the stem of one of the young inner stalks.

ably arrived on rafts of vegetation during the break with continental Africa some 165 million years ago. With little to threaten these early species they began to evolve along evolutionary paths quite different from those followed by their mainland cousins, who had to contend with a large variety of predators in order to survive. With the arrival of man some of these early species became extinct as their habitats were cleared for agriculture and animals were hunted for food. Despite this, however, of the 200,000 species living on the island, 150,000 are found nowhere else in the world.

It is estimated that a quarter of Madagascar is burnt each year to prepare for agriculture. In the process many natural habitats are destroyed and the loss of forested area will in time lead to the development of wasteland and the extinction of indigenous species. The Government is attempting to tackle the problem, and has set up a number of national parks, reserves and protected areas.

Flora

Some estimates suggest that the range of floral species on Madagascar lies between 7,000-12,000 and that although mainland Africa has many in common with Madagascar, close to 80% of these species are endemic to the island. Vegetation on Madagascar, like the climate and landscape, varies dramatically from region to region.

The Eastern Region incorporates the E coast, the Highlands and a small part of N W Madagascar. On the E coast, below 800 m, rainfall totals range from 2,000 mm - 3,500 mm a year. Low altitude evergreen rainforest stretches from Fort Dauphin to Vohemar. Estimates suggest that tree densities in these forests are 3 times greater than those found in similar rainforests in other continents. Stratified tree canopies cut out much of the available light which significantly retards the development of undergrowth. The upper canopy is dominated by a number of tree species which include euphorbiaceae, sapindaceae, rubiaceaae (including wild coffee), palms, and ebenaceae (which includes ebony among its many species). Among a number of epiphytes, the comet orchid (*Angraecum sesquipedale*) is quite common. On the coastal fringe large barringtonia trees, bishop hat fruits and coconut palms are found. In recent years, however, pressures on low altitude rainforests have begun to take their toll and the areas are diminishing leaving the only significant stands around Baie d'Antongil and on the Masoale Peninsula. Much of the rest of the eastern coast is occupied by grassland where Traveller's Palm (*Ravenala madagascariensis*), the symbol of Madagascar, are common. Traveller's Palm is not a true palm but related to the strelitzia (bird of Paradise flower). On forest fringes indigenous species like canarium, and 2 guava species, *Psiadia altissima* and *Haronga madagascariensis*, provide locals with a valuable drug source used in local medicines.

The North West region is dominated by moist montane forest found between 800m and 2000m. The forest canopy is lower, species are fewer but epiphytes are abundant and include a variety of orchids (many of which are served by their own particular species of moth), ferns, mosses and the occasional strangler fig (lauracea ocotea). As altitude increases the forest canopy decreases allowing more light through the canopy stimulating the growth of species in the undergrowth. The best examples of upland moist montane forest are situated around Montagne d'Ambre National Park, and at this altitude tree species include Dalbergia rosewood and Weinmannia.

In the Highlands, the central domain is dominated by grasslands and Inselberg rock formations, where Pachypodium Euphorbia and aloe plants predominate. Highland altitude montane forests occur between 1,000-2,000m. The forest is covered with moss, lichens and numerous epiphytes, ferns and orchids whilst the undergrowth is dominated by Ericaceous species. At higher altitudes above 2000m impenetrable evergreen woody plants cover the landscape.

The western region is split into the Western Domain and the Southern Domain. Whilst 80% of the western region is covered by secondary or wooded grasslands, dry deciduous forests corresponding to those found in the dry tropics also persist in the Western Domain. These forests are found in clay and sandy soils and extend from Diego Suarez to just S of Isalo. The forest is less dense than forests found to the E. Tamarind trees are found along rivers while further inland baobabs are more common. Another species endemic to the area is the flamboyant, (flame tree), *Delonix regia*. In the Southern Domain, the spiny forests of S W Madagascar are home to a variety of drought-resistant succulents. These plants have small leaves which are designed to reduce water loss through transpiration and large stems which are used to store water which help the plant survive during the dry season. There are 9 species grouped into 4 types endemic to Madagascar. Alluaudia (6 species) and didierea (2 species) are the most common. The Alluandia group of succulents belongs to the genus Euphorbia whose 31 species range from small shrubs to large trees (the tallest being *Euphorbia enterophora* at 20m). There are 9 species of Pachypodium (whose trunks are adapted for water storage) found throughout Madagascar. Although the pachypodium is not related to the baobab, *Pachypodium rosulatum* is often referred to as "little baobab". Leaf succulents are also abundant, one of the most interesting comes from the genus kalanchoe and grows buds around the leaf margins which then form as individual plants (an adaptation to increase survival).

Noteworthy endemic flora species include the Rosy Periwinkle (extracts from the plant have been used to help combat leukaemia; *Uapaca bojeri* (a fire resistant tree); and more than 6 distinct species of boabab (only one species is found in continental Africa). The scope for new drug exploration using Madagascar plant species is considerable and there is considerable concern that the species be protected.

Fauna

Madagascar wildlife is quite distinct from wildlife found on the African continent. There are 5 orders of indigenous land mammal: Primates (lemurs), Rodentia (rodents), Carnivora (carnivores), Chiroptera (bats) and Insectivora (tenrecs/shrews).

Lemurs are undoubtedly the most famous mammal on Madagascar. The name Lemur is derived from the Latin

Lemures "ghost" because of its elusive appearance in the jungle. Lemurs evolved some 55 million years ago and while other descendants of the ancestral primate evolved into monkeys, lemurs developed a greater intelligence and eyesight. They are Prosimians, a rare suborder of primates and are related to the bush babies of Africa and Lories of Asia. Today there are somewhere in the region of 30 species though a recent discovery has noted the existence of a further 3 species, including the golden bamboo lemur Hapalemur aureus of Ranomafana and the golden crowned sifaka Propithecus tattersalli. Of the other species which remain, half are nocturnal and half diurnal. Most diurnal lemurs are dominated by the females, live in troops and sunbathe in the morning to raise their body temperature as they have a slow metabolic rate. One of the strangest families of lemur is the Aye Aye. It has bat-like ears, rat-like teeth, dog-like nose, a squirrel-like tail and unusual hands with a skeleton-like middle finger used to prise grubs from the bark of trees. Rural people believe the animal is a herald of death and they are killed if seen near villages. Though its habitat is threatened, numbers have increased since they were introduced to the Island of Nosy Be in 1966.

Another mammal common to Madagascar are tenrecs, who are insect eaters. These mammals, often described as Malagasy hedgehogs, are thought to have been the first mammals to arrive on the islands. There are at present around 30 species of tenrecs and they fall into 2 sub families, the nocturnal Oryzoryctinae (25 species) and the diurnal Tenrecinae (5 species). Nocturnal Oryzoryctinae species are generally soft-furred and vary in size from the 6cm shrew-like *Microgale cowani* to the 20cm *Limnogale mergulus*, an aquatic tenrec. Diurnal tenrecs are predominantly prickly and less timid. The largest diurnal tenrec, the *Tenrec ecaudatus* or (common tenrec), is found throughout Madagascar and the Comores and is famed for producing around 32 young per litter. Most tenrecs enter a state of torpor during the dry season in order to survive during this lean period.

There are 28 species of Chiroptera, or bat, 9 of which are endemic to Madagascar. The largest is a fruit bat *Pteropus rufus* or flying fox which is related to a species found in Australia (although not, interestingly, in continental Africa).

Eight species of Carnivora are found in Madagascar, all of which belong to the Viverridae family (related to the Mongoose and civet). There are 3 sub-families Fossinae, Galidiinae and Crypotoprocta. The Fossinae are represented by the striped civet *Fossa fossana* or Madagascar genet, and the *Eupleres gaudoti*, which is becoming rare. The Galidiinae comprise 5 species of which the most common is the ring-tailed mongoose, *Galida elegans*. Two other species are only found around Lac Tsimanampetsotsa, one of which is *Galidictus grandidieri* (largely nocturnal and secretive). The last subfamily, Crypotoprocta, has only one species *Crypotoprocta ferox* (roughly the size of an otter). The animal uses its retractable claws to catch its prey which includes lemurs, birds, and reptiles.

There are around 450 amphibian species in Madagascar, all are frogs and only 2 are not endemic. The best place to see these frogs is in the reserves of the Eastern forest and Ranomatana. Most of the 235 species of reptile are endemic, the largest being the increasingly rare Nile crocodile Crocodilus nilotius. Lizards inhabit the island and number 184 species and include geckos and chameleons. Both the world's smallest chameleon, *Brookesia minima* (3cm), and the world's largest, *Chamaeleo oustaleti* (65cm) are found in Madagascar. Madagascar chameleons are also unique since they lay eggs, rather than live young, when giving birth. There are around 65 species of snake, none of which are poisonous,the most common being the do and the boa. There are 4 species of freshwater turtles and 5 species of land tortoise but pressure on both species has increased, and the ploughshare tortoise (*Geichelone yniphora*) has been pushed to the verge of extinction as its colourful shell is being hunted and sold. The species now survives around Cap St Andre. Other land tortoises have been threatened by introduced animals which prey on them. Encouraging signs have been the introduction of successful breeding programmes set up in areas like Ampijoroa.

Madagascar has surprisingly few birds and forests are unusually silent without bird chatter. Of the 256 species, 198 originated in Madagascar and 106 endemic. The endemic varieties are Mesithornitidae, Brachypteraciidae, Leptosomidae, Philepittidae and Vangidae but there are others that belong to other families like the egret, heron, ibis, duck and several birds of prey. Rare birds of prey include the Madagascar serpent eagle (*Eutriorchis astur*), the Madagascar sea eagle (*Haliaeetus vociferoides*) and the Madagascar sparrow hawk (*Accipiter madagascariensis*). Madagascar's most famous bird, Aepyornis maximus, which laid huge eggs 30 cm long, became extinct in the seventeenth century.

History

There is a degree of confusion as to the time the first settlers arrived. Some suggest they were from Indonesia in the fourth century AD, others argue that the date is probably closer to the third century BC. Since there is no evidence of Buddhism in Malagasy culture, the first Indonesian migrants must have arrived in Madagascar before the introduction of Buddhism, which reached Indonesia in the fourth century AD. Early settlers traded along the paths of the prevailing winds. Migrants arrived from the N, and the oldest archaeological findings are in the NW. As population spread, tribes emerged, accentuated by the differences in the original migrants. Since people from the coastal regions remain very different from those who inhabit the highlands, one can assume there were several migrations both from South East Asia and Africa.

Arabic influence

Islam reached Madagascar in the twelfth century via the Comores and Arabic groups settled in the N W coastal regions. The Muslims (known as *Antalaotra* "people of the sea") controlled ocean-going trade whilst the Malagasy generally concentrated their efforts on the domestic economy. By the fifteenth century Madagascar was producing and trading in gold, iron, wood, tortoise shell and cattle.

European arrival

Although Marco Polo and the Arabs

Marco Polo On Madagascar

Madagascar is a large and beautiful island, 4 thousand miles in extent. Its inhabitants are all Muslim, and live by trade. Every day they slaughter a large number of camels for food. In this island, as in Zanzibar which lies to the N of it, there ar more elephants than anywhere else in the world, and there are found also leopards, lions, giraffes and wild asses.

In the island is found the 'Griffin' or 'Roc', which is not, as related, half-bird, half-lion, but is rather a giant eagle which covers with its wings a span of thirty paces, and carries elephants in its talons; these it drops down from a height and then feeds on the crushed flesh.

Travels 1299

King Radama I

Robert Farquhar was appointed governor of Mauritius in 1810. It was immediately clear that his island was heavily dependent on Madagascar for food, particularly rice and beef. A French slave-trader who had penetrated the dense forest of the coastal stip and eluded the hostile inhabitants of Madagscar, wrote of an enlightened civilsation on the central plateau. As conquest of Madagscar, because of its size, tough inhabitants and difficult terrain, was out of the question, Farquhar resolved to make an alliance with the people of the interior. He despatched a French trader Chardeneaux, in 1816 to make approaches.

The central people, the Merina, had by this time been consolidated by Ramboasalama. He had settled a thousand warriors and their wives to create Tananarivo (now Antananarivo) the 'City of the Thousand'. Ramaboasalama died in 1809, and the kingdom passed to his 17 year-old son, Radama.

Radama, now 24, was taken with Chardeneaux's proposals, and he sent a group of his relatives and officials back with the Frenchman to Mauritius to learn about European discoveries. Under Sergeant James Hasty a party of about 50 craftsmen and soldiers returned to Madagascar, and, with their help, Radama set about conquering the rest of the island. His first success was to defeat the Betsimasavaka around the port of Tamatave.

On the back of this triumph, Radama signed a treaty with the British. The 4 articles called for friendship with the British; an end to slave trading; US$2,000 a year compensation to Radama for ending slaving; and Radama to supress the Black Pirates.

Ten young Malagasy were sent to England to learn about gunpowder and firearms. The London Missionary Society (LMS) established a station in Tamatave, and were given permission to build a church and a school in Tananarivo. More craftsmen were sent out from England to teach metal-work, leather-tanning and carpentry. The Malagasy language was transliterated into the Roman alphabet, a printing press was set up, and an output of schoolbooks and religous tracts got under way. Both trial by ordeal, and infanticide for children born at inauspicious times, were abolished.

In 1922 Farquhar returned to England, and he never in fact met his protegé. At this juncture, Radama was busy engaging the Skalava on the W coast. The campaign was a mixed success. Although many cattle and women were carried back to Tananarivo, a third of the expeditionary force of 75,000 perished from fever and starvation. In 1923, Radama got his confidence back by giving the Betsimisakava on the E coast another working over, and the next year he went back to the N W and this time thoroughly hammered the Salakava, taking Majunga. The next year was allocated to mopping up the remaining groups around the island, and when the half-dozen remaining French at Fort Dauphin were sent packing to Ile Ste Marie, the 33 year-old Radama found himself with all the main island under his control.

Radama was fluent in both English and French, and could read and write in both languages. He led the way in literacy, and by 1925 the LMS had established over a hundred schools with 4,000 pupils, and another 600 apprentices were learning trades. The redoubtable Sergeant Hasty, who had masterminded Radama's military conquests, died of fever in 1826. In 1828, at the age of 36, Radama died, victim, it was said, of his punishing campaigns and the unlimited drink and women they had provided. The Merina people were aghast, for they knew they would never find another remotely like him.

knew of Madagascar's existence, it was not until 1500 that the island was recorded by the Portuguese explorer, Diego Dias. Arriving on St Lawrence's day, Aug 10th, the Portuguese called the Island St Laurent. Many Arab coastal communities suffered at the hands of the Portuguese and trading became difficult. By the sixteenth century, however, Islamic influences heralded the establishment of hierarchical societies and kingdoms. The first kingdoms to emerge were the Menabe and Boina to the W, both Sakalava, and they grew rapidly. Despite attempts by the French and British to establish themselves, the coastal tribes succeeded in keeping them at bay. The Sakalava extended their kingdoms W and N-westwards while the Betsimisaraka grew eastwards along the coast. The Merina tribe under Ramboasalama, an ambitious and capable king, soon emerged as the dominant tribe. When he died his son Radama I took over and continued to expand the kingdom, forming alliances with European powers along the way. He acquired help from Britain. To ensure a balance between European political alliances a Frenchman was made governor of the East Coast. By his death Radama controlled virtually all of the main island.

When Radama I died his widowed wife, Ranavalona I, took over, killing all possible rivals to the throne. Under Ranavalona Christianity was outlawed (1835) and European links were relaxed. In 1861 she died and her son Radama II succeeded, Christianity was revived and relations with Europe improved. The last 2 monarchs of Madagascar, Ranavalona II (1868-83) and Ranavalona III (1883-95) wielded little effective power.

Colonial period

In 1896 the French and British signed a treaty agreeing that Madagascar be assigned to France, in return for Zanzibar being assigned to Britain. France assumed control of Madagascar with relative ease, forcing Ranavalona III to flee into exile to Reunion. He died in Algiers in 1917, and his remains were returned to Madagascar to be buried at Rova in 1938.

Nationalist groups began to emerge. The first to do so was the VVS (Vy Vato Sakelika "stone iron network") but in 1915, shortly after its formation, its leaders were imprisoned. In 1942 Britain invaded and control passed from Vichy to de Gaulle. In 1947 nationalist demonstrations saw much blood shed and an estimated 80,000 people lost their lives.

Independence

In 1958 a pro-French domestic administration was established under Philibert Tsiranana and in 1960 Madagascar acquired its independence. Throughout the 1970s social discontent grew and in 1972 the military stepped in under General Ramantsoa (85% of commercial life was still at this point in time in French hands). In 1975 Colonel Ratsimandrava took over but was assassinated shortly after. Following his death, Lt. Commander Didier Ratsiraka assumed power, and introduced a socialist development strategy in which key elements of the economy were nationalised. Economic and military support were received from the Soviet Union and North Korea. A new constitution was established in which the Front Nationale pour la Defence de la Revolution (FNDR) was the only legal political organisation. Other parties were absorbed into FNDR, with Ratsiraka heading the Avant-garde de la Revolution Malagache (AREMA) faction.

The years following 1975 were marked by social unrest and a severe decline in economic fortunes. In 1985 there were clashes between middle-class vigilante groups who practised martial arts (Kung Fu) as their means of defence, and unemployed urban youths. In 1986-7 the Government was in crisis and the

IMF pressurised Ratsiraka to introduce reforms. In 1989 Ratsiraka was re-elected, although the election was restricted to members of FNDR. In 1990 the FNDR was effectively abolished, and multi-party politics was restored. Several new parties were formed, with Albert Zafy, a professor of medicine co-ordinating pressure on Ratsiraka to resign through Force Vive (FV), an opposition coalition.

In 1991 there was a general strike, and widespread discontent culminated in a large crowd marching on the Presidential Palace. The demonstrators were fired upon, and there were numerous deaths. Pressure increased from international donors and the army for Ratsiraka to go. In 1991, an interim administration was formed to oversee the introduction of a new constitution, with Ratsiraka remaining as a non-executive President serving as head of State. In presidential elections in 1993, Zafy was elected President.

Art and crafts

Music Malagasy music is based on the dance rhythms of Salegy from Sakalava; Tsapika from Fort Dauphin; Basese from the N; Singaoma and Watsa Watsa from mainland Africa; and the creole Sega from Mauritius, Reunion and the Seychelles. A variety of instruments are used but unique ones include the valiha (strings strung around a tubular wooden sounding box); the cordophone (with a calabash resonator); the kabosy (a small Malagasy ukelele guitar); the sodina (a traditional recorder); the kiloloka (a small bamboo whistle producing a single note); the katiboky (a xylophone usually played by women); and 2 types of drum, langorona and amponga which are played using sticks.

People

The inhabitants of Madagascar are known as the Malagasy (sometimes pronounced "Malagash"). Recent evidence suggests early settlers were from Indonesia and Malaya and came to Madagascar some 2,000 years ago. Later immigrants from the African continent gave the Islands a strong African element along the coast, while in the highlands Merino people still display many of their original Indonesian characteristics. Despite the various tribes, the country shares a common language and as mobility of the population has increased, so tribal differences have become less pronounced. Most inhabitants live on the eastern coast and Highlands whilst western areas remain sparsely populated. There is no great population pressure on the land.

Beliefs and customs

Most Malagasy people believe in the power of dead ancestors (*razana*) who are thought to continue to share in family life. In remembering their ancestors, the ancestors will thrive in the spirit world and will help those living. The dictates of razana must be obeyed in a complex system of *fady* or taboos. Fady vary from not eating pork to not whistling. Courtesy demands that visitors follow these observances, especially in country areas where traditions tend to be stronger. Special care needs to be taken when visiting burial sites and tombs.

Luck Heaps

It is said that on every pathway in Madagscar is a pile of stones. As a traveller approaches the edge of unfamiliar territory, or embarks on a journey with an ucerain outcome, he adds a pebble to the pile, whispering '*fanataovana*'. Literally this means 'may it come true' and refers to unspoken hopes for a safe return and a successful outcome.

There is also a belief in a sense of destiny (*vintana*) which links traditional Africa and Islam, for example through the religious significance and status of zebu cattle. *Vintana* is related to times, whereas *fady* involves actions or behaviour. Therefore each period of time has either bad or good omens and those who foresee *Vintana* are *Famiadihana*, similar to astrologers.

Vintana decrees that Sun is God's day therefore work done will succeed. Mon is a hard day but work done will last. Tue is an easy day, too easy for death, and therefore no burials take place. Wed is the day of no return and though good for funerals (*famadihana*) one should not leave home. Thu is good for weddings. Fri is a fat day and Sat a noble day. Since *vintana* has roots in astrology, those with opposing Vintanas should not marry since bad luck will prevail.

In rural areas divine healers (*ombiasy*) use both spiritual power and herbal medicines to cure illness. Others known as *mpisikidy* use amulets, stones and beads to cure people whilst evil witch doctors (*mpamorika*) use poisons.

The Malagasy believe that once dead a person becomes more powerful. They also believe that dead bodies and the possessions of the dead are polluted. This is the reason that the departed's possessions are placed on their tomb. The tomb is regarded as the spirit's home and therefore when the living want to make contact with a dead person, the bones are exhumed. Tribes in southern Madagascar carve commemorative wooden stelae (pillars which depict scenes from the life and work of the deceased). In the Highlands bones of the dead are from time to time exhumed in the "turning of the bones" ceremony. Much rejoicing occurs as the bones draped in a fresh shroud (*lamba mena*) are taken around the town, shown new developments and kept informed on recent events before being returned to the family tomb. This practise is known as *famadihana* and usually only occurs during Jun to Sep.

Ethnic groups

Although the Malagasy share a common language and culture there are 18 different tribes on the Island each with their own territory (*tanindrazana* "land of the Ancestors "). The largest tribe are the **Merina** ("those from the country where one can see far", indicating Malayo-Polynesian origin), living on the high plateau in and around Antananorivo. By the nineteenth century the tribe had managed to unite most of the main island under a central administration. The tribe used to be stratified into 3 groups of people the Andriana (nobles),the Hova (free men) and the Andevo (serfs) but this does not really exist anymore. The tribe also introduced the *famadihana* ritual onto the islands, a ritual later absorbed by other tribes in Madagascar.

Another highland tribe are the **Betsileo** ("the invincible"). They live around Fianarantsoa and Ambositra and practise wet rice cultivation on terraced hillsides. Originally divided into 4 kingdoms, Lalangina, Arindrano, Isandra and Manandriana, they fell to the Merinos in the early 1800s.

The second largest group, on the E coast, are the **Betsimisaraka** ("the inseparables") living in the Tamatave-Antalaha region. Traditionally seafarers and sedentary agriculturists, they were used as slaves by the Europeans in the eighteenth century. They believe in *angatra* (ghosts), *zazavavy an-drano* (mermaids) and *kalamoro* (little wild men of the woods).

South of the Betsimisaraka tribal region live the **Antambahoaka** (those of the people), mostly around Mananjary, and they are a small group. Thought to be descendants from Arabia, they are knowledgeable in astronomy, divination and medicines. Neighbouring the Antambahoaka are the **Antaimoro** ("people of the coast"), living around Vohipeno

Black Pirates

In the early eighteenth century, the chiefs of the N W coast of Madagascar would band together every Aug to Oct in the Bay of Bombatok, by Majunga. They were each required to provide men and canoes, and any spoils were divided accordingly. The normal contingent was 300 outriggers, each with thirty men, though on occasion a force of 40,000 put to sea in 1,500 canoes

In skirmishing in the Mozambique channel, what they lacked in firepower through being unable to mount cannon on their outriggers, they made up in manoeuvrability and numbers. European and Arab traders supplied muskets, and for twenty years they ravaged the coast of the mainland from Cape Delgado down to the legendary goldfields of Sofala. European ships were regularly surrounded and overpowered, and sea captains lived in dread of being becalmed in the Mozambique channel and seeing a swarm of canoes appearing over the horizon. The unfortunate Comores, en route to the coast, were regularly ransacked as a passing diversion. They were finally eliminated in 1824 when the Merina king, Radama I, in observing the terms of his treaty with the British to eliminate the Black Pirates, defeated the Skalava at the second attempt, and took Majunga.

and Manakara. They still use Arabic sura (writings) passed down from their Middle Eastern ancestors. Verses of the koran are used as amulets and they abide by a cast system similar to that found in India.

The **Sakalava** ("people of the long valley"), found along the western coast of Madagascar were once the dominant tribal group but no longer, failing to unite among themselves against the Merina. Originally a southern tribe, they expanded along the W coast and up to northern areas of Madagascar such as Nosy Be. By the eighteenth century, after much inter-kingdom strife, they separated into the Menabe kingdom (around Morondava in the S) and the Boina kingdom (around Majunga in the N). Most raise cattle and exhibit African characteristics such as attaching a symbolic significance to gold and falling into the *tromba* (trance state, or spirit possession).

To the NW live the **Tsimihety** ("those who do not cut their hair"). This tribe migrated from the E coast and along the way intermarried with Sakalava. The Sakalava cut their hair to mourn the death of a Sakalava king but, to demonstrate their independence, the Tsimihety do not.

Other groups include the **Antaifasy**, **Antaisaka** and **Antanosy** who inhabit the S eastern coast; the **Mahafaly** and **Antandroy** who live in southern Madagascar; pockets of **Tanala**, **Zafimaniry**, **Bezanozano** and **Sihanaka** who live inland on the eastern side of the Island. Communities of **Mokoa** and **Vezo** are scattered along the W coast; **Ste Mariens** inhabit the Island of Ste Marien; and the **Bara** live on the dry plateau regions of southern Madagascar.

Religion Catholic and Protestant missionaries introduced Christianity to Madagascar during the colonial era, and there are also followers of Hinduism and Islam. While Christianity predominates, there is a noticeable marriage of traditional beliefs, customs and rituals with Christianity.

Modern Madagascar

Politics

Traditional antagonism exists between the highland Merina, essentially the ruling elite following the conquest of Madagascar by Radama I, and the "co-tiers", the peoples of the coastal areas. There is also resentment of the numbers of Metropolitan French, Indians and Chinese who are prominent in economic and commercial life.

Against this background, Madagascar has found it extemely difficult to establish the institutions of stable government. There have been 4 non-constitutional changes since 1960. The longest administration, the military government of Didier Ratsiraka, a "côtier", was from 1975 to 1991. However, his regime was subjected to regular violence, rioting and attempted coups.

The atmosphere clearly changed in 1989 with the collapse of the Eastern Bloc, and it was no longer possible for Ratsiraka, by drawing on Soviet support, to defy pressure for democratic reforms from the West. Ratsiraka attempted to cling to power in a democratic context by pressuring for a federal constitution, calculating that his support, as a cotier, was particularly strong in the regions. In this he was unsuccessful, and the new arrangements, endorsed by a referendum in 1992, was for a unitary system, with a President as Head of State, a National Assembly elected by proportional representation, and the chief executive being the Prime Minister elected by the Assembly. Although Ratsiraka was successful in persuading the transitional government to allow him to stand for President, he was soundly beaten in peaceful and internationally-monitored elections by Albert Zafy.

The elections to the National Assembly were contested by numerous parties. Cartel HVR, a section of FV obtained 45 seats; another party, MFM, that had opposed Ratsiraka, won 16; and the pro-Ratsiraka party secured 11. Francisque Ravony, a lawyer, deputy Prime Minister in the transitional government, and supported by President Zafay and the business community, was elected Prime Minister by the National Assembly. So far the transition to a civilian multi-party system appears to have proceeded smoothly. However, these are early days, and the key to continuing stability is restoration of economic recovery.

Economics

Recent economic policy has been characterised by 2 sharp reversals of direction. The mixed economy established under the French persisted in the early year of Independence. However, Madagascar withdrew from the Franc Zone in 1973 and the introduction of a programme of nationalisation in 1975 reduced business confidence and discouraged foreign investment. Following IMF pressure in 1982 a partial policy reversal has taken place, accompanied by devaluations, de-controlling of rice prices and termination of the government's monopoly in rice purchase. Despite this policy reversal, economic recovery has been hampered by political instability.

Economic structure

Estimates for 1994 give a population of 13.1mn. Population density varies from 30 people per sq km on the central plateau to 2 per sq km on the western coast. The average density has risen from 16 per sq km in 1982 to 22.3per sq km in 1994. The population has increased at 3.03% over the period 1980-91. Around 25% of the people live in urban areas. In all these features, Madagascar is fairly typical of the economies of Africa.

Madagascar's GDP is about average for the region at US$2,070 mn in 1991 but the country's living standards, with US$ 210 per person, puts it in the low-income group of countries. With agriculture generating 33% of GDP, industry 14% and services 53%, Madagascar appears to have a heavy reliance on services.Private consumption of 92% of GDP, government consumption at 9% and investment of 8%, indicate an economy under considerable stress, where priority is given to day-to-day survival with little for creating future capacity.

Exports contribute 17% of GDP while imports comprise 267%. Coffee made up 44% of export earnings, vanilla 16% and cloves 11%.

In 1989, the percentage of primary-aged children in school was 92%. A further 19% of the secondary age group were in schools, double the regional average, while 3% of 20-24 year olds were in higher education. Adult literacy was very high, at 80% in 1990. This is one of the best education records in Africa. Life expectancy at 51 years, is comparable with the rest of Africa, but health provision is good, with 4 times as many doctors than is the average for Africa. Daily average nutrition is above the minimum for healthy existence.

Overall, Madagascar is a low-income country with substantial dependence on sevices for generating GDP and on agriculture to generate export earnings. Health and educational provision are above average.

Economic performance

Economic growth has been slow with GDP growing by only 1.1% a year from 1980-91. Living standards fell during the same period with GDP per head falling by -2.5% a year. Growth in the agricultural sector was 2.4%, but the industrial and service sectors expanded much more slowly, at 0.9% and 0.2% respectively. Export volumes increased by 0.3% a year, while import volumes expanded at 0.5% a year.Inflation over this period averaged 16.8% a year, which is less than the regional rate, but about average for Africa.

Overall, Madagascar's economic performance has been poor in the 1980s despite efforts to reform the economy. Production has not kept pace with population expansion in any sector.

Recent economic developments

President Zafy is to continue the IMF and World Bank economic reform programme which was first introduced in 1982.This has involved substantial devaluation of the currency, deregulation of domestic prices, and liberalisation of imports. The trade balance is typically in deficit, but export values peaked in 1980 at US$437mn and had declined to US$344 mn in 1991. Imports have consequently been compressed from US$764 mn in 1980 to US$445m. Production of the main export, coffee, has remained stagnant. Ageing coffee tree stocks and poor roads, which resulted in 20% of the crop remaining unharvested, were responsible for the poor performance. The budget deficit of around 6% of GDP is too high to allow inflation to dip below 10% a year.

Madagascar had US$3,381 mn of outstanding external debt in 1991, giving rise to a ratio of debt service to export earnings of around 32%. This has been kept to manageable proportions by virtue of debt forgiveness by France and Germany. The level of aid receipts is high, and is a reflection of Madagascar's low-income status and the concern of France to maintain an influence.

Madagascar withdrew from the Franc Zone in 1973, and the currency appreciated up to 1980, from which time the Malagasy franc has steadily depreciated. Substantial devaluations have resulted in the currency depreciating from FMG 676 = US$1 in 1986 to FMG 3346 = US$1 in 1994.

Current projects financed by the donor community include port improvements, water projects, rice and sugar schemes, electricity, and oil exploration.

Economic outlook

Madagascar has no significant mineral deposits, but the soil is fertile, and there is every reason to expect that with political stability, economic reforms and donor support, that the agriculture sector will expand substantially faster than the rate of population increase. The boom in coffee prices at the end of 1994 will give a big boost to the economy. For the future, prospects will depend on imaginative exploitation of Madagascar's unique tourist attractions, and the ability to attract foreign investment to provide employment for the comparatively well-educated work-force.

Comparative Economic And Social Data

	Madagascar	East Africa	Africa	Industrial countries
Population and land				
Population, mid year, millions, 1994	13.1	12.2	10.2	40.0
Urban population, %, 1991	25	30.5	30	75
Population growth rate, % per year, 1980-91	3.0	3.1	3.1	0.8
Land area, thou. sq. kilom.	587	486	486	1,628
Population density, persons per sq km. 1994	2.3.	24.2	20.4	24.3
Economy: production and income				
GDP, US$ millions, 1991	2,488	2,650	3,561	550,099
GNP per head, US$, 1991	210	250	389	12,960
Economy: supply structure				
Agriculture, % of GDP, 1991	33	43	35	3
Industry, % of GDP, 1991	14	15	27	35
Services, % of GDP, 1991	53	42	38	61
Economy: demand structure				
Private consumption, % of GDP, 1991	92	77	73	62
Gross domestic investment, % of GDP, 1991	8	16	16	21
Government Consumption, % of GDP, 1991	9	15	14	17
Exports, % of GDP, 1991	17	16	23	17
Imports, % of GDP, 1991	26	24	26	17
Economy: performance				
GDP growth, % per year, 1980-91	1.1	1.6	-0.6	2.5
GDP per head growth, % per year, 1980-91	-2.5	-1.7	-3.7	1.7
Agriculture growth, % per year, 1980-91	2.4	1.1	0.0	2.5
Industry growth, % per year, 1980-91	0.9	1.1	-1.0	2.5
Services growth, % per year, 1980-91	0.2	2.5	-0.5	2.6
Exports growth, % per year, 1980-91	0.3	0.7	-1.9	3.3
Imports growth, % per year, 1980-91	0.5	0.2	-6.9	4.3
Economy: other				
Inflation rate, % per year, 1980-91	16.8	23.6	16.7	5.3
Aid, net inflow, % of GDP, 1991	16.4	11.5	6.3	-
Debt service, % of Exports, 1991	32.0	18	20.6	-
Budget Surplus (+), Deficit (-), 1991	-5.9	-3.0	-2.8	-5.1
Education				
Primary, % of 6-11 group, 1990	92	62	76	102
Secondary, % of 12-17 group, 1990	19	15	22	93
Higher, % of 20-24 group, 1990	3	1.2	1.9	39
Adult literacy rate, %, 1990	80	41	39	99
Health and nutrition				
Life expectancy, years, 1991	51	50	50	76
Calorie supply, daily per head, 1991	2,3156	2,111	2,096	3,357
Population per doctor, 1990	8,130	35,986	24,185	550

Notes: 'Africa' excludes South Africa. Dates are for the country in question, and do not always correspond with the Regional, African and Industrial averages.

ANTANANARIVO

The capital of Madagascar lies in the middle of Merina territory. Legend has it that a Merina King, Andrianjaka, took refuge from the Vazimba on one of the sacred hills of Imerina. There he built a fort with one thousand supporters, hence the name Antananarivo "town of a thousand men". As the Merina went through an expansionist era under Andrianampoinimerina in the eighteenth century, so the town's strength and influence grew. The Europeans modified traditional building techniques introducing slate roofing, verandahs,and brick buildings which have remained part of the architectural style ever since. By 1895 the French had established a strong presence in Antananarivo, building new areas to the city. Today the town looks very European, has a population estimated at 2 million, and is encircled by paddy fields.

Places of interest

The **Queen's Palace** (Rova) Within the Queen's Palace compound are in fact a number of palaces. The main structure, the *Queen's Palace,* or *Manjakamiadana*, "where it is easy to reign", was originally wooden and was known as the wooden Palais d'Argent (Silver Palace) because the timbers were fastened with silver nails - these have now been replaced by iron ones. The palace was built for Queen Ranavalona I by Jean Laborde (1839-40) on the site of Andrianampoinimerina's old Palace. A single wooden pillar, said to have been dragged by a thousand slaves from Madagascar's eastern coast, supports the building and symbolises a single monarch supporting the people. In 1868, on the orders of Ranavalona I, James Cameron built a stone façade to surround the Palace. In recent recent years the Palace has been closed for renovation work. In the main courtyard lie the royal tombs of Merina Kings Andrianampoinimerina, Radama I, II and Queens Ranavalona I, II & III and Rasoherina. Behind these tombs are tombs of 7 Antananarivo regional Chiefs.

To the S of the Palace compound is a second large palace, the **Manampisoa** ("excess beauty"), built in 1866 by an Englishman William Pool it displays many interesting exhibits ranging from jewellery, weapons and traditional ceremonial objects to musical instruments, displayed on the first floor. Between the main Palace and the Church (also built by William Pool) lies the royal mortuary. Here Ranavalona I's bier is on display.

Ruins are all that remain of the Prime

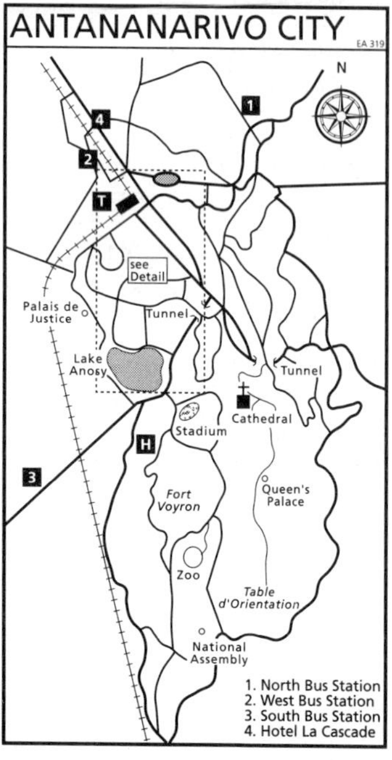

Minister's old residence, formerly the palace of Ranavolona I, situated behind the wooden Palace d'Argent. It was destroyed by French cannons during the siege of 1895.

The **White Hill**. Near the Rova (palace) through Ambohimitsimbina "where one must be careful", past the Ambohipotsy Church (completed in 1868 and the oldest church in Antananarivo) is the site where Christians were thrown to their deaths during the reign of Ranavalona I. Their white bones, collected at the base of the hill, give it its name. Open Tue to Fri 1000-1200 and 1400-1700; Sat 1400-1700; Sun 0900-1200 and 1400-1700. Admission: non residents US$4, residents US$1. Apply for photography permit 24hrs in advance of your visit.

Zoo

Open Thu-Sun and public holidays 0800-1100 and 1400-1700. Free entry. The zoo is a little run down. The main entrance is Acadamie Malgache gate at the bottom of Lalana Fernand Kasanga.

Academie Malgache Museum

Open Thu-Sun and public holidays 0800-1100 and 1400-1700. Free entry. This museum is in the zoo grounds and exhibits include a vertebrae of a dinosaur discovered near Majunga in 1907, a preserved coelacanth (see page 679), various skeletal remains, and displays on village life, funeral art and tombs. There is also a vivarium with lemurs, chameleons, and snakes.

The Museum of Art and Archaeology

Situated on the corner of La Reunion and Lalona Dok Villette, opposite Maison de la Reunion. Open Tue-Sun 1430-1730. The Museum exhibits include skeletal remains of extinct animals, old photographs, art carvings and porcelain pots.

Local information

Price guides:
A+ Over US$100;
A US$40-100; **B** US$20-40; **C** US$10-20;
D US$5-10; **E** Under US$5.

● Where to stay

A+ *Hilton*, just off Lalana Ranaivo Jules, T 26063, two bars. Two restaurants shops, casino, swimming pool and tennis.

A *Palace Hôtel*, ave de L'Independence, T 25663, F 33943, high standard and excellent facilities. **A** *Colbert*, Làlana Jean Ralaimongo, T 20202 F 34012. Two restaurants. High standard facilities. Comfortable atmosphere. **A** *Hôtel de France* ave de Independence, T 20293/21304, F 20108. Good facilities. Italian and local food. **A** *Solimotel* Làlana Dok Ravoahangy Andrianavalona Joseph, T 25040, on the outer part of the city centre, to the S W.

B *Shanghai*, Làlana Jean Jaures, T 31472. All rooms own bathroom. Restaurant (Chinese food).

C *Terminus*, ave de L'Independence, T 20376. Variety of rooms available, with or without bathrooms. **C** *Pavillon de Jade*, Làlana Ranarivelo, T 20273. To the E of the railway station. Rooms with own bathroooms. Good value. **C** *Central*, Làlana Ratianarivo, T 22794. Range of rooms available. **C** *Glacier*, ave de L'Independence, T 20260. Range of rooms available. Restaurant. **C** *Valhila*, Arabe Grandidier Rabahevitra, T 24795. Shared bathrooms. **C** *Select*, ave de L'Independence, T 21001. Central Some facilities communal. **C** *Anjary*, Làlana Dok Ranaivo, T 24409. Modern, good value.

D *Le Karthala*, Làlana Andriandahifotsy, T

Crow Alarms

Surrounding the old centre of Antanarivo are groves of fig trees, palnted by Ramboasalama, Reigning Chief of the Hova in 1790. The figs provided roosting places for large numbers of crows, which Ramboasalama fed with daily provisions of rice. When Antanarivo was subject to surprise attacks the birds would raise the alarm with their crowing, and even, it is said, help in the defence by diving to attack the raiders.

24895. Shared bathrooms. Comfortable Colonial atmosphere. **D** ***Nishate***, Làlana Radama I, T 26872/34872. Shared bathrooms. **D** ***Mellis***, Làlana Ghandi, T 23425. Range of rooms available. Communal facilities. **D** ***Au Bolidor Lapasoa***, Arabe Andrianampoinimerina, T 26941. Communal facilaities. **D** ***Hôtel du Lac***, Làlana Rasamimanana, T 28251/24542. Fairly central. Range of rooms, some with own bathrooms. Pleasant location. **D** ***Parine***, Làlana Radama I, T 23830. Shared bathrooms. Good value. **D** ***Roger***, Làlana Benyowski, T 30969.

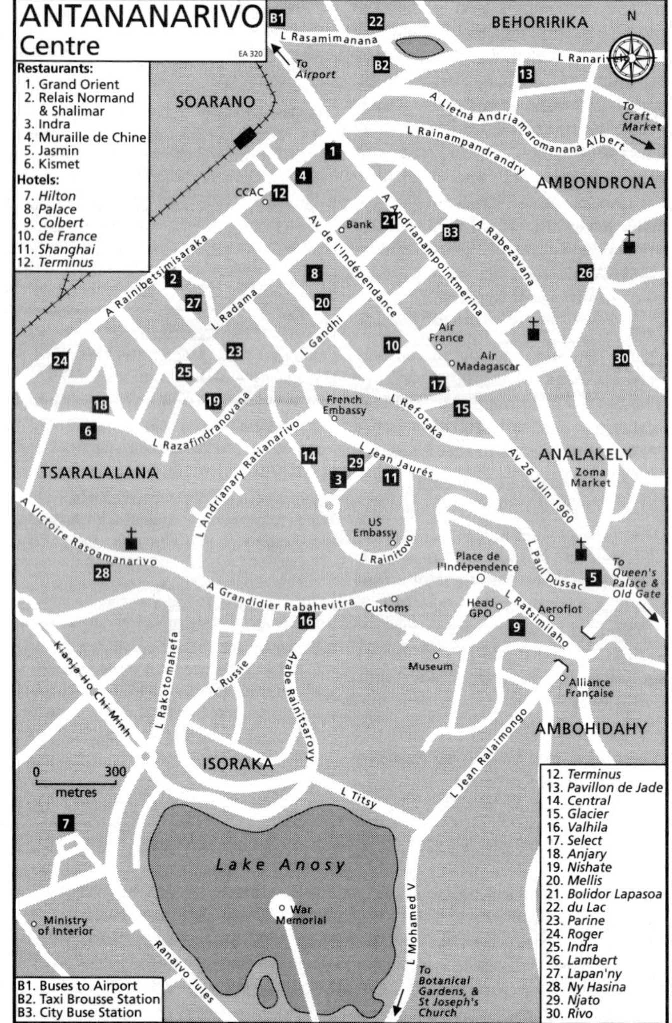

Shared bathrooms. Reasonable value.

E *Indra*, Làlana Radama I, T 32241. Shared bathrooms. Good value. Restaurant. **E** *Lambert*, Làlana Radinandriampandry, T 22992. Shared bathrooms. Restaurant. **E** *Lapan'ny Vahiny*, Làlana Mahafaka. Shared bathrooms. Fairly basic. **E** *Auberge de la Jeunesse*, Làlana Ranavalona III. Just to the S of city centre. Youth Hostel. Dormitory-style accommodation. **E** *Ny Hasina*, Arabe Grandidier Rabahevitra. Some more expensive rooms with own bathrooms. Restaurant. Well run. **E** *Njato*, just off Làlana Jean Jaures, T 28021. Central Good value. Malagasy atmosphere. **E** *Rivo*, Làlana Radinandriampandry. Shared bathrooms. Restaurant.

Where to eat

Price guide:
♦♦♦♦Over US$10; ♦♦♦US$5-10; ♦♦US$2-5; ♦Under US$2

♦♦♦♦*La Taverne* at the Hôtel Colbert has good quality cuisine. Buffet on Sun.

♦♦♦*La Rotonde*, rue 19 Besaret, T 20788. East of centre. French cuisine. High standard. ♦♦♦*L'Aquarium*, Mahavoky Besarety, T 22266. To east of city centre. Specialises in seafood. ♦♦♦*Shanghai Restaurant*, rue Raintovo at *Shanghai Hotel*. Sound Chinese fare. ♦♦♦*Restaurant Grand Orient*, near Railway Station on Kianja Ambiky. Chinese food. Resident pianist. ♦♦♦*Relais Normand*, Arabe Rainbetsimisaraka. Mostly French and international food. ♦♦♦*Hotel de France*, ave de Independence. Serves pizzas. ♦♦♦*Shalimar*, Arabe Rainbetsimisaraka. Good Indian restaurant. ♦♦♦*Indra*, Làlana Radama I, T 32241. Indian cuisine.

♦♦*Muraille de Chine*, Arabe Rainibetsimisaraka. Good quality. ♦♦*Restaurant Jasmin*, 8 Rue Paul Dussac behind the post office on Araben ny 26 Jona 1960, T 34296. Chinese food. ♦♦*La Pradelle*, Ambatoroka, T 32651. South E of the city and provides a good view of the Queens Palace. ♦♦*Kismet*, opposite *Anjaray Hotel*. Mediterranean food.

Entertainment

Just past the station, near the *Hotel Terminus* on Arabe ny Fahaleovantena, is the *Centre Cultural Albert Camus* which puts on plays, films, concerts and various other events. *The American Cultural Centre* has a library and shows films. *Alliance Français* Làlana Ranavalona III. Has a library, and has a programme of cultural events. *Theatre Municipal* Isotry district, western section of city centre. Theatrical performances in Malagasy. *Hira Gosy a Malagasy* show of mime, dance, drama and opera to depict a situation which occurs in everyday life. They used to be held in an area at Isotry but now it occurs in different locations.

Night Life

Independence Ave has quite a considerable café society. There are terrace cafés at the Hôtel de France, Hôtel Terminus, Hôtel Glacier and Hôtel Colbert. They are all popular with local girls. *Calumet Club*, near Station. *Le Kaleidoscope*, lively disco popular with young people. *Le Caveau*, Arabe Grandidier Rabahevitra. *Acapulco Piano Bar*, located in *Le Pub*. Comfortable meeting place. *Papillon Bar*, located in *Hilton Hotel*. Live music. *Cocktail et Reves*, located in Faravohitra above the market. *TGIF*, run by US Diplomatic Corp at the Marine House in Invadry, T 21257/20956. This is essentially a private event, but they are usually happy to see new faces if you telephone to inquire.

Airlines

Air Madagascar, Head Office 31 Arabe ny Fahaleovantena, T 22222. **Air France**, Arabe ny Fahaleovantena. **Aeroflot**, Làlana Ratsimilaho, near the Central Post Office.

Art & Craft

Besides the Fri market there is *La Terrace* on Ave de l'Independence. Jewellers are found along Lanana Ratsimilaho (uptown). Gemstones can be bought from *Le Quartz* on the route Circulaire E of town.

Bookshops

Libraire de Madagascar near *Hôtel de France* on Arabe ny Fahaleovantena and *Toutel'Ecole* on Làlana Indira Gandhi.

Embassies (E) and Consulates (C)

Algeria (E), 5 rue Robert Ducrocq BP 734 Behorika 101, Antananarivo, T 21123 Tlx 22373. **China** (E), *Ancien Hotel Panorama*, BP 1658, 101 Antananarivo. **Egypt** (E), 47 ave Lenine, BP 4082, Ankadifotsky, 101 Antananarivo, T 25233, Tlx 22364. **France** (E), 3 rue Jean Jaures, Bp 204, 101 Antananarivo, T 23700, Tlx 22201. **Germany** (E), 101 route Circulaire, BP 516, Ambodirotra, T 23802 Tlx 22203. **India** (E), 4 lalana Emile Rajaonson, BP 1787, 101 Antananarivo, T 23334, Tlx 22484. **Indonesia** (E), 15 rue Radama I, Tsaralalana, 101 Antananarivo, T 24915, Tlx 22387. **Iran**

(E), route circulaire, Lot II L43 ter, 101 Antananarivo, T 28639. **Italy**, 22 Rue Pasteur Rabary, BP 16, Ankidivato, T 21217, Tlx 22293. **Japan** (E), 8 rue du Dr Villette, BP 3863, Isoraka, 101 Antananarivo, T 26102, F 21769, Tlx 22308. **Korea**, Democratic People's Republic (E) Ambohibao, T 44442, Tlx 22494. **Netherlands** (E), Immeuble ny Havana 67 Ha, BP 167, T 277 4927370. **Libya** (E), Lot IIB, 37A route Circulaire Ampandrana-Ouest, 101 Antananarivo, T 21892. **Mauritius** (C), Ambohitsoa. **Russia** (E), Ampefiloha, Lot O, BP 4006, T 27070. **Seychelles** (C), BP 1071 Analakely. **Spain** (E), Antananarivo. **Switzerland** (E), BP 118, 101 Antananarivo, T 22846, Tlx 22300. **Thailand** (E), Antanarivo. **UK** (E), Immeuble 'Ny Havana', Cité de 67 Ha, BP 167, 101 Antananarivo, T 27749, F 26690, Tlx 22459. **USA**, 14-16 rue Rainitovo, Antsahavola, BP 620, 101 Antananarivo, T 21257, F 34539, Tlx 22202.

● Hospitals
Military Hospital, T 40341. Missionaires de Marie, T 23554.

● Libraries
National Library in the *Hilton Hotel*, Anosy Antananarivo. ***English Language Learning Centre***, on Lalana Havana Antsahabe, Antananarivo, T 27554. ***United States Cultural Centre***, Lalana Dok Raz Randramazo Antananarivo Open 0900-1200 and 1400-1800, closed on Sun.

● Local Transport
Bus Flat fare around US$0.10. There are several competing companies. Main departures from Independence Ave. **Taxi** Fares between US$1-3 around town, but it is necessary to bargain. Surcharge after dark. To airport, around US$8. **Rickshaw** (*pousse pousse*) Around US$0.25 a trip.

● Shopping
Large Fri **market** (*zoma*) on Arabe ny Fahaleovantena and is the place to buy Malagasy crafts, particularly behind the burnt out town hall (*Hôtel de Ville*). Clothes are found on the *Hôtel de France* side and books near *Hôtel Glacier*. **Supermarkets** There is a Prisunic on Arabe Grandidier Rabahevitra in uptown Antananarivo and various others dotted around.

● Sports Facilities
Swimming Pool next to the American Cultural Centre. **Sauna** 8 rue Fumaroli (T 26395). **Golf** Out of town at Ambodhidratrimo.

● Vehicle Hire
Car Hire Avis, T 20435/340800. **Clovis Arthur**, T 32847. **Aventour**, T 31761. **Tropi Car**, T 331681/44019. **Comet**, T 34257. **Sambava Voyages**, T 30570. **Espace**, T 26297/27296 for the W.

Bicycle Hire Mountain bikes available to hire from **Madagascar Wheels**, Lot II A 23 Andravoahangy-Ambony, T 33547.

● Tourist Office
Director du Tourisme, T 26298. *Madagascar Airtours* in *Hilton*.

● Transport
Train Two departures a day for **Antsirabe**, US$3 1st class, US$2 2nd class, journey takes 4 hrs. One departure a day to **Tamatave**, US$7 1st class, US$4 2nd class, journey takes 12 hrs. One departure a day to **Andasibe**, US$3 1st, US$2 2nd, journey takes 6 hrs. One departure a day to **Ambatondrazaka** US$5 1st US$3 2nd, journey takes 10 hrs.

Ticket Office open at the Station between 1500-1700 and an hr before trains depart. **Taxi-brousse** (minibuses) and **Taxi-be** (Peugeot station wagons) There are 2 main stations (*gares routières*), providing transport to all parts of Madagascar. Very cheap, about US$1.50 for 100km. **North** Làlana Dok Raphael Raboto, in Ambonivona near Andravoahangy market Serves the N and E. For Tamatave, Majunga and Diego Suarez. **South** Làlana Pastora Rahajason, in the S W of the city. Serves the S and W. For Antsaribe and Fianarantsoa.

Excursions from Antananarivo

Ambohimanga

Lies 20km N of Antananarivo and one of the 12 sacred hills of Imerina. Entrance to the town is via the eastern gate. The Ambatomitsangana, a stone, now lies beside it. In former times this was rolled across the entrance at nightfall. There are 6 other gates to the village. The Fidasiana square was the site of the first royal palace. Beyond this lies the Palace, Rova Andrianamapoinimerina. The Palace is wooden, like the one in Antananarivo, and is supported by a single pillar. In its grounds is the Palace built for Ranavalona II. There is a café in the Palace compound. Further North lies the sacred Lac Amparihy which at one time supplied the royal baths. There is a restaurant in town serving traditional food.

It is accessible by taxi-brousse from Antananarivo (they leave from the N gare routiere Ambonivona near Andravoahangy market).

Antsahadinta

Situated some 20 km SW of Antananarivo this site served as a place of exile and there are several tombs. The Presidential Palace at Iavolona is 12 km to the S.

Ambatolampy

Located S of Antananarivo,and is a popular weekend retreat, where there is trout fishing. Close by (46km) is the third largest mountain in Madagascar, Tsinjoarivo (2,643m) where Queen Rasoherinal's country Palace lies, with great views amid good hiking country. There are Merina tombs nearby. **C** *Rendezvous des Pecheurs*, comfortable lodging which will arrange fishing expeditions. Restaurant.

Ambodhidratrimo

The first town NW of Antananarivo towards Majunga. The town is on another sacred hill and has a Rova (palace). Beyond the town is a new golf course (T 29295). The airport also lies along the Antananarivo-Majunga road at Ivato.

- **Where to stay** C *Auberge Au Cheval Blanc*, T 44646. Own bathrooms. Free transfer to and from the airport. C *Auberge d'Alsace*, T 44656. Some rooms with own bathrooms. C *Motel au Transit*, T 45012. Some bungalows and suites.

- **Car Hire** Available from *Motel au Transit*.

Andramasina

Located 40km S of Antananarivo. Close by are the Sisaony falls. D *Fara Sy Fara*.

Ampefy

140 km W of Antananarivo. Pleasant location on the edge of **Lake Kavitaha**. Also a good place from which to explore **Lake Itasy**. There are some falls on the Lily River about 40 km W of Ampefy. **D** *Kavitaha*, T 4. Pleasant location overlooking Lake. Good value. **E** *Village Touristique*, Bungalow accommodation. Basic but sound.

Antsirabe

Located 170 Km S of Antanarivo. Norwegian missionaries settled here in 1872 attracted by the cool climate and hot springs. Previously a prison town, the arrival of Europeans influenced the town's character and architecture. Market day is on Saturdays and for those wishing to visit the town's thermal baths, it is best to do so in Oct-Nov before the rains.

Local information

● Where to stay

B *Hotel des Thermes*, T 48761. Cosy bar. Good restaurant. Tennis available, and the pool opens in warm months. **B** *Diamant*, T 48840. Some rooms with own bathrooms. Restaurant. Tahiti disco upstairs.

C *Villa Nirima*, T 48669. Communal facilites. **C** *Aloalo* Own bathrooms. **C** *Baobab*, some cheaper rooms without hot water. Good restaurant. No alcohol. **C** *Soafytel*, T 48055. Rooms with hot water. Breakfast included.

D *Trianon*, T 48881. Shared bathrooms. Generous restaurant. Colonial atmosphere. **D** *Niavo*, T 48467. Shared bathrooms. Pleasant setting.

● Places to eat

♦♦♦*Hotel des Thermes* Sun brunch buffet is good value. ♦♦♦*Restauranta la Halte*, T 48994. Good standard. ♦♦♦*Le Fleuve Parfume* Vietnamese food. ♦♦♦*Meraj* Indian food.

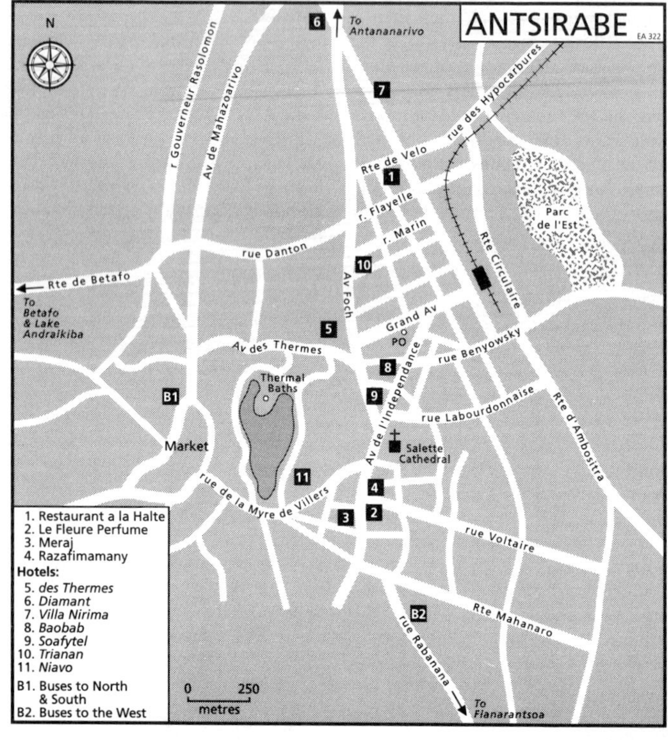

♦♦*Razafimamony Grill* Opposite market. Local food.

● Transport

Local transport Plenty of rickshaws (*pousse pousse*). Bus system which serves local towns.

Car hire Villa Nirima (T 48597/48669). **Bicycle hire** Behind daily market. US$8 per day. **Riding** Horses can be hired at *Hotel des Thermes* for excursions to the lakes.
Rail 2 departures a day for *Antananarivo*, US$3 1st class, US$2 2nd class, journey takes 4 hrs. **Road** Taxi-brousse takes 7 hrs and costs US$2; taxi-be costs about US$2.50.

The Lakes

These are close enough to allow excursions from Antsirabe.

Lake Andraikiba lies 6km W of Antsirabe. As legend has it, a local prince, who found it hard to decide which of 2 women he should marry, decided the first to swim across the lake would be his wife. Unfortunately one of the women was pregnant with his child and drowned trying to cross the river. Locals now say that the lake is haunted by the beautiful young woman who emerges from the lake only to disappear when people approach.

Lake Tritriva is a volcanic lake 12km S W of Antsirabe. There are 2 trees with intertwined branches which are situated on a ledge above the water's edge. The legend is that they are 2 lovers, forbidden to marry by their parents, who committed suicide by drowning themselves in the lake. It is said that if you cut the trees, they bleed.

Ambositra

About 100 km S of Antsirabe is the centre of Madagascar's wood carving industry. Wood carvings are usually done by Zafimaniry people. Société Jean et Frere has good quality carvings. Also Arts Zafimaniry which is opposite the Catholic Church, open 0730-1115 and 1415-1730.

● Where to stay **C** *Grande Hotel* A little dilapidated. Comfortable Colonial atmosphere. **D** *Voilette* Pleasant accommodation. Good restaurant.

Fianarantsoa

Further along the RN7 southwards from Ambositra is Fianarantsoa ("Place of good learning"). The town is built on a hill; founded in 1830, it became the region's capital in 1870. The upper town is the old town and has various buildings of antiquity. The Catholic Cathedral of Ambozotany, built in 1871, is located in the place Mgr Givelet and commands a view of Lake Anosy. The lower (new) town was mostly built after 1895 in the Colonial period. It has a population of around 150,000

Local Information

● Where to stay

C *Soafia*, T 50353. Rather grand hotel with a range of accommodation, some more expensive. It has a Salon de The and a Ballroom. Swimming pool under construction. **C** *Modern du Betsileso* (*Chez Papillion*), T 50003/50553. Own bathrooms. Good quality hotel. Excellent restaurant

D *Tsara Guest House*, T 50206. Pleasant location with surrounding gardens. **D** *Cotsoyannis*, T 51486. Shared bathrooms.

E *Escale*, T 50031. Shared bathrooms. Noisy disco.

● Places to eat

♦♦♦*Chez Papillon* French cuisine. Good standard. ♦♦♦*Restaurant Bleu* Chinese food. ♦♦♦*Maharajah* rue Printsy Ramaharo. Indian food.

♦♦*Le Panda* Chinese food. Reasonable standard.

● Tourist Office

(Syndicat d'Initiative) near the *Hotel Modern du Betsileso*.

● Transport

Air The town has an airport connected to Antananarivo (US$70, 4 flights weekly).

Rail Connected to Manakara terminus (approximately 7hrs) and is a memorable journey through interesting scenery, and more comfortable than by road.

Road Taxi-brousse from Antananarivo (US$5).

Excursions

Wine tasting is available at ***Isandra Estate*** 30km N W of Fianarantsoa and the ***Famoriana Estate*** just past Isorana.

Ranomafana National Park

Located about 60 km to the NE of Fianarantsoa. The main attraction used to be the thermal springs here. In 1986 the Golden bamboo Lemur was discovered in the area. Visitors are not allowed into the park without a guide and permit, US$12 obtained from Eaux et Forets in Ranomafana. The guide's fee is US$6. Camping is available in the park for those with tents. You can walk in but transport to the park and back is advisable since the park entrance is 7km away. A museum and gift shop are near the entrance, Open Mon-Fri.

• **Where to stay** **D** *Station Thermal de Ranomafana* BP 13, T 1. A little run down. **E** *Ravenala* Reasonable. Good value.

Ambalavao

56km SW of Fianarantsoa. Narrow streets, overhanging balconies, and very attractive. It is the home of Antaimoro paper, with dried flowers set in the fibres, first introduced into Madagascar with the arrival of Islam. The open air factory is signposted. A shop in the premises allows you to buy the finished product. The town is also famous for silk and to the N lies the Soavida vineyard which is open to visitors.

• **Where to stay** **E** *Tsi Kivy* Rather simple.

Andringitra and Pic Boby

Moving S this area is famous for the Andringitra Massif and Madagascar's second highest peak, Pic Boby (2,658m). The area has been declared a reserve, guides can be hired to take visitors around the reserve and it is a good trekking area.

SOUTH WEST - TULÉAR AND FORT DAUPHIN

The S amongst other things is known for its spiny forests, the Berenty nature reserve and its magnificent beaches, most of which are situated around Fort Dauphin. During the sixteenth and seventeenth centuries St Augstine Bay just S of Tulear thrived through the spice trade. The British tried to establish a colony in St Augustine but failed and left in 1646. Tribes along the coast are predominantly Mahafaly, Antanosy and Antandroy and inland, Bara. Southern tribes have African characteristics and own Zebu cattle. They remember the dead by highlighting the deceased's life in the form of wood carvings (*aloalo*) or colourful paintings covering the tomb. In addition Zebu skulls are sometimes placed on tombs, the number represents how wealthy the deceased was, and pillars or stones lie at each side of the tomb. The Antandroy carvings and paintings, which represent the deceased's life, do not lie over the grave, which is situated elsewhere.

Miandrivazo

On the Mahajilo river in the northernmost district in Toliara Province. Located 200 km W of Antsirabe The town is the starting point for excursions along **Tsiribihina River**, taking 2-5 days. 150km in either a motor boat or dug-out canoe. Viewing wildlife by canoe is preferable, as the wildlife are less disturbed, and easier to sight. Trips available Apr to Oct.

• **Where to stay** D *Relais de Miandrivazo* Overlooking town square, T 3. Shared bathrooms. Comfortable colonial building. **E** *Bemaraha* Restaurant. Simple accommodation and uncomplicated food.

• **Transport** Taxi-brousse from Antsirabe takes 10 hrs and costs US$5, from Morondava takes a day and costs US$8

Morondava

Small town on the coast between Tuléar and Majunga, around 700km from Ananarivo, the centre of the Sakalava people. In town there is an avenue of baobabs running N to Belo sur Tsiribihina. Erotic Sakalava sculptures on traditional tomb sites can be found in the district.

Local information

● Where to stay

C *Oasis* South of town, slightly back from the beach, T 52160. A/c. Own bathrooms. Restaurant. Bar. Pleasant gardens.

D *Les Bougainvilliers*, south of town, T 52163, a/c Bungalows. Range of accommodation available. Good restaurant. **D** *Nosy Kely* (Chez Cucco) South of town, on the shore, T 52319. Bungalows. Own bathrooms. Good restaurant with Italian food. **D** *Village Touristique*, T 52163. Bungalows

● Places to eat

♦♦*Carré d'As*, restaurant Part of Village Touristique Malagsy and international food. ♦♦*Renala*, on shore just to N of centre, T 521 74. Seafood. ♦♦*Etoile de Mer*, south of town. Seafood.

● Transport

Air Four flights a week to from *Antanaarivo*. Fare around US$100 single.

Road Taxi-brousse from *Antananarivo*, allocate 2 days to the journey, cost US$12.

Sea Boat from *Morombe*. Small sailing boat, takes 2 days, costs US$25. You must take your own provisions.

Belo sur Tsiribihina

Small beachside village, located 75 km N of Morondava. Famed for its *Fitampoha* ceremony held every 5 yrs (last one 1993). The ceremony involves turning (see page 721) Sakalava relics and it is *fady* during the ceremony to touch river water. The *zomba*, opposite the post office, contains these relics. The town was where the Sakalava were finally defeated by the forces of Radama I in 1818.

• **Where to stay D** *Hôtel du Menabe*, T 10. Shared lavatory, own shower. Old Colonial building. Comfortable. **E** *Firaisana* Shared bathrooms. Simple, but good value.

Ihosy

This town lies in the middle of Bara territory. The roads to Ihosy are poor and if you are travelling from Fianarantsoa can take up to 9hrs in bad weather, 5 hrs in good.

• **Where to stay D** *Zahamotel* 1 km from town, T 83. Bungalow accommodation. Restaurant. Money changing facilities. **D** *Relais Bara*, T 17. Opposite the Post Office. Quite comfortable.

Ranohira

Located 97km S W of Ihosy, and is a base for those visiting the Isalo National Park and hiking in the area.

• **Where to stay D** *Berny*, T 6. Shared bathrooms. No running water or electricity. Restaurant. **D** *Hotel les Joyeux Lemuriens* Reasonably new. Good standard; **D** *Touristique de l'Isalo*, T 18. Shared bathrooms. **E** *Camping* in grounds of *Hotel Berny*.

Isalo National Park

Sandstone formations are notable. A small stream runs through the Park and has formed an oasis. There is a clean deep pool here with a natural stone bridge, a waterfall and elephant's foot (*Pachydodium rosulatum*) growing on the rocks nearby. Other attractions include a trek to swim in the Piscine Naturalle and a visit to the Canyon de Singes (Valley of Monkeys).

Permits can be obtained from Direction des Eaux et Fôrets in Tulear or Antananarivo, or in the park office in Ranohira. Tents can be hired in Ranohira and guides (about US$4 a day) are available from the Park Ranger's Office, Department des Eaux et Fôrets in Ranohira.

Tuléar (Toliara)

Located in Toliara Province, this town of around 75,000 people lies 10km N of Tropic of Capricorn. Early attempts to establish a colony at St Augustine Bay by the British proved unsuccessful and it wasn't until 1859 that the French established a trading post on the Fiherenana River, designing and building the town of Tulear around 1895. Tulear provides a base for trekking with a base from which to explore several parks and reserves in the area, and the beaches to the N and S of the town. Tuléar has some interesting Mahofaly tombs. Traditional music is played at the Galecha next to the *Plaza Hotel* or the Zaza Club. T.

Excursions from Tuléar

Madagascar Air Office in the *Plazza Hotel*. Arrange tours and day trips to St Augustine and Nosy Ve *Safari Vezo* BP 427 (T 41381). Organise trips down the Onilahy River; excursions to Lac Tsimanampetsotsa which has excellent bird-life; trips by sea to Morombe, 200 km to the N.

Local information

● Where to stay

B *Capricorn* ave de Belemboka. (T 42620) On outskirts of town centre. (T 41495) Best hotel in town. a/c. Good restaurant.

C *Plazza* rue Marius Jatop On the shore. (T 41900/1) a/c. Hot water. Good facilities. Restaurant. Pleasant garden setting. Beach poor, just mudfalts. Range of accommodation available.

D *Chez Alain* close to *taxi-brousse* stand on the road to the airport. (T 41527). Shared lavatory, own shower. No hot water. Restaurant. Good value; **D** *Centrale* Blvd Philibert Tsiranaa (T 42884) Shared lavatory, own shower. Garden; **D** *La Pirogue* rue Marius Jatop On the shore. (T 41537) Own bathroom. Beach poor, just mudflats. Range of accommodation available.

E *Soavadia* Off eastern end of Blvd Gallieni, opposite the taxi-brousse stand on the road to the airport. Shared lavatory, own shower.

● Places to eat

♦♦*La Cabane*, Blvd Lyantey. Specialises in seafood. ♦♦*Maharadjah*, Blvd Philibert Tsiranaa. Indian cuisine. ♦♦*L'Etoile de Mer*, Blvd Lyantey. Specialises in seafood. ♦♦*Resto du Sud*, off eastern end of Blvd Gallieni, opposite the

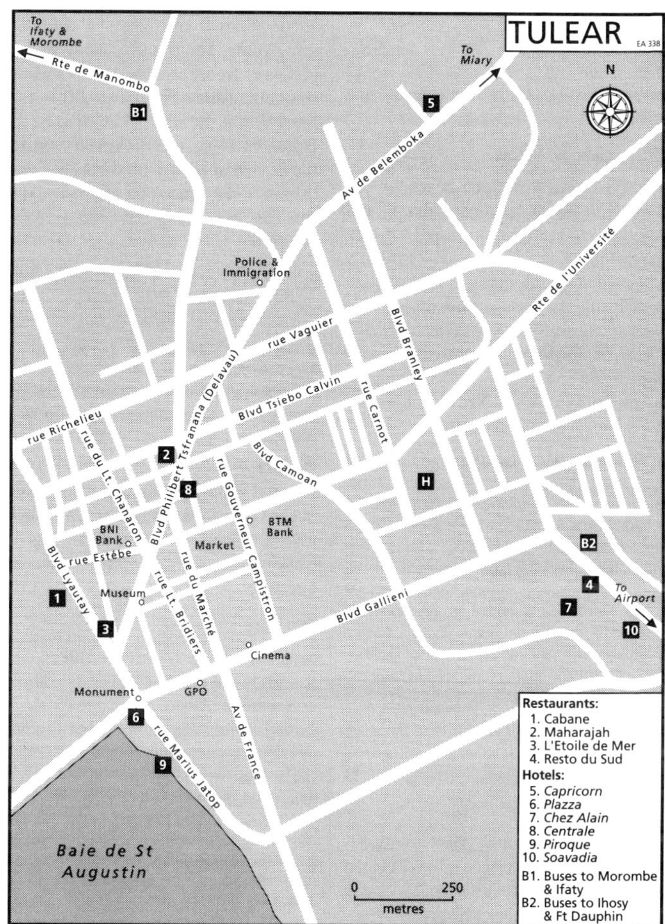

taxi-brousse stand on the road to the airport. Vietnamese food.

● **Bank**

Banky Ny Indostria Blvd Delavau. Open Mon-Fri 0800-1100 and 1400-1600.

● **Entertainment**

Disco *Plazza* rue Marius Jatop. On the shore. *Le Calypso* Blvd Lyantey. *Club Zaza* Blvd Lyantey.

Cinema *Cinéma Tropic* Blvd Gallieni.

● **Post Office**

Blvd Gallieni. Open Mon-Fri 0800-1200 and 1400-1800; and 0800-1200 Sat.

● **Travel and Tour Agents**

Air Madagascar (T 41585) Open Mon-Fri 0730-1300 and Sat 0730-1030. **Madagascar AirTours** (T 41585). **Vezo Safari** BP 427 (T 41381) Offers boat trips and accommodation at Anakao beach to the S.

● **Transport**

Air Four flights each week to connect **An-**

tananarivo, single US$160.

Road Luxury buses run Tue from **Antananarivo** US$13. Otherwise fairly regular taxi-brousse at US$12, with the trip taking 2 days.

Ifaty (Mora Mora)

This is the nearest good beach, 26 km from Tuléar. There is good diving and snorkelling, although hired diving equipment needs to be carefully checked as maintenance is a little rough and ready. At **Sarondrano**, 30 km S of Tuléar are a number of caves in the sea cliffs. **St Augustin** (Anantsono) lies 35 km to the S of Tuléar, and is the site of an attempt to found a British settlement in the seventeenth century.

• **Where to stay A** *Lakana Vezo* To the S, 8 km along coast, T 42620. Reasonable standard. Specialises in diving and snorkelling. **C** *Mora Mora* BP 41, T 41071. Colonial style accommodation in bungalows. Reasonable restaurant. Facilities for deep-sea fishing, snorkling and diving. Excursions arranged to **D** *Zahamotel* Close to centre. a/c. Restaurant. **D** *Dunes* To the S, 3 km along coast, T 42885. Restaurant. Tennis. Reasonably new. **D** *Bamboo Club*, just to N, T 42717. Restaurant. Well-run.

• **Transport Road** From **Tuléar** there are taxi-brousse costing US$0.50. A transfer direct from the airport at Tuléar costs US$12.

Morombe

The name means "Big Beach", and it is situated on a desolate coast line. Located 250 km N of Tuléar. The town has a Bank and Air Madagascar Office.

• **Where to stay C** *Croix du Sud* BP 12, T 18. Most comfortable accommodation in town. **C** *Baobab* Bungalow accommodation. **E** *Mozambic* Located near *Hotel Croix du Sud*. Restaurant.

• **Transport Air** There are flights from Tuléar once a week, costing around US$50. **Road** Takes about a day by taxi-brousse, and costs around US$5.

Anakao

South of Onilahy River, and located about 55km from Tuléar by the most direct route. The Island of **Nosy Ve**, just offshore from Anakao,has excellent snorkelling and a fine variety of birdlife. Nosy Ve was the site of a landing by the Dutch in 1595, and became a base for the French in 1888 in preparation establishing a settlement on the mainland. This was eventually achieved, in 1897, at Tuléar.

• **Where to stay C** *Safari Vezo* Near Anakao, T 41381. Beach bungalows. Full board is very good value.

• **Transport Road** *Taxi-brousse* to St Augustin, then canoe across the Onilahy river to Soalara, and *taxi-brousse* on to Anakao. **Sea** Canoe with outboard motor from Tuléar is US$8.

Bezaha

Located about 110 km S E from Tuléar in the Onilahy River valley. Small town with hot springs. E *Taheza* (Chez Pageot) Centre of town, T 19. Simple and comfortable.

Betioky

Situated 130km S E from Tulear. The town is in the heart of Mahafaly country and there tombs are decorated by *alo alo* carved totems. *Bara* tombs also situated nearby are painted with scenes depicting events in the life of the deceased. More classical tombs are decorated with *alo alo* and carved zebu, and wrestlers.

• **Where to stay D** *Mamirano* Shared bathrooms. Choice of bungalows or rooms. **E** *Mahafaly* Fairly basic.

Beza Mahafaly Special Reserve

In the Onilahy valley 30km E from Betioky. spiny forest with lemurs, ringtails and sifakas. Accommodation in cabins run by Research Station in the Reserve. Bring your own provisions. Permits from Eaux et Forêts in Antananarivo. Agro Forestry has started up in the area, administered by the University of Antananarivo.

• **Tansport Air** There are weekly flights from Antananarivo. **Road** *Taxi-brousse* from Tuléar.

Fort Dauphin (Taolanaro)

Founded in 1643 by Sieur Pronis (representing the Société de l'Orient) who took control of the peninsular and built a Fort named after the Dauphin (later to be Louis XIV). In 1665 the French East India Company took control of Fort Dauphin but in1674 a vicious attack by the Antanosy forced the few remaining French to flee.

Linaona Beach

Pic Louis This is the mountain that stands behind the town to the N W. It is possible to climb the mountain (529m) in about half a day. There are 2 trails, one from near the Roman Catholic Mission past the airport to the W, the other from near the sisal factory on the road

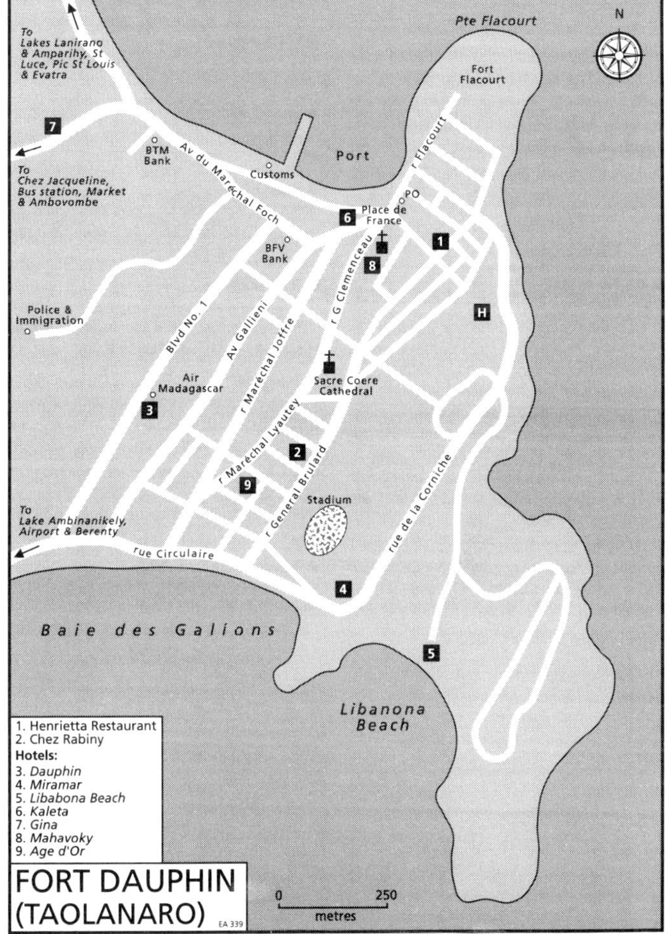

going N to Ste Luce.

Portuguese Fort Located 6km from Fort Dauphin is the fort built in 1504 by shipwrecked sailors.Trips arranged by Madagascar Airtours. US$12 for half a day.

Botanical Gardens Located 15 km N of Fort Dauphin on the road to Ste Luce.

Baie Sainte Luce Lies 65 km N E of Fort Dauphin, where the French first landed in 1638. Excursions are available.

Berenty Reserve This comprises an area of protected forest, located 80km W of Fort Dauphin. There is a wide variety of wildlife here especially the ring-tailed lemurs and sifakas. Visits to the Reserve can be arranged through *Hotel Dauphin* in Fort Dauphin. A day trip costs US$30, with an overnight stay US$105.

Local information

● Where to stay

C *The Dauphin* (and Galian Annexe) Blvd No 1, T 21192. Garden and crocodile pool (netted over). Trips to Berenty Reserve arranged. **C** *Miramar* Overlooking the bay, southern side of promontory, T 21048. Swimming pool. Very popular. **C** *Libanona Beach*, southern side of promontory, T 21378. Pleasant location. Excursions organised. **C** *Kaleta*, rue Blondlat, by harbour, T 21287/21397. Some rooms with bath, some with showers, some with sea view. Excursions available.

D *Gina*, route No 13 to N of town centre, T 21266. Thatched bungalows. Restaurant. **D** *Mahavoky*, Town centre, opposite Catholic Cathedral, T 21332. Shared bathrooms. Hot water. Restaurant. Free transfer for guests to Airport. Good value.

E *Maison Age d'Or*, rue Marechal Lyautey, close to Cathedral. Shared bathrooms.

● Places to eat

♦♦*Chez Jacqueline* route No 13 to N W of town centre. Chinese cuisine. ♦♦*Gina* route No 13 to N of town centre, T 21266. French and Chinese cuisine.

♦*Henrietta* Old market, just S of Post Office. Good inexpensive food.. ♦*Chez Rabiny Salon de Thé* rue General Bruland.

● Entertainment

Panorama Bar Disco North end of Ave du Maréchal Foch.

● Banks

On Ave du Maréchal Foch. Open Mon-Fri 0800-1100 and1400-1600.

● Post Office

Near intersect of Rue George Clemenceau and Ave Flacourt. Open Mon-Fri 0800-1200 and 1400-1800; Sat 0800-1200.

● Transport hire

Air Fort Services ave Gallieni, T 21234/21264, F 21224. Hire out bikes and vehicles. *Mahavoky* rents out bikes at US$2 a day.

● Transport

Air Four flights a week from Antananarivo, costing US$160. Weekly flights from Tulear (US$100).

Road Taxi-brousse from **Antananarivo** costing US$20, and you should allocate 3 days for the trip. From **Tuléar** takes 2 days and costs US$8.

● Travel Agents

SHTM, *Hotel Miramar*, T 21192. *Air Fort Services*, ave Gallieni, T 21234/21264, F 21224.

EAST COAST – NORTH AND SOUTH OF TAMATAVE

The area experiences harsh weather, and is celebrated for its rainforests. In coastal waters sharks are numerous, and it is important to swim in protected areas. In the eighteenth century the region was unified under King Ratsimilaho (son of an English pirate, educated in Britain) and by 1754 his rule extended from Masoala peninsula to Mananjary.

Tamatave (Toamasina)

The name means "salty water". The town grew up to serve the pirate community, and in the late eighteenth century the French controlled the port. By 1811, the British Governor of Mauritius, in an attempt to crush slavery in the Indian ocean, successfully invaded the port and installed a garrison. It was returned to the French in 1815, but fell to the Merina in 1822. In 1845 British and French forces attacked the town but were unsuccessful. King Ranavalona had the heads of those who died impaled on stakes (they remained there until 1854) to remind the French and British of their failure. The settlement continued to grow around the port and by 1883 the French had retaken the town. Tamatave prospered by acting as the conduit for foodstuffs grown in the Highlands and exported to Mauritius. Throughout the era there was a strong colonial influence on architecture, and many grand residences, now a little shabby, remain. Today the town is popular with both locals and foreigners, the **Bazar be** market and the **Zoo** at the eastern end of Rue la Réunion are notable attractions.

Pangalanes Canal Extraordinary inland waterway that runs through lagoons inland from Farafangana 550km to the S to Tamatave. The canal exits to the sea just to the N of the town centre, and there is a bridge where the Blvd Ratsimilano passes over it.

Ile aux Prunes 1 hr by boat for fishing and snorkelling. Trips arranged by *Hotel de Neptune*.

Jardin d'Essai Ivoloina Botanical gardens. 13km N of town toward Foulpointe. A little dilapidated. Open 1200-1700 and weekends 0900-1700.

Local information

● Where to stay

A *Neptune*, 35 Blvd Ratsimilaho, T 32226, F 32426. Bar, restaurant. Swimming pool.

B *Noor*, Blvd Mal, T 33845. Some rooms with a/c, some with fans. **B** *Joffre*, Blvd Joffre, T 32390. Pleasant colonial atmosphere. **B** *Flamboyants*, Av de la Liberation, T 32350. A/c. Restaurant with high standard cuisine.

D *Pax*, 7 Rue de la Pondriere, T 32976. Own showers. **D** *Etoile Rouge*, 13 Rue de la Tassigny, T 32290. Restaurant. Good value. **D** *Darafify* North of town, T 32618. Chalets in local style. Good restaurant.

E *L'Escale*, blvd Foch, T 32587. Good value. **E** *Plage*, blvd de la Liberation, T 32090). Range of facilities.

● Places to eat

♦♦♦♦*Oasis*, Blvd Joffre High standard.

♦♦♦*Fortuna*, rue de la Batterie, T 33828. Chinese food. Open 1200-1400 and 1800-2100. Good standard. ♦♦♦*Adam and Eve*, Blvd Joffre American-style hamburgers and french fries. *La Revea* for snacks on beach front.

♦*Salon de Thé Saify*, Blvd Joffre.

● Banks

Arabe ny Fahalaevantena. Open 0800-1100 and 1400-1600, not weekends.

● Entertainment

Disco *Queen's Club*, Blvd Joffre. *La Chouette*, rue du Commerce. *Neptune*, Blvd Ratsimilaho.

● Post Office

Arabe ny Fahalaevantena, opposite old Town Hall. Open Mon-Fri 0800-1200 and 1400-1800; Sat 0800-1200.

● Transport

Air Services on daily basis to **Antananarivo**,

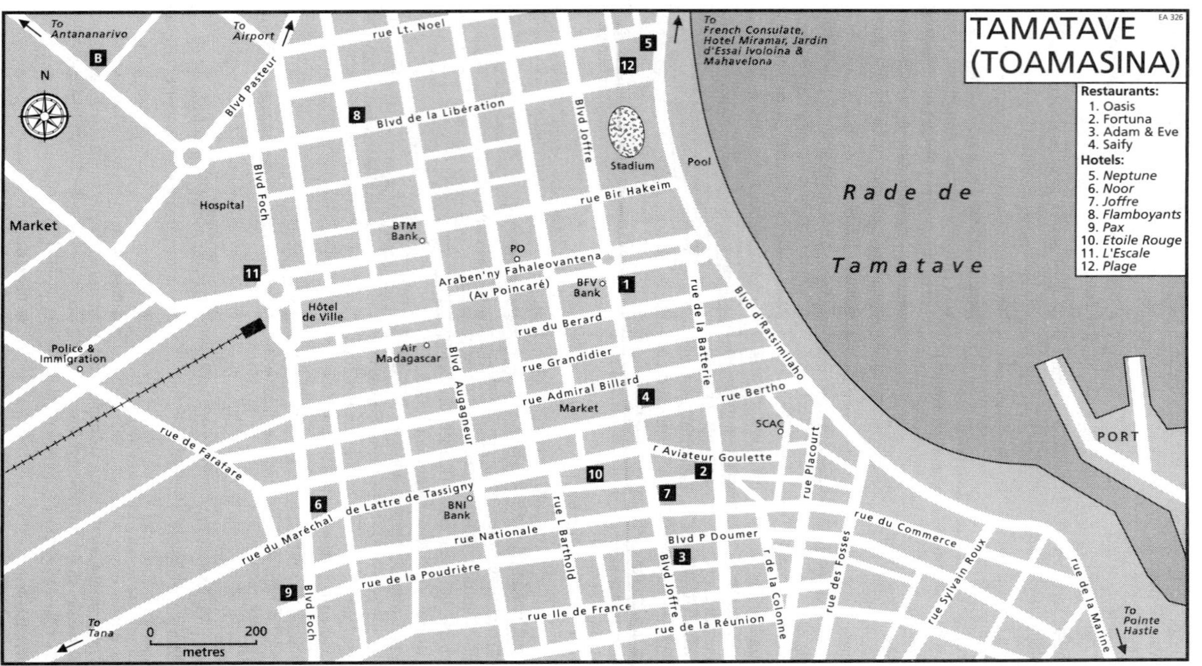
TAMATAVE (TOAMASINA)
EA 326
Restaurants:
1. Oasis
2. Fortuna
3. Adam & Eve
4. Saify
Hotels:
5. Neptune
6. Noor
7. Joffre
8. Flamboyants
9. Pax
10. Etoile Rouge
11. L'Escale
12. Plage
Rade de Tamatave
PORT
To Pointe Hastie
rue de la Marine
rue Sylvain Roux
rue du Commerce
rue des Fosses
rue Placourt
r de la Colonne
Blvd d'Ratsimilaho
To French Consulate, Hotel Miramar, Jardin d'Essai Ivoloina & Mahavelona
Pool
Stadium
rue Bir Hakeim
Blvd Joffre
rue de la Batterie
rue Bertho
SCAC
r Aviateur Goulette
Blvd P Doumer
rue de la Réunion
BFV Bank
rue du Berard
rue Grandidier
rue Admiral Billard
Market
rue L Barthold
rue Ile de France
PO
Araben'ny Fahaleovantena (Av Poincaré)
Blvd Augagneur
rue Nationale
BNI Bank
rue du Maréchal de Lattre de Tassigny
rue de la Poudrière
rue Lt. Noel
Blvd de la Libération
BTM Bank
Air Madagascar
Hôtel de Ville
Blvd Foch
To Airport
Blvd Pasteur
Hospital
rue de Farafare
0 200 metres
To Antananarivo
B
N
Police & Immigration
Market
To Tana

US$60 single. Also services to **Ile Ste Marie**, **Maroantsetra**, **Diego Suarez** and other inland destinations. **Air Madagascar**, Office Open Mon-Fri 0700-1100 and 1400-1600 and Sat 0700-1100.

Road Deluxe bus leaves from the *Colbert Hotel* in **Anatanarivo** Mon, Wed, Fri, costing US$18, tickets can be reserved ticket in advance in Antananarivo. *Taxi-brousse* station is on rue de la Liberté, to the N W of the centre, fare to Ananarivo is around US$9, and takes about 6 hrs. Road travel can be prolonged in wet weather.

Sea SCAC Marine Transport Co ferry the *Rapiko* runs a weekly service N up the coast to **Ile St Marie**, **Mananara** and **Maroantsetra**. Head office on Rue de Barriere between Rue de Billard and Rue Grandidier, for bookings, although tickets can be bought on board.

Train Leaves for **Antananarivo** 0600 daily arrives around 1900 with stops (36 in all) along the way. 1st class US$6.50; 2nd class US$3.50. Departs Anatanarivo at 0600, arrives Tamatave at 1700.

● **Vehicle hire**

Somacotour, T 33545. Bike and moped hire. **Garage Rachid** blvd Joffre. Car hire. **Aventour** rue Bir Hakeim, T 32261. Car hire.

North of Tamatave

The route N up the coast from Tamatave is sealed as far as Soanierana Ivongo, and there is then a track going further N to Mananara Nord, a distance of about 250 km. The coast has a series of small beach resorts and villages, and crossings to Ile Ste Marie can be made from Soanierana Ivongo and Manompana.

Foulpointe (Mahavelona)

Located 60km N of Tamatave. This was the initial site of French settlement on the E coast before re-locating at Tuléar. Of interest in the town is an old circular Merina **Fortress** guarded by British cannons. Entrance US$2.50.

● **Where to stay A** *Manda Beach*, T 32243. Quite new and high standard. Swimming pool. **D** *Au Gentil Pêcheur* Bungalow accommodation. Good Restaurant.

Mahambo

Is about 30 km N of Foulepointe. The sea is safe for swimming, as the reef protects the beach.

● **Where to stay D** *Le Récif*, T 43525. Bungalow accommodation. Good restaurant. **D** *Motel Le Gite*, T 43525. Bungalow accommodation, good value. **D** *Le Dola* Fairly modern. Chalets.

Fénérive (Fenoarivo Atsinanana)

Lies about 10 km N of Mahambo and was at one time the capital of the Betsimisaraka empire. Quite a pleasantly laid out settlement, with good beaches just to outside of town, both to the N and the S.

● **Where to stay E** *Tsarahely*, T 116. Shared bathrooms. **E** *Mandrosa* Shared bathrooms. Some rooms without electricity. **E** *Doany*, T 64. Simple shower, communal lavatories.

Soanierana Ivongo

A further 60km N of Fénérive. Its main aspect is that it provides a sailing point for Ile Ste Marie.

● **Where to stay E** *Tsiriry* Shared bathrooms. Basic.

Manompana

About 50 km N of Soanierana Ivongo, where you take a boat to Ile St Marie.

● **Where to stay E** *Antsikara* Shared bathrooms. **E** *Manompana* Shared bathrooms. Very simple.

Mananara Nord

lies at the southern end of the Baie d'Antongil. It is the main base for **Mananara National Park.**

● **Where to stay D** *Aye Aye* Opposite the airport. Shared bathrooms. Large rooms. Good restaurant. **D** *Chez Roger* Town centre. Pleasant location in garden.

The Mananara National Park

Recently set up a little S of Mananara Nord. It covers approximately 1400 sq km, and includes Mananara town. The objective is to try and create a sustainable reserve where local people benefit from controlled tourism (tourism at present is minimal). The reserve offers visitors one of the best places to see the Aye

Aye Lemur. It is also possible to visit **Aye Aye Island** (Rogers Island). Chez Rogers is the only hotel at present allowed to take visitors to Aye Aye Island (about US$6 per person).

● **Transport**

Air There are flights from Tamatave to Mananara and between Mananara and Madritsara to the W.

Road There are *taxi-brousse* running along this route. You should be prepared to make the trip up to Mananara (300 km) in several stages.

Ile Sainte Marie (Nosy Boraha)

Lies 8 km off the coast, and is 57 km from N to S and about 7km at its widest point. Originally called Island of Abraham it was renamed Ile Saint Marie in the seventeenth century by European sailors and was notorious as a pirate base. In 1750 it was given to France as a marriage gift to Jean Onesime Filet who married King Ratsimilaho's daughter, Princess Bety. After Jean's death Bety ceded the Island to France and moved to Mauritius. In 1896 the Island became part of Madagascar but its inhabitants still held the rights to French citizenship.

The Island is some 60km long and relatively undeveloped as far as tourism is concerned. The main crop is cloves, and coffee and vanilla are also grown. People speak French more than Malagasy. The Island has several good beaches and it is possible to swim safely since reefs keep out sharks.

Ambodifotatra

The capital, lies on the W coast, and is a town of about 2,000 people. There is a granite **Fort** which was built by the French in 1853. The **Church** is the oldest in Madagascar, and was built in 1857. The **Pirate Cemetery** is 2km S of the town. **L'Ilot Madame** is reached by a causeway from Ambodifotatra. Here the French East India Company established its offices. They now house the local adminstration.

Ile aux Nattes

Located off the southern tip of the island. Reached by outrigger canoe at a

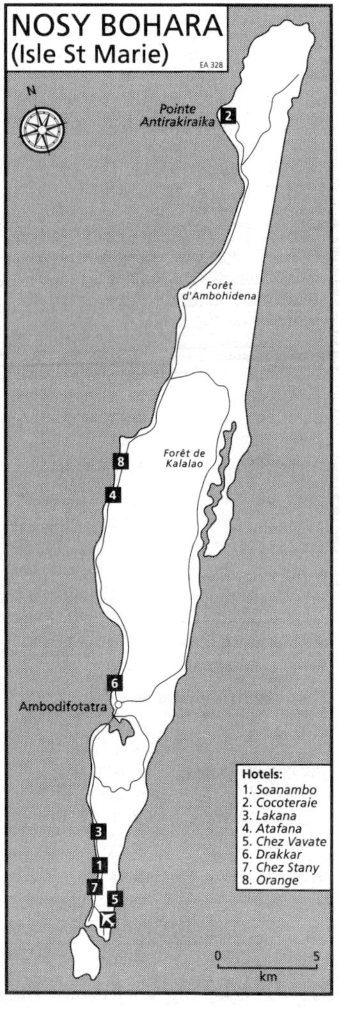

cost of US$0.50 per person. It is possible to eat or stay in the simple accommodation at E *Chez Napoleon* or E *Nautilus* (Cez Fabien).

Local information

● Where to stay

B *Soanambo* 3km from Airport, 10km from Ambodifotatra, T 40. Wide range watersports include sailing and windsurfing. Swimming pool. Reservations at *Hotel Colbert* in Antananarivo.

C *Cocoteraie II* and **D** *La Cocoteraie* North of the island, 35 km from Ambodifotatra. Boat goes there from *Hotel Soanambo*, (owned by same people). Shared bathrooms. Quiet beach. Cocoteraie II are timber bungalows. **C** *Lakana* Located 7km S of Ambodifotatra, T 46. Bamboo bungalows perched along a jetty Shared bathrooms.

D *Atafana*, 10 km N of Ambodifotatra, situated in a cove. Bungalows. Some own shower. Communal lavatories. Restaurant. Good value. **D** *Chez Vavate*, near Airstrip, 12km S of Ambodifotatra. Pleasant atmosphere. Men with wheel barrow meet flight to carry your luggage 1.5km to the hotel. Good restaurant. **D** *Le Drakkar*, 1 km N of Ambodifotatra. Bamboo bungalows Shared bathrooms. Colonial main building. Good restaurant.

E *Stany's Bugalows* (Chez Stany) about 10 km S of Ambodifotatra. Excellent location. Good restaurant. **E** *Hotel Orange*, situated 10 km N of town. Pleasant location. Good value.

● Transport

Air From Antananarivo (US$85) 5 flights a week; or from Tamatave (US$40) 4 flights a week. It is wise to book well in advance to ensure a place, and once you arrive reconfirm your return flight at Air Madagascar office.

Sea From *Tamatave*, SCAC Marine Transport Co runs a cargo and passenger ferry, the "Rapiko" which offers a weekly service N up the coast to Ambodifotatra on Ile St Marie (US$6, 10 hrs); and then on to Mananara and Maroantsetra. Departs Tamatave 0530 Wed, returns from Ambodifotatra 0500 Fri. Office of SMAC in Tamatave on Rue de Barriere. Tickets can be bought on board, but it is wisest to book.

From Manompana the ferry "Vedette Alize" departs around 0500 on Tue and Fri and costs US$8. Returns from Ambodifotatra 0500 Mon and Thu. From Soianiera Ivongo a crossing is made by cabin cruiser, costing US$30. Departs Wed and also Mon when busy. Sodextours, T Ste Marie 25.

● Vehicle hire

Most hotels have bikes to rent out (US$2 a day). Motorbikes (US$40 a day) and mopeds (US$30 a day) can be hired from *Hotel Soanambo*.

South West of Tamatave to Lake Alaotra

This route leads first down to Brickaville, from where it is possible to strike inland to Perinet and Moramanga, and thence N to Lac Alaotra. The railway runs along all this route. In addition there is the **Pangalanes Canal**, with a rich bird life, along the coast as far as Brickaville.

Brickaville Located some 80 km S of Tamatave, where the rail line and the road cross the Rianila River. When the rail line was first opened in 1909, it teminated at Brickaville, and freight was shipped by the Pangalanes Canal to Tamatave. E *Florida*, very simple.

Ambila Lemaitso Where the railway from Brickaville reaches the coast. E *Les Everglades*, T 1. Located between the beach and the canal. E *Rélais Malaky*, T 3.

Andranokoditra Fashionable resort for residents of Antananarivo by **Lac Ampitabe** on the Pangalanes Canal, 60 km S of Tamataye. B *Bushhouse*, bookings T Antananarivo 20454/33185, F Atntananarivo 25117. Good watersports. Nature reserve. Reptile farm. C *Pangalanes*, bookings T Tamatave 33403/32177. Range of accommodation. Will arrange transfer from station, or boat from Tamatave.

Perinet is 60km as the crow flies inland from Brickaville, but rather move by train and road as they twist and turn to climb up to the Highlands D *Buffet de la Gare*, Chalet bungalows. E *Camping* is available at *Hotel Buffet de la Gare*, where tents can be hired.

Perinet Analamazoatra Nature Reserve

A nature reserve, home to the Indri Indri Lemur family, which has panda bear characteristics. Also many lemurs and extensive birdlife. Permit required from Eaux et Forêts, Antananarivo. Guides available.

Moramanga

This town is at the junction where the railway line branches off to Lac Alaotra. It also provides accommodation for those visiting the **Perinet Analamazoatra** reserve.

• **Where to stay** **C** *Grand Hôtel*, T 62016. Bungalow or apartments. **D** *Emeraude*, T 62157. Hot water. Comfortable. **E** *Maitso an'Ala*. Simple and inexpensive.

Ambatondrazaka Penultimate stop on the line which terminates at Ambatsoratra, 20 km N on the edge of the Lake. There is no suitable accommodation at Ambatsoratra, so Ambatondrazaka is the most suitable base for exploring the Lake. D *Voahirana*, BP 65, T 81208. Comfortable. D *Max*, close to station. E *Hôtel du Plaisir*, simple and inexpensive.

Lake Alaotra

This is the largest Lake in Madagascar, with a surface area of 220 sq km. It is the home to endemic water fowl. Hiking is possible, but the terrain is difficult and you need to be well prepared. Guided tours can be arranged through *Hotel Voahirana* in Ambatondrazaka.

South of Tamatave to Manakara

In principle it is possible to travel down the waterway of the Pangalanes Canal, use *taxi-brousse* along the coast tracks, or hug the shore in a outrigger canoe, for a further 520 km from Brickaville to Farafangana. Otherwise the access is via Fianarantsoa from which there is the railway line to Manakara, and a sealed road to Mananjary which continues down the coast, through Manakara to Vangaindrano.

Vatomandry

Located 60 km S of Brickaville. Graphite is mined nearby and shipped by canal to Tamatave.

• **Where to stay** **D** *Derrien*, T 17. Situated on the shore. Reasonable. **E** *Fotsy*, thatched bungalows. **E** *Tsimialona*, T 54. Rather simple.

• **Travel** There are also flights from Tamatave(US$60) and Mhanoro (US$25).The road is generally not passable in the wet season. The less wet months are Sept to Jan, and Apr, May. The section of the canal is navigable, and it is possible to hire a ride on a boat.

Mahanoro

Around 240 km S of Tamatave. Small town with some coffee and cloves produced.

• **Where to stay** **E** *Hotel des Pangalanes* Simple shelter. **E** *Huo Wai*. Uncomplicated but adequate.

• **Transport** Access by road easiest Sept to Jan, and Apr, May, or by boat along the canal all year round.

Masomelika situated a further 50 km S of Mahanoro, and **Nosy Varika** is another 50 km S again. They both have small lodging houses. Boat along the canal is possible all year round. Tracks are better Sept to Jan, and Apr, May.

Manajary

Location of the circumcision ceremony carried out by Antambahoaka people every 7 yrs (last one 1993).

• **Where to stay** **C** *Jardin de la Mer* On the shore, T 940. Quite large and well-run. Restaurant. **E** *Solimotel*, Blvd Maritime, T 94250) Fairly simple. **E** *Rakotobe*, T 94327. Inexpensive but adequate.

• **Transport** Accessed most easily along sealed roads by *taxi-brousse* from Fianarantsoa (US$4) and Manakara (US$3). Flights from Antanarivo (US$70) and from Manakara (US$40) There is an unsealed track from Nosy Varika, and the canal from Nosy Varika and Manakara.

Manakara

This is Madagascar's second largest port, after Tamatave. It owes its prominence to the fact that it is the seaboard terminus of the Fianarantsoa- Côte Est (FCE) railway. The Manakara River runs through the town, parallel to the shore for part of the way. The old part of town, Mankara Be, has considerable charm with tree-lined streets and Colonial buildings. The post office and banks are in the old part of town, the railway station and taxi-brousse stand across the river in the newer section. **Vohipeno** is located 35 km to the S of Manakara, and is the centre for the Antaimoro people, a Shirazi people. They transcribed Malgasy into Arabic script and texts continue to be produced in this form today, known as *sorabe*. There are no hotels in Vohipeno.

• **Where to stay C** *Eden Sidi* Located 12 km N of town. BP 80 Ambinagny, T 21202/3. Bungalow-style Range of accommodation, some cheaper. Fine beach location. Good restaurant. Transport from town US$2. **D** *Hôtel Mankara* Located in old part of town, T 21141. Lavatories communal, some rooms with own shower. Fine location and great character. Good standard restaurant. **D** *Sidi* Close to taxi-brousse station in new part of town, T 21202. Range of rooms and facilities. Not particularly good value.

• **Transport Air** There are flights to and from **Mananajary** (US$40) to the N and then on to Antananarivo; and to **Faranfangana** (US$40) to the S, and then on to Fort Dauphin.

Rail Daily train link (170km), each way, to **Fianarantsoa**, leaving Manakara at 1200 and arriving at 2400, fare US$4 1st class, US$2.50 2nd class. Departs Fianarantsoa at 0600, and arrives 1300 at Manakara.

Road Taxi brousse to **Fianarantsoa** costs US$1.50 and takes 4 hrs. To **Vohipeno** a taxi-brousse costs US$0.75 and takes about an hr.

Farafangana

This is the southern terminus of the Pangalanes Canal. It still retains some of its colonial charm. The Manombo Special Reserve is about 30 km S on the route to Vangaindrano, and is an area of coastal marshland with rich birdlife.

• **Where to stay D** *Tulipes Rouges*, T 91186. Shared bathrooms. Colonial building of some character. chinese restaurant **E** *Rose Rouge*, T 91154. Shared bathrooms. Restaurant with Indian food. **E** *Rélais d'Agnambahy* Close to the taxi-brousse stand. Shared bathrooms.

• **Transport Air** There are flights to and from **Manakara** (US$40) to the N and then on to Mananjary and Antananarivo; and to **Fort Dauphin** (US$80) to the S. **Road** taxi-brousse N to **Vohipeno** US$0.75 and takes an hr; S to **Vangaindrano** is US$1.50, and takes just over 2 hrs.

Vangraindrano

At the southern end of the sealed road that runs S from Mananjary. Located on the Mananara River, and is the main town of the Antaisaka people. It is an agricultural market town, with coffee, bananas and rice grown in the surrounding area.

• **Where to stay E** *Chez Camélia* Shared bathrooms. Rather simple.

• **Transport** North to **Farafangana** is straightforward by *taxi-brousse*, US$1.50, and takes just over 2 hrs. There are unsealed tracks to **Fort Dauphin**, passing through **Mantanenina**, but it is 3 day journey in all, and little public transport along the 220km. Hiring rides on trucks is possible in the drier months of Sept to Jan, and Apr, May.

THE NORTH – DIEGO SUAREZ AND NOSY BE

Homeland of the Antankarana people. The presence of the Tasaratanana Massif (Madagascar highest peak at 2,880m) causes heavy rainfall over the attractive island of Nosy Be. Diego Suarez experiences a 7 month dry season before 90% of rain falls during Dec-Apr.

Diego Suarez (Antsiranana)

The town of about 60,000 people lies 1,194km from Antananarivo, and is surrrounded by hills. Named after the Portuguese sea captain who first sighted it in 1543. In 1885 the French exploited the deep harbour and installed a military base to protect their interests in the region. The British captured it in 1942 from the Vichy French government to ensure it did not fall to the Japanese. South of the town, following route de l'Ankarana, is the **War Cemetery** for those killed in 1942. In the 1972 disturbances French troops withdrew from Madagascar and the town suffered considerable damage. Today Diego Suarez has a very cosmopolitan atmosphere.

Local information

● Where to stay

B *Hotel de la Poste*, near Clemenceau Sq, T 21453. Best in town. Pleasant views. **B** *Paradis du Nord*, overlooks market, T 21405. Some a/c Sat night disco.

C *Fian-Tsilaka*, 13 Blvd Etienne, T 22348. Some rooms with own bathrooms. Good restaurant. **C** *Fiadanana*, T 22348. Fans. Some studios. Good value.

D *Nouvel*, rue Colbert, T 22262. Restaurant. Night club.

● Places to eat

♦♦♦*La Venilla*, rue Surcouf. Malagasy dishes of high standard, plus international food. ♦♦♦*Restaurant Hortensia*, Rue Colbert. International cuisine.

♦♦*L'Extreme Orient*, ave Lally Tollendal. Chinese food. ♦♦*Libertalia* rue Colbert. Food from the Far East.

● Nightlife

Nouvel rue Colbert; *5/5* rue Colbert; *Tropical* rue Lafayette.

● Travel Agencies

Agence Colbert rue Colbert. *Air Madagascar* rue Surcouf.

● Vehicle Hire

Nathalic Lozere 9 Rue Français de Mahy (T 21908) Cars (4 wheel drive), motorbikes. **Quatro Evasion** Off Place Foch (T 21955) Cars, motorbikes.

Excursions

Ramena Beach 20km E of town. Safe swimming. E *Au Bon Coin*. Restaurant. Boat trips can be organised.

Lac Sacre, 80km S of Diego, is the sacred lake of Anivorano. There is a local story that long ago Anivorano lay in a desert. A thirsty traveller arrived at the village but was refused water, as there was a drought. The visitor left, but warned the local people they would soon have water enough. As he left the village it was flooded, and the local people turned into crocodiles.

Montagne d'Ambre National Park

The mountain itself is 1,474m high. The Park opened in 1958 and was Madagascar's first National Park. Permits can be collected from the World Wildlife Fund (WWF) rue Surcouf, opposite the Air Madagascar office. The park provides the visitor with one of the best examples of upland moist forest and experiences a micro climate with a rainy season from Dec to May. Sanfords Lemurs (*Lemur fulvus sanfordi*) and the crowned Lemur (*Lemur Coronatus*) can be seen. The mouse tenrec (*Microgale parvula*) is endemic to the area. There are 2 waterfalls in the Park, Grand Cascade and Petite Cascade. Guides are available.

It is important to come prepared for the forest, with stout footwear and long socks to guard against leeches. **E** *Camping* is available at a site near Petite Cascade.

Ankarana Reserve

80km S of Diego Suarez is the relatively small limestone Ankarana Massif where typical limestone karst scenery predominates. Some of the caves are burial sites and are sacred. Every 7 years the Tsangatsaina ceremony is held to give thanks for the successful return of the Antakarana people to their homeland. There are 2 stages of this ceremony held

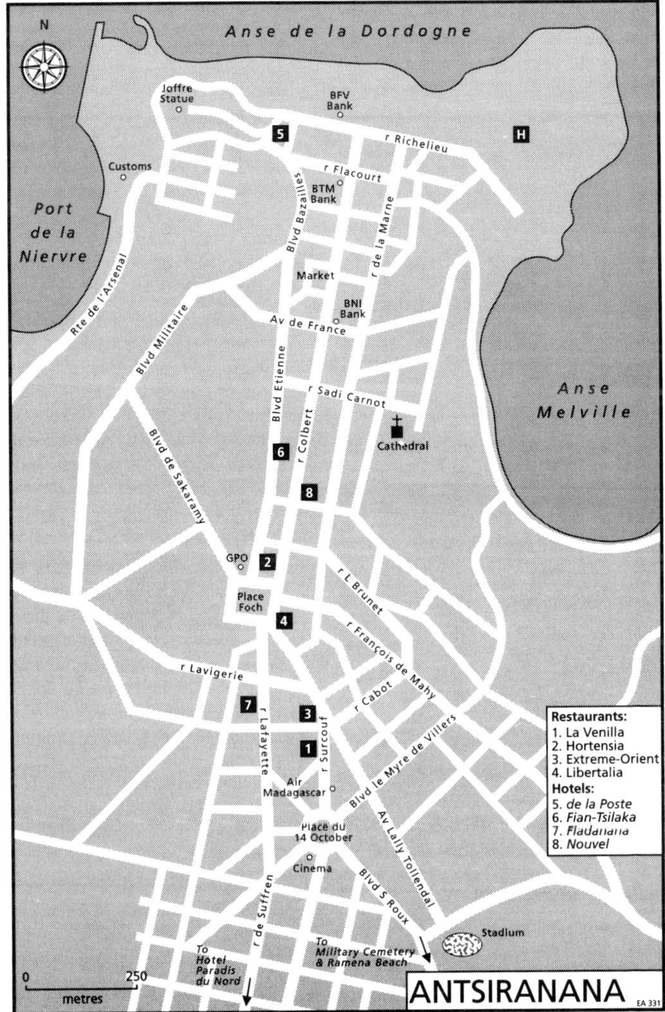

a year apart. The first part involves visiting the homeland of the ancestors, Nosy Mitsio, which ends with a visit to the first Antakarana king to ask his blessing for the ceremony to continue the next year. The second part involves acquiring 2 sacred trees, representing male and female, and these are then brought to Ambatoharanana. Here they are jointed together to form a flag pole, the 2 parts represent the continuity of the monarchy and the unity of the people.

For those interested in caving, locals will direct you to the largest cave Grotte d'Andrafiabe.

• **Transport Air** Flights to and from **Antananarivo** (US$150, daily). **Majunga** (US$100). **Tamatave** (US$120). **Sambava** (US$60). **Nosy Be** (US$40); and **Vohémar** (US$40). **Road** Taxi-brousse stand on route de l'Ankarana, S of the centre. To **Vohéma**, US$7,

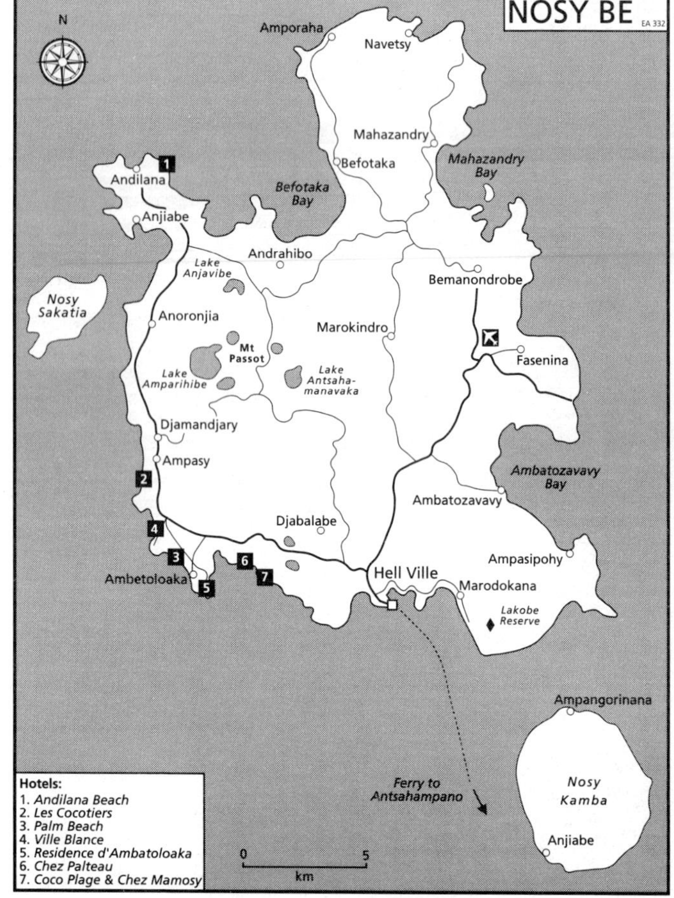

20 hrs (goes via Ambilobe); to **Ambanja** (for Nosy Be) US$4, 6 hrs; to **Antananarivo** US$20, 3 days.

Nosy Be

About 200 km SW of Diego Suarez. Originally inhabited by Atakarana and later, in the seventeenth century, by Sakalava. In 1649 the British tried but failed to set up a British colony on the Island. During the 1800s Sakalava residents were faced by expansionist ambitions of the Merina but they managed to repel a Merina invasion. In 1841 the Island came under French rule. To the S E lie ruins of an Indian settlement built by shipwrecked sailors. The Island has some good roads and is a very popular tourist resort, with a good climate, fine beaches, and the scent everywhere of *ylang-ylang* flowers.

• **Transport Air** Flights from **Antananarivo** (US$140, 5 flights a week). **Majunga** (US$80). **Diego Suarez** (US$40, 5 flights a week). **Ambajana** (US$20). It is important to remember to book well in advance if travelling in peak periods. **Sea** Cargo boats from **Majunga** (US$8, takes 2 days), irregular. Ramzana Aly, rue Nicholas in Majunga. **Road** Taxi-brousses run from **Diego Suarez** to Ambanja on the mainland. Taxis leave from outside *Hotel de Ville* for Antsahampano, the ferry port. From

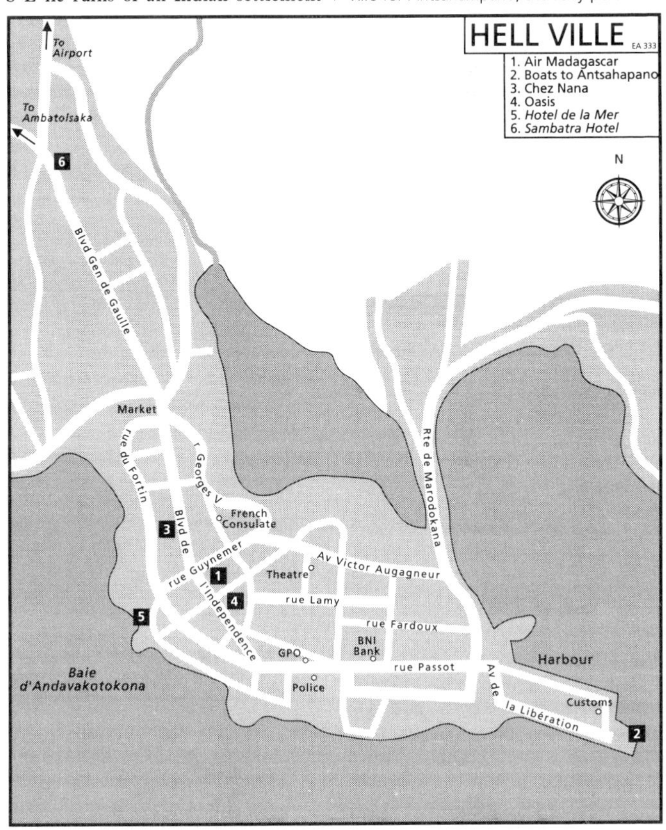

there take a ferry to Nosy Be (times of ferries posted outside *Hotel Patricia*).

Hell-Ville

The capital of Nosy Be, named after Admiral de Hell. There is a pleasant tree-lined square and scattered colonial buildings.

Local information

● Where to stay

C ***Hotel de la Mer***, blvd du Docteur Mauclair, T 61353. Good location on beach overlooking bay to W of town centre.

D ***Sambatra*** Inexpensive and good value.

● Places to eat

♦♦***Classic*** International food. Good value. ♦♦***Oasis Salon de Thé***. Pleasant café.

● Beach hotels

The main beach area is at Ambatolaoka, about 10km W of Hell-Ville.

A ***Andilana Beach***, north W of Hell-Ville, about 25 km distant, T 61176, a/c Swimming pool. Tennis. Pleasant location; **A** ***Les Cocotiers*** Ambatolaoka, T 61314. Bungalows. Very popular; **A** ***Palm Beach***, Ambatolaoka. Swimming pool. Casino. **A** ***Villa Blanche*** Ambatolaoka, T Antananarivo 22854.

B ***Résidence Ambatolaoka***, Ambatolaoka, T 61068/61368. Own bathrooms.

C ***Chez Pulteau***, Ambatolaoka. Fine location and excellent restaurant. Good value. **C** ***Coco Plage*** Ambatolaoka, T 61353. Good location on beach.

E ***Chez Mamosy***, Ambatolaoka. Shared bathrooms.

● Airline Office

Madagascar Air has its office at *Andilana Beach Hotel*.

● Vehicle Hire

Villa Blanche Motorbikes are available to hire. **Societe Nossi Be Auto** (T 61150) Cars and mopeds.

Excursions

Lokobe Guided tour of forest and visit to small village, accessed by out-rigger canoe. Local food of high standard provided. Cost around US$20. Hotels will arrange.

Nosy Kamba (Nosy Ambariovato) This island has volcanic origins, and is located to the S E of Nosy Be, between the island and the mainland. A variety of Lemurs inhabit the island, particularly the black lemur. Waters around the island are good for diving. D *Lemuriens*, BP 185, Nosy Be. E *Madio*, BP 207, Nosy Be.

Nosy Tanikely Located 10 km S of Hell-Ville Home to a lighthouse, its keeper, island wildlife and a beach. The island is a marine reserve so fires, and fishing are prohibited, but diving is allowed.

Tours to other small islands around Nosy Be can be arranged by local tour companies: *Round Liberty Ranch*, Rue Galleieni, Hell-Ville, T 61036. *Andilana Beach*, T 61176. also Antananarivo, T 22631. *Les Cocotiers*, Ambatolaoka, T 61314. *Nosy Be Charters*, Hell-Ville, T 61053. *Sambava Voyages* Deep sea fishing trips.

North East Coast: Diego Suarez to Maroantsetra

This part of the country gets plenty of rainfall, and the high land running back from the coastal strip is extremely fertile. This is the centre of Madagascar's vanilla industry, with coffee and rice also grown. The towns along the coast have pleasing old Colonial centres from which spices were exported to Europe, and food to Mauritius.

Vohémar

Small town on attractive cove with mountains behind. Originally a Shirazi town (see page 278), but the original inhabitants were driven out by the Sakalava. Local production of items from soapstone.

● Where to stay **D** ***Sol y Mar***, Beach location, T 46. Bungalows Restaurant. Good value. **E** ***Poisson d'Or***. Sound accommodation. Good restaurant.

● Transport **Air** From **Diego Suarez** (US$40). **Road** *Taxi-brousse* from **Diego Suarez**, US$7, 20 hrs (goes via Ambilobe; to **Savamba** US$3.

Sambava

Small town with an attractive location and an old colonial section. Coffee, vanilla and cloves are grown, and vanilla is processed at a local factory.

● **Where to stay** **C** *Carrefour* On the beach, T 60, a/c. Restaurant. **D** *las Palmas* Close to beach, T 87, a/c. Own bathrooms Good value. Organises excursions. **D** *Orchidea Beach* Bungalows on the beach, T 128. Restaurant with Italian cuisine. Good value in charming setting. **D** *Nouvel*, T 66. Own bathrooms, some rooms cheaper with communal facilities. Pleasant seting in a garden. Good restaurant.

● **Excursions** *Sambava Voyages* Near Air Madagascar office, T 110.

● **Transport** **Air** From **Diego Suarez** (US$60); from **Antananarivo** (US$160); from **Maroantsetra** (US$35). **Road** *Taxi-brousse* N to **Vohémar** US$3; S to ***Antahala*** (US$3).

Andapa

About 75km inland from Sambava. Surrounded by cultivation of rice, vanilla and coffee. Very attractive route from Sambava.

● **Where to stay** **D** *Vatosoa*, T 39. Comfortable and well-run. Organises excursions. Chinese cuisine.

● **Transport** *Taxi-brousse* from Sambava. Takes aroound 3 hrs, and costs (US$3).

Antahala

Centre of Madagascar's vanilla industry. Pleasant town with a nice beach and a colonial port. There is a hill behind the town.

Masoala Peninsula The area is covered in rainforest and excellent for trekking. It has 2 rare lemurs. It is possible to trek across it from Antahala to Maroanatsetra, taking around 5 days. Guides can be engaged at Antahala.

● **Where to stay** **D** *Hôtel du Centre*, T 81167. Shared bathrooms. Restaurant. Comfortable. **D** *Ocean Plage*, located on shore, T 81205. Bungalows. Own bathrooms.

● **Transport** **Air** Flights to **Tamatave** (US$70), **Maroantsetra** (US$30), **Diego Suarez** (US$80), **Mananara** (US$30). **Road** Taxi-brousse N to **Sambava** (US$3). **Sea** Cargo boats run from Antalaha to Tamatave calling at **Ile St Marie**, fare around US$8 amd takes 3 days to Ste Marie. Small boats run down to **Maroantsetra** costing US$5.

Maroantsetra

This town receives more rain than any other in Madagascar, but has a large amount of wildlife and trekking through the rain forest is possible.

Nosy Mangabe Island Permit to visit required from Eaux et Forêts in Antananarivo. If you wish to stay on the island, you need to bring a tent. The Island has Aye Aye and a variety of wild life including the snake *Pseudoxrhopus heterus*. Beaches are beautiful but there is danger from sharks.

● **Where to stay** **D** *Motel Coco Beach*, T 18. Beach bungalows, some with own bathrooms. Excursions arranged. **D** *Le Tropical* Bungalows on stilts. Shared bathrooms. Pleasant atmosphere. Boat excursions available.

● **Transport** **Air** Flights to **Savamba** (US$35); **Antahala** (US$30); **Tamatave** (US$60); **Mananara** (US$30). **Road**. There is a road to Mananara to the S, but it is not in use. **Sea** Small boat to Antahala US$5; to Mananara US$4.

NORTH WEST COAST - MAJUNGA

Dominated by the Sakalava people who emerged from the S W during the seventeenth century, they were the largest and most powerful grouping for some time. By the eighteenth century, however, the empire had split into Menabe in the S and Boina in the N. This division left the Sakalava weak and it was soon under Merina control, and later French colonisation.

The people in western Madagascar are predominantly from African backgrounds. Their African ancestors migrated from the mainland bringing African traditions and language which have influence today, such as *tramba* "possession of the spirit". Language has also been influenced by Bantu dialect. The Sakalava do not practise second burial but their tombs often have erotic paintings representing rebirth and sexuality. Royality relics are washed every 10 years in Sep (next occasion is 1998).

Majunga (Mahajanga)

Majunga was first settled in 1745. In 1895 the French occupied the town, their first step towards a conquest of Madagascar. The town's importance grew through its port, attracting Arab, Malagasy and European traders. For many years the town acted as the unofficial capital of the Comores and today more Comoriens live in Majunga than Moroni. Majunga also has a large Indian population who arrived during the colonial period, partly to provide labour after the abolition of slavery, and partly to trade. It is now a fairly busy town of about 100,000 people.

Arabic architectural influence is visible in parts of the town especially around the old commercial centre. One of the town's famed possessions is a sacred baobab tree on Ave de France that is thought to be over 700 years old.

Local information

● Where to stay

A *Zahal Motel*, Amborovy beach, 8 km from centre, T 2324, a/c. Bungalows. Good beach.

C *Les Roches Rouges*, blvd Marcoz, N of town centre, T 23871, a/c. Own bathrooms. Swimming pool. Tennis. Excursions available; **C** *Kanto*, blvd Marcoz 1km N of town, T 22978, a/c. Some cheaper rooms in old part with communal facilities. Overlooks the sea. Chez Carron bungalows at Village Touristique on beach. **C** *Hotel de France*, rue du Maréchal Joffre, T 23781, a/c. Own bathrooms. Colonial building. Bar. Some cheaper rooms with shared bathrooms.

D *Bombetoka*, blvd Marcoz. Overlooks sea. Good restaurant.

E *Chez Madame Chabaud* ,ave Philbert Tsiranana. Shared bathrooms. Good restaurant.

● Places to eat

♦♦*Chez Chabaud*, ave Philbert Tsiranana. Local and international food. ♦♦*Le Vietnamien*, rue du Maréchal Joffre. Far Eastern cuisine. ♦♦*Pakiza Restaurant*, ave de la republique. Malagsy food. ♦♦*Sampan d'Or*, rue Georges. Chinese food.

♦*Bhavna Salon de Thé*, rue Georges. Indian food.

● Airline

Air Madagascar, Ave Gillon, T 2421.

● Banks

BNI rue du Maréchal Joffre and **BTM** on corner of Rue Georges and Ave de la Liberation.

● Entertainment

Cinema *Ritz*, Ave de la Republique.

● Nightlife

Le Ravinala, ave Jule Aubourg, on waterfront. *Sasa Club*, rue Nicholas.

● Post Office

Rue du Colonel Barre open Mon-Fri 0800-1200 and 1400-1800, Sat 0800-1200.

● Useful addresses

French Consulate, Rue Edouard VII Open Mon-Wed and Fri 0800-1200. Visas for Mayotte.

● Travel Agents

Transtour for car hire and chartering of yachts.

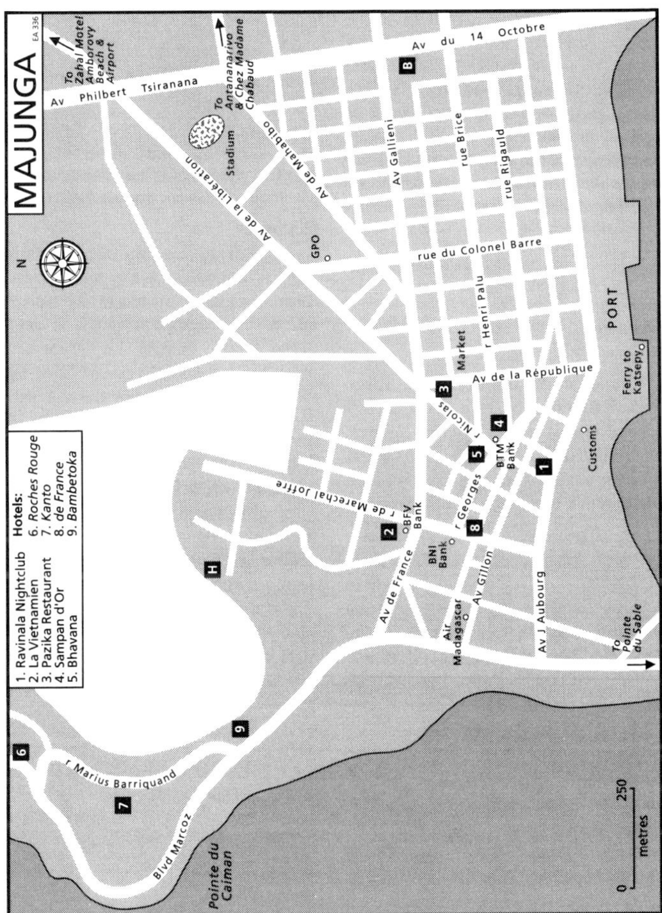

Crosieres, Ambarika (T 22054) has yachts to charter.

Excursions

Amborovy Beach Approx 6km from town and is a pleasant coastal location where *Zahal Motel* is located.

Cirque Rouge is a large natural amphitheatre 12 km from Manjunga, good for camping.

Katsepy Charming village across the bay. Ferry "Avotra" which makes the trip twice a day, takes 1 hr, costs US$0.75. D *Chez Madame Chabaud*, Bungalows. Own bathrooms. some cheaper rooms with shared bathrooms. Excellent food.

● **Transport**

Road *Taxi brousse* to **Antananarivo** take roughly 15 hrs to cover the 560 km and leave from ave Philbert Tsiranana in Majunga, and costs about US$5. There are also taxi-be (Peugeot 504s) and buses, which are slightly more expensive. From Antananarivo, *taxi-brousse* leave from the stand on Làlana Dok Raphael Raboto to the noth W of the centre.

Air Flights to **Antananarivo** (US$100, 6 a week); **Diego Suarez** (US$100); **Nosy Be** (US$80); **Soalala** (US$35).

Sea Cargo boats to **Nosy Be** (US$8, takes 2 days), irregular. Ramzaana Aly rue Nicholas, BP 60, Majunga. Boats to **Comores** SCTT, rue du Maréchal Joffre. Fare around US$75. Larger boats, the "Ylang Ylang" and the "Chongui", based in Comores, also service this route, costing US$60 single.

Mitsinjo

A pleasant small town, about 50 km W of Majunga, on the Mahavavy River. **Lake Kinkony** close by is Madagascar's second largest lake, 150 sq km in area, with significant bird life. No regular accommodation, but it is usually possible to rent a room in a private house.

From Mitsinjo you can visit **Soalala**, a further 50 km along the coast where there are a number of Islamic sites, thought to have been founded by 2 Princesses from Mayotte. It is possible to camp on the beach and buy fish from local fishermen. The Agents pour la Protection de la Nature (APN) have an office at the Eaux et Forêts, and are able to help those wishing to visit **Sada** where the Angonoka tortoise live.

• **Transport Air** Service to **Soalala** from **Majunga** (US$45) **Road** Ferry from **Majunga** across to Katsepy, and then *taxi-brousse* to Mitsinjo (US$0.50) and **Soalala** (US$1).

Marovoay

Located 50 kms E of Majunga the name means "where there are many crocodiles". Originally Sakakava, it was conquered by the Merina and later came under French control. Important as a port. Today colonial presence still felt through the old buildings. River trips can be arranged from here.

• **Where to stay E** *Tiana*, T 61.

Antkarafantsika Forest Reserve

Located 100km S E of Manjunga along the road to Antananarivo. Filled with wildlife, very good for birdwatching. A permit is required from Eaux et Forêts in Antananarivo or Majunga. It is possible to camp or stay at the Research Station in the reserve. **Transport** *Taxi-brousse* from Majunga.

INFORMATION FOR VISITORS

Contents

Before you go

Entry requirements

● **Visas**

Visas are needed by anyone planning to visit Madagascar, and can be acquired from Madagascar Embassies and Consulates as either a single (1 month) or double (3 month) entry visas. Some consulates require an inbound ticket into the country before they issue a visa. Four photgraphs are required. The cost varies, depending on where the application is made - from US$7.50 in Mauritius to US$45 in the UK. Visas are usually processed in 48hrs and in London are issued while you wait.

Visas can be renewed in Madagascar. Make sure you have cashed a plausible amount of money before applying for an extension.

Visa extensions can be obtained at Ministry of the Interior, Làlana Ranaivo Jules, Anosy, 101 Antanarivo (T 23084), which is just to the W of Lac Anosy. Alternatively visas can be extended at central police station in any of the provincial capitals: Tuléar, Diego Suarez, Fianaratsoa, Tamatave and Majunga.

Other visas for France (Mayotte) or Reunion see list of representatives below found in Antananarivo.

● **Vaccinations**

If you are arriving from Africa you will need to show yellow fever and cholera vaccination certificates. (see Health, below 758).

● **Madagascar Representation Overseas**

Comores (C), route de Mitsamiloui Moroni. **France** (E), 4 Avenue Raphael 75016 Paris. **Germany** (E), Rolandstrabe 48, 5300 Bonn Bad Godesburg. **Kenya** (C), Kenya Air Madagascar, Nairobi *Hilton*. **Mauritius** (E), 6 Queen Mary Avenue Floreal. **Reunion** (C), 51 rue Juliette Dodu 97461 St Denis. **Seychelles** (C), Independence House Victoria. **United Kingdom** (C), 16 Lanark Mansions, Pennard Road, London W12 UK. **United States**, Mission to the United Nations 801 Second Ave Suite 404 New York 10017.

● **Overseas Representation in Madagascar**

See Antanarivo, page 729. **France** also has consulates in Fianarantsoa (Rue Verdun); Manjunga (Rue Edouard VII); Tamatave (Rue de la Convention); Diego Suarez (Rue Benyowski).

● **Tourist information**

There is no Tourist Office on Madagascar but *Madagascar Airtours* office in the Hilton Anosy Antananarivo, T 24192, will be able to help you. The company also offers package tours around the Island.

● **Travel Agents**

Transcontinental, 10 Araben ny Fahaleovantena Antananarivo, T 22398. *Madagascar Tourist Bureau* (a private company) Immeuble La Pargola Antananarivo, T 22364. *Direction du Tourisme*, BP 610 Antananarivo, T 26298. For maps and brochures.

When to go

● **Best Time to Visit**

May-Sept is best. Oct to Apr is the rainy season and travel by road can be difficult.

Health

● Staying healthy
If you are arriving from Africa you will need to show yellow fever and cholera vaccination certificates on entry. Other vaccinations which are recommended include Typhoid, Tetanus, Polio, Hepatitis A and Rabies. Make sure you also take Malaria pills and if you are planning to travel cheaply, a mosquito net is essential. See general Health Section, page 21.

Money

● Currency
The unit of currency is the Malagasy Franc (MGF). Rate of exchange in 1994 MGF 1,892 = US$1. Everyone entering Madagascar, on arrival, is required to complete a currency declaration form. It is important to declare all currency and traveller's cheques as this will be checked on your departure. The amount of currency on arrival, currency exchanges and departure currency must tally. Once you have filled in the form make sure it is stamped. When changing foreign currency make sure to keep a receipt for each transaction since you will be asked to show these receipts on departure.

The importation of Malagasy Francs is limited to F5000 (export is illegal). There are no limits to foreign currency brought into the country but it must all be declared. You cannot change MGF back into foreign currency.

● Credit cards
Limited use, accepted by large hotels, airlines and travel agents. ***American Express Representative***, *Madagascar Airtours, Hilton Hotel,* T 24192. Anosy Antananarivo. *Madagascar Airtours* also represents American Express in the main towns.

● Cost of Living
Budget travellers, staying in the simplest lodgings, eating in restaurants serving local food, and travelling by *taxi-brousse* or train, can get by on US$20 a day. Indeed it is quite possible to stay in some quite charming, simple places, particularly around the coast, on this daily expenditure.

Modest travellers, staying in hotels with fans or air conditioning, and hot water, travelling by taxi-be, and sampling a variety of restaurants, will find it costs perhaps US$40 a day.

Luxury travellers, staying in the best hotels with air-conditioning and swimming pools, travelling by air, and eating in the best restaurants in town, will spend US$150 a day.

● Banks
There are 5 banks in Madagascar: the Banque Malagache de L'Océan Indian (BMOI); Banky Fampandrosoana ny Varota (BFV); Union Commercial Bank (UCB); Bankin'ny Tantsaha Mpamokatra (BTM); Banky ny Indostria - Credit Lyonnais Madagascar (BNI).

Opening Hrs are 0800-1100 and 1400-1600 (Mon-Fri)

Getting there

● By air
Low season Jan-Jun; medium season mid-Sept to mid-Dec; high season Jul to mid-Sept and mid-Dec to end-Dec.

● From Europe
Cheapest fares from **Aeroflot** via Moscow (Wed outward, Fri return), from US$700 return. These flights are very heavily booked. Via Paris with **Air Madagascar/Air France** on Mon via Jeddah, Thu, Fri via Nairobi from US$1,500 return. Alternative is to buy a flight to Nairobi and then buy an excursion ticket from there to Antananarivo (Thu outward, Fri return) operated by Air Madagascar & Air Mauritius, from US$320 return.

● From Africa
Flights from **Johannesburg** with South African Airways; from **Nairobi** (Kenya) with Air Madagascar & Air Mauritius; **Lusaka** (Zambia) with Air France; **Lilongwe** (Malawi) with Air France; **Moroni** and **Dzaoudzi** (Comoros) with Air Madagascar; **St Denis** (Réunion) with Air France and Air Madagascar; **Plaisance** (Mauritius) with Air Mauritius; **Mahé** (Seychelles) with Kenya Airways and British Airways.

● Specialist Agencies
For discounted fares, see page 737.

● Air Madagascar Offices Overseas
France 7 Ave de L'Opera Paris 75001, T 42603051. **Germany**, Herzog-Rudolf Strasse 3, 8000 Munchen 22, T 231801. **Switzerland**, c/o ATASH. 34 Neumuehlequai 8035 Zurich, T 362 77700.

● Airline Offices in Madagascar
See Antananarivo, page 729

● Airport Information
Airport Departure Tax: Regional (Indian Ocean) US$12; Inter-continental US$16.

● **Transport to town**
There is an airport bus to the city centre, costing US$2. Timetables are found in the airport and Air Madagascar office. Departs Air Madagascar office, 31 Arabe ny Fahaleovantena, Sat-Wed; Grand Orient Restaurant, close to the railway staion, on Thu & Fri. Taxis are also available for US$9.

● **By Sea**
A comfortable option is the MV Mauritius Pride which is planning to introduce a sailing to Madagascar. Boats (*boutres*) run from Anjouan and Dzaoudzi in Comoros to Majunga, fare about US$70.

● **Customs**
On entry, arrivals are allowed one bottle of alcohol; 500 cigarettes or 25 cigars; 10 rolls of film.

When you arrive

● **Conduct**
Madagascar is a very relaxed atmosphere for travellers, and observance of common courtesies will ensure that you do not offend. Burial places, tombs and remains require particular reserve and respect.

● **Electricity**
Two pin sockets (round). Adaptors are advised. Big towns are usually on 220 volts, but some old rural supplies are still 110 volts.

● **Hours of business**
Most shops closed on Sat & Sun. Government Offices Mon-Fri 0830-1530. Lunch breaks are long so be prepared.

● **Safety**
Madagascar is a safe place for visitors. It is not wise, however to walk around at night in poorly lit or isolated places in Antananarivo. Beware of snatch thieves in crowded areas such as market places.

● **Time**
3hrs ahead of GMT.

Where to stay

● **Hotels**
There is plenty of accommodation, at a very reasonable price. It is seldom the case that places are full - the busiest times are mid-Dec to mid-Jan; Easter; Jul-Aug. Accommodation is more expensive in Antananarivo and Nosy Be. The large hotels may require payment in foreign currency. Simple accommodation used by Malagasy is very cheap, and usually costs under US$1 a night.

Hotel Classifications

A+	Over US$100 a night. International standards and decor, a/c, self contained rooms, swimming pool, restaurants, bars, business services.
A	US$40-100. First class standards. Air-conditioning, attached bathrooms. Restaurants and bars. Swimming pool.
B	US$20-40. Tourist class. Comfortable with a/c or fans, attached barthrooms. Restaurant, bar, public rooms.
C	US$10-20. Budget. Fans. Shared bathroom facilities.
D	US$5-10. Guest house. No fan. Shared bathroom. Cold water.
E	Under US$5. Basic guest house. Simple bed. No soap or towels. No wardrobe. Shared bathroom facilities. Erratic cold water supply. No fans or mosquito nets.

Restaurant Classifications

♦♦♦♦	Over US$10 for a meal. A 3 course meal in a restaurant with pleasant decor. Beers, wines and spirits available.
♦♦♦♦	US$5-10 for a meal. Two courses. Comfortable surroundings.
♦♦	US$2-5 for a meal. Probably only a single course. Surroundings spartan but adequate.
♦	Under US$2. Single course. Often makeshift surroundings such as a street kiosk with simple benches and tables.

Food and drink

● **Food**
Traditional food includes rice, stewed meat, fish, or chicken with boiled *brede* (green vegetables). On the coast seafood is popular whilst further inland cassava and manioc form the base of local diets. One of the most common traditional sweets is made with peanuts, rice and sugar wrapped in banana leaves and cooked.

● **Drink**
The local beers are *Three Horses* and *Beeks Brau*, and a bottle costs about US$0.50. In the Highlands, around Fianarantsoa, wine is produced, and it is quite drinkable. They are mostly

reds, and include ***Lazan'i Betsileo***, ***Beau Vallon*** and ***Coteauz d'Ambalavao***.

Local drinks include *tokoa gasy*, a rather fierce rum; *litchel*, a spirit with a sweet flavour made from lychees; *betsabetsa* made from fermented molasses; *trembo* made from fermented coconut milk; and *punch au coco*, from coconut milk and rum.

There are a plenty of soft drinks, and a mineral water, *Eau Vive*.

Getting around

Air

All the major towns, and many smaller ones are served by Air Madagascar, which is owned partly by the government and partly by Air France. In all, over 50 destinations are served. Fares from Antanarivo to the provincial capitals are: Tamatave US$63; Diégo Suarez US$172; Majunga US$98; Tuléar US$160; Fort Dauphin US$160.

Train

There is approximately 1,100km of railway in Madagascar. One track runs from Antananarivo to Tamatave with a branch line to Moramanga, Morarano Sud and Ambatosorata on Lac Alaotra and S via Antsirabe to Vinaninkarena.

The other line of 170 km runs from Fianarantsoa to Manakara port.

If you are travelling first class you will probably have to pay in foreign currency.

It is possible to hire a Micheline (single carriage train, running on tyres. Trips are limited to 7 days though this is negotiable. Trains are slower than road transport, but they are a comfortable way to travel.

Sea and Canal

Boats ply around the coast; to the islands of Nosy Be and Ile Ste Marie; and along the Panganales Canal, the 600 km of inland waterway, linking the lagoons on the E coast between Tamatave and Farafangana.

Fares on *boutres* (powered boats) should cost around US$1 for 10km. Outrigger canoes (*pirogues*) can also be hired and cost US$8 per day (be prepared to bargain).

Road

Only one tenth of Madagascar's 40,000 km roads is paved. There are 2 types of taxi: the ***taxi be*** is an 8 seater Peugeot 504; the ***taxi-brousse*** is a minibus (usually overcrowded). Buses operate in and around Antananarivo. In the towns rickshaws (*pouse pousse*) are available.

Communications

Language

The official languages in Madagascar are French and Malagasy. In administrative quarters French predominates, though in some rural areas only a few people speak French. Malagasy belongs to the Malayo-Polynesian family of languages and has incorporated vari-

Malagasy Express

In early times the main routes round the island were narrow footpaths, often over very hilly terrain.. For transport the Malagasy developed a type of panquin or sedan chair called the *filanjana*. It consisted of 2 poles about 2m long with a leather-padded iron-frame chair with foot-rests slung between them, a sunshade, a rainproof apron and some pouches for luggage. Women had a special, fully-enclosed version with a sort of hammock of plaited sheepskin and a cloth roof.

Four men, running, carried the *filanjana* on their shoulders, with a spare team running behind. A change of bearers took place every few minutes with the relief team running under the poles and lifting the *filanjana* off without breaking stride. The teams would cover 42 miles in a 7 hr day. Goods were carried on a pole with a bundle at each end by a runner and a relief man. Messages went by relays of runners who could cover 60 miles in a day.

Oxen were occasionally used for riding, with saddles and bridles. Later, Europeans introduced horses and carts. Although carrying heavier loads, they were slow and ill-suited to the hillier areas.

ous words derived from English, French and Swahili. Malagasy was first transcribed in an Arabic-derived alphabet in the sixteenth century. The London Missionary Society transcribed the language into the Roman alphabet in the 1820s.

● Post Office

Open Mon-Fri, 0800-1200 and 1400-1800. Telegrams, International phone-calls and Poste Restante Mon-Sat 0700-1900 and Sun 0800-1100 from 2nd floor, Central Post Office, Anatanarivo.

● Telephone Services

Domestic phone service is generally unreliable, and there are few public telephones. Post Offices often have telephone services. International calls are most easily made from Antanarivo.

Entertainment

In 1990, state control of the media was relaxed. Newspapers can be published without prior authorisation. Private radio and television stations can operate, although these are meant to operate in conjunction with the government or its agencies.

● Newspapers

Taranta, French language daily newspaper, government controlled; *Imongo Vaovao*, Malagasy language daily newspaper, government controlled; *Madagascar Tribune*, independent daily published in both French and Malagasy; *Maresaka*, independent daily published in Malagasy; *Midi-Madagscar*, independent daily published in French.

● Radio

Radio Madagascar State-owned, broadcasts in French and Malagasy.

● Television

Télévision Malagasy State-owned, programmes in French and Malagasy.

Holidays and festivals

1 Jan	New Year's Day
29 Mar	National Day
Mar/Apr	Easter Monday
1 May	International Labour Day
May/Jun	Ascension Day
26 Jun	Independence Day
15 Aug	Assumption
1 Nov	All Saints' Day
25 Dec	Christmas Day
30 Dec	Republic Day

Further reading

● General

Heseltine, N. 1971 *Madagascar* London: Pall Mall.

Brown, M. 1978 *Madagascar Rediscovered*. London: Damien Tunnacliffe.

● Natural History

Preston-Mafham, K. 1991. *Madagascar: A Natural History*, Oxford & New York: Facts on File.

Langrand, O 1990 *Field Guide to the Birds of Madagascar*, Yale: Yale University Press

Haltenorth, T. and Diller, H 1080, *Field Guide to the Mammals of Africa including Madagascar*, London: William Collins.

● Travellers' Tales

Attenborough, D. 1961. *Zoo Quest to Madagascar* London: Lutterworth. Durrell, G 1983. *Ark on the Move*, New York: Coward-McCann. Murphy, D. 1985. *Muddling Through in Madagascar*, London: John Murray.

Drysdale, H. 1991 *Dancing with the Dead: A Journey Through Zanzibar and Madagascar.* London: Hamish Hamilton.

● Other Guides

Bradt, H. 1992. *Guide to Madagascar* Chalfont St Peter: Bradt Publications.

RÉUNION

Introduction

Réunion is a small, rocky island in the Indian Ocean, that was uninhabited until the arrival of the French in 1642. Apart from a brief spell in the early nineteeth century when it fell to the British, it has remained in French hands ever since. Lack of a good natural harbour impeded its development, but despite that, it has prospered as the main base of France in the Indian Ocean. Its present status is that of a Department of France, sending representatives to sit in the assemblies in Paris. As a consequence of its status, it receives substantial financial transfers from France. The mainstays of the economy are tourism, sugar and exotic spices and oils.

The population is cosmopolitan, made up of Creoles (the descendents of African slaves), a substantial French community, Indians and Chinese. There is a fine white sand beach area on the W coast, although not all the shoreline is quite as attractive, with much being black powdered lava. A major attraction for tourists is the range of volcanic mountains in the centre of the island (one recently active), with rich vegetation, providing the setting for some magnificent hikes between a network of simple but comfortable lodges.

Contents

Maps

Environment

Geography

The island is one of the Mascarene Islands (the others being Mauritius and Rodrigues) and lies some 800km E of Madagascar and 200 km SW of Mauritius. The island is small, being approximately 60 km from N to S and a little more from E to W. Réunion is volcanic in origin and still active with Piton de la Fournaise last erupting in 1992. The island covers 2,512 sq km and although larger than neighbouring Mauritius, it is much less densely populated.

The western half of Réunion is dominated by a major mountain range and the SE by a smaller one. Three huge natural amphitheatres, the cirques of Cilaos, Mafate and Salazie are located in the centre of the island, as is the highest point, Piton des Neiges (3,069m). The SE half of the island harbours the only remaining active volcano Piton de la Fournaise (2,631m). The island has been through several volcanic eras and layers of lava

form the bedrock of the island, each layer representative of a different period of activity. There are no recorded mineral deposits.

Soils are generally poor, ferrosol soil is the most fertile despite its low organic matter content. The younger andasol soils, on the other hand, despite having a high organic matter content, are not particularly fertile. Steep slopes on the island add to the problems of cultivation.

Climate

The island experiences a tropical climate though regional variations can be significant. The windward side of the island, the eastern coast, has a wetter, more humid climate than the leeward W coast which is noticeably drier. Rain falls for most of the year over the eastern side of the island whilst western regions experience more marked wet and dry seasons. The rainy season is between Nov and Apr, with Jan to end of Mar being the wettest period. The summer months fall between Nov and Apr, and at this time of the year the hot and humid weather can often cause cyclones. Winter falls between Apr and Sep and is fairly dry. Temperatures during the summer months on the coast reach 28°C whilst further inland, in the mountainous areas, summer temperatures only reach 18°C. In winter coastal temperatures rarely fall below 21°C but inland temperatures of 12°C are not uncommon, and above 2,000m temperatures can fall below 0°C.

Flora

The island exhibits a wide range of flora.

Cyclones

When the temperature is high over warm sea water, the moist air spirals as it rises to form a cyclone. In the southern hemisphere the main season for cyclones is Jan to Apr. The centre, the 'eye of the storm', perhaps 20 km across, is calm, with very low pressure, but circling around it are vicious winds of up to 200 km an hour. The spiral is clockwise in the southern hemisphere, and anti-clockwise in the northern. The whole storm travels at around 300 km in a day, toward the W.

On reaching land, the cyclone ravages the coastal belt, but dies out when there is no longer warm sea water to provide the water vapour essential to sustain it. Brillaint red sunsets, winds from unusual directions, and intervals between waves 3 times longer than normal are signs of a cyclone's impending arrival. It moves fairly slowly, at about 20 km an hour, and always to the W. A steamship armed with a barometer and a experienced skipper experienced in reading the sea swells that reveal the path of the storm, is able to take evasive action. Sailing vessels could often to little in the face of a cyclone, and in the summer months skippers of tall ships avoided the Indian Ocean like the plague.

Every year, on average, as long as memory goes back, 8 cylones have ravaged these waters, and battered the tiny island scattered across them.

In the W around St Paul and Le Port dry grasslands predominate. Some fine stands of mesothermic (middle temperature) forest can be found on La Plaine des Palmistes and the Cirques in and around Salazie. Lower altitude megathermic (high temperature) forests are found largely in the eastern parts of the island around St Philippe, St Rose and most notably around Marche Longe, a botanical reserve. Among the tree species found in mesothermic forests are Tamarin des hauts, which thrive between 1,300m and 1,900m. Tree species found between La Possession and St Pierre include bois d'olive, bois rouge, benjoin, natte, and reinette. High altitude forests exist around Enclos at la Fournaise and are known as Bois des Couleurs. Trees here include grande natte (*Mimusops petiolaris* or *maxima*) and petite natte (*Labourdonnaisia* or *Mimusops callophylloides*), tan rouge (*Weinmannia tinctoria*) and benjoin (*Terminalia angustifolia*), used widely in reforestation projects. Approximately 60% of the island's indigenous flora are endemic and there are currently about 120 species of orchid in Réunion. The Office National des Forets (ONF) is involved in afforestation projects throughout Réunion.

Fauna

The only indigenous mammals are thought to be fruit bats and include the white-stomached *Taphozous mauritianus*, the free-tailed bat (*Tadarida acetobulosus*), and the chauve souris des hautes (*Scotophilus borbonicus*). Deer, hares and rats and hedgehogs have all been introduced to the island.

Birdlife

A great variety of birds visit the island. The merle blanc (*Coracina newtoni*), known by Creoles as 'tuit tuit', is endemic, and although rare, the bird can be seen on the Plaine des Chicots. Other birds include the Mascarene paradise flycatcher with its violet head, which the Creoles believe has seen the Virgin Mary; and the tec-tec (*Saxicola borbonensis*), another endemic species. More common bird species include the bellier (*Ploceus spilonotus*) which inhabits palm trees, and 2 species introduced from the Indian sub-continent, the zel blanc or mainate commun (a member of the martin family), specially introduced to rid the island of grasshoppers; and the white-tailed tropical seabird, paille en queue. The only bird of prey on the Island is the Réunion harrier (*Cicus maillardi*), a buzzard.

History

Réunion was certainly known to Arab seafarers in the Indian Ocean prior to the earliest recorded European visitor, a Portuguese explorer Pedro de Mascarenhas in 1513, on a voyage to India, who named the island Mascarin. In 1648 the French East India Company banished a party of mutineers to the island, and they became the first settlers. In 1649 it was renamed Ile Bourbon, after the French King at the time. By the latter part of the 1680s the island had become a base for pirates. Coffee was introduced, and in an effort to get it established, in 1717 it became compulsory for farmers to grow the crop. By 1740 coffee had become so successful that slaves were drafted in from Africa and India to work on the estates. In 1764 the island became the property of the French Crown as the French East India company felt they were no longer able to administer effectively. After the French Revolution the island was renamed Réunion by the Colonial Assembly.

The island was captured by the British in 1810, but was returned to France in the treaty of Paris of 1815, and was renamed Ile Bourbon. During the early part of the 1800s the island was hit by a series of cyclones which devastated the coffee estates. Sugar cane, more resistant to the ravages of the tropical storms, was introduced by the British and began to played a larger part in Réunion's development. In 1848 France abolished slavery and indentured labour was brought from Indo-China and East Africa. However, with the opening of the Suez Canal Réunion no longer became a staging post on the route from Europe to India, and this adversely affected development. Increasing competition from Mauritian sugar caused Réunion to diversify into vanilla, ylang ylang, geranium oil and tobacco.

After the First World War sugar production recovered but the disruption of shipping in the Second War meant the crop could not be exported, and the sugar industry collapsed. In 1946 the island was granted Department status, coming under the Departément Français d'Outre Mer (DOM).

Culture and life

People

The island of Réunion is cosmopolitan. African and Creoles (descendents of slaves who have inter-married) 35% of the population, Europeans 30%, Hindus 25% whilst Muslims and Chinese comprise 5% each. Réunion has fewer Indian immigrants than Mauritius and more white immigrants who originated

The Solitaire

This bird was a smaller version of the dodo, found only on Réunion and Rodrigues. The name came from the fact that the early visitors observed that they always appeared to be alone, never in pairs or groups. They were described as being the size of a goose, having white feathering with black at the tips of the wings and the tail, a long neck and a large beak.

Unlike the dodo they could fly, but not very well, and they are now extinct. In 1867, the adminstrator of Rodrigues, George Jenner, excavated in a cave where some bones had been discovered and unearthed some complete solitaire skeletons.

from France.

By far the largest religion in Réunion is Christianity. Other religions followed include Hinduism and Islam whilst some of the Chinese community are Buddhists.

Art and craft

The *séga*, a dance brought by the African slaves from Madagascar, is popular in Réunion, although it has developed slightly from neighbouring Mauritius, incorporating some elements of European ballroom dancing. Another dance originating from Africa is the *maloya*, a more languid dance than the *séga*.

Traditional instruments include the *bob* with calabash resonator and bow, similar to the *jejolava* of Madagascar; the *kayanb*, a rattle similar to the *maravane* found in Mauritius; and the *rouleur* a 2 handed drum.

Notable poets include Marius Leblond and Ary Leblond, the latter acting for a while as Conservator of the Musée de la France d'Outre Mer. These men were not related: their names are artistic pseudonyms.

Crafts are not particularly distinctive, although there are good examples of basketry and wood carving produced.

Modern Réunion

Politics

Réunion is administered by a Prefect, appointed by France, and an elected council legislates on local issues. The Prefect is responsible to the French Minister for Departments and Territories Overseas (DOM-TOM). There are 3 elected Deputies representing Réunion in the French National Assembly in Paris, and 2 members are sent to the Senate. Plans for an assembly in Réunion and a larger measure of decentralisation were abandoned in 1982 following the failure of these proposals to pass through the French National Assembly.

In 1972 a series of strikes were called, resulting in a general strike in 1973 in protest against unemployment and the rise in rice prices. In 1974-76 a sugar modernisation plan was introduced, and this served to alleviate some of the discontent. In 1978 the OAU called for the independence of Réunion and condemned its occupation by a colonial power, rather overlooking the fact that the island was uninhabited prior to the arrival of the French. Few islanders want independence, and the fact of the matter is that their status as a Département brings them substantial financial inflows and political stability.

Economics

As it is regarded as part of France (the currency is the French Franc), economic data for Réuninon as an entity on its own is meagre. Although the statistics presented are sometimes relates to earlier periods, they nevertheless present a reasonable picture of economic life on the island in comparison with other African countries.

Economic and social structure

GDP in 1984 was US$1,708m, and this is quite a surprising size – medium in the African context – given the population of 600,000. GNP per head is the highest in Africa at US$3,580, mainly as a result of French assistance. In 1983 the economy had a low dependence on agriculture which generated only 8% of GDP, while the industrial sector generated 13% and 79% was generated by the service sector, which includes the government departments and the tourist sector. Private consumption at 99% of GDP in 1983 was one of the highest rates in Africa. Investment of 22% was also higher than most African countries while government consumption was 18%. These high proportions, adding up to over 100% of GDP, are only possible because of French financial inflows.

Exports comprised about 14% of GDP in 1983, and this is about the average for the region, though below the African average. Imports, however, were 53% of GDP in 1983, and this is made possible by the financial transfers from France. Merchandise exports are mainly sugar, which made 75% in 1984, and rum which made up 4%. Imports in 1984 comprised foodstuffs 25%, machinery 25%, manufactures 23%, intermediate goods 16% and fuel 11%. France takes 61% of Réunion's exports and provides 65% of her imports.

Educational provision, as might be expected in an upper middle-income country, is good, with primary enrolment rates in 1981 of 116%, secondary at 51%, and 6% enrolled in higher education. These rates are markedly better than elsewhere in Africa. Health provision would also appear to be good, with

COMPARATIVE ECONOMIC AND SOCIAL DATA

	Réunion	East Africa	Africa	Industrial Countries
Population & land				
Population, mid year, millions, 1991	0.641	12.2	10.2	40.0
Urban Population, %, 1982	41	301	30	75
Population Growth Rate, % per year, 1974-83	1.6	3.1	3.1	0.8
Land Area, thou. sq. km.	2.5	486	486	1,628
Population Density, persons per sq km., 1988	256.4	24.2	20.4	24.3
Economy: production & income				
GDP, US$ millions, 1984	1,708	2,650	3,561	550,099
GNP per head, US$, 1984	3,580	250	389	12,960
Economy: supply structure				
Agriculture, % of GDP, 1983	8	43	35	3
Industry, % of GDP, 1983	13	15	27	35
Services, % of GDP, 1983	79	42	38	61
Economy: demand structure				
Private Consumption, % of GDP, 1983	99	77	73	62
Gross Domestic Investment, % of GDP, 1983	22	16	16	21
Government Consumption, % of GDP, 1983	18	15	14	17
Exports, % of GDP, 1983	14	16	23	17
Imports, % of GDP, 1983	53	24	26	17
Economy: performance				
GDP growth, % per year, 1974-83	5.2	1.6	-0.6	2.5
GDP per head growth, % per year, 1974-83	3.6	-1.7	-3.7	1.7
Agriculture growth, % per year, 1974-83	4.7	1.1	0.0	2.5
Industry growth, % per year, 1974-83	4.4	1.1	-1.0	2.5
Services growth, % per year, 1974-83	5.4	2.5	-0.5	2.6
Exports growth, % per year, 1974-83	5.0	0.7	-1.9	3.3
Imports growth, % per year, 1974-83	11.5	0.2	-6.9	4.3
Economy: other				
Inflation Rate, % per year, 1974-83	9.4	23.6	16.7	5.3
Education				
Primary, % of 6-11 group, 1981	116	62	76	102
Secondary, % of 12-17 group, 1981	51	15	22	93
Higher, % of 20-24 group, 1981	6	1.2	1.9	39
Health & nutrition				
Life Expectancy, years, 1991	72	50	50	76
Population per doctor, 1977	1,360	35,986	24,185	550

Notes: 'Africa' excludes South Africa. Dates are for the country in question, and do not always correspond with the Regional, African and Industrial averages.

one doctor for every 1,360 people in 1981. This is seventeen times better provision than the African average.

Economic performance

Figures are only available for the 4 years 1980-83, and in this period GDP grew at 4.6% a year. This implies a rate of expansion of GDP per head at 2.6% a year, and this is considerably better than elsewhere in the region.

All sectors appear to have expanded steadily, with agriculture growing at 4.7% a year in the period 1974-83, industry at 4.4% a year and services at 5.4%. These growth rates are all very much better than elsewhere in Africa.

Export volumes expanded at 5.0% a year in the 1974-83 period, again, well above the African average. Import volumes as a result of expanding tourism revenues and financial transfers from France have expanded at 11.5% a year in the same period. Inflation has been modest, at 8.6% a year for 1980-87.

Recent economic developments

GDP and GDP per head growth rate have been lower in the first part of the 1980s compared with the latter half of the 1970s. However, inflation performance has been better in the 1980s, and the most recent figures for 1986 and 1987 show the impact of recent monetary and fiscal discipline imposed by France with annual rate of price increase below 3%.

The French franc is the currency used, and this depreciated against the US dollar in the early 1980s, being FFr 4.23 = US$ 1 in 1980 and FFr 8.99 = US$1 in 1985. Subsequently, the weakness of the dollar has brought about an appreciation, with the exchange rate standing at FFr 5.56= US$1 in 1994.

Merchandise exports in dollar terms reached their peak in 1979, but declined by 34% up to 1984 despite the depreciation of the franc which would have raised domestic prices to producers. Merchandise imports peaked in dollar terms in 1980, and they fell by 12% up to 1984.

Economic outlook

As long as Réunion remains as part of France it will remain politically stable, encouraging foreign investment in the tourist sector, and its economic outlook will remain secure. In the immediate future its prospects will improve as the world moves out of recession bringing more tourists.

ST DENIS

This is the administrative centre of Réunion. It is located on the N coast, and has a population of 121,000. The town was founded by Etienne Regnault in 1669, and was named after his boat, becoming the seat of government in 1738. There are some handsome colonial buildings in the town, particularly along rue de Paris.

Places of interest

La Barachois During the 18th and 19th centuries the French established a port here until shipping moved to the Le Port area. Today the sea front park plays host to evening boule players whilst cafés dotted along the waterfront make for a pleasant evening drink. There is also a monument in the park to the French aviator Roland Garros, born in Réunion in 1888. Besides being the first pilot to cross the Mediterranean he devised a method for firing through a propeller with a machine gun.

Maison de la Montagne An attractive colonial building, also serving as a tourist office for trekking in the mountains. T 21 75 84.

Museum Léon Dierx Named after Léon Dierx, a poet and artist who lived and worked in Réunion 1858-1912. The museum has a fine collection of modern art mostly donated by an art dealer Ambroise Vollard, and includes work by Cezanne, Matisse, Picasso, Degas and Gaugin, as well as by local arstists. Open 1000-1200 and 1500-1800 except Tue when it is open from 1000-1700. Entrance free.

Jardin de I'Etat & Natural History Museum Originally the Jardin Royal the garden became the Jardin de I'Etat in 1948. In the a grounds monuments pays tribute to Pierre Poivre (the 'Peter Piper' of the tongue-twister) who lived in Mauritius and but introduced a great many agricultural products to Réunion, including pepper and cinnamon. The museum contains examples of living and extinct specimens, most notably a coelacanth (see page 769) and an aquarium. Open 1000-1600, entrance free.

Hindu Temple This is a Tamil temple dedicated to Shiva on rue du Marechal Leclerc, and is a particularly colourful building.

Excursions

Half way between St Denis and La Possession is **La Grande Chaloupe** where the British landed in 1810.

Le Brule an 800m high hill lying S of St Denis is a popular destination, and is a good centre for hiking. The waterfall **Cascade Maniquet** is 5km from Brule village. It is possible to walk from Brule to **La Roche Ecrite** (2,277 m) stopping for the night at Plaine des Chicots. From La Roche Ecrite there are magnificent views of the Cirques of Mafate and Salazie. Early morning is the best time to visit, since later in the day La Roche Ecrite tends to become obscured by cloud. **La Montagne** is another hill district behind St Denis, in good hiking country. There are gîtes where hikers can lodge in all these districts (see below).

Local information

● Where to stay

A+ *Meridien*, 2 rue Doret, T 218020. The hotel is the best on the island with excellent facilities. Piano bar. Swimming pool, disco,tennis. **A+** *Creole*, 14 rue du Stade, T 304343, F 301818, Sports centre, swimming pool, nightclub.

A *Le Bourbon*, Rampes St Francois, just S of the town, T 407240. Swimming pool. Organises deep-sea fishing expeditions. **A** *Ascotel*, 20 Rue Charles Gounod, T 418282, 2 restaurants. Popular with group bookings. **A** *Astorea*, 16 rue Juliette Dodu, T 200558. Good value in this range. **A** *Central*, 37 rue de la Compagnie, T 211808. Located in the heart of town.

B *Hotel de L'Ocean*, 10 boulevard de l'Ocean,

to the E of the centre, T 414308. Modern building. a/c. **B** *Les Mascareignes*, 3 rue Lafferiere, T 211528. Quiet area. Good value. **B** *Mme Roche*, 39 rue General de Gaulle, T 213289. Comfortable, popular, and often full. **B** *Le Vieux Carthage*, 13 rue des Limites, T 206718. Very popular. Good value. **B** *Pension Amanda*, 20 rue Amedee Bedier, behind St Jacques Church, T 208076.

C *Pension du Centre*, 272 rue du Marcechal Leclerc, T 417302. Some self-catering.

D *Pension Roger*, 22 rue Mazagran, T 412438. Dormitory accommodation. Good value.

● Gîtes outside St Denis

Le Brule D *Mme Slyvaine Robert*, 105 Route des Azelees, T 230015. More expensive if you are not in a group and only staying a night or 2.

La Roche Ecrite D *Plaine des Chicots*, at the

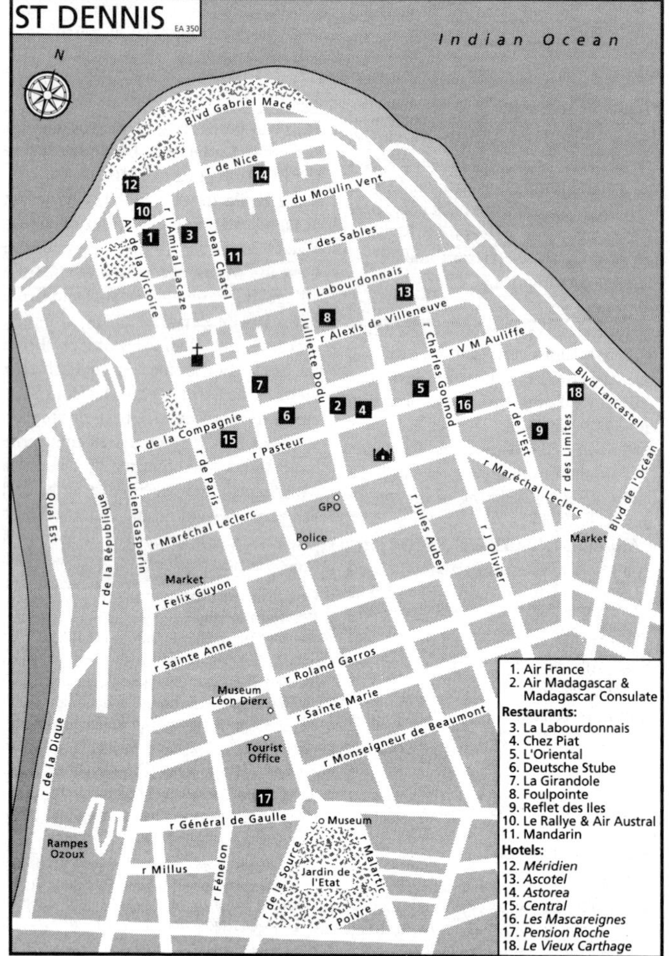

foot of the peak, T 217584. Bunk bed accommodation.

La Montagne C *Home Fleuri de Cendrillon*, 48 route des Palmiers, T 236328. Minimum stay of 3 nights.

Places to eat

♦♦♦♦*La Labourdonnais*, 14 rue l'Amiral Lacaze, T 214426. French cuisine. High quality food and surroundings. ♦♦♦♦*Le Pavillon d'Or*, 224 rue du Marechal Leclerc, T 215650. Chinese food. Excellent standard. ♦♦♦♦*Chez Piat*, 60 rue Pasteur, T 214576. French food. Closed Sun & Mon. ♦♦♦♦*Restaurant l'Oriental*, rue Pasteur Chinese food. ♦♦♦♦*Deutsche Stube*, 34 rue de la Compagnie. German menu. ♦♦♦♦*Vesuvio*, rue du Marechal Leclerc. Italian food.

♦♦♦*Le Pekinois*, Ave de Villeneuve. Chinese food. ♦♦♦*La Capricorne*, at the Airport, T 488170. International menu. Not particularly good value. ♦♦♦*La Belle Etoile*, Ravine des Chevres les Bas, T 534078. Chinese cuisine. Closed Wed and Sun. ♦♦♦*La Girandole* 173 rue Jean Chatel, 213160. French menu. Good value. Closed Sun. ♦♦♦*Le Foulpointe*, corner of rue J Dodu and Ave de Villeneuve. Chinese food. ♦♦♦*Le Reflet des Iles*, 27 rue de l'Est, T 217382. Creole cooking. ♦♦♦*La Bambara*, 160 rue Monthyon. Creole menu. Good standard. ♦♦♦*Le Rallye*, Ave de la Victorie. Terrace cafe. Pleasant atmosphere.

♦♦*Palais du Mandarin*, rue Jean Chatel. Chinese food. Good value.

Entertainment

Cinema *Salle François Truffaut*, centre Réunionnais d'Action Culturelle (CRAC). Jardin de l'Etat, T 216975. Art cinema. **Ritz** rue Juliette Dodu. Popular films; **Plaza** rue Pasteur. Popular films.

Discos *La Locomotive*, *Hotel Meridien*. *Le First*, 88 rue Juliette Dodu. Tue-Sat. *Les Thermes*, 111 rue Juliette Dodu. *Ti-bird*, 1 rue de Nice. Open all night.

Jazz *Le Shanker*, 20 rue de Nice. *Le Jamboree*, 61 Rue Monthyon.

Gambling Casino at *Hotel Meridien* 2 rue Doret, T 218020.

Tourist information

Syndicat d'Initiative, 48 rue Ste Marie, T 418300. Also at Airport. **Centre Réunionnais d'Action Culturelle (CRAC)**, Jardin de l'Etat, T 216975. **Maison de la Montagne**, 10 Place Sarda Garriga, T 217584. **RUN magazine**, listing of events for tourists.

Banks

Banque de la Réunion (BR), 27 rue Jean-Chatel, T 400123, F 400061, Tlx 916134. **Credit Agricole (CA)**, Rue Felix Guyon, T 408181, F 408140, Tlx 916139. **Banque Français Commerciale Océan Indien (BFCOI)**, 60 rue Alexis de Villeneuve, T 405555, F 413909, Tlx 916162. **Banque Nationale de Paris Intercontinentale**, 67 rue Juliette Dodu, T 403030, F 413909, Tlx 916133. Opening hrs Mon-Fri 0800-1600.

Libraries

The Central Library is near the Bus station the corner of Rue Labourdonnais and Rue Joffre in St Denis.

Bookshops

Tend to stock mainly books in French and French newspapers and magazines. *Librairie de la Réunion* on Ave de la Victoria has some English books.

Local travel

Bus The city bus terminal is at Weekly or monthly passes are available. Students are eligible for discounts.

Car hire **RFS**, rue Labourdonnais St Denis, T 200962. **Budget**, rue Stanislas Guimart T 296000. Also office at airport. **ADA**, Blvd St Denis, T 2159 01, F 212318.

Airline offices

Air France, 7 Ave de la victoire, T 410123. **Air Madagascar**, Rue juliette Dodu, T 210521. **Air Mauritius**, 3 rue de la Victoire, T 413300.

Tour operators and travel agents

Bourbon Voyages, 14 rue Rontaunay, St Denis, T 216818. **American Express** representative. Well organised. *Comete Voyages*, corner rue Jules- Auber and rue du Moulin Vent, St Denis, T 213100. Helicopter trips arranged. *Nouvelles Frontiers*, 92 rue Alexis de Villeneuve, St Denis, T 215454.

Transport

Bus There are buses to *St Pierre* and stops on the way, travelling W round the coast roads. There are buses travelling E to *St Benoît* and intermediate destinations. Connection *en route* for all other parts of the island.

EAST COAST

Ste Marie

About 10 km E of St Denis, Réunion's Airport is nearby. During the 18th century, the crew of a ship foundering off the coast prayed to St Mary and were saved. The survivors built a chapel and named the town Ste Marie. The Rivière des Pluies flows close by and there is a local shrine called **La Vierge Noire** (the Black virgin).

Ste Suzanne

A village on the coast 20 km E of St Denis. There is a lighthouse at Bel Air. Close by is **Cascade Niagara** a 30m waterfall and its pool is good for swimming. There is an 18th century mansion in a large garden, surrounded by a sugar plantation which can be visited – contact M Chassagne, T 523281.

• **Where to stay C** *Mme Caladama*, rue Raymond Verges, Quartier Français, T 461143. Comfortable. **D** *M Payet*, Quartier Français, T 461078. Rate is for a group booking (7 persons) staying a week.

St André

Located 30 km E of St Denis, about 3km from the coast. Much of Réunion's Indian population live here. In the past their ancestors worked on the surrounding sugar plantations.

Places of interest

La Maison de la Vanille, T 460014, is an old Creole building with fine lawns and gardens. Open to the public and tours are available. Ruins are all that remain of the old church of **Champs Borne** which was struck by a cyclone in the 1940s. There is an art and craft centre opposite. Close by is a **Tamil Temple**, where, during the Hindu festival of *cavadee* (Feb or Mar) firewalking ceremonies take place.

Local information

• Where to stay

C *Pension les Pluies d'Or*, 3 allee Sapories la Cressoniere, T 461816. Restaurant serves Creole food. **C** *Mme De Palmas*, 174 bras des Chevrettes, T 470007, Chambre d'Hôte. **C** *Mme Cadet*, 96 rue du Stade, T 465637. Small, with good homely food.

• Places to eat

♦♦♦*Le Ficus Nitida*, Pont Minot serves a variety of cuisines. ♦♦*Chez Sully*, Pont Minot Cafe style, with light meals.

• Tourist office

Office Municipal du Tourisme de St André, 68 Commercial centre, rue de la Gare. T 469163.

Bras Panon

The town and surrounding land is famous for its Vanilla crop, the co-op (open Mon-Fri 0800-1300 and 1400-1600) here has an informative programme, including a short film, which explains all the different stages the crop passes through.

Rivière des Roches and Cascade de la Paix To get to the pool and waterfall follow the main road heading S, go over the Rivière des Roches bridge and follow the road up the valley. Carry along this road for 5km until you reach the falls.

• **Accommodation C** *Ferme Auberge*, 6 chemin Rivière du Mat, T 515376. **D** *Camping*, Rivière des Roches, T 515859.

St Benoît

Located on the coast by the Rivière des Marsouins, the area is agricultural and some fishing occurs along the river. The Syndicat d'Initiative, 21 route Nationale, St Benoît, T 51 5062, can organise visits to sugar mills and other sites close to town.

Roughly 5 km from St Benoît heading along the road to Plaine des Palmistes is an 18th century Creole house **Domaine de La Confiance**, set in gardens. There is an old sugar mill in the grounds but this no longer functions. Today the owner has introduced a table d'hôte (fixed price menu). Open all week except Sun.

South from St Benoît on the coast road is **St Anne** famous for a baroque-style church. Covered in decorations of fruits and flowers, the church was the inspiration of Father Dobemberger who died in 1948.

The road from St Benoît towards Takamaka passes by the Rivière des Marsouins, and the journey is spectacular. Nearby the **Cascade de l'Arc en Ciel** can be visited by foot or the cable car which starts at the car par. A dam above the waterfall has 2 hydro-electric power stations.

Following the road to St Pierre out of St Benoît is **Le Grand Etang** the largest fresh water lake on Réunion. There is fishing in the lake but you need a permit.

• **Where to stay B** *Hotel Le Bouvet*, 75 route National, T 501496. By the sea. **C** *Gîte de Group Diana*, Route de Cambourg, Piton Arnaud les Hauts, T 535496. **C** *Mme Guichard*, Les Orange, St Anne, T 510345.

• **Places to eat** ♦♦♦♦*Domaine de La Confiance*, 5km from St Benoît heading along the road to Plaine des Palmistes. Table d'hôte menu in colonial surroundings.

♦♦♦*Café de Chine*, Place du Maré, T 501247. Chinese cuisine. Good standard.

Ste Rose

The area experiences the highest rainfall in Réunion, producing bananas and vanilla. Fishing plays an important part in the local economy. A monument to Captain Corbett the English commander killed whilst fighting the French at the battle of St Denis in 1810, stands in the town.

The village of **Piton Ste Rose**, 5 km S of Ste Rose was covered by a lava flow in 1977, and although lava entered the village church it stopped short of the altar. Local people believe this to be a miracle, especially as nobody died in the eruption, and have renamed the church **Notre Dame de Lava**. Another waterfall **Anse des Cascade** lies between Ste Rose and Bois Blanc, plunging off the cliffs directly into the sea. From Bois Blanc heading towards Le Grand Brule there is a statue, the **Vierge au Parasol**, where an umbrella over the Virgin Mary sympolises protection from the volcano.

• **Where to stay B** *Mme Adam de Villiers*, 206 route National la Roseraie, T 472133. Restaurant, with table d'hôte menu.

• **Places to eat** ♦♦♦*L'Anse des Cascades*, Piton St Rose, T 472133. Lunch only. Closed on Wed.

• **Transport Bus** There are regular services from St Benoît N round the coast to *St Denis*; from St Benoît S round the coast roads to *St Pierre*; from St Benoît, across country, via Plaines des Palmistes, Plaines des Cafres and Le Tampon to *St Pierre*.

SOUTH COAST

Between Ste Rose and St Philippe are some dramatic examples of lava flows. The area is known as **Le Grande Brûlé** ('large burn'). The most recent lava flow to reach the sea along this stretch occurred in 1976. The last eruption, in 1992, was not as severe as 1986 when several hundred people were evacuated, and scores of homes destroyed. There are also some beaches along this stretch of coastline though they are not as popular as those found on the W coast.

At the southern section of Le Grand Brûlé, along a turning inland signposted Symboise pour Volcan et Oiseaux, is **Les Sentinelles** a sculpture created by a Réunion artist Jean Cluade Mayo. It is possible to climb **Piton de la Fournaise** volcano, the hike being quite manageable in a day. Just before you reach St Philippe in the S E corner, you pass the **Point de la Table**, created by an eruption on the 23 Mar 1986, adding approximately 20 ha to the island.

St Philippe

This small town is supported by agriculture and fishing, and **Le Baril** is the nearby resort area. There are four **wells** sunk into the lava. It has never been satisfactorily explained who constructed them and for what reason. The Puits Anglais can be found on the coast road W of St Philippe, the Puits Arabes lies E of St Philippe and the Puits des Français toward Cap Méchant. The fourth is Puits du Tremblet. The **Nature Trail** (Sentier Botanique) starts from Mare Longue. There is a garden here open to visitors (0830-1230 and 1430-1700). Other forest trails are from Le Baril; from Basse Vallée to Cap Méchant and Puits des Français; and from Langevin to Plain des Sables. Office du Tourism de St Phillipe, T 371043, will advise on hiking in the area.

• **Where to stay** **B** *Hotel le Baril*, T 370104. Located on shore at Le Baril. Restaurant with Chinese food. **C** *Mme Marcelle Trebel*, Route Nationale 2, Le Baril, T 370151. Small Chambre d'hôte, with fixed price menu. Good value.

• **Places to eat** ♦♦♦*La Canot St Phillipe*, T 370036. Creole food. ♦♦♦*Le Cap Méchant*, Basse Vallée, T 370061. Creole and Chinese food. ♦♦♦*L'Etoile de Mer*, Basse Vallée, T 370460. Emphasis on seafood.

St Joseph

The town is sited by the estuary of the Rivière des Remparts. An agricultural area, the region is the centre of the island's vetiver (a grass used for making mats, the roots containing a fragrant oil) and geranium growing. Walking in the area is particularly good, It is possible to hike up the Rivière Langevin to the waterfall at Grande Ravine, and up the Rivière des Remparts to Nez de Boeuf.

• **Where to stay** **B** *Mme Chan Sang*, T 561444. Cheaper by the week. **C** *Mme Turpin*, Deuxieme Village, La Crete, T 372703. **C** *Mme Grondin*, T 565166. Gîte accommodation. Rate is by the week, for a group. More expensive, otherwise.

• **Places to eat** ♦♦♦♦*Le Manapany*, T 265558. Excellent cuisine. Swimming area nearby. ♦♦♦*Le Lezard Vert*, serves Creole food. ♦♦♦*Le Tajine*, Vincendo, T 562130, French and African food.

St Pierre

The main town of the S, with a population of 60,000 and follows St Denis and St Paul as the third largest commune in Réunion. Has some fine old buildings, there is a fairly wide choice of accommodation, and a good selection of eating places offering a wide variety of cuisines.

Places of interest

A most impressive building is the **Hôtel de Ville** (Town Hall) on the square at the northern end of rue due Port, close to the harbour. It dates from the 18th century, and has recently been restored. It is possible to be shown around. The old **Railway Station** stands on the beach front, and is now used as a library. The grave of an African bandit **Le Sitarane** in the cemetery on Blvd Hubert Delisle is marked with a black cross, and serves as a shrine where people wish for misfortune to happen to others.

There is an active **cock-fighting** venue in St Pierre, at 192 rue du 4 à Chaux, and the programme fights can be obtained from the Syndicat d'Initiative de St Pierre 27 rue Archambaud, T 250236.

Local information

● **Where to stay**

A *Hotel Sterne*, Blvd Hubert Delisle, T 257000. Faces the sea. Good restaurant. **A** *Le Suffren*, 14 rue Suffren, T 351910. Close to sea front. Discounts for students. Popular. **A** *Hotel Hibiscus*, 56 Blvd Hubert Delisle, T 351310. Close to beach.

B *Hotel Star*, 88 Conde Ravine des Cabris T 272069. Reasonable value. **B** *Hotel Tropic*, 2 rue Auguste Babet, T 259070. A/c. Overlooks river. **B** *Demotel Residence Club*, 8 Ave des Lataniers, Grand Bois. T 311160. Bungalow accommodation. Swimming pool. **B** *Pension Touristique*, 27 rue du Four à Chaux T 256487. Studio accommodation also available Shared bathrooms.

B *M Lebon*, 11 chemin Maurice Techer, Ravines des Cabris. T 497378. Restaurant.

C *Mme Decanonville*, 17 rue Auguste Babet, T 250462. Some chalet accommodation, some dormitory-style. Good value. **C** *Mme Malet*, 52 Allee des Aubepines, Bassin-Plat. T 256190. Good value.

● **Places to eat**

♦♦♦♦*Le Margouillat*, Blvd Hubert Delisle. ♦♦♦♦*Le Flamboyant*, T 350215, French cuisine. ♦♦♦♦*L'Osteria*, rue Marius. Italian food. ♦♦♦♦*Baguette d'Or*, rue M Ghandi. Vietnamese menu.

♦♦♦*Le Grec*, 23 rue Auguste Babet. Greek food. ♦♦♦*Le Penelope*, rue M & A Leblond Local and Creole food.

♦♦♦*Restaurant Le Cantonnais*, rue des Bons Enfants. Chinese food.

● **Entertainment**

Cinema *Rex*, Rue Désiré Barquisseau.

Discos *Blue Moon*, Bvad Hubert Delisle Fri and Sat from 2200. *Queen's Club*, 2 Rue Auguste Babet.

● **Tourist office**

Syndicat d'Initiative de St Pierre, 27 rue Archambaud, T 250236.

● **Banks**

Rue des Bons Enfants and Rue Victor Vigoureux. (Hours 0800-1600).

● **Post office**

On Rue des Bons Enfants (open 0730-1600, Sat 0800-1200)

● **Transport**

Road Bus station is on corner of rue du Four à Chaux and rue François Isautier. There are regular buses to running roud the coast to both the E and the W, and inland to Le Tampon.

St Louis

The fifth largest town in Réunion. **Notre Dame du Rosaire** is the oldest church on the island, dating from the eighteenth century. The lake at **Etang du Gol** is about 2 km away, and is a local beauty spot. North of the town is the village of **Les Makes**, used by many visitors as a base for hiking to **La Plaine du Bois des Nefles** and **La Fenêtre** – 'the window' – so named so because of the views.

● **Where to stay** **C** *M Eurveilher*, 6 lot Safer Montplaisir, T 37 82 77. Comfrotable and sound. **C** *M Leperlier*, 41 rue Paul Herman, Les Makes, T 378217. Good base for hikes in the countryside near Les Makes.

Etang-Salé-les-Bains

Just 6 km of St Louis is Etang-Salé-les-Bains, a small quiet town a little inland. The beaches on the nearby coast are black lava sand, and not as popular as those further round the coast to the N with white sand. The *Syndicate d'Initiative de l'Etang-Salé-les-Bains*, T 266732, is a source of information for visitors along this stretch of coast. There is a **bird sanctuary** between Etang-Salé-les-Bains and Etang-Salé-les-Hauts, and a **Golf Club** close by, T 263339.

● **Where to stay** **C** *M Savigny*, Ravine Sheunon, T 263109. **Camping** T 263382.

• **Places to eat** ♦♦♦*La Louisiane*, Creole cuisine. Closed Wed, Thu, Sun. ♦♦♦*L'Ete Indien*. Varied menu with some curry dishes, and some international food.

Les Avirons

The town, a couple of kilometres inland, acts as a base for visiting the hills around the town. Replicas of colonial furniture and cane chairs are manufactured here. North of the town is **Tévelave** village and **Fôret de Tévelave**. Between Les Avirons and St Leu are several blow-holes (souffleur).

• **Where to stay C** *Mme Turpin*, Tévelave, T 38 04 21. Small, wise to book ahead. Good value. **C** *M Jery Vitry*, Tévelave, T 38 03 07. Gîte rented by the week. **C** *Mme Augustine Cadet*, Les Avirons, T 380134. Close to beach.

• **Transport Bus** There are regular services from St Pierre N round the coast to St Denis; from St Pierre S round the coast roads to St Benoît; from St Pierre across country, via Le Tampon, Plaines des Cafres and Plaines des Palmisteso St Benoît.

WEST COAST

The route W from St Denis starts unpromisingly with the rather undistinguished small town of **La Possession**, and then the rather grim docks and industrial area of **Le Port**. The Cirques inland, however, provide a grand backdrop. The best beaches in Réunion, with white sand (the others are black lava sand) are on the W coast. St Paul is a medium sized town with historic interest, and the main beach resort area runs from here down to **St Lue**, where the sand reverts again to being black.

La Possession

Is 15 km to the W of St Denis, and is a somewhat straggling village. In 1887 a railway was built linking St Denis and La Possession. Today the train connects La Possession and La Grande Chaloupe and there are plans to restore the line to St Denis as a tourist attraction.

• **Where to stay** B *Latanaiers*, 102 rue Raymond Mondon, T 22 23 23. Fairly modern.

• **Places to eat** ♦♦♦♦*Lions de Lyon*, 10 rue Camp Magliore, T 222141. Particularly expensive, but excellent standard cuisine, typical of Lyon. ♦♦♦♦*Le Viet Nam*, 301 La Corniche, T 222832. High quality Vietnamese cuisine. ♦♦♦♦*Hai Phong*, rue Raymond Mondon La Possession. Vietnamese food.

Le Port

This is the smallest commune on the island, 20 km to the W of St Denis, and the place where the French first took the island in the name of the French King, in 1640. The site is now devoted entirely to the docks and an industrial area.

• **Places to eat** ♦♦♦*L'Ebene*, rue du General de Gaulle. Serves African and French food. ♦♦♦*Chez George*, specialises in Creole, Greek and German food.

St Paul

The town is Réunion's oldest town, and the largest after St Denis, with a population of 72,000. It served as a regional administrative centre until the French under Labourdonnais decided to move the government to Mauritius in 1735.

Places of interest

There are a number of colonial buildings around the town and one of the best examples is the old **French East India Building** built in 1767 now serving as the Town Hall. Cannons and coconut trees line the shore. There is a **Hindu Temple** dedicated to Lord Shiva on rue St Louis.

The **Mariners' Cemetery** (Cimetière Marin) is to the S of town, on the shore, off rue des Filaos. It contains the grave of the poet Leconte de Lisle (1818-1894) and one of most notorious Indian Ocean pirates, Oliver Levasseur, nicknamed 'The Buzzard', executed in 1730.

Grotte des Premiers Français ('Cave of the First Frenchman') is in the cliffs opposite the Mariners' Cemetery, and was the initial shelter of the muineers banished to Réunion in 1648, who became the first settlers. The **Grotte de Notre Dame de Lourdes** close by acts as an alternative pilgrimage for those unable to visit Lourdes.

It is possible to hike to **Tours des Roches** which has attractive scenery and to **Ravine du Bernica Gorges**, the site where, according to legend, 'The Buzzard' buried a haul of treasure.

Local information

● **Where to stay**

B *Pension Marie Christine*, Chaussee Royale, T 22 56 53. B *Leconte Delisle*, rue Lambert, T 45 43 92.

● **Places to eat**

(Note that most restaurants close at weekends)

♦♦♦♦*Le Mangoustan*, rue des Rosiers, La Plaine. Creole food. ♦♦♦♦*Le Mandarinier*, Chaussee Royale. Chinese food. ♦♦♦♦*Le Petit Jardin*, rue Leconte de Lisle. Creole food. ♦♦♦*Leconte Delisle*, rue Lambert. International menu. Open weekends. ***Hong Kong*, rue Marius and Ary Leblond. Chinese food.

***Le Poisson Rouge*, rue Leconte de Lisle. Creole food. ***Etoile des Neiges*, rue Leconte de Lisle. Chinese food

● **Vehicle hire**

Au Bas Prix, rue Suffren, T 45 43 36, F 22 54 27. Car hire. **Moto Flash**, rue Marius & Ary Leblond. Rents motorbikes and mopeds.

St-Gilles-Les Bains

The Lagoon from Toucan Canot to Souris Chaude is popular especially at weekends and attracts surfers from all over the island. It is possible to hire boards and get lessons from surfing clubs in the area). Being a major tourist resort it has extensive watersports facilities. **Hermitage les Bains Aqua Parc** has water slides (open all week and weekends except Mon-Tue). The **Jardin d'Eden** is a botanical garden close by (open Tue-Sat 0930-1230 and 1430-1800; Sun and holidays 1000-1800).

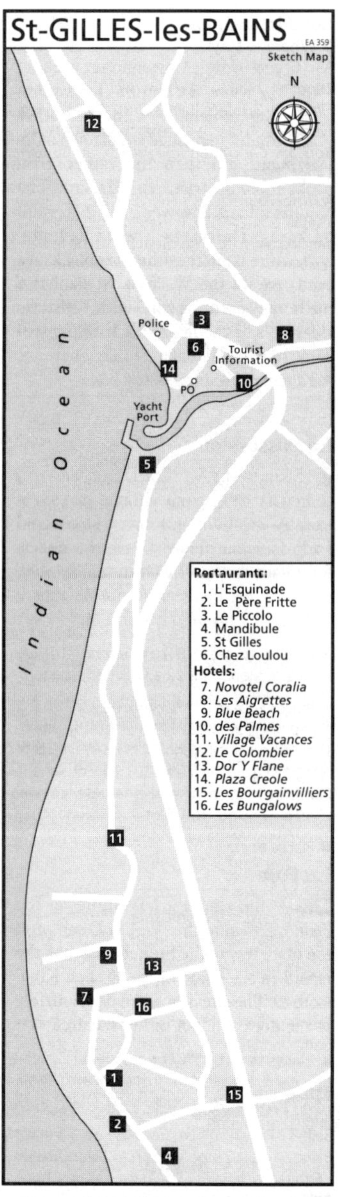

Le Maido Standing at 2,204m, this site provides one of the best views on the island. An early start is advised since cloud or haze can obscure the view as it gets hotter. If you plan to trek to **Cirque de Mafate** from here be sure you are prepared and set off very early since there is no accommodation en route.

Nearby at St Gilles les Hauts is the **Musée de Villèle**, T 227334, built in 1787, the house originally belonged to Mme Panon Desbassyns, a sugar and coffee estate owner, who died in 1846. One of the exhibits is a clock which was presented to Mme Desbassyns by Napoleon. Other pieces include furniture, china and tapestries. Part of the museum depicts life on plantations in the 18th century. Open 0930-1200 and 1400-1700 Closed Tue. Free admission.

Close to St-Gilles-les-Hauts is **L'Eperon,** renowned for its art and crafts shops.

Local information

● Where to stay

A+ ***Grand Hotel Mascareignes***, Boucan Canot, T 243624. **A+** ***Novotel Coralia Les Filaos***, St-Gilles-les-Baines, T 24 44 44. Has a live bands on Mon with a barbeque. **A+** ***Hotel Boucan Canot***, on the beach at Boucan Canot, T 24 41 20.

A ***Hotel Aigrettes***, Chemin Bottard, St-Gilles-les-Baines, T 245555. Presents traditional folk-dancing. **A** ***Hotel Blue Beach***, Ave de la Mer, Les Filaos, T 245025. **A** ***Hotel Swalibo***, rue des Salines, La-Saline-les-Bains, T 241097. **A** ***Hotel des Palmes***, rue du General de Gaulle, St Gilles de Bains, T 24 43 89. Good value in this range.

B ***Village Vacances Familles***, St-Gilles-les-Baines, T 240464. **B** ***Le Colombier***, rue Eugene Dayot, Grand Fond, T 240062. **B** ***Dor Y Flane***, Ave de la Mer, St -Gilles-les-Bains, T 24 44 19. A/c available. Self-catering facilities. **B** ***La Plaza Creole***, les Roches Noire St-Gilles-les-Baines, T 244284. **B** ***Le Bougainvilliers***, ruelle des Bougainvilliers, St-Gilles-les-Baines, T 24 44 76. Close to beach. Swimming pool. **B** ***Auberge Cadet des Iles***, rue Lacaussade, La-Saline-les-Bains, T 24 63 73. Self-catering available. **B** ***M Lougnon***, Rte du Maido Petite France, T 32 44 26. Also has gîtes to rent.

C ***Mme Magdeleine***, Petite France, T 32 53 50. **C** ***Mme Grondin***, Le Bernica, St-Gilles-les-Hauts, T 22 74 15. Also has gîtes to rent in Tan Rouge and Bernica. **C** ***Mme Malliot***, Eperon, St-Gilles-les-Hauts, T 55 69 83. **C** ***Les Bungalows***, Ave des Badamiers, T 24 46 06.

Camping in La-Saline-les-Bains and at L'Ermitage, T 24 42 35.

● Places to eat

There is a wide range of places to eat in the area.

♦♦♦♦***Le Jardin du Flibustier***, L'Ermitage-les-Bains. High standard cuisine. ♦♦♦♦***Les Trois Roches***, L'Ermitage-les-Bains. Creole food. ♦♦♦♦***L'Italiano***, St-Gilles-les-Baines. Italian food. ♦♦♦♦***L'Esquinade***, L'Ermitage-les-Bains. Creole food. ♦♦♦♦***Alpha Centre de Peche*** Harbour, St-Gilles-les-Baines. Seafood speciality.

♦♦♦***Le Pere Frite***, L'Ermitage-les-Bains. Creole food. ♦♦♦***Le Piccolo***, High street,St-Gilles-les-Baines. Pizzas. ♦♦♦***Le Coralys***, St-Gilles-les-Baines. Italian food. ♦♦♦***La Mandibule***, L'Ermitage-les-Bains. Pleasant atmosphere. ♦♦♦***Le St Gilles***, Harbour, St-Gilles-les-Baines. International menu. ♦♦♦***L'Espadon*** Plage, Trou d'Eeau. Closed Sun and Mon.

♦♦***Chez Loulou***, General de Gaulle, St-Gilles-les-Baines. Café style. ♦♦***Le Chaland***, close to the Aqua Parc, L'Ermitage-les-Bains. Creole food. ♦♦***Le Bourbon***, General de Gaulle, St-Gilles-les-Baines. Light meals.

● Entertainment

Gambling Casino in *Novotel Coralia* St-Gilles-les-Baines, T 244700.

Discos *Le Swing*, at Grand Fond near the turn off to St-Gilles-les-Hauts. ***Le Lovers***, T 336733, on the way to L'Eperon. ***Le Circus***, T 245018 L'Ermitage-les-Bains. ***Moulin du Tango***, T 245390, L'Ermitage-les-Bains.

● Car hire

(All offices on rue du General de Gaulle, St-Gilles-les-Baines. All these firms have offices at Airport where vehicles can be left.) *Citer Foucque*; *Europcar*; *Inter Rent* ; *ERL*.

● Moterbike and bicycle hire

(Both offices on rue du General de Gaulle, St-Gilles-les-Baines) *L'Ile en Moto* Rents mopeds; *Locacycles* Rents bicycles and motorbikes.

St Leu

Small fishing village. The beaches begin to be white sand a little N of here (rather than black lava). The **Hôtel de Ville**, was constructed by the French East India Company, and dates from around 1760. The **Notre Dame de la Salette**, was built in 1859 during an outbreak of cholera in Réunion and is credited with having saved the town from the epidemic.

Ferme Corail is a turtle farm 2 km N of St Leu. It is managed by the Societé Bourbon Naise d'Aquaculture. The opening hours are from 0800-1200 and 1400-1700 daily. Entry adults US$2 and Children US$1. The farm is a large affair and has turtles from all over including Seychelles, Mauritius and Madagascar. The shop sells items crafted from turtle shell.

Conservatoire Botanique de Mascarin A new garden planning to conserve endemic plants, T 24 92 27.

Stella Matutina The sugar factory here

closed in 1978 but has now reopened as a Museum. Exhibitions on display illustrate the importance of agriculture on the island from the early days of coffee and sugar cane through to the present range of spices, geraniums and other aromatic plants. Closed Mon. Admission US$5.

• **Where to stay** **B** *Village Vacances Familles*, well run. **B** *Mme Rangapin*, 132 ch Dubuisson, T 344251. **B** *Villa Celinette*, 29 lot le Liere, T 347712. Self-catering. **C** *Mme Maillot*, 4 Chemin des Hortensias, Chaloupe St Leu T 548292. Small. Table d'hôte. **C** *M Cadet*, 20 Chemin Payet, La Chaloupe St Leu, T 548500.

• **Camping** Site at St Leu is only open in Aug. Very popular. Enquire at the town Hall Service du Garde Champetre, T 348003.

• **Places to eat** ♦♦♦*La Palais d'Asie*, rue du General Lambert. Chinese food. ♦♦♦*L'Ocean*, St Lue. On the shore. Creole food.

• **Transport** **Bus** There are regular services from St-Gilles-les-Bains N to *St Denis;* and S to *St Pierre*.

THE CIRQUES

There are 3 great natural amphitheatres formed by the volcanic activity that created Réunion. They all have their own particular charms: Mafete is the most wild; Salazie is the most developed, with wonderful dawns breaking above the rim of the crater; Cilaos has the famous thermal springs in the mountain spa. Each Cirque is most easily accessed from the coast, the departure points for the trek inland being La Possession in the N W for Mafete; St André in the N E fro Salazie; and St Louis in the S for Cilaos. Once in the Cirques, however, it is possible to trek from one to another.

Cirque Mafate

This is the least accessible of the Cirques, and remains largely untouched by tourism. The surrounding area has several gîtes that cater for trekkers.

Dos d'Ane is the village used as an access point for those walking to Cirque de Mafate. It is important to note that there is no public transport to the village, which is about 20 km from La Possession. For those not keen to continue up to the Mafate Cirque there is a viewpoint close to the village and various picnic spots dotted around. There are a couple of small guest houses: **B** *M Techer*, T 320004. **C** M Axel Nativel, T 320147 and a restaurant ♦♦♦*Le Porteau Vert*.

Marla is the highest village on the island (1540m). Most trekkers pass through the village. Travel N to the **Rivière des Galets** and then on to **La Nouvelle**, the capital of Mafate. You can take a stay here in La Nouvelle and there are a number of gîtes to choose from **C** *Sylvain Begue*, T 438277. **C** *La Nouvelle*, T 436177. **C** *Cesar Manrique*, T 434316.

Roche Plate is a small village with a general store and a gîte **C** *Roche Plate*.

Ilet a Bourse village provides trekkers with a useful stop over from either Le Belier, Aurere or Grand Place. There is a Gîte which is of a good standard.

Grand Place town next to the Rivière des Galets has a gîte **C** *Cayenne* run by the local priest

Aurere village lies in the northern part of the cirque, from here there are some great views. There is a **C** *Gîte* but it has no cooking facilities. The Bras des Merles, close by, has a lookout point.

- **Transport Bus** Regular buses to La Possession, and then a day's hike up to Dos d'Ane. alternative access is from Cirque Cilaos (see page 784) or Cirque Salaziae (see page 781).

Cirque de Salazie

The Cirque is approached from St Andre on the N coast. The first town on the road is Salazie. There is little promising accommodation in Salazie, and most visitors make their base for exploration in Hell-Bourg or Grand Ilet.

Salazie

This is a mountainous area and there are several gorges which the road passes through on its way to Salazie town, the biggest settlement in the Cirque de Salazie. Towards Hell-Bourg below the turn off to Grand Ilet there are the **Cascade du Voile de la Mariée** 'Falls of the Bridal Veil. Information for travellers from the **Syndicat d'Initiative**, located in the town hall, T 47 50 09.

Hell-Bourg

Hell-Bourg (named after governor Admiral de Hell) is a pleasant town displaying some interesting examples of Creole architecture. There is also the old **Spa** which played a major role when the town was famous as a thermal resort, but today the springs have long since dried up. This is the main centre for excursions round the Cirque.

Excursions from Hell-Bourg include **Les Trois Cascades**, along the road to **Ilet à Vidot**. On leaving the town there is a path off to the left for the falls. **Belouve** is an hour's walk from Hell-Bourg, and the remains of an old cable car can be seen beside the forest road to Belouve. Accommodation at **D** *Gîte de Montagne*.

• **Where to stay A** *Le Relais des Cimes*, rue General de Gaulle, T 47 81 58. Facilities include sauna and sporting activities such as canoeing. **C** *Mme Laurent*, Rond Point, T 478060. **C** *Mme Parisot*, rue General de Gaulle, T 478148. **D** *Auberge de Jeunesse*, rue de la Gaulle, T 47 826 5. You need to be a member of a youth hostel association, or join on the spot for around US$15. Dormitory accommodation and self-catering facilities. Splendid old Creole mansion.

• **Places to eat** ♦♦♦♦*Le Relais des Cimes*, rue General de Gaulle, T 47 81 58. Fixed-price menus of good standard. ♦♦♦*Le Chou Chou*, Town centre, T 23 54 21. Fixed-price menu.

Grande Ilet

Near Salazie at the base of the cirque. The village contains the only wooden church in Réunion.

• **Where to stay and places to eat** 2 small chambres d'hôte, also providing table d'hôte meals, are: **C** *Mme C Nourry*, T 23 51 27. **C** *Mme J M Grondin*, T 23 52 29.

• **Transport Bus** Regular service from St André at the coast to Salazie, some going on to Hell-Bourg, and some to Grand Ilet. Fare US$3.50.

Cirque Ciloas

This is probably the most popular Cirque to hike around, its beauty is unsurpassed even in Réunion. The area is famed for its thermals which originally established Cilaos as a spa town, and which still attract visitors for their curing properties. There is a local wine, and an aperitif, *Isabelle*.

Trek to Roche Plate

The walk begins in Cilaos and heads towards **Ilet Cordes**, but takes the right fork about 4 km from Ciloas, at the turning to Ilet à Cordes. On this path there are a number of waterfalls including **La Chapelle**, and **Cascade du Bras Rouge**. Past the waterfalls, the track passes **Col du Taibit** (2,083m) with **Marla** at the foot. From Marla it is possible to follow follow the course of the Rivière des Galets past Les Trois Roches to Roche Plate. An alternative route passes through **La Nouvelle** instead of Les Trois Roches, but is a bit more strenuous. From La Nouvelle it is possible to carry on N to **Aurere** and to **Dos d'Ane** in the NW amid very picturesque scenery.

Ciloas

Ciloas is a charming mountain resort and spa, with lakes. It is famous for its embroidery work which can be bought where it is produced at the **Maison de la Broderie**. Woodcarvings and local art work is widely available. and there is a studio selling craft studio on rue Winceslas. To the N of the town is the road to the small nearby village of **Bras Sec**, which lies E of Cilaos, and the track which doubles back to to **Ilet à Cordes.**

Local information

● Where to stay

A *Hotel des Thermes*, just off route des Sources, T 277001. Facilities include tennis courts. **A** *Hotel Le Vieux Cep*, chemin des Trois Mares, T 317189.

B *Hotel du Cirque*, rue du Pere Boiteau. T 317068. Chinese and Creole food in the restaurant. **B** *Le Petit Randonneur*, rue du Pere Boiteau, T 31 79 55, friendly atmosphere. **B** *Les Fleurs Jaunes*, (Village Vacances Familles) route Hopital, T 31 71 39. More expensive at weekends. **B** *Gîte Auberge*, T 317829. Some communal accommodation much cheaper. **C** *Hotel le Marla*, Mare-a-Jones, T 317233. Cheaper rooms with communal facilities. Fixed-price menu.

Camping at **E** *Camping de Cilaos*, T 277741. Bar. Restaurant. Very busy in European holiday seasons. Also 2 **D** *Huts* with dormitory accommodation.

● Entertainment

Discos *La Caverne*, by lake at the northern

end of town. *Tilt 3*, off chemin des Trois Mares.

Cinema Route des Sources. Shows films at weekends and during the holiday periods.

● Sport (participant)

Swimming, pool Off rue Victorine Séry. Hours Thu, Fri 1100-1200; Wed,Sat 1030-1200 and 1400-1600. US$1,50 adults, US$1 children.

● Sport (spectator)

Soccer, Stadium on Rue due Stade. Matches most Sundays.

● Tourist information

Sindicat d'Intitiative. Rue des Ecoles, T 27 78 03.

● Transport

Bus from St Louis and is US$3 one-way. *Taxi-collectif* from St Louis is US$5.

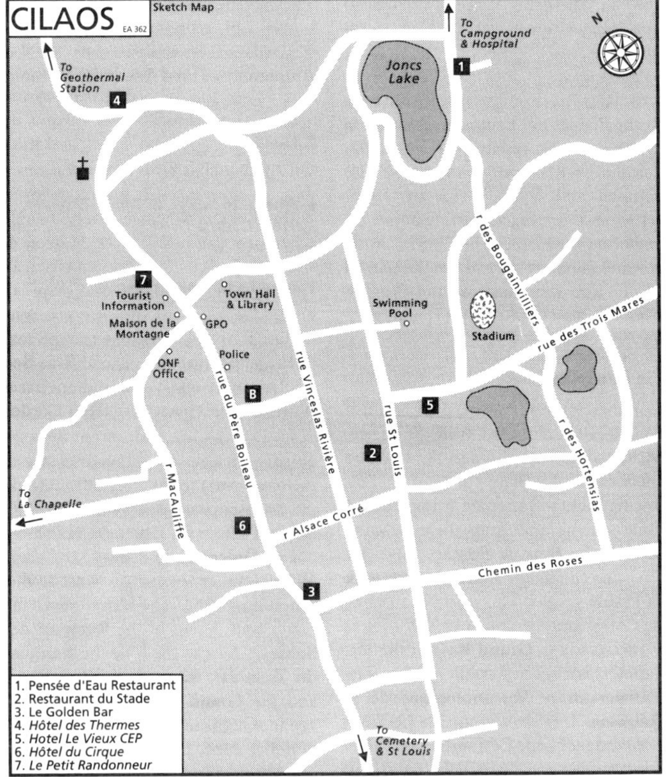

THE PLAINES AND THE VOLCANO

To the SE of Réunion lie 2 less mountainous areas, Plaines de Cafres and Plaines de Palmistes, which run between St Louis in the S to St Benoît in the N E. They lie between the Cirques in the western central part of the country and the recently active volcano. The name 'Cafre' is thought to be a degeneration of 'kaffir' a Dutch term for blacks, and a reference to the fact that escaped slaves (*marrons*) hid out in the area. There are no longer many palm trees in the Plaines des Palmistes. Piton de la Fournaise, the recently active (1992) volcano of Réunion, is in the SE. Le Tampon and Entre Deux are larger settlements serving as starting points for exploring the Plaines, the Cirques or the volcano. Some of the villages are named by the km posts marking the distance from the coast (eg Le Vingt Deuxième).

Le Tampon

Commercial centre with a population of 50,000, 10 km inland from St Pierre. Most people pass through the town on their way to La Plaine des Cafres. Following Route Nationale 3 towards Le Quatorzième and from there heading towards Le Bras de Pontho, there are fine views along the route of the **Bras de la Plaine** gorges. The road N to Plaine de Cafres and then turning N W to Bois Court, leads to **Grand Basin** ('the lost valley'), with a waterfall nearby. The **L'Observatoire Volcanologique de la Réunion**, T 275461, is outside Le Vingt Septième towards Le Tampon.

• **Where to stay A** *Hotel Le Paille en Queue*, 25 rue H Delisle, T 274760. **B** *Le Chalet Enchante*, T 270790. Swimming pool. **C** *Hotel Relais du Tampon*, 83 rue Sarda Garriga T 279530. **C** *Mme Mangue*, 64 Chemin Jamerosas T 273685.

• **Places to eat** ♦♦♦♦*Les Orchidées*, French and Creole cuisine. High standard. ♦♦♦♦*L'Auberge Alsacienne*, dishes from Alsace.

• **Entertainment Cinema** *Eden* rue H Delisle. **Disco** *Hotel Le Maria*.

Entre Deux

This small town lies between 2 rivers, the Bras de la Plaine and the Bras de Cilaos. The settlement grew with the help of the coffee industry, but as coffee declined so did the town. Today fruit and tobacco are the main crops. From the town to **Le Dimitile** and **Cirque de Cilaos** it is a good day's trek, and from the top there is a great panorama.

• **Where to stay B** *Mme Grondin*, T 395189. **C** *Mme Corre*, T 395343. **C** *Mme Fontaine*, T 395121.

Piton de la Fournaise

For a hike up to the summit, it is wise to start as early as possible, take protection from the sun, sufficient water, rehydration packs, waterproofs, some warm clothing and if possible a first aid kit. Since fog and cloud often descend quickly, stick close together and keep to the paths and take all precautions (people do disappear every year on the volcano). There are 2 larger craters on the massif **Dolomieu** and **Bory**, and some other smaller ones, of which **Zoe** erupted in 1992. The oldest surviving crater wall is that of the **Rempart des Sables**, whilst to the E lie the **Rempart du Tremblet**, **Rempart du Bois Blanc** and the **Grand Brule**. It is wisest to spend a night in the **C** *Gîte du Volcano*, at Bellecombe, T 212896, before setting off to the summit, some 14km away. The path to the craters turns right down the **Enclos Fouque**, continues past the **Formica Leo** to reach **Chapelle de Rosemont**. The circuit passes **Cratere Bory** (2,632m), **Piton de la Fournaise** (2,510m) and **Cratere Dolomieu** (2,366m).

The Plaines

In the centre of Plaines de Cafres, about 12 km N E of Entre-Deux is **Grand Bassin** where there is a waterfall nearby in a deep gorge. To the N E of Le Tampon is **Notre Dame de la Paix,** a small village with a notable beauty spot looking out over the valley.

Roughly 2 km from Le Premier in Plaines des Palmistes is **Cascade Biberon**, with a pool under the falls that is large enough to swim in.

Local information

● Where to stay in the Plaines

B *Hotel L'Allemand*, Le Vingt Troisième, T 27 51 27. **B** *Auberge du Volcano*, Le Vingt Septième, T 27 50 91. Very popular.

C *Jean-Louis Lacouture*, Le Vingt-Deuxième, T 59 04 91. **C** *La Diligence*, Le Vingt Huitième, T 59 10 10. Bungalow accommodation. Excursions and treks arranged. Restaurant. **C** *Mme Anne Tenon*, Le Vingt Quatrième, T 591041. **C** *M Guy Hoareau*, Grand Ferme, T 571044. Gîte accommodation. **C** *Mme Joseph Victor Payet*, Petit Tampon, T 27 09 92. Gîte accommodation. **C** *Mme Louise Magnan*, Bois Court, T 27 56 91. Restaurant Taureau Noir. **C** *S & T Mussard*, Chemin Notre Dame de la Paix, T 27 57 59. Farm accommodation. **C** *Mme Sery Picard*, Grand Bassin, T 275102. Gîte accommodation.

D *Mme Sery*, Grand Basin, T 59 10 34. Gîte accommodation.

Camping Bois Court

● Places to eat in the Plaines

♦♦♦*Auberge du Volcano*, Le Vingt Septième. Creole food. Closed Mon and Sun. ♦♦♦*Hotel La Diligence*, Le Vingt Huitième. French and Creole food, ♦♦♦*Le Tourne-Broche*, Vingt Huitième Creole food. ♦♦♦*La Soucoupe Volante*, Trentième Creole food. ♦♦♦*Chez Cocotier*, Le Vingt Troisième. French and Creole food.

● Entertainment

Disco *Ouragan*, Bois Court; *Twist*, Soucoupe-Voante, Plaines des Palmistes.

● Transport

Bus Regular services across the Plaines. Costs about US$5 from St Pierre to St Benoît.

INFORMATION FOR VISITORS

Contents

Before you go

Entry requirements

● Visas

Those who belong to the EU do not need visas. EU citizens who wish to stay for more than 3 months are allowed to do so but must first obtain a *permit de sejour*. Those who do not belong to the EU need visas (which are issued only if you have an outward bound ticket). It is advisable that visitors enquire and obtain visas for Réunion in their own countries since in Moroni, Comoros, for example, they take close to a month to process (although in Port Louis, Mauritius visas are processed as you wait).

● Vaccinations

Visitors require Cholera and Yellow Fever certificates if arriving from an infected area, for example, another African country.

● Réunion representation overseas

As Réunion is a Département of France, it is represented by French Embassies in the various capitals around the world.

● Overseas representation in Réunion

Madagascar (consulate) 51 rue J Dodu, T 210521. Open 0800-1200 and 1400-1600. **South Africa** (consulate) 18 rue de la Compaignie. T 215005. **United Kingdom** (consulate) 2 rue de la Diague, T 210619. **Germany** (consulate) 18 rue Papangue, St Clotilde, T 281302.

● Tourist information in Réunion

Syndicat d'Initiative 48 rue Ste Marie St Denis, T 41 83 00. This is the main office and best for general enquiries. Regional offices tend to specialise on local attractions and facilities. The office will provide information on a trekking,water sports,Diving facilities etc. and advise you on which agencies to approach, otherwise check for advertisements in the newspapers.

Maison de la Montagne 10 Place Sarda Garriga, St Denis Open Mon-Thu 0900-1730, other days open until 1600. Provide informtion on trekking routes and facilities in the mountains.

Run is a magazine which publishes the programme of events in Réunion.

● Tourist information overseas

For information on Réunion contact French Tourist bureaux around the world. **Australia**, Kindersley House 33 Bligh St Sydney NSW 2000, T 02 231 5244. **France**, 3 rue du Faubourg St Honore, 75008 Paris T 1 42 66 33 80 and T 1 40 75 02 79. **UK**, French Tourist Bureau 178 Piccadilly, London WIV OAL, T 071 493 6594. **USA**, 610 5th Ave, New York, T 900 990 0040.

● Travel and tour agents

See entry under St Denis, page 771

● Best time to visit

Dry season Apr to Oct with Apr and Jun probably the best time to visit. French school holidays are from Jul to Sept, making the main resort area round St-Gilles-les-Bains very busy, and the small gîtes providing accommodation in the mountains tend to get booked up. Aug is particularly popular, as is Christmas and New Year.

● **Health**

Water is everywhere safe to drink. Malaria has been eradicated, but it is wise to take anti-malaria tablets – there are mosquitoes, and it is possible that they might transmit malaria from another visitor. See Health Section, page 21) and Vaccinations, page 786.

Money

The unit of currency is the French Franc. Foreign currency can be changed easily. Euro Cheques are best cashed at *Credit Agricole* Rue Felix Guyon, St Denis (they also allow visa cash withdrawals over the counter). Open 1000-1900 Mon-Sat; Sun 1300-1900.

● **Credit cards**

American Express representative on Réunion is *Bourbon Voyages* 14 rue Rontaunay, St Denis, T 216818. Major hotels also exchange currency and travellers cheques, most offer a 24 hour service, but commission is generally higher than at a bank. Major credit cards are accepted in most large establishments and visa and credit card cash dispensers have been introduced.

Major credit cards are accepted in large shops and hotels, and by airlines and travel agents.

● **Cost of living**

Accommodation for the visitor is moderate in terms of price. There is little that is very cheap. The chambre d'hôte and gîte accommodation is good value and very reasonable. Food tends to be more expensive than elsewhere in the Indian Ocean, and bus travel is also dearer.

Getting there

● **Air**

There are direct flights to all the Indian Ocean countries, 3 African countries, but only to France in Europe.

Indian Ocean Comoros, Madagascar, Mauritius, Mayotte, Seychelles.

Africa Djibouti, Kenya, South Africa.

Middle East Saudi Arabia

Europe France

Direct flights from Europe are expensive, and budget travellers should consider a cheap excursion flight to Nairobi, and a connection via Kenya Airways to Réunion.

Airline Offices, see page 771.

Specialist Agencies for discounted fares, see page 14.

● **Sea**

The *MV Mauritius Pride* ferries to and from Mauritius (US$32 one-way). For yacht to Mauritius *Ylang Ylang*, T 244118, 48 rue General du Gaulle, St-Gilles-les-Bains. Other yacht travel, Claire Caroline Croisières 402 Menciol Bras des Chevrettes, St Andre, T 462574.

When you arrive

Airport information Gillot airport is 11 km to the E. There is no airport departure tax.

Transport to town Taxi from St Denis to Gillot airport is US$11. There is a bus, but it stops on the road outside the airport. Bus fare to St Denis is US$1.

● **Conduct**

Conventions of dress and behaviour are similar to those in Europe.

● **Electricity**

220 volts with European-style 2-pin plugs.

● **Hours of business**

0900-1200 and 1430-1800. Shops are closed on Sun.

● **Official time**

Réunion is 4 hours ahead of GMT.

● **Safety**

There is a good record of law and order in Réunion, and visitors need not feel anxious about walking around alone or after dark.

Where to stay

Hotels in Réunion are comfortable and moderately priced. There are only a few in the luxurious class, in St Denis, the capital; and St-Gilles-Les-Bains, the main beach resort.

Chambres d'hôte are family-run guest houses that are regulated to maintain standards. They are good value, with rates at US$15 for a single room, and US$10 per person in a double, and includes a contintental breakfast. Evening meals are substantial and cost US$11. Bookings can be made through tourist offices.

Pensions de famille are boarding houses found in the main towns, St Denis, St Pierre, Le Tampon and St Louis. There are inexpensive, but vary considerably in quality. The better establishments are usually fairly well booked up with with long-stay guests.

Rural gîtes are self-catering and can be hired for a group, for a period. Mostly in the S and the Plaines area in the S E. Rates vary according

HOTEL CLASSIFICATIONS

A+ Over US$100 a night. International standards and decor, a/c, self contained rooms, swimming pool, restaurants, bars, business services.

A US$40-100. First class standards. Air-conditioning, attached bathrooms. Restaurants and bars. Swimming pool.

B US$20-40. Tourist class. Comfortable with a/c or fans, attached barthrooms. Restaurant, bar, public rooms.

C US$10-20. Budget. Fans. Shared bathroom facilities.

D US$5-10. Guest house. No fan. Shared bathroom. Cold water.

E Under US$5. Basic guest house. Simple bed. No soap or towels. No wardrobe. Shared bathroom facilities. Erratic cold water supply. No fans or mosquito nets.

RESTAURANT CLASSIFICATIONS

♦♦♦♦ Over US$10 for a meal. A 3 course meal in a restaurant with pleasant decor. Beers, wines and spirits available.

♦♦♦♦ US$5-10 for a meal. Two courses. Comfortable surroundings.

♦♦ US$2-5 for a meal. Probably only a single course. Surroundings spartan but adequate.

♦ Under US$2. Single course. Often makeshift surroundings such as a street kiosk with simple benches and tables.

to length of stay, and size of group, and are around US$5 – US$10 per person per night if the place is filled. They can be booked through *Agence Régionale du Tourisme et des Loisirs (ARTL)* 2 Ave de la Victoire, St Denis. T 210041.

Mountain gîtes are cabins for hikers, with dormitory accommodation. They are about US$6.50 per person per night, and there is a security deposit of US$6 against leaving the place in good order. It is only possible to stay for 2 nights consecutively in each gîte. Places can be booked through tourist offices.

Food and drink

● Food

Eating is more expensive than in other Indian Ocean Islands, and it is difficult to buy a meal for under US$5. Fixed-price menu meals are between US$8 and US$13. *Table d'hôte* establishments (usually, but not always, chambre d'hôte premises at well) give very good value for a meal, with wine and local liqueurs, at around US$11. Budget travellers are best advised to do as much self-catering at possible.

● Drink

The local water is fine, but there are plenty of bottled waters on sale. Most wine is imported. The local wine made in Cilaos is rather heavy and sweet. Plenty of imported beers are available. The local brewery produces *Bière Bourbon* at about US$1 for a third of a litre bottle.

Getting around

● Air

The island is too small to require internal air travel, although there are helicopter sight-seeing tours of the Cirques and the volcano, for between US$100 and US$250, from Réunion Air Services Rue Mât-de-Pavillon, St Denis, T 219540.

● Road

Bus There is an efficient bus service on the routes between the main towns. The buses run to a timetable, it is well worth obtaining a copy of the schedule from one of the tourist offices or the main bus station on Blvd Joffre in St Denis. The service is roughly every 2 hours on the busiest routes, and every 4 hours on the less-used. The buses are not as cheap as elswhere in the Indian Ocean at roughly US$0.50 a km, but they are superior vehicles.

● Vehicle hire

Cars Although all the major agencies exist i.e. Avis, Europcar, Budget and Hertz there are a wealth of other local cheaper firms to choose from. A variety of firms have offices at the Gillot Airport.

Motorbike and bicycle hire is available in St Denis see page 778 and Ste-Gille-les-Bains.

● Other local transport

Taxis Plenty of taxis in the main towns.

Taxi collectifs These are shared taxis operating in the country areas. They are minibuses or converted station wagons, and they run to timetables. Cost is about US$0.50 a km.

Communications

● Language

The official language is French but Réunion Creole is widely spoken. English, though taught in schools, is not commonly used.

Postal services

Central Office is on the of rue du Marechal Leclerc and rue Juliette Dodu, St Denis. Open 0730-1800 Mon-Fri; Sat 0800-1200. Poste Restante at the Boites de Commerce door.

Telephone services

Some public telephones tend only to accept phone cards available in shops and post offices.

Entertainment

Centre Réunionnais d'Action Culturelle (CRAC) Jardin de l'Etat, St Denis, T 216975, publishes a monthly listing of all cultural events. It is free, and available at the large hotels, tourist offices and travel agents.

Cinemas

There are cinemas in the main towns, showing mainly adventure, glamour, and martial arts films in French. Some programmes of Indian films.

Newspapers

3 daily papers, all in French. *Journal de l'Ile de la Réunion* is slightly more up-market, with a big Sunday edition; *Quotidien de la Réunion* is the most popular with the largest circulation; *Témoignages* is the paper of the Réunion Communist party.

There are several periodicals, among which are: *Cahiers de la Réunion et de l'Océan Indien*, which is published monthly and focusses on regional affairs; *L'Economie à la Réunion*, which appears every 2 months and surveys business and economic issues; *Le Journal de la Nature*, a wildlife magazine; *Télé 7 Jours Réunion*, comes out each week and carries carries details of radio and TV programmmes.

Radio

RFO is the main service. In the last few years a number of private radio stations have come into operation, many with specialist slants. *Société Nationale de Radio Télévision Française d'Outre-Mer (RFO)* Government-owned. *Télé Free-DOM* Privately-owned. Programmes listed in *Télé 7 Jours Réunion* (weekly).

Sporting events

Soccer is the main team sport, and there are matches at the stadia in the main town on Sundays.

Television

Réunion has had a television service since 1990. *Société Nationale de Radio Télévision Française d'Outre-Mer (RFO)* Government-owned. Operates 2 television channels. Télé Free-DOM. *Antenne Réunion* Privately-owned. 5 hours of programmes each day. *Canal Réunion* Privately-owned. Subscription channel which transmits 12 hours a day. *Télé Free-DOM* Privately-owned. Programmes listed in *Télé 7 Jours Réunion* (weekly).

Holidays and festivals

Public holidays

1 Jan	New Year's Day
1 May	International Labour Day
8 May	Victory Day
May	Ascension
Jun	Bank Holiday
14 Jul	Bastille Day
15 Aug	Assumption
11 Nov	Armistice Day
25 Dec	Christmas Day

The Railway

When the main harbour of Réunion was moved from St Denis (never more than an unsheltered roadstead) to Le Port in 1867, work began on a railway linking the docks to the capital. The terrain was very difficult, but the only alternative at the time for hauling the sugar crop was by bullock cart over unsealed roads. Eventually the line was extended round the E coast to St Benoît, and from there across the Plaines to St Pierre.

The line is spectacular. There is a tunnel 10 km long, the third longest land tunnel in the world. The bridge over the Rivière des Galets is 380m long, and the span crossing the Rivière du Mat is 480m.

With the construction of roads able to take the sugar freight, the railway became uneconomical. A short section of the line, between La Possession and La Grande Chaloupe, is still in operation, and there are plans to extend it as a tourist attraction.

● Festivals

These are in the nature of harvest festivals for particular crops, and also serve as local agriculatural shows.

Date	*Celebration*	*Location*
Jan	Honey	Le Tampon
Apr	Rope	St Benoît
May	Chou Chou	Hell-Bourg
May	Vanilla	Bras Panon
Jun	Guava	Plaines des Palmistes
Jul	Sugar Cane	Ste Rose
Aug	Wood	St Louis
Aug	Saffron	St Joseph
Sep/Oct	Flowers	Le Tampon
Nov	Rose	St Benoît
Nov	Lentils	Cilaos
Nov	Mangosteens	St Benoît
Dec	Lychees	St Denis
Dec	Garlic	Petite Ile

● Fairs

Date	*Location*
Jul	St Paul
Dec	St Pierre

The exact dates of the Festivals and Fairs, and details on activities planned can be obtained from *Syndicat d'Initiative* 48 rue Ste Marie, St Denis, T 41 83 00. or in *RUN* magazine.

Further Reading

● Reading on Réunion

Bulpin, T. V. (undated, but *circa* 1954). *Islands in a Forgotten Sea.* Howard Timmins. Entertaining popular history of the Indian Ocean Islands, with a chapter on Réunion. Illustrations by A. A. Telford.

MAURITIUS

Introduction

The island is small, being about 60 km from N to S, and 45 km from E to W. It has a long and chequered history from the arrival of the Portuguese in the 16th century when the island was uninhabited, through periods of Dutch settlement, French and British rule, and then independence. French influence remains strong. Added to their continuing presence was the influx of slaves to work the plantations, followed by the immigration of Indian and Chinese labourers, artisans and traders.

The economy was originally heavily dependent on sugar, but Mauritius has diversified by establishing a very strong manufacturing sector, and by developing its tourist attractions. It has one of the most successful economies in all of the developing world. Mauritius has maintained a healthy multiparty democracy since independence.

At the superb coastal resorts, windsurfing, waterskiing, snorkelling and surfing and sailing are all available. Diving to view marine life and coral formations is particularly good. Deep sea game fishing is excellent. It is possible to hunt deer, wild boar and hare.

Exchange Rate 1994: MR 17.7 = US$1

Contents

Maps

Environment

Geography

The island of Mauritius, one of the Mascarene Islands, lies some 800 km E of Madagascar and covers an area of approx 1900 square km. The other islands belonging to Mauritius are St Brandon (460 km NE), Agalega (1,100 km N), Rodrigues and outer islands (560 km NE of Mauritius). The Mascarene islands include Réunion, which is administered by France. They are volcanic in origin and part of a chain which extends to the Islands of the Seychelles, evolving some 8 million years ago during the Miocene period.

The central part of Mauritius is dominated by a highland plateau which continues to rise forming rugged terrain towards the SW where Piton de la Petite Rivière (standing at 828m, the highest point of Mauritius) is situated before sloping down towards the NE coast. The other hill ranges which lead off the high plateau are the Montagne Bambous which extends eastwards and the Moke Range which surrounds Port Louis. Northern and northeastern areas of the island are relatively flat.

Today there are no active volcanoes on Mauritius, all that remains are relics of eruptions long since past. Extinct craters like the Trou aux Cerfs crater and

Grand Bassin lake are the most prominent volcanic formations. Elsewhere, however, smaller, less dramatic pyramidal formations are reminiscent of an ancient volcanic era. The SW has numerous river systems which are largely derived from the mountains in that area. The high plateau area has 2 main river systems running through the region, the Grande Rivière Sud Est (the country's largest) and the Grande Rivière Nord Ouest.

Being volcanic, the island has basaltic bedrock, and although there are some alluvial deposits and limestone, much of the island is covered with volcanically derived soils. The island itself is surrounded by a coral reef with small unprotected coastal strips on the S coast and the northern part of Black River.

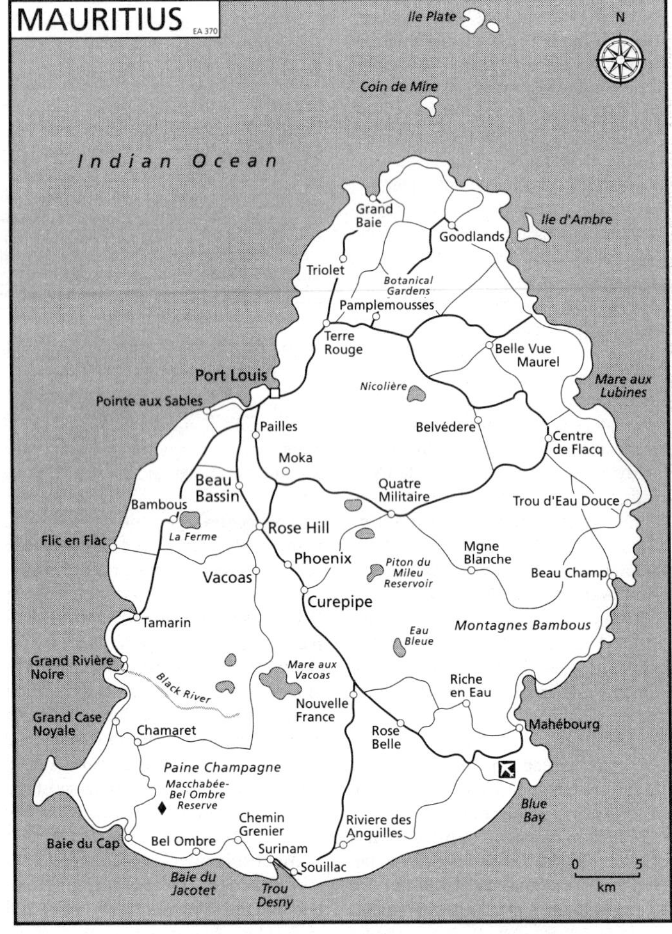

Climate

The Island is affected by the SE trade winds which cause rain to fall predominantly over the SE and central plateau. There is a single rainy monsoon season, Jan to May.

The hottest months are from Jan through to Apr when temperatures of 30°C are not uncommon on the coast. It is during this period that cyclones (see page 818) are most likely to strike the region. Nov to Apr is generally considered the summer. Winter, although the climate is comfortably warm by non-tropical standards, arrives from Jul and lasts through to Sep. During this period, day time temperatures average 25° but at night-fall these fall to 15°.

The central highlands experience the coolest temperatures in Mauritius, which can fall to 10°C in the winter. However usual winter temperatures average 15°C and summer temperatures 24°C. On the coast temperatures range from 21°C in winter to 28°C in summer.

Nature

Flora

Originally the Island had a wide variety of indigenous plant species of which a large proportion were endemic to Mauritius. In recent years, however, pressure from agriculturists and the introduction of new plants has significantly reduced the number of indigenous species. Forested land has been severely affected; it is thought that today less than 1% of this land has been left undisturbed. To combat the problem the Mauritian Wildlife Appeal Fund and Royal Society of Arts and Science have joined forces and cornered off land to be protected from animals. Rare species have been planted in these reserves to encourage their spread.

Amongst the rarer species are ebony trees which exist in small pockets around the Black River district. On the coastal fringes casuarinas (*Casuarina equisetifolia*) and eucalyptus predominate though even eucalyptus species such as tambalacoque (the dodo tree) are becoming rarer. Other unusual species include the Indian banyan, and the flamboyant with its brilliant red flower which was introduced from South America at the end of the last century. Since the island is tropical you would expect coconut trees to line the shores. These do not occur naturally, though they have been planted in some of the beach resorts. One of the places where one can see a significant amount of endemic flora is in the Royal Botanic Gardens at Pamplemousses.

Fauna

Unlike Madagascar, Mauritius has little in the way of fauna and the only indigenous mammal is a fruit bat (*Pteropus rubricollis*) found largely in forests to the SW. There are 2 endemic species of the boa snake family. These are the *Bolyeria multicarinata* and the *Casarea dussumieri*, and they are a protected species on Ile Ronde.

Non-indigenous species include Java deer, (brought by the Dutch from Asia) and the Macaque monkey (introduced by the Portuguese from Asia).

Birds

The most famous species of bird to inhabit Mauritius was the dodo (*Raphus cucculatus*) which became extinct some time around 1700. Some particularly rare birds inhabit the island and include the Mauritius kestrel (*Falco punctatus*) of which only a handful remain; the pink pigeon (*Columba mayeri*); and the the Mauritius ring-necked parakeet (*Psittacula echo*). Other rare birds include the Mauritius cuckoo-shrike (*Coracina typicus*); the fody, known as the cardinal or banana bird (*Foudia rubra*); the fly catcher, oiseau de la vierge (*Terpsiphone bourbonnensis*) and the olive white-eye (*Zosterops chloronotos*).

More common species include the Air Mauritius symbol, the paille-en-queue, with a long red or white tail

The Dodo

The dodo (*Raphus Cucullatus*), a species endemic to Réunion and Mauritius, was found on the islands in great numbers by the earliest visitors. It was a pigeon-like bird, but about the size of a turkey, and weighed up to 20 kilos, with short stubby wings, and a small fluffy tail. The wings were yellowy-white, the breast white, and it had a large, black, powerful, hooked beak which it used to ward off attackers and to grind up the seeds of the vacoa tree that comprised its main food.

The dodo was unable to fly, and was described as so fat that it could barely walk, making it easy to catch. It made good eating for sea-farers accustomed to getting by on ships' biscuit and salted meat.

The dodo laid a single large egg on a pile of grass, and this served to make it even more vulnerable. The Portuguese had introduced wild hogs to ensure a future food supply, and together with the rats that escaped off the ships, they ate the eggs and the young. Some dodos were brought to Europe, but none survived. No dodos were reported after the departure of the Dutch in 1710.

In 1985 a local schoolmaster, George Clark excavated in a site close to the present airport in SE of the island, where a farmer had found skeletons preserved ina marsh. Enough bones were recovered to make up 2 complete dodo skeletons, one from the British Museum and the other for the Natural History Museum at the Mauritius Institute in Port Louis.

(*Phaethon lepturus* and *Paethon rubricauda*); the white pic-pic (*Zosterops borbonica*); and the red-whiskered bulbul (*Pycnonotus jocosus*).

Organisations such as the Mauritius Kestrel Conservation program (first started in 1973) and the Mauritius Wildlife Appeal Fund (now protecting the echo parakeet) are working to protect and encourage breeding of these rarer species.

Marine life

There is a huge variety of marine life in Mauritian waters and the coral gardens are among the best in the world, with good areas being off the S coast at Le Morne in the W and Blue Bay to the E. Particularly attractive specimens are the trumpet fish with its quick, agile swimming, and the boxfish with an unusual movement of its fins, similar to rowing.

The waters round the island are especially rich in molluscs. Among the prettiest that can be seen on the shores are cowries, of which there are over a hundred species; mitre shells, of which there are over 130 species; and 4 types of harp shell. A comprehensive collection of both rare and common shells is to be found at the Mauritius Institute Museum.

History

The earliest documented reference to Mauritius is to be found in early Arabic texts of the fourteenth century. As yet no archaeological findings have been uncovered to indicate the island was inhabited during that era. The first European, a Portuguese sailor by the name of Domingo Fernandez landed on the island in 1511. He named the island Ilha do Cirne (Island of the swan) but no settlement was established until 1638 when the Dutch founded Van Warwijk Haven (today Vieux Grand Port). The Dutch harvested the island's forest hardwoods, such as ebony, and introduced sugar cane. In 1658 they left the island, returned again in 1664 but in 1710 finally departed to concentrate their efforts on The Cape of Good Hope.

French Settlement

In 1715 the French claimed the islands

and a settlement was established in 1721. The island, known as Ile de France, was to be controlled by the Compagnie des Indes Orientales (French East India Company). In 1735, under Bertrand Francois Mahe de Labourdonnais the port facilities were expanded and the island's infrastructure developed. De Labourdonnais played a significant role in naval campaigns, harassing the shipping lanes to British India which passed through the area after rounding the Cape of Good Hope. However the governor of Pondicherry, Dupleix, accused him of collaborating with the British and he was sent to the Bastille.

As war continued so the islands reserves were plundered to support French naval campaigns. In 1763 the Island was sold to by the company to the French crown who made Pierre Poivre (of nursery rhyme fame for having picked a peck – a measure of volume equal to 9 litres – of pickled peppers) the first administrator of the islands in 1746. Poivre encouraged the spice trade, banned the felling of trees and passed laws improving the conditions of the island's slaves. The sugar cane industry grew steadily. With the advent of the French Revolution in mainland France the islanders dismissed their governor. Despite demands from France to outlaw slavery it persisted, and during this period the island enjoyed considerable autonomy. The British attacked in 1810 and, despite losing the naval battle at

The Battle Of Grand Port

In the early years of the nineteenth century, Captain Nesbit Willoughby harrassed the French on Ile de France (Mauritius) unmercifully. His classic manoeuvre was 'cutting out' – gliding into a harbour on a moonless night, overpowering the suprised crews of the French vessels and sailing the prizes out.

In Mar 1910 Willouhgby managed to attack and seize the fortified island, Ile du Passage, which guarded the approach through the reef to Grand Port. He then hoisted the French flag on the fort and on his own ship, the *Néréidé*. A flotilla of 5 French ships was lured in, running the gauntlet between the guns of the *Néréidé*, and the battery on the island. Four managed to battle through to the haven between Mahebourg and the old Dutch settlement at Vieux Grande Port. The fifth, *Windham* backed off to seek sanctuary in Black River. Willoughby gave chase, entered the river mouth in small boats, stormed the *Windham* and sailed back with their prize to Grand Port.

From 5pm on 22 Mar a mighty battle ensued, with the British making their assault against the well-protectd squadron in the port. Despite his unfavourable position, Willoughby risked everything in the attack. 2 of the British ships were hampered by running aground, and this restricted their ability to bring their guns to bear on the French. By 10pm that night, Willoughby's flagship, *Néréidé*, had been battered into submission, but darkness prevented the signal of their surrender, by lowering the colours, being noticed, and the bombardment continued. The last British ship hauled down its flag at 5pm the next day.

The French paid a high price for their victory with 36 killed and 112 wounded, but the British losses were appalling. One ship was destroyed by fire, 2 were blown apart when their magazines exploded, and the other 2, including the *Néréidé*, where taken by the French. The British losses were 105 killed and 169 wounded. The *Néréidé* suffered 92 killed and 137 wounded, out of a complement of 281 men, with Willoughby himself losing an eye.

Grand Port (see box) forced the French to retreat to Port Louis where they surrendered. The terms were generous, and the French were allowed to continue in agriculture, land-owning and trade as before, but under the British flag.

British Administration

In 1814 the Treaty of Paris was signed formally recognising the island and its dependencies (apart from Reunion which remained French) as British. The island was renamed Mauritius and remained British for 150 years. The domestic economy remained largely in the hands of French land-owners who had decided to stay on after the islands were ceded to Britain. Cheap labour and slavery remained until its abolition in 1835, after which freed slaves worked as paid labour, but not under noticeably improved conditions. The opening of the Suez Canal in 1869 meant significant amounts of traders heading E bypassed the islands. Sugar continued to be the mainstay of the economy.

In 1901 Gandhi visited the islands spreading his message of self awareness to the Indian community. Political activity grew during the early 1900s and came to a head in 1921 during the election campaign when there was pressure for the island to be returned to France. Universal suffrage was introduced in 1958.

By the 1960s the main political parties were established. The Mauritius Labour Party (MLP) drew support, in the main, by the Hindu community. The Parti Mauricien Sociale Democrate (PMSD) was supported by whites and Creoles. The Muslim Action Committee (CAM) was Muslim-based. After the first elections in 1959, the leader of the MLP, Seewoosagur Ramgoolam, became chief minister, though no party had an overall majority. Mauritius became officially independent on Mar 12 1968, with a coalition government under Ramgoolam as prime minister, while becoming a member of the Commonwealth.

Independence

In 1969 the PMDS and CAM joined forces to oppose a new party, the Mouvement Militant Mauricien (MMM). Growing unrest continued however and in 1971 a state of emergency was declared and some MMM members jailed. The 1972 elections were subsequently cancelled and later held in 1976 where the MMM gained 34 seats. In 1982 the MMM joined forces with the Parti Socialiste Mauricien (PSM) a splinter-group from the Labour party. Ramgoolam (the MLP leader) became governor general, and the leader of the PSM, Anerood Jugnauth became prime minister. In 1982 unsatisfied members of the MMM joined the PSM to form the Mouvement Socialiste Militant (MSM) and went on to win the 1983 elections under Jugnauth.

Despite the death of Ramgoolam and a heroin scandal involving 4 government deputies, MSM were successful again in 1991, with Cassam Utem, the new president.

Culture and life

People

Mauritians are representatives of a great many cultures. The descendants of the slaves and people of mixed background are usually referred to as Creoles, and make up about 28% of the total. Indo-Mauritians represent a little over 70%. Franco-Mauritians (French who have not inter-married), comprise 2% of the Island's population.

Religion

Hindus comprise 50% and Muslims make up around 17%. Most Muslims are Sunni but there some Shiites. Buddhism is followed by some Mauritians of Chinese origin. The rest are Christians and Creole followers of traditional religions.

Music and dance

Sega is a traditional dance of the Creole. It was originally performed by couples to the accompaniment of traditional string instruments and rhythmic drumming. The dance dates back to the days of slavery when there were only a few women. Each woman would partner several men, finally choosing one on the basis of his skill in the dance. Today the dance has been modernised with electric instruments, but still maintains its sensual characteristics. On Rodrigues Island it is still possible to see the *sega* danced to the music of traditional instruments. Some of the hotels present displays of *sega* dancing for tourists.

Teemeedee is a firewalking ceremony, and can be seen, from time to time, at Hindu temples through out the island. The participants prepare by fasting and ritual bathing, before walking on a bed of glowing charcoal embers. In other ceremonies, devotees will climb a ladder of swords.

Cavadee is a Hindu ceremony taking place in the early part of the year. The *cavadee* is a display of flowers and palm fronds with vessels of milk, which is carried in procession to the temple. Participants pierce their tongues and cheeks with needles, and try to ensure that the milk is delivered at the temple without going sour.

Chinese New Year is celebrated in Jan or Feb, and there are processions with ceremonial dragons, fireworks and decorations.

Paintings, in a wide range of local styles, are on display in the Max Boulle Gallery (Rose Hill) and Port Louis Art Gallery (on the corner of Malefille St and Poudriere St).

Literature is sponsored by the *Academie Mauricienne* at the Carnegie Institute in Curepipe, T 676 4042. Members have compiled collections of poems, memoirs and local stories. The most celebrated Mauritian literary figure was the poet Robert Edward Hart (1891-1954), who wrote in French. His home in Souillac (see page 815) has now become a museum.

Information on cultural events can be obtained from the *Mauritius Government Tourist Office* (MGTO), Emmanuel Anquetil Building, Sir S Ramgoolam St, Port Louis, T 201 1703, Tlx 4249. A leaflet with the programme of events is published by MGTO, and is available at most of the large hotels.

Modern Mauritius

Politics

Mauritius has a stable multiparty parliamentary democracy that is the envy of most developing countries. The Governor General's role is largely ceremonial, representing the British monarch who is Head of State. Efforts to make Mauritius a republic have not been successful.

The Legislative Assembly is based on the Westminster model, with a Speaker and 70 members. There a are 62 directly elected seats (3 for each of 20 constituencies in Mauritius Island and 2 for Rodgrigues). The remaining 8 seats go to the 'best losers' in the elections, a system designed to assist representation of minority groups.

Coalitions are the main feature of government. Despite the shifting alliances and continual intrigue, they have been highly successful in avoiding extreme policies and in bringing about the consensus that has been the foundation of the outstanding economic success of the country since independence.

Economics

Although a small country in terms of geographical size and population, and

SUGAR

Dutch settlers introduced sugar in 1639 from their colonies in the East Indies to the settlement at Vieux Grand Port on the S E coast. The first sugar factory was established at Villebague. Rollers, powered by windmills, slaves or oxen crushed the cane, and the juice (*molasses*) was boiled in vats using dried crushed cane stalks (*bagasse*) as fuel. As water was boiled off, the molasses became syrupy, and when cooled it crystallised into unrefined brown sugar.

A steam engine, with *bagasse* as fuel, was first used to drive a mill in 1822 at Quatre Cocos in Flacq. Thereafter the other forms of power were gradually phased out.

Governor Farquhar encouraged sugar production when the British took control in 1810. When the duty on Mauritian sugar was lifted in 1825, putting it on an equal footing with sugar from the Caribbean, there was a big expansion. By 1900, sugar production was at its peak with 250 sugar mills in operation, 90% of the land devoted to sugar cane, and the crop grown by both large estates and small farmers.

By 1960, the dependence of Mauritius on sugar was a matter of concern. Population was increasing, but the cultivated area could not be expanded. There were fears that sugar prices would steadily fall on world markets, and this added to the anxiety. Fortunately Mauritius had a well-educated, skilled, enterprising and thrifty population. This, in conjunction with encouragement to foreign investment, enabled the economy to establish a modern manufacturing sector, and this, together with tourism, has spearheaded the current economic success.

There are now only 19 sugar estates and mills, although there are still around 40,000 small growers. A restored mill of the early years can be visited in the Botanic Gardens at Pamplemousses (see page 806), and some of the remaining sugar estates can be toured (see page 817).

despite having only good beaches and no significant mineral resources, Mauritius has had an outstanding period of economic success since independence. Living standards have risen faster in Mauritius in the last thirty years than in any country in the world, with the single exception of mineral-rich Botswana. This has been achieved entirely by the skill and industry of her people.

Economic and social structure

Population in 1994 was just over a million, but with only 2 thousand square km of land, the population density was 555 a square kilometre, very high indeed, and a factor that caused despair in evaluating the economic prospects of Mauritius in the 1960s. Population growth is low at 1.0% a year, and the level of urbanisation at 41% is high in the African context. The urban population is growing at only 1.3% a year, and the impact of the population on society is well under control.

GDP in 1991 was estimated at US$ 2,253 mn, and despite the small population this makes the economy about average in size for East Africa. GNP per head was estimated at US$ 2,410 mn, which places Mauritius at the top end of the lower middle-income group of countries. Only Botswana, Gabon, Mayotte, South Africa and Seychelles in Africa have higher GNP per head.

Agriculture generated 11% of GDP in 1991, and this is fairly representative of countries in the lower middle-income group. Industry generates 33% of GDP, and the services sector 56%, and, again, this is reasonably typical of countries in the same income grouping as Mauritius.

On the demand side, consumption has comprises 65% of GDP, investment 28% and government consumption 12%. The investment ratio is higher and the government consumption ratio slightly lower than the average for lower middle-income countries.

The small size of the Mauritian economy demands that there be a heavy reliance on international markets. Exports represented 64% of GDP, and this is about triple the trade dependence of the average lower middle-income country. The main exports are manufactured (56%) and sugar (36%).

A survey in 1990 set the literacy rate at 85%. Primary enrolments were 106%, and secondary were 52% in 1990. These levels of educational provision are fairly representative of a lower middle-income country. The surprise is the provision of tertiary education, where enrolments are 2% of the relevant age group. Enrolments in lower-middle-income countries are typically around the 17% level.

Life expectancy in 1990 was 70 years. There was one physician in 1983 for every 1,900 people. Daily calorie supply was 25% above the minimum. These are among the best health and nutrition provisions in Africa, and better than the average for the lower middle-income group.

Overall, Mauritius is a small economy at the upper end of the lower middle-income group. It has a small agricultural sector by African standards, and relatively large industrial and services sectors. There is a heavy trade dependence, where manufactures are the main export. Educational provision, with the exception of the tertiary sector, and health delivery are as good as, or better than, countries in the same lower-middle-income group.

Economic performance

GDP grew at 6.7% a year in 1980-91, and a low rate of population growth at 1% a year allowed GNP per head to expand at 6.1% a year. This was the best performance in the world for this period apart from China.

All sectors grew impressively, with agriculture at 3.2% a year, expanding comfortably faster than the population. The main engine of growth has been the industrial sector, growing at 10.1% a year, and within industry, manufacturing has grown at 11.2% a year. The services sector has grown at 5.8% a year, and this is slower than the overall rate of expansion of the economy. These performance figures are significantly better than the average for the lower middle-income group of countries.

The performance of the trade sector has enabled the producing sectors to expand rapidly. Export volumes grew at 9.9% for the period 1980-91, and this places Mauritius among the top half-dozen countries in the world for 1980s export performance. Terms of trade have moved 4% in favour of Mauritius since 1980, and this, together with the export performance, has enabled import volumes to expand by 10.8% a year.

Inflation has averaged 8.1% in the period 1980-91, and this is a better price stability performance than most of Africa, and certainly for the lower middle-income group which contains several very high inflation South American economies. Good inflation performance has come about through low levels of government expenditure and a balance budget.

Overall, Mauritius has had an extremely good record of economic performance ranging across all sectors of the economy, with the export and manufacturing sector records being particularly good.

Recent economic developments

Mauritius was in receipt of 2 structural adjustment loans from the World Bank in 1981 and 1983, and in 1987 received US$ 61 mn in industrial sector adjustment loans. An IMF credit of US$ 58.2 mn expired in Aug 1986, and it is felt that the balance of payments is now strong enough not to require further IMF support. Economic policy has strengthened the reliance of Mauritius on market forces with the establishment of a successful export processing zone, considerable tariff cuts on imports and removal of sales tax. Growth of manufactured exports and tourism have been particularly strong features of good GDP performance. Inflation has steadily fallen since 1980 when prices rose by 42%. Merchandise imports have been greater than exports by some 20% or so

Comparative Economic And Social Data

	Mauritius	East Africa	Africa	Industrial countries
Population and land				
Population, mid year, millions, 1994	1.1	12.2	10.2	40.0
Urban population, %, 1985	41	30.5	30	75
Population growth rate, % per year, 1980-91	1.0	3.1	3.1	0.8
Land area, thou. sq. kilom.	2	486	486	1,628
Population density, persons per sq kilom., 1994	550	24.2	20.4	24.3
Economy: production and Income				
GDP, US$ millions, 1991	2,253	2,650	3,561	550,099
GNP per head, US$, 1991	2,410	250	389	12,960
Economy: supply structure				
Agriculture, % of GDP, 1991	11	43	35	3
Industry, % of GDP, 1991	33	15	27	35
Services, % of GDP, 1991	56	42	38	61
Economy: demand structure				
Private consumption, % of GDP, 1991	65	77	73	62
Gross domestic investment, % of GDP, 1991	28	16	16	21
Government consumption, % of GDP, 1991	12	15	14	17
Exports, % of GDP, 1991	64	16	23	17
Imports, % of GDP, 1991	69	24	26	17
Economy: performance				
GDP growth, % per year, 1980-91	6.7	1.6	-0.6	2.5
GDP per head growth, % per year, 1980-91	6.1	-1.7	-3.7	1.7
Agriculture growth, % per year, 1980-91	3.2	1.1	0.0	2.5
Industry growth, % per year, 1980-91	10.1	1.1	-1.0	2.5
Services growth, % per year, 1980-91	5.8	2.5	-0.5	2.6
Exports growth, % per year, 1980-91	9.9	0.7	-1.9	3.3
Imports growth, % per year, 1980-91	10.8	0.2	-6.9	4.3
Economy: other				
Inflation rate, % per year, 1980-91	8.1	23.6	16.7	5.3
Aid, net inflow, % of GDP, 1991	2.5	11.5	6.3	-
Debt service, % of exports, 1991	8.8	18	20.6	-
Budget surplus (+), deficit (-), 1991	0.0	-3.0	-2.8	-5.1
Education				
Primary, % of 6-11 group, 1990	106	62	76	102
Secondary, % of 12-17 group, 1990	52	15	22	93
Higher, % of 20-24 group, 1990	2	1.2	1.9	39
Adult literacy rate, %, 1990	86	41	39	99
Health & nutrition				
Life expectancy, years, 1990	70	50	50	76
Calorie supply, daily per head, 1987	2,897	2,111	2,096	3,357
Population per doctor, 1987	1,900	35,986	24,185	550

Notes: 'Africa' excludes South Africa. Dates are for the country in question, and do not always correspond with the Regional, African and Industrial averages.

in the 1980s. However, good export performance appears to have resulted in a balance of trade surpluses, and a balanced budget has been necessary to prevent foreign exchange earnings expanding the money supply. Imports were compressed by declining export revenues up to 1983, but thereafter have expanded as export earnings have increased. Mauritius had US$961 mn outstanding in external debts in 1991, and a ratio of debt service payments to export earnings for goods and services of 8.8%. Expanding export earnings have manged to make the debt service ratio quite manageable without rescheduling.The rupee has steadily depreciated since 1980 when it stood at MR 7.68 = US$1 to MR 18.4 = US$1 in 1994. This has served to encourage export performance.

The World Bank is lending US$30 mn for electricity and hydro-electricity schemes and a further US$30 mn for sugar sector rehabilitation. France and the EU are providing US$12 mn for roads, and Japan US$ 3.5 mn for fisheries. Saudi Arabia is lending US$2.3 mn for sewerage improvements, and the US is providing US$4.7 mn in wheat and rice shipments to compensate for falls in sugar earnings.

Foreign investment has been vigorous with the establishment of the export processing zone. Textiles have attracted commercial loans from the European Investment Bank and the World Bank's private sector lending arm, the International Finance Corporation of US$16.7 mn. Spectrum of the US has raised US$130 mn in commercial loans for 2 Boeing 767 aircraft for Air Mauritius; Malaysian business interests are reported to be investing US$50 mn in banking, hotels, garment manufacture and palm-oil processing; Speyside Electronics from the UK is setting up a factory; and Lonrho is establishing 6 industrial sites.

Economic outlook

There is every reason to expect Mauritius to maintain its high level of political stability, and for this to provide a sound foundation for continuing exceptionally good growth performance. This optimistic outlook can only be enhanced by the fact that the world economy now appears to be coming out of recession.

PORT LOUIS

In 1735 Labourdonnais transferred the capital to Port Louis where it has remained ever since and was named by the French after King Louis XV of France in 1772. In former times, Fort William and Fort George protected the harbour from possible invasion, but today these forts lie in ruins.

Currently the population is around 150,000. The commercial area of the town lies E of the Place d'Armes.

Places of interest

Mauritius Institute North end of Poudriere St, facing onto Company Gdns. (Opens at 0900-1600, and Sat 0900-1200. Closed Wed & Sun). There is no fee to enter; publications are on sale. Handsome library on first floor, with reference section and archives on Mauritius. Special lectures and exhibitions staged.

Natural History Museum Ground floor of Mauritius Institute, same opening hours. Exhibits include examples of extinct birds including the dodo, the Bourbon crested starling and numerous fauna still living today.

Company Gardens Intersection of Poudriere St and Chausse St. Built during Labourdonnais era and belonged to the French East India Company until 1765, today the property of the town (acquired in 1791). In the garden grounds several statues lie testament to prominent members of Mauritian society including poets, authors and journalists.

Theatre de Port Louis Corner of Sir William Newton and Seewoosagur Ramgoolam St, behind Government House. Originally built in 1822, a handsome building that has been carefully restored. Not much used for performances.

Merchant Navy Club Joseph Riviere St. Handsome colonial building of some style. Founded in 1857 as a sailors' hostel, is now a members club.

The Market Between Farquhar and Queen St, close to Sir William Newton St. (Open Mon-Fri 0500-1700 and Sat & Sun 0500-1200). Regularly burns down but always re-opens for business. Besides meat and fruit and vegetables you can also buy leather goods here (bargain).

Jummah Mosque At intersection of Queen St and Jummah Mosque St, middle of Port Louis Chinatown. The eighteenth century mosque is the largest on the island (open to non-Muslims 0930-1200 except Thu-Fri).

Fort Adelaide At S end of Jummah Mosque St. The fort was built by 1840 and named after Queen Adelaide, wife of William IV of England. There are often *son et lumière* displays here.

Champ de Mars Racecourse (Hippodrome) At the southern end of Pope Hennessy St. Racing season is from May-Oct. In the grounds is a statue of Edward VII (built by Prosper d'Epinay) and close by lies General Malartic's tomb (governor 1792-1800).

St Louis Catholic Cathedral (1929) is on Pope Hennessey St. The **Bishop's Palace** (1852) stands behind the Cathedral, a rather charming tropical building with verandahs.

Port Louis Historical Museum Open Mon-Fri 1000-1500, Sat 1000-1200. Entry free. Situated on Old Colonial St, this Creole building dates back to 1927 and houses old paintings, maps and letters. The heart of Robert Edward lies preserved in a jar.

Père Laval's Shrine Jaques Desire Laval graduated in medicine before becoming a missionary. He lived a very simple life, relentless in his work to help the poor and needy. He spent 23 years in Mauritius and in that time converted

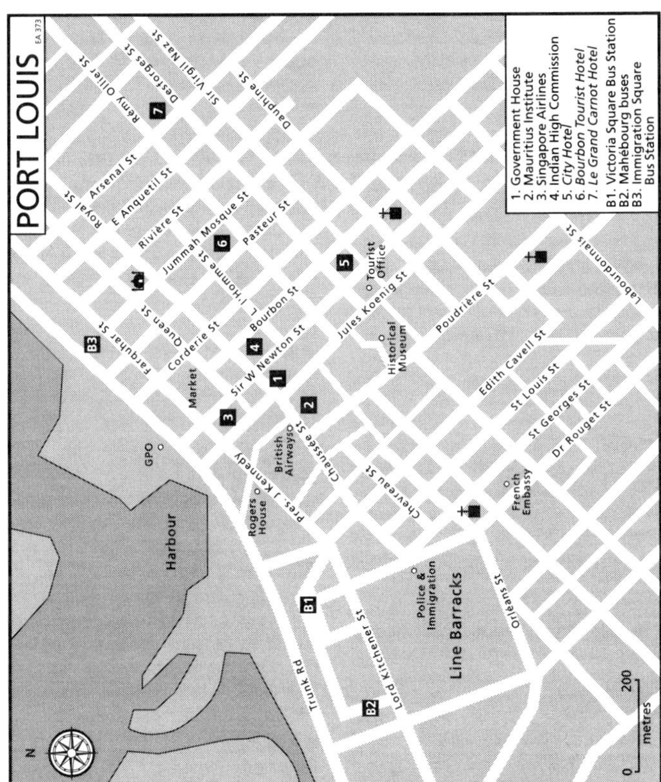

many to Christianity. He died in 1864 and is revered by Mauritians regardless of religion and in early Sep thousands of people make the pilgrimage to his grave at Ste Croix. Often those who visit the shrine pray that they might receive a miracle.

Local information

● Where to stay

B *City*, Sir Seewoosagur Ramgoolam St, near the Tourist Office, T 208 5340, Tlx 4405. Most comfortable hotel in city centre.

C *Palais d'Or*, Jummah Mosque St, T 242 5231. All rooms a/c. **C** *Moderne*, 36 Joseph Riviere St, T 240 2382. Includes breakfast. **C** *Bourbon Tourist*, Jummah Mosque St, T 240 4407. Bar. Good restaurant. A/c in some rooms. Own bathroom. Good value. **C** *Le Grand Carnot*, 17 Dr Edouard Laurent St, T 240 3054. Includes breakfast. Quiet area. **C** *Le Rossignol*, Jules Koenig St, T 212 1983. Includes breakfast. Some rooms have balconies. Good value. **C** *National*, Pope Hennessy St, T 242 0453. Oldest hotel in Port Louis (1925), and little changed by the passage of time.

D *Tandoori Tourist*, Victoria Sq, near bus station, T 212 2131. Good restaurant. Own bathroom. Noisy, but otherwise good value. **D** *France Tourist*, Joseph Riviere St. Reasonably central. Bar on first floor verandah. Sound.

● Places to eat

Le Carri Poule, Place d'Armes. Serves Creole and Indian cuisine. Open to 2400. Closed Sun. High standard. ♦♦♦♦*La Flore Mauricienne*, Intendance St near Parliament House. French and Creole food. Well-run establishment. Separate self-service section. Smart cafe on street. ♦♦♦♦*Lai Min*, Royal St. Chinese cuisine. Good standard. A/c. Takeaway service on ground floor.

♦♦♦*Cordon Bleu*, Farquar St. Open 0900-1730. International menu. ♦♦♦*La Bonne Marmite*, Sir William Newton St. Open only for lunch. Closed weekends. Well run and smart. Also cafe on ground floor. ♦♦♦*La Flore Orientale*, Sir S Ramgoolam St. First floor. Pleasant location. Asian food, with French flavour. ♦♦♦*Nobby's Paddock*, Edith Cavell St. International food, mostly grills. Closes 1730, open later on race days. ♦♦♦*La Palmeraie*, Sir C Antelme St. Lunches only. French cuisine. Good atmosphere in a covered courtyard. ♦♦♦*La Partrimoine*, on Rue Labourdonnais, Indian and Creole. Open 1000 to 2200. Closed Mon. ♦♦♦*Palais d'Or*, Jummah Mosque St T 242 5231. Chinese food. Quite lively. ♦♦♦*Shamrock*, Corner Royal St and Corderie St. 1100-2100. Mostly Chinese, but does serve other dishes. Pleasant location. ♦♦♦*Snow White*, corner Queen St and Sir William Newton St. Chinese and International menu. Neat and well-run.

♦♦*Tandoori Restaurant*, Victoria Sq. Near bus station. T 212 213. Open to 2000. Good standard with varied menu. Comfortable atmosphere. ♦♦*Cambuse*, St George St. Local food in pleasant patio surroundings. ♦♦*Le Ciel Bleu*, J Riviere St. Simple cuisine, rather spartan atmosphere. ♦♦*Kwang Chow*, corner Queen St and Emmanuel Anquetil St. Sound Chinese food. ♦♦*National*, Pope Hennessy St. Chinese food, plus some international dishes. Only open lunchtime. Unique atmosphere of 1930s Mauritius. ♦♦*Paloma*, L'Homme St. 1100-2000. Chinese food. Old style establishment. ♦♦*The Underground*, Bourbon St. Good value. International menu. ♦♦*Luxor Palace*, Edith Cavill St. Local food. Good value. ♦♦*Champs Elysée*, Victoria Sq. Varied menu. Good value. ♦♦*Chez Kayoum Snack Bar*, Church St. ♦♦*Foong Shing Remy*, Ollier St.

♦*Moontaza*, Victoria Sq. Simple Indian-style meals. ♦*Namaste*, Intersection Farquhar St and Louis Pasteur St. Simple but good value. Lunches only. ♦*ONU*, Royal St. Lively establishment. ♦*The Providence*, Sir S Ramgoolam St. Varied menu. Stays open late. ♦*The Taj*, Sir William Newton St. Indian style.

● Airline offices

Air France, Rogers House, 5 President Kennedy St, T 208 6801. **Air India**, Rogers House, 5 President Kennedy St, T 208 3739. **Air Madagascar**, Rogers House, 5 President Kennedy St, T 208 6801. **Air Mauritius**, PO Box 441, Rogers House, 5 President Kennedy St, T 208 7700, Tlx 4415. **British Airways**, Chaussée St, T 208 5411. **Cathay Pacific**, Chaussée St. **Lufthansa**, 18 Edith Cavell St, T 208 0861. **Singapore Airlines**, 5 Duke of Edinburgh Ave, T 208 68012. **South African Airways**, Rogers House, 5 President Kennedy St, T 208 6801. **Zambia Airways**, 18 Edith Cavell, St T 208 0861.

● Banks

Barclays Bank, Queens St, T 208 2801. **Mauritius Commercial Bank**, on Royal St, T 208 2801. Hours 1000-1400 Mon-Fri; 0930-1130 on Sat.

American Express Representative is **Mauritius Travel & Tourist Bureau**, T 208 2041, Tlx 4338, on the corner of Sir William Newton Street and Royal St.

● Bars

ONU Bar, Royal St. Classic waterfront style. *Jolie Madame Bar*, corner of Suffren and Churchill St. Serves snacks. *Tan Yan Bar*, Farquar St. Busy area. Fairly basic. *Rocking Boat Pub*, L'Homme St. English style. Closes at 1600. *Chez Ah Nee*, Victoria Sq. Serves some food.

● Bookshops

Librairie du Trèfle, Royal St. New books and books on Mauritius. *Librairie Bourbon*, Rue Bourbon. Secondhand books.

● Cinema

Rex, Sir Seewoosagur Ramgoolam St. *Luna Park*, John Pope Hennessy St. *Majestic*, Poudriere St.

● Curios and crafts

Emporium d'Art, Royal St. Has good selection of local craft work, including model ships and minature reproductions of the colonoila houses of Mauritius. *L'Argonaute*, Sir William Newton St. Decorative sea-shells, coral, shark-tooth jewellery, tortoiseshell ware.

● Gambling

L'Amicale Chinese Gaming House, corner of Royal St and Joseph Riviere St. Open 1900-0200 Mon-Fri. 1300-0200 Sun. Only Chinese games.

Lady Gomm And The Penny Red

Mauritius was the first British colony to issue its own postage stamps, in 1847. A postal service had been in operation since 1811, soon after the British take-over, but British stamps had been used up till then.

The first 1,000 stamps were printed by a local watch-maker, Joseph Barnard in Port Louis. He engraved a couple of copper dies, inked them up by hand and printed the stamps one at a time, 500 at a penny, in red, for internal mail, and 500, at tuppence, in blue for overseas. By mistake he engraved 'Post Office' on this first batch instead of 'Post Paid'. The unsold faulty stamps were withdrawn, and the mistake corrected for the subsequent printings.

However, Lady Gomm, wife of the governor, had bought a big batch of the penny-red stamps to send invitations to a grand ball at the governor's mansion, Le Reduit. As a result, many of the faulty stamps got into circulation, and many recipients of invitations kept them in their envelopes as souvenirs of the ball. Quite a few of the overseas stamps, as they were a novelty, were also kept.

Of the thousand printed, 15 penny-reds and 12 tuppenny blue survive. They are worth over US$200,000 each.

● Hospital

Jeetoo Hospital, Volcy Pougnet St, Port Louis, T 212 3201.

● Post Office

The main office is located at the harbour end of Sir William Newton St (opening hrs of post offices Mon-Fri 0800-1115 and 1200-1600, Sat 0800-1145).

● Religion

The main Islamic centre is **Jummah Mosque**, just to the E of the city centre, at the intersection of Jummah Mosque St and Royal St. **St Louis Cathedral**, (Catholic), is off Dauphine St, and **St James Cathedral**, (Anglican), is at the southern end of Poudrie St.

● Theatre

Theatre de Port Louis, corner of Sir William Newton and Seewoosagur Ramgoolam St, behind Government House. Irregular performances.

● Travel and tour agents

Air International Travel and Tours, Georges St, T 208 0101. *Atlas Travel Services*, Sir S Rangoolam St, T 208 5555, Tlx 4277. *Atom Travel Agency*, 22 Royal St, T 208 0164, Tlx 43352. *Budget Holidays*, 42 Edith Cavell St, T 212 5486, Tlx 4353. *Chinese Travel Agency*, 6 Jummah Mosque St, T 208 0196. *Concorde Travel and Tours*, La Chaussée, T 208 5041, Tlx 4305. *Mauritius Air Travel and Tours Agency*, Sir S Ramgoolam St, T 202 5026, Tlx 4593. *Mauritius Travel and Tourist Bureau (MTTB)*, Royal St, T 208 2041, Tlx 4338. *MauriTours*, 10 Sir William Newton St, T 208 5241/121 4712, Tlx 4349/4650/4279. *Silver Wings Travel*, 21 Louis Pasteur St, T 2026405, Tlx 4228. *Skyline Travel and Tours*, 3 Eugene Laurent St, T208 5038, Tlx 4553. *Stella Travel Agents*, 17 Bourbon St, T 208 0259, Tlx 4325. *Sun Travel & Tours*, 2 St Georges St, T 202 1639. *White Sand Travel*, La Chaussée, T 202 3712, Tlx 4217.

● Tourist Information

Mauritius Government Tourist Office **(MGTO)**, Emmanuel Anquetil Building, Sir S Ramgoolam St, Port Louis, T 201 1703, Tlx 4249.

● Transport

Air Airport An express bus goes to Mahebourg from Port Louis; it will drop you off at the Airport (service ends early evening, 2hr journey). Otherwise use taxi.

Road Southern and Western destinations (Rose Hill, Curepipe and the plateau towns) leave from Victoria Square terminus. **North or eastern**, destinations from Immigration Square. **Baie du Tombeau**, Ste Croix and northern parts of town from Labourdonnais Square terminus. **Pointe aux Sables**, leave from Dumas St near Victoria square.

AROUND THE ISLAND

NORTH TO CAP MALHEUREUX

The North is split into 2 districts, **Pamplemousse** which encompasses the northern suburbs of Port Louis and goes on to cover NW Mauritius, and **Rivière du Rempart** which covers NE Mauritius. Pamplemousse has plenty of fine beaches and therefore benefits a great deal from tourism. In the NW on the other hand the beaches are less good.

Baie du Tombeau

This resort in Pamplemousse district is about 10 km N of Port Louis. The bay has been responsible for a great many shipwrecks. The first victims were a Dutch convoy in 1615. Numerous dives in 1980 brought up a large haul of finely preserved porcelain dating back to 1518. The area attracts treasure seekers though little has been found since.

• **Where to stay** **A** *Corotel*, T 247 2355. Private balconies. Includes breakfast. **B** *Le Cactus*, T 2472485. Own bathroom. Friendly atmosphere. **B** *Baie des Cocotiers*, T 247 2442/62, F 247 2463. Self-catering. **B** *Arc en Ciel*, T 247 2616/7. Inclusive of breakfast. Disco. **C** *Pension Cheval du Mer*, T 263 8433. Includes breakfast. Comfortable. **C** *Le Capri*, T 247 2533. Good value. Capricorn Disco on Sat. **B** *Arc en Ciel*, T 247 2616/7. Inclusive of breakfast. Disco.

Pamplemousse

Close to Port Louis, 11 km to the NE, the location is named after the orchards of shaddock trees, producing a fruit known as *pampelmoes*, rather like a grapefruit, growing up to 10 kilos in weight, which were introduced here from Java by the Dutch.

Royal Botanic Gardens The site was established by a French settler in 1729 and named Mon Plaisir. It was bought in 1735 by Governor Mahe de Labourdonnais who built his residence here and began developing the gardens, particularly with plants from Europe. The property was later sold to the French East India company but in 1770 Pierre Poivre, the island's Administrator acquired the property and created botanical gardens in the grounds. When the British took control of the island in 1810, the gardens were taken over by the government. A period of neglect followed until James Duncan was appointed Director from 1849 to 1864. Duncan consolidated the gardens, and, in particular, established the Royal Palms along the main avenue. The gardens are open every day, 0600-1800. It is possible to drive round except on Sundays, although a more graceful mode is a bicycle rickshaw that takes 2 and can be hired for US$3 an hour.

Chateau Mon Plaisir is not the former home of Labourdonnais, but was built by the British some time later. The first Prime Minister and later Governor General, Sir Seewoosagur Ramgoolam, was cremated here. It is not currently open to the public. The **Old Sugar Mill** nearby is a reproduction. The **Church of St François** dates from 1759, and is the oldest place of worship in Mauritius. The churchyard contains the tombs of several prominent Mauritians.

• **Hospital** *Sir Sewoosagur Ramgoolam National Hospital*, T 264 1661.

• **Transport** Buses from Immigration Square for Grand Gaube and several other NE destinations pass through Pamplemousse.

Baie aux Tortues

The tortoises, after which the bay is named, are few. Baie de L'Arsenal, a secluded cove, lies N of Baie du Tombeau, near Balaclava (Creole for 'black lava'). The ruins of the French **Arsenal** now lie in the grounds of *Hotel Maritim*, they can be visited – ask at the hotel.

• **Where to stay** **A+** *Maritim*, T 2615600, F 261 6749. Very luxurious. The hotel is on an excellent beach. **A+** *Hyatt Regency*, T 261 5757, F 2615709.

Trou Aux Biches

Luxurious resort area, about 20 km N of Port Louis. The name does not translate very well, being literally the 'hole of the does', that is, the drinking pool of the female deer. The beach is excellent, there is a golf course close by, and some of the beaches are public.

• **Where to stay** **A+** *Trou aux Biches Village*, T 2616562/63, F 261 66111. Luxurious. Golf course and casino. **A+** *PLM Azur*, just N toward Pointe aux Canonniers. T 261 6070, F 261 6749. Luxurious. Range of water sports. Squash courts. **A** *Mon Choisy Villas*, just N toward Pointe aux Canonniers. T 2638771. A/c Some studio rooms. Rather expensive for the facilities available. **A** *Casuarina Village*, T 261 5653/54/55, F 261 6111. Some self-catering bungalow accommodation. Pool. Tennis. Beach across the road. **B** *Residence C'est Ici*, T 261 7380. Bungalow-style with some self-catering. **B** *Etoile de Mer*, T 2616561. Close to the aquarium. Some self-catering. Outdoor restaurant. **B** *Rhapsodie*, T263 8771, F 263 8274. Apartment-style accommodation. **C** *Aquamarine*, T261 6923. Some self-catering. Good value. **C** *Le Grande Bleu*, T 261 5812/13. Some self-catering. Some rooms a/c. Restaurant. **C** *La Sirene*, T 261 6026. Small, close to the beach. Good value.

• **Places to eat** ♦♦♦♦*La Lagon Bleu*, French cuisine, to a high standard. ♦♦♦♦*Le Pescatore*, good quality seafood. ♦♦♦*Le Corsaire*, mainly French, but also serves international dishes. ♦♦♦*Lagoona*, opposite La Sirene, French cuisine and seafood. ♦♦♦*L'Exotique*, Creole and European food. ♦♦*Alambik*, above grocery store, opposite Aquarium. Chinese food. Reasonable.

• **Transport** Bus leaves from Immigration Sq, Port Louis (bus to Malheureux). Takes a little over half an hour, last bus back 1840.

Point Canonniers

This promontory gets its name from the fact that an artillery battery was positioned here to cover the entrance to Grand Baie.

• **Where to stay** **A+** *Le Cannonier*, T 263 7999, F 263 7864. Luxury hotel. Bar/disco on beach. **A** *Le Colonial Coconut*, T 263 8720, F 263 7116. New, and well appointed. **B** *Sea Breeze Apartments*, T 208 7449. 2 room apartments. **C** *Sea Point Bungalows*, T 696 4804, F 686 7380. On beach, bungalow-style. Some self-catering. *Club Mediterranée*, T 263 8509. Allows day visitors. Attractive botanical gardens. Nightclub, floor shows and disco. Advisable to telephone – the establishment caters primarily for package tourists from Europe.

• **Places to eat** ♦♦♦♦*Le Bateau Ivre*. Seafood. High standard. ♦♦♦*Palais Orient* Chinese cuisine. Reasonable. ♦♦♦*Trattoria Azzurra*, Italian food. Relaxed atmosphere.

Grand Baie

Very popular tourist resort area, particularly for local people, in the Rivière de Rempart district. There are plenty of hotels, restaurants, and beach activities. The atmosphere is relaxed, however. Nearby **Pereybere** is quieter and less developed, and often visited by those staying at Grand Baie who want more seclusion. Excursions can be arranged to the islands of **Coin de Mire** and **Ile Plate** off Cap Malheureux. *Grand Baie News* is a weekly sheet with a host of information on amenities and events in the area, and is available at all the main hotels and at Grand Baie Travel & Tours (see below). Yachts can be chartered for the day, you can join a cruise, or arrange deep-sea fishing (again see Grand Baie Travel & Tours, see page 808).

Local information

● Where to stay

A+ *Royal Palm*, T 263 8353, F 263 8455. Luxurious. Although built in 1895, the style is colonial and the atmosphere opulent. Part of Beachcomber group. **A+** *Merville Beach*, T 263 8621, F 263 8146. Metropole group. All facilities of a high standard. **A+** *Pullman*, T 263 7800/7810, F 263 7888. High-class hotel. **A** *Verandah Bungalow Village*, T 263 8015/6, F 263 7369. Some self-catering, studios. Pleasant surroundings, in the style of a Creole village. **B** *Les Orchidees*, good value in this category. **C** *Auberge Ile de France*, T 263

85433. Centre of town. Colonial style atmosphere. **C** *Auberge Miko*, T 263 7048. Near Les Orchidees. Good value. **C** *Les Palmiers*, T 263 8464. Just back from the main beach road. Apartments, self-catering. Some studios. **C** *Paradis de l'Ocean*, apartments, self-catering. **C** *Sunny Bay*, T 263 7434, F 263 7434. Self-catering. **C** *La Residence*, T 240 4774. Self-catering. Good value. **D** *Villa Floralies*, T 263 8269. Self-catering Good value for shared rooms. **D** *La Terrasse*, right by the fish market, on esplanade.

Self-catering apartments Widely available in the area, and an economical option for longer stays or family groups. It is possible for a family of 4 to rent an apartment for around US$30 a day. *Grand Baie Travel & Tours* (GBTT), Royal Rd, T 2638273, F 2638274, act as agents for flats and apartments to rent around the area.

● **Places to eat**
♦♦♦♦*Sakura*, Japanese food. Nothing special, but caters to particular market. ♦♦♦*Assiette*, Chinese food. Good standard. ♦♦♦*Le Grillon*, mostly seafood, but other grills also served. ♦♦♦*La Mediterranée*, seafood to quite good standard. ♦♦♦*La Charette*, mainly Indian food, but some international dishes. ♦♦♦*Le Capitaine*, Indian food. Reasonable standard ♦♦*L'Esplanade*, pizzas, crepes and seafood. ♦♦*La Jonque*, Chinese food. ♦♦*Le Tamarinier*, Creole food. ♦♦*Veranda*, Creole food. Good value. ♦*Chez Patty Patisserie*.

● **Banks**
Mauritius Commercial Bank, Esplanade near Grand Baie Stores. Open for foreign exchange dealings Mon-Sat 0800-1800, Sun 0900-1200 and 1230-1430. **Barclays Bank**, Esplanade, near fish market. 1000-1400 Mon-Sat, 0930-1130 Sat. The large hotels will change travellers' cheques 24 hours a day, but at a rather unfavourable rate.

● **Nightlife**
The main hotels offer live bands and floorshows. *Eden Disco*, is on the road that runs back from the shore next to *Auberge Ile de France* in the centre of town. *Number One*, disco is close to the fish market on the esplanade.

● **Shopping**
Grand Bay Stores, in the centre of town has a wide selection of goods. *Librairie Papyrus*, Bookshop with local and foreign newspapers. *Galerie Helene de Senneville*, has a range of good quality local craft. *La Gallerie des Matieres d'Art*, Run by National Handicrafts Centre, and is good value.

● **Tour operator and travel agent**
Grand Baie Travel & Tours (GBTT) Royal Rd, centre of town, near road to Goodlands. T 263 8273, F 263 8274. Act as agents for flats and apartments to rent around the area. Boat trips can be arranged to the nearby islands of Coin de Mire and Ile Plate. Yacht charter, cruises, deep-sea fishing. Bicycle, motor-bike and car hire.

● **Transport**
Local Car hire Beach Car, T 263 8759. **Grand Baie Contract Cars**, T 26385664. **Avis**, T 263 7600 and **Europcar**, T 2637948. It is possible to hire an older car cheaply – most small restaurants or garages will know someone who will arrange things. **Motorcycle hire** *Charette Restaurant* (US$10 a day). **Bicycle hire** *Charette Restaurant*, near fish market. **Grand Bay Yacht Club**, further round bay to the N, near *Pullman Hotel*, (US$2 a day).

Road Bus going to Cap Malheureux leaves Immigration square, Port Louis frequently, costs US$0.25, takes close to an hour, stops elsewhere on route. A taxi from Port Louis will cost US$7.

Pereybere

About 2 km further N from Grand Baie. Quiet bay located between 2 promontories, Pointe d'Eglise and Point d'Azur. A rather less expensive place to stay than Grand Baie. **Vieux Moulin** is the site of an old windmill, with the Flowers of the World gift shop located there, specialising in designs made out of fresh and dried blooms.

● **Where to stay** **A** *Villa-Francia*, T 423 7134 (UK Rep: Mr S Appiah T 071 281 0033/081 889 7589). Self-catering villa, three bedrooms, lounge, TV, fridge etc. Five minutes walk from beach. **C** *Jolicoeur Guest House*, T 263 8202. Off road that runs back from the esplanade close to Pointe d'Eglise. Good value and popular. **C** *Casa Florida*, T 263 7371, F 4547336. Off road that runs back from the esplanade, close to Pointe d'Eglise. Bungalow-style. Some self-catering. **C** *Krissy's Apartments*, T 263 8859. Self-catering. A/c. **C** *Fred's Apartments*, T 263 8830, F 263 8830. Off road that runs back from the esplanade, close to Pointe d'Eglise. Self-catering. **C** *Pereybere Beach Apartments*, T 263 8679. Central location. **C** *Etoile du Nord*, T 263 8303. Well located in the centre of the bay. **C** *Sylvilla Pension*, T 263 8303. Studios and apartments. A little noisy. **C** *Motel Panarama*, T 263 8641/2. Comfortable, but unprepossessing.

Excursions and car, motorcycle, bicycle hire through *Etoile du Nord*, T 263 8303. in centre of bay.

● **Places to eat** ♦♦♦*La Sapinière*, good location overlooking bay. Mainly Chinese, but some international dishes. Cocktail bar. ♦♦*Cafe Pereybere*, opposite Pointe d'Eglise. Mainly Chinese. Good value. ♦♦*Cafeteria Pereybere*, beach side of main road. Mainly Chinese.

● **Transport** Bus going to Cap Malheureux leaves Immigration square, Port Louis frequently, costs US$0.30, takes just over an hour, stops elsewhere on route. A taxi from Port Louis will cost US$9.

Cap Malheureux

This is the most northerly point on the main island, about 22 km from Port Louis. The **Notre Dame Trice** Roman Catholic church is located close to the shore. Grand Gaube is close by the church of St Michel, to which pilgrimages are made.

The Islands of **Coin de Mire** (or Gunner's Quoin – named after the wedge used to alter the elevation of canons), **Ile Plate** (Flat Island), **Ile Ronde** (Round Island) and **Ile aux Serpents** (Serpent Island, sometimes known as Parasol Island – a bird sanctuary, and uninhabited) can all be visited.

● **Where to stay** **A+** *La Maison*, T 263 8974, F 263 7009. Very pleasant, has 5 rooms on the waterfront, car and yacht available as well. **A** *Kuxville Beach Cottages*, T 263 7913/263 8836. Roughly 1.5 km from the Cap. Apartments, bungalows and studios. No restaurant. No a/c. Well liked by regular visitors from Europe. Good value for 3 persons in a double room with an extra bed. **B** *Les Mascareignes*, T 263 7373/74, F 263 7372. 2 km from Cap. Good value. **B** *Coin de Mire Village*, T 263 7302/04, F 212 1361. Attractive surroundings. Studios and apartments. Italian restaurant. More luxurious suites available.

● **Places to eat** ♦♦*Le Coin de Mire*, Chinese and Creole food.

Grande Gaube

About 6 km SE of Cap Malheureux. The Creole for bay is *gaube*. Quite a pleasant location, but rather quiet. Inland some 5 km is the industrial town of Goodlands.

● **Where to stay** **A+** *Le Grand Gaube*, T 283 9350, F 283 9420. Pleasant location. **A** *Island View Club*, T 283 9544, F 283 9233. Bungalows. Swimming pool. **B** *Archipel Bungalows*, T 242 1271/72/73, F 208 1035.

● **Places to eat** *The Nomad*, Italian, Middle Eastern and Creole food.

● **Transport** Buses from Immigration Square, Port Louis.

Poudre d'Or

A beach area about 7 km to the S of Grand Gaube. A monument, erected in 1944, commemorates those who died in 1744 in the *St Geran*, which foundered off this coast. The shipwreck inspired Bernardin de St Pierre's love story, *Paul et Virginie*.

Visits to the uninhabited islands of **Ile d'Ambre** and **Ile Bernache** can be organised; ask at the Poudre d'or police station.

● **Transport** Buses from Immigration Square, Port Louis.

CENTRAL: MOKA AND PLAINES WILHEMS

This area covers the districts of Moka and Plaines Wilhelms. **Moka** is best known for being the academic centre of Mauritius, but is also includes the rather bleak centre of the island. **Plaines Wilhelms** contains a group of towns that are the main urban concentration on the island, and more than a third of the population live there. The 20 km from Port Louis to Curepipe is quite heavily built-up, and the main original towns, Beau Bassin, Rose Hill, Quatre Bornes have merged into one complex and Phoenix, Floreal, Vacoas and Curepipe into another.

Moka

Situated just 12 km S of port Louis, Moka with a population of 55,000 is the home of the main institutions of higher learning in Mauritius, and some historic buildings. The countryside is pleasant around Moka with neatly cultivated tea plantations, and Piton du Mileau, a craggy peak.

Places of interest

University of Mauritius Located close to the Governor's residence, Le Reduit. It is centred on the College of Agriculture established in 1928. At that time Mauritius relied heavily on sugar production for its exports. In 1965 it became a fully-fledged University, with a wide range of subjects now offered, although its size (1,500 students) is quite small. The **Mahatma Gandhi Institute** is a specialised centre covering African and Indian studies, as Mauritius sees itself as mid-way between the 2 continents. Mahatma Gandhi embraced the 2 cultures, having been born in India and worked in South Africa. Gandhi visited Mauritius in 1901.

Le Reduit was begun in 1748, initially as a stronghold for French officials in the event of the island being invaded. It was extended later, and from 1788 became an official residence of the Governor. It was from here in 1874 that the English governor's wife, Lady Gomm, sent invitations to a ball using the famous Blue Stamp (see Box, page 805). Visitors are allowed to the extensive gardens 0930-1200 Mon-Sat. The house is only open to visitors for a few days each year.

Eureka Creole House A two-storey house which is now a museum, built in 1830. In 1856 it was bought at an auction by Eugene Leclezio who cried 'Eureka' and so it was named. In 1986 it became a museum and has many colonial antiquities and artefacts. The house is open to visitors Mon-Sat 0900-1200 and 0900-1200 on public holidays. Lunch is available if you book in advance. T 433 4951.

Domaine Les Pailles This is an historical reconstruction. There is a working replica sugar mill with cane brought in by oxcart. Organised tours are available, and it is possible to go horse-riding.

Travelling 12 km E from Moka there is the **Quartier Militaire**, a post that was strategically based in the centre of the island, partly to provide refuge against the attacks from the community of escaped slaves (*marron*). It is possible, though difficult, to climb the rocky **Pieton du Milieu** peak (585m). The track to the summit leaves from the pumping station at the Pieton du Mileau Reservoir.

Local information

● Where to stay

There are no hotels in Moka, and most visitors stay in nearby (4 km away) Quatre Bornes (see below).

● Places to eat

♦♦♦♦*Cannelle Rouge*, Clo St Louis, here it may be necessary to book in advance. ♦♦♦*Le Lodge*, International menu. ♦♦♦♦*Le Pavillion des Guibies*, French cuisine. Good standard.

● Entertainment

Le Jazz Club des Ecuries du Domaine, T 208 1998. Jazz every Fri at 2100.

● Transport

Road Bus to Curepipe from Port Louis along the M2 motorway. Fare from Port Louis US$0.30.

Quatre Bornes

Beau Bassin town is largely made up of official institutions, though the **Balfour Gardens**, with a waterfall, provide the visitor with a pleasant site to walk around (open 1000-1800 except Wed). **La Tour Blanche** is a stylish house near the Gardens, in which Charles Darwin stayed during his visit in 1836. Rose Hill, close by, has the **Max Moutia Museum**, **Max Boulle Art Gallery** and **Plaza Theatre**, with an ornately decorated interior. The **British Council** with library and offices is nearby. Quatre Bornes has a **Hindu Temple** at the base of Corps de Garde mountain, and an open market on Wed and Sat.

Local information

● Where to stay

A *Gold Crest*, T 454 5945, F 454 9599. Suites available. Good standard hotel. **B** *El Monaco*, T 425 2608, F 425 1072. Popular hotel with garden. **B** *The Garden House*, T 424 1214, F 4241214. Good standard guest house. **B** *Riverside*, T 464 4957, F 464 5553. Old hotel with some character. **D** *Auberge de Quatre Bornes*, T 424 2163. Shared bathrooms. **D** *Le Gibier*, T 424 6072. Shared bathrooms. Straightforward, but good value.

● Places to eat

♦♦♦♦*Restaurant Ah Fat*, Chinese cuisine. Good standard, rec. ♦♦♦♦*Blue Mauritius*, Commercial Centre, Rosehill. 1100-0100 Closed Thu. Night-club/restaurant. ♦♦♦*Rolly's Steak House*, St Jean Rd, Quatre Bornes. Closed Mon. ♦♦♦*Mandarin*, Royal Rd, Vacoas. *Green Dragon*, on 2nd floor of Palladium disco at Trianon. Closed Mon. ♦♦*Govinda*, Vegetarian. St Jean Rd, Quatre Bornes. Closed Tue.

● Travel and tour agents

Mauritours, 5 Venkatasananda St, Rose Hill T 4541666, Tlx 4349/4560 and St Jean Rd. Quatre Bornes T 424 7034/5, Tlx 4349/4560.

● Transport

Buses from Victoria Sq bus station in **Port Louis**. Bus station in **Rose Hill**, at Margeot Sq; in **Quatre Bornes** at Jules Koenig Sq. Fare to Port Louis US$0.40.

Curepipe

Phoenix, to the E on the the route S from Port Louis, houses a lot of industrial companies with the **Labourers' Quarters** at Trianon, protected buildings, and an interesting example of early housing for migrant labour.

Vacoas is a mainly residential area, with some horticultural production. It is named after the pandanus screw-pines from Malaysia that grew in the district.

Floreal was established during the period of Governor Hesketh Bell 1916-1924. It is a residential and diplomatic district, with large houses set in extensive gardens. Several embassies are located here.

Curepipe The name means pipe cleaner – it is said early travellers stopped here to scrape out their pipes and to have a smoke. It is the centre of the tea and model boat industries. The **Town Hall** on Elizabeth Ave is a colonial building dating from 1902. There are some gardens and a lake, with a **Statue of Paul and Virginie**, and the **Carnegie Library**. One attraction is the crater of **Trou aux Cerfs** (605m), which is quite deep, and the crater floor is covered in woodland. The **Sir Seewoosagur Ramgoolam Botanical Gardens** are S of the crater. The gardens are small, with a lake and well maintained. The making of replica sailing vessels is a speciality of Mauritius, and a workshop that can be visited, **Voilers de l'Ocean Model Ships**, is in Sir Celicourt Antelme St, Cuerepipe, S of the town centre.

SW of Curepipe, about 6 km away, is the reservoir **Mare au Vacaos**. It is possible to ascend to the top of the dam, and to view the sluice gates. There is another reservoir, Marie Longeue just over 2 km W, and it can be reached along a track through attractive countryside. On the road from Curepipe to Marie au Vacuos, at La Marie is the **Matthew Flinders Memorial**. A third reservoir, **Tamarind Falls** can be reached 5 km along a turnoff from the B3 road going S from Vacaos, but permission to visit must be obtained from the Forestry Department. There are 7 waterfalls from the reservoir.

Local information

● Where to stay

A *The Continental*, Sir Winston Churchill St, T 675 3434. A/c. Suites are available. Fairly new. **C** *The Shanghai*, Sir Winston Churchill St, T 676 1965. Own bathrooms. **C** *Hong Kong*, Elizabeth Ave, T 676 5582. Central. Own bathrooms. **C** *Welcome*, Royal Rd, N of the centre, T 676 1469. Neat and well-run. **C** *L'Auberge de Madelon*, Sir John Pope Hennessy St, T 676 2550. Some rooms with own bathroom.

● **Places to eat**
♦♦♦♦*Au Gourmet*, Bernadin de St Pierre Ave, T 6761871. Open 1800-2400. French cuisine. Handsome surroundings in restored colonial house. ♦♦♦*Tropicana*, Mahebourg Main Rd, T 676 3286. European menu. ♦♦♦*La Nouvelle Potiniere*, Sir Winston Churchill St, T 6762648. ♦♦♦*Nobby's Restaurant*, Royal Rd, T 676 1318. Closed Sun. Creole and European food. ♦♦*Le Bonne Bouffe*, Sir John Pope Hennessy St, Curepipe. Inexpensive cheap take-away food. ♦♦*Le Pot de Terre*, Royal Rd, T 672204. Open 0730-1800. Snacks, coffee and light meals.

● **Banks**
Barclays. **Mauritius Commercial Bank**. **Banque National de Paris**. **State Commercial Bank**. All on Mahebourg Main Rd. Open 1000-1400 Mon-Fri, 0930-1130 Sat. **Foreign Exchange Bureau**, at Mauritius Commercial Bank 0900-1700 Mon-Sat.

● **Cinemas**
Mostly Indian, adventure and martial arts, *Ritz*, Chateauneuf St. *Novelty*, Sir J H Jerningham St.

● **Gambling**
Casine de Maurice, De la Teste De Buch St, close to the Town Hall. 1400-0200 Mon-Sat, 2000-0200 Sun.

● **Hospital**
Medical and Surgical Centre, Floreal, T 686 2307. Private clinic.

● **Post Office**
Off Chateauneuf St, behind bus station (0800-1115 and 1200-1600 Mon-Fri; 0800-1145 Sat).

● **Shopping**
Main arcades are at the *Continental Hotel* on Sir Winston Churchill St. and off Chateauneuf St. High standard stores at both locations. (0900-1800, except Thu and Sat 0900-1200, closed Sun.)

● **Sport (participant)**
Gymkana Club, At Vacoas. Golf, tennis, swimming pool, snooker. Temporary membership is available.

● **Transport**
Road Buses from Victoria Sq bus station in **Port Louis**. Bus station in **Curepipe**, in Ian Palach Sq. Fare to Port Louis US$0.50.

EAST COAST: FLACQ

The name is a degeneration of the Dutch word *vlakte*, meaning plain. The Dutch settlers exploited the area for its ebony timber. Later the area became a centre for sugar production. Hotels have now grown up around the coast to take advantage of the excellent beaches.

The main route from Port Louis, the A2, goes N of Moka, and passes through Bon Accueil on the way to Centre de Flaq. The **Court House and Post Office** are housed in a French colonial building that is preserved.

The road S to Mahebourg and the Airport runs along the shore and the Grande Riviere Sud-Est passes through a dramatic gorge over which there is a road bridge.

Poste de Flacq

Situated a short distance (1 km) inland from the bay. There is a **Hindu Temple** at Poste de Flacq.

● **Where to stay** **A+** *Belle Mare Plage*, T 413 2515, F 413 2993. Beautiful beach. 18 hole golf course. **A+** *St Geran*, T 413 2825, F 413 2983. Suites available. Beach superb. Casino. Tennis. 9-hole golf course. Swimming pool. One of the *Sun International hotels*. **A** *Sandy Bay*, T 413 2880, F 413 2054. Pleasant beach. Fairly new, but not particularly well designed. **A** *Le Kestrel*, north of the bay toward Poste Lafayette, T 413 9336. Pleasant atmosphere.

● **Places to eat** ♦♦♦*Chez Manuel* In the village of St Julien between Centre de Flacq and Bon Accueil. Chinese food of good standard.

Trou d'Eau Douce

This is a fishing village, originally settled by the Dutch. *Le Touessrok Hotel* has an inspired design by Maurice Giraud, a Mauritian architect. There is a public ferry to **Ile aux Cerfs**, (Island of Stags) with wild deer, a small zoo and fine beaches.

● **Where to stay** **A+** *Le Touessrok*, T 419 2451, F 419 2025. Not on beach itself but adjoins Ile aux Cerfs to which there is a ferry.

Swimming pool and water sports. Disco from 2300 (Not Sun). Architecturally very stylish. **A** *Silver Beach*, T 419 2600. **A** *Residence Valmarin*, T 2638771, F 2638274. Self-catering. Pool. **B** *Blue Ocean Resort*, Self-catering. Good value.

• **Places to eat** ♦♦♦*La Chaumiere*, On Ile aux Cerfs. Creole food.

Belle Mare

The **Prison** and **Old Sugar Factory** are protected buildings.

• **Where to stay** **A** *Le Flamboyant*, T 413 2036, F 208 8328. Well appointed. **A** *Emeraude Beach*, T 413 2107, F 413 2109. Good beach. **A** *Le Surcouf Village*, T 419 2800, F 212 1361. Apartments.

• **Transport Bus** from Immigration Square in Port Louis to Centre de Flacq (US$0.30). Local buses then to Belle Mare, Trous d'Eau Douce. A taxi instead of a local bus costs US$3-4. There are also buses to Flacq from Quatre Bornes and Curepipe in the W; Mahebourg to the S; and Grande Gaube in the N.

WEST COAST: BLACK RIVER

The Black river district is the poorest and least populated in Mauritius. The district is home to the Black River Gorges and National Park and is renowned for game fishing off the coast.

Pointe aux Sables

Popular weekend destination close to Port Louis, being 5 km away, mostly for day trips. It also has a reputation as a red light district. The beach is not particularly good.

• **Where to stay** **C** *Sun and Sea*, on the beach, T 234 4494. Verandah with columns, and a white tower. Terrace restaurant. Lively bar, popular with local girls. **C** *Venus Holiday Resort*, T 234 4089. Bungalow accommodation.

• **Bars and Nightclubs** *Golden Moon Night Club*, T 234 4089. Dancing every night. Popular with local girls. *Beach Bar*, rooms available by the hour. Popular with local girls.

• **Transport** Bus for Pointe aux Sables leaves from Dumas St, Port Louis, close to Victoria Sq.

Flic en Flac and Wolmar

The name is thought to be a degeneration of the Dutch for 'Free and Flat'. Another interpretion is that it is the sound of a drum played with the fingers. The town is a holiday centre about 20 km from Port Louis, with a fine coastline, quite well developed. About 1 km S is the resort of Wolmar.

There is some good sea diving, with **Cathedral Cave**, 27m down, a particular attraction.

Inland from the resort, 4 km towards Tamarin, is **Casela Bird Park** (0900-1800, closes an hour earlier Apr-Sep; entrance US$2 adults, US$0.50 children) with a zoo, shop and a cafe. There are 2,500 birds including some rare pink pigeons, in an extensive aviary area. Some of the animals are imported.

• **Where to stay (Flic en Flac)** **A** *Manisda*, T 453 8550, F 453 8562. Swimming pool and restaurant. **A** *Klondike Village Vacances*, T 453 8333, F 453 8337. Some self-catering bungalows. Swimming pool. Popular. **A** *Villas Caroline*, T 453 8411, F 453 8144. A/c. Some self-catering. Good standard. Pleasant surroundings. Diving facilities. **B** *Flic en Flac*, T 453 8537/38. Some a/c. **B** *C & A Bungalows*, T 425 7575. Self-catering. **C** *Little Acorn*, T 453 8431. Self-catering. On main road. Beach close by. Good value. **C** *Easy World Apartments*, T 453 8557. Self-catering.

• **Where to stay (Wolmar)** **A+** *Sofitel Imperial*, T 453 8700, F 453 8320. Oriental style. Tennis and 9-hole golf course. **A+** *La Pirogue Sun*, T 453 8441, F 453 8449. Luxurious setting. Casino. A *pirogue* is a dugout canoe, and the roof of the hotel resembles the sail. **A** *Le Pearle Beach*, T 453 8429, F 208 8077. A/c **A** *Villa Sand 'n Dory*, T 453 8420, F 208 5385. Some self-catering.

• **Places to eat** ♦♦♦*Sea Breeze*, T 453 8413. On main road in Flic en Flac. 1130-1430 and 1800-2000, closed Tue. International cuisine. ♦♦*Mer de Chine*, located on shore, Flic en Flac. 1100-2200. Chinese food. ♦♦*Leslie Snack*, good food, with extensive menu. Just before Flic en Flac.

• **Entertainment** *Sega* dancing, usually Sat, at *Villas Caroline* (Flic en Flac).

• **Gambling** Casino at *La Pirogue Sun Hotel*, T 453 8441, F 453 8449.

• **Sport** Diving, arranged through *Villas Caroline* (Flic en Flac) or La Pirogue (Wolmar).

• **Transport Bus from Quatre Bornes, no direct buses from Port Louis.**

Tamarin

Resort with reasonable beaches. There is a break in the reef which allows surfing – the waves are better in the cooler weather months, from Jun to Aug. **Tamarin Falls Reservoir** is 10 km inland (see page 811). Between Tamarin and Grande Riviere Noire is the **Shellorama Museum**, with a large collection of sea-shells.

• **Where to stay B** *Tamarin Hotel*, T 683 6581, F 683 6927. Bungalows in well-kept gardens. A/c. Verandah restaurant. Patio bar. Swimming pool. Very good value. **C** *Saraja Guest House*, Anthurium Ave. Rooms Rs 250. **C** *Edouard Laganes Bungalows*, T 683445. Some self-catering bungalows.

• **Places to eat** ************La Bonne Chute*, 3 km from Grande Rivere Noire, opposite Shellorama Museum. 1000-2200, closed Sun. French seafood cuisine. Unprepossessing exterior, but good reputation.

• **Bicycle hire** *Edouard Laganes Bungalows*, T 68 3445.

Grande Riviere Noire

Name arises from the black lava cliffs through which the river flows. **Black River Bay** is the deep sea fishing centre in Mauritius – the beach is not exceptional. The bay, with an island, lies between 2 promontories just to the S of Grande Riviere Noire. The more southerly of these, about 10 km from Grande Riviere Noire, is the **Le Morne Brabant** peninsula, with a distinctive rocky peak, 2 luxury hotels and high-class restaurants.

A martello tower, **La Preneuse,** built by the French, and dating before 1810, overlooks the bay. 2 islands, **Ile aux Benitiers**, in the bay, and **Ilot Fourneau**, S of the Le Morne Brabant peninsula, can be visited. The **Black River Aviary** can be visited, but only by prior arrangement. The **Yemen** estate is a wilderness area with deer and birdlife.

The rocky peak **Le Morne**, 556m high, is located on the peninsula at the most westerly point on the main island. It was a refuge for run-away slaves (*marron*). The slaves feared that the soldiers, actually coming to tell them that slavery had been abolished, were intent on their recapture, and they threw themselves from the peak. The name means 'mournful' – relating it is said to this episode. It is possible to climb, but permission needs to be sought from the Tourist Office in St Louis (see page CR).

About 7 km S and inland from Grande Rivere Noire there is a natural riverpool ('La Salle de Bains de Madame') at **Chamarel**. The **Cascade Chamarel**, is a 100m high waterfall. A geological curiosity of the area is the different coloured rock strata caused by uneven cooling of molten lava. The area is in the centre of the Mauritian coffee area. Further inland is the **Plaine Champagne**, a plateau at an altitude of 737m. There are vantage points for viewing the coast, and another cascade at **Alexandra Falls**.

Just inland of the southern corner of the Black River district is the mountainous area of Mauritius, with Little Black River Mountain (828m), the highest in Mauritius. It is possible to climb in the **Black River Mountains**. There is abundant birdlife, deer and monkeys, and the area is covered by the largest nature reserve in Mauritius, the **Maccabe Forest**.

• **Where to stay (Grande Riviere Noire) A** *Club Centre du Peche*, T 683 6522. Specialises in deep-sea fishing, and is the home of the International Marlin Championships each year. Many trophies and exhibits. **B** *Riviere Noire*, T 683 6547. Swimming pool. Diving. Deep-sea fishing. Disco. **C** ***Les Bouganvillears***, T 683 6525. Located on the coast. Sound guest house.

• **Where to stay (Le Morne Brabant) A+** ***Meridien Brabant***, and ***Meridien Paradis***, T 683 6775, F 683 6786. Both operated by *Beachcomber* group. *Paradis* has a disco and casino, *Brabant* is a little more sedate. Watersports. Deep-sea fishing. Diving. Tennis. Squash. 9-hole golf cours. Horse-riding.

• **Places to eat (Le Morne Brabant)** ♦♦♦♦***Blue Marlin Restaurant***, situated between the 2 *Meridien hotels* on the Le Morne Brabant peninsula. Emphasis on seafood. ♦♦♦***Le Domino Restaurant***, Le Morne Brabant peninsula. International menu.

SOUTH – SAVANNE & GRAND PORT

The main towns in the southern area are **Souillac**, in Savanne district, and to the W, **Mahebourg** in Grand Port district. It is not a particularly popular tourist area. There are several large sugar plantations, some of which can be visited through MauriTours (see page 805). Part of the terrain is highly forested and mountainous in the northern part of the region, and in the higher districts there is some tea growing. The airport is at Plaisance in the SE corner of the island, some 40 km from the capital, Port Louis. It was here in 1875 that remains of the Dodo were found (see page 818).

Souillac

Small fishing town named after Vicomte de Souillac, governor of Mauritius in the late eighteenth century. The better beaches are 20 km to the W toward **Baie du Cap**. Closer is **Le Gris Gris**, just to the E of Souillac. It dangerous for swimming, but has a headland, **Le Roche Qui Pleure**, which gives a good view over the ocean.

Telfair Gardens were established in Souillac by a British plantation owner, Charles Telfair, who arrived in 1810 to take over the sugar estates established by the French in 1776, at Bel Ombre, 14 km to the W of the town. The coastal location has made it difficult to grow some of the more exotic but delicate plants and trees.

The **Robert Edward Hart Memorial Museum** is dedicated to the Mauritian poet, with a background that was part French, part Irish, who lived 1891-1954. His house, **Le Nef**, which has been made into the museum, is between Souillac and Gris Gris. It is a simple cotttage on the shore, with coral walls and a corrugated iron roof. His writing materials and personal belongings are on display. Open to visitors 0900-1800, closed Tue, Fri and Public Holidays. The poet was made a Chevalier de la Legion d'Honneur by France in 1950 and awarded an OBE by Britain in 1949.

Rochester Falls are 4 km to the N of Souillac, not particularly high, but quite a spectacle, and a cool and pleasant place for a short excursion.

Bel Air is an old sugar plantation, between Souillac and Riviere des Anguilles, originally established by the French in 1804. It has fine gardens which run down to the shore and a series of pools and small cascades. It can be visted through MauriTours (see page 805).

Riviere des Anguilles (Eel River), a small country village, is 7 km to the NE of Souillac. Just to the S of Riviere des Anguilles is Senneville, the location of **La Vanille Crocodile Park**. On display are Nile crocodiles (That have been introduced) as well as a variety of other animals. Open daily 0930-1700. A café serves snacks and drinks.

Bel Ombre is about 14 km W of Souillac, and is the site of the the **Trevessa Monument**, dedicated to survivors of the *SS Trevessa*, which sank in 1923 on its way to Australia, over 2,500 km from Mauritius. The sixteen survivors spent 25 days at sea in an open boat before making a landfall at this point.

Grand Bassin is a crater lake, 700m above sea level, 12 km to the NW of

Souillac. Local belief is that it is replenished with waters from an underground channel which links the lake with the Ganges river in India. It has a great significance for Hindus who have erected several temples on the shore, and know the waters as *Ganga Talab* (Lake of the Ganges).

• **Where to stay B** *Villa Pointe aux Roches*, is 5 km W of Souillac, T 626 2507. Restaurant. Bar. Excellent coastal location. **C** *Gris Gris Restaurant*, 3 km E of Souillac. Mainly a food establishment, but does have some rooms.

• **Transport Buses** run regularly on the route from Baie du Cap, through Souillac to Mahebourg.

Mahebourg

This is a town of some 20,000, although its development has languished as emphasis has been focussed on Port Louis. There is a strong Creole influence here, with a relaxed and comfortable atmosphere. It is an inexpensive place to stay, with a variety of moderately-priced hotels in the town.

The best beach is **Blue Bay**, about 6 km S round the coast from Mahebourg, Excursions can be made to **Ile des deux Cocos**, where there is a summer residence for the governor, through *La Croix du Sud Hotel*, Pointe Jerome, T 631 9505, F 631 9603.

Places of interest

Housed in a handsome chateau built in 1722 by Lean de Robillard by the River La Chaux on the edge of the town, is the **Naval Museum.** It contains relics from various wrecked ships including the *St Gerain* and the *SS Trevessa*, as well as maps, paintings, and other historical exhibits. The museum is open 0900-1600 daily except Tue, Thu, Sun and Public Holidays; entrance is free.

Ile aux Aigrettes is located just off-shore, S-E of Mahebourg. In 1985 the island became a nature reserve and The Mauritian Wildlife Appeal Fund (MWAF) has begun to introduce species and strengthen the existing ecosystem. Rare Mauritian species, often bred abroad, are reared here and later reintroduced into the wild. They hope to introduce the island to small numbers of tourists who, by paying to enter the reserve, will help sustain the work.

The French fort on **Ile de la Passe** on the edge of one of the gaps in the reef, is about 5 km off-shore, and commands the bay just across from Vieux Grand Port. Excursions can be arranged through the larger *Mahebourg hotels*.

Across the bay from Mahebourg, and about 7 km N on the coastal road is **Vieux Grand Port**. This is the site of the original Dutch settlement, who first arrived in 1598, and named in Warwyck Bay. They made 2 attempts to establish a settlement here before leaving in 1710 to concentrate their efforts on Cape Colony in South Africa. The French renamed it Port Bourbon, but began to decline with the establishing of Port Louis as the premier harbour on the island. In 1804, Governor Decaen decided to move the settlement to Mahebourg, named after Mahe de Labourdonnais, which he felt was better protected, and the old site of Vieux Grand Port was abandoned. The ruins of the old settlement can be seen.

There is a cemetery for Dutch settlers at nearby **Lion Mountain** just to the N. The mountain can be climbed in about half a day.

At **Fernay**, to the E is a set of monuments to the Dutch, recording their arrival, and the introduction of sugar cane from Java in the Dutch East Indies (now Indonesia).

Further N, about 20 km on a winding coastal road from Mahebourg, is **Pointe de Diable**. Here the French installed cannons in the period from 1750-1810 to cover the 2 gaps in the reef that allowed access to Grand Port. The remains of these batteries can be seen, and the site is a national monument.

About 14 km SW of Mahebourg is **Le**

Souffleur, a tidal waterspout caused by the tide rushing in through a break in the reef and into a channel in the rocks. When conditions are right, Le Souffleur has been known to spout 20m into the air. Access is through the town of L'Escalier, and it is necessary to get a permit (no charge) to visit from the Savinia Estate office in L'Escalier (the waterspout is in the grounds of a sugar plantation). Visits are possible Mon-Fri 0700-1600 and Sat 0700-1200.

On the old road from Mahebourg to Curepipe is **Le Val**, a nature park and estate with extensive gardens. The location is splendid, surrounded by mountains on 3 sides, with a vista that opens to the sea. **Riche en Eau**, also on this road, is an old plantation mansion associated with a sugar estate, now a national monument.

Local information

● Where to stay (Mahebourg)

B *Les Aigrettes* (*Blue Bay Hotel*), T 631 9094. Restaurant planned should be completed, looks like a castle. **C** *Auberge L'Aquarelle*, Sivananda St, T 631 9479. Overlooks sea. Terrace resaurant. Bar. Garden. Occasional entertainment. **C** *Auberge Sea Fever*, Sivananda St, (road to Blue Bay) T 631 9218. **C** *Monte Carlo Guest House*, Sivananda St (road to Blue Bay), T 631 9514. Rather charming old-style guest house. It is popular, and it is wise to book. **C** *Pension St Tropez*, Sivananda St (road to Blue Bay), southern end of town, T 631 9646. Faces the sea. Shared bathrooms in most rooms. **D** *Auberge Le Coralier* (*Auberge Diane*), Sivananda St (road to Blue Bay), T 631 9728. Restaurant. **D** *Le Commodore*, Sivananda St (road to Blue Bay), T 631 1670. Good value. **D** *Pension Notre Dame*, Rue du Souffleur, southern end of town, T 631 9582. Shared bathrooms. Part of a convent. Very hospitable, run by nuns. It is wise to phone ahead and reserve a place.

● Camping

At *Auberge L'Aquarelle*, Sivananda St, T 631 9479.

● Where to stay (Mahebourg environs)

A+ *Shandrani*, (used to be *Beachcomber Club*), Blue Bay, T 637 3511. Based on the oldest beach hotel in Mauritius, Le Chaland. Watersports. Disco. **A** *La Croix du Sud*, Pointe Jerome, Blue Bay, T 631 9505, F 631 9603. Cottage-style accommodation. Water sports, bikes hired and excursions organised. **A** *Chante Mer*, T 631 9688. Family-run establishment. **B** *Villa Le Guerlande*, T 631 9225. Self-catering bungalows in garden with sea view. **B** *The Blue Lagoon Beach*, situated on Blue Bay roughly 6 km from Mahebourg, T 631 9529, F 6319045. Swimming pool. Beach bar. Regular entertainment. Good value, but more expensive in peak periods.

● Places to eat

♦♦*Chez Joe*, Sivananda St (road to Blue Bay), T 631 9728. Chinese cuisine. ♦♦*Chez Jacqueline*, Sivananda St (road to Blue Bay), T 631 1670. Local menu. ♦♦*Monte Carlo*, Rue du Bouchon at southern end of town. Local cuisine with emphasis on seafood.

● Entertainment

Cinema *Mahe Cinema*, Rue Marianne. *Odeon Cinema*, Rue de la Maurice. Both show mainly Indian, martial arts and action movies.

Discos *Mo Gate*, *Shandrani Hotel* (used to be *Beachcomber Club*), T 637 3511. Situated on Blue Bay roughly 6 km from Mahebourg. *Blue Lagoon Beach Hotel*, Blue Bay, 6 km from Mahebourg, T 631 9529, F 631 9045.

Gambling *Starlight*, Rue des Flamards. Chinese gaming. Bar.

Other *Blue Lagoon Beach Hotel*, (see above) variety of entertainments, including martial arts displays, Sega dancing.

● Car and bicycle hire

Arnulphy Car Hire, T 631 9806, F 631 9991. *Pension St Tropez*, T 631 9646.

● Tour agent

Domaine du Chasseur (LP), T 6319259, F 2080076.

● Transport

Bus Frequent service to and from Curepipe, also sevices to Vieux Grand Port to the N, and then on to Centre de Flacq; and W to Souillac. **Taxi** From airport costs about US$5.

RODRIGUES AND ISLANDS

Rodrigues lying approximately 600 km E of Mauritius and covering an area of 108 square km, is a volcanic island and one which remains little visited. Unlike Mauritius the island has a strong African rather than Indian population.

Climatically the island has unpredictable weather being a small landmass and cyclones can be fierce.

Flora

The plant life on the island is similar to that found in Mauritius. Endemic varieties include mango wood *(Bois mangue)*, papaya wood *(Bois papaya)*, and the wild coffee plant 'cafe marron' (*Ramosmania heterophylla*). These are all protected species.

Fauna

The Golden Bat (*Pteropus rodericensis*), a fruit bat, is the only endemic mammal on the island. An extinct bird, the Rodrigues solitaire, a flightless dodo (Pezophaps solitaria) was present on the island until 1800 when it became extinct. Surviving endemic bird species includes the Rodrigues fody (*Foudia flavicans*) and the Rodrigues brush warbler (*Bebrornis rodericana*), both species seen around Port Mathurin and the Cascade Pigeon area. Visiting sea birds include the common and small nody members of the Paille en queue.

History

The Portuguese first sighted the island in 1528, and it was named after its discoverer, Diego Rodrigues. The Dutch were the first to set foot on the soil in 1601, but did not establish any settlement. Nine protestant exiles from France arrived during the Dutch period, but only remained 2 years. The French made an unsuccessful attempt to establish a settlement in 1725, and the first permanent base was set up only in 1792.

The British used Rodrigues as a base from 1794, establishing good relations with the settlers. Cattle and slaves were imported from Madagascar, and it was from here that the assault of 1810 was launched which resulted in British capture of Ile de France (Mauritius). In 1814 Rodrigues was formally handed over to the British by the Treaty of Paris, the troops withdrew, and the beginnings of settlement got under way. Toward the end of the eighteenth century the population crept up to 3,000 with the beginning of significant Indian and Chinese immigration, with these communities becoming paricularly strong in commercial life. During this period Rodrigues was

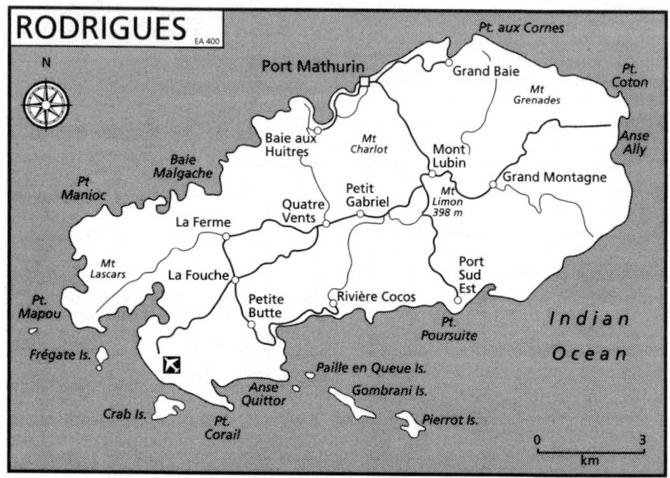

administered from Mauritius, and in 1968 became part of the newly independent country.

The island has 2 political parties the first, Socialist Organisation du Peuple Rodriguais (OPR), was formed in 1976 the other, the more conservative of the 2, Rassemblement du Peuple Rodrigues (RPR) was formed in 1986.

People

The population is now close to 40,000, with quite a high population density at 375 persons a square kilometre (compared, however, with the very high density of 550 per sq km on the main island of Mauritius).

The original islanders are decendents of African slaves (from Madagascar), and have intermarried with the European settlers. Rodriguan traditional beliefs mirror those followed in Madagascar. The population is split into 2 groups 'blacks' who make up a little over 80% of the inhabitants and 'reds', those from mixed backgrounds, predominantly found around Port Mathurin. The main religion is Catholicism.

Language

The main languages are Kreol (lingua franca of Rodrigues), French and a little English.

Traditional food

Much the same as Mauritius though corn is eaten a lot as are sweet potatoes and manioc. Seafood is served with the staple diet.

Port Mathurin

This is the main town, neat, fairly quiet, with wooden single-storey buildings. There are some public gardens by the jetty on the waterfront, a war memorial, and the market nearby. The **Residence** of the administrator, built in 1873, is on Jenner St, with a cannon outside. On the other side of Morrison St is the **Noor ud-Deen Mosque**, with 6 small minarets, recently restored.

The E and SE coasts have good beaches, particularly **Pointe Cotton**, **Anse Ally**, **St Francois**, and **Baie de L'Est**. Others include **Trou d'Argent**, **Anse Vascoas** and **Petit Gravier** (S). Beware swimming can be dangerous (currents).

Caverne Patate (limestone caves) lie to the S-W of Rodrigues and can visited, but you must have a permit (no charge) to do so, available from Adminstration House, Jenner St, Port Mathurin which has to be presented to the guardian of the caves. The caves are extensive, over 500 m of caverns, and the guide leads the way with a burning brand through stalagtites and stalagmites.

Ile aux Cocos (a nature reserve) and **Ile aux Sables** (both about 1 km offshore to the W); **Diamond Island**, and **Booby Island** (to the N) can be visited. You need a permit for Ile aux Cocos from Adminstration House, Jenner St, Port Mathurin (US$17). Tours are organised by HenriTour and Ebony (see page 820).

Local information

● Where to stay

A+ *Cotton Bay*, Point Coton on superb beach, T 831 3000. Swimming pool. Restaurant. Bar.

C *Relais Pointe Venus*, T 831 1577. Colonial building with verandah Shared bathrooms. A little dilapidated. **C** *Pension Les Filaos*, to the E on the extension of Jenner St, about 1 km from the town, T 831 1644. Shared bathrooms. Restaurant. Excursions are available. **C** *Pension Ciel d'Ete*, Jenner St, T 831 1587. Shared bathrooms. Good value. Excursions and car hire available.

D *Pension Beau Soleil*, Victoria St, T 8311 673. Car rental. Excursions arranged.

● Places to eat

Ebony Restaurant. ♦♦*Restaurant du Port*, Duncan St, eastern end. Local cuisine, with Lagon Bleu. ♦♦*Victoria Restaurant*, Victoria St. Rather charming with thatched roof. Local menu.

● Banks

Barclays Bank, Jenner St, T 831 1553. **State Commercial Bank**, Ricard St. **Indian Ocean International Bank**, open 0800-1430 (Mon-Fri), 0800-1115 Sat.

● Post Office
Mann St Port Mathurin.

● Telephone
The Overseas Tecommunications Office is on Mont Venus, just outside Port Mathurin T 831 1724. Open 0800-2200 (0800-1300 Sat and Sun).

● Travel and tour agents
Henritours, T 831 1823 and *Ebony*, T 831 1640. Rent vehicles and motorcycles. *Mauri-Tours*, Sir William Newton St, Port Louis, T 263 3078. Arranges tours to Rdorigues.

● Transport
Local Most transport on the island is from local villages into Port Mathurin in the morning, and out again in the afternoon. Buses stop running after mid-afternoon.

Air The island has daily flights from Mauritius by *Air Mauritius*, Ricard St, Port Mathurin, T 831 1632. For non-Mauritians, a return for 30 days is US$200 (about half this for residents). Travel agents in Mauritius can sometimes offer packages with accommodation which are good value (see page 808). There is no regular transport from the airport and it is necessary to arrange a ride in a hotel or government shuttle.

Sea Cargo boats to the island depart on an irregular basis. The *MV Mauritius Pride*, T 241 2550, F 242 5245. Makes 2 trips per month and takes 2 days, staying 7 days. Tickets from *Island Service Limited*, Dr Ferriere St, Port Louis, (US$107 return first class; US$40 second; US$23 third). *Concorde Travel and Tours*, La Chaussée, Port Louis, T 208 5041, Tlx 4305. Can arrange charter boat trips to the island.

Other islands

St Brandon (Cargados Garayos)

This group of small islands lies 370 km NE of Mauritius. Fishing, salting and drying are the main economic activities. It is a pretty archipelago, but very remote. The coral atoll is a diving centre. If you wish to visit, the Mauritian Fishing Development Ltd in Port Loius, T 208 0299. can help.

Agalega

Comprises Southern and Northern Islands, lying 1,200 km N of Mauritius. Population is about 300, and the main economic activity is coconut production. They are low lying islands sighted by the Portuguese in 1501. In the mid 1700s France claimed the island, control of the island went through several hands, until 1975 when it came under Mauritian governmental control.

Tromelin

A small island 480 km the W. There is some turtle-farming and a weather station. In 1761, there was a shipwreck on the reef. The survivors, 122 in number, struggled ashore. The Europeans managed to build a boat and reach Madagascar, leaving the slaves behind. Fifteen years later, a French visitor rescued the remaining 98 survivors.

Chagos Archipelago

These are a remote group 2,000 km to the NW of Mauritius. In 1965 there were perhaps 2,000 inhabitants, producing coconuts and fish. One of the groups of islands, **Diego Garcia**, had at one time been a leper colony for Mauritius, but this ended when the British took control in 1810. At the time of independence in Mauritius, the archipelago was taken over by the British, and the British Indian Ocean Territory created. The ferry service ended, the company producing copra ceased production, and gradually the inhabitants left. Diego Garcia was leased to the USA as a military base, and in 1982, compensation was paid to the departed islanders.

● **Transport** From Seychelles there are flights to **Agalega** (see page elles. The other islands can only be visited by chartered boat.

NATURE RESERVES AND HUNTING

There are 18 areas of Mauritius designated as reserves. As the islands are small and densely populated, none of the reserves is very extensive, the largest being Maccabée-Bel Ombre, which is about 12 km N to S, and 8 km wide. A good guide to rambles and climbs in the reserves is Marsh R. V. R. 1976. *Mountains of Mauritius: a Climber's Guide*.

The reserves fall into 4 groups:

Mainland Bois Sec, Cabinet, Combo, Corps de Garde, Grouley Père, Maccabée Bel Ombre, Les Mares, Perrier, Le Pouce.

North coast: Round Island, Serpent Island, Flat Island, Gabriel Island and Gunner's Quoin.

East coast: Marianne Islet and Aigrette Isle.

Rodrigues: Cocos Island and Sables Island.

Aigrette Isle: Close to Mahebourg off the E coast. Seabirds and marine life.

Bois Sec Small forest reserve in the SW.

Cabinet In Palines Wilhelms in the W central area. Contains Tamarind Falls.

Cocos Island Off western coast of Rodrigues. Seabirds and marine life.

Combo North of Souillac in S. Forest reserve with small animal and birds.

Corps de Grande Mountain reserve in Black River region, in the W central part of the mainland. Overlooks la Ferme Reservoir. Bird life, and a good hiking area.

Flat Island About 12 km off the N coast, with a lighthouse. Seabirds and marine life. Water is particularly clear and good for snorkelling.

Gabriel Island About 12 km off the N coast. Seabirds and marine life.

Gouley Père Small reserve in the SW. Bird life, small animals and good hiking.

Gunner's Quoin A rocky island which has a wedge shape when seen from the side. About 12 km off the N coast. Seabirds and marine life.

Maccabée Bel Ombre Forest with both lowland and upland vegetation. In the period Sep-Jan the trees and plants are in flower. Rich birdlife with several of the species unique to Mauritius, most notably the Pink Pigeon and the Cardinal Bird (see page 793). There are several good hikes and climbs.

Les Mares Small forest reserve in the SW.

Marriane Island Off the E coast, about 10 km from Mahebourg. Bird and marine life.

Perrier Central location close to Curepipe. Forest location with several endemic bird species.

Le Pouce Mountain reserve, close to Port Louis. Can be climbed in about half a day.

Round Island Off the N coast, about 20 km from Cap Malheureux. Bird, marine life, lizards (some endemic) and snakes.

Sable Island Off western coast of Rodrigues. Seabirds and marine life.

Serpent Island (Parasol Island) Rocky outcrop near Round Island off the N coast. Bird sanctuary.

Hunting Deer hunting takes place during the season from Jun-Sep, at locations on the E coast and in the SW. Wild boar and hares can be hunted all year round. Expeditions can be arranged through *MauriTours*, 10 Sir William Newton St, T 208 5241/121/4712, Tlx 4349/4650/4279.

INFORMATION FOR VISITORS

Contents

Before you go

Entry requirements

● Visas

If you are a member of the EU or the British Commonwealth (Portugal exception), all you need is a ticket to show your outward journey.

If you are not in either of these categories then you need a visa (which is free). The government does not recognise a Taiwan passport. Visitors are allowed to stay in Mauritius for a period of 1 month, if you wish to stay longer you can acquire an extension (again free). Applications for visa extension should be made in person to the Passport and Immigration Office in Line Barracks, Port Louis T 208 1212) Open 1000-1200 Mon-Fri. Applications take 2 weeks to process.

● Vaccinations

You need Cholera and Yellow Fever certificates if you arrive from an infected area i.e. Africa. See Health Section, see page 823).

● Mauritian Representation Overseas

Australia, High Commission, 43 Hampton Circuit, Yarralumla, ACT 2600, T 06 281 1203. **Belgium**, Embassy 68 Rue Bollandistes, Etterbeek, 1040 Brussels, T 733 9988. **Egypt**, Embassy 72 Abdel Moneim Riad St, Agouza, Cairo. T 346 4659. **France**, Embassy 68 blvd de Courcelles 75017 Paris, France T 01 42 27 30 19. **India**, High Commission, 5 Kautilya Marg Chanakyapuri, New Delhi 110021, T 301 1112/3. **Madagascar**, Embassy Lot No VI 2113 bis, Ambatoroka, Antananarivo, T 02 32157. **Pakistan**, Embassy House No 27, Street No 26, Sector F-6/2 Islamabad, T 823345/823235. **United** ***Kingdom***, High Commission, 32/33 Elvaston Place, London SW7, T 071 581 0294/5. **USA**, Embassy Suite 134, Van Ness Centre, 4301 Conneticut Ave, NW, Washington DC 20008, T 202 244 1491/2.

● Overseas Representation in Mauritius

(E Embassy; HC High Commission; C Consulate. **Australia** (HC), Rogers House, 5 President John F Kennedy St, Port Louis, T 208 1700. **Austria** (C), Rogers House, 5 President John F Kennedy St, Port Louis, T 208 6801. **Belgium** (C), Blyth Brothers, New Quay St, Port Louis, T 208 1241. **Brazil** (C), Harel Mallac Building, Edith Cavell St, Port Louis, T 208 0861. **Canada** (C), Blanche Birger Ltd, J Koenig St, Port Louis, T 208 0821. **China** (E), Rogers House, 5 President John F Kennedy St, Port Louis, T 254 9111. **Egypt** (E), George V Avenue Floreal, T 675 5012. **Finland** (C), Rogers House, 5 President John F Kennedy St, Port Louis, T 208 6801. **France** (E), St George St, Port Louis, T 208 3755. You can acquire tourist visas here (US$10 each) for Reunion and Mayotte. **Germany** (C), 60 Sir Seewoosagur Ramgoolam St, Port Louis, T 240 7425. **India** (HC), Borada Building, Sir William Newton St, Port Louis, T 208 3775. **Japan** (C), Blyth Brothers, New Quay St, Port Louis, T 208 1241. **Madagascar** (E), Rue Guiot Pasceau St, Floreal, T 686 5015/6. Office open Mon-Fri 0900-1600. Visas take 3 days. **Netherlands** (C), Blyth Brothers, New Quay St, Port Louis, T 208 1241. **Norway** (C), Rogers House, 5 President John F Kennedy St, Port Louis, T 208 6801. **Pakistan** (HC), Anglo-Mauritius Building, Jules Koening St Port

Louis, T 208 2786. **Portugal** (C), Harel Mallac Building, Edith Cavell St, Port Louis, T 208 0861. **Russia** (E), Queen Mary Ave, Floreal, T 675 5533. **Seychelles** (C), Peat Marwick Building, Leoville l'Homme St, Port Louis. **Sweden** (C), Rogers House, 5 President John F Kennedy St, Port Louis, T 208 6801. **Switzerland** (C), 2 J Koenig St, Port Louis, T 212 4086. **United Kingdom** (HC), George V Avenue, Floreal, T 208 9850. **USA** (E), Rogers House, 5 President John F Kennedy St, Port Louis, T212 3219.

● Tourist information (Mauritius)

See Port Louis, **see page 805** ; Rodrigues, **see page 820**.

● Tourist information (Overseas)

In addition to the agencies listed below, *Air Mauritius*, offices around the world provide information for tourists, and they are listed above. **Australia**, Mauritius Travel and Tourist Bureau, 106 Sugarloaf Crescent. Castlecrag, NSW 2068, T 02 958 0378. **France**, CORP 41, Rue Ybry, 92200 Neuilly, T 475 812 40, Tlx 610029. **Germany**, Mauritius Information Bureau Goethestrasse 22, D-6000 Frankfurt, Main 1, T 089 290 03930. **Italy**, Foro Buonaparte 46, 20121 Milan, T 865984/879157. **Switzerland**, Kirchenweg 5, CH 8632 Zurich, T 515025, Tlx 815282. **United Kingdom** (MGTO), 49 Conduit St, London, W1R 9FB, T 071 437 7508/9. **USA**, Mauritius Tourist Information, 15 Penn Plaza, 415 Seventh Ave, New york, NY 10001, New York, T 212 239 8367.

● Travel and tour agents

Agents are listed under Port Louis (see page 805); Rose Hill and Quatre Bornes (see page 811).

When to go

High seasons for tourism are Dec and Jan The main harvest and flower season), and mid-Jun to mid-Sep (dry, but not too hot). Low seasons are Feb to mid-Jun (Feb and Mar can be hot and humid) and mid-Sep to Nov.

Health

Water is safe to drink. People with delicate stomachs, however, might consider restricting themselves to bottled water if visiting for a short period. Malaria has been eradicated, but it is wise to take anti-malaria tablets – there are mosquitoes, and it is possible that they might transmit malaria from another visitor. See Health Section, page 21.

Money

● Credit cards

All major credit cards are accepted by large hotels, the main travel agents and the airlines. American Express Representative ***Mauritius Travel and Tourist Bureau (MTTB)***, Royal St, T 208 2041, Tlx 4338.

● Currency

Unit of currency Rupee (MR), divided into 100 cents.

● Exchange rate

The exchange rate fluctuates, but remains fairly stable. There has tended to be a slight depreciation of the Rupee each year. Exchange Rate 1994: MR 17.7 = US$1.

● Travellers cheques

A minimal charge is made for cashing travellers cheques. There is no black market in foreign currency. No limit on amount of foreign exchange that can be brought in and out of the country. Credit cards are accepted by airlines, travel agents, and the larger hotels.

● Cost of living

The luxurious beach hotels used by many visitors are expensive. The budget traveller can, however, get by on US$20 a day for accommodation, food and travel. This involves staying in modest hotels in the towns used by local people (taking day-trips to the beach – never more than a few km away), eating in local restaurants and cafes, and travelling by bus.

Getting there

● Air from Africa

Comoros, flights by Air Mauritius. **Kenya**, two flights a week from Nairobi by Air Mauritius. **Madagascar**, two flights a week from Antananarivo by Air Mauritius. **Reunion**, several flights each week by Air France and Air Mauritius. **Seychelles**, flights by Air France and British Airways. **South Africa**, daily flights from Johannesburg and Durban by Air Mauritius and South African Airways. **Tanzania**, two flights a week from Dar es Salaam by Lufthansa. **Zambia**, weekly flights from Lusaka by Zambia Airways.

Europe France, direct flights from Paris by Air France and Air Mauritius. **Germany**, direct flights from Frankfurt by Lufthansa and from Munich by Air Mauritius. **Italy**, direct flights from Rome by Air Mauritius. **Switzerland**, direct flights from Zurich by Air Mauritius. **United Kingdom**, direct flights from London by British Airways and Air Mauritius.

Asia India, direct flights from Bombay by Air India and Air Mauritius. **Singapore**, two flights a week from Singapore Airlines and Air Mauritius.

● Air Mauritius Offices Overseas

Australia, Suite 1204, MLC Centre, Martin Place, Sydney, NSW 2001, T 22 17 300, Tlx 178117. **Belgium**, 7 Rue de Lausane, Boite 9, 1060 Brussels, T 539 00 12, Tlx 24 507. **France**, 8, Rue Halevy, 75009 Paris, T 47 42 75 02, Tlx 209189. **Germany**, Herzog Rudolf Strasse 3, 800 Munchen 22, T 23 18 01 30, Tlx 528 504 and Bockenheimer Landstrasse 68, Frankfurt, T 069 720253, Tlx 416865. **India**, Air India Building, Nariman Point, Bombay, T 2028474. **Italy**, Via Barberinis 68, 00187 Rome, T 474 2051-5, Tlx 625363. and Via P Da Cannobia, 10, 20022 Milan. **Kenya**, PO Box 45270, Union Towers Building, Nairobi, T 29166/7, Tlx 22855. **Singapore**, 135 Cecil St, Singapore 0106, T 2223033, F 2259726, Tlx 42226/42129. **South Africa**, 701 Carlton Towers, Commissioner St, Johannesburg 2000, T 3311918/9, Tlx 48-6668 and 320 West St Durban 4001, T 304 6681/82. **Sweden**, Birger Jarlsgatan 2, 11434 Stockholm, T 7230645, Tlx 19481. **Switzerland**, 1-3 Rue sde Chantepoulet, 1201 Geneva, T 320560, Tlx 27502/23670 and Neumuehlequai 34, CH-8006 Zurich, T 816 33 35, Tlx 825640. **United Kingdom**, 49 Conduit St, London, W1R 9FB, T 071 434 4375/79, Tlx 24469. **USA**, Roosevelt Hotel, 45th St, Madison Ave, New York, NY 10017, T 808 9038/661 9600.

● Discount air fares

See page 14.

● Customs

Duty-free allowances are: 200 cigarettes or 50 cigars or 0.25 kg of tobacco; 75 cl of spirits; 2 ltrs wine or beer; 25 cl of toilet water.

When you arrive

● Airport information

The airport is located at the SE corner of the main island at Plaisance, about 45 km from the capital Port Louis. Departure tax US$7.

Transport to town There are buses to Mahebourg and Curepipe, from which onward connections can be made. A taxi to Port Louis is US$17.

Airline offices See under Port Louis, page 804.

Sea The MV Mauritius Pride runs between Mauritius and Reunion (US$32 one-way) and a service is planned to Madagascar. CTC Cruise Lines, London, UK, T 071 930 5833, F 071 839 2483. Visit Mauritius as part of cruise itineraries.

● Conduct

Since there are significant numbers of Hindus and Muslims in Mauritius, it is courteous to restrict bathing to designated beaches. Nude bathing is illegal.

It is expected that men will wear collars and ties (though not necessarily a jacket) for formal meetings, with safari suits also being acceptable. Women are expected to be dressed appropriately for formal meetings, particularly not in holiday or beach-wear. Some effort is always appreciated if making a social visit – it is taken as a mark of respect to the host.

● Electricity

220 v. Continental 2-pin sockets in older establishments. Newer buildings have 3 square-pin sockets. A universal adapter is desirable – if necessary one can be bought locally.

● Business hours

Government offices and businesses Mon-Fri 0900-1600. Businesses also 0900-1200 on Sat. Shop hours 0900-1700. On Sat many shops and cafes close at noon. Some shops open Sun morning. Some restaurants close before 1800. Bank hours, see below; Post Office hours, see under Postal Services, below.

● Bank hours

1000-1400 Mon-Fri; Sat 0930-1130. 24 hour foreign exchange bureau at Plaisance Airport. Large hotel with change currency and travellers cheques 24 hours, but at a slightly less good rate than the banks.

● Official time

4 hrs ahead of GMT.

● Safety

There is a good record of law and order in Mauritius, and vistors need not feel anxious about walking around alone or after dark.

Where to stay

● Accommodation

Lodging can certainly be obtained at a budget price in Mauritius, it is sometimes a good idea to have a sheet sleeping bag.

Self-catering **apartments**, are an economical alternative to hotels for family groups or longer-stay visitors. They are available in several beach resorts, but particularly around Grand Bay in the N. It is possible for a family of 4 to rent an apartment for around US$30 a day. *Grand Baie Travel & Tours* (GBTT), Royal Rd, T 2638273, F 2638274, act as agents for flats and apartments to rent.

At the airport there is an accommodation desk that can be used to book a hotel, and which will arrange a transfer.

● Camping

There are no formal camp-sites, but the odd small hotel in the beach resorts will allow camping in its grounds – you will need to bring your own tent. It is quite possible to camp on an informal basis on public beaches in all except the most exclusive beach resorts.

Food and drink

● Food

There is a wide variety of cuisine available, covering local Creole dishes, Indian, Chinese, and European cooking, the latter with a strong French influence.

HOTEL CLASSIFICATIONS

A+	Over US$100 a night. International standards and decor, a/c, self contained rooms, swimming pool, restaurants, bars, business services.
A	US$40-100. First class standards. Air-conditioning, attached bathrooms. Restaurants and bars. Swimming pool.
B	US$20-40. Tourist class. Comfortable with a/c or fans, attached barthrooms. Restaurant, bar, public rooms.
C	US$10-20. Budget. Fans. Shared bathroom facilities.
D	US$5-10. Guest house. No fan. Shared bathroom. Cold water.
E	Under US$5. Basic guest house. Simple bed. No soap or towels. No wardrobe. Shared bathroom facilities. Erratic cold water supply. No fans or mosquito nets.

RESTAURANT CLASSIFICATIONS

♦♦♦♦	Over US$10 for a meal. A 3 course meal in a restaurant with pleasant decor. Beers, wines and spirits available.
♦♦♦♦	US$5-10 for a meal. Two courses. Comfortable surroundings.
♦♦	US$2-5 for a meal. Probably only a single course. Surroundings spartan but adequate.
♦	Under US$2. Single course. Often make-shift surroundings such as a street kiosk with simple benches and tables.

Local Creole dishes include curries, stews with vegetables (*daube*), served with rice and salad. Small snacks, (*gadjacks*), can be bought in bars, and are rather similar to Spanish *tapas*.

Street cuisine is widely available, including Indian, Chinese and Creole items, and is very cheap. Although the facilities are rudimentary, the food is quite safe for visitors.

● Drink

For many years *arrack* was a favourite drink of local people, made from the sap of the palm, fermented and distilled. It is difficult to find nowadays.

A local soft drink is *Alooda*, milky and sweet, served cold, and sold on street corners.

Locally produced **beers** include lagers, *Phoenix* and *Stella* (the lighter of the 2), and Guinness, brewed in Mauritius under licence. There are 2 popular locally produced **spirits**, *Rum of Mauritius* and *Green Island Rum*, and specialist rums such as *Mainstay Dry Cane Spirit*, *Old Mill Rum* and *Vieux Rhum de L'Ile de France*. Grape juice is imported to make a range of reasonable priced wines, and local wines are made from lychees and papayas.

A full range of imported wines, beers and spirits is available, particularly beers and wines from South Africa.

Getting around

● Air

The island is so small that there is little demand for internal air services except to Rodrigues and the outer islands (see page 804).

Air Mauritius, PO Box 441, Rogers House, 5 President Kennedy St, T 208 7700, Tlx 4415. Offers helicopter flights for between US$100 and US$200 for short trips round the island. These trips depart from the airport or from one of the large hotels.

● Bicycle hire

Often available through hotels. Around US$2 a day.

● Bus

Services regular and cheap (under US$.02 a km). Rural buses stop running at 1730, and town buses at 2000.

● Car hire

Port Louis Avis, Al Madina St, T 208 1624. **Hertz**, T 675 1453. **Europcar**, T 208 9258 and **Sunny Beach Tours**, T 240 5245.

Central **Kevtrav**, Quatre Bornes, T 454 5760. **Mask Touring**, *Gold Crest Hotel*, St Jean Rd, Quatre Bornes, T 4546975. **Hertz**, Royal Road, Curepipe, T 676 1453.

North Coast **Beach Car**, Marcellement Swan, Pereybere, T 263 8239. **Budget Car**, Grand Gaube, T 263 9337.

● Motorcycle hire
Grand Baie Travel & Tours (GBTT), Royal Rd, centre of town, near road to Goodlands, T 2638273, F 2638274. Around US$10 a day.

● Sea
There is a regular sailing to **Rodrigues** twice a month, and it is possible to charter boats (see page 820).

● Taxis
Recognisable by white number plates. Taxi trips are about US$0.50 a km. It is wise to agree a fare before getting in. **Taxi trains** look the same but carry more people (a shared taxi), and are correspondingly cheaper.

Communications

● Language
The official language is English. The main languages in use are Creole, a pidgin version of French, and this is spoken by 54% of the population. French is widely used, as is English; also Chinese and some languages from India. It is not easy for visitors to communicate with local people in Creole as the accent is difficult, and it is hard to relate the spoken word to the written language.

● Postal services
Hours 0800-1115 and 1200-1600 Mon-Fri, 0800-1115 on Sat. **Post Restante**, services can be arranged through General Post Office, Quay St, Port Louis, T 208 2851. Alternatively, American Express cardholders can use Mauritius Travel and Tourist Bureau (MTTB) Royal St, Port Louis, T 208 2041, Tlx 4338.

● Telephone services
Overseas calls can be made at OTS, Rogers House, 5 President John F Kennedy St, Port Louis, T 208 1036. Hours 0830-1730 Mon-Fri, 0830-1400 Sat. A 24 hr services is available at the OTS office at Cassis, 1 km W of the city centre. International calls through hotels often cost 3 times as much as calls made through OTS.

Entertainment

● Cinemas
Most of the large towns will have a cinema (there are 3 in Port Louis). Programmes are mainly Indian, martial arts and, and adventure movies. Films are also shown from time to time by the *British Council*, Royal Rd, Rose Hill, T 424 2034 and *Alliance Francaise*, Bell Village, Floreal, T 675 2949.

● Newspapers
The 2 daily papers are published in French: *L'Express* and *Le Mauricien*, a significant reflection of the way in which French influence has endured despite the presence of the British for 180 years and English being the official language. The only English language paper is a weekly, the *Mauritian Times*.

● Radio
One service, run by the Mauritius Broadcasting Corporation. Programmes are in Creole, English, French, and Hindi.

RAILWAYS

William Stevenson became governor in 1857, and in 1858 initiated a survey for a railway. In 1861, a British firm, Brassey and Wythes were commissioned to build the lines. the northern line opening in 1864 and the Midland line in 1865. There was then a pause to assess how financially viable they would be. They were so successful that a line to Savanne in the S was built in 1879 and the Moka branch was opened in 1880. Most of the traffic was the shipping of sugar and canes from the plantations and mills scattered round the island to Port Louis for export.

The railway ceased operation in 1964 when the road network became well enough developed to take the sugar traffic. However, the path of the old lines can still be seen around the country, and almost all the iron bridges that carried the lines over the many rivers of the island have remained intact.

● Theatre

Occasional performances at ***Theatre de Port Louis***, Sir William Newton St, T 212 1090. ***Plaza Theatre***, Royal Rd, Rose Hill, T 424 1145.

● Sporting events

Horse Racing, at Champ de Mars in Port Louis, on Sats, May to Nov. **Soccer**, is played in all the main towns. The principal venue is the George V Stadium in Curepipe.

● Television

The service was introduced in 1965, run by the government-owned Mauritius Broadcasting Corporation. Relays to Rodrigues began in 1987. There are broadcasts from early afternoon through to late night. Programmes are in Creole,English, French, and Hindi.

Holidays and festivals

● Official Public Holidays

(If a holiday falls on a Sun, the Mon is taken as the holiday. Sat is usually a half working day.)

- **1 Jan** New Year's Day
- **2 Jan** New Year
- **Jan/Feb** Chinese New Year (Fireworks and feasting)
- **Jan/Feb** *Cavadee* (Hindu Tamil festival with processions and body piercing)
- **Feb/ Mar** *Maha Shivaratree* (Hindu festival with procession to Vacoas Lake, (see page 811)
- **12 Mar** Independence Day
- **Mar/Apr** Ougadi (Telegu New Year)
- **1 May** Labour Day (International holiday for working people)
- **Aug/Sep** Gunesh Chaturthi (Tamil festival)
- **Oct/Nov** Diwali (Hindu festival of light)
- **1 Nov** All Saints' Day (Christian festival)
- **25 Dec** Christmas Day (Christian festival)
- **Variable** Id El Fitr (Islamic festival of Ramadhan, with fasting)

● Festivals

(Employees are allowed holidays for 2 religious festivals each year)

- **Jan** Sankranti (Harvest festival for Hindu Tamils)
- **Mar** Holi (Hindu festival with participants spraying paint on each other)
- **Mar** Mehraj Shariff (Islamic festival)
- **Apr** Varashu Pirappu (Tamil New Year)
- **Apr** Shabbe Baraat (Islamic festival)
- **Mar/Apr** Good Friday
- **Mar/Apr** Easter Monday
- **May** Seemadee Appana Parsa (Telegu religious festival)
- **May** Sittarai Cavadee (Hindu Tamil religious festival)
- **May/Jun** Corpus Christi (Christian festival)
- **Aug** Id El Adha (Islamic festival)
- **Aug** Raksha Bandhan (Hindu festival)
- **Aug** Assumption Day (Christian festival)
- **Sep** Laval Day (Death of Father Laval, Catholic missionary in Mauritius)
- **Oct** Autumn (Chinese celebration)
- **Nov** Yaum Un Nabi (Islamic festival devoted to the Prophet Mohammed)
- **Nov** Ganga Asnan (Hindu festival of bathing and cleansing)
- **26 Dec** Boxing Day (Traditional British holiday)

Further reading

● History

Toussaint, A. 1966. *The History of the Indian Ocean* London: Routeledge & Kegan Paul. Scholarly history; Riviere, L. 1982. *Historical Dictionary of Mauritius* London: Scarecrow Press. Thorough coverage of people, issues and events; Bulpin, T. V. (undated, but *circa* 1954). *Islands in a Forgotten Sea.* Howard Timmins. Entertaining popular history of the Indian Ocean Islands, with particular emphais on Mauritius. Illustrations by A. A. Telford.

● Natural History

Atacia, M. 1984. *Sea Fishes of Mauritius*; Michel, C. 1986. *Birds of Mauritius;* Michel, C. 1985. *Marine Molluscs of Mauritius*; Ventor, A. J. 1988. *Underwater Mauritius.*

● Travellers' Tales

Mark Twain 1897. *More Tramps Abroad;* Durrell, G. 1979. *Golden Bats and Pink Pigeons.*

● Fiction

De St Pierre, B. 1788. *Paul et Viginie.* (English translation by Hein, R.). Editions de L'Océan Indien. Celebrated love story set in eighteenth century Mauritius; Conrad, J. 'A Smile of Fortune'. Short story set in Mauritius.

● Guides

Ellis, R. 1990. *Guide to Mauritius.* Chalfont St Peter: Bradt Publications. Well-informed guide which successfully transmits an enthusiasm for Mauritius. Special section of advice for business people; Marsh R. V. R. 1976. *Mountains of Mauritius: a Climber's Guide.*

SEYCHELLES

INTRODUCTION

The Seychelles consist of a scattered group of over a hundred islands and atolls in the western Indian Ocean. Despite being close to the equator the climate is pleasant, varying at sea level from 24°C to 29°C. There is a hot season from December to May and a cool season from June to November. The islands are exceptionally beautiful and rise steeply from the surrounding coral reefs, with marvellous beaches of white sand fringed by palm trees backed by mountains of thick vegetation.

The tourist sector is well developed, and there are many first-rate hotels. The beaches are splendid for swimming, and the clear waters are ideal for observing marine life. Seychelles people are friendly, and the Islands are very safe for visitors. However, the Seychelles are expensive and the budget traveller must expect to allow about three times the amount for daily expenditures as compared with Comores, Madagascar, and Mauritius. In addition, the remote location of the Islands make them costly to access.

Exchange Rate August 1994 R 4.8 = US$1

CONTENTS

Maps

Environment

Geography

The Seychelles, comprising 115 islands in all, are situated just south of the equator and cover an area of 450 sq km. Unlike Reunion and Mauritius which are volcanic in origin, the Seychelles appears to have been formed from shift in layers of the earth's crust some 650 million years ago. The larger islands are granite in origin while smaller less-inhabited islands are usually coral atolls. The inner islands of Mahé (155 sq km), Praslin (38 sq km), Silhouette (20 sq km) and La Digue (10 sq km) are the largest.

Climate

The Islands experience an equatorial climate. The wet season is from December to May while the dry season begins in June and lasts through to November. January is the wettest month with around 375mm of rainfall while August only receives 75mm of rain . Temperatures generally range from 24°C to 31°C and humidity levels do not often rise above 80%. Since the Islands are spread out, climatic variations do exist. The Aldabra Islands, for example, 1,220km south of Mahé receive around 1800mm of rain a year while Mahé receives close to 3000mm. Rainfall variations do also exist on a local scale, but only on the larger islands. The islands are out of the cyclone belt.

Flora

Perhaps the most famous floral species in the Seychelles is the coco de mer (*Lodoicea maldivicas*) which is found only on the Islands of Praslin, Curieuse and Silhouette and is best seen in the Vallée de Mai on Praslin. It is here that the last remaining stands of virgin forest can be found. Other rare species include the bois de fer, Wright's gardenia (*Gardenia annae*) and the very unusual and rare jellyfish tree (*Medusagyne oppositifolia*). In addition, the islands have a few carnivorous plants such as the insect pitcher, a number of palm varieties which include lataniers and palmis varieties and endemic pandanus species. The islands also share a wide variety of exotic flora including frangipani, bougainvilliea, orchids and many more.

Fauna

The only mammal indigenous to the islands are the *Pteropus Seychellensis* fruit bats. Other small animals such as flying foxes and tenrecs (insect eaters) have all been introduced. There are also snakes, geckos, a Chamaeleon (*Chamaeleo tigris*) and four different types of frog which includes the *Sooglossus gardinieri* which, fully grown, measures just 2 cm . Although at one time the only remaining area in the Seychelles inhabited by giant tortoises (*Testudo gigantea*), which fully grown weigh an average 450-500 kilos, was the Aldabra Islands, they have, over the years, been re-introduced to other Islands.

Birds

The Islands have a wide variety of visiting bird species which include herons, gulls, sunbirds, sparrows, and plovers. Indigenous species are common and many Islands have their own endemic species, birds endemic to Mahé include the Seychelles Kestrel, the banana bird (*Zosterops modesta*) and the bare-legged scops owl, on Fregate the toc-toc (*Foudia seychellarum*) is endemic whilst the magpie robin is also found on Aride. Praslin

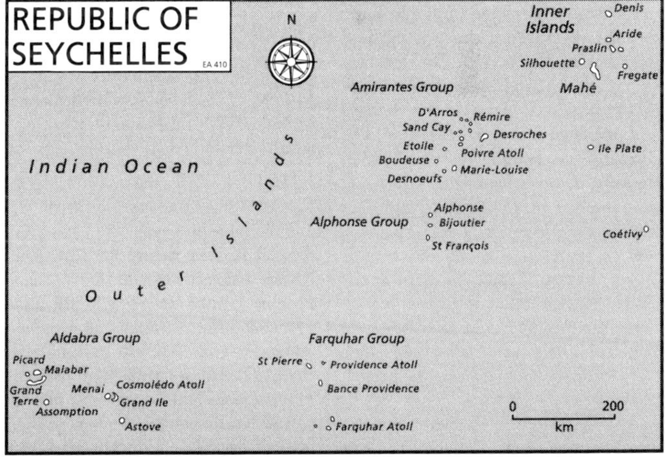

has its Black Parrot (*Coracopsis nigra*) and the Seychelles sunbird (*Otus insularis*) whilst the Paradise flycatcher (*Tchitrea corvina*) remains endemic to La Digue. Other birds found throughout the Seychelles include a host of owls, the cattle egret *Bubulcus ibis seychellarum* and the Seychelles blue pigeon (*Alectroenas pulcherrima*).

Marine Life

The Islands enjoy a developed marine ecology and several areas have been set aside as marine reserves. Besides the wide variety of fish and corals common to the Indian Ocean Islands, the Seychelles is a popular area for the Green turtle (*Chelonia mydas*) other common turtles found in Seychelle waters are the Hawksbill, Ridley and loggerhead turtles. Unfortunately in recent years these animals have come under increasing pressure from poachers and there are fears for their safety. It is hoped with the development of marine reserves and increasing awareness, poaching levels may decrease. There are also three types of endemic terrapin (box turtle).

History

Although the Islands had been known to the Arab traders and pirates well before the seventeenth century, the first recorded landing occurred in 1609 by a ship of the British East India Company. Pirates began using the Islands as a base and one such Oliver Le Vasseura "The Buzzard" is thought to have hidden treasure in the islands that has never been found. In 1742 the governor of Mauritius, Mahé de Labourdonnais, sent a representative of the French crown, Lazare Picault, to map the Islands. Lazare later returned having named the main Island after Mahé de Labourdonnais and in 1756 the Islands were formally taken over by the French crown.

The Islands were named Séchelles after the then French Finance Minister Jean Moreceau de Séchelles and the first settlement was established in August 27th 1770. During the early days the settlers were encouraged by Peter Poivre from Mauritius to cultivate spices, and cinnamon, cloves and nutmeg were established. In 1790 the Island declared its independence from France but this was short-lived and French rule was re-established a year later. In 1794 the Islands, then under a new governor Jean Baptiste Queau de Quinssy surrendered the Islands to the hostile British to avoid bloodshed, although visiting French ships were welcomed when the British had departed. At the Treaty of Paris in 1814 the Seychelles were ceded to the British. In an effort to provide continuity and stability, Quinssy was asked to stay on as governor. He changed his name to Quincy, and he remained in the Seychelles until his death in 1827.

Under British rule the Islands were left very much to themselves. With the abolition of slavery in 1835, the emancipated slaves were unwilling to work on plantations. The owners showed no inclination to recruit labour from India, and although there was some immigration, shortage of labour caused the economy to suffer. The opening of the Suez Canal placed the Seychelles on the new route to Mauritius, and exports of vanilla, copra and guano were developed. In 1903 the Seychelles were declared a crown colony (until then they had been administered from Mauritius) but French remained the main language.

In the 1960s universal suffrage was granted and the Legislative Council increased in size. Before long two main Parties were established, the Seychelles Peoples United Party (SPUP) under France René and the anti-independence lobbyists, the Seychelles Democratic Party under James Mancham. Although Mancham won the 1966 elections the SPUP persuaded him, under growing general pressure for independence, to form a coalition with René a minister. On June 26 1976 Seychelles acquired its Independence. In 1977 René seized control in a coup, and the Seychelles People's Progressive Front (SPPF) was established as the only legal political party. A number of mercenaries, posing as a South African rugby club, made an unsuccessful coup attempt in 1982. Later that year there was an army mutiny, quickly suppressed, and in 1985 another coup, this time engineered by army officers, was foiled. Discontent continued to be widespread, forcing René to legalise opposition parties in 1991. In 1992 elections were held and won by René and the SPPF.

People

The population comprises a wide mix, and African, European, Indian and Chinese immigrants have intermarried and created a people of light skin colour. The society has few castes, either social or racial, and interracial marriages are fully accepted. In the early 1990s the population was about 68,000, with most living on Mahé, some 5,000 on Praslin and 2,000 on la Digue. The attitude of the local people to tourists has improved, with a resentment to visitors in the post-colonial days dwindling with the realisation of the financial benefits.

Most of the people of the Seychelles are Christian, with Catholics making up over 90%. Other religions have less of a following but still play a significant part in Seychelles society. Traditional voodoo or witchcraft still exists, the use of amulets and charms is common, and sorcery, although banned in 1958, is still practised.

Culture and Life

The Islands have a local dance known as the *moutia* and the *sega* common on Reunion and Mauritius is also performed in the Seychelles. Traditional crafts include woodcarving, weaving, basketwork and model boatbuilding, with training and marketing undertaken by the Compagnie pour le Développement de l'Artisanat (Codevar).

Modern Seychelles

Politics

After Independence in 1976, Seychelles had a coalition government that was ousted by a coup in 1977. Subsequently President Albert René established single-party rule, and succeeded in remaining in power despite several coup attempts, and the introduction of multiparty elections in 1993. The introduction of socialist reforms and the expectations that these would be reversed in a coup damaged business confidence and deterred foreign investment. Economic strategy has effectively remained unchanged, with consistent reliance on a mixed economy, despite a declaration of President René in favour of a more socialist strategy.

Overall, Seychelles' stability record must be judged poor. There is continued concern that one of the regular coup attempts mounted from outside the country will be successful, although there is now less anxiety that the René government will introduce radical changes.

Economics

As Seychelles is a small economy, some of the data relating to economic performance is not collected regularly and some of the figures are not very recent. However, the data that is available allows a fairly clear picture of the economy to emerge.

Economic and social structure

With a GDP of US$373 mn in 1991, the Islands have one of the smallest economies in Africa. However, GNP per head was around US$5,110. Only Réunion and Mayotte in Africa (and they both have special status making them part of

France) have a higher living standard. Agriculture, which includes fishing, generated only 7% of GDP in 1984, compared to 16% for industry, with limited manufacturing, fish processing being the most important development in this sector. The service sector, dominated by the tourist industry, generates 77% of GDP.

On the demand side, private consumption was 60% of GDP in 1984. Investment was 21%, while government consumption at 31% was one of the highest in the region.

Exports were 64% of GDP in 1984 and this is well above both the regional and African averages of 16% and 23% respectively. Imports were equivalent to 76% of GDP while the regional and African averages are about one third of that figure. Such a high dependence on trade is inescapable when a small domestic market does not allow manufacturing and heavy industry at a sufficiently large scale to be efficient. In 1987, the main commodity exports were fish, 80%, and copra, 9%.

Primary enrolment was 113% in 1982, one of the highest in Africa. The percentage of secondary-aged population in school was 31%, double the regional average, while 16% of the 20-24 age group were in tertiary education, by far the highest ratio in Africa. The resources devoted to Education has achieved an adult literacy rate of 89% in 1991, over twice the Africa average.

Provision of health services is also very good with a life expectancy of 71 years, one of the best in Africa. Provision of doctors and nurses in 1975 was also extremely good with 2,170 people per doctor. Daily average calorie supply was 2,368 in 1983, about 12% better than the African average.

Overall, Seychelles is a small economy in the upper-middle-income group, with most GDP generated by the services sector which has a large tourist component. Dependence on international trade is high. Educational, health and nutrition provision are good.

Economic Performance

GDP growth for 1973-82 was 6.3% a year, implying GDP per head growth of 4.8%. The industrial sector grew fastest, at 8%, a high growth rate for an African economy, as was the 6.9% a year growth in the service sector. Agricultural growth was negative, -0.6%, though in recent years the government has made efforts to stimulate growth in this sector and the fishing industry has expanded significantly. Export volume growth was also good, with a 10.1% annual increase, while imports grew by 10.5%. Inflation over the 1980-91 period ran at an average of 3.5% a year, one of the lowest rates in Africa.

Overall, Seychelles has had good economic performance, with GDP and GDP per head rising leading to improved living standards. Price stability has been good.

Recent Economic Developments

The government has increased its participation in the economy since 1977 by taking majority shareholdings in certain enterprises. There are a number of state farms, some hotels have been acquired, and parastatals have been set up to run utilities, market commodities and control imports. State acquisition and intervention, however, appears to be extended in an *ad hoc* manner, and there is considerable encouragement to private foreign investment. Two minor parastatals were abolished in 1987, and some printing parastatals rationalised. At the same time, investment in other parastatals has increased, notably Air Seychelles and the Seychelles Marketing Board. The development strategy is mainly concerned to maintain balance on external payments, and to ensure that debt service can be maintained. To this end the tourist industry is of vital importance as the main foreign exchange earner, and private foreign investment is an important element in sustaining Seychelles' position as an attractive tourist destination.

In the 1980s Seychelles found it difficult to sustain the rapid growth of GDP achieved in the 1970s. Much depends on the fortunes of the tourist sector which is very sensitive to rumours of political instability and decisions of major airlines concerning both scheduled and charter flights. Inflation performance has improved. Annual price rises were consistently above 10% up to 1982, but inflation has declined to under 5% a year currently.

Seychelles runs a substantial trade deficit, with earnings for merchandise exports estimated at US$15 mn in 1989,

Comparative Economic And Social Data

	Seychelles	East Africa	Africa	Industrial Countries
Population & Land				
Population, mid year, millions, 1994	0.073	12.2	10.2	40.0
Urban population, %, 1985	26	30.5	30	75
Population growth rate, % per year, 1980-91	1.2	3.1	3.1	0.8
Land area, 000 sq km	0.450	486	486	1,628
Population density, persons per sq km, 1994	162.2	24.2	20.4	24.3
Economy: Production & Income				
GDP, US$ millions, 1991	373	2,650	3,561	550,099
GNP per head, US$, 1991	5,110	250	389	12,960
Economy: Supply Structure				
Agriculture, % of GDP, 1984	7	43	35	3
Industry, % of GDP, 1984	16	15	27	35
Services, % of GDP, 1984	77	42	38	61
Economy: Demand Structure				
Private consumption, % of GDP, 1984	60	77	73	62
Gross domestic investment, % of GDP, 1984	21	16	16	21
Government consumption, % of GDP, 1984	31	15	14	17
Exports, % of GDP, 1984	64	16	23	17
Imports, % of GDP, 1984	76	24	26	17
Economy: Performance				
GDP growth, % per year, 1973-82	6.3	1.6	-0.6	2.5
GDP per head growth, % per year, 1973-82	4.8	-1.7	-3.7	1.7
Agriculture growth, % per year, 1973-82	-0.6	1.1	0.0	2.5
Industry growth, % per year, 1973-82	8.0	1.1	-1.0	2.5
Services growth, % per year, 1973-82	6.9	2.5	-0.5	2.6
Exports growth, % per year, 1973-82	10.1	0.7	-1.9	3.3
Imports growth, % per year, 1973-82	10.5	0.2	-6.9	4.3
Economy: Other				
Inflation rate, % per year, 1980-91	3.5	23.6	16.7	5.3
Aid, net inflow, % of GDP, 1991	6.7	11.5	6.3	-
Debt Service, % of exports, 1984	4.3	18	20.6	-
Education				
Primary, % of 6-11 group, 1982	116	62	76	102
Secondary, % of 12-17 group, 1982	31	15	22	93
Tertiary, % of 20-24 group, 1982	16	1.2	1.9	39
Adult literacy rate, %, 1990	89	41	39	99
Health & Nutrition				
Life expectancy, years, 1991	71	50	50	76
Calorie supply, daily per head, 1989	2,368	2,111	2,096	3,357
Population per doctor, 1987	2,170	35,986	24,185	550

Notes: 'Africa' excludes South Africa. Dates are for the country in question, and do not always correspond with the regional, African and industrial averages.

while imports were US$160mn. Seychelles' external debt was estimated at US$US 124m in 1987. As Seychelles is an upper-middle-income country, this is mostly commercial debt or loans not made at the highly concessionary rates extended to the very poorest countries. Debt servicing is low at 4.3% of exports of goods and services. The exchange rate depreciated gently from 1980 when it stood at R6.39 = US$1 to R7.13 = US$US 1 in 1985. Thereafter, the weakening of the US dollar has seen an appreciation to R5.2 = US$1 in 1994.

The upper-middle income status enjoyed by Seychelles restricts the amount of concessionary lending it receives. Main lending commitment have been US$12.7 mn from the African Development Bank for water supply, and US$3.3 mn from France for sewerage. France gave over half of the total US$20.1 mn bilateral aid in 1987 with only another US$4.7 mn coming from multilateral sources.

Private investment has included the establishment of an international airline, which has raised US$2.9 mn, most of it locally. The International Finance Corporation of the World Bank is lending US$7.6 mn for hotel development. Intercontinental Hotels are to manage the project, and are investing US$0.5 mn. Enterprise Oil of the UK have taken up an option to explore for oil off-shore to the south of the Seychelles.

Economic Outlook

Seychelles' prospects depend on sustaining the levels of earnings from tourism, and achieving expansion. This will doubtless be helped by the improved world economic conditions in the last part of the 1990s. The other important factor is the ability to avoid political instability, and it remains to be seen how robust the new multi-party system proves to be.

VICTORIA

About half the population of Mahé live in the capital, but with a population of around 30,000, it is still small. The city centre has buildings from the Colonial period, particularly along Revolution Ave and Lodge St. The Clock Tower at the intersection of Independence Ave and Albert St is a replica of one on Vauxhall Bridge in London, and commemorates the break from Mauritius in 1903, when Seychelles acquired the status of a Crown Colony. The Post Office and the Court House, both Colonial buildings, are close to the Clock Tower, as is the Statue of Peter Poivre, who introduced spices from Mauritius in 1770. On Independence Ave, running east from the Clock Tower, are the Craft Market, and the National Museum. At the roundabout is the Twa Zwazo monument, with three birds representing the influence of the cultures of Europe, Africa and Asia on the Seychelles.

Turning south at the Twa Zwazo monument leads past the **Zomn Lib** monument (which commemorates the Independence of the Seychelles in 1975), and the **Yacht Club**, on the inner harbour. A small park, **Jardin des Infants**, is just before the roundabout from which the road leads to the airport. The new **National Library** faces on to the roundabout, and the parliament, **Maison du Peuple**, is just to the east.

Turning north up Francis Rachel St, the **People's Stadium**, the main sporting venue, is on the right. Off to the left, on rue de la Poudriere, is the new **Mosque**. This road winds round past **State House**, which was constructed in 1913 as the governor's residence.

To the north of the Clock tower is **St Paul's Anglican Cathedral**, part of which dates from 1857, and which was consecrated as a Cathedral in 1973. Just to the north is Market St, and the **Sir Selwyn Clarke Market**. On Quincy St, at the western end of Market St is the **Hindu Temple**. The **Catholic Cathedral** is on Oliver Maradan St, and contains the celebrated clock that chimes twice -once, it is said, to wake the sleepy citizens of the capital, and a second time to inform them of the hour. Close by is **Capuchin House**, the Bishop's residence, with verandahs and columns, built in 1933 and in an architectural style drawn from Portugal.

Places of interest

National Museum Located on Independence Ave. There is a collection of natural history items and historical exhibits. The **Possession Stone** is situated in the entrance. It was originally laid in the gardens surrounding the Governor's Residence in 1756 to mark French possession of the Seychelles. In 1894, with the Islands now under British control, there was an attempt by the French to remove the Stone and ship it to Paris. The boat carrying the Stone was intercepted at Aden, and it was returned. In

Louis Xvii

It is said that the son of Louis XVI and Marie Antoinette, born in 1785, was smuggled from Paris to the Seychelles during the French Revolution. The Governor of the Islands was aware if his identity, but allowed the fugiteve to be brought up under an assumed name, Poiret. At his death in 1856, his origins were revealed, but it has never been satisfactorily established that Poiret was Louis XVI, and that his descendents are the heirs to the French crown.

Spice Tragedy

In 1768 the French arrived in the Seychelles and in 1770 the first settlers were installed. Land grants were made, and botanical gardens established at Anse Royale in 1772. Spice plants were brought from Ile de France (Mauritius) under the direction of Peter Poivre.

The French lived in perpetual fear that the British would attack the island, capture the spice plants that had been brought from South East Asian and painstakingly adapted to local conditions and undermine French monopoly of the Indian Ocean spice trade. As a precaution they piled brushwood round the plantations so that the plants could be burnt at a moment's notice if there was a sudden attack.

Alas, they were to fall victims of a tragic bluff. In May 1780 a French slave-trader, flying British colours just in case the island had already fallen to the enemy, entered harbour. In panic the inhabitants torched the spices, and only the cinnamon plants survived the blaze.

1964 it was removed from State House and installed in the Museum. Opening hours Mon-Fri 0900-1700 and Sat 0900-1200. Entrance free.

Bel Air Cemetery At the end of Bel Air Rd. Not particularly well maintained. It has the grave of a local giant, reputed to be 3m in height. It is said that his stature so alarmed local people that he was poisoned, in 1870, when still in his teens.

A pillar, marking his height, stands by the grave. Other graves in the cemetery are said to include those of pirates who used the Seychelles as a base in the seventeenth century.

Botanical Gardens Situated off Chemin Mont Fleuri to the south of the city centre. Founded by Antoine Gillot from Mauritius in 1771, under the direction of Peter Poivre. There is a collection of tropical trees, in which the palms are well represented. Orchids are displayed in a special garden, there is a giant tortoise, and a café. Open every day 0900-1800. Entrance free, but entry to the orchid display is US$2.

Seychelles People's United Party (SPUP) Museum On Francis Rachel St, at the party headquarters. The current President, Albert Rene founded the party in 1964. There are exhibits relating to the party's history, and a display of items from the coup of 1977 in which Albert Rene overthrew James Mancham.

La Bastille A Colonial house on the road north of Victoria to Anse Etoile. It houses the National Archives and Museum, with many historical documents and a newspaper collection. There is a statue of Queen Victoria that at one time stood outside the Court House near the Clock Tower. The National Archives and Museum are due to be re-located in the new National Library on Francis Rachel St.

Local information

● Where to stay

A *Auberge Louis XVII*, about 3km south of the centre on Mont Fleuri Rd, T 44411, F 44428. Bungalow-style. a/c. Swimming pool. Bar. Restaurant. Gardens. Excellent views. **A** *Mountain Rise Hotel*, on Chemin Sans Souci, around 2 km south of the centre, T 225145 F 225503. Good location. Swimming pool. Gardens. Restaurant, excellent Creole and international menu, open to non-residents. Excursions, water sports and marine viewing arranged. **A** *Sunrise Guest House*, Mont Fleuri Rd, south of the centre, T 224560, a/c. Restaurant, Chinese and Creole. At lower end of A-range. Good value. **A** *Harbour View Guest House*, Mont Fleuri Rd, T 322473. Fairly small. Restaurant. Lower end of A-range. **A** *Hilltop Guest House*, Chemin St Louis, T 323553. Restaurant. bar. Lower end of the

A-range. **A** ***Pension Bel Air***, Bel Air Rd, T 224416, F 224923. Fairly close to centre. Colonial building. Restaurant. Arranges marine excursions.

B ***Beaufond Lane Guest House***, Mont Fleuri Rd, south of the town centre, T 322408. Reasonably close to centre. a/c. **B** ***La Louis Lodge***, Eureka Relais des Iles. Located 4 km south of the centre on Chemin la Misere, T 44349. Comfortable and well appointed. Situation allows good views out over Victoria and toward St Anne Island. **B** ***Michel Holiday Appartements***, Le Rocher, south of centre, T 344540. Rate is for two people sharing a studio – it is possble to squeeze in two children at no extra cost. Reasonable value.

● Places to eat

♦♦♦♦***Marie Antoinette***, Chemin St Louis, T 323942. Creole menu. Handsome setting in Colonial house with gardens. Open 1200-1500 and 1900-2200. Closed Sun.

♦♦♦♦***King Wah***, Benezet St, T 323658. Chinese food. Reasonable standard. ♦♦♦♦***Pirates Arms***, Independence Ave, T 225001. Café, opening out onto street. International menu. Central, with good atmosphere. Closed Sun. ♦♦♦♦***Mandarin***, Revolution Ave. Chinese food. Good standard. ♦♦♦♦***L'Amiral***, Independence Ave. International menu.

♦♦♦***Marmite***, Revolution Ave. International menu. ♦♦♦***Bon Appetit***, Francis Rachel St. Take-away meals. ♦♦♦***Sandy's***, Revolution Ave. Take-away meals.

● Airlines

British Airways, Kingsgate House, Independence Ave, T 224910. **Kenya Airways**, Revolution Ave, T 322989. **Air Seychelles**, Victoria House, Independence Ave, T 321548. **Air France**, Victoria House, Independence Ave, T 322414. **Aeroflot**, Independence Ave.

● Banks

Several located on Independence Ave. Hours

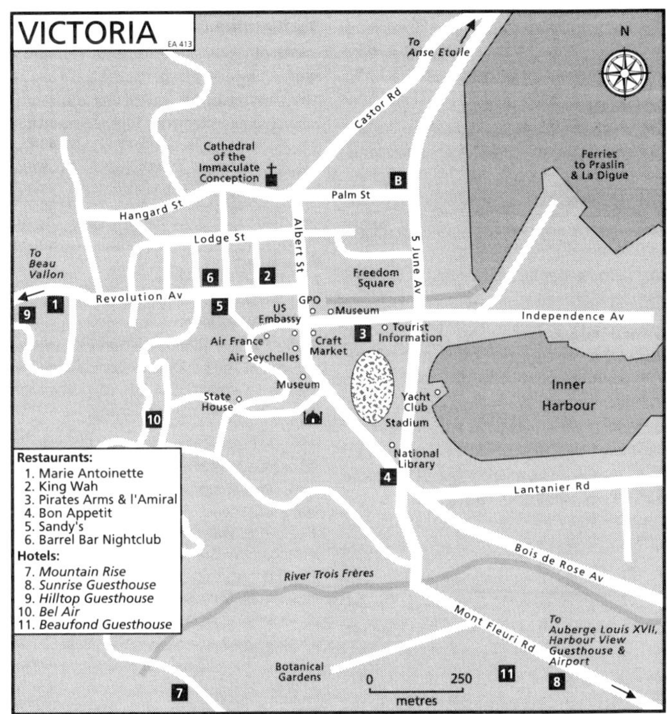

Mon-Fri 0830-1230 and 1400-1530; Sat 0800-1130.

Embassies (E), High Commissions (HC) and Consulates (C)

Belgium (C), Huteau Lane. **Cuba** (E), Liberation Ave. **Denmark** (E), Bel Air. **India** (HC), Le Chantier. **Madagascar** (C), Independence House, Independence Ave. **Norway** (C), Victoria House, State House Ave. **UK** (HC), Victoria House, State House Ave, T 225225. USA (E), Victoria House, State House Ave, T 225256.

Entertainment

Discos *Love Nut*, Off Albert St. *Barrel Bar*, Revolution Ave.

Theatre Occasional performances at the *Polytechnic*, Mont Fleuri, south of the centre, by the National Cultural Troupe, and visiting companies. Programmes and booking from *Seychelles Artistic Productions*, Independence Ave, T 225170.

Cinema *Deepam*, Albert St. Western films. *Centre Culturel Francais*, Independence Ave, T 322268. Three different film programmes per week.

Hospitals

Mont Fleuri Hospital, Mont Fleuri Rd, T 234400. Charge of US$15 for visitors for a consultation.

Libraries

National Library, Francis Rachel St Open Mon-Fri 0830-1700, Sat 0830-1145. *American Cultural Centre*, Francis Rachel St Open Mon-Fri 1130-1530.

Local transport

Bus Station is at corner of Palm St and 5th June Ave. Bus to airport is US$0.60.

Car Hire Sunshine, T 3246710. **Eden's Rentacar**, T 323359. **RAM Car Hire**, T 323442. **Jean's Car Hire**, T 322278.

Taxi stand is on Albert St. Fares are US$3 for the first km and US$0.60 thereafter.

Post Office

Central Post Office Independence Ave.

Religion

Mosque Rue de la Poudriere. **Catholic Cathedral**, Oliver Maradan St. **Anglican Cathedral**, Albert St. **Hindu Temple**, Quincy St.

Shopping

Craft Centre, Independence Ave. Wood carvings, basketry, batiks, mother of pearl items. *Victoria House Shopping Arcade*, Francis Rachel St. Shops with wide variety of imported items.

Bookshops *SPACE*, Albert St Books, magazines, imported newspapers, Government publications. *Information Office*, 5 June Ave. Maps.

Telecommunications

Cable and Wireless, Francis Rachel St. Open 24 hours. International telephone calls, faxes, telexes, telegrams.

Tourist Office

Seychelles Tourist Board, Independence Ave, T 225333

Travel Agents & Tour Operators

Masons's Travel, Revolution Ave, T 322642, F 225273. *Travel Services Seychelles*, Victoria House, Independence Ave, T 322414, F 321366. *Bunson's Travel*, Revolution Ave, T 322682. *National Travel Agency*, Kingsgate House, Independence Ave, T 224900, F 225111.

Transport

Air There are regular flights to **Praslin** ($30, takes 15 mins) and **Fregate Island** ($30, 15 mins); **Bird Island** ($80, 30 mins); **Desroches** ($80, 1 hour). Flights to **Denis Island** are included in the package excursion price. Taxi to airport is around US$10. The airport is about 8km to the south east of Victoria.

Boat There are boats Mon-Fri to **Praslin**, they take 3 hours and cost US$10. Also to **La Digue**, Mon-Fri, taking just over 3 hours and costing US$10.

MAHE

The island contains the capital, Victoria, and a population of around 60,000. It is the largest and most populated of the Seychelles group. Granite hills run along the spine of the island which is 27km from north to south and 10km at its widest. The highest point is Morne Seychois, at 905m, and it rises up behind Victoria. The island is surrounded by fine beaches. Victoria is the only significant urban area, all the other centres being villages.

The northern part of the island is the most developed, and is more mountainous. **Beau Vallon** beach is a notable tourist area with a cluster of shops and hotels. It has good sand along the shore, and a break in the reef allows quite large waves. It is an easy walk from Victoria, about 4 km. The east coast has attractive, fairly quiet beaches, and the bay at **Anse Royale** is particularly pretty. The southern tip of the island is closed off. The west coast is quite secluded, but breaks in the reef can lead to some heavy seas, and some beaches are not suitable for swimming.

Places of interest

Morne Seychellois National Park There are two tracks running through the Park, which was first designated in 1973.

The first begins at Sans Souci and ascends to the **Trois Freres** peaks at 699m. The track is marked by posts, and can be awkward in the rain. It is possible to carry on past the peaks to Beau Vallon. The summit is often encased in mist, but there is a fine view on a clear day.

The other routes is from Danzilles, and runs west through the edge of the park to **Anse Major**. There is an Agricultural Research Station on the site of a former Catholic Mission at Anse Major. The trail on to Baie Ternay from Anse Major is closed.

The highest peak in Mahé is **Morne Seychellois** (905m), sited in the Park. It can be climbed, but a permit is required from the Tourist Office on Independence Ave in Victoria, T 225333. The services of a guide, which can be arranged through the Tourist Office, is advisable unless you have some climbing experience.

Bel Ombre Treasure Site A British resident, Reginald Cruise-Wilkins, was convinced, on the basis of a map obtained from an elderly Norwegian mariner, that the Levasseur's treasure (see page 839) is concealed at Bel Ombre. He searched the site for forty years, and although some coins have been unearthed, the hoard remains undiscovered. The site is marked off on the beach, and there are tentative plans to begin exploration again.

Kreol Fleurage Located about 5km north of Victoria at Anse Nord D'Est. This is a perfume and fragrant oils dis-

The Buzzard's Treasure

Olivier Levasseur, known as "The Buzzard", was a pirate who operated in the Indian Ocean in the eighteenth century. One of his most valuable prizes, laden with gold, was the Portuguese caravelle, *Vierge au Cap*. As a final defiant gesture at his execution in Reunion in 1730, Levasseur is reputed to have tossed a scrap of paper to the crowd which contained clues as to the whereabouts of the hoard. A site at Bel Ombre on Mahé is thought to match the descriptions on scraps of evidence that have been collected on the treasure site. Despite excavations, nothing has been found.

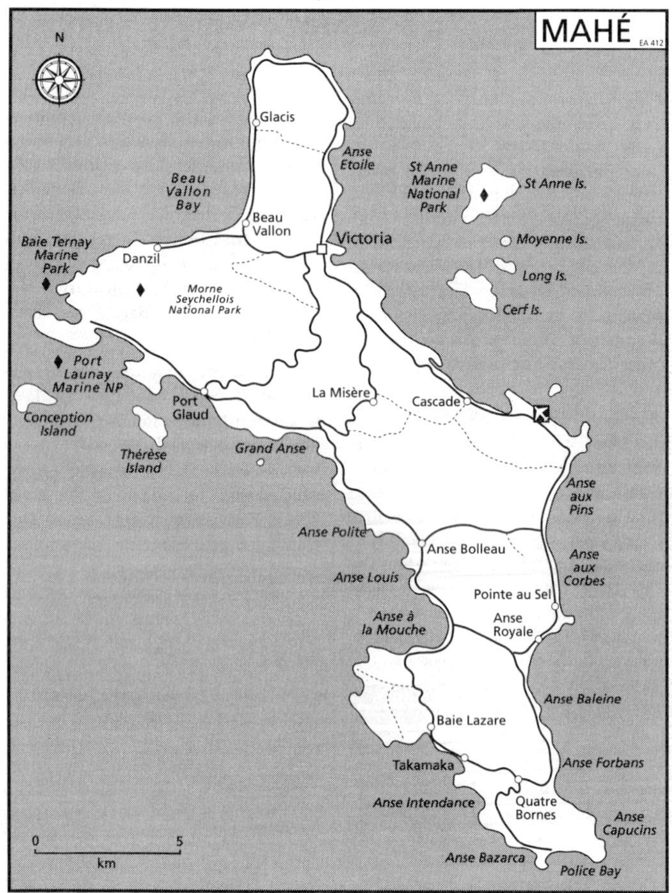

tillery. Small phials of perfumes and essences can be purchased.

La Gogue Reservoir Lies between Anse Etoile and Glacis. It makes for a pleasant walk into the hills, and can be accessed from Anse Etoile by road. The route from Glacis is a footpath only.

Sauzier Falls Close to Port Glaud, and about 1km inland along the path that runs beside the church opposite L'Islette. The falls are very pretty, and it is possible to swim in the pool.

Coppiola Peak This can be rached from the Chemin Sans Souci road, with the turn-off about 3 km from Victoria. The ascent is quite steep, and the granite summit is at an altitude of 510m. The trail is marked by posts, and there are good views from the top.

Tea Factory Located on the Chemin Sans Souci road, between Victoria and Port Glaud. A selection of spice-flavoured teas are on sale, there is a café, and it is possible to visit the plantation.

Open Mon-Sat 0800-1600.

Morne Blanc This can be climbed from the Chemin Sans Souci road. The trail is blazed by yellow paint markings, and is quite steep in parts, to the summit at 667m.

Riviere Cascade Trail runs from Cascade, near the airport, and divides to go west to La Misere, or east to Anse Faure. There are waterfalls along the stream, and the two routes are each about 6km.

Marine Parks. Two bays on the main island in the north, on the fringes of Morne Seychellois National Park, at Baie Ternay and Port Launay, have been designated Marine National Parks. The waters are particularly good for snorkelling. There are no formal facilities.

La Brulee This is a 501m peak, accessed from the Chemin Montagne Posee road in the southern part of the island. The rail begins among forest vegetation and streams, and there are good views from the summit.

Craft Village Located at Anse aux Pins on the east coast. Has displays of batik, pottery, wood-carvings and mother-of-pearl work for sale. Craftsmen can be observed at work, there is a café, and the village is centred on a rather fine restored colonial mansion.

National Theatre At Anse Royale on the west coast. Performances by local and visiting companies.

Michael Adams' studio Situated at Anse aux Poules Bleues on the west coast. Adams is a water-colourist, and he specialises on local landscapes. Paintings, prints and line-drawings are displayed, and are for sale.

Val d'Andorre In the southern part of the island there are two routes from Baie Lazare on the west coast. One, Chemin Val d'Ender, crosses to the east coast at Anse Baleine. The other, Chemin Dame le Roi, forking off from it after about 2km, back to Anse Soleil. At Val d'Andorre, near the junction, is a pottery studio with items for sale.

Local information

● Where to stay – North coast

A+ *Vista Bay*, near northern point, T 247351, F 247642. Modern, reasonably large. Good facilities. **A+** *Sunset Beach Hotel*, Glacis, T 247227, F 247521. Range of accommodation, all fairly luxurious. **A+** *Northolme Hotel*, between Glacis and Beau Vallon, T 247222. Reasonably large, comfortable, and with good views. The oldest hotel in the Seychelles. Compton MacKenzie and Alec Waugh have stayed here. **A+** *Vacoa Village*, Beau Vallon, T 261130, F 247606. Self-catering studios and apartments. Swimming pool and gardens. Imaginative architectural style. **A+** *Coral Strand*, Beau Vallon, T 247036, F 247517. Busy, modern style. Most guests on package holidays. Swimming pool and pool bar. Restaurant. Popular with non-residents. **A+** *Beau Vallon Bay Hotel*, Beau Vallon, T 247141, F 247107. Large hotel, mostly catering for package tourists. Restaurants. Bars. Casino. Tennis. Water sports. Diving. Entertainment programme. Popular with non-residents. **A+** *Fisherman's Cove* (*Le Meridien*), Bel Ombre, T 247252, F 247450. Thatched chalets. Swimming pool. Garden. Range of expensive suites available. **A+** *Auberge Sun*, Danzilles, T 247550. Thatched bungalows in pleasant location. Restaurant.

A *Sea Breeze*, Pointe Conan, T 241021, a/c. Modern style. Chalets with verandahs. Restaurant. **A** *Jade House*, Anse Etoile, T 241489, F 241888, a/c. Fairly small. Restaurant. **A** *Manresa*, Anse Etoile, T 241388. Some a/c. Rooms with balconies. Restaurant. Bar. **A** *Coco d'Or* Beau Vallon, T 247331, F 247454. Fairly small. Located away from beach. **A** *Panorama*, Beau Vallon, T 247300. Comfortable modern house. Restaurant. **A** *Beau Vallon Bungalows*, Beau Vallon, T 247382. At lower end of A-range. **A** *Villa Madonna*, Beau Vallon, T 247403. Homely and good value – at lower end of the A-range. Located away from beach. **A** *Villa Napoleon*, Beau Vallon, T 247133. Small guest house. Lower end of A-range. **A** *Le Tamarinier*, Bel Ombre, T 247611/429, F 247711. Small and modern, set back from the beach.

B *Calypha*, Anse Etoile, T 241157. Modern style. Verandah. Fine location. Excellent value. **B** *North Point*, northernmost point of island, T 242339. More expensive for single occupancy. Some self-catering bungalows. Good value. **B** *Chez Jean* (Villa Carol), near northernmost point, T 241445, F 225430. Comfortable and good value. **B** *Les Manguiers*, near northernmost point. (T 241455) House and double rooms for rent. More expensive for single occupancy. **B** *Pti Payot*, Beau Vallon, T 261447. Self-catering chalets. More expensive for less than 3 persons in chalet. Pleasant garden and good views. **B** *Bel Ombre Villas*, Bel Ombre, T 247616. Villas more expensive for less than four persons sharing, set back from beach. Good value. **B** *Le Niol*, Chemin St Louis, between Victoria and Beau Vallon, T 323262. Small and rather spartan.

● East Coast

A+ *Reef Hotel*, Anse aux Pins, T 376251, F 267606, a/c. Swimming pool. Tennis. Golf. Sailing and watersports. Good entertainment.

A *Carefree*, close to airport, just past Point Larue, T 376237. Quite small. a/c. Restaurant. **A** *Casuarina*, Anse aux Pins, T 376211. Based on old colonial house. Medium size. Swimming pool. Restaurant. **A** *Residence Bouganville*, Anse Baleine, T 371334. Old colonial house. Lower end of A-range. Restaurant. Bar. Good value and fairly stylish. **A** *La Roussette*, Anse aux Pins, T 376245. Bungalows with verandahs. a/c Restaurant. Bar.

B *La Retraite*, Anse aux Pins, T 376816. Small, but comfortable. Good value. **B** *Lalla Panzi*, Anse aux Pins, T 376411. Small guesthouse.

● West Coast

A+ *Meridien Barbarons*, Grande Anse, T 378253, F 378484. Large modern hotel on good beach site. Restaurants, bars. Swimming pool. **A+** *Equator*, Grande Anse, T 378228/12, F 378244. Large hotel on spectacular site on cliffs. Restaurants, bars, swimming pool. **A+** *Seychelles Sheraton* (*Mahe Beach Hotel*), about 1km south of Port Glaud, T 378451, F 378517. Large hotel, multi-story, concrete. a/c. Restaurants, bars. Swimming pool. **A+** *Chateau d'Eau*, Grande Anse, T 378339. Small and fairly exclusive guesthouse. Located in grounds of Meridien Barbarons.

A *L'Islette*, on island of L'Islette, north of Port Glaud, 200m offshore, T 378229. Small, with thatched bungalows. Restaurant, popular with non-residents. Fine location. **A** *Auberge d'Anse Boileau*, Anse Boileau, T 376660. Bungalow-style. Quite small. Good restaurant. **A** *Lazare Picault*, Baie Lazare, T 371117. Thatched bungalows. Restaurant. **A** *Plantation Club*, Pointe Lazare, T 371588, F 371517. Large complex. a/c. Swimming pool. Bar. Restaurant. Casino.

B *Blue Lagoon*, Anse a la Mouche, T 371197. Self-catering bungalows. Sailing and watersports.

● Places to eat – North

♦♦♦♦*Kyoto*, Anse Etoile, T 241337. Japanese restaurant. Reasonable standard, but quite expensive. Closed on Sun. ♦♦♦♦*La Perle Noire*, Beau Vallon, T 247046. French and Creole cuisine. ♦♦♦♦*La Goelette*, Bel Ombre, set back from the beach, T 247414. This is the training school for the Seychelles Tourist Board. Usually something exotic on the menu. Open only for lunch. ♦♦♦♦*Le Corsaire*, Bel Ombre, T 247141. Located on the beach. Mostly French cuisine. Quite expensive. Closed Mon. ♦♦♦♦*Lobster Pot*, Anse Etoile. Seafood. Quite expensive. ♦♦♦♦*Etoile de Mer*, (Kakatwa) Anse Etoile. Accent on French cuisine and seafood.

♦♦♦*La Fontaine*, Beau Vallon. Creole cuisine. ♦♦♦*Baobab Pizzeria*, Beau Vallon, T 247167. Other Italian food as well as pizza. Location on the beach. Popular and invariably busy.

● East coast

♦♦♦♦*Katiolo*, Anse Faure, T 376453. Creole cuisine and seafood. Disco. ♦♦♦♦*Ty-Foo*, Anse aux Corbes, T 371485. Creole and Chinese food. Friendly atmosphere. Popular. Open to 2400. ♦♦♦♦*Kaz Kreol*, Anse Royale, T 371680. Creole cuisine and seafood.

● West coast

♦♦♦♦*Oscar au Captaine Rouge*, Anse a la Mouche, T 371224. French cuisine. High standard. Closed Wed. ♦♦♦♦*La Sirene*, Anse aux Poules Bleus. (T 371339) Creole food. Beach location. ♦♦♦♦*Anse Gaulettes*, Baie Lazare. Creole and Chinese food. ♦♦♦♦*Sundown*, Port Glaud, T 378352. Creole food. Situated on the shore. ♦♦♦♦*La Marie Galante*, Grande Anse, T 378455. Creole food. ♦♦♦♦*Reduit Restaurant*, Anse Takamaka. Creole food.

♦♦♦*Chez Batiste*, Anse Takamaka, T 371535. Creole food. Good value. ♦♦♦*Anchor Cafe & Pizza*, Anse a la Mouche. Hamburgers, snacks.

● Local travel

Bus Regular services round the island during the day, with departures at about hourly intervals, and a more limited service up to midnight. Fares are US$0.50 to US$1.

Taxi Fares are US$3 for the first km and

US$0.60 thereafter.

Car Hire Victoria Car Hire, Anse aux Pins, East Coast, T 376314; **MS Car Rental**, Anse aux Corbes, East Coast, T 376522.

● **Transport**
See for Victoria, see page 838.

St Marine National Park

There are 6 small islands about 5km to the east of Victoria, and the area around them has been designated a Marine National Park. Snorkelling and viewing in glass-bottomed boats is particularly good.

The largest island, **St Anne**, was the site of the first settlement in 1770, and contains the ruins of an old whaling station, but is closed to visitors. **Cachee Island**, a small nature reserve to the south of the group, and **Long Island**, where there is a prison, are also closed to visitors.

Moyenne Island has some nature walks, there is a bar, the *Jolly Roger*, and ♦♦♦♦*Maison Moyenne*, T 322414. Serving Creole food in a stylish colonial mansion.

Round Island is very small, in the centre of the group, contains the **National Parks Visitor's Centre**, and was at one time the site of a leper colony. One of the old colony buildings houses ♦♦♦♦*Chez Gaby*, T 224209, a high-class restaurant serving mostly seafood in Creole style, at lunchtimes.

Cerf Island is the largest island in the group after St Anne, and offers some walks up the island's peak (108m) and round the shore. ♦♦♦♦*Beach Shed*, T 322126, serves lunch to people on day excursions.

● **Transport** See tour operators in Victoria, page 838, for day excursions, about US$40 per person, with lunch.

Therese Island

This is a small island about 1km off the west coast of Mahe. It is owned by the *Seychelles Sheraton* (*Mahe Beach Hotel*), about 1km south of Port Glaud (T 378451 F 378517), which runs day excursions to the island for about US$60 per person. There are facilities for watersports, diving and deep-sea fishing. **Conception Island** is 1km further west, but is not visitable as it is difficult to make a landing there.

Silhouette Island

Located 20 km to the west of Mahe, this is a granite island with several peaks, the highest being Mont Daubin at 740km. There is an old **Copra Mill** at La Passe on the east coast, by the jetty, which can be visited. The remains of an early settlement, possibly Shirazi, can be seen close to **Pointe Zeng Zeng** on the east coast. There is a good climb to **Mont Pot a Eau** (621m) from La Passe. It is possible to hike across the island by way of the route just to the south of the **Gratte Fesse** peak, or by following on from the route that leads to Mont Pot a Eau, to **Grande Barbe** on the west coast. Other walks are round the shore, north from La Presse to Grebeau on the north coast and then on to **Pointe Etienne**, about 8km in all.

● **Where to stay A+** *Silhouette Island Lodge*, T 224003, F 244178. Offers exclusive bungalow accommodation.

● **Transport** Tour agents in Victoria (see page 838) arrange day trips for around US$95 per person, including lunch. A trip from Victoria takes 2-3 hours, from Bel Ombre on the west coast 1-2 hours.

PRASLIN

An exceptionally attractive island, 12km long and 5km wide, about 35km to the north east of Mahe. The island is granite, and the peaks are less high, the tallest being 367m. Praslin has only around 7,000 inhabitants, and there are no real urban areas, just small settlements and villages.

In the **Vallee de Mai** is found the *coco de mer*, an unusual species, unique to the Seychelles. The beaches round the island are excellent, and **Anse Lazio** on the north coast, where a break in the reef lets in rollers, is exceptional.

The island was originally named Ile de Palme in 1774 by Lazare Picault, a French mariner. It was formally claimed for France in 1768, and a "possession stone" laid in Anse Possession bay. The island was later renamed in honour of the French Minister of State, Duc de Praslin.

Places of Interest

Vallee de Mai National Park Quite exquisite area, small, covering about 4 sq km, in the southern half of the island. Apart from the coco de mer there are many other palms, red pineapple, wild coffee, and allspice. For visitors, there are a number of well-marked trails and guides to the plants and wildlife. Open daily 0830-1750. Entry US$5, children under 12 free.

St Pierre A small island off Anse Volbert on the east coast. A good site for snorkelling. Trips run form Anse Volbert for around US$8.

Chauve Souris Island Less than 1km off Anse Volbert, and can be reached by wading at low tide. A good site for exploring rock pools and snorkelling.

Grand Fond A peak of 340m in the northern half of the island. There are trails to the summit from Anse Possession, Anse Lazio and Grande Anse.

Local information

● Where to stay

A+ *Flying Dutchman*, Grande Anse, west coast, T 233337 F 247606. Thatched bungalows. **A+** *Maison des Palmes*, Grande Anse, west coast, T 233411, F 233880. Thatched bungalows. Good restaurant, barbeques on Wed, local food and entertainment on Sat, popular with non-residents. **A+** *Coco de Mer*, Anse Cimitiere, south west coast, T 233900, F 2333919. Chalets on the beach. Expensive. Pleasant gardens. Watersports. Restaurant. Bars. Regular entertainment. **A+** *Chateau de Feuilles*, Pointe Cabris, south east corner, T 233316 F 233916) Range of accommodation available in secluded site. Expensive. **A+** *Praslin Beach*, Anse Volbert, east coast, T 232222, F 247606. Quite large. Self catering. Swimming pool. Wind-surfing, deep-sea fishing, diving. **A+** *Cote d'Or*, Anse Volbert, east coast, T 232200, F 232130. Medium-size, mostly occupied by Italian package visitors. **A+** *Chauve Souris Island Lodge*, Island off Anse Volbert on east coast, T 232003, F 232130. Small, rather exclusive lodge. Expensive. **A+** *Village du Pecheur*, Anse Volbert, east coast, T 232030, F 232185. Fairly small. Restaurant and bar. Popular with non-residents. **A+** *Paradise Sun*, Anse Volbert, east coast, T 232255, F 232019. Expensive. Excursions available. **A+** *L'Archipel*, Anse Gouvernement, east coast, T 232242, F 232072. Bungalows in pleasing garden, by a good section of beach. Expensive. Watersports available. **A+** *La Reserve*, Anse Petite Cour, east coast, T 232211, F 232166. Some bungalows. Pleasant tropical setting. Restaurant.

A *Islanders*, Anse Kerlan, north west coast. (T 233224) Small establishment. Some self-catering. Very accommodating for families. At lower end of A-range. Good value. **A** *Laurier*, Anse Volbert, east coast, T 232241. Small, and new, with choice of rooms or chalets. More expensive for shorter stays or single occupancy, but otherwise good value. **A** *Duc de Praslin*, Anse Volbert, east coast, T 232252. Small, chalet accommodation. **A** *Cabanes des Pecheurs*, Grande Anse, west coast, T 233320. Bungalows with verandahs. Small. Lower end of A-range. **A** *Indian Ocean Fishing Club*, Grande Anse, west coast, T 233324, F 233911. Medium size. Ocean excursions and fishing

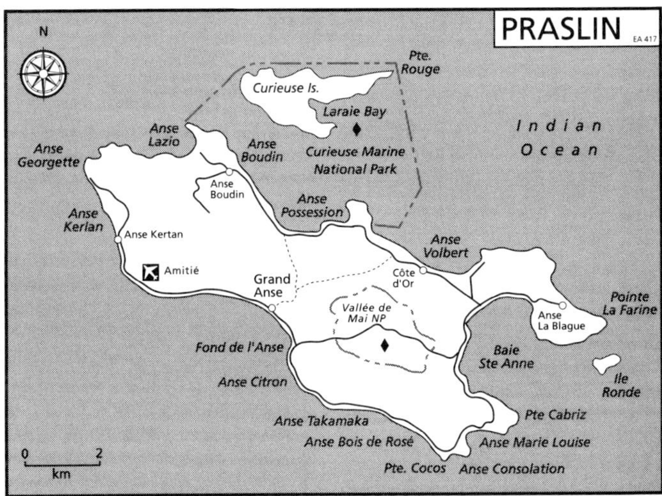

arranged. **A** ***Brittania***, Grande Anse, west coast, T 233215, F 233944. At lower end of A-range. Reasonable value. Restaurant. **A** ***Villa de Mer***, Grande Anse, west coast, T 233972, F 233015. Self-catering chalets. Lower end of A-range. Good value. **A** ***Colibri***, Point Cabris, south east corner, T 233902. Small guest-house. Good location on pleasant beach. Lower end of A-range, and good value.

B *Beach Villas*, Grande Anse, west coast, T 233445. Small. Bungalows. Ocean excursions arranged. Good value. **B** *Orange Tree*, Baie St Anne, south east coast, T 233248. Fine elevated location above bay. Friendly, small and good value.

● Places to eat

♦♦♦♦*Bon Bon Plume*, Anse Lazio, north coast. (T 232136) Specialises in seafood. Expensive, but high standard. ♦♦♦♦*Laurier*, Anse Volbert, east coast. (T 233241) International menu, with emphasis on French cuisine. ♦♦♦♦*Rocky Bay*, Petite Anse, close to most easterly point. charming location, diners are ferried to restaurant by boat. ♦♦♦♦*Le Roches*, Anse Citron, west coast. Emphasis on seafood in Creole and French style. Closed Sun. ♦♦♦♦*Britannia*, Grand Anse International menu, with good seafood.

● Local travel

Bus Regular hourly service round the island from 0600 to 1800, with fares US$0.50 to US$1. **Taxi** Cost US$3.50 for first km and US$1 per km thereafter.

● Travel Agents & Tour Operators

Travel Services Seychelles Grande Anse, T 233438/41. *Mason's Travel*, Grande Anse, T 233211. *National Travel*, Grande Anse, T 233223.

● Transport

Air There are frequent flights to and from **Mahe**, costing US$70 one way, and taking 15 mins.

Boat Regular ferries to **Mahe**, taking just over 3 hours and costing US$10. To **La Digue** there are regular ferries taking 30 mins and costing US$6. The ferries leave from Baie St Anne on Praslin.

● Vehicle Hire

Bicycles, Indian Ocean Fishing Club, Grande Anse. (T 233324 F 233911) US$5 half-day, US$10 full-day. **Car** **Solace Car Hire**, Grande Anse, T 233525). **Prestige Car Hire**, Grande Anse, T 233226; **Austral Car Hire**, Anse Volbert, T 232015.

Cousin Island Special Reserve

Situated 2.5 km south west off Praslin Island, the island was turned into a nature reserve in 1968 by the International Council for Bird Preservation (ICBP). It is small, less than 1 sq km, but the birdlife is really quite exceptional.

There is no accommodation, but it is possible to visit the island, 20 mins by boat, for guided tours. A day trip costs around US$60 and can be arranged through the travel agencies in Praslin (see page 845).Information on the bird conservation strategy from ICPB, 219c Huntingdon Road, Cambridge, CB3 ODL, UK (T 02223-277318)

South west of Cousin Island, and about 2km way is **Cousine Island**, privately owned, and not visitable.

Curieuse Island

Situated roughly 1.5km north west of Praslin, just over 3km wide and 1 km from north to south. The highest point is 172m. The south coast was the site of a **Leper Colony** from 1833 to 1965, and the ruins /can be seen. The home of the colony director, a handsome Colonial mansion with a verandah, now a national monument.

The surrounding waters are designated as the Curieuse Marine National Park. The island is home to a tortoise and turtle preservation project, and a number of giant tortoises have been brought from Aldabra to breed. There is no accommodation on the island, but day trips can be organised from Praslin through travel agents.

Aride Island

Small granite island located 10km north of Praslin. Acquired in 1973 by the Royal Society for Nature Conservation (RSNC), and run as a nature reserve. Common species on the Island include the noddys, frigate birds, terns, tropic birds and shearwaters.

There is no accommodation on the island for visitors.

- **Transport** Day trips are possible from Apr to Oct, (at other times of the year, the seas make landing difficult) when there are excursions operated most days by the travel agents in Praslin (see page 845), costing US$70.

INNER ISLANDS

These are the islands that are reasonably easily accessed from the main islands, Mahé and Praslin. La Digue is fairly popular, and there is a regular ferry service linking it to both Mahé and Praslin.

La Digue

Small island, 5km by 3km, just 5km east of Praslin. First settled in 1798, it still has few inhabitants, numbering about 2,000. Granite hills rising to 333m. Once a major coconut producer, now mainly given over to tourism. Fairly sleepy atmosphere – there are no sealed roads, and no airstrip. Superb beaches, among the best being **Anse Patales** on the northern tip, and nearby **Anse Gaulettes** on the east coast.

Places of Interest

L'Union Estate Coconut plantation and copra factory at L'Union just about 1 km south of the church at Anse la Reunion on the west coast. Tours are available (US$2). Open Mon-Fri 0700-1600.

Veuve Reserve Small bird sanctuary adjoining the south side of the road toward La Digue Peak. The main attraction is the Black Paradise Flycatcher (*Terpsiphone corvina*), found only in the Seychelles. It is known as the 'widow' (*veuve*) by the local people because of its black plumage.

Mare Soupage (Terrapin Pools) It is possible to walk from La Passe on the east coast to Grande Anse on the west shore. En route there is a Colonial cemetery, and a marshy area Mare Soupape, containing swampland wildlife including the yellow-bellied and star-bellied terrapins.

Anse Cocos (Coconut Beach) There is also a track from Grande Anse, hugging the shore, to Anse Fourmis. At Anse Cocos, just over 1km from Grande Anse, there are the remains of a copra processing plant and the shoreside shipping post. Beyond Anse Cocos the track involves some scrambling over rocks, but it's quite manageable.

La Digue Island Peak Approach is from Anse la Reunion on the west coast. It is about 3km from the shore, and the highest

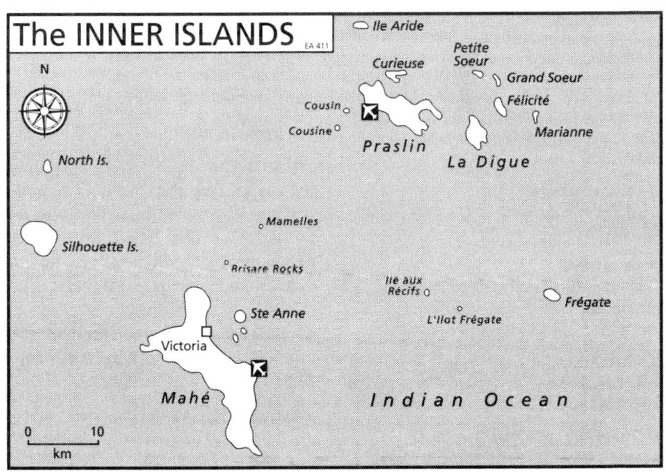

point at 333m is along a ridge that runs at right angles to the track up from the coast.

Local information

● Where to stay

A+ *Patatran Village*, Anse Patates, right at the northern tip, T 234333, F 234244. Small collection of chalets, on an excellent beach. Restaurant. **A+** *La Digue Island Lodge*, Anse Reunion, on the west coast, T 234233. Complex of renovated colonial houses and newer chalets. Restaurant, bars. Swimming pool. Diving, marine excursions arranged.

A *Choppy's Bungalows*, La Passe, T 234334. Pair of bungalows on the beach. Restaurant and bar, set back from the beach. **A** *Anse Severe Bungalow*, Anse Severe, west coast, near northern tip, T 247354. Good value for families, and close to excellent beaches.

B *Le Romarin*, just under 1km along the track from La Passe that runs inland toward Belle Vue, T 234334. Small guesthouse. Good value. **B** *Le Sitronnel*, just under 1km along the track from La Passe that runs inland toward Belle Vue, T 234115. Small guesthouse. Slightly more expensive for single occupancy. **B** *Bernique Guest House*, just under 1km along the track from La Passe that runs inland toward Belle Vue, T 234229. Choice of rooms in Colonial house or bungalows. Good restaurant. Entertainment on Tue and Sat.

C *Chateau St Cloud*, just over 1km along the track from La Passe that runs inland toward Belle Vue, T 234346. Rooms in colonial mansion. Exceptional value.

● Banks

Barclays, Anse Reunion, west coast. Open Mon-Fri 0800-1100 and 1300-1500. **Seychelles Savings Bank**, La Passe, west coast. Open Mon-Fri 0815-1300 and 1400-1530, Sat 0900-1100.

● Leisure Activities

Diving, *La Digue Island Lodge*, Anse La Reunion, west coast.

● Local travel

Taxi Rate is US$3.50 for first km and then US$1 per km. **Bicycle** Hire costs around US$5 a day, and is available in La Passe.

● Post Office

At la Passe, on the west coast. Mon-Fri 0800-100 and 1300-1500.

● Travel Agents & Tour Operators

Mason's Travel, La Passe; *National Travel*, La Reunion; *Travel Services Seychelles*, La Passe.

● Transport

There is no airstrip on La Digue, and the only access is by boat. There are regular ferry services from **Mahe** (the sea can be heavy May-Oct) costing US$10, and taking just over 3 hours, though more in bad weather. From **Praslin** the journey is under an hour and costs US$6.

Felicite Island

Situated roughly 3km north east of La Digue, a little over 2km wide, and a 1km from north to south. Moderately hilly, with two peaks in the NW just over 100m.

Abdullah Khan, Sultan of Perak in Malaysia, was exiled here in 1875 after apparently being involved in the death of the British Consul in Perak. There are two large converted former plantation houses on the Island comprising the main accommodation. There are some pleasant walks over island. The **Ile aux Cocos** is close by but is currently closed to tourists after the coral was damaged.

● **Where to stay A+** *Felicite Island Lodge*, east coast by the main village (Bookings through La Digue Island Lodge, T 234232, F 234132). Full board, drinks and boat transfer. a/c. Tennis. Fishing and marine viewing arranged. Idyllic, exclusive, isolated and expensive.

● **Transport** Transfer by boat from La Digue takes about 30 mins. Day trips are organised by La Digue Island Lodge (see above) and cost about US$60 per person.

Fregate Island

Situated around 20km south of La Digue the Island is privately owned. The Island is named after the frigate bird which is no longer a visitor. There are a two endemic species, the Magpie robin and the Tenebrionid beetle (*Pulposipes herculeanus*). Some pleasant and adventurous walks can be taken and there are good beaches to explore such as Grand Anse, Anse Victorin, and Anse Parc.

● **Where to stay A+** *The Plantation House*, T 224789) Fine old colonial dwelling. Bookings can be made from Fregate office (T 323123/24789 F

225169) on Revolution Av Victoria.

• **Transport** There are daily flights from Mahe ($80 return). Day trips for US$120 per person through Mahe travel agents (see page 838).

Bird Island

The French name is IIe aux Vaches from the sea cows (dugong) that once inhabited the waters. Small island coral island 95km north of Mahe and is visited by large numbers of birds. The Island's other visitors, which also breed in the area, are turtles. Fine beaches, snorkelling, swimming, bird-watching and a giant 152 year old tortoise.

• **Where to stay A+** *Bird Island Lodge*, T 324925/344449. Chalet accommodations include return air flight. The daily rate is lower for longer stays.

• **Transport** There are flights daily from Mahe, about US$100 return.

Dennis Island

Named in 1773 after Denis de Troubriand, a French navigator, the island is coral and lies roughly 80km from Mahe, east of Bird Island. Today it is owned by Pierre Burkhardt who still has a coconut plantation in operation. To the north of the island there lies a light house and a couple of deserted prisons. Deep-sea fishing is available, as well as tennis and golf. Time is one hour ahead of the Seychelles. There are no day trips, and the island owner markets holidays there on the basis of their exclusivity.

• **Where to stay A+** *Denis Island Lodge*, T 344143, F 344405. Minimum three day stay is usually required.

• **Transport** There is a daily flight to the island's airstrip, fare being about US$120 return.

OUTER ISLANDS

There are a number of small, often uninhabited, islands which can be visited, although their inaccessibility makes travel expensive. There are three main sets of islands (besides the Inner Islands Mahe group) and these are the Farquhar, Amirantes and the Aldabra groups.

Most of the Islands in this region are coconut and copra producers. The Island Development Company (IDC) owns many of the Islands and those wishing to make independent visits need to request permission to do so from the IDC, PO Box 638, New Port Area, Victoria (T 224640). It is possible to travel on the IDC fleet of three boats travelling to deliver supplies and collect copra.

Amirantes Group

This is the largest group, first sighted by the Portuguese explorer Vasco de Gama in 1501 it is situated in a cluster around 300km south west of Mahe. Marine Charter Association (T 322126 fax 224679) and others in Victoria hire yachts to visit. Most of the the 28 islands in this group are uninhabited. **D'Arros Island** is privately-owned, has no accommodation is covered by coconut plantations and lies roughly 35km North of Poivre. **St Josephs** is a little larger that the rest, and has a few inhabitants producing copra. **Poivre Island Atoll** is where it is believed Louis XVII lived under an assumed name (see page 835). Named after Pierre Poivre of Mauritius. The island has some inhabitants, and is accessible at high tide by boat from Des Roches Island. Popular with yacht visitors. **Desnoeufs Island** is a regular nesting ground for many sea birds.

Desnoeufs Island is a small island, about 5 km long and under 1 km wide. Excellent beaches with fishing, diving, watersports, and excursions are possible to other islands in the Amirantes group. There is a small village with a church.

• **Where to stay** A+ *Desroches Island Lodge*, T 229002. Chalets, in a rather simple style.

• **Transport** There are three flights a week, and the air fare is around US$200.

Farquhar Group

This group lies 400km south west of the Amirantes and 700km from Mahe. Named after the the governor of Mauri-

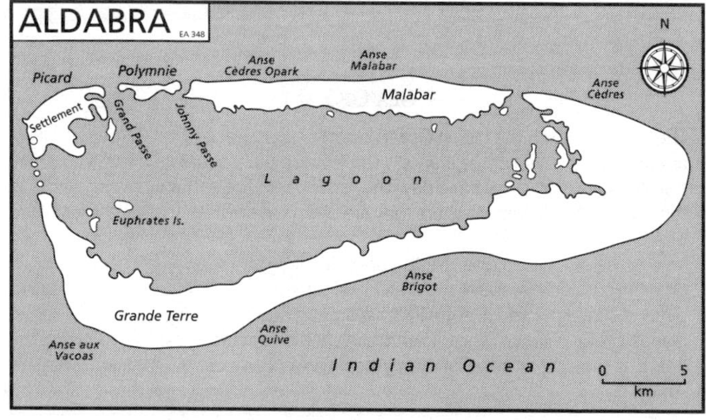

tius, Sir Robert Farquhar. The islands remained dependencies of Mauritius until 1921 when they were handed over to the Seychelles. Of the northern islands in this group **Providence**, has a few inhabitants tending coconuts and fishing, **St Pierre** and **Bancs Providence** are uninhabited. The islands to the south part, make up **Farquhar Atoll**. North Island and South Island have a handful of people, engaged in fishing and farming with a little copra for export. North Island is served by an airstrip.

Aldabra Group

These Islands lie 1000km from Mahe and 400km from Madagascar. The group consists of Aldabra Atoll, Cosmoledo Atoll, Assomption Island and Astove Island.

Aldabra Atoll The Atoll covers a land area of 154 sq km and consists of four main islands, **Picard**, **Polymnieli**, **Malabar** and **Grand Terre** which encircle a large tidal lagoon. Aldabra has been declared a world heritage site by UNESCO and has a great variety of endemic fauna on it, such as the giant tortoise (*Testudo gigantea*), the white-throated rail bird which cannot fly, and many others. There is also the robber crab which has strong claws which it uses to break open coconuts to eat the flesh inside.

Cosmoledo Atoll is a great nesting site for birds 120km south west of Aldabra Atoll. The Islands are uninhabited.

Assomption Island lies 27km south of the Aldabra Atoll. Guano, a fertiliser from decomposed bird droppings, was once mined here, and has resulted in the clearance and destruction of much vegetation. The coral atoll is extremely attractive and a good spot for diving and snorkelling. There is now an airstrip on the northern side of the island and some bungalow accommodation. Bookings can be made through travel agents in Mahé (see page 838) and Praslin (see page 838).

Astove Island is located 35km to the south of Cosmoledo Atoll and has a small population. There is no accommodation, but there is an airstrip.

- **Transport** The construction of the airstrip and the completion of the accommodation on Assomption is expected to lead to some regular flights. It is possible to charter boats in Mahe or Praslin, but very expensive.

SEA OF ZANJ

The water in which the Indian Ocean islands lie was first known to Arab mariners as Bahr el Zanj - "Sea of the Blacks". The whole area is marked by strong currents, travelling at around 150 km a day. They arrive from the east and sweep across to the coast of Madagascar, where they are deflected north to the Seychelles island of Aldabra.

The balmy waters give rise to corals, forming atolls (circular coaral reefs). In time the corals grow above the water line, the coral dies, silt, sand and bird-droppings accumulate, and eventually it becomes covered with vegetation. The larger islands are the result of vocanic eruptions, the one exception being Madagascar, which is thought to have originally been part of the continental land mass of Africa.

INFORMATION FOR VISITORS

Contents

Before you go

Entry requirements

● Visas

Visas are not required by any visitor. All that is necessary is to present immigration officials on arrival with an outward bound air ticket, a valid passport, an adequate amount of money and an address (name of expected hotel residence) in the Seychelles at which you can be contacted in case of emergency. If all these conditions are met then you will be issued a tourist visa for 1 month. Those visitors arriving by boat are issued a shorter stay tourist visa valid for 2 weeks.

Visas can be extended for three months free of charge (two photographs required), and thereafter for around US$40 per three months. Applications to The Immigration Service, Independent House, Independence Avenue, Victoria, Seychelles. (T 322881).

● Vaccinations

No vaccinations are required for the Seychelles.

● Seychelles Representation Overseas (E) Embassy; (HC) High Commission; (C) Consulate

Australia (C), 271 Canning Road, Les Murdie, Perth, WA 6076. **France** (E), 53 rue Francois Premier, 75008 Paris France, T 47237702. **Germany** (C), Jungfernstieg 7, 2000 Hambourg 36. **Japan** (C), Nagoya Denki Gakuen, Wakamizu, Chikusa, Nagoya, Japan. **Kenya** (C), Po Box 20400, Nairobi. **Madagascar** (C), BP 1071, Analakely, Antannarivo. **Mauritius** (C), Peat Marwick, Leoville L'Homme St, Port Louis. **UK** (HC), 2nd floor, Eros House, 111 Baker St, London WIM 1FE, T 071 224 1660. **USA** (E), Suite 927F, 820 Second Avenue, New York.

● Overseas Representation in Madagascar (E) Embassy; (HC) High Commission; (C) Consulate

See Victoria, page 838, and: **China** (E), Plaisance, Mahé. **Cyprus** (C), Anse aux Pins, Mahé. France (E) Arpent vert, Mont Fleuri, Mahé (T 224523). **Germany** (C), Chemin Mont Fleuri, Mont Fleuri, Mahé, T 322306. **Mauritius** (C), Anse aux pins, Mahé. **Monaco** (C), Chateau de Feuilles, Praslin. **Netherlands** (C), *Sunset Beach Hotel*, Gacis, PO Box 372, Mahé, T 261200. **Switzerland** (C), Sancta Maria Estate, Anse à la Mouche, Mahé. **Russia** (E), le Noil, Mahé.

● Tourist Office

Seychelles Tourist Board, Independence House PO BOX 92 Victoria, T 22881 F 21612.

● Tourist Offices Overseas

France, 32 rue de Pothieu, 7500 Paris, T (01) 42898533. **Germany**, Kleine Bockenheimer Strasse 18A, D-6000 Frankfurt Am Main 1, T 292 064. **UK** 2nd Floor, Eros House, 111 Baker St , London W1M 1FE, T 071 224 1670. **USA**, 820 Second Ave, Suite 927, New York, NY 10017, T 6879766.

When to go

● Best time to visit

There is a hot season from December to May, and the weather is best then.

Health

● Staying healthy

There are no particular health hazards. See Health Section, page 21.

Money

● Currency

Currency in Seychelles is the Rupee (R). The value is allowed to float against other currencies, but its value is fairly stable. Only R100 can be taken out, but Rupees can be reconverted to other currencies on leaving. There are a wide selection of banks, and bureau de change. Large hotels will also change money.

● Cost of Living

Budget travellers, staying in the cheaper guest houses, eating in restaurants serving local food, and travelling by ferry between the main Islands, can get by on US$60 a day.

Modest travellers, staying in hotels with fans or air conditioning, and hot water, travelling by ferry, and sampling a variety of restaurants, will find it costs perhaps US$100 a day.

Luxury travellers, staying in the best hotels with air-conditioning and swimming pools, travelling by air to exotic islands, and eating in the best restaurants in town, will spend in excess of US$200 a day.

● Credit Cards

Credit cards are widely accepted, particularly by large hotels, airlines and travel agents. **American Express** Travel Services Seychelles Victoria House, Victoria, T 322414, F 321326. Bank Hours Mon-Fri 0830 to 1300 and Sat 0830-1100.

Getting there

● Air

Europe There are regular scheduled flights by Air France, British Airways, Air Seychelles and Aeroflot. The cheapest excursion fare is from US$700 on Aeroflot, and US$900 with the other lines.

Africa Nairobi twice a week (Kenya Airways) sgl US$280, rtn US$351; **Johannesburg** once a week (Air Seychelles) sgl US$480, rtn US$590.

Indian Ocean Mauritius four flights a week (British Airways & Air France) sgl US$330, rtn US$400; **Réunion** twice a week (Air France) sgl US$650, rtn US$780; Antananarivo, **Madagascar** once a week (Air France) sgl US$535, rtn U$S650.

Specialist Agencies For discounted fares, see page 14.

● Sea

There are no passenger ferries/services to the Islands but cruise liners regularly visit. For those with a spirit of adventure the Seychelles is a popular spot for yachts, if you are lucky you might be able to crew on one.

● Customs

Duty free 1 litre spirits; 1 litre wine; 200 cigarettes or 250 gms tobacco; 125ml perfume; 250 ml toilet water. **Export** Shells, corals, turtles, tortoises and coco de mer nuts require permission.

When you arrive

● Airport Information

Departure tax US$12.

● Conduct

Seychelles is a cosmopolitan society, and visitors need observe only the normal courtesies and proprieties. It is unwise to photograph government buildings, military installations, radio and TV stations or tranmitters, airfields.

● Electricity

240 volts. Three pin square plugs. Adaptor is advised.

● Hours of Business

Offices Mon-Fri 0830 - 1200 and 1300-1600. Shops Mon-Sat 0830 - 1200 and 1300-1700.

● Safety

Seychelles are very safe for visitors. There is some petty theft, and it is unwise to leave belongings unattended, or where locks can be easily broken.

● Time

Seychelles 4 hrs ahead of GMT.

● Weights and Measures

Official system is metric. Local markets will often use British pounds (2.2 lbs = 1kg)

Where to stay

● Hotels

Rates in tourist hotels vary: **High Season** is mid-Dec to mid-Jan; Easter; July and August. All accommodation is controlled by the Seychelles Tourist Board (STB), and regulation keeps prices high. Local people are reluctant to risk acting illegally by renting out a room.

Hotel Classifications

A+ Over US$100 a night. International standards and decor, a/c, self contained rooms, swimming pool, restaurants, bars, business services.

A US$40-100. First class standards. Air-conditioning, attached bathrooms. Restaurants and bars. Swimming pool.

B US$20-40. Tourist class. Comfortable with a/c or fans, attached barthrooms. Restaurant, bar, public rooms.

C US$10-20. Budget. Fans. Shared bathroom facilities.

D US$5-10. Guest house. No fan. Shared bathroom. Cold water.

E Under US$5. Basic guest house. Simple bed. No soap or towels. No wardrobe. Shared bathroom facilities. Erratic cold water supply. No fans or mosquito nets.

Restaurant Classifications

♦♦♦♦ Over US$10 for a meal. A 3 course meal in a restaurant with pleasant decor. Beers, wines and spirits available.

♦♦♦♦ US$5-10 for a meal. Two courses. Comfortable surroundings.

♦♦ US$2-5 for a meal. Probably only a single course. Surroundings spartan but adequate.

♦ Under US$2. Single course. Often makeshift surroundings such as a street kiosk with simple benches and tables.

There are luxury hotels; guesthouses & smaller hotels; and a few self-catering units. It is possible to rent houses and flats on a long term basis for around US$700 a month.

Camping is forbidden.

Food and drink

● **Cuisine**

The specialities of the Island centre on seafood, and a wide variety is available. The local cuisine is Créole, the food developed by the groups that have inter-married with descendants of slaves brought from mainland Africa. A variety of spiced fish, chicken and sometimes pork stews, perhaps curried, is typically accompanied by rice, and *bréde,* a green vegetables. Local vegetables include yams (sweet potatoes), irish potatoes, cassava and breadfruit. Fruits include custard apples, guavas and passion fruit.

Drink

On Mahé, Praslin and La Digue the water is quite safe to drink. There is a local bottled water *Eau de Val Riche*. There are imported soft drinks, and there is a local soft drink manufacturer, *Seypearl*.

There are two locally produced brands of lager beer, *Seybrew* and *EKU*, as well as plenty of imported beers, particularly from France, South Africa and Kenya.

Imported wines are available. Local alcoholic drinks include *Toddy* made from the coconut palm; *Bacca Rum* from molasses; and *Lapuree* from fermented fruit juice.

Getting around

● **Air**

Air Seychelles operates scheduled flights linking **Mahé** with **Praslin**, **Frégate Island**, **Bird Island**, and **Denis Island**.

Bus There is a bus service, running to timetables, on the bigger islands.

● **Car Hire**

Available on **Mahé** and **Praslin**.

● **Ferries**

There are ferries linking **Mahé** with **Praslin**; **Mahé** with **La Digue**; **Praslin** with **La Digue**. (See **Transport** under these islands).

● **Road**

Taxi The fares standards have been set by the government and are about US$3 per km.

Communications

● **Language**

While English is the dominant language, French and Creol are also widely spoken. The latter has been actively encouraged by the government of late and was rewarded with something akin to official status in the early 1980s, and now can be read in many newspapers.

● **Postal Services**

Post Restante, Central Post Office, Independence Ave, Victoria. Free service.

● **Telephone Services**

Telephone connections are good and direct dialling is possible. Overseas calls from hotels may cost up to three times the normal charge. **Cable and Wireless**, Francis Rachel St, Victoria, is open 24 hrs for international calls, telgrams, telexes and faxes.

Entertainment

● Cinemas

There is a cinema, *Deepam*, in Victoria on Mahé, and there are regular showings of films by the *American Cultural Centre* and the *Centre Culturel Français*, both in Victoria. Video films are widely available, and most hotels will have a player.

● Music

Local band play regularly at the large hotels. Occasional concerts at the *American Cultural Centre* and the *Centre Culturel Français*.

● Newspapers

The daily paper is the government-owned *Nation*, which is mainly in English, but does contain items in French and Créole. It carries all the main announcements of cultural events, sport, entertainment and the radio and TV programmes.

● Radio

SBC broadcasts in French, English and Créole.

● Sport

Soccer is played regularly, and there is a league involving teams from Mahé and Praslin. The national stadium is in Victoria. **Netball** and **hockey** are also popular.

● Television

There is one government controlled station, Seychelles Broadcasting Corporation (SBC). Programmes are transmitted in English, French and Créole, in the evenings only.

Holidays and festivals

1 & 2 Jan	New Year
Mar/Apr	Good Friday and Easter Monday
1 May	Labour Day
5 Jun	Liberation Day
29 Jun	Independence Day
May/Jun	Corpus Christi
15 Aug	Assumption
1 Nov	All Saints' Day
8 Dec	Immaculate Conception
25 Dec	Christmas Day
15 Aug	*La Digue* Festival

Further reading

● General

Thomas, A 1968. *Forgotten Eden* London: Longmans. Toussaint, A.1966. *History of the Indian Ocean* London: Routledge & Kegan Paul.

● Natural History

Friedmann, F. 1986. *Flowers and Trees of the Seychelles*. Mahé: Government of Seychelles. Venter, A. 1972. *Underwater Seychelles* London: Verhoef. Penny, M 1974. *Birds of the Seychelles and Outlying Islands* London: Collins. Smith, J. L. B. and Smith, M. M. 1963. *The Fishes of the Seychelles*. Grahamstown: Rhodes University Press.

● Travellers' Tales

Waugh. A. 1954. *Where the Clocks Chime Twice*. London: Chapman and Hall. Travis, W. *Beyond the Reefs* London: Century Travellers.

Index of maps

Index

A

B

C

N

KILDARE COUNTY LIBRARY
A048019

LEABHARLANN
CO. CILL DARA